Second edition

Business Information Systems
Technology, Development and Management for the e-business

Paul Bocij
Dave Chaffey
Andrew Greasley
Simon Hickie

Edited by
Dave Chaffey

FT Prentice Hall
FINANCIAL TIMES

An imprint of **Pearson Education**

Harlow, England • London • New York • Boston • San Francisco • Toronto • Sydney • Singapore • Hong Kong
Tokyo • Seoul • Taipei • New Delhi • Cape Town • Madrid • Mexico City • Amsterdam • Munich • Paris • Milan

Pearson Education Limited
Edinburgh Gate
Harlow
Essex CM20 2JE
England

and Associated Companies throughout the world

Visit us on the World Wide Web at:
www.pearsoneduc.com

First published 1999
Second edition 2003

© Pearson Education Limited 2003

ISBN 0 273 65540 X

British Library Cataloguing-in-Publication Data
A catalogue record for this book can be obtained from the British Library.

Library of Congress Cataloging-in-Publication Data

Business Information Systems: Technology, Development, and Management for the
e-business / Paul Bocij ...
    p. cm.
  Includes bibliographical references and index.
  ISBN 0-273-65540-X
  1. Business--Computer network resources. 2. Business information services. 3.
Electronic commerce.

  HF54.56 .B867 2002
  650'.0285--dc21

                           2002025248

10 9 8 7 6 5 4
07 06 05 04 03

Typeset by 30 in 9/12pt Stone Serif
Printed by Ashford Colour Press Ltd., Gosport.

Business Information Systems

We work with leading authors to develop the strongest educational materials in Business Information, bringing cutting-edge thinking and best learning practice to a global market.

Under a range of well-known imprints, including Financial Times Prentice Hall, we craft high quality print and electronic publications which help readers to understand and apply their content, whether studying or at work.

To find out more about the complete range of our publishing, please visit us on the World Wide Web at: www.pearsoneduc.com

Brief contents

Contents

Part 2
Business information systems development

▶ Introduction

Writing in *The Economist* of 16 June 1990, John Browning stated that:

> *Information Technology is no longer a business resource; it has become the business environment.*

Through the 1990s, and into the new millennium, the validity of this statement has been supported by the ever increasing global expenditure on the information technology (IT) which is used to build information systems (IS) (Fig. 1). What is less clear, is how well IT has supported increases in production.

With the prominence of the concept of e-business and the increased use of business information systems (BIS) within organisations, the need for all working professionals to have a good knowledge of IT and IS has also increased. With the vast, rapidly changing choice of IS available, important business skills are understanding and assessing the range of options available, and then choosing the solution best suited to the business problem or opportunity. This is, essentially, our aim in writing this book: to provide a source of knowledge that will explain how the right systems can be chosen by a business, then developed appropriately and managed effectively.

Despite the rising expenditure on IS, surveys also show that the potential of IS is often not delivered, often due to problems in the management, analysis, design or implementation of the system. The intention in this book is to acknowledge that there are great difficulties with developing and using IS and to explain the measures that can be taken to try and minimise these difficulties in order to make the systems successful.

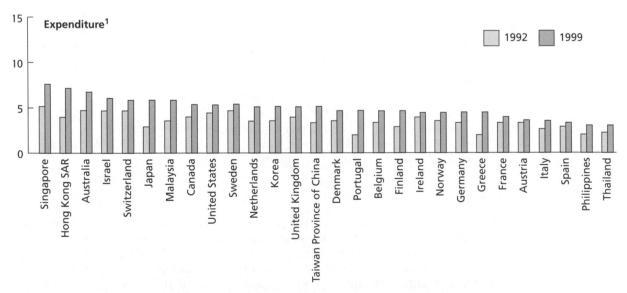

Figure 1 Information technology (IT) expenditure as proportion of Gross Domestic Product (information technology expenditure comprises hardware, software and telecommunications equipment, but not services)

Source: 'World Economic Outlook The Information Technology Revolution, October 2001', in World Economic and Financial Surveys, http://www.imf.org/external/pubs/ft/weo/2001/02/pdf/chapter3.pdf, International Monetary Fund (2001)

The opportunities and risks afforded by investment in business information systems are highlighted by a survey of 599 Chief Information Officers in 'Top 500' companies in the UK, USA and Australia (PricewaterhouseCoopers, 2001). The benefits are summarised as follows:

> Three quarters of respondents reported that investment in data management had delivered a positive impact across their business. Almost 60% had cut their processing costs and well over 40% had managed to boost sales through better analysis of customer data.

However, the difficulty in achieving these benefits is illustrated through a third of companies reporting delay or scrapping of new information systems. This clearly indicates the need for effective systems development processes as described in Part 2 of this book.

▶ Why study business information systems?

Information systems form an integral part of modern organisations and businesses. Computer-based IS are now used to support all aspects of an organisation's normal functions and activities.

New technology creates new opportunities for forward-thinking companies. Higher levels of automation, high-speed communications and improved access to information can all provide significant benefits to a modern business organisation. However, the benefits of new and emerging technologies can only be realised once they have been harnessed and directed towards an organisation's goals.

The hybrid manager

The traditional view of managers is as functional specialists having specialised knowledge and expertise in a particular area, such as finance. The modern business environment requires a new kind of manager, often called a *hybrid manager*. The hybrid manager combines management and business skills with expertise in the areas of IT and IS. This type of manager is able to undertake a wide variety of roles and can operate across functional areas. The study of IS plays an important part in the development of an individual so that they may become a competent and effective manager as well as providing prospective managers with important problem-solving skills that can be applied to range of situations and problems. Specifically, the hybrid manager will need to:

- define the IS strategy for their workgroup, department or company;
- identify potential uses of IS to improve company performance;
- select and then acquire new IS from appropriate suppliers;
- oversee the development and implementation of these new systems;
- manage the IS to ensure they are effective in delivering information of the appropriate quality to users.

▶ Aims

This book is intended to provide a comprehensive, yet accessible, guide to choosing the right systems for an organisation, developing them appropriately and managing them effectively. The book was conceived as a single source book that undergraduate business students would refer to throughout their course, without the need to purchase a separate book for different topics such as IT; information management; systems analysis and design; and strategy development. It covers, in detail, the software and hardware technologies which form IS, the activities involved in acquiring and building new IS, and the elements of strategy required to manage IS effectively.

Key skills necessary to participate in the implementation of IT in businesses are developed, and these skills, which form the main themes of the book are:

● understanding of the terms used to describe the components of BIS to assist in selection of systems and suppliers;
● assessing how BIS applications can support different areas of an organisation;
● managing IS development projects;
● systems analysis and design;
● developing an IS or e-business strategy and managing its implementation.

The book assumes no prior knowledge of IS or IT. New concepts and terms are defined as simply as possible, with clear definitions given in the margins of the book. It explains the importance of information in developing a company business strategy and assisting decision making. The use of relevant hardware and software components of computer systems are defined and explained in the context of a range of business applications. The book also explains the benefit of specialised innovative applications such as the Internet and intranets; office automation using groupware and workflow products such as Lotus Notes, and marketing analysis using tools such as data warehouses and geographical information systems. The application of IS to business process re-engineering and initiatives is also described.

After using the book as part of IS modules on their course, students will be able to:

● evaluate and select IT solutions for deployment within different functional parts of a business to achieve benefits for the business;
● actively participate in IT projects, applying skills such as selection of suppliers, procurement of hardware and software, systems analysis and design, and project management;
● communicate effectively with IT specialists when collaborating on a task or project;
● use IT to access a wide range of information sources for research and acquisition of knowledge.

▶ Changes for the second edition

The logical structure of the first edition has been retained, but many changes have been incorporated based on lecturer and student feedback. The most significant change for the second edition is the integration of more material on the concept of e-business throughout the book. The main changes are as follows:

● New chapters on e-business applications (Chapter 6) and management (Chapter 14) have been included.
● E-business concepts and topics have been integrated into many chapters. Particular topics which are covered in more depth include the e-business concept (Chapter 1), knowledge management (Chapter 1), new digital technologies such as mobile and interactive TV access (Chapter 5), drivers and barriers impacting e-business adoption (Chapter 6), user-centred design for the web (Chapter 11), and legal and ethical issues of Internet usage (Chapters 15 and 17).
● The majority of cases have been updated by articles from the *Financial Times* and *Computer Weekly*, many of which relate to e-business topics.
● Systems theory has now been integrated into the introductory chapters while other chapters have been simplified to ensure a succinct coverage of key topics.
● Navigation within chapters has been improved through a redesigned page at the start of each chapter including a summary of the management context plus clear cross-referencing to the main sections and case studies.

The structure of this book

The book is divided into three parts, each covering a different aspect of how BIS are used within organisations to help achieve competitive advantage:

- *Part 1* focuses on the hardware and software technologies, known collectively as IT, which make up IS. It is intended for introductory courses in IT and BIS.
- *Part 2* explains how IS are acquired and developed by considering the activities involved with each of the stages of developing an IS. This part is intended for more advanced courses in systems analysis and design.
- *Part 3* describes how IS need to be managed, and a strategy developed, to ensure they effectively support the mission of the business. This part is appropriate for courses which consider the strategic management of IS.

Each part is self-contained and is the equivalent of what might be covered in a single module, or course, in a programme of study.

Part 1: Introduction to business information systems

Part 1 introduces the basic concepts of BIS. Its main focus is the technology that forms BIS, but it starts by reviewing the importance of information and what makes good-quality information. Many people who work in the IT industry tend to believe it is the technology part of IT that is important, whereas most business people will tell you it is the information part of IT that is crucial to business performance. As Philip Evans and Thomas Wurster, writing in the *Harvard Business Review* of September 1997 put it:

> ... *every business is an information business...information is the glue that holds together the structure of all businesses.*

To enable a business user to communicate effectively with their suppliers of IT, a knowledge of the often bewildering terminology, used to describe the components of IS, and a basic idea of how these components interact is important. To aid understanding, basic concepts and characteristics of IS are reviewed in Chapter 2. Hardware, software, communications and networking technologies are then described in subsequent chapters.

The different aspects of IT are introduced as follows:

- *Chapter 1: Basic concepts – understanding information* provides an introduction to how information is used within a business, introduction to the e-business concept.
- *Chapter 2: Basic concepts – an introduction to business information systems* introduces the different types of BIS and how they can be used to gain strategic advantage.
- *Chapter 3: Hardware* describes the issues in the selection of different hardware components of IS which are used to capture, process, store and output information.
- *Chapter 4: Software* reviews the selection and use of general-purpose applications software such as word processors, spreadsheets and databases, which are often referred to as productivity software.
- *Chapter 5: Networks, telecommunications and the Internet* explains how BIS are linked using telecommunications links which form networks within and between businesses.
- *Chapter 6: E-business applications* explains the concept of e-business in more detail and illustrates how technologies are applied in different types of business. The business applications are considered from several perspectives: how IS support decision making at different levels of the organisation such as at senior management level and an operational level; how IS are used in different functional areas of an organisation to support different processes such as sales order processing, manufacturing or recruitment.

Part 2: Business information systems development

Part 2 focuses on how BIS are acquired and built. A basic understanding of this is necessary to every business user of BIS so that they can appreciate the context of their use of the system and this can be of particular importance when they are involved in testing or using a new system since they will need to understand the reason for introducing new systems as will as their limitations. A more detailed understanding of building BIS is important to users and managers who are responsible for, or are involved in a systems development project. In this case they will need to know the different stages of systems development to help plan the project or work with the developers of the system. They will also need to be aware of the different alternatives for sourcing IS, such as buying pre-written 'off-the-shelf' systems or specially written 'bespoke' systems, to decide which is best for their company or department.

This book provides a reference framework known as the systems development lifecycle which puts all the activities involved with building a system into a business context. Chapters give guidelines on how best to approach system development, giving examples of activities that need to occur in order to avoid any pitfalls and enabling a quality system to be produced which meets the needs of the users and the business. The chapters in Part 2 are sequenced in the order in which activities occur in the systems development lifecycle:

- *Chapter 7: An introduction to acquiring and developing BIS* gives an introduction to alternatives for acquiring new systems. It also introduces the software development lifecycle which acts as a framework for the next chapters.
- *Chapter 8: Initiating systems development* covers the initiation phase of system development when the need for the new system and the feasibility of different development methods are assessed.
- *Chapter 9: BIS project management* describes how project management can be used to ensure the new system is built within the time and budget constraints, while also providing the features and quality required by the business and end-users.
- *Chapter 10: Systems analysis* details system analysis techniques including methods of capturing the requirements for the system, and then summarising them using different diagramming techniques.
- *Chapter 11: Systems design* reviews different aspects of the design of IS from overall architectural or system design to aspects of detailed design, such as database and user interface design.
- *Chapter 12: System build, implementation and maintenance* describes the final stages of a systems development project when the system is released to end-users, following programming, testing and installation, and is then maintained.

Part 3: Business information systems management

Part 3 considers issues involved with the management of IS within an organisation. Of these, probably the most important is ensuring that the strategy defined is consistent with the mission and objectives of the business. Techniques for achieving this are reviewed, together with trends in IS strategy, such as location of IS within a large company and outsourcing IS management to third-party companies. Key issues in implementing the strategy are detailed in the areas of ensuring IS are secure; managing end-user facilities such as desktop PCs, development tools and the help desk; managing a company intranet and its Internet presence and ensuring the company is acting within moral, ethical and legal guidelines.

The chapters are structured as follows:

- *Chapter 13: BIS strategy* stresses the importance of basing the IS strategy on the business strategy and looks at alternative techniques for achieving this. Setting investment levels and locating the IS function are also considered.
- *Chapter 14: Managing e-business* explores strategic issues such as how the Internet is integrated into existing strategy and discusses implementation and operational issues of creating and maintaining service levels such that the competitiveness of business does not suffer through problems with the e-business infrastructure.
- *Chapter 15: Managing information security* describes how information and systems can be protected through controls from threats such as destruction, failure or loss as part of business continuity planning.
- *Chapter 16: End-user computing – providing end-user services* explains why managing use of systems and, in particular, development by end-users is a significant trend in IS.
- *Chapter 17: Ethical, legal and moral constraints on information systems* discusses the importance of protecting personal data and other ethical, moral and legal requirements which must be met by the IS manager.

▶ Who should use this book?

The book discusses key aspects of BIS development and management for students who need to understand the application of IT to assist businesses. It is designed for college students, undergraduate degree and postgraduate students taking courses with modules giving a grounding in the practical IT skills of selection, implementation, management and use of business information systems (BIS). The main types of reader will be:

- *Undergraduates taking general business courses* such as Business Administration and Business Studies or *specialised business courses* such as Accounting, Marketing, Tourism and Human Resources Management.
- *Undergraduates on computer science courses* in Business Information Systems or e-commerce which involve the study of business applications of information technology and the management of the development of IS.
- *Students at college aiming for vocational qualifications* such as the HNC/HND in Business Management or Computer Studies.
- *Postgraduates students on MBA, Certificate in Management, Diploma in Management Studies or specialist masters degrees* which involve courses on information management or IS strategy or electives in e-business and e-commerce.

Managers in industry involved in the development and use of IS who will also find the practical sections in this book of use are:

- *Business analysts* working with customers to identify business problems and propose solutions.
- *Systems analysts and software designers* specifying how the solution will be implemented.
- *'Hands-on' managers* responsible for implementing IT solutions either as a supplier or a client.

▶ What does it offer to lecturers teaching these courses?

The book is intended to be a comprehensive guide to the business applications, development and management of BIS. As such, it can be used across several modules to help integrate different modules. Lecturers will find the book has a good range of excellent case studies to support their teaching. These include industry case studies of the applications of BIS together with problems encountered and simplified practical exercises for systems analysis and design. Web references are given in the text to important information sources for particular topics.

▶ Student learning features

A range of features have been incorporated into this book to help the reader get the most out of it. They have been designed to assist understanding, reinforce learning and help readers find information easily. The features are described in the order you will encounter them.

At the start of each chapter:

- *Chapter introductions*: succinct summaries of why the topic is relevant to the management of IS and its content and structure.
- *Learning objectives*: lists describing what readers should learn through reading the chapters and completing the exercises.
- *Links to other chapters*: a summary of related information in other chapters.

In each chapter:

- *Definitions*: when significant terms are first introduced the main text contains explanations and succinct definitions in the margin for easy reference.
- *Web links*: where appropriate, web addresses are given as reference sources to provide further information on a particular topic. They are provided in the main text where they are directly relevant as well as at the end of the chapter.
- *Case studies*: real-world examples of how technologies are used to support businesses. Case studies are taken from around the world but there is a particular emphasis on the UK and Europe. They are referred to from related material within the text they support. Questions at the end of the case study are intended to highlight the main learning points from each case study.
- *Mini case studies*: short examples which give a more detailed example, or explanation, than is practical in the main text. They do not contain supplementary questions.
- *Activities*: exercises in the main text which give the opportunity to practice and apply the concepts and techniques described in the text.
- *'Focus on' sections*: used to consider topical issues of IS in more detail. Such sections may be used to support the essay or discussion-style questions, or may provide areas for further student research, perhaps giving ideas for student dissertations and projects.
- *Chapter summaries*: intended as revision aids which summarise the main learning points from chapters.

At the end of each chapter:

- *Self-assessment exercises*: short questions which will test understanding of terms and concepts described in the chapters.
- *Discussion questions*: require longer essay-style answers discussing themes from the chapters, and can be used for essays or as debate questions in seminars.
- *Essay questions*: conventional essay questions.
- *Examination questions*: typical short-answer questions which would be encountered in an exam and can also be used for revision.
- *References*: these give details of books, articles or papers referred to within the chapter.
- *Further reading*: supplementary text or papers on the main themes of the chapter. Where appropriate a brief commentary is provided on recommended supplementary reading on the main themes of the chapters.
- *Web links*: extensive lists of relevant web sites and particular articles together with a brief description of what information is available.

At the end of the book:

- *Glossary*: a list of all definitions of key terms and phrases used within the main text.
- *Index*: all key words, abbreviations and authors referred to in the main text.

▶ Support material

The following free supplementary materials are available via the Pearson Education Companion website. This site contains advice, comment, support materials and hyperlinks to reference sites relevant to the text. There is a password-protected area for lecturers only. The web site address is: www.booksites.net/chaffey

References

PricewaterhouseCoopers (2001) Global Data Management Survey 2001. PricewaterhouseCoopers, New York. Available online at: www.pwcglobal.com www.pwcglobal.com/extweb/ncsurvres.nsf/DocID/E68F3408A463BD2980256A180064B96A

Companion website

A Companion website accompanies
BUSINESS INFORMATION SYSTEMS, 2nd edition
by Bocij, Chaffey, Greasley and Hickie

Visit the Business Information Systems Companion website at
www.booksites.net/chaffey to find valuable teaching and learning material
including:

For students
- Study material designed to help you improve your understanding
- Multiple choice questions for every chapter, to help reinforce learning
- A host of links to useful websites, including:
  - professional computing magazines
  - perspectives from industry analysts and management consultants
  - case study materials
- Glossary of key terms in BIS

For lecturers:
- A secure, password protected site with teaching material
- Downloadable PowerPoint slides to assist in lecturing
- A bank of further multiple choice questions for use in student assessment
- Complete, downloadable Lecturer's Guide and teaching Handbook, incorporating:
  - teaching hints for specific materials
  - suggested answers for all assignments in the book
  - further exercises and case studies for tutorial sessions
  - suggested extended assignments

This site will also have a syllabus manager, search functions, and email results functions.

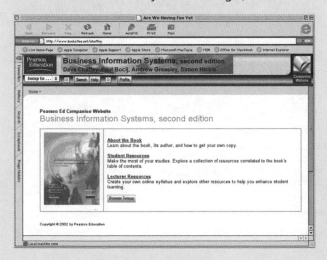

Guided tour

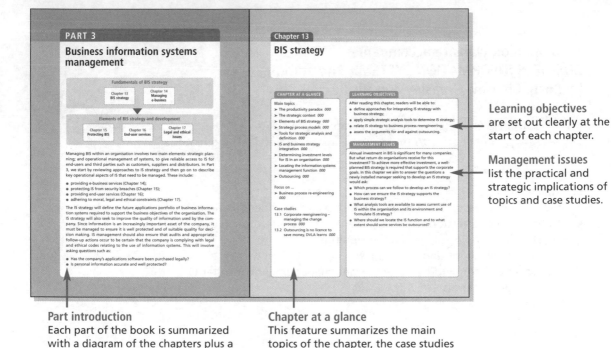

Learning objectives are set out clearly at the start of each chapter.

Management issues list the practical and strategic implications of topics and case studies.

Part introduction
Each part of the book is summarized with a diagram of the chapters plus a brief introduction to the main themes that follow.

Chapter at a glance
This feature summarizes the main topics of the chapter, the case studies and the 'focus on' issues.

Case studies are integrated throughout the text, illustrating topical examples of businesss information systems in practice. Questions reinforce the issues.

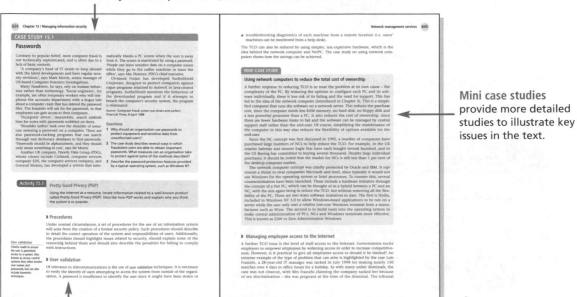

Mini case studies provide more detailed studies to illustrate key issues in the text.

Activites give the opportunity to practice and apply the concepts and techniques described in the text.

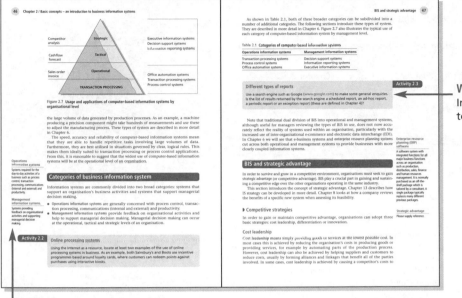

Weblinks
In-text weblinks direct users to relevant websites.

Definitions
explain and define new terms in the margin for easy reference.

Exercises
Self-assessment exercises, discussion questions, essay questions and examinations questions provide extensive opportunities for testing.

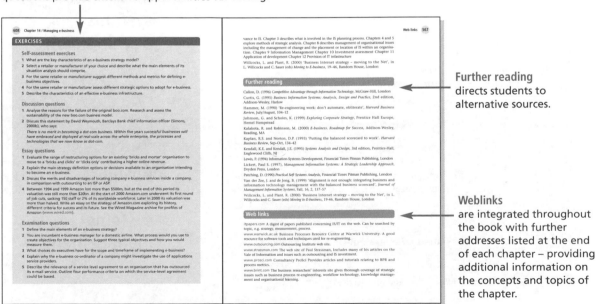

Further reading
directs students to alternative sources.

Weblinks
are integrated throughout the book with further addresses listed at the end of each chapter – providing additional information on the concepts and topics of the chapter.

Plan of the book

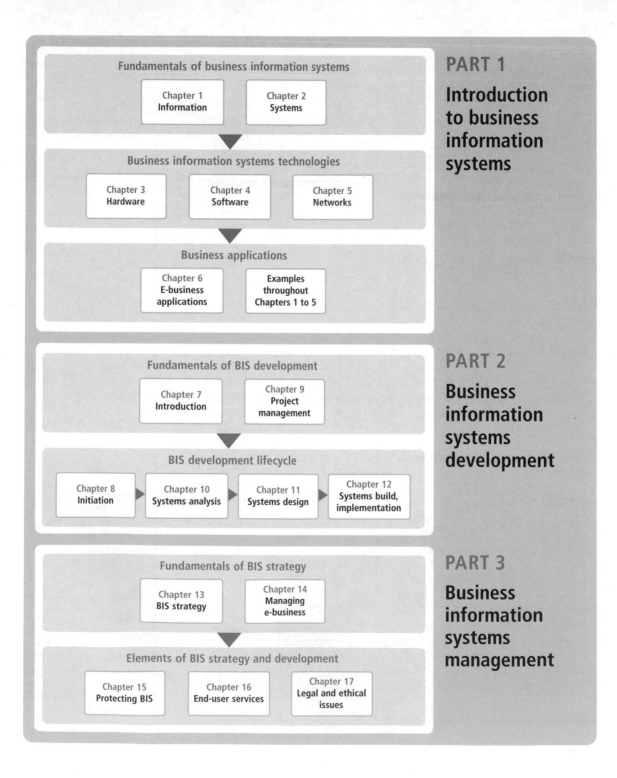

Fundamentals of business information systems

| Chapter 1 Information | Chapter 2 Systems |

Business information systems technologies

| Chapter 3 Hardware | Chapter 4 Software | Chapter 5 Networks |

Business applications

| Chapter 6 E-business applications | Examples throughout Chapters 1 to 5 |

PART 1

Introduction to business information systems

Fundamentals of BIS development

| Chapter 7 Introduction | Chapter 9 Project management |

BIS development lifecycle

| Chapter 8 Initiation | Chapter 10 Systems analysis | Chapter 11 Systems design | Chapter 12 Systems build, implementation |

PART 2

Business information systems development

Fundamentals of BIS strategy

| Chapter 13 BIS strategy | Chapter 14 Managing e-business |

Elements of BIS strategy and development

| Chapter 15 Protecting BIS | Chapter 16 End-user services | Chapter 17 Legal and ethical issues |

PART 3

Business information systems management

About the authors

Dave Chaffey, BSc, PhD, MCIM has extensive experience of working in industry on corporate information systems projects for companies such as Ford Europe, WH Smith, North West Water and the Halifax Bank in roles varying from business/systems analyst, programmer and trainer to project manager. He is currently senior lecturer in Business Information Systems in the Derbyshire Business School at the University of Derby. He is involved in teaching at undergraduate and postgraduate levels including a first-year undergraduate module in Information Systems for Business, HND module in Managing Business Computing, MBA module in Information Management, MSc in Strategic Management and more specialist postgraduate modules in e-business and information strategy and e-commerce communications. Dave has also been course director for Chartered Institute of Marketing seminars in e-marketing since 1997 and is an examiner for the e-marketing professional development award. He is author or co-author of five business books including *Groupware, Workflow and Intranets; Internet Marketing Strategy, Implementation and Practice; E-business and E-commerce Management and eMarketing eXcellence*. Dave has compiled a regularly updated web site of resources at www.marketing-online.co.uk to support students and delegates attending courses and reading these books.

Paul Bocij is a graduate of the University of Nottingham and the University of Derby. He is an experienced lecturer, having worked for a wide variety of institutions, including universities, colleges and numerous commercial organisations. His commercial experience includes time spent in the fields of programming, management, training and consultancy. Some of his previous clients for consultancy services such as technical writing, training and software development include Cashco, British Red Cross, Barclaycard, Ministry of Defence, WROX Press, Bank of Ireland, JCB, Cardiff NHS Trust, Youth Hostels Association and many others. As a professional writer, he has produced or contributed to more than twenty books, including a number of academic texts. In addition, he is the author of numerous articles, magazine columns, academic papers, training guides and other materials related to Information Systems and Information Technology. More recently, he has begun to develop a range of Internet-based learning materials for adult learners and undergraduates. This work has also included co-authorship of the online course that accompanies this book. He is an active researcher and his research interests are largely concerned with the impact of technology on society, with a particular emphasis on deviant forms of behaviour, such as harassment. He is also interested in the use of educational technology in higher education, especially in areas such as the use of computer-based assessment systems. At present, he operates a successful IT service company, specialising in the provision of education, training and technical writing services.

Andrew Greasley is a lecturer in Information Systems, Operational Research and Statistics in the Operations and Information Management Group at Aston Business School, Aston University. His research area is the application of discrete-event simulation modelling for process improvement. He has over ten years' experience of building simulation models for industrial clients in the public and private sectors. He has published papers in journals such as the *International Journal of Operations and Production Management, Journal of the Operational Research Society*, and *SIMULATION*. He is author of the text *Operations Management in Business* published by Nelson Thornes Ltd. He is a member of the European Operations Management Association (EUROMA) and the Society for Computer Simulation International.

Simon Hickie is a senior lecturer in Business Information Systems in the Derbyshire Business School. He studied Economics and Politics at Keele University, and took his PGCE at Leicester University. After teaching Economics for two years, he retrained in 1980 as a commercial computer programmer. During a ten-year career working for a variety of organisations including the NAAFI, Hogg Robinson and Kenner Parker he undertook a variety of roles including analyst programmer, systems programmer, project manager and training consultant, before returning to education in 1990 as a senior lecturer in Information Systems in the department of Mathematics and Computing at the University of Sunderland. He moved to the University of Derby in 1992. He is module leader of the business analysis and systems design and information systems management modules and MSc Strategic Management strategic information management module. In addition to his teaching role, he is also a Senior Academic Counsellor, Head of Operations for the second stage of the University's Combined Subject Programme and Head of Programme for combined business subjects within the Derbyshire Business School.

Acknowledgements

The authors would like to thank the assistance of the team at Pearson Education in the compilation of this book. Thanks also go to the team of reviewers for their constructive comments which have helped develop the book. The book has also been shaped by discussion with colleagues in the Derbyshire Business School and the School of Mathematics and Computing. Valuable feedback has also been obtained from students completing exercises and case studies. We thank everyone who has contributed in this way.

List of reviewers

The following people contributed to the first edition of this book by commenting on the initial plan, or by providing detailed feedback on the entire manuscript:

Linda Charnley	Robert Gordon University
Neil Doherty	Loughborough University
Glenn Hardaker	University of Huddersfield
Alan Hunt	Robert Gordon University
Chris Percy	Oxford Brookes University
David Rowe	Kingston University
Daune West	University of Paisley

For this second edition, in addition to the invaluable feedback provided by a full review panel, the publishers and authors would particularly like to thank the following people for their insightful and constructive feedback on the new manuscript as it was written:

Professor Mogens Kuehn Pedersen	Copenhagen Business School
Rebecca Chandler-Wilde	Lead Tutor, Henley Management College
Lisa Jackson	Lecturer at the Department of Informatics, Halmstad University
Roger Hammond	Senior Lecturer, University of Gloucester Business School

Publisher's acknowledgements

We are grateful to the following for permission to reproduce copyright material:

Figure 1.0 reproduced from Figure 3 from Chapter 3 from 'World Economic Outlook The Information Technology Revolution, October 2001', in World Economic and Financial Surveys, http://www.imf.org/external/pubs/ft/weo/2001/pdf/chapter3.pdf, International Monetary Fund (2001); Table 5.4 adapted and republished with permission from CRC Press LLC from 'Road Map to the E-Revolution', Kampas, P.J., in Information Systems Management, Vol. 17, No.3, 2001, Auerbach Publications, permission conveyed through Copyright Clearance Center, Inc.; Figure 6.7 reproduced from 'Percentage of online purchasers who have bought category online in the 6 months to November 2001', from The Internet Monitor, BMRB, November 2001, Copyright © 2001 BMRB International; Figures 6.8 and 6.9 reproduced from 'E-Commerce Inquiry to Business', in E-Commerce and Business, 29 'Economic trends' No. 572, July 2001, Office for National Statistics, (Williams, M., 2001), © Crown Copyright 2001. Crown Copyright material is reproduced with the permission of the Controller of Her Majesty's Stationery Office and the Queen's Printer for Scotland; Figures 6.26 and 6.27 reproduced from screenshots of a PowerPlay demonstration (2002), from www.cognos.com, reproduced by kind permission of Cognos, Copyright © 2002 Cognos Incorporated; Figure 11.26 reproduced from screenshot of RS Components Web Site, www.rswww.com, Copyright © 2000 RS Components Ltd.; Figure 11.30 reproduced from screenshot of Sainsbury's to You Web site, www.sainsburystoyou.co.uk, reproduced by kind permission of Sainsbury's Supermarkets Ltd., Copyright © 2000 Sainsbury's Supermarkets Ltd., Figure 11.31 reproduced from screenshot of Cisco Systems website, 'Cisco Connection Online', at www.cisco.com. These materials have been reproduced by Pearson Education with the permission of Cisco Systems, Inc. COPYRIGHT © CISCO SYSTEMS, INC. ALL RIGHTS RESERVED; Titles of Figures 11.26, 11.28, 11.30 & 11.31 from Figures 11.11, 11.14, 11.16 & 11.17 from E-Business and E-Commerce Management, Pearson Education, (Chaffey, D., 2001); Table 13.2 from ITNET survey 'UK Outsourcing Market by Sector', from ITNET Index, www.itnetplc.com, ITNET plc (1999); Table 13.4 adapted from '1998 Global Survey of Chief Information Executives', Deloitte Consulting Group, (1998); Table 13.5 reprinted from Long Range Planning, October 1995, Vol. 28, No. 5, Feeney, D., Fitzgerald, G., and Willcocks, L., 'Outsourcing IT: The Strategic Implications', pp. 59–71, Copyright © 1995 Elsevier Science, with permission from Elsevier Science; Table in Ch 13, p. 82 adapted from 'Top 10 Reasons Companies Outsource', 'Survey of Current and Potential End-Users, The Outsourcing Institute Membership, 1998', 'Top Ten Outsourcing Survey', http://www.outsourcing.com, reproduced by kind permission of The Outsourcing Institute, Copyright © 1998 The Outsourcing Institute, Jericho, NY; Table 14.7 from table 'Variation in download and availability of top UK sites, February 2002, from www.keynote.com and Keynote Europe Ltd., Copyright © 2002 Keynote Systems Inc. Keynote Systems Inc. (Nasdaq "KEYN"), The Internet Performance Authority®, is the world wide leader in Internet performance services that enable corporate enterprises to monitor, benchmark, test diagnose and improve the quality of service of their e-business applications. Keynote Systems, Inc. was founded in 1995 and is headquartered in San Mateo, California. The European headquarter is based in London; Table 15.1 from table from 'Why do we need controls? A catalogue of major computer-related security incidents for 2000', in Computer Weekly, 11 January 2001, Reed Business Information, Copyright © 2001 Reed Business Information.

British Computer Society for an extract from their Code of Conduct; Commerce One for an extract of XML that appears on their web site; Reed Business Information Limited for extracts from Computer Weekly; and VNU Business Publications for an extract from 'Focus on corporate re-engineering – managing the change process' by David Harvey, published in Computing, 1st October 1996.

In some instances we have been unable to trace the owners of copyright material, and we would appreciate any information that would enable us to do so.

PART 1

Introduction to business Information systems

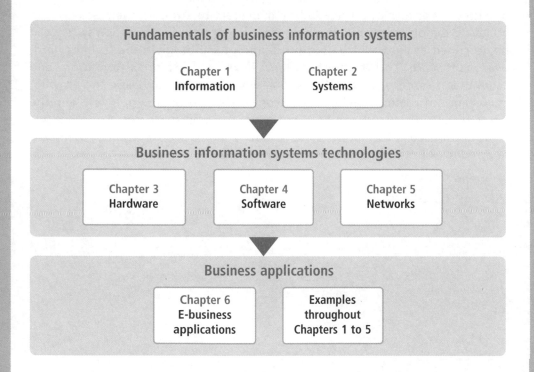

Fundamentals of business information systems

| Chapter 1 Information | Chapter 2 Systems |

Business information systems technologies

| Chapter 3 Hardware | Chapter 4 Software | Chapter 5 Networks |

Business applications

| Chapter 6 E-business applications | Examples throughout Chapters 1 to 5 |

When beginning the study of the use of information systems (IS) in business, it is important to understand a number of concepts drawn from a variety of different fields. In order to create, improve and manage business information systems (BIS), one must combine an understanding of information, systems concepts, business organisations and information technology (IT). Part 1 is intended as an introductory section to IS which provides a background supporting further study in Parts 2 and 3. In addition to explaining basic terms and concepts, Part 1 shows, through examples in Chapters 3, 4, 5 and 6, why IS are vital to business today. The role of BIS in transforming organisations through the application of electronic commerce and electronic business is also introduced in Part 1 in chapters 1, 5, and 6.

Understanding the terms and components that define IS is necessary in order that business users can communicate with the IT suppliers building and maintaining their systems. All systems involve transforming inputs such as data into outputs such as information by a transformation process. The UK Academy for Information Systems defines information systems as follows:

> *Information systems are the means by which organisations and people, using information technologies, gather, process, store, use and disseminate information.*

In simpler terms, a business information system can be described as a system that provides the information needed by managers to support their activities in achieving the objectives of a business. A computer-based information system can be described as an IS which uses information technology in the form of hardware, software and communications links. The term information and communication technology (ICT) is sometimes used to emphasise the growing importance of communications technology such as local area networks and the Internet. Note that an IS can be paper-based or computer-based. For simplicity, computer-based information systems and business information systems are referred to as BIS throughout this book.

Chapter 1

Basic concepts – understanding information

LEARNING OBJECTIVES

After reading this chapter, readers will be able to:
- distinguish between data, information and knowledge;
- describe and evaluate information quality in terms of its characteristics;
- classify decisions by type and organisational level;
- identify the information needed to support decisions made at different organisational levels.

MANAGEMENT ISSUES

The purpose of business information systems (BIS) is to produce high-quality information that can be used to support the activities of an organisation and its business partners. In order to gain a good understanding of BIS, managers must first understand the nature of information and how effective decisions are made. From a managerial perspective, this chapter addresses the following areas:

- the importance of managing information and knowledge as a key organisational asset.
- the transformation process from data to information of high quality;
- the process and constraints of decision making;
- the different kinds of decisions that managers make and how these affect the organisation.

Links to other chapters

Chapter 2	builds upon the concepts described within this chapter and introduces new ideas, such as BIS.
Chapter 6	gives examples of how decision support systems assist decision making.
Chapter 10	describes the techniques used in analysing information flows within an organisation.
Chapter 13	reviews the ways in which information systems can support an organisation's business strategy.
Chapter 15	considers techniques for increasing the security of information.

Introduction

The general aim of this chapter is to introduce readers to the basic concepts needed to gain a thorough understanding of business information systems (BIS). However, before looking at BIS themselves, it is important to understand something of the nature of information. For BIS to be effective, the quality of information provided is vital. In this chapter we look at how we can assess and improve the quality of data and information. The topics covered are intended to give readers an understanding of:

● the nature of data, information and knowledge;
● the value of information;
● the characteristics that can be used to describe information quality;
● information in the context of the e-business environment;
● managerial decision making, including the characteristics of decisions at different organisational levels;
● the information needed to support decision making.

Data and information

Much of a manager's work involves ensuring information flows in an organisation are efficient and using information to make decisions. Increasingly, this information is captured in digital form by BIS and is shared throughout the organisation and beyond. Many organisations are active in learning how best to use this information to achieve competitive advantage. Bill Gates has said: '*I think people still underestimate in the decade ahead how much digital approaches will change the way they work and the way they live*' (Gates, 2001). In this chapter we provide an insight into the natures of data, information and knowledge to provide a foundation for how we can harness them through BIS.

▶ What is data?

Data

A collection of non-random facts recorded by observation or research.

Data are raw facts or observations that are considered to have little or no value until they have been processed and transformed into information. Unrelated items of data are considered to be essentially without meaning and are often described as 'noise'. It is only when data has been placed in some form of context that it becomes meaningful to a manager.

There are several definitions for data that are in common use:

(a) *a series of non-random symbols, numbers, values or words;*
(b) *a series of facts obtained by observation or research and recorded;*
(c) *a collection of non-random facts;*
(d) *the record of an event or fact.*

> **Examples of data include:**
> - today's date;
> - measurements taken on a production line;
> - records of a business transactions such as a single visit to a web site.

Data can exist naturally or can be created artificially. Naturally occurring data need only to be recorded. Managers have to put in place procedures and tools to ensure data are recorded. For example, to ensure a call centre operator includes the postcode of every customer this can be written into their script and a validation check performed to check these data have been entered into the system.

Artificial data are often produced as a by-product of a business process. Processing an organisation's accounts, for example, might produce the number of sales made in a particular month.

 ▶ **What is information?**

As with the concept of data, there are several definitions of information that are in common use:

(a) *data that have been processed so that they are meaningful;*
(b) *data that have been processed for a purpose;*
(c) *data that have been interpreted and understood by the recipient.*

Information
Data that have been processed so that they are meaningful.

Three important points can be drawn from these definitions. First, there is a clear and logical process that is used to produce information. This process involves collecting data and then subjecting them to a **transformation process** in order to create information. The concept of a transformation process will be discussed in more detail in the next section. Secondly, information involves placing data in some form of meaningful context, so that they can be understood and acted upon. Thirdly, information is produced for a purpose, to serve an **information need** of some kind. The concept of an information need is described in more detail later on.

Transformation process
A transformation process is used to convert inputs into outputs.

Information need
Information is produced to meet a specific purpose or requirement.

> **Some examples of information include:**
> - a bank statement;
> - a sales forecast;
> - a telephone directory;
> - graphs of trends in visitor numbers to a web site.

A somewhat different view of information can be examined by introducing an additional definition:

Information acts to reduce uncertainty about a situation or event.

Although uncertainty can never be eliminated entirely, it can be *reduced* significantly. Information can help to eliminate some possibilities or make others seem more likely. Managerial decision making can be improved by using information to reduce uncertainty. Information is said to influence decision behaviour, the way in which people make decisions. Managerial decision making is dealt with in more detail in a later section.

To summarise the key points made in the preceding section. Information:

- involves transforming data using a defined process;
- involves placing data in some form of meaningful context;
- is produced in response to an information need and therefore serves a specific purpose;
- helps to reduce uncertainty, thereby improving decision behaviour.

Creating information

Processing data is necessary to place them into a meaningful context so that they can be easily understood by the recipient. Figure 1.1 illustrates the conversion of data into information.

Data process

A process used to convert data into information. Examples include summarising, classifying and sorting.

A number of different **data processes** can be used to transform data into information. Data processes are sometimes also known as 'transformation processes'. The next section describes a range of common data processes.

▶ Data processes

Some examples of data processes include the following:

- *Classification.* This involves placing data into categories, for example categorising an expense as either a fixed or a variable cost.
- *Rearranging/sorting.* This involves organising data so that items are grouped together or placed into a particular order. Employee data, for example, might be sorted according to last name or payroll number.
- *Aggregating.* This involves summarising data, for example by calculating averages, totals or subtotals.
- *Performing calculations.* An example might be calculating an employee's gross pay by multiplying the number of hours worked by the hourly rate of pay.
- *Selection.* This involves choosing or discarding items of data based on a set of selection criteria. A sales organisation, for example, might create a list of potential customers by selecting those with incomes above a certain level.

It is worth noting that any action that serves to place data into a meaningful context can be considered a valid data process. In addition, several processes may be used in combination to produce information.

Figure 1.1 Transforming data into information using a data process

Activity 1.1

Data v information

From the point of view of a student at university, which of the following might be examples of information? Which might be examples of data?

(a) the date
(b) a bank statement
(c) the number 1355.76
(d) a National Insurance number
(e) a balance sheet
(f) a bus timetable
(g) a car registration plate

▶ Value of information

It is often possible to measure the value of information directly. The **tangible value** of information is often measured in terms of financial value. An example might be the use of inventory information to improve stock control procedures. A simple calculation can be used to determine the value of a given item or collection of information:

Value of information – Cost of gathering information

However, in many cases, it is not possible to calculate the value of information directly. Although it is certain that the information is of benefit to the owner, it is difficult – or even impossible – to quantify its value. In such cases, the information is said to have **intangible value**. A good example might involve attempting to measure the extent to which information can improve decision behaviour. Such a calculation might appear as shown below:

Improvements in decision behaviour – Cost of gathering information

There can be little doubt that the ability to make better decisions can be of great value to any organisation. However, one cannot readily quantify any improvements in decision making since a large number of other factors must also be taken in account. We will see in later chapters that this makes performing a cost–benefit analysis for BIS difficult (Chapters 8, 13).

Tangible value
A value or benefit that can be measured directly, usually in monetary terms.

Intangible value
A value or benefit that is difficult or impossible to quantify.

Activity 1.2

Tangible and intangible information

When information is used effectively, it can bring about many of the improvements listed below. State and explain why each of the items listed illustrates a tangible or intangible value of information.

(a) improved inventory control;
(b) enhanced customer service;
(c) increased production;
(d) reduced administration costs;
(e) greater customer loyalty;
(f) enhanced public image.

Activity 1.3	Information value
	Using the Internet as a resource, find three case studies of the value of information in the context of a business organisation. As an example, you might locate a news story in *Computer Weekly* (www.cw360.com) describing the savings made as a result of implementing a new stock control system.

◗ Sources of information

Formal communication

Formal communication involves presenting information in a structured and consistent manner.

Informal communication

This describes less well structured information that is transmitted by informal means, such as casual conversations between members of staff.

BIS should support both formal and informal communication. **Formal communications** can include reports and accounting statements. **Informal communications** can include conversations and notes.

Formal communication

Information transmitted by formal communication tends to be presented in a consistent manner. Company reports, for example, will often use the same basic format. This allows the recipient to locate items of interest quickly and easily. Since formal communications tend to be presented in a more structured manner, they are also more likely to present a more comprehensive view of the situations or circumstances they describe. In addition, the information transmitted in this way is likely to be accurate and relevant, since it is normally created for a specific purpose.

> BIS can be used to help apply a 'house style' for standard documents. Memos, reports and other documents are produced by making use of the templates that are found in most modern word processing packages. These templates contain the basic structure of a given document and what information to include and exclude and can be compared to completing a standard form.

However, formal communication also has several disadvantages. The structure imposed on information is often inflexible, sometimes limiting its type, form and content. In addition, formal communications often overlook information obtained by informal means. This can affect the decision-making process, reducing the quality and accuracy of any decisions made. Finally, formal communications often ignore group and social mechanisms. A formal report, for example, might marginalise or ignore staff opinions, causing offence and leading to reduced morale.

Informal communication

Informal communication is always present in an organisation, regardless of its size or nature. Information of this kind can be considered a valuable resource and one of the aims of knowledge management (described later in this chapter) is to harness it to work for the benefit of the organisation. Perhaps the most common means by which informal communication takes place is by word of mouth. In a sales organisation, for example, a casual conversation between a salesperson and a client might yield information that can be used to enhance a product or find new ways of making it more attractive to customers. If this information is not recorded the feedback will not be available to the new product development group.

Informal communication tends to offer a high degree of flexibility since there is more freedom to choose how information is structured and presented. Information

Informal communication

Consider the role of informal communication within an organisation such as a local government department or hospital.

1 In what ways can informal communication support the day-to-day activities of the organisation?
2 How important is the role of informal communication within the organisation? Could the organisation function effectively if informal communication was restricted?
3 How can informal communication be controlled or harnessed for the benefit of the organisation?
4 What negative results might occur if overly strict controls are imposed upon informal communication?

obtained in this way also tends to be highly detailed, although it may often contain inaccuracies and may not be entirely relevant.

The scope of information obtained in this way is often very narrow, relevant only to localised problems and situations. However, even at a local level, this can improve problem solving and decision making since it allows managers to gain a more detailed and in-depth understanding of a given situation.

One of the major disadvantages of informal communication is that it cannot deal with large volumes of information. Furthermore, as a means of communication, it is relatively slow and inefficient. Informal communication can also be highly selective, for example a person taking part in a conversation may be able to restrict what information is transmitted and who is able to receive it.

Case Study 1.1 considers how the Boots company uses customer information to improve the products and services offered to the public. The adoption of **customer relationship management** (CRM) techniques demonstrates how information gathered during the course of a company's usual business can be used to increase profitability whilst also making sure that customer needs are met more closely.

Customer relationship management (CRM)
A company aims to achieve long-term business relationships with its customers for mutual benefit.

CASE STUDY 1.1

Boots Insight team analyse customer data

Boots is nurturing its customers by strengthening its commitment to its Advantage Card loyalty scheme and launching a joint venture health e-business, Digital Wellbeing. Lindsay Nicolle reports:

'Being able to accurately monitor, interpret, second-guess or even know precisely the ins and outs of every customer's shopping behaviour is a retailer's dream. The first step along this road is to put in place appropriate IT systems and business processes and then follow up with multimedia, multi-channel communications with customers to ultimately create a personalised sales relationship.'

Boots the Chemist is in hot pursuit of this nirvana – but not in reaction to the rise of so-called customer relationship management (CRM), argues senior IT project manager Ian Radmore.

Radmore calls CRM 'a red herring'. 'Boots was becoming customer-centric long before the CRM buzzword came along', he says. 'CRM is only about developing the business so that it pays more than lip service to what the customer wants and still makes money, and that's always been as true for us as for anyone. It's just good business sense.'

Radmore adds, 'We will become more multimedia and multi-contact in our relationship with customers through phones, digital TV and the Internet but that's only because it's the kind of communication that customers are going to want with us, and it's a while away yet. Customers don't suddenly migrate overnight – it's a cultural thing. But it's certainly something we think about in relation to our in-store kiosks – how they can be tied in with other activities.'

Boots' network of Advantage Point in-store kiosks housed in some 380 stores nationwide, delivers personalised offers to Advantage Card holders. The loyalty scheme is a strong foundation on which Boots can build a knowledgeable and mutually satisfying relationship with its customers.

The card was launched nationally in 1997 and in its first 18 months had a 4% impact on the retailer's sales. Today, of Boots' 27 million customers, more than 12 million are Advantage Card holders and 10 million are active users. These customers account for more than 40% of transactions in Boots' 1,400 chemist shops and 300 Boots Opticians UK stores. On average, cardholders spend 50% more than non-cardholders.

Crawford Davidson, head of Boots Advantage Card, says, 'Having introduced the Advantage Point kiosks, we must now look forward and see how we can replicate that contact in a multimedia, multicontact environment. Ultimately, the customer will be the one to select the way in which he or she chooses to contact the brand.'

In September 2000, Boots strengthened its commitment to its card and to mining customer loyalty for mutual benefit with the launch of a combined credit and loyalty smartcard supported by Egg. The card was the first of its type in Europe, with smart chip technology managing the Advantage Card loyalty scheme and simultaneous Europay, Mastercard and Visa payment.

The smartcard presents new opportunities for electronic marketing through Boots' in-store kiosks. Customers can add the points earned on their credit card to their loyalty account, and service their accounts.

In an initiative designed to export the Boots brand to new media and reach customers in new ways, last month the company officially announced an e-business joint venture with Granada Media – the formation of an independent Internet and broadband company designed to be Britain's leading e-business for health, beauty and well-being.

The new company, called Digital Wellbeing, also provides an interactive forum for individuals to exchange personal experience and consult experts online, on air and by phone.

The market for health and beauty products is one of the world's largest growth areas. In the UK alone, and excluding the National Health Service, sales of health and beauty products and services amount to £11bn a year, according to research by Verdict.

By creating a strong new media contender in consumer health and beauty in the UK and with 10,000 products available, Wellbeing intends to become the natural platform for all those with an interest in wellbeing, including professional associations, government bodies, commercial organisations and interest groups.

Wellbeing was launched with an information and transactional Web site together with an interactive digital television channel. Described as a personalised health service, it enables customers to enjoy secure delivery of information, services and products through whatever access service they choose, be it digital TV, PC or laptop and, as they develop, mobile and handheld devices.

As broadband technology becomes available to every home and office, Wellbeing will increasingly integrate the TV channel with the Web site, adding to the interactivity and offering a growing range of products and personalised services, says Boots.

Sixty per cent of the new venture is owned by Boots with Granada Media taking the rest, and its operating cost in the first year to 31 March 2001 is expected to be £18m.

Steve Russell, chief executive of Boots, says, 'This new, innovative company will be Boots' primary initiative in consumer e-commerce. Within a few years, we would anticipate new revenues equivalent to around 2% of Boots the Chemists' current UK sales. In the digital world, we will create a store of unlimited scale, going far beyond our current offer.'

Revenues will flow from the sale of products and services, from broadcast and online advertising and from TV programmes and online sponsorship.

Meanwhile, the data on customer buying behaviour that Wellbeing will generate will be pooled with that gathered from traditional in-store card transactions, other anonymous point-of-sale data and third-party data from Experian. Together these inputs will provide invaluable, 3D-style insights into what customers want from the company.

Boots has a special Insight team, a group of 25 people dedicated to analysing data gathered from card transactions and skilled in customer segmentation, clustering and predictive modelling. They use Boots' Customer Data Analysis System (CDAS) to help the retailer delve into new areas of business, provide further information points and enhance product offerings.

Using the IBM-based business intelligence solution, the team knows which customers buy more products, the demographics of high purchasing customer segments and specific patterns among customers, as well as subtle data, such as specific moments when customer behaviour can be positively influenced.

'Discerning which customers have the potential to become more valuable is a complex and interesting area our new system has opened up', says Helen James, head of customer and marketing insight.

But proving the value of such insights is a hard thing to measure, admits Radmore. 'It's extremely

▶

difficult, but the number of things the Insight team is increasingly getting involved in probably demonstrates how much value it has to the business in terms of helping the decision-making process,' Radmore says. 'It's a very important support tool.'

The team's work has already reaped rewards in photographic sales, says Radmore. 'We targeted kiosk offers at different types of usage to encourage broader take-up of photographic offers and that's been quite successful. Also – and significantly for CRM – when we have to do product recalls, we can easily identify individual purchasers, which means we can provide a comprehensive service: not something we could do otherwise.'

The way Boots merchandises its stores plays a big part in drawing customers in and keeping them there. To this end, customer data has been used to reveal which product categories contain 'hooks' and which are mainly 'basket fillers'. Boots has used Advantage Card analysis to understand the role of its store categories and whether they attract people to the store or encourage customers to fill their baskets once inside the particular location.

Armed with actionable data, Boots then makes informed decisions about category strategies while the Insight team links specific tactics to the overall corporate marketing strategy.

'Although we're still refining our approach, we're consistent in thinking of categories as a means of making shopping easier and more orderly', says James. 'In the long run, we think this philosophy will help us with customer retention and value.'

With the help of business intelligence capabilities, Boots has created a model that looks at financial impacts as well as customer behaviour. This will help the Insight team entice existing customers to spend more money on items and products that they already buy, as well as determine which customers have the potential to buy from new categories. The idea is to understand how customers shop and which products should be linked to promote additional purchases.

'One of the techniques we use involves determining the items that people tend to buy at the same time and using that knowledge to position products in the store', says Radmore.

'Making shopping easy and intuitive for customers is the goal. We've determined which products logically fit together and, in some cases, which offerings might be eliminated from the product mix and layout all together.'

By designing retail stores based on the buying behaviour of Boots' most valuable customer segment, the team hopes to encourage top customers to continue buying and to positively impact the behaviour of other customer segments. In addition, the information gathered about what increases customer value and lifts customer spending will be used to target marketing to specific customer segments.

The information generated by the team has also made additional and important strides in helping Boots deal with its supply chain. Boots' marketeers and buyers now have more informed conversations with suppliers about the customers who buy their products.

'Three communities of users at Boots access the data contained in the CDAS system – the team of analysts access the data regularly and deeply, the direct marketing team uses the database to create lists of people for particular campaigns and the category teams are able to access customer data to help with everyday decision-making, such as product development and promotional activity', says Radmore.

'Actionable data is accessible to key decision makers – extending the impact of the data beyond the outputs that a team of analysts can provide', adds Radmore

The system supplies flexible, structured reports to more than 70 business end-users, who use the data to perform their own analysis and track their own initiatives.

DSS Agent from MicroStrategy and BI/Query from Andyne are used for most queries. Eventually, CDAS will hold 1 Tbyte of data, including more than two years of individual cardholder transaction records and a selection of non-cardholder sales records.

Boots still has some way to go to create a multi-channel, multi-contact CRM-style system that is end-to-end across the business. But the foundations being laid are wide-ranging and rooted in a strategy to improve customer service, not just to apply technology for technology's sake.

The company sees good business as making choices to enhance the shopping experience – but if its strategy also boosts profits at the expense of diverse competitors, that will also be welcome.

Source: Lindsay Nicolle, 'Interactive being', courtesy of *Computer Weekly*, 2 May 2001

Questions

Conduct any additional research needed and then answer the following questions.

1 Why do some consider customer relationship management (CRM) a 'red herring'?

2 Advantage and Digital Wellbeing allow Boots to collect a great deal of information about customers. What benefits does the company gain from this information?

3 How do customers benefit from allowing Boots to gather information about them?

Qualities of information

Information can be said to have a number of different characteristics that can be used to describe its quality. The differences between 'good' and 'bad' information can be identified by considering whether or not it has some or all of the **attributes of information quality**.

Lucey (1997) provides a list of characteristics likely to be present in information considered to be of good quality. However, others, such as O'Brien (2001), take a more organised approach and describe the attributes of information quality as being divided into three basic categories: time, content and form. Table 1.1 summarises information characteristics that can be used to assess quality. Note that each column is independent; reading down each column lists the attributes associated with a particular factor.

Attributes of information quality
A group of characteristics by which the quality of information can be assessed, normally grouped into categories of time, content and form.

Table 1.1 **Summary of attributes of information quality**

Time	Content	Form	Additional characteristics
Timeliness	Accuracy	Clarity	Confidence in source
Currency	Relevance	Detail	Reliability
Frequency	Completeness	Order	Appropriate
Time period	Conciseness	Presentation	Received by correct person
	Scope	Media	Sent by correct channels

◗ Time dimension

Time dimension
Characteristics of information quality such as timeliness, currency and frequency which are related to the time of collection and review.

The **time dimension** describes the time period that the information deals with and the frequency at which the information is received.

● *Timeliness*. The information should be available when needed. If information is provided too early, it may no longer be current when used. If the information is supplied too late, it will be of no use.
● *Currency*. The information should reflect current circumstances when provided. One can go further and suggest that in addition to being up-to-date the information should also indicate those areas or circumstances liable to change by the time the information is used.
● *Frequency*. In addition to being available when needed, information should also be available as often as needed. This normally means that information should be supplied at regular intervals, for example, some organisations may require weekly sales reports whilst others need only monthly reports.
● *Time period*. The information should cover the correct time period. A sales forecast, for example, might include information concerning past performance, current performance and predicted performance so that the recipient has a view of past, present and future circumstances.

◗ Content dimension

Content dimension
Characteristics of information quality such as accuracy, relevance and conciseness which are related to the scope and contents of the information.

The **content dimension** describes the scope and contents of the information.

● *Accuracy*. Information that contains errors has only limited value to an organisation.
● *Relevance*. The information supplied should be relevant to a particular situation and should meet the information needs of the recipient. Extraneous detail can compromise other attributes of information quality, such as conciseness.

- *Completeness*. All of the information required to meet the information needs of the recipient should be provided. Incomplete information can compromise other attributes of information quality, such as scope and accuracy.
- *Conciseness*. Only information relevant to the information needs of the recipient should be supplied. In addition, the information should be provided in the most compact form possible. As an example, sales figures are normally provided in the form of a graph or table – it would be unusual for them to be supplied as a descriptive passage of text.
- *Scope*. The scope of the information supplied should be appropriate to the information needs of the recipient. The recipient's information needs will determine whether the information should concern organisational or external situations and whether it should focus on a specific area or provide a more general overview.

◗ Form dimension

The form dimension describes how the information is presented to the recipient.

Form dimension
Characteristics of information quality related to how the information is presented to the recipient.

- *Clarity*. The information should be presented in a form that is appropriate to the intended recipient. The recipient should be able to locate specific items quickly and should be able to understand the information easily.
- *Detail*. The information should contain the correct level of detail in order to meet the recipient's information needs. For example, in some cases highly detailed information will be required whilst in others only a summary will be necessary.
- *Order*. Information should be provided in the correct order. As an example, management reports normally contain a brief summary at the beginning. This allows a manager to locate and understand the most important aspects of the report before examining it at a high level of detail.
- *Presentation*. The information should be presented in a form that is appropriate to the intended recipient. Different methods can be used to make information clearer and more accessible to the recipient, for example it is common to present numerical information in the form of a graph or table.
- *Media*. Information should be presented using the correct media. Formal information, for example, is often presented in the form of a printed report, whereas a presentation might make use of a slide projector.

◗ Additional characteristics

In addition to the attributes described above, one might also add several others.

Of particular importance is *confidence* in the source of the information received. Recipients are more likely to accept and trust the information they obtain if it is received from a source that has been accurate and reliable in the past.

A further attribute of information quality is that of *reliability*. It can be argued that recipients should be confident that they can rely upon information being available when required and that the information will be of a consistent quality in terms of other attributes of information quality, such as accuracy and conciseness.

The widespread use of computer-based information systems raises a number of issues related to the sheer quantity of information that is freely available via sources such as the Internet. In addition, the use of computer-based information systems also raises concerns in relation to security. In view of this, one might suggest that a further attribute of information quality is that the information provided should be *appropriate* to the recipient's activities. This might restrict information from being supplied if it is of a confidential nature or beyond the duties or responsibilities of a person's role.

It also seems natural to suggest that some confirmation that the information has been *received by the correct person* is required. Unless the information has been received and acted upon, then it is of no value. Thus, it can be suggested that an additional attribute of information quality is that it can be verified that the information has been received and understood.

Finally, it can be argued that another attribute of information quality is that that information should be capable of being transmitted via the *correct channels*. Most organisations have formal policies and procedures for dealing with particular situations. For example, a complaint against a member of staff is normally presented in a written form and travels upwards through the management hierarchy until it is received by the correct person. If the information were to be sent in any other way, for example by word of mouth, it might not reach its destination or might become garbled during the journey.

Activity 1.5   **Information quality**

Visit the web sites of two different online booksellers. For each example, assess whether the information provided about a particular book is of 'good' or 'poor' quality. Explain your reasoning with reference to the characteristics of information described in this chapter, and in particular Table 1.1. Does the information provided differentiate between the offerings of the companies?

The business environment

All business organisations operate within an environment that influences the way in which the organisation operates. Legislation, for example, will act to control some of the organisation's activities. However, the actions of an organisation may also influence parts of the environment. For example, companies may launch an advertising campaign designed to draw customers away from a competitor. John Browning, writing in *The Economist* in 1990, acknowledged that IT had gone far beyond being a support service, but had become part of the environment when he wrote:

> *Information Technology is no longer a business resource; it has become the business environment.*

Figure 1.2 illustrates some of the elements that may influence the way in which an organisation operates. For managers, utilising information about the external environment is vital to decision making. BIS need to provide information from both the micro-environment and the macro-environment.

▶ Internal business resources

Business resource base
The resources that a company has available to it which are made up of physical and conceptual resources known as tangible and intangible assets.

To operate within the business environment, organisations use a **business resource base** which supports their activities. The resource base consists of tangible or physical resources and intangible or conceptual resources.

BIS can be applied to make best use of physical and conceptual resources to help an organisation to reduce costs, improve productivity and enhance overall efficiency.

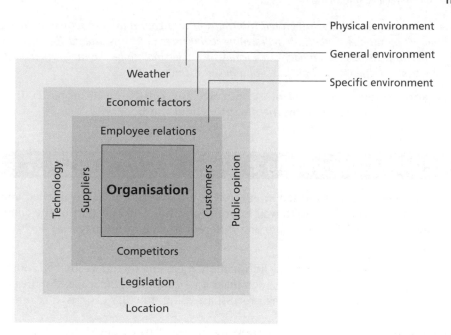

Figure 1.2 **The business environment of an organisation and the main factors that influence it**

◗ Tangible assets (physical resource base)

Physical resources are often known as *tangible assets* and are normally directed towards the production of a product or service. Examples of physical resources include money, land, plant and labour power. The hardware and software comprising BIS are also physical resources

Physical resources
....
Tangible assets or resources owned by a company such as land, buildings and plant.

◗ Intangible assets (conceptual resource base)

Conceptual resources are often known as *intangible assets* and are normally used to support an organisation's activities, for example by helping managers to make better decisions. Examples of intangible resources include experience, motivation, knowledge, ideas and judgement. The data and information that is part of a BIS (business information system) are a valuable intangible resource which must be protected.

Conceptual resources
....
Non-physical resources or intangible assets owned by a company, such as organisational knowledge.

> Intangible assets on average account for over 20% of the market capitalisation of UK high-technology companies, according to a study by Taylor Johnson Garrett, a City law firm.
>
> *Source*: Courtesy of *Computer Weekly*, 22 March 2001

◗ The e-business concept

Increasingly, business communications both within an organisation and between an organisation and its environment are achieved through BIS. This has given rise to the concept of e-business. E-business involves increasing the efficiency of information flows and business processes within an organisation and with other partners such as customers, suppliers, distributors and other intermediaries. The UK Department of Trade and Industry (2000) explains e-business as follows:

Electronic business (e-business)
....
All electronically mediated information exchanges, both within an organisation and with external stakeholders supporting the range of business processes.

> [W]hen a business has fully integrated information and communications technologies (ICTs) into its operations, potentially redesigning its business processes around ICT or completely reinventing its business model ... e-business is understood to be the integration of all these activities with the internal processes of a business through ICT.

E-business and the related concept of e-commerce are considered in more detail in Chapters 2, 5 and 6 and are common themes throughout this book.

Managerial decision making

In order for an organisation to function effectively, all activities must be planned and monitored by managers according to well-informed decisions. In this part of the chapter we review the role of BIS in supporting different aspects of managerial decision making as follows:

1 An introduction to how managers use information, including their decision behaviour.
2 The three key levels of managerial decision making – operational, tactical and strategic.
3 A description of the decision-making process, assessing how BIS can assist at different stages of this process.
4 A section on decision-making theory showing how structured decisions can be formally described in order to incorporate them into BIS.
5 The final section on knowledge management illustrating how businesses are looking to manage information that can be used to assist less clearly structured decision making.

▶ The information requirements of managers

Henri Fayol (1841–1925) devised a classic definition of management that is still widely used in both industry and academia:

> To manage is to forecast and plan, to organise, to command, to coordinate and to control.

Fayol's definition should make it clear that much of a manager's work involves making decisions about the best way to achieve the organisation's objectives and that there is a direct link between a manager's decision-making and planning activities. A forecast, for example, is created to help managers decide what actions are necessary to prepare the organisation for the future. The success of *all* of the activities described in Fayol's definition depend upon access to high-quality information. It is here that BIS have a role, as a means of supporting the manager's work by providing the information he or she needs. The next sections discuss managerial decision making in more detail.

Max Weber's (1864–1920) view of a *bureaucratic form* of organisation suggests that as an organisation grows in size and complexity, it becomes more difficult to control. For Weber, an ideal organisation displayed a number of characteristics, such as well-defined hierarchy or legitimate authority, the division of labour based on functional specialism and the existence of rules and procedures to deal with all situations and decisions. Large organisations, such as public utilities, often adopt some or all of the characteristics of a bureaucracy.

As organisations grow in size or complexity, the importance of effective and efficient management increases. In turn, greater reliance is placed upon the BIS used by the organisation. Put simply, as an organisation becomes larger, effective information systems become critical to continued survival.

❱ Decision behaviour

The way in which managers make decisions, and the factors that influence those decisions, are often described as **decision behaviour**.

Decisions can be classed as structured or unstructured (sometimes referred to as programmable and non-programmable decisions). In reality, however, many decisions fall somewhere in between the two extremes and are known as *semi-structured decisions*.

Structured decisions tend to involve situations where the rules and constraints governing the decision are known. They tend to involve routine or repetitive situations where the number of possible courses of action is relatively small. A good example involves stock control. The decision to reorder a given item will be governed by a fairly simple set of rules and constraints. When the amount of stock held falls below a certain point, a fixed quantity of new stock will be ordered.

Unstructured decisions tend to involve more complex situations, where the rules governing the decision are complicated or unknown. Such decisions tend to be made infrequently and rely heavily on the experience, judgement and knowledge of the decision maker. A good example of an unstructured decision might be whether or not an organisation should open a new branch in a particular area.

The behaviour of a manager will influence the way in which he or she absorbs information and reaches a decision. This is often referred to as a person's **cognitive style**. A manager's cognitive style will fall between analytical and intuitive styles.

The analytical manager typically displays a high level of analytical thought and is able to provide detailed justifications for any decisions made. He or she tends to prefer quantitative information as the basis for a decision and will often overlook any qualitative information received. This type of manager examines situations in fine detail and often overlooks the wider issues that might influence a decision.

> Data are often described as 'hard data' or 'soft data'.
>
> Hard data, also known as **quantitative data**, tend to make use of figures, such as statistics. Hard data are often collected in order to measure or *quantify* an object or situation.
>
> Soft data, often known as **qualitative data**, tend to focus on describing the *qualities* or characteristics of an object or situation. Interviews, for example, are often used to collect qualitative data related to a person's opinions or beliefs.

The intuitive manager relies heavily on prior experience, judgement and intuition. He or she tends to examine situations as a whole, adopting a holistic view that takes into account the wide range of factors that might influence a decision. This kind of manager will also be more willing to accept qualitative information when making a decision.

It should be evident that a manager with an analytical cognitive style is likely to be most effective when making structured decisions. Intuitive managers are likely to be most effective when making unstructured decisions. Systems to assist in decision making are described in Chapter 6.

❱ Levels of managerial decision making

The characteristics of the decisions taken in an organisation vary according to the level at which they are taken. Figure 1.3 shows the distribution of managerial responsibility within a typical organisation. As can be seen, the largest proportion of managers is located at the operational level of the organisation. The smallest proportion of managers, typically less than 10 per cent, is located at the strategic level.

Decision behaviour
Describes the process and factors involved when people make decisions.

Structured decisions
Situations where the rules and constraints governing the decision are known.

Unstructured decisions
Complex situations, where the rules governing the decision are complicated or unknown.

Cognitive style
This describes the way in which a manager absorbs information and reaches decisions. A manager's cognitive style will fall between analytical and intuitive styles.

Quantitative data
Includes use of figures, such as statistics. Also known as *hard data*, often collected in order to measure or quantify an object or situation.

Qualitative data
Describe without the use of figures, the qualities or characteristics of an object or situation. Also known as *soft data*.

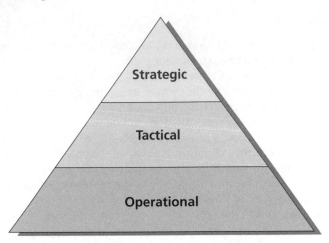

Figure 1.3 **Levels of managerial decision taking**

- At the *strategic* level, managers are largely concerned with long-term organisational planning. Decisions tend to be unstructured and are made infrequently. However, the decisions made at this level are likely to have a large impact on the organisation as a whole and cannot be reversed easily. An example of a decision taken at the strategic level might be a choice of new markets to move into.
- At the *tactical* level managers are largely concerned with medium-term planning. Managers monitor the performance of the organisation, control budgets, allocate resources and set policies. Decisions taken at this level are used to set medium-term goals that form stages leading to the accomplishment of the organisation's strategic objectives. An example of a decision taken at the tactical level might be setting a departmental budget.
- At the *operational* level managers deal with short-term planning and the day-to-day control of the organisation's activities. The decisions taken at this level direct the organisation's efforts towards meeting the medium-term goals, abiding by the budgets, policies and procedures set at the tactical level. Operational decisions tend to be highly structured and have little impact on the organisation as a whole. An example of a decision taken at the *operational* level might be setting a daily or weekly production schedule.

Example of decision types

Structured decisions: operational planning
- How should we process a sales order?
- How do we perform quality control? For example, measure conformance of product (is it within quality limits on a control chart?). If outside limits, then system will reject part.

Semi-structured decision: tactical planning
- How do we target our most profitable customers and what are their characteristics?
- Which foreign markets should we target?
- What is the best pricing structure for this product?

Unstructured decision: strategic planning
- Which business area should the organisation be in?
- How should the organisation be structured?
- What should our distribution channels be?

A direct relationship exists between the management level at which a decision is taken and the characteristics of the information required to support decision making. Tables 1.2 and 1.3 illustrate how the characteristics of the information needed by managers change according to the type of decision being made.

Table 1.2 Decision characteristics and management level

Management level	Decision			
	Type of decision	Time scale	Impact on organisation	frequency of decisions
Strategic	Unstructured	Long	Large	Infrequent
Tactical	↔	Medium	Medium	↔
Operational	Structured	Short	Small	Frequent

Table 1.3 Information characteristics for decisions by management levels

Management level	Information					
	Time period	Frequency	Source	Certainty	Scope	Detail
Strategic	Wide	Infrequent	External	Less certain	Wide	Summarised
Tactical	↔	↔	↔	↔	↔	↔
Operational	Narrow	Frequent	Internal	More certain	Narrow	Detailed

Activity 1.6

Organisation-level decisions

Classify the following decisions by type (structured, semi-structured, unstructured) and organisational level (strategic, tactical, operational). In addition, determine whether or not the decision-making process could be automated, and if possible describe the name or type of BIS used.

(a) At what level should we set the budget for next year?
(b) Does this customer qualify for a discount on a large order?
(c) How should we deal with a takeover bid?
(d) Should we employ more staff to cope with an urgent order?
(e) Should we expand abroad?
(f) Should we launch an advertising campaign?
(g) Should we take a short-term loan to help our current cash flow position?
(h) What new markets should we move into?
(i) What should we do about a faulty machine?

In Chapter 2, Figure 2.3 and in Chapter 6 we consider how particular types of BIS are used to support activities at the three different levels of operational, tactical and strategic.

▶ The decision-making process

The work of H. Simon (1977) provides a framework from which to examine the way in which managerial decisions are made. Although presented in a modified form, this framework can be used to show how the act of making a decision involves moving through five stages. Each stage must be completed before it is possible to move on to the next. As you read about each stage, consider to what extent BIS are effective in supporting it. Table 1.4 provides an overview of the decision making process.

Table 1.4 A model of decision making

Stage	Activities
Intelligence	● Awareness that a problem exists
	● Awareness that a decision must be made
Design	● Identify all possible solutions
	● Examine possible solutions
	● Examine implications of all possible solutions
Choice	● Select best solution
Implementation	● Implement solution
Evaluation	● Evaluate effectiveness or success of decision

The *intelligence* stage involves gathering information concerning the decision to be made. It recognises that managers must be made aware that a problem exists before any action can be taken. Once a problem has been identified, information is collected in order to achieve a thorough understanding of the problem and the circumstances in which it arose. Unless this understanding is achieved, managers may take an inappropriate approach to the problem, resulting in a less efficient or ineffective solution.

In the *design* stage, as many as possible of the potential solutions to the problem are identified and evaluated. At this point, the decision maker will begin to discard unsatisfactory solutions in order to reduce the number of alternatives as far as possible. The solution that will be implemented is then chosen during the *selection* stage.

Having made a decision, the action required to achieve a resolution to the problem is taken in the *implementation* stage. Following implementation, the *evaluation* stage considers how successful the solution has been. If further action is required, the decision maker returns to the intelligence stage and examines the problem again.

This model can be used to highlight two important points. First, it is important to recognise that information plays a critical part in arriving at an effective and successful decision. In the design stage, for example, it is essential to examine the implications of each possible solution. Unless the decision maker has access to adequate information, he or she may reject or accept possible solutions for the wrong reasons.

Secondly, the information required to support the decision-making process is determined by the decision itself. In other words, *decision needs determine information needs.*

Information need

The object of producing information is to meet a specific purpose or requirement.

> An information need can be thought of as a specific requirement for information. As an example, when a student sits an examination, he or she is asked to meet an information need by providing answers (information) to a series of specific questions.

Case Study 1.2 looks at how technology can be used to obtain valuable information that can be used to support a company's business activities. It also highlights a number of issues related to information quality and decision making.

The impact of agents on corporate intelligence

Often answers to business questions reside in data sources that cannot be found easily. Intelligent agents may be the answer.

A disproportionate amount of time is currently invested in digesting and evaluating information, only to discover that it is of little or no use. A large proportion of this irrelevant information comes from the typical abuse of distribution lists or cc'd e-mails – just compare the number of e-mails instantly deleted to those kept for a very rough indication to the scale of this problem.

Another side of this information equation relates to data and intelligence discovery; how to find answers to questions rapidly and with the minimal amount of data retrieval effort. In an ideal situation, employees would spend the vast majority of their time analysing key information or implementing changes and decisions, and not constructing queries or wading through pages of printed reports to find just a couple of lines of data. In order to reach such a situation, a level of control and autonomy must be devolved to some kind of third party or parties – namely intelligent agents.

Intelligent agents

Intelligent agents, or 'bots', are appearing in a variety of scenarios and situations, many of which are consumer-based. For example, shopbots, such as kelkoo.com, are helping to direct on-line shoppers to the cheapest destination sites for commodities, such as books, CDs, videos, computers, and electronics. Use of the shopbot cuts down on the time it would take to perform price comparisons across retailers and also leads to the best deal available.

Other commercial applications of intelligent agents include:

- *Auctions*: Bots will become particularly sophisticated in the world of on-line auctions. Companies such as eBay and QXL support auctions for any number of goods. These auctions are still manual, in that the bidder places a bid and the auctioneer co-ordinates all activities. This will change. Bots will soon be placing our bids in multiple auctions, ensuring that customers do not pay over the odds for an item. Auctions will also become much more sophisticated, with items being bundled and sold in ways we cannot even imagine right now.
- *Dynamic Pricing*: The Internet will become a huge battleground with billions of bots all trying to outsmart each other. The bots will not only have to contend with each other, but they will have to deal with much more complex purchasing methods. Will you allow your bots to participate in aggregate buying, where the more orders are placed for an item, the cheaper it becomes? How about inverse auctions, where the price is initially high, and the first bidder gets the goods? Agents will haggle, bid, and transact without user intervention.
- *Searching*: Intelligent agents, as we have already discussed, will make information discovery more intuitive and rapid. This could be in terms of the retrieval of a particular Web page or document based directly on keywords, or through more 'intelligent', contextual, information filtering. For example, Copernic is an intelligent meta-search application, which has been developed to access multiple search engines simultaneously. The user no longer needs to visit the Web site to use AltaVista, Excite, Yahoo!, Google, or MSN, et al, as he or she can access the information held by these search engines by a higher level infomediary.

As consumers, we will not want to know about the mechanisms involved in buying an item, we will have to leave that to the bots. Just in the same way that we do not generally know the internal workings of a TV, so we will not need to understand the internal workings of our bots. Whether an item was purchased through an inverse auction, aggregate buying, or just a simple fixed-price purchase, will not interest us.

Enterprise agents

At first glance it may appear that enterprise use of agents is not as well documented and developed, however, in essence, they have been around for many years. Such agents have often been defined as software processes that can be trained to manage information on a user's behalf. In this case, a typical example could include an e-mail system capable of auto-reply and auto-forward. Now with the developments in artificial intelligence and rules derived from knowledge-based systems, software agents are set to go beyond simple automation and making low-level decisions.

Once again this technological field is assuming importance. It is evolving rapidly, due to the constant upgrading of client/server networks and Object-Orientation software, creating an environment suitable for agent software. Designed to be self-contained, they are ideal component building blocks. Although much of the early development work has been university-based, there is a focus on creating industry standards relevant to business modelling.

A dictionary definition of an agent is as 'being anyone or thing that acts in representation for another party, ostensibly to produce an effect, but generally to benefit the represented party'. Intelligence is defined as 'that which has the capacity to acquire and apply knowledge with rational decision-making'. Due to the complex nature of today's computer systems, there is a need for smart software that can be trained to initiate actions arising from system states, or changes in data-based parameters, pertaining to the particular needs of the user.

Typically, agents are used to perform routine and laborious searching of Web sites or network databases. As applications expand, the take-up will be fast and immediate, but there are serious debates on just how far down the decision-making spectrum an agent will be allowed to go before human interaction is brought back on-line.

The attributes of intelligent agents are defined by various terminologies, but must encompass the following:

- *Degree of Autonomy* – Analogous to the human state of 'doing it my way', the intelligent agent must have autonomy to make decisions to complete its objectives.
- *Communication* – Again, taking the human analogy, an agent must be able to communicate with third parties or external sources in a two-way process. Typically, these may be other agents or information warehouses. These communications may be singular or part of a more complex problem but generally independent of protocols.
- *Reasoning* – This is where the intelligent agent distinguishes itself from automatic software systems. Once again, modelling the human system, it must be able to make evaluations in regard to its objectives. To achieve that end, an intelligent agent has to interrogate and understand the environment in which it is based. There must be an ability to make rational decisions in response to its own 'belief structure'.
- *Learning Ability* – Again, analogous with humanity, an agent must similarly have the capacity for acquisition of extra knowledge by 'learning'. In that respect, an agent sits within a framework of other agents, allowing each to operate independently, yet being part of a larger problem-solving environment. The knowledge base has to be reusable and be capable of being extended or adapted to allow for tailor-made applications and to link to other agents.

Defining the constraints of an agent is difficult, as each agent is in a different environment with differing levels of knowledge and capability, and may not see the environment in the same way. One important dimension that really needs further analysis is that of trust. Autonomous agents with sensitive information must represent the beneficiary and act for the user's own good. Security issues therefore need to be addressed, for example, credit card details used to complete transactions.

On a more simplistic level, imaging software has a read and learn agent that has an ability to learn and make informed guesses. The question arises whether it is merely an add-on to a software package (a glorified macro in simple terms). In the early stages, the answer was probably, yes.

Now, however, consider the scenario of an intelligent agent monitoring time scheduling for the sales and marketing departments, and being activated in response to an upcoming quarterly meeting. From its knowledge of sales meetings in the past, a sales report is generated from other intelligent agents, within the report handling software, using typical inputs. These inputs may be acquired by triggering other data mining agents on the network to source out specific information from accounts, order processing, or external sources (World Wide Web, data warehousing). All necessary personnel would be advised by their scheduling agent of an upcoming meeting, organise the room booking, and print the reports to each participant. Thus, without positive intervention, a set of procedures and problems have been overcome.

As to how each intelligent agent achieves the tasks is not relevant and is system independent. Consider the car engine management system and its agents varying between manufacturers, yet the required solution of forward momentum is achieved.

Examples

The following is a list of application areas where agent technology can be deployed:

- *Systems and Network Management* – Intelligent agents can be employed in order to enhance systems management software. For example, they can be designed to monitor, filter, and take, according to predefined parameters.
- *Mobile Data Access and Management* – Server-side agents can be used to handle remote user requests (multiple times if necessary) and process relevant data at the source, before transferring the minimal amount of data to the user.
- *E-mail and Messaging* – Agent technology is now widely used in messaging software, such as e-mail, to help users manage the influx of messages. For

example, the agent can be used to prioritise and organise e-mails, according to predefined rules.

- *Business Process Automation* – Agents can also be used in a workflow/process automation scenario, to route documents/messages/data, etc., throughout the organisation, based upon user wishes or demands.
- *Collaboration* – A great deal of emphasis is now placed on information-sharing and teamwork, made possible through advances in networking technology. Many Groupware products take advantage of agent technology to perform routine tasks automatically for the user. For example, agents can interact with other agents to manage the users' calendars when booking appointments.
- *E-Commerce* – Agents can be used to improve the sales process by routing customers through a Web site, for example, providing advice and handling queries, and of course for monitoring activity and browser conversion rates. In addition, intelligent agents can also be used by customers to seek out the best deals on a virtual shopping list. The next stage will see both selling and buying agents completing transactions on behalf of their owners.
- *Information and Data Management* – Information access and management is a massive area of great importance. The exploding volume of data that has been made available to users has, in essence, become a victim of its own popularity – it is now virtually impossible to 'make out the woods from the trees'. Intelligent agents can assist users primarily with searching and filtering data, but also with prioritising, routing, distribution, and analysis. This is a particular area that, the Butler Group analysts believes, is poised for rapid growth.

Agents as an aid to decision-making

Perhaps the issue to be addressed next is exactly how intelligent agents can be used to improve the decision-making capabilities of individuals, and hence the organisation as a whole. Intelligent agents, or bots, are very much interwoven with the concept of intelligence, as they act to give information a purpose: to improve decision-making. Before delving deeper into the lives of bots and intelligent agents, it is worth taking a mental step back to look at the way information is used within the organisation.

Enterprise data and information comes from a vast range of discrete sources. Unifying these streams into one coherent strategy can be complex to achieve and difficult to manage. Modern applications and systems are extremely proficient in the generation and processing of data. However, the level of granularity that can now be recorded, combined with the transaction volumes that are characteristic of e-business, results in spiralling volumes of data. In order for the organisation to leverage its data resources, it must be able to rationalise and interrogate all of its data from disparate sources on-the-fly.

One of the greatest challenges facing businesses today, therefore, remains how to access, manage, and distribute the business information locked away in their corporate databases, and secreted in the minds of their employees – intellectual capital. As the world moves from an industrial society to an information society, the value and volume of corporate information is growing exponentially. The sheer volume of information that is available has created an environment in which separating critical business information from the inconsequential has become increasingly complex. What is needed is a more pragmatic, flexible, and altogether more intelligent approach to enterprise data and information management. Truly intelligent businesses need to radically revamp their processes and strategies, by placing information at the centre of everything they do.

There is a danger in artificially creating conceptual boundaries where none really exist. For example, between unstructured data and structured data, between internal data and external data, and between Business Intelligence (BI) and Knowledge Management (KM). Of course technical boundaries and restrictions are prevalent and well documented, but modern technology is designed to mask complexity from the user. For too long, too much has been made about the differences in the origin or format of data and information. Data is data, no matter where it comes from or where it resides. Many different tools and techniques have been developed for exploiting data and information, but this is merely a question of exploiting the most appropriate technology.

Human intelligence is derived from many sources, which include structured data in the form of books, Web pages, or CD-ROMs, and unstructured data from videos, films, music, teachers, parents, and all kinds of personal interactions. However, when we call upon this intelligence we do not make a conscious decision that depends on where the data first came from – we are far more sophisticated than that. We are able to combine elements of all the above types of medium, forever expanding and developing our intelligence. This is the way that intelligent organisations should operate – by assimilating data and information from a range of sources and in a range of formats, to maximise intellectual capital, and cultivate the ability to make rapid and accurate decisions. With this is mind, it is clear to see that various forms of intelligent agent can help data and information management and distribution.

▶

Exception reporting and alerts

Exception reporting is now accepted as an incredibly valuable method of reporting key business events that warrant some form of intervention. In certain cases, for example in a manufacturing organisation, it may be necessary to halt a particular process until a problem or issue has been resolved. Exception reporting can be based upon any number of pre-defined parameters, complex calculations, trends, or patterns, and employs agent technology to 'watch' over the necessary data sources.

Clearly there will be a degree of skill involved in directing the agent at the relevant data sources, setting the parameters and rules, and also the course of action to be taken if and when the exception occurs. A very simple example of this kind of methodology is a thermostat. When the temperature reaches an upper limit the heat source is turned off and is restarted when a lower limit is reached. Organisations and processes are far more complex than this; however, the 'if-then-else' logic is the same.

As agent technology becomes more sophisticated, the level of autonomy that is given to the agents will increase. For instance, they could incorporate neural network technology so that the agent 'learns' the appropriate cause of action. They are also becoming more functional, for example, by having the ability to deliver alerts and messages to a range of devices, such as PCs, Personal Digital Assistants (PDAs), mobile phones (including Wireless Application Protocol (WAP) phones), and pagers. The alerts may contain different levels of information depending, not only on the nature of the exception, but on the device that the information is being delivered to. There is clearly little point in attempting to deliver a large file to a WAP phone. Intelligent agents can also be used for the execution of standard reports, say on a daily, weekly, or monthly basis, the results of which can also be delivered in a way that suits their human owner.

The majority of Business Intelligence vendors incorporate Exception Reporting into their offerings, however, rather interestingly, this tends to be without giving mention to the use of agent technology. Perhaps it is felt that use of terms such as 'bots' and 'agents' do not sit well with their audience? It is more conceivable that, because the term 'agent' is often abused, vendors would rather stay clear of it altogether. The benefits of this kind of technology relate to the ability of the agents to analyse vast amounts of data, continuously if required. This means that less time is spent by analysts constructing, developing, and executing reports, freeing them up to concentrate on the real job of interpreting results, amending processes, and making strategic and tactical decisions.

Specifically, the use of intelligent agents removes the burden and reliance on key individuals, who have to retain and maintain a model of all of the data sources on the network – a task that becomes exponentially more intensive as the organisation expands to include numerous internal and external databases.

Data mining and data discovery

Agents are also being implemented to perform intensive data mining. The possibilities of this technology are huge, especially for knowledge discovery and knowledge management. Agents can be designed to automate acquisition, generation, and exploitation of knowledge and information from heterogeneous sources, such as text, video, and audio sources. This is not just limited to internal data sources, as open sources, such as the Internet, can also be patrolled by agents. Relevant information can then be returned, and indexed, before being passed to a knowledge repository.

Although difficult to prove, it is believed that only a tiny fraction of available enterprise data and information is utilised correctly. Very often the answers to questions reside in data sources that have been forgotten or remain undiscovered. Agents are ideally suited to mining data; they do not get bored by repetition, can work faster and for longer hours with greater accuracy, and are cheaper to employ over time.

Rather than working in disparate remote situations, the likelihood is that multiple intelligent agents will be deployed to work together, according to a multi-agent architecture.

Data can exist in many forms, each of which requires the development of a special agent designed to find, acquire, interpret, and extract the data into a usable and common format.

The use of agents in data acquisition and discovery is commonplace throughout the Internet – search engines and meta search engines play a key role in aiding navigation. Similarly, agents can be used for competitive intelligence, by continually monitoring news-feeds and information in the public domain. More recently, through solutions provided by the likes of Autonomy [www.autonomy.com], organisations are turning their focus inwards, to improve their internal information retrieval capabilities.

Conclusion

The use of intelligent agents within businesses will increase dramatically over the next few years. They will become subsumed into everyday life to such a degree that it will become difficult to know exactly when an agent is being utilised. What is more, agents will learn to work together, providing businesses with a battalion of loyal, committed, and reliable troops. Not only will agents have to inter-face with humans, but also with applications. They will be able to carry out a constant vigil on disparate areas such as on security, performance, and Web site traffic monitoring. Through the use of Artificial Intelligence, they will be taught the actions to be taken based upon the change of state of certain attributes or parameters.

Although dependent on state-of-the-art technology, the impact that such bots have is not felt in technical terms, but in the empowerment of customers and transparency of information. Shopbots have a dra-matic impact on transaction costs, making it possible for customers to transcend organisational boundaries.

The next step will be to utilise an interface and infrastructure, such as an Enterprise Information Portal (EIP), to co-ordinate and unify the use of an agent. Not only will this aid management and con-trol, but it will help to blend areas that are often considered to be disparate, such as BI, KM, and Customer Relationship Management (CRM). As a consequence, agents will perform a key function in helping to control information supply and demand;

however, it is unlikely that they will ever reach a sufficiently high level of intelligence and rational to replace many of the roles played by humans.

This Concept Paper is reproduced from Butler Group's Business Intelligence Research and Advisory Service. Visit www.butlergroup.com for more infor-mation about the Butler Group.

Source: Ian Charlesworth, 'The impact of agents on corporate intelligence', courtesy of *Computer Weekly*, 27 April 2001

Questions

1 What is an intelligent agent?

2 'A disproportionate amount of time is currently invested in digesting and evaluating information, only to discover that it is of little or no use.' Using the case study as a source of reference, explain why this might be. Your answer should refer to concepts related to the attributes of information quality.

3 What are the major limitations of intelligent agents?

4 In what ways might a typical home computer user make use of intelligent agents?

Intelligent agents

Activity 1.7

Using the Internet as a resource, locate at least two examples of how intelligent agent software is being used in business. Tip: find supplier sites using a search engine such as Google (www.google.com) using keywords from Case Study 1.1 or news sources such as the FT (www.ft.com) or Moreover (www.moreover.com).

Decision-making theory

Decision-making theory is important in defining how structured decisions or busi-ness rules based on quantitative data are incorporated into BIS. A **business rule** defines the actions that need to occur in a business when a particular situation arises. For example, a business rule may state that if a customer requests credit and they have a history of defaulting on payments, then credit will not be issued. A business rule is broken down into an event that triggers a rule and test conditions that result in defined actions.

Decision making involves selecting the correct action from a series of choices. The business rules governing the correct action may be complex, so we use diagrams and tables to help take the decision in a structured way and to ensure the rules are defined correctly for when they are implemented as program code in software. Consider the example of the business rule for when a company checks credit for a customer. This can be broken down as follows:

> **Business rule**
> A rule defines the actions that need to occur in a business when a particular situation arises. For example a business rule may state that if a customer requests credit and they have a history of defaulting on payments, then credit will not be issued. A business rule is broken down into an event which triggers a rule with test conditions which result in defined actions.

1 *Name of event or process*   Credit request
2 *Condition (question when event occurs)*   Is credit OK?
3 *Alternative results*   Yes or No
4 *Alternative actions*   If Yes: Continue   If No: Refuse order

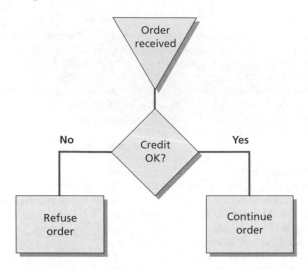

Figure 1.4 Decision tree notation for checking credit

requesting credit. There is then a question that needs to be answered. In this case there are two alternative results: the customer is either creditworthy or not. Different actions will need different actions. In this case, if the customer is creditworthy the order can continue, if not the order will be refused.

In this example there is a single condition or question. However, most business rules will involve several questions and these can be misinterpreted if they are not clearly defined. In more complex cases we use a combination of **decision trees** and **decision tables**. Decision trees are usually drawn first and then the corresponding decision table is based on the decision tree. This is the approach used in the examples below.

A decision tree is a diagram showing the sequence of events and decisions that occur in a process. It shows the different business rules using flow chart notation. The simple decision tree for the rule above is shown in Figure 1.4.

A decision table is a matrix showing all the alternative outcomes of different decisions that occur when certain input conditions are met. It shows the different components of the decision in a tabular form, as in Figure 1.5.

A decision table for the credit checking example is shown in Figure 1.6.

To understand more about the application of decision trees and decision rules, a fuller example is required. The credit checking example above is extended to include other decisions that are required when a sales order is received from a customer. Figure 1.7 shows the decision tree for the sales order process. The first question is whether the customer has sent payment with the order. If they have, then the next question to ask is, are the items in stock? If they are, then the order can be dispatched to the customer. If not, the orders must be put on hold until the items are available. If the customer has not sent payment with the order, then the third question about the customer's credit is asked. If the customer's credit is acceptable, then the order can proceed and the question about the availability of items must be asked.

Decision tree

A diagram showing the sequence of events, decisions and consequent actions that occur in a decision-making process.

Decision table

A matrix showing all the alternative outcomes of different decisions which occur when certain input conditions occur.

Condition or rule	Condition entry
Action	Action entry

Figure 1.5 Framework for a decision table

Rule: Is credit OK?	Yes	No
Action: *Continue*: accept order *Terminate*: refuse order	X	X

Figure 1.6 Decision table for the credit checking example

Figure 1.8 shows the decision table for this example. The five rules correspond to the five final outcomes at the end of each branch of the tree in Figure 1.7. The upper part of the table shows the three test conditions and the relevant Yes/No outcomes for each of the rules. The lower part of the diagram shows the corresponding outcomes. For example, for rule 3, the outcome or action will be to refuse the order if the customer has not provided payment with the order and they are not creditworthy.

Once decision tables for the business rules have been produced, these act as a summary for the business rule that will be enacted by the information system. The corresponding program code for this example is shown in the box. Structured English is a method of design described in Chapter 12.

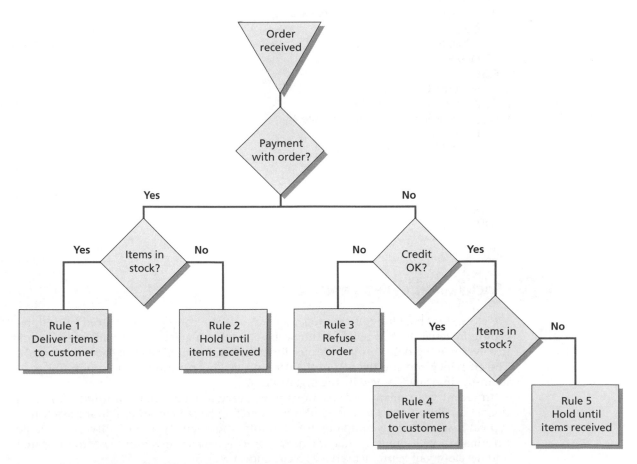

Figure 1.7 Decision tree indicating decisions involved in a sales order processing system

		Rules				
		1	2	3	4	5
Test conditions	Payment with order	Y	Y	N	N	N
	Items in stock	Y	N	–	Y	N
	Credit OK?	–	–	N	Y	Y
Actions dependent on conditions	Deliver item to customer	X			X	
	Hold order until items received		X			X
	Refuse order			X		

Figure 1.8 **Decision table for Figure 1.7**

Structured English program code for implementing the decision table in Figure 1.8

```
IF Payment_with order? THEN
     IF items_in_stock? THEN
          Deliver item to customer (Rule 1)
     ELSE
          Hold_until_received (Rule 2)
     ENDIF
ELSE
     IF credit_OK? THEN
     IF items_in_stock? THEN
          Deliver item to customer (Rule 4)
     ELSE
          Hold_until_received (Rule 5)
     ENDIF
     ELSE
          Refuse order (Rule 3)
     ENDIF
ENDIF
```

F *Focus on* knowledge management

We close this chapter by linking together some of the concepts introduced in the preceding material. By this point, it should be clear that a great deal of a manager's work involves making decisions in order to direct an organisation's efforts towards its goals. The efficiency and effectiveness of the decision-making process depends upon the quality of the information held by the organisation.

In recent years, many organisations have come to realise that information has an impact on almost every activity and must therefore be seen as an important asset. In a typical manufacturing company, for example, the quantity and quality of available information will influence manufacturing processes, sales, inventory control, research and development, customer service levels, and so on.

This realisation has led to a renewed emphasis on ensuring that **knowledge** of how to utilise information resources is used as effectively as possible (e.g. Choo, 1996; Davenport et al., 1998). **Knowledge management** (KM) has been adopted as a new term to describe a broad range of activities related to ensuring that an organisation makes the best use of its information resources. New roles have been created to foster KM. Many US companies now have chief knowledge officers (CKOs), specialist managers have become knowledge workers and knowledge engineers are used to design systems through eliciting knowledge from specialists.

Knowledge management has an important role within any organisation, but particularly for the e-business since success is critically dependent on staff knowledge about all aspects of the micro-environment such as customers, suppliers, intermediaries, competitors and how to shape internal processes to best deliver customer value. With the move towards globalisation and the need for a rapid response to changing market conditions knowledge transfer is a key to competitiveness. Knowledge management is also important where turnover of staff is high. As Saunders (2000) puts it:

Every day, knowledge essential to your business walks out of your door, and much of it never comes back. Employees leave, customers come and go and their knowledge leaves with them. This information drain costs you time, money and customers.

The concept of knowledge is more difficult to state than that of data or information. However, knowledge can be regarded as the next level of sophistication or business value in the cycle from data through information to knowledge. Consider a retail manager analysing their sales figures. Raw data on sales figures will simply consist of the figures in each individual shop for a given month. We can use a BIS to present these data within the context of sales compared to previous months as information. This information might include trends from previous years, sales against budget and maps of sales for different regions. However, this information is of little value if the manager does not know how to act in response to it. Managers apply their knowledge to decide how to respond if the sales in one region are much lower than others, or if one store is under-performing against budget. Thus knowledge is the processing of information and is a skill based on previous understanding, procedures and experience. Knowledge management seeks to share this experience within a company.

Theorists have identified two different types of knowledge, and different approaches can be used to disseminate this type of knowledge within an organisation:

1 **Explicit** – details of processes and procedures. Explicit knowledge can be readily detailed in procedural manuals and databases. Examples include records of meetings between sales representatives and key customers, procedures for dealing with customer service queries and management reporting processes.
2 **Tacit** – less tangible than explicit knowledge, this is experience on how to react to a situation when many different variables are involved. It is more difficult to encapsulate this knowledge, which often resides in the heads of employees. Techniques for sharing this knowledge include learning stories and histories. Examples include knowing how to react when changes occur in the marketplace, such as a competitor launching a new product or a major customer defecting. Knowing how to analyse and respond to information in management reports depends on tacit knowledge. To acquire tacit knowledge may rely on sharing knowledge with partners outside the company or others in different sectors. So knowledge management should not be considered solely as confining corporate knowledge within the firewalls.

It follows that one goal of knowledge management is to turn tacit knowledge into explicit knowledge which can then be shared between employees and used to train new employees.

Knowledge
Applying managerial experience to problem solving.

Knowledge management
Techniques and tools for collecting, managing and disseminating knowledge within an organisation.

Explicit knowledge
Knowledge that can be readily expressed and recorded within information systems.

Tacit knowledge
Mainly intangible knowledge that is typically intuitive and not recorded since it is part of the human mind.

The reasons organisations are enthusiastically adopting knowledge management are highlighted by a 1999 International Data Corp. survey. The main reasons for adoption given by 355 US IS manager respondents were:

- improving profit/growing revenue (67%)
- retaining key talent/expertise (54%)
- increasing customer retention and/or satisfaction (52%)
- defending market share against new entrants (44%)
- gaining faster time to market with products (39%)
- penetrating new market segments (39%)
- reducing costs (38%)
- developing new products/services (35%).

It is evident that although employee retention is important, knowledge management is also seen as a competitive force for acquiring and retaining customers.

Applications of knowledge management are described in more detail in Chapters 4 and 6; they include:

- *Business intelligence (BI)* (sometimes known as 'corporate intelligence' or 'competitive intelligence'). This describes approaches towards gathering a range of information to ensure that an organisation is able to keep pace with competitors. The information gathered might cover areas such as new advances in technology, market conditions, customer data (see 'data mining' below) and the actions of competitors. Leading management consultants invest in capturing and disseminating approaches to different projects to learn from past projects. Hansen et al. (1999) estimate that during the late 1990s consulting companies such as Accenture and Ernst & Young each spent more than $500 million on knowledge management.
- *Document image processing (DIP)*. This involves converting printed documents into an electronic form. One of the advantages of DIP is that documents can be searched quickly and easily in order to locate specific items of information.
- *Data mining*. This involves analysing a body of corporate data in order to discover patterns or trends that are not immediately obvious. The results of data mining can bring many benefits, for example the potential to launch a new product or service might be identified.

As should be apparent from the examples given here, many activities related to knowledge management depend almost entirely on technology. Both data mining and DIP, for example, would be impossible without the use of modern computer technology. However, one cannot apply technology to best effect without a good understanding of certain fundamental concepts. For instance, improving the effectiveness of the decisions taken within an organisation requires managers to have a good understanding of the decision-making process. Similarly, ensuring an organisation remains competitive requires managers to understand how technology can provide competitive advantage. Chapter 2 explores areas such as systems theory and competitive advantage.

▶ Competitive intelligence

Competitive intelligence (CI)
A process that transforms disaggregated information into relevant, accurate and usable strategic knowledge about competitors' position, performance, capabilities and intentions.

We will take **competitive intelligence or CI** as an example of a typical application of knowledge management. The Competitive Intelligence handbook (www.combsinc.com) presents different definitions of CI, for example:

The objective of competitor intelligence is not to steal a competitor's trade secrets or other proprietary property, but rather to gather in a systematic, overt (i.e., legal) manner a wide range of information that when collated and analysed provides a fuller understanding of a competitor firm's structure, culture, behaviour, capabilities and weaknesses.

MINI CASE STUDY

Novartis select Autonomy for Knowledge Management

John McCulloch, Manager, Executive Information Systems says:

Novartis is a world leader in pharmaceuticals, healthcare, agribusiness and nutrition. That means we handle a vast amount of complex information daily, both from internal and external sources. Until now, that has cost us a great deal of time and money in manual processes, but Autonomy's technology can automate the whole process from start to finish. We are delighted to be bringing the technology on board.

Novartis implemented Autonomy Portal-in-a-Box™ to provide an automated infrastructure for the handling and personalization of the complex information generated internally as well as research papers, market intelligence and breaking news from outside. The system not only aggregates and personalizes an enormous amount of content without incurring large labour costs in the form of staff to read, manually tag and hyperlink each piece of information, but also dynamically and continuously understands individual needs and preferences in order to deliver compelling and timely content.

Personalization occurs by automatic profiling of employees by analysing the ideas in the text they read and write in company documents, e-mail and web sites visited. Important information is automatically delivered to top managers by alert flashing icon, based on their interests and professional expertise as soon as it is available, without the user having to waste valuable time actively searching for it.

Source: Autonomy web site (www.autonomy.com)

Competitor intelligence is the analytical process that transforms disaggregated competitor intelligence into relevant, accurate and usable strategic knowledge about competitors, position, performance, capabilities and intentions.

Now complete Activity 1.8 to gain an appreciation of typical managers' requirements for inputs, processes and outputs for such as system.

Competitive intelligence and customer knowledge

Activity 1.8

The marketing department of a construction company is planning the creation of a competitive intelligence system. Its aim is to capture and disseminate information about 30 key competitors and also existing or potential customers served by account representatives.

You are designing the system. Working in groups, agree an approach for:

1 Capturing data (who is involved, what information they need to collect).
2 Entering data (who is responsible for this, how they evaluate and categorise the different types of information entered).
3 Output requirements. Using the framework for quality of information in Table 1.1, what are the requirements in terms of types of content, frequency, who can access the data and filtering according to different criteria?
4 What types of hardware and software may be required for the system (reference to later chapters may be needed to answer this)?

To read more about competitive intelligence visit the web sites listed at the end of the chapter.

Summary

1 Data can be described as a collection of non-random facts obtained by observation or research

2 Information can be described as data that have been processed so that they are meaningful. An alternative view of information suggests that it acts to reduce uncertainty about a situation or event.

3 Information can have tangible or intangible value. One view suggests that the value of information can be measured in terms of the improvements it brings to managerial decision making.

4 The quality of information can be described by using the attributes of information quality.

5 The functions of management include forecasting, planning, organisation, coordination and control. One of the key management functions that information systems seek to support is managerial decision making.

6 Decisions can be structured, semi-structured or unstructured. A simple model of decision making includes five stages: intelligence, design, choice, implementation and evaluation. Decisions can be taken at a strategic, tactical or operational level. The characteristics of a decision will vary according to the organisational level at which it is made.

7 'Knowledge management' is a term used to describe how organisations attempt to make the best use of the information resources at their disposal. It is part of 'e-business', a concept that describes the use of information and communications technology to increase the efficiency of information flows within an organisation and with its partners.

EXERCISES

Self-assessment exercises

1 What are the three dimensions of information quality?

2 How can the value of information be measured?

3 What are the functions of management?

4 What are the stages involved in making a decision?

5 How will a manager's cognitive style affect the decisions he or she makes?

6 Explain how the concept of knowledge management relates to data and information.

7 What differences in perspective about managerial decision making are introduced by the e-business concept?

Discussion questions

1 Some people argue that employees should be restricted in terms of the information they have access to in the course of their duties. Others argue that they are able to work more efficiently if they have access to *all* of an organisation's information resources. Using relevant examples, make a case for one side of this argument.

2 It has been said that decision needs should determine information needs. Is this always true or is there a case for an organisation gathering *all* available data and information?

▶

3 Select an article of your choice from a newspaper, journal or magazine. Analyse the information contained within the article using concepts related to the attributes of information quality. Use the web links provided at the end of this chapter to locate suitable articles.

4 'Knowledge management is nothing new, it is merely a repackaging of existing information management techniques.' Discuss.

Essay questions

1 Select an organisation you are familiar with. Identify at least one major decision that the organisation has taken recently. Describe the decision-making process that took place, paying particular attention to the following points:

   (a) describe how managers became aware that a problem existed and that a decision was required;
   (b) describe what information was gathered so that managers could achieve a good understanding of the problem;
   (c) provide examples of any alternative solutions that were considered and explain why these were eventually rejected;
   (d) explain why the final solution was selected and describe how it was implemented;
   (e) discuss how the solution was evaluated and whether or not it was successful.

2 The survival of a large organisation depends upon access to high-quality information. Discuss this statement, providing relevant examples where necessary.

3 The Microsoft Corporation is arguably the most successful company in the world. Conduct any research necessary to complete the following tasks:

   (a) Provide an overview of the company and its activities.
   (b) Selecting appropriate examples, describe the company's physical and conceptual resource bases.
   (c) Identify and describe some of the factors in the company's business environment. Provide examples of factors that act either to support or obstruct the company's activities.

4 Write a report on how knowledge management could enhance an organisation of your choice.

Examination questions

1 It is generally agreed that one of the key functions of management is decision making. Using specific examples, you are required to:

   (a) describe the types of decisions that managers are required to take;
   (b) explain the stages involved in making a decision;
   (c) describe the characteristics of decisions taken at different levels in an organisation.

2 An understanding of the nature of information is fundamental to the study of information systems. Using specific examples, you are required to:

   (a) define information;
   (b) describe the characteristics that will be present in information of high quality;
   (c) describe how the value of information can be determined.

3 Information can be transmitted via formal and informal means. Using specific examples, you are required to:

   (a) describe the advantages and disadvantages of each method;
   (b) discuss each method in terms of the attributes of information quality that are likely to be present.

4 In relation to the concept of knowledge management:

   (a) Explain how knowledge differs from information.
   (b) Describe two ways of classifying knowledge.
   (c) Give an example of a business application for each of your answers in (b).

References

Choo, C. (1996) 'The knowing organization: how organizations use information to construct meaning, create knowledge and make decisions', *International Journal of Information Management*, 16, 5, 329–40

Davenport, T., DeLong, D. and Beers, M. (1998) 'Successful knowledge management projects', *Sloan Management Review*. Winter, 39, 2, 43–57

DTI (2000) Business in the Information Age – International Benchmarking Study 2000. UK Department of Trade and Industry. Available online at: www.ukonlineforbusiness.gov.uk

Gates, B. (2001) Speech at Tech Ed 2001, Tuesday, 19 June, 2001, www.microsoft.com/billgates/speeches/2001/06-19teched.asp

Hansen, M., Nohria, N. and Tierney, T. (1999) 'What's your strategy for measuring knowledge?', *Harvard Business Review*, May–June, 106–16

Lucey, T. (1997) *Management Information Systems*, 7th edition, DP Publications, London

O'Brien, J. (2001) *Introduction to Information Systems*, 10th edition, McGraw-Hill, New York

Saunders, R. (2000) Managing knowledge, *Harvard Management Communication Letter*. June 2000, 3–5

Simon, H. (1977) T*he New Science of Management Decision*, Prentice-Hall, Englewood Cliffs, NJ

Further reading

Chaffey, D. (2002) *E-Business and E-Commerce Management: Strategy, Implementation and Applications*, Financial Times Prentice Hall, Harlow. Chapter 1 introduces the e-business concept. Chapter 10 discusses approaches to knowledge management within organisations

Curtis, G. and Cobham, D. (2001) *Business Information Systems: Analysis, Design and Practice*, 4th edition, Financial Times Prentice Hall, Harlow. Chapter 1 deals with concepts related to information, systems theory and management information systems

Laudon, K. and Laudon, J. (2002) *Management Information Systems*, 7th edition, Pearson Education, Upper Saddle River, NJ. Chapter 5 covers concepts related to data and information, the functions of management and managerial decision making. In addition, Chapter 16 deals with the use of computer-based information systems to improve managerial decision making

O'Brien, J. (2001) *Introduction to Information Systems*, 10th edition, McGraw-Hill, New York. Chapter 1 deals with basic concepts, such as systems theory

Sveiby, K.-E. (1997–2001) *The New Organizational Wealth: Managing and Measuring Knowledge-based Assets*, Berrett-Koehler. Book updated on author's web site (www.sveiby.com.au/KnowledgeManagement.html)

Web links

News sources for finding case studies about organisations

www.findarticles.com FindArticles provides searching through many newspapers, business magazines and some journals.

www.moreover.com Moreover provides searching through the world's newspapers. Particularly good for recent stories.

www.ft.com The *Financial Times* web site provides access to news stories from some 3000 publications. The searchable archive of news stories is a wonderful resource for a wide range of research activities.

www.guardian.co.uk The *Guardian's* web site provides excellent news coverage and a wide variety of additional services.

www.reuters.com The official site for Reuters. Provides coverage of international news and financial information.

www.worldnews.com News stories from around the world. Major stories are categorised by city, e.g. New York, London, etc. Some stories are accompanied by multimedia, such as Real Audio sound files. The site can be searched for items of interest.

news.bbc.co.uk The highly respected news service of the BBC. Coverage includes multimedia elements, such as sound and video.

www.infobeat.com Allows the creation of a personalised newspaper. Although the content received cannot be customised to a great extent, it nevertheless demonstrates the concept of delivering up-to-date, personalised information via the Internet.

www.mindtools.com/page2.html The Mind Tools site provides a series of brief articles that describe common approaches to problem solving in plain language.

www.mapnp.org/library/prsn-prd/prb-bsc.htm A paper on approaches to problem solving. Contains links to related articles, such as group problem solving.

www.eb.co.uk The *Encyclopedia Britannica* web site.

Knowledge management and competitive intelligence

www.brint.com A Business Researcher's Interests is an extensive portal with articles on e-business, e-commerce, knowledge management, change management and IS strategy.

www.sveiby.com.au/KnowledgeManagement.html Karl-Erik Sveiby has a regularly updated definition of different views of knowledge management; the FAQ 'What is Knowledge Management?' is recommended.

www.knowledgespace.com Andersen Knowledgespace is an external initiative to enable customers to access a wide range of market information for different sectors. A test drive will highlight some of the available features.

www.kmcentral.com Knowledge Management Central provides practical advice and support for business professionals working on knowledge management issues and projects.

www.competia.com Competia is a portal and online community for competitive intelligence and strategic planning professionals.

www.combsinc.com Competitive Intelligence Handbook.

www.fuld.com Fuld and Co. Internet Intelligence Index lists over 600 sites that are sources for competitive intelligence.

www.marketing-online.co.uk Internet marketing sources, with a section on competitive intelligence sources.

www.scip.org/ci Society of Competitive Intelligence Professionals has a good overview of CI concepts.

Chapter 2

Basic concepts – an introduction to business information systems

LEARNING OBJECTIVES

After reading this chapter, readers will be able to:
● identify systems and their components;
● identify and describe the behaviour of systems;
● identify types of BIS, distinguishing them by category and the organisational level at which they are used;
● identify basic strategies and methods used to gain competitive advantage through the use of BIS.

MANAGEMENT ISSUES

Systems theory is a powerful tool that can be used to analyse systems at a high level of detail. It can be applied to a range of situations, from examining an organisation as a whole to analysing a specific task carried out by an individual employee. From a managerial perspective, this chapter addresses the following areas:
● how systems theory is used as a means of defining problems and situations so that they can be understood more easily and BIS can be developed to support them;
● by understanding BIS, managers can maximise an organisation's use of technology;
● how BIS can help achieve competitive advantage.

Links to other chapters

Chapter 1   provides an introduction to concepts related to data, information and managerial decision making.

Chapter 6   describes how BIS support the functional areas of business.

Chapter 13   looks in more detail at developing a company strategy for introducing and using information systems effectively.

Introduction

This chapter builds upon the concepts introduced in Chapter 1 and introduces the features of systems. The topics covered are intended to give readers an understanding of:

- the basic characteristics of systems
- the behaviour of systems
- types of information systems
- applications for information systems
- applying information systems for competitive advantage.

Introduction to systems

Systems theory provides a powerful means of analysing and improving business processes. It can be applied to a wide variety of different areas and is one of the fundamental concepts required to gain a good understanding of the managerial application of BIS.

Systems theory
The study of the behaviour and interactions within and between systems.

▶ What is a system?

A **system** can be defined as a collection of interrelated components that work together towards a collective goal. The function of a system is to receive inputs and transform these into outputs. Figure 2.1 illustrates the organisation of the input–process–output model. Note that though natural systems such as the solar system may not have an obvious goal, business systems usually have multiple goals such as profit or improving the quality of a product.

System
A collection of interrelated components that work together towards a collective goal.

An example will help to illustrate this concept and aid understanding. In Chapter 1, the concept of a transformation process was used to explain how data can be converted into information. Using the model shown in the diagram, it can be said that data are used as the input for a process that creates information as an output.

However, this model illustrates a system that is essentially static. The performance of the system cannot be adjusted and there are no checks to ensure that it works correctly. In order to monitor the performance of the system, some kind of feedback mechanism is required. In addition, control must be exerted to correct any problems that occur and ensure that the system is fulfilling its purpose.

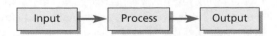

Figure 2.1 A basic model of a transformation process

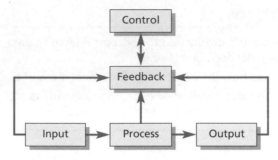

Figure 2.2 A generic model of a system

If these additional components are added to the basic model of the system, it can be illustrated as shown in Figure 2.2. The model shown in the diagram is sometimes referred to as an **adaptive system**, in order to signify that it has the ability to monitor and regulate its own performance.

Adaptive system

A system with the ability to monitor and regulate its own performance.

▶ System components

At this point, it can now be argued that a generic system includes five components: input, process, output, feedback and control. Each of these components can now be described in more detail.

Input

The raw materials for a *process* that will produce a particular *output*.

Process

Inputs are turned into outputs by a transformation process.

Output

A product that is created by a system.

Feedback mechanism

Provides information on the performance of a system which can be used to adjust its behaviour.

Control

If alterations are needed to the system, adjustments are made by a control mechanism.

System objective

All components of a system should be related to one another by a common objective.

- The **input** to a system can be thought of as the raw materials for a process that will produce a particular output. Inputs can take many forms and are not necessarily purely physical in nature. Examples of inputs might include data, knowledge, raw materials, machinery and premises.
- Inputs are turned into outputs by subjecting them to a transformation **process**. The concept of a transformation process was described in Chapter 1.
- The **output** is the finished product created by the system. Again, the outputs produced by a system can take many forms. Examples might include information, products and services.
- Information on the performance of the system is gathered by a **feedback mechanism** (sometimes known as a 'feedback loop'). Customer feedback on a web site is an example of a feedback mechanism.
- If alterations are needed to the system, adjustments are made by some form of **control mechanism**. In general, control is exerted as the result of feedback information regarding the performance of the system. The function of the control component is to ensure that the system is working to fulfil its objective (which is normally the creation of a specific output). Control tends to be exerted by adjusting the process and input components of the system until the correct output is achieved.

▶ Other system characteristics

All systems share these characteristics:

1 *The components of a system work towards a collective goal*. This is known as the system's **objective**. The objective of a system is normally very specific and can often be expressed in a single sentence. As an example, the objective of a car might be expressed simply as: to transport people and goods to a specified location.

2 *Systems do not operate in complete isolation.* They are contained within an **environment** that contains other systems and external agencies. The scope of a system is defined by its **boundary**. Everything outside of the boundary is part of the system's environment, everything within the boundary forms part of the system itself. The boundary also marks the **interface** between a system and its environment. The interface describes exchanges between a system and the environment or other systems.

3 *Systems can be complex and can be made up of other, smaller systems.* These are known as **subsystems**. Systems composed of one or more subsystems are sometimes referred to as **suprasystems**. The objective of a subsystem is to support the larger objective of the suprasystem. For an organisation the subsystems such as marketing and finance would lie within the systems boundary while the following elements would lie outside as part of the business environment:

- customers
- sales channel/distributors
- suppliers
- competitors
- partners
- government and legislation
- the economy.

An organisation will interact with all these elements which are beyond the system boundary in the environment. We refer to this as an **open system**. Most information systems will fall into this category since they will accept input and will react to it. Totally **closed** systems which do not interact with their environment are unusual.

4 *Subsystems in an information system interact by exchanging information.* This is known as the interface between systems. For information systems and business systems having clearly defined interfaces is important to an efficient organisation. For example, sales orders must be passed from the sales subsystem to the finance subsystem and the distribution subsystem in a clear repeatable way. If this does not happen orders may be lost or delayed and customer service will decline.

5 *The linkage or coupling between subsystems varies.* The degree of **coupling** defines how closely linked different subsystems are. It is a fundamental principle of systems theory and BIS design that subsystems should be loosely coupled.

Systems or subsystems that are highly dependent on one another are known as *close-coupled* systems. In such cases, the outputs of one system are the direct inputs of another. As an example, consider the way in which an examination system might operate. The letter that confirms a student's grade could be said to be the result of two subsystems working together very closely. One subsystem ensures that all examination scripts are marked and that a list of final results is produced. The second subsystem produces the letter of confirmation as its output. However, the letter of confirmation can only be produced once all marks have been confirmed and recorded. Thus, the output of the marking subsystem becomes the input to the subsystem that creates the confirmation letter.

The 'Just In Time' method used by a number of manufacturing organisations also illustrates a close-coupled system well. This method involves holding as few parts or raw materials as possible. In order to ensure that production is not halted, parts must be supplied 'just in time' to be used in the manufacturing process. Unless the manufacturing organisation has very close links with its suppliers, this approach cannot work effectively.

Decoupled systems (or subsystems) are less dependent on one another than coupled systems and so are more able to deal with unexpected situations or events. Such

---

Environment

The surroundings of a system, beyond its boundary.

Boundary

The interface between a system and its environment.

Interface

Defines exchanges between a system and its environment, or other systems.

Subsystem

Large systems can be composed of one or more smaller systems known as subsystems.

Suprasystem

A larger system made up of one or more smaller systems (*subsystems*).

Open system

Interaction occurs with elements beyond the system boundary.

Closed system

No or limited interaction occurs with the environment.

Coupling

Defines how closely linked different subsystems are. Loose coupling means that the modules pass only the minimum of information between them and do not share data and program code. Close-coupled systems are highly dependent on each other.

systems tend to have higher levels of autonomy, being allowed more freedom to plan and control their activities. Although decoupled systems are more flexible and adaptive than close-coupled systems, this very flexibility increases the possibility that inefficiencies might occur. The traditional method of production where material is held 'in-hand' as inventory is decoupled. In this arrangement it is not necessary for production to match sales so closely, but this results in higher costs of holding inventory.

6 *Systems are hierarchical.* Systems are made up of subsystems that may themselves be made up of other subsystems. From this, one should realise that the parts of a system are dependent on one another in some way. This **interdependence** means that a change to one part of a system leads to or results from changes to one or more other parts.

Interdependence

Interdependence means that a change to one part of a system leads to or results from changes to one or more other parts.

❱ Control in organisational systems

Figure 2.3 shows the relationship between different parts of an organisation and how they are related according to systems theory. The control mechanism is indicated by the arrowed line from the output back to the input.

The role of the BIS is to provide information to management which will enable them to make decisions which ensure that the organisation is controlled. The organisation will be in control if it is meeting the needs of the environment (Figure 1.2).

Open-loop control systems in business

Open-loop control system

An open-loop control system is one in which there is an attempt to reach the system objective, but no control action to modify the inputs or process is taken once the process has begun.

Figure 2.4 shows a generic **open-loop system**. An open-loop control system is one in which there is an attempt to reach the system objective, but no action is taken to modify the process or its input to achieve the targets once the process has begun. Open-loop systems have no mechanism for ensuring goals are met once the process is under way, for example, a decision to manufacture to a predicted market demand. In an open-loop system no changes would be made in reaction to, for example, a decision by a major competitor to cut its price.

Open-loop systems are inadequate in an organisational context because of the complexity of organisational systems and their environments. In other words, open-loop systems would only be successful in attaining the system objectives in cases where we could plan with certainty the events that would take place during the system's process.

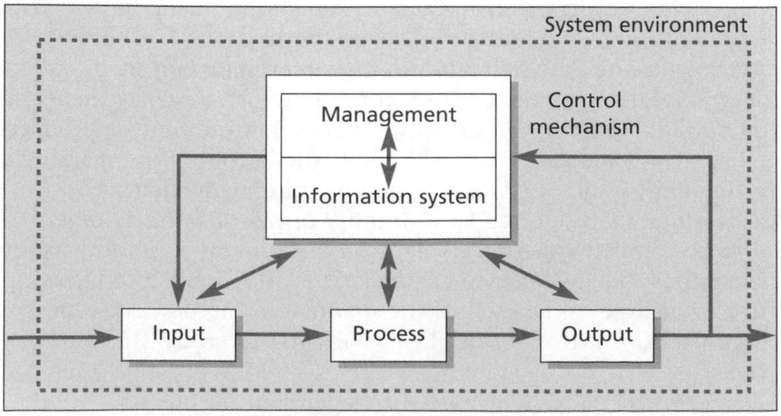

Figure 2.3 **Business information systems as an organisational control mechanism**

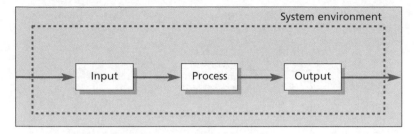

Figure 2.4 **A generic open-loop system**

Closed-loop control systems in business

Two types of control mechanism that can be employed in this situation are **feedback control** and **feedforward control**.

Feedback control systems generally provide a relatively cheap method of reactive control and provide an effective method of bringing a system back under control. Figure 2.5 shows a generic closed-loop system.

Feedforward systems (Figure 10.6) provide a pro-active way of overcoming the timing delays associated with feedback systems but depend upon the accuracy of the plans on which they are based. Feedforward control systems attempt to overcome the overcorrection and time-delay disadvantages of feedback systems by incorporating a prediction element in the control feedback loop. Feedforward systems are not as common as feedback systems in business settings. Examples include inventory control systems which work to a planned sales level or material usage rate. Elements of project management can also be seen as feedforward control where plans are made for resource requirements over time.

Feedback control

The output achieved is monitored and compared to the desired output and corrective action is taken if a deviation exists.

Feedforward control

The environment and system process are both monitored in order to provide corrective action if it is likely that the system goal will not be met.

❚ Positive and negative feedback

Negative feedback is used to describe the act of reversing any discrepancy between desired and actual output. Thus in a business setting a budget overspend would be responded to with actions leading to a reduction in this variance. A business example is rapid sales growth requiring increased production levels leading to increased sales. A situation of positive feedback is unsustainable and some corrective action arising either

Positive and negative feedback

Negative feedback is used to describe the act of reversing any discrepancy between desired and actual output. Positive feedback responds to a variance between desired and actual output by increasing that variance.

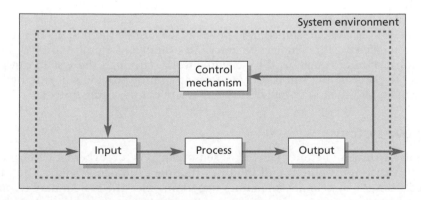

Figure 2.5 **A generic closed-loop feedback control system**

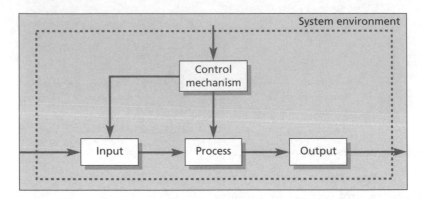

Figure 2.6 A generic closed-loop feedforward control system

from within the system or from the environment will occur. For the example of increasing sales and production, the business may meet cashflow problems with expanding too fast.

The major difficulty with negative feedback systems is the potential for delays in the feedback control loop. Thus the effect of a change in inputs to bring about a change in output may not be observed until after a period of time. This can lead to an output level that oscillates around the desired output because of overcorrection of input values during the feedback delay period. For example, the delay between the setting of interest rates and their effect on the output goal of a level of inflation can lead to a situation of overcompensation in either direction.

Different types of systems

In this final section on systems theory, we introduce some common terms for describing types of systems which you may encounter in business.

◗ Deterministic and probabilistic systems

In a *deterministic* system (sometimes known as *mechanistic*), all of the system's outputs can be predicted by examining its inputs. An example of a deterministic system is an electronic calculator, where the results of carrying out a calculation can be predicted with complete accuracy.

In a *probabilistic* system (sometimes known as *stochastic*), the outputs of the system cannot be predicted with complete accuracy. An example of a probabilistic system is a production planning system used to schedule work. Although the system can predict how long the production run is *likely* to take, it cannot provide a precise figure. An example of an information system of this type is a sales forecasting system.

◗ Adaptive systems

Adaptive system

In general, an adaptive system has the ability to monitor and regulate its own performance. In many cases, an adaptive system will be able to respond fully to changes in its environment by modifying its behaviour.

An **adaptive system** (sometimes known as 'self-organising' or 'cybernetic') responds to changes in the environment and modifies its operation accordingly. The outputs obtained from the system are sometimes uncertain since the system may respond to the same stimuli in a different way. Examples of adaptive systems include human beings, plants and business organisations.

▶ Hard and soft systems

A *hard system* has an explicit objective and is governed by fixed rules and procedures such as those encountered for structured decision making (Chapter 1). The conditions in the system's environment tend to be stable and therefore more predictable. In turn, the system's outputs can be predicted more easily and its performance can be measured objectively. An example of a hard system is a production line.

A *soft system* operates in a relatively unpredictable environment where conditions may be uncertain or liable to rapid change. Soft systems usually involve people or socio-technical situations. The next section describes a specific methodology used for dealing with these kinds of situations.

Business information systems

In this section, we introduce the concept of a business information system and consider the characteristics of computer-based information systems.

▶ What is a business information system?

Having examined concepts related to information, systems theory and decision making, it is possible to combine these to suggest a basic definition of a **business information system**:

> *A business information system is a group of interrelated components that work collectively to carry out input, processing, output, storage and control actions in order to convert data into information products that can be used to support forecasting, planning, control, coordination, decision making and operational activities in an organisation.*

It should be noted that alternative definitions exist and it is worth taking a brief look at some aspects of these definitions.

Business information systems

This describes information systems used to support the functional areas of business. For example, an organisation might use specialised information systems to support sales, marketing and human resource management activities.

- Many definitions refer to 'data resources' that are converted into 'information products'. This underlines the notion that data form part of an organisation's intangible resource base and that the information derived from them is provided in a finished, useful form. The importance of information as a business resource is highlighted by Evans and Wurster (1997) who said: 'every business is an information business … information is the glue that holds together the structure of all businesses'.

- Many definitions also specify that information systems involve the use of *information technology*. However, this can be disputed since it is possible to provide many examples of information systems that do not involve information technology at all. A simple example of such a 'manual' information system is a set of accounting ledgers.

- Some definitions specify that information systems are used only to support decision making. Again, this can be disputed since it is apparent that managers make use of information in a number of other ways, for example as feedback on various aspects of a company's performance.

- Although some definitions refer to organisations in general, others specify that they are concerned only with business organisations. However, it can be argued that it is sometimes very difficult to distinguish between profit-making and non-profit-making organisations.

Resources that support BIS

BIS typically rely on five basic resources: people, hardware, software, communications and data.

1 *People resources*. People resources include the users of an information system and those who develop, maintain and operate the system. Examples of people resources might include managers, data entry clerks and technical support staff.

2 *Hardware resources*. The term hardware resources refers to all types of machines, not just computer hardware. Telephones, fax machines, switchboards are all valid examples of hardware. The term also covers any media used by these machines, such as magnetic disks or paper. These resources are described in Chapter 3.

3 *Software resources*. In the same way, the term software resources does not only refer to computer programs and the media on which they are stored. The term can also be used to describe the procedures used by people. Within this context, examples of software include instruction manuals and company policies. These resources are described in Chapter 4.

4 *Communications resources*. Resources are also required to enable different systems to transfer data. These include networks and the hardware and software needed to support them. These resources are described in Chapter 5.

5 *Data resources*. Data resources describes all of the data that an organisation has access to, regardless of its form. Computer databases, paper files and measurements taken by sensors on a production line are all examples of data resources.

Activity 2.1

Example of information systems

What information systems might be found in your newsagent? For each system identified, list the people, hardware, communications, software and data resources involved.

▌ Information technology

The terms 'information systems' (IS) and 'information technology' (IT) are often used interchangeably. This is an error, because the scope of the terms is different. The stress in IT is on the technology while IS not only refers to the technology, but also incorporates how it is applied and managed to contribute to the business. For this reason, we refer to BIS throughout this book. Approaches to management of IS and IT as part of BIS strategy development are discussed in more detail in Chapter 13.

▌ Computer-based information systems

Computer-based information system
An information system that makes use of Information Technology in order to create management information.

In modern organisations, most BIS make extensive use of information technology, such as personal computers. The reasons why computerised BIS have become widespread are evident in their advantages.

▌ Some advantages of processing by computer

- *Speed*. Computers can process millions of instructions each second, allowing them to complete a given task in a very short time.

- *Accuracy*. The result of a calculation carried out by a computer is likely to be completely accurate. In addition, errors that a human might make, such as a typing error, can be reduced or eliminated entirely.
- *Reliability*. In many organisations, computer-based information systems operate for twenty-four hours a day and are only ever halted for repairs or routine maintenance.
- *Programmability*. Although most computer-based information systems are created to fulfil a particular function, the ability to modify the software that controls them provides a high degree of flexibility. Even the simplest personal computer, for example, can be used to create letters, produce cash flow forecasts or manipulate databases.

These advantages combine to give major benefits to a business, as described on p. 53 in the section *Information systems for strategic advantage*.

There are, however, some disadvantages to computer-based BIS:

- *Judgement/experience*. Despite advances in artificial intelligence techniques and expert systems, computer-based information systems are incapable of solving problems using their own judgement and experience.
- *Improvisation/flexibility*. In general, computer-based information systems are unable to react to unexpected situations and events. Additionally, since most systems are created to fulfil a particular function, it can be difficult to modify them to meet new or changed requirements.
- *Innovation*. Computers lack the creativity of a human being. They are unable to think in the abstract and are therefore restricted in their ability to discover new ways of improving processes or solving problems.
- *Intuition*. Human intuition can play an important part in all certain social situations. For example, one might use intuition to gauge the emotional state of a person before deciding whether or not to give them bad news. BIS cannot use intuition in this way and are therefore unsuitable for certain kinds of situations.
- *Qualitative information*. Managers often make unstructured decisions based on the recommendations of others. Their confidence in the person they are dealing with often has a major influence on the decision itself. Once again, BIS cannot act upon qualitative information of this kind.

▶ Business applications of BIS

In Chapter 1 it was shown how the characteristics of the decisions taken by managers vary according to organisational level from operational to strategic. The problems and decisions dealt with at the operational level of an organisation tend to have a high degree of structure. Frequent access to highly detailed information is often required to support the decision-making process. Since BIS are well suited to such situations, they are more common at this organisational level than at the strategic level where unstructured decision making based on qualitative data is more common.

Figure 2.7 illustrates areas of applications for BIS in a typical organisation. Note that there will be fewer applications and therefore lower levels of usage at the strategic level. A need for higher levels of automation and the structure of the tasks carried out mean that highest levels of usage will be at the operational level.

The key operational activities referred to in Figure 2.7 include **data processing** or handling the large volumes of data that arise from an organisation's daily activities. Although 'data processing' describes a wide range of activities, the most common are transaction processing and process control.

Transaction processing involves dealing with the sales and purchase transactions that an organisation carries out in the course of its normal activities. Banks, for example, handle millions of deposits and withdrawals each day. **Process control systems** deal with

Data processing
The transformation of the large volumes of data that arise from an organisation's daily activities into information for decision making.

Transaction processing
Processing the sales and purchase transactions that an organisation carries out in the course of its normal activities.

Process control systems
Systems which manage manufacturing and other production processes.

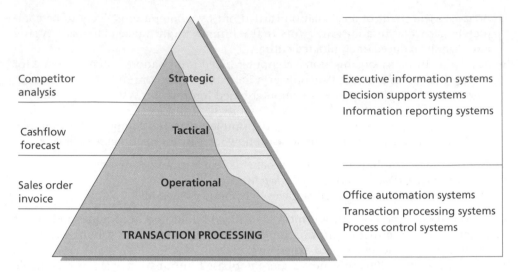

Figure 2.7 Usage and applications of computer-based information systems by organisational level (shading denotes usage of BIS)

the large volume of data generated by production processes. As an example, a machine producing a precision component might take hundreds of measurements and use these to adjust the manufacturing process. These types of system are described in more detail in Chapter 6.

The speed, accuracy and reliability of computer-based information systems mean that they are able to handle repetitive tasks involving large volumes of data. Furthermore, they are best utilised in situations governed by clear, logical rules. This makes them ideally suited to transaction processing or process control applications. From this, it is reasonable to suggest that the widest use of computer-based information systems will be at the operational level of an organisation.

Categories of business information system

Information systems are commonly divided into two broad categories: systems that support an organisation's business activities and systems that support managerial decision making.

- **Operations information systems** are generally concerned with process control, transaction processing, communications (internal and external) and productivity.
- **Management information systems** provide feedback on organisational activities and help to support managerial decision making. Managerial decision making can occur at the operational, tactical and strategic levels of an organisation.

Operations information systems
Systems required for the day-to-day activities of a business such as process control, transaction processing, communications (internal and external) and productivity.

Management information systems.
Systems providing feedback on organisational activities and supporting managerial decision making.

Activity 2.2	**Online processing systems**

Using the Internet as a resource, locate at least two examples of the use of online processing systems in business. As an example, both Sainsbury's and Boots use incentive programmes based around loyalty cards, where customers can redeem points against purchases using interactive kiosks.

As shown in Table 2.1, both of these broader categories can be subdivided into a number of additional categories. The following sections introduce these types of system. They are described in more detail in Chapter 6. Figure 2.7 also illustrates the typical use of each category of computer-based information system by management level.

Table 2.1 Categories of computer-based information systems

Operations information systems	Management information systems
Transaction processing systems	Decision support systems
Process control systems	Information reporting systems
Office automation systems	Executive information systems

Activity 2.3

Different types of reports

Use a search engine such as Google (www.google.com) to make some general enquiries. Is the list of results returned by the search engine a scheduled report, an ad hoc report, a periodic report or an exception report (these are defined in Chapter 4)?

Note that traditional dual division of BIS into operational and management systems, although useful for managers reviewing the types of BIS in use, does not now accurately reflect the reality of systems used within an organisation, particularly with the increased use of inter-organisational e-commerce and electronic data interchange (EDI). In Chapter 6 we will see that e-business systems and **enterprise resource planning systems** cut across both operational and management systems to provide businesses with more closely coupled information systems.

BIS and strategic advantage

In order to survive and grow in a competitive environment, organisations must seek to gain **strategic advantage** (or competitive advantage). BIS play a crucial part in gaining and sustaining a competitive edge over the other organisations operating in the same industry.

This section introduces the concept of strategic advantage. Chapter 13 describes how IS strategy can be developed in more detail. Chapter 8 looks at how a company reviews the benefits of a specific new system when assessing its feasibility.

◗ Competitive strategies

In order to gain or maintain competitive advantage, organisations can adopt three basic strategies: cost leadership, differentiation or innovation.

Cost leadership

Cost leadership means simply providing goods or services at the lowest possible cost. In most cases this is achieved by reducing the organisation's costs in producing goods or providing services, for example by automating parts of the production process. However, cost leadership can also be achieved by helping suppliers and customers to reduce costs, usually by forming alliances and linkages that benefit all of the parties involved. In some cases, cost leadership is achieved by causing a competitor's costs to

Enterprise resource planning (ERP) software
A software system with integrated functions for all major business functions across an organisation such as production, distribution, sales, finance and human resources management. It is normally purchased as an off-the-shelf package which is tailored by a consultant. A single package typically replaces many different previous packages.

Strategic advantage
Organisations gain benefits through developing distinctive competencies.

increase, for example by introducing new product features that will be expensive for a competitor to duplicate. Using Internet technologies for e-business can assist in achieving cost leadership. For example, the airline easyJet has dramatically reduced staff costs through transferring over 90% of their ticketing online.

Product differentiation

Differentiation involves creating a distinction between the organisation's products and those of its competitors. In many cases, differentiation is used to concentrate on a specific niche in the market so that the company can focus on particular goods and services. A car manufacturer, such as Rolls Royce, provides a good example of product differentiation. The cars produced by Rolls Royce are perceived as luxury items that indicate status and importance in society. They are considered far superior to standard production models in terms of quality, reliability and comfort. By creating this image, Rolls-Royce has succeeded in differentiating its products from those of its competitors. An e-commerce-related example of differentiation is that of a newspaper personalising content for its readers according to their preferences and then making it available via alerts on e-mail or mobile phone.

Innovation

Innovation is concerned with finding new ways to approach an organisation's activities. Examples of innovation include improving existing products or creating new ones, forging strategic linkages, improving production processes and entering new markets. Case Study 2.1 shows how a company can innovate and develop a variety of methods for retaining competitive advantage. The case study also highlights how *responsiveness* to the market environment and the *flexibility* to be able to respond are important capabilities of a company.

CASE STUDY 2.1

Battle of the e-grocers

Gareth Coslett explains how Tesco.com is battling to be your first port of call when you want to fill up your e-trolley.

John Browett could be ranked alongside the giant panda or the black rhino as an endangered species. He is a member of one of the tiniest subsects of the e-commerce world: the rare genus known as e-profit makers.

And the former Cambridge zoology student has as good a case as any to be billed as the king of the jungle. As chief executive of Tesco.com, he is heading up one of Europe's largest online retailers and the biggest e-grocer in the world.

Just 18 months after a full roll-out into 240 Tesco stores in the UK, the grocery business is already making a profit. No embarrassed finger-jabbing at sales projections, no demographic justification for current loss-making strategies, Tesco's Internet shopping and home delivery service is already in the black on the grocery side.

The constant addition of new product categories such as electrical goods, financial services, mother and baby goods, clothes and home entertainment – plus the losses from the mail order business and overseas expansion – mean that the overall Tesco.com business is still making a loss. But Browett says it is just a matter of time before his business produces positive returns.

'The reason we report losses is that we put in all the start-up losses for all the other e-commerce initiatives that we have. But the grocery business is profitable. It is not the same as store profitability, but it has only been fully going for 18 months. Our objective for that business – and we expect to achieve it fairly straightforwardly – is to have profit margins that are the same as, if not higher than, the stores', he says.

The relationship with stores has always been a thorny one for online food retailers. The fear that e-commerce will cannibalise sales from bricks-and-

▶

mortar outlets has held back development for many retailers. Tesco took a gamble in launching into e-commerce and, Browett says, it paid off.

'Half our sales on the Internet are new to Tesco, so half are cannibalised. That is a really exceptional performance. It means that I can build a new business while keeping existing customers happy.

'We always knew that this was a device to increase market share. It is a new service, it adds value to customers and enables us to access customers we could not otherwise get to. We think there is a very big advantage to being first in this.'

The size of his business and its rate of growth is sending shock waves through Tesco's traditional competitors such as Sainsbury's, Safeway and Asda, which have all proved reluctant to roll out a full service before working out how to turn a profit.

Tesco's online service is handling 60,000 orders per week, producing a turnover of more than £5m per week in groceries alone, and has 750,000 registered users in the UK. The grocery service covers 90% of the UK population and the average spend per order is £85. The business has doubled in size in the last six months and Browett is confident that the Tesco.com steamroller will power forward.

'We have capacity within our system to do up to £2bn worth of turnover. That is based on the capacity within our stores and what we currently know, but there is no reason why it should not go beyond that.

'It has surprised everybody that there is £250m worth of business to be done in grocery home shopping. If it doubled every year for the next five years then we could handle it, but faster growth than that would be difficult.'

There is also huge scope for overseas development. In markets where Tesco already has stores, the UK business model is being adopted: Tesco.com launched in Ireland last month and is hitting South Korea next year, with Taiwan also pencilled in for the future.

In countries where it has no presence, Tesco is looking to set up joint ventures with other retailers to combine their store portfolio with Tesco's e-commerce business model. Its first priority market is an audacious coals-to-Newcastle play: 'We're focusing on North America at the moment. We're going through the list and have got some promising leads', says Browett.

His level-headed approach is the result of a textbook business upbringing: Cambridge student; five years cutting his teeth in the City; excelled at the best MBA in the US; think-tank role at the Boston Consulting Group; groomed for the top at Tesco – arguably the UK's best-run company in arguably the UK's most cut-throat business environment.

Here is a man not averse to dipping into a business manual or two.

'In our business model we have created a classic "strategy versus tactics" environment. We set a strategy for our development team and all they do is think about how to actually make the business better, simpler and cheaper.

'Tesco.com has its own board and is run as a separate business, but it obviously taps into the advantages that the mainstream Tesco business has, such as the power of the brand, the chance to use our stores to promote the service – half of all UK households come through our doors every 12 weeks – and the buying power and contacts that Tesco has.

'We are running a real business, so our day-to-day problems are in managing the cost lines properly and improving the quality of the service. We worked on the economic model for three years before we launched in December 1996. We were not ready for a full roll-out until 1999, so it has taken us a long time to work out how to make it robust and profitable.'

Browett is proud of the fact that existing Tesco staff have largely been behind its success – a team of just six people was working on the project when the first Internet order was taken four years ago. A total of 70 people now work on the business.

'We have developed a lot of people internally. We have not spent a lot of time going out into the market to get whizzkids. The reason for that is two-fold. One is that the Tesco people are good and they know the business well. The other is that it is not actually that complicated when you get down to the fundamentals.

'The mistake that lots of people make with Internet businesses is that they say they are IT businesses when in fact they are not. A lot of the Internet start-ups have failed because they were not run by people who actually knew what the underlying business process was going to look like. The IT is only a facilitator; it is not an end in itself.

'The way we do our IT is we have a core group of people who work on key projects, but we then outsource quite a lot of tasks such as code writing to contractors, consultants and even the Tesco IT department. When you are developing the business, you need different skills at different times. There is no way we could go out and hire a snapshot of all the people we need because we know it will change in six months' time. We need to think fast on our feet.'

He says that most of the £35m capital expenditure being invested in Tesco.com last year is into IT – particularly into the fully automated in-store picking system which features a PC on each trolley that tells the pickers where to go next after scanning each item.

Browett says Tesco.com's success has been built on getting the basics right. This pragmatic capitalist

▶

is scathing about some of the hot air talked in the dotcom arena, but argues that the bursting of the e-bubble will not affect 'well-rooted' businesses such as his own.

'All that has happened with pure plays is that the fundamentals of business have come back into practice. I think that is healthy for the market because there were too many people running around with business plans which were unachievable and were not going to deliver value to the customers. They were reliant on putting prices up over time rather than working out what the business model is today.

'It's better to have well-executed, well-run businesses that are making money on the Internet rather than people who are not giving value to customers and not going to achieve their long-term promises.'

He lists e-Bay, Dell and Charles Schwab as the e-commerce operations that he most admires. 'They have created completely new business models, they have fashioned a successful business out of something that just wasn't there before. But I would argue that what we have done with grocery home shopping is as big a change to the market as what Dell did with its straight-through delivery. Both have fundamentally changed the competitive structures of their industry.'

As for his competitors in grocery home shopping, Browett says, 'We do not fear anybody. Nobody seems to have hit on an economic model that actually works – you can tell that by the fact that their sales are not closing up on us. But we don't take our lead for granted. Tesco has traditionally been paranoid number two and that is how it became number one. That is how it will stay number one – you cannot rest on your laurels.'

Battling through the technology constraints

Tesco is striving to make the online shopping experience a more enjoyable, efficient experience. One recent innovation is the introduction of Express Shopper, a new facility which allows shoppers to type in their shopping list, click a 'go shopping' button and then be transported to the aisles where items are stored so they do not have to search.

John Browett believes that faster, further-reaching Internet technology will revolutionise e-commerce and the potential for retailers to reach customers. 'Broadband will make a dramatic impact on the Internet and its usability. Always-on is also going to significantly improve uptake', he says.

'We all know the Internet experience can be frustrating. But the question is about time – will the new technology take 10 years or three years to reach the mass market?'

He concedes he must work within the constraints of the system for the time being but, once the public does have access to the technology, he fully intends to exploit it. 'We will be able to improve the customer offer by streaming videos directly through to people. We will be able to do things on the Web site that are not possible at the moment – the design and usability and product shots are obvious areas.'

But he is cautious of investing too heavily in technology supporting platforms such as digital television and Wap-enabled mobile phones. 'Digital TV and m-commerce are more appropriate for non-food than food shopping. The problem with the new platforms is that the platform owners want to get a very high percentages of sales. Platform owners are looking at i-mode in Japan and seeing that they are getting 9%, so they say they will get 8%.

'This percentage out of any retail business is very high – the only retail businesses that can afford it are the high-margin ones such as luxury goods and clothing. No one else has the margins. So they are cutting off the options for any major discount operation to work on those.

'In digital television, no-one has explained to me how the customer offer can be made attractive for retailing. Take the "normal household" – what is the rest of the family going to watch when one individual is doing the shopping? It is lean back, not lean forward, and is hard to present the data in the right format. The modems on digital TV, frankly, are not fast enough. It will be a while before we see it having a major impact on a data-intensive process like grocery shopping.'

Source: Gareth Coslett, 'Battle of the e-grocers', courtesy of *Computer Weekly*, 21 January 2001

Questions

1 Half of Tesco.com's sales are cannibalised. What does this mean?

2 Why do you think Tesco.com has become successful as an online retailer?

3 Tesco.com is confident that it will remain 'number one' for the foreseeable future. What competitive factors might help it to achieve this ambition?

▶ Value chain analysis

Michael Porter's work includes the concept of a value chain: a series of connected activities that add value to a organisation's products or services. An analysis of an organisation's value chain can indicate which areas might provide an organisation with a competitive advantage.

To understand value chain analysis we need also to consider an organisation's supply chain. **Supply chain management (SCM)** is the coordination of all supply activities of an organisation from its suppliers through to production of goods and services and their delivery to its customers. The **value chain** is a related concept that describes the different value-adding activities that connect a company's supply side with its demand side. We can identify an internal value chain within the boundaries of an organisation and an external value chain where these activities are performed by partners. Traditional value chain analysis (Fig. 2.8(a)) distinguishes between primary activities that contribute directly to getting goods and services to the customer (such as inbound logistics, including procurement, manufacturing, marketing and delivery to buyers, support and servicing after sale) and support activities which provide the inputs and infrastructure that allow the primary activities to take place. Support activities include finance, human resources and information systems. It can be argued that, with the advent of e-business, the support activities offer much more than support, indeed having effective information systems and management of human resources is critical to the primary activities. Note that in the era of e-business a company will manage many interrelated value chains, so part of e-business strategy development (Chapter 13) is **value network** creation and maintenance.

Evans and Wurster (1997) describe how information can impact the value chain in three ways:

1 *Reach* – a business can share information with more stakeholders or gain a larger audience at relatively low cost.

Supply chain management
The coordination of all supply activities of an organisation from its suppliers and partners to its customers.

Value chain
A model for analysis of how supply chain activities can add value to products and services delivered to the customer.

Value network
The links between an organisation and its strategic and non-strategic partners that form its external value chain.

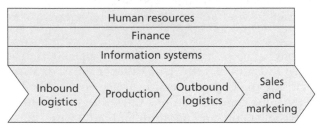

Secondary value chain activities

Primary value chain activities

(a)

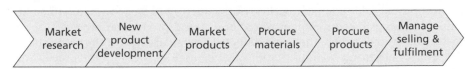

Revised value chain model

(b)

Figure 2.8 Alternative models of the value chain: (a) traditional value chain model, (b) revised value chain model
Source: Chaffey (2002)

2 *Customisation* – information can be more readily tailored for sharing with a large number of partners. Dell's Premier Pages extranet enables them to provide customised sales and order histories for large accounts.

3 *Dialogue* – interaction between the parties is two-way rather than the traditional push of information. For example, it is possible for a supplier to anticipate a retailer's product requirements from examining their inventory forecast rather than awaiting a faxed order.

The Internet technologies described in Chapter 5 can also reduce production times and costs by increasing the flow of information and so integrating different value-chain activities. Through doing this the value chain can be made more efficient and services can be delivered to customers more readily. Rayport and Sviokla (1996) contend that the Internet enables value to be created by gathering, organising, selecting, synthesising and distributing information. They refer to a separate parallel virtual value chain mirroring the physical value chain. The virtual value chain involves electronic commerce being used to mediate traditional value-chain activities such as market research, procurement, logistics, manufacture, marketing and distributing. The processing is machine-based or virtual rather than paper-based. The situation is not truly virtual in that human intervention is still required in many value-chain activities such as procurement. The 'virtuality' of the virtual value chain will increase as software agents increasingly perform these activities.

Restructuring the internal value chain

Traditional models of the value chain (such as Fig. 2.8(a)) have been re-evaluated with the advent of global electronic communications. It can be suggested that there are some key weaknesses in the traditional value chain model:

● It is most applicable to manufacturing of physical products as opposed to services.
● It is a one-way chain involving pushing products to the customer; it does not highlight the importance of understanding customer needs through market research and responsiveness through innovation and new product development.
● The internal value chain referred to does not emphasise the importance of value networks.

A revised form of the value chain has been suggested by Deise et al. (2000); an adaptation of this model is presented in Figure 2.8 (b). This value chain starts with the market research process, emphasising the importance of real-time environment scanning made possible through electronic communications links with distributors and customers. For example, leading e-tailers now monitor, on an hourly basis, how customers are responding to promotional offers on their web site and review competitors' offers and then revise them accordingly. Similarly, manufacturers such as Cisco have feedback forms and forums on their site that enable them to collect information from customers and channel partners that can feed through to new product development. When new product development occurs, the marketing strategy will be refined and at the same time steps taken to obtain the resources and production processes necessary to create, store and distribute the new product. Through analysis of the value chain and looking at how electronic communications can be used to speed up the process, manufacturers have been able to significantly reduce time to market from conception of a new product idea through to launch on the market. For example, car manufacturers have reduced time to market from over 5 years to 18 months.

In addition to changes in the efficiency of value-chain activities, electronic commerce also has implications for whether these activities are achieved internally or externally (outsourced). These changes have been referred to as value-chain disaggregation (Kalakota and Robinson, 2000) or deconstruction (Timmers, 1999) and value-chain reaggregation (Kalakota and Robinson, 2000) or reconstruction (Timmers, 1999). Value-chain disaggregation can occur through deconstructing the primary activities of the value chain. Each of the elements can be approached in a new way, for instance by working differently with suppliers. In value-chain reaggregation the value chain is streamlined to increase efficiency between each of the value-chain stages. Indeed, Timmers (1999) notes that the conventional wisdom of the value chain as a separate series of discrete steps may no longer be tenable as steps such as inbound logistics and operations become more tightly integrated through technology.

The value stream

The **value stream** is a closely related concept to the value chain. The difference is that it considers different types of tasks that are involved with adding value and looks at how the efficiency of these tasks can be improved. How BIS can enhance the value stream is readily apparent from this definition from Womack and Jones (1998), which identifies three different areas where efficiency can be increased, and costs reduced:

Value stream
The combination of actions required to deliver value to the customer as products and services.

> *the set of all the specific actions required to bring a specific product through the three critical management tasks of any business:*

1 the problem-solving task (the processes of new product development and production launch)
2 the information management task (the processes of order taking, scheduling to delivery)
3 the physical transformation task (the processes of transforming raw materials to finished product delivered to customers).

The benefits of using BIS can also be identified by applying the equation of Deise et al. (2000) which is intended to highlight the components of customer value:

$$Customer\ value\ (brand\ perception) = \frac{Product\ quality \times Service\ quality}{Price \times Fulfilment\ time}$$

By reducing new product development and production times and costs, organisations can then either increase customer value by decreasing fulfilment time or if they wish decrease price, and/or increase product and service quality. Clearly e-commerce plays a key role in decreasing time to market and production times and costs.

Assessing customer value   Activity 2.4

Assess the applicability of the equation of Deise, *et al.* (2000) by reviewing how these companies can use BIS to add customer value:

● manufacturer of fast-moving consumer goods (FMCG)
● a supermarket
● a newspaper.

▶ Using information systems for strategic advantage

BIS can be also used to counter the five competitive forces of their environment described by Porter (1980). Examples of how this can be achieved are given in Chapter 13. The five forces are:

(a) the threat of new entrants,
(b) the bargaining power of suppliers,

(c) the bargaining power of customers,

(d) the threat of substitute products or services,

(e) rivalry among existing competitors.

Porter's work can also be used to identify a number of ways in which BIS can be used to achieve competitive advantage. These include:

(a) improving operational efficiency,

(b) raising barriers to entry,

(c) locking in customers and suppliers,

(d) promoting business innovation,

(e) increasing switching costs,

(f) leverage.

Figure 2.9 summarises the main ways in which computer-based information systems can be used to achieve competitive advantage.

Improving operational efficiency

One of the most common ways of using computer-based information systems to achieve competitive advantage is by using them to improve *operational efficiency*. As an example, consider a typical manufacturing company wishing to adopt a cost leadership strategy. In a primary activity, such as production, an inventory control system might be used to manage stock levels, reducing storage and transportation costs. In addition, support activities, such as management and administration, might achieve higher levels of productivity through the introduction of office automation systems. The organisation might also realise additional benefits from this kind of approach, such as improved customer service.

Barriers to entry

In many industries, organisations have improved operational efficiency by investing heavily in BIS. Often, the systems employed are extremely complex and require ongoing maintenance and development. This means that newcomers to the industry must be prepared to make a large initial expenditure so that they can acquire the computer-based information systems they need to be able to compete effectively. The level of expenditure needed may be so high that an *entry barrier* is created that deters or prevents the new competitor from entering the industry. Investing heavily in

Figure 2.9 Applying computer-based information systems for competitive advantage

computer-based information systems may also deter existing competitors, since they too must invest in their information systems in order to maintain or improve their position in the industry. New technologies can decrease barriers to entry. For example, electronic banking removed the requirement for a branch network, meaning that new entrants such as First e (www.first-e.com) entered the market in 1999. However, the barriers to entry were high and existing companies were successful in fighting off this new challenge – First e ceased trading in 2001.

Locking in customers and suppliers

Linking an organisation's computer-based information systems to those of its customers and suppliers can help to strengthen business relationships. As an example, computer-based information systems can be used to provide higher levels of customer service, thereby encouraging clients to remain loyal to the company.

Close integration with a supplier's information systems can result in a number of business benefits, which include:

(a) the availability of raw materials or parts is more certain,
(b) cost savings can be realised through reduced administration overheads,
(c) suppliers are less likely to abandon the business relationship,
(d) the organisation can negotiate favourable terms and prices,
(e) competitors are excluded from the business relationship.

Chaffey (2002) describes how Shell Chemical has developed SIMON (Shell Inventory Managed Order Network) to reduce costs and improve ordering performance for its customers.

However, it should be noted that achieving high levels of integration can also have some significant disadvantages. Perhaps the single largest disadvantage is that the organisation may come to rely upon a relatively small number of suppliers. This reliance might lead to some suppliers' taking advantage of the relationship, for example by raising prices.

Promoting business innovation

Investing in computer-based information systems often helps to stimulate business innovation. Introducing a new process control system, for example, might ultimately result in the development of new product features or new product lines.

Organisations that have invested in building effective computer-based information systems are well placed to support business innovation. Such organisations are likely to have established a resource base that can be drawn upon to develop new ideas.

On the other hand, an organisation that has failed to invest adequately in its information systems may lack essential resources, such as hardware, software and trained personnel, and be unable to explore new methods.

Increasing switching costs

In general, an organisation that has invested time, money and effort in developing a computer-based information system will be reluctant to bear the *switching costs* of moving to a new system. In addition to the cost of new hardware and software, a range of other costs can be incurred. These might include costs connected with:

(a) converting data for use with the new system,
(b) training staff,
(c) interruptions to the company's operations,
(d) lost opportunities to gain new business.

When an organisation links its information systems to those of its suppliers or customers, it will often ensure that switching costs are as high as possible. In this way, the supplier or customer is discouraged from switching to a competitor's system and competitors are excluded from the business relationship.

Leverage

Access to a resource base of this kind can provide a number of other benefits to an organisation as well as innovation. First, the organisation is equipped so that it can take advantage of any opportunities that arise in the business environment. Secondly, the organisation can begin to develop new products and services by maximising its use of existing resources. As an example, a travel agent might create a mailing list from its customer database so that they can offer customers new products or services, such as travel insurance or car rental.

Finally, the organisation may use its resources to gain competitive advantage through **information leadership**. Information leadership involves enhancing a product or service with an organisation's specialised information or expertise.

Information leadership
....
Enhancing a product or service using an organisation's specialised information or expertise.

MINI CASE STUDY

Capital One develop information leadership

As products become commoditised, it is often said that how companies use information is the key to competing successfully in the marketplace. Dave Buch, director at Capital One, has said: 'Back in 1987 we figured that our business is nothing to do about credit cards, it's about information. *Capital One is now a $14 billion company with 12 million customers.*'

In some cases, organisations achieve information leadership by selling information or expertise in the form of a separate product. A good example might be selling a mailing list created from an organisation's customer database.

We can see many of the approaches described in this chapter, in the e-business strategies adopted by many organisations. As explained in Chapter 1, e-business involves making use of the Internet to improve internal and external communications and automate various business processes. As an example, selling products via the Internet allows companies to reduce labour and administrative costs, whilst simultaneously increasing the size of the potential customer base. As a summary to Chapter 2, Case Study 2.2 illustrates different ways in which small and medium enterprises (SMEs) are using Internet technologies for competitive advantage.

CASE STUDY 2.2

SMEs use e-commerce for competitive advantage

'As it is, we are only just here and we may yet go under. Without e-commerce, we wouldn't be here at all.'

Graham Waters is no dotcom entrepreneur and his firm, Pentwyn Splicers of Pontypool, south Wales, is no Internet startup. Yet when UK orders for the company's splicers – used to produce knot-free joints in yarns for carpets and hosiery – fell by 60

per cent in two years, Mr Waters was prepared to consider anything.

'Two-thirds of our turnover came from the UK. Then the UK textile industry hit a brick wall. We knew there could be new customers overseas but we are a small firm. We couldn't even afford a discount air fare to send someone to the Far East to find sales leads', says Mr Waters.

But when the University of Cardiff and BT selected Pentwyn Splicers as a case study for the adoption of e-commerce by small businesses, Mr Waters began to consider the Internet as a new sales channel.

'If you are given a technology such as the Internet . . . you should push it to the limit. If you are a small business, you should sit down and find out what it can do, and then what it can do for you.'

The firm, with half a dozen staff, now relies on overseas sales from Thailand, Korea and Poland for 70 per cent of its £300,000 annual turnover. The majority of fresh leads arrive by e-mail via its web site (www.splicer.co.uk). The site's domain name was kept generic to present it as a source of industry information rather than as a corporate web brochure.

The same idea was used to create 'tags' that identify the web site's content for search engines when overseas buyers seek suppliers.

As well as increased sales, the firm believes, the opportunity to improve customer service – by publishing updated equipment manuals and spares information online and ensuring rapid replies to e-mail – will give it an edge over larger rival suppliers that do not offer the same range of services online.

But Mr Waters has blunt advice for small companies looking to imitate his web site, which he created using 'a £100 Microsoft package' and 'a lot of my own time'.

'I would very positively say: "Don't even think of doing it yourself".' And there is the rub. Most small traders successfully operating on the web argue that a strong degree of personal commitment from the top is essential. However, knowing how much effort, money and – more importantly – time to invest in an online offshoot is extremely difficult.

Civil Defence Supply, a Lincoln company that exports riot shields and pepper sprays via the Internet to police and state officials, including to the US Department of Defense, has championed the use of the internet in an effort to increase sales.

Director Gerard Bauer says his brother and fellow director, Erin, oversaw Internet strategy: 'We learnt by our mistakes – but it takes one person really to get behind it.'

As enthusiasm for internet start-ups has faded and estimates of electronic trading have fallen, other small companies have found themselves with a website that has neither delivered customers nor enhanced productivity.

'There were a lot of businesses that jumped in last year without thinking whether they needed a web site or whether they could afford to maintain and run it', says Mark Abrahams of Myratech, a Birmingham web design company, which largely services small to medium-sized companies.

'A lot of our work now is on second sites for companies that either tried to do it themselves or went to a provider that couldn't meet their needs', adds Mike Pearce, managing director of Business Internet in Derby.

The situation is compounded by the heterogeneity of the small to medium-sized enterprises sector, which encompasses very different degrees of technology awareness. For a sophisticated minority, particularly in the creative, media or technology industries, high-speed Internet connections and streaming video over the internet are concerns. Others are still trying to get to grips with e-mail.

At first glance, there is no shortage of advisers from the public and private sectors to provide guidance. As part of its commitment to double the number of SMEs trading online (defined as both initiating and completing transactions online) to 1m by the end of 2002, the government has created a 'UK online for business' programme.

The programme has 300 advisers in the UK providing face-to-face assessments. It offers printed and Internet-based material, including case studies to encourage SMEs to assess how their businesses could benefit from going online.

Spurred by fear of a saturated corporate market for information technology, software providers to big business such as Oracle, the database company, are identifying SMEs with modified versions of software to handle sales figures, accounts and purchasing distributed via the Internet.

Ian Smith, UK managing director of Oracle, says: 'Technology is becoming pervasive in the workplace, yet there is a predicted future shortfall of 1m trained information technology people in the UK. No SME is going to be able to retain an IT worker in that labour market. It makes sense for them to rent software via the Internet and to do away with the need for an IT person altogether.'

Yet Jenny Searle, director of UK Online for Business, says SMEs have traditionally been a low priority for IT vendors because of the fragmented nature of the sector and a lack of suitable products for small companies.

Ms Searle says: 'What SMEs lack above all is time to strategise and the IT management skills to make the best use of the technology they have already bought.

'We are not aiming to get 100 per cent of SMEs UK online. They have to use the Internet as an organic part of their business and adapt their business processes to reflect that. It is a commercial decision for them.'

▶

Mr Bauer, of Civil Defence Supply, agrees. 'The danger is that people think of the Internet as something in itself, rather than only another way to reach customers or to organise business', he says.

Mike Pearce believes the series of high-profile closures of dotcom startups has not seriously affected confidence in the internet and now that hype about the sector has faded, companies can make better decisions. As Mr Pearce puts it: 'Most SMEs don't really identify with the Boo.coms of this world.'

Questions

1 Summarise the business benefits of Internet adoption for the companies mentioned in the article.

2 Describe the success factors for each company.

3 Summarise the difficulties in developing an online presence according to the article.

Source: Carlos Grande, 'Inside track enterprises: SMEs and e-commerce', *Financial Times*, 19 April 2001

Summary

1 A system is composed of a group of interrelated components that work towards a common goal. These components include inputs, processes, outputs, feedback and control. A system also has a boundary that separates it from the environment. Systems can be made up of one or more smaller subsystems.

2 An information system converts data into information products. This information is used to support the activities of managers. Information systems make use of people resources, hardware resources, software resources and data resources.

3 Computer-based information systems take advantage of the benefits of information technology and are often grouped into two broad categories. Operations information systems are concerned with process control, transaction processing and productivity. Management information systems provide feedback on organisational activities and support managerial decision making. Computer-based information systems are referred to as 'information systems' in the remainder of the book for simplicity.

4 Operations information systems include transaction processing systems, process control systems and office automation systems.

5 Management information systems include information reporting systems, decision support systems and executive information systems.

6 Other categories of computer-based information systems include expert systems, business information systems, end-user computing systems and strategic information systems.

7 In order to gain strategic advantage, companies will often adopt one of three basic competitive strategies: cost leadership, product differentiation or business innovation. BIS and e-business systems can be used to support attempts to gain competitive advantage through a number of different approaches. These include improving operational efficiency, raising entry barriers, creating high switching costs and gaining information leadership.

EXERCISES

Self-assessment exercises

1 Answer the following questions in relation to your college or university:

   (a) What are the institution's objectives?
   (b) Identify a range of typical inputs, processes and outputs.
   (c) What feedback mechanisms are in place and what kinds of information do they produce?
   (d) What control mechanisms exist?

2 In what ways can information systems support a manager's activities?

3 How can computer-based information systems help an organisation to achieve a strategic advantage over its competitors?

4 Match each term to the correct statement.

   (a) input   1. provides information concerning the performance of a system
   (b) process   2. describes exchanges between the system and its environment
   (c) output   3. converts raw materials into a finished product
   (d) feedback   4. contains everything outside of the system
   (e) control   5. defines the scope of the system
   (f) boundary   6. examples include raw materials, energy and labour power
   (g) environment   7. examples include information, a product and service
   (h) interface   8. adjusts the performance of the system

5 Describe how a business could be divided into a number of subsystems.

Discussion questions

1 Can each of the following be described as a system? For each item, try to identify at least two inputs, processes and outputs. In addition, what feedback and control mechanisms exist?

   ● a human being
   ● a plant
   ● a house
   ● a country
   ● a computer.

2 A small company is considering the purchase of a computer and accounting software to help it keep track of its finances. In general, what are the benefits of processing by computer? What other benefits might the company gain by taking this step?

3 Locate an annual report or article that describes a large organisation, such as a supermarket chain. From the information contained in the annual report, identify and describe the information systems that the company might use.

Essay questions

1 Use the Internet to research the SABRE system produced by American Airlines. This system demonstrates how BIS can be used to gain strategic advantage. Provide an analysis of this system. Your response should include discussion of the following areas:

   (a) Describe how the overall approach adopted by American Airlines incorporated the basic competitive strategies of cost leadership, innovation and product differentiation.
   (b) In what ways did SABRE provide American Airlines with a competitive advantage? Your analysis should refer to concepts related to the strategic use of information systems, for example entry barriers.

▶

(c) Although SABRE was undoubtedly successful, American Airlines was not able to maintain its competitive advantage beyond the late 1980s. What factors played a part in the erosion of the company's lead over its competitors and how did the company react?

2 Select an organisation you are familiar with. You may choose a department within a large organisation, if you wish. Analyse the structure and behaviour of the organisation using systems concepts. Your response should include the following elements:

(a) Identify and describe at least two examples of the following: inputs, processes, outputs, feedback and control.

(b) Identify and describe two decisions that will be taken at the strategic, tactical and operational levels of the organisation.

(c) For each of the decisions described, identify at least two items of information that may be required. Describe some of the characteristics that each item of information will have.

4 Draw a diagram illustrating the subsystems occurring in a hospital. Label the inputs and outputs of each subsystem. Which subsystems are most closely coupled?

Examination questions

1 Information systems play a critical part in supporting a company's activities. Using specific examples, you are required to:

(a) define an information system;

(b) describe the categories of computer-based information systems, providing relevant business examples for each category identified;

(c) explain how computer-based information systems can support managers at each level of an organisation.

2 Computer-based information systems are critical to an organisation's survival in the modern competitive environment. Discuss this statement with reference to the following:

(a) Porter's competitive forces model and the basic competitive strategies that can be used to gain advantage;

(b) how computer-based information systems can support these strategies;

(c) how an organisation's information resources can be used to create information leadership.

3 Large retail organisations employ a wide variety of computer-based information systems in order to support their activities. Considering a large supermarket chain, such as Sainsbury's, you are required to:

(a) Define the term 'computer-based information system'.

(b) Identify the types of computer-based information systems that are likely to be found within a typical branch. Your response should describe the function of each system identified and the category to which it belongs.

(c) Selecting one of the systems identified in (a), describe the system in more detail, identifying the hardware, software, data and people resources it employs.

4 Draw a diagram illustrating the main components of a generic system.

5 Explain why feedback and control are important in business information systems.

References

Chaffey, D. (2002) *E-Business and E-Commerce Management*, Financial Times Prentice Hall, Harlow

Deise, M., Nowikow, C., King, P. and Wright, A. (2000) *Executive's Guide to E-business. From Tactics to Strategy*, Wiley, New York

Evans, P. and Wurster. T. (1997) 'Strategy and the New Economics of Information', *Harvard Business Review*, Sept–Oct, 70–82

Kalakota, R. and Robinson, M. (2000) *E-business. Roadmap for Success*, Addison-Wesley, Reading, MA

Porter, M. (1980), *Competitive Strategy*, Free Press, New York

Rayport, J. and Sviokla, J. (1996) 'Exploiting the virtual value-chain', *The Mckinsey Quarterly*, 1, 20–37

Timmers, P. (1999) *Electronic Commerce Strategies and Models for Business-to-Business Trading*, Wiley, Chichester

Womack, J. and Jones, D. (1998) *Lean Thinking*, Touchstone–Simon and Schuster, London

Further reading

Chaffey, D. (2002) *E-Business and E-Commerce Management: Strategy, Implementation and Applications*. Financial Times/Prentice Hall, Harlow. Chapter 1 introduces the types of competitive advantage achievable by e-business. Part 2 explains strategic approaches to achieving competitive advantage

Curtis, G. and Cobham, D. (2002) *Business Information Systems: Analysis, Design and Practice*, 4th edition, Pearson Education, Harlow. Chapter 1 deals with concepts related to information, systems theory and management information systems. Chapter 2 deals with issues related to strategy and planning

Elliott, G. and Starking, S. (1998) *Business Information Technology: Systems, Theory and Practice*, Pearson Education, Harlow. Chapter 2 deals with systems theory

Evans, P. and Wurster. T. (1997) 'Strategy and the new economics of information', *Harvard Business Review*, Sept–Oct, 70–82. Provides an overview of the way in which the Internet impacts the value chain and the sharing of information between organisations

O'Brien J. (2001) *Introduction to Information Systems*, 10th edition, McGraw-Hill, New York. This is an accessible and structured text. Chapter 1 deals with basic concepts, such as systems theory. The material takes an alternative view of information systems, attempting to define them in terms of various resources, such as people and hardware. Chapter 8 deals with decision support systems, executive information systems and management information systems

Web links

The links in this chapter provide references to articles describing competitive advantage.

www.webcmo.com/index.htm?u=/report/success/report1.htm The *Journal of Web Marketing Research* provides an interesting survey on competitive advantage related to online marketing business.

www.strategy-business.com/casestudy/ The *Journal of Strategy and Business* provides a good range of up-to-date case studies related to competitive advantage. Also offers a variety of informative articles.

gartner5.gartnerweb.com/btj/static/help/quick_start.html Gartner's *Business Technology Journal* provides access to articles, surveys and case studies. However, you must become a member to use the site, although (at the time of writing) registration is free.

www.watsonwyatt.com/homepage/GI/RESEARCH/compedge-tm.htm A summary of a report from Watson Wyatt that looks at how competitive advantage can be gained by managing and developing employees effectively. The summary contains some interesting research findings and general information.

www.mcb.co.uk/services/conferen/oct95/bledi/backgrnd.htm A research paper that discusses inter-organisational information systems and their importance as means of forging strategic links with suppliers. Particular emphasis is given to EDI (electronic data interchange).

Chapter 3

Hardware

LEARNING OBJECTIVES

After reading this chapter, readers will be able to:
- categorise the type of computer system that a business uses;
- recognise the different components of a computer;
- specify the components needed for the purchase of a personal computer;
- define the criteria for selection of hardware.

MANAGEMENT ISSUES

Whilst it is unnecessary for managers to have an in-depth knowledge of computers, it is important for them to have an understanding of modern technology. Such an understanding can help to make sure that managers communicate with suppliers and apply technology effectively to an organisation. From a managerial perspective, this chapter addresses the following areas:

- Learning the characteristics of input, output and storage devices will allow managers to select the correct equipment for a given application.
- An understanding of selection criteria will allow managers to specify equipment in terms of required quality and functionality.
- An increased understanding of computers will help managers to see how technology can be used to improve existing business processes and identify potential applications.

Links to other chapters

Chapter 4   focuses on computer software and describes a number of common applications.

Chapter 5   provides a detailed view of networks and communications.

Chapter 11   gives detail on client/server technology and the network computer.

Introduction

The aim of this chapter is to provide readers with a basic grasp of the often complex and technical language used to describe the computer hardware which is part of information systems. A knowledge of this language is necessary to help business users communicate with technical staff when discussing their requirements for new systems. An appreciation of how the different components of a computer interact is also useful when you are trying to understand problems that occur with hardware. For example, if your PC is running too slowly, what are the potential reasons for this? Finally, departmental managers (or home users) will need to specify the hardware requirements for their personal use or their staff. Specification of hardware 'kit' is not possible without a grasp of the terminology and an idea of what represents a basic specification, and what an advanced specification.

The chapter is structured according to the main parts of a computer system such as input, output, storage and processing. For each part we explain the purpose of different hardware and the key issues in selecting this type of hardware. Different categories of computer system are introduced at the start of the chapter.

Components of a computer system

Some of the concepts explained in earlier chapters can be used to explain the notion of a computer system. Chapter 2 described a system as a collection of interrelated components that work together towards a collective goal. It was also said that business information systems (BIS) can be defined as systems whose purpose is to convert data into information. We can think of a **computer system** as consisting of a number of interrelated components that work together with the aim of converting data into information. In a computer system,

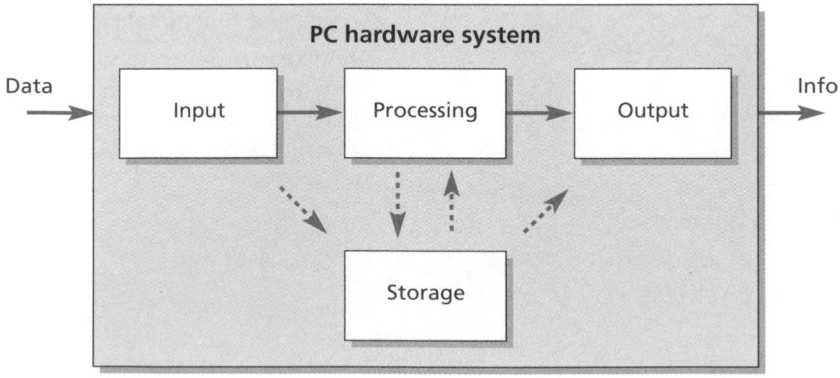

Computer system
Interrelated components including hardware and software that work together with the aim of converting data into information.

Figure 3.1 **Basic hardware components of a computer system**

processing is carried out electronically, usually with little or no intervention from a human user. The components of a computer system include **hardware** and software. This chapter considers hardware in depth, whilst Chapter 4 focuses on software.

Hardware
The physical components of a computer system: input devices, memory, central processing unit, output devices and storage devices.

▶ Computer hardware

Hardware describes the physical components of a computer system. The hardware of a computer system can be said to consist of different elements whose relationship is shown from a systems theory perspective in Figure 3.1. Data are input, then processed

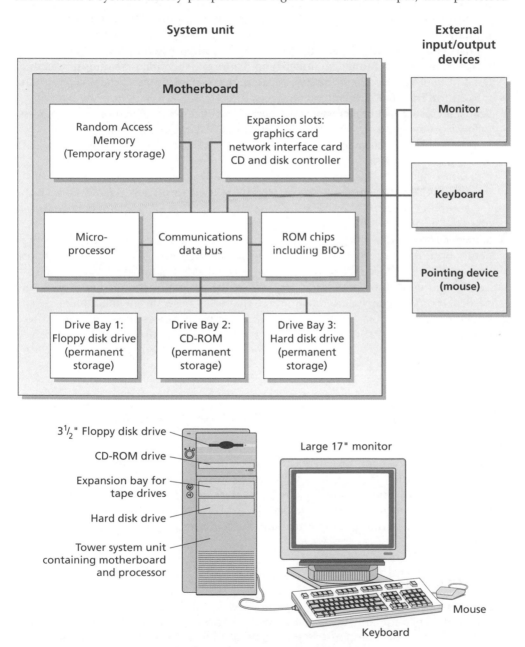

Figure 3.2 **A personal computer labelled with the typical components**

according to software instructions, then output to the screen, for example, as information. Information that needs to be stored permanently will be placed in storage. This chapter is structured by describing the options available for each of these elements and assessing the criteria used for purchase decisions. Figure 3.2 shows the familiar physical appearance of a personal computer system.

The main components of a computer system, shown in Figures 3.1 and 3.2 can be conveniently grouped as follows:

Input device

Hardware used to enter data, information or instructions into a computer-based information system.

Central processing unit (CPU)

The processor found in a computer system that controls all of the computer's main functions and enables users to execute programs or process data.

Memory

A temporary means of storing data awaiting processing, instructions used to process data or control the computer system, and data or information that has been processed.

Storage devices

A permanent means of storing data and programs until they are required.

Output devices

Translate the results of processing – output – into a human readable form.

- **Input devices**. Input devices are used to capture or enter data into the computer. Before data can be used within a computer system, it is usually necessary to convert them into a format that supports processing by computer. Most data are held in human-sensible form, that is, in a format that makes them directly accessible to human beings. A bank statement, for example, contains text and numbers that are relatively easy for a human to understand. However, such data are almost meaningless to the electronic components of a computer system. Input devices convert data into a form that makes them machine-sensible.

- **Central processing unit or processor**. The central processing unit (CPU) performs processing by carrying out instructions given in the form of computer programs.

- Primary storage or **memory**. Memory is used as a temporary means of storage data and instructions. Memory is used to store:
  (a) data awaiting processing,
  (b) instructions loaded fom software which are used to process data or control the computer system,
  (c) data or information that has been processed.

- **Storage devices**. Storage devices provide a means of storing data and programs permanently until they are required. As an example, a program can be stored on a hard disk drive until it is needed. When the program is activated, it is transferred from the storage device into the computer's memory. When the program has ended or is no longer needed, it can be removed from memory so that other programs or data can be used.

- **Output devices**. Output devices translate the results of processing – output – into a human-readable form. The results of a calculation, for example, might be displayed on a screen or sent to a printer. An output device may also transfer data requiring further processing to a storage device.

Major categories of computers

We can begin to understand more of the technology by looking at the ways in which computers themselves can be categorised. A traditional view of computer technology suggests three basic categories of computer: mainframe, minicomputer and microcomputer. We will briefly examine the characteristics of each category, in order to understand more of how industry makes use of computer technology. The physical forms of these different types of system and some newer types of computers are illustrated in Figure 3.3.

❱ Mainframe

Mainframe

Mainframes are powerful computers used for large-scale data processing.

A traditional view of **mainframe** computers saw them as large, extremely powerful machines designed for large-scale data-processing activities. The use of mainframe computers in industry, once responsible for the multi-billion dollar revenues of companies such as IBM, Tandem, Amdahl and Hitachi, has declined steadily over the past two

PDA   Laptop/Notebook   Desktop

Tower   Server (mini)   Mainframe

Figure 3.3 **Different forms of computer system**

decades. Now IBM is the sole supplier. Advances in technology have enabled smaller, less expensive systems to compete with mainframes in terms of speed and power. A modern personal computer, for example, could be considered many times more powerful than one of the very earliest mainframe systems.

In many organisations, mainframe computers are considered **legacy systems**, meaning that while managers recognise that the existing system may not be entirely adequate to meet the company's needs, a changeover would be difficult – or even impossible – to implement. This can be for a number of different reasons:

Legacy system
A system which has been superseded by new technologies or business practices.

- So much has been invested in developing and maintaining the mainframe system that a move towards more modern technology would be prohibited by the costs involved.
- The data and information produced by the mainframe system are critical to the company's operations. Since any changes might disrupt the company's activities, any new systems that are introduced are made compatible with the older mainframe system. In turn, this reinforces the need to retain the existing mainframe system.
- The links between the existing mainframe system and the company's major business activities are so strong that it is not possible to introduce new systems a little at a time. This can mean that the cost of introducing new systems across the entire organisation is too high. Furthermore, the risk of disruption to the company's activities may be so high that it is considered unacceptable.

Activity 3.1

Legacy systems

Although use of mainframe computers has declined quite sharply since the middle of the 1980s, many are still in use today. In many cases, retaining an existing mainframe system may be considered more cost-effective than introducing a new system. As an example, consider a public utility that provides a service to a relatively stable base of customers. What are the arguments both for and against retaining the current mainframe system?

Activity 3.2

Benefits of mainframes

Using the Internet as a resource, locate examples of companies currently selling mainframes. From promotional material and case studies explain how the mainframe is suited to certain applications.

▶ Minicomputers and servers

Minicomputer

Minicomputers offer an intermediate stage between the power of mainframe systems and the relatively low cost of microcomputer systems.

The **minicomputer** combines some of the characteristics of the mainframe computer and the microcomputer. Today, they are often referred to as servers by companies such as Sun and Hewlett-Packard. Different types of server may have different functions, such as managing a network or hosting a database. Further information on how different types of servers are used by e-business are given in Chapter 5.

Activity 3.3

Minicomputers and servers

Using the Internet as a resource, locate two examples of companies that are currently selling minicomputers or servers. From promotional material and case studies explain how servers are suited to certain applications.

Microcomputer

Microcomputers are considered less powerful than minicomputers and mainframes, but are more flexible and relatively inexpensive to purchase.

Client/server

The client/server architecture consists of client computers such as PCs sharing resources such as a database stored on a more powerful server computers.

IBM-compatible

The modern personal computer found in most business organisations developed from a family of personal computers launched by IBM in the early 1980s.

Apple Macintosh

A family of personal computers produced by Apple Computers.

Workstation

A powerful terminal or personal computer system, usually applied to specialised applications, such as computer-aided design (CAD).

▶ Microcomputers

The **microcomputer** makes use of more modern technology to provide relatively powerful computing facilities at low cost. Microcomputers are now often referred to as the 'client' machine which receives services and data from a 'server' machine. This **client/server** architecture is described in Chapter 5 as a common type of communications structure. Some of the major characteristics of the microcomputer are as follows:

● In physical size a microcomputer is far smaller than a minicomputer.
● Microcomputers are widely used and provide the best price and performance of the types of computer.
● Since microcomputers are inexpensive, they are more accessible than mainframes or minicomputers. A typical microcomputer will be within the means of a small business or an individual.
● Microcomputers are extremely flexible and are considered general-purpose machines capable of being used for a wide variety of applications. However, they are generally seen as being unsuitable for applications involving large volumes of data processing such as transaction processing (Chapter 6).
● Microcomputers are considered easier to use than mainframes or minicomputers. Users require little technical knowledge and can be trained quickly and at low cost.
● Technical and non-technical users are able to develop applications quickly and easily.

In industry, several types of microcomputer are in common use. The **IBM-compatible** or personal computer (PC) , is considered the standard for general business use. The **Apple Macintosh** or iMac is often used for professional desktop publishing applications, such as the production of newspapers. **Workstations**, such as those produced by Sun, are typically used in the area of computer graphics. Typical applications include computer-aided design (CAD) and animation.

Types of microcomputers

◗ Desktop

As its name suggests, the **desktop computer** is intended for office use and supports the day-to-day activities of an organisation's employees. These machines tend to be placed in a fixed location and connected permanently to items such as printers, scanners and other devices. The desktop computer is the most common type of microcomputer and is found in the majority of organisations.

Desktop computers tend to have a modular design, that is, they are made up of components that can be removed or replaced individually. This means that repairs can be carried out quickly and easily. Since components are relatively inexpensive, it is possible to upgrade desktop machines at low cost. Many expansion devices can be fitted internally, protecting the device from accidental damage and helping to reduce its cost.

The case used to house the motherboard and other components of a computer system also contains the computer's **power supply unit** (PSU) and cooling fan. The PSU converts AC current into DC current, regulating the amount of power supplied to the motherboard and any other devices installed within the case. The cooling fan ensures an even flow of air through the case so that heat can be dissipated quickly and efficiently. In addition to the desktop case (Fig. 3.3) there are other forms of case:

- A *mini tower case* is narrow and tall, designed to be placed alongside the monitor or beneath a desk. These cases provide more room for expansion devices but tend to require more space on the desktop.
- The *full tower case* is the largest type of case available and is normally placed on the floor next to a desk or table. Since a typical full tower case is intended to house a large number of expansion devices, it tends to have a larger power supply and can include a more powerful cooling fan.

◗ Portable

The **portable computer** is largely self-contained, featuring its own power supply, keyboard, pointing device and visual display unit. Modern portables tend to weigh very little and fit easily into a briefcase.

> Portable computers are often described as 'notebooks' or 'sub-notebooks'. A **notebook** or *laptop* is approximately the size of an A4 writing pad. The size of a **sub-notebook** can vary considerably: some feature keyboards that can be used in the normal way, others have keyboards so small that a special pointing device is needed to press keys.

Some typical applications for portable computers include:

- Collecting data from a number of different locations. Salespeople, for example, might record order details and other information as they visit different clients.
- Remote working. Portable computers allow users to work in a variety of different locations and situations, for example an employee travelling to work might use a portable so that they can complete a task that had been started in the office. Dockable computers are laptop PCs that may be integrated with a desktop network

Desktop computer
Intended for office use to support the day-to-day activities of an organisation's employees.

Power supply unit (PSU)
All modern personal computers feature a power supply unit used to convert AC current into DC current. The PSU regulates the amount of power supplied to the motherboard and any other devices installed within the case.

Portable computer
A self-contained computer with integrated power supply, keyboard, pointing device and visual display unit to facilitate carrying.

Notebook
A small portable computer, which is approximately the size of a sheet of A4 paper.

Sub-notebook
A small portable computer which is usually significantly smaller than a notebook due to a small screen and keyboard.

access point that also provides a conventional monitor and keyboard; this allows 'hot-desking' which is popular for workers who are not regularly in the office.

- Communications. Many portable computers contain telecommunications facilities that can be used to send and receive information in a variety of forms. A manager, for example, might compose and send a fax message whilst travelling.

Although they are undoubtedly useful, some common criticisms of portable computers include:

- Portable computers often have a limited battery life, sometimes offering only as little as two hours of continuous use before the battery needs to be recharged.
- The limited expansion capacity of a portable computer means that it is often not possible to install additional devices, such as CD-ROM drives. Expansion is often achieved by installing devices externally through the use of special cards.
- Many users find portable computers unsuitable for anything more than occasional use. Poor display units, small keyboards and clumsy pointing devices can sometimes make prolonged use of a portable computer very uncomfortable.

▶ Organiser/PDA

Personal digital assistant (PDA)
A hand-held device, often no larger than a pocket calculator with functions such as address book, appointment scheduler and calculator.

A **personal digital assistant (PDA)** can be thought of as a sophisticated personal organiser. A PDA is normally a hand-held device, often no larger than a pocket calculator. The purpose of the PDA is to help users manage their time more efficiently and effectively. The typical functions of a PDA can include: address book, appointment scheduler, calculator, expenses tracking, currency conversion, alarm clock, world time display and a variety of other features that allow users to store notes, such as to-do lists. More sophisticated models such as the PalmPilot or Pocket PC may include a more powerful range of tools, including communications, spreadsheet and word processing applications.

PDAs have several advantages over portable computers. First, they are relatively inexpensive to purchase. Secondly, they have a comparatively long battery life and there is often no need to purchase expensive rechargeable batteries. Thirdly, since they have a rather limited range of functions, they tend to be easier to use than their larger counterparts. However, PDAs are considered to have only limited functionality and are therefore not appropriate to some applications.

▶ Network computer (NC)

Network computer (NC)
A computer providing access to a network system, which to reduce cost features limited disk storage, less powerful processor and less memory.

A relatively recent development has been the introduction of inexpensive **network computers** by a number of leading manufacturers. Network computers are targeted at two distinct segments of the personal computer market: home users reluctant to purchase more expensive personal computers, and organisations seeking to reduce the costs associated with computer-based information systems.

Net PC
A hybrid between a traditional PC and an NC, it will usually feature no floppy or hard drive and limited memory and processor since it will use the power of the server to provide applications.

Since the concept of the NC was introduced a further variant on this type of limited PC has been proposed. These are known as **Net PCs** and can be thought of as hybrid between a PC and an NC, with the aim again being to reduce the cost of ownership.

The philosophy behind the network computer is that it should be inexpensive to manufacture, purchase and maintain. For this reason, a typical network computer will feature limited disk storage, memory and expansion potential. In addition, the computer may also feature an older, less powerful processor than its desktop counterpart.

The purpose of the network computer is to provide access to a network system, such as an intranet or the Internet, at minimal cost. Since the network computer is able to call upon the resources of the network server, only limited processing power is required. Simple tasks can be carried out by the network computer itself. More complex tasks, such as those that make intensive use of a computer's processor, are dealt with by the network server and the results are passed back to the network computer. In a similar way, since software applications and data can be accessed via the network, only minimal storage capacity is required. This type of network architecture is often described as **thin client** and the design of such an architecture is described in more detail in Chapter 11.

Network computers are popular with cost-conscious IS managers since they potentially reduce the **total cost of ownership** (TCO) associated with computer systems. The cost of ownership describes a range of different expenses incurred by purchasing and maintaining a computer system. Such costs include the original cost of the hardware and software, upgrades, maintenance, technical support and training. TCO is discussed further in Chapter 16 with regard to the cost of providing end-user services. Network computers act to reduce the cost of ownership in several ways:

- The initial purchase costs of hardware and software are low.
- Since network computers can be managed via a central network server, administration costs can be reduced. Network computers are often described as offering the potential to achieve **zero administration**, a point where the centralised management and control of the computers attached to a network server makes administration costs potentially negligible.
- Since the network computer contains fewer components than a conventional personal computer, it is less expensive to maintain, repair and replace.
- As network computers are often used for a relatively small number of applications, training and support costs can be reduced. As an example, a business organisation might purchase network computers for the sole purpose of data entry. Similarly, home users are likely to purchase network computers as a means of accessing the Internet.

The Panalpina case study gives an example of an international company that has committed itself to NCs for the reduced costs they promise.

Thin client

In a network system, this describes an architecture where the bulk of the processing is carried out by a central server.

Total cost of ownership (TCO)

TCO refers to the total cost for a company operating a computer. This includes not only the purchase or leasing cost, but also the cost of all the services needed to support the end-user.

Zero administration

The point where centralised management and control of the computers attached to a network server makes administration costs almost negligible.

MINI CASE STUDY

Panalpina use network computers to reduce costs

Panalpina of Switzerland, a freight forwarding company with a turnover of over £2 billion, is converting two-thirds of its 9,500 users worldwide from PCs to network computers. Most users are located at ports or airports. The work is straightforward data entry, logging the arrival or departure of shipments. This does not require a state-of-the-art PC. Panalpina now uses Winframe software from Citrix which allows multiple-user sessions on the NC 'thin clients' to be run on a Microsoft Windows NT-based server. The Data General Aviion servers need about 8 Mb per user. All the processing occurs on the server with only screen updates and user events such as key presses and mouse clicks needing to be transmitted over the network. Cost reductions are anticipated on hardware purchase and reduced cost of support through the simplicity of the thin clients.

CASE STUDY 3.1

Network computers

FT

Although the network computer initially failed, it helped to initiate the introduction of the Windows terminal and is destined to eventually return as a mobile device.

In April 1996, the personal computer was famously described as 'a ridiculous device' by Larry Ellison, chief executive officer of Oracle Corporation. His vision of a 'network computer' as a replacement for the PC has not caught on, but he initiated an important change in the way PCs are managed, which resulted in the introduction of 'Windows terminals' or 'thin clients'.

The network computer was designed as a low cost intelligent device to access a network. Once connected to the network, it downloads into its memory a new range of small applications written in the Java programming language, called 'applets'.

'The network computer as championed by Oracle and Sun Microsystems is dead and buried, because the software to make it work was never delivered', says Tom Austin, research fellow at Gartner Group, the independent analysts. 'Although it will re-emerge in about three years, part of the concept has already succeeded in the form of the Windows Terminal.'

The Windows terminal is an even lower cost 'dumb' device that displays a full Windows application that is located on a network server.

'A few years ago we all used terminals, which Microsoft thought were one of the ultimate evils of an earlier era', comments Mr Austin. 'In early 1997, they did an about face and outflanked Oracle and Sun by licensing terminal display technology from Citrix. The Windows terminal is alive and doing rather well.'

Gartner Group estimates that there are about 10m users of the Windows terminal. Nine million are actually using old personal computers which can no longer run the latest software themselves, but have enough power to act as terminals to display it. The rest are using purpose-designed devices from companies such as Network Computing Devices and Wyse.

George Koncikowski, global program manager for Unisys e-@ction Application Delivery, says: 'The biggest advantage of the Windows terminal is that it allows users the same rich interactive interface they already use on their desktop. The network computer was always exactly the right idea with its focus on the network, but it happened at the wrong time.'

According to Mr Koncikowski, the infrastructure was not evolved enough, downloading applets had enormous network implications, it required a lot of redevelopment of applications and interfaces and there was no way to incorporate Windows applications into it.

'If there had been a very smooth path from an existing Microsoft desktop environment to the network computer, it would have caught on', says Nigel Beighton, technology delivery director at Cap Gemini, the Paris-based management consulting and information technology group. 'After its launch, the network computer hit Year 2000 work and now organisations are occupied with electronic business, so they have higher priorities. Our clients are comfortable with their Microsoft desktop and the management tools for distributed environments are reducing costs, so they are unwilling to face the risk of moving away.'

Before the network computer reappears, Gartner Group is forecasting an explosion of mass access devices in about 2003. These are consumer-orientated commodity devices that are either free or so inexpensive they are almost disposable. They include internet screenphones, personal digital assistants, e-Book readers and set-top boxes.

'After it happens, the chief executive will ask why his organisation is spending money on expensive end-user PC devices when employees are bringing commodity devices into work', Mr Austin predicts. 'It will drive a renaissance in network computing models from "one size fits all" to mass produced task-oriented devices.'

Last November, Mr Ellison introduced version two of the network computer, now aimed at consumers. 'It was scheduled to be $500, but the PC industry made an astounding response and now PCs are down to $500, but the network computer is now down to $199', he said. 'The old one worked fine on a network but not at home. This one has an operating system and browser that boots off the CD-ROM. I'd like to say I invented this, but we stole the idea from Sony. To upgrade it, you just take out the CD and put in a new one – like changing music.'

Whereas Mr Beighton feels there are too many conflicting priorities for the network computer to enter the corporate desktop, he believes that the new generation of mobile computing devices will become network computers – because local processing will be required for word processing, spreadsheets and databases. 'The mobile device, especially personal digital assistants with a Bluetooth radio chip for mobile communication, is the future of the network computer', he says.

▶

Traver Gruen-Kennedy, head of business development at Citrix, says the promise of network computing was to make it easier for the end-user to connect to a network, by a cable or wirelessly. They can do it from anywhere using any simple inexpensive device to work with their data in the manner they wish.

'The hardware really doesn't matter, as long as it is light, easy to use and comes on instantly and is available in a variety of form factors', he says. 'It is really about giving users the choice, convenience and control they want.'

One obstacle in the path of new devices is that many users have an emotional attachment to PCs. 'We have the concept that the bigger the PC on your desk, the more important you are', says Mr Koncikowski. 'What users don't realise with these devices is you are not trading a device for a device,

but a device for a service, in which all your data and applications are managed for you. They are not the economy version of the PC, which is the way the industry has been pitching it, but the premium version that important people will want.'

Source: R. Newing, FT IT Review: 'Expected to rise again like the phoenix: Network Computer', *Financial Times*, 5 April 2000

Questions

Conduct any additional research that is necessary so that you can answer the following questions.

1 What are the attractions of network computers and similar devices to business organisations?

2 Why did network computers fail to become popular?

3 The case study implies that there is a difference between a network computer and a thin client. Can you explain this difference?

Input devices

Input devices (Fig. 3.4) are used to enter data or instructions. 'Device' is used in this context to refer to an individual piece of hardware with a specific function. Mouse and keyboard are examples of input devices. Before looking at some of the devices available, it is worth making some observations:

● It should be noted that modern computers make use of a wide variety of input devices since data flowing in to the organisation may take a number of different forms.

● The choice of an input device will often depend upon the quantity of data to be entered. Entering data on a small scale is normally carried out by human operators, using a number of familiar input devices, such as the mouse or keyboard. However, large-scale data input may require the use of more specialised input devices. In many cases, a **direct capture** device will be used to acquire and store data automatically. Generally, the data are captured at the source and stored with little or no human

Direct capture
A method of acquiring and storing data automatically with little or no human intervention.

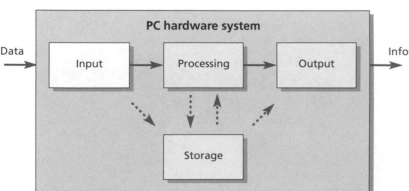

Figure 3.4 Input devices in context

intervention. Data obtained from sensors on a production line, for example, might be stored and then processed automatically.

● A computer-based information system will seldom make use of only a single input device. Even a typical personal computer will often feature several different methods for data entry, such as keyboard, mouse, joystick and sound card.

There are a wide variety of types of input device, note the business applications of the following:

Keyboard/keypad

The keyboard remains the most common input device and its basic design has remained largely unchanged for more than a century.

A common criticism of the keyboard is that inexperienced users find it difficult and uncomfortable to use. In answer to this, new keyboard designs have appeared that attempt to make them easier to use. **Natural (or ergonomic) keyboards** have the keys arranged so that users can locate them more quickly and easily and is shaped to make prolonged use more comfortable.

Mouse

Computers featuring a **graphical user interface** often require the use of a **mouse** or other **pointing device**. Although there are many different kinds of mouse, all use the same basic method of operation: moving the mouse over a flat surface causes a corresponding movement to a small pointer on the screen (Fig. 3.5). The operating system software (Chapter 4) translates direction and rate of movement of the mouse to movement of the on-screen cursor.

Lightpen

A **lightpen** is a pointing device that can be used to control applications by pointing to items on the screen. Lightpens are also used for applications involving graphics, such as drawing packages, since images can be drawn directly onto the screen.

Trackball

A **trackball** is a pointing device that is controlled by rotating a small ball with the fingertips or the palm of the hand. Moving the ball causes corresponding movement to a small pointer on the screen. Buttons are used to select items in the same way as with the mouse.

Natural keyboard

Keys are arranged so that users can locate them more quickly and easily in a way that makes prolonged use more comfortable.

Graphical user interface (GUI)

Allows the user to control the operation of a computer program or item of computer hardware using a pointing device, such as a mouse by selecting options from icons and menu options.

Mouse

A pointing device found on most modern personal computers.

Pointing device

An input device that allows the user to control the movement of a small pointer displayed on the screen that is used to select options.

Lightpen

A pointing device used to control applications by pointing to items on the screen.

Trackball

A trackball is a pointing device that is controlled by rotating a small ball with the fingertips or palm of the hand.

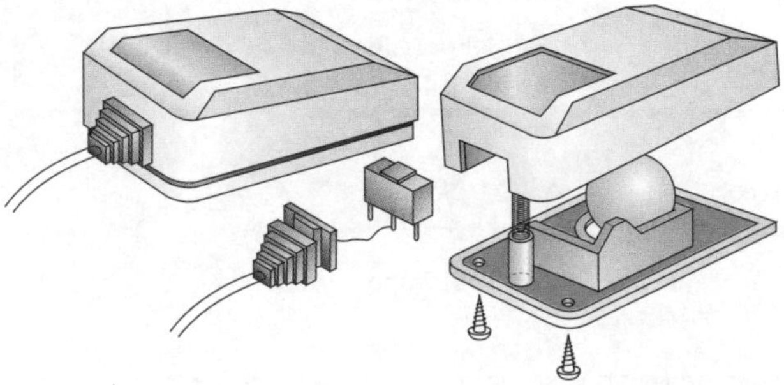

Figure 3.5 **The mouse**

Joystick

The joystick is one of the most common input devices available and is primarily used for leisure activities, such as playing computer games.

Optical scanner

The **optical scanner** is now widely used in business for capturing graphics and text from printed documents. Images captured in this way are normally incorporated into word processing or desktop publishing documents or are part of workflow management systems (Chapter 6).

Optical scanners can also be used to perform data entry by converting printed documents into text files that can be used by word processing packages and other programs. **Optical character recognition** (OCR) involves using software that attempts to recognise individual characters. As a scanned image is processed, the program creates a text file containing all of the characters recognised. This file can then be edited further using a word processor, text editor or some other suitable program since recognition is not 100% accurate. For example, the letter 'i' is sometimes recognised as 'l'.

A variation on optical character recognition is **optical mark recognition** (OMR), which involves detecting and recognising simple marks made on a document.

> **Optical scanner**
> An input device used to capture graphics and text from printed documents.
>
> **Optical character recognition (OCR)**
> Software that attempts to recognise individual characters.
>
> **Optical mark recognition (OMR)**
> Detection and recognition of simple marks made on a document.

MINI CASE STUDY

Optical mark recognition

Public examinations, such as the GCSE qualifications that students take at school, often involve a multiple-choice paper. Students record their answers on a special sheet, usually by filling in small boxes corresponding to their choices.

The answer sheet used by students is a special document that has been prepared so that it can be used with an optical mark reader. The size and position of the boxes on the sheet, for example, have been designed so that the optical mark reader can process the sheet quickly and accurately.

The optical mark readers used by examination bodies are almost completely automatic and are able to deal with hundreds of answer sheets each hour. However, although this simplifies the process of marking the papers from the many thousands of examinations sat each year, problems can still arise. Common problems include equipment breakdowns, damaged answer sheets and answer sheets that have been completed incorrectly.

Bar code reader

A **bar code** (Fig. 3.6) is a means of displaying a unique identification number as a series of thick and thin lines. The sequence and width of the lines in the bar code can be translated into a sequence of digits. Bar code numbers are normally produced according to a specific method. The **Universal Product Code**, for example, is a standard method for creating and using bar codes.

A **bar code reader** measures the intensity of a light beam reflected from the printed bar code to identify the digits making up the unique identification number. The digits making up the identification number are also printed at the foot of the bar code.

The most common example of the use of the bar code reader in industry is the supermarket checkout. However, bar codes are also used in a variety of other situations including manual inspection and update of stock levels on inventory control systems;

> **Bar code**
> A means of displaying a unique identification number as a series of thick and thin lines.
>
> **Universal product code**
> A standard for defining bar codes used frequently in retailing.
>
> **Bar code reader**
> Measures the intensity of a light beam reflected from a printed bar code to identify the digits making up a unique identification number.

Figure 3.6 Examples of different formats for bar codes

identification of patients in hospitals by bracelets to enable retrieval of patient information; bar codes on magazines and newspapers are used to record sales of particular titles, which helps vendors, distributors and publishers to monitor trends and plan possible promotions.

Touch screen

The **touch screen** is a transparent, pressure-sensitive covering that is attached to the screen of the monitor. Users make selections and control programs by pressing onto the screen. Although touch screens are simple to use, they are comparatively expensive and require special software to operate.

Common applications for touch screens are interactive kiosks and bookings systems. An **interactive kiosk** allows a user to purchase items or browse through a list of products by pressing buttons or other controls shown on the screen. Such kiosks are often found in banks, music stores, supermarkets and large catalogue stores. Many bookings systems, such as those used by airlines, theatres and travel agents, also make use of touch screens.

Graphics tablet

A **graphics tablet** is used in the same way as a writing pad. A stylus is used to draw images on a rigid pad located near to the computer. As the user draws with the stylus, the image is duplicated on the computer's display. Although graphics tablets can be used to control programs and select items shown on the screen, they are most often used for professional graphics applications.

Video capture card

The **video capture card** records and stores video sequences (motion video) when connected to a digital video camera or other device. A playback device, for example a video cassette recorder, is connected to the video capture card and special software is used to capture, edit and manipulate video sequences. Once a motion video sequence has been processed, it can then be output to a television, video cassette recorder or other device.

Microphone/sound card

A **sound card** can be used to capture sound, music and speech from a variety of sources. Sound can be captured at a very high quality; even the most inexpensive sound cards are capable of producing results similar in quality to a CD recording. A business application is the use of **voice recognition** software to dictate text directly into a word processing document. In many cases, a special microphone is required in order to ensure that the user's voice is not obscured by background noise. In addition, the software used normally

---

Touch screen

A transparent, pressure-sensitive covering that is attached to the screen of the monitor. Users make selections and control programs by pressing onto the screen.

Interactive kiosk

A typical application for touch screen systems, an interactive kiosk allows a user to purchase items or browse through a list of products by pressing buttons or other controls shown on the screen.

Graphics tablet

Used in the same way as a writing pad; a stylus is used to draw images on a rigid pad located near to the computer.

Video capture card

The video capture card records and stores video sequences (motion video).

Sound card

A sound card allows a personal computer to play speech, music and other sounds. A sound card can also be used to capture sound, music and speech from a variety of sources.

Voice recognition

The facility to control a computer program or carry out data entry through spoken commands via a microphone connected to a sound card.

requires 'training' so that it can adapt to a user's accent or the way in which they pronounce particular words. Even with this training, recognition rates are unlikely to exceed 95%, so some modifications are usually required after recognition. Voice recognition packages also provide limited control over a graphical user interface.

The addition of a sound card and CD-ROM device provide a computer with **multimedia** facilities.

Digital camera

The **digital camera** captures and stores still images. Images are held in the camera's memory or stored on disk until they can be transferred to a personal computer.

> The individual dots that make up an image are known as 'pixels'. Early digital cameras were only able to capture images at a size of 320 by 200, giving approximately 64000 individual pixels. Later models allowed images to be captured at sizes of up to 1024 by 768, giving approximately 780000 pixels. Even this quality is considered inadequate for professional applications. The latest digital cameras measure quality in terms of millions of pixels, or megapixels. These models typically offer an image quality of 3.5 megapixels or higher.

Magnetic ink character recognition (MICR). This involves capturing data that has been printed using a special magnetic ink. This technology is normally associated with the banking industry, especially cheque processing. Some of the details on a cheque, such as the cheque number, are printed in a special typeface using magnetic ink. The shape of each character means that it can be recognised by its magnetic field.

Selecting input devices

It is important to select an appropriate means of data entry in order to ensure that any computerised system works as efficiently as possible. The collection of data on a very large scale, for example, usually requires an approach that involves automating the process as far as possible. When selecting keyboard and mouse for a new PC, although these are provided as standard, it may be worth paying extra for superior quality versions to reduce the risk of repetitive strain injury (RSI). However, the selection of an input device is usually based upon three basic criteria: volume, speed and accuracy.

▶ Volume

Some input devices are unsuitable for dealing with large volumes of data. An electricity company, for example, would be unlikely to use manual data entry methods to record the details of payments made by customers. Instead, this data would be collected using more sophisticated methods, such as optical mark recognition (OMR) or optical character recognition (OCR). On the other hand, a small business dealing with far fewer transactions might prefer to enter data using the keyboard as an input device.

Multimedia
A combination of several media under the control of an interactive computer program including text, graphics, sound, video and animation.

Digital camera
A digital camera captures and stores still images in a camera's memory until they can be transferred to a personal computer. The image is recorded using a charge-coupled device which recognises the different colours and intensity of light in the image.

Magnetic ink character recognition (MICR)
Capture and recognition of data that has been printed using a special magnetic ink.

❯ Speed

If large volumes of data need to be entered, speed and accuracy may be important considerations for many business applications. It would be unrealistic, for example, to enter text into a word processor using only the mouse. Similarly, the electricity company mentioned earlier would be unlikely to employ data entry clerks in order to record payment details – OCR and OMR can be many thousands of times faster than manual data entry methods.

❯ Accuracy

In some business applications it is essential to ensure that data entry is completely accurate. In engineering, for example, sensing devices are often required to measure components with an accuracy of plus or minus 0.01 cm. Obviously, if there are any errors in the data recorded this may mean that components need to be scrapped.

In many cases, it may be acceptable if an input device generates a certain number of errors. This is often referred to as the **error rate** and the acceptable level will vary according to the input device being used and the business application. Optical character recognition, for example, is generally considered a comparatively unreliable means of entering data. At present, a typical OCR software package will have an error rate of between five and ten per cent.

Error rate

The frequency of errors which occur when using an input device to recognise patterns.

❯ Other criteria

Other considerations when selecting an input device might also include:

● *Complexity of data.* Some methods are unsuitable for entering data of a complex nature. In many cases, data may need to be interpreted or altered before they are entered. In entering a letter into a word processor, for example, a secretary may need to interpret shorthand notes or alter words and phrases as the document is typed.
● *Cost.* Although some methods offer high levels of speed and accuracy, an organisation may be unwilling or unable to purchase the hardware and software required. In such cases an alternative means of data entry may be required.
● *Frequency of data entry.* Some types of data entry may be carried out on an infrequent or ad hoc basis. In these cases, the acquisition of new or specialised input devices may not be justifiable.

Activity 3.4

Selecting input devices

Using the criteria described in this section, select the most suitable type of input device to perform these functions:

● entry of an application for a loan, received on a paper form, into an operational system for processing loan applications;
● entry of details of a house for entry into a system for an estate agents;
● entry of details collected in a ward visit by a hospital consultant;
● a field map from a geologist's survey into a mapping system.

CASE STUDY 3.2

Document image processing at Royal Sun Alliance

Royal Sun Alliance streamlined its correspondence scanning process in customer services and doubled productivity, Julia Vowler reports.

Business process re-engineering is a big subject, and those that undertake it know that it is usually a big undertaking.

But they also know that every business process consists of a host of smaller ones, and that small improvements made along the way to each can total quite significantly. At times, one small improvement can even stop a log-jam building up and slowing down the whole process.

That was the case at insurance giant Royal Sun Alliance (RSA) where productivity in customer service was being held up at one small, but significant point – transforming the 1.7 million items of mail received annually into computer-storable images to feed into the company's workflow systems. Such was the volume of paper arriving at the RSA's central post location in Birmingham that staff were having to pull out all the stops, constantly, just to maintain throughput.

'The pressure was on and they were struggling to keep up', says Phil Surley, system team manager at RSA. 'We were running at something close to full capacity. It was definitely a problem.'

The critical rate limiting factor was the speed at which the 30 existing scanners could operate. Each incoming piece of paper had to be fed in, scanned, turned over and scanned again, one at a time.

'Now we've streamlined the process', says Surley, 'productivity has doubled.'

Installing two high-speed duplex Kodak K3500 scanners controlled by ActionPoint's Input Accel software, RSA can now scan incoming mail in batches, both sides simultaneously, imaging 100 pages a minute.

Staff at workstations check the document image that appears on their screen for an index criterion, such as policy number, and key it in as part of the image file. The software checks against other systems, such as claims processing, to ensure the number is valid, and then sends it by high speed communications links to RSA's datacentre in Horsham where it joins the several hundred gigabytes of stored document images in IBM's mainframe-based ImagePlus that feeds the workflow system.

The result is that for each customer there is an electronic file with all correspondence, status and actions. But every improvement leaves room for further improvement.

Surley, a keen hill walker, has a personal campaign to keep trees where nature put them, and not let them creep into RSA as waste paper.

'The new system allows us to make significant improvements to processing and productivity easily and quickly', he says.

The insurance giant is also working on an electronic format for outgoing letters, working off the PC that generates it, and incoming faxes that are transferred directly into the imaging system.

Source: Julia Vowler, 'Small change doubles produtivity at RSA', courtesy of *Computer Weekly*, 21 September 2000

Questions

1 What factors would have been taken into account by RSA when selecting new optical scanners for the company's central post location in Birmingham?

2 What obvious problem exists with the company's solution and how might this be dealt with?

3 Can you think of two more examples of applications for the system described in the case study?

Output devices

Output devices (Fig. 3.7) display the results of computer processing. Before looking at some of the devices available, it is worth making some observations:

- The output produced by some devices is temporary in nature. A display shown on a monitor, for example, is lost when a new image is shown or the computer system is switched off. On the other hand, a report produced on a printer is more permanent and may last for many years.
- Some forms of output may be used as the input for another process. Photographs, sounds and video sequences, for example, might be combined during the production of a training package or demonstration programme.

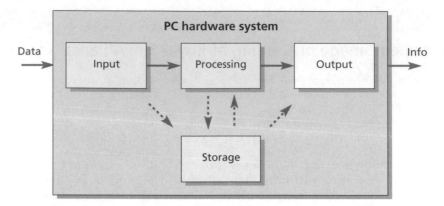

Figure 3.7 Output devices in context

- Business organisations have a wide range of requirements in terms of the *form* of the information they produce. These requirements mean that there are a large variety of specialised output devices available.
- A computer-based information system will seldom make use of only a single output device. Even a typical personal computer will often feature several different output devices, such as monitor, sound card and printer.

▶ Display devices

Visual display unit (VDU)

A monitor connected to a computer system, traditionally used to describe character-based terminals.

The most common output device is almost certainly the *monitor*, formerly referred to as **visual display unit** (VDU) or dumb terminal, that is attached to all personal computer systems.

The monitor has several advantages over other forms of output device.

- Information can be shown instantly with only a negligible delay between the information becoming available and its being displayed. In addition, the monitor is one of only a small number of devices that allows users to view the progress of an activity as it occurs.
- As standard components of a computer system, monitors are relatively inexpensive to purchase, repair or replace.
- The monitor is particularly suited to displaying certain kinds of information, for example charts and graphics.
- The cost of using the monitor as an output device is very low. Unlike printers, for example, a monitor does not require consumables, such as paper. In turn, this means that wastage does not occur.

Resolution

The 'fineness' of the image that can be displayed expressed as number of pixels (picture elements) – the individual dots that make up an image on the screen.

Monitors are available in a range of shapes and sizes. Smaller computer systems may feature units with a 14" diagonal or 17" screen measured across the diagonal, whilst a graphics workstation may have a screen measuring 21" or more. Systems used for desktop publishing may have monitors shaped to provide an accurate representation of an A4 page, whilst multimedia systems may feature internal speakers or other hardware. Portable computers tend to make use of liquid crystal displays (LCDs), similar to the much smaller displays found on pocket calculators. Recent advances in LCD technology mean that large flat-screen LCD monitors are starting to appear on the market.

The quality of a monitor's display can be described in several ways:

1 *Resolution*. The **resolution** of the monitor describes the fineness of the image that can be displayed. Resolution is often expressed in terms of pixels (picture elements) – the

individual dots that make up an image on the screen. Various standards exist that describe the resolutions that a monitor should be capable of displaying. A 14" or 15" VGA monitor, for example, is able to display an image that is 640 by 480 pixels in size. As screen sizes become larger, it becomes possible to display much higher resolutions. A 15" monitor should be capable of displaying 800 by 600 pixels or 1024 by 768 pixels. A typical 17" monitor can display images up to 1600 by 1200 pixels in size.

2 *Colour depth*. The number of colours that can be displayed on the screen are also related to resolution. In Microsoft Windows, the typical number of colours that can be selected through the Control Panel ranges from 2 (monochrome) through 16,256 to 32 million.

> The number of colours that can be displayed on the screen becomes almost meaningless beyond a certain point. Since the human eye can only distinguish between a few hundred shades of the same colour, the ability to display several thousand shades is of little practical importance.

Dot pitch
A method of gauging the quality of a monitor's display that involves measuring the distance between the pixels on the screen.

3 *Dot pitch*. Another method of gauging the quality of a monitor's display involves measuring the distance – known as the **dot pitch** – between the pixels on the screen. The smaller the distance between pixels, the finer the image will appear. A dot pitch of 0.28 mm is standard and will normally appear sharp and clear.

Refresh rate
A method of gauging the quality of a monitor's display that involves measuring the number of times the image is drawn upon the screen each second.

4 *Refresh rate*. A third indicator of image quality relates to the way in which an image is displayed on the monitor. The number of times the image is drawn upon the screen each second is known as the **refresh rate** and is measured in hertz. A refresh rate of 60 Hz, for example, means that the image will be drawn upon the screen 60 times each second. However, as screen size and the complexity of the display increases, it becomes difficult for some monitors to refresh the image at a high enough rate. Some monitors attempt to refresh the screen in two stages, alternately updating each half of the screen. This often results in a flickering effect that can cause difficulties, such as eyestrain, for some users.

Interlaced display
Each complete image shown on a monitor's display is drawn in two steps.

Activity 3.5

Changing your monitor's display settings

If you use a PC running Microsoft Windows, choose Display from the Control Panel available via the Settings section of the Start Menu. Referring to the section above, examine the options available to configure and improve your monitor's output.

Non-interlaced display
The monitor refreshes the display in a single pass.

> An **interlaced** display is one where each complete image is drawn in two steps. A **non-interlaced** monitor refreshes the display in a single pass. A good-quality monitor is normally capable of supporting a non-interlaced display at a refresh rate of 70 Hz or more.

Video projector
A computer system can be connected directly to a projector so that output is directed to a projection screen.

Another way of producing a large display for presentations is by making use of a **data or video projector**. A computer system can be connected directly to a projector so that output is directed to a projection screen.

Plotter
A plotter uses a number of different coloured pens to draw lines upon the paper as it moves through the machine.

▶ Printers and plotters

Since many users are involved in selecting printers these are described in a seperate section. A **plotter** uses a number of different coloured pens to draw lines upon the paper as it moves through the machine. Although capable of producing characters, the quality of the text created is often very poor. Plotters are primarily used to create technical drawings, such as engineering diagrams and to record the progress of continuous monitoring.

▶ Other output devices

In addition to the items described in this section, a wide variety of other output devices are also available. Some examples include the following:

- *Sound.* In addition to music and sound output via speakers, a sound card can be used to output information in a variety of other forms. Two common examples include voice annotations and speech synthesis.
- *MIDI devices.* The ability to link devices to a personal computer via **MIDI** (musical instrument digital interface) connections allows users to send information directly to one or more musical instruments.
- *Microfilm.* **Computer output to microfilm (COM)**, also known as 'computer output microform', is often used to archive large quantities of information for future reference. Information is processed via a personal computer and sent directly to a device that produces microfilm negatives.

MIDI (musical instrument digital interface)

MIDI connections allow users to control musical instruments or synthesise any sounds or effects required in order to play the music.

Computer output to microfilm (COM)

Information is processed via a computer and sent directly to a device that produces microfilm negatives.

Selecting output devices

The selection of an inappropriate output device can incur unnecessary costs and lead to a variety of other problems. Some of the factors that should be considered when selecting an output device include appropriateness, permanence, speed, response time and cost.

▶ Appropriateness

An output device should be appropriate to the type of information produced as the result of a business process. A plotter, for example, provides an efficient means of producing large technical diagrams, but would not be an appropriate means of printing a business letter.

▶ Permanence

It is often necessary to make a permanent record of the results of a given activity, for example an organisation will normally retain a copy of a business letter sent to a client.

▶ Response time

Many activities require constant and immediate feedback. The user of a word processor, for example, needs to see the results of their actions at all times – in other words, the **response time** between action and feedback must be very small.

Response time

The time it takes for a maintenance provider to fix a problem.

▶ Speed

In many applications, the speed of the output device can be of critical importance. As an example, consider a mailmerge operation, where personalised letters are produced by inserting the names and addresses of customers into a standard document. Although generating each letter may take only a matter of seconds, printing each copy can take considerably longer. The time taken to complete the process will depend heavily on the speed of the output device: the slower the device (in this case, the printer), the longer the overall time taken to complete the task.

▶ Cost

The operating costs of certain output devices can be extremely low. The monitor, for example, costs relatively little to purchase, maintain and operate. However, other output devices, for example printers, incur costs each time they are used.

Activity 3.6

Selecting output devices

Using the criteria described in this section and using numerical specifications, select the most suitable type of screen output device and configuration to perform these functions:

- a business analyst involved in using a spreadsheet to model a company's financial performance;
- a student using a PC to produce assignments;
- a web site designer;
- a personal assistant to the director.

Focus on printers   **F**

In this section we describe the main printers used for business and home use and criteria for selecting them.

▶ Laser printer

A laser is used to charge sections of a rotating drum. The pattern of charged and uncharged areas on the drum corresponds to the image that will be printed. As the drum rotates, particles of dry toner powder are picked up. Heat is used to transfer the toner powder to the paper.

Some advantages of the laser printer are as follows:

- *Print quality*. Laser printers are capable of producing documents at a quality appropriate for business correspondence.
- *Speed*. A typical laser printer will be able to print at a rate of between 4 and 12 pages per minute. This compares well against other printing methods, for example a typical inkjet printer may only be capable of printing 1–2 pages per minute.
- *Volume*. Laser printers are normally capable of dealing with large volumes of work. Manufacturers often provide ratings for their printers that describe the typical workload appropriate for a given model. Whereas a dot-matrix printer may be suitable for a workload of 500 pages per month, it is not unusual to find laser printers capable of a workload of 5,000 pages or higher per month.
- *Noise*. Laser printers are almost completely silent in operation.

However, laser printers also suffer from a number of disadvantages:

- *Cost of printing*. The cost of printing via a laser printer is considered high. One reason for this is that all documents – including drafts – are printed at a high quality.

Laser printer
A laser is used to charge sections of a rotating drum which is then used to print using toner powder achieving a combination of speed with high print quality.

- *Colour printing*. A typical laser printer is not capable of printing in colour. Although special colour laser printers are available, these cost thousands of pounds and are expensive to use and maintain. They have, however, largely replaced other forms of colour printing such as wax printers and dye sublimation printers.
- *Cost*. Laser printers are considered expensive to purchase in comparison with other types of printer.

Inkjet printer

Although initially considered expensive and unreliable, inkjet printers have rapidly gained acceptance and are now found in many organisations and homes. Changes in technology have resulted in models that are inexpensive to purchase, reliable in operation and capable of excellent results.

Inkjet printer

An inkjet printer uses a print-head containing 50 or more small nozzles that squirt ink onto paper by varying electrostatic charges produced by the printer.

An **inkjet printer** uses a print-head containing 50 or more small nozzles. Each nozzle can be controlled individually by electrostatic charges produced by the printer. Characters are formed by squirting small droplets of ink directly onto the paper. Bubble jet printers work in a similar manner but transfer the character by melting the ink droplets onto the paper.

Some advantages of inkjet printers include:

- *Cost*. Inkjet printers can be purchased at low cost and are relatively inexpensive to operate.
- *Reliability*. Since inkjet printers have very few moving parts, they are considered reliable and robust.
- *Colour printing*. Inkjet printers provide a relatively inexpensive means of printing in colour at an acceptable quality.
- *Versatility*. Inkjet printers are able to produce a variety of different documents, including overhead transparencies, cards, labels and envelopes.
- *Noise*. Inkjet printers are almost completely silent in operation.

Some of the disadvantages of inkjet printers include the following:

- *Permanence*. The ink used by some printers is not waterproof, meaning that documents can become smudged or blurred easily.
- *Print quality*. Printing at the highest possible quality requires the use of special paper. This increases the cost of printing significantly.
- *Speed*. Although considerably faster than dot-matrix printers, inkjet printers are still unable to compete with laser printers in terms of speed. Colour printing can be particularly slow, with some models taking 6–8 minutes to produce a single page.

Dot-matrix printers

Dot-matrix printer

A character is transferred to the paper by striking pins against an ink ribbon.

The **dot-matrix printer** arranges a series of pins (usually from 8 to 24) to form the shape of a required character. The character is transferred to the paper by striking the pins against an ink ribbon. This form of printing is known as *impact printing*. Dot-matrix printing is now only commonly used when carbon copies of a document need to be created. Similarly, the daisywheel printer, now seldom used, functions in much the same way as a conventional typewriter.

Selecting a printer

A number of factors should be considered when selecting a printer for business use. The aim should be to acquire equipment that meets the business needs of the organisation and ensures high print quality at minimum cost. Some of the factors that should be considered include printing costs, print quality, speed, volume, any requirement to print in colour, and paper handling. Each of these factors is described in the following sections.

Printing costs

The cost of printing is normally described in terms of **cost per page**. Two separate figures are usually given for the cost per page: the typical cost of a page containing only text and the typical cost of a page containing a large graphic image.

The cost per page provides a simple means of determining the overall running costs of a given printer. The figures given usually refer to the costs of *consumables* such as ink and replacement components (toner cartridges, drums and so on).

In general, laser printers and inkjet printers have slightly higher costs per page than other types. However, this is largely due to the fact these printers print at very high qualities. The cost per page tends to rise dramatically when printing in colour is carried out. In some cases, the cost per page can increase by a factor of more than ten.

Cost per page
Figures refer to the costs of consumables such as ink and replacement components (toner cartridges, drums and so on).

Print quality

Print quality is normally measured in **dots per inch** (dpi). This describes the number of individual dots that can be printed within a space of one square inch. Quality is normally compared against professional typesetting, such as the equipment used to produce a book or magazine. A typeset document is normally produced at a quality of between 1200 and 1500 dpi. However, since business documents seldom need to be produced to this standard, the typical 600 dpi quality provided by a laser printer is considered acceptable for business correspondence, reports and other documents.

Dots per inch (DPI)
This describes the number of individual dots that can be printed within a space of one square inch.

Paper handling

Many organisations require the capability to print on envelopes, overhead transparencies and card. In general, only inkjet and laser printers offer this facility. In addition, some laser and inkjet printers have special paper feeders that allow batches of envelopes or labels to be printed at a time.

The quantity of paper that a printer can hold is also an important factor when selecting a business printer for workgroup printing since a large paper capacity will reduce the need to refill the printer constantly.

Colour printing

At present, inkjet printers offer the best compromise between print quality and cost when producing documents in colour. Although other printers, such as colour laser printers, are capable of producing better results, the purchase and consumable costs can be prohibitive.

Volume

The volume of printing that will be carried out using a particular printer has implications for running costs, maintenance costs and reliability. Manufacturers often provide ratings for their printers that describe the typical workload appropriate for a given model. This value is often described in terms of **pages per month**. An inkjet printer, for example, might be described as appropriate for home use where the average monthly workload is likely to be less than 1000 pages per month. A laser printer might achieve 8000 pages per month.

Pages per month (ppm)
Manufacturers often provide ratings for their printers that describe the typical workload appropriate for a given model.

A common problem experienced by organisations using inkjet printers concerns increased printing costs. Many organisations acquire inkjet printers so that they have the facility to print documents in colour. In many cases this is seen as a facility that will be used infrequently, for specific documents on specific occasions. However, employees often overuse this facility, even printing internal and draft documents in colour. The result is often twofold: printing costs increase dramatically (sometimes by a factor of up to 20) and the working life of the printer is reduced significantly.

Speed

The speed of a printer can have a major impact on the work carried out within an organisation. Delays in printing documents can promote bottlenecks within administrative processes and are wasteful in terms of labour power. As an example, consider a household or motor insurance company. Such companies often print documents on demand, for example, a motor insurance quotation may be printed as the customer waits at the service counter. Clearly, printing the document quickly and efficiently has implications for customer service and company image.

Pages per minute (ppm)
A simple means of measuring the speed of a printer.

Printing speeds are usually measured in **pages per minute** (ppm). Typical examples of printing speeds are 1–2 ppm for an inkjet and 8 ppm and above for a laser printer.

Activity 3.7

Selecting printers

Using the criteria described in this section, select the most suitable type of printer for these applications:

Primary storage
Data and instructions are loaded into memory such as random access memory. Such storage is temporary.

- a student on a business course with a limited budget
- a shared workgroup printer for 10 people
- proofing magazines
- printing duplicate copies of invoices.

Secondary storage
Floppy disks and hard disks are secondary storage which provides permanent storage.

Storage devices

Storage devices (Fig. 3.8) are used to store programs, data awaiting processing and the information resulting from computer processing. Storage devices are categorised as **primary storage** when the data is loaded into computer memory or **secondary storage** when

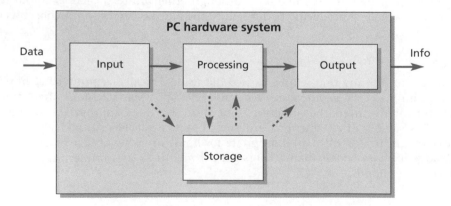

Figure 3.8 **Storage devices in context**

the data is stored on a separate device where the information will be retained even if the machine is switched off. This distinction is similar to that between human short-term and long-term memory. Floppy and hard disks are examples of secondary storage.

A brief description of several storage-device concepts will support an understanding of the sections that follow:

● Storage devices can have varying degrees of functionality in terms of their ability to record data. At one end of the spectrum, a **read-only** device can only be used to access

Read-only

A device that can only be used to access data that is already present on the media and is unable to write data.

Units of data measurement

The capacity of a storage device is often measured in terms of kilobytes, megabytes and gigabytes. The following may help readers to understand these units.

● A bit is a single binary digit and represents a 0 (zero) or a 1. The bit is the smallest unit of measurement.
● A byte is made up of eight bits and represents a value between 0 and 255. A byte can be thought of as the amount of space required to hold a single character.
● A kilobyte (kb) is approximately 1000 bytes, or the equivalent of 1000 characters.
● A megabyte (Mb) is approximately 1000 Kb, or the equivalent of one million characters.
● A gigabyte (Gb) is approximately 1000 Mb, of the equivalent of one billion characters.

The list below puts these numbers in context:

1 *One character such as 'a'?*
   A byte

2 *A typewritten page?*
   2 kilobytes. (Kilobyte = 1000 bytes)

3 *A low-resolution photograph?*
   100 Kb. (Kilobyte = 1000 bytes).

4 *The complete works of Shakespeare?*
   5 megabytes. (Megabyte = 1 000 000 bytes)

5 *A standard CD-ROM?*
   640 megabytes. (Megabyte = 1 000 000 bytes)

6 *A pickup truck filled with documents?*
   1 gigabyte. (Gigabyte = 1 000 000 000 bytes)

7 *The works of Beethoven in digital audio format?*
   50 gigabytes

8 *50 000 trees made into paper and printed as documents?*
   1 terabyte. (Terabyte = 1 000 000 000 000 bytes)

9 *The printed collection of the US Library of Congress?*
   10 terabytes. (Terabyte = 1 000 000 000 000 bytes)

10 *All printed material?*
    200 petabytes. (Petabyte = 1 000 000 000 000 000 bytes)

11 *All words ever spoken by human beings?*
    5 exabytes. (Exabyte = 1 000 000 000 000 000 000 bytes)

12 *Words possibly spoken by all beings in the Universe?*
    Zettabyte = 1 000 000 000 000 000 000 000 bytes)
    Yottabyte = 1 000 000 000 000 000 000 000 000 bytes)

Source: Roy Williams of Caltech (www.ccsf.caltech.edu/~roy/dataquan/)

Bit

A single binary digit representing a (0) zero or a 1.

Byte

Made up of eight bits and represents the amount of space required to hold a single character.

Kilobyte (Kb)

Approximately 1000 bytes, or the equivalent of 1000 characters.

Megabyte (Mb)

Approximately 1000 Kb, or the equivalent of one million characters.

Gigabyte (Gb)

Approximately 1000 Mb, of the equivalent of one billion characters.

WORM (write once, read many)

A storage device allows data to be written only once. Once the data have been written, they cannot be changed or erased.

data. A CD-ROM drive, for example, is unable to write data to a CD. A **WORM** (write once read many) storage device allows data to be written only once. Once the data have been written, they cannot be changed or erased. Fortunately, the majority of storage devices allow data to be written, erased and re-written as often as required.

- The media used to hold data can be fixed or removable. Removable media, such as floppy disks, tend to be portable. Fixed media, such as a hard disk drive, have limited storage capacity but often allow speedy access to data.

◗ Secondary storage – floppy disk

These are usually referred to as the 'A: drive' on PCs.

Floppy disk

Consists of a plastic disk, coated with a magnetic covering and enclosed within a rigid plastic case.

Early floppy disks were enclosed within a cover made of thin card, hence the term 'floppy disk'. A modern **floppy disk** consists of a plastic disk, coated with a magnetic covering and enclosed within a rigid plastic case. Floppy disks are available in a number of different sizes and with varying capacities. At present, the most common type is the high-density 3.5" floppy disk.

The two major advantages of the floppy disk are as follows:

- The floppy disk drive is a common, standardised means of storing data and floppy disk drives can be found on the majority of personal computers.
- Floppy disks are portable between computer systems, allowing users to transfer relatively small amounts of data between machines.

Some of the major disadvantages of the floppy disk include:

- Floppy disks are relatively delicate, being susceptible to dust, magnetic fields, liquid spills and other forms of accidental damage.
- The storage capacity of the floppy disk is considered small. A standard 3.5" disk is capable of storing 1.44 Mb of data, the equivalent of approximately 350 pages of text.
- The floppy disk drive is considered relatively slow: it can take several minutes to read or write data to a disk.

◗ Secondary storage – hard disk drive

Hard disk

A magnetic medium that stores data upon a number of rigid platters that are rotated at very high speeds.

Hard disk drives are a standard feature of a modern personal computer. They are used to store the computer's operating system, application software and data.

These are usually referred to as the 'C: drive' on PCs. On servers, network drives based on hard disks are typically denoted by a letter in the range F to Z.

A hard disk drive (Fig. 3.9) stores data upon a number of rigid platters that are rotated at very high speeds. Since the magnetic read/write heads float above the surface of the platter at a distance of a few microns, the drive mechanism is enclosed within a vacuum to protect against dust and other contaminants.

The major advantages of the hard disk drive are as follows:

- Hard disk drives tend to have large storage capacities, with typical capacities varying from 6 Gb to more than 60 Gb, equivalent to between 14 million and 140 million pages of text.
- A hard disk drive is considered a fast means of storing and retrieving data, for example a modern drive can be hundreds of times faster than a floppy disk drive.
- The hard disk drive is a standard component of a personal computer system. As such they are relatively inexpensive to purchase or replace.

The major disadvantages of the hard disk drive are as follow:

- Hard disk drives are seen as delicate devices that are easily damaged. They are particularly susceptible to damage from sudden shocks and excessive vibration.

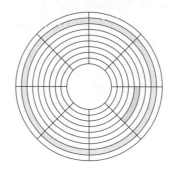

Currently
4-20Gb for
home PCs

Figure 3.9 Different views of the platters and sectors on hard disk drives

- In general, a hard disk drive is considered to be a fixed part of a computer system and is not portable. However, it should be noted that removable hard disk drives exist and that these are rapidly becoming popular.

▶ Secondary storage – removable disks

Removable disk drives have become popular in response to the need for portable storage devices with larger capacities than the traditional floppy disk. A removable disk drive combines some of the advantages of the hard disk drive and the floppy disk drive. An example of a removable disk drive is the Iomega ZIP or Jazz drive; these are capable of storing 100 Mb of data or more

▶ Secondary storage – CD-ROM

The **CD-ROM** drive arose from the audio compact disc player and began to gain popularity during the late 1980s. The acronym CD-ROM stands for 'compact disc – read-only memory', denoting the fact that CD-ROM discs are read-only devices; data cannot be written to a CD-ROM by a conventional player.

The data on a **compact disc** are encoded as a series of dips and raised areas. These two states represent binary data – the same number system used by microprocessors. The player shines a laser beam onto the surface of the disc and measures the light that is reflected back. The intensity of the light that is reflected back enables the player to distinguish individual binary digits.

The two major advantages of the compact disc are:

- A compact disc has a very high storage capacity. A standard disc is able to store 650 Mb of data. This is equivalent to approximately 2 million pages of text or 74 minutes of high-quality music.
- The costs associated with CD-ROM storage are typically very low. CD-ROM drives are inexpensive and can be repaired or replaced easily.

CD-ROM
....
A computer storage device offering a relatively high capacity. The acronym CD-ROM stands for Compact Disc – Read Only Memory, denoting the fact that CD-ROM discs are read only devices.

Compact disc (CD)
....
The media used by CD-ROM players. The data on a compact disc is encoded as a series of dips and raised areas.

Some of the disadvantages of the CD-ROM include:

- Compact discs are relatively fragile. They are easily damaged, for example by accidental scratches or exposure to heat.
- CD-ROM is relatively slow in comparison to other storage devices, such as the hard disk drive.
- CD-ROM is a read-only medium. Although listed as a disadvantage, this can sometimes be seen as an advantage since unauthorised changes and accidental erasure of data can be prevented.

CD-R (CD-recordable)
Can both read conventional compact discs and also write data to special 'gold' discs.

A variation on the traditional CD-ROM drive is the **CD-recordable** (CDR) drive. These drives can not only read conventional compact discs but can also write data to special gold or silver-coloured discs. Compact discs produced in this way are known as write-once discs (WORM), that is, once data has been stored on the disc it cannot be altered or erased.

CDRW
In addition to providing the functionality of the CDR drive, the CDRW drive also allows the use of special compact disc media that can be written and erased many times.

A more recent development is the **CD re-writable** (CDRW) drive. In addition to providing the functionality of the CDR drive, the CDRW drive also allows the use of special compact disc media that can be written and erased many times. It is a cost-effective method of data backup of volumes previously only possible through tape backup. However, discs produced in this way are not always compatible with standard CD-ROM drives.

▶ Secondary storage – DVD

Digital versatile disc (DVD)
Similar to CD-ROM but with higher storage capacities, typically between 4Gb and 7Gb which is accessed at higher speeds.

Digital versatile disc (DVD) players began to gain popularity in 1997 and are now fitted as a standard component of many new personal computers. Although superficially similar to CD-ROM, DVD offers two important benefits to users. First, the discs used by a DVD player offer extremely high storage capacities, typically between 4 and 7 Gb. Secondly, data held on DVD can be accessed at very high speeds. One of the most common applications for DVD is as a distribution medium for full-length feature films.

▶ Secondary storage – magnetic tape

Tape streamer
A common form of storage device that uses magnetic tape as a storage medium.

Magnetic tape has been a common form of storage media for more than three decades. The most common form of storage device based on magnetic tape is the **tape streamer**. A tape streamer is normally installed as an internal device, similar to a floppy disk drive or CD-ROM drive. The tape streamer uses small plastic cartridges filled with magnetic tape. Since each cartridge tends to have a relatively small storage capacity, it is often necessary to use several in order to store large data files.

The major characteristics of magnetic tape include:

- Magnetic tape allows only sequential access – data can only be accessed in strict order.
- The costs associated with the use of magnetic tape as a storage medium are extremely low.
- Storage devices based on magnetic tape are considered extremely slow. In view of this, they are mainly used for archiving and backup applications.
- Magnetic tape is relatively fragile and is easily damaged.

Digital audio tape (DAT)
A storage medium that combines some of the characteristics of magnetic tape and compact disc.

A range of new devices based on magnetic tape have begun to appear over the past few years. The majority of these devices make use of **digital audio tape** (DAT) or even ordinary video cassettes. Digital audio tape couples higher storage capacities with improved speed. However, at present, storage devices based on DAT remain costly and are often beyond the reach of small organisations.

❱ Primary storage – memory

Computer memory can take a number of different forms and is found within many of the devices that go to form part of a computer-based information system. Computers, printers, graphics cards, modems and many other devices all make use of various kinds of memory 'chips'. Although relatively expensive, memory is the fastest form of storage available.

There are two broad categories of computer memory: volatile and non-volatile. The contents of **volatile** memory are lost when the power to the device is switched off. On the other hand, non-volatile memory retains its contents until changed in some way.

Volatile memory
....
Anything held in memory is lost once the power to the computer system is switched off.

A digital camera is just one device that makes use of non-volatile memory. The memory found in a personal computer is considered volatile, that is, anything held in memory is lost once the power to the computer system is switched off. However, non-volatile memory retains its contents until altered or erased. Typically, non-volatile memory is housed in a small expansion card that be inserted into a special slot on a digital camera, portable computer or other device.

Non-volatile memory
....
Non-volatile memory retains its contents until altered or erased.

Random access memory (RAM) is used as working storage, holding instructions and data that are waiting to be processed. The contents of RAM are volatile, that is, any data held is lost when the power to the computer system is switched off. A typical computer system will feature 128 or 256 Mb of RAM. In general, the more RAM a computer system is equipped with, the faster it will operate and the more powerful it will be in terms of the complexity of the programs it can run. RAM is also found in a number of other devices, for example in a printer RAM is used to store an image of the document to be printed.

Random access memory (RAM)
....
RAM is used as volatile, working storage by a computer, holding instructions and data that are waiting to be processed.

The contents of **read-only memory** (ROM) are fixed and cannot be altered. ROM is also non-volatile, making it ideal as a means of storing the information needed for a device to function properly. In a computer system, for example, the basic information needed so that the computer can access disk drives and control peripherals is stored in ROM. This prevents users from accidentally deleting or altering information essential to the computer's operation.

Read-only memory (ROM)
....
The contents of ROM are fixed and can not be altered. ROM is non-volatile.

Some other forms of computer memory include the following:

- An **EPROM** (eraseable programmable read-only memory) is a type of ROM that retains its contents until they are changed using a special device (known as a 'burner').
- VRAM (video random access memory) is a type of memory that has been optimised in order to speed up operations that involve graphics.
- CMOS, NMOS and PMOS memory are used as semi-permanent means of storage in a variety of different devices. Similar to EPROMs in many ways, a major difference is that no special device is needed to alter the contents of the memory. As an example, this kind of memory is generally used in computer systems as a means of storing any special settings needed to control the operation of the computer or a peripheral. This approach allows users to add or remove devices quickly and easily.

EPROM (eraseable programmable read-only memory)
....
This is a form of ROM memory that retains its contents until changed using a special device known as a 'burner'.

It is worth highlighting the wide range of ways in which computer memory is used. In a domestic environment, for example, one might find memory chips in television sets, satellite receivers, video cassette recorders, burglar alarm systems, alarm clocks, washing machines, microwave ovens, hi-fi equipment and a variety of other devices.

In terms of a computer-based information system, the following examples illustrate the range of applications to which computer memory can be put:

- In a modem, ROM is used to store the commands used to control communications and any special settings the user has specified.

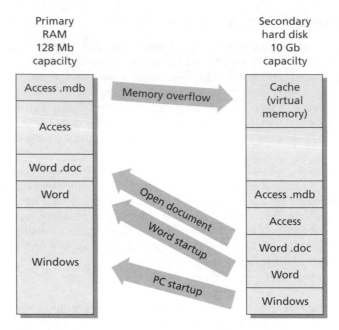

Figure 3.10 Relationship between primary and secondary storage on a PC

- In a laser printer, special ROM cards can be used to expand the printer's range of typefaces. Additional RAM can also be added to speed up printing or allow the printing of more complex documents.

Cache memory
....
Used to improve performance by anticipating the data and instructions needed by the processor. The required data is retrieved and held in the cache, ready to be transferred directly to the processor when required.

- In a computer system, **cache memory** is used to improve performance by anticipating the data and instructions that will be needed by the processor. The required data are retrieved and held in the cache, ready to be transferred directly to the processor when required. By removing the need for data to be retrieved from the computer's much slower main memory (RAM), the overall speed of the system is improved. The *hit rate* describes how often a correct prediction has been made in terms of the data needed by the processor. In general, the higher the hit rate, the greater the increase in performance.

- Another form of cache memory used on a PC is the virtual memory created on the hard disk when the RAM capacity is exceeded. An example of a situation in which this might occur is indicated in Figure 3.10. Initially software such as Windows and Word together with associated documents are loaded from hard disk to RAM (memory) according to the user's selections. Once too many programs are running in the RAM, additional temporary storage on the hard disk is used. This is cache or virtual memory. Note that although this enables the PC to continue operating, it slows considerably since accessing the virtual memory on the hard disk is significantly slower than accessing the primary RAM. This indicates the importance of investing in sufficient RAM to avoid the need to use the slower virtual memory.

Selecting storage devices

The selection of a storage device will normally be based upon speed, storage capacity and cost. However, the importance of these factors will vary according to the function being performed, for example speed might be considered of little importance when making a backup of data overnight. Table 3.1 summarises some of the characteristics of several typical storage devices.

Table 3.1 Comparison between storage media and devices

Storage medium	Speed	Cost	Capacity	Permanent
Magnetic tape	Very slow	Very low	Very high	No
Floppy disk	Slow	Low	Very low	No
Hard disk drive	Fast	Low	Very high	No
CD-ROM	Slow	Low	Very high	Yes
Memory	Very fast	High	Low	No/yes

◗ Speed

Many of the tasks carried out by a computer-based information system require large quantities of data to be processed quickly and efficiently. In many cases, the overall time taken to complete an action will depend upon the speed of the storage device used.

The speed of a storage device is usually measured in terms of its access time (sometimes known as 'seek time') and data transfer rate. The **access time** refers to the average time taken to locate a specific item of data. Access times are normally given in milliseconds, for example a typical hard disk drive might have an access time of 11 ms.

The **data transfer rate** describes how quickly the device is able to read continuous blocks of data. This figure is normally expressed in terms of kilobytes or megabytes. A typical data transfer rate for a CD-ROM drive, for example, might be given as 900 kb per second, whilst a hard disk drive might transfer more than 6 Mb per second.

Access time
The average time taken to locate a specific item of data.

Data transfer rate
The rate at which a device is able to read continuous blocks of data.

◗ Capacity

The storage capacity of a given device will be measured in kilobytes, megabytes or gigabytes, for example a standard CD-ROM has a storage capacity of 650 Mb. Some storage devices, such as a hard disk drive, will have a fixed storage capacity whilst others will use removable media that provide an almost unlimited amount of data storage. In general, a fixed storage device will operate faster than one that uses removable media. In addition, many applications generate large data files that can not be stored conveniently on removable media. A database file, for example, can easily exceed the capacity of a floppy disk or removable disk.

◗ Cost of storage

The costs associated with storage devices are normally given in terms of **cost per megabyte**. In some cases, the cost per megabyte is based upon the cost of the hardware, in others it is based upon the cost of media. Two simple examples should help to make this clearer:

Cost per megabyte
A simple means of gauging the costs associated with a given storage device.

- A hard disk drive has a fixed capacity, so the cost per megabyte can be calculated by simply dividing the cost of the hard drive by its storage capacity.
- A floppy disk drive uses removable media with a capacity of 1.44 Mb. The cost per megabyte would be calculated by dividing the cost of a single floppy disk by 1.44.

◗ Other factors

A number of other factors should be taken into consideration when selecting a storage device. Amongst these are the following:

- The *reliability* of a storage device can be an important factor in many circumstances, for example a hardware failure might prevent all access to important business data. Furthermore, errors introduced when storing or reading data might also have serious consequences. For example, a small error on a magnetic tape cartridge might lead to the loss of all of the data held on the cartridge.

- *Permanence* of storage is important if there is a need to protect data from being deleted or altered. A more permanent form of storage can also be desirable if the data held are unlikely to change often. Reference materials, for example, are often distributed on CD-ROM.

- It may often be necessary to take *security* measures to prevent data from being stolen or damaged. Removable media, such as floppy disks, can be transported easily from one location to another. Whilst this can provide added security, it can also increase risk of theft. Fixed devices, such as hard disk drives, are less vulnerable but also less versatile.

Activity 3.8

Hardware selection

Using the criteria described in this section, select the most suitable type of storage device (with numerical specifications) to perform these functions:

- a backup device for a student working on their dissertation;
- a backup device for a designer transferring large files between their home and work offices;
- a graphic designer who requires large graphics to be held in memory;
- web pages on a web server.

Processors

Processor

Uses instructions from software to control the different components of a PC.

The **central processing unit** (CPU) – or processor – found within a computer consists of two components: a *control unit* and an *arithmetic logic unit* (ALU). The control unit fetches instructions from software that has been loaded into memory, decodes them and then executes them. The control unit controls the operation of all hardware, including all input/output operations. The ALU carries out arithmetical calculations, for example addition, and can also make comparisons between values. An often used analogy is to compare the processor to the human brain – which has a similar control function over the other parts of the body. The brain controls bodily function according to stimuli monitored by different sensory organs of the body. The analogy is not entirely appropriate since the human brain is of course a very complex part of the human system, also containing permanent and volatile memory functions for example!

The speed of a processor will depend upon a number of different factors. Two such factors are clock speed and bus width. The **clock speed** determines how many instruc-

Clock speed

Measured in MHz (megahertz, or millions of pulses per second). The clock speed is governed by a quartz-crystal circuit.

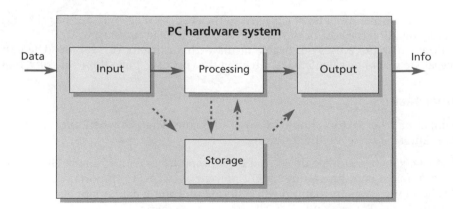

Figure 3.11 **The processor in context**

tions per second the processor can execute. The **bus width** describes how many pieces of data can be transmitted at one time. In both cases, the higher the value, the more powerful the processor. Clock speed and bandwidth values can be helpful when attempting to compare processors in order to select the most appropriate. For example, clock speeds for the Pentium range of processors have varied from 60 MHz in early versions through to several GHz in more recent versions (Table 3.2).

Bus width
Describes how many pieces of data can be transmitted or received at one time by the bus connecting the processor to other components of the PC.

Table 3.2 **Historical improvements in processor capability**

Date	Name	Transistors and microns	Clock speed in MHz	MIPS (millions of instructions per second)
1974	8080	6k, 6	2	0.64
1979	8088	29k, 3	5	0.33
1982	'286	134k, 1.5	6	1
1985	'386	275k, 1.5	16	5
1993	Pentium	3.1M, 0.8	60	100
1997	Pentium II	7.5M, 0.35	233	400
1999	Pentium III	9.5M, 0.25	450	1000
2001	Pentium 4	42M, 0.18	1500	1500

Most IBM-compatible personal computers are based upon a series of processors manufactured by Intel and several of its competitors. Older systems may feature early Pentium processors such as the Pentium II, whilst more up-to-date computers may use a more recent Pentium-class processor such as a Pentium III or Pentium 4. Over recent years, Intel has faced increased competition from rivals such as AMD. Competitors such as AMD manufacture processors that are compatible with the various types of Pentium processors but tend to market them at lower prices. The Athlon and Duron processors manufactured by AMD, for example, are broadly equivalent to Pentium processors operating at 1 GHz and above.

Intel's first microprocessor, the 4004, ran at 108 kilohertz (108,000 hertz), compared to the Pentium® 4 processor's initial speed of 1.5 gigahertz (1.5 billion hertz). If automobile speed had increased similarly over the same period, you could now drive from San Francisco to New York in about 13 seconds.

Source: Intel processor museum (www.intel.com)

It is important to recognise that not all aspects of performance of a computer are governed by the processor. As a general rule, the faster the processor, the faster and more efficient the computer. However, referring back to the section on virtual memory, RAM capacity, hard-disk speed and graphics cards can also have a significant impact on overall system speed.

Activity 3.9

Selecting processors

Since this book was published, the clock speed of processors will have increased significantly. Using a site that reviews hardware such as CNet (www.cnet.com) or ZDNet (www.zdnet.com) select the best processor specifications for:

- an entry level ('cheap and cheerful' basic PC);
- a high-end PC for a graphics designer;
- a web server.

Other components of a personal computer

The preceding sections have already described a wide variety of the input, output and storage devices that can form part of a computer system. In this section, we look at a range of other components found in a typical personal computer.

▶ Graphics card

A graphics card enables a computer to display text or graphics on a monitor. The graphics card prepares and stores the image in memory prior to showing it on the screen. When the image is complete, it is transmitted to the monitor and displayed. A graphics card may produce and display images more than 60 times per second.

The amount of memory available to a graphics card determines the maximum resolution of the image and how many colours can be displayed. All graphics cards support the **VGA** (video graphics array) standard which specifies a maximum image size of 640 by 320 pixels, displayed in 16 colours. A VGA display can be achieved with just 256 kb of memory but larger images with more colours can require 1 Mb of memory or more. Many graphics cards are supplied with 16 Mb, 32 Mb or even 64 Mb of memory, allowing them to display very complex images at large sizes.

Table 3.3 illustrates some of the most common graphics standards, indicating the highest resolution and maximum number of colours possible. Note that the table is arranged in approximate order of age, from oldest to newest.

VGA (video graphics array)

A common standard for graphics cards. All graphics cards support the VGA (video graphics array) standard which specifies a maximum image size of 640 by 320 pixels, displayed in 16 colours.

Graphics accelerator card

A type of graphics card containing its own memory and featuring a coprocessor.

3DFx graphics card

A type of graphics card that features a sophisticated coprocessor used to manipulate an image so that it appears more realistic.

Motherboard

The motherboard is the main circuit board within a computer and houses the processor, memory, expansion slots and a number of connectors used for attaching additional devices, such as a hard disk drive.

BIOS (basic input/output system)

Housed in a memory chip on the computer's motherboard, the BIOS contains software that controls all of the computer's most basic activities.

Table 3.3 **PC graphics standards**

Standard	Highest resolution	Maximum colours
MDA	Text only	2
Hercules	720 by 348	2
CGA	640 by 200	2
EGA	640 by 350	16
VGA	640 by 480	16
XGA	1024 by 768	65 000
SVGA	1600 by 1200	16 million

Many graphics cards contain a graphics coprocessor that is used to carry out graphics calculations. This can help to improve the speed of the computer as some of the burden on the CPU is removed. Graphics cards that use a graphics coprocessor are often called **graphics accelerator cards**.

A growing trend towards more detailed graphics has spurred development of 3DFx graphics cards that manipulate an image so that it appears more realistic. Although the term **3DFx** was originally used to identify the products made by a specific manufacturer, the term now encompasses all graphics cards capable of producing the sophisticated effects required by various leisure and business software packages.

▶ Motherboard

The **motherboard** (Fig. 3.12) is the main circuit board within a computer and houses the processor, memory, expansion slots and a number of connectors used for attaching additional devices, such as a hard disk drive. Any device that forms part of the motherboard is able to communicate with the processor directly.

On a personal computer, the motherboard will contain a ROM chip that holds the computer's BIOS. The **BIOS** (basic input/output system) contains software that controls all of the computer's most basic activities. It is the BIOS that allows the keyboard, dis-

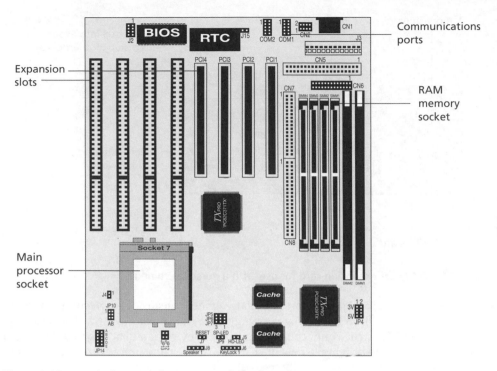

Figure 3.12 A typical personal computer motherboard

play, hard disk drives, serial ports and other devices to function. The BIOS is stored in ROM so that it is always available and cannot be accidentally damaged or erased.

Storage devices, such as hard disk drives, are attached via the motherboard's I/O (input/output) connections. At least two **serial ports** are also supported, allowing mouse, modems, printers and a range of other devices to be connected. In addition, a **parallel port** is normally used to connect a printer, scanner or other device.

Expansion slots allow additional devices to be connected to the computer. Expansion slots are described in more detail in the next section. A computer's capabilities can be extended by adding special circuit boards (known as **expansion cards**) to the motherboard (Fig. 3.13). Common expansion cards include graphics cards, modems and sound cards. A typical computer will feature up to six expansion slots.

A motherboard will normally support expansion devices conforming to several different standards, such as PCI or USB. Some of the most common standards include the following:

● The **ISA** (Industry Standard Architecture) and **EISA** (Extended Industry Standard Architecture) standards were the first to be widely adopted by manufacturers. Expansion cards based on these standards tend to offer relatively poor performance. ISA and EISA are seldom found on modern personal computers since they declined in popularity after the introduction of PCI and USB standards.
● The **PCI** (Peripheral Component Interconnect) standard allows devices to communicate with the processor at high speeds. PCI expansion cards can also support **Plug and Play** (PnP), where new devices can be configured automatically without the user needing to enter settings or make other changes. Almost every new computer system features at least four PCI expansion slots.
● **SCSI** (Small Computer System Interface) devices are able to transmit data at very high speeds. In addition, up to seven separate devices can be attached to a single SCSI interface simultaneously. Connecting several devices in sequence is known as *daisychaining*. Common SCSI devices include scanners, hard disk drives, CDR units and printers.

Serial port

A type of connector that allows various devices to be attached to a computer system. Examples of common serial devices might include a mouse, modem or printer.

Parallel port

A type of connector that allows various devices to be attached to a computer system. Examples of common parallel devices include printers and external storage devices.

Expansion slot

A slot on the computer's motherboard which can accommodate expansion cards.

Expansion card

Expansion cards can be used to extend a computer's capabilities by adding new devices to the system.

ISA (Industry Standard Architecture)

This describes a common standard governing the way in which an expansion card interacts with a computer's motherboard and CPU.

EISA (Extended Industry Standard Architecture)

This describes a common standard governing the way in which an expansion card interacts with a computer's motherboard and CPU.

PCI (Peripheral Component Interconnect)

This describes a common standard governing the way in which an expansion card interacts with a computer's motherboard and CPU.

Plug and Play (PnP)

This describes a means by which expansion cards can be added to a computer system and configured automatically without the user needing to enter settings or make other changes. See *Expansion card.*

SCSI (Small Computer System Interface)
This describes a common standard governing the way in which an expansion card interacts with a computer's motherboard and CPU.

USB (universal serial bus)
This describes a relatively new standard that governs the way in which an expansion card interacts with a computer's motherboard and CPU.

Hot plugging
This describes the ability to add or remove new devices whilst the computer is running and have the operation system automatically recognise any changes made.

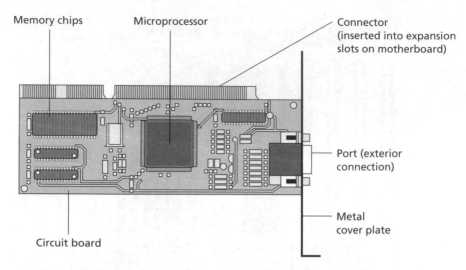

Figure 3.13 A typical expansion card for use with a personal computer

● The USB (Universal Serial Bus) port is a relatively new means of connecting devices to a computer. In addition to offering very high data transmission speeds, USB also supports Plug and Play, the connection of up to 127 devices, and **hot plugging**. The latter is the ability to add or remove new devices whilst the computer is running and have the operating system automatically recognise any changes made.

It should also be pointed out that new devices need not be installed inside the computer. Some expansion cards merely add a new interface, allowing devices to be

---

Activity 3.10

Identification of hardware types

To check your knowledge of the different types of hardware introduced in this chapter, match the descriptions of software above with the specific types of software below.

Hardware descriptions

1 Store programs and data in a PC when it is powered down.
2 Store data for fast access when the computer is running.
3 Access 25 000 clipart samples for incorporating into presentations.
4 Backing up company financial data.
5 Automatically reading the ISBN of a book.
6 Performing calculations of company profit and loss.
7 Obtaining hard copy of a spreadsheet to discuss with your accountant.
8 Connecting to the Internet.
9 Taking data home to analyse on your PC.
10 Joining five PCs together.
11 Storing data to share between users on five networked PCs.

Hardware types

(a) 256 Megabytes of RAM; **(b)** HP Laserjet; **(c)** floppy disk; **(d)** fax-modem;
(e) CD-ROM; **(f)** bar code reader; **(g)** Intel Pentium processor; **(h)** CDRW or tape streamer; **(i)** local area network (LAN); **(j)** server; **(k)** 20 Gigabyte hard disk drive

attached outside of the case via a connecting cable. Furthermore, many devices can be connected to the computer via its serial or parallel ports. An external modem, for example, can be connected to a serial port or USB port via a special cable.

Focus on managing technological change   F

A major difficulty for companies wishing to apply information systems to help their businesses is how often technology changes. The speed of this change occurs through the competitiveness of the IT industry. If the leading vendors do not introduce new products, they can quickly be overtaken by smaller companies, or even startups. Witness the speed at which Microsoft moved from being a small player to topple IBM as one of the world's leading software companies.

Moore's law

Gordon Moore, co-founder of Intel, predicted in 1965 that the transistor density of semiconductor chips would double roughly every 18 months. This prediction has actually happened as we have moved from different generations of processors, such as from 8086 to 80286 and through to the Pentium 4.

The problem of change refers to hardware, software and entire business information systems, but it is perhaps best evidenced by the speed in change of processors. Improvements in processing power are indicated by *Moore's law*.

Alongside this increase in the capacity and speed of processors, the capacity and speed of primary RAM storage and secondary magnetic disk storage have also increased dramatically, allowing larger, more complex, software to be run. The hardware improvements have permitted more complex software to be built, and this in turn requires newer hardware, since software designers tend to design new systems for the fastest machines available. To some extent, the speed of change in other hardware and software is governed by the rate at which processing power increases.

20 000 000 – the number of times cheaper that computing grew, between 1940 and 2000, according to David Mowery, economic historian at University of California, Berkeley.

How do these technical changes affect a business? Many managers would answer that they result in unnecessary expense and disruption. While this may be true, managers do not have to adopt the latest technologies if they do not believe that they are delivering benefits. So why are new technologies adopted? The reason may often be fear: fear that if your competitor has upgraded to the latest Intel version, or Windows or e-business system, then they may have a competitive advantage. If you perceive that your competitor has, or may develop, a competitive advantage, then this is a powerful incentive to invest in new systems.

Much of this investment cycle may be driven by uncertainty and the fear of falling behind. Industry figures seem to suggest that companies overestimate the benefits that new systems can give them and underestimate the risk of project failure. The productivity paradox, which was popularised by Strassman (1997), seemed to suggest that there is little or no correlation between a company's investment in information systems and its business performance measured in terms of profitability or stock returns (see Chapter 13 for further discussion).

▶ Techniques for dealing with technological change

There is a continuum of approaches for how managers deal with technological change. The approaches are informed by considering the typical pattern for the diffusion of innovation summarised by Rogers (1983). Figure 3.14 illustrates a typical curve for adoption of any innovation by consumers or businesses, whether it be a new processor, a new form of storage such as DVD, or a new business concept such as e-business. One adoption approach is to be an early adopter, who always tries to be the first to make use of new technologies to gain a competitive advantage. The second is to use a more conservative, 'wait-and-see' approach and not use new technology until its benefits have been successfully demonstrated by other companies in your sector. Of course, there is a continuum here and most companies would seek to position themselves somewhere between the two extremes.

Activity 3.11   **Adoption of transactional e-commerce for sales**

Referring to Figure 3.14, suggest and explain the current state of e-commerce adoption for e-commerce sales for different types of business according to size and industrial sector. Use the sources of Internet usage data available under student resources at www.marketing-online.co.uk.

The problem with being an early adopter is that the leading edge of development is often also referred to as the 'bleeding edge' of technology due to the risk of failure. New systems may have many bugs, may integrate poorly with the existing system or may simply not live up to their promise. The counterargument to this is that, although the risks of adoption are high, so are the rewards, since you may gain an edge on your rivals. American Airlines gained a considerable advantage over its rivals when it first introduced the SABRE customer reservation system; similarly, the banks that first introduced new techniques such as auto-teller machines and phone banking facilities also managed to increase market share. The examples in the box give examples of people and organisations that have been too conservative – not envisaging the benefits of new hardware or technology approaches.

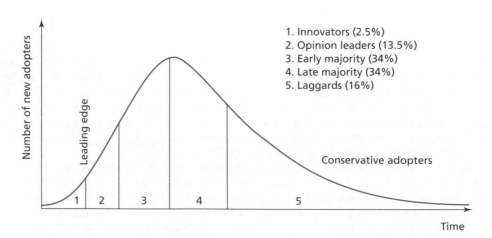

1. Innovators (2.5%)
2. Opinion leaders (13.5%)
3. Early majority (34%)
4. Late majority (34%)
5. Laggards (16%)

Figure 3.14 Typical diffusion of innovation curve

Reported quotations from conservative technology adopters

'This "telephone" has too many shortcomings to be seriously considered as a means of communication. The device is inherently of no value to us.'
Western Union internal memo, 1876.

'Who the hell wants to hear actors talk?'
H.M. Warner, Warner Brothers, 1927.

'I think there is a world market for maybe five computers.'
Thomas Watson, chairman of IBM, 1943.

'There is no reason anyone would want a computer in their home.'
Ken Olson, Founder of DEC, 1977.

◗ Keeping pace with PC software and hardware

There is a tendency for hardware vendors to retain their entry-level price as technology improves. For $1000 or £1000 the specification that is available has increased dramatically over the past five years. Yet this price bracket seems to be that most commonly used in business adverts. The result of this is that a business manager may over-specify the equipment needed for end-users. Does an administration assistant really need the latest-generation PC with a very fast processor and full memory complement for simple word-processing?

A further problem is upgrading to new versions of operating systems and applications software. For example, a company such as Microsoft needs to produce new versions of software every few years to maintain its revenue stream. The question for the business user is, do we really need these latest versions? Companies will often find that the benefits of the new software are marginal and the costs and disruption of upgrading may be significant. Remember that costs will not only include upgrading to the software, but upgrades to hardware such as RAM and processors to run the new software, and also training for staff. For these reasons, in August 1995 when Microsoft introduced Windows 95, many companies decided to continue using Windows 3.1 and DOS for their operating system since it fulfils the main functions required. Similarly when Microsoft introduced Windows XP and Office XP suites for word-processing and spreadsheets, many companies decided to keep using their existing software because they perceived that the benefits were marginal and would probably be exceeded by the costs.

Hardware for networks and communications

The majority of the computer systems purchased by large organisations are intended to form part of a network system. One of the most important benefits gained from introducing a network system is the ability to share hardware, software and data resources. In addition, a network allows users to work collaboratively and improves communication within the organisation.

This section introduces some of the hardware components needed in order to establish a network system. Chapter 5 describes networks and telecommunications in more detail.

Focus on selecting hardware suppliers   **F**

For the medium-to-large organisation the process of hardware selection is often rigorous in order to achieve the best combination of cost and quality. The process of selecting a supplier for hardware is often known as *vendor analysis*. Here we relate this to a structured means of comparing potential suppliers of hardware in order to select the most appropriate. Chapters 7 and 8 also consider the issue of selection from a different perspective: that of selecting the best source for an information system.

▶ Tenders

Although the purchase of small items can normally be carried out quickly and easily, larger purchases may involve the organisation in producing a tender document. A **tender document** is an invitation to suppliers, asking them to bid for the right to supply an organisation's hardware, software and other requirements. An organisation selects a supplier by examining each response to the *invitation to tender* in detail. When several suppliers compete for the same contract, this is known as *competitive tendering*.

Tender documents will also often ask for important information about potential suppliers. Obtaining this information can be critical in selecting the right supplier. Some of the items requested might include the size of the organisation (staffing, premises, turnover, etc.), number of years of experience, details of any major projects undertaken and details of any previous customers who may be willing to provide references.

In general, organisations will invite a number of potential suppliers to compete against one another for the tender. The number of suppliers chosen will depend on a number of factors, such as the overall size of the project. Choosing too many suppliers can be time consuming and wasteful of company resources; choosing too few does not allow the company to consider all 'good' suppliers.

> **Tender document**
>
> A document used as an invitation to suppliers, asking them to bid for the right to supply an organisation's hardware, software and other requirements.

▶ Evaluating proposals

There are three basic criteria for evaluating a supplier's proposals. These are based on technical, cost and support issues.

Technical issues

Technical issues refer to the extent to which the proposal satisfies the hardware and software requirements set out in the tender document or statement of requirements. They include:

- *Performance*. It is important to determine whether or not hardware will perform as specified. The performance of a new computer, for example, may be adequate when used as a standalone machine but may degrade when the machine is used as part of a network.
- *Compatibility*. In addition to checking that hardware items actually work properly when used together, it is also important to ensure that equipment is compatible with the company's existing systems, particularly any software packages already in use. Furthermore, compatibility with the organisation's plans for future development is also of importance, as is the capability to take advantage of changes in technology, for example the introduction of new processors.

Costs

Cost issues describe the overall cost of the project, including: installation, ongoing maintenance and factors involving methods of finance.

Consideration must be given to the different costs associated with the purchase of a new computer system. The **initial cost** of a computer system covers the purchase of hardware, installation and training. **Ongoing costs** include insurance and maintenance and are paid over the life of the system. Ongoing costs are known as the 'total cost of ownership' (TCO). This issue is of great relevance to the manager of end-use computing since it also covers other support costs. It is described in more detail in Chapter 15.

> **Initial cost**
>
> Purchase, installation and training.
>
> **Ongoing costs**
>
> Maintence costs of consumables, repairs and upgrades.

Since most hardware becomes out of date after approximately three years, it is important to consider the initial cost in comparison with the business value of the new system. Simply, the value of the system must be equal to or greater than the costs involved.

Support issues

These describe the reputation of the supplier in terms of their ability to provide adequate support, training, advice, repairs and maintenance.

Some of the criteria that can be used to evaluate a supplier include the following.

- *Training*. Suppliers should be able to offer a range of training courses that cater for mixed abilities and enable users to reach different levels of competence.
- *Maintenance*. Many organisations require suppliers to guarantee that important repairs are carried out within a fixed time limit. An organisation might require a supplier to guarantee a *response time* of a few hours for a vital system, but might be willing to allow longer times for less important equipment.
- *Implementation*. The extent of the service offered by a supplier may be of importance when purchasing large or complex systems. Instead of placing work with several suppliers, it is often advantageous to select a single supplier that is capable of performing most or all of the work required. The purchase of a network system, for example, will require a number of tasks to be performed, including the installation of network cabling, software configuration, data conversion, training and ongoing maintenance. The use of a single supplier can help to ensure that the project runs more smoothly and simplifies the division of responsibilities.
- *Backup facilities*. Many suppliers provide a variety of backup and recovery services for their clients. At a basic level, this can involve little more than arranging for copies of important data files to be made on a regular basis. However, many organisations, such as major banks and insurance companies, require more extensive facilities. A **backup** or **disaster recovery site**, for example, reproduces an organisation's computing facilities in order to provide a measure of protection against a major breakdown. In the event of a breakdown, the organisation's activities can be transferred to the backup site with a minimum of disruption.

▶ Evaluation methods

There are two main methods for evaluating supplier proposals.

Benchmarking

Benchmarks are the results of a range of tests carried out on hardware or software. As an example, the retrieval speed from large databases is often measured. By carrying out benchmark tests on a range of hardware items, comparisons can be made between specific items of hardware. In turn, this information can be used to select the most appropriate supplier.

Scoring systems

Here, the requirements of the organisation are used to devise a list of criteria for the selection of a given piece of hardware or a supplier. The *relative* importance of each factor is determined by a weighting factor. Each item or supplier is assigned a series of scores based on the criteria in the *weighted ranking table*. The total score for each item or supplier is calculated and used as the basis for final selection. Evaluation methods for information systems are described in Chapter 8.

Backup site
Reproduces an organisation's computing facilities in order to provide a measure of protection against a major breakdown.

Disaster recovery company
These maintain copies of import ant data on behalf of an organisation. They may also provide a service which can immediately supply replacement systems.

Benchmarks
This describes the process of testing the performance of computer equipment. Having carried out a series of benchmark tests, the results can be compared against similar items in order to make the best selection.

Scoring system
A means of selecting hardware, software and suppliers using a point-scoring system.

Summary

1 A computer system consists of a number of interrelated components that work together with the aim of converting data into information. In a computer-based information system, processing is carried out electronically, usually with little or no intervention from a human user.

2 Hardware is the physical components of a computer system. The hardware of a computer system can be said to consist of input devices, memory, central processing unit, output devices and storage devices.

3 Major categories of computers include mainframes, minicomputers and microcomputers.

4 The main hardware components of a computer system are:

- Input devices are used to enter data, information or instructions. Typical input devices include: mouse, keyboard, optical scanner, trackball, joystick, bar code reader, touch screen, graphics tablet, video capture card, sound card and digital camera.
- Output devices display the results of computer processing. Examples include visual display unit, printer, plotter, microfilm and sound card.
- Storage devices are used to store programs, data awaiting processing and the information resulting from computer processing. Examples of secondary storage devices which retain data even when a PC is switched off include floppy disk drives, hard disk drives, CD-ROM, DVD, magnetic tape and digital audio tape. Computer memory provides permanent or temporary storage of data. The contents of volatile memory are lost when the power to the device is switched off. On the other hand, non-volatile memory retains its contents until changed in some way. The two main categories of computer memory are random access memory (RAM) (primary memory) and read-only memory (ROM).
- The processor, which is used to execute software instructions and perform calculations.

5 A personal computer consists of a number of components, including: microprocessor (CPU), graphics card, motherboard and casing.

6 Tendering is a common method by which organisations select suppliers for hardware. Responses to tender documents are analysed in order to select an appropriate supplier. Other common methods for selecting hardware include benchmarking and scoring systems.

EXERCISES

Self-assessment exercises

1 Which type of printing technology is best suited to the production of the following documents?

(a) a business letter
(b) a program listing
(c) a chart or diagram, printed in colour
(d) an internal memorandum
(e) an engineering diagram.

2 Which input device is best suited to the following tasks?

(a) entering the details of bank cheques
(b) entering data from multiple-choice test papers
(c) entering data from labels or price tags
(d) entering a diagram, picture or photograph
(e) entering the text of a letter.

3 Describe some of the major characteristics of mainframes, minicomputers and personal computers.

4 How can network computers help to reduce the cost of ownership?

5 List at least three common pointing devices.

6 What is the meaning of each abbreviation or acronym listed below? Provide a brief explanation for each of the items listed.

(a) MICR   (f) OCR
(b) RAM   (g) COM
(c) BIOS   (h) PDA
(d) CD-ROM   (i) ROM
(e) CPU   (j) DVD

Discussion questions

1 Will network computers and thin clients make personal computers obsolete? Using relevant examples, make a case for one side of this argument.

2 You intend to purchase a personal computer to help with your studies. You have decided to create a weighted ranking table to help you choose a suitable system. What criteria should be used for selection and how should each item be weighted?

3 Despite still being functional, an obsolete computer system is of little value to a business organisation. Organisations should continually upgrade or replace systems in order to keep abreast of changes in technology. Make a case in favour of or against this argument.

Essay questions

1 IBM's AS/400 series of minicomputers is one of the most popular systems available and is used by an extremely wide range of organisations. Conduct any research necessary to complete the following tasks:

(a) Provide an overview of the costs associated with the purchase and installation of a minicomputer system, such as the AS/400.
(b) Provide an overview of the variety of applications for which the AS/400 system is used. Provide relevant examples where necessary.
(c) In your opinion, what features of the AS/400 range may have contributed to its popularity?

2 You have been asked to produce a guide to buying a personal computer by a fellow student on your course. The student has a budget for hardware of £1 500. Avoiding technical terms as far as possible, produce a guide that addresses the following:

(a) Produce a detailed specification for a personal computer system. You should describe the system in terms of the input, output and storage devices needed. Justify any choices made and explain any technical terms used.
(b) Select at least two computer systems that meet the requirements specified. Evaluate each of the systems in turn and make a recommendation to the student.
(c) Provide a realistic costing for the chosen system. Ensure that any ongoing costs are included.

3 Voice recognition systems have begun to gain popularity with both business and home users. However, such systems still suffer from a number of limitations that restrict their overall effectiveness. Conduct any research necessary to produce a report that addresses the following tasks:

(a) Provide an overview of voice recognition technology and describe how such systems operate.
(b) Provide a balanced view of the advantages, disadvantages, strengths and limitations of voice recognition systems.
(c) Explain some of the uses to which voice recognition systems can be applied. Pay particular attention to the business applications for this technology.

Examination questions

1 A small business organisation wishes to purchase a number of personal computers and has issued a tender document to a number of suppliers. Using relevant examples, provide an overview of the technical, support and cost issues that should be considered when evaluating supplier proposals.

2 A modern supermarket will make extensive use of technology to support all of its activities. Considering an organisation such as ASDA or Sainsbury's, describe the range of input, output, storage and processing devices that might be used within a typical branch. For each item identified, provide a brief description of its purpose and any benefits gained from its use.

3 Considering a typical IBM-compatible personal computer, you are required to:

(a) Identify the main components of a personal computer system. For each item identified, provide a brief description of its purpose.

(b) Using relevant examples, describe some of the methods that can be used to assess the performance and quality of key components.

(c) In addition to the initial cost of the personal computer itself, a number of other expenses are likely to be incurred. Using relevant examples, provide an overview of these additional costs.

References

Chaffey, D. (2002) *E-Business and E-Commerce Management*, Financial Times Prentice Hall, Harlow

Rogers, E. (1983) *Diffusion of Innovations*, 3rd edition, Free Press, New York

Strassman, P. (1997) *The Squandered Computer*, Information Economics Press, New Haven, CT

Further reading

Clifton, H. and Sutcliffe, A. (2000) *Business Information Systems*, 6th edition, Financial Times Prentice Hall, Harlow. Chapter 2 deals with a variety of topics including computer architecture, office automation and telecommunications. Chapter 3 deals with computer hardware with particular emphasis on input and output devices

Curtis, G. and Cobham, D. (2002) *Business Information Systems: Analysis, Design and Practice*, 4th edition, Pearson Education, Harlow. Chapter 3 deals with hardware and software

O'Brien, J. (2001) *Introduction to Information Systems*, 10th edition, McGrawHill, New York. This is an accessible and structured text. Chapter 2 deals with hardware

Sinclair, I. (1999) *Build and Upgrade Your Own PC*, Newnes, Oxford. A good way of learning about computer hardware is by looking at how to build, repair or upgrade personal computers. This book is written in a clear style and contains some very explanations of computer hardware

Web links

www.euro.dell.com/countries/uk/enu/gen/default.htm Dell is one of the world's leading manufacturers of personal computers.

www.timecomputers.com/indexmain.html Time Computers is one of the UK's largest manufacturers and suppliers of personal computers. The site includes a brief 'jargon buster' section that explains some common terms.

www.tiny.com/uk/index.html Like others, the Tiny Computers site provides an interactive service that allows you to customise a personal computer to your needs. Once satisfied with the specification, you can view information on prices and order online.

www.hp.com/ Hewlett Packard is one of the world's largest manufacturers of personal computers, laser printers and inkjet printers.

www.intel.com/ The Intel web site holds a great deal of information concerning microprocessors. Intel manufacture the Pentium II and Pentium III range of processors.

www.intel.com/intel/intelis/museum/exhibit/hist_micro/hof/hof_main.htm The Museum section is best for explaining the development of processors and explains pictures of each.

www.amd.com/ AMD manufactures the Athlon and Duron series of processors.

www.3dfx.com 3DFx are responsible for an extremely popular range of graphics cards. The site contains information on the cards themselves, as well as other useful snippets, such as which software products are supported.

www.stjohnsprep.org/htdocs/sjp_lnks/babel1.htm BABEL is a comprehensive list of acronyms related to information technology.

wombat.doc.ic.ac.uk/foldoc/index.html Online dictionary of computing.

www.le.ac.uk/cc/iss/glossary/ccgl.html Online glossary of terms from University of Leicester.

jac.sbs.ohio-state.edu/co140au98/topics/intro/personal_computers.htm Provides a good overview of how computers work.

www.askjeeves.co.uk A generic search tool that allows questions to be asked in plain language. Ideal for asking questions such as 'How do hard disks work?'.

education.indiana.edu/~w200/HyperTextbook/comp_wrk/topic.html Brief tutorial on how computers work. Organised in a similar way to this chapter. Some of the information is a little dated, but there are some good explanations and links to additional documents.

www.digitalcentury.com/encyclo/update/comp_hd.html A history of computing. Contains links to other useful articles, including biographies.

www.intel.com/technology/itj/ The Intel Technology Journal provides some useful articles dealing with microprocessors and other areas of technology.

www.howstuffworks.com/ A great deal of general material but contains relevant features on microprocessors, the Internet and more.

www.whatis.com This site is effectively a glossary giving succinct definitions of terms relating to hardware and software.

www.tomshardware.com Despite the name, this site is a detailed well-laid-out site giving detailed reviews on areas such as RAM and hard disks.

www.tutorialfind.com/tutorials Access to a wide range of tutorials on a wide range of subjects including hardware, operating systems, programming and web development.

www.wired.com Wired is one of the oldest and most respected titles to provide up-to-date news on technology and related subjects.

www.21stcentury.co.uk Online publication covering all areas of science and technology.

Chapter 4

Software

LEARNING OBJECTIVES

After reading this chapter, readers will be able to:

- explain the purpose of software applications in different categories;
- describe the features found in a variety of modern applications software packages;
- identify some of the advantages and disadvantages associated with a variety of common applications;
- describe some of the ways in which applications software supports the activities of a business organisation.

MANAGEMENT ISSUES

In Chapter 3, it was suggested that an understanding of computer technology can help managers to ensure that such technology is applied effectively. The same argument applies to the area of software. From a managerial perspective, this chapter addresses the following areas:

- All major organisations make use of common applications, such as word processing and database software. An understanding of the factors involved with selecting these applications is required by all managers.
- An understanding of the range of software applications available will help managers to see potential applications relevant to a given organisation or industry.
- An understanding of recent developments in the software industry, such as the emergence of the XML, will help managers to develop long-term plans for the organisation's use of technology.

Links to other chapters

Chapter 3	describes the computer hardware required to enable the efficient and productive use of computer software.
Chapter 6	describes functional information systems and applications-specific software, providing a view of how computer hardware and software can be used to support specific business activities.
Chapter 8	contains a review of techniques for evaluating BIS from different suppliers which can also be applied to software.
Chapter 10	considers data analysis for relational database management systems.
Chapter 11	describes design techniques for relational database management systems.
Chapter 16	describes how to manage Internet access and corporate intranets.

Introduction

This chapter builds upon the concepts introduced in Chapter 3 and provides an overview of the common software packages used in business. The material addresses two separate themes: a review of the features common to a range of modern software applications, and the way in which software can be used to support the business activities of an organisation.

The topics covered are intended to give readers an understanding of:

● categories of computer software,
● categories of applications software,
● the features found within a range of common software packages,
● the ways in which computer software can support the activities of a business organisation.

The chapter focuses on general-purpose applications software such as word processors and spreadsheets which is sometimes referred to as 'productivity software'. Software for specific business applications is described in detail in Chapter 6.

It is intended that this chapter provide readers with an *overview* of the available features in different categories of applications software, not be a user guide! Readers will, of course, obtain experience of the use of the software through practical experience. There are many excellent books available that can help readers to learn how to use business applications such as word processors and spreadsheets. The *Dummies* series of books, for example, are invaluable guides to areas such as word processing, spreadsheets, databases and the Internet.

Categories of software

Software can be defined as a series of detailed instructions that control the operation of a computer system. Software exists as *programs* which are developed by computer programmers. Software is less tangible than hardware – the instructions comprise program code that is translated into binary instructions (a series of 0 and 1 digits) for the processor hardware.

There are two major categories of software: systems software and applications software. Managers purchasing new BIS have to specify their requirements for both categories. Figure 4.1 illustrates the major categories of information systems software.

Software
....
A series of detailed instructions that control the operation of a computer system. Software exists as programs that are developed by computer programmers.

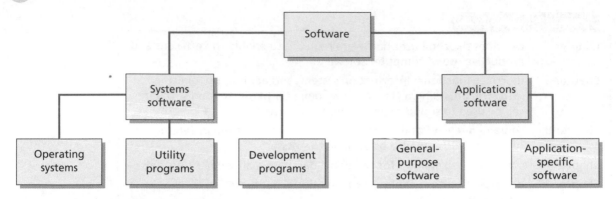

Figure 4.1 **Categories of computer software**

❱ Systems software

Systems software
This form of software manages and controls the operation of the computer system as it performs tasks on behalf of the user.

Operating system (OS)
Software that interacts with the hardware of the computer in order to manage and direct the computer's resources.

Systems software manages and controls the operation of the computer system as it performs tasks on behalf of the user. Systems software consists of three basic categories: operating systems, development programs and utility programs.

Operating systems

The **operating system** interacts with the hardware of the computer by monitoring and sending instructions to manage and direct the computer's resources. Figure 4.2 indicates the relationship between the operating system, the hardware and other types of software for a typical computer system. The components can be considered as different layers, with information being passed between the layers as the user interacts with the application. The operating system functions as an intermediary between the functions the user needs to perform, for example a spreadsheet calculation, and how these translate to and from the hardware in the form of responding to mouse clicks and displaying information on the screen. For most operating systems such as Microsoft DOS there is a text-based operating system and a GUI (graphical user interface) operating environment such as Windows 3.1. In Windows ME and Windows XP the text-based operating

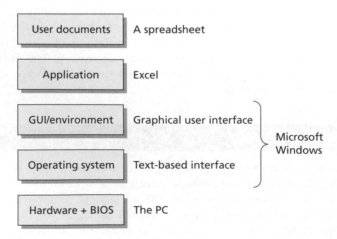

Figure 4.2 **Diagram showing the relationships between the different types of software and hardware**

system is normally not evident but remains present. Note that when a PC first starts the BIOS stored in ROM (Chapter 3) is used to start the operating system loading.

The basic functions of the operating system include: allocating and managing system resources, scheduling the use of resources and monitoring the activities of the computer system. Examples of these functions include the following:

- controlling access to storage devices, for example disk drives;
- coordinating and controlling peripheral devices, for example printers;
- allowing users to input data and issue instructions, for example by allowing data to be entered via keyboard;
- coordinating and controlling the operation of programs, for example by scheduling processor time;
- managing the computer's memory (including management of virtual memory as shown in Figure 3.10);
- performing file management and access control, for example by allowing certain users to create, view or delete files;
- dealing with errors, for example by displaying a message to the user if a fault is detected within a hardware component.

Operating systems can be controlled by either a text-based or a graphical interface. A text-based interface uses a **command line interpreter** (CLI) to accept instructions from the user. Instructions are entered as brief statements via the keyboard, for example COPY C:\AUTOEXEC.BAT A: would instruct the operating system to copy a file called AUTOEXEC.BAT from the computer's hard disk drive to a floppy disk. MS-DOS (Microsoft Disk Operating System) is an example of an operating system that uses a CLI.

A **graphical user interface** (GUI) allows users to enter instructions using a mouse. The mouse is used to issue instructions using menus and icons. The term **WIMP** (windows, icons, mouse and pull-down menus) is often used to describe this kind of environment. Examples of operating systems using a GUI are OS/2, Windows ME and Windows 2000.

Operating systems for PCs such as Windows ME are normally 'bundled' when a computer is purchased. This is also true for some applications software.

Operating environments describe programs intended to simplify the way in which users work with the operating system. Early versions of Windows, for example, provided a graphical user interface that removed the need for users to work with the more complex aspects of MS-DOS.

Network software

In general, the **network operating system** (NOS) used by an organisation will provide the majority of facilities required to support workgroup computing. For example, the NOS will allow a network manager to define a group of users as belonging to a particular workgroup. Some of the typical services provided by the NOS include:

- A centralised storage space can be created on the network system for the exclusive use of workgroup members.
- The security features of the NOS can be used to restrict access to documents and other data by those outside of the workgroup.
- The workgroup can be given network privileges that allow individual members access to resources and facilities that are not normally available to others. For example, many organisations with only limited Internet and e-mail facilities restrict access to key members of staff.

NOS are now often integrated with operating systems such as Microsoft Windows 2000 and UNIX, but Novell Netware is still commonly used on PC-based networks in conjunction with Microsoft Windows.

Network operating software is described in more detail Chapter 5.

Command line interpreter (CLI)
Passes instructions from a user to a computer program as instructions from a user in the form of brief statements entered via the keyboard.

Graphical user interface (GUI)
Provides a means for a user to control a computer program using a mouse to issue instructions using menus and icons.

WIMP
Windows, Icons, Mouse and Pull-down menus (WIMP) is often used to describe a GUI environment.

Operating environment
Programs intended to simplify the way in which users work with the operating system. Early versions of *Windows*, for example, provided a graphical user interface that removed the need for users to work with the more complex aspects of MS-DOS.

Network operating system (NOS)
This describes the software needed to operate and manage a network system.

Utility programs

Utility programs

Utility programs provide a range of tools that support the operation and management of a computer system.

Utility programs provide a range of tools that support the operation and management of a computer system. Programs that monitor system performance or provide security controls are examples of utility programs.

Development programs

Development programs

Allow users to develop their own software in order to carry out processing tasks.

Development programs allow users to develop their own software in order to carry out processing tasks using programming languages.

Programming languages can be described in terms of their historical position in the development of computer programming systems. Table 4.1 shows that increasingly languages have been usable by business users.

Applications software

A set of programs that enable users to perform specific information processing activities that may be general-purpose or application-specific.

▶ Applications software

Applications software can be defined as a set of programs that enable users to perform specific information-processing activities. Applications software can be divided into two broad categories: general-purpose and application-specific.

Table 4.1 The development of different programming languages

Generation	Characteristics and advantages	Main disadvantages
First generation	Early computer systems were programmed using machine language that consisted of strings of binary digits.	Programs were considered expensive to develop as they took extremely long periods of time to design, code and test.
Second generation	Assembly language represented an attempt to simplify the process of creating computer programs. Symbols and abbreviations were used to create sequences of instructions. An assembler or low-level language was used to translate a completed assembly language program into the machine code required by the computer.	Relatively slow for certain tasks, such as those involving large-scale data processing. Remained difficult to create large or complex programs using assembly language.
Third generation	Provided a more natural means of developing programs by enabling users to create programs made up of English-like statements. Such programming languages are still in use today and are known as 'high-level languages'. Languages such as COBOL, Fortran, C++ and Java allowed users to develop programs quickly and easily,	Resulting applications were sometimes slow and inefficient.
Fourth generation	A drive towards even greater ease of use resulted in the development of new programming systems designed to allow even non-technical users to develop their own applications. The focus of such tools as Microsoft Visual Basic was on ease of use and the rapid development of applications. Examples of common programming tools include report generators, query languages and application generators.	Some programming knowledge is still necessary.
Fifth generation	Developments in this area may result in programming systems that accept a spoken question from a user and then generate a computer program intended to produce the required information.	Artificial intelligence techniques are still not sufficiently developed to make this a practical reality.

General-purpose applications

General-purpose applications are programs that can be used to carry out a wide range of common tasks. A word processor, for example, is capable of producing a variety of documents that are suitable for many different purposes. This type of application is often referred to as **productivity software** since it helps improve the efficiency of an individual.

The next sections in this chapter will describe the use of some general-purpose applications software in more detail for each of these business tasks that are carried out in an office:

- *Document production and graphics software.* This involves the creation of various internal and external documents, including letters, reports, invoices, notes and minutes of meetings. Various types of software can be used to support these activities, including text editors, word processors and desktop publishing packages.
- *Spreadsheets – software for processing numerical information.* All organisations require the means to store, organise and analyse numerical data. The spreadsheet program represents the most common means of carrying out these tasks.
- *Databases – software for storage and retrieval of information.* All organisations require the means to store, organise and retrieve information. Electronic database packages represent the most common means of carrying out these tasks.
- *Multimedia software.* Multimedia involves the user interacting with a computer using media such as text, sound, animation and video. Its main business applications are computer-based training and customer service in retail applications.
- *Software for using the Internet.* This describes activities involving internal and external communications. Significant examples include electronic mail (e-mail) and the use of web browsers to find information on the World Wide Web.
- *Management applications of productivity software.* Software for personal information management and team working.

Productivity software
This describes a category of computer software that aims to support users in performing a variety of common tasks.

Application-specific software

Application-specific software comprises programs intended to serve a specific purpose or carry out a clearly defined information processing task. Software designed to carry out payroll processing or manage accounts is an example of an application-specific program.

Application-specific packages such as software for use in the accounting or marketing function or enterprise resource planning software used across the organisation are described in Chapter 6.

The interaction between hardware and software

Develop an explanation of the purpose of and interaction between hardware, systems software and applications software to someone who is unfamiliar with them. To help the explanation use an example based on the creation of a spreadsheet to calculate wages based on hours worked and refer to Figure 4.2. Start your description with when the PC is first switched on.

Activity 4.1

Document production software

One of the most common activities in a business organisation is the production of documents for internal or external use. Internal documents, such as an inter-office memo, are generally used to support communications within an organisation. External documents, such as a sales brochure, are generally used to support communications with customers, suppliers and other agencies.

The requirements for internal and external documents are often very different. The appearance of an internal document, for example, is seldom important since the document's main purpose is to convey information quickly and efficiently. However, since the appearance of an external document can have an impact on an organisation's image and reputation, a great deal of emphasis is often placed upon presentation.

Activity 4.2

Internal and external documents

Internal documents can include inter-office memos, reports and summaries, such as minutes of meetings. External documents can include invoices, sales brochures and correspondence. Using these examples, identify some of the other characteristics of internal and external documents. Are any of the characteristics identified common to both internal and external documents?

Word processor

Provides the ability to enter, edit, store and print text and layout different elements of a document.

Office automation systems

In business organisations, productivity software is often used to reduce the time needed to complete routine administrative tasks, such as producing documents or organising meetings. By attempting to automate many of the activities carried out within a typical office, organisations seek to improve efficiency, reduce costs and enhance internal communications. Computer-based information systems used in this way are generally referred to as office automation systems.

Groupware

Software which enables information and decision making to be shared by people collaborating within and between businesses.

Electronic meeting systems

This describes a category of Office Automation Systems that seeks to improve communications between individuals and groups. Examples of these systems include those that support teleconferencing, teleworking and group work.

A modern view of document production views technology used in three basic ways: word processing, desk top publishing and document management.

- **Word processing** is concerned with entering or editing text, with emphasis on the *content* of the document. Word processing allows the production of simple documents but gives more limited control over layout.
- *Desktop publishing* is concerned with the overall *appearance* of documents, placing a great deal of emphasis on features that provide control over the layout and presentation of a document.
- *Document management* involves managing documents such as company procedures, letters from customers or invoices from suppliers which are circulated to people throughout an organisation. It is an important business application and is described in more detail in Chapter 6.

The distinctions between different categories of document production software have become blurred. A modern word processor, for example, will often have much of the functionality of a desktop publishing program. Similarly, many desktop publishing packages now have sophisticated text editing features and no longer rely on users' preparing the different elements of a document in advance.

Case Study 4.1 indicates how document management can help to improve the efficiency of various administrative processes. Note that the paperless office is a concept that has been suggested for more than twenty years, but has failed to materialise in many organisations. Computer-based information systems used in this way are generally referred to as **office automation systems**. Applications of these systems and the software used to support them are described in Chapter 6

The functions of office automation systems are commonly provided by groupware. **Groupware** can be defined as a category of software used to support the activities of workgroups. In general, groupware applications fall within two basic categories: electronic communications systems, supporting internal and external communications, and **electronic meeting systems**.

❿ Word processing

A word processor provides the ability to enter, edit, store and print text. In addition, word processing packages allow users to alter the layout of documents and often provide a variety of formatting tools.

CASE STUDY 4.1

The paperless office

When two decades ago Xerox announced that by the year 2000, we would live in a paperless world, many sceptics doubted this statement. The sceptics were right. But are we doomed to deal with piles of paper forever? Will Garside reports.

The concept behind the paperless office is sound. Essentially paper forms would be replaced by electronic equivalents and stored in huge, fully indexed databases. Where paper was used, it would be photographically scanned and smart software would turn the output into editable documents. In the paperless office, instead of documents being pushed around internal mail systems or via postal services, email would rule with high quality printers reconstituting the original documents from their electronic form when necessary.

'To some degree, we are seeing the fruits of this ideal now, with the growth and acceptance of email', says Nick Turner, marketing director of Mandoforms – a specialist in electronic forms. Turner adds: 'Even now, many of the barriers that prevented a total switch over to electronic media are starting to be removed. With the electronic signature finally becoming law, many more documents can be electronically processed without the requirement of a secondary paper copy, a legacy of our archaic law.'

But even if the paperless office can actually become a reality, what are the benefits for businesses?

'One of our customers, Alliance and Leicester, is using our electronic form software to create smart forms', states Turner, adding 'If you consider a typical mortgage form will have over 100 different questions, the possibility of entering incorrect data is very high. As a legally binding document, even accidentally putting in the wrong information could be deemed as an attempted criminal act.'

Mandoforms' developer tool has built-in validation software, which checks if the items like dates and amounts are structurally correct. The software will also alter a form depending on the person filling it out. 'For example', explains Turner, 'if you are filling out a car insurance form and you specify that you're over 65 and the sole user of the vehicle as the first couple of questions, any questions related to additional insured drivers or aimed at under 25 drivers would be removed from the form.'

This type of smart form is on the increase. Alliance and Leicester alone has sent out over 40,000 forms this year and have reported high levels of user satisfaction. The main problem with forms is that someone normally has to read them to decide what action to take based on the content. However with technologies like XML, forms themselves can become smarter.

'By using XML, we can now make our Mandoforms almost intelligent. For example, if you filled in an expense request form, which claimed money from various departmental budgets, the form itself would be aware of which departmental finance systems it would need to transfer the relevant contents too. The form effectively delivers itself.'

Mandoforms is still constantly developing many of the advanced functions for its system, and plans to incorporate XML next year.

The prime mover behind the paperless philosophy has always been Xerox. Though its approach is less evangelical than previously, it is still working toward the need to make all business communication – whether electronic or on paper – as efficient as possible.

Andy Muskett, a senior solution manager at Xerox, says 'Maybe the totally paperless office is not a viable solution but we are helping several large corporate companies to use the Internet and document management technologies to help manage paper.'

However, Xerox has not admitted defeat just yet. Considering that Xerox's Palo Alto Research Centre (PARC) had a hand in developing the photographic scanner, fax machine, Ethernet networking and the graphical user interface (some years before the advent of Windows), its track record is impressive. Xerox currently spends in excess of a billion dollars per year on R&D. With a large portion of this spending going towards document management solutions it is in a good position to speak about the future.

One project currently under development is to create 'placeless documents', which are identified by content as opposed to location. These documents would fit nicely with prototype data interfaces more appropriate to their environment than computers (including electronic books and programmable 'data boards' instead of paper). The ultimate conclusion of this research could see documents that flow from person to organisation and groups and adapt themselves to the device on which they are displayed.

Xerox is also working on making document management highly interactive. The Presto system is a prototype document management system providing what Xerox researchers term as 'rich interaction' with documents. Essentially this allows documents to be sorted and ordered according to more user-specific document attributes, such as 'Word file', 'published paper', 'shared with Jim', 'about Presto' or 'currently in progress'. Recognising the multiple different roles that a single document might play, these attributes allow users to rapidly reorganise their document space for the task at hand.

The Presto system is still under development although some of the technology has been released for Xerox Workflo document management software, which allows the implementation of company-wide policies for managing the movement of documents between departments and individuals.

Another academic project known as 'haystack' (as in 'needle in a ...') has been occupying researchers at MIT for the last 2 years. It involves a method of indexing content, irrespective of location, and then learning from user searches to create a flexible indexing process. The fruits of haystack are starting to be seen in Internet search engines that can now index billions of web pages using more than just the meta tags.

Both these projects assume that paper documents are not going to be around in the distant future. But Robert Packington's advice for businesses that want to manage their growing paper mountain is simple: 'Don't try and change everything overnight, take one department and work out what you want to achieve.' As a director of Image Integrators Ltd, one of the UK's oldest document management companies, Packington has a long history working with both small business and large retail companies such as McVities and Bernard Matthews. 'Many of the elements needed to both manage paper and electronic documents are often already within a business. What we provide is the glue to create a solution', he adds.

Most electronic documents already contain space for additional information required for a document management system. Microsoft Word documents for example can have a complex set of properties to define author, revision number, attachments and file links that can be used within a document management system. Many scanners already ship with OCR software while the majority of enterprise databases such as Oracle 8I and Microsoft SQL can quite happily index and manage whole documents as opposed to just text and numbers.

Packington is naturally enthusiastic about a total document management solution. 'We have customers, such as Bernard Matthews, that have switched the majority of their paper invoices, POD, and delivery notes completely to an electronic equivalent but if you visit these companies you will still see quite a bit of paper on each person's desk. Essentially, they still print out paper, not out of necessity but for situations when it's more convenient then having to logon to the document management system – essentially the permanent version is always indexed on the system.'

The idea of digitising paper and switching to electronic forms is perceived as expensive, and for the small business trying to gauge the value of a new system it is also difficult. 'As an industry we need to be more accessible to smaller business and the Internet offers us a method of providing document management for a wider audience', claims Packington.

Image Integrator and several other document management companies are starting to offer ASP services to cater for both SME and larger enterprises. In the ASP model, the customer can rent all the scanning, software and communication equipment required to run a document management solution on a monthly basis. After document scanning or electronic form creation, documents are sent to the ASP's data centre via the Internet or leased line. Within the data centre, the company's documents are stored, indexed and served up on request. Each time a document is processed, a small payment of a few pence is deducted from the customer's account. This ASP model makes it very easy to discern the cost of the solution and provides a very scalable option for those testing the water of the paperless office.

But does Packington believe that even with the ASP option, the smart forms and the electronic signature, that the paperless office is ever achievable?

'Personally no', he admits. 'Even though we are a document management company, my desk always has a few pieces of paper on it – correspondence and reports mostly. Paper is a great medium and although we may see less of it than before, the completely paperless office is definitely a pipe dream.'

Source: Will Garside, 'Whatever happened to the paperless office?', courtesy of *Computer Weekly*, 20 December 2000

Questions

1 What benefits have the companies described in the case study gained by turning towards technology?

2 How can XML help to make electronic forms 'smarter'?

3 What is the 'paperless office'? Can applications such as document management software genuinely achieve such a goal?

Overview

Early word processors produced effects, such as bold or italics, by inserting special codes into the text. This made it difficult to see how the finished document would appear until it was printed. One of the most important features of a modern word processor is the provision of a WYSIWYG display (pronounced 'whizzywig'), where What You See Is What You Get.

Features of a word processor

The sheer range of features provided by a typical word processing program is a reflection upon the diverse requirements of modern business organisations. Many features are underutilised because many packages are so 'feature-rich' it is difficult to know which features are available. This section is intended to give a brief overview of features available in order that these terms be familiar when encountered in business.

1 *Editing*. All word processing programs allow users to enter, edit, copy, move and delete text. The process of entering or correcting text is known as **editing**.

2 *Text alignment*. As users type text and move towards the end of a line, the program automatically moves to the beginning of a new line. The spacing between words and characters is also adjusted so that the appearance of the text is improved. This is known as **word wrap**.

A word processor allows the user to control text alignment, that is, the layout of the margins on the page. Text alignment is often called **justification**. Text that is flush with the left margin but has a ragged right margin is known as *left-justified* (sometimes also known as 'unjustified'). Text that is flush with the right margin but has a ragged left margin is known as *right-justified*. Text that is flush with both margins is *fully justified* (it is said to have *full justification*).

Editing
....
The process of entering or correcting text is known as editing.

Word wrap
....
In a word processor, as users type text and move towards the end of a line, the program automatically moves to the beginning of a new line.

Justification
....
In a word processor, the alignment of text with the left and right margins can be controlled by specifying the justification.

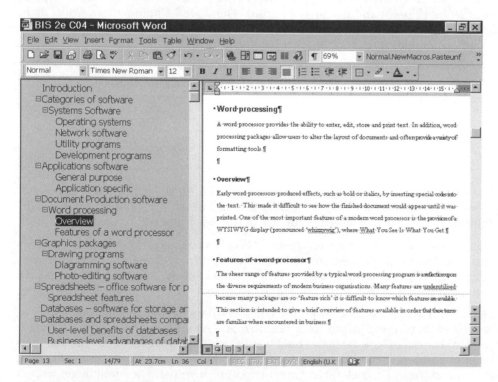

Figure 4.3 Microsoft's Word for Windows showing the use of a document map

> This paragraph is **left-justified**. Note that the text is flush with the *left* margin but has a ragged *right* margin. In contrast, the text in this book is *fully justified*.

> This paragraph is **right-justified**. Note that the text is flush with the *right* margin but has a ragged *left* margin. In contrast, the text in this book is *fully justified*.

3 *Block operations*. All word processing packages allow users to manipulate blocks of text in a number of ways. Once a block of text has been marked, it can be moved, deleted, copied or formatted. One powerful feature of a word processor is the ability to *cut and paste* blocks of text. A marked block can be removed from a document (cut) but held in the computer's memory. One or more copies can then be pasted into a new position in the same document (paste). This can be used to move whole sections of a document from one place to another or to make several copies of a block of text.

4 *Search and replace*. Programs such as Word for Windows allow the user to search an entire document for a specific word or phrase. Once the text has been located, it can be deleted or replaced with something else. This is called a search and replace operation. Text can be replaced *globally*, where every occurrence of the specified text is replaced automatically, or *with confirmation*, where the user is asked whether or not to replace each piece of text as it is found.

Font
....
The typeface used in a document is referred to as the font. The size of the characters used is referred to as the point size.

5 *Text formatting and style*. Most word processing packages allow users to specify the style, font and point size of text. *Style* refers to text effects such as bold, italics and underlined. The typeface used in a document is referred to as the **font**. The size of the characters used is referred to as the *point size*. For example, text in the body of a document may be 10 point and headings 14 point. There are 72 points to a vertical inch. Heading styles can be standardised for each document within a company to achieve standard communications.

> This text uses the *Arial* font, which is similar to the Helvetica styles used for newspaper headlines.

> ```
> This text uses the Courier font found on typewriters.
> ```

The word processor allows users to specify the layout of the pages in the document. *Page layout* is normally performed by setting the sizes of the top, bottom, left and right margins of the page and by selecting the size of the paper that will be used.

6 *Headers and footers*. A header is a piece of text that will appear at the top of every page of the document. Headers are typically used to print a chapter heading or title at the top of each page. A footer appears at the bottom of each page. Footers are typically used to print page numbers at the bottom of every page.

7 *Mailmerge*. Packages such as Word for Windows allow sets of personalised letters to be produced by merging information taken from a separate data file with a standard document. For example, a database could be used to hold the names and addresses of a number of business clients. A standard letter could be produced with blanks where the name and address of the client are meant to appear. When the mailmerge process begins, each name and address would be inserted in the document and printed. Mailmerge is not restricted to names and addresses; any kind of data can be merged into a standard document. This allows mailmerge to be used for applications ranging from the production of invoices to personalised newsletters.

7 *Import and export*. Many word processors allow documents to be opened or saved in a number of formats. The process of saving a file in a format compatible with another package is known as **exporting**. The process of loading a file created with another package is known as **importing**.

Most modern word processing packages allow users to incorporate graphics and tables of figures into their documents. As an example, Word for Windows can import pictures from a range of sources. Some of the most common picture file formats are GIF, PNG, WMF, JPG, TIFF, and PCX.

8 *Language tools*. Almost every major package now supports *spellchecking*, *grammar checking* and a *thesaurus* function. Many recent word processing programs offer an *autocorrect* feature that attempts to correct spellings as the user types. Common misspellings such as entering 'teh' instead of 'the' are detected and changed automatically by the program.

9 *Drawing tools*. Many packages provide a variety of drawing tools, allowing users to add lines, shapes or graphic files to their documents.

10 *Tables*. Packages allow users to produce tables containing a specified number of rows and columns. Tables created in this way often provide some of the functionality of a spreadsheet program, although this functionality is often limited.

11 *Programming applications*. A **macro** is a sequence of instructions that can be used to automate complex or repetitive tasks. Macros can be used to emulate a sequence of keys pressed on the keyboard or can be programmed so that they can carry out more complicated processes. For example, a company name and address could be prepared as a macro. Modern packages often feature entire programming languages that can be used to handle extremely complex tasks. Word for Windows, for example, contains Visual Basic for Applications – a complete implementation of the Visual Basic programming language which is available in all the Microsoft Office programs described in this chapter.

Export
The process of saving a file in a format compatible with another software package is known as exporting.

Import
The process of loading a file created with another package is known as importing.

Macro
A sequence of instructions that can be used to automate complex or repetitive tasks.

Activity 4.3

Word processing

We have described some of the key features of a word processor. How should the owner–manager of a small business with 10 staff using word-processor software ensure they work efficiently to produce good-quality standard internal and external documents?

Graphics packages

Traditionally, graphics packages have been divided into three basic categories: drawing (or paint) packages, design packages and presentation software. However, it has become common to include two other categories of graphics software: diagramming packages and photo-editing programs.

▶ Drawing programs

Paint programs serve the same purpose as a sketchpad or easel and enable users to produce drawings using a variety of different techniques.

A combination of tools allows users to create drawings made up of freehand lines and regular shapes. Amongst the tools available are:

Paint programs
Serve the same purpose as a sketch pad or easel and enable users to produce drawings using a variety of different techniques.

- A palette of drawing tools can be used to mimic the effects of drawing with different materials including pens, spray cans, brushes and charcoal.
- Selection tools can be used to copy, erase or resize sections of a drawing.
- Painting tools let users apply shading and colours to areas or shapes.
- Text tools allow users to add text to a drawing. Users can specify the typeface, size, colour and style of the text.
- Special tools provide a range of sophisticated features. A colour replacement tool, for example, can be used to change one colour for another within a specific section of the image.

One of the distinctions that can be made between drawing packages involves the type of image that can be produced. In general, paint packages are said to produce bitmap images whilst drawing packages are said to create vector images.

A **bit map** image is made of up of small dots (*pixels*) arranged in a grid. The finer the grid, the higher the **resolution** of the image. A newspaper photograph, for example, might offer a resolution of 100 dpi, whilst a photograph reproduced in a textbook might have a resolution of 1200 dpi. Although bitmap images are suited for certain types of images, such as photographs, they suffer from two main disadvantages. First, the overall quality of the image cannot be maintained if it is resized. Secondly, bitmap images can require a great deal of storage space, depending on the number of colours contained in the image and its resolution.

Vector graphics are made up of shapes, rather than individual dots. Mathematical formulae determine the size, position and colour of the shapes that make up a given image. Since far less information needs to be recorded about the contents of a vector image, they require comparatively little storage space. In addition, vector images can be resized with great precision and without loss of quality. Since it can be difficult to produce highly detailed images, vector graphics are often used for diagrams and relatively simple drawings.

▶ Diagramming software

The need to produce a wide variety of business-related charts and diagrams has resulted in the emergence of numerous diagramming packages. Aimed at business users, the majority of these packages assume little technical knowledge and rely on menus, icons and palettes of tools in order to construct diagrams.

In order to produce a chart or diagram, users select shapes and symbols from a library of pre-prepared materials. The libraries used by these programs are often called *stencils* or 'stamps', reflecting the idea that users are not expected to draw each required shape manually. Having arranged a number of shapes in order, users can then add text, lines and other elements to complete the diagram.

Diagramming programs such as Visio tend to offer a relatively limited number of stencils from which users can select, although additional stencils can be obtained from various sources. All packages cater for a range of common business diagrams. A typical package will provide stencils that enable users to produce flow charts, office layouts, organisational charts, network diagrams, project timelines and block diagrams.

▶ Photo-editing software

The growth in the use of optical scanners and video capture devices has resulted in a need for tools that can be used to edit and manipulate photographic images. **Photo-editing packages** enable users to capture, view and edit scanned images.

Bit map image

Small dots (pixels) arranged in a grid to form an image. The finer the grid, the higher the resolution of the image.

Resolution

The resolution of the monitor describes the fineness of the image that can be displayed. Resolution is often expressed in terms of pixels (picture elements) – the individual dots that make up an image on the screen.

Vector image

Image made up of lines and shapes, rather than individual dots. Mathematical formulae determine the size, position and colour of the shapes that make up a given image.

Photo-editing packages

Photo-editing packages enable users to capture, view and edit scanned images.

Although the majority of photo-editing programs provide many of the features found in paint packages, most provide more sophisticated tools intended especially for use with scanned images. Two typical examples are:

- Capture features enable a user to acquire images directly from an optical scanner or digital camera attached to the computer system, removing the need for the user to control two separate programs.
- **Filters** can be used to apply a range of special effects to an image. As an example, filters can be used sharpen a blurred image or alter brightness and contrast.

Filter

In a spreadsheet or database, a filter can be used to remove data from the screen temporarily. Filters do not alter or delete data but simply hide any unwanted items.

Spreadsheets – office software for processing numerical information

Spreadsheet packages are used for a variety of different purposes. Some examples include the following:

- *Financial applications*. Common applications include the production of cashflow forecasts, accounting statements, invoices, purchase orders, sales orders, quotations, managing expenses and project management.
- *Modelling and simulation*. In general, **modelling** involves creating a numerical representation of an *existing* situation or set of circumstances, whilst *simulation* involves *predicting* new situations or circumstances. In both cases, a *model* is produced that provides a numerical representation of the situation or circumstances being studied. A cashflow forecast, for example, is a numerical model that attempts to predict the financial state of a business over a given period of time. Once a model has been constructed, it can be manipulated so that users can see how changes to parts of the model influence the whole. As an example, a user might change the level of sales in a cashflow forecast to see how overall profit and loss would be affected. This ability to manipulate models is often referred to as **what if? analysis** and is considered one of the spreadsheet's most powerful features.
- *Statistical analysis*. All spreadsheet programs provide a wide range of tools that can be used to analyse numerical information in a number of ways. Two simple examples can be used to illustrate the range of facilities available.
  - (a) **Goal seeking** describes a way of automatically changing the values in a formula until a desired result is achieved. As an example, a user might enter a formula that calculates the profit made on sales of various items. Goal seeking could then be used to calculate the level of sales needed to produce a specified level of profit.
  - (b) Many programs offer a *descriptive statistics* feature which can be used to generate various summaries relating to a block of data. The spreadsheet performs a simple analysis and creates a set of descriptive statistics automatically. The results are presented in table format and include values such as maximum, minimum, mean, average, standard deviation, sum, count and variance.

Spreadsheet

A program designed to store and manipulate values, numbers and text in an efficient and useful way.

Modelling

Modelling involves creating a numerical representation of an *existing* situation or set of circumstances, whilst simulation involves *predicting* new situations or circumstances.

What if? analysis

This describes the ability see the predicted effect of a change made to a numerical model.

Goal seeking

In a spreadsheet, goal seeking describes a way of automatically changing the values in a formula until a desired result is achieved.

> We use the term *formulas* to distinguish those used by spreadsheets from traditional mathematical formulae.

All modern spreadsheet programs originate from the original Visicalc program launched in 1979 by Bricklin, Frankston and Fylstra. The program was originally created as a means of carrying out repetitive calculations for the Harvard Business School. Although created for the Apple II computer system, the program rapidly gained in popularity and became one of the best-selling software products of all time.

The interest shown in the Visicalc package prompted the Lotus Development Corporation to develop a version of the program for IBM-compatible computer systems. The release of Lotus 1-2-3 in 1982 is often credited as being responsible for the widespread acceptance of personal computers in business.

> Both Visicalc and Lotus 1-2-3 are often held as being the first *killer apps*. This term describes a program that offers a service so valuable that the purchase of a computer system is warranted in order to be able to use the software. More recently, the same term has begun to be used to describe an application that is superior to all similar products.

▶ Spreadsheet features

Spreadsheet
A program designed to store and manipulate values, numbers and text in an efficient and useful way.

Worksheet
An individual area or sheet for entering data in a spreadsheet program.

We can describe a **spreadsheet** as a program designed to store and manipulate values, numbers and text in an efficient and useful way. As with word processors, we give a brief refresher of the terms used to describe spreadsheets:

1 *Worksheets and cells*. The work area in a spreadsheet program is called the **worksheet**. A worksheet is a grid made up of *cells*. Each cell is uniquely identifiable by its horizontal (row) and vertical (column) coordinates. A cell can contain text, numbers or a formula that relates to information held in another cell. For example, a cell could contain any of these pieces of data:

```
127
'Cash Flow Forecast'
+A12 (a reference to another cell)
```

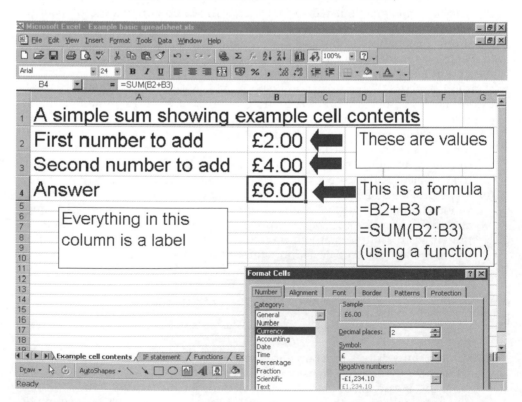

Figure 4.4 **Organisation of a spreadsheet worksheet showing example formula**

Figure 4.4 shows how a worksheet is organised. Cell coordinates are traditionally given in the form of column–row, for example the very first cell in a worksheet is A1, in column A and row 1.

One of the most important features of a spreadsheet is its ability to update the entire worksheet each time a change is made. For example, imagine that the cell at B4 contains information based on the contents of the cells at B2 and B3. Changing the contents of B2 and B3 causes the computer to update the worksheet, placing a new value in B4 automatically.

2 *Formulas*. Another important feature of the spreadsheet is that users can manipulate the contents of cells using formulas. A **formula** is a calculation that is entered by the user and performed automatically by the spreadsheet program. They are denoted to the spreadsheet by starting with =, + or @. Formulas can be used to manipulate the values held in cells by referring to their coordinates. An example is given in Figure 4.4; if B2 holds 2 and B3 holds 4, then placing the formula =B2+B3 in B4 can be interpreted as 'take whatever is in B2 (in this case, 2), add it to the contents of B3 (in this case, 4) and place the result in B4' – giving a result of 6 in B4.

Formula

In a spreadsheet, a formula is a calculation that is entered by the user and performed automatically by the spreadsheet program.

3 *Functions*. A spreadsheet **function** is a built-in command that carries out a calculation or action automatically. As an example, in Microsoft Excel, the AVERAGE function returns the average of a series of numbers.

All spreadsheet programs contain a number of built-in functions that can be used to simplify the construction of a worksheet. Functions are normally divided into categories so that users can locate them easily. Some typical categories include:

Function

In a spreadsheet, a function is a built-in command that carries out a calculation or action automatically.

	A	B	C	D	E	F	G	H
C15			DERBY MACHINERY LTD - CASH FLOW FOR YEAR (£)					
1								
2	DATA INPUT TABLE							
3								
4		Jan	Feb	Mar	Apr	May	Jun	Jul
5	Sales Profile by Month	5	10	15	20	25	25	25
6								
7		£						
8	Selling Price per Unit	500						
9	Materials per Unit	90						
10	Labour per Unit	80						
11	Overheads per Unit	60						
12	Salaries per Month	5000						
13	Opening Cash	30000						
14								
15			DERBY MACHI					
16		Jan	Feb	Mar	Apr	May	Jun	Jul
17								
18	Income (Sales)	=B5*B8	=C5*B8	=D5*B8	=E5*B8	=F5*B8	=G5*B8	=H5*B8
19								
20	Expenditure:							
21	Materials		=B5*$B9	=C5*$B9	=D5*$B9	=E5*$B9	=F5*$B9	=G5*$B9
22	Labour	=B5*$B10	=C5*$B10	=D5*$B10	=E5*$B10	=F5*$B10	=G5*$B10	=H5*$B10
23	Overheads	=B5*$B11	=C5*$B11	=D5*$B11	=E5*$B11	=F5*$B11	=G5*$B11	=H5*$B1
24	Salaries	=$B12	=$B12	=$B12	=$B12	=$B12	=$B12	=$B12
25	Total Expenditure	=SUM(B21:B24)	=SUM(C21:C24)	=SUM(D21:D24)	=SUM(E21:E24)	=SUM(F21:F24)	=SUM(G21:G24)	=SUM(H21

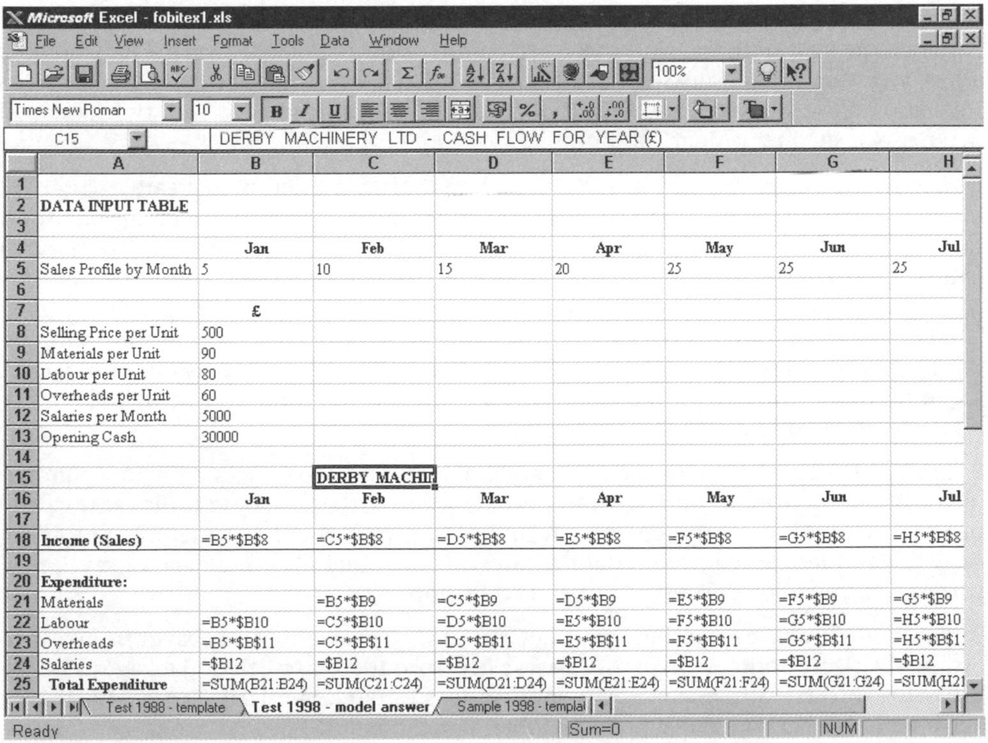

Figure 4.5 Microsoft's Excel for Windows 95 showing a worksheet being used for cashflow analysis

- *Date and time*. These allow users to perform calculations dealing with dates, for example, a user might wish to calculate the number of working days between two dates.
- *Database*. Typical functions include the ability to sort rows or columns into a specified order. Although spreadsheet programs are clearly unable to offer the functionality of a specialised database program, all programs offer the basic functions of queries, filters and sorting.
- *Financial*. These provide a variety of financial and accounting functions, such as the ability to calculate loan repayments based on factors such as the interest rate and the amount borrowed.
- *Logical*. These allow users to create formulas that perform calculations according to whether or not specific conditions have been met. As an example, a worksheet used to create invoices might generate a different total according to whether or not the customer is required to pay VAT.
- *Lookup and reference*. These provide a range of functions that can be used to create more sophisticated worksheets. As an example, a user might wish to create a formula that looks up a value from a table.
- *Mathematics*. These include mathematical functions, such as factorials, exponential numbers, square roots, and trigonometrical functions
- *Statistical*. These allow users to produce statistical information, such as frequency distributions.

4 *Automatic features*. Many programs allow users to enter part of a formula, completing the rest of it automatically. The *autosum* feature, for example, is found in a number of different programs and automates the generation of totals. In order to use this feature, the user selects the cells to be added and then chooses the autosum feature. The program then generates the formula needed to add the numbers together automatically.

5 *Formatting*. All spreadsheet programs provide a variety of tools that can be used to enhance the appearance of worksheets. A built-in range of *numeric formats*, for example, allow users to display values as currency or to a fixed number of decimal places. Users may also adjust the width and height of rows and columns, use different typefaces and make use of shading, colour and lines.

6 *Charts*. An integral feature of spreadsheet programs is the ability to create a variety of different charts based upon the data held in the worksheet. Modern programs provide a range of different chart types, including bar charts, pie charts, line graphs and area charts. Most packages also offer a range of specialist chart types in order to cater for users with particular requirements. A good example of a such a chart type is the *combination chart* which can be used to show two or more sets of data in a single diagram.

The charts created by spreadsheet programs are often described as *live* or *dynamic*, meaning that if the data in the worksheet are altered, the chart will be updated automatically in order to reflect the changes made.

7 *Data analysis tools*. The majority of modern spreadsheet packages contain a number of tools designed to automate common data analysis tasks. These tools remove the need for users to memorise complex formulae and perform all calculations automatically. Examples of common data analysis tools include: analysis of variance, correlation, covariance, *T*-test, *Z*-test and regression.

8 *Import and export*. Spreadsheet programs are able to deal with data drawn from a variety of different sources. In many cases, files produced by other packages can be imported directly into a worksheet with no loss of data. Similarly, spreadsheets also allow data to be exported in a variety of different formats.

Occasionally, it may be necessary to convert data into a form that can be used by the spreadsheet program. A common file format used to transfer data between spreadsheet packages and other programs is known as **comma-separated (or -delimited) values** (CSV). A CSV file is a simple text file made up of items enclosed within quotation marks and separated by commas. The use of commas and quotation marks enables the spreadsheet program to identify individual items.

9 *Workbooks.* Early spreadsheet programs allowed users to work with only a single worksheet at a time. In order to make use of information stored on a different worksheet, special commands were needed to access the disk file containing the data required. This often resulted in applications that were unnecessarily complex, slow to operate and prone to errors.

Modern packages enable a user to organise groups of worksheets within a single **workbook**. In addition, several workbooks can be opened at the same time. This facility allows users to carry out large or complex tasks more easily and quickly. Two examples may help to make this clearer:

- An organisation wishes to analyse monthly sales data. The data for each month can be stored on separate worksheets within a single workbook. Although the data held on each worksheet can be analysed separately, users can also employ special formulas and functions to examine the workbook as a whole. The total sales for the year, for example, could be obtained by using a formula that adds together the monthly totals taken from each worksheet in the workbook.
- An organisation uses two workbooks to store data on sales and expenses respectively. The data from both workbooks can be combined within a third workbook to produce information related to profitability. Only the third workbook needs to be open in order to carry out any calculations required, but all three workbooks can be open simultaneously if required.

An important feature of modern spreadsheet packages is the ability to create *views* on the data held in a worksheet or workbook. The use of views enables users to focus on specific sections of the worksheet by displaying data in a predetermined way. As an example, a manager might wish to view only the summary information held in a worksheet. In order to cater for this, a view could be created that displays only the required information, hiding all other data from sight.

As mentioned earlier, once a worksheet has been constructed it can be used to perform what if? analysis by changing some of the values stored. The task of keeping track of the changes made to the worksheet can be simplified by making use of *scenarios*. The user begins by constructing the basic model to be used for the analysis and stores it under a given name. The worksheet can then be altered repeatedly until the user obtains results they consider important. Each time a new set of results is obtained, the user can save these by storing the worksheet as a new scenario. They can then continue to alter the worksheet or can restore the original data to begin a new analysis. After the analysis has been completed, the user can access any of the scenarios stored and compare these to the original worksheet.

240 Comma-separated values (CSV)

A simple text file made up of items enclosed within quotation marks and separated by commas in order to assist conversion between programs.

Workbook

In a spreadsheet program, this describes a collection of worksheets.

The sheer size of the workspace available to a spreadsheet user means that functions providing quick and efficient navigation are essential.

Although the capacity of a spreadsheet program will be limited by available memory and storage space, a typical workbook can contain 256 worksheets and a typical worksheet can contain 16 384 rows by 256 columns. This means that a worksheet can contain up to 4 194 304 cells and that a workbook can contain up to 1 073 741 824 cells.

Case Study 4.2 looks at how spreadsheets are used for financial planning. The material highlights some of the disadvantages associated with spreadsheets and suggests some alternative approaches.

CASE STUDY 4.2

Spreadsheets for planning and accounting

By clinging to outdated spreadsheet technology managers are causing major problems, write Max Penny.

The big five accountancy firms have warned that the inappropriate use of spreadsheets can result in catastrophic consequences, yet every day hundreds of thousands of executives bypass their multimillion pound enterprise resource planning (ERP) systems and spend their time tinkering with the same data in a spreadsheet.

Research by the 'big five' has found that computational errors, mainly buried in spreadsheets, alone result in costs to business amounting to hundreds of millions of pounds.

Finding a technology that gives managers all the benefits of spreadsheets without the dangers is now becoming mission-critical. A number of of large organisations have established think-tanks to address the dilemma and some are quietly piloting new-technology solutions.

Neil Hogg, a partner with Arthur Andersen's Business Modelling Group, gets a good overview of what companies are using for financial modelling and how well these 'solutions' do the job.

'The majority use desktop spreadsheets even though they adopt enterprise-scale solutions for most other key systems', he explains. 'Nevertheless, when it comes to "designing the future" managers like to build models and play with them on their desk, it is a personal thing. And even organisations that do actively use enterprise solutions such as ERP find the plan that quantifies future business strategy is either derived from, or presented in, a spreadsheet.'

Hogg says that, to many users, none of the 'abbreviations' – ERP, MIS, CRM, etc. – feel right. It is not that they can't use them, it is just that they prefer spreadsheets.

'The good old spreadsheet may solve the immediate problem but it highlights a variety of strategic planning issues', Hogg warns. 'Some of the biggest problems come from the "simple" model and the "ambitious" model, where literally hundreds of millions, and sometimes billions of pounds, are at stake.'

Barry Pettifor, a director at PriceWaterhouseCoopers (PWC) takes a similar view. 'PWC sees a huge variety of financial plans from customers,' he says. 'The models we see are getting more complex and the strategic issues raised by spreadsheeting remain. If anything, things are getting worse. On the one hand, we can see simple errors leading to potentially really bad decisions and, on the other, we see companies wasting huge amounts of money reinventing wheels.'

Pettifor believes that many of the spreadsheeters are way behind the times. 'Everything we see people build is a hand-crafted piece of personal mathematical art – doing it this way is inefficient and expensive. We are always looking at new technologies that can address this problem. Things have to change in terms of more robust tools and management processes', he says.

The pain experienced in using spreadsheets has triggered the development of database-centric solutions. The established suppliers in this field, such as Hyperion and Comshare, have made good progress into the Fortune 500 companies but are barely noticeable in the greater scheme of things. A decade after they first appeared, they still count their customer base in tens of thousands. By contrast, the big five accountancy firms estimate there are more than 30 million business-planning spreadsheeters.

With such criticisms and the lack of desktop penetration there are opportunities for new players. Indeed, the challengers are already on the horizon.

A common thread between the two first challengers to appear is that they are calling their new breed of technology an 'object planner'. Object planners are end-user technologies for building financial plans and models from objects or components. The objects hold both the end-user calculations and the end-user data. In object-planning terms, a plan is merely a loosely associated set of objects. Behind the scenes, the object planner may be connected to a database.

An object plan might, for instance, comprise sales, marketing, departmental and staff objects. The dimensions of data held 'inside' the objects are unrestricted, as is the relative timing of events modelled by the objects and the structure that associates the objects.

Defining and creating objects and new formulas is a low-skill end-user task, and the objects will be compatible with a company's existing chart of accounts and database. Plans can be instantly consolidated regardless of content.

Both Hyperion and Comshare express the view that object-based planning systems using database back-ends are interesting and feasible but were unwilling to comment on any plans they may have in this area.

The UK's first object-based planning technology has been built by a company called Brixx. Gary Simon, senior partner at Deloitte and Touche, has seen it and was impressed. 'Overall, Brixx is an amazing tool for the corporate planner. The challenge for Brixx is to enable enterprise deployment of the system over the Web so that more users can enjoy the benefits of this powerful application', he says.

Hogg has looked at object-oriented (OO) planning as an alternative to spreadsheets. 'We started looking at OO business planning two years ago', he says. 'Since then, we have been busy building and experimenting with a library of object-based reusable components. By comparison with spreadsheets, these technologies are new – even the most mature is only three years old – but we can demonstrate that the approach addresses many of the key strategic issues.

'Using the example of a large organisation with 50 business planners using a wild assortment of spreadsheets', Hogg says, 'in spreadsheeting terms, rolling out an upgrade to specific cells across diverse spreadsheet applications simply will not work. However', he adds, 'if everyone's business models conform to an underlying object standard, the task becomes trivial.

'We think that businesses should take a fresh look at all their spreadsheet applications and question whether the job is being done right or whether the right job is being done', Hogg says.

The first factor to identify is whether there is any threat posed. Hogg says that if a model is personal, used only by the author, then it should not be seen as a threat. If it is shared, by which he means viewed or edited by users other than the author, the situation should be reviewed.

The job then becomes one of deciding on some simple metrics and costings for assessing the economic impact of your findings. This is purposefully a gross simplification but it tells you whether you should take a closer look at how your company builds its financial models and plans.

Some spreadsheets will demand action, others will have a negligible effect and can be discounted – but none should be ignored.

Source: Max Penny, 'Accountancy managers insist on using outdated spreadsheets', courtesy of *Computer Weekly*, 23 November 2000

Questions

1 The case study refers to spreadsheet 'models' when describing how managers work with spreadsheets. Is this an appropriate term, or should the word 'simulation' be used instead?

2 The case study suggests that managers are placing too much reliance on spreadsheet models. What criticisms of spreadsheet models are given by the case study?

3 The case study suggests that there has been a great deal of resistance to the introduction of database-centric planning systems. Why do you think organisations have been slow to adopt such systems?

Databases – software for storage and retrieval of information

Prior to the introduction of electronic database systems, almost all of the information an organisation needed to store was organised using manual filing systems. Typical methods included filing cabinets and card index records. Although manual filing systems are still used widely today, electronic databases are also commonplace and are considered to provide a number of important benefits to business organisations. Since databases are so important in storing data for information systems the analysis and design need to create databases is covered extensively in Chapters 10 and 11.

We can understand something more of electronic databases by first considering the disadvantages of manual filing systems. Some of the most common disadvantages of manual filing systems include:

● The way in which information is organised largely determines the uses to which it can be put. For example, if a list of customers is stored in alphabetical order by name, it becomes difficult to view customers by location.
● It is often difficult to retrieve specific items of information quickly.
● It might not be possible to add, amend or delete the information held in a manual record without creating a new copy of the record.

● It is sometimes difficult to classify information so that it can be stored in the correct location. This can make it difficult to locate specific items at a later date.

● If the information is used regularly by a number of different individuals or departments, multiple copies of manual files may need to be maintained. This is a major information management problem since a number of difficulties arise from the duplication of data. Some examples include:

   (a) Extra expense is incurred in terms of the additional storage space and labour power required to maintain files.

   (b) Changes made to one set of files may not be reflected in all copies. This can mean that some files contain outdated information, whilst others may contain new or additional details.

   (c) If a standardised filing system is used, this may not suit the needs of all users. On the other hand, the use of different filing systems creates problems in maintaining files and locating information.

The use of an electronic databases can remove all of the difficulties outlined above. We can suggest that an electronic database offers the following advantages:

Data mining

This involves searching organisational databases in order to uncover hidden patterns or relationships in groups of data.

● A database will allow users to organise information in a variety of different ways. The initial order in which records are placed is often unimportant, as information can be reorganised quickly and easily. This allows an organisation to maximise its usage of the information it holds, through techniques such as **data mining**.

● The powerful search facilities provided by electronic database programs can be used to locate and retrieve information many thousands of times faster than by manual methods.

● An electronic database provides facilities for users to add, amend or delete records as required. Additional features simplify data entry and assist in managing the information held. As an example, adding groups of similar records can be simplified by making multiple copies of an existing entry. Each copy can then be edited as needed. This removes the need for the data entry operator to enter the details of each record in full.

● Sophisticated indexing features mean that the same basic information can be stored under a number of different categories. This provides great flexibility and allows users to locate, retrieve and organise information as needed.

● Databases used throughout a company are usually accessed by many different users across a network system. Some of the advantages of this approach include:

   (a) Since the unnecessary duplication of information is minimised, the costs involved in maintaining records are reduced, although often separate databases can give rise to similar problems to those of duplicated paper records.

   (b) Any changes made to the information held in the database are reflected to all users, ensuring consistency at all times.

   (c) Although information is held in a structured manner, the database software will normally provide sufficient flexibility to meet the different requirements of individual users and departments.

Database

A collection of related information stored in an organised way so that specific items can be selected and retrieved quickly.

To summarise, a **database** can be defined as a collection of related information. The information held in the database is stored in an organised way so that specific items can be selected and retrieved quickly. A database need not involve the use of technology – examples of manual databases include telephone directories, address books, diaries and card index files.

▶ Databases and spreadsheets compared

Databases are often thought of as unnecessarily complicated by those who are familiar with using spreadsheets. Despite this, databases are widely used for information management in business and are at the heart of many business applications such as accounting packages, enterprise resource planning systems, workflow systems and transactional e-commerce facilities (Chapter 6).

▶ User-level benefits of databases

If a spreadsheet is produced on a 'one-off' basis for a particular problem, this will be quicker than producing an equivalent database. But imagine that the reporting problem is larger and you regularly have to produce several different reports each month. Although this could be completed using the spreadsheet, certain advantages will occur for the database:

1 It is easier to run a predetermined report for each month than printing out the relevant part of a spreadsheet
2 Errors are arguably less likely to be produced in a standard database report, but can be hidden within a spreadsheet cell.
3 Data can be summarised more readily in a report or query.
4 Ad hoc queries can be used to find information information more rapidly.

These benefits occur due to the *report* and *query* functions of databases which are not core features of spreadsheets and are not, therefore, so sophisticated.

Databases are also superior for *entry* of data. Forms such as that in Figure 4.6 can be provided to users; these allow them to enter data for a single transaction without having to see all the other items. The figure illustrates a data entry form for the car dealership example.

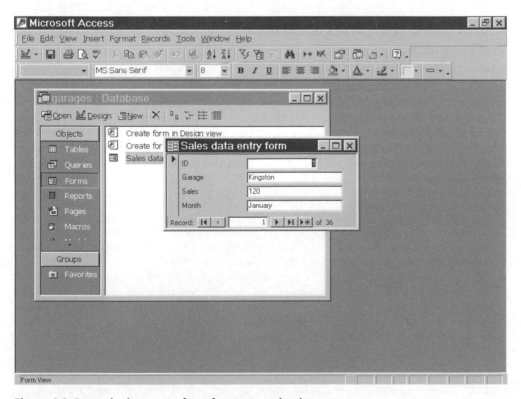

Figure 4.6 **Example data entry form for garages database**

▶ Business-level advantages of databases

The main business benefits of databases derive from the way that databases are designed for sharing information. They are superior for:

- *multi-user access* – allowing different people in the business access to the same data simultaneously such as a manager and another member of staff accessing a single customer's data;
- *distributed access* – users in different departments of the business can readily access data;
- *speed* – for accessing large volumes of information, such as the customers of a bank, only databases are designed to produce reports or access the information rapidly about a single customer;
- *data quality* – sophisticated validation checks can be performed when data are entered to ensure their integrity;
- *security* – access to different types of data can readily be limited to different members of staff. In a car dealership database, for example, the manager of a single branch could be restricted to sales data for their branch;
- *space efficiency* – by splitting up a database into different tables when it is designed, less space is needed, as will be seen in the section on normalisation (Chapter 11).

Despite the many advantages of databases, there are certain information management applications where spreadsheets are more appropriate since it is:

- easier and faster to create a spreadsheet structure;
- easier and faster to enter data using facilities such as auto-filling the months;
- easier to perform numeric modelling;
- easier and faster to produce total and average sales summary data.

▶ An overview of the types of database

Database management system (DBMS)

One or more computer programs that allow users to enter, store, organise, manipulate and retrieve data from a database.

Field

The data in an electronic database are organised by fields and records. A field is a single item of information, such as a name or a quantity.

Record

In an electronic database, a record is a collection of *related* fields. See *Field*.

Table

In an electronic database, data are organised within structures known as tables. A table is a collection of many records.

The information held in an electronic database is accessed via a **database management system** (DBMS). A DBMS can be defined as one or more computer programs that allow users to enter, store, organise, manipulate and retrieve data in a database. For many users, the terms *database* and *database management system* are interchangeable, although the definitions given here demonstrate that this is not the case.

The data in an electronic database are organised by fields and records. A **field** is a single item of information, such as a name or a quantity. A **record** is a collection of *related* fields and a **table** is a collection of related fields. Two examples can be used to illustrate these terms:

- An address book typically stores three items of information: a name, an address and a telephone number. Each of these types of information can be thought of as a *field*. Since the name, address and telephone number of a specific person are related to one another, these constitute a *record*. Together, all of the entries in the address book form a *table*, and in this case the *database* has a single table.
- Consider a filing cabinet used to store information on sales or orders. The cabinet itself is the database, since it holds *all* the information on sales. Each drawer represents a *table* in which related information is stored and each document inside the cabinet is a *record*, since each holds details on a particular sales order. The details of the order, such as the customer who has placed it and the value of the order, can be thought of as fields.

In order to identify a specific item of information within a database, all records must contain a unique identifier, normally called the *key field*. The record key usually takes the form of a number or code and will be different for each record in the database.

Defining the best design for a database is a common business activity covered in more detail in Chapter 11 with an example of a how a Microsoft Access database can be used for storing sales orders. The role of key fields in managing relational databases is also covered in more detail at that point.

A number of national databases store information on every adult in the country. Each of these systems uses a unique identifier to distinguish between specific individuals. As an example, all UK adults have a unique National Insurance number that can used to track pension contributions and entitlement to welfare benefits. Other unique identifiers used by national databases include: driving licence reference number, passport number and NHS number.

◗ Approaches to file processing

Three basic approaches have become popular for the design of electronic databases: file processing, database management systems and relational database management systems. The following provides a brief overview of each of these approaches.

File processing

Early data processing systems were based around numerous files containing large amounts of data related to daily business transactions. As a result, many organisations found themselves in a position where they held large amounts of valuable data but were unable to maximise their use of them. A major problem stemmed from the fact that the data held were often stored in different formats, for example completely different structures might be used to store details of sales and purchases. In order to make use of this data, it was usually necessary to create specialised computer programs, often at great expense.

This type of database is sometimes described as having a **flat file** structure. A flat file database can be described as being self-contained since it contains only one type of record – or *table* – and cannot access data held in other database files.

Free-form database

A **free-form** database allows users to store information in the form of brief notes or passages of text. Each item held can be placed within a category or assigned one or more key words. Information is organised and retrieved by using categories or key words.

A modern variation on free-form databases is the hypertext database. In a **hypertext** database information is stored as series of objects and can consist of text, graphics, numerical data and multimedia data. Any object can be linked to any other, allowing users to store disparate information in an organised manner.

A good example of a free-form database is the help files found within most software packages. An example of a hypertext database is the pages available via any given site on the World Wide Web.

◗ Database management systems

The introduction of database management systems altered the way in which organisations managed their data resources. Although data were still held separately from the programs that made use of them, this new approach offered greater flexibility whilst reducing development and operating costs. Some of the major characteristics of the database management system (DBMS) approach included:

Flat file database
....
A self-contained database that only contains one type of record – or table – and can not access data held in other database files.

Free-form database
....
Allows users to store information in the form of unstructured notes or passages of text. Information is organised and retrieved by using categories or key words.

Hypertext database
....
Information is stored as series of objects that can consist of text, graphics, numerical data and multimedia data. Objects are linked allowing users to store disparate information in an organised manner.

- Programs included a range of general-purpose tools and utilities for producing reports or extracting data. This meant that comparatively little development was needed in order to undertake new tasks.
- The availability of general-purpose tools enabled non-technical users to access data. Users were able to analyse data, extract records and produce reports with little support from technical staff.
- The use of a DBMS encouraged organisations to introduce standards for developing and operating their databases. As an example, many organisations developed standards governing the structure of any new data files created.

We will now review the main types of database management system.

Relational database management systems

The popularity of the **relational database management system** (RDBMS) approach grew from a need to share data resources across the entire organisation. In the past, it had been normal to concentrate resources in a small number of specific areas. For example, an organisation's accounting and stock control functions often dealt with the largest number of business transactions and were seen as having the greatest need of the organisation's information technology resources. In the same way, these functions were also seen as having the greatest need of the organisation's data resources. However, as companies aimed to become more efficient and reduce costs it became essential to ensure the widest possible access to organisational data resources. In addition, organisations were also beginning to receive increased demands for information from users and managers.

The RDBMS approach can be seen as an extension of the DBMS approach with the additional benefits to be gained by sharing data across an organisation and the ability to combine data from several different sources. As an example, it is possible to reduce stockholding costs by linking together an organisation's production and stock control functions. Such an approach would allow stock levels to be adjusted continuously by examining production levels. In this way, stocks of raw materials can be increased or decreased according to actual usage. In the same way, production scheduling might be improved by inspecting stock levels at regular intervals.

Relational databases enable data to be stored within a number of different tables. They are the most widely used type of database. Separate record designs can be used to store data dealing with different subjects. For example, a database used for stock control might use separate record designs to store information concerning items stocked, reorder levels and supplier details.

The tables within a relational database can be linked together using one or more **record keys**. As mentioned earlier, all database records must contain a unique record key that can be used to identify a specific record. In a relational database, this is often called the **primary key**. However, records can also contain other keys to help locate data stored in another table. The record keys contained in each table can used to establish one or more **relationships** between tables. By using record keys in combination – a **compound key** – it is possible to retrieve data from several tables at once. Note that a field used to locate information in another, related table is often called a **foreign key**.

Figure 4.7 illustrates how records can be linked together using record keys. The diagram illustrates a simple relational database containing two tables: one holding details of an employee's pay, the other holding personal information, such as the employee's address. The database is to be used to generate a pay slips for all employees. In order to accomplish this, the DBMS would carry out the following actions for each record in the Personal Details table:

1 Locate a record within the Personal Details table. The unique primary key can be used to identify a specific employee.

Relational database management system (RDBMS)

An extension of a DBMS that allows data to be combined from a variety of sources.

Relational databases

Data are stored within a number of different tables with each dealing with different subjects that are related (linked) using key fields.

Record key

Identifies a specific record within a database, usually takes the form of a number or code and will be different for each record in the database.

Primary key

The tables within a relational database can be linked together using one or more record keys. All records must contain a unique record key called the primary key.

Relationship

In a relational database, data can be combined from several different sources by defining relationships between tables.

Compound key

In a relational database, it is possible to retrieve data from several tables at once by using record keys in combination, often known as a compound key.

Foreign (secondary) key fields

These fields are used to link tables together by referring to the primary key in another database table.

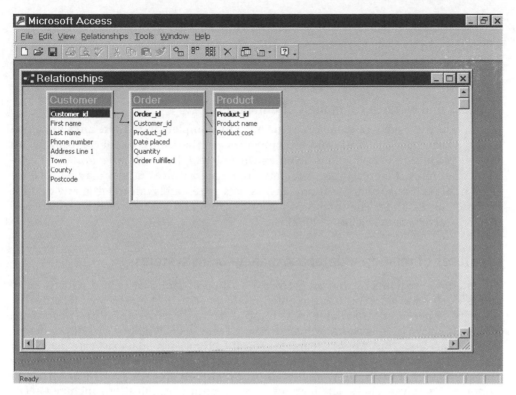

Figure 4.7 **An example of how key fields are used to link information from different database tables**

2 Extract any information required from the Personal Details record, such as the employee's name and address.

3 The secondary key identifies a unique record in the Pay Details table. Since the secondary key in the Personal Details table matches the primary key in the Pay Details table, the DBMS can locate the specific record required.

4 The information required from the Pay Details table is extracted and the pay slip is printed.

A more detailed explanation of database terminology and applications based on a case study is provided in Chapter 11.

The object-oriented approach

An **object-oriented** approach to database design employs the concept of reusable objects in order to develop sophisticated or complex applications. An *object* combines data structures with any functions needed to manipulate the object or the data it holds. As an example, an object called Employee might be created to store details of staff. The object would contain a data structure that allowed basic details such as name, address, age, etc. to be stored. In addition, the object would also contain facilities that allow various actions to be performed, such as changing an employee's address.

This object-oriented approach offers several important advantages:

● Since objects are self-contained, they are easy to manage, for example changes can be made to an individual object without necessarily altering any other part of the system.

● New objects can be created quickly and easily from existing ones. Continuing with the example given previously, the Employee object might be used as the basis for a

Object-oriented database

The database is made up of objects combining data structures with functions needed to manipulate the object or the data it holds.

new object entitled Manager. Only minor changes would be needed to complete the new object since it would already share all of the features of Employee.

● Objects can be copied or transferred into new systems with little difficulty. Since the object already contains any functions needed to make use of it, it can be used immediately within the new system.

Network and hierarchical models of databases

Mention of these types of databases is included for completeness. These are alternatives to the relational model and were its competitors in the 1980s. In the 1990s, the vast majority of business applications became RDBMS-based, but with object-oriented techniques being used increasingly. The network or hierarchical model may be used for some high-performance applications such as data warehouses (although many of these are based on RDBMS). The interested reader can read an overview of the network and hierarchical databases in Curtis (2002).

▶ Features of relational database management systems

All database programs enable users to create and edit tables or record structures. In addition, all packages allow users to enter, modify, delete, sort and extract records. The majority of packages also enable users to print data in a variety of different formats. Microsoft Access is the best-known database used on the PC (Figure 4.7). Others include Borland Paradox, Lotus Approach and Microsoft FoxPro. These databases are mainly for personal or departmental use by a small number of users. Where databases are used by a large number of users, they are hosted on a mainframe or on a UNIX or Microsoft Windows NT server. These databases for 'mission-critical' applications include Oracle, Informix, Sybase, Microsoft SQL Server and IBM DB2.

The majority of modern database programs support the creation of relational databases containing several linked tables. Although tables can be used in isolation, they can also be used to combine together information drawn from one or more other tables.

Many programs also provide the ability to link tables together automatically. Microsoft Access, for example, provides an interactive facility to analyse one or more tables and create any required relationships.

Data entry form

In an electronic database, a data entry form provides a convenient means of viewing, entering, editing and deleting records.

Index

Stores information concerning the order of the records in the database. The index lists the locations of records but does not alter the actual order of the database.

All major database programs enable users to create and modify **data entry forms**. A data entry form provides a convenient means of viewing, entering, editing and deleting records (Fig. 4.7).

An **index** stores information concerning the order of the records in the database. The index lists the locations of records but does not alter the actual order in the database. This can be made clearer by using the index of a book as a simple analogy: the index allows users to find a specific piece of information quickly and easily, regardless of how the material in the book is organised.

Indexes are commonly used to increase the speed with which records can be located or sorted. Multiple indexes can be created so that the records in the database can be sorted in a variety of ways.

All modern database programs provide a range of sophisticated security features. Examples of some of the most common features available include:

● *Encryption*. Data can be encoded so that it appears meaningless until decoded. Passwords provide control over the encryption and decryption process.

● *Recovery*. Many programs contain tools that allow damaged database files to be repaired. In the event that a file cannot be repaired, additional tools may be available that allow users to retrieve as much data as possible from the damaged file.

● *Passwords*. Access to specific files or tables can be restricted through the use of passwords. Several passwords can be used to limit what parts of the database different users can view or alter. As an example, a data entry clerk might be assigned a password that prevents changes being made to the structure of a table or the format or a report.

All major database packages allow users to generate a wide variety of *reports*. Many programs are capable of creating simple reports automatically. In addition, many programs allow users to perform calculations and other actions as the report is produced. This enables additional information, such as subtotals, to be calculated and included in the report whenever required.

A **query** enables a user to locate, sort, update or extract records from the database. Users design a query by specifying the conditions that must be met in order for a record to be selected. In many programs, the creation of a query is an interactive process, where users respond to a series of questions in order to generate the required design.

> **Query**
> Extracts data according to a set of conditions specified by the user.

There are two basic types of query: selection queries and update queries:

- A *selection query* can be used to locate and display any records meeting a set of specified conditions. None of the data held in the database are altered; any records not meeting the conditions set are simply hidden from view temporarily.
- An **update query** (sometimes known as an 'action query') can be used to modify records in a variety of ways. Records are selected for alteration according to a set of conditions specified by the user. Common actions performed by update queries include:
  (a) updating values held in fields, for example by carrying out a calculation;
  (b) deleting any records no longer required;
  (c) appending new records to the database;
  (d) generating new tables containing selected records or summary information.

> **Update query**
> An update query can be used to change records, tables and reports held in a database management system.

It is worth noting that the majority of database programs make use of a special **structured query language (SQL)** in order to create queries. SQL is described in more detail further on in this section.

> **Structured query language (SQL)**
> A form of programming language that provides a standardised method for retrieving information from databases.

A **filter** allows users to view the information held in a database in a variety of ways. Filters can be used to sort data into different orders, display only selected fields or display only selected records. In many ways, filters can be thought of as combining some of the features of both indexes and selection queries. It is worth noting that filters do not alter any of the data held in the database.

> **Filter**
> In a spreadsheet or database, a filter can be used to remove data from the screen temporarily. This allows users to work with a specific group of records. Filters do not alter or delete data but simply hide any unwanted items.

Structured query language (SQL) provides a standardised method for retrieving information from databases. Although traditionally used to manage large databases held on mainframes and minicomputers, it has become a widely used and popular tool for personal computer database packages. One of the reasons for this popularity is that SQL supports multi-user databases that operate across network systems.

SQL programs are created by producing a series of statements containing special key words. The example below shows a simple SQL query designed to search the Student Record table and display records for students with a Last Name of 'Jones'.

```
SELECT DISTINCTROW [Student Record].[Last Name]
FROM [Student Record]
WHERE (((([Student Record].[Last Name])='Jones'));
```

Users are often unaware that queries created using the interactive design tools provided by many modern database packages are converted into SQL programs before being executed. In Microsoft Access, for example, a mouse is used to design a query on the screen. However, the query is translated into equivalent SQL statements before it is executed.

In common with many other types of application software, most modern database packages include a *macro language* or a programming tool that can be used to handle extremely complex tasks.

The majority of modern database programs contain a number of tools designed to automate common *data analysis* tasks. The ability to generate charts and graphs, for example, is a common feature amongst programs.

Database programs are able to deal with data drawn from a variety of different sources. In many cases, files produced by other packages can be *imported* directly into a database with no loss of data. In addition, some programs are capable of producing table designs automatically, based on the content of the file being imported.

The ability of a database program to *export* data in a variety of formats is used extensively in a variety of applications. Mailmerge operations, for example, often make use of data drawn from customer records held in an organisation's sales database.

Activity 4.4

Forms, queries and reports

Using a package such as Microsoft Access, create a simple database that can be used to store the names and addresses of your friends and colleagues. Make sure that the database includes the following features:

● a simple data entry form that can be used to add, edit or delete records;
● at least one query, for example a query to list all people living in a certain city;
● at least one report, for example a report to show the telephone number of every person listed in the database.

Management applications of productivity software

Productivity software is general-purpose applications, aimed at supporting users in performing a variety of common tasks. In addition to the productivity applications such as word processors and spreadsheets, more specialist management applications are also possible. Office software such as Microsoft Office combines software both for document creation and for data analysis with team-working tools such as shared diaries. Such packages are now also intended to support knowledge management (Chapter 1) with built-in facilities or through integration with other software.

❱ Managing time and projects

One of the principal activities of a business organisation is managing resources so that tasks are completed as quickly and efficiently as possible. It can be argued that the most important organisational resources are the skills and abilities of employees. For this reason, a major category of business applications is devoted to maximising the use of employee time. This type of software can be subdivided into a number of other categories:

● *Packages for managing tasks and projects*. These programs allow managers to schedule tasks, allocate resources and monitor progress. Typical applications include project management programs and scheduling software. How they are applied is described in Chapter 9.
● *Packages for individual time management and organising personal information*. These programs help managers to make more effective use of their time by helping them to schedule appointments, organise meetings and record important information. Typical applications include personal information managers (PIMs) and contact management software.

    A **personal information manager** can be thought as an electronic personal organiser. The program allows users to store, organise and retrieve personal information such as appointments, personal expenses, telephone numbers and addresses, reminders

Personal information manager (PIM)
A program that allows users to store, organise and retrieve personal information.

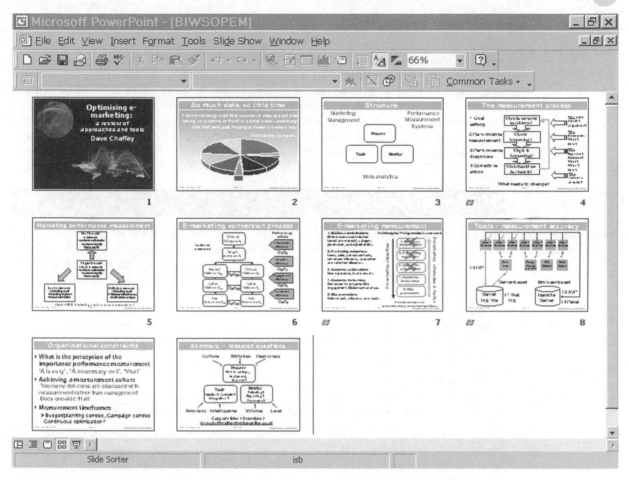

Figure 4.8 Microsoft's Powerpoint for Windows showing the 'Slide Sorter' view which can be used when preparing a presentation

and to-do lists. Generally, a PIM is made up of several individual applications that are linked together by a menu system.

Contact managers can be used to maintain lists of information relating to customers, suppliers and other important individuals or organisations. Such programs are commonly used by sales organisations to assist in building and maintaining business relationships between customers and individual members of staff.

- *Network software*. This describes the software used to establish workgroups on an organisation's network system. The programs used provide the basic infrastructure for workgroup computing.
- *Scheduling software*. This describes programs that help to organise the activities of the workgroup. Typical applications include calendars, scheduling programs and workflow software.

A *workgroup* can be defined as a group of individuals working together on a given task. Each member of the workgroup will be attached to the organisation's network system so that tasks can be organised and information can be shared with other members.

Contact manager
This describes a software application that can be used to maintain lists of information relating to customers, suppliers and other important individuals or organisations.

◗ Presentation packages

Interactive presentations are commonly used for a number of purposes including staff training and briefings and as sales tools. Presentation software enables users to create, edit and deliver presentations via a computer system. At a simple level, presentations can consist of nothing more than a series of simple *slides* displayed on a computer monitor. More sophisticated presentations can incorporate multimedia, such as video sequences, and can allow users to interact with the material presented. Although primarily concerned with the creation of slides, many programs also support the creation of speaker notes, handouts and overhead transparencies.

Multimedia software

Multimedia software
Uses text, sound, animation or video to interact with the user.

Multimedia is the term used to describe software which (together with appropriate hardware) can interact with the user through different techniques such as text, sound, animation or video. The type of hardware required to support multimedia was briefly described in Chapter 3. It includes sound and video cards and capture using microphones and video cameras.

Multimedia software is most common in home computers, but also has business applications. These include training courses and product promotions that are distributed on CD-ROM. Multimedia and computer-based training (CBT) have been demonstrated to be more effective than simple presentations since studies show we remember:

- 10% of what we see
- 30% of what we see and hear
- 50% of what we see, hear and do (through interaction or role plays).

Multimedia functions can be incorporated into both general-purpose software and application-specific software. For example a word processor or e-mail can incorporate multimedia elements such as a commentary or video from a manager who has reviewed a document.

An example of a business application of multimedia is the CBT system used by Accenture in the United States. This company has developed an interactive training package that provides the consultant with different challenges according to the client they are working with. Video images and audio of the client describing their requirements are shown and the trainee has to use these and supporting documentation to recommend the best solution. CBT is also used in more hazardous environments such as for rail or construction-site workers to reduce the cost and risk of such training.

Information kiosk
A multimedia system usually integrated with a touch screen to provide information for retail or community applications such as libraries or local government.

Multimedia is also used for **information kiosks**. These are used for retail applications in shops or supermarkets. They usually consist of a PC mounted in a stand which is accessed by a touch screen and will often make use of multimedia. They have the appeal that they can be consulted when sales staff are not available, and they are used to provide information rather than giving a 'hard sell'. It remains to be seen whether they become widely used, since many customers may still prefer to speak to a member of staff. It is estimated that there are over 100 000 kiosks in the USA.

Before turning to look at software for communications and the Internet, it is worth considering some of the business issues related to purchase and use of software applications. Case Study 4.3 looks at an alternative model of software development and distribution. Chapter 7 looks at approaches towards the acquisition of software and services in general, whilst Chapter 14 looks at outsourcing as a means of obtaining software and services at reduced cost.

CASE STUDY 4.3

Open-source software

The recent plague of Microsoft-hosted computer viruses has caused an international charity to consider moving to Linux-based PC systems.

Kerry Scott, IT director for ActionAid, faced with a migration to Windows 2000 or Linux, said the low implementation costs of Linux with a Gnome user interface compared favourably to Windows.

Microsoft offers large discounts to charities but this only saves on the initial purchase.

'There are large hidden costs with Microsoft with the need to buy anti-virus software', Scott said. 'We are now seeing the cost of viruses in downloading and installing updates on each desktop.

'Most viruses are targeting Outlook and the message seems to be "avoid Microsoft and avoid viruses".'

Scott admitted that Linux was not as easy to install as Windows, despite improvements by distributors such as RedHat and SuSe. He is also aware that the choice of software is primarily limited to Sun's open-sourced Staroffice productivity suite rather than Microsoft Office, so no decision will be made until the end of this year when a plan will be submitted to ActionAid's chief technical officer.

Mark Simmons, a senior analyst at Bloor Research, said, 'It's a good idea to take time to evaluate Linux

and, if the user is happy, it should provide a cheaper and more resilient platform.

'Where viruses are concerned, Microsoft is the focus at the moment but it may only be a matter of time before Linux attracts attention. In its favour, Linux has a worldwide base of thousands of developers to build better firewalls and security protection.'

ActionAid, which addresses problems associated with poverty in the Third World, has an estimated 300 desktops in the UK and more than 1,000 worldwide. Scott said many of its users are in the poorest countries where IT support is difficult to find whatever the operating system.

Source: 'Charity looks to Linux on cost and security', *Computer Weekly*, 22 March 2001

Questions

Conduct any additional research that may be necessary in order to answer the following questions.

1 What is open-source software?

2 Using the case study as an initial source of reference, identify the advantages and disadvantages of open-source software.

3 The adoption of open-source software is a practical and moral necessity for not-for-profit organisations. Provide an argument in favour of or against this statement.

Software for using the Internet

The networking concepts behind the **Internet**, a description of how it functions, and how it has developed as a business tool are reviewed in Chapter 5. Here we introduce the main types of personal user software that are used to access the Internet – the web browser and e-mail. Internet-based e-business applications are described in Chapter 6.

Internet
A global network system made up of many smaller systems.

❱ Internet-access software applications

Over its lifetime, many tools have been developed to help find, send and receive information across the Internet. Web browsers used to access the World Wide Web are actually one of the most recent applications. These tools are summarised in Table 4.2. In this section we will briefly discuss the relevance of some of the more commonly used tools to the modern organisation. The other tools have either been superseded by the use of the World Wide Web or are of less relevance from a business perspective. Note that many of the other tools such as e-mail, IRC and newsgroups, that formerly needed special software to access them, are now available through web browsers across the WWW, for example the Hotmail (www.hotmail.com) and Yahoo!Mail (www.yahoo.com) services.

Table 4.2 **Applications of different Internet tools**

Internet tool	Summary
Electronic mail or e-mail	Sending messages or documents, such as news about a new product or sales promotion between individuals. A primitive form of 'push' channel.
Internet relay chat (IRC)	This is a synchronous communications tool that allows a text-based 'chat' between different users who are logged on at the same time. Of limited use for business or marketing purposes.
Usenet newsgroups	A widely used electronic bulletin board used to discuss a particular topic such as a sport, hobby or business area. Traditionally accessed by special newsreader software, can now be accessed via a web browser from www.google.com.
FTP file transfer	The file transfer protocol is used as a standard for moving files across the Internet. FTP is available as a feature of web browsers that is used for marketing applications such as downloading files such as product price lists or specifications. Also used to update HTML files on web sites by uploading.
Gophers, Archie and WAIS	These tools were important before the advent of the web for storing and searching documents on the Internet. They have largely been superseded by the web which provides better searching and more sophisticated document publishing.
Telnet	This allows remote access to computer systems. For example, a retailer could check to see whether an item was in stock in a warehouse using a telnet application.
Push channel	Information is broadcast over the Internet or an intranet and received using a web browser or special program for which a subscription to this channel has been set up. This technique is still used for automated software distribution, but has not proved popular as a method for accessing web content by users
World Wide Web	Widely used for publishing information and running business applications over the Internet.

▶ Electronic mail or e-mail

Electronic mail (e-mail)
The transmission of a message over a communications network.

E-mail is well known as a method of sending and receiving electronic messages. It has been available across the Internet for over 20 years. E-mails are typically written and read in a special mail reader program that in a large company is often part of a groupware package such as Lotus Notes, Microsoft Exchange or Novell Groupwise. Smaller companies or individuals may use lower-cost or free mail programs such as Microsoft Outlook Express, Eudora or Pegasus mail. A relatively recent innovation is the use of web sites which provide free e-mail facilities and do not require any special software other than a web browser.

E-mail is now vital as a method of communicating internally and externally with customers, suppliers and partners. Since many e-mails are received and sent by companies, management of e-mail is a major management issue for the e-business. This is discussed further in Chapter 16. For example, ZDNet (2000) reported that Dell receives 50 000 e-mail messages a month and 100 000 order-status requests a month from customers. It is thought that globally 4 billion e-mail messages and 300 million SMS messages are sent daily. For Dutch electronics company Philips International 110 000 users within the firm create 7 million e-mails and 700 Gb of data a week. A large company with an average of 8000 corporate e-mail users spends more than £1 million a year as users try to find and retrieve old e-mail messages, often from archives.

SMS (short mesage service)
A standard for transferring text messages between mobile services.

E-mail management involves developing procedures and using systems to ensure that inbound and outbound e-mails are processed efficiently. **Inbound e-mail** should be routed to the correct person. E-mails may be sent from a customer to a company requesting information such as product specifications or quotations. Autoresponders or mail-bots are used to notify customers that their response is being dealt with. For example, an e-mail sent to products@company_name.com could automatically dispatch a summary of a company's products. **Outbound e-mail** may be used on an ad hoc basis or as part of a standardised method of keeping customers informed, such as through a regular e-mail newsletter. Managing inbound and outbound e-mail is an important issue for customer service delivery.

In a business organisation, e-mail can be used to support both internal and external communications. Examples of two typical applications for e-mail are as follow:

- *Internal communications*. Many organisations use e-mail instead of internal memos or telephone calls. One of the advantages of using e-mail in this way is that messages are stored automatically until the user comes to access them. In addition, a great deal of information, such as the date and time of the message, can be included in the message automatically.
- Teleworking. It is estimated that as much as five per cent of the UK workforce uses teleworking. E-mail enables people to stay in contact with clients, colleagues and employers. In addition, it allows teleworkers to send or receive work-related materials quickly and easily. Teleworking is considered further in Chapter 19.

> A *teleworker* is a person who works from home, using technology as a means of communicating with employers, clients and other persons. Teleworkers send or receive materials using a variety of different methods including e-mail and fax machines.

Advantages of e-mail

Some of the major advantages of e-mail can be summarised as follows:

- *Speed*. E-mail messages can be transmitted very quickly. A typical message containing 400 words, for example, can be transmitted in under a second. As a means of communication, e-mail is considered extremely fast with some messages able to reach their destinations in minutes.

> Since e-mail is considered to be an extremely fast method of communication, users often use the derisory term 'snail mail' to refer to the conventional postal system.

- *Cost*. The cost of sending or receiving messages is considered very low. Hundreds of messages can be sent or received for the cost of a brief telephone call, making e-mail far cheaper than the postal service. For this reason, many companies have adopted e-mail marketing strategies.
- *Multiple copies*. E-mail allows multiple copies of the same basic message to be created and transmitted. Using some of the functions of the directory, groups of people can be contacted by assigning an **alias** (sometimes known as a *nickname*), for example, the name of a department might be used as an alias for all of the people working there.
- *Auditing*. Even the simplest e-mail package will provide a number of features that allow users to *audit* their messages. Most programs allow users to keep copies of any messages they produce, automatically marking them with the date and time they were created.

Inbound e-mail
E-mail received from outside the organisation such as customer and supplier enquiries.

Outbound e-mail
E-mail sent from the company to other organisations.

Teleworking
A teleworker is a person who works from home, using technology as a means of communicating with employers, clients and other persons.

Alias
The process of sending e-mail messages to specific individuals or groups of users can be simplified by making use of an alias or nickname.

- *Sharing data*. E-mail messages can be used to transmit data files to other users. Files can be *attached* to messages and transmitted in the usual way. All types of data can be sent in this way including word processor files, spreadsheet data, graphics and database files.
- *Multimedia*. The latest e-mail packages allow users to include multimedia elements in their messages. Messages can include a variety of different elements including graphics, video, hyperlinks to information on the Internet, and sound files.
- *Groupwork*. E-mail supports groupwork and remote working

Disadvantages of e-mail

Some of the major disadvantages of e-mail can be summarised as follows:

- *Routing*. E-mail messages seldom take the most direct route to their destinations. A message sent from Manchester to London, for example, might travel through Leicester, Birmingham and Nottingham before reaching its final destination. This can lead to a number of difficulties:
  - (a) the time taken to receive the message can be long. Instant messaging such as Yahoo! Instant Messenger is increasingly used to overcome this deficiency;
  - (b) there are more opportunities for the message to become lost or garbled;
  - (c) there are more opportunities for messages to be intercepted.
- *Cost*. In order to send or receive e-mail, organisations must have access to the correct hardware and software. The expense of buying new equipment, such as modems, can mean that it is beyond the reach of smaller companies.

A survey by analysts Gartner has found that:

- employees spend on average 49 minutes each day managing e-mail;
- 24 per cent of staff spend more than an hour each day dealing with e-mail;
- only 27 per cent of the e-mail received by staff requires their immediate attention;
- 34 per cent of internal business email is unnecessary

Source: ZDNet, 2 May 2001 (www.zdnet.com)

Spam

Unwanted messages, such as advertisements, are received by most e-mail users. The act of sending out these messages is usually called spamming.

File attachment

E-mail messages can be used to transmit data files to other users. Files can be attached to messages and transmitted in the usual way.

Offline

When a user is not connected to their Internet account, they are said to be offline.

Online

When a user is connected to their Internet account, usually by a modem link, they are said to be online.

- *Technical issues*. Since using an e-mail service requires a certain level of technical knowledge: novice users may find it difficult to operate the hardware and software involved. This can place a burden on an organisation in terms of training and technical support requirements. E-mail services can be outsourced to reduce this problem.
- *Spam*. Unwanted messages, such as advertisements, are received by most e-mail users. The act of sending out these messages is usually called **spamming**. Dealing with unwanted or unnecessary e-mail messages can place a great burden on an organisation's resources.
- *Security*. Unless encrypted, e-mail messages can be intercepted relatively easily. This makes e-mail unsuitable for sending confidential information unless special precautions are taken.

Features of an e-mail package

1 **Attachments**. Although messages sent by e-mail are usually composed of text alone, additional files can be 'attached' to an e-mail message so that users can send programs, data files and other materials with their messages.

2 *Composition tools*. E-mail messages can be composed **online** or **offline**. They can also be posted immediately (immediate delivery) or can have delivery deferred. All packages pro-

vide an editor that allows users to enter the text of a new message. More sophisticated programs will have many of the features of a word processor, for example spell-checking.

3 *Viewing tools*. All e-mail programs are designed to collect new messages and allow users to view them on the screen. Most programs also allow users to print the contents of a message or copy the text into another program, such as a word processor.

4 *Filters*. Filters provide the ability to mark messages for special attention. A filter searches for key words or phrases in a message. Any messages matching the filter conditions can be dealt with automatically. Filters can be used to: highlight messages for special attention, delete messages automatically, copy or move messages to another location or reply to incoming messages automatically.

5 *Management tools*. Most packages provide facilities for archiving, copying, moving, deleting and grouping messages. *Mail boxes* can be created to hold messages from certain people or concerning a particular subject.

6 *Encryption*. Many programs provide the facility to encode messages so that only the intended recipients can read them. This is known as encryption.

7 *Managing addresses*. An alias usually consists of a description and the e-mail addresses of those grouped under the alias. Groups of aliases can be stored within the **address book** tool found within most e-mail packages. The address book enables to users to create, delete, edit and organise aliases.

8 *Signature files*. A **signature file** contains information that can be automatically added to the end of an e-mail message. The signature file is normally a simple text file that can be created or edited using a text editor or similar program. Most e-mail programs allow users to have a number of different signature files.

▶ The World Wide Web and web browsers

The **World Wide Web**, or 'web' for short, is a medium for publishing information on the Internet in an easy-to-use form. If we take the analogy of television, then the Internet would be equivalent to the broadcasting equipment such as masts and transmitters, and the World Wide Web is equivalent to the content of different TV programmes. The medium is based on a standard document format known as **HTML** (hypertext mark up language) which can be thought of as similar to a word-processing format. It is significant since it offers *hyperlinks* which allow users to readily move from one document to another – the process known as 'surfing'.

The World Wide Web (WWW) is accessed using a **web browser**. Since they have been designed for ease of use, WWW pages feature sections of text that include hypertext links and graphics. Figure 4.9 shows the Microsoft Explorer web browser being used to access a web site to find information about Internet marketing. The other main browser is Netscape Navigator.

Features of a web browser

The interface used by a web browser makes use of **hypertext** linking techniques. A hypertext is a document that includes highlighted words or phrases. These highlighted sections represent *links* to other documents or sections of the same document. Clicking the mouse above one of these links causes it to be activated. A link can be used to move to another document, transfer a file, view a section of video, listen to a sound file or carry out a number of other actions.

Address book

A way of grouping e-mail addresses in a similar way to a phone book.

Signature file

Information such as an address and phone number that can be automatically added to the end of an e-mail message.

World Wide Web (WWW)

Interlinked documents on the Internet made up of pages containing text, graphics and other elements.

Hypertext Markup Language (HTML)

WWW pages are mainly created by producing documents containing HTML commands that are special tags (or codes) to control how the WWW page will appear when displayed in a web browser.

Web browser program

Enables users to navigate through the information available and display any pages of interest.

Hypertext

Hypertext is highlighted words or phrases that represent links to other documents activated by clicking the mouse.

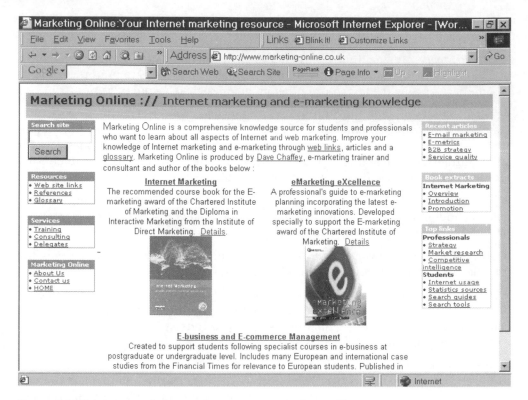

Figure 4.9 Web browser being used to access Marketing Online (www.marketing-online.co.uk)

As users move through a hypertext document, their actions are recorded automatically by the program being used. Users can access the *history* of their movements and jump backwards or forwards through all of the documents they have viewed.

All web browsers provide users with a variety of tools that enable them to navigate through often complex collections of WWW pages. Some of the most common tools include:

- *Navigation buttons*. These enable users to move backwards and forwards through the list of pages previously viewed. Additional command buttons include:
  (a) Stop. This cancels the action currently being taken.
  (b) Home. Users are able to designate a specific WWW page as a 'home page' which is displayed each time the web browser runs. The user can return to the home page at any time by using the appropriate command button.
  (c) Search. Many pages provide access to **search engines** that can be used to locate specific information on the Internet. This command causes the web browser to load a WWW page that provides access to one or more search engines.
- *History*. All web browsers maintain a list of pages previously viewed by the user. The user is able to display the list and can revisit any of the pages previously viewed.
- *Address bar*. Users are able to enter the location of a WWW page or file via the address bar.

Search engine
Key words are entered to locate information stored on the Internet.

In order to increase the speed and efficiency with which a web browser functions, a temporary storage space is used to store copies of any pages that the user has viewed. If the user returns to a given location, the web browser retrieves the required page from the temporary storage space, rather than transferring a fresh copy from a remote computer. The use of a **cache** in this way improves the speed with which previously viewed pages can be displayed.

> The transmission of information across the Internet is often described as being based around either pull or push technology. **Pull technology** describes information sent out as a result of receiving a specific request, for example a page is delivered to a web browser in response to a specific request from the user. **Push technology** describes information that is sent without a user's specifically requesting it, for example a customised news service received by subscribing to a channel or e-mail.

All web browsers allow users to maintain a directory of WWW sites. The directory will enable users to add, edit, delete and organise addresses in the form of **bookmarks**.

As organisations seek to apply the Internet to business applications, renewed emphasis has been placed on matters concerning security and privacy. As an example, many users and organisations cite security concerns as a reason for not taking up developments such as e-commerce. In order to address these concerns, many web browsers now provide a range of security features that can be used alone or in combination to offer varying levels of security. Some common features include the following:

- *Digital ID*. A **digital ID** provides a means of confirming the identity of a specific user through the use of a small data file called a **personal certificate**. The certificate contains encrypted information relating to the user's identity. Since the user's web browser is able to transmit or receive personal certificates, they are able to verify the identity of a third party or confirm their own identity to that party.
- *Certificates*. A **site certificate** contains information regarding the identity of a particular site on the Internet. As with personal certificates, the site certificate is encrypted to protect the information it contains. Web browsers automatically maintain a list of certificates concerning sites designated as being trustworthy by the user or organisation. When the web browser accesses a given site on the Internet, the corresponding certificate is checked to ensure the authenticity of the site. If the information in the certificate is invalid or out of date, a suitable warning is issued.
- *Ratings*. Many browsers support the use of **ratings** in order to restrict access to inappropriate content, for example pornography. The majority of ratings schemes are voluntary and are based on four basic criteria: language, nudity, sex and violence. When a web browser is used to access a site belonging to a given scheme, the site's ratings are checked against the list of criteria set within the browser. If a site does not meet the criteria specified within the browser, access to the site is denied.
- *Applets*. WWW pages can contain small programs that are activated when a page is accessed. Such programs can take a variety of forms and can include complete, self-contained applications known as **applets**. As an example, a page may have been created to display an animation sequence by activating an appropriate applet after the page has finished loading. Although such programs are generally considered harmless, they can represent a potential security risk to an organisation or individual. As a result, all web browsers provide control over the operation of any applets embedded in a WWW page.

A **plug-in** is a small program or accessory that can be used to extend a web browser's capabilities. For example, a number of different plug-ins exist that allow a web browser to display video or animation sequences.

Cache
A temporary storage space is used to store copies of any pages that the user has viewed for rapid access if the user revisits a site.

Pull technology
Information sent out as a result of receiving a specific request, for example a page is delivered to a web browser in response to a specific request from the user.

Push technology
Information that is sent without a user specifically requesting it, for example a customised news service received by subscribing to a channel.

Bookmarks
All web browsers allow users to maintain a directory of WWW sites. The directory will enable users to add, edit, delete and organise addresses in the form of bookmarks.

Digital ID
Provides a means of confirming the identity of a specific user through the use of a small data file called a personal certificate.

Personal certificate
A data file containing encrypted information relating to the user's identity.

Site certificate
Contains information regarding the identity of a particular site on the Internet. The site certificate is encrypted to protect the information it contains.

Ratings
Used to restrict access to certain content. If a site does not meet the criteria specified within the browser, access to the site is denied.

Applets
Small programs with limited functions typically running from within a web browser.

Plug-in
A small program or accessory that is installed permanently to extend a web browser's capabilities.

The use of plug-ins offers two main advantages. First, users are able to select which plug-ins they require and can install only those needed to meet a specific requirement. This acts to reduce storage space requirements and prevents unnecessary or unwanted changes being made to the user's computer system. Secondly, the functionality of some plug-ins can be extended to the user's computer system as a whole. From the point of view of a company hosting the web page they have the major disadvantage that their customer will not be able to view the content unless they go through the process of downloading and setting up the plug-in.

All modern web browsers are capable of executing special commands that have been embedded within the body of a WWW page. These **scripts** can be used to control the appearance of the page or can provide additional facilities, such as on-screen clocks and timers.

Many scripts are produced using a special programming language known as **Java**. Java, a derivative of the C++ programming language, can be used to create small applications that run when users display a WWW page or activate a control shown on the screen. One of the major advantages of Java is that applications are *platform-independent*, meaning that they can be used with any system equipped with the correct software. This allows applications created using one particular kind of system to work on other systems without modification.

A brief introduction to HTML

Many web browsers provide facilities that allow users to construct their own WWW pages using a special authoring language known as **hypertext mark up language** (HTML). What are the basic elements of an HTML page? First, we need *tags* to tell the browser this is an HTML page: this is performed by the <HTML> tag. Second, we need tags to show the header and body of the page. This is performed <HEAD> and <BODY> tags. Within the <HEAD> part of the HTML document it is possible (but not essential) to add the <TITLE> tag to indicate the text to appear in the title bar of the browser. Within the part of the document tagged by <BODY> </BODY> any text will be displayed as shown below. Comments are denoted by the Comment tag <!-- -->. Formatting of text can be applied through tags such as <B></B> which denote bold text.

<HTML> tag	Denotes an HTML document.
<HEAD> tag	The header part of an HTML document containing titles, meta tags and scripts.
<TITLE> tag	The text that appears in the browser title bar.
<BODY> tag	The main part of an HTML document containing content.
Comment tag <!-- -->	Used to document code, text does not appear in browser.

HTML code	Browser display
| ```
<HTML>
<HEAD>
<TITLE>The B2C Company</TITLE>
</HEAD>
<BODY> <!--Main content starts here-->
Welcome to the web site of the <B>B2C Company</B>
</BODY>
</HTML>
``` | Welcome to the web site of the **B2C Company** |

Script

Program instructions within a web page used to control the appearance of the page or provide additional facilities.

Java

Java is a derivative of the C++ programming language and can be used to create small applications that run when users display a WWW page or activate a control shown on the screen.

HTML (hypertext markup language)

HTML is the method used to create web pages and documents. The HTML code used to construct pages has codes or tags such as <TITLE> to indicate to the browser what is displayed.
```

Extensible markup language (XML)

Since 1999 a great deal of attention has been paid to the use of the extensible markup language (XML) for business applications. Both HTML and XML share SGML (standard generalised markup language) as a common ancestor. However, whilst HTML is used primarily for the creation of WWW pages, XML is intended to serve a wider variety of applications. In simple terms, XML is a data description language that allows documents to store any kind of information. The 'extensible' part of XML refers to an ability to create new language elements (or whole new languages) using standard XML elements. An XML document created using one application can be used with other programs without the need to convert it or process it in any other way.

The nature of XML means that it is ideal for applications that require information to be shared between business organisations. For example, many organisations have already adopted XML as a core element of their EDI systems. Since XML documents are easily transferred between operating systems and applications software, XML lends itself to applications that include web portals, e-commerce, e-procurement, m-commerce, mobile Internet, groupwork and database development. A Forrester Research survey of B2B companies (Yates et al., 2000) showed that over half were already using unspecified XML, with 20% using industry-specific XML standards; 49% still used EDI, but this was expected to fall to 4% within two years.

Some of the advantages of XML include the following:

- XML is supported by a wide range of existing applications. All modern web browsers, for example, support XML. This means that XML documents can be created and distributed without the need to purchase or install additional software.

- A large number of development packages already feature support for XML. Such packages range from conventional programming languages, such as Visual Basic, to web authoring software, such as Front Page.

- XML is extremely flexible. If a feature does not exist, it can be created and added to the 'core' language. This enables XML to be used for an extremely wide range of purposes, from controlling the content of a web page to sophisticated database applications.

- XML can be used across a wide range of technologies. In terms of information technology, XML can be used across different processors and operating systems with little difficulty. This means, for example, that the same basic material can be used on Windows computers, UNIX systems and even WAP mobile phones.

- Since XML allows extremely flexible data structures to be created, it can be used to work with any existing legacy data owned by an organisation.

- XML is considered simpler to use than alternatives such as SGML.

- XML files are often compatible with many existing applications that are based on SGML (although the reverse is not necessarily true).

Many large organisations have already begun to adopt applications that use XML as a medium for storing and transmitting data. Furthermore, as organisations move towards distributed computing, using the Internet to enable communications, we are likely to see an even greater emphasis placed on the use of XML. As an example, much of Microsoft's strategy for the next five years is based around the development of applications that make use of XML. Clearly, as the world's largest supplier of productivity software, operating systems and programming languages, Microsoft's initiative will have a profound effect on the software industry and on business organisations in general.

▶

Example XML for Online Marketplace catalogue

This example is taken from the Commerce One (www.commerceone.net) xCBL 3.0 standard for publishing catalogue data. It can be seen that specific tags are used to identify:

- product ID
- manufacturer
- long and short description
- attributes of product and associated picture.

There is no pricing information in this example.

```
<CatalogData>
<Product>
<Action Value='Delete'/>
<ProductID>118003-008</ProductID>
</Product>
<Product Type='Good' SchemaCategoryRef='C43171801'>
<ProductID>140141-002</ProductID>
<UOM><UOMCoded>EA</UOMCoded></UOM>
<Manufacturer>Compaq</Manufacturer>
<LeadTime>2</LeadTime>
<CountryOfOrigin>
<Country><CountryCoded>US</CountryCoded></Country>
</CountryOfOrigin>
<ShortDescription xml:lang='en'>Armada M700 PIII 500
12GB</ShortDescription>
<LongDescription xml:lang='en'>
This light, thin powerhouse delivers no-compromise performance in a sub-five pound form
factor. Size and Weight(HxWxD): 12.4 X 9.8 X 1.1 in 4.3 - 4.9 lbs (depending on
configuration) Processor: 500-MHZ Intel Pentium III Processor with 256K integrated
cache Memory: 128MB of RAM, expandable to 576MB Hard Drive: 12.0GB Removable
SMART Hard Drive Display Graphics: 14.1-inch color TFT with 1024 x 768 resolution
(up to 16M colors internal) Communication: Mini-PCI V.90 Modem/Nic Combo Operating
System: Dual Installation of Microsoft Windows 95 &amp; Microsoft Windows 98
</LongDescription>
<ProductAttachment>
<AttachmentURL>file:\5931.jpg</AttachmentURL>
<AttachmentPurpose>PicName</AttachmentPurpose>
<AttachmentMIMEType>jpg</AttachmentMIMEType>
</ProductAttachment>
<ObjectAttribute>
<AttributeID> Processor Speed</AttributeID>
<AttributeValue>500MHZ</AttributeValue>
</ObjectAttribute>
<ObjectAttribute>
<AttributeID>Battery Life</AttributeID>
<AttributeValue>6 hours</AttributeValue>
</ObjectAttribute>
</Product>
```

Source: www.commerceone.com/download/xCBL3ForContent.pdf

Activity 4.5

Using the simple web-page design tools included with packages such as Internet Explorer and Netscape Navigator, produce a simple web page containing your c.v. If possible, make use of colour, different typefaces, graphics, horizontal lines, bullet points and other features. When you have created the page, save it and then view it from within the web browser. View the source for the web page so that you can see how the design of your page has been translated into HTML.

Focus on finding information on the Internet

▶ Purpose

Many new users of the Internet are discouraged when they first use it, since, although it appears useful, it often proves difficult to find relevant information. There are several billion web pages containing information, so it is natural that useful information will be difficult to find, but there are techniques to make it easier. In this focus section we present a tutorial in which we review a number of methods for locating particular web pages and describe approaches that use criteria to locate the information you need.

Information can be found on the World Wide Web in four main ways:

- typing in the web address of a known page (URL);
- search engines such as Google, Altavista or Hotbot;
- directories (or web catalogues/indexes) such as Yahoo;
- web guides (a relatively new concept from US, including www.about.com and www.4anything.com);
- 'surfing'.

Note that both search engines and directory services are now available at single-gateway sites known as **portals**.

To learn about the different types of search engines go to www.searchengine watch.com.

We will look at each of these techniques in turn.

Portal

Sites which provide the main method of access to other web sites through providing services to locate information on the WWW are now commonly referred to as portals. Such portals are often set to the default or home page of the user's web browser. Examples of portals include Yahoo (www.yahoo.com), Microsoft's MSN (www.msn.com) and the Netscape Netcenter (home.netscape.com).

▶ Web 'addresses' or URLs (universal resource locators)

The preferred method of reaching a web site is by typing the web address or URL directly into the web browser (if you know it!). While it may be obvious for a company such as IBM (www.ibm.com), it is less obvious for a company with a longer name such as 'The Alliance and Leicester Building Society' (www.allianceandleicester.co.uk).

Web addresses must start with 'http://' as given below, and any '.' or '/' must be in the correct position.

Tip
You don't need to type the http:// prefix in modern browsers.

Starting the web browser

Using the Windows Start menu choose Internet Explorer, Netscape Communicator or Navigator. Type in the web address such as www.bt.com into the *address* (Internet Explorer) or *location* (Netscape Navigator) box (after double clicking on it to highlight the existing text).

Web addresses | **Activity 4.6**

Try the following:

- www.telegraph.co.uk
- www.bbc.co.uk (for this try menu option File, Open or Ctrl O)
- www.altavista.com

▶ Search engines

Search engines provide an index of all words stored on the World Wide Web. Keywords typed in by the end-user are matched against the index and the user is given a list of all corresponding web pages containing the keywords. By clicking on a hyperlink the user is taken to the relevant web page.

This example uses 'Google', one of the most common search engines. Imagine you wanted to find out information on holidays available in Spain. You could start by typing in a general word such as 'holiday'. The problem with a non-specific search is that there is such a large volume of information on the web. This search would return references to over a million web pages. To use the web efficiently it is necessary to know the syntax provided by search engines to narrow down the search. For example, +'holiday inn' +'Costa del Sol' returns fewer pages, since we have indicated through the '+' symbol that both phrases must be present and, by enclosing in quotes, that the words must appear in the order shown.

Information on the main search engines or portals and how they work is provided by www.searchenginewatch.com. Searchenginewatch lists the main portals as:

AOL Search	Uses Open Directory and Inktomi	search.aol.com
AltaVista	One of the largest SEs plus Open Directory	www.altavista.com
Ask Jeeves	Database matches previous questions, plus metasearch	www.askjeeves.com
Direct Hit	A 'popularity engine' based on clicks on previous searches	www.directhit.com
Excite	Popular medium-sized index	www.excite.com
FAST Search	Norwegian company aiming to index the entire web	www.alltheweb.com
Go / Infoseek	Disney's portal. Infoseek SE plus searcher-produced directory	www.go.com
GoTo	Companies pay to be listed higher	www.goto.com
Google	Uses link referral (site-to-site) popularity to rate sites	www.google.com
HotBot	Combination of Direct Hit and Inktomi, rates well in tests	www.hotbot.com
IWon	Inktomi-based directory and SE offering prizes	www.iwon.com
Inktomi	Used as a basis for other SEs, e.g. Hotbot: can't access direct	www.inktomi.com
LookSmart	Human-compiled directory	www.looksmart.com
Lycos	Combination of Direct Hit and Open Directory, own Hotbot.	www.lycos.com
MSN Search	Combination of LookSmart, Altavista Direct Hit, RealNames	search.msn.com
Netscape Search	Open Directory and Netscape and Google SE	search.netscape.com
Northern Light	One of largest indexes, including 'the invisible web'	www.northernlight.com
Open Directory	Uses volunteer editors – widely used by other sites	www.dmoz.org
RealNames	Matches to established names paid for by companies	www.realnames.com
Snap	A challenger to Yahoo! and Looksmart owned by Cnet/NBC	www.snap.com
WebCrawler	Small index	www.webcrawler.com
Yahoo!	1 million-site directory supplemented by Inktomi search	www.yahoo.com

You may find it easier to use meta-search engines than submit your search phrase to several search engines. Examples include Mamma (www.mamma.com) and Meta Fetcher (www.metafetcher.com) or Ask Jeeves (www.askjeeves.co.uk). Also check the UK- and Europe-specific search engines at Searchenginewatch.

Tips (Google syntax)

- Use several words (or synonyms) to narrow down the search: London Fire
- Use quotes to define a phrase: 'Fire of London'
- Use + and – to include or exclude words: +'Fire of London' +1666 -Wren

Search engine

This example uses Google, one of the most effective search engines for studying. Imagine you wanted to find out information on car insurance.

Tip: Use several keywords

You could start by typing in a general word such as 'insurance'. The problem with a non-specific search is that there is such a large volume of information on the web. The search above would return references to several million web pages.

Tip: Use quotes to define a phrase

To narrow down a search it is best to use several key words. In this example you could type 'car insurance' for the UK or 'auto insurance' for the USA. Google works better than most browsers in this area since its advanced search gives options for all of the words, any of the words or the exact phrase.

Tip: Get to know the advanced search syntax of your preferred search engine

To use the web efficiently it is necessary to know the syntax provided by search engines to narrow down the search. For example, if we were looking for special discounts on car insurance for women drivers from a UK-based insurer we could type +'car insurance' +'ladies' + domain:uk. This returns fewer pages (see example below), since we have indicated through the '+' symbol that both phrases must be present and through enclosing in quotes that the words must appear in the order shown. Domain:uk indicates that we are only interested in sites based in the UK. '-' can be used before a keyword to exclude this keyword from a search.

If you typed in these keywords into Google.com: +'car insurance' + 'ladies' + site:.uk, you would receive this type of information:

> **Searched the web for + 'car insurance' + ladies + site:.uk**
>
> Result 1–10 of about 7,690.
>
> **A list of top 10 links then follows.**

To experiment with the syntax, see how many words are returned by Google for each of the following:

- 'car insurance'
- car insurance
- car insurance ladies
- 'car insurance ladies'

MINI CASE STUDY

Google increases relevance of search by using PageRank technique

The most effective search engines for users changes through time as methods for indexing and retrieving pages are improved. Searchenginewatch (www.searchenginewatch com) is an independent site that collects reviews of the merits of different search engines and summarises data on their popularity. Published data indicate that Altavista has declined in importance while Yahoo! (www.yahoo.com) and Microsoft Network (www.msn.com) are dominant at the time of writing. Google (www.google.com) is, however, rapidly increasing in popularity due to a reputation for achieving good-quality matches for keywords entered by the user. Google uses an inovative technique referred to as PageRank. Essentially a site that has more links to it from other sites is considered more relevant than a site that has fewer links. Each link effectively acts as a vote for that site, with greater weighting for popular sites that have many links to them. In addition, Google uses standard techniques such as ranking the pages presented to the user based on the frequency with which the search keywords occur in the text, how near they are to the top of the document, and whether they appear in titles, headings or meta tags (hidden keywords inserted in the web page for the purpose of search engines).

Given the importance of search engines as a tool for finding information on the World Wide Web, it is vital for marketers to ensure their sites are listed as highly as possible for relevant keywords. Specialist search engine optimisation companies are available to help achieve this.

▶ Web catalogues or directories

Web directories provide a structured listing of web sites. They are grouped according to categories such as business, entertainment or sport. Each category is then subdivided further, for example into football, rugby, swimming, etc. It can be confusing because directories are now included with what are thought of as search engines such as Yahoo! and Hotbot.

Web catalogues such as www.yahoo.com work differently from search engines in that they have a hierarchy of information stored under different categories. For example, to find a UK travel agent specialising in cheap flights you would move down the hierarchy to select:

Regional:Countries:United Kingdom:
Business:Companies:Travel:Agents:Direct

This would then lead you to the site of www.cheapflights.co.uk. 'The best source for bargain air tickets from the United Kingdom.'

Tips: Yahoo
- Use www.yahoo.co.uk site for speed.
- Restrict choices by selecting 'UK only'.
- Use categories rather than search facilities.

▶ Web guides

These are a relatively new concept and can be considered to be an extension of directories. They consist of structured information about a particular topic providing articles,

Web catalogues

1 Type in the name of a pop group or football team or other interest and search through the catalogue for it.

2 Now find this position in the hierarchy starting at the top. For example Regional:Countries:United Kingdom:Recreation and Sport:Sport:Football:FA Carling Premiership:Clubs:Arsenal FC

3 Or try this one to see which newspapers are online: /Regional/Countries/United_Kingdom/News_and_Media/:Newspapers

definitions, links and news about a particular topic, for example e-commerce, procurement, marketing or human resources management. They have the benefit that they are edited by a human who will create a structure and rate information so that only relevant material is included.

The two main web guides are www.about.com and www.4anything.com. They are US-oriented, but are a useful supplementary resource for researching a topic. Try using them to help with your next assignment! For now, go to www.about.com and visit marketing.about.com by typing the keyword marketing and then going to this category site.

▶ Navigating or 'surfing'

Try all of these methods:

1 Click on blue, underlined <u>'hyperlinks'</u> to move from one page to the next.

2 Use **Back** or **Forward** buttons to move between pages visited already (a right mouse click gives these options, or pressing the ALT key plus the left or right arrow key also does this).

3 Use **Go** menu to move to previous choices.

4 Use **Go**, **Open History Folder** (Internet Explorer), **Communicator**, **History** (Netscape Navigator) to move to previous choices.

5 In Internet Explorer use **Favorites**, **Add To Favorites** (Internet Explorer), **Communicator**, **Bookmark**, **Add Bookmarks** (Netscape Navigator) to retain a page for revisiting later. These are personal bookmarks retained on the hard disk.

6 Use **Edit**, **Find** to search for a word in the page that is currently loaded.

▶ Other techniques of finding information

At this point, we can turn to look at a range of software applications that have started to have an impact on the use of the Internet by organisations. Although it is not possible to deal with all of the applications currently available, the following material demonstrates some of the significant developments that have taken place recently.

Three areas have been selected in order to highlight some of the user applications that are likely to see rapid growth over the next few years. These are the use of meta-search tools, offline readers and intelligent agents.

Meta-search tools

Most readers will be familiar with special WWW pages that allow a search engine to be accessed by a web browser. Traditional search engines work are sometimes considered to be inefficient since they work with a single catalogue of data. Since many catalogues only represent a relatively small proportion of the pages available via the Internet, a traditional search tool will often fail to return any results. Furthermore, many search engines are prone to returning irrelevant or no-longer-current data.

A meta-search engine, such as Ask Jeeves (http://www.askjeeves.com), performs searches across a number of individual search engines. The results of these searches are collated and processed further to remove duplicate items. As a consequence, the list of results returned to the user is often more comprehensive and up-to-date. However, although meta-search engines are undoubtedly useful, users often face further difficulty in locating the information they need, for example a link to a page may no longer be current, or too many results may have been returned.

In order to provide more flexibility and control over the process of searching the Internet, a number of specialised search tools have begun to appear. These meta-search programs combine the ability to search a number of traditional search engines simultaneously with a variety of relatively sophisticated analytical tools. Some of the features offered by a typical meta-search program include:

- Hyperlinks can be validated so that no time is wasted in attempting to load pages or access web sites that no longer exist.
- Searches can be saved (with or without any results that were previously returned).
- Searches can be scheduled so that they are carried out automatically at any time chosen by the user.
- Users can select a group of search engines to work with. Some programs group search engines into a number of categories, such as news, financial information and so on.
- The depth of a search can be specified by the user. 'Depth' refers to the number of results that should be returned by a given search engine.
- Users can specify the type of search to be performed. For example, it is possible to use sophisticated search criteria such as the NEAR operator.
- The results of a search can be sorted into different orders, according to factors such as relevance, the date of each page, and so on. Results can also be filtered to remove unwanted items.
- The results of a search cother applications.
- The pages located by a search can be downloaded automatically, saving the users the effort of having to handle each page manually.

A good example of a meta-search program is Copernic (http://www.copernic.com). The package allows users to work with more than 90 categories of search engines, providing access to a total of more than 1000 individual search engines.

In general, meta-search programs offer two significant benefits: they allow information drawn from a wide variety of sources to be combined into a single, coherent whole, and they reduce the time needed to locate important information. These attributes mean that meta-search programs can be of great value in areas such as business intelligence and data mining. It is also worth pointing out that the techniques employed by meta-search programs can be integrated into an organisation's web site or intranet. This allows the benefits of such tools to be extended beyond the company to customers and suppliers.

Offline readers

An important development in terms of software for the Internet has been the growth in popularity of offline readers (sometimes called 'offline browsers'). An offline reader allows a single page, a group of pages, or an entire web site to be copied to the user's hard disk drive. Pages are saved complete with graphics, animations, scripts and any other relevant data. Where possible, the links on the pages downloaded are converted so that they relate to the pages stored on the hard disk drive. The user can browse the downloaded data as if they were looking at the original web site. Whilst web browsers provide a rudimentary offline browsing facility, the facilities offered by dedicated offline readers open up a range of possibilities.

For most organisations, an offline browser can be of great use in gathering business intelligence. As an example, the offline browser can be made to download an entire set of web sites at regular intervals. This would be useful, for example, for monitoring a competitor's web site(s) in order to keep track of the competitor's actions. The same approach can be used to monitor groups of sites related to industry news services, suppliers and other agencies.

Many offline readers provide the ability to monitor changes to a web site over time. Each time the web site is downloaded, the program checks to see if a given page already exists. If the page already exists, and it has not been modified, it will not be stored. Organisations can use this facility in order to build up a historical view of a given competitor or market sector. As an example, this feature might be used to track financial information, with a view to conducting further analysis in order to identify any trends or patterns.

Whilst the ability to monitor web sites over a period of time allows for a crude form of data mining, some sophisticated offline readers are now starting to incorporate more powerful data mining tools. The main aim of these tools is to simplify the process of finding and extracting important information from what may amount to thousands of individual files. Offline Explorer by MetaProducts (http://www.metaproducts.com) is a good example of a powerful offline reader that incorporates the ability to carry out simple data mining through the use of a third-party analysis tool.

Intelligent agents

Although a great deal has been written about the use of intelligent **agents**, we must regard this area of software development as being still in its infancy. An intelligent agent is a semi-autonomous computer program capable of carrying out one or more tasks specified by the user. In general, an intelligent agent can be thought of as a software 'robot'. The robot is instructed to carry out a task and then left to its own devices. When the task has been completed, the robot presents the results to the user. Two factors set intelligent agents apart from other software applications such as meta-search tools:

Agent
The term agent is used to describe a specialised program that automatically searches the Internet for information meeting a user's requirements.

- they can be programmed to carry out a wide variety of tasks;
- intelligent agents have a limited ability to deal with difficult situations or unexpected problems.

At present, there are few commercial packages available that offer the power and sophistication one would expect of this kind of tool. Of the packages available, a common criticism is that they are little more than Internet-enabled programming languages. However, given the potential benefits of intelligent agents, we can expect to see significant progress made within the next five years.

There are numerous applications for which intelligent agents might be used. Some examples include:

- An agent can be programmed to access news services around the world and locate stories of interest to a specific user.
- An agent can be programmed to search for a specific product and return details of companies that can meet the customer's specific requirements in terms of price, payment options, delivery times and so on.
- An agent can be programmed to search the Internet for every occurrence of a competitor's name. Sophisticated rules can be used to place information in order of importance and the agent can be made to ignore repeated, redundant or unimportant information.

NetStepper is a good example of intelligent agent software for the Internet. The company describes the package as allowing users to treat the Internet as a personalised database. Simple agents can be created to carry out tasks that include downloading files, accessing web pages, converting data and sending e-mail.

Activity 4.9

Different software types

To check your knowledge of the different types of software introduced in this chapter, match the descriptions of software above with the specific types of software below.

Software descriptions

1 Allows you to create and edit company reports.
2 Finds information for an assignment from the World Wide Web.
3 The use of icons, bars, buttons and other image displays to get things done.
4 Sends information to a computer user in another country.
5 Creates and displays a worksheet for analysis.
6 Manages and supports the maintenance and retrieval of structured data.
7 Manages and supports telecommunications on a network of computers.
8 Detects and removes viruses.
9 A program or set of programs that controls the computer hardware.

Software types

(a) Spreadsheet; **(b)** graphical user interface (GUI); **(c)** operating system; **(d)** a search engine such as Google accessed through a web browser; **(e)** Norton Anti-Virus Kit; **(f)** word processor; **(g)** e-mail package; **(h)** Novell Netware (a network operating system); **(i)** relational database management system (RDBMS)

Summary

1 Software can be defined as a series of detailed instructions that control the operation of a computer system. There are two major categories of software: systems software and applications software.

2 Systems software manages and controls the operation of the computer system as it performs tasks on behalf of the user. Operating systems interact with the hardware of the computer at a very low level in order to manage and direct the computer's resources.

3 Applications software can be defined as a set of programs that enable users to perform specific information processing activities. Applications software can be divided into two broad categories: general purpose productivity software and application-specific.

4 Productivity software describes general-purpose applications that aim to support users in performing a variety of common tasks. In business organisations, productivity software is often used to reduce the time needed to complete routine administrative tasks, such as producing documents or organising meetings. Computer-based information systems used in this way are generally referred to as 'office automation systems'.

5 The three main types of productivity software are:

- A word processor provides the ability to enter, edit, store and print text. In addition, word-processing packages allow users to alter the layout of documents and often provide a variety of formatting tools.
- Spreadsheet programs are designed to store and manipulate values, numbers and text in an efficient and useful way.
- The data in a database are organised by fields and records. A field is a single item of information, such as a name or a quantity. A record is a collection of related fields. A database can be defined as a collection of related information. The information held in an electronic database is accessed via a database management system (DBMS). A DBMS can be defined as one or more computer programs that allow users to enter, store, organise, manipulate and retrieve data from a database. A relational database can consist of numerous record designs – tables – and can combine information drawn from several tables. A key field can be used to identify individual records within an electronic database or to create relationships between different tables.

6 The Internet provides a variety of opportunities for organisations to carry out business activities. These include competitor research, product research, customer support, advertising and promotion, and e-commerce. The World Wide Web (WWW) is a part of the Internet that can be accessed using a web browser. A web browser provides the means to search for and retrieve information quickly and easily.

7 E-mail (electronic mail) can be defined as the transmission of a message over a communications network. Messages can be entered via the keyboard or taken from files stored on disk. E-mail programs provide the ability to create, edit, organise, transmit and receive e-mail messages.

8 Office automation systems consist of five basic categories: electronic publishing systems, electronic communications systems, electronic meeting systems, image processing systems and office management systems.

9 Management applications consist of personal information managers (PIMs), project management software, contact managers and groupware applications.

EXERCISES

Self-assessment exercises

1 Produce your own definitions of the following terms:
  (a) software
  (b) operating system
  (c) graphical user interface
  (d) productivity software
  (e) personal information manager.

2 Describe the five basic categories of office automation systems.

3 What is data mining and how can it bring benefits to a business organisation?

4 In an electronic database, what are the differences between queries and filters?

5 Describe the different approaches to file processing. What are the major characteristics, advantages and disadvantages of each?

Discussion questions

1 In recent years the developers of encryption programs have been placed under pressure to provide government agencies with a means of decrypting messages sent by e-mail. It has been

argued that such facilities are essential in order to combat terrorism and organised crime. However, civil liberties organisations feel that government agencies may abuse their power and begin to monitor e-mail traffic on a massive scale. Prepare a case for one side of this argument.

2 A wide range of factors should be considered before purchasing applications software. Construct a list of selection criteria and place these in order of importance. Justify each item on the list.

3 Why do you think XML is considered to be of great importance to business organisations?

Essay questions

1 Select two competing software packages as the basis for a detailed comparison. Produce a report that addresses the following tasks:
   (a) Using relevant examples, describe the major features of each package.
   (b) Considering the range of features offered by each package, indicate how these might be of benefit to a business organisation.
   (c) Which package would be more likely to meet the needs of a business organisation? Provide a detailed rationale for your choice.

2 Conduct any required research and produce a report that addresses the following tasks:
   (a) Provide an overview of how organisations can conduct business transactions over the Internet.
   (b) Discuss the advantages and disadvantages of using the Internet as a business tool.
   (c) Issues related to security are of great concern to many organisations. Discuss the major security problems faced by organisations conducting business over the Internet.

3 As a student, you are required to produce essays and reports containing graphics, diagrams and charts. You may also be required to take part in seminars and presentations. As your course progresses you are likely to recognise a need to store information obtained through research. Produce a report that addresses the following areas:
   (a) Considering the tasks described above, identify a range of applications software that can be used to support your studies.
   (b) Discuss the ways in which the applications you have identified can help to improve your studies or enhance the quality of your work.
   (c) Identify and discuss any other ways in which the applications identified may be of benefit.

4 Discuss the use of specialised software for the Internet in terms of its value to business organisations. Refer to applications such as meta-search engines and intelligent agents in your response.

Examination questions

1 Interest in commercial uses for the Internet has grown rapidly over the past five years. You are required to carry out the following tasks:
   (a) Using relevant examples, describe the range of business applications to which the Internet can be applied.
   (b) Using relevant examples, discuss the costs, technical problems and organisational issues associated with making use of the Internet as a business tool.
   (c) Using relevant examples, discuss the potential benefits to an organisation of using the World Wide Web as a business tool.

2 You have been approached for advice by the manager of a small company. The manager wishes to purchase a number of software packages in order to improve the productivity of staff. Prepare a guide that can be used by the manager when selecting appropriate applications.

3 Groupware improves productivity, enhances communication and reduces costs. Using relevant examples, provide a balanced discussion of this statement.

References

Curtis, G. (2002) *Business Information Systems: Analysis, Design and Practice*, 4th edition, Pearson Education, Harlow

Yates, S., Rutstein, C. and Voce, C. (2000) *Demystifying B2B Integration*, Forrester Research Report, September

ZdNet (2000) www.zdnet.co.uk/itweek/specials/2000/ecommerce2

Further reading

Kennedy, A. (2000) *The Internet. The Rough Guide*, Rough Guides, London. An accessible guide to using the web and e-mail

Rolland, C., Feng, M. and Chen, Y. (eds) (1998) *Information Systems in the WWW Environment*, Chapman and Hall, London. A collection of materials that deals with areas related to the Internet, such as collaborative working, e-commerce and searching for information

Web links

www.irt.org Articles on web-related technology, such as CGI, PHP, SSI, etc.

www.tutorialfind.com/tutorials Access to a wide range of tutorials on a wide range of subjects including hardware, operating systems, programming and web development.

www.pcwebopaedia.com An online encyclopaedia of computer-related acronyms and terms. Each entry is accompanied by a concise explanation and additional web links.

www.hotfiles.com ZDNet provides access to a large library of software including shareware, freeware and commercial (demonstration) packages.

www.comspec.com/ctlg Online directory of hardware and software catalogues. Allows users to search by company name or product.

sunsite.ust.hk/homepage/vendors.html Online directory of hardware and software companies. Offers links directly to the web site of each company.

www.microsoft.com Microsoft are the world's largest software company. Use this site to locate information on products such as Windows (all versions), MS Office, Internet Explorer and Visual Basic.

www.lotus.com Lotus Corporation is the publisher of Lotus 1-2-3 (spreadsheet), Organizer and SmartSuite, an integrated suite of business applications.

www.corel.com Corel are well known for Corel Draw, a sophisticated art package. In addition, the company markets Corel Office, an integrated suite of business applications.

www.ca.com Computer Associates is one of the largest software publishers in the world. They publish a wide range of business applications, including project planning software, database applications and applications generators.

www.seagatesoftware.com/homepage Seagate markets both hardware and software. With regard to software, Seagate publishes a range of data analysis products, including Crystal Reports.

Networks, telecommunications and the Internet

LEARNING OBJECTIVES

After reading this chapter, readers will be able to:

● specify which components of a communications system are necessary to exchange information within and between businesses;

● explain the basic components and terminology of networks, including the Internet;

● identify the benefits available through the introduction of computer networks;

● identify the advantages and disadvantages of the client/server architecture in comparison with traditional approaches;

● explain the broad implications of the Internet on the marketplace.

MANAGEMENT ISSUES

As organisations become increasingly dependent on networking technologies, managers need to be aware of the business benefits of deploying and updating networks and the risks if they are mismanaged. A basic grasp of the terminology is required for discussing networks with solution providers. From a managerial perspective, this chapter addresses the following questions:

● What are the business benefits of networks?

● What are the basic concepts and terminology associated with the Internet and other networks?

● How does the Internet change marketplace structures?

● How are network components selected?

Links to other chapters

The chapter focuses on the physical components of networks and how they can be structured.

Chapter 1   describes the qualities of the business information shared and transported via networks.

Chapter 3   covers software for network management including network operating systems, and also software that makes use of networks such as groupware and e-mail.

Chapter 6   reviews business applications of Internet-based networks.

Chapter 14   examines the strategic management of Internet-based networks.

Introduction

For the modern business to operate effectively, the links connecting its people and their computers are vital. The network links provide the channels for information to flow continuously between people working in different departments of an organisation, or in different organisations. This allows people to collaborate much more efficiently than before the advent of networks when information flow was irregular and unreliable. These links also allow hardware such as printers and faxes to be shared more cost-effectively.

As with many aspects of technology, jargon is rife when describing the different parts of and types of network. As an example of the many three-letter acronyms (TLAs), networks of different scales are referred to as LAN, WAN, VAN, VPN and PBX! Here, we will try to filter out the jargon to highlight the terms you need to know when understanding and specifying information systems for a business.

In this chapter, we trace the use of computer networks from the global network of the Internet through to small-scale networks. We look at the components that form a network and how to specify a suitable architecture for the modern business.

Introduction to computer networks

◗ What are computer networks?

We can describe the links that transfer information between different parts of an information system on different scales. At the smallest scale, links are etched in silicon between the different components of a microchip. At a larger scale, all the components of a PC, such as the hard disk, CD-ROM and main processor, are connected by internal cables. In this chapter, we consider links at a larger scale still, that is, between computers and other hardware devices such as printers, scanners and separate storage devices. These links between computers and other hardware form a computer network.

A **computer network** can be defined as: 'a communications system that links two or more computers and peripheral devices and enables transfer of data between the components'.

As we shall see, computer networks are themselves constructed on different scales. Small-scale networks within a workgroup or single office are known as **local-area networks (LANs)**. Larger-scale networks which are national or international are known as **wide-area networks (WANs)**. The Internet is the best known example of a wide area network.

Computer network

A computer network can be defined as a communication system that links two or more computers and peripheral devices and enables transfer of data between the components.

Local-area network (LAN)

A computer network that spans a limited geographic area, typically a single office or building.

Wide-area network (WAN)

Networks covering a large area which connect businesses in different parts of the same city, different parts of a country or different countries.

❱ Telecommunications

On a national or global scale, communications technology such as satellite and microwave transmissions are important in linking businesses. To transfer information electronically, companies create **telecommunications** systems. These systems consist of both the hardware and the software necessary to set up these links. Telecommunications enable a business that operates from different locations to run as a single unit. This means that the same information and control structures do not need to be repeated at each company office. Instead, information can be managed centrally and control maintained from a central location. As well as improving internal communications in a company, telecommunications also allow companies to collaborate using electronic data interchange or web-based e-procurement with partners such as suppliers. Similarly, customers can transact with the company using the Internet.

Telecommunications
The method by which data and information are transmitted between different locations.

❱ What are the business benefits of networks?

Networks are vital to a business. They are important for the cost savings and improved communications that arise from an internal network. Beyond this, they are truly vital, because they help a business reach out and connect with its customers, suppliers and collaborators. Through doing this a company can order new raw materials more rapidly and cheaply from its suppliers and can keep in touch with the needs of its customers.

Figure 5.1 indicates the links that may exist between different partners. In some industries, such as the travel industry, travel agents and suppliers (such as the airlines) have made use of telecommunications links for over 20 years. In other sectors, however, most communications have been over the phone or in person, until more recently. The potential for e-business has been made by possible by the use of the Internet technologies explained in later sections to reduce the cost and complexity of linking companies.

When computers and telecommunications are integrated, they can provide many advantages. Take the simple example of a humble e-mail sent to a customer or colleague. This costs only a few pence and can be sent to any location in the world immediately. As well as the low cost and fast delivery, it can be integrated to work with the users' other information needs, perhaps by supplying a spreadsheet as an attachment.

We will now look at the benefits that networks provide in more detail.

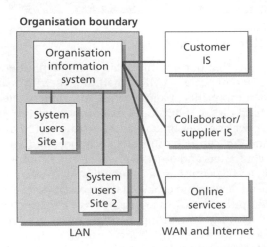

Figure 5.1 **Communications links between different stakeholders in an industry**

1 *Reduces cost compared to traditional communications.* Costs can be reduced in various ways depending on the type of communication required. If information has to be sent to another location, the cost of sending is very low compared to using a letter or even a fax. If face-to-face communication is needed to exchange information or solve a problem, then the traditional approach would be to jump into a car or on to a plane. Telecommunications now make this less necessary. Meetings can be conducted by conferencing, which not only includes video conferencing, but also sharing ideas through writing on whiteboards or running shared software. Money is saved on transport and accommodation but, perhaps more significantly, the time it takes for people to travel to the meeting is also saved.

2 *Reduces time for information transfer.* The benefits of shorter times for messages to arrive are obvious, but more subtle benefits can also occur through the rapid transfer of information. It is now possible for the global company to operate 24 hours a day by taking advantage of people working in different time zones. If someone is working on a product design in New Zealand, for example, they can dispatch it for review in Europe at the end of their working day. The review can then be conducted in Europe while the other team members are asleep and will be ready for review the next morning. Using this simple method product designs could be accelerated significantly. Customer service queries can also be turned around more quickly through the use of telecommunications.

3 *Enables sharing and dissemination of company information.* Opportunities to share information are lost when it is locked in a filing cabinet or stored on an individual's PC. By placing information on a server, either as a file or within a database, it can be made accessible to all departments that need it and the flow of information in the company is improved. This has proved to be one of the big benefits of intranets. A company selling through agents worldwide can provide information such as prices or technical specifications over an intranet. This information is always up to date, as there is no delay while price lists are reproduced and transported to the agents. Of course, this approach also helps in reducing costs. Intranets are described in detail in Chapter 17.

4 *Enables sharing of hardware resources such as printers, backup, processing power.* An obvious benefit of setting up a network is that it enables the cost of equipment such as printers, faxes, modems or scanners to be shared between members of a workgroup. Printers are the most obvious item that can be shared within a business. Workgroup printers may be shared between small teams of three or four or up to twenty or so people, but a more powerful printer would be required in the latter case. For a printer shared by many people, it is usual to use a print server to schedule the jobs and store them while they are pending. Through storing information on a server, the security of the users' data can be increased by attaching a tape or optical backup device to the server and performing regular backups. Other administrative tasks are also made easier by centralising more complex equipment.

5 *Promotes new ways of working.* As well as the tangible benefits, introducing networks can facilitate a different approach to running a business. Setting up an internal network makes it possible to use group-working tools. Setting up a wide area network makes electronic data interchange with suppliers possible.

6 *Operates geographically separate businesses as one.* Through using wide area communications technology, it is possible to rationalise the operations of a company that originally operated as separate business units in different geographic locations, perhaps with their own working practices, procedures and reporting mechanisms. Linked business units can use common ways of working. Sharing of information on best practices can also occur.

Table 5.1 A summary of the key advantages and disadvantages of network technology

Advantages	Disadvantages
1 Lower transaction costs due to less human input	1 Overreliance on networks for mission-critical applications
2 Improved sharing of information and hardware resources	2 Cost of initial setup and administration
3 Reduced costs through sharing hardware and software	3 Disruption during initial setup and maintenance
4 Reduced time for communication compared with traditional methods such as postal mail	4 Reduced security due to more external access points to the network on wide-area networks and the Internet
5 Increased security of data which is backed up on file servers. Increased security through restricting access via user names and passwords	

MINI CASE STUDY

Federal Express turns IS 'inside out' using communications technology

To a global company such as Federal Express, communications are an integral part of the business operation. FedEx was one of the first major companies to make use of the Internet to allow customers to arrange a delivery and then track its progress to its destination (see Fig. 5.2).

To enable progress monitoring and to schedule delivery of a package, FedEx makes use of satellite communications to link its many offices around the world.

These developments demonstrate how FedEx and now many of the other parcel companies have turned their information systems 'inside out' to face their customers. The original system involved FedEx customers phoning a call centre where staff used various IS to assemble an answer and, if necessary, phone back. Now the *customer* operates the new IS and this has cut transaction costs significantly from $25 to 25 cents in round figures. Similarly, United Parcel Services reports that it has saved on 500 000 phone calls per month.

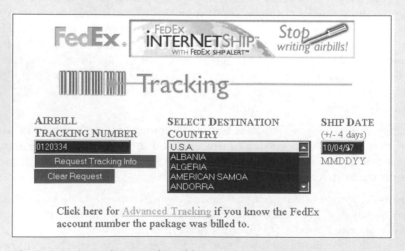

Figure 5.2 The FedEx parcel tracking page

7 *Restructures relationships with partners*. In the same way that different groups or businesses within a company can work more effectively together, different companies can also collaborate better. This may occur, for example, when new products are being designed or when a manufacturer is ordering goods from its suppliers. This is an important issue within e-business applications and is described in Chapter 6.

To balance against the many benefits, there are, of course, disadvantages with introducing networks. The main disadvantages are:

1 The initial setup cost may be high, and there may be a considerable period before the costs are paid off.
2 When implementing or updating the network there may be considerable practical difficulties. Deploying cabling can be very disruptive to staff doing their daily work.
3 In the long term, companies become reliant on networks, and breaks in service can be very disruptive. For this reason investment in network maintenance is vital.
4 Security is reduced through introducing a network, since there are more access points to sensitive data. Data may also be intercepted when it is transferred from one site to another.

Despite these disadvantages, most companies still proceed with implementation and take care to reduce the risks of disruption and security breaches. In doing so, further costs will be introduced. Table 5.1 summarises the advantages and disadvantages of networks.

Network components

In this section we examine how to specify the often confusingly named components that are necessary to set up a network. We start by looking the client/server architecture of the modern information system and why this has been adopted by businesses. We will then examine each of the components in turn and look at how they fit together and the important factors in their selection.

▶ The client/server model of computing

The **client/server** architecture consists of client computers such as PCs sharing resources such as a database stored on more powerful server computers. Processing can be shared between the clients and the servers.

Client/server architecture is significant since most modern networked information systems are based on this structure. The client/server model involves a series of clients, typically desktop PCs, which are the access points for end-user applications. As is shown in Figure 5.3, the clients are connected to a more powerful PC or Unix server computer via a local-area network within one site of a company, or a wide-area network connecting different sites and/or companies. The network is made up of both telecommunications processors to help route the information and the channels and media which carry the information.

The server is a more powerful computer that is usually used to store the application and the data shared by the users. When a user wants to run a program on a PC in a client/server system, the applications, such as a word processor, will usually be stored on the hard disk of the server and then loaded into the memory of the client PC, running or 'executing' on the processor of the client. The document the user creates would be saved back to the hard disk of the server. This is only one alternative. One of the benefits of client/server is that there are many choices for sharing the workload between resources. The system designers can decide to distribute data and processing across both servers and

Client/server
....
The client/server architecture consists of client computers such as PCs sharing resources such as a database stored on more powerful server computers.

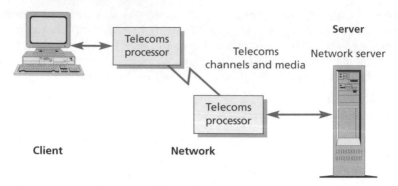

Figure 5.3 **Components of a client/server system**

client computers, as described in Chapter 11. There we also explain how different functions can be partitioned between client and server and the merits of using 'thin' or 'fat' clients, applications on the former being smaller and easier to maintain.

To summarise, the main components of a client/server system are shown in Figure 5.3 and can be defined as follows:

● Client software is the interface by which the end-user accesses the software. It includes both the operating system, such as Windows 95, and the applications software, such as word processors. Increasingly, web-based browsers are being used as clients on a company intranet.
● Server software is used to store information, administer the system and provide links to other company systems. Again, this may be a web server or a database server.
● The application development environment provides interactive programming tools to develop applications through the application programming interface (API) of the package.
● The infrastructure or plumbing of the system. This is based on local- and wide-area networking techniques and consists of the telecommunication processors and media.

Why use client/server?

The adoption of the client/server architecture was part of a trend to 'downsize' from large mainframes with arrays of user terminals which had limited functionality. This latter type of architecture was widespread in businesses during the 1970s and 1980s. The client/server model represented a radically new architecture compared to the traditional, centralised method of a mainframe, with its character-based 'dumb terminals' which dated back nearly to the birth of computers. Rather than all the tasks involved in program execution (other than display) occurring on the mainframe, client/server gives the opportunity for them to be shared between a central server and clients. This gives the potential for faster execution, as processing is distributed across many clients.

Cost savings were originally used to drive the introduction of client/server. PC-based servers were much cheaper than mainframes, although the client PCs were more expensive than dumb terminals. The overall savings were dramatic. These savings were coupled with additional benefits of ease of use of the new clients compared with the older terminals. The clients used new graphical user interfaces which were easier to use thanks to a mouse, and the graphics could improve analysis of business data. Customisation of the client is also possible – the end-user is empowered through being able to develop their own applications and view data to their preference. With queries occurring on the back end, this reduces the amount of network traffic that is required. Centralised control of the user administration and data security and archiving can still be retained.

With these advantages, there are also a host of system management problems which were not envisaged when client/server was first adopted. These have been partly responsible for the reduced costs promised with this 'downsizing' not materialising. To some extent there is now a backlash, in which the new network-centric model is being suggested as a means of reducing these management problems. These disbenefits include:

1 *High cost of ownership.* Although the purchase price for a PC is relatively low, the extra potential for running different applications and modifications by end-users means that there is much more that can go wrong in comparison with a dumb terminal. More support staff are required to solve problems resulting from the complex hardware and software. The annual cost of ownership of a PC is now estimated by the Gartner Group to be $8000, which is about four times the purchase price. The cost of ownership of a dumb (text-based) terminal is approximately $2000. The issue of reducing what is known as the 'total cost of ownership' is considered further in Chapter 15.

2 *Instability.* Client/server technology is often complex and involves integrating different hardware and software components from many different companies. Given this, client/server systems may be less reliable than mainframe systems. EuropCar suffered three days of system downtime in the early 1990s, which was thought to have led to the loss of $300 000 of rental business. This downtime occurred after migration from a mainframe to a client/server system.

3 *Performance.* For some mission-critical applications, a smaller server cannot deliver the power required. In a travel agency business, for example, this will give rise to longer queues and poorer customer service. For this reason, many banks and travel agents have retained their mainframe-based systems where performance is critical. The use of a PC can also cause delays at the client end, as the screen takes a long time to redraw graphics compared to a teletext terminal.

4 *Lack of worker focus.* Although PCs can potentially empower end-users, the freedom of choice can also lead to non-productive time-wasting, as users rearrange the colours and wallpaper on their desktop rather than performing their regular tasks!

Despite these difficulties, the compelling arguments of ease of use and flexibility of client/server still remain. The empowerment of the end-user to develop their own applications and to use and share the data as they see fit is now considered to be the main benefit of client/server.

▶ Servers

Servers are vital to an information system, since they regulate the flow of information around the network in the way that a heart controls the flow of blood around the body. Network servers run the network operating system (NOS), the software that is used to manage the network, and are often used to store large volumes of data. The server and NOS together perform the following functions:

Server
A server is a powerful computer used to control the management of a network. It may have a specific function such as storing user files or a database or managing a printer.

- *Maintain security* – access to information in files is restricted according to the user name and password issued to users of the network.
- *Sharing of peripheral devices* connected to the network, such as printers and tape drives. These are often attached directly to the server.
- *Sharing of applications* such as word processors, which do not then need to be stored on the hard drive of the end-user's computer. The cost of buying applications can be reduced through buying a 'site licence'.
- *Sharing of information* – access to this data is maintained by the NOS and it is stored within the hard drive of a server as files or as part of a database.

Both applications and data can be managed better when they are stored on a managed server. It is easier to audit who uses which applications and to ensure the security of the data. Data quality can also be managed more effectively.

For the larger network of perhaps 20 people or more, the functions described above may be split between several servers to share the load. There may be a separate file server, print server, password server and database server. In very large companies there will be many servers used for data storage. These will all be linked by the network to ensure that the data are accessible by everyone. They will also be responsible for ensuring through a process known as **replication** that the same version of data exists on different servers. With the use of many servers, an opportunity exists to spread the computing workload across these servers rather than overloading a single central machine, which is what happened in the days of the mainframe. The sharing of functions across several computers is known as 'distributed computing'. An example of distributed computing is given in Chapter 19.

The different types of server are summarised in Table 5.2.

Replication

Ensures that the versions of data stored on different servers are consistent. Software is used to check changes made to data on each server. Changes are transmitted to all other servers.

Table 5.2 **Types of server**

Type of server	Purpose
Network	Contains functions to manage the network resources and control user access
File	This term is sometimes used to refer to network server functions. It can also indicate that users' files such as documents and spreadsheets are stored on the network server
Print	Dedicated print servers have a queue of all documents for which print requests have been made, often combined with file or network servers
Fax	Used to route incoming and outgoing faxes received and sent from the user's desktop
Mail	Stores and forwards e-mail messages
Database	Used to store data and provide the software to process data queries supplied by users, often accessed by structured query language (SQL)
Application	Used to store programs such as spreadsheet or bespoke applications run by end-users on their PCs. This removes the need to store each application on every user's hard disk
Communications	Manages connections with other networks in a WAN configuration. Sometimes known as 'gateways' and attached to other gateway devices such as routers and firewall servers.

When creating an information system, there are a number of critical functions which must be designed in to the server. These are important requirements which must be checked with server vendors, database vendors and operating systems vendors. They are:

- *Performance.* The server should be fast enough to handle all the requests from users attached to the network. A margin should be built in to accommodate future growth in users and network traffic. This means specifying a suitable amount of memory (for example, a PC server might need 512 Mb RAM minimum on a PC-based server), a fast hard disk and, less importantly, a fast processor.
- *Capacity.* When initially specified, the hard disk capacity should be large enough that it will not need to be upgraded in the near future.
- *Resilience/fault tolerance.* If there is a problem affecting the hardware, such as a power surge or a problem with the hard disk, it is important that the whole network does not 'crash' because of this. Preventive measures should be taken, such as installing an uninterruptible power supply or running two disks in parallel (disk mirroring or RAID – redundant array of inexpensive disks).

- *Clustering* is used to spread the load across different servers, so improving reliability and performance. It involves linking several servers together via a high-speed link such as fibre-optic cabling. This can enable parallel processing, where tasks are shared between processors, and also storage mirroring, where duplicate copies of data are stored on different servers to improve performance and reduce the risk of one server failing.

Servers can be specified as powerful PCs running an operating system such as Windows NT or Novell Netware, or they can run the UNIX operating system, from companies such as Sun, IBM or Hewlett-Packard.

▶ End-user computers or terminals

The access points for users of a network are known variously as clients, nodes, workstations or, most commonly, plain PCs. It is best to use the term 'client PC', as this helps distinguish clients from servers which may also be PC-based. To work on the network each client must have networking software such as Novell Netware or TCP/IP installed (see later section). Of course, a physical connection to the network is also required. For a PC on an office LAN, this is provided by a *network interface card* in one of the PC's slots. The card is then attached to the network cabling. For a PC at home which is linked to the Internet, the network card is replaced by a modem.

▶ Data communications equipment or telecommunications processors

As well as the physical cables that link the computers, there are also other important components of the complete telecommunications system that have to be purchased by a business. These are the pieces of hardware that are used to link the servers and clients and different networks together. These devices can be thought of as connectors located between client computers and servers. Collectively, these processors can be called telecommunications connectors or gateways, but they are usually referred to by their specific names, such as hubs, multiplexers, bridges and routers. In a company that needs to use gateway devices, a specialist is required to maintain them. Modems and network interface cards also fit into this category.

Modems

The **modem (modulator–demodulator)** is a common feature of many personal computers. A modem allows users to send and receive data via an ordinary telephone line. A modem works by converting data between digital and analogue form. The modem receives **analogue** data transmitted via a telephone line and converts this into **digital** data so that the computer can make use of it. Similarly, the modem converts outgoing digital data into an analogue signal before transmitting it.

The main application for the modem is for **dial-up networking (DUN)** facilities. This allows users to access a network at a **remote location** via a modem. Most home computer users, for example, access the Internet via dial-up networking.

A **fax-modem** combines the capabilities of a modem with the ability to send and receive fax transmissions. Incoming fax messages can be displayed on the screen or sent directly to a printer. Outgoing messages can be composed within a word processor or other package and transmitted automatically. Alternatively, an optical scanner can be used to read in an existing document and convert it into a form suitable for transmission.

Voice modems offer greater flexibility by combining voice, fax and data facilities. At a simple level, a voice modem can be used as a speaker phone or answering machine. However, the more sophisticated applications possible have made **voice–data integration** (sometimes known as computer telephony) extremely popular with business organisations in a very short time. Some examples of common applications include:

Modem (modulator-demodulator)

A modem is a communications device that allows users to ordinary telephone line. See also *Fax-modem*.

Digital

Digital data can only represent a finite number of discrete values. For example, at the most basic level, a computer recognises only the values 0 (zero) and 1. Any values between 0 and 1, for example 0.15, cannot be represented.

Analogue

Analogue data is continuous in that an infinite number of values *between* two given points can be represented. As an example, the hands of a clock are able to represent every single possible time of the day.

Dial-up networking (DUN)

Dial-up networking software allows users to access a network at a remote location via a modem. Most home computer users, for example, access the Internet via dial-up networking.

Remote location

Remote location describes a means of accessing a network from a distant location. A modem and specialised software allows users to send and receive information from home or an office when travelling. A sales representative, for example, might use remote access to review current prices and stock levels before meeting a client.

Fax-modem

A fax-modem combines the capabilities of a modem with the ability to send and receive fax transmissions.

Voice modem

Voice modems offer
greater flexibility than
conventional modems by
combining voice, fax and
data facilities. At a simple
level, a voice modem can
be used as a speaker
phone or answering
machine.

Voice–data integration

Sometimes known as
computer telephony. A
combination of different
communications
technologies that provide
a range of sophisticated
facilities, for example
automated call-switching,
telephone answering
services and fax-on-
demand. See
Fax-on-demand.

Fax-on-demand

A service that allows users
to select from a range of
documents by using the
keys on the telephone
handset. Once a
document has been
selected, the system
automatically telephones
the user's fax machine
and transmits the
document.

Cable modem

These devices allow users
to make use of the fibre-
optic cables that are
installed by cable
television companies.
They offer very high data
transfer rates, up to a
theoretical maximum of
30 Mbps.

Baud

A simple means of
measuring the
performance of a modem
or other device. Early
modems operated at
speeds of 1200 baud, the
equivalent of
approximately 100
characters per second.
Data transmission rates
can also be expressed in
bits per second (bps). In
general, the higher the
baud rate or bps value,
the faster and more
efficient the device.

- Automated call-switching allows the modem to intercept all incoming telephone calls and route them to appropriate locations. A fax, for example, might be stored on the computer's hard disk and also printed automatically so that it is available as soon as the user returns.
- A variation on answering systems is a **fax-on-demand** service which allows users to select from a range of documents by using the keys on the telephone handset. Once a document has been selected, the system automatically telephones the user's fax machine and transmits the document. Many organisations use fax-on-demand for dealing with common customer support queries, issuing price lists and making product information available to customers.

Cable modems make use of the fibre-optic cables that have been installed by cable television companies. Services tend to be restricted to heavily populated areas, such as cities and large towns. Cable modems offer very high data transfer rates, up to a theoretical maximum of 30 Mbps. In reality, however, most services restrict speeds to 512 kbps for downloads and 128 kbps for uploads.

The speed of a modem is measured in **bauds** or **bits per second** (bps). Early modems operated at speeds of 1200 baud, the equivalent of approximately 100 characters per second. At present, the highest speed supported by a typical modem is 56 600 bps, equivalent to approximately 4700 characters per second. The speed at which data are transmitted can be improved by making use of data compression techniques that attempt to place data in a form that requires less space than usual. However, the modem that receives the data must use a compatible protocol in order to decompress data sent in this format. As more individuals and organisations gain access to high speed services (known as **broadband services**), data transfer speeds have started to be measured in terms of thousands (kbps) or millions (Mbps) of bits per second.

A number of applications require high data transfer rates in order to function effectively. Video conferencing, for example, requires large quantities of data to be transmitted simultaneously to several users. However, the limitations of conventional telephone lines restrict the maximum speed with which data can be transmitted. Some of the alternatives to the modem and conventional telephone line include the following:

- Digital telephone exchanges support an **integrated services digital network (ISDN)** standard that allows data transfer rates that are up to five times faster than a 56 600 bps modem. An ISDN telephone line provides two separate 'channels', allowing simultaneous voice and data transmissions. Since ISDN lines transmit digital data, a modem is not required to make use of the service. Instead, a special terminal adaptor (often called an 'ISDN modem') is used to pass data between the computer and the ISDN line.
- The introduction of **asymmetric digital subscriber line (ADSL)** services makes use of existing telephone lines to provide very high data transfer rates. Although the bandwidth offered by such services is usually shared by a number of users, ADSL offers many of the benefits associated with ISDN and the potential of data transfer rates of up to 6 Mbps.
- A relatively recent development has been the introduction of systems that make use of satellite communications in order to receive data at very high speeds. Many services, for example, make use of a conventional modem to send requests for data, such as an Internet page. The requested data are received via a satellite link at speeds of up to 400 kbps, approximately four times faster than an ISDN link. Such systems are used to beam back news stories from remote locations.

Devices allowing the transmission of data via ordinary electricity cables are expected to appear by the end of the decade. The use of the national electricity grid offers the potential of permanent, high-speed communications links at very low cost. Although the effectiveness of this technology has already been proven, it remains to be seen if a commercially successful service can be established in Europe.

Hubs

Hubs are used to connect up to 20 PCs to a network in a convenient way using patch cables (which look similar to phone cables and sockets) running between the back of each PC and the hub. The hub may then be attached to a server or a backbone connection leading to the server.

Bridges and routers

These are used to connect different LANs and transfer data packets from one network to the next. They can be used to connect similar types of LAN. They also offer filtering services to restrict local traffic to one side of the bridge, thus reducing traffic overall. Routers can select the best route for packets to be transmitted and are also used on the Internet backbones and wide area network to achieve this. Although these devices used to be distinct, they are now produced as hybrids which share functions.

Companies attached to the Internet usually use a router as a gateway to attach their internal network to the Internet. This is often combined with a 'firewall', which is intended to reduce the risk of someone from outside the company gaining unauthorised access to company data. Firewalls are described in more detail in Chapter 17.

Repeaters

Over a long transmission distance, signal distortion may occur. Repeaters are necessary to increase transmission distances by regenerating signals and retransmitting them.

Data service units and channel service units

These devices are used to connect to digital communications lines by converting signals received from bridges, routers and multiplexers.

Broadband
A relatively high-capacity, high-speed transmission medium such as cable.

ISDN (integrated services digital network)
ISDN represents a standard for communications that allows data transfer rates that are up to five times faster than a 56 600 bps modem. An ISDN telephone line provides two separate 'channels' allowing simultaneous voice and data transmissions. Since ISDN lines transmit digital data, a modem is not required to make use of the service. Instead, a special terminal adapter (often called an ISDN modem) is used to pass data between the computer and the ISDN line. See *Modem and Baud rate.*

Activity 5.1

Transmission of data through different hardware and network components

Describe the order in which a message passes from one piece of hardware to the next when a home user in the UK sends an e-mail via the Internet to someone in a large corporation in the USA. You should refer to the following terms:

(a) mail server;
(b) client PC;
(c) modem;
(d) hub;
(e) network cable;
(f) network card;
(g) gateway server (telecommunications processor);
(h) router.

Treat the Internet transmission as a single stage.

Asymmetric digital subscriber line (ADSL)
A relatively new development in telecommunications that makes use of conventional telephone lines to provide extremely high data transmission rates.

▶ Telecommunications channels

Telecommunications channels are the different media used to carry information between different locations. These include traditional cables and wires known as *guided media*, and wires and more recent innovations such as satellite and microwave which are *unguided media*.

Telecommunications channels
The media by which data are transmitted. Cables and wires are known as guided media and microwave and satellite links are known as unguided media.

We will now examine the benefits and applications of these different media. When doing this, the main factors that need to be considered are the physical characteristics, data transmission method, performance and cost.

Characteristics of guided media

The main types of cabling used in LANs are based on copper cabling. Data are transmitted along this by applying at one end a voltage, which is received at the other. A positive voltage represents a binary one and a negative voltage represents a binary zero. There are two main types of twisted copper cabling used in networks. Insulated straight cabling is not suitable except for very short distances such as between a computer and a printer. The two types are:

● *Twisted-pair (often used for 10Base-T Ethernet).* Twisted-pair cabling consists of twisted copper wire covered by an insulator. The two wires form a circuit over which data can be transmitted. The twisting is intended to reduce interference. Shielding using braided metal may also be used to reduce external interference. A cable may have more than one pair. Twisted-pair cabling was traditionally used for telephones.
● *Co-axial (used for Thin 10Base-2 Ethernet).* Co-axial cable consists of a single solid copper core surrounded by an insulator and a braided metal shield. 'Co-ax' can be used to connect devices over longer distances than twisted-pair. It is possibly best known as the means used to connect an antenna to a television set. However, it has largely been superseded for office LAN environments, since twisted pair has now been refined to offer faster speeds than co-axial.

Fibre-optic is a relatively new transmission medium, and consists of thousands of fibres of pure silicon dioxide. Packets are transmitted along fibre-optic cables using light or photons emitted from a light-emitting diode at one end of the cable; detection is by a photo-sensitive cell at the other end. Fibre-optic cables give very high transmission rates since the cable has very low resistance. This is well known as a method by which cable TV is delivered to homes.

Characteristics of unguided or wireless media

For wide-area network cables are still commonly used, but they are being superseded by the use of unguided media. This method uses signals transmitted through air and space from a transmitter to a receiver. It tends to be faster than wired methods. Wireless transmissions can be used for different business applications at different scales:

● *Wireless infra-red transmission* can be used for sending data between a portable PC or personal digital assistant (PDA) and a desktop computer. This saves downloading files by floppy disk or serial cable. It is useful for salespeople or engineers who are away from base frequently but need to upload the data they have collected in the field from their mobile computer to their desktop computer. Recent laser printers from Hewlett-Packard can now also receive documents for printing via wireless infra-red transmission from desktop or laptop computers that do not need to be connected to the printer.
● *Wireless transmission* can also be used locally to form a wireless LAN. Here a microwave or narrow-band radio transmitter and receiver may be used to connect different buildings. Wireless LANs are often used across college campuses. They have the benefit that the cost of laying cabling is not incurred. This makes them particularly suitable where it is not clear whether a link is needed in the long term.
● *Microwave transmission* can be used to beam information through the atmosphere. The maximum distance that can separate microwave transmitters is 45 km, since the signal follows a straight line and the curvature of the earth limits transmission dis-

tance. This can make microwave an expensive method of transmitting data, but the cost can be reduced if it is combined with satellite methods.

● *Satellite transmission* operates at two orbit levels, high orbit at 22 300 miles in a geostationary orbit and at a lower orbit. Messages are sent from a transceiver at one location on the earth's surface and are bounced off the satellite to another transceiver. Because of the distances involved, this can give a time delay of up to a quarter of a second, which is evident in interviews conducted by satellite. A range of frequencies can be used. Satellite applications include television, telephone and data transmission.

CASE STUDY 5.1

Choosing the right Internet connection

FT

The majority of small-to medium-sized enterprises (SMEs) do not have the expert staff, the time or the money to manage and maintain the computing equipment and applications needed to foster growth and keep themselves competitive.

Instead, many SMEs must focus on developing the core business, rather than attempt to keep up with rapid changes in IT systems.

In this scenario, the application service provider (ASP) model should in theory come into its own. However, connecting ASPs to SMEs is problematic, given the general lack of affordable and accessible broadband communications networks. Typically, SMEs are geographically scattered, exacerbating the connectivity problem

ASPs have to make it easy for companies to outsource their applications by providing fully managed high-speed networks and bundled packages for fixed monthly or annual fees. Lisa Danielsson, a consultant at Schema, says: 'Big ASPs with a substantial market presence will deliver end-to-end connectivity, while smaller companies may outsource network connections. There are lots of variables for ASPs – and it's not until corporations adopt this model that SMEs will jump.'

To work effectively, ASPs must guarantee security, provide resilience and service level agreements (SLAs), over relatively cheap broadband networks. ASPs must either lease capacity from, or partner with, a telco which has high-speed local loop capacity and backbone connectivity.

'Networks are the biggest potential weakness in the model', says David Mills, commercial vice-president of Futurelink, a US-based ASP. 'Partnering with a telco extends our reach, provides back-up, and delivers SLAs.'

By exploiting relationships with customers, telcos are also moving into retail and wholesale ASP markets and generating extra revenues. Together, Cable & Wireless and Compaq have created a global offering for SMEs bundling networks, equipment and popular business applications.

'Customers want to buy a complete solution, including fully managed networks and receive one predictable bill for ASP services and network costs', says Stuart Keeping, C&W's vice president for global marketing. 'Local access is still a barrier to ASP adoption, especially with smaller businesses. Digital Subscriber Line (DSL) technology will help, as will wireless, and greater pressures to reduce bandwidth prices.'

Typically, only large industrial estates or metropolitan areas have direct access to the vast capacity of fibre optic cables. Peter Boland, Nortel Networks' vice president for personal internet, explains: 'It's easy to run fibre through an industrial estate. Each fibre can be split between 32 different SMEs for optical ethernet connections.'

Outside such high-density areas, the options are more limited and can be costly. For most SMEs, connection will be via DSL running on the almost ubiquitous twisted copper pairs, but availability is still patchy in most countries outside the US. Offering the same capacity in both directions, SDSL (Symmetric DSL) is likely to be the best option for business applications although consumer ADSL (Asymmetric DSL) is sufficient for smaller companies.

Commercial DSL roll-outs are starting in Europe. In the belief that there will be an evolutionary use of high-speed networks, France Telecom will provide ADSL and different business packages to more than 85 per cent of SMEs by the end of 2002.

Etienne Bostsarron, marketing manager of France Telecom's Oeleane unit, says: 'ASPs are at the top maturity of the market. A large percentage of French SMEs are not yet connected to the internet and often their first connection is via consumer services to establish e-mail.'

Broadband cable operators plan to use DSL and/or wireless to extend their reach outside franchise areas. Stephen Rowles, NTL's deputy group managing direc-

▶

tor, suggests it is very difficult for ASPs to develop until there is local loop bandwidth. And he believes the model has not taken off as expected. 'America is the clue to success. DSL in the US is starting to come into its own now.'

Leased lines or virtual private networks (VPNs), are expensive options for smaller SMEs (around £100 monthly per user in the UK), but bandwidth and security are guaranteed. Despite high connection costs, companies may save on equipment, maintenance, licensing fees, security insurance and upgrades while benefiting from advanced applications.

David Tanner, administrative director at Seabrooks, the British international freight forwarder, pays £50,000 annually for applications and connectivity. 'The cost factors for the VPN made us think, but on analysis, the potential savings makes ASP services free. We estimate that over five years we will save between 50–70 per cent of the cost of running applications ourselves.'

Other technology options are also available. Offering huge capacity and falling prices, satellite networks are global, reliable, quick and easy to install. Astra, Gilat and Hughes are among operators offering robust two-way satellite connections. Not yet widely available, broadband wireless is a maturing technology.

A different model is offered by US-based Citrix, which specialises in server-based computing. This reduces required bandwidth by loading applications on servers and viewing them on personal computers. Roger Baskerville, director of business development, explains: 'Only mouse movements and screen clicks are transmitted between user and server, so little data is transferred. Most business applications can run over a 9.6 [kilobits per second] link although the system is optimised to run at 19.2Kbps.'

SMEs typically use applications which involve capturing data and distributing it around the organisation, for which the ASP model is well suited and which may not require high capacity connections. Graphics or video-intensive applications are better done locally, rather than outsourced to an ASP.

'The biggest issue for most SMEs, especially if they operate in more than one country, is the delay involved in getting quick connections from telcos', says Nick Goss, technical director at Digica, the UK application and infrastructure provider. 'SMEs could get an ISDN [integrated services digital network] line which can be installed at the pilot stage, giving them time to buy the real required bandwidth.'

Richard Medcalf, a senior consultant at Analysys, believes a key enabler for SMEs is a flat-fee 'always on' connection, but he agrees there are availability problems.

'Broadband networks are not being rolled out as fast as expected because the market has dried up, and incumbent telcos worldwide have dragged their heels', he says.

'Hosting applications and using broadband as a platform to deliver software has to be the future of telecoms networks, but it will take time.'

Questions

1 Using the article and research using the Internet assess the different options for a small–medium company to connect to the Internet

2 From the article and the relevant section in the text briefly define what an ASP is and explain the benefits and disadvantages for an SME.

Source: Priscilla Awde, 'Finding the correct connections is seldom a straightforward task', FTIT, 4 July 2001

▶ Transmission methods

Transmission of data can be achieved in a variety of ways. Of those methods given below, the difference between analogue and digital signals is the important one to grasp.

Signal type

Analogue
Analogue transmissions send data in a continuous wave-form.

Digital
Digital transmissions send binary data as a series of ones and zeros.

The two alternative methods of transmission are analogue and digital. An **analogue** signal represents a message by using a continuous wave-form which is carried by a cable such as a phone line. Here analogue transmission is used to carry voice, data or fax. Analogue is less suitable for higher capacity needs such as video, since its 'bandwidth' is limited (see below). A **digital** signal is not continuous, consisting of binary data sent in pulses of ones and zeros. This is achieved by varying the voltage of the line from a high to a low state. Digital transmissions are used where higher bandwidth is available. They have the dual advantages that no conversion from digital to analogue is necessary before sending, and the quality is better since distortion does not occur when the signal is boosted when long-distance transmission is required.

Communications method

Data transmission can occur in different modes according to how the individual characters are transmitted. Asynchronous communication occurs when transmission of data occurs one character at a time with control bits to either side. Synchronous communication occurs when groups of characters are sent as **packets** and both the sending and receiving device synchronise data using a timer.

Packets are units of data that are exchanged between different devices over communications media. The entire message to be sent is broken down into smaller packets, since if an error occurs in transmission, only the packet with the error needs to be retransmitted.

Packets
Units of data that are exchanged between different devices over communications media. An entrie message is broken down into smaller packets.

Transmission modes

When all end-user computers were character-based terminals, the terms 'simplex' and 'duplex' were commonly used to refer to the transmission mode. Today, these terms are unimportant to end-users or business managers. For the record, the differences are:

- *Simplex* refers to a one-way transmission.
- *Half-duplex* refers to a two-way transmission, but only one way at a given time.
- *Full-duplex* refers to a simultaneous two-way transmission.

The terms have now dropped out of common usage since LANs became predominant and most digital networks achieve full-duplex mode with simultaneous data flow in both directions.

Transmission speed

The speed at which data can be transferred from A to B is governed by the channel capacity, which is measured in bits per second (bps). Transmission of a single bit in a second is equivalent to one baud, a binary event. Rates are usually measured in terms of thousands of bits/second (kbit/sec), millions of bits/second (Mbit/sec) or billions of bits per second (Gbit/sec).

A general term often used for describing capacity is **bandwidth**. The technical definition of bandwidth is that it is a measure of capacity given by the difference between the lowest and highest frequencies available for a given medium. This range of frequencies is measured in hertz. For example, bandwidths in the 500 to 929 MHz range are used for TV and radio broadcasts.

Bandwidth
Bandwidth indicates the data transfer rates that can be achieved using given media. It is measured in bits per second.

Bandwidth is commonly used in a general sense to describe the data transfer rate. A good way to think of bandwidth as a measure is that it is similar to the diameter of a pipe along which a fluid is flowing. The larger the width of pipe, the higher capacity of water or data that can be transmitted. So the bandwidth of a 10 Mbit/sec LAN is much higher than the bandwidth available over analogue lines with a 28.8 kbit/sec modem.

Table 5.3 summarises the characteristics of the different transmission media that we have considered.

Table 5.3 A summary of characteristics for different transmission media

Characteristic	Twisted-pair	Co-axial	Fibre-optic	Microwave radio	Satellite
Maximum data transfer rate	4 Mbit/s	140 Mbit/s	10 000 Mbit/s	100 Mbit/s	100 Mbit/s
Installation	Easy	Moderate	Difficult	Difficult	Difficult
Cost	Low	Moderate	High	High	High
Maintenance	Moderate	Low	Low	Low	–

Activity 5.2

Data transmission speeds

Rank the following in terms of their data transmission speeds:

(a) Ethernet LAN (10 Mbit/sec);
(b) modem attached to a phone line (28 800 baud);
(c) ISDN2 link to the home operating at 128 kbit/sec;
(d) fibre-optic cable used for video conferencing at a speed of 10Gbit/sec.

◗ Network operating systems

Network operating system (NOS)
The software necessary to control the access to and flow of information around a network. It is used to implement the different levels in the OSI model.

The final component that is needed to make all the other components work in unison is a **network operating system (NOS)**. This is systems software necessary to control the access to and flow of information around a network. It is used to implement the different levels in the *OSI models* (see below: Focus on Internet standards). It provides the following functions:

- access control or security through providing user accounts with user names and passwords;
- file and data sharing of data stored on a database server or file server;
- communication between users via e-mail, diary systems or workgroup software such as Lotus Notes;
- sharing of devices, enabling, for example, the backup to tape of data on the server, or printer sharing.

The most widely used NOS for a PC-based LAN are Novell Netware and IBM LAN Manager. However, NOS features are now being built into standard operating systems such as Microsoft Windows, and this is increasingly being adopted by companies. For Unix-based servers the NOS is a component of the operating system. Unix is used by many medium and large companies operating servers from companies such as Sun Microsystems, Hewlett-Packard and IBM. It is often thought to offer better stability than Windows NT since it is a long-established NOS.

◗ Middleware

Middleware
A type of software that acts as a layer between other software to assist in data transfer between incompatible systems.

Middleware is a specialised type of software which allows different software applications to communicate. It acts as a layer between other software to assist in data transfer between incompatible systems. It is often described as the 'glue' that binds the software applications to the systems software. It is important in a networked world, since it provides translation services between software running on different types of computer systems in different companies. An example of middleware is gateway software which enables an internal e-mail system such as Lotus cc:Mail to send messages to other e-mail systems via the Internet. Middleware is also necessary to enable a single software application such as sales order processing to access different types of database, such as Oracle, Informix or Microsoft SQL Server, which a large company may use. Middleware to assist in communications can be categorised according to a seven-layer model known as the OSI model.

Specific networking standards

Other network standards define transmission for particular types of network. These are briefly covered in this section for reference purposes, since they are used frequently in industry when new communications facilities for a company are being installed. These standards include:

- *ISDN (integrated services digital network)*. This is used for sending digital data over telephone networks. In the UK speeds of 64 or 128 kbps are possible, making it suitable for exchange of voice, data, images and short video sequences.
- *ADSL (asynchronous digital subscribed line)*. Offers many of the benefits associated with ISDN and the potential of data transfer rates of up to 6 Mbps.
- *SMDS (switched multimegabit data service)*. This provides a higher speed than ISDN. It is often used in metropolitan areas of Europe for linking branches of shops or financial service providers with the regional office. It provides an extension of LAN communication methods across a city.
- *ATM (asynchronous transfer mode)*. ATM is applicable to both local- and wide-area networks and has been touted as the way forward for providing the high-speed services required by businesses for supporting multimedia such as video conferencing. It achieves this by accommodating bursts in traffic and so more packets. To provide the bandwidth needed, ATM is coupled with fibre-optic cables.
- *X.25*. X.25 is a packet-switching network allowing communication across a wide area network. Although it is well established for use in light traffic between remote sites, it is not practical for real-time data or video. The maximum speed of the standard is 2 Mbit/sec, compared to a maximum of 600 Mbit/sec with ATM.
- *Ethernet network*. The Ethernet standard was developed jointly by Xerox, Digital and Intel in the 1980s. It is implemented most commonly using 10Base-T twisted-pair or 10Base-2 co-axial cable to implement a bus or star LAN topology.
- *X.400*. This message-handling system standard is important in allowing different types of e-mail systems to interoperate. This is particularly important for large companies that have many incompatible mail systems, each of which would require a gateway product to talk to the others. With X.400, gateways are no longer required.
- *X.500*. This defines a standard for directory services. For the global organisation, this is important as it defines a hierarchy for locating staff and equipment efficiently. Once implemented it will effectively give a global phone directory which will make finding a person's e-mail address easier. The information most relevant to each site is stored locally to make it quicker to access.

The evolution of networking technology

It is instructive to examine the progression of commercial networks applications. The trends illustrate why networks are important and some of the issues that govern their structure.

The 1960s – mainframes and dumb terminals

In the 1960s those companies that had computer systems were using mainframes. A central mainframe was connected to terminals by a simple network. The main function of these aptly named 'dumb terminals' consisted of the display and input of character information. Limited information was transmitted over the network.

Characterised by being cost-driven and technology-limited.

The 1970s – minicomputers

In the 1970s the trend to downsizing was under way and cheaper minicomputers such as the DEC PDP-11 and VAX became popular. It was during this period that wide-area networks started to be used for specialist functions such as air-travel reservation and banking.

Characterised by being cost-driven, technology enabled through use of microchips.

The 1980s – the IBM PC and Apple Macintosh

With the introduction of the PC in the early 1980s, networking faced a setback. PCs were often deployed as standalone, non-networked machines. While this often gave the user more freedom to develop applications such as spreadsheet models, it meant that information sharing was limited, with a failure to add value to the business through information. This was known as the period of the 'trainer net', as file sharing occurred by people walking from one machine to the next. The opportunities for sharing devices such as printers and storage devices were also often missed.

Characterised by being led by technology and by the desire for increased user autonomy.

It was not long before these limitations were realised and a rapid increase in the adoption of the PC LAN occurred. Managed by early versions of network operating systems such as Novell Netware and IBM LAN Manager, these gave all the benefits of printing, file sharing and security which had been lost with the standalone PC.

Characterised by being driven by cost and by the desire for e-mail and file sharing.

In the 1980s large numbers of companies were starting to communicate with their suppliers and overseas operations via wide-area networks.

The 1990s – the client/server architecture and global networks

As the popularity of LANs increased, the benefits of a client/server architecture became clear and the introduction of first-generation **client/server** architecture with centralised data and mainly local processing occurred. This gradually became more sophisticated with the introduction of second-generation client/server with a distributed architecture where data and processing are shared between several computers over a LAN or WAN.

In the mid-1990s, IP networks started to be used widely as the basis for business applications. With increasing concerns about the cost of PC ownership, we are now seeing a reversion to centralisation of processing power and administrative functions with the introduction of network computers (NCs) and Net PCs (see Chapters 3 and 15) which have lower specifications than PCs.

Characterised by being collaboration- and cost-reduction-driven.

The 2000s – ubiquitous IP networks and application service providers (ASPs)

The use of IP networks to deliver e-business applications is a major trend in network technology. The term 'IP' is explained in the Focus on Internet Standards section. Some business applications are now hosted by **application service providers** (see later section for an explanation).

Characterised by standards-based technology increasing information sharing.

The Internet

▶ What is the Internet?

The **Internet** allows communication between millions of connected computers worldwide. Information is transmitted from client PCs whose users request services to server computers that hold information and host business applications that deliver the services in response to requests. As such, the Internet is a large-scale client/server system. By end 2001, Cyberatlas compilations estimated that, worldwide, there were 445 million Internet users (see www.cyberatlas.com). The client PCs within homes and businesses are connected to the Internet via local **internet service providers (ISPs)** which, in turn, are linked to larger ISPs with connection to the major national and international

Client/server

The client/server architecture consists of client computers such as PCs sharing resources such as a database stored on more powerful server computers.

Application service provider

An application server provides a business application service across the Internet from a server remote from the user.

The Internet

The Internet refers to the physical network that links computers across the globe. It consists of the infrastructure of network servers and communication links between them that are used to hold and transport information between the client PCs and web servers.

Internet service provider (ISP)

A provider enabling home or business users a connection to access the Internet. They can also host web-based applications.

infrastructure or backbones (Fig. 5.4). In the UK, at the London Internet Exchange in the Docklands area of east London, a facility exists to connect multiple **backbones** of the major ISPs within the UK onto a single high-speed link out of the UK into Europe and through to the rest of the world. These high-speed links can be thought of as the motorways on the 'information superhighway' while the links provided from ISPs to consumers are equivalent to slow country roads.

A variety of end-user tools are available to exchange information over the Internet – web browsers and e-mail are the best known. They are outlined in Table 4.2. As we will see in the next section, although the Internet has existed for around 30 years, it is only since the early 1990s when the web browser was first widely adopted that the use of the Internet by business has grown dramatically. An overview of adoption of the Internet by consumers and businesses is given in Chapter 6.

Backbones

High-speed communications links used to enable Internet communications across a country and internationally.

▶ Development of the Internet

The simplest way in which the Internet can be described is as a global network system made up of smaller systems. Estimates suggest that it is composed of approximately 2.5 million individual network systems distributed across the world. The history and origin of the Internet as a business tool is surprising since it has taken a relatively long time to become an essential part of business. The Internet was conceived by the Defense Advanced Research Projects Agency (DARPA), an American intelligence organisation, in 1969. The Internet began to achieve its current form in 1987, growing from systems developed by DARPA and the National Science Foundation (NSF). Figure 5.5 shows

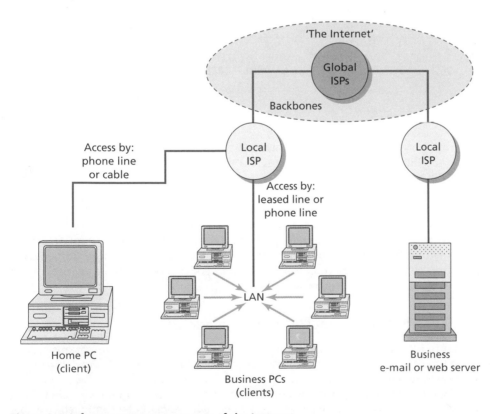

Figure 5.4 Infrastructure components of the Internet
Source: Chaffey (2002)

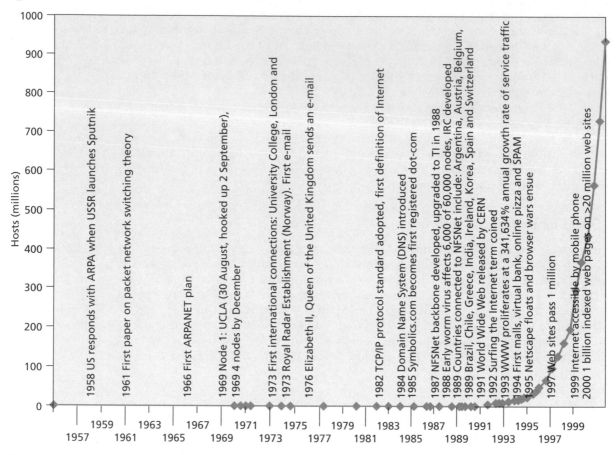

Figure 5.5 An Internet timeline

Source: Chaffey (2002)

some significant events in the development of the Internet, starting with the lauch of the Soviet satellite which issued a challenge to the US administration. Read Gillies and Cailliau (2000) for a detailed description of the history of the Internet.

The Internet is only the latest of a series of developments of how the human race has used technology to disseminate information. Kampas (2000) identifies ten stages that are part of five 'megawaves' of change. The first six stages are summarised in Table 5.4. It is evident that many of the major advancements in the use of information have happened within the last hundred years. This indicates that the difficulty of managing technological change is likely to continue. Kampas goes on to speculate on the impact of access to lower-cost, higher-bandwidth technologies.

Business-to-consumer (B2C)

Commercial transactions are between an organisation and consumers.

Business-to-business (B2B)

Commercial transactions are between an organisation and other organisations.

▶ Business and consumer models of Internet access

It is useful to identify e-business opportunities in terms of whether an organisation is using the Internet to transact with consumers (**business-to-consumer – B2C**) or other businesses (**business-to-business – B2B**).

Business-to-business transactions predominate over the Internet, in terms of value, if not frequency. For example, a report by analyst eMarketer (www.emarketer.com) predicted that B2B e-commerce would account for 79 per cent of total e-commerce by the end of 2000,

Table 5.4 **Six stages of advances in the dissemination of information**

Stage	Enabling technology	Killer applications and impact
1. Documentation 3500 BC to AD 1452	Written language and the development of clay tablets in Mesopotamia	Taxes, laws and accounting giving rise to the development of civilisation and commerce
2. Mass publication 1452 to 1946	The Gutenberg press of movable metal type	Demand for religious and scientific texts resulting in scientific advances and ideological conflicts
3. Automation 1946 to 1978	Electric power and switching technologies (vacuum tubes and transistors)	Code breaking and scientific calculations. Start of information age
4. Mass interaction 1978 to 1985	Microprocessor and personal computer	Spreadsheets and word processing
5. Infrastructuralisation 1985 to 1993	Local and wide-area networks, graphical user interfaces	E-mail and enterprise resource planning
6. Mass communication 1993 to c. 2005	Internet, World Wide Web, Java	Mass information access for communications and purchasing

Source: Adapted and republished with permission from CRC Press LLC from '*Roadmap to the E-Revolution*', Kampas, P.J., in *Information Systems Managements*, Vol. 17, No. 3, 2001, Auerbach Publications, permission conveyed through Copyright Clearance Center, Inc.

82 per cent by end 2001, 85 per cent by 2002 and 87 per cent by 2003. Figure 5.6 helps explain why this is the case. It shows that there are many more opportunities for B2B trans-actions than B2C, both between an organisation and its suppliers, together with intermediaries, and through distributors such as agents and wholesalers with customers. Additionally, as explained in Chapter 6 there is a higher level of access to the Internet among businesses than among consumers, and a greater propensity to use it for purchasing.

Figure 5.7 gives examples of different companies operating in the business-to-con-sumer (B2C) and business-to-business (B2B) spheres. Figure 5.7 also presents two

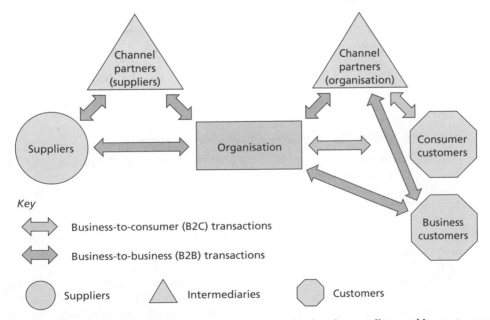

Figure 5.6 **B2B and B2C interactions between an organisation, its suppliers and its customers**
Source: Chaffey (2002)

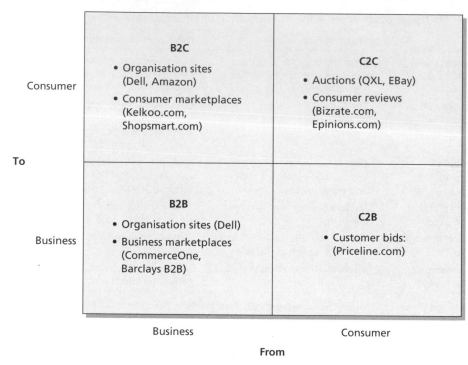

Figure 5.7 Summary of transaction alternatives between businesses and consumers
Source: Chaffey (2002)

additional types of transaction: that where consumers transact directly with consumers (C2C) and that where they initiate trading with business (C2B). Note that the terms C2C and C2B are less widely used (e.g. *Economist*, 2000), but they do highlight significant differences between Internet-based commerce and earlier forms of commerce. Consumer-to-consumer interactions were relatively rare, but, as Figure 5.6 shows, are now very common in the form of online auctions and communities. Indeed, Hoffman and Novak (1996) suggest that C2C interactions are such a key characteristic of the Internet that it is important for companies to take them into account. As well as the models shown in Figure 5.7, it has been suggested that employees should be considered as a separate type of interaction through the use of intranets – this is sometime referred to as employee-to-employee or E2E.

The role of the Internet in restructuring business relationships

The relationship between a company and its channel partners shown in Figure 5.6 can be dramatically altered by the opportunities afforded by the Internet. This occurs because the Internet offers a means of bypassing some of the channel partners. This process is known as **disintermediation** or 'cutting out the middleman'.

Figure 5.8 illustrates disintermediation in a graphical form for a simplified retail channel. Further intermediaries such as additional distributors may occur in a business-to-business market. Figure 5.8(a) shows the former position where a company markets and sells it products by 'pushing' them through a sales channel. Figure 5.8(b) and (c) show two different type of disintermediation in which the wholesaler (b) or the wholesaler and retailer (c) are bypassed, allowing the producer to sell and promote direct to the consumer. The benefits of disintermediation to the producer are clear – it is able to remove the sales and infrastructure cost of selling through the channel. Benjamin and Weigand (1995) cal-

Disintermediation

The removal of intermediaries such as distributors or brokers that formerly linked a company to its customers.

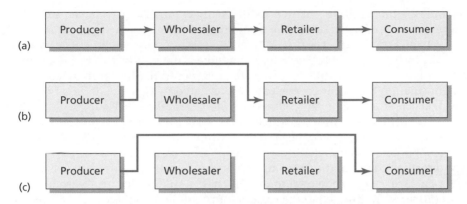

(a)

(b)

(c)

Figure 5.8 Disintermediation of a consumer distribution channel showing (a) the original situation, (b) disintermediation omitting the wholesaler and (c) disintermediation omitting both wholesaler and retailer
Source: Chaffey (2002)

culate that, using the sale of quality shirts as an example, it is possible to make cost savings of 28 per cent in the case of (b) and 62 per cent for case (c). Some of these cost savings can be passed on to the customer in the form of cost reductions.

At the start of business hype about the Internet in the mid-1990s there was much speculation that widespread disintermediation would see the failure of many intermediary

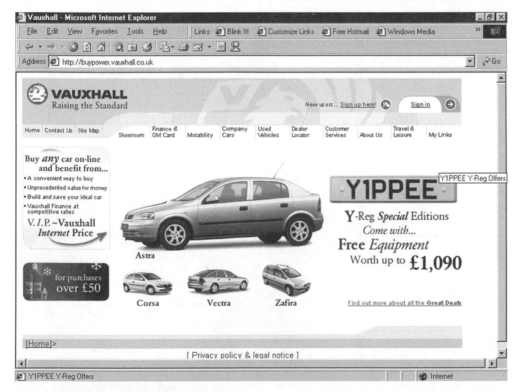

Figure 5.9 Vauxhall e-commerce site
Source: buypower.vauxhall.co.uk

companies as direct selling occurred. While many companies have taken advantage of distintermediation, the results have sometimes been less than spectacular. Vauxhall (www.vauxhall.co.uk), the UK part of General Motors,. started selling its cars direct to customers in the mid-1990s (Fig. 5.9), but despite a major advertising campaign, only several hundred cars were sold direct over the Internet in the first year. In fact, although disintermediation has occurred, the pattern illustrated in Figure 5.10 has also occurred. Let us take the example of car insurance in the UK market. In Figure 5.10 (a) we start with the traditional situation in which many sales were through brokers such as the Automobile Association (www.theaa.co.uk). With disintermediation (Fig. 5.10 (b)) there was the opportunity to sell direct, initially via call centres as with Direct Line (www.directline.co.uk) and then complemented by a transactional web site as was the case for Eagle Star (www.eaglestar.co.uk). Purchasers still needed assistance in the selection of products and this led to the creation of new intermediaries, a process referred to as **re-intermediation** (Fig. 5.10 (c)). In the UK Screentrade (www.screentrade.co.uk) was established as a broker to enable different companies to sell insurance direct. Note that in 2001 its owners, Misys, sold the service because the cost of marketing and operations exceeded the brokering revenues from referring customers to the insurers.

Re-intermediation

The creation of new intermediaries between customers and suppliers providing services such as supplier search and product evaluation.

What are the implications of re-intermediation for the e-commerce manager? First, it is necessary to make sure that your company, as a supplier, is represented with the new intermediaries operating within your chosen market sector. This implies the need to integrate, using the Internet, databases containing price information with those of different intermediaries. Secondly, it is important to monitor the prices of other suppliers within this sector (possibly by using the intermediary web site for this purpose). Thirdly, it may be appropriate to create your own intermediary, for example DIY chain B&Q has set up its own intermediary to help budding DIYers, but it is positioned sepa-

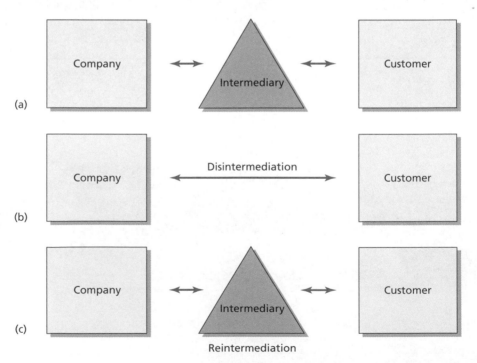

Figure 5.10 The move to re-intermediation: (a) original situation, (b) disintermediation, (c) re-intermediation

Source: Chaffey (2002)

rately from its owners. Such tactics to counter or take advantage of re-intermediation are sometimes known as **countermediation**.

Countermediation
Creation of a new intermediary by an established company

Activity 5.3

Re-intermediation in practice

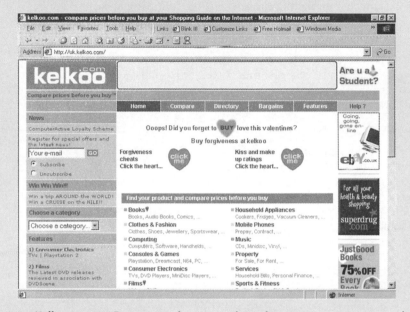

Figure 5.11 **Kelkoo.com, a European price comparison site**

Purpose

To provide an example of the services provided by 'cybermediaries' and explore their viability as businesses.

1 Visit the Kelkoo web site (www.kelkoo.com), shown in Figure 5.11, and search for this book, a CD or anything else you fancy. Explain the service that is being offered to customers.
2 Write down the different revenue opportunities for this site (some may be evident from the site, but others may not; write down your ideas also).
3 Given that there be other competing sites in this intermediary category such as Shopsmart (www.shopsmart.com), assess the future of this online business using press releases and comments from other sites such as Moreover (www.moreover.com).

Intranets and extranets

The majority of Internet services are available to any business or consumer who has access to the Internet. However, many e-business applications that access sensitive company information require access to be limited to favoured individuals or third parties. If information is limited to those inside an organisation, this is an **intranet**. If access is extended to some others, but not everyone beyond the organisation, this is an **extranet**. The relationship between these terms is illustrated in Figure 5.12. Extranets can be accessed by authorised people outside the company such as collaborators, suppliers or major customers, but information is not available to everyone with an Internet

Intranet
A private network within a single company using Internet standards to enable employees to share information using e-mail and web publishing.

Extranet
Formed by extending the intranet beyond a company to customers, suppliers and collaborators.

connection – only those with password access. Note that the term 'intranet' is some-times loosely used to refer to an extranet.

Intranet applications

Intranets are used extensively for supporting the marketing function. They are also used to support core supply-chain management activities as described in the next section on extranets. A marketing intranet has the following advantages:

- reduced product lifecycles – as information on product development and marketing campaigns is rationalised we can get products to markets faster;
- reduced costs through higher productivity, and savings on hard copy;
- better customer service – responsive and personalised support with staff accessing customer information via the web;
- distribution of information through remote offices nationally or globally.

Intranets are also used for sharing these types of information:

- staff phone directories;
- staff procedures or quality manuals;
- information for agents such as product specifications, current list and discounted prices, competitor information, factory schedules, and stocking levels, all this information normally has to be updated frequently and can be costly;
- staff bulletin or newsletter;
- training courses.

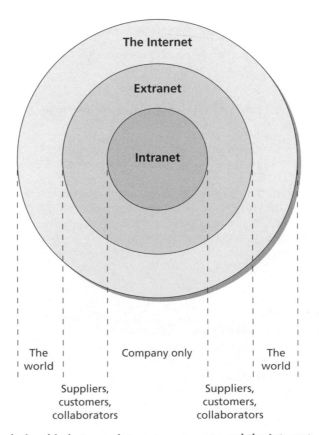

Figure 5.12 **The relationship between intranets, extranets and the Internet**

Extranet applications

Extranets are used extensively to support supply chain management as resources are ordered from suppliers and transformed into products and services delivered to customers. At Marshall Industries, for example, when a new customer order is received across the extranet it automatically triggers a scheduling order for the warehouse (transferred by intranet), an order acknowledgement for the customer and a shipping status when the order ships (Mougayer, 1998). To enable different applications within a company, such as a sales ordering system and an inventory control system that interoperate with each other and databases in other companies, requires an internal company intranet to be created that can then communicate across an extranet with applications on another company intranet.

MINI CASE STUDY

The Mecalux extranet

Mecalux (www.mecalux.com), based in Barcelona, is involved in the design, manufacture and assembly of storage systems, from simple slotted angle racks to sophisticated self-supporting warehouses. Since it was formed in 1996, this Spanish company has expanded and it now has offices in Argentina, Germany, the UK, France, Portugal, Singapore and Mexico. One of the challenges of this expansion was to improve communications between its representatives around the world and to supply them with the information needed to improve customer service. The management team decided they wanted to create a paperless company where information flows freely between all locations around the world to make it easier for the engineers to have the information necessary to respond to any customer's requirements. The extranet created to solve this problem has, for example, enabled representatives in Singapore to tap into data held on the server in Spain to check the availability of the product and get the specifications (such as measurements and price) to a local customer in the shortest possible time-frame. The solution also permits technicians and engineers to collaborate on ideas and work together on future designs from anywhere in the world.

Figure 5.13 shows the range of technologies that companies use to allow customers to order according to a DTI (2000) survey. It is evident that the humble e-mail is the most common form of ordering method. Web-based ordering, where a user enters their order details into a form is the second most common method of ordering and is used by over 50 per cent of companies in the sample countries. Note that this ordering can vary in sophistication from a simple form that is converted into an e-mail without secure payment through to a secure integrated catalogue and merchant server ordering system. The lower proportion of companies that have adopted EDI and extranet methods of ordering indicates that these approaches are mainly limited to the largest companies involved with B2B trading.

Firewalls

Firewalls are necessary when we are creating an intranet or extranet to ensure that outside access to the confidential information does not occur. Firewalls are usually created as software mounted on a separate server at the point where the company is connected to the Internet. Firewall software can then be configured to only accept links from trusted domains representing other offices in the company. A firewall has implications

Firewall
A specialised software application mounted on a server at the point where the company is connected to the Internet. Its purpose is to prevent unauthorised access into the company from outsiders.

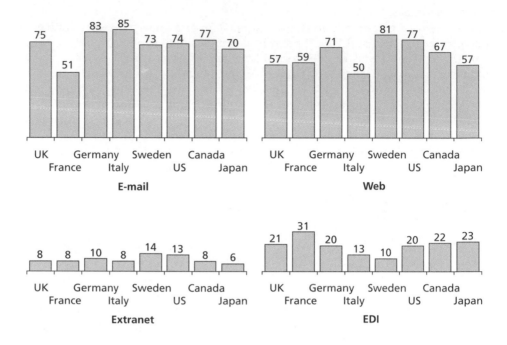

Base: All respondents allowing customers to order online weighted by number of employees

Figure 5.13 Use of different technologies for online ordering
Source: DTI (2000)

for e-marketing since staff accessing a web site from work may not be able to access some content such as graphics plug-ins.

The use of firewalls within the infrastructure of a company is illustrated in Figure 5.14. It is evident that multiple firewalls are used to protect information of the company. The information made available to third parties over the Internet and extranet is partitioned by another firewall using what is referred to as the 'demilitarised zone' (DMZ). Corporate data on the intranet is then mounted on other servers inside the company.

◗ Applications service providers

Application server
An application server provides a business application on a server remote from the user.

Application service providers (ASPs) offer great potential for reducing the cost of administering information systems. An **application server** can be considered to be a relatively new application of a three-tier client–server approach (see Chapter 12 for a description) consisting of a graphical user interface server, an application or business logic server, and a database or transaction server. Links to legacy application databases and transaction management applications are part of this final tier.

Traditionally, companies have employed their own information systems support staff to manage different types of business applications such as e-mail. An applications service provider offers an alternative where the e-mail application is hosted remotely or off-site by a server operated by an ASP. For example, *ITWeek* (2000), reported that Opus group, a marketing agency with 60 staff, outsourced management of its Microsoft Exchange (e-mail and groupware) package to ASP NetStore (www.netstore.com). The quoted price was £19.95 in 2000. Other application services include Microsoft Office or accounting packages. On a larger scale, Pizza Hut, KFC and Taco Bell signed a $50 million contract to provide operational systems to their 6545 restaurants in over 100 countries. The oper-

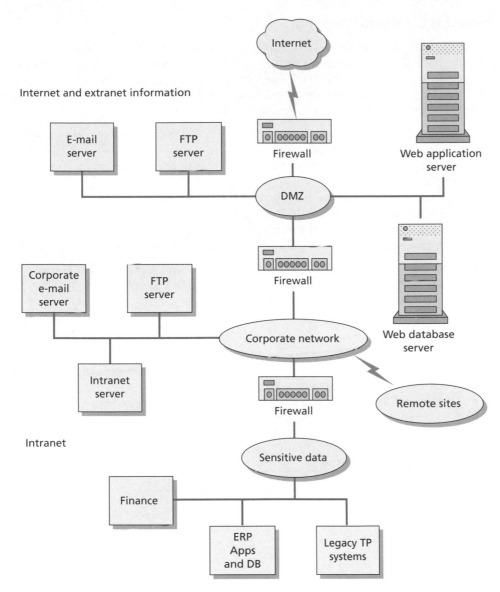

Figure 5.14 An example of the use of firewalls to increase security within an e-business infrastructure

Source: Chaffey (2002)

ational systems include labour, inventory management, supplier ordering and perform-ance reporting. The investment enables standardisation of back-office systems across the company and brings cost reductions since no back-office server is required in each outlet. The A-services venture (www.cwas.net) from Cable and Wireless, Microsoft and Compaq offers services such as Office for £175 per user per year, but also includes a low-specification PC, and network connection, plus 24-hour support. This is effectively out-sourcing of IS infrastructure using a new model enabled by the Internet. A further example of an ASP is where Red Sheriff (www.redsheriff.com) provides a service to com-panies to monitor the customer activity on their web site. The customer logs into the Red Sheriff web server in Australia to access reports on their web site.

▶ What is the World Wide Web?

The **World Wide Web**, introduced in Chapter 4, provides a standard method for exchanging and publishing information on the Internet. The medium is based on standard document formats such as HTML (hypertext markup language) which can be thought of as similar to a word-processing format such as that used for Microsoft Word documents. This standard has been widely adopted because:

● it offers **hyperlinks** which allow users to readily move from one document or web site to another – the process known as 'surfing';
● HTML supports a wide range of formatting, making documents easy to read on different access devices;
● graphics and animations can be integrated into web pages;
● interaction is possible through HTML-based forms that enable customers to supply their personal details for more information on a product, perform searches, ask questions or make comments.

It is the combination of web browsers and HTML that has proved so successful in establishing widespread business use of the Internet. The use of these tools provides a range of benefits including the following:

● It is easy to use since navigation between documents is enabled by clicking on hyperlinks or images. This soon becomes a very intuitive way of navigation which is similar across all web sites and applications.
● It can provide a graphical environment supporting multimedia which is popular with users and gives a visual medium for advertising.
● The standardisation of tools and growth in demand means information can be exchanged with many businesses and consumers.

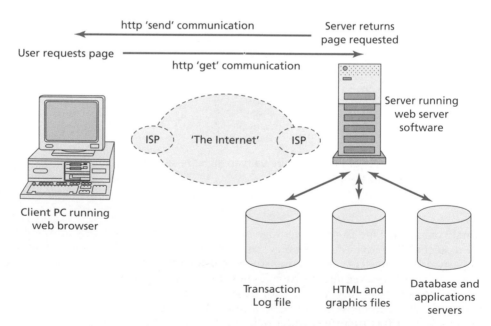

Figure 5.15 Information exchange between a web browser and web server
Source: Chaffey (2002)

Web browsers and servers

Web browsers are software used to access the information on the WWW that is stored on **web servers**. Web servers are used to store, manage and supply the information on the WWW. The main web browsers are Microsoft Internet Explorer and Netscape Navigator or Communicator. Browsers display the text and graphics accessed from web sites and provide tools for managing information from web sites.

Figure 5.15 indicates the process by which web browsers communicate with web servers. A request from the client PC is executed when the user types in a web address, clicks on a hyperlink or fills in an online form such as a search. This request is then sent to the ISP and routed across the Internet to the destination server using the mechanism described in the section on **protocols**. The server then returns the requested web page if it is a **static** (fixed) page, or if it requires reference to a database, such as a request for product information, it will pass the query on to a database server and will then return this to the customer as a **dynamically created web page**. Information on all page requests is stored in a **transaction log file** which records the page requested, the time it was made and the source of the enquiry.

Focus on how the Internet works – Internet standards   F

We have introduced the general terms and concepts that describe the operation of the Internet and World Wide Web. In this section we look in more detail at the standards that have been adopted to enable transfer of information. Knowledge of these terms is useful for anyone involved in the management of e-commerce since discussion with suppliers may involve them.

▶ Networking standards

Internet standards are important since they are at the heart of definitions of the Internet. According to Leiner et al. (2000), on 24 October 1995 the Federal Networking Council unanimously passed a resolution defining the term 'Internet':

> *'Internet' refers to the global information system that – (i) is logically linked together by a globally unique address space based on the Internet Protocol (IP) or its subsequent extensions/follow-ons; (ii) is able to support communications using the Transmission Control Protocol/Internet Protocol (TCP/IP) suite or its subsequent extensions/follow-ons, and/or other IP-compatible protocols; and (iii) provides, uses or makes accessible, either publicly or privately, high level services layered on the communications and related infrastructure described herein.*

TCP/IP development was led by Robert Kahn and Vince Cerf in the late 1960s and early 1970s and, according to Leiner et al. (2000), four ground rules controlled Kahn's early work on this protocol. These four ground rules highlight the operation of the TCP/IP protocol:

1 Distinct networks would be able to communicate seamlessly with other networks.
2 Communications would be on a best-effort basis, i.e. if a data packet didn't reach the final destination, it would be retransmitted from the source until successful receipt.
3 Black boxes would be used to connect the networks; these are the gateways and routers produced by companies such as Cisco and 3Com. There would be no information retained by the gateways in order to keep them simple.
4 There would be no global control of transmissions, these would be governed by the requester and sender of information.

Web browsers
Browsers such as Microsoft Internet Explorer provide an easy method of accessing and viewing information stored as web documents on different servers.

Web servers
Store and present the web pages accessed by web browsers.

Protocol
The Internet functions using a series of standard protocols which allow different computers to communicate with each other.

Static web page
A page on the web server that is invariant.

Dynamic web page
A page that is created in real time, often with reference to a database query, in response to a user request.

Transaction log files
A web server file that records all page requests from site visitors.

TCP/IP
The transmission control protocol is a transport-layer protocol that moves data between applications. The Internet protocol is a network-layer protocol that moves data between host computers.

It can be seen that simplicity, speed and independence from control were at the heart of the development of the TCP/IP standards.

The data transmissions standards of the Internet such as TCP/IP are part of a larger set of standards known as the open systems interconnection (OSI) model. This defines a layered model that enables servers to communicate with other servers and clients. When implemented in software, the combined layers are referred to as a 'protocol stack'. The seven layers of the OSI model are:

- *Application*. The program such as a web browser that creates and receives messages.
- *Presentation*. These protocols are usually part of the operating system.
- *Session*. This includes data-transfer protocols such as SMTP, HTTP and FTP.
- *Transport*. This layer ensures the integrity of data transmitted. Examples include the Internet transmission control protocol and Novell SPX.
- *Network*. Defines protocols for opening and maintaining links between servers. The best known are the Internet protocol (IP) and Novell IPX.
- *Data link*. Defines the rules for sending and receiving information.
- *Physical layer*. Low-level description of physical transmission methods.

The postal service is a good analogy for the transmission of data around the Internet using the TCP/IP protocol. Before we send mail, we always need to add a destination address. Likewise, the IP protocol acts as an addressed envelope that is used to address a message to the appropriate IP address of the receiver (Fig. 5.16).

The Internet is a packet-switched network that uses TCP/IP as its protocol. This means that, as messages or packets are sent, there is no part of the network that is dedicated to them. This is like the fact that when your letters and parcels are sent by post they are mixed with letters and parcels from other people. The alternative type of network is the circuit switched network such as phone systems where the line is dedicated to the user for the duration of the call. Taking the analogy further, the transmission media of the Internet such as telephone lines, satellite links and optical cables are the equivalent of the vans, trains and planes that are used to carry post. Transmission

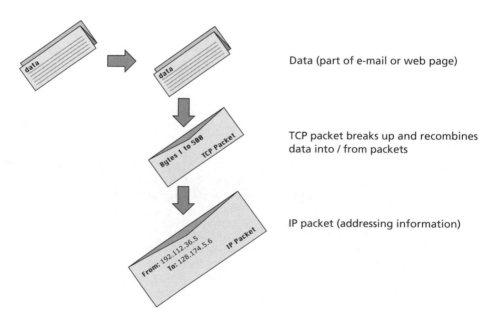

Figure 5.16 The TCP/IP protocol
Source: Chaffey (2002)

media for the Internet include analogue media such as phone lines and faster, digital media such as integrated service digital network (ISDN) technology and more recently asynchronous digital subscriber line (ADSL), as mentioned in Case Study 5.1.

In addition to the transmission media, components of the network are also required to direct or route the packets or messages via the most efficient route. On the Internet these are referred to as 'routers' or 'hubs', and are manufactured by companies such as Cisco and 3Com. The routers are the equivalent of postal sorting offices which decide the best route for mail to take. They do not plan the entire route of the message, but rather direct it to the next router that seems most appropriate given the destination and current network traffic.

Some addressing information goes at the beginning of your message; this information gives the network enough information to deliver the packet of data. The **IP address** of a receiving server is usually in the form 207.68.156.58, which is a numerical representation of a better known form such as www.microsoft.com. Each IP address is unique to a given organisation, server or client, in a similar way to postal codes referring to a small number of houses. The first number refers to the top-level domain in the network, in this case **.com**. The remaining numbers are used to refer to a particular organisation.

IP address
The unique numerical address of a computer.

Once the Internet message is addressed, the postal analogy is not so apt since related information is not sent across the Internet in one large message. For reasons of efficiency, information sent across IP networks is broken up into separate parts called **packets**. The information within a packet is usually between 1 and 1500 characters long. This helps to route information most efficiently and fairly with different packets sent by different people gaining equal priority. The transmission control protocol, TCP, performs the task of splitting up the original message into packets on dispatch and reassembling it on receipt. Combining TCP and IP, you can think of an addressed IP envelope containing a TCP envelope which in turn contains part of the original message that has been split into a packet (Fig. 5.16).

Packet
Each Internet message such as an e-mail or http request is broken down into smaller parts for ease of transmission.

▶ The HTTP protocol

HTTP, the hypertext transfer protocol is a standard used to allow web browsers and servers to transfer requests for delivery of web pages and their embedded graphics. When you click on a link while viewing a web site, the web browser you are using will request information from the server computer hosting the web site using the http protocol. Since this protocol is important for delivering the web pages, the letters http:// are used to prefix all web addresses. HTTP messages are divided into HTTP 'get' messages for requesting and web page and HTTP 'send' messages as shown in Figure 5.17. The web pages and graphics transferred in this way are transferred as packets, which is why web pages do not usually download gradually, but come in jumps as different groups of packets arrive.

HTTP (hypertext transfer protocol)
HTTP or Hypertext transfer protocol is a standard that defines the way information is transmitted across the Internet between web browsers and web servers.

The inventor of http, Tim Berners Lee describes its purpose as follows (Berners Lee, 1999):

> HTTP rules define things like which computer speaks first, and how they speak in turn. When two computers agree they can talk, they have to find a common way to represent their data so they can share it.

▶ Uniform resource locators (URL)

Web addresses refer to particular pages on a web server which is hosted by a company or organisation. The technical name for web addresses is **uniform or universal resource locators (URLs)**. URLs can be thought of as a standard method of addressing similar to post codes that make it straightforward to find the name of a site.

Uniform (universal) resource locators (URL)
A web address used to locate a web page on a web server.

Web addresses are usually prefixed by 'http://' to denote the http protocol that is explained above. Web addresses always start with 'http://', so references to web sites in this book and in most promotional material from companies omit this part of the URL. Indeed, when using modern versions of web browsers, it is not necessary to type this in as part of the web page location since it is added automatically by the web browser. Although the vast majority of sites start with 'www', this is not universal, so it is necessary to specify this.

Web addresses are structured in a standard way as follows:

http://www.domain-name.extension/filename.html

❱ Domain names

The domain name refers to the name of the web server and is usually selected to be the same as the name of the company, and the extension will indicate its type. The extension is known as the global top-level domain (gTLD). There are also some 250 country-code top-level domains (ccTLD).

Some common gTLDs are:

● **.com** represents an international or American company such as http://www.travel-agency.com
● **.co.uk** represents a company based in the UK such as http://www.thomascook.co.uk
● **.ac.uk** for a UK university (e.g. http://www.derby.ac.uk)
● **.org.uk** or **.org** are for not-for-profit organisations (e.g. www.greenpeace.org)
● **.net** for a network provider such as www.virgin.net

The 'filename.html' part of the web address refers to an individual web page, for example 'products.html' for a web page summarising a company's products. When a web address is typed in without a filename, for example www.bt.com, the browser automatically assumes the user is looking for the home page, which by convention is referred to as index.html. When creating sites, it is therefore vital to name the home page index.html. The file index.html can also be placed in sub-directories to ease access to information. For example, to access a support page a customer would type www.bt.com/support.

Note that gTLDs are continuously under review and in 2000 Icann, the Internet Corporation for Assigned Names and Numbers (www.icann.org) granted seven new gTLDs. Available from June 2001 are .biz for business, .name to be used by individuals, .museum, .pro for professionals, .aero for aviation, .coop for cooperatives and .info. Some of the proposed gTLDs refused included '.sex', '.shoes', '.kids' and '.xxx'. The introduction of these names, while increasing choice where .com names have already been assigned, may make finding the URL of a company more difficult – it may less often be sufficient to take the name of the company and add '.com'. According to another view, existing companies such as Amazon will attempt to register with the new domain such as '.biz' which will not help to increase the availability of gTLD names.

Icann is involved in domain name arbitration. Its first case involved an individual who offered the name WorldWrestlingFederation.com to the World Wrestling Federation. The WWF won since it was considered the individual was 'cybersquatting'. In another case, Penguin books stated that it had a claim to www.penguin.org which had been registered by an individual. But in this Penguin lost since the respondent argued convincingly that he was known as Penguin and his wife as Mrs Penguin!

The long-term solution to the difficulty for users in matching company and brand names with URLs seem to be lookup systems. One such system is RealNames (www.real-names.com) which has been integrated into search engines such as Altavista.com. RealNames was established in 1998. Centraal, the company that operates RealNames, will register company names and brands for $100 and it offers a searching service to consumers where the consumer types a company or product they are looking for and its search engine will then list matches. In March 1999 there were 15 000 registered companies or brands registered with RealNames and 3 million other companies.

Domain name registration

If a company wants to establish a web presence they need to register a domain name that is unique to them. Domain names can be registered via an ISP or at more favourable rates direct from the domain name services:

1 InterNIC – www.internic.net. Registration and information about sites in the .com, .org and .net domains.
2 Nomination – www.nomination.uk.com. This is an alternative registration service for the UK, allowing you to register in the uk.com domain.
3 Nominet – www.nominet.org.uk. This is the main co.uk site.

◗ Web page standards

The main web page standards introduced in Chapter 4 are **HTML (hypertext markup language)** and, for data exchange, **XML (extensible markup language)**. Figure 5.17 gives an example of an HTML page as source and how it is rendered on screen.

HTML (hypertext markup language)
HTML is a standard format used to define the text and layout of web pages. HTML files usually have the extension .html or .htm.

XML or extensible markup language
A standard for transferring structured data, unlike HTML which is purely presentational.

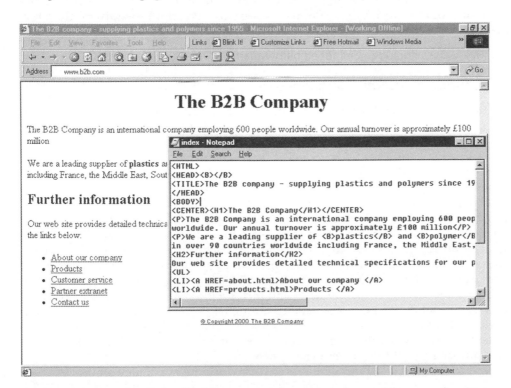

Figure 5.17 Home page index.html for an example company in a web browser showing HTML source in text editor
Source: Chaffey (2002)

Graphical images (GIF and JPEG files)

GIF (graphics interchange format)

A graphics format and compression algorithm best used for simple graphics.

JPEG (joint photographics experts group)

A graphics format and compression algorithm best used for photographs.

Graphics produced by graphic designers or captured using digital cameras can be readily incorporated into web pages as images. **GIF (graphics interchange format)** and **JPEG (joint photographics experts group)** refer to two standard file formats most commonly used to present images on web pages. GIF files are limited to 256 colours and are best used for small simple graphics such as banner adverts while JPEG are best used for larger images such as photographs where image quality is important. Both formats use image compression technology to minimise the size of downloaded files.

Animated graphical information (GIFs and plug-ins)

Plug-ins

An add-on program to a web browser providing extra functionality such as animation.

GIF files can also be used for interactive banner adverts. **Plug-ins** are additional programs, sometimes referred to as 'helper applications', and work in association with the web browser to provide features not present in the basic web browser. The best-known plug-ins are probably that for Adobe Acrobat which is used to display documents in .pdf format (www.adobe.com) and the Macromedia Flash and Shockwave products for producing interactive graphics (www.macromedia.com).

▶ Audio and video standards

Streaming media

Sound and video that can be experienced within a web browser without the need to download a complete file.

Traditionally sound and video (or 'rich' media) have been stored as the Microsoft standards .wav and .avi. A newer sound format for music is MP3. These formats are used on some web sites, but they are not appropriate for sites such as the BBC (www.bbc.co.uk), since the user would have to wait for the whole clip to download before hearing or viewing it. Streaming media are now used for many multimedia sites since they enable video or audio to start playing within a few seconds – it is not necessary for the whole file to be downloaded before it can be played. Formats for **streaming media** have been established by Real Networks (www.realnetworks.com).

▶ The future of Internet infrastructure

For many first-time and regular users, the Internet is seen as frustrating because of its speed. Of course, the poor performance is, to an extent, a consequence of the success of the Internet in attracting over half a billion users. Action to improve this situation takes the form of projects by government departments such as education and defence together with business initiatives. The Internet 2 project is coordinated by the University Corporation for Advanced Internet Development (UCAID), an association formed by 34 international universities in 1996. UCAID's Internet 2 project is directed at software aspects of the infrastructure. These include the concept of 'teleimmersion' where different people can occupy virtual space from different locations. The development of broadband access will also enable improved use of multimedia. On a more fundamental level, UCAID is reviewing how improvements in the standards of the Internet such as Ipv6 can be used in Internet 2. IPv6 is a revision of the IP protocol that is intended to give better performance and increase the number of addresses available. This could enable, for example, walking through a prototype building to discuss its merits. Other initiatives from the United States include new high-speed network backbones such as Abilene, the National Science Foundation's Very High Speed Backbone Network Service (VBNS) and new defence networks.

Focus on new access devices   **F**

There are an increasing number of new technologies by which customers can access content across the Internet or other wide-area networks such as wireless phone-type devices or interactive digital TV. The Internet Monitor from MORI (www.e-mori.co.uk) showed that in the UK in March 2000 the number of households with access to interactive TV exceeded the number of Internet users. This is a pattern likely to be repeated elsewhere, although access does not necessarily equate to use.

These new technology developments pose a difficult dilemma for organisations responding to e-commerce since often, to be competitive, the investment decision must be made before the extent of its impact is apparent. These issues apply in particular to business-to-consumer companies such as media owners and retailers since the content made available for new access devices has mainly been targeted at consumers. Imagine you are the e-commerce manager at this type of company; what would be the benefits and drawbacks of updating your e-commerce systems to support these new platforms? The benefits of deciding to invest could include:

- early-mover advantage
- learning about the technology
- customer acquisition
- customer retention
- improving corporate or brand image.

However, it will be difficult to estimate the number of new customers who may be acquired, and profitability of the project may sacrificed to achieve the other benefits above. As new technologies become available, companies need to assess the technology, understand the services that may be relevant to their customers and work out a strategy and implementation plan. It also becomes necessary to support development across multiple platforms, for example retailers such as WH Smith Online use a database to generate book catalogue content for display on web, mobile or interactive digital TV platforms.

Although it may appear that there is a divergence in access devices from PC to phone, to PDA, to TV, in the long term most commentators expect **technology convergence** to occur.

Mougayer (1998) identifies different types of convergence:

Technology convergence
A trend in which different hardware devices such as TVs, computers and phones merge and have similar functions.

- *infrastructure convergence* – this is the increase in the number of delivery media channels for the Internet, such as phone lines, microwave (mobile phones), cable and satellite. These are now often being used in combination;
- *information appliance (technology) convergence* – the use of different hardware devices to access and deliver the content of the Internet;
- *supplier convergence* – the overlap between suppliers such as Internet service providers, online access providers and more traditional media suppliers such as the telcos and cable companies.

We will now briefly consider the technology and business implications for two of the main new access devices – mobile or wireless and interactive digital TV.

▶ Mobile or wireless access devices

Mobile technologies are not new – it has been possible for many years to access the Internet for e-mail using a laptop connected via a modem. The need for a large device to access the Internet was overcome with the development of personal digital assistants (PDAs) such as the Palm Computing Palm VII or Psion which accessed the Internet via a wireless connection.

The characteristics that mobile or wireless connections offer to their users can be summarised by the supposedly idyllic image used in many adverts of a user accessing the Internet via a laptop or phone from a field, riverbank or mountaintop. They provide ubiquity (can be accessed from anywhere), reachability (their users can be reached when not in their normal location) and convenience (it is not necessary to have access to a power supply or fixed-line connection). In addition to these obvious benefits, there are additional benefits that are less obvious: they provide security – each user can be authenticated since each wireless device has a unique identification code; their location can be used to tailor content and they provide a degree of privacy compared with a desktop PC – looking for jobs on a wireless device might be better than under the gaze of a boss. An additional advantage that will shortly be available is that of instant access or being 'always on'; here there is no need to dial up a wireless connection.

In addition to offering voice-calls, mobile phones have increasingly been used for e-mail and **short message service (SMS)**. SMS is effectively a simple form of e-mail that enables messages to be transferred between mobile phones. In early 2000, it was estimated that there were over 2 billion SMS messages exchanged each month. These consist of voice, mail notifications, alerts about news or messages direct between phone users.

In 1999 the first of a new generation of mobile phones such as the Nokia 7110 were introduced; these offered the opportunity to access the Internet. They are known as **wireless application protocol or WAP** phones, or in more common parlance web-enabled or Internet phones. What these phones offer is the facility to access information on web sites that has been specially tailored for display on the small screens of mobile phones. There is a tremendous amount of hype about these phones since they provide all the benefits that have been provided by the World Wide Web, but in a mobile form.

Wireless application protocol (WAP)
WAP is a technical standard for transferring information to wireless devices, such as mobile phones.

How does WAP work?

Figure 5.18 summarises the hardware requirements for a WAP system. A user needs a WAP-enabled handset which is used to type in WAP web addresses. WAP pages are then accessed using wireless techniques from a WAP gateway that is connected to a traditional web server where the WAP pages are hosted. Portals from the mobile phone companies or new phone portals will be used to configure services on the phone such as setting up SMS.

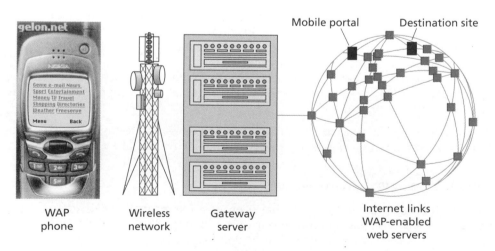

| WAP phone | Wireless network | Gateway server | Internet links WAP-enabled web servers |

Figure 5.18 Hardware and software infrastructure for WAP system
Source: Chaffey (2002)

As Figure 5.19 shows, the different parts of the standard are consistent with those for the Internet. For example, there are layers for security and starting and finishing a transaction. The equivalent of the HTML authoring layer is the 'Wireless Application Environment'. Development of applications for this environment uses a markup language similar to HTML known as the wireless markup language or WML.

Pages are written in **wireless markup language (WML)**. This is similar to HTML, but it introduces new concepts in accordance with the medium. To speed access, each WML file is referred to a 'deck' and consists of several cards that can be displayed sequentially without reconnecting. For more information on the technology see www.anywhereyougo.com

Wireless markup language (WML)
Standard for displaying mobile pages such as transferred by WAP.

Demand for services

In the UK in early 2000, WAP mobiles such as the Nokia 7110 were available from suppliers such as BT Cellnet, Orange and Vodafone. Virgin was planning an emulation service for existing phones. Demand for the services appears to be high, with many consumers reporting that they were unable to purchase in early 2000. Durlacher Research reported that demand for WAP as a percentage of all mobiles was likely to climb from 9% at the end of 2000 to 22% in 2001 to 85% in 2003.

Transactional and informational services for consumers have been delivered. Consumer applications to date include retail (WH Smith Online books, the Carphone Warehouse), ticketing (lastminute.com), broking, banking (the Woolwich), gambling (Ladbrokes), bill payment and job searching. Some informational services based on personalisation such as that of Excite UK and Yahoo! have also been launched. These

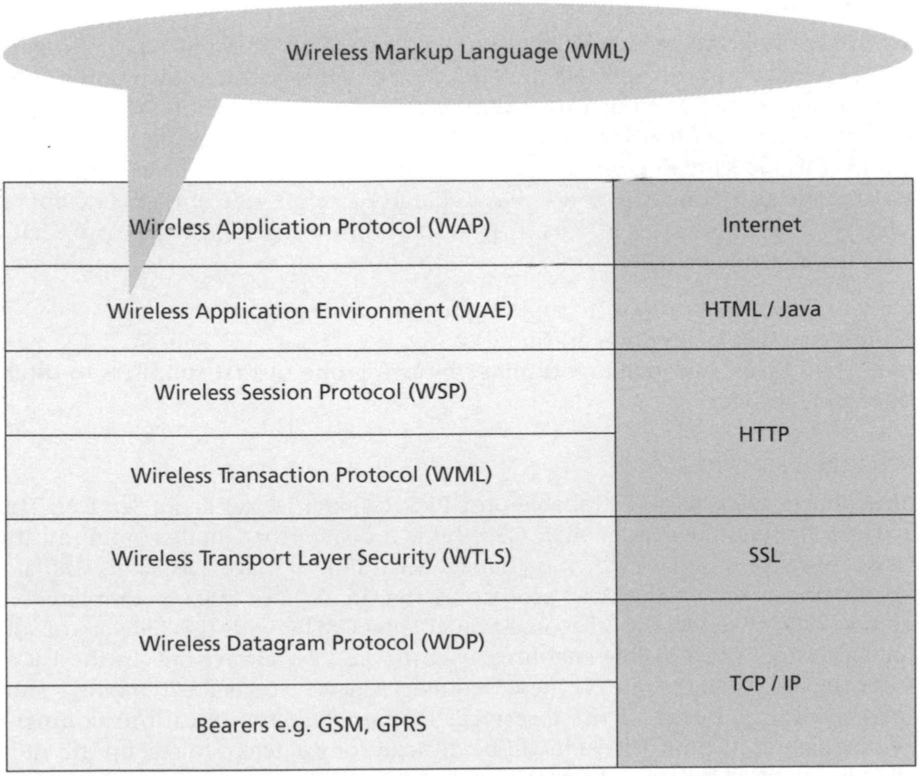

Wireless Markup Language (WML)	
Wireless Application Protocol (WAP)	Internet
Wireless Application Environment (WAE)	HTML / Java
Wireless Session Protocol (WSP)	HTTP
Wireless Transaction Protocol (WML)	
Wireless Transport Layer Security (WTLS)	SSL
Wireless Datagram Protocol (WDP)	TCP / IP
Bearers e.g. GSM, GPRS	

Figure 5.19 Different protocol layers of the WAP standard
Source: Chaffey (2002)

include information such as sports news, stock prices, news, cinemas, weather, horoscopes and reminders.

Services for businesses delivered by WAP are currently less developed, but are forecast by Durlacher to centre on supply-chain integration where there will be facilities to place orders, check stock availability, give notification of dispatch and track orders.

MINI CASE STUDY

Guinness uses SMS to reach a young audience

Revolution (2001a) described how brand owner Diageo used Nightfly 30 SMS channels described as 'your mobile nightlife guide' to reach 18–24-year-old users. On St Patricks Day (17 March 2001), a promotion went out to the 3612 Nightfly users in Nottingham who had opted to receive drinks promotions; 92% were aged between 18 and 29 and 63% were male. Two alerts were involved in the promotion, one a week in advance and one on the day – each listing the bars and clubs where the promotions were available. Follow-up research suggested that sales had increased substantially, with 43.7% of those influenced to purchase Guinness! Ellie Calver, brand manager at Guinness, was quoted as saying: 'the results were very encouraging and it looks as if this might be an exciting addition to the marketing mix, particularly for informing customers about below-the-line activity'.

Strategies for mobile commerce

Different types of strategy can be identified for two main different types of organisations. For portal and media owners the options are to migrate their own portal to WAP or SMS (the option followed by Excite and *The* Guardian) or to partner with other WAP portals and provide content for these. Revenue models may include sponsorship or subscription for individual content items or on a subscription basis. Options for advertising are also being explored – www.247europe.com is one of the first companies to offer WAP-based advertisemsents. For destination sites such as banks and retailers, the options available include:

- marketing communications (to support purchase and support);
- e-commerce (sale of products on site);
- brand building – improve brand image by being one of first suppliers to offer an innovative service.

Future mobile services

In 2001 new services became available on GPRS (General Packet Radio Service). This is approximately five times faster than GSM (global system for mobile communication) and is an 'always-on' service which is charged according to usage. Display is still largely text-based and based on the WAP protocol. Later, in 2002 or 2003 a completely new generation (3G) of services will become available by UMTS; with this delivery of sound and images should be possible enabling instant access or 'always-on'. In the UK auctions for the licence to operate on these frequencies have exceeded £20 billion – such is the perceived importance of these services to the telecommunications companies. Many commentators now believe it will be difficult for the telcos to recoup this money and this has resulted in large falls in their share prices.

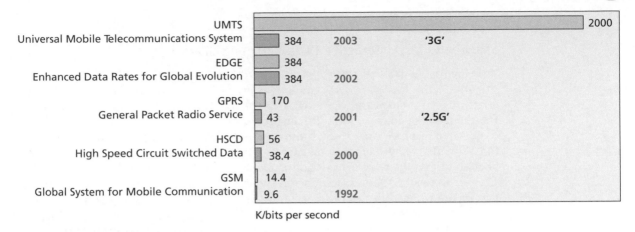

Figure 5.20 Mobile access technologies
Source: Chaffey (2002)

Figure 5.20 summarises these new standards for accessing the mobile Internet. For each new technology there is an envelope between the lowest and highest possible transmission speeds. Very often the hype is based on the upper limit, but with implementation only the lower limit is achieved.

▶ Interactive digital television

Interactive digital technology (iDTV) has now been used in Europe for several years to deliver broadcasting to homes and offer new interactive services. In France, Canal Plus launched iDTV in 1996, Television par satellite launched in 1997 and Spain, Italy and Germany have had these facilities since 1996 or 1997. It offers similar e-commerce facilities to the Internet, but is provided with a simpler interface that can be operated from a remote control. IDTV has a limited number of suppliers compared to the Internet since start-up costs are higher. The amount of information available from providers is lower because of limited bandwidth on site.

In the UK there are several providers. For example, Sky Digital can be viewed by over 5 million subscribers and initially had content from banks such as HSBC and Woolwich, retailers such as Woolworths, Dixons and Carphone Warehouse. This is known as a 'walled garden service' since it is not open access like the Internet. Although there are few reported figures of the overall use of these services, individual examples indicate some early success: HSBC registered 80 000 customers within 3 weeks, of whom 20 000 were new. Domino Pizza had 10 000 requests in its first 10 days. In 2002 several retailers stopped their use of Sky service, citing high costs. Cable providers Ntl, Telewest and Digital terrestrial ITV digital are the other main providers.

How does interactive digital TV work?

Figure 5.21 shows that a set-top box is an important component of the interactive digital TV system. This is used to receive and decode the message from a satellite dish or cable that is then displayed on a conventional TV. The set-top box also includes a modem that is used to pass back selections made on the interactive shopping channel to the company across the Internet.

Sharwood's tests interactive TV as marketing channel

This campaign ran for three months on the ntl: platform and offered Virgin Atlantic flights and Sharwood's coupons as prizes. Revolution (2001b) reported that Sharwood's were looking to use iDTV to reach a different demographic, audience test the medium and also promote the brand.

Creative in phase one of the campaign used 'Take your tastebuds on an adventure with Sharwood's' emblazoned across a colourful banner, but this was changed later on so that the banner read 'Korma Blimey!' and this doubled click-through.

Users were asked three questions on the microsite about Sharwood's products as part of the competition in order to promote registration and data capture. Further information about recipes was also available.

Results were reported as 2175 entries and 1.37 million page impressions after 12 959 click-throughs. Phase one of the banner campaign achieved an average click-through of 1.25% and phase two saw 1.37%.

When a company decides how to respond to iDTV several levels of commitment can be identified:

- *promotion* – using interactive ads
- *content* – repurpose web site
- *content* – new interactive services
- *e-commerce* – perhaps for a limited range of products.

Other new digital access devices may affect the future infrastructure requirements. These include digital home storage. Its promoters are describing this as '*the biggest change in conventional broadcasting since the industry began*'. Variously referred to as personal video

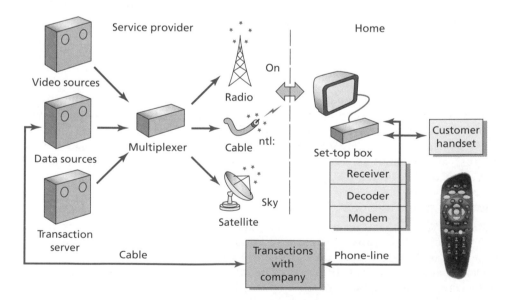

Figure 5.21 Components of an interactive digital TV system
Source: Chaffey (2002)

recorders, home media servers or content refrigerators, they all involve recording a TV programme direct to a magnetic disk which gives 20 hours of recording time. Examples are TiVo and ReplayTV. These offer the opportunity to pause a programme while it is transmitted, record it and return to it later. It may also be possible to filter out adverts.

CASE STUDY 5.2

What went wrong with WAP?

Wireless commerce has a credibility problem and WAP is a big part of that problem. Wireless Application Protocol is the technology that once promised to catapult Europe into the digital age by bringing interactive services to a potential market of more than 250m owners of mobile phones.

But this vision of wireless commerce has failed to take root and WAP has taken much of the blame. Only 12m Europeans had WAP phones at the end of 2000, according to Durlacher, the London-based investment bank. Worse news still, once the novelty has worn off, these people rarely visit any of the 10,000 WAP-enabled websites or 7.8m WAP pages that exist today. 'Whilst most of these end-users will use their WAP browsers, we do not expect that their usage will be high', says Durlacher. A survey of Swedish WAP phone owners found that only 6 per cent use the WAP functionality regularly. T-Mobil, Germany's largest mobile operator, reports that its WAP users spend only 17 minutes online per month. This creates a vicious circle: if usage stays low, it makes little sense to spend large sums creating content for WAP, particularly given today's more cautious investment climate. So what has gone wrong with WAP?

Experts say the technology should not be held solely responsible. 'WAP is just a simple protocol and it's not fair to just blame the technology', says Tomas Franzén, chief executive of AU-System, a Swedish company that developed the WAP browser used by Ericsson and others. 'There were just too many expectations placed on technology.'

The WAP protocol is not the only way to handle data on mobile devices. In Japan, NTT DoCoMo has created a market of 20m with its rival i-mode technology. In the US, the popularity of wireless devices such as the Palm VII organiser has led many developers to use HDML, another rival standard. 'Wireless commerce should not be seen as WAP-centric', says Karl Andersson, vice-president of m-commerce for Scandinavia at Cap Gemini Ernst & Young, the IT services company.

Just one of many standards

The Nordic region has the highest wireless penetration in the world and many m-commerce services are available – Helsinki even allows its motorists to pay for their parking space using their mobile phone. However, most of these services were developed using SMS, the simple text-only messaging technology that is built into every mobile phone. 'There are many examples of text-based services that are generating revenues for operators', says Mr Andersson. Despite the success of SMS, i-mode and other alternatives to WAP, the future of Europe's fledgling wireless commerce market has become inextricably linked to WAP. So, when users complained that early WAP services failed to live up to expectations, the WAP standard got much of the blame. Most complaints centred on the achingly slow speeds when accessing WAP services over today's GSM networks.

This problem may be solved with new, higher-speed, cellular networks based on GPRS technology, and then on third-generation UMTS telephony. The first GPRS mobile phones will be available this year, but many operators and handset manufacturers have got cold feet over GPRS and it may not become widely available until 2002. UMTS will not appear until 2003–2004.

Other complaints have focused on difficulty in viewing content such as web pages on the diminutive screens of WAP phones. In a study carried out by the Nielsen Norman Group, a US research firm, people who had used WAP services for a week were asked whether they were likely to still be using a WAP phone one year later. A resounding 70 per cent answered no. 'WAP is not ready for prime time yet, nor do users expect it to be usable any time soon', concluded Marc Ramsay and Jakob Nielsen, authors of the report.

The drubbing given to WAP has poured cold water on the feverish expectations of Europe's m-commerce industry, which once had a vision of WAP opening a cornucopia of revenue-generating services such as stock alerts, ticketing or wireless banking. Wireless Commerce (WCL), a Finnish start-up, believes there is still a bright future for these types of service, particularly in Finland, where mobile phones already outnumber fixed lines. But WAP is unlikely to be part of that future. 'We are not often asked for WAP services by the operators as WAP is not used very much in Finland', says Hannu Vähäsaari, managing director of WCL. 'The thinking behind WAP is very good but it was just too early.' WCL has developed various m-commerce services, including a travel alert service for Railtrack, the UK train network operator, and mobile auctions for eTori, a Finnish website. These services were developed principally for SMS, which Mr Vähäsaari believes is sufficient to handle most if not all of the data services that operators want to offer today.

Compared with the sophisticated graphics capabilities of WAP – soon to be enhanced with colour – SMS may seem basic, but that is part of its attraction, according to Mr Vähäsaari. 'SMS is a very robust way to do wireless business today', he says. SMS works well, whereas developers of WAP applications have to contend with multiple versions of the WAP standard and idiosyncrasies in how WAP is implemented by the handset manufacturers. Jinny Software, an Irish start-up, is another fan of SMS. It has created an SMS-based banking service for AIB, the big Irish bank, among other customers. 'SMS is blooming all over Europe and you can do some pretty clever things with SMS', says Ciazan Carey, head of m-commerce at Jinny. Earlier this year, Jinny was acquired by Acotel, an Italian company, for $14m (£9.7m) in cash. Acotel plans to use Jinny's SMS technology to develop and host SMS applications for Telecom Italia Mobile, which means a potential market of 35m GSM users in Italy and around the world.

Wireless commerce continues to generate great interest in Europe, as this deal demonstrates. However, the WAP backlash has had its effect and companies are turning to SMS, an established and trusted technology, to unlock the market's potential, at least for the next couple of years. 'In contrast to SMS, WAP has not built up goodwill because its benefits currently simply do not outweigh its inconvenience', says Durlacher. There could be 72m WAP-enabled phones in Europe by the end of 2003, predicts Durlacher, but it will be SMS, not WAP, that produces most of the data and content revenues that these users generate.

Source: Geoff Nairn, *Connectis*, 29 May 2001

Questions

1 Describe the evidence for the failure of WAP and explain reasons for this according to the article.

2 What are the lessons of the relative failure of WAP for a manager? How you would advise a manager at a news magazine publisher to assess the relevance of the next generation of wireless technology such as 3G?

Other wide-area networks

▶ Wide-area network (WAN)

Wide-area network (WAN)

Networks covering a large area which connect to businesses in different parts of the same city, different parts of a country of different countries.

These are large in extent and may connect offices in different parts of the same city, different parts of a country or even different countries (Fig. 5.22). The WAN will connect many servers at each site. When we connect from a PC at one site to a server at another site, we talk about connecting to a 'remote' server across a WAN. If there is a large international coverage, it will be referred to as a global network. If the WAN enables communication across the whole company, it is referred to as the 'enterprise network' or 'enterprise-wide network'. Companies usually pay for their own 'leased lines' or communications links between different sites. Virtual private networks and value-added networks, which are described later, provide cheaper alternatives where the communications links are shared.

Often the network used to connect remote sites is the public telephone, referred to as POTS or 'plain old telephone system'. A company can also lease private or dedicated lines from a telecommunications supplier to connect sites, or can set up links using microwave or satellite methods.

Other terms are also used to refer to the extent of a network. Many colleges and universities will have campus networks which connect different buildings making up the campus. Large cities such as London or New York often have a high-speed metropolitan area network to connect businesses within the city. Singapore has developed the concept of the 'intelligent island' in which businesses of the city are connected by a very high-speed network.

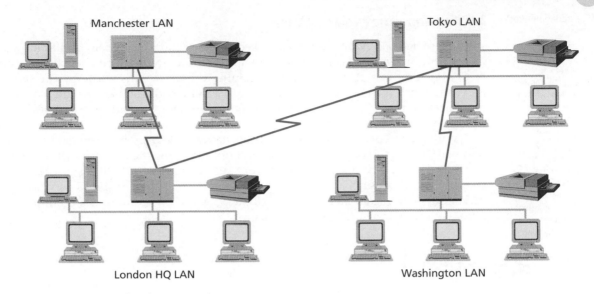

Figure 5.22 **A wide-area network (WAN)**

The virtual organisation

The virtual organisation is now touted by many authors as the shape of the future business. A virtual organisation makes use of networking to set up communication between its employees, suppliers and customers in such a way that there are no physical boundaries or constraints on the company. Employees may work any-where in the world and customers are able to purchase tailored products from any location. The absence of any rigid boundary or hierarchy within the organisation should lead to a more responsive and flexible company. This extends to 'virtual products' where mass production is replaced by the ability to tailor the product to the customer's need.

A hypothetical example is of a 'virtual shoe company' which contracts seven other companies to:

- research the shoe market;
- design shoes;
- make shoes;
- advertise shoes;
- transport to retailers;
- sell shoes;
- do the accounts.

The Internet and a wide-area network are used to set up the links between the play-ers in the virtual organisation. Software such as e-mail, groupware and workflow are used to aid collaboration between people in the organisation.

▶ Value-added networks (VANs)

Value-added networks (VANs)

Value-added networks (VANs) give a subscription service enabling companies to transmit data securely across a shared network.

Value-added networks (VAN) are so named because they allow a company to minimise its investment in wide-area communications while still receiving all the benefits this can bring. The cost of setting up and maintaining the network is borne by the service provider, which then rents out the network to a number of companies. This works out more cheaply than if a company had leased its own point-to-point private lines, but it is not as secure.

Virtual private network (VPN)

A data network that makes use of the public telecommunication infrasructure and Internet, but information remains secure by the use of security procedures.

A similar concept to VAN is **virtual private networks (VPNs)**. These are data networks that make use of the public telecommunications infrastructure and Internet, but information remains secure by the use of what is known as a 'tunnelling protocol' and security procedures such as 'firewalls', which are described in Chapter 17. A virtual private network can again be contrasted with a system of owned or leased point-to-point lines that can only be used by one company.

F Focus on EDI

Electronic data interchange (EDI)

The exchange, using digital media, of structured business information, particularly for sales transactions such as purchase orders and invoices between buyers and sellers.

Transactional e-commerce predates PCs and the World Wide Web by some margin. In the 1960s, **electronic data interchange (EDI)** and **electronic funds transfer (EFT)** over secure private networks became established modes of intra- and inter-company transaction. The idea of standardised document exchange can be traced back to the 1948 Berlin Airlift, where a standard form was required for efficient management of items flown to Berlin from many locations. This was followed by electronic transmission in the 1960s in the US transport industries. The EDIFACT (Electronic Data Interchange for Administration, Commerce and Transport) standard was later produced by a joint United Nations/European committee to facilitate international trading. There is also a similar X12 EDI standard developed by the ANSI Accredited Standards Committee.

Electronic funds transfer (EFT)

Automated digital transmission of money between organisations and banks.

Clark (1998) considers that EDI is best understood as the replacement of paper-based purchase orders with electronic equivalents, but its applications are wider than this. The types of documents exchanged by EDI include business transactions such as orders, invoices, delivery advices and payment instructions as part of EFT. There may also be pure information transactions such as a product specification, for example engineering drawings or price lists. Clark (1998) defines EDI as:

> the exchange of documents in standardised electronic form, between organisations, in an automated manner, directly from a computer application in one organisation to an application in another.

DTI (2000) describes EDI as follows:

> Electronic data interchange (EDI) is the computer-to-computer exchange of structured data, sent in a form that allows for automatic processing with no manual intervention. This is usually carried out over specialist EDI networks.

Financial EDI

Aspect of electronic payment mechanism involving transfer of funds from the bank of a buyer to a seller.

It is apparent from these definitions that EDI is one form, or a subset, of electronic commerce. A key point is that direct communication occurs between applications (rather than between computers). This requires information systems to achieve the data processing, data management associated with EDI, and integration with associated information systems such as sales order processing and inventory control systems.

Internet EDI

Use of EDI data standards delivered across non-proprietary IP networks.

According to IDC (1999), revenues for EDI network services were already at $1.1 billion in 1999 and are forecast to reach over $2 billion by 2003. EDI is developing through new standards and integration with Internet technologies to achieve **Internet EDI**. IDC (1999) predicts that Internet EDI's share of EDI revenues will climb from 12%

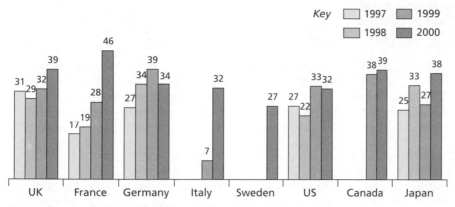

Figure 5.23 Businesses that use EDI (%)
Source: DTI survey, 2000

to 41% over the same period. The international benchmarking survey (Fig. 5.23) suggests that EDI is increasing in most countries. Such data should be treated with caution since respondents may not be clear on the strict meaning of EDI.

Internet EDI enables EDI to be implemented at lower costs since rather than using proprietary, so-called **value-added networks (VANs)**, it uses the same EDI standard documents such as that for a purchase order illustrated below, but using lower cost transmission techniques through **virtual private networks (VPNs)** or the public Internet. Reported cost savings are up to 90% (www.edi-insider.com 1996). EDI Insider estimated that this cost differential would cause an increase from the 80 000 companies in the United States using EDI in 1996 to hundreds of thousands. Internet EDI also includes EDI structured documents being exchanged by e-mail or in a more automated form using FTP.

Value-added network (VAN)
....
A secure wide-area network that uses proprietary rather than Internet technology.

Virtual private network (VPN)
....
A secure, encrypted (tunnelled) connection between two points using the Internet, typically created by ISPs for organisations wanting to conduct secure Internet trading.

◗ Benefits and limitations of EDI

The benefits of EDI are the same as those for Internet-based electronic commerce between organisations. The benefits of using EDI to streamline business processes include:

- more rapid fulfilment of orders. Reduced lead times are achieved through reduced times in placing and receiving order, reduced times of information in transit and integration with other processes;
- fewer errors in data entry and less time spent by the buyer and supplier on exception handling;
- reduced costs resulting from reduced staff time, material savings such as paper and forms and improved inventory control.

Early EDI solutions were expensive to implement. Despite efforts to create national and international standards for document formats, they were based on proprietary technologies which tended to lock a company into that supplier since each EDI link tended to be set up specifically for a single supplier and buyer. This made it difficult to switch the connection to another supplier. If a company was multi-sourcing rather than single-sourcing then separate EDI standards might be needed for each supplier. Internet EDI tends to reduce these disadvantages.

MINI CASE STUDY

Flymo and EDI

Flymo, the largest lawnmower manufacturer in the UK, is typical of many companies that have moved from EDI to Internet EDI. Traditionally, it has used EDI for linking to the largest retailers, such as the DIY superstore where the trading volume and the potential cost savings required it. Smaller retailers, however, could not order electronically, because they could not afford the cost of setting up dedicated links to Flymo. This meant, however that Flymo had the expense of processing and re-keying paper and fax-based documents. With the advent of the Internet-based e-commerce, Flymo could create an Internet EDI system that solved their administrative overheads, but was also affordable for the smaller retailer. Supplier IBM created what is known as the 'Internet for dealers network'. This gives the retailers two facilities. The first is a CD-ROM for offline ordering, which can be used to enter orders offline. They then open up a transmit form screen and the data is transmitted in a similar format to the traditional EDI links. The dealers can also log on to the extranet with their user name and password and place an order, check the status of previous orders, make invoice enquiries, and view their full account history.

Although EDI was established before Internet-based e-commerce became widespread, it appears to have a future. The volume of Internet EDI is increasing rapidly and revision of EDI standards to be compatible with XML (XML/EDI standards proposed by the XML EDI group (www.xmledi.com)) should guarantee its continued use. The use of XML by B2B exchanges such as CommerceOne and Microsoft Biznet is essentially an extension of EDI.

▶ How does EDI work?

EDI has standard specifications based on traditional paper or fax documents or forms for transactions such as purchase orders and invoices. EDI standards can be integrated into a range of software from purchasing systems to sales order processing systems or ERP (see Chapter 6). Transmission of the EDI documents can be achieved through a VAN, Internet EDI, FTP, or even e-mail. To gain an appreciation of the way EDI specifications work see the box 'Example EDI specification for a purchase order'. This shows that for each type of transaction, in this case a purchase order, different codes are used to denote different items such as item, required delivery date and location.

Example EDI specification for a purchase order

This definition of a purchase order is based on the international standard: ASC X12 850 Purchase Order. Each standard such as this is based on its own specific syntax. It is broken down into *segments* or blocks of information made up of different *data elements* that have their own code. The specification includes data elements such as the currency (CUR), delivery location (N1-4), shipment dates and times (DTM) and line item product details (PO1).

Purchase order specification

1   ISA – Interchange Control Header
2   GS – Functional Group Header (for Combination set)
3   ST – Indicates the start of a transaction set
4   BEG – Beginning of Purchase Order
5   NTE – Note Segment
6   CUR – Currency

7	REF – Reference Numbers	
8	FOB – FOB Related Instructions (shipment payer)	
9	SSS – Special Services	
10	CSH – Header Sale Condition	
11	DTM – Date/Time Reference	
12	PWK – Paperwork	
13	TD5 – Carrier Details	
14	N1 – Name Information	
15	N2 – Additional Name Information	
16	N3 – Address Information	
17	N4 – Geographic Location	
18	PO1 – Baseline Item Data	
19	PWK – Paperwork	
20	PKG – Marking, Packaging, Loading	
21	REF – Reference Numbers	
22	IT8 – Conditions of Sale	
23	SDQ – Destination Quantity	
24	DTM – Date/Time Reference	
25	SCH – Line Item Schedule	
26	N1 – Name Information	
27	N2 – Additional Name Information	
28	N3 – Address Information	
29	N4 – Geographic Location	
30	REF – Reference Numbers	
31	FOB – FOB Related Instructions	
32	TD5 – Carrier Details	
33	CTT – Transaction Totals	
34	SE – Transaction Set Trailer	
35	GE – Functional Group Trailer	
36	IEA – Interchange Control Trailer	

Purchase order example based on the specification above

```
ISA*00* *00*
*01*007061617*01*00507479*930906*2018*U*00303*000007023*0*P**^
GS*BS*007061617*005070479*930906*2025*1225*X*003030^
ST*850*121653^
BEG*00*NE*MOG009364501**950910*CSW11095^
NTE*GEN*FOR ILLUSTRATION PURPOSES ONLY^
CUR*BY*USA^
REF*PR*1234567890^
FOB*PC^
SSS*C*ZZ*ID^
CSH*SC^
DTM*071*950915*1100*CD*19^
TD5**2*YFSY*M*ROUTING*****CD*2^
N1*ST**92*H98111A1^
N3*DEPARTMENT MI5*6565 WELLS AVENUE^
N4*STE GENEVIEVE*MO*636951465*USA^
PO1*1*3*EA***BP*K6200^
CTT*1*3^
SE*16*121653^
GE*1*1225^
IEA*1*000007023^
```

Source: e-business solution provider MISG (www.misg.com/products/edi_guidelines/edi_guidelineS.html)

Smaller-scale networks

❯ Local-area network (LAN)

Local-area network (LAN)

A computer network that spans a limited geographic area, typically a single office or building.

A **local-area network (LAN)** consists of a single network segment or several connected segments that are limited in extent, hence local. A network segment defines a group of clients that are attached to the same hub or network interface card linked to a single server. The term 'local' can be interpreted in different ways. LANs are usually limited to a company occupying a single building, but could equally connect several buildings across a larger company site. Faster, higher-capacity links such as fibre-optic cables connecting different LANs or network segments are sometimes referred to as 'backbones'. Such networks may just have a single server if the company is of fewer than, say, 20 people. Larger companies with hundreds of employees are very likely to have several central servers and possibly departmental servers also. A LAN is used to share computer resources between different members of a company or workgroup. For example, a printer sharer allows several computers to be attached to a single printer, thus reducing costs. Manual printer sharers are controlled by turning a dial to indicate which computer will be used to send data to the printer. Automatic printer sharers detect any data sent to the printer and configure themselves accordingly.

A simple network that links three PC workstations with a shared server and printer is shown in Figure 5.24. This is an example of a LAN that might serve a workgroup or a small company. Here the computers and the printer are the main components of the network, with the cables and network cards forming other components. We will explain servers in more detail later. For now, consider them as a more powerful computer that is used to store data and help the other PCs communicate. The final component needed to make the network function, which is not shown on the diagram, is the communications software that enables all the components to work together.

A small-scale or workgroup network gives the following benefits by enabling:

- workers to share common information which is typically stored on the server;
- communication between workers, perhaps through e-mail or a shared diary system;

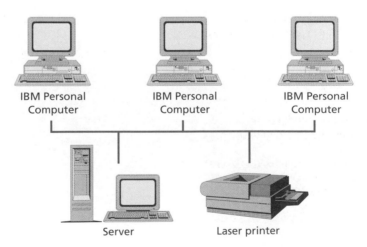

Figure 5.24 A small workgroup network connecting a single server to three PCs and a laser printer

● sharing of various facilities such as printing, hard disk storage or software applications on the server.

The capability to share devices and applications also gives the additional major benefit of cost reduction.

▶ Peer-to-peer networking

A **peer-to-peer network** is a simple type of local-area network which provides sharing of files and peripherals between PCs.

'Peer-to-peer' refers to the capability of any computer on a local-area network to share resources, in particular files and peripherals, with others. It is particularly appropriate for small workgroups where central control from a server is less necessary. Both Windows for Workgroups and Windows 95 provide these capabilities. For example, a user can, with permission, share across the network a file stored on another user's hard disk. With a peer-to-peer arrangement, data will be distributed and therefore difficult to backup and secure.

PCs can also be connected with a serial cable using the serial ports on each machine. This enables files to be transferred between, for example, a laptop and a desktop PC. This facility is available through Windows 95 or 98 or through specialised software such as Laplink.

Peer-to-peer network
A simple type of local-area network which provides sharing of files and peripherals between PCs.

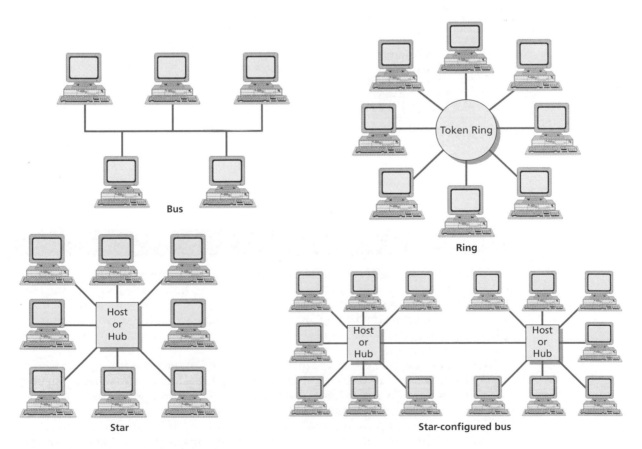

Bus

Ring

Star

Star-configured bus

Figure 5.25 Local-area network topologies

▶ Private branch exchange (PBX)

A **private branch exchange (PBX)** enables switching between phones or voice and data using existing telephone lines. This can be used for printer sharing, for example.

▶ Layouts for company networks

The physical layout of a LAN is known as a **network topology**. Bus, star, ring and combinations are most common.

There are a number of different arrangements for connecting the clients to the server in a local area network. These are known by the description of the layout or topology: bus, star or ring. The layouts of the arrangements are shown in Figure 5.25. When building a network for a company, the topology adopted will form part of the specification for the company performing installation of the network. The topology chosen and the media used to implement it will affect the network cost and performance, so these aspects are referred to in the description below. The advantages of the different types of topology are summarised in Table 5.5.

Table 5.5 Summary of the characteristics, advantages and disadvantages of the main local-area network topologies

Topology	Characteristics	Advantage	Disadvantage
Bus or linear	Simple. Based on co-axial Ethernet cable, e.g. twisted pair 10Base-T.	Easy to install and manage for small workgroup	Breaks in the cable disrupt the whole network
Star	Each PC is connected via a cable to a central location Each PC is not usually connected directly to the server, but via a hub.	Provide protection from cable breaks	Dependent on central host
Ring	A continuous ring of network cable, e.g. token ring. The word 'token' refers to a packet of data which is passed from one node to the next.	Suitable for large data volumes and mission-critical applications	Higher initial cost and time for installation

Specifying and building networks

There are three key factors in deciding which network system to purchase. These are the performance or speed that the system can deliver, how stable it is, and the cost. Most network managers receive frequent complaints about network downtime and slow performance when loading applications or data across the network. Naturally, when upgrading or specifying a new network, these will be targeted as the most important areas to improve.

When implementing communications systems, one of the main factors is the extent of the disruption to staff who are already working. This is usually minimised by making the changes out of working hours, over the weekend or during the night. A further problem is the lead time for all the different hardware and software to be delivered. This needs advanced planning. Once the new network has been installed, there may also be a lengthy period when the stability of the links is checked and optimised.

Managing Internet-based networks effectively is vital to the e-business. This is covered in Chapter 16.

Summary

1 Computer networks are built on different scales, from those limited to a single location (LAN) to national or international wide-area networks known as WAN. Table 5.6 summarises the different types.

2 Most PC-based networks are based on a client/server architecture in which there are a number of PC clients that share resources and communicate via a more powerful server computer. Client/server networks can be arranged in a number of different topologies, such as bus, star and ring.

3 The main components of a network are the server and client computers which are linked to peripheral devices such as printers. The hardware is connected by guided media such as cables or, on a larger scale, unguided satellite and microwave. Telecommunications processors or gateways are required to translate information as it is passed from the hardware devices to the media. A network operating system such as Unix, Windows NT or Novell Netware is necessary to control the hardware and provide facilities such as security and file and printer sharing.

4 Through using networks, companies can exchange information more rapidly and reduce costs by removing the need for human resources. The advantages of faster communication are not only internal, but extend to improving links with customers, suppliers, collaborators and even competitors.

5 The Internet is a global communications network that is used to transmit the information published on the World Wide Web (WWW) in a standard format based on hypertext markup language (HTML) using different standard protocols such as HTTP and TCP/IP.

6 Companies deliver e-business services to employees and partners through web servers which are often hosted at third-party companies known as Internet service providers (ISP). Web servers will be linked to applications servers, database servers and legacy applications to deliver these services.

7 Consumers and business use these e-business services through web browser software with connections to the Internet also managed by an ISP through which they can access web servers.

8 Intranets are private networks used inside companies to share information. Internet-based tools such as e-mail, FTP and the World Wide Web are all used as the method of sharing this information. Not all Internet users can access intranets since access is restricted by firewalls and password controls. Extranets are similar to intranets, but they are extended beyond the company to third parties such as suppliers, distributors or selected customers.

9 Standards to enable delivery of information include:

- communications standards such as TCP/IP and HTTP;
- text information standards such as HTML, XML and WML;
- graphical information standards such as GIF and JPEG;
- multimedia standards such as Shockwave, Flash and streaming audio and video.

Table 5.6 **Summary of the applications of different scales of network**

Scale of network	Description	Business application
Peer-to-peer	A simple network enabling sharing of files and devices	Small company or local workgroups in a single department
Local-area network	One or several servers accessed by client computers and used for sharing peripheral devices such as printers	Network at a single company site
Wide-area network	LANs at different sites are linked via leased lines which will often use microwave or satellite transmission	National company with several offices or multinational company; company wanting to perform EDI with its suppliers
Internet	A global arrangement of wide area networks	Companies needing to communicate with many other companies via e-mail or accessing web servers

EXERCISES

Self-assessment exercises

1 Specify the components required for a client/server based LAN for a company of 10 people.

2 Distinguish between a local-area network (LAN) and a wide-area network (WAN).

3 What are the main business benefits delivered by a local-area computer network?

4 What are the main components of a telecommunications system?

5 What is the purpose of a network operating system?

6 What is the difference between the Internet and the World Wide Web?

7 Describe the two main functions of an Internet service provider (ISP). How do they differ from applications service providers?

8 Distinguish between intranets, extranets and the Internet.

9 Describe the standards involved when a web page is served from a web server to a user's web browser.

Discussion questions

1 Do you think that the introduction of client/server systems has been worthwhile to businesses?

2 There are many possible benefits of company-wide networks. Is it possible for them to be achieved without changing working practices?

3 Discuss the merits and disadvantages of locating company e-business services inside a company, in comparison with outsourcing to an ISP or ASP.

Essay questions

1 You are a newly installed IT manager in a company with 100 staff. You want to convince the directors of the benefits of adopting a local-area network across the whole company. How would you present your case?

2 Explain the benefits that a company deciding to downsize to a client server/architecture as part of its IT strategy could derive. What management initiatives will be necessary to ensure that the introduction of the new system is a success?

3 You are consultant to a small retailer interested in setting up a transactional e-commerce site. Create a summary guide for the company about the stages that are necessary in the creation of a web site and the management issues involved.

Examination questions

1 Name three ways in which installing a local-area network can reduce costs. Explain how this is achieved.

2 Which features would you need to specify for a company network for a company of 100 people working at a single site?

3 Computer networks exist on different scales. Distinguish between the following types:

   (a) local-area network;
   (b) wide-area network;
   (c) metropolitan-area network;
   (d) value-added network.

4 Explain, with the aid of diagrams, the difference between the following network topologies:

   (a) star;
   (b) bus;
   (c) ring.

5 Distinguish between the following different types of servers:

   (a) network;
   (b) applications;
   (c) database.

6 What are the advantages of the following types of media? Is each more likely to be found in a local- or wide-area network?

   (a) copper cable;
   (b) fibre-optic;
   (c) satellite;
   (d) microwave.

7 Networked communications in business occur through wide-area networks and local-area networks.

   (a) How do the two types of network differ?
   (b) What is the difference between a local-area network and an intranet?

8 You have been tasked with arranging Internet access for other employees in your company. Summarise the hardware and software needed.

9 How would you explain to a friend what they need to purchase to access the World Wide Web using the Internet? Explain the hardware and software needed.

10 Explain the term 'electronic data interchange'. What is its relevance to companies now that the Internet is widely used for data exchange?

References

Benjamin, R. and Weigand, R. (1995) Electronic markets and virtual value-chains on the information superhighway. *Sloan Management Review*. Winter, 62–72

DTI (2000) *Business in the Information Age – International Benchmarking Study 2000*. UK Department of Trade and Industry. Based on 6000 phone interviews across businesses of all sizes in eight countries. Statistics update: available online at: www.ukonlineforbusiness.gov.uk

Economist (2000) 'E-commerce survey. Define and sell', Supplement, 26 February, pp. 6–12

Gillies, J. and Cailliau, R. (2000) *How the Web Was Born*, Oxford University Press, New York. Another readable book on the whole history of the Internet

Hoffman, D.L. and Novak, T.P. (1996) 'Marketing in hypermedia computer-mediated environments: conceptual foundations', *Journal of Marketing*, 60 (July) 50–68

IDC (1999) *Reinventing EDI: Electronic Data Interchange Services Market Review and Forecast*, 1998–2003, International Data Corporation, Framingham, MA, www.idcresearch.com

IT Week (2000) 'Why small firms still shun ASPs', 13 November, p. 74

Kampas, P. (2000) 'Road map to the e-revolution', *Information Systems Management Journal*, Spring, 8–22

Leiner, B., Cerf, V., Clark, D., Kahn, R., Kleinrock, L., Lynch, D., Postel, J., Roberts, J. and Wolff, S. (2000) A Brief History of the Internet. Published by the Internet Society at www.isoc.org/internet-history/brief.html. Continuously updated document

Mougayer, W. (1998) *Opening Digital Markets – Battle Plans and Strategies for Internet Commerce*, 2nd edition. CommerceNet Press, McGraw-Hill, New York

Revolution (2001a) 'The night belongs to text messages', *Revolution*, 16 May, 30-2. (www. revolutionmagazine.com)

Revolution (2001b) 'Campaign of the week', *Revolution*, 16 May, 38. (www.revolution-magazine.com)

Further reading

Berners Lee, T. (1999) *Weaving the Web. The Past, Present and Future of the World Wide Web by its Inventor*, Orion Publishing, London. A fascinating, readable description of how the concept of the web was developed by the author, with his thoughts on its future development

Chaffey, D. (2002) *E-Business and E-Commerce Management*, Financial Times Prentice Hall, Harlow

Clarke, R. (1998) *Electronic Data Interchange (EDI): An Introduction*, www.anu.edu.au/people/Roger.Clarke/EC/EDIIntro.html

Gillies, J. and Cailliau, R. (2000) *How the Web Was Born*, Oxford University Press, New York. Another readable book on the whole history of the Internet

Hawyrszkiewycz, I. (1997) *Designing the Networked Enterprise*, Artech House, Boston. This book explains how networks can be implemented and describes the impact on the organisation at operational and strategic levels. It focuses more on the human and organisational issues rather than giving technical details

Held, G. (1998) *Understanding Data Communications: From Fundamentals to Networking*, 2nd edition, Wiley, Chichester. This book complements that by Hawyrszkiewycz since it has comprehensive coverage of different communications technologies

Leiner, B., Cerf, V., Clark, D., Kahn, R., Kleinrock, L., Lynch, D., Postel, J., Roberts, J. and Wolff, S. (2001) A Brief History of the Internet. Published by the Internet Society at www.isoc.org/internet-history/brief.html. Continuously updated document

Laudon, K. and Laudon, J. (1995) *Management Information Systems: Organization and Technology*, 4th edition, Prentice Hall International, London. A summary of how telecommunications are used in business is given in Chapters 9 and 10

Sheldon, T. (1994) *LAN Times Encyclopedia of Networking*, Osborne-McGraw-Hill, Berkeley, CA. Useful summaries of networking terms, with good use of diagrams

Web links

www.isoc.org/internet-history/brief.html A brief history of the Internet. Updated history by key players in its design – Barry M. Leiner, Vinton G. Cerf, David D. Clark.

www.ittoolbox.com Guidelines, articles on E-business, ERP, CRM and data warehousing.

www.rosettanet.org Organisation promoting exchange of B2B data.

www.howstuffworks.com Good explanations with diagrams of many Internet technologies.

www.whatis.com Succinct explanations of technical terms.

www.xmledi.com/.net Organisation promoting use of XML to support EDI.

www.xml.com XML resources.

www.virginbiz.net Portal to enable SMEs to move online. Explains stages and tools involved in plain language.

www.ukonlineforbusiness.gov.uk Government portal.

Wireless media

Examples of the WML language are available at www.anywhereyougo.com

Technical details are available at www.wapforum.org

To see how WAP phones work, visit the emulators at www.gelon.net or www.phone.com

A portal about wireless communication is available at www.mcommerceworld.com

E-business applications

LEARNING OBJECTIVES

Learning objectives
After reading this chapter, readers will be able to:
● describe e-business and evaluate its relevance to an organisation
● appreciate the importance of transaction processing systems, process control and office automation systems to the operational management of a business;
● select an appropriate system for decision support at tactical and strategic levels of an organisation;
● assess the potential for using business information systems in different parts of an organisation.

MANAGEMENT ISSUES

As the use and importance of BIS in an organisation increases, the organisation moves towards an electronic business or e-business. From a managerial perspective, this chapter addresses the following questions:
● What is e-business?
● What is the relevance of e-business to an organisation?
● What are the specific applications used in an e-business? What are their benefits?
● How does e-business differ from previous use of business information systems?

Links to other chapters

Links to other chapters

Chapter 2	Introduces the different types of BIS used within the e-business.
Chapters 4 and 5	Some of the technologies in this chapter are introduced briefly in Chapters 4 and 5, which provide an introduction to the different types of software and communications technology.
Chapter 14	Assesses e-business strategy and management.

Introduction

The value of business information systems (BIS) to an organisation is dependent on how the hardware, software and network technologies described in the previous chapters are applied to support the organisation's objectives. This is achieved through deployment of specific business applications that support different organisational processes and functions. The extensive use of business information systems (BIS) throughout an organisation is now commonly referred to as **electronic business** or e-business. This concept, which emerged at the turn of the millennium, is explored in terms of its relevance to the modern organisation.

In the first part of this chapter we review the significance of e-business, and in the second part, we review different applications of BIS in different parts of the e-business organisation.

Introducing e-business

E-business is now a well-established management term, but what precisely does it mean, how does it differ from e-commerce and what organisational benefits can it bring? These questions need to be answered by any management team looking to harness the power of Internet-based BIS. A better understanding of the terms illustrates the scope and scale of potential business applications. Let us start from the definition by IBM (www.ibm.com/e-business), who were one of the first solution providers to coin the term:

> *e-business (e' biz' nis) – the transformation of key business processes through the use of Internet technologies.*

Electronic business (e-business)
All electronically mediated information exchanges, both within an organisation and with external stakeholders supporting the range of business processes.

The processes that can be enhanced by e-business are standard business processes that occur within any organisation. Arthur Andersen (www.globalbestpractices.com) have developed standard definitions of business processes as part of their Global Best Practices knowledge base. There are seven main operating organisational processes:

1 Understand markets and customers.
2 Develop vision and strategy.
3 Design products and services.
4 Market and sell.
5 Produce and deliver services.
6 Produce and deliver services (services organisation).
7 Invoice and service customer.

There are also six support and management processes:

1 Develop and manage human resources.
2 Manage information.
3 Manage financial and physical resources.
4 Execute environmental management programme.
5 Manage external relationships.
6 Manage improvement and change.

You will recognise many of these processes as part of the value chain which includes research and development, marketing, manufacturing and inbound and outbound logistics. Essentially, e-business is aimed at using information and communications technology to integrate and enhance all these processes. In a value-chain context, the efficiency of processes is enhanced, which should result in lower-cost, higher-quality products so giving the customer better value. We will review specific benefits of e-business in more detail in a later section.

▶ E-commerce defined

Electronic commerce (E-commerce)
All electronically mediated information exchanges between an organisation and its external stakeholders.

Electronic commerce (e-commerce) is often thought to simply refer to buying and selling using the Internet: people immediately think of consumer retail purchases from companies such as Amazon. But, e-commerce involves much more than electronically mediated financial transactions between organisations and customers. Many commentators refer to e-commerce as *all* electronically mediated transactions between an organisation and any third party it deals with. By this definition, non-financial transactions such as customer requests for further information would also be considered to be part of e-commerce. Kalakota and Whinston (1997) refer to a range of different perspectives for e-commerce:

1 *A communications perspective* – the delivery of information, products/services or payment by electronic means.
2 *A business process perspective* – the application of technology towards the automation of business transactions and workflows.
3 *A service perspective* – enabling cost cutting at the same time as increasing the speed and quality of service delivery.
4 *An online perspective* – the buying and selling of products and information online.

Zwass (1998) uses a broad definition of e-commerce. He refers to it as:

> *the sharing of business information, maintaining business relationships, and conducting business transactions by means of telecommunications networks.*

The UK government also uses a broad definition:

> *E-commerce is the exchange of information across electronic networks, at any stage in the supply chain, whether within an organisation, between businesses, between businesses and consumers, or between the public and private sector, whether paid or unpaid.*
>
> E-commerce@its.best.uk, 1999

All these definitions imply that electronic commerce is not solely restricted to the actual buying and selling of products, but also covers pre-sale and post-sales activities across the supply chain.

When evaluating the impact of e-commerce on an organisation, it is instructive to identify opportunities for buy-side and sell-side e-commerce transactions as depicted in Figure 6.1, since business information systems with different functionality will need to

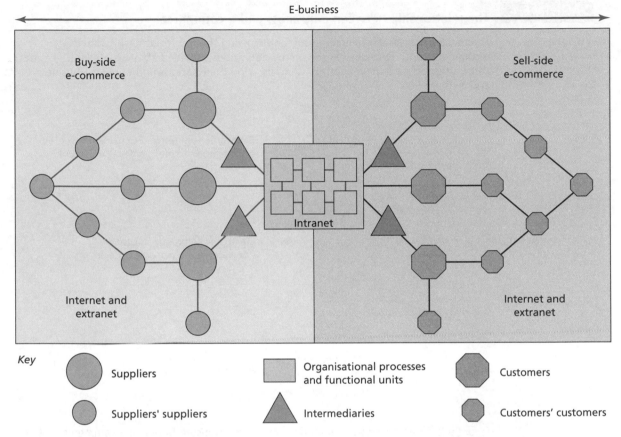

Figure 6.1 Buy-side and sell-side e-commerce
Source: Chaffey (2002)

be created to accommodate transactions with buyers and suppliers. **Buy-side e-commerce** refers to transactions to procure resources needed by an organisation from its suppliers. **Sell-side e-commerce** refers to transactions involved with selling products to an organisation's customers. Case Study 6.1 illustrates the potential for sell-side e-commerce amongst SMEs.

In addition to buy-side and sell-side transactions, Figure 6.1 also shows the internal (or inside) transactions that are part of e-business. These are operational transactions that are part of the internal value chain. They include transactions related to the buy-side such as procurement and sell-side-related transactions such as dealing with customer enquiries as well as basic administrative functions related to employee leave and pay.

Figure 6.2 (c) illustrates that *e-commerce* can perhaps best be conceived as a subset of *e-business*, and this is the perspective we will use in this book. However, since the interpretation in Figure 6.2(b) is equally valid, what is important within any given company is that managers involved with the implementation of e-commerce/e-business are agreed on the scope of what they are trying to achieve!

Buy-side e-commerce
E-commerce transactions between a purchasing organisation and its suppliers.

Sell-side e-commerce
E-commerce transactions between a supplier organisation and its customers.

Activity 6.1

The relationship between e-business and e-commerce

Figure 6.2 provides a convenient tool for discussing the interrelationship between e-commerce and e-business. Based on the definitions provided above, state which of the three alternatives is most appropriate to describe the relationship between e-business and e-commerce.

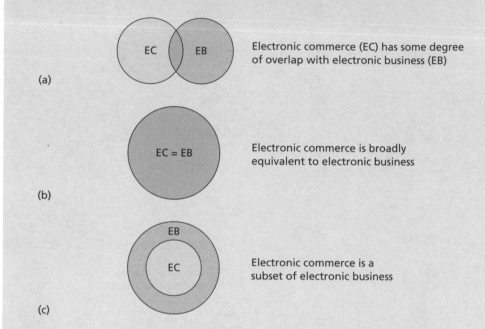

(a) Electronic commerce (EC) has some degree of overlap with electronic business (EB)

(b) Electronic commerce is broadly equivalent to electronic business

(c) Electronic commerce is a subset of electronic business

Figure 6.2 Three alternative definitions of the relationship between e-commerce and e-business

How significant is e-business

As managers, we need to assess the impact of e-commerce and e-business on our marketplace and organisations. How should we respond? How much do we need to invest? What are our priorities and how quickly do we need to act? Answering these questions is an essential part of formulating an e-business strategy – this is considered in more detail in Chapter 13.

We will assess the significance of e-business by asking three further questions:

1 What are the adoption levels by access?
2 What are adoption levels by type of usage?
3 What are the adoption levels for e-commerce transactions?

Question 1: What are the adoption levels by access?

Adoption levels

The proportion of the population/businesses that have access to the Internet, are influenced by it or purchase using it.

As part of the environment analysis of developing an e-business strategy, organisations will need to conduct or access marketing research to determine the current levels of access to the Internet. The relevant data will concern either consumer adoption or business adoption. For the categories of access to the Internet we reviewed in Chapter 5 we need to know *consumer adoption levels* for businesses involved in B2C, C2C or C2B transactions and *business adoption levels* for businesses involved in B2B transactions. For B2B organisations, managers need a picture of current and forecast adoption both for

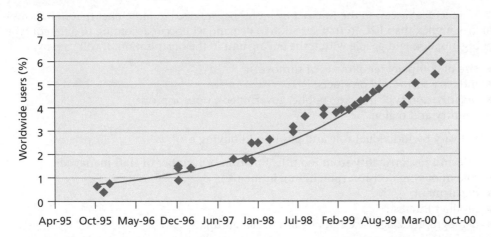

Figure 6.3 Percentage of global population with Internet access (based on Nua compilations at www.nua.ie/surveys**)**

Source: Chaffey (2002)

their customers (sell-side) and their suppliers (buy-side). Initially, we are interested simply in the proportion of individuals or organisations that have access or have a connection to the Internet.

E-commerce provides a global marketplace, and this means we must review access and usage of the Internet channel at many different geographic levels: worldwide and between and within countries.

On a worldwide basis, a relatively small proportion of the population has access to the Internet. Figure 6.3 shows that despite rapid growth from the mid-1990s to about 400 million users by the end of 2000 this only represents less than 10% of the population. A different compilation of Internet users by Cyberatlas (http://cyberatlas.internet.com/big-picture/stats-toolbox/article) suggested that this is still less than 10% of the world's population, but the total is expected to grow to 1 billion by 2005. Access levels in developed countries are much higher, now exceeding 50% in many countries. For example, the UK National Statistics Omnibus Survey for June 2001 showed over half of adults have now used the Internet at some time.

Since the numbers are increasing rapidly, complete Activity 6.2 to update yourself on consumer and business adoption in your country.

Activity 6.2

The scale of e-commerce

Purpose

To examine estimates of the current and future size of e-commerce trade and critically review the validity of these estimates.

Activity

Nua and Cyberatlas are two content aggregator sites that compile estimates from different industry analysts of e-commerce activity in different sectors and in different geographic markets. Visit Nua (www.nua.ie/surveys) and Cyberatlas (www.cyberatlas.com).

Also visit the web site of the International Telecommunications Union (ITU) (www.itu.int/ti/industryoverview/index.htm). Choose Internet indicators. This presents data on Internet and PC penetration in over 200 countries.

If we look at access to the Internet by businesses we need to remember that B2B access is more complex than B2C in that variation in demand will occur according to different types of organisation and people within the buying unit in the organisation. It will vary by:

● size of company (employees or turnover);
● industry sector and products;
● organisation type (private, public, government, not for profit);
● country and region.

It will vary by individual role and position in buying unit:

● role and responsibility from job title, function or number of staff managed;
● role in buying decision (purchasing influence);
● department;
● product interest;
● demographics: age, sex and possibly social group.

When a company analyses the potential of the Internet as a selling tool it needs to research all of these variables. For instance, many companies may have Internet access from research and development, but do the purchasing managers have Internet access? DTI (2000) is an international benchmarking study that reviews factors that affect access levels by country (Fig. 6.4).

▶ Factors governing Internet adoption

It is useful for managers to understand the different factors that affect how many people actively use the Internet. If these are understood for customers in a target market, action can be taken to overcome some of the perceived risks. For example, marketing communications can be used to explain benefits of the customer being online or to reduce fears about ease of use or security. Chaffey et al. (2000) suggest that the following factors are important in governing adoption:

1 *Cost of access*. This is certainly a barrier for those who do not already own a home computer – a major expenditure for many households. The other main costs are the cost of using an ISP to connect to the Internet and the cost of using the media to connect (telephone or cable charges). Free access will certainly increase adoption and usage.

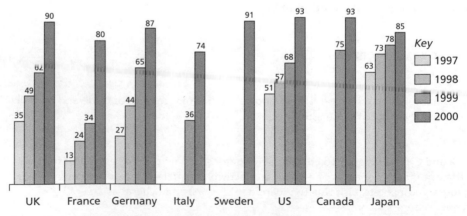

Base: All respondents weighted by number of employees

Figure 6.4 **Percentage of businesses with Internet access**
Source: DTI (2000)

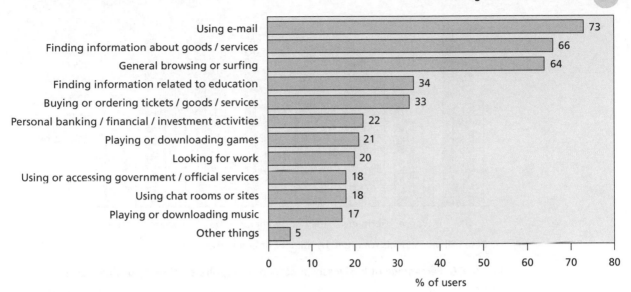

Figure 6.5 Popularity of online activities in the UK
Source: ONS (2000)

2 *Value proposition.* Customers need to perceive a need to be online – what can the Internet offer that other media cannot? Examples of value proposition include access to more supplier information and possibly lower prices by using online B2B auctions.
3 *Ease of use.* This includes the ease of first connecting to the Internet using the ISP and the ease of using the web once connected.
4 *Security.* While this is only, in reality, a problem for those who shop online, the perception generated by news stories may be that if you are connected to the Internet then your personal details and credit card details may not be secure. It will probably take many years for this fear to diminish as using the Internet slowly becomes established as a standard way of purchasing goods.
5 *Fear of the unknown.* Many will simply have a general fear of the technology and the new media which is not surprising since much of the news about the Internet non-adopters will have heard will concern pornography, fraud and privacy infringements.

Question 2: What are adoption levels by type of usage?

Research presented in Figure 6.5 shows that socialising, shopping and browsing, being entertained and being educated are typical reasons people give for going online. So, socialising through e-mail and chat rooms is the so-called killer application in the B2C markets. The second most popular activity is finding out about products. This is significant, since for many companies where direct sale of products is not practical via the Internet, customers may still be active in supplier selection as part of their buying decision. Take car manufacturers. Research in the USA suggests although less than one per cent of consumers are prepared to buy online, over half visit car supplier sites when making their decision. Investment in web sites to support this is therefore important.

Although Figure 6.4 suggests that many businesses access the Internet, we also need to ask whether it is used for identifying suppliers. Figure 6.6 indicates that for many companies the Internet is important in identifying online suppliers, with the majority identifying some suppliers online, especially in the larger companies.

Organisations defining an e-business strategy need to define the appropriate level of Internet adoption by their organisation. For example, with sell-side e-commerce, is the Internet used as a simple promotional tool, a brand building tool, a customer service tool or a full transactional service? Similarly, for buy-side e-commerce, is the Internet

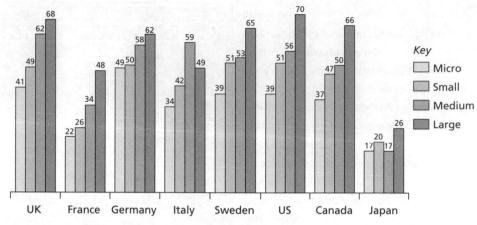

Base: All respondents weighted by number of employees

Figure 6.6 **Percentage of businesses that identify suppliers online by business size**
Source: DTI (2000)

used as a means of selecting suppliers, are B2B exchanges and auctions used or is online tendering involved? Evolutionary stage models, reviewed in Chapter 14, have been developed to assist companies in taking these decisions.

Question 3: What are adoption levels for purchasing (transactional e-commerce)?

For consumers, Figure 6.7 shows that in developed countries, online purchasing is increasingly popular – it is undertaken by over a third of Internet users. Of course, popularity is dependent on the type of product purchased; Figure 6.7 shows the typical variation in a developed country.

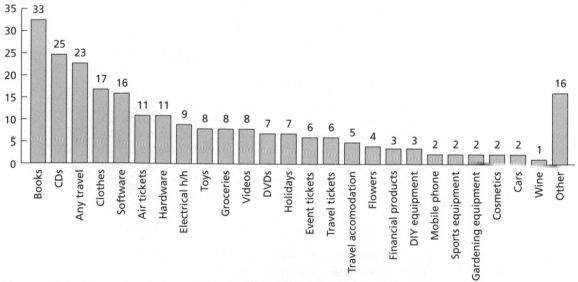

There are 9.9 million online shoppers (54% of internet users aged 15+)
Base size is 576.

Figure 6.7 **Percentage of UK online purchasers in the 6 months to November 2001**

Source: Reproduced from '*Percentage of online purchasers who have bought category online in the 6 months to November 2001*', from *The Internet Monitor*, BMRB, November 2001, Copyright © 2001 BMRB International.

De Kare-Silver (2000) suggests a simple test ('The Electronic Shopping Test') that can be applied to determine the propensity for online purchase of a product. He says that the factors that should be considered are:

1 *Product characteristics*. Does the product need to be physically tried or touched before it is bought?
2 *Familiarity and confidence*. Considers the degree the consumer recognises and trusts the product or brand.
3 *Consumer attributes*. These shape the buyer's behaviour – are they amenable to online purchases in terms of access to the technology and skills available and do they no longer wish to shop for a product in a traditional retail environment?

Typical results from his evaluation are:

- groceries (27/50)
- mortgages (15/50)
- travel (31/50)
- books (38/50).

De Kare-Silver states that any product scoring over 20 has good e-commerce potential, since the score for consumer attributes is likely to increase through time. Given this, he suggests companies will regularly need to review the score for their products.

Activity 6.3

The electronic shopping test

Explain the variation in online purchases for different products shown in Figure 6.7 using the Electronic Shopping Test.

For businesses, a similar effect operates, with only certain products being particularly suitable for online sale (or purchase). Figure 6.8 shows that, in the UK, although a significant number of businesses already use or are planning to use the Internet for sales in the year of the survey, there are a significant proportion that do not. This contrasts

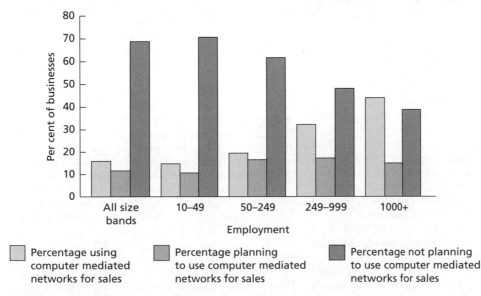

Figure 6.8 **Internet usage for sales**
Source: © Crown Copyright 2001

with high levels of Internet access within all sizes of business, suggesting that for businesses one of the main roles of the Internet will be informing buying decisions rather than making online purchases. Note that the proportion not planning to use the Internet for sales decreases in the larger companies.

In terms of access device and purchase method Figure 6.8 indicates that e-mail and the web are widely used for online purchases, with extranets and EDI less important since these are the preserve of larger companies. Case Study 6.1 reviews factors influencing adoption of e-business amongst European SMEs.

CASE STUDY 6.1

European SME adoption of e-business

Small- and medium-sized enterprises (SMEs) are an awkward bunch. They encompass every stereotype imaginable, ranging in size from one-man bands to organisations of up to 250 or 500 employees, depending on the definition used. Where does small become medium? Is it based on number of employees, turnover, or other criteria? However difficult to target and individualist they may be, SMEs are the engine of growth in Europe, Asia and the US. From sleepy, family-owned concerns to lean, entrepreneurial go-getters eager to give the multinationals a run for their money, they come in all shapes and sizes.

Some carve out their own niche – often by occupying profitable but marginal activities that are too small for corporations to bother with. Others want to compete with established companies, and still others want to expand and become dominant players in their own field.

SMEs have proved notoriously difficult to co-ordinate en masse. Expensive government initiatives to encourage exports and efforts to form effective lobby groups have had limited results. And the internet, which could be a useful, profitable tool for these businesses, has failed to attract anything approaching the numbers that were predicted a couple of years ago.

In March 2000, only one in seven SMEs – about 100,000 companies across Europe – was using the internet to sell goods, cut costs and deliver services, according to a report by International Data Corporation (IDC), commissioned by Cisco, the US telecommunications equipment supplier. This contrasts with predictions made nine months to a year earlier that European SMEs would cater for 70 per cent of the market for internet services and 70 per cent of the growth in data revenues by mid-2000. 'This is partly to do with the over-optimistic predictions for everything to do with the internet at that time', says Paul Barnes, head of service provision at Netdecisions, an international digital solutions provider that advises companies on internet strategies. There is a parallel with the business-to-consumer (B2C) expectations for dotcoms in that period, he notes.

The dizzy assumptions that almost everyone who owned a PC would eventually shop online proved invalid due to a host of reasons, including worries over privacy and security and a general lack of readiness to deal with this brave new world. 'Much of the same applies to SMEs', says Mr Barnes. 'Basically, they are a conservative breed and many probably felt that all the hype about the internet just didn't relate to them. Lots of bright, young things were setting up dotcoms with piles of venture capital money while SMEs struggled to get an overdraft from the bank.' Simon Manley, an associate partner at Financial Dynamics, a business communications company in London, agrees.

He also notes that technology is still a 'big barrier' for SMEs. 'There are too many acronyms, software solutions and gizmos. It's baffling for a small family business anywhere.' Mr Manley says it is not surprising that SMEs have been reluctant to trust their hard-earned money to new, unknown and strangely named technology companies that might not be around in a few months' time. And anyway, where is the need for expensive supply chain management software when you know all your suppliers, talk to them on the phone every day and have been dealing with them for years? 'Small businesses are often too busy just getting on with running their daily affairs, doing accounts, sorting out their tax, buying, selling and juggling the multitude of other things they have to do each day', says Mr Barnes.

'There is not much extra time for getting new technology, building an internet presence and managing a whole new – and unknown – dimension to your business.'

Reticence reigns

This sentiment is borne out by a recent report on SMEs and their telecoms providers. Conducted by the UK telecommunications watchdog, Oftel, the independent survey, highlights the reticence of UK small businesses to change their telecoms service provider, despite a more open, competitive market where many special deals are on offer. The November 2000 survey, covering 701 SMEs throughout the UK with a minimum turnover of £50,000 (€80,300), reveals a generally high awareness of services available from British Telecommunications, cable operators and other indirect suppliers. However, further highlighting the importance of size, the survey shows that medium-sized businesses are twice as likely as smaller establishments to change their telecoms provider and explore new services.

The internet pattern is similar. The earlier IDC survey of 2,500 SMEs across Europe showed that 66 per cent of businesses with fewer than 250 employees had access to the internet, compared with 76 per cent for companies employing more than 500. But out of the 66 per cent, far fewer were using the internet to generate sales and only 6.6 per cent of the smaller concerns had the facility to carry out online transactions. UK Department of Trade and Industry figures also bear out the differences in the SME sector, with companies of fewer than 100 employees half as likely to have a website as larger concerns. Businesses with nine or fewer staff are one-sixth as likely.

The conservative approach among smaller SMEs is similar throughout Europe. 'In France, it's very difficult to make company heads generally aware of the need to use the internet', was the conclusion of one delegate to the latest meeting to discuss smaller companies and the internet organised by Medef, the French employers' federation. CGPME (French acronym for General Confederation of Smaller Companies, a trade body for SMEs) believes that only around half of companies with sales of under €38m (£23.7m) currently use the internet. Emmanuel Colcombet, chairman of CBT Consultants and a specialist SME consultant in Paris, notes that implementing an internet strategy initially generates fixed costs without producing any immediate gain. 'It is a slow process, since reserves of productivity are scattered throughout the company's production and marketing chain', he says, which may be one explanation for the reticence of certain smaller company bosses in France.

A survey by Sage, the accountancy software supplier, conducted in the US, UK, France and Germany in October and November last year, found mixed results. While SMEs in the US were generally more aware and had a higher level of internet presence, there were varying levels of appreciating the implications for business and dealing with suppliers. When presented with the statement 'I know that e-commerce is more than just buying and selling, but I don't yet fully understand the implications of it for my company', more than half the companies in all four countries agreed with it – the highest proportion in France.

While SMEs across the four countries were generally aware of the possibilities of e-commerce, there were obvious signs of confusion about how best to go about it. 'A lot of SMEs need some hand-holding', says Nigel Hudson, UK marketing manager at Sage. 'It's mostly about moving from a state of knowledge into action.'

What's stopping them?

Supporting the UK Department of Trade and Industry 'online for business' initiative, Sage has just launched a nationwide programme of free, interactive workshops. Entitled 'What's Stopping You?', the short seminars address concerns that SMEs may have about the internet and show them how their business might take advantage of what it has to offer.

Sage, the UK's market leader in accounting and business software for personal computers, is convinced that 'last year was not the right time for SMEs and the internet. The moment is now', says Mr Hudson. This was evident from Sage's European research involving 800 SMEs. The interviews were conducted initially in April last year, with follow-ups in July and September/October. Each 'wave' of the survey showed rising levels of interest and awareness. Among other indications of SME internet-unreadiness last year was the collapse of Work24, the £30m (€48.2m) internet portal for small businesses established by Scottish Power and the Royal Bank of Scotland.

The portal closed in February this year after only seven months of operations. Its closure shook a host of blue-chip names which had been spending increasing amounts on targeting SMEs. It raised the question that if two established businesses with strong brands, a large customer base of SMEs and existing supplier relationships could not create a viable business, what hope was there for the others? Out of a predicted 150,000 online registrations, Work24 attracted only 10,000 and far fewer actual trading customers, despite spending £15m (€24m) on technology, customer support infrastructure and marketing.

There have been parallels in expected SME participation in online marketplaces, widely billed as platforms for smaller businesses to participate in e-commerce, gain new business and reduce costs. They are just not there in any meaningful numbers, as eZoka found out. The company, which targets members of SME associations and electronic marketplaces licensing its e-procurement software, identified a potential 392,000 users but has marketed to only 50,000 and converted only about 1 per cent of this number into trading customers.

Concerns about trading online, particularly in B2B marketplaces, are most acute in Germany, where the Mittelstand – 3m mostly family-run, small- and medium-sized manufacturing companies – account for half the country's industrial turnover and provide 80 per cent of all jobs. However, French companies are not far behind in their shyness of marketplaces, according to the Sage survey.

Ghost from the past

Part of this hesitancy is due to a hangover from electronic data interchange (EDI) networks, the first generation of e-commerce systems, which are often associated with big purchasing organisations, such as supermarkets, exerting pressure on their small suppliers in the buying chain. Many SMEs still hold the view that electronic exchanges are designed primarily to help large organisations improve their procurement systems at the expense of small suppliers. However, on the flip side, B2B commerce has introduced certain small companies to the web because of the pressure from the large multinationals. In France, many small auto-parts suppliers have moved on to the internet, and are now benefiting from it, because of pressure from their 'big account' customers.

The US Federal Trade Commission, the European Commission and the German Cartel Office are all keeping a watchful eye on B2B activities, particularly marketplaces. The Commission has also been actively canvassing SMEs about the problems they face in the internal market and doing business in Europe on all levels through its Business Feedback Mechanism.

A recent report by American Express predicts a large rise in the number of medium-sized companies conducting B2B trade online during this year. Some 40 per cent of US companies – with an annual turnover of between $5m (£3.5m) and $500m (£350m) – buy goods online and a further 20 per cent expect to step up their online purchasing this year. European predictions, although scaled back from the heights of two years ago, still expect big things from small companies. London Economics, the UK economics consultancy, estimates that SMEs in the UK could save between £18bn (€29bn) and £24bn (€38.5bn) a year by sourcing goods over the internet.

Hans Martens, managing director of the Brussels-based Martens International Consulting, is broadly upbeat about the prospects for all businesses trading in the European Union. Specialising in technical assistance, industrial and European affairs, he has designed numerous training programmes on the workings of the EU. He is particularly upbeat about the potential for e-trade, e-commerce and SMEs. 'E-commerce gets any business a home market of 300m people with no currency transactions and no barriers to trade', he says. He expects the launch of euro notes and coins at the end of this year to dramatically improve opportunities for e-commerce.

Sifting through the figures, the signs are that the web is slowly becoming an essential tool of development for smaller companies. This can range from creating a simple site to setting up a trading platform as an important strategic development. The latter appeals more to companies that manufacture finished products, according to Jean-François Roubaud, vice-chairman of the French CGPME, and responsible for economic and tax matters.

The web opens up potentially enormous markets for consumer products of all types, Mr Roubaud says, acknowledging that some businesses are more suited to remote-selling than others. This is the case for computer products, for example, since almost all computer users are also web surfers – it explains the explosion in online computer sales. Dell, for example, markets more than 50 per cent of its products via the web.

Arguments for and against

The internet is also a valuable tool for companies wishing to improve communication with their different partners – customers, suppliers, professional organisations, etc. – which is perhaps why so many telecoms companies, software providers, banks, consultants and other parties have not given up on it. But Richard Cartland, managing director of Virginbiz, a UK portal for SMEs spun off from the Virgin.net group, acknowledges that all the positive arguments for SMEs using the internet can equally be viewed as negative: their fragmentation, for example, often understates their vast yet unharnessed business muscle.

Mr Cartland is an advocate of the 'one-stop shop' approach – providing small businesses with all the tools to build websites, get online, trade and manage their finances. He doesn't see the point of just having a 'shop front' on the internet without all the server-based products to make it a real e-business concern. 'The main obstacle is the learning curve, but sometimes it is as simple as having someone explain the benefits in plain language', he says. 'Businesses need to know things like "what is it going to do for me" or "how much is it going to cost?"'

Mr Cartland concedes that there are high customer acquisition costs for SMEs – which was part of Work24's downfall – because of their diversity. But he argues that reasonable monthly fees for services are more acceptable and in tune with SME business planning than huge, one-off fees. 'The set-up cost can be a huge barrier to an SME', he says. He is borderline evangelical about the potential benefits of SMEs moving on to the web and says there is so much they could utilise, research and exploit, if only they knew about it.

▶

Slowly, it seems, businesses are taking this on board. 'The internet allows us to synchronise information – for example, it helped us resolve problems arising from the great distances between our agencies', says Michel Hervé, chairman of Hervé Thermique, a French air-conditioning engineering and maintenance company. He says the internet also helps lower barriers between employees within the company, particularly between technical and sales staff, since it gives everyone a better idea of the global picture.

Whatever the sector or the size of the company, the internet allows an improvement in internal organisation and better decision-making, says Mr Roubaud of CGPME, who is also chairman of Delamare, a roofing, plumbing and heating specialist. This might concern implementing the French 35-hour working week law, or creating employee savings schemes, for example. Likewise, some administrative problems, such as tax – from May this year, French companies generating sales of more than €15.2m (£9.5m) have had to declare and pay VAT online – or centralised sourcing of office supplies will be best handled on the web.

Banking on it

In the field of general services, banks such as Société Générale, Crédit Agricole and BNP Paribas are increasingly participating in the creation of B2B marketplaces for their clients. The aim is to generate new sources of revenue to compensate for the irreversible loss of financial intermediation fees every time a client starts settling transactions (procurement or sales) online. Following the collapse of Work24 in the UK, many banks are still eyeing the SME potential for e-commerce but are reviewing the portal model. BarclaysB2B, the £30m (€48m) venture to provide internet services for business, expects to receive zero 'portal' revenue this year from its site and has dropped its plan to become a leading portal for SMEs. Jointly owned by Barclays Bank and Accenture (formerly Andersen Consulting), it is instead focusing on web services, such as electronic tendering, order settlement and hosted software. In other words, it is abandoning the concept of attracting maximum users to drive advertising and bulk purchasing deals in favour of deeper relationships with fewer customers. Given their special relationship with smaller company bosses, bankers are increasingly seeking to enrich and diversify online services, according to Jean-Eric Mercier, vice-president at the Paris operation of consultants AT Kearney.

In addition to resolving traditional financing and cash-management problems, banks can also give their customers strategic advantages such as access to the bank's network of information about a given

sector, simulating a sales campaign, helping put together a business plan and assisting in the search for partners. Here, the internet clearly demonstrates its importance for smaller companies, giving them access to decision-making tools that were hitherto available only to larger companies.

Over and above problems of internal organisation and commercial strategy, the spread of the internet is likely to contribute to the restructuring of Europe's industrial fabric. As Mr Colcombet of CBT Consultants observes, the internet can remove the isolation of many SMEs and lead to alliances between companies active in the same or related fields. Such alliances are already being formed through the link system available on almost all trading sites.

Virtual communities

Regionally grouped 'internet business communities' are also emerging, particularly in larger towns and cities where virtual shopping precincts mirror their bricks-and-mortar establishments in the high street. Once again, the 'trickle-down' effect comes into play with online directories, cross-links and additional information giving smaller companies the chance to compete with much larger concerns.

In a small rural village in England, for example, the local pub, pétanque league, sports clubs and craft businesses all have links from their websites to others in the village, as well as to the village website. 'It has generated cross-business', says Ross Moynihan, the landlord of the Cricketers pub in the village of Weston, but he concedes that this is difficult to measure, although the number of hits on the website has been rising steadily, as has custom.

Harriet Kelsall, who produces hand-crafted jewellery in a converted barn and won the regional new business of the year award last year, has linked her site to that of the Cricketers. How many people come to buy her river pearl earrings and then go on for a meal at the pub is hard to establish, but both are happy. Nigel Blyth has a simple philosophy about integrating small businesses with the internet. 'I see the requirement for it. But first of all you have to have established a successful business without it.'

Mr Blyth is managing director and owner of Eximedia, a business based in London and Suffolk that started out in 1988 as a computer supplies provider. It has since grown into an £8m-a-year (€12.8m) business that meets all aspects of office purchasing from hardware to furniture to stationery. The internet element of the business is very new, although Eximedia planned its online presence for more than two years and spent a lot of money in the process.

Mr Blyth examined a number of online models before deciding to outsource the Eximedia site to a design and marketing company that would create an overall, modern image to distinguish it from competing sites. The aim is to provide a convenient business-to-business store for existing registered trade customers who are quoted tailored discounts of up to 30 per cent. Eventually Eximedia, which employs 30 people, plans to offer as many as 60,000 products over the internet. 'We've gone on to the internet because our customers have asked for this facility.' Mr Blyth says it is important for small business sites to include a contact phone number and a map, which are invariably absent from the sites of much larger companies. Many people like to hear a voice on the end of the phone after they have done their web search, he adds.

The indications are strong that SMEs are becoming much more web-wise, says Mr Barnes of Netdecisions.

The telecoms companies, technology providers, banks, portals and governments are all aware of the business potential that smaller businesses can unleash through the internet. And, somewhat slowly, so are the SMEs.

Source: Annie Counsell, 'Small is the next big thing', *Connectis*, 25 May 2001

Questions

1 Summarise the current usage of the Internet by SMEs according to the article. Use online resources to find specific figures for your country.

2 Discuss the reasons for the lower than expected take-up of Internet services amongst SMEs.

3 Identify the factors that will be important in determining the future use of the Internet by SMEs.

Drivers and barriers of e-business adoption

◗ Drivers for e-business adoption

A useful framework for understanding the reasons for e-business adoption is provided by the supply chain and value chain concepts that were introduced in Chapter 2. Information systems, and in particular electronic communications, can be used to impact supply chain management in a number of ways. Electronic commerce can:

1 *Increase reach to overseas customers or niche markets. Benefit – increased revenue potential.* Increased revenue can arise through using a basic or e-commerce-enabled web site to reach a larger customer base and also by encouraging loyalty and repeat purchases amongst existing customers.

2 *Increase efficiency of individual processes. Benefit: reduced cycle time and cost per order.* Here the cycle time to completion of a process and the resources needed to execute it are reduced. If a company adopts e-procurement this will result in a faster cycle time and cost per order as described later in the chapter.

3 *Reduce complexity of the supply chain. Benefit: reduced cost of channel distribution and sale.* This occurs through a process of disintermediation, as explained in Chapter 5. Here the company will offer the facility to sell direct from its e-commerce site rather than through distributors or retailers.

4 *Improve data integration between elements of the supply chain. Benefit: reduced cost of paper processing.* The company can share information with its suppliers on the demand for its products to optimise the supply process in a similar way to that described for Tesco in Case Study 6.2.

5 *Reduce cost through outsourcing. Benefits: lower costs through price competition and reduced spend on manufacturing capacity and holding capacity. Better service quality through contractual arrangements?* The company can outsource or use virtual integration to transfer assets and costs such as inventory holding costs to third-party companies. Technology is also an enabler in forming value networks, and in making it faster to change suppliers on the basis of cost and quality.

6 *Innovation. Benefit: Better customer responsiveness.* It may be possible to offer new products or new ways of ordering and servicing products to customers. For example, a

B2B company may use e-commerce to enable its customers to specify the mixture of chemical compounds and additives used to formulate their plastics and refer to a history of previous formulations.

Figure 6.9 summarises the reasons for benefits given by business respondents according to size. It is apparent that reduced costs and increased reach are the most commonly cited benefits. Note that larger companies' customers seem to be more convinced by the benefits of e-commerce.

An alternative perspective on benefits of e-commerce is to look at the benefits that technology can deliver to customers at the end of the supply chain. For the customers of a B2B company these could include:

- increased convenience through 24 hours a day, 7 days a week, 365 days a year ordering;
- increased choice of supplier leading to lower costs;
- faster lead times and lower costs through reduced inventory holding;
- the facility to tailor products more readily;
- increased information about products and transactions such as technical data sheets and order histories.

Drivers were rated out of 4 by e-commerce adopters where 4 = very important and 1 = unimportant, in a recent international benchmarking study (DTI, 2000). Two main types of driver were identified. Cost/efficiency drivers are internally influenced – here e-business is driven by a desire to reduce costs or lead times. Competitiveness drivers are external influences from the marketplace such as customer demand for new services and competitors' offering alternative services. The different drivers were rated as follows.

Cost/efficiency drivers:
1 increasing speed with which supplies can be obtained (2.76);
2 increasing speed with which goods can be dispatched (2.63);
3 reduced sales and purchasing costs (2.65);
4 reduced operating costs (2.73).

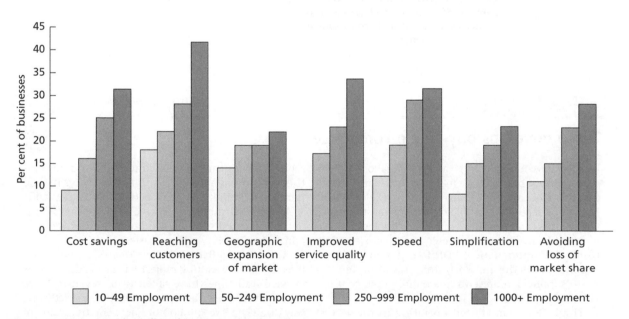

Figure 6.9 Perceived benefits of making sales by e-commerce
Source: © Crown Copyright 2001

Competitiveness drivers:

5　customer demand (2.86);
6　improving the range and quality of services offered (2.83);
7　avoid losing market share to businesses already using e-commerce (2.7).

This survey suggests that the internal cost/efficiency drivers and external competitiveness drivers are of similar importance. The survey also reports on scores for non-adopters, and, unsurprisingly, all these benefits are rated significantly lower.

As part of strategy development benefits need to be turned into specific objectives. Here it is useful to identify both tangible benefits (for which monetary savings or revenues can be identified) and intangible benefits (for which it is more difficult to calculate cost savings). The types of potential benefits are summarised in Table 6.1.

Table 6.1 Benefits from e-business

Tangible benefits	Intangible benefits
Increased sales from new sales leads giving rise to increased revenue from: ● new customers, new markets; ● existing customers (repeat-selling); ● existing customers (cross-selling). Marketing cost reductions from: ● reduced time in customer service; ● online sales; ● reduced printing and distribution costs of marketing communications. Supply-chain cost reductions from: ● reduced levels of inventory; ● increased competition from suppliers; ● shorter cycle time in ordering. Administrative cost reductions from: ● more efficient routine business processes such as recruitment, invoice payment and holiday authorisation.	● Corporate image communication ● Enhance brand ● More rapid, more responsive marketing communications including PR ● Faster product development lifecycle enabling faster response to market needs ● Improved customer service ● Learning for the future ● Meeting customer expectations to have a web site ● Identifying new partners, supporting existing partners better ● Better management of marketing information and customer information ● Feedback from customers on products.

CASE STUDY 6.2

Tesco develops buy-side e-commerce

Retailers have long sought greater collaboration in their supply chains, but few have managed to achieve it. One that has is Tesco, the UK's largest grocery retailer, which has built a reputation as one of Europe's most innovative retailers in its use of information technology.

As with many retailers, Tesco has long used electronic data interchange (EDI) to order goods from suppliers and the network links 1,300 of Tesco's 2,000 suppliers, representing around 96 per cent by volume of goods sold in Tesco stores.

The EDI system started operating in the 1980s and its use was initially limited to streamlining store replenishment. In 1989, Tesco took its first steps on the road to collaboration and began using its EDI network to help its suppliers better forecast demand.

About 350 suppliers receive EDI messages with details of actual store demand, depot stockholdings and Tesco's weekly sales forecasts.

According to Barry Knichel, Tesco's supply chain director, this forecasting project has been successful as average lead times have fallen from seven to three days. 'Nevertheless, the information flow is strictly one way', he says. 'We still do not know the true value of this sales data because we never get any feedback.'

In 1997, Tesco thus started its Tesco Information Exchange (Tie) project in an attempt to achieve much more sophisticated two-way collaboration in its supply chain.

'This really was a big development for us', he says. 'The guiding principle was to combine our retailing knowledge with the product knowledge of our suppliers.'

A large Tesco store may carry 50,000 products while a supplier will have at most 200. An important aim of the Tie project was thus to shift responsibility for managing products down to the relevant supplier.

'Suppliers clearly have a better understanding of their specific product lines, so if you can engage the supplier to manage the supply chain you are going to get much better product availability and reduce your inventory', says Jorge Castillo, head of retail business for GE Information Services, which developed the extranet technology behind Tie.

Suppliers pay from £100 to £100,000 to join Tie, depending on their size. This then allows them to access the Tie web site and view daily electronic point-of-sale (Pos) data from Tesco stores.

According to Mr Castillo, Tie lets suppliers monitor changes in demand almost in real time and so

gives them more time to react. 'Before, Tesco's suppliers would not have seen a problem until Tesco got on the phone to them', he says. 'Now, it is the suppliers who get on the phone to Tesco and they can see much earlier on if a product is not selling well.'

The data can be analysed in a number of ways to allow suppliers to see how sales perform by distribution centre, by individual store or even by TV region – important for promotions.

The management of promotions is a complex process requiring close co-operation between supplier and retailer. However, it has traditionally been difficult to do well because of the lack of shared data to support collaborative decisions.

'Promotions can be a nightmare', says Mr Knichel. Tesco and GEIS added a promotions management module to the service in 1999. It allows retailers and suppliers to collaborate in all stages of the promotion: initial commercial planning, supply chain planning, execution and final evaluation.

According to St Ivel, one of Tesco's bigger food suppliers, Tie has saved 30 per cent of its annual promotional costs.

More than 600 suppliers, representing 70 per cent of Tesco's business, are using Tie today and Tesco aims to

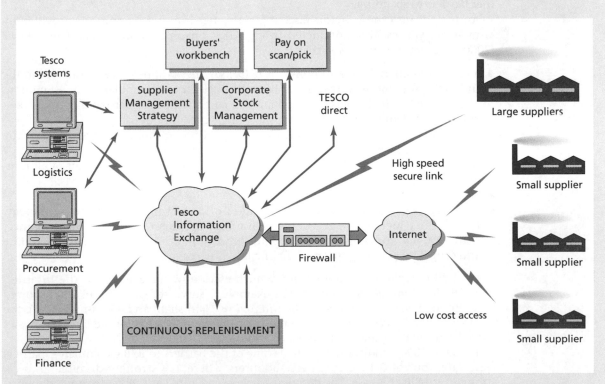

Figure 6.10 Infrastructure for Tesco Information Exchange (Tie)
Source: Tesco web site

have all its suppliers onboard by the end of 2000. Around 40 suppliers are participating in the most recent addition to the Tie system, a collaborative data module.

This aims to allow 'seamless' planning in which the planning data on the screen is jointly filled in by both retailer and supplier. Mr Knichel sees this as radical change for the retail industry as suppliers and retailers have traditionally worked to separate agendas.

He feels Tie has much potential to streamline Tesco's supply chain and to help suppliers improve their service levels and promotions. But retailing is a traditional industry and many suppliers are set in their ways.

'Only two suppliers have fundamentally changed the way they work as a result of Tie. Nevertheless, they can bring products to market much faster than any of their competitors', he says.

Source: Geoffrey Nairn, 'Survey – FT-IT review: demand', *Financial Times*, 3 May 2000

Questions

1   What benefits does Tesco's information exchange offer to the retailer and its suppliers?

2   What differences have the use of Tie added over the original EDI system?

3   Discuss reasons why only two of Tesco's suppliers have fundamentally altered the way they work as a result of Tie.

◗ Barriers to e-business adoption

While there are many tangible and intangible benefits of developing an e-business, before adoption organisations need, of course, to evaluate the many difficulties that may arise from e-business success. The most significant of these barriers are those that stifle demand for e-commerce services. Fear of not achieving a satisfactory return on investment in e-commerce is one of the major benefits. We saw in a previous section that levels of Internet access are one barrier, but for those with access there may be further barriers to spending.

An insight into these factors affecting consumer Internet adoption is provided by annual market research conducted by the UK Consumer Association. The *Which?* (2000) Internet survey showed that:

● a large proportion of current non-users (51%) say they will never get connected to the Internet. This amounts to 15 million adults out of a total population of 60 million. This highlights the barriers to adoption, with cost and poor understanding of the benefits of the Internet being the reasons most often cited for not using the service;

● the reluctance to go online increases with age, 85% of those over 55 saying in the 1999 survey they will never be connected to the Internet;

● when asked, in the 1999 survey, why they would remain non-users, half of all non-users said they did not believe that the Internet was relevant to their needs;

● 30% have resisted because of the cost;

● 16% have resisted because they are afraid of or do not understand the technology. Part of the reluctance to access the technology appears to be based on ignorance, with 25% not knowing that a computer (or set-top box) is necessary to get online and only 37% knowing that a telephone line is necessary.

For B2B companies, although many businesses now have access to the Internet, access within companies is uneven. For example, a survey of UK SMEs in 2000 showed that although 90% have access to the Internet (87% in small and 95% in medium), the number of employees with access to the Internet was only 41% for medium businesses and 46% in small businesses (Durlacher, 2000).

The DTI (2000) study also evaluated some of the barriers to B2B e-commerce. Barriers were rated out of 5 by e-commerce adopters where 1 = strongly disagree and 5 = strongly agree in this case. The different barriers were rated as follows by non-adopters:

● no tangible benefits (3.51);

● e-commerce is not relevant to the business (3.6);

- the technology costs are too high (3.5);
- concern about fraud (3.11);
- concern about confidentiality (3.22).

Note that security is not the main barrier – as perhaps expected, it is lack of imperative.

To summarise, the main barriers for adoption are cost, lack of perceived need and fears about security and technology.

Introduction to e-business applications

The remainder of this chapter looks at specific examples of e-business applications by looking at options for deploying different types of BIS in an organisation. As part of BIS strategy development (Chapter 13) every organisation will assess its current business information systems **applications portfolio**. The strategy will then define how this needs to be revised to achieve the BIS strategy objectives.

We will explore different models for assessing the BIS applications portfolio in Chapter 13, but in this chapter we use a simple division of BIS applications based on the different levels of management decision making introduced in Chapter 2. First, we will consider *operational* information systems. These include transaction processing systems and those used for manufacturing and office automation. We then look at how decision support systems can be used for tactical and strategic planning. Finally, we will briefly review how different types of software are used in different functional areas of a business, such as finance and accounting, human resources and marketing.

Applications portfolio
The range of BIS applications deployed in an organisation.

▶ Operational systems

Operational systems are used for the tasks involved in the daily running of a business. Their performance is often vital to an organisation and they are sometimes described as mission critical or strategic information systems. We consider three types of operational systems:

1 *Transaction processing systems (TPS)*. These are used to manage the exchange of information and funds between a company and third parties such as customers, suppliers and distributors.
2 *Office automation systems (OAS)*. OAS are used to manage the administrative functions in an office environment and are often critical to service-based industries.
3 *Process control systems*. These are important in manufacturing industries for controlling the manufacture of goods.

▶ Transaction processing systems (TPS)

Transaction processing systems (TPS) perform the frequent routine external and internal transactions that serve the operational level of the organisation. These are effectively e-commerce transactions involving recording events within a business or between the business the third parties which incorporate the exchange of information regarding different services. Examples of these transactions include:

Transaction processing systems (TPS)
Manage the frequent external and internal transactions such as orders for goods and services that serve the operational level of the organisation.

- customers placing orders for products and services from a company, such as making a holiday booking;
- a company placing orders with a supplier for components from which to make its products;
- payment for goods or services received by a third party;

- a customer visiting a supermarket to shop (see the mini-case study on retail applications of TPS by Sainsbury's);
- a customer ringing a call centre of a bank to pay their bills;
- a withdrawal of money from an auto-teller machine.

Although the functions undertaken by the TPS are routine and repetitive, they usually perform a vital function in the organisation.

Figure 6.11 shows the typical components of a transaction processing system. Data are usually input by being keyed in to on-screen data entry forms such as those used when orders are placed by phone. For retail applications, customer transactions are recorded through bar-code technology.

Storage and retrieval are often handled by a database management system, except where high performance is required, in which case a transaction monitor linked to a standard file system may be used. Transactions will typically occur across a local-area network within a retail branch or bank environment, with real-time processing and data transfer occurring across a wide area network with a central mainframe computer. Sometimes data on transactions such as loyalty card purchases is stored locally in the supermarket on a local server in real time and then uploaded by a batch system (when the store is closed) to head office. This arrangement is shown in Figure 6.12. Other information such as supply requests may be transmitted on demand in real time. Links with suppliers occur through EDI, which is described in Chapter 5.

There are two main types of transaction systems in operation. Batch systems, as the name suggests, collect information on transactions in batches before it is processed at times of lower transaction rates (such as overnight). Real-time systems process information immediately. These are two design alternatives compared in Chapter 11.

Information from the transaction processing system is accessed in the branch and in the head office using online reporting, for example to find stock availability, or by offline reporting, where information is stored in a separate system for detailed analysis. This is the approach used for data warehouses, which are described later in the chapter.

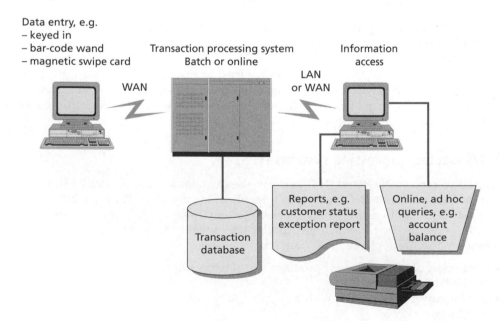

Figure 6.11 Key elements of a transaction processing system

Because the TPS give direct contact with customers and suppliers beyond the boundary of an organisation, if it fails it becomes immediately apparent to the organisation's customers (think about the consequences of a failure of an airline reservation system!). Therefore these are often mission-critical systems which must be reliable and secure. Another reason for such applications being mission-critical is that data captured by the TPS is used to monitor the performance of the organisation.

The Sainsbury's case study shows that for some organisations there will be many TPS in operation which have become essential to the needs of the organisation.

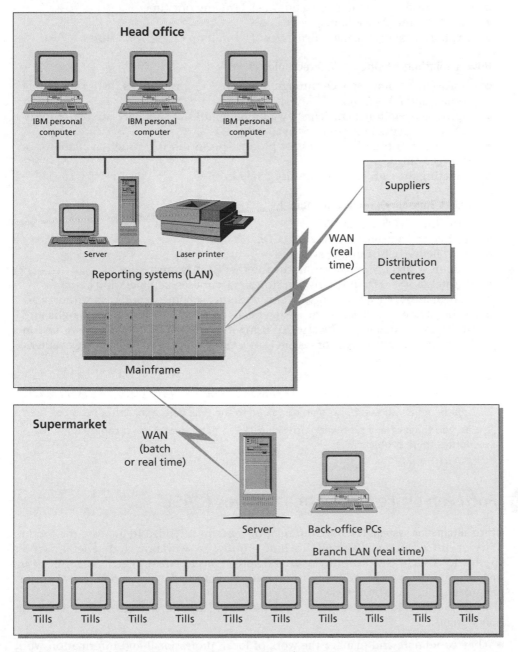

Figure 6.12 Network architecture for a retail transaction processing system

MINI CASE STUDY

Retail applications of TPS by Sainsbury's

This case study of UK retailer Sainsbury's considers the different ways in which a retailer may make use of TPS.

The company and its customer service objectives

- 17 000 commodities
- aim is for no more than 5 to be unavailable at any one time
- order lead time 24–48 hours
- distribution centres manage deliveries of 11 million cases to 335 stores.

How is Sainsbury's helped by TPS technology?

- Improved customer service through more choice, lower prices, better quality of produce and full shelves.
- Improved operational efficiency by automatic links to suppliers and better information on product demand and availability.
- Assessment of the effectiveness of product promotions through availability of better information.
- Marketing through customer loyalty schemes.

How does Sainsbury's use technologies?

- At the till – EPOS and EFTPOS
- On shelves – auto-price-changing LCDs
- On trolleys – 'self-scanning systems'
- At home – direct wine sales from the Internet BarclaySquare site
- At warehouses – EDI links between stores, warehouses, suppliers and banks
- For banking – TPS are vital to providing customer statements and cash withdrawals
- In the marketing department – the effectiveness of marketing campaigns and loyalty card schemes can be assessed using information on transactions stored in data warehouses. This type of system is covered in more detail later in the chapter.

Questions

1 Draw a diagram summarising the links between all the parties who access Sainsbury's TPS.
2 What benefits will Sainsbury's gain compared to the time before the introduction of TPS?
3 Can you think of any problems with using TPS so extensively? What can be done to counter these problems?

F *Focus on* office automation systems (OAS)

Office automation systems (OAS)
Are intended to increase the productivity of office workers. Examples include groupware, workflow and general-purpose applications such as word processors and spreadsheets.

Office automation systems (OAS) are information systems intended to increase the productivity of office workers. Examples include groupware, workflow and general-purpose applications such as word processors and spreadsheets. Mission critical applications such as groupware and workflow can be considered to be key for supporting the internal processes of the e-business.

Laudon and Laudon (1996) state three critical organisational roles for office automation systems:

- They coordinate and manage the work of local, professional and information workers within the organisation.

- They link the work being performed across all levels and functions of the organisation.
- They couple the organisation to the external environment, including to its clients and suppliers; when you call an organisation, you call an office.

These roles emphasise the fact that the office should be seen as more than a typing area but rather as a centre for the exchange of organisational knowledge. Activities undertaken in offices include document management, collaborative work and the management of project activities.

Personal OAS technologies have been introduced in Chapter 4. These applications included desktop publishing (DTP), for producing, for example, drafts of promotional marketing material such as brochures and flyers; personal information managers (PIM), for managing tasks and contacts; and project management software, to assist the management and control of projects. In this section we focus on groupware and workflow management systems, which are most significant in office automation systems, involving teams of people. They are the cornerstone of many 'in-side e-commerce' e-business systems.

Groupware

Groupware is software that enables information to be shared by people collaborating on solving problems. This could include activities such as the scheduling and running of meetings, sharing documents and communicating over a distance. Groupware assists teams of people in working together because it provides the 'three Cs' of communication, collaboration and coordination:

- *Communication* is the core groupware feature which allows information to be shared or sent to others using electronic mail. Groupware for conferencing is sometimes known as computer-mediated communication (CMC) software.
- *Collaboration* is the act of joint cooperation in solving a business problem or undertaking a task. Groupware may reduce some of the problems of traditional meetings, such as finding a place and a time to meet, a lack of available information or even dominance by one forceful individual in a meeting. Groupware improves the efficiency of decision making and its effectiveness by encouraging contributions from all group members. As a result, the study of groupware is known as computer-supported collaborative work (CSCW).
- *Coordination* is the act of making sure that a team is working effectively and meeting its goals. This includes distributing tasks to team members, reviewing their performance and perhaps steering an electronic meeting.

When people exchange information simultaneously, as is the case with real-time chat or a telephone conversation, this is said to be **synchronous**. When collaborators send messages that can be accessed at a later time, these are said to be **asynchronous**. Asynchronous exchange occurs with e-mail and discussion groups.

A further reason that groupware has become a useful business tool is that it can be used for collaboration within and between companies when face-to-face contact is impossible. Employees can continue to communicate and work on joint projects even when they are in different locations or in different time zones. The asynchronous use of groupware is one of its key benefits. When considering the benefits of collaborative systems, it is useful to categorise them according to the quadrant in which they lie on a grid showing how people can work together in time and space (Table 6.2).

Groupware
Software that enables information and decision making to be shared by people collaborating within and between businesses.

Synchronous
When people exchange information simultaneously as is the case with real-time chat or a telephone conversation this is said to be synchronous.

Asynchronous
When collaborators send messages that can be accessed at a later time these are said to be asynchronous. Asynchronous exchange occurs with e-mail and discussion groups.

Table 6.2 Different uses of collaborative systems classified in time and space

	Synchronous	Asynchronous
Same location	Same time, same place Example: meeting support software	Different time, same place Example: workflow systems
Different location	Same time, different place Example: video conferencing	Different time, different place Example: e-mail and discussion groups

Software applications associated with groupware are summarised in Table 6.3.

Table 6.3 Main groupware functions

Groupware function	Application
E-mail and messaging	E-mail, electronic forms processing
Document management and information sharing	Improved information dissemination
Collaborative authoring	Team development of documents
Conferencing	Text conferencing, video conferencing, whiteboarding
Time management	Calendar and group scheduling
Groupware management and decision support	Remote and distributed access facilities including replication and access control
Ad hoc workflow	Loosely coupled collaboration
Structured workflow	Structured management of tasks

Normally, applications such as electronic calendars and e-mail are purchased as separate software packages. However, some software provides an integrated package of groupware functions. One such package is Lotus Notes, which is based on a database that allows the sharing of text, graphics, sound and video data. The system can run on a local-area network (LAN) or a wide-area network (WAN) and so allows information to be shared over distance. Communication between users is automatically logged by Notes for reference. This facility can be used to increase customer service by retrieving previous interactions between organisational members and customers in a variety of formats in response to a customer request. The other main integrated groupware packages are Novell Groupwise and Microsoft Exchange. These are similar to e-mail software in that they have an inbox of messages (Fig. 6.13), but they also provide calendar and worklist facilities and document management.

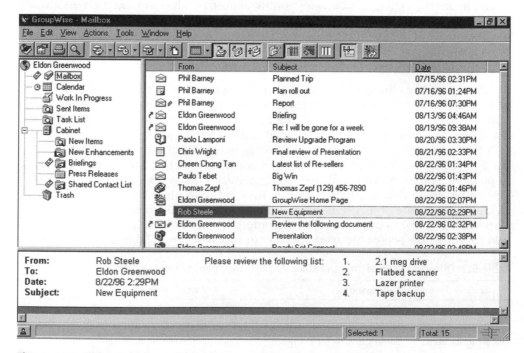

Figure 6.13 Universal inbox of Novell Groupwise groupware product

The use of groupware applications has been revolutionised by the adoption of intranets as part of the move to e-business. Many groupware products are now available through web browsers that enable e-mail, for example, to be sent and reviewed. The e-business uses groupware tools to assist processes such as purchasing. Figure 6.14 shows an e-mail generated by an electronic procurement system as part of a workflow; it shows that a manager has approved the purchase requisition.

Document imaging processing (DIP)

DIP systems attempt to alleviate the problems caused by paper-based systems, including the cost of handling large amounts of paperwork and the time wasted searching for paper documents. DIP systems convert documents (and images) into a digital format which allows storage, retrieval and manipulation of the document on computer. The document is converted using a scanner which can be either handheld and passed over a document, or a flat-bed type where a document is placed on a glass sheet and a scanner reader passes under it. It is then indexed and stored on high-capacity magnetic or optical storage. The main components of a DIP system are shown in Figure 6.15. Figure 6.16 shows document management software as an integrated part of an e-procurement system. Here a paper invoice from a supplier (on the left) has been scanned into the system and is compared with the original electronic order information (on the right).

Document imaging processing (DIP)
DIP systems are used in industry to convert printed documents into an electronic format so that they can be stored, organised and retrieved more easily.

Electronic document management systems (EDMS)

EDMS are used for the management of large procedural documents which are required in organisations for managing their products and services. For example, the aircraft manufacturer Boeing has a service manual for each aircraft containing thousands of pages (see case study). To write and update this is a significant undertaking because of

Electronic document management systems (EDMS)
Systems that convert documents into a digital format which allows storage, retrieval and manipulation of the document on computer.

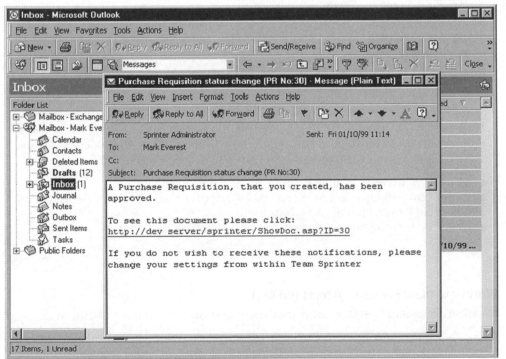

Figure 6.14 E-mail notification of requisition approval (with permission of Tranmit)
Source: Chaffey (2002)

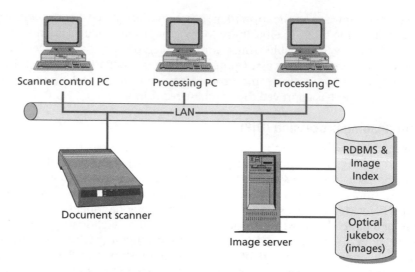

Figure 6.15 Components of a document image processing system

the volume of material and the number of authors. EDMS are intended to help in the task of managing the document lifecycle of:

- write;
- review and annotate;
- modify;
- publish;
- distribute;
- update and repeat the cycle.

MINI CASE STUDY

Boeing uses EDMS for managing technical information

At Boeing there are 10 500 users of an EDMS system to update and access information about Boeing Standards, each of which defines a design or manufacturing process. There are 70 000 pages of information on over 10 000 processes. Boeing has used the Interleaf EDMS to implement this system by scanning in previous documents and using OCR to convert them to electronic text. The main savings have been:

- 31 per cent decrease in time to locate a standards document;
- 63 per cent reduction in rework caused by inaccurate or out-of-date documents;
- 6 per cent elimination of paper distribution;
- return on investment 96 per cent (payback period of five years).

Source: Myers-Tierney, L. and Campbell, I. (1996)

Workflow management (WFM)
Systems for the automation of the movement and processing of information in a business according to a set of procedural rules.

Workflow management systems (WFMS)

Workflow management (WFM) is defined by the Workflow Management Coalition as:

> *the automation of a business process, in whole or part during which documents, information or tasks are passed from one participant to another for action, according to a set of procedural rules.*

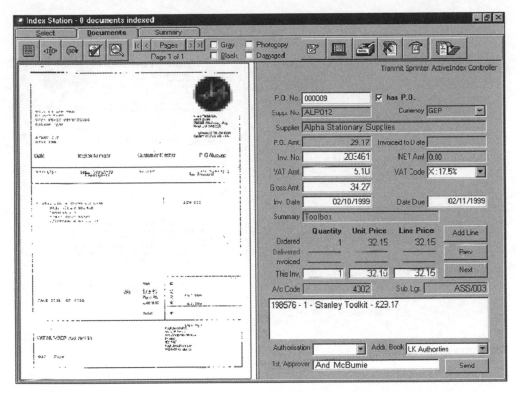

Figure 6.16 Document management software for reconciling supplier invoice with purchase order data

Source: Chaffey (2002)

Workflow systems are used to automate business processes by providing a *structured* framework to support the process. Workflows help manage business processes by ensuring that tasks are prioritised to be performed:

> *as soon as possible*
> *by the right people*
> *in the right order.*

This gives a consistent, uniform approach for improved efficiency and better customer service. Workflow software provides functions to:

- assign tasks to people;
- remind people about their tasks which are part of a workflow queue;
- allow collaboration between people sharing tasks;
- retrieve information needed to complete the task, such as a customer's personal details;
- provide an overview for supervisors of the status of each task and the team's performance.

Workflow and groupware systems are often used to support re-engineering. BPR (business process re-engineering) is discussed in detail in Chapter 13. Today, these workflow systems are typical of e-business systems.

Workflow is usually used in conjunction with DIP technology to improve efficiency by automatically routeing documents to the correct person to deal with them. Each person is given a list of tasks or documents on which to work, from what is known as the workflow queue. Figure 6.17 gives an example of an integrated DIP/workflow system used for a customer service application to action a letter of complaint.

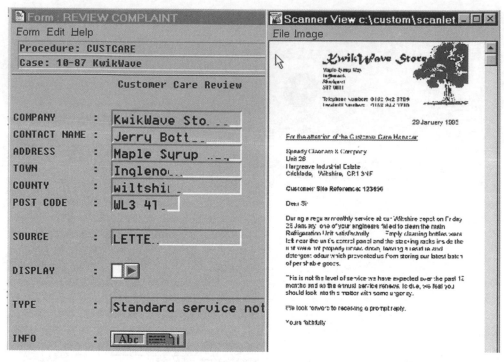

Figure 6.17 **Example of a workflow application from Staffware**

WFMS can be particularly effective when they replace a large paper-based system, and substantial amounts of time can be saved by eliminating lengthy searches for documents. Another improvement area is for customer service applications, such as at a call centre when a document can be called up instantaneously in response to a customer request. The drawbacks associated with the technology include the expense of installation and the problem of integration with existing computer network systems. In order to gain the full benefits from WFMS, it is also necessary to re-engineer or redesign the paper-based workflow in order to avoid simply automating inefficient processes.

WFM is most closely associated with large companies such as banks and insurance companies which deal with a large number of complex, paper-based transactions. These transactions need to be dealt with in a structured way and use structured or production workflow systems to manage them.

Small and medium companies are making increasing use of workflow for administrative tasks. These involve fewer transactions and can be managed by less costly software which is based on an e-mail system. Example applications for this administrative or forms-based workflow include authorisation of travel claims or holidays or payment of an invoice. In the latter example, the details of the invoice could be typed into the workflow system by a clerk. The workflow system will then forward the details of the invoice to a senior manager for authorisation. When this has occurred, the authorised invoice will automatically be sent back to the clerk for payment. This process will occur entirely electronically through routeing of forms.

Figure 6.18 illustrates the different categories of workflow software according to the degree of structured working they support. *Production* systems are highly structured and are used in call centres, for example, for assessing insurance claims or issuing new policies. *Administrative* workflow is more widely used, for routine administration such as processing a travel claim. *Ad hoc* workflow overlaps with groupware applications, such as in a group design of a new product.

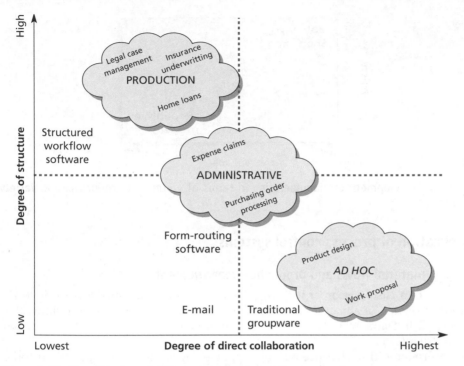

Figure 6.18 Classification of different types of workflow systems

Process control systems for operations management

Process control systems are used to support and control manufacturing processes. Operations management involves the transformation of inputs, such as raw materials, equipment and labour, into outputs in the form of goods and services. All organisations undertake this process, even if they may not have an identifiable operations function.

Business applications of operations management which need to be supported by information systems include product design, planning for resource requirements, location decisions, layout design, job design, quality control and business planning.

Traditionally, information systems for manufacturing were thought of in terms of automation of *repetitive*, uniform products such as foodstuffs on a production line. While this was true when information systems were first introduced, there is a strong trend to specialised tailoring of products or *mass customisation* to an individual customer's needs (Fig. 6.19).

Figure 6.19 shows the three main types of production facility that information systems can be used to support:

- *Repetitive*. Production-line-type systems producing a standard product such as the Model T Ford car (this is the equivalent of packaged software).
- *Job shop*. Production of individual 'jobs' for individual customers according to their specific requirements (this is the equivalent of bespoke software).
- *Batch*. Intermediate between the two, a batch of identical products produced before changing the production setup for the next batch of systems.

Process control information systems have provided the flexibility to enable all three types to be automated.

Process control systems
Used to manage manufacturing-type processes.

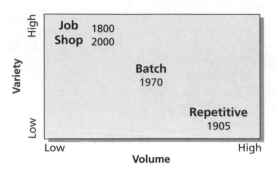

Figure 6.19 Development of manufacturing in terms of volume of production and variety of product

▶ Application of process control systems

Managing material flows and production management

The receipt of a customer order will trigger a series of information flows through the operations function of a manufacturing company. These are shown as a simplified flow process chart in Figure 6.20. Flow process charts are described in the context of system design in Chapter 11.

The information flow that needs to be supported by an IS begins with the customer order, which will normally provide information on the product required, the quantity and the date when the order is required. An order management system should enable the status of customer orders to be checked continually. Information should be available on the progress of the order through the production process and the reason for any delays (e.g. equipment breakdown, awaiting a raw material shipment).

A production plan determines the sequence in which work generated by orders is performed by the production system. The orders are not processed in the order that they are received but are rearranged according to their required due dates and the amount of resources they require.

A detailed breakdown of the order in terms of its components and an examination of components held in stock provides the information required for activating the ordering of additional components. In addition to material availability, equipment availability must be determined. Maintenance records need to be consulted and the

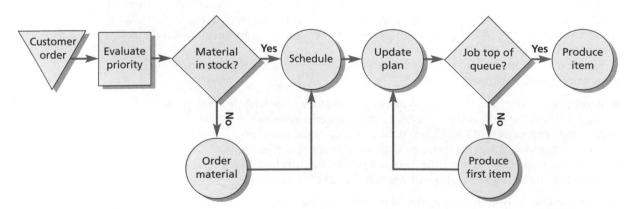

Figure 6.20 Simplified flow process chart for a production management system

equipment may not be available due to routine maintenance or breakdown. Also, special tools may be required to process a particular component.

Scheduling concerns the order and quantity of components that are processed through the production system on a day-to-day or operational basis. In order to form a schedule, information on labour availability and the routeing of the order through the system is required. Scheduling issues are usually considered under the three main types of production system that are put into the context of variety and volume in Figure 6.19: repetitive, job shop and batch.

When the goods have passed through the production process they are held as finished goods inventory. Information on finished goods inventory is used to form a shipping schedule for delivery to customers (in service operations, storage of the finished service is not usually feasible).

Materials management

Three approaches to materials management will be described. Materials requirements planning (MRP) aims to ensure that just the right amount of each item is held at the right time in order to meet the needs of the manufacturing schedule. Just-in-time (JIT) production uses a 'pull' mechanism that provides a trigger when demand occurs and then attempts to supply that demand. Optimised production technology (OPT) focuses on the system bottleneck, that is, the production stage with the lowest level of capacity which is the limiting factor on the speed of the flow of goods to the customer.

MRP requires information from three main sources. The master production schedule (MPS) identifies what products are needed and when they are needed based on customer orders held and a forecast of future demand. The bill of materials (BOM) file provides a list of the components required to create each product, and the inventory status file (ISF) provides information on the current stock level of each component. From this information, the MRP system will indicate when an order should be placed.

The JIT approach implements a 'pull'-type system called the 'kanban' production control system. The idea is that parts are requested in the system only when needed by 'pulling' them from the subsequent operation that requires more work. To implement this system, a kanban (Japanese for 'card' or 'sign') is used to pass through the production system information such as part identification, quantity and the location of the next work centre. The kanban authorises the production and movement of material through the pull system.

The OPT system is based on the identification of bottlenecks within the production process. The idea is that the output of the whole production process is determined by the output of the bottleneck machine. Thus the bottleneck should pace production and determine the amount of work done at non-bottleneck resources.

Product/service design and development

Good design of products and services is an essential element in satisfying customer needs. The success of the design process is primarily dependent on the relationship between the marketing, design and operations functions of the organisation. Information requirements are:

● market research to evaluate customer needs;
● demand forecasts;
● component costings;
● technical specification of the product.

In order to reduce time to market for new designs, the concept of concurrent design can be implemented. This replaces the traditional sequential design process when work is undertaken within functional business areas. Instead, the contributors to the design effort work together as a team (groupware can assist in this). This means improved communications and enables different stages of the design process to occur simultaneously. Another concept is design for manufacture (DFM), which aims to improve design and reduce costs through such techniques as simplification, standardisation and modularisation of the product design (Slack et al., 1995).

Facility design

Facility design concerns how capacity will be supplied by the organisation to meet market demand, that is, it involves the design of production facilities, often using CAD/CAM software which is defined in the next section. Information requirements are:

- external sources on the state of competition and risks associated with not undertaking a task in-house;
- facility location needs to consider long-range demand forecasts and information on the cost of land, the availability of appropriately skilled labour, transportation links and the quality of local education and training services.

Materials requirements planning (MRP) software

Materials requirements planning (MRP) Software
Used to plan the production of goods in a manufacturing organisation by obtaining components, scheduling operations and controlling production.

Materials requirements planning (MRP) software is used to plan the production of goods in a manufacturing organisation by obtaining components, scheduling operations and controlling production. Dedicated MRP software provides input screens, a database and reporting facilities required of a production system. Information required by the system includes the master production schedule which states what needs producing, the bill of materials or component list and the inventory status file (ISF) giving the current component stock levels. A typical structure for an MRP system is shown in Figure 6.21. For large numbers of components a computerised system is essential. The MRP system will automatically generate a series of purchase orders for components along with the timing of their release to the production process, in order to ensure that customer order due dates are met. A development of the MRP system termed MRP II integrates the information system with other functional areas in the business such as finance and marketing, for instance the incorporation of cost data through integration with the financial accounting system.

Computer-aided design (CAD)

Computer-aided design (CAD)
Provides interactive graphics that assist in the development of product and service designs. Connects to a database allowing designs to be recalled and developed easily.

CAD provides interactive graphics that assist in the development of product and service designs. It also connects to a database, allowing designs to be recalled and developed easily.

Computer-aided manufacture (CAM)

Computer-aided manufacture (CAM)
CAM involves the use of computers directly to control production equipment and indirectly to support manufacturing operations.

CAM involves the use of computers, directly to control production equipment and indirectly to support manufacturing operations. Direct CAM applications link a computer directly to production equipment in order to monitor and control the actual production process. An example is a computerised numerical control (CNC) machine which reads instructions for making parts from tape or disk. Indirect CAM applications include MRP, quality control and inventory control systems.

CAD/CAM

The successful design of a component must consider not only design issues in achieving customer requirements, but also the ability of the production system to manufacture the design. CAD/CAM systems improve the design process by enabling information exchange between the CAD and CAM systems by using a common database containing information on items such as component lists, routeings and tool design.

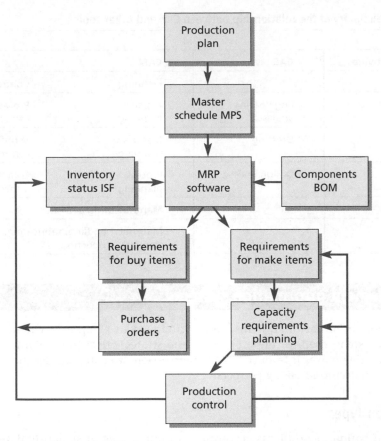

Figure 6.21　Flow of control and information requirements for a typical MRP system

Computer-integrated manufacture (CIM)

CIM aims to integrate information for manufacturing and external activities, such as order entry and accounting, to enable the transformation of a product idea into a delivered product at minimum time and cost. CIM incorporates design activities such as CAD/CAM and operational activities such as MRP, FMS and inventory control. One of the main challenges in the implementation of CIM is integrating equipment from different manufacturers on a common network. In order to overcome this a data communication standard, called Manufacturing Automation Protocol (MAP), has been evolved. CIM covers all aspects of the overall process of production in a business. Its aims, through process automation, are to simplify production processes and product design, automate using robots and process control computers and integrate inventory holding and stock control and costings through the accounting information system. Table 6.4 summarises some of the tools discussed which form part of CIM.

Computer-integrated manufacture (CIM)
Aims to integrate information for manufacturing and external activities such as order entry and accounting to enable the transformation of a product idea into a delivered product at minimum time and cost.

Flexible manufacturing systems (FMS)

Each such system is a group of machines with programmable controllers linked by an automated materials handling system and integrated by an information system that enables a variety of parts with similar processing requirements to be manufactured. FMS are most suited to batch production systems which have intermediate amounts of variety and volume of output. The system aims to use computer control to produce a variety of output quickly.

Table 6.4 **Summary of the relationship between CIM and other tools**

Business activities	CAD	CAM	
		Planning	Control
Procurement	Engineering analysis	Capacity planning	Process control
Accounting	Drafting	Materials planning	Shopfloor control
Order entry	Design review	Process planning	Computer-aided inspection
Payroll		Manufacturing activities	
Billing etc.		Materials handling, fabrication, assembly, inspection	

Management information systems

Management information systems were introduced in Chapter 2 where they were defined as systems used to support tactical and strategic decision making. Basic decision-making theory was introduced in Chapter 1. Here we will consider the application of MIS from a decision-making perspective.

▶ Decision types

The identification of problems according to their degree of structure dates back to Garry and Scott-Morton (1971), but it still provides a useful framework for defining decision types (Fig. 6.22).

Figure 6.22 indicates that at the operational level, structured decisions predominate and these are commonly supported by TPS. Decision support systems are mainly used to support the tactical, semi-structured decisions that need to be made as part of the evaluation and planning of the business. Executive information systems are targeted at strategic decision making, which often involves unstructured decisions.

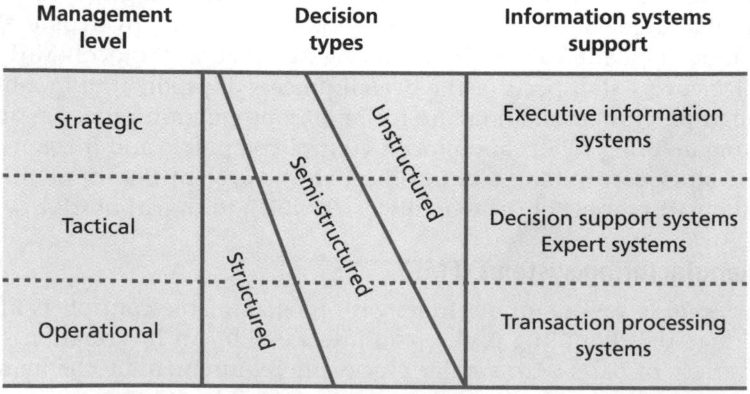

Figure 6.22 **Classification of decisions by decision type and their relation to different types of system**

It should be noted that there is considerable overlap between strategic and tactical and structured and unstructured. Similarly, there is overlap between the types of systems used to support these different levels. For example, decision support systems can also be used in a strategic capacity or in an operational capacity.

◗ Decision support systems

Decision support systems (DSS) provide information and models in a form to facilitate tactical and strategic decision making. They are information systems that support management decision making by integrating:

- company performance data;
- business rules based on decision tables;
- analytical tools and models for forecasting and planning;
- an easy-to-use graphical user interface.

Decision support systems (DSS)
....
Provide information and models in a form to facilitate tactical and strategic decision making involving semi-structured and unstructured decisions.

They are often developed by end-users and are departmental rather than corporate systems. DSS tend to be used for ad hoc queries rather than regular reporting. The technology varies particularly rapidly in this area and the newest developments such as data warehouses attest to this. They are frequently used as a marketing tool, with applications such as:

- forecasting sales through geodemographic analysis;
- optimising distribution networks, using a model to select the best retail locations;
- optimising product mixes.

When used by teams of people to make decisions, they are sometimes known as GDSS or group decision support systems. DSS are often implemented as specialised types of information systems such as data warehousing, expert systems, geographical information systems or even spreadsheet models. We will explore some of these in more detail below.

Functions of a decision support system

Sprague (1980) suggests the following main objectives for a DSS:

1 The DSS should provide support for decision making, but in particular semi-structured and unstructured decisions.
2 The DSS should not focus on a single level of management decision making, such as tactical. Rather, it should integrate across all levels in recognition of the overlap between operational, tactical and strategic decisions.
3 The DSS should support all phases of the decision-making process outlined above.
4 The DSS should be easy to use.

Decision support system components

Watson and Sprague (1993) identify three main components in a decision support system. These are:

1 *Dialogue*. This component is used for achieving interaction with the user so they can formulate queries and models and review results. Essentially, it is the user interface. It is often difficult to devise an effective user interface for a DSS since there is a trade-off between simplicity and flexibility. Simplicity is needed since some managers may not be frequent users of decision support systems. Flexibility is required to allow a range of different questions to be asked and to enable data to be displayed in different ways. The problem is that as more flexibility and options are built into the system, it becomes more difficult to use.
2 *Data*. Data sources are, of course, critical to DSS. Information may need to be collected from a range of sources such as operational systems (for sales performance),

financial accounting systems (for financial performance), or document sources such as internal documents or those available on the Internet.

3 *Model*. The model component provides an analysis capability for the DSS. A financial model, for example, may predict for given inputs what the future profitability of a company will be if it continues on the present course.

Analysis techniques available for a salesforce management problem

Here, we will briefly review commonly used expressions for describing analysis using DSS in relation to a simple example. A company has recognised that there is a positive correlation between the number of sales staff and revenue generated. Through setting up a simple model in a spreadsheet based on this relationship, it is possible to perform the following types of analysis:

1 *What-if? analysis*. Changing a series of variables to see the effect, e.g. what if we increase our salesforce by 10 per cent? The corresponding forecast increase in sales will readily be calculated by the spreadsheet.

2 *Sensitivity analysis*. This is a structured what-if? analysis where we change a single variable repeatedly to see the effects, e.g. increase salesforce in increments of 1 per cent.

3 *Goal-seeking analysis*. This is the reverse of what-if? Here we change variables governing the value of the goal until it is achieved, e.g. by what percentage do we need to increase the salesforce to achieve a growth in sales of £100 000?

4 *Optimisation analysis and simulation*. Change a number of variables to find the optimal solution through, for example, linear programming, e.g. which is the best mix of increasing advertising and salesforce to achieve a set increase in sales?

5 *Data mining*. This approach is used with data warehouses (see below) to try to identify a relationship between variables in order to assist decision making. It will involve statistical techniques such as multiple linear regression where a number of variables are compared to identify patterns.

Types of decision support system

There is a bewildering array of terms used to describe software developed to help solve unstructured and semi-structured problems. These include artificial intelligence, expert systems, neural networks, fuzzy logic, data mining, business intelligence (BI) systems, knowledge-based systems and intelligent knowledge-based systems. All of these types of software have the same broad aim – to assist decision making by using software to mimic the way decisions are made by experts in their own field.

Artificial intelligence (AI) is the term given to research into how computers can reproduce human intelligence. Many of the terms above, such as expert systems and neural networks, are specialist areas of artificial intelligence from which business applications have been produced. Further business applications of AI include voice recognition and security applications such as retinal scanning.

A useful method of considering different types of DSS is to consider the different types of problem they can solve (Luconi et al., 1986). The problems are considered in terms of four elements:

- the data;
- the problem-solving procedures;
- the goals and constraints;
- the flexibility of strategies among the procedures.

Artificial intelligence (AI)

The study of how computers can reproduce human intelligence.

The types of problem are:

- Type I problems are structured in all of the four elements above.
- Type II problems have some incomplete data and partly understood goals and constraints.
- Type III problems are those in which rules can be defined in a knowledge base and the software can then solve problems of a similar type.
- Type IV problems have aspects of both Type II and Type III problems.

Which types of DSS can be used for solving these types of problems? Type I problems are usually incorporated into operational systems as part of the program logic and do not require a specific DSS. The Pareto Partners case study with credit checking falls into this category. Type III problems can be solved by a classical expert system and Types II and IV require a hybrid approach, which may involve modern techniques such as data mining, neural networks and genetic programming as described by Goonatilake and Khebbal (1995). We will now consider some of these types of system in more detail.

Expert systems

Expert systems are used to represent the knowledge and decision-making skills of specialists so that non-specialists can take decisions. They encapsulate the knowledge of experts by providing tools for the acquisition of knowledge and representation of rules and their enactment as decisions. They need to contain information relevant to taking the decision. This is often referred to as the *knowledge base* and includes the rules on which the decisions are based. An important distinction between expert systems and other information systems that are used for decision making is that the suggested actions are not based only on rules and algorithms. Instead, they also use heuristic techniques that may involve searching through different 'rules of thumb' that recommend the best action. The different rules are applied using a separate module of the expert system, known as the *inference engine*. This uses specialist techniques such as forward chaining and backward chaining, explained briefly in the Pareto study.

The relationship between these different components of the expert system is shown in Figure 6.23. The *user interface* program, sometimes referred to as the 'expert system shell', is used to build rules and ask questions of the system.

Applications of expert systems include:

- gold prospecting!
- medical diagnosis;
- credit decisions and insurance underwriting;
- product design, management and testing.

Expert systems
Used to represent the knowledge decision-making skills of specialists so that non-specialists can take decisions.

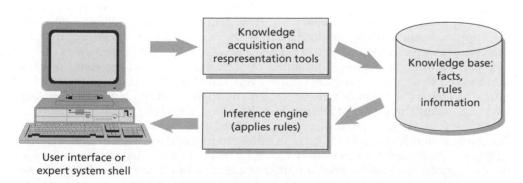

Figure 6.23 **Components of an expert system**

MINI CASE STUDY

Pareto Partners use expert systems to manage over £130 million in global financial markets

Investment company Pareto has invested over £1 million in an expert system which manages many times that amount in investments. The system uses hybrid techniques according to the type of problem that is being solved. It uses fuzzy logic based on reasoning and imprecise values such as low, medium or high. For other scenarios it uses case-based reasoning relating to previous examples and standard forward and backward chaining techniques, employing about 2000 rules based on the expertise of leading financial analysts.

In financial markets, the amount of profit required is usually proportional to the risks that a company is prepared to take. This risk:return ratio is therefore a programmable parameter of Pareto's system.

To date, *Computer Bulletin* reported in March 1998 that the system had achieved a return of 3.4 per cent, which matches the performance of the top quarter of human investment managers. The magazine also notes that such a system is unlikely to succumb to the stress of decision making in this high-pressured situation. It is difficult for a human manager to remember the number of investment opportunities and past trends. If a manager manages funds in 10–15 markets with 10–20 variables for each of three sources of variables, then this is equivalent to millions of combinations.

In medicine, expert systems have recorded some success in diagnosing illnesses that might not have been recognised by doctors because of their obscurity. In a medical expert system such as MYCIN which was used to identify the treatment for blood disorders, the symptoms of a condition are entered into the expert system, which then compares them with all the known symptoms of different ailments in a knowledge base and gives a diagnosis. The knowledge base consists of facts or expert knowledge, in this case the symptoms and also a series of rules that match the symptom to the problem.

Expert systems are used quite widely in the financial services industry for assessing the risk of investing in a particular share or futures market (see case study) or in personal finance or issuing a loan. For example, if a customer wants a loan they will give personal details about their employment history and where they have lived, and an expert system will assess what the credit risk is based on this pattern of behaviour in their existing customer base. The degree of sophistication of this risk assessment could vary from assessing the individual on a series of rules or a more advanced system using neural networks. The rules-based approach might state, for example, that credit cannot be issued if an individual has not lived in a particular location for less than six months over the last five years or if the amount of the loan is greater than 10 per cent of their salary. With a neural network approach, the software would learn from the history of previous customers what characteristics represented a bad credit risk and assess according to these criteria.

Expert systems (ES) achieved prominence during the 1980s as the result of work summarised by Scott-Morton (1991). Since this time they have not been applied as widely as forecast, often only being used in niche applications such as credit broking. Their use to date and predicted future use are described in Chapter 19.

More recent AI-type systems have been referred to as *intelligent hybrid systems* by Goonatilake and Khebbal (1995). These differ from expert systems in that they are adaptive – they often have the ability to modify their decision-making capabilities as their knowledge base is expanded, in other words they can 'learn'. **Neural networks** are systems that use a similar process to biological intelligence to learn problem-solving skills by 'training' or exposure to a wide range of problems. The learning occurs through interactions between nodes, which are similar to the neurons of the brain. Neural networks work in a similar way to brain neurons, which gives them the capacity to learn through exposure to different patterns. For example, a neural network could be used for a photofit application if it learnt the characteristics of different types of people. As an example of the way in which neural networks can be applied to business applications, consider a bank processing Visa credit card transactions. Of all the transactions that occur, a proportion will be fraudulent. By learning from past transactions, both legal and fraudulent, a neural network will be able to predict the likelihood of fraud on an account. Barclays Bank installed such a system in the UK in 1997, and it was soon recognising over £100,000 of fraudulent transactions each month.

Another type of adaptive system is a *genetic algorithm*. This uses successive iterations of a problem-solving algorithm to improve the quality of decision taken by the software. A further method, known as *fuzzy logic*, is often combined with neural networks in a hybrid system.

Expert systems have not been widely adopted in industry, although they are widely used in some areas such as financial risk assessment. Since most business users are unlikely to be involved in the specification or use of expert systems, they are not covered further here. The interested reader should refer to Curtis (1998) for a summary of different techniques for representing and processing knowledge in expert systems, or Turban (1995) for a complete text on expert systems and decision support.

▶ Executive information systems (EIS)

EIS or executive support systems provide senior managers with a system to assist them in taking strategic and tactical decisions. Their purpose is to analyse, compare and highlight trends to help govern the strategic direction of a company. They are commonly integrated with operational systems, giving managers the facility to 'drill down' to find out further information on a problem.

In the USA the terms 'business intelligence' and 'online analytical processing' (OLAP) are often used for these types of applications by analysts such as the Gartner Group and vendors such as Cognos and Business Objects. These terms and the data warehouses described in the next section are also starting to supersede EIS in the rest of the world.

Business intelligence software is a general term to describe the market for a range of decision support systems, including EIS, DSS and data-warehouse software and including application of expert systems and data-mining techniques to interpret data.

Online analytical processing (OLAP) is a synonym for a data warehouse. It refers to the ability to analyse in real time the type of multidimensional information stored in data warehouses. 'Online' indicates that users can formulate their own queries, compared to standard paper reports. The originator of OLAP, Dr E. Codd, defines it as the dynamic synthesis, analysis and consolidation of large volumes of multidimensional data.

EIS are intended as decision support tools for senior managers. Since these strategic decisions are based on a wide range of input information, they always need to be well integrated with operational systems in a business. Some important features of EIS are:

● They provide summary information to enable monitoring of business performance. This is often achieved through measures known as critical success factors or key performance indicators (KPIs). These will be displayed in an easy-to-interpret form such as a graph showing their variation through time. If a KPI falls below a critical preset value, the system will notify the manager through a visible or audible warning.
● They are used mainly for strategic decision making, but may also provide features that relate to tactical decision making.
● They provide a drill-down feature which gives a manager the opportunity to find out more information necessary to take a decision or discover the source of a problem.

Neural networks

Systems that use a similar process to biological intelligence to learn problem-solving skills by 'training' or exposure to a wide range of problems.

Executive Information Systems (EIS)

Provide senior managers with a system to assist them in taking strategic and tactical decisions. Their purpose is to analyse, compare and highlight trends to help govern the strategic direction of company.

Business Intelligence software

A general term to describe the market for a range of decision support systems including EIS, DSS and data-warehouse software.

Online Analytical Processing (OLAP)

Refers to the ability to analyse in real time the type of multidimensional information stored in data warehouses.

For example, a manager with a multinational manufacturing problem might find from the EIS that a particular country is underperforming in production. He could then drill down to see which particular factory was responsible for this.

● They provide analysis tools.
● They must be integrated with other facilities to help manage the solving of problems and the daily running of the business. These include electronic mail and scheduling and calendar facilities.
● They integrate data from a wide variety of information sources, including company and external sources such as market and competitor information.
● They have to be designed according to the needs of managers who do not use computers frequently. They should be intuitive and easy to learn.

All these facilities require integration with operational data. Since this information is commonly stored in ERP systems (see p. 275), these are often integrated with EIS or have EIS functions built in.

Data warehouses, data marts and data mining

Data warehouses

Large database systems containing detailed company data on sales transactions which are analysed to assist in improving the marketing and financial performance of companies.

Data warehouses are large database systems (often measured in gigabytes or terabytes (terabyte = 1000 billion bytes)) containing detailed company data on sales transactions which are analysed to assist in improving the marketing and financial performance of companies.

Data warehouses form a category of business intelligence software that has been adopted by many companies for analysis of transactions to help improve their competitiveness. A good example is that in Case Study 1.1 where retailer Boots analyses the transactions of its loyalty card users. This amounts to 500 000 product transactions each day. Such has been their popularity, that the term data warehouse has to a great extent

---

Keys to success for a data warehouse

In a 1998 white paper by US analysts IDC, Graham and Notarfonzo listed five keys to success. These are:

1 Ensure end-user's needs are fully defined.
2 Ensure business requirements are fully defined.
3 Develop enterprise-level data models and business rules.
4 Include individuals from affected departments in the development teams.
5 Promote use of the warehouse internally.

The top five pitfalls they identified are:

1 Raising users' expectations higher than you can deliver.
2 Letting the project scope become unmanageable.
3 Underusing the warehouse.
4 Letting management interest wane.
5 Not fully developing business requirements.

In a report by analysts The Meta Group, *Data Warehouse Opportunities 1997/98: an In-depth Analysis of the Key Market Trends*, a survey indicated the following key challenges to implementing the data warehouse (by % of respondents):

● 35–40%: Data quality;
● 30–35%: Transforming/scrubbing legacy data, managing end-user expectations;
● 20–25%: Managing management expectations, business rule analysis, managing meta-data (data about data);
● 15–20%: Database performance tuning/scaling, ROI justification;
● 10–15%: Time to load/refresh data;
● 5–10%: Security, maintenance.

displaced EIS in software purchases for strategic and tactical decision making. **Data marts** are a newer development. This term defines a smaller, departmental version which may be easier to manage than a company-scale data warehouse. Data marts do not aim to hold information across an entire company, but rather focus on one department.

William Inmon is often known as the father of the data warehouse. He defines a data warehouse as:

> *A subject oriented, integrated, time variant, and non-volatile collection of data in support of management's decision making process.*

It is worth considering each of the characteristics of the definition in more detail:

- *'Subject-oriented'* – examples of subjects that are commonly held in data warehouses for analysis are customer and product.
- *'Integrated'* – an important principle of data warehouses is that information is collected from diverse sources within an organisation and brought together to enable integrated analysis.
- *'Non-volatile'* – data are transferred from operational information systems such as sales order processing systems into a data warehouse where the information is static – it is not updated.
- *'In support of management's decision making process'* – this final point emphasises the purpose of the data warehouse.

Figure 6.24 indicates the structure of a data warehouse. It can be seen that the data warehouse takes information from operational systems (which record sales or transactions with customers) and transfers this information into a repository for decision making, which happens across the network via a web-based client, or a specific client from a BI software vendor such as Cognos Powerplay.

BI and data warehousing software are used in three main ways:

1 For analysing large volumes of product sales information to identify problem areas where sales targets are not being achieved. The data may be 'sliced and diced' by different dimensions to spot particular problems. These include by product segment, by

Data marts

These are small scale data warehouses which do not aim to hold information across an entire company, but rather focus on one department.

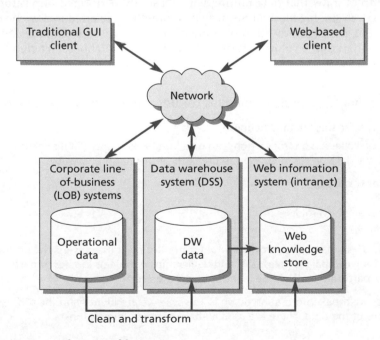

Figure 6.24 Data warehouse architecture

geographical area, by time period (monthly, quarterly, yearly), by salesperson and by customer type (for example, age and sociodemographic group for retail consumers).

2 For data mining. This identifies trends in the data, allowing marketing managers to optimise the product mix. For example, if a credit card company is experiencing a high 'churn rate' of customers moving to other brands, data mining could be used to identify the characteristics of these customers and then suggest a method or alternative product that could be offered to alleviate this.

3 For forecasting and performing what-if? scenarios. Using this type of software the company can vary the characteristics of its products or the customers it targets and see the likely impacts on future sales.

Data mining
An attempt to identify relationships between variables in data warehouses in order to assist decision making.

Data mining of data warehouses is an attempt to identify a relationship between variables in order to assist decision making. It will involve statistical techniques such as multiple linear regression where a number of variables are compared to identify patterns.

Data mining is used to identify patterns or trends in the data in data warehouses which can be used for improved profitability. The well-known Wal-Mart example shows that these patterns would often not be evident without computer analysis. Rather than asking direct questions such as: 'Who are the top 20 per cent of our customers?', more open questions will be asked such as: 'What are the characteristics of the top 20 per cent of our customers?'. Through understanding customers better, their needs can be better met. Particular data mining techniques include:

- *Identifying associations* – a shopping basket analysis by a chemist revealed an association of shoppers who purchase condoms and foot powder. It is not clear how this information can be used.
- *Identifying sequences* – shows the sequence in which actions occur, e.g. path or click-stream analysis of a web site.
- *Classifications* – patterns, e.g. identifying groups of web site users who display similar visitor patterns.
- *Clustering* – finding groups of facts that were previously unknown.
- *Forecasting* – using sales histories to forecast future sales.

These examples show that data mining is increasingly performed on visitor data collected using web-site log-file analysis, which is sometimes referred to as web analytics.

Activity 6.4 gives an indication of some of the specialised techniques necessary to deal with analysis of the volume of data stored in a data warehouse, referred to as multidimensional data.

Activity 6.4

Data warehouse analysis techniques for describing multidimensional data

Example 1: a car sales data warehouse

Information collected on transactions can often be broken down in different ways. Say that we have data on car sales. We can break this information down by:

- time car was sold;
- model;
- location at which sold;
- salesperson;

and so on. This type of breakdown is vital for marketing staff to assess the performance of advertising campaigns, sales staff and dealerships. Problems in sales of particular models or particular staff can be identified and then rectified.

Whenever we break information down in this way we are identifying the different *dimensions* of the data. There are usually three common dimensions:

- time period;
- product or market segment;
- geographic location where the product was sold (or where consumers originate).

The example in Figure 6.25 shows how these three dimensions form a cube, with each individual cube effectively representing one combination of data. The small cube represents all four-wheel-drive vehicles in Quarter 1 of 1998 sold into a particular postal sector.

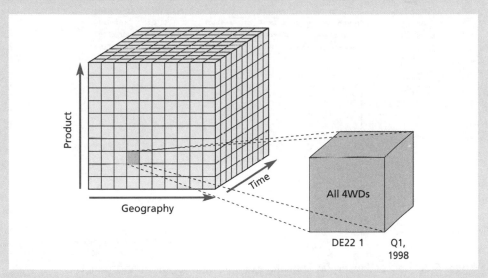

Figure 6.25 Example of multidimensional data cube for vehicle sales

When designing data warehouses, each dimension and its division into categories can be shown on a diagram, as in Table 6.5.

Table 6.5 Designing a data warehouse

	Dimensions					
	All time periods (85)	All locations (4306)	All products (35)	Age groups (8)	Economic groups (6)	Genders (3)
Categories	Year 5	Regions 6	Segments 5	8	ABC1 C2DE 6	3
	Quarter 20	Postal areas 200	Models 30			
	Month 60	Postal districts 1500	(Paint colours 100)			
		Postal sectors 2000	(Plus competitor segments)			
		Dealerships + DARs (plus sales staff not shown) 300 × 2				

Measures:
Forecast sales, Budget sales, Actual sales, Budget variance (calc), Forecast variance (calc), Market share. For each of 6 measures, number of data items are: $85 \times 4306 \times 35 \times 8 \times 6 \times 3 = 1.8$ billion. Assume 4 bytes per item, $6 \times 4 \times 1.8$ billion = approx 40 gigabytes.

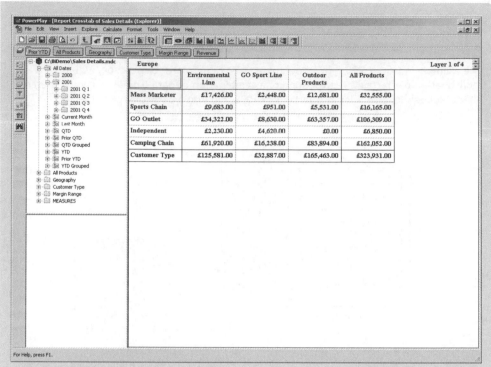

Figure 6.26 Cognos Powerplay showing example data for outdoor products
Source: Reproduced by kind permission of Cognos, Copyright © 2002 Cognos Incorporated

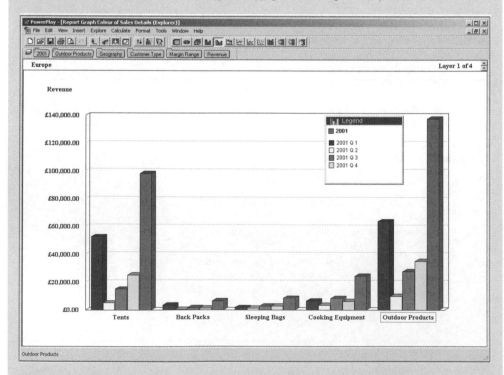

Figure 6.27 Cognos Powerplay showing graphed sales of outdoor products
Source: Reproduced by kind permission of Cognos, Copyright © 2002 Cognos Incorporated

Note that measures such as sales figures and market share, which are all broken down into the different dimensions, are shown along the bottom of the table. This table can also be used to assess the information storage requirements.

Example 2: a retail data warehouse for camping equipment

This example shows two different views on this data. The first (Fig. 6.26) tabulates sales for a particular product range – outdoor products in 2001 for the North American market. It can be seen from the categories dialogue box that it is possible to choose different views of the data according to the category. Cognos Powerplay is a widely used tool for analysis of complex, multidimensional data.

The view of the data in Figure 6.27 shows the same data in graphical form. Sales variations in the five products for the five different quarters are clearly evident.

Hammergren (1996) gives a good treatment of some of the techniques of data analysis described in this case study.

Activity

For the second example of outdoor equipment, develop a matrix showing the dimensions and categories of information in the same form as that for the car sales matrix. List your assumptions where insufficient information is available.

Multidimensional data are data broken down in the analysis used for building a data warehouse. For sales data the common dimensions are time period, product types and geographic location. Dimensions are broken down into categories. For time these could be months, quarters or years. Data describing data are known as **metadata**.

Multidimensional data
Data broken down in analysis for a data warehouse into dimensions such as time period, product segment and the geographical location. Dimensions are broken down into categories. For time these could be months, quarters or years.

Metadata
Reference data describing the structure and content of data in a data warehouse are known as metadata.

Functional and departmental applications

In the final section of this chapter we will review how information systems can be used in four key functional parts of an organisation: the procurement, human resources, marketing and finance functions. These examples have been chosen since they usually require application-specific software.

▶ E-procurement – procurement information systems

Procurement has not traditionally been a significant topic for management study in comparison with other areas such as marketing, operations or strategy. The concept of e-business has, however, highlighted its importance as a strategic issue since introducing **electronic procurement** or e-procurement can achieve significant savings and other benefits which directly impact the customer.

The growing importance of e-procurement was highlighted by a Tranmit (1999) report that showed that around 90% of companies said that they plan to implement an electronic procurement management system within the next five years, with the majority identifying cost savings as their primary goal. The biggest barrier to automation is integration of these systems with existing financial systems, according to 60% of the respondents. Furthermore, the survey suggested that only 13% of these businesses have computerised the procurement process and integrated it with other financial processes; 25% of organisations continue to rely on entirely paper-based procurement. The majority

Electronic procurement (e-procurement)
The electronic integration and management of all procurement activities including purchase request, authorisation, ordering, delivery and payment between a purchaser and a supplier.

(62%) continue to rely on a mixture of electronically supported and manual processes. The respondents in the survey were procurement directors and senior managers in 112 UK organisations with an annual turnover of more than £30 million who were approached to establish the adoption levels, drivers and barriers for e-procurement.

Procurement refers to all activities involved with obtaining items from a supplier, which includes purchasing, but also inbound logistics such as transportation, goods-in and warehousing before the item is used. The key procurement activities and associated information flows within an organisation are shown in Figure 6.28. In this chapter we focus on these activities, which include searching and specification of product by the end-user, purchasing by the buyer, payment, and receipt and distribution of goods within a warehouse.

◗ Drivers of e-procurement

E-procurement should be directed at improving performance for each of the 'five rights of purchasing' (Baily et al., 1994), which are sourcing items:

- at the right price;
- delivered at the right time;
- of the right quality;
- of the right quantity;
- from the right source.

Case Study 6.3 illustrates many of the reasons why many companies are now introducing e-procurement. The primary driver is cost reduction, in this case from an average of £60 per order to £10 per order. In many cases the cost of ordering exceeds the value of the product purchased. Savings may also be made through the need for less material in inventory because of faster purchase cycle times.

Kluge (1997) considers procurement to be a strategic issue since, as the figures above show, significant savings can be made, and these cost reductions should increase with greater profitability. Kluge (1997) reports on a survey of electronics companies in which there was a

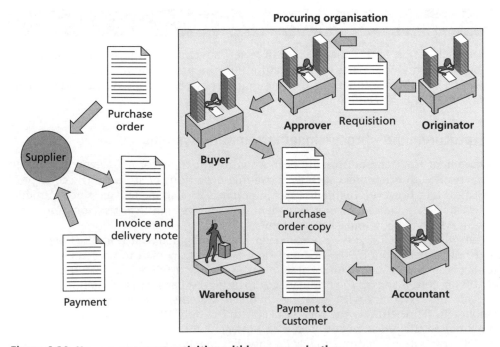

Figure 6.28 Key procurement activities within an organisation
Source: Chaffey (2002)

19% difference in profitability between the most successful and least successful companies. Of this difference, 13% was due to differences in the cost of goods sold, of which between 40 and 70% were accounted for by differences in the cost of purchased goods and services.

Direct cost reductions are achieved through efficiencies in the process, as shown by examples in Chapter 10. Process efficiencies result in less staff time spent in searching and ordering products and reconciling deliveries with invoices. Savings also occur through automated validation of pre-approved spending budgets for individuals or departments, leading to fewer people processing each order, and in less time. It is also possible to reduce the cost of physical materials such as specially printed order forms and invoices. There are also indirect benefits from e-procurement: cycle times between order and use of supplies can be reduced. In addition, e-procurement may enable greater flexibility in ordering goods from different suppliers according to best value. This is particularly true for **electronic B2B marketplaces** (Chapter 13). E-procurement also tends to change the role of buyers in the purchasing department. By removing administrative tasks such as placing orders and reconciling deliveries and invoices with purchase orders, buyers can spend more time on value-adding activities. Such activities may include more time spent with key suppliers to improve product delivery and costs or analysis and control of purchasing behaviour.

Electronic B2B marketplace
An intermediary facilitating electronic trade of goods beween buyers and suppliers.

CASE STUDY 6.3

Cambridge Consultants reduce costs through e-procurement

Introduction
Cambridge Consultants offers technical product design and development services to commerce and industry. It has over 300 employees, all based in Cambridge, 200 of whom are engineers, consultants, and technicians. They work on products in health care, industrial consumer development (ICD), and telecommunications, information, media and electronics (TIME). Although it is not a volume manufacturer, Cambridge Consultants must design to production standards. This means building several production prototypes for each project. With 120 projects in hand at any one time, Cambridge needs a diverse range of components every day.

Purchasing is centralised across the company and controlled by its Purchasing Manager, Francis Pullen. Because of its varied and often unique requirements, Cambridge has a supplier base of nearly 4,000 companies, with 20 new ones added each month. Some of these companies are providing items so specialized that Cambridge purchases from them no more than twice a year. Of the total, only 400 are preferred suppliers. Of those, just 10% – 1% of the overall supplier base – have been graded key supplier by Cambridge. That number includes RS Components. Francis Pullen says, 'We charge our clients by the hour, so if a product is faulty or late we have engineers waiting for new parts to arrive. This doesn't align with our fast time to market business proposition. RS Components' guarantee of service and range of products fits in with our business ethos.'

The existing purchasing process
Pullen has seen many changes and improvements in the company's purchasing process as its suppliers have used new technology to introduce new services. The first was moving to CD-ROM from the paper-based catalogue. Next was an online purchasing card – an account card with detailed line item billing, passwords and controls. Using industry standard guidelines from the Chartered Institute of Purchasing and Supply (CIPS), Francis Pullen analysed the internal cost of raising an order. This took into account every step, from the engineer raising a paper requisition, through processing by purchasing, the cost of handling the delivery once it arrived, invoice matching and clearance and even the physical cost of a four-part purchase order form. The whole process involved between eight and ten people and cost the company anywhere from £60 to £120, depending on the complexity of the order.

The main cost is in requisitioning, when engineers and consultants spend their revenue-producing time in identifying their needs and raising paperwork. (Centralised purchasing, by contrast, is very efficient, costing around £50 an order.)

Using the RS purchase card removes the need for engineers and consultants to raise a paper requisition. This makes low-value ordering much more cost efficient. Invoice matching costs are also reduced, since the purchase card statement lists all purchases made each month.

Although the purchase card is undoubtedly an advance, on its own it does not allow costs to be assigned to jobs in the system each day. The purchase card statement takes a month to arrive, giving rise to an equivalent lag in showing the real costs on internal project accounts.

The e-procurement process

To enable the company to order online immediately, RS put Cambridge's pre-Internet trading records on the Web server. Purchasing agreements and controls were thus automatically set up on the Internet order form, including correct pricing and special payment terms.

The benefit was instantly apparent. The use of the RS purchase card when ordering from the Web site, meant that the complete order was automatically collated, with all controls in place. Accuracy was assured and the purchase process was speeded up with the cost per transaction reduced significantly.

Pullen describes the change this has had on Cambridge's purchasing process. 'For the first time in our purchasing history, our financial controllers saw the benefit of distributed purchasing because of the cost savings, reassured by the central purchasing controls as back up.

'This has benefited us enormously. We have allowed three department heads to have their own purchasing cards, so that they can order independently from the Web site.

'We have implemented a very efficient electronic workflow requisition system which is initiated by the purchase card holders and mailed to central purchasing. The orders are held in a mailbox and checked against physical delivery. This has cut out two layers of order activity.

'In purchasing, we no longer spend our time passing on orders that they have raised, and there is no generation of paper during the order process. It doesn't just save time and money – it's also far more environmentally friendly. Passing on low value orders each day adds very little value, so devolving this function back to our internal customers frees up our time in purchasing to work on higher value tasks.'

Benefits for staff

Francis Pullen continues: 'Our internal customers are also much happier. We leave at 6 pm but the engineers will often work late if they are on a deadline. Because they can order off the Web site from their desks (everyone at Cambridge has Internet access), they can add items to the order right up until RS's 8 pm deadline without our involvement. We maintain control because of the reporting functions on the site.

'Phase 2 of the rswww.com design has also made it possible for multiple orders to be opened during the day and then put against different cost centres internally.'

Results

In the year to June 1999, Cambridge Consultants placed 1,200 orders with RS Components, totalling more than £62,000 in value. Of those transactions, 95% went via the Internet. Average order value over the Internet was £34 and accounted for £43,000 of the total business done. The remaining 60 orders were placed though traditional channels but had an average value of £317.

The cost to Cambridge of raising a paper-based order was identified as being £60. Using the combination of the RS purchasing card and rswww.com, this has been reduced to £10 an order. Over a year, this represents a saving of £57,000 to Cambridge. The net effect, therefore, is that its purchases from RS Components now cost it a mere £5,000 a year!

Francis Pullen again: 'RS has demonstrated its commitment to its customers in spending time and investing money in developing a world-class purchasing system that delivers tangible customer cost savings and benefits. We have welcomed their innovative approach to purchasing and believe they are way ahead of their competition in this sector.'

Source: RS Components white paper (www.rswww.com)

Questions

1 Given the scale of the purchasing operation at Cambridge Consultants, what benefits do you think e-procurement has brought?

2 Why are procurement costs currently as high as £60 to £100 per order?

3 How are procurement costs reduced through e-procurement?

4 What staff benefits occur for Cambridge Consultants as a result of e-procurement?

▶ Risks and impacts of e-procurement

The Tranmit (1999) report indicated that in the UK and throughout Europe, adoption of e-procurement is low, with less than a fifth of large companies adopting this technology. It may be possible to explain low adoption through a consideration of the risks and impacts involved with e-procurement. A PricewaterhouseCoopers survey of 400 senior European business leaders indicates that security concerns and lack of faith in trading partners are the most significant factors holding back e-procurement (Porter, 2000). Although 62% said they expected 30% of procurement to be online by the end of 2001, the typical online spend in early 2000 was 5%. Porter states that authentication of identity is the main issue. He says:

> *People need to be satisfied about who they are dealing with. They need to know that their messages have not been intercepted or corrupted on the way, and most importantly they are legally non-repudiable – meaning that the other party can't walk away from it in a court of law.*

He goes on to say that the security fears are well founded with nearly two-thirds of companies relying solely on password protection when dealing with suppliers. Trusted third-party certification is required for the level of trust to increase. While the Internet may give the impression of making it readily possible to swap between suppliers and use new suppliers, two-thirds of those interviewed said building a trusted relationship with suppliers is necessary before they would trade using the Internet.

If the cost savings referred to earlier in the chapter are to be achieved it may be necessary to redeploy staff, or in the worst case make them redundant. For a medium-sized company such as Cambridge Consultants the purchasing team of five people was reduced to four. The threat of redundancy or redeployment is likely to lead to resistance to the introduction of the system, and this needs to be managed. The purchasing manager will have to carefully explain the reasons for introducing the new system, emphasising the benefits to the company as a whole and how it should enable more variety to be introduced to the buying role.

Since the cost savings of e-procurement are achieved through empowerment of originators throughout the business to directly purchase their own items rather than through purchasing there is a risk that some originators may take advantage of this. This is known as 'maverick' or 'off-contract' purchasing, and it has always happened to some extent. Maverick purchasing occurs when items are ordered that are unnecessary or too expensive. Proponents of e-procurement argue that better controls can be put in place than previously.

A further risk, typical of many e-business implementations, is the difficulty in integrating information systems. Figure 6.29 shows how different types of information system cover different parts of the procurement cycle. The different types of systems are shown below.

- *Stock control system* – this relates mainly to production-related procurement; the system highlights when reordering is required when the number in stock falls below reorder thresholds.
- *CD- or web-based catalogue* – paper catalogues have been replaced by electronic forms that make it quicker to find suppliers.
- *E-mail- or database-based workflow systems* integrate the entry of the order by the originator, approval by manager and placement by buyer. The order is routed from one person to the next and will wait in their inbox for actioning. Such systems may be extended to accounting systems.
- *Order-entry on web site* – the buyer often has the opportunity to order directly on the supplier web site, but this will involve rekeying and there is no integration with systems for requisitioning or accounting
- *Accounting systems* – networked accounting systems enable staff in the buying department to enter an order which can then be used by accounting staff to make payment when the invoice arrives
- *Integrated e-procurement or ERP systems* – these aim to integrate all the facilities above and will also include integration with suppliers systems. Figure 6.29 shows document management software as an integrated part of an e-procurement system. Here a paper invoice from a supplier (on the left) has been scanned into the system and is compared to the original electronic order information (on the right).

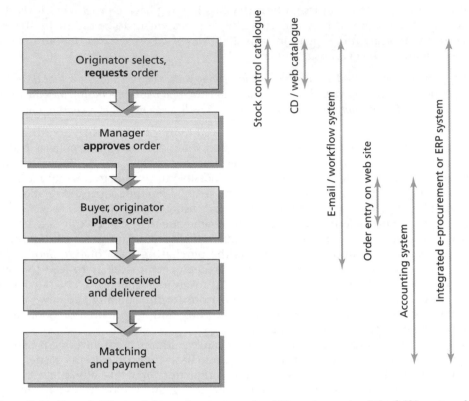

Figure 6.29 Use of different information systems for different aspects of the fulfilment cycle
Source: Chaffey (2002)

▶ Human resource management (HRM) information systems

Human resource
management (HRM)
....
Management that
ensures the employees of
the organisation have the
required skills and tools in
order to meet the
strategic goals of the
organisation.

Human resource management (HRM) is about ensuring that the employees of the organisation have the required skills and tools in order to meet its strategic goals. The management of an organisation's human resources is critical to its success. The development of an organisation's human resources is particularly important in a service company, where employees are more likely to be required to provide customer contact. Human resource decisions and information systems support will be required both within the central human resource function and by managers of the functional areas of the business. Organisations need a supply of trained and qualified personnel in order to achieve their goals. Human resource management (HRM) is about ensuring that the employees of the organisation have the required skills and tools in order to meet its strategic goals.

Objectives of HRM software

The main role of HRM software is to act as a storage and retrieval system maintaining large volumes of data on employee and job specifications. This data will be required for applications such as routine reports for government agencies, information for recruitment and selection, and more sophisticated forecasting models for workforce planning.

Information needs for human resources systems

The main activities of the HR function and the information needed to support them are:

- *Job analysis and design.* HR systems need to contain job descriptions describing the purpose, tasks and responsibilities of that job and job specifications describing the skills, knowledge and other characteristics required of workers in order to undertake the tasks specified in the job description.
- *Job management.* This includes recording of employee development through appraisals, training, salary and benefits planning. The government will also require human resource information to be available from all organisations to comply with laws governing such areas as health and safety legislation, equal opportunities regulations and employee sickness history.
- *Recruitment.* In large organisations workflow systems are used for managing the thousands of applications for jobs. Such systems will help structure interviewing and in sending out letters.

Software for HRM information systems

A database provides a central feature of HRM systems and will contain information on such areas as name, address, job title and attendance for each employee in the organisation and other information required to construct job description and applicant files. With this information it should be possible to use a database management system to match applicant and current employee details to a job specification. The database could also be used in areas such as the identification of training needs and producing details of employees for government agencies. Unfortunately, some HR databases have been constructed within the HR function and are not compatible with such areas as payroll. This leads to problems of duplication and ensuring that data is up to date. Small companies could develop their own databases, but more often small, medium and large companies will buy an off-the-shelf package based on a database.

An example of an HRM database

Single *record* per employee in main employee table. *Fields* within the employee *table* to include:

- surname, forename, next of kin;
- date of birth;
- address;
- National Insurance number;
- position – job description;
- department;
- salary;
- tax code;
- start date.

Links to other *tables*:

- training records;
- assessment/performance appraisal details;
- payroll.

The terms table, field and record were introduced in Chapter 3. Database design is discussed further in Chapters 10 and 11.

▶ Marketing information systems

The word *marketing* has two distinct meanings in terms of modern management practice. It describes:

1 The range of specialist marketing functions carried out within many organisations. Such functions include market research, brand/product management, public relations and customer service.
2 An approach or concept that can be used as the guiding philosophy for all functions and activities of an organisation. Such a philosophy encompasses all aspects of a business. Business strategy is guided by an organisation's market and competitor focus and everyone in an organisation should be required to have a customer focus in their job.

The modern marketing concept unites these two meanings and stresses that marketing encompasses the range of organisational functions and processes that deliver products and services to customers and other key stakeholders, such as employees and financial institutions. Increasingly, the importance of marketing is being recognised both as a vital function and as a guiding management philosophy. Marketing has to be seen as the essential focus of all activities within an organisation.

Given the importance of marketing to an organisation, many companies make use of information systems to assist in mission-critical activities such as customer sales – sell-side e-commerce is a major component of e-business. The benefits of this type of transactional e-commerce system have been described in earlier sections.

In this section we will mainly consider information systems that are used within the marketing department to assist in running the marketing function.

Marketing information systems support decision making at the operational, tactical and strategic levels. At the operational level, distribution information systems and telemarketing systems offer assistance in day-to-day activities and provide information to areas such as inventory and customer credit systems. Tactical marketing systems provide assistance in such areas as product pricing and sales management information systems. At the strategic level, information from sales forecasting, marketing research and competitive tracking systems helps management plan and develop new products.

Marketing information systems
Support decision making at the operational, tactical and strategic levels necessary to manage the marketing function.

Application areas for marketing information systems

The following types of marketing information system can be identified:

● *Sell-side e-commerce systems and customer relationship management systems*. These were discussed earlier in the chapter in the discussion of e-business.
● *Sales force automation (SFA) systems*. Employees involved in the sales area are required to identify potential customers, negotiate the sale of goods and services with those customers, and provide a follow-up service. Systems are available to support each of these tasks. Prospect information systems provide lists of potential customers by categories such as product range or geographic area. Databases can also be used to assist in the selling process. Telemarketing and direct mail systems will incorporate a database to enable storage and extraction of the large amounts of required when dealing with extensive client lists. Siebel (www.siebel.com) is a well-known supplier of SFA systems.
● *Distribution information systems*. Speed of delivery is often an important aspect of service to the customer. In order to provide this, it is important that tracking systems be in place which can locate products during the distribution process. These tracking systems may incorporate technology such as mobile and satellite communications and pen-based computing.

- *Sales and campaign management information systems*. The sales management information system provides information in support of decision making at the tactical level. It will hold information on such aspects as sales performance by geographic area, product group and salesperson. This information can be used to determine sales effort in different areas and products and level of bonus payments to an individual salesperson. This information can be used as the basis for a marketing plan based around an advertising and promotion scheme aimed at a particular customer segment (e.g. targeting of designer-label drinks at people in the 18–25 age range).

- *Sales forecasting information systems*. At a strategic level, it is necessary to provide sales forecast data in order to help form the long-range strategic plan. Sales forecast data is essential so that demand can be met and resources employed in the correct areas. For instance, marketing needs to inform other functions such as operations of predicted demand, so that they can organise their resources to meet this demand. The information system is required because of the range of data that goes into the forecast and the need continually to update the database so the forecast is as accurate as possible.

- *Marketing research and analysis information systems*. In order to ensure that there is a demand for the organisation's goods and services, it is necessary to undertake market research. For a new product, this may include information on demographic changes and customer feedback from questionnaires and interviews indicating customer preferences. For existing products, it will involve analysis of sales using business intelligence software such as data warehouses, described in the section on decision support software.

- *Competitive intelligence (CI systems)*. Knowledge of competitor prices, products, sales and promotions is an important factor in the development of a marketing strategy. For example, the organisation would need to consider its reaction to a competitor moving to build market share. Such information is increasingly managed via the company intranet

- *Telemarketing software*. This software is designed to dial the telephone numbers of potential customers automatically based on customer files maintained in a database. The software will also allow notes to be stored on customer requests, generate follow-up letters and display information gathered on the customer for reference as the call is taking place. Telephone call centres use computer-integrated telephony (CIT) to sell direct product lines such as insurance and personal finance. CIT is also used to provide customer service via helpdesk and advice services. The software can be integrated with a workflow system that provides automatic management of customer requests (e.g. automation of activities such as letter generation). Using historical data, the software can also be used to predict workload levels over time and thus aid management in workforce planning.

- *Geographical information systems (GIS)*. A **geographical information system** (GIS) uses maps to display information about different areas. They are commonly used for performance analysis by marketing staff. Performance of distribution channels such as branches can be shown by colour coding them. Colour-coded areas on the map can be used to show variation in the demand of customers for products or the characteristics of people living in different areas, such as average disposable income. Figure 6.30 shows an example of the application of a GIS. The locations of banks are shown – the dark areas indicate where the bank is performing well and lighter areas where the bank is underperforming. The performance ratio here can be thought of as market share. Marketing analysts can review this in an attempt to correct problems in areas of underperformance. For example, there appears to be an opportunity in the south of the area to open a new branch.

Geographical information system (GIS)

Uses maps to display information about different geographic locations such as catchments or branches. They are commonly used for performance analysis by marketing staff.

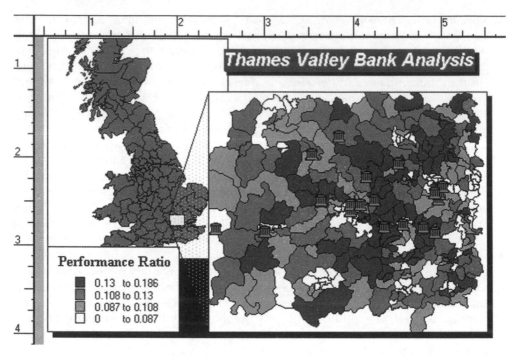

Figure 6.30 Data view from MapInfo geographical information system showing performance analysis for a bank

▶ Accounting information systems

Accounting information systems are used for the financial activities that take place in any organisation. These include the operation of sales order processing systems, payroll, budgeting and reporting of the financial condition of the organisation. Other functions include the management of capital investment and general cashflow management.

Operational accounting systems focus on daily recording of business transactions, that is, the flow of funds through an organisation. All businesses require this basic information. In larger businesses these systems will be linked to other operational functions, such as sales order processing and inventory.

Management accounting systems enable planning and control of business finance. These are sometimes referred to as financial information systems and will be linked to executive information systems.

Application areas for accounting information systems

Most companies use an integrated accounting system that covers a number of application areas, as shown in Figure 6.31. The essential modules are accounts receivable, accounts payable and the general ledger. Many companies will look to extend these to related areas such as sales order processing and payroll.

- *Sales order processing.* The SOP system is particularly important, as it records sales transactions and supplies documents to other areas such as stock control and manufacturing. There might also be links to payroll to calculate such elements as bonus payments to salespeople on receipt of a customer order. The accounts receivable system contains customer information such as sales made, payments made and account balances for overdue payments. These can be used to halt the extension of

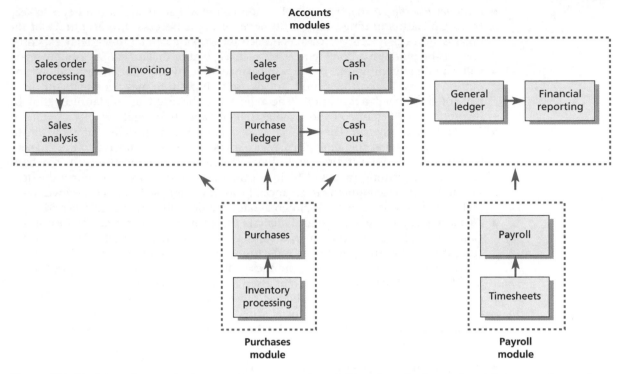

Figure 6.31 Modules of a standard accounting system, plus additional purchasing, sales order processing and payroll modules

further credit until the balances have been cleared. The system may also be searched to identify customers who have purchased certain items – a list of them is then used as the basis for a mailing list for promotional purposes. The accounts payable system contains information regarding the firm's creditors (as opposed to customers for the accounts receivable). The system provides information on which a schedule of supplier payments can be made and thus ensures that payments can be made as late as possible (to optimise cashflow) without losing discounts offered from suppliers for prompt payment.

- *Inventory*. The inventory system maintains stock levels by recording when stock is used for sales orders. A reorder point (ROP) system will generate an order for stock once the level of a stock item falls below a certain number of units. Other time-based systems will replenish stocks after a predetermined time interval.

- *Payroll*. The payroll system processes payments to employees, including deductions for such items as National Insurance and income tax. Many organisations will have electronic links to banks for direct deposit to employee accounts rather than issuing pay cheques.

- *Budgeting systems*. Budgets are an important control tool for management. A predetermined budgeted amount is periodically compared to the actual expenditure and any difference noted as a variance. This comparison of allocations (budgeted amounts) against actuals (amounts spent or received) can be reported to management. The identification of a variance will normally instigate a discussion and may lead to corrective action being taken to eliminate any adverse variance. Budgets for areas or departments can be aggregated or brought together to form a functional or organisational budget statement for higher-level decision making.

- *Cashflow reporting.* A major cause of business failure is inadequate cash reserves to keep the organisation functioning. Cashflow reporting is necessary to keep track of the organisation's cash reserves. Cash is needed for working capital (day-to-day expenses) and for the purchase of long-term assets such as plant or machinery. A cashflow report will contain a running total of the cash balance from information on cash inflows and outflows for each reporting period. An adverse cash position may necessitate the deferring of a planned acquisition. The report can be used as a planning tool by incorporating different cost and revenue scenarios and studying the results.
- *Capital budgeting system.* The financial system should contain tools that allow for the evaluation of capital spending plans. Major investments are compared to the financial return that the organisation could have gained from placing the cash in a bank account and accruing interest. The investment evaluation may also inform the decision to buy or lease equipment. Financial measures often used to assess an investment include net present value (NPV), internal rate of return (IRR) and payback period.
- *Financial analysis system.* Financial analysts use a variety of performance measures to gauge the financial position of an organisation. These include such measures as the current ratio, inventory turnover and earnings per share (Dyson, 1997). An information system can be used to generate these values automatically using figures stored in a database of such items as current assets and current liabilities.
- *Forecasting systems.* By projecting budget statements into the future, an organisation is able to forecast its potential financial state. These forecasts will need to incorporate economic and market forecasts in order that sales and cost data can be estimated.

▶ Accounting information systems software

Spreadsheets

Owing to their flexibility in numerical analysis and the incorporation of built-in facilities for statistical and numerical analysis, spreadsheets are an ideal medium in which to conduct financial analysis. For instance, a budget or cashflow forecast can be compiled by the addition of relevant items under income and expenses headings. If a spreadsheet template is constructed, consisting of the headings for the relevant items to be included, it is simply a matter of the user entering the appropriate amounts into the spreadsheet cells. Cashflow forecasts are an essential financial statement in any business. Bank managers can be forewarned of the probable requirement for overdraft facilities. The forecasts are of particular importance to start-up businesses where they can be used to support applications for additional funding from potential money lenders.

Once the cashflow statement has been entered, any values can easily be changed and the spreadsheet cell values will be updated to reflect the new cash position.

Accounting packages

A vast number of accounting software packages are available which can produce invoice statements, monthly budget statements and other financial items needed to run a small or medium-sized organisation.

The requirements for accounting information systems will differ from other types of system in which issues such as ease of use and performance will usually be considered important. In accounting systems, accuracy and reliability are paramount.

Financial modelling packages

While accounting packages tend to be restricted to operational systems, financial modelling packages are also available for decision making at the strategic and tactical levels of an organisation. These provide the following types of facilities for strategic planning:

- corporate financial forecasting models;
- merger and acquisition strategy.

Facilities for tactical planning include:

- annual budgets – cashflow, capital, tax planning;
- new product assessments – ROCE (return on capital employed).

They can also be used for operational financial management issues such as:

- funds management – cash and securities, shares;
- cost accounting and project cost monitoring;
- tax accounting.

Systems to provide these functions tend to be available as modules of the high-end accounting packages. Such software allows the decision maker to hold financial models of the organisation in order to construct 'what-if?' analysis. It has the advantage of providing more guidance than a spreadsheet does on building financial models.

▶ Enterprise resource planning (ERP) systems

We complete this chapter by considering enterprise resource planning (ERP) software. This is appropriate since ERP systems were the forerunner of the e-business concept. Indeed, many leading ERP solutions providers such as SAP and Baan now refer to themselves as e-business providers. ERP systems provide a single solution from a single supplier with integrated functions for major business functions from across the value chain such as production, distribution, sales, finance and human resources management. They are normally purchased as an off-the-shelf package which is then tailored. The main reason for implementing an ERP system is explained by Figure 6.32. It compares an ERP application with the previous company arrangement of separate data silos and applications (sometimes known as 'information islands') in different parts of the company. The

Enterprise resource planning applications (ERP) software
Provides functions for managing business areas such as production, distribution, sales, finance and human resources management.

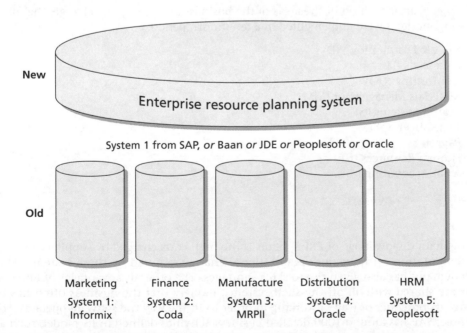

Figure 6.32 **ERP application in comparison to separate functional applications**

problem of information silos arose as decentralisation of BIS selection became devolved, with the end-users in individual departments making their own purchasing decisions. This often led to separate applications from different vendors in different departments, often with poor data transfer between applications.

The benefits of the ERP approach include:

● integration of all internal and external value-chain processes, resulting in increased customer value as explained in earlier sections;
● better sharing of information within the organisation since all modules of the system are compatible;
● reduced cost of buying from a single supplier;
● simplified support and maintenance through a single supplier;
● use of 'best-of-breed' solution applied by other companies.

MINI CASE STUDY

Yorkshire Water revises Business Processes

As part of the move to e-business, Yorkshire Water implemented SAP R/3 and SAP Business-to-Business Procurement with the aim of increasing the efficiency of business processes, e-procurement, and improved supplier management. Systems development manager Dave Murphy explains how change was achieved: 'We ran a whole series of different computer systems which had been written by our own staff in the late eighties. They were heavily tailored to Yorkshire Water's needs and they were held together by bits of string and sticky tape. SAP was chosen as the result of a selection procedure since around 87% of business requirements were fulfilled by the software.' Murphy says: 'To bridge the gap between 87% and 100%, Yorkshire Water preferred to adapt its business processes rather than the software. We didn't customise the software package because we realised that these business changes were a good thing.'

To give an indication of the areas of the business affected by the change, the following modules were implemented in a ten month period:

● Sales & Distribution (SD)
● Financials (FI)
● Controlling (CO)
● Materials Management (MM)
● Project System (PS)
● Time Sheet (CATS)
● Payroll
● Human Resources (HR)
● Asset Accounting (AA).

Source: SAP web site (www.sap.com/uk)

The main disadvantage of ERP systems is the high costs charged by suppliers and the implementation of the major organisational change required by these systems. This high demand has also given rise to skills shortages. The other disadvantages of ERP systems are shared with all off-the-shelf systems, namely that the business often has to change its processes or way of working in order to fit the way the software operates. For example, SAP has around 1000 detailed business activities defined in its model, such as 'post an accounting entry'. This may not present a problem if a company is intending to re-engineer its processes, since then the ERP software can provide a framework – as is the Yorkshire Water case study.

Owing to the high cost of ERP solutions, only medium–large companies can afford the software and the consultants, which will often total millions of pounds. Smaller companies can take advantage of the features of integrated accounting packages such as Sage which now provide modules beyond those of the basic accounting package.

Summary

1 Electronic commerce traditionally refers to electronically mediated buying and selling.

2 Sell-side e-commerce involves all electronic business transactions between an organisation and its customers, while buy-side e-commerce involves transactions between an organisation and its suppliers.

3 'Electronic business' is a broader term referring to how technology can benefit all internal business processes and interactions with third parties. This includes buy-side and sell-side e-commerce and the internal value chain.

4 The main business drivers for introducing e-commerce and e-business are opportunities for increased revenues and reducing costs, but many other benefits can be identified that improve customer service and corporate image.

5 Adoption of the Internet is limited by lack of imperative, cost of access and security fears.

6 Operational information systems are often critical to the success of a business, since their efficiency directly affects customer experience, profitability and cashflow. Operational systems include:

● transaction processing systems for managing transactions such as customer orders, supplier purchases and payment;
● office automation systems such as groupware and workflow systems, which enable office workers to collaborate on administration and customer service;
● process control systems for manufacturing.

7 Decision support systems are tools for assisting decision making at tactical and strategic levels within an organisation. The main tools available are:

● expert systems which enable non-specialists to take unstructured decisions outside their area of expertise;
● executive information systems for giving senior managers an overview of the business, with monitoring facilities to alert them to a problem and then provide drill-down to find the source of a problem;
● data warehouses, providing a repository for transaction data with analysis tools for marketing-driven optimisation of company performance.

8 Business applications have traditionally served the functional areas of an organisation, such as:

● human resources;
● accounting;
● production;
● inbound and outbound logistics;
● marketing and sales.

9 In large companies, applications in these functional areas are gradually being replaced by enterprise resource planning applications that provide functionality applicable across the organisation. In smaller companies, accounting systems are being extended to use in other areas such as payroll, purchase ordering and inventory management.

EXERCISES

Self-assessment exercises

1 Distinguish between e-commerce and e-business and explain what are meant by buy-side and sell-side e-commerce.

2 Summarise the consumer and business adoption levels in your country. Outline the reasons why a business may wish to adopt e-commerce. What seem to be the main barriers to adoption for businesses and consumers?

3 Summarise the impact of the introduction of e-business on different aspects of an organisation.

4 Describe the purpose of workflow management and groupware in an e-business context.

5 Evaluate the role of transaction processing systems in an organisation.

6 How can information systems support the manufacturing process?

7 Explain how decision support systems can support different parts of an organisation.

8 Which information systems tools can be used to support the marketing function?

9 Explain the reasons for the adoption of enterprise resource planning systems by organisations.

Discussion questions

1 Discuss the following statement with reference to how an organisation should react to the Internet. 'Is the Internet a typhoon force, a ten times force, or is it a bit of wind? Or is it a force that fundamentally alters our business?' (Andy Grove, Chairman of Intel).

2 Data warehouses are only the latest in a long line of reporting tools. They will not make a significant impact on business. Discuss.

3 Workflow systems are currently mainly in large organisations. This is likely to remain the case. Discuss.

4 Neural networks, fuzzy logic and genetic programming are some of the latest artificial intelligence ideas. Are they likely to remain lab-based products, or is there potential for their use in industry?

5 Enterprise resource planning software is likely to replace packages used in a single area of the organisation, such as accounting, logistics, production and marketing. Discuss.

Essay questions

1 Write a report on how a organisation can evaluate the impact of the Internet on their business

2 Review the changing tools available for decision making at a strategic level within the organisation. What does this mean for senior managers?

3 Was the promise of expert systems in the 1980s delivered in the 1990s? Justify your answer.

4 How must transaction processing systems be managed, given their mission-critical role in many organisations?

5 Critically assess the importance of data warehouses to large organisations. Are they relevant for the small or medium enterprise?

6 Do you believe that the advantages of enterprise resource planning applications outweigh their disadvantages? Illustrate your answer with reference to company examples.

Examination questions

1 Explain the relationship between the concepts of e-commerce and e-business.

2 Distinguish between buy-side and sell-side e-commerce and give an example of the application of each.

3 Summarise three reasons why a company may wish to introduce e-commerce.

4 Describe three of the main barriers to adoption of e-commerce by consumers and suggest how a company could counter these.

5 What is the purpose of data warehouses?

6 How can workflow software and groupware assist in re-engineering an organisation?

7 What special precautions need to be taken when using IT for managing human resources?

8 Define an enterprise resource planning application. Name two main disadvantages of this type of approach.

References

Baily, P., Farmer, D., Jessop, D. and Jones, D. (1994) *Purchasing Principles and Management*, Pitman, London

BMRB (2001) BMRB International's Internet Monitor, February. Published at www.bmrb.co.uk

Chaffey, D. (2002) *E-Business and E-Commerce Management*, Financial Times Prentice Hall, Harlow

Chaffey, D., Mayer, R., Johnston, K. and Ellis-Chadwick, F. (2000) *Internet Marketing: Strategy, Implementation and Practice*, Financial Times Prentice Hall, Harlow

Curtis, G. (1998) *Business Information Systems, Analysis, Design and Practice*, 3rd edition, Addison-Wesley, Harlow

de Kare-Silver, M. (2000) *eShock 2000*, Macmillan, Basingstoke

DTI (2000) *Business in the Information Age – International Benchmarking Study 2000*. UK Department of Trade and Industry. Based on 6000 phone interviews across businesses of all sizes in eight countries. Statistics update: available online at: www.ukonlineforbusiness.gov.uk

Durlacher (2000) 'E-commerce developments in the SME sector', *Durlacher Quarterly Internet Report*, August

Dyson, J. (1997) *Accounting for Non-accounting Students*, Financial Times Pitman Publishing, London

Garry, A.G. and Scott-Morton, M. (1971) 'A framework for Management Information Systems', Sloan Management Review, 12, 55–70

Goonatilake, S. and Khebbal, S. (1995) 'Intelligent hybrid systems: issues, classifications and future directions', in S. Goonatilake and S. Khebbal (eds) *Intelligent Hybrid Systems*, Wiley, New York

Hammergren, T. (1996) *Data Warehousing: Building the Corporate Knowledgebase*, International Thomson Computer Press, London

Kalakota, R. and Whinston, A. (1997) *Electronic Commerce. A Manager's Guide*, Addison-Wesley, Reading, MA

Kluge, J. (1997) Reducing the cost of goods sold: role of complexity, design relationships. *McKinsey Quarterly*, 2, 212–15

Laudon, K. and Laudon, J. (1996) *Management Information Systems: Organization and Technology*, 3rd edition, Macmillan, Upper Saddle River, NJ

Luconi, F.L., Malone, T.W. and Scott-Morton, M. (1986) 'Expert systems: the next challenge for managers', *Sloan Management Review*, 27, 3–14

Myers-Tierney, L. and Campbell, I (1996) *The Business Case for Electronic Document Management*, International Data Corp., Framingham, MA

ONS (2000) National Statistics Omnibus Survey – October at www.statistics.gov.uk/press_release/Archive.asp

ONS (2001) E-commerce and Business. Economic Trends' Office for Narional Statistics, Author Magdalen Williams

Potter, C. (2000) Trust... Not built at e-speed: trust issues in B2B e-procurement, PricewaterhouseCoopers Report, July 2000, London, available online at www.statistics.gov.uk/themes/economy/articles/general/extracts/downloads/e_commerce_inquiry_2000.pdf

Scott-Morton, M. (1991) *The Corporation of the 1990s: Information Technology and Organizational Transformation*, Oxford University Press, Oxford

Slack, N., Chambers, S., Harland, C., Harrison, A. and Johnston, R. (1995) *Operations Management*, Financial Times Pitman Publishing, London

Sprague, R. (1980) 'A framework for the development of decision support systems', *MIS Quarterly*, 4, 4

Tranmit (1999) *Procurement Management Systems: a Corporate Black Hole, A survey of technology trends and attitudes in British industry*, Tranmit, UK

Turban, E. (1995) *Decision Support and Expert Systems*, 4th edition, Prentice-Hall, Englewood Cliffs, NJ

Watson, H.J. and Sprague, R.H. (1993) 'The components of an architecture for DSS', in R.H. Sprague, and H.J. Watson (eds) *Decision Support Systems: Putting Theory into Practice*, 3rd edition, Prentice Hall, Hemel Hempstead

Which? (2000) 'Annual Internet user survey', 7 November

Zwass, V. (1998) 'Structure and macro-level impacts of electronic commerce: from technological infrastructure to electronic marketplaces', in K. Kendall, (ed.) *Emerging Information Technologies*, Sage, Thousand Oaks, CA

Further reading

Chaffey, D. (1998) Groupware, *Workflow and Intranets: Reengineering the Enterprise with Collaborative Software*, Digital Press, Woburn, MA

Chaffey, D., Mayer, R., Johnston, K. and Ellis-Chadwick, F. (2000) *Internet Marketing: Strategy, Implementation and Practice*, Financial Times Prentice Hall, Harlow

Coleman, D. (1995) Groupware: *Technologies and Applications*, Prentice-Hall, Englewood Cliffs, NJ

Dudman, J. (1998) 'So you want a data warehouse? Boardroom briefing', *Computer Weekly*, 14 May

Georgakopoulos, D., Hornick, M. and Sheth, A. (1995) 'An overview of workflow management: from process modelling to workflow automation infrastructure', *Distributed and Parallel databases*, 3, 119–53

Kalakota, R. and Robinson, M. (2000) *E-business. Roadmap for Success*, Addison-Wesley, Reading, MA. E-procurement is considered in Chapter 9, which states procurement to be a senior manager issue and describes implementation of e-procurement from both buy-side and sell-side perspectives

Krooenke, D. and Hatch, R. (1993) *Business Information Systems*, McGraw-Hill, New York

O'Brien, J. (1993) *Management Information Systems: A Managerial End User Perspective*, 2nd edition, Richard D. Irwin, Boston. Part 3 (Chapters 8–12) provides good detail on business applications of different types of information systems

O'Hicks, J. (1993) *Management Information Systems: A User Perspective*, 3rd edition, West Publishing, St. Paul, MN

Workflow Management Coalition (WfMC) (1996). 'Reference model. Version 1', in *The Workflow Management Coalition Specification. Terminology and glossary*, Workflow Management Coalition, Avenue Marcel Thiry 204, 1200 Brussels

Web links

E-business

Sites giving general information on market characteristics of the Internet

www.nua.ie/surveys Nua Internet Surveys summarises the majority of reports by analysts on e-commerce developments and reports on company and consumer adoption of Internet and characteristics in Europe and worldwide.

www.cyberatlas.com CyberAtlas gives a similar service to Nua, but with more of a US focus.

www.europeprofile.com EuropeProfile summarises adoption across business with monthly reports on particular markets.

www.marketing-online.co.uk Marketing Online is a collection of web resources created by Dave Chaffey.

www.e-consultancy.com E-consultancy.com is an excellent online digest of consultant and analyst reports.

Magazines

www.e-businessreview.co.uk E-business review is a monthly for IS managers from the publishers of *Computer Weekly*.

www.revolutionmagazine.com Revolution magazine has a web site for monthly UK magazine on new media – mainly sell-side e-commerce.

www.net-profit.co.uk Net Profit is a monthly UK-based newsletter on Internet commerce with a European focus.

Workflow

www.ed.ac.uk/WfMC This Workflow Management Coalition site contains extensive technical papers explaining how workflows are defined. It also contains introductory papers on the purpose and components of workflow systems.

www.waria.com WARIA is another significant industry body which again has good industry support and is active in promoting conferences and sharing experience and documentation. It has been less active in promoting standards.

www.aiim.org The Document Management Alliance (DMA) is a task force created by AIIM in April 1995, attempting to create a uniform approach to the design, implementation and management of enterprise-wide document management systems.

Business intelligence

www.data-warehouse.com. A resource centre for data warehousing techniques.

www.dw-institute.com. The Data Warehousing Institute.

www.cognos.com Provider of PowerPlay.

www.businessobjects.com

www.oracle.com Is an additional module to the Oracle database.

www.essbase.com

E-procurement

purchasing.about.com The Purchasing web guide on About.com gives an excellent collection of links on the benefits *and* disadvantages of e-procurement. See also ecommerce.about.com

www.ariba.com Guidelines on B2B E-commerce procurement.

www.cips.org.uk The Chartered Institute of Purchasing and Supply (CIPS) is the industry body in the UK.

PART 2

Business information systems development

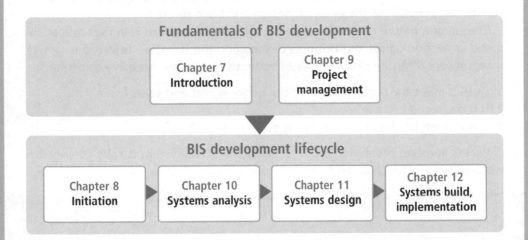

Fundamentals of BIS development

Chapter 7
Introduction

Chapter 9
Project management

BIS development lifecycle

Chapter 8
Initiation

Chapter 10
Systems analysis

Chapter 11
Systems design

Chapter 12
Systems build, implementation

Part 2 focuses on how business information systems are acquired and built. An understanding of building BIS is important to users and managers who are responsible for, or are involved in, a systems development project. Such managers need to understand the activities involved in different stages of systems development to help plan the project or work with the developers of the system. They will also need to be aware of the alternatives for sourcing IS such as buying a pre-written off-the-shelf system or a specially written bespoke system, in order to decide which is best for their company or department.

To build a good quality BIS, a company will follow a process that has defined stages with clear objectives and deliverables at each stage. Part 2 describes the typical activities involved when a new system is built. These stages form what is commonly referred to as the *systems development lifecycle* (SDLC):

- *initiation*: a startup phase that usually occurs in response to a business problem or opportunity;
- *feasibility*: an attempt to determine whether the proposed systems development will be viable;
- *systems analysis*: to determine what the system is required to do;
- *systems design*: to specify how the system will deliver the stated requirements;
- *systems build*: the design is transformed into a physical system by programming, testing and creation of databases;
- *systems implementation and changeover*: the organisation moves from installing and testing the information system to operating in a live business environment;

▶ ● *Review and maintenance*: the success of the system is measured against the original requirements, and modifications are made over its lifetime.

Note that as errors are found, or new requirements arise, it is necessary to revisit previous stages. Iterative models such as the spiral model are used to show the cyclical nature of system development where several prototypes are built; this involves repeating the analysis, design and build phases.

The unique nature of systems development projects, which is in part due to the speed of technological and business change and the iteration referred to above, makes it very difficult to develop a system that satisfies the three key constraints:

1 Does it meet the requirements of the business and end-users?
2 Is it delivered on time?
3 Has it been produced within the allocated budget?

Part 2 involves reviewing each stage of the SDLC systematically to consider what action can be taken to ensure the project objectives are met.

Chapter 7

An introduction to acquiring and developing BIS

LEARNING OBJECTIVES

After reading this chapter, readers will be able to:
● evaluate the different alternatives for acquiring BIS;
● distinguish between the typical stages involved in building BIS;
● explain the purpose of each stage in building a system;
● select the best alternative type of approach or methodology for building a BIS.

MANAGEMENT ISSUES

Managers need to select the optimal method for introducing a new BIS once an opportunity is identified. From a managerial perspective, this chapter addresses the following questions:
● What are the alternatives for systems acquisition and how is the most suitable approach selected?
● What alternative models are there for the different stages for introducing a BIS? Which is most appropriate?
● Which activities need to occur at each stage for the project to be successful?

Links to other chapters

This chapter provides a framework for all subsequent chapters in Part 2.

Chapter 8   describes the startup – the *initiation* phase or *feasibility study* of an information systems development project.

Chapter 9   reviews methods for controlling the progress of the development through *project management* techniques.

Chapter 10   describes techniques for *analysis* of user and system requirements.

Chapter 11   covers techniques for systems *design*.

Chapter 12   examines the final phases of system development – *build and implementation*.

Chapter 16   describes the end-user development method of acquisition in more detail.

Introduction

This chapter provides the foundation for subsequent chapters in Part 2 by taking a broad look at the main activities involved in acquiring and building new business information systems. The word 'acquire' is used deliberately here, since 'development' implies the writing of a system. However, since many business applications can be purchased off the shelf without the need for any development activity, 'acquisition' more precisely defines the process we are going to outline here.

This chapter will start by considering alternative approaches to the acquisition of new computer-based information systems, ranging from purchasing off-the-shelf applications through to creating new bespoke systems.

BIS acquisition describes the method of obtaining an information system for a business. The main choices are off-the-shelf (packaged), bespoke applications developed by an in-house IT department or a software house, or end-user developed systems.

We will then review the traditional **systems development lifecycle (SDLC)**, sometimes known as the 'waterfall model' of systems development. This defines the different SDLC stages involved in developing a new system. Any BIS project follows a logical series of development phases. Typical stages are: initiation, feasibility study, analysis of business requirements, systems design, system build and implementation and, finally, review and maintenance. The stages will be summarised in this chapter in preparation for a more detailed description in subsequent chapters.

Lastly, we will look at some of the different methodologies for building systems to establish which are the most appropriate for different types of business and system. The methodologies to be covered include traditional structured methods (using the example of Structured Systems Analysis and Design Methodology – SSADM) through to more modern approaches involving prototyping and rapid applications development (RAD).

BIS acquisition

The process of evaluating and implementation for a BIS.

Systems development lifecycle (SDLC)

Any information systems project follows a logical series of development phases. These are known as the systems development lifecycle.

SDLC stages

Initiation, feasibility study, analysis of business requirements, systems design, system build and implementation and, finally, review and maintenance.

Methods of software acquisition

Many texts deal admirably with the range of tools and techniques available to the systems analyst for bespoke systems development. However, bespoke development is only one method of software acquisition. In fact for many businesses, especially small and medium-sized enterprises, bespoke applications development is not a viable option because of the costs and practical difficulties involved. It is necessary, therefore, to begin by looking at the range of acquisition methods and consider which is most appropriate for the needs of a particular business.

There are three main methods for acquiring the information system necessary to support a particular business need. These are bespoke development, off-the-shelf software and end-user development.

▶ Bespoke development

Bespoke development is the term for when an information system is developed 'from scratch' by an information systems professional to suit the business requirements of the application.

Here a new BIS will be developed from scratch by a team of information systems professionals. The IS professionals will either work for the business, in which case we refer to this as 'in-house' bespoke development, or for a third party such as a software house, in which case we say that the software development has been 'outsourced'. Bespoke development has the benefit of producing software tailored to the precise requirements of the business. On the downside, there are a number of difficulties:

- *Expense*. Bespoke development is the most expensive way of developing new information systems.
- *Time*. Bespoke development, especially when using formal structured development methodologies, is notorious for time overruns, with delays of months or years not uncommon.
- *Quality*. Bespoke software is not usually free from bugs; software bugs can range from the trivial to the catastrophic, the latter often attributable to poor analysis of requirements.

▶ Purchasing 'off-the-shelf' software

Off-the-shelf purchase of packaged software is an acquisition method that involves direct purchase of a pre-written application used by more than one company.

This type of software is pre-written and is available for a whole variety of hardware platforms from PCs to mainframes. Off-the-shelf software is written to offer a broad functionality that will suit a wide range of different businesses. This broad range of functions has the benefit of fitting the requirements of a large number of businesses. It also may offer too many features for any particular business, which may then feel that it is paying for things it will not use. At the same time, it may require businesses to process information in a particular way that is at odds with the way they normally do business. Alternatively, a certain off-the-shelf software package may not offer sufficient features. For example, a well-known accounting package in the UK only offered an eight-character code for the customer's order number, though it would appear that some 50 per cent of UK companies use longer order number codes. The major benefit, however, of off-the-shelf software packages is their low cost when compared with acquiring bespoke software with the same level of functionality. In addition, because packaged software has been developed for a commercial market, it is less likely to suffer from the bugs that afflict bespoke software.

In a *tailored off-the-shelf purchase*, pre-written software is purchased from a supplier, but it is possible to configure it to be specific to the company. In a *component off-the-shelf purchase*, different modules may be purchased from different suppliers and built together. Visual Basic controls for graphing is a good example of a component that can be added to an off-the-shelf application.

Bespoke development
An IS is developed 'from scratch' by an IS professional to suit the business requirements of the application.

Off the shelf purchase
An acqusition method that involves direct purchase of a pre-written application used by more than one company.

▶ End-user-developed software

End-user-developed software

Software written by non-IS professionals i.e. the business users.

End-user-developed software is software written by non-IS professionals, i.e. the business users.

Senn (1995) estimated that 50 to 75 per cent of all computing applications will be classed as end-user applications (as distinct from institutional applications) and that many of these systems will be developed by end-users (i.e. non-IT professionals).

Enterprise resource planning or *institutional applications* are those that affect general corporate activities, cut across more than one department or functional area, or systems that involve organisational data held in corporate databases. Examples include accounting systems, sales order processing systems and materials requirements planning.

End-user applications are more limited in scope. Applications may be departmental or personal in nature and are usually output- or report-oriented rather than input-driven. These applications may either be written by IT professionals or by the end-users themselves. If the latter is the case, they are often referred to as *end-user-developed applications*.

Such systems may be simple (e.g. a spreadsheet or a small PC database) or less commonly they may be more sophisticated (e.g. a production planning system based on sales forecast data from several branches of the same organisation). Such applications are typically for individual or departmental use, although in the case of the second example the system may have company-wide relevance. The main benefit of end-user-developed software is that it is normally used by those who develop it, and so the requirements are not subject to mistranslation or the provision of over-sophisticated solutions. The negative side to this is that in some cases inappropriate software development tools might be used (such as complicated spreadsheets instead of the construction of a database). A further significant concern with end-user development is that software may be riddled with bugs as a consequence of corner cutting (poor or non-existent design, little or no testing, or no documentation). The end-user development approach is described in more detail in Chapter 16.

There are also a number of hybrid approaches to acquisition. A group of organisations in the same business or activity area may have information systems requirements that individually may be very expensive to develop. A solution may be for a bespoke system to be developed by a third party, which allows the development costs to be spread among all the organisations involved. Good examples here are a university student records system and various systems used in police forces across the UK.

Similarly, an off-the-shelf package may provide 80 per cent of the required features, but others may need to be added through some bespoke development by either IS/IT professionals or by end-users.

▶ Hybrid approaches to systems acquisition

The approaches to systems acquisition described above are not mutually exclusive for a given project or within an organisation. Where the software is generic to all businesses, as is the case with systems software and office productivity packages, off-the-shelf software will be purchased. Where the business has more specific needs and wishes to achieve a competitive advantage, bespoke and tailored approaches to acquisition will be used. Case Study 7.1 illustrates a hybrid approach. With e-business systems there is often a need to integrate in-house legacy systems and systems purchased from different vendors. This uses a building block approach of different components including data sources that are integrated together. This is referred to as **enterprise application integration (EAI)**, and achieving this is a significant challenge facing project managers and systems designers. Such managers and developers require flexibility from suppliers to provide what were known in the 1990s as 'open systems' which can be used in combination. As

Enterprise application integration (EAI)

Software used to facilitate communications between business applications including data transfer and control.

Sprott (2000) puts it, '*Tomorrow's customers will demand the ability to buy, reuse, and build their competitive edge solutions: can the package vendors adapt in time?*'

◗ Factors affecting software acquisition

There are a number of factors that will influence the choice of acquisition method. Three critical ones are time, cost and quality considerations.

If an organisation has a pressing problem that requires a new information system quickly, it is probable that a package or tailored package will be sought. An example here is a business which may have been operating an old legacy system and in order to become Year 2000 compliant saw 'buying' rather than 'making' as the only realistic solution. Similarly, an organisation that needs a 'quality systems solution' may well consider the packaged software route, especially if its requirements are straightforward.

The different acquisition options have different strengths when considered in terms of the three critical criteria. Table 7.1 shows how the alternatives compare in terms of these three criteria. Quality of the delivered product is considered from two respects: the number of bugs or errors found and the suitability of the software in meeting the requirements of the business user. Note that good quality in terms of the number of bugs that typically occur for packaged software may coincide with poor quality in terms of the business fit.

Table 7.1 **An evaluation of alternatives for BIS acquisition**

Acquisition option	Delivery time	Cost	Quality: Bugs	Quality: Fits business needs
Bespoke in-house	Poor	Poor	Poor	Good
Bespoke software house	Good	Very poor	Medium	Medium
End-user development	Poor	Medium	Poor	Good
Tailored – off the shelf	Good	Good	Good	Medium
Standard – off the shelf	Very good	Very good	Very good	Poor

The benefit of packaged software occurs because the cost of developing and debugging the software is shared between more than one company. This results in lower costs and fewer bugs than bespoke development for a single company. The use of packaged software by more than one company is also its greatest weakness, since its features must suit the typical company. As a consequence, it may not meet the needs of an individual company.

Other factors affecting software acquisition include the following:

● *Organisation size.* A small or medium-sized business will inevitably have relatively limited resources for the purchasing of information systems and information technology (IS/IT). This suggests that there will be a tendency for such organisations to favour the purchase of off-the-shelf packages or possibly end-user applications development.

● *In-house IS/IT expertise.* Where little in-house IS/IT expertise exists, either in the form of IS/IT professionals or experienced end-users, there will be a need to use third parties in the acquisition of new business information systems. These may include software vendors for off-the-shelf software packages, the use of consultants and/or software houses. Precisely what form of third party is used will depend on the other factors discussed here.

- *Complexity of the required information system.* Where a business information system requirement is particularly complex, or for an unusual application not available as a packaged solution, it is possible that one may view bespoke software (either developed in-house or by a third party) as the only viable solution. However, complexity does not necessarily equate to 'uniqueness'. For example, one could regard a materials requirements planning system or a complete accounting system as complex, but many packages exist for a variety of hardware platforms. Therefore, complexity is not necessarily an indicator that an off-the-shelf package should be ruled out.
- *Uniqueness of the business or business area to be supported.* The higher the degree of uniqueness that exists in the area to be supported, the less likely it is that a suitable off-the-shelf package can be found. This is clearly an indicator, therefore, for bespoke development of some kind. As before, we must not confuse uniqueness with complexity. It may well be feasible for a non-IS/IT specialist to develop a solution using tools available to end-user developers. Of course, if the required system is complex and also carries a high degree of uniqueness, then bespoke development by IS/IT professionals is probably the best acquisition method.
- *IS/IT expertise among end-users.* A certain degree of IS/IT literacy and expertise is necessary if end-users are to be able to develop information systems. In addition, such literacy is desirable when selecting suitable off-the-shelf packaged software, as it can help the business focus more clearly on its precise requirements from both a functional and a technological perspective. If an organisation has little end-user IS/IT expertise of its own, but has its own IS/IT department, it will be very much dependent on solutions provided by IS/IT professionals with or without third-party support.
- *Linkages with existing applications software.* Where new business software needs to integrate very tightly with existing information systems, there is a higher probability that at least some bespoke development work will need to be done to integrate the two systems. Also, a high degree of integration may imply that the new information system has to be developed in a bespoke fashion in order to achieve the desired level of integration. Having said that, many software vendors supply packages for different business areas which integrate very well with each other. For example, on the IBM AS/400 hardware platform alone, it is possible to find single vendors such as JD Edwards or JBA which will supply a sales order processing system, an accounting system, a warehouse management system, a payroll and personnel system and a manufacturing system, all of which can be purchased separately or together and which operate in a fully integrated manner as enterprise resource planning applications (Chapters 6 and 19).

By looking at combinations of the above, it is possible to come up with a 'best-fit' acquisition method. Figure 7.1 illustrates the relationship between the complexity of the required application (as driven by the business needs) and the uniqueness of the application under consideration. The reader should note that bespoke development may be performed either by in-house IS/IT specialists or by a third party.

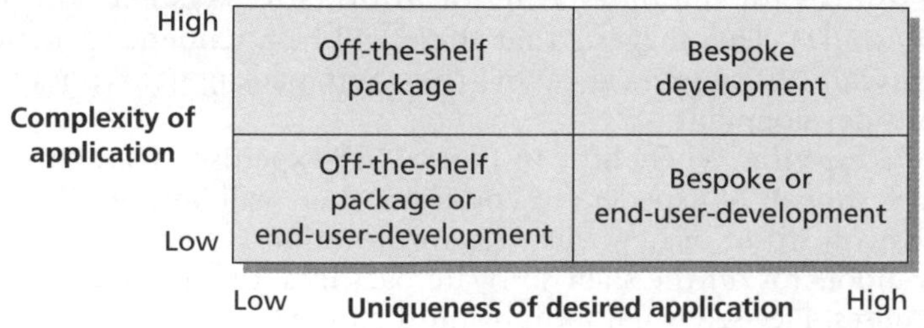

	Low uniqueness	High uniqueness
High complexity	Off-the-shelf package	Bespoke development
Low complexity	Off-the-shelf package or end-user-development	Bespoke or end-user-development

Complexity of application (High / Low)

Uniqueness of desired application (Low / High)

Figure 7.1 Application complexity versus uniqueness

Similar relationships can be established with other pairs of selection acquisition factors. For example, when comparing the expertise of end-users in developing applications with the complexity of the desired application, a relatively simple information system may need professional IT staff involvement if the end-users do not have sufficient IS/IT capability.

CASE STUDY 7.1

Direct Line reviews systems acquisition approaches

Richard Beal is a 49-year-old IT director living in the centre of London and commuting to the outlying district of Croydon every working day. His morning starts with a lightning appraisal of post and e-mail messages from IT companies. He estimates that 50 product brochures and sales pitches pass his desk each day.

'I scan these documents for about three seconds before they go into the bin or are deleted. About one in 100 catches my eye.'

The reason why Mr Beal's attention is so in demand – and why he has so little time for the frantic sales machine of the IT industry – is because he is group IT director for Direct Line, a financial services organisation wholly owned by the Royal Bank of Scotland.

Since 1985, Direct Line has been selling car insurance to the public over the telephone and now has 2.3m UK customers for that business plus another 900,000 subscribers to services it has added to the original offering.

This operation is an obvious attraction for the endless stream of software companies that feel their product would fit perfectly into a high profile success story such as Direct Line.

But under Mr Beal the Direct Line business has a policy of starting software projects at home. He says: 'Some companies offer CRM products as if they are a kind of magic. But they gloss over the reality of CRM.'

Mr Beal believes the key to effective CRM lies in not trying to enforce one single view of the customer. Direct Line owns a huge database of customer information but this does not come from one of the IT industry's leading suppliers of complex database software. It was built in-house by Mr Beal's programmers.

He talks of the Japanese kaizen or continuous improvement approach which in his world involves not one huge team of call centre agents employing a single approach to callers, but small groups of staff trying out different ways of handling calls.

The strategic goal of this CRM project is cross-selling. Direct Line has expanded into home insurance and now offers loans via the internet. It needs the ability to spot a loan application that comes from a member of the public who might also benefit from one of its credit card schemes.

Faced with an expanding portfolio of products, Mr Beal has broken the Direct Line habit of relying on internal development resources and bought a suite of software from Chordiant, a US CRM program supplier.

While Direct Line can take a customer through financial products and offer quotes over the internet today, it will begin offering a full service internet loans facility next month.

Chordiant claims its software can allow the customer to bounce between web contact and a telephone conversation. This flexibility is the key to converting queries into sales.

'We have found that people want a hybrid', says Mr Beal. 'They will commence an inquiry over the internet but do not feel comfortable carrying out the whole transaction online.' He admits that the initial Directloan.com service generated 500,000 quotes 'but a small percentage of these were converted into sales online'.

Direct Line is about to sell cars over the internet. It is using a UK distributor to supply and deliver vehicles while Direct Line customers gather information on cars and order them from its web site.

Following its purchase of the Green Flag roadside assistance company, it can now use Chordiant's facility embodied in the call centre to cross-sell breakdown services to car insurance customers.

Neil Morgan, Chordiant's marketing director for Europe, claims that with his software it does not matter which particular communications medium the end-customer wants to use. 'Chordiant finds the background information that is relevant to that caller but makes it available to the call centre agent whether they are using a web contact or a phone call. And this happens in real time.'

So a change to the call centre response mechanism for telephone queries is instantly reflected in the web interface for queries, too. For Mr Beal and his staff at Direct Line this is vital.

'He wants his business managers to be able to make a special offer on one type of financial product without having to rewrite software right across the call centre. Direct Line is the epitome of why people would buy Chordiant. We offer a consistent experience over different channels.'

Chordiant software needs a powerful hardware engine – a Sun server that offers the processing ability of a large mainframe computer in the case of Direct Line. Installing this capability costs between £1m and £5m.

Mr Morgan admits that Direct Line was not an easy sale. 'They did a very intensive evaluation. Anyone in the business knows that Direct Line's original system was handcrafted and they are known for doing their own thing.' It took a detailed study before Direct Line broke with tradition and called in an external CRM software supplier.

'They put us right under the microscope before they signed', says Mr Morgan. The flexibility that Direct Line is writing into its call centres is about more than conventional web access.

It will be able to transfer the same customer interaction to internet-enabled phones and digital TV without any extension of its contract with Chordiant. Mr Beal is planning for the long term, and is using CRM technology to build on Direct Line's success in winning more than 3m customers.

Source: Michael Dempsey, 'Direct Line: Strategic goal of this CRM project is cross-selling', Financial services case study, www.ft.com/ftsurveys/spb2f2.htm, 7 June 2000

Questions

1 Summarise the different systems acquisition approaches used in Direct Line.

2 Explain the reasons given for these approaches.

3 What do you think made Direct Line 'break with tradition' and purchase the Chordiant package.

The traditional waterfall model

Waterfall model
Outlines the series of steps that should occur when building an information system. The steps usually occur in a predefined order with a review at the end of each stage before the next can be started.

The **Waterfall model** outlines the series of steps that should occur when building a BIS. These steps usually occur in a predefined order with a review at the end of each stage before the next can be started. It is possible to read half a dozen different texts on this topic and come across six different ways of describing the elements within this model. Not only will there be a different number of steps in each alternative model, but there will also be differences between the names given to each of the stages. For example, in one text the term 'implementation' may refer to the process of programming, testing and data conversion, while in another the same term may refer to the process by which a developed and tested system becomes a live, operational system. During the course of this chapter, therefore, a consistent and clear approach to the naming of the individual elements will be adopted and reference will also be made to other terms that the reader might encounter when reading other texts.

The purpose of the waterfall model of systems development is to divide the development process up into a series of manageable parts that relate to each other in an organised way. In addition, some tasks will have to be completed before others can commence. For example, it will not be possible for a programmer to start writing a program until the design specification for that program is complete. The waterfall model is a simple representation of what actually happens during a systems development project, but it provides a good framework for introducing information systems development, since all of the activities that are identified in the model occur in a typical project. We will examine more realistic models later in the chapter.

▶ The systems development lifecycle

An alternative representation of the waterfall model is the systems development lifecycle (SDLC). This model was developed and launched by the National Computing Centre in the UK in 1969. Until then, the emphasis in systems development was on programming. It was recognised, however, that many systems being developed at that time failed to meet user needs, because they were either functionally inadequate or too

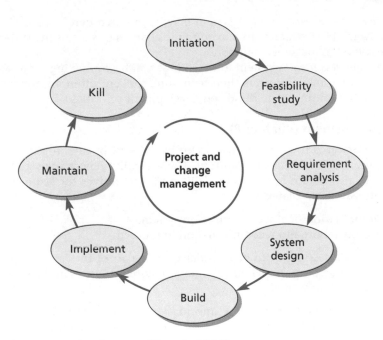

Figure 7.2 **The systems development lifecycle (SDLC)**

inflexible to meet changing business needs. The SDLC approach recognises that systems are developed in a series of steps or phases and that each phase needs to be completed before the next one commences. Recognition is also given to the fact that the programming activity (part of the build phase) should only commence once user requirements have been determined and the system design produced. Figure 7.2 illustrates the normal steps found in the systems development lifecycle. It should be compared with the waterfall model shown in Figure 7.3.

Within the diagram it will be noted that in addition to the lifecycle phases, the concepts of project management and change management have been added. This reinforces the notion that information systems projects do not take place by chance, but that they must be carefully managed carefully.

We will now summarise the basic steps that most systems development projects follow.

Initiation (Chapter 8)

Initiation phase is the initiation or startup phase and is the first phase in an information systems development project. Its aims are to establish whether the project is feasible and then prepare to ensure the project is successful. The intiation phase context is:

- *Input*: creative thought and/or systematic evaluation of IS needs.
- *Output*: idea for initiation of a new information system.

The initiation phase contains the stimulus from which the need to develop a new BIS arises. This stimulus may come about as a result of some external event such as a change in legislation, or it may arise from a desire internally to develop an information system that better supports the business needs of the organisation. The source of this initiation process may be one of the following:

- *Managing director or other senior management*. Systems initiated from this point are likely to have the support necessary for successful development.

Intiation phase

The startup phase in an IS development project. Its aims are to establish whether the project is feasible and then prepare to ensure the project is successful.

Initiation phase context

Input: creative thought and/or systematic evaluation of IS needs. Output: idea for initiation of a new information system.

- *Information systems department.* A system may be initiated here as part of the organisation's overall IS/IT strategy; to maximise the chances of success the system will still need high-level management support.
- *Functional business area.* A system initiated here will be competing for attention with all other development projects then being undertaken; often an organisation will have a steering committee to decide on development priorities.

Feasibility assessment (Chapter 8)

Feasibility assessment

An activity at the start of the project to ensure that the project is a viable business proposition. The feasibility report analyses the need for and impact of the system and considers different alternatives for acquiring software.

Feasibility assessment is the activity that occurs at the start of the project to ensure that the project is a viable business proposition. The feasibility report analyses the need for and impact of the system and considers different alternatives for acquiring software. The **feasibility assessment context** is:

Input: idea for initiation of a new information system.
Output: feasibility report and recommendation to proceed.

The feasibility assessment can be considered to be part of the *initiation phase*. It will establish whether a computer-based information system fits certain feasibility criteria. Three criteria are usually cited:

Feasibility assessment context

Input: idea for initiation of a new information system.
Output: feasibility report and recommendation to proceed.

1 It must be established whether the information system is *technically feasible*. To be technically feasible, either the technology exists or it can be created to support the required system.
2 To be *economically feasible*, an information system must generate more in the way of benefits than the cost needed to produce it. One of the problems here is that benefits are often difficult to quantify in monetary terms, while costs are far easier to estimate.
3 Assuming that a proposed information system is both technically and economically feasible, an assessment must be made of whether the project is *operationally and organisationally feasible*. By operationally feasible, we mean that the system must be capable of performing within the required speed, volume, usability and reliability parameters. Also, to be feasible for the organisation, the proposed information system must either be capable of running alongside work patterns or existing work patterns must be capable of being adapted or re-engineered to run alongside the new information system. Organisational feasibility will involve a review of how the potential users' skill sets and attitudes will affect the system.

Systems analysis

The capture of the business requirements of a system from talking to or observing end-users and using other information sources such as existing system documentation. Defines *what* the system will do.

Part of the feasibility process may be the invitation to tender for some or all of the information system elements. These may include application software, hardware, communications technology or systems software. Different alternatives from different vendors will then be assessed.

The output from this step (and, therefore, the input to the next step of the model) is a stage review and a feasibility report, which will recommend either that the project proceeds or that the project is reassessed in some way.

Systems analysis (Chapter 10)

Systems analysis context

Input: terms of reference in feasibility report describing outline requirements.
Output: detailed requirements specification summarising system functions. Supported by diagrams showing the information flow and processes that are required.

Systems analysis is the capture of the business requirements of a system from talking to or observing end-users and using other information sources such as existing system documentation. The **systems analysis context** is:

Input: terms of reference in feasibility report describing outline requirements.
Output: detailed requirements specification summarising system functions. Supported by diagrams showing the information flow and processes that are required.

Once a proposed information system is agreed to be feasible, it is necessary to carry out the detailed work of assessing the precise requirements that the intended users have for the new system. Note that the *systems analysis* step is sometimes referred to as the 'requirements determination' step or the 'systems study' step. There are three main tasks within this phase.

First, it is necessary to gain an understanding of how the *current* information system (computerised or paper-based) works. Second, a diagrammatic model of the current system workings is produced to ensure that IT professionals and system users are in agreement. Finally, a set of requirements for the new information system is produced. The requirements specification will define:

- the features that the new system is required to contain (e.g. the ability for end-users to be able to design their own reports);
- the scope of the system under consideration (for example, is the system intended for just one functional area of the business or is it to embrace all business activities?);
- the intended users of the new system;
- system performance standards, including response times, batch processing times (if required) and reliability needs;
- environment requirements such as physical working environment, operating system and hardware on which the system will run.

In this last task, it may be desirable to produce another diagrammatic model, this time of the *required* information system.

If at any point it is discovered that the requirements of the system as articulated by the prospective users appear to be unfeasible in some way, it will be necessary to revisit the feasibility step and perform an additional analysis of the possible options.

The output from this step in the model will be a user requirements analysis document which details *what* the proposed system must do.

Systems design (Chapter 11)

The **systems design** phase defines how the system will work in key areas of user interface, program modules, security and database transactions. The **systems design context** is:

Input: requirements specification.
Output: detailed design specification .

The input to this stage is a breakdown of the requirements that the proposed information system is to deliver. The task of the systems design stage is to convert those requirements into a number of design alternatives from which the best will be selected. The design step therefore deals with *how* the proposed information system will deliver what is required.

Some texts and methodologies make a distinction between 'systems design' and 'detailed design'. Systems design is broader in scope and will deal with such matters as:

- choosing an appropriate database management system;
- establishing general systems security standards;
- deciding on methods of system navigation (e.g. menu systems and graphical user interfaces);
- general standards for printed report production;
- screen design standards for input and output;
- data capture requirements;
- data storage requirements.

Detailed design, on the other hand, will result in a blueprint for individual system modules which will be used in the systems build phase that follows. Detailed design will further define some of the aspects of system design referred to above.

Systems design
Defines *how* the system will work in key areas of user interface, program modules, security and database structure and transactions.

Systems design context
Input: requirements specification.
Output: detailed design specification.

If at any point during the design step it becomes obvious that the requirements as presented in the analysis step do not have a design solution (e.g. because of conflicting or incomplete requirements), it will be necessary to revisit the analysis step and determine more precisely what the new information system is to do in those particular respects.

System build (Chapter 12)

System build is the creation of software by programmers. It involves writing the software code (programming), building release versions of the software, constructing and populating the database and testing by programmers and end-users. Writing of documentation and training may also occur at this stage. The **system build context** is:

Input: requirements and design specification
Output: working software, user guides and system documentation

The term 'build' is one that we shall be using in addition to the more usual and ambiguous term 'implementation' which is found in many texts and methodologies. This step embraces three substeps: physical database construction, programming and testing.

Physical database construction involves the conversion of the database design from the previous step into the required tables and indexes of a relational database. The programming substep involves the construction of computer code that will handle data capture, storage, processing and output. In addition, it will be necessary to program various other operational attributes of the required system (e.g. those that stem from control design). Alongside and subsequent to the programming substep, various forms of testing will take place.

The output from the build stage will be an information system that has been tested and is available for final data conversion or take-on and live operation.

If during the build phase it appears from testing that the system does not meet the original requirements as determined during the analysis step, then it will be necessary to revisit the design step to see whether any errors were made in interpreting the systems requirements. If the design brief was correctly interpreted but the system still contains errors in the delivery of the perceived requirements, it will be necessary to revisit the analysis to determine the systems requirements more precisely.

▶ System implementation and changeover

System implementation covers practical issues such as making sure the hardware and network infrastructure for a new system are in place; testing of the system; and also human issues of how best to educate and train staff who will be using or affected by the new system. Implementation also involves the transition or changeover from the old system to the new. The **system implementation context** is:

- *Input*: working system, not tested by users.
- *Output*: signed-off, operational information system installed in all locations.

This step in the waterfall model deals with preparing for and making the change from old to new information systems. As one might expect, the systems implementation step is fraught with difficulties. Here, it will be discovered whether all the previous steps have combined to deliver an information system that does what the users actually want and that also works properly. Data will be converted from old information systems or directly entered into the new database. Finally, the new system will become operational straight away, or in phases, or after a period of parallel running. If errors are encountered at the live running stage it may be possible for the system to continue in operation while the errors are corrected. Alternatively, it may be necessary to suspend

---

System build

Describes the creation of software by programmers. It involves writing the software code (programming), building release versions of the software, constructing and populating the database and testing by programmers and end-users. Writing of documentation and training may also occur at this stage.

System build context

Input: requirements and design specification
Output: working software, user guides and system documentation.

System implementation

Involves the transition or changeover from the old system to the new and the preparation for this such as making sure the hardware and network infrastructure for a new system are in place; testing of the system; and also human issues of how best to educate and train staff who will be using or affected by the new system.

System implementation context

Input: working system, not tested by users.
Output: signed off, operational information system installed in all locations.

the operation of the new system while the most significant errors are fixed. Such error correction may require any of the previous steps to be revisited, depending on the nature and severity of the error(s).

It will be clear from this short discussion that the later in the systems development process errors are discovered, the higher is the cost of putting them right. The worst-case scenario is probably for a system to have reached the live running stage only for it to be discovered that the required system was never really feasible in the first place. Recent cases bear this out, including the London Ambulance Service and the early version of the London Stock Exchange electronic trading system. Many millions of pounds were spent on developing systems that had to be abandoned because they proved unworkable in a live running situation.

Review and maintenance (Chapter 12)

Once an information system is operating under live running conditions, it will be inevitable that changes will be required over time. The maintenance phase involves two different types of maintenance. The first, known as 'unproductive maintenance', stems from errors or oversights in the original systems development which, while not preventing the system operating to an acceptable level, are still necessary to correct for it to conform with the original specification. The second form of maintenance involves the addition of new features and facilities that extend the scope and functionality of the information system. In the early days, these may take the form of 'nice-to-haves' or 'bells and whistles' which were not deemed to be essential to the system at changeover time. Over the longer term, the system will be adapted and modified to meet changing business requirements. An activity known as the post-implementation review should also be undertaken. This should take place about six months after the system changeover and should review what was planned for the information system against what actually happened. Lessons learned from this exercise will be extremely valuable when the next system is developed.

Post implementation review
A meeting that occurs after a system is operational to review the success of the project and learn lessons for the future.

❿ The sequence of phases in the waterfall model

At each stage in the development process we have seen a number of activities that need to take place and also opportunities for things to go wrong! It is important, therefore, to emphasise the importance of the review that takes place at the end of each stage. Work should not commence on the next stage unless it can be shown that the current stage has been satisfactorily completed.

The waterfall model can now be summarised using Figure 7.3. It will be seen that each step follows in sequence from the one above. Each step, apart from the first, also has a link back to the previous stage, to correct problems discovered at an earlier stage. If during a development project it frequently becomes necessary to revisit a previous stage, it may be a sign that a stage has not been properly reviewed before the next one is started.

Sometimes, if a major problem is discovered it may be necessary to revisit several stages. For example, consider if the user acceptance testing at the changeover or implementation phase identifies a significant user requirement that has been overlooked. This will need each of the analysis, design and build phases to be revisited. Potentially, the feasibility will also need to be reassessed.

The need to revisit previous phases has given rise to alternative models of systems development, such as Boehm's spiral model and rapid application development which are described later in this chapter.

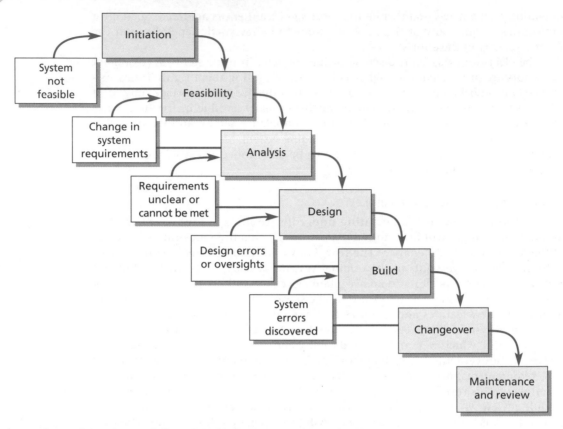

Figure 7.3 **The traditional waterfall model of information systems development**

The traditional waterfall model and BIS acquisition

The traditional waterfall model as described above implies that the system is being acquired using a bespoke development approach. Bespoke development, whether in-house or by a third party, traditionally follows all the steps described above. However, as we have seen, there are methods of information system acquisition that do not require the development of bespoke solutions. Which steps within the traditional waterfall model are required for these alternative methods of software acquisition? We will consider each acquisition method in turn.

Bespoke development

It is in this form of BIS acquisition that the traditional waterfall method is most evident. Different information systems development methodologies have different approaches to achieving the same overall objective, that is, the acquisition of business information systems that deliver real business benefits by providing the information needed to make better business decisions.

In this chapter, the waterfall model is not discussed in any detail with respect to **bespoke development** since subsequent chapters deal with each step of the model in more detail. However, it is worth making the following points:

Bespoke development
An IS is developed 'from scratch' by an IS professional to suit the business requirements of the application.

- Bespoke development is much more expensive than alternative software acquisition methods – the software that is produced is unique and must be tailored to the precise needs of the users.
- The time taken to develop a new, bespoke computer-based information system is significantly longer than the period needed to purchase an off-the-shelf software package. That said, there have been recent developments in a method known as 'rapid applications development' which claims to reduce substantially the time taken to develop bespoke software.
- There will be situations where bespoke development provides the only realistic way of producing the required software – high degrees of organisational or application uniqueness or the need to integrate a new information system very tightly with existing applications are common reasons for this.

▶ Purchase of an off-the-shelf package

- *Initiation.* This step clearly applies regardless of the acquisition method: there must be some kind of stimulus which creates the notion that a computer-based information system is needed to respond to a business opportunity or problem.
- *Feasibility.* Again, this step must be followed. Indeed, it is during the feasibility step that an investigation will be undertaken into the technical aspects of the required system and a make-or-buy decision will be made. A 'buy' decision indicates that a solution is probably available off the shelf; a 'make' decision indicates that a bespoke solution is probably required because of a combination of factors, as discussed above.
- *Analysis.* This is as important a step in the acquisition of off-the-shelf software as it is in building bespoke software solutions. System requirements must be determined and catalogued so that they can be compared with the features offered by the package.
- *Design.* It is here that significant differences are found when compared with bespoke software design. An off-the-shelf package will have been designed with many different businesses in mind and will offer a range of features to satisfy most requirements. The 'how' aspect of software acquisition has, therefore, already been determined and the system subsequently built. The task for the purchaser of an off-the-shelf package is to compare the design features required (e.g. menu systems, database design or user interface design) against those offered by different packages.
- *Build.* With an off-the-shelf package, the system has already been built by the vendor. As part of the feature set offered by a package, there may be an ability to customise aspects of the software product by setting certain parameters. For example, an accounting package may be set up either to interface with a sales order processing system from the same vendor, or to offer the ability to interface with a package offered by another supplier or with a bespoke system. There will also need to be a testing phase where all the relevant features of the package are run in a simulated live environment. This might, for example, be done in parallel with existing information processing activities.
- *Implementation/changeover.* As with a bespoke software solution, data will have to be converted or entered from old computer or paper-based information system. One of the benefits of purchasing off-the-shelf software is that the product should be free from major bugs and errors. The purchaser should be confident, therefore, that the software product will work as specified from the outset.
- *Maintenance and review.* Maintenance and enhancements of the software will differ from those in a bespoke solution. Whereas bespoke software can be enhanced over time by the developer (either in-house or by a third party), an off-the-shelf package will differ in a number of ways. Enhancements to the package will normally be made available by the vendor as a new release. Sometimes it is possible for a business

organisation to build its own enhancements or 'add-ons' to the package. There is a danger that such bespoke amendments to standard packages may be lost if the organisation buys a new release of the software. In addition, maintenance is usually covered by a separate maintenance agreement after the original guarantee period. Annual maintenance costs can vary from 10 to 20 per cent of the original software purchase price. There may be differential pricing depending on whether the maintenance agreement is to cover simply 'bug fixing' or whether it is to entitle the user to the latest version of the software at no or little additional cost. As with the bespoke solution, a post-implementation review should be undertaken.

▶ End-user development

End-user-developed software

Software written by non-IS professionals, i.e. the business users.

End-user applications development is in line with the steps normally covered during the bespoke development process. The main difference is that end-user-developed applications are usually on a much smaller scale than those developed for corporate use. However, many of the tools and techniques associated with large-scale corporate bespoke development still have a role, albeit a more limited one, in end-user-developed information systems. As before, each step in the waterfall model will be discussed separately. The advantages and disadvantages of end-user development are described in detail in Chapter 16.

- *Initiation.* The stimulus for end-user information system development will typically come from a personal or departmental requirement which can be satisfied by employing easy-to-use end-user development tools. Such systems may be standalone with no linkages to any other end-user or corporate system, or they may use databases and database extracts from corporate information systems (perhaps with additional database tables created by the user) and manipulate the data in order to produce information not previously made available. In the latter case, the data may already exist in the corporate database, but the processing necessary to produce the information has not been included as a core part of the application.
- *Feasibility.* Part of the feasibility exercise is for the user to be sure that the necessary and appropriate end-user development tools exist or can be acquired in order to proceed with the development. A second aspect is an analysis of the cost involved in end-user developed software: while an end-user is producing software, their 'normal' tasks either remain undone or have to be done by someone else. Therefore, end-user applications development needs to be justified on economic grounds.
- *Analysis.* One of the benefits is that an end-user need not present information systems requirements to an IS/IT specialist for subsequent development. This therefore reduces the risk of mistranslating information systems requirements and increases the probability that the developed system is what the user actually wants. The end-user may still find it useful to apply some of the tools associated with the analysis phase such as those discussed in Chapter 11, although clearly they will be used on a much smaller scale.
- *Design.* End-user-developed software has a tendency to be developed more on a 'trial and error' basis than through the use of formal design techniques. When it works well, this can result in the faster development of applications software. The downside is that poor design may result in a system that at best does not work quite as it should and at worst a system that actually results in incorrect information being produced. Incorrect information can have various results, ranging from short-term irritation to corporate decision-making errors with large financial consequences. One of the most useful tools in end-user design is entity relationship modelling, which should be used in conjunction with logical and physical database design. The proba-

bility is that if the database design and associated data validation rules are correct, then the system is more likely to produce the information that is required.

- *Build*. Recent improvements in the availability of inexpensive development tools such as Visual Basic for the PC have made it much easier for the end-user developer to build systems without recourse to difficult programming techniques. As end-user development is now much easier than it was five years ago, emphasis can be placed on the functionality which the system is to offer. Also, development times are speeded up, and this provides for the effective use of iterative prototyping in this step.

- *Implementation/changeover*. This step is less critical than for company-wide information systems. Data is either locally generated or extracted from central databases, where it can be assumed that the data is validated and verified as correct. In fact, the term 'changeover' is probably not a good one in this context – 'live running' may be a better one. It is quite possible that an end-user-developed system is capable of producing useful information even before it becomes a 'live' product. A risk is that end-user-developed software may not have been tested sufficiently thoroughly and this raises an important question of the management of such software. We will deal with this in Chapter 16.

- *Maintenance and review*. All software has to be maintained in some way. In many respects, the maintenance of end-user developed software is more problematic than for other forms of software acquisition. This is because end-user-developed systems are often not documented and they may employ obscure techniques in their construction.

End-user development is discussed in more detail in Chapter 16.

Focus on the waterfall model and SSADM   **F**

Systems Analysis and Design Method (SSADM) is a methodology that defines the methods of analysis and design that should occur in a large-scale software development project. It is used extensively in the UK, particularly in government and public organisations.

> **Systems Analysis and Design Method (SSADM)**
> ....
> A methodology that defines the methods of analysis and design that should occur in a large-scale software development project. It is used extensively in the UK, particularly in government and public organisations.

Structured Systems Analysis and Design Methodology (SSADM) is one of over 1000 brand-name methodologies (Jayaratna, 1994). We will focus on SSADM because it is one of the most widely used formal methodologies in the UK today. Indeed, SSADM must be used for any government systems development projects, usually alongside the PRINCE project management method (Chapter 9).

SSADM focuses on the feasibility, analysis and design aspects of the systems development lifecycle. It provides fewer guidelines on the changeover and maintenance aspects of an IS project.

Describing SSADM in some detail highlights the methodical approach required for large-scale projects which some may refer to as bureaucratic. It also illustrates the contrast with alternative techniques such as RAD.

SSADM has a five-module framework within which are seven stages. Each stage has its own activities and the required deliverables are clearly mapped out for each. It is not possible to go into a great degree of detail here. Texts such as Eva (1992) and Weaver (1993) deal with the methodology in a comprehensive manner. However, we will discuss the essentials of each module and associated stage(s) in turn.

▶ Feasibility study

Stage 0 – Feasibility

The project will already have been through a planning or initiation stage, so it is necessary at this point to determine whether it is technically and economically feasible. The feasibility study is broken down into four steps:

- *prepare for feasibility study* by assessing the scope of the project;
- *define the problem* (what should the new system do that the present one does not);
- *select the best feasibility option* from those available (typically up to five business options and a similar number of technical options);
- *assemble the feasibility report*, including a rationale for the selected option.

The output from this stage, the feasibility report, now provides the input for the next module – requirements analysis.

▶ Requirements analysis

This module is broken down into two stages: investigation of current environment and business system options.

Stage 1 – Investigation of current environment

This stage is critically important because it is used to gain a full understanding of what is required of the new system. Any errors or omissions made at this stage will be reflected in the rest of the systems development process. The following steps are taken:

- *Establish analysis framework*. The scope of the project is reassessed and then planned accordingly.
- *Investigate and define requirements*. Broad requirements will have been defined at the feasibility stage: these are now expanded into a detailed catalogue of systems requirements.
- *Investigate current processing*. The feasibility study will have created an initial data flow diagram which is now expanded to embrace all the existing processes.
- *Investigate current data*. A logical data model is developed so that the organisation can obtain a clear picture of which attributes the data entities contain and how they relate to each other. Entity and attribute are defined in Chapter 12.
- *Derive logical view of current services*. This involves the revision of the logical data model so that it reflects the business logic of the system under consideration rather than its current physical implementation.
- *Assemble investigation results*. This is the last step in the analysis of the current system environment. The analysts will check for consistency and completeness before proceeding to the next stage.

Stage 2 – Business systems options

This stage comprises two steps, the objectives of which are to agree what the functionality of the new system should be. A number of possible systems solutions for the perceived business requirements are formulated and the impacts and benefits of each will be evaluated. The solution selected will be the one that most closely matches the requirements of the business. The two steps are:

- *Define business systems options*. Activities here will include the establishment of minimum systems requirements, the development in skeleton form of alternatives, the production of a short list of options, and finally a full evaluation of each alternative short-listed option, including a cost–benefit analysis, impact analysis and system development and integration plan for each.

- *Select business system option*. The precise way in which this is done will vary between organisations. The objective is the same, however: for appropriate user managers to select the business system option from the evidence presented by the analysis team.

▶ Requirements specification

This module has one stage which in turn is split into eight discrete steps.

Stage 3 – Definition of requirements

- *Define required system processing*. Here, the features of the existing system that are to remain a part of the new system are added to the details contained in the requirements catalogue.
- *Develop required data model*. Redundant elements from the data model of the existing system are removed (if any exist) and additional required elements are added. In addition, the relationships between old and new entities are reviewed.
- *Derive system functions*. Here, the processes that will have been identified and incorporated in the data flow diagrams are identified more precisely and properly documented.
- *Enhance required data model*. The required data model developed earlier is now enhanced by carrying out relational data analysis and normalisation (Chapter 12); the result should be a set of tables which can be implemented using a relational database management system.
- *Develop specification prototypes*. This involves the creation of prototypes for selected parts of the specification so that precise requirements can be validated with the intended end-users; such elements as menus, sample data entry screens and reports may be constructed.
- *Develop processing specifications*. The analyst at this stage is concerned with illustrating the effect of time on data subjected to various actions (i.e. creation, reading, updating and deleting); two tools that are used here are entity life history analysis and effect correspondence diagrams. These are tools used by the professional systems analyst and it is beyond the scope of this book to deal with them in detail.
- *Confirm system objectives*. The penultimate task is to carry out a formal review of the system requirements to ensure that the final requirements specification which follows is complete and fully understood by users and developers alike.
- *Assemble requirements specification*. Finally, the various components (including the required system logical data model, function definitions, requirements catalogue and other items) are assembled into the final requirements specification document, which then provides the input into the next module and stage.

▶ Logical system specification

Stage 4 – Technical system options

- *Define technical system options*. Here, any constraints on the choice of technical environments are established (e.g. security, performance, ease of upgrade).
- *Select technical system options*. The appropriate technical option is selected; it must conform with the required strategic and operational criteria which have already been established.

Stage 5 – Logical design

This stage can take place at the same time as Stage 4. Here, the process of developing the systems specification is continued, with the outcome being a set of implementable components. The individual steps are as follows:

- *Define user dialogues*. This is concerned with defining the ways in which the user will interact with the system (e.g. menus and systems navigation).
- *Define update processes*. Here, the definition of transactions which will change data are established (entity life histories are used to support this step).
- *Define enquiry processes*. In addition to navigation and updating, users will wish to perform enquiries on the data held in the system.
- *Assemble logical design*. This is essentially a consistency and completeness check.

Once the logical design is complete and has been 'signed off', the final stage can be tackled.

◗ Physical design

Stage 6 – Physical design

This stage is concerned with the delivery of the final blueprint from which the system can be developed and implemented. There are seven steps to be completed:

- *Prepare for physical design*. The implementation environment is studied, applications development standards drawn up and a physical design strategy agreed.
- *Create physical data design*. The required logical data model (LDM) is used as a base for this and the business-specific data design is produced.
- *Create function component implementation map*. The components of each systems function are drawn up. This includes their relationship with the physical function components (the actual business activities) which they support.
- *Optimise physical data design*. The physical data design is tested against the required performance objectives and optimised if necessary.
- *Complete function specification design*. This will be for any function components that required programming.
- *Consolidate process data interface*. The process data interface is located between the physical database design and the process design. This helps the mapping of the database to the processing requirements (especially important when the database has been altered or the processing requirements have been modified).
- *Assemble physical design*. This stage and the whole SSADM lifecycle are completed with this step. A number of products are delivered, including the function definitions, the optimised physical data design, the requirements catalogue and space and timing estimates.

◗ SSADM and the waterfall model – a summary

Although complex, SSADM as a methodology only covers part of the systems development process (as the name of the methodology suggests, the emphasis is on analysis and design). However, given the importance of having systems requirements determined correctly before further development takes place, this is perhaps understandable. We will now turn our attention to what the traditionalists would regard as the very antithesis of a 'proper' structured methodology, that is, rapid applications development. Before this, refer to Case Study 7.2 which summarises the acquisition options available to a business.

CASE STUDY 7.2

Lascelles Fine Foods

Lascelles Fine Foods (LFFL) is a fictitious example of a long-established company operating in the food industry. The company has its administrative headquarters in Ashville and manufactures on an adjacent site. All customer deliveries are from the Ashville-based warehouse. In addition, LFFL purchases finished and semi-finished food products from other manufacturers which it then finishes before resale.

The company has enjoyed steady growth in recent years and is now seeking to capitalise on the current fashion for quality and healthy food products. LFFL's turnover is £16 million with net profitability of 6.3 per cent of turnover. It is hoping to gain a competitive edge by providing quality food products which meet all present and anticipated quality standards and to this end will be applying for BS5750 accreditation within the next six months. It is hoping to increase turnover by 10 per cent a per year after inflation over the next five years and increase net profitability to 9 per cent of turnover over the same period.

LFFL's main operations are divided into four main areas:

- sales and marketing;
- warehousing and distribution;
- manufacturing;
- finance.

All information recording and internal communication is paper based and relies on a range of preprinted documents which are then used as appropriate.

The sales department
LFFL has a diverse customer base, ranging from small health food shops to major supermarket chains. Orders can be one of two types: standard orders placed in advance for delivery in a specific week or priority orders placed for immediate delivery.

Orders are placed either directly through sales office 'account handlers' or through field sales persons (each customer has one sales person). Each customer is allocated an account handler who acts as the main liaison point within LFFL. Besides receiving orders, the account handler is responsible for cash collection, ensuring satisfactory progress of the order and handling day-to-day queries. Customers are also placed into sales categories based on geographic location, volume of business and type of customer (e.g. specialist store vs supermarket chain). The sales director is apt to change his mind about which category a customer is in and which category means what.

Order processing
Once an order is taken, it is recorded on a preprinted order form. One copy is retained by the sales department and two copies are sent to warehousing and distribution.

Warehousing and distribution sort all order forms into date order. When an order is due to be delivered, products are picked from the warehouse and loaded into the appropriate vehicle.

When an order is delivered, it is accompanied by a consignment note and an invoice. The customer is required to check the delivery against the invoice and note any errors on the consignment note. The delivery driver returns with a signed copy of the consignment note and if any errors are noted a corrected invoice is sent to the customer.

Warehousing and distribution
LFFL stores finished products, bought-in products and raw materials in the warehouse. The warehouse is divided into three areas:

- the general zone, comprising a high-rise bulk storage area with a floor-level picking area;
- the cool zone, comprising low-level storage at 2 to 4° C.
- the frozen zone, with temperatures held to −18° C.

In addition to their role in the order processing cycle, other activities are also performed:

- internal warehouse movements from high-rise locations to ground-level areas and vice versa;
- receiving products and raw materials from suppliers and returned products from customers;
- issuing raw materials to manufacturing in response to submitted requisition forms;
- receiving finished products from manufacturing and any unused raw materials.

Information about quantities of finished goods and raw materials in stock is recorded in a card file, which has to be searched manually for the appropriate entry when updating is required.

Manufacturing
Manufacturing ranges in complexity from simple repackaging of bulk-purchased materials to complex mixing and cooking activities.

▶

Recipes are recorded on 7" by 5" cards and include details of the required ingredients as well as the processing which is to take place.

Finance

LFFL's finance department is divided into three areas:

- accounts payable – when LFFL makes purchases, suppliers will invoice them; LFFL uses a manual purchase ledger to manage these accounts;
- financial accounting – management of all monies flowing in and out of the company together with compliance with legal accounting requirements;
- management accounting – internal accounting information necessary to manage the business more effectively.

The accounts receivable area is handled by the account handlers who use a manual sales ledger and make a weekly return to the finance department on the state of their customers' accounts.

Specific business issues

There are a number of specific issues which relate to the activities of each department. These are detailed below.

Sales

- The status of an order cannot easily be determined without pestering the warehouse.
- Many customer complaints occur due to delivery of wrong products, orders delivered too late, incomplete orders and faulty products.
- Warehousing does not deliver the most important orders first – small orders are often given priority over larger orders from major retailers.
- Orders often cannot be delivered on time because manufacturing produces too late and in insufficient quantity.

Warehousing and distribution

- Many items have a limited shelf life – warehousing often fails to rotate the stock properly.
- Actual stock levels are rarely in step with the recorded stock levels – this may be due to pilfering, poor update of stock records or both.
- The sales department often accepts priority orders for products which are not in stock.
- Manufacturing bypasses the normal requisition procedures and simply takes raw materials as required – it also often fails to return unused materials to warehousing.

Finance

- The sales returns from the account handlers are often incomplete.

- There are several bad debts which cannot be recovered – this is attributed to poor credit control procedures.
- Management accounting is very difficult due to a general lack of accurate information from other departments.
- Financial accounts are often published late due to lack of accurate information.

Manufacturing

- Warehousing is slow to respond to requests for raw materials, thus necessitating correct procedures being bypassed (especially when the sales department is applying pressure).
- Lack of accurate forecasting makes it difficult for production to be planned ahead and adequate supplies of raw materials to be secured.

General

- There is a rapid turnover of staff, especially in the sales area where the pressure from customers can be intense. In addition, field sales personnel are apt to make promises which cannot be kept and new sales personnel are often thrown in at the deep end with little formal training for their jobs.
- There is a high level of sickness in the warehousing and distribution area, due mainly to inadequate provision of lifting equipment.
- There is a perceived lack of management and technical support which has resulted in a general lowering of morale.

Future plans

The managing director, Clive Moor, has indicated that he would like to replace the existing paper-based systems with 'computers of some kind'. With such a move, he is hoping to improve on the communication of information at all levels in the organisation. However, Mr Moor knows little about computer hardware or applications software except that it seems to cost rather a lot.

In order to proceed with the computerisation programme, Mr Moor has asked the following senior managers to produce a plan:

- Paula Barlow – Finance director
- Terry Watson – Sales and marketing director
- Peter Jackson – Manufacturing operations director
- Frances Clarke – Warehousing and distribution director

However, these directors have varying degrees of enthusiasm for the project, together with a desire to minimise the risk of damage or exposure within their own departments. One of the key decisions which must be made will be how LFFL acquires the necessary applications software. One option will be to hire relevant IT staff and build bespoke applications, while another will be to purchase off-the-shelf packages. Yet another option will be for end-users to develop their own applications. This last option may prove awkward, since there is very little IT expertise among the end-users.

Questions

1 Which method(s) of business systems software acquisition would you recommend to LFFL? Explain and justify your answer.

2 Assuming that LFFL decides to go down the route of purchasing off-the-shelf packages, what steps do you recommend it takes to ensure that the applications which are selected meet their requirements?

Rapid applications development (RAD)

The evidence from project failures for projects in the 1980s and 1990s implies that traditional structured methodologies have a tendency to deliver systems that arrive too late and therefore no longer meet their original requirements. Traditional methods can fail in a number of ways:

- *A gap of understanding between users and developers.* Users tend to know less about what is possible and practical from a technology perspective, while developers may be less aware of the underlying business decision-making issues which lie behind the systems development requirement.
- *Tendency of developers to isolate themselves from users.* Historically, systems developers have been able to hide behind a wall of jargon, thus rendering the user community at an immediate disadvantage when discussing IS/IT issues. While some jargon may be necessary if points are to be made succinctly, it is often used to obscure poor progress with a particular development project. The tendency for isolation is enhanced by physical separation of some computer staff in their own air-conditioned computer rooms. Developers might argue in their defence that users also have their own domain-specific jargon which adds to the problem of deciphering requirements.
- *Quality measured by closeness of product to specification.* This is a fundamental difficulty – the observation that 'the system does exactly what the specification said it would do' hides the fact that the system may still not deliver the information that the users need for decision-making purposes. The real focus should be on a comparison of the deliverables with the requirements, rather than of deliverables with a specification that was a reflection of a perceived need at a particular point in time.
- *Long development times.* A glance back at the previous section on SSADM and the waterfall model will reveal that the processes of analysis and design can be very laborious and time consuming. Development times are not helped by the fact that an organisation may be facing rapidly changing business conditions and requirements may similarly be changing. There is a real risk of the 'moving goal-posts' syndrome causing havoc with a traditional approach to systems development.
- *Business needs change during the development process.* This is alluded to above. A method is needed where successive iterations in the development process are possible so that the latest requirements can be incorporated.
- *What users get isn't necessarily what they want.* The first a user may see of a new information system is at the testing or training stage. At this point, it will be seen whether the system as delivered by the IS/IT professionals is what the user actually needs. An appropriate analogy here is the purchase of a house or car simply on the basis of discussions with an estate agent or a garage, rather than by actually visiting the house or driving the car. It is unlikely that something purchased in this way will

result in a satisfied customer and there is no reason to suppose that information systems developed in a similar way will be any more successful.

Not only is there pressure from end-user management for faster systems development, IS/IT departments themselves increasingly recognise the need to make more effective use of limited human resources within their departments while at the same time quickly delivering systems that confer business benefits. All this is in a climate of rapid business change and, therefore, rapidly changing information needs. **Rapid applications development (RAD)** is a possible solution to these problems and pressures. This uses **prototyping** to involve users and increase development speed.

Rapid applications development (RAD) is a method of developing information systems which uses prototyping to achieve user involvement and faster development compared to traditional methodologies such as SSADM.

Rapid applications development (RAD)
A method of developing information systems which uses prototyping to achieve user involvement and faster development compared to traditional methodologies such as SSADM.

Prototyping
A prototype is a preliminary version of part or a framework of all of an information system which can be reviewed by end-users. Prototyping is an iterative process where users suggest modifications before further prototypes and the final information system is built.

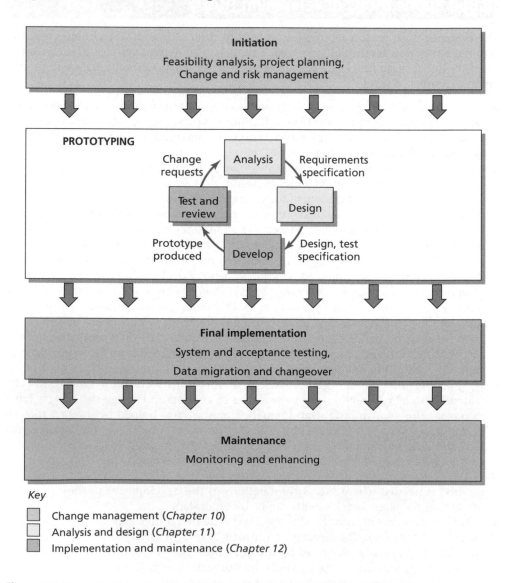

Figure 7.4 The role of prototyping within the systems development lifecycle
Source: Chaffey (2002)

Prototyping produces a preliminary version of part or a framework of all of an information system which can be reviewed by end-users. Prototyping is an iterative process where users suggest modifications before further prototypes and the final information system are built.

Case Study 7.3 illustrates the benefits that can be derived from a RAD approach. It also hints at some disadvantages, such as the lack of a methodology to support RAD which can lead to a casual approach to a project. A later section on the dynamic systems development method (page 312) shows how this deficiency is being made good.

Since modern systems development using prototyping is an iterative approach, the sequential models defined in Figures 7.2 and 7.3 are a simplification of the actual process. Figure 7.4 gives a more realistic representation of systems development. It is apparent that all the phases within the SDLC are still present, but that the activities of analysis, design, test and review repeat within the prototyping phase.

CASE STUDY 7.3

Lloyds Bank Insurance Services applies RAD

When marketing people spot a business opportunity, it is often IT people who have to think and act the fastest.

Systems have to be put in place that meet the stipulated deadline, that work first time, and that fulfil the expectations of users. Otherwise the opportunity could be lost forever.

That was the situation facing the computer team at Lloyds Bank Insurance Services when a new product called MUDI (Mortgage Unemployment Disability Insurance) required a telesales quotation system that had to be fully operational by October 2nd.

Yet it was already mid-August when David Jacklin, IT Development Manager, LBIS, was informed of the need for a new application. It was a moment he remembers well. 'I faced the classic dilemma of no available resource within my team and an immovable deadline', he recalls.

However, in spite of that initial reaction and against some unexpected odds, the race against time was won. The insurance broker's objective was achieved with the help of a hard-working software house, a development environment toolset, and a fast-track approach called RAD (Rapid Application Development). In fact, the entire development took just five weeks.

Reason for the urgency at the LBIS headquarters in Haywards Heath, West Sussex was a government decision to amend the rules relating to the payment of mortgage cover out of social security in the event of a house-owner being made redundant. This opened a new insurance window which the company was determined to exploit.

LBIS, a subsidiary of Lloyds Bank and Abbey Life, is a firm of independent brokers dealing in life assurance, pensions and general insurance. Annual turnover is £100 million and 800 people are employed at Haywards Heath and six regional offices. A significant proportion of the company's business is generated through a business unit called Lloyds Bank Insurance Direct.

This is essentially a telemarketing organisation based in Bournemouth. About 70 per cent of its business comes via branches of Lloyds Bank, where advisors take an enquirer's details and ring LBID for a quote. The remaining 30 per cent is from people responding to direct mail of advertisements and telephoning in direct.

A simple version of MUDI was, in fact, available at the bank branches. But there were no facilities for accurate underwriting and anyone taking up the policy paid a straight £6.50 per £100 of cover (i.e. if the monthly mortgage payment was £300, the premium was £19.50). The new system would incorporate a complex screen replacing the existing simple paper form, providing the flexibility to quote premiums appropriate to the enquirer ranging from £4.40 to £9.40 per £100 of cover.

But first the new system had to be built. There already existed another application at Bournemouth – BIQS (Building Insurance Quotations Service) – but this ran under DOS, so what would almost certainly be a Windows system could not merely be tagged on.

Jacklin and his team had been looking at development toolsets and the RAD concept earlier in the summer. They had been particularly attracted by a RAD specialist, MDA Computing, and had already met the Croydon-based software house at the end of July.

Suddenly, with the new business-critical requirement looming, the need for RAD became urgent.

▶

'We had no hesitation going back to MDA. They obviously knew what they were talking about and we were in urgent need of a system', says Jacklin.

Some of the main attractions of RAD included the delivery of a workable first version within a very short timescale, testing that is integrated within the development cycle, flexibility of the specification, and user involvement throughout the whole process.

Within days, Jacklin and his colleagues had agreed with MDA the RAD methods to be used. The software house underlined the need for an appropriate development environment, and recommended Enterprise Developer. This versatile toolset from Symantec had all the advanced features of a second generation client/server development system, and this was precisely what the LBIS team sought.

Such systems are repository-based and scaleable, and – specially important according to Jacklin – are driven by business rules so that future changes are easily made as business needs change. MDA evaluates every tool that comes on to the client/server market and felt that Enterprise Developer offered the best set of second generation facilities.

Next step was a demonstration of the Symantec toolset at MDA, 'The demo convinced us. We had looked at other development tools but they did not seem meaty enough for our needs. And although MDA had never built anything with Enterprise Developer they were clearly keen to do so.' Following that demo and an agreement of project scope, work began on August 24th.

The key requirement was for a front-end system that would enable telesales staff at 30 screens to capture a caller's details and generate an immediate MUDI quotation. The system would be in Windows 3.1 and GUI based, essentially a classic PC LAN application. It would run a Compaq server using Novell.

However, MDA's first task was systems analysis. At the early stage, LBIS had not formulated all their needs – not even the design of the 'forms' that would appear on the screen. So MDA used RAD techniques to work out what the requirements would be, and spent three days at LBID in Bournemouth prototyping the forms on screen using Enterprise Developer. The software house also had to allay fears, among a user-team with little experience of Windows, about mouse-driven systems.

In order to get the project started, the use of a Watcom database was assumed. However, following discussions within LBIS, it was decided that for strategic and operational support reasons the use of Oracle was preferred.

MDA had to accommodate a new database in already tight development cycle. The ability to adapt to the fresh circumstances and still deliver the system on time was a big tribute to the software house's RAD methods and the Symantec toolset. (In fact, there were minor compatibility problems which disappeared when LBIS upgraded to Enterprise Developer 2.5 at the beginning of November.)

The system was delivered in the last week of September for final testing in readiness to go live the following Monday. By then, LBIS's own technical team had adjusted the BIQS system so that the telesales people could flip to it from MUDI, depending on the caller's needs, with a simple keyboard Alt/Tab depression.

On 'live' day, the telesales team processed 200 customer quotations with scarcely a hitch. Jacklin, MDA and Symantec had every right to feel pleased with themselves. A business need had demanded IT support, and that support was implemented on time.

Now the end-users, equipped with telephone headsets, enter personal details which affect ratings, such as sex, post code and occupation, on to a GUI screen. The quotation then appears on the same screen. There are five other, supporting screens labelled status, comments, letter print, rating and search for existing customer.

A happy Jacklin concludes, 'Here was a software house that gave us what we needed. They were always confident they could do something with Enterprise Developer and within time. There was no slippage despite it being their first real use of the Symantec product and despite the change in database midway through. I think that says something for Enterprise Developer too. And we went live on the big day.

'We like RAD and we shall use it again. In a market-oriented organisation like LBIS, we always have a need to react to business changes quickly, and I suspect that within 18 months we could need a system to handle all six of our insurance products.'

He adds, 'The system has allowed LBIS to launch a more competitive product than would otherwise have been possible, and we have sold more than we would have done. It had to be in at the right time or we would have missed the boat. From a technical point of view, it forced us to go to Windows which was always our eventual intention. All this, and the system will pay for itself before Christmas!'

Source: This case study was taken with permission from the DSDM web site, www.dsdm.org

Questions

1 Why and how did the company choose the RAD approach used for this project?

2 What disadvantages of the RAD method can you identify from the study?

3 Do you think that Lloyds can be confident that future RAD projects will be successful?

❯ The spiral model

The **spiral model** is an iterative systems development model developed by Boehm (1988) which incorporates risk assessment.

The spiral model was developed in recognition of the fact that systems development projects tend to repeat the stages of analysis, design and code as part of the prototyping process. Each spiral consists of four main activities, as shown in Figure 7.5 The activities are:

1 *Planning*. Setting project objectives, defining alternatives.
2 *Risk analysis*. Analysis of alternatives and the identification and solution of risks.
3 *Engineering*. Equivalent to the build phase of the SDLC with coding and testing.
4 *Customer evaluation*. Testing of the product by customers.

It can be seen from Figure 7.5 that the model is closely related to RAD, since it implies iterative development with a review possible after each iteration or spiral, which corresponds to the production of one prototype or incremental version. Before the first spiral starts the requirements plan is produced, so it can be seen that the spiral model does not detail the initiation and analysis phase of the SDLC, focusing on design and build.

Although the spiral model has not been applied widely in industry, proponents of this model argue that it includes the best features of both the classic SDLC and the prototyping approach. It also adds validation of requirements and design, together with risk analysis, which is often overlooked in RAD projects.

Spiral model
....
An iterative systems development model in which the stages of analysis, design, code and review repeat as new features for the system are identified.

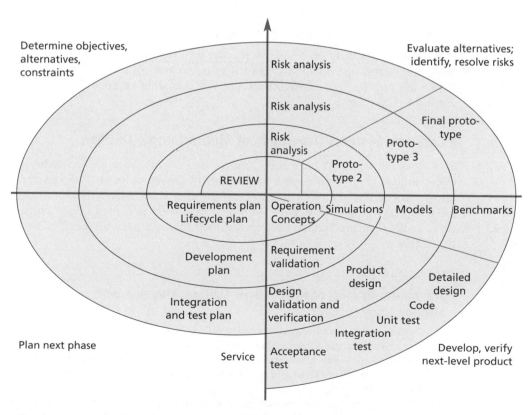

Figure 7.5 Boehm's spiral model of systems development

▶ The Capability Maturity Model for Software development

Another influential model for best practice in the development of BIS is the **Capability Maturity Model for Software** from Carnegie Mellon University (Carnegie Mellon, 2001). This model, which has been revised throughout the 1990s and into the new millennium, challenges organisations to review their process of systems development. It provides a framework for managers to assess the current sophistication of their process for systems development. There are five stages to the model. These are described by the institute as:

1 *Initial.* The software process is characterized as ad hoc, and occasionally even chaotic. Few processes are defined, and success depends on individual effort and heroics.
2 *Repeatable.* Basic project management processes are established to track cost, schedule, and functionality. The necessary process discipline is in place to repeat earlier successes on projects with similar applications.
3 *Defined.* The software process for both management and engineering activities is documented, standardized, and integrated into a standard software process for the organization. All projects use an approved, tailored version of the organization's standard software process for developing and maintaining software.
4 *Managed.* Detailed measures of the software process and product quality are collected. Both the software process and products are quantitatively understood and controlled.
5 *Optimizing.* Continuous process improvement is enabled by quantitative feedback from the process and from piloting innovative ideas and technologies.
   Predictability, effectiveness, and control of an organization's software processes are believed to improve as the organization moves up these five levels. While not rigorous, the empirical evidence to date supports this belief.

Published maturity levels (www.sei.cmu.edu/sema/pub_ml.html) show that today many large specialist organisations such as NASA and information systems consultants have achieved the higher levels. However, many smaller companies have processes that are still at stage 1 or 2.

▶ Dynamic Systems Development Methodology (DSDM)

The ideas behind RAD have been around for several years, but a methodology that encapsulates its principles has only recently emerged. In the UK, an organisation known as the DSDM Consortium has put together a set of underlying principles. These are given in full below, together with a commentary provided by the consortium. In total, **DSDM (Dynamic Systems Development Methodology)** has nine key principles, shown in the box.

Capability Maturity Model for Software (CMM or SW – CMM)
A model for judging the maturity of the software processes of an organisation and for identifying the key practices that are required to increase the maturity of these processes.

Dynamic Systems Development Methodology (DSDM)
A methodology that describes how RAD can be approached.

> #### The nine principles of the Dynamic Systems Development Methodology (DSDM)
>
> I   *Active user involvement is imperative.* DSDM is a user-centred approach. If users are not closely involved throughout the development life-cycle, delays will occur as decisions are made. Users no longer sit outside the development team acting as suppliers of information and reviewers of results but are active participants in the development process.
>
> II   *DSDM teams must be empowered to make decisions.* DSDM teams consist of both developers and users. They must be able to make decisions as requirements are refined and possibly changed. They must be able to agree that certain levels of

▶

functionality, usability, etc. are acceptable without frequent recourse to higher level management.

III   *The focus is on frequent delivery of products.* A product-based approach is more flexible than an activity-based one. The work of a DSDM team is concentrated on products that can be delivered in an agreed period of time. This enables the team to select the best approach to achieving the products required in the time available. By keeping each period of time short, the team can easily decide which activities are necessary and sufficient to achieve the right products.

IV   *Fitness for business purpose is the essential criterion for acceptance of deliverables.* The focus of DSDM is on delivering the business functionality at the required time. The system can be more rigorously engineered later if such an approach is acceptable. Traditionally the focus has been on satisfying the contents of a requirements document and conforming to previous deliverables, while losing sight of the fact that the requirements are often inaccurate and the previous deliverables are flawed.

V   *Iterative and incremental development is necessary to converge on an accurate business solution.* DSDM allows systems to evolve incrementally. Therefore the developers can make full use of feedback from the users. Moreover partial solutions can be delivered to satisfy immediate business needs. Iteration is inherent in all software development. DSDM recognises this and, by making it explicit, strengthens the use of iteration. When rework is not explicitly recognised in a development life-cycle, the return to previously 'completed' work is surrounded by controlling procedures which slow development down. Since rework is built into the DSDM process, the development can proceed more quickly during iteration.

VI   *All changes during development are reversible.* Backtracking is a feature of DSDM. However in some circumstances it may be easier to reconstruct than to backtrack. This depends on the nature of the change and the environment in which it was made.

VII   *Requirements are baselined at a high level.* Baselining high-level requirements means 'freezing' and agreeing the purpose and scope of the system at a level which allows for detailed investigation of what the requirements imply. Further baselines can be established later in the development.

VIII   *Testing is integrated throughout the life-cycle.* Testing is not treated as a separate activity. As the system is developed incrementally, it is also tested and reviewed by both developers and users to ensure that the development is moving forward; not only in the right business direction, but that it is technically sound. Early in DSDM, the testing focus is on understanding the business needs and priorities. Towards the end of a project, the focus is on assuring users and developers that the whole system operates effectively.

IX   *A collaborative and co-operative approach between all stakeholders is essential.* The nature of DSDM projects means that low-level requirements are not necessarily fixed when the developers are originally approached to carry out the work. Hence the short term direction that a project takes must be quickly decided without recourse to restrictive change control procedures. When development is procured from an external supplier, both the vendor and the purchaser organisations should aim for as efficient a process as possible while allowing for flexibility during both the pre-contract phase and when the contracted work is carried out.

Source: www.dsdm.org

Avison and Fitzgerald (1995) outline an approach to rapid applications development which embraces many of the principles outlined above. For them, the RAD approach:

- is based on evolutionary/prototyping rather than the traditional lifecycle approach;
- identifies key users and involves them in workshops at the early stages of development;
- obtains commitment from the business users;

- requires the use of CASE (computer-aided software engineering) tools for system building.

Typical RAD activities include:

- joint requirements planning (JRP) to determine high-level management requirements;
- joint applications design (JAD) using prototyping tools to explore processes, interfaces, screens, reports, dialogues etc., which are then developed and modelled using entity modelling, dataflow diagrams, action diagrams and function decomposition diagrams;
- transformation of user designs to detailed design and code generation, often with the assistance of CASE tools;
- a cut-over phase involving more testing, functional-level training, training for organisational change and adaptation, conversion, parallel running and, finally, live running.

The result of the rapid applications development approach should be new information systems that more closely meet the requirements of the intended users, not least because the requirements will not have changed significantly over a relatively short development timescale.

Summary

1 Acquisition refers to the approach for sourcing BIS. Alternative acquisition methods include:

- *off-the-shelf* – purchased from a software vendor;
- *bespoke* – 'built from scratch';
- *end-user-developed* – self explanatory.

Complex and organisation-wide BIS such as e-business systems often require hybrid sourcing approaches and enterprise applications integration of different components from different vendors.

2 A useful model for the stages of a BIS acquisition project is the systems development lifecycle model (SDLC). The stages described in later sections of Part 2 are:

- *initiation* – identification of opportunity or problem to be solved by BIS;
- *feasibility* – assessing cost-benefit and acquisition alternatives;
- *analysis* – assessing the user and business requirements;
- *design* – producing a specification for the approach of producing a structure for the BIS;
- *build* – coding, documenting, data migration, testing;
- *implementation* – installation, testing, changeover;
- *maintenance and review* – live system review and update.

3 End-user development tends to neglect the feasibility, analysis, design and testing phases. The design and build phases are relatively insignificant for off-the-shelf acquisition.

4 The classic stage model of system acquisition has experienced problems of insufficient user involvement – leading to poor delivery of business-user requirements and a protracted lifecycle which may also result in loss of competitive advantage or budget overruns.

5 RAD and prototyping approaches encapsulated in the Dynamic Systems Development Methodology (DSDM) are aimed at solving the problems of the stage models. The key characteristics of this approach are an iterative approach with frequent delivery of prototypes coupled with user involvement throughout the project.

EXERCISES

Self-assessment exercises

1 Explain what the main similarities and differences are between bespoke development and end-user development.

2 Why would a small business be more constrained in its choice of software acquisition method than a large one?

3 What are the main differences between the analysis and design steps of the traditional waterfall model of systems development?

4 What are the main components of the system build stage?

5 Explain how the application of the waterfall model differs between (a) the purchase of an off-the-shelf package and (b) an end-user-developed application.

6 Briefly review the main advantages and disadvantages of bespoke development when compared with off-the-shelf packages.

7 Identify the main stages involved in SSADM. Which stages of the traditional waterfall model do they relate to?

8 How does rapid applications development differ from SSADM as a means of producing 'quality' software?

Discussion questions

1 The rise of rapid applications development is mainly a response to the failure of traditional systems development methodologies to deliver the right system at the right price and at the right time. Discuss.

2 End-user applications development would be far less popular if central IS/IT departments did not have such a large applications development backlog. Discuss.

3 Do you think it is true that the existence of so many information systems problems attributed to the 'millennium bug' is primarily a reflection of poor systems development techniques?

Essay questions

1 What do you believe to be the main differences between large and small organisations in deciding the best approach for information systems acquisition?

2 In what circumstances do you think that SSADM would be (a) appropriate and (b) inappropriate when carrying out systems analysis and design?

3 In what circumstances do you think that rapid applications development would be (a) appropriate and (b) inappropriate when carrying out systems analysis and design?

4 Is the end-user development approach to business software development something which you think should be encouraged, or do you believe that applications software for business is best left to information systems professionals?

Examination questions

1 Explain the terms 'bespoke development', 'off-the-shelf package' and 'end-user computing'. Illustrate your answer with some of the reasons cited in favour of each of these methods of application software acquisition.

2 Give three advantages usually associated with prototyping.

3 During a bespoke development project, the systems development lifecycle will include a number of steps from requirements analysis, design and system. Which of these steps is relevant to an off-the shelf system? Which activities might be involved?

4 Explain how the spiral model of systems development which can be applied to RAD differs from the traditional waterfall model. Which do you believe represents the best method of developing information systems?

References

Avison, D.E. and Fitzgerald, G. (1995) *Information Systems Development: Methodologies, Techniques and Tools*, Blackwell, Oxford

Boehm, B. (1988) 'A spiral model of software development and enhancement', *IEEE Computer*, 21, 5, May, 61–72

Carnegie Mellon (2001) Research Report. CMMISM for Systems Engineering/Software Engineering/Integrated Product and Process Development, Version 1.02, Staged Representation (CMMI-SE/SW/IPPD, V1.02, Staged). Available online at www.sei.cmu.edu/pub/documents/00.reports/pdf/00tr030.pdf. See also www.sei.cmu.edu/cmm/cmm.html

Chaffey, D. (2002) *E-business and E-commerce Management*, Financial Times Prentice Hall, Harlow

Eva, M. (1992) *SSADM Version 4: A User's Guide*, McGraw-Hill, London

Jayaratna, N. (1994) *Understanding and Evaluating Methodologies NIMSAD, a Systematic Framework*, McGraw-Hill, London

Senn, J. (1995) *Information Technology in Business Principles, Practices and Opportunities*, Prentice-Hall, Englewood Cliffs, NJ

Sprott, D. (2000) 'Componentizing the Enterprise application packages', *Communications of the ACM*, April, 43, 4, 63–9

Weaver, P.L. (1993) *Practical SSADM Version 4: A Complete Tutorial Guide*, Financial Times Pitman Publishing, London

Further reading

Curtis, G. and Cobham, D. (2001), *Business Information Systems: Analysis, Design And Practice*, 4th edition, Financial Times Prentice Hall, Harlow, Essex

Kendall, K.E. and Kendall, J.E. (1995) *Systems Analysis and Design*, 3rd edition, Prentice-Hall, Englewood Cliffs, NJ

Kerr, J. and Hunter, R. (1996) *Rapid Development: Taming Wild Software Schedules*, Microsoft Press, Redman, WA

Lewis, P. (1994) *Information-Systems Development*, Financial Times Pitman Publishing, London

Martin, J. (1990) *Rapid Applications Development*, Macmillan, London

Stapleton, J. (1998) *DSDM: The Method in Practice*, Addison Wesley, Harlow, Essex

Web links

www.sei.cmu.edu Carnegie Mellon Software Engineering Institute.

www.sei.cmu.edu/publications/articles/index.html In-depth guidelines on achieving improvements in systems development including the Capability Maturity model.
www.sei.cmu.edu/cmm/cmm.html

www.cw360.com Computer Weekly CW360 is a good source of case studies of different acquisitions approaches and problems of project management.

www.eds.com/case_studies/cs_home.shtml Case studies from major BIS consultant EDS illustrate many of the issues of systems analysis, design and implementation.

www.yourdon.com Ed Yourdon's web site is a good collection of up-to-date papers about problems of information systems development from one of the gurus of software development, many taken from *Software Development* magazine (www.sdmagazine.com).

www.fdic.gov/regulations/information/index.html FDIC: The Federal Financial Institutions Examination Council (FFIEC) handbook for conducting examinations of banks' and savings associations' information systems is relevant since it recommends appropriate approaches and activities to different stages of building banking systems which also apply to other systems.

www.research.ibm.com/journal/ The *IBM Systems Journal* and the *Journal of Research and Development* have many cases and articles on analysis and design related to e-business concepts such as knowledge management and security.

www.intranetjournal.com/itadvisor/ Intranet journal has case studies on systems analysis and design specific to intranets.

Initiating systems development

LEARNING OBJECTIVES

After reading this chapter, readers will be able to:

- explain the importance of conducting a structured initiation phase for a BIS acquisition project;
- identify typical tangible and intangible costs and benefits associated with the introduction of an information system;
- apply different techniques to select the most appropriate options from different software, hardware and supplier alternatives;
- describe the importance of contracts to a successful outcome to information systems projects.

MANAGEMENT ISSUES

The senior management team sponsoring a new BIS must ensure that the project is (a) necessary, i.e. will contribute to business performance, and (b) that it is managed effectively. The initiation and feasibility phase of the systems development lifecycle is directed at achieving these two aims. From a managerial perspective, this chapter addresses the following questions:

- How should we assess the feasibility of a project?
- What are the stages and techniques that can be applied to assess feasibility?
- How can the return on investment of a BIS project be assessed?

Links to other chapters

The chapter focuses on the startup phase of systems development projects.

Chapter 7   describes alternative acquisition methods such as bespoke and off-the-shelf development.

Chapter 9   describes how to manage a project to ensure that the quality of the system is maintained throughout the project.

Chapter 14   also considers cost–benefit analysis in relation to the overall investment that a company makes in IS rather than individual systems. Critical success factors for the new system are described in more detail. Outsourcing of information systems development and management is also described.

Introduction

Many information systems projects fail. Often they overrun in time or budget, or they not deliver the benefits expected. A survey conducted between November 2000 and January 2001 of 599 Chief Information Officers in 'Top 500' companies in the UK, USA and Australia showed that there are still significant challenges when implementing information systems projects – one third of companies had experienced a delay or scrapping of new information system (PricewaterhouseCoopers, 2001).

These failures are often the result of errors made during the systems development project, but other systems projects are set to fail right from the start because the planned systems are unnecessary or not capable of delivering what the business needs. This is often the case if a feasibility study has not been carried out as part of the **initiation or startup phase** of the project. This chapter describes all the activities that need to occur at the start of a project to minimise the risk of failure later.

The initiation phase is the first phase in an information systems development project. Its aims are to establish whether the project is feasible and to prepare to ensure that the project is successful.

The **feasibility study** is the activity that occurs at the start of the project to ensure that the project is a viable business proposition. The feasibility report analyses the need for and impact of the system and considers different alternatives for acquiring software is normally considered to be part of the initiation phase.

A feasibility study normally occurs as part of the initiation phase (or as a separate phase after initiation) as a preliminary investigation intended to establish whether a business opportunity or problem can be solved through introducing a new information system. It is often also referred to as defining the 'terms of reference' for the project.

Initiation phase
The first phase in an information systems development project. Its aims are to establish whether the project is feasible and prepare to ensure the project is successful.

Feasibility study
The activity that occurs at the start of the project to ensure that the project is a viable business proposition. The feasibility report analyses the need for and impact of the system and considers different alternatives for acquiring software.

▶ Activities involved in project initiation

The purpose of the initiation stage is to assess whether an information systems development project will have a successful outcome. The key activity in a feasibility assessment is a cost–benefit analysis to check that the benefits provided by the system will outweigh the costs. Other factors such as the effect on staff will also be considered and the scope of the project will be defined. The activities that occur during the initiation stage are summarised in Table 8.1.

Table 8.1 **Principal activities during the initiation phase of an IS project**

Activity	Purpose
1 **Assess feasibility**	This is the most important aspect of the initiation stage. It involves performing a cost–benefit analysis and considering non-monetary considerations such as the effect that the new system will have on staff. An overall feasibility study may be conducted to establish the business reasons for proceeding, followed by a comparison of alternative technical solutions from different suppliers.
2 **Define business objectives and outline systems requirements**	Check that the system is aligned with business needs by defining critical success factors (CSFs) that must be achieved by incorporation of particular features.
3 **Evaluate acquisition alternatives**	This evaluation will cover different aspects such as cost, suitability and performance of systems from different suppliers, which may be either bespoke or 'off the shelf'.
4 **Define scope**	This involves specifying system boundaries describing which parts of the organisation will be affected by the system. Will it be used in a single department, across the whole organisation or beyond with suppliers?
5 **Define responsibilities**	Since a large input to a project in areas such as defining the requirements and undertaking testing is from managers and users of the final system, time for their input must be set aside. Responsibilities of the system developers will also be specified.
6 **Assess risks**	Identify potential problems which may cause the project to fail, such as skills shortages or changes to the company's market. What precautions can be taken to ensure that the project doesn't fail?
7 **Identify constraints and develop project plan**	Use estimating and planning to develop an initial project plan. This will preview project size and complexity to establish a preliminary budget and timescale, which will be refined once the go-ahead for the project is given.

Note that the initiation phase may involve two separate phases of feasibility analysis. In the first, overall feasibility may be established by establishing the needs and objectives for the system. If it is decided that the project is worthwhile, a more detailed evaluation of available solutions from different vendors will occur.

Figure 8.1 shows a typical sequence of activities that occur at the initiation stage of a project. For a large-scale project the feasibility report will normally be considered by a panel comprising senior staff in the company, such as the managing director, finance director, IS director or manager, and representatives of departments or processes that will use the system. For a smaller-scale project, the departmental manager may be the only person involved if he or she holds the budget. This should be discouraged, since there may be other systems already in the organisation that meet the needs or conflict with the proposed system. Independent review by someone with an overview, such as the IS manager, can avoid this problem.

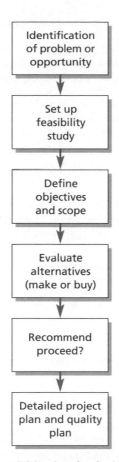

Figure 8.1 Sequence of main activities involved with project initiation

Reasons for project initiation

A project is usually initiated by a company in response to a business problem or opportunity in order to gain competitive advantage. Some examples of such benefits were introduced in Chapter 2. When a company is considering the benefits that can arise through implementing an information system, a useful framework is provided by the '5 Cs' of Senn (1995), updated here to include customer service as another important factor. This framework covers the following benefits:

1 *Cost reduction*. Cost reduction is often the key driver for the introduction of new systems. This factor is relatively easy to quantify and is readily understood by the managing director and finance manager. Different aspects of quantifying cost are given in the section on cost–benefit analysis.

2 *Capability*. A new information system can provide a new capability to achieve something that has not previously been possible. For example, establishing an Internet presence through a web site gives a new sales channel capability. Information systems can also be enhanced to improve an existing capability where capacity has become limited. For example, business expansion may produce workloads with which current systems cannot cope – a growing company may find that its existing systems can no longer handle the quantity of orders received. An improved capability can be provided by increasing the amount of storage of an existing system or upgrading the software to a version with new features.

3 *Communication.* One of the aims of e-business is improving internal, intranet-based communication and external communication with customers, suppliers and other partners.

4 *Customer service.* Customer service can be directly improved by introducing 'customer-facing' systems which are used directly by customers or in their presence. A bank might use these to reduce the length of queues, and so improve customer service. Customer service can also be enhanced indirectly: a company could purchase an improved sales order processing system that reduces the time taken to order and deliver a product to the customer.

5 *Control.* Control can be improved through better information delivery for managers. A sales manager who has weekly reports on the performance of his or her sales force is in a better position to exercise control than a manager who receives the figures monthly.

6 *Competitive advantage.* If information systems can give a company the edge over its rivals through the benefits above, a competitive advantage may be achieved. For example, travel agent Thomas Cook (www.thomascook.com) was one of the first in its sector to introduce an Internet booking service. Increasingly, competitive advantage is transitory as competitors copy innovation.

A further useful indication of the need for a new system is to ask: *What would be the consequence of not having the proposed information system?* A summary of the types of benefit that a company can achieve is given in Table 8.2. This gives examples of how a car manufacturing company might use information technology to gain benefits.

It is evident from Table 8.2 that any new information system will give multiple benefits. In addition to the benefits given in the table, other benefits include better decision making and reduced error and wastage in existing manual processes through automation.

Table 8.2 Common benefits of introducing information systems, with examples of how they might assist a car manufacturer

Benefit	Achieved through
1 Cost reduction	'Deskilling' or using information systems and robots to reduce the number of staff required. Computer-aided design and manufacture can help reduce the time and cost from concept to production
2 Capability	A new capability to build specific cars for customers
3 Communications	A network can be set up linking the head office of the company and dealerships to assist in ordering new cars and monitoring the sales performance of the individual dealership
4 Customer service	Through integrated manufacturing a customer can specify his or her exact requirements for a car which will then be produced within a week
5 Control	Improved information can be delivered for management decision making and to assist control
6 Competitive advantage	Reduced time to market and improved build quality can be delivered through automation

Benefits of BIS

Select a company or organisation with which you are familiar. Rank in order of importance the benefits that developing a new BIS, such as an e-commerce system, could deliver to the business or a particular department. You should give an explanation of why you have placed each benefit factor where you have.

Alignment of information systems with the business strategy

When undertaking the feasibility study, as part of the initiation phase it is important to check that there is a strong alignment between the benefits that the new information system will provide and the overall business strategy. This may seem an obvious point, but it is stressed since the culture and structure of many organisations do not support this. If some departments such as marketing have a strong influence on the board, then their systems may be more likely to be accepted from those from another area such as production.

Another reason that poor alignment may occur is when the IS department has sole responsibility for which systems are developed. Traditionally most companies have an area with responsibility for IT, but it is often seen as a support service in the same way as, for example, estates management. Owing to this, the IT department does not integrate with or understand other business functions and tends to be isolated. This problem is compounded if there is no IT director on the board of the company (or at least another director with responsibility for IT).

Many companies are now changing this situation and this enables the IS strategy to support and be responsive to the business strategy. Developing a culture where the other functions of the business represent internal customers to the IS/IT function also helps in this transition. The main techniques for achieving this alignment include a top-down approach to IS strategy, where the mission and objectives of the company are translated into a portfolio of information systems required by the company. Whether alignment occurs should be assessed as part of the feasibility to the organisation. The feasibility review panel should also ask the question: *Is this system consistent with and supportive of the mission and objectives of the company?*

Other techniques such as the application of critical success factors are also relevant. The issue of aligning systems with objectives and choosing systems to affect the organisation is discussed in more detail, from a strategic viewpoint, in Chapter 14.

▶ Critical success factors

The use of **critical success factors (CSFs)** is valuable in helping to align new systems with business objectives. Critical success factors are those factors that determine whether business objectives will be achieved. **Key performance indicators (KPIs)** are then used to set targets for CSFs and assess whether these have been achieved. An example of this approach is illustrated by Reicheld and Schefter (2000). They reported that Dell Computer has created a customer experience council that has researched key loyalty drivers or CSFs which determine whether customers will be retained by Dell as repeat customers. The business objectives and corresponding CSFs and KPIs are shown in Table 8.3.

BIS play a significant role in achieving these CSFs since:

1 BIS are required indirectly to collect data about the CSFs and report them throughout the organisation, so corrective action can be taken when targets are not achieved.
2 BIS may be used to directly achieve the CSFs.

Critical success factors (CSFs)
Must be present to achieve strategic business objectives.

Key performance indicator (KPI)
A specific measure used to determine the progress in achieving critical success factors.

Table 8.3 Relationship between loyalty drivers and measures to assess their success at Dell Computer

Business objective	Critical success factor and KPI
1 **Improve order fulfilment**	Ship to target. KPI: percentage of systems that ship on time exactly as the customer specified
2 **Increase product performance**	Initial field incident rate. KPI: frequency of problems experienced by customers
3 **Enhance post-sale service and support**	On-time, first-time fix. KPI: percentage of problems fixed on the first visit by a service representative who arrives at the time promised

---

Activity 8.2

Critical success factors

Suggest how Dell Computer may use BIS to:

(a) collect and report the CSFs and KPIs in Table 8.3;
(b) achieve the business objectives and KPIs in Table 8.3.

After identification of CSFs during initiation, development of a system should be targeted specifically at meeting KPIs at all SDLC phases. For example, the analysis stage will question which functionality, data inputs and outputs the system requires to meet these objectives. The testing stage will involve benefits-based testing to check that the system has the features to deliver the intended benefits. CSFs are also used to inform BIS strategy, as described in Chapter 13.

Economic feasibility – the cost–benefit analysis

Assessing costs and benefits is not an exact science. A fundamental problem is that it is not easy to measure each benefit and cost accurately. Even where the benefits and costs are quantifiable, the figures used are only based on an estimate predicting several years into the future. This section outlines how cost–benefit analysis occurs at the start of a project to implement a new BIS.

All feasibility assessments for information systems development should include a cost–benefit analysis. Although this may seem obvious, some companies miss out this stage because other factors are driving the development such as the need to counter a competitor threat or respond to customer demand. The creation of e-commerce systems by grocers is an example of this – here the cost of setup and maintenance may be greater than the revenue achieved through increased sales. The marketing manager may, however, want to proceed with such a strategic initiative to gain experience aimed at ensuring success in the future when this form of channel becomes more widely used. In the UK, for early adopters such as Tesco and Sainsbury's this approach has proved appropriate, but for others such as Safeway, Somerfield and Budgen the costs have exceeded the benefit.

The business analyst undertaking a cost–benefit analysis will identify both **tangible and intangible costs and benefits**. When a cost or benefit is tangible, it is possible to set a definite numeric value against an item such as the cost of installing a new network. It is not possible to place a numeric value on intangible costs and benefits. Note that for some factors it may be difficult to establish whether the benefit is tangible or intangible. For example, although it is difficult to measure the benefit of general improvements in data

Tangible costs
A measure of cost can be calculated for each tangible cost.

Intangible costs
A monetary value cannot be placed on an intangible cost.

Tangible benefits
A definite measure of improvement can be calculated for each tangible benefit.

Intangible benefits
It is not possible to measure intangible benefits.

quality, it would be possible to measure specific aspects of quality such as the time the new system takes to deliver information to the users.

Tangible costs are a measure of cost that can be calculated for each item of expenditure on BIS. For example, the purchase price of new hardware needed to run new software is a tangible cost. A monetary value cannot be placed on an intangible cost: the disruption and possible user resistance that will occur due to implementing a new system will have an effect on overall company performance, but they are difficult to measure.

A definite measure of improvement can be calculated for each tangible benefit. A reduction in customer waiting time in a bank because of a new information system is an example of a tangible benefit. It is not possible to measure an intangible benefit. For example, the improved decision-making capability provided by a decision support system would be difficult to cost.

▶ Assessing costs

A range of costs must be included in the feasibility study. These include:

- hardware and software purchase costs;
- systems development staff costs if a bespoke or tailored solution is chosen;
- installation costs including cabling, physically moving equipment and bringing in new furniture to house the computers;
- migration costs such as transferring data from an existing system to the new system or running the new and original systems in parallel until the reliability of the new system is established;
- operating costs including maintenance costs of hardware such as replacing parts or upgrading to new versions of software. Staff costs in maintaining the hardware and software and trouble-shooting any problems must also be factored in. Operating costs may also include an environmental audit of the amount of energy and consumables used;
- training costs;
- wider organisational costs, for example redundancy payments may need to be made if computerisation leads to loss of jobs.

Note that these costs include not only the initial cost of purchase, but also the ongoing maintenance cost. These are considerable for information systems and will often exceed the initial cost of purchase.

It is worth noting that there is a growing realisation that the cost of ownership of a software or hardware product is potentially much higher than the purchase cost. This is mainly due to the cost of troubleshooting software bugs and hardware faults, phone support, installing upgrades and paying for support and/or upgrades from the vendor. In the mid-1990s the Gartner Group showed that the total cost of ownership (TCO, see Chapter 16) for a PC may be as high as $8,000 per year, reducing to $2,000 per year for a simpler thin client such as a network computer. The cost of ownership of the selected software–hardware combination should obviously also be factored into your cost–benefit analysis. The cost of training and education and documentation of staff should also be included with standard development costs of paying analysts and programmers.

Radosevich (1999) summarises typical cost metrics as external and internal labour, hardware, software, travel and training, support and testing. She notes that most companies estimate these costs after determining the business requirements and scope since costs are based on the tasks in the work breakdown structure as explained in Chapter 9.

Activity 8.3

Typical BIS costs and benefits

The following are examples of costs and benefits:

- Software purchase cost
- User resistance
- Reduction in working hours
- Improved decision making
- Hardware purchase cost
- New working practices
- Sales increase
- Broader planning horizons
- Implementation costs
- Disruption during implementation

- Training costs
- Reduction in customer complaints
- Better data integration
- Reduction in maintenance costs
- Better data quality
- Hardware and software maintenance and consumable costs
- Reduction in inventory levels
- Better cash flow

Assess where they should be in the grid below:

Costs		Benefits	
Tangible	Intangible	Tangible	Intangible

▶ Assessing benefits

While information systems costs are relatively easy to identify, the benefits are harder to quantify since they are often intangible and will occur in the future. Benefits from a new system can be considered in terms of improvements to business processes and the quality of information used to support these processes. Common benefits include reduced costs of operating processes and greater efficiency leading to faster completion of tasks such as serving a customer.

Parker and Benson (1988) recommend a structured approach to identifying tangible benefits. This involves considering the cost of performing a business process *before* introduction of a new system and comparing this to the cost *after* implementation. Costs may include staff time, materials and equipment. This result will indicate either a tangible benefit through cost reduction or an added cost of using the new system.

Intangible benefits will include improvements to the quality of information, as described in Chapter 1. A new information system should enable information quality to be improved in some of the following ways:

- improved accuracy;
- improved availability and timeliness;
- improved usability (easier to understand and then act on information);
- improved utilisation;
- improved security of information.

▶ Using financial measures to assess the viability of a new system

The balance between costs and benefits can be assessed using a variety of financial measurements. These techniques may be familiar from the study of accounting, since these measures can be applied to the assessment of the return on any investment for any capital investment. The techniques are reviewed briefly here and the reader is referred to an accounting text or the coverage in Robson (1997).

Once the costs and benefits have been identified and quantified, it is normal to calculate their value in present-day monetary terms since the costs and benefits will be incurred in the future. Monetary benefits achieved in the future will be worth less than when the project was started due to the effect of inflation. To take this into account, discounted cashflow calculations such as net present value or internal rate of return are performed. In these the future benefits are discounted assuming a fixed or variable level of interest rate. These techniques are described in Robson (1997) and measurement of costs and benefits is described in more detail in Remenyi (1995).

Return on investment (RoI)

This is the simplest measure and it is widely used in IS feasibility assessments. The **RoI** is calculated by dividing the benefit by the investment amount and is expressed as a percentage:

$$RoI = 100 \times \frac{Benefit \ldots value}{Investment \ldots value}$$

Where: *Benefit value* = return – cost

Return on investment (RoI)
....
An indication of the returns provided by an IS. Calculated by dividing the benefit by the amount of investment. Expressed as a percentage.

The Gartner Group suggests that a RoI of more than twice the current cost of borrowing is usually viable. Currently RoIs of 20 per cent or more are usually viable (this is, of course, dependent on the prevailing interest rate).

Although this appears to be a simple measure that is easy to calculate, there is no standard of how it is applied over the duration of the investment. To counter this, Robson (1997) suggests that the RoI should be calculated using the annual benefit value. Analysts such as the Gartner Group calculate the RoI over an arbitrary four-year period, while others calculate it over the expected lifetime of the project.

Net present value (NPV)

A problem with the RoI measure is that it is often (but not always) calculated without considering how the future value varies through time. For the calculation to be meaningful, the future value should be discounted so that it is expressed in terms of its value today. This is known as a *discounted cashflow* (DCF). The **NPV** can be calculated with a standard spreadsheet function:

$$NPV = \sum_{i=1,n} \frac{Value^i}{(1 + rate)^n}$$

Net present value (NPV)
....
A measure of the return from a system which takes into account the variation in monetary value through time.

where: *Value* = cashflows, starting with investment as negative cashflow
n = number of periods (usually years)
Rate = company cost of capital (discount rate).

If the NPV is positive, the estimate suggests that the company will achieve a return and it may decide to invest. An NPV that is negative suggests no return on the investment and the project is unlikely to go ahead.

Internal rate of return (IRR)

IRR is also a discounted cashflow technique, considering the NPV from a different perspective. The IRR calculation yields the *interest rate that will produce an NPV of zero*. Robson suggests that this method can be used to compare different potential projects. Project A with an IRR of 15 per cent is more favourable than Project B with an IRR of 5 per cent. In this example, 10 per cent might be set as the cutoff rate for feasible projects.

Payback period

This metric is also usually considered together with ROI, NPV and IRR, since it provides additional information not available in these other measures. The payback period is the period in which, after the initial investment, the company has not achieved a net benefit. This is apparent from Figure 8.2, which shows through the dashed curve that it will be after the benefits start accruing that the payback will be achieved. BIS often have payback periods of the order of several years, when the initial development and investment may take over a year. Two alternatives may have a similar RoI or NPV, but one project could have a much shorter payback period, so it is important to use a combination of the methods covered here.

Before leaving this topic, it should be noted that the measures reviewed are purely financial and should not be used in isolation. It is important to consider other factors, such as the intangible benefits and the risks expected for the different alternatives. Parker and Benson (1988) coined the term 'information economics', which provides a methodology for evaluating these other factors.

▶ Different types of feasibility

As well as considering the costs and benefits of a project, the feasibility study will also consider other aspects of feasibility. These factors will usually be reviewed for each of the possible solutions that have been proposed. The alternative solutions may be from different hardware or software vendors, or they may be different technical solutions that have been proposed.

The different aspects of feasibility are commonly referred to as economic, technical, operational and organisational.

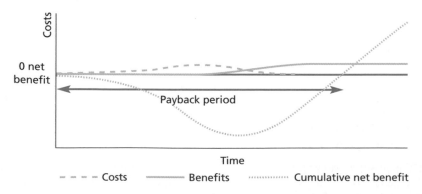

Figure 8.2 Graph showing the relationship between systems development cost and benefit value through time and their effect on cumulative net benefit

Discounted cashflow calculations for an e-commerce system development project

This activity illustrates the types of tangible costs and benefits that should be considered when building an information system and shows how the benefits and costs vary over time.

You should build a spreadsheet to assess the installation of an e-commerce system.

The measures you should use to assess the investment are:

● Payback period
● Return on Investment
● Net Present value

Complete the following stages to perform the calculation:

Stage 1: Costs

By referring to the costs in Table 8.4, complete the costs spreadsheet model Table 8.5 by filling in the question marks (?).

Table 8.4 **Costs input table**

	Hours	Rate
Project Manager	300	£50
Analyst	400	£40
Developer	800	£30
Other staff costs		£15
Hardware		£10,000
Software		£20,000
Installation		£5,000
Training		£15,000
Maintenance p.a.		£12,000

Table 8.5 **Costs spreadsheet model**

Costs	Year 0	Year 1	Year 2	Year 3
Project Mgr	?			
Analyst	?			
Developer	?			
Hardware	?			
Software	?			
Installation	?			
Training (other staff)	?			
Maintenance		?	?	?
Totals	?	?	?	?

Stage 2: Benefits

By referring to Table 8.6, complete the benefits spreadsheet model Table 8.7 (you will need to fill in the ?s).

▶

Table 8.6 Benefits input table

Reduced processing costs (p.a.)	£500		
Reduced inventory costs (p.a.)	£10,000		
Sales (Years 1 to 3)	£50,000	£100,000	£150,000
Fewer returns (p.a)	£10,000		
Discount rate	**15%**		

Table 8.7 Benefits spreadsheet model

	Year 0	Year 1	Year 2	Year 3
Reduced costs		?	?	?
Reduced inventory		?	?	?
Sales		?	?	?
Fewer returns		?	?	?
Totals		?	?	?

Stage 3: Discounted cashflow calculations

Finally, complete the DCF (Table 8.8) by referring to the costs and benefits spreadsheet models (Table 8.5 and Table 8.7).

Table 8.8 Discounted cashflow calculations

	Year 0	Year 1	Year 2	Year 3
Benefits–costs	?	?	?	?
Discounted benefits–costs		?	?	?
Cumulative benefits–costs		?	?	?
Cumulative (NPV) – initial		?	?	?

Payback period (months) _____?_____ = Initial Costs/(Savings – Operating Costs)

RoI (at year 3) _____?_____ = Savings (benefits)/Costs

NPV (at year 3) _____?_____ = Sum Net Income – Initial Costs

Economic feasibility

Economic feasibility
An assessment of the costs and benefits of different solutions to select that which gives the best value. (Will the new system cost more than the expected benefits?)

Economic feasibility is the analysis of the different costs and benefits of implementing the new system, as described above.

Technical feasibility

Technical feasibility
Evaluates to what degree the proposed solutions will work as required and whether the right people and tools are available to implement the solution. (Will it work?)

Technical feasibility refers to the analysis of possible technical problems in the different solutions and who is appropriate to solve them. Technical feasibility can involve asking a series of questions to determine whether a computer system is the right tool for solving a problem. Some tasks may only be conducted using a human operator. The types of questions asked are:

● Can the system deliver the performance required? For example, a transaction processing system such as a national lottery must be able to deliver thousands of transactions a second.

- Can the system support the type of decision making required (particularly support for semi-structured or unstructured decisions)?
- Does the system deliver the necessary level of security?

A technical feasibility assessment will aim to determine whether the proposed solution will work at all. In some cases, such as for an accounting system, there will be an obvious product that will fulfil the outline requirements. In others, such as for a specialised manufacturing facility, a fairly detailed analysis of requirements and a high-level design of the system may be necessary to assess alternatives before it is possible to decide on the feasibility. If this is the case then the initiation stage will be protracted and costly.

Most problems are technically feasible, the important question is 'How much will the solution cost'? Some solutions may be possible, but will require expensive hardware, software or development staff. So technical feasibility needs to be conducted before economic feasibility to assess these costs.

Operational feasibility

Operational feasibility will review how the introduction of the new system will affect working practices on a day-to-day basis. For example, detailed estimates will be made of whether the system usability and response times are sufficient for the expected volume of customer transactions. At this stage, a check will be made as to whether the proposed system will be able to deliver the features and functions required. There is close linkage between operational and organisational feasibility, and they are sometimes considered together.

Operational feasibility
An assessment of how the new system will affect the daily working practices within the organisation. (Is the system workable on a day-to-day basis?)

Organisational feasibility

Organisational feasibility considers how closely the solution matches the needs of the organisation and identifies problems that may arise in this area. Organisational feasibility will involve a review of how the potential users' skill sets and attitudes will affect the system. Problems may include resistance to change from end-users, particularly those who don't have experience of using computer systems. If resistance to change from staff is anticipated, then steps should be taken to ensure that this does not happen. Such measures include training and educating staff by explaining why the system is being introduced (Chapter 12). If potential users are not familiar with using computers, then training must occur.

Organisational feasibility
Reviews how well the solution meets the needs of the business and anticipates problems such as hostility to the system if insufficient training occurs. (Considers the effect of change, given a company's culture and politics)

Organisational feasibility is a particularly important consideration for large-scale systems that will be deployed across an organisation. Examples are e-business and enterprise resource planning systems that substantially change working practices through re-engineering business processes. In these cases, the new system may affect the balance of power of different functional parts of the organisation. These implications should also be included as part of the organisational feasibility assessment. A new system may well also affect the communication channels and control mechanisms within an organisation and any detrimental effects on these should be established.

Organisational feasibility will also assess how well the proposed system fits in with the company's overall business and IS strategy (Chapter 13).

Note that since operational and organisational feasibility are not technical factors, they are sometimes ignored, which can cause a failure in implementation of what is a technically sound solution.

▶ Risk management

Risk management
Aims to anticipate the future risks of an information systems project and to put in place measures to counter or eliminate these risks.

Risk assessment can be used at the start of a project to determine the level of risk and develop plans for reducing this risk. **Risk management** involves the following stages:

Activity 8.5

A feasibility analysis for Lascelles Fine Foods

This activity is based on Case Study 7.2 where acquisition alternatives were considered for this company.

Produce a feasibility analysis of the alternative methods of acquiring application software as they relate to LFFL. You should pay particular attention to the operational, organisational, economic and technical feasibility of each one. You should conclude with a recommendation on how LFFL should best proceed to the next phase of the information systems acquisition process.

1 Identify risks, including their probabilities and impacts.
2 Identify possible solutions to these risks.
3 Implement the solutions, targeting the highest-impact, most likely risks.

Risk assessment has been considered in detail by Boehm (1991). Boehm views risk identification as listing possible factors that might jeopardise a project's success.

Risks can be placed into six broad categories, according to Ward and Griffiths (1996). These can be used as a framework for identifying risk within a project. Each will have a different impact depending on the nature of the system being developed.

1 *Project size.* A large, complex project will be more difficult to manage and complete on time than a small one; this will be owing to its having a larger number of individual tasks and interdependencies within the project and the need to have more individuals working on it (thus increasing the level of coordination required). In addition, with a large project there is more to be lost if the project fails since it is expected to deliver major business benefits (or it would never have been undertaken in the first place!).

2 *Project complexity.* Complexity may also cause the project to overrun. Note that although a project may be large, the business problem and/or the technology involved may be quite straightforward. Complexity will be dependent on:

● the variety of business functions that are going to be affected (with implications for the organisational change management process);
● integration with other information systems (with implications for the technical change management process);
● technical complexity within the system itself (perhaps due to the need to use only recently developed technology that has not been used before within the organisation).

3 *People issues.* These relate to the extent to which senior management are committed to and involved in the project. The right blend of business and technical skills must be found and effective communication between business users and systems deliverers must occur. An example of risk in this category is whether there may be a skills shortage – programmers with the right skill set are not available and there is a lack of input from the end-users.

4 *Project control.* This refers to the rigour with which the time, cost and quality aspects of the project are controlled. Elements in this will include the setting of project milestones, IS/IT standards, systems development and project management methodologies, budgetary control and change management. A rigidly planned project may fail to accommodate unexpected changes, so flexibility is important. Risk will lie in the accuracy of the planning process and the extent to which changes can be accommodated. Risks in this category are if sample data are unavailable or hardware is ordered late. These may be the responsibility of others, but it is still up to the project manager to make things happen.

5 *Novelty*. If a large amount of business change is needed to allow the project to be implemented or the technical solution contains a great deal of innovation, the risks can become very high. A further potential risk to be aware of is the 'moving goalposts syndrome'– the business needs or the technologies to be used are changing so rapidly that the system may not deliver what is required. However, if the project under consideration is intended to deliver significant competitive advantage, it may be necessary to incur such risks. This is the common problem of the balance between risk and reward.

6 *Requirements stability*. The greater the degree of certainty (business and technical), the lower the level of risk associated with the project. A situation where requirements are fluid or hard to pin down means that the project will be harder to cost and the anticipated benefits harder to match against those costs. In addition, a dynamic business environment may mean that fundamental business needs change relatively quickly and this will be reflected in changing systems requirements.

In summary, risk assessment will involve balancing the risks and costs likely to be incurred against the anticipated business benefits.

Acquisition choices and methods

Part of the feasibility stage is to decide on the method of acquisition. This will usually occur after the need and requirements for the system have been established. The make-or-buy decision will occur, and different suppliers of either off-the-shelf or bespoke solutions will be evaluated, as has been described in Chapter 7. The economic, technical and operational feasibility will be evaluated for each of the suppliers after a tender or request for proposals has been sent out to the suppliers. If a company decides to use a third party to develop its information systems or provide other IS services, this is known as *outsourcing* (Chapter 14). This is usually a strategic initiative which involves the outsourcing company in developing more than one system.

Example request for proposals for a BIS

Executive summary (two pages). Includes company description, acquisition mission statement, ROI requirement, preferred technology strategy, acquisition timing.

Administrative information (three pages). Includes procurement timeline, short-list requirements, proposal submission preparation guidelines, evaluation criteria checklist.

Business case (six pages). Includes business benefit, description of current operations, expectations, critical success factors.

Technical case (fifteen pages). This section acts as an acceptance list for the buyer. Includes overview of current IS operations, expectations for the new IS operations, system functional specs, expected system response time, document management requirements, integration requirements, exception handling, hardware requirements, software requirements, mass storage specifications.

Management (three pages). Can be reserved for short-list vendors to complete. Includes system acceptance criteria, project management plan, site preparation plan, training plan and schedule, delivery and installation plan and schedule, systems maintenance plan, documentation (description and pricing), qualification and experience (number of installations etc.), customer references, financial report.

Agreement (one page). Asks for vendor's pricing breakdown, itemised by definitions, so you can easily compare vendor to vendor.

▶ **Summarising system requirements**

If we decide to go ahead after the initial feasibility study, the next stage for a major implementation for a large organisation will be to issue an invitation to tender a document, brief or **request for proposals** – an RFP. The RFP is a specification drawn up to assist in selecting the supplier and software. An example structure of an RFP is shown in the box. The purchaser will fill in the first four sections and different vendors will fill in the last two sections. For a smaller company or system, alternative suppliers will also need to be assessed, but the effort spent on selection will be scaled down.

Request for proposals (REP)
....
A specification drawn up to assist in selecting the supplier and software.

 F *Focus on* **techniques for comparing systems**

When purchasing a system, structured decision making is required to ensure that the best option is selected. Three simple methods for making product or supplier decisions are given below.

MINI CASE STUDY

Feature checklist for comparing three different groupware products

Three products are compared according to

- features provided;
- operating systems supported for the server platform;
- operating systems supported for the client (end) user.

These systems are compared using Table 8.9. Price for different options could also be shown in a table such as this, together with more detailed features, such as, does the e-mail have an address book for the whole company or does it support file attachments?

From inspection of the table, it can be seen that Product A and Product C fulfil most of the criteria. Product B would be unsuitable for a company that had a range of existing computers running different operating systems. Since Products A and B are similar and cannot be distinguished using this table, a more detailed evaluation of these two could then occur after excluding Product B. A different example of a more detailed evaluation for a business system is described below.

Table 8.9 Feature comparison for three groupware products

Criteria	Product A	Product B	Product C
Server platforms			
Windows 2000	Yes	Yes	Yes
Novell Netware	Yes	No	Yes
Sun Solaris (Unix)	Yes	No	No
Client platforms			
Windows 2000	Yes	Yes	Yes
MacOS	Yes	No	Yes
Features			
E-mail	Yes	Yes	Yes
Scheduling	Yes	No	Yes
Document management	Yes	No	Yes
Internet access	Yes	No	Yes

Detailed weighted analysis of fleet vehicle management sofware

Table 8.10 shows a real analysis for three products from different suppliers that were compared across many factors to establish which was most suitable. This type of detailed analysis is usually conducted when a new system costs tens or hundreds of thousands of pounds. The grand total shows that Supplier 3 is the clear winner, and this is the project that was chosen and successfully implemented.

Table 8.10 **Detailed weighted analysis for fleet management software**

Decision criteria	Weighting factor	Supplier 1 score	Supplier 2 score	Supplier 3 score
A Individual module functionality (summary)				
Fleet maintenance job control	100	80	86	98
Schedule of rates	100	79	84	85
Stores/purchasing	100	72	71	86
Subtotal	**300**	**231**	**241**	**269**
General functionality				
Fully integrated core modules	100	60	60	60
Integrated job ticket and stores	100	30	40	80
Data maintained online	80	56	56	56
Flexibility to accommodate SOR	80	40	40	68
Data take-on from existing systems	80	64	64	64
Powerful ad hoc reporting	70	28	56	56
Performance monitoring	60	30	36	42
Links to office automation systems	60	42	42	42
Interface with financial ledger	60	32	40	42
Training manuals and documentation	60	30	36	36
Subtotal	**750**	**412**	**470**	**576**
B Technical considerations				
Effective data security procedures	80	56	56	56
Runs in an open environment	80	56	56	56
Ease of use and performance	80	48	48	56
Subtotal	**240**	**160**	**160**	**168**
Other considerations				
Financial considerations	60	36	48	54
Support maintenance	60	36	30	42
Local government user base	50	30	30	30
Confidence in supplier	50	25	25	35
Subtotal	**220**	**127**	**133**	**161**
Grand total	**1510**	**930**	**1004**	**1174**

Questions

1 Review the different categories and the criteria within them. Do you think that the weighting factors are valid? For example, consider module functionality, reporting, documentation, ease of use and financial considerations.

2 Look in detail at the values for each product. Comment on the basis for deciding on individual scores.

3 Given possible deficiencies in 1 and 2 above, comment on the suitability of this technique for making a decision. Would you use it and why? What would you do differently?

▶ Feature checklist – first-cut exclusion

This is used initially to exclude products that are perhaps missing a key function or do not support the operating system you use. The humble feature checklist is the most easily applied and useful tool. The case study shows a typical checklist, which might be available in a magazine such as *PC Magazine* (www.zdnet.com), comparing three off-the-shelf software products.

▶ Feature checklist – detailed ranking

The main deficiency of simple checklists is that they do not attach relative importance to features. To extend them, give each feature a weighting of, say, between 0 and 100 points for each factor and then add up the scores for the different products. Activity 8.6 shows a detailed analysis using a range of factors to decide on which supplier to use.

▶ Final selection using benchmarking

Once a company has narrowed down its selection of software using feature checklists to two or three contenders, a number of possibilities are available to make the final decision. These can be quite costly for both purchaser and supplier. First, it is possible to benchmark against other organisations that are performing similar tasks to you – what are their experiences, what performance is the software achieving, are they an independent reference site?

Second, if it is a large order, you can ask the suppliers to provide the software and test important functions using example process scenarios from your company. Table 8.11 gives such scenarios for using a groupware product.

Table 8.11 Five example scenarios for selecting a groupware package

Function to test	Scenario
1 Administration. Add new user	How readily can a new user be added to system or their personal details changed? How easy to set up the client (end-user) PC?
2 All staff or workgroup e-mail broadcast	How easy is it to set up a list of all staff, or those in a workgroup you need to e-mail and then reuse?
3 Create a new document using a structured form giving name of company, attendees, date of meeting and report of meeting	A report database containing a summary of all meetings with a key client needs to be updated by a salesperson.
4 Circulate minutes of meeting to participants	How easy is this to achieve?
5 Information query and retrieval	You have your customer contacts stored in a groupware system. A customer rings reporting a problem with their salesperson. How quick is it to find the customer and salesperson and retrieve the information required?

▶ Which factors should be used when selecting systems?

When comparing software, cost is an obvious constraint on any purchase, but since this is often a fixed constraint, it is often best to evaluate software on other factors to narrow the choice and then decide finally on cost where contenders are similar in other respects. Eight key factors in deciding on systems are shown in the box.

Eight key factors in selecting systems

1 **Functionality.** Does the software have the features described to support the business requirements?

2 **Ease of use.** For both end-users and initial setup and administration.

3 **Performance.** For different functions such as data retrieval and screen display. If used in a customer-facing situation, this will be a critical factor.

4 **Compatibility *or* interoperability.** How well does your solution integrate with other products? This includes what you are using now and what you will be using based on your strategic direction.

5 **Security.** This includes how easy it is to set up access control for different users and the physical robustness of methods for restricting access to information.

6 **Stability *or* reliability of product.** Early versions of products often have bugs and you will experience a great deal of downtime and support calls, hence the saying 'never buy one dot zero' (Version 1.0).

7 **Prospects for long-term support of product.** If the vendor company is small or likely to be taken over by a predator, will the product exist in three years' time? Is the company responsive in issuing patches and new features for the product? Is the company forming strategic alliances with other key vendors which will improve the product's features and interoperability?

8 **Extensibility.** Will the product grow? Are the features available to accommodate your future needs? Are the features available in the initial purchase or will you have to integrate with software from another vendor? As a rule of thumb, it is best if you can single-source software, or use as few vendors as possible: the system will have greater reliability than making different modules interoperate.

Functionality

A term used to describe whether software has the features necessary to support the business requirements.

Compatibility

Software compatibility defines whether one type of software will work with another. For example will a word processor run Windows 3.1 or Windows 95? Data compatibility defines whether data can be exported from one package and imported for use into another. For example, can a word-processor file from one package be used in another?

Interoperability

A general term used to describe how easily different components of a system can be integrated.

Activity 8.7

Comparing selection factors for different systems

Referring to the eight key factors for selecting software, discuss in a group, the order of importance of these factors for each of these different types of business information system:

- an accounting system;
- a system controlling a production line;
- a system for booking customers on to coach trips;
- a system to support investment in company shares;
- an HR management system.

Create a table comparing the different factors for each system. Explain similarities and differences.

❱ Assessing products from different suppliers

Some businesses make the mistake of limiting an assessment of new software to its technical merits or features. This is unwise, since software purchase is a long-term commitment and a company is reliant on the support provided by the vendor. A small, 'startup' company may provide a good range of features in its products, but it is likely to have fewer staff responsible for ensuring quality of the software and providing after sales support.

In an article in *Computing* (8 May 1988), Simon Rigden, general manager of ERP specialist JD Edwards, claimed: 'People need to move away from ticklists and start looking more closely at the credibility of the vendor.' The article also suggested that many companies take too long in deciding because they evaluate too many suppliers. Some should be excluded early on, through basic criteria such as their record or financial stability. A survey of 200 UK companies by consultants Tate Bramald showed that three-quarters listed up to eight vendors and half of them then spend more than six months deciding.

A further risk is that the vendor may fail or be taken over by a larger company and no support or upgrade versions will be available.

▶ Contract negotiation

An appropriate contract is vital when outsourcing to a third-party systems development or any information systems function. This may include custom or bespoke software, amendments to off-the-shelf software and outsourcing or facilities management (FM). In essence, contracts define which activities should happen and when, and who is reponsible for them. For example, the supplier should deliver Prototype 1 by 1 October, and review should be completed by 28 November. Both the customer and the suppliers benefit from a reduced risk of failure.

The value of having a well-defined contract is illustrated by failures that have occurred when they are not in place. For example, in the mid-1990s, the UK police terminated a fingerprint system development after two years in development, claiming £10 million in costs. The supplier, IBM, then counter-claimed £19 million on the basis of the client not having made their requirements clear. A protracted legal battle followed before agreement was reached.

Contracts should define the following main parameters:

1 business requirements and features of system;
2 deliverables such as hardware, software and documentation;
3 timescales and milestones for different modules;
4 how the project is managed;
5 division of responsibilities between different suppliers and the customer;
6 costs and method of payment;
7 long-term support of system.

Contracts are particularly difficult to establish for information systems projects for the following reasons:

● It is difficult to specify the requirements in detail at the outset of the project when the contract is signed. Varying functional requirements can lead to project overruns.
● Establishing acceptable performance at the outset is difficult because this depends on the combination of hardware and software.
● Many different suppliers are involved and it is often not clear where responsibilities for fixing problems may lie.
● After the project is finished, critical errors can potentially occur and a support contract is required to ensure that they are remedied rapidly.
● If a supplier's business fails, the system may be unmaintainable without the software program, which may need to be put into safekeeping with a third party in a source code escrow agreement.

▶ Contents of a typical IS product contract

A typical contract will be made up of the following sections or schedules, as well as general clauses on confidentiality, intellectual property (who owns the rights to the software), indemnity, law and jurisdiction.

Schedule 1: Product specification and acceptance

This is usually the most involved section, since it will detail the features of the software and acceptance criteria. These will include the completion of all key features with an acceptable level of error and ensure that functions such as reporting occur rapidly enough.

Schedule 2: Input to project from client

This information is sometimes omitted since most activities are conducted by the provider. The activities essential to the completion of the project may include time for writing and reviewing requirements and prototypes; time for user acceptance testing (UAT); time for training; supply of test data; possibly supply of hardware and systems software (if purchased by buying department of company); support from internal IS function and project management.

Schedule 3: Services to be supplied by contractor

Each deliverable should be linked to a milestone and a specific payment to help avoid slippage in the project. Milestones should include deliverables from both client and supplier. Frequent monthly milestones should be set.

Schedule 4: Support of system and warranty

A service-level agreement should state how problems are 'escalated' within suppliers (passed up through the hierarchy so as to be resolved), and should define acceptable times for response according to the severity of the problem. The fault-logging system and contact points such as a helpdesk may also be defined.

Schedule 5: Project plan

An outline project plan showing key deliverables and milestones should be part of the contract. Responsibility for project management will be identified for both parties and regular meetings defined.

Schedule 6: Payment method

The two main methods of payment are fixed price, which tends to be favoured by the client since it has better visibility of costs, and time and materials, which is usually preferred by the supplier. Timing of payments should be tied into milestones (when they are known as 'phased payments'). Suppliers may prefer regular monthly payments. Penalty clauses or liquidated damages may be stipulated where the supplier loses part of its payment if it delivers late or risk and reward clauses which provide financial incentives if it delivers early.

CASE STUDY 8.1 HERE

Blue Circle assess alternative Enterprise Resource Planning Systems

Industrial giant Blue Circle Industries is taking its first steps towards creating a single pan-European IT and business infrastructure, with a £4.6 million investment in Enterprise Resource Planning (ERP).

Yet despite the importance of the project, its Swedish supplier, Intentia, is virtually unknown in the UK. Blue Circle Industries (BCI) IT director Roger Ellis says that until last year he'd never heard of the company.

So what persuaded one of the UK's leading industrial conglomerates to invest in Intentia's Movex suite and, in the process, to put critical business systems for its heating and boiler manufacturing divisions into the hands of a low-profile ERP supplier?

Ellis says that Intentia's commitment to BCI's business plan was crucial: 'Intentia may not be the largest or best-known of the many vendors we reviewed, but it has grasped the business issues and has an unparalleled enthusiasm to work closely with us.'

Blue Circle's heating division comprises three companies in France, Germany and the UK: Finimetal, Broetgae and Potterton Myson. Acquired over a number of years, each company has its own IT infrastructure, a mixture of mainframes, Micro-VAX, Alpha and outsourcing services, none of which had previously communicated effectively.

'The main reason for investing in new software and hardware was to get these systems to talk to each other, making data sharing easier and more cost-effective', says Ellis.

'The commercial rationale is to run the companies as pan-European centres of excellence, rather than autonomous business units.

'When we decided to change the business structure, it had a significant impact on IT, while the year 2000 issue was also a key element. We had to do something to make the systems compliant, more effective, and to achieve a lower cost of ownership.'

The change involves moving to the AS/400 platform with E 640 machines installed in the UK and Germany and an E 620 in France. Apart from the central servers, 24 9402-model AS/400s will be installed in each warehouse across Germany to deal with the demands of BCI's wholesale business.

'When our French subsidiary suggested Intentia as a supplier, I was sceptical', admits Ellis. 'I felt it was fine for France, but had doubts about rolling the Movex suite across the rest of Europe. But we talked with Intentia, which has a high profile outside the UK, and decided to undertake a two-month review.

The more I looked at the company, the more I liked it', he adds.

Ellis acknowledges that choosing an ERP supplier isn't easy, especially as functionality is broadly similar across all suppliers. So what convinced him to take the Intentia route and install a raft of AS/400s?

'We were more concerned about getting the right product than focusing on a single platform. The only technical requirement was the ability to run under NT, now or in the near future', says Ellis.

'In talks with Intentia, Baan and JD Edwards, we concluded that all three had very good products, but Intentia had the edge. It is big enough to engender confidence, but small enough to develop a close working relationship', Ellis says.

Intentia took the initiative, according to Ellis. 'The other companies would have done the same things, but I would have had to get them to do it. For example, we said we wanted this to be a pan-European project, so each of Intentia's managing directors attended our discussion meetings.

'They all demonstrated top-level commitment to the pan-European aspect from the start. Bjorn Algkvist – Intentia's founder and chief executive – also took a personal interest in the deal and attended many meetings.'

Ellis says Intentia's track record of long-term client relationships and its accessible chief executive helped during contract negotiation.

'We got lots of detail into the contract and found that Intentia was very flexible', he adds.

Intentia UK managing director Mike Nutter stresses that Intentia's contracts often run for '15 years or more'.

'Unlike many of our competitors, we don't have several partners per country or region. We focus on building a one-partner relationship per country, rather than working with a host of consultants and integrators', says Nutter.

'Our business strategy is to invest in research and development, rather than high-profile marketing, and most of our business comes through recommendation. It's a different business model, but we now have over 4000 sites worldwide.'

Intentia's commitment to the project and the fact that it is undertaking all implementation and modification were other key factors in BCI's decision, says Ellis.

'They're not bringing in consultants or third-party integrators, and they're working directly with our project managers,' he adds.

BCI's French and German subsidiaries are installing Movex modules – logistics, production, finance, marketing, sales and personnel administration – and Intentia is customising the system for the German wholesale business.

The UK is installing everything except the sales module, preferring to keep its in-house sales system. Intentia will handle all system modifications, providing extra function for Potterton Myson's spares and services business.

Nutter makes no bones about the nature of an ERP installation: 'Customer resource is a real issue with ERP and when we put in one hour's work, we expect three or four hours' work from the customer. They must be committed, and that must come from the top. It's the customer's project, not ours.'

Costing ERP projects is always a thorny issue, and Ellis says that there was some hard negotiating by both parties. Nutter advocates target pricing rather than fixed pricing, arguing that benefits and penalties should be shared between the vendor and customer.

In BCI's case, Ellis explains that target pricing means that 'payment schedules are dependent on how well the product performs. We have agreed a pricing structure for the overall purchase and mandatory modifications in Germany, but local modifications and issues like training will be negotiated in situ.'

The sheer diversity of IT across BCI is a reflection of growth by acquisition. Until recently, BCI companies were autonomous units servicing their own markets.

The three national subsidiaries intend to collaborate much more closely, targeting the wider European market. To do this effectively, all subsidiaries must access each other's product lead times and schedules to create improved information flows for business efficiency and manufacturing.

The chief executive of the heating division, Frank McKay, was brought in to improve performance levels of the company. He says that a central theme of the restructuring programme is to 'secure superior cost, quality and service levels through greater integration of the companies'.

McKay adds: 'It is essential to meet European and global competition, and the creation of a single IT infrastructure is vital to support this integrated business approach.'

ERP systems are somewhat notorious for running late, and consultants stress that time spent detailing the project and defining its objectives in advance can save money further down the line.

Ellis says that the review and decision periods were not easy: 'We had the thankless and challenging task of building consensus across three countries. We spent a lot of time in discussion and arguments, which delayed us for about four or five months.

'What didn't help was that Intentia's competitors realised they probably weren't going to get the contract and attempted to spoil the deal, which created more debate.

'It's the first time BCI has undertaken a multinational project like this, and it was a complicated negotiating process, both internally and with Intentia and IBM.'

The review-to-decision process ran from May to October. 'Most of this was internal soul-searching characterised by robust debates and negotiations', comments Ellis.

The French subsidiary kicked off implementation in November 1997. The UK and Germany subsidiaries aimed for a January 1998 start.

'It was a bad month to start', says Ellis, 'because of year-end issues, and realistically it was February before we were very focused. It's still early days. Part of the system will be complete by the end of 1998, and the implementation should be finished by May 1999 at the latest, which allows us some time for slippage.'

BCI has established a pan-European steering group which will monitor and review the project. Ellis says: 'We have three levels of management and plan to build in a fourth. Apart from the steering group, each country has a full-time project manager, along with a part-time manager from Intentia. The monthly steering group meetings are attended by the main players from each company, including the managing and financial directors.

'We have local business co-ordinators with IBM and Intentia, so that if any issues need urgent attention, I can call the nominated contacts directly.

'The top-level management committee is not in place yet, but we plan to have senior review meetings every four months, attended by myself, our financial director and chief executive, and Intentia's chief executive. Hopefully, it will be no more than a rubber-stamp committee, but the point is that it's staffed by real heavyweights.'

Ellis says that he's hugely impressed by Intentia's software and its commitment to BCI's business. He would be 'very surprised' if the system were to fall down, but it's a business project and BCI has 'contractual clauses defining actions and responsibilities', Ellis adds.

The next phase in BCI's restructuring involves developing a wider communications strategy. Ellis says: 'We don't have dedicated lines between countries, but the UK has an extensive network built on our other business interests.

'We might look at using the Internet, but we're not ready to get into phase two yet, and we need to consider many issues before making any moves on the communications front', adds Ellis.

ERP vendors have a poor reputation for delivering all their promises, but Ellis is pretty confident that Intentia software will deliver significant business benefits for BCI. He does, however, have one reservation: 'I wish Intentia would do more to get its name known in the UK'.

Source: Computing, 16 April 1998

Questions

1 Into which category of acquisition does Blue Circle fit?

2 Why did Blue Circle choose the Intentia solution rather than one of the better-known solutions?

3 What best practices can you identify for successful acquisition and implementation?

4 Can you identify any problems with this approach? Which source for the system would you have chosen if supplied with this information?

Summary

Stage summary: initiation

Purpose:	Determine viability of systems and technique used to acquire it
Key activities:	Feasibility study
Input:	Idea for new system or problem with existing system
Output:	Feasibility study, recommendation to proceed

The case study on Blue Circle illustrates the type of feasibility assessment that can occur when political factors are also considered during feasibility analysis. Other key points are:

1 The initiation phase is the first stage of the system development lifecycle.

2 The initiation phase is generally considered to consist of two main activities: the generation of the idea for a new system and assessing the feasibility of introducing a new system. Feasibility assessment should occur for all projects, whatever the acquisition method.

3 Feasibility assessment will involve comparing different alternatives in terms of their:

● *economic feasibility* – the cost–benefit analysis;
● *technical feasibility* – evaluation of the merits of different alternatives in terms of practicality;
● *operational feasibility* – will the system meet the needs of the business and end-users?
● *organisational feasibility* – do the staff have the skills to use the system and how will their attitudes affect the acceptance of the system?

4 There is a range of financial measures for assessing the financial viability of a new system. These should take into account the time-varying nature of costs and benefits by using discounted cashflow techniques. Non-financial measures should not be neglected.

5 A contract for the supply of the system should be negotiated at the outset; this minimises the risk of project failure and provides adequate support for when the system becomes operational.

EXERCISES

Self-assessment exercises

1 What is the purpose of the initiation phase of a project?

2 What is meant by the terms 'intangible' and 'tangible benefit'?

3 Identify each of the following as tangible or intangible benefits or costs:

   (a) purchase of a server for data storage with a new information system;
   (b) reduced waiting time for customers when querying the progress of an order;
   (c) disruption caused by installation of a new company network;
   (d) reduced inventory holding period resulting from a new stock management system.

4 Summarise the differences between economic, operational, technical and organisational feasibility.

5 What do you understand by the term 'risk assessment' and how can it be applied to assist an information systems development project?

6 What is the purpose and outline contents of a 'request for proposal' or 'invitation to tender' document?

7 What are the key factors that a company will consider when choosing software from different suppliers?

8 What are the main items that should be specified in an information systems contract?

Discussion questions

1 To what extent is the failure of many information system projects a consequence of too little time being spent on the initiation stage?

2 'The techniques that are available for comparing different software packages or systems from different suppliers must be applied rigorously.' Discuss.

Essay questions

1 Examine the main consequences for an information systems project if the initiation stage is omitted.

2 A company is intending to purchase accounting software for 100 staff and is considering three different packages. It is currently using a Microsoft Windows 3.1-based application, but wants to move to using a Microsoft Windows NT-based application. Give a full account of the factors it should consider when making the comparison. Which do you consider are the most important factors?

3 Risk assessment is a valuable tool for the project manager. What does this technique involve and which future risks might be identified at different stages in a systems development project?

4 Write a short feasibility or initiation report for a new e-commerce site or an enhancement to an existing site incorporating the elements of initiation referred to in this chapter. It can refer to a fictitious company, a small company you are familiar with, or a larger company whose sites you can visit.

   Your answer should not be limited to exploring economic, operational, organisational and technical feasibility, but should include all the aspects of initiation planning covered in this chapter.

Examination questions

1 What is the purpose of establishing the following types of feasibility:

   (a) operational;
   (b) organisational;

    (c) technical;

    (d) economic.

2 Give three reasons for a company's initiating an information systems project. Give a brief example of each.

3 Define information systems outsourcing.

4 Give examples of two tangible costs and two intangible costs that may be incurred during an information systems development project.

5 What are the most important factors you would consider when comparing alternative software packages?

References

Boehm, B. (1991) 'Software risk management: principles and practices', *IEEE Software*, 8, 1, January, 32–41

Parker, M. and Benson, R. (1988) *Information Economics: Linking Business Performance to Information Technology*, Prentice-Hall, Englewood Cliffs, NJ

PricewaterhouseCoopers (2001) *Global Data Management Survey 2001*, PricewaterhouseCoopers, New York. Available online at www.pwcglobal.com

Radosevich, L. (1999) 'Measuring up – project management successfully', *CIO Magazine*, 15 September. Available in archive at www.cio.com

Reicheld, F. and Schefter, P. (2000) 'E-loyalty: your secret weapon on the Web', *Harvard Business Review*, July–August 2000, 105–13

Remenyi, D. (1995) *The Effective Measurement and Management of IT Costs and Benefits*, Butterworth–Heinemann, Oxford

Robson, W. (1997) *Strategic Management and Information Systems: an Integrated Approach*, Financial Times Pitman Publishing, London

Senn, J. (1995) *Information Technology in Business Principles, Practices and Opportunities*, Prentice-Hall, Englewood Cliffs, NJ

Ward, J. and Griffiths, P.M. (1996) *Strategic Planning for Information Systems*, John Wiley, Chichester

Further reading

Radosevich, L. (1999) 'Measuring up – project management successfully', *CIO Magazine*, 15 September. Available in archive at www.cio.com. An accessible introduction to factors influencing project metrics that need to be considered during the initiation of a project

Sandison, H. (1992) 'Introduction to software development contracts', in D. Allen and K. Davis, (eds) *Allen and Davis on Computer Contracting: a User's Guide with Forms and Strategies*, Prentice Hall, London

Web links

www.cio.com CIO.com for chief information officers and IS staff has many articles related to analysis and design topics in different research centres such as security (www.cio.com/research/security), CRM (www.cio.com/research/crm/) and infrastructure (www.cio.com/research/infrastructure).

www.360.com *Computer Weekly* is a weekly IS professionals' trade paper with UK/Europe focus has many case studies on practical problems of analysis, design and implementation.

www.eds.com/case_studies/cs_home.shtml Case studies from major BIS consultant EDS illustrate many of the issues of systems analysis, design and implementation.

www.research.ibm.com/journal *IBM Systems Journal* and the *Journal of Research and Development* have many cases and articles on analysis and design related to e-business concepts such as knowledge management, security.

www.intranetjournal.com/itadvisor Intranet journal has case studies on systems analysis and design specific to intranets.

www.fdic.gov/regulations/information/index.html FDIC: The Federal Financial Institutions Examination Council (FFIEC) handbook for conducting examinations of banks' and savings associations' information systems is interesting since it recommends appropriate approaches and activities to different stages of building banking systems which also apply to other systems.

knowledge.wharton.upenn.edu/category.cfm?catid=14 Managing Technology at Wharton articles cover a range of technology management issues including evaluation of feasibility and return on investment.

BIS project management

LEARNING OBJECTIVES

After reading this chapter, readers will be able to:

● understand the main elements of the project management approach;

● relate the concept of project management to the creation of BIS;

● assess the significance of the different tasks of the project manager;

● outline different techniques for project management.

MANAGEMENT ISSUES

Managers need to ensure that their BIS projects will be completed satisfactorily, whether they are directly responsible, or if the project management is delegated to another person in the organisation, or an external contractor. From a managerial perspective, this chapter addresses the following questions:

● What are the success criteria for a BIS project?

● What are the attributes of a successful project manager?

● Which project management activities and techniques should be performed by the project manager for a successful outcome?

Links to other chapters

The preparation of a preliminary project plan will occur during the initiation phase of a systems development project which was described in Chapter 8. After the project has been given the go-ahead, a more detailed project plan will be generated using the techniques described in this chapter. The project plan will specify the activities and the resources needed to complete the subsequent stages of the project lifecycle. These are analysis (Chapter 10), design (Chapter 11) and build and implementation (Chapter 12).

Introduction

Projects are unique, one-time operations designed to accomplish a specific set of objectives in a limited timeframe. Examples of projects include a building construction or introducing a new service or product to the market. In this chapter we focus on providing the technical knowledge that is necessary to manage information systems projects. Large information systems projects like construction projects may consist of many activities and must therefore be carefully planned and coordinated if a project is to meet cost, time and quality targets. The quality target is to implement the desired features with as few errors as possible.

Successful project management for information systems is very difficult to achieve. A recent extensive study reported by Bicknell (1998) has confirmed the parlous state of systems development projects. The US consultancy group Standish has analysed 23 000 projects of a range of sizes completed in 1997 and 1998 and found that:

- 28 per cent failed to complete;
- 46 per cent were 'challenged' by cost and/or time overruns;
- 26 per cent were completed within the constraints of cost/time and delivering and anticipated benefits.

More recently, a survey conducted between November 2000 and January 2001 of 599 Chief Information Officers in 'Top 500' companies in the UK, USA and Australia showed that there are still significant challenges when information systems projects are implemented (PricewaterhouseCoopers, 2001). A third of companies had experienced a delay or scrapping of new information systems. This clearly indicates a serious problem that shows the difficulty in IS project management and the need for effective project managers.

The three key objectives of project management are shown in Figure 9.1. The job of project managers is difficult since they are under pressure to increase the quality of the information system within the constraints of fixed costs, budget and resources. Often it

Projects
Projects are unique, one-time operations designed to accomplish a specific set of objectives in a limited timeframe.

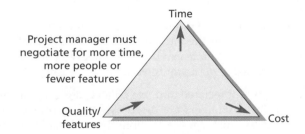

Figure 9.1 **Three key elements of project management**

is necessary to make a compromise between the features that are implemented and the time and resources available – if the business user wants a particular new feature, then the cost and duration will increase or other features will have to be omitted.

While it is difficult to control and plan all aspects of a BIS development project, the chance of success can be increased by anticipating potential problems and by applying corrective strategies. The PRINCE methodology is reviewed since it is used to assist in the delivery of BIS projects to time, cost and quality objectives. Network analysis techniques are also reviewed in this chapter, since they can be used to assist project planning and control activities by enabling the effects of project changes to be analysed.

The project management process

When undertaking a BIS project, the project manager will be held responsible for delivery of the project to the traditional objectives of time, cost and quality. Many BIS have the attributes of a large-scale project in that they consume a relatively large amount of resources, take a long time to complete and involve interactions between different parts of the organisation. To manage a project of this size and complexity requires a good overview of the status of the project in order to keep track of progress and anticipate problems. The use of a structured project management process can greatly improve the performance of IS projects, which have become well known for their tendency to run over budget or be late (Bicknell, 1996; Kaye, 1997; Mouler, 1996; Warren, 1996).

▶ Context: where in the SDLC does project planning occur?

Project managers need to control projects, and to achieve this they tend to use frameworks based on previous projects they have managed. The systems development lifecycle (SDLC) or waterfall model introduced in Chapter 7 provides such a framework. The majority of project plans will divide the project plan according to the SDLC phases.

An *initial project plan* will usually be developed at the initiation phase (Chapter 8). This will normally be a high-level analysis that does not involve the detailed identification of the tasks that need to occur as part of the project. It may produce estimates for the number of weeks involved in each phase, such as analysis and design, and for the modules of the system, such as data-entry and reporting modules. If the project receives the go-ahead, a more *detailed project plan* will be produced before or as the project starts. This will involve a much more detailed identification of all the tasks that need to occur. These will usually be measured to the nearest day or hour and can be used as the basis for controlling and managing the project. The detailed project plan will not be produced until after the project has commenced, for two reasons:

1 It is not practical to assess the detailed project plan until the project starts, since the cost of producing a detailed project plan may be too high for it to be discarded if the project is unfeasible.
2 A detailed project plan cannot be produced until the analysis phase has started, since estimates are usually based on the amount of work needed at the design and build phases of the project. This estimate can only be produced *once the requirements for the system have been established at the analysis phase*.

These points are often not appreciated and, we believe, are a significant reason for the failure of projects. Project managers are often asked to produce an estimate of the amount of time required to finish a project before the analysis phase, when insufficient information is at their disposal. Their answer should be:

I can give you an initial estimate and project plan based on similar projects of this scale at the initiation phase. I cannot give you a detailed, accurate project plan until the analysis is complete and the needs of the users and the business have been assessed. A detailed estimate can then be produced according to the amount of time it is likely to take to implement the users' requirements.

Case Study 9.1 illustrates the importance of project management throughout the SDLC. It also highlights the diversity of issues that must be managed, including business, technical, human, organisational and political issues.

CASE STUDY 9.1

Project management issues for an e-business portal

In the new information economy, every organisation has different information needs as it seeks to outperform its competitors. Within each organisation, every user also has different needs for information. Their needs also rapidly change over time as the business environment evolves.

Finally, the information they need to access is held in a wide variety of different sources. This means that implementation is an essential ingredient of any portal project and the concept of a so-called portal in a box an impossible dream confined to marketing departments.

However, implementation of portals is a new and inexact science that is closely related to implementation of management information, decision support and data warehouse systems, whose histories are littered with failures.

As with management information systems, portal projects lend themselves very well to prototyping. This involves a limited number of users being given limited functionality and access to limited information in a live system. As they use this to help with everyday tasks, their feedback is used to extend gradually the functionality, information and user base.

'The main challenge is to quickly identify a clear set of benefits that supports the business objectives and use them to drive implementation', advises Frank Wolfsteiner, a senior manager at Deloitte Consulting, a management consultancy. 'Projects must not lose sight of them and get carried away by the technology. We find that technology is often driving solutions, not benefits realisation.'

The user interface is generally provided by the IT department, because of its skills in interface building, information connectivity and integration of services. However, it often lacks the business skills to identify both the critical business needs and the implementation barriers.

'You cannot underestimate the business issues', advises Kathleen Hall, senior industry analyst at Giga Information Group, the analyst. 'There are many political issues in giving users access to information.'

The IT department might provide a basic portal and give users access to tools that enable them to customise their own screens and add new information. In practice, it is frequently left to so-called power users and business analysts to create an effective portal.

'You need somebody who is knowledgeable about the business and the type of information available', says David Parlby, lead partner for workforce solutions at KPMG Consulting, the management consultancy. 'They must be good with technology, but not at the plumbing level. They need to be able to gain access to information, format it and manipulate it to meet their own needs. They can do the same for those managers who don't have the time or the appetite to delve into it themselves.'

Even if the correct portal application is designed, there are still considerable technical issues to be addressed in accessing the necessary data. These include both the quality of the data and definition of the information.

'Some people think that if they implement a portal they have all the information, but it is a presentation tool and doesn't generate information or make processes any better', says Mr Wolfsteiner.

'You can implement the front end fairly easily and display more information, but it is an enormous effort to provide that information. The major implementation challenge is the quality, accessibility and reliability of information in back end systems and processes. There is a lot of work to do and this is often underestimated.'

Even if the data is cleaned and made accessible, different departments and their systems have different definitions of data. Users may not be aware that terms such as sales and week in other systems may have different definitions to their own.

Cultural issues are also important in a successful implementation. 'Using a portal requires a change in

▶

mindset', says Mr Parlby. 'The organisation must encourage people to use the portal as their first port of call. [Portals] give a much greater range in terms of applications and information that can be accessed, but users must not be allowed to short circuit the system or delegate using it to their secretary.'

He points out that with portals, success depends on achieving a significant degree of user adoption. He advises using software to track who is using what functionality. Identifying uses that are popular helps with forward planning of new functionality.

Conversely, low usage of important functionality should generate initiatives to increase user adoption. Another aspect to be considered is remote and offline access, enabling portals to remain productive while users are travelling.

Users will want to be able to access the same services remotely and may want key information to be available offline. With always on mobile access now becoming available, however, offline use may become much less of an issue.

Implementing a portal is a major challenge if it is to be successful. As Mr Wolfsteiner points out, a portal does not create information, it just tailors it better and gets it to the right person.

Getting access to that information requires work on improving data quality and definitions and improving back-end systems and processes. It needs business understanding of the organisation's strategy and objectives, together with the skills to convert this into an application.

Most of all, it needs an understanding of the cultural and political barriers to be overcome. 'Portals can enable organisations to be more productive by ensuring that employees access and use the right information most efficiently, but technology cannot do it alone', warns Gytis Barzdukas, global product manager for portals at Microsoft.

'Even the best technology is not a cure all and the human element cannot be understated.'

Source: Rod Newing, 'Implementation – how the human factor affects portals implementation', FTIT specials.ft.com/ftit/may2001/FT373UTC6MC.html, 1 May 2001

Question

The article states '*implementation of management information, decision support and data warehouse systems … are littered with failures*'. Review the article and list the different actions it suggests that a project manager could take to avoid project failure. Thinking back to Chapter 7 on systems acquisition, relate each action to a particular stage of the systems development lifecycle.

❱ Why do projects fail?

Lytinen and Hirscheim (1987) researched the reasons for information systems projects failing. They identified five broad areas which still hold true today:

- *Technical failure* stemming from poor technical quality – this is the responsibility of the organisation's IS function.
- *Data failure* due to (a) poor data design, processing errors and poor data management; and (b) poor user procedures and poor data quality control at the input stage. Responsibility for the former lies with the IS function, while that for the latter lies with the end-users themselves.
- *User failure* to use the system to its maximum capability – may be due to an unwillingness to train staff or user management failure to allow their staff full involvement in the systems development process.
- *Organisational failure*, where an individual system may work in its own right but fails to meet organisational needs as a whole (e.g. while a system might offer satisfactory operational information, it fails to provide usable management information). This results from senior management's a failure to align IS to overall organisational needs.
- *Failure in the business environment*. This can stem from systems that are inappropriate to the market environment, failure in IS not being adaptable to a changing business environment (often rapid change occurs), or a system not coping with the volume and speed of the underlying business transactions.

It is apparent that a diverse range of problems can cause projects to fail, ranging from technical problems to people management problems.

It is the responsibility of the project manager to ensure that these types of problems do not occur, by anticipating them and then taking the necessary actions to resolve them. This will involve risk management techniques, described in Chapter 8. Case Study 9.2 shows the type of problems that occur, the reasons behind them and the attributes the project manager must possess to be able to manage projects successfully.

CASE STUDY 9.2

Falling at the final hurdle

IT projects continue to run over time and over budget, resulting in systems that do not match business or end-user requirements, or stall before they are finished. The only possible fault one can call common to all failures is inadequate, to a greater or lesser extent, management of those projects. And that in turn means blame must be laid fairly and squarely on the shoulders of the project manager responsible. In mitigation, the design and implementation of IT systems is horrendously complicated, involving a highly complex matrix of technologies and business interdependencies, which are shifting at different rates across several management planes. But that is still no excuse for such failures. The reasons IT projects fail, to whatever extent, remain the same as always: the inability to specify user requirements, manage the number of requested changes, or limit the scope of change as the project progresses. There are many other issues behind failed projects, including in-house politics, deadline-centric cultures and new legislation emerging during the project.

Good project management, however, is about taking account of change up-front, and building in risk management and contingency planning buffers. It is about setting realistic duration and cost estimates, and not being afraid to tell the chief executive that his pet project cannot be finished in the six months he expects, even if being so honest puts your job at risk. Since none of this is rocket science, it begs the question as to why IT projects continue to fail. 'It's because there's too often a lack of an agreed requirements specification', says Dennis Gower, a founding member of the Association of Project Managers. 'At least 50% of the time of the contract should be to find out precisely what users and departments require, it's that important.'

Anne Bentley, a business consultant with project management software house Artemis agrees: 'The actual specification of what's wanted by the department is often not concise or clear, which means costs won't be clear, estimated timescales will be out, and soon the whole thing goes wrong'. In addition, says John Pocock, commercial director at software implementation specialist Druid: 'A lot of the failure is down to the fact that users aren't fully aware of the change that the company has embarked upon on their behalf. Pressure on any project manager to change the scope is fierce, and while there may be formal change management processes in place, he can still get swamped.'

If that all sounds obvious, it is because the people explaining the issues are all project management professionals. Many of those managing end-to-end IT projects, however, are not. Not only that, but the companies they work for have no sense of project management on a corporate basis, spanning all business operations. This state of affairs is changing. With the onset of recession at the start of the decade, corporate minds were focused on monetary constraint and efficiency improvements in existing systems. The number of new projects lessened, and those that were given the go-ahead were, often for the first time, highly scrutinised from a non-IT perspective.

Focus was sharpened on professional project management skills, regardless of whether they came from outside the organisation through consultants, or through in-house training and development programmes. During the past three years, institutes and groups, such as the Association of Project Managers, have emerged. 'The use of project management hasn't been good in the past', admits James Baker, responsible for setting up the BCS's project management group. 'But in the past five years there's been a dramatic upturn in training, qualifications and attention to project control, and its role in organisations as a whole.'

Unfortunately, this trend has taken 30 years to arrive, with relatively recent disasters such as those at the Stock Exchange, the London Ambulance Service and British Gas still fresh in the mind. One of the key reasons for this, believes Baker, has been the huge divide between users and IT shops, the latter delivering what they thought the user required, and users naively expecting systems the IT department could not deliver. 'With IT systems now very much a business issue', adds Baker, 'those gaps may be closing, but there remain crucial issues regarding managing projects. There's an argument that technology always

▶

has a solution to technology problems, but you can't necessarily find solutions to people problems, the management of which accounts for perhaps 80% of successfully managed projects.'

If the right people are involved, the chances of success increase exponentially. But what constitutes an ideal project manager is debatable. To some, it is a combination of having a listening ear with the ability to rule with a rod of steel, while having the requisite project management skills. For others, such as long-time project manager Ervin Munir, now projects director with AMS, there is much emphasis on imperturbability. 'In some firms personal success is based on meeting dates, and if slippages are perceived, it leads to situations where the project manager is unwilling to tell the truth.' Munir relates an instance in his career, which has featured Currys, Dixons and Burger King, when he was given six months to complete a project which his own analysis showed would take a year. 'I had to decide whether to keep quiet or tell the truth', he recalls. 'In the end I stuck to my guns, and the users were pleased with the final result. And that's what all project managers should be able to do.'

For Neil McEvoy, a director at consultancy Hyperion, a key attribute is the ability to manage expectations and balance resources and skills against those expectations. 'When things go wrong because business requirements change, that's when the real skill of project managers come in.' With more project management courses and certification schemes, the prospect of an improved UK base of skilled professionals seems certain. 'Certification', says McEvoy, 'can arm people with a basic toolkit. But most problems are about managing relationships, so all the training in the world will be of little use if the project manager has no instinctive feel for people.'

And there is more, adds Druid's Pocock: 'Project managers need to be methodical, but also intuitive and able to understand real issues. It's an art and a skill.' But UK organisations have shown historically that they are not particularly adept at mixing those attributes. At least with a growing body of professional project managers to call on, the prospects for doing so successfully are enhanced.

Source: Courtesy of *Computer Weekly*, 8 May 1997

Questions

1 What reasons does the case study indicate are responsible for project failure?

2 What steps can be taken to reduce the risk of project failure?

3 What does the experienced project manager Ervin Munir suggest that project managers should do when faced with unrealistic deadlines? What skills and attributes should the project manager possess according to Neil McEvoy?

▌ Project organisation

In order that a project is clearly defined and meets its objectives it is important to define the roles of the staff involved and how those roles are organised within a particular project. The principal roles encountered in a project are outlined below. Note that these roles may be known by other names or be undertaken by more than one person or roles may be combined and allocated to a single person, depending on the organisational context and the size of the project.

Project sponsor

The project sponsor role is to provide a justification of the project to senior management. The role includes defining project objectives and time, cost and quality performance measures. The role also involves obtaining finance and appointing a project manager. The project sponsor is accountable for the success or failure of the project in meeting its *business* objectives.

Project manager

Appointed by the project sponsor the project manager role is to provide day-to-day management and ensure *project* objectives are met. This involves selection and management of the project team, monitoring of the time, cost and quality performance measures and informing the project sponsor and senior management of progress. In larger projects the project manager may delegate certain areas of the project (e.g. programming) to team leaders for day-to-day management.

Project user

The project user is the person or group of people who will be utilising the outcome of the information systems project. The user(s) should be involved in the definition and implementation of the system to ensure successful ongoing usage.

Other major roles that may be defined in the project include the following.

Quality manager

This role involves defining a plan containing procedures that ensure quality targets are met. Quality can be defined as 'conformance to customer requirements'. Total quality management (TQM) attempts to establish a culture that supports quality. The European Foundation for Quality Management (EFQM) has provided a model that allows an organisation to quantify its progress towards a total quality business. For more information on quality management in relation to IS projects see Cadle and Yeates (2001).

Risk manager

All projects contain some risk that the investment made will not achieve the required business obejctives. Risk management has become increasingly important in providing processes that attempt to reduce risk in complex and uncertain projects (see Chapter 8 for more details on risk management).

In many situations the project is organised by the main roles of project sponsor, project manager and project user. However, in complex or larger projects other organisational bodies may be encountered. A *steering committee* brings together a variety of interested people such as users, functional staff (e.g. finance, purchasing) and project managers in order that all stakeholder views are taken into consideration. At a lower level *user groups* may be instituted to represent the views of multiple potential users.

Steps in project management

Before the planning process can commence, the project manager will need to determine not only the business aims of the project but also the constraints under which they must be achieved. Major constraints include the overall budget for project development, the timescale for project completion, staffing availability, and hardware and software requirements for system development and running of the live system. These questions form the framework for the project and it is important that they be addressed at the beginning of the project planning process. It is usual, however, to only prepare detailed plans of the early stages of the project at this point.

The project management process includes the following main elements:

- estimate;
- schedule/plan;
- monitoring and control;
- documentation.

◗ Estimation

The first task in project management is to identify the activities involved in the project. **Estimation** allows the project manager to plan for the resources required for project execution through establishing the number and size of tasks that need to be completed in the project. This is achieved by breaking down the project repeatedly into smaller tasks until a manageable chunk of one to two days' work is defined. Each task is given its own cost, time and quality objectives. It is then essential that responsibility be assigned to achieving these objectives for each particular task. This procedure should produce a **work breakdown structure (WBS)** that shows the hierarchical relationship between the project tasks. It is an important part of estimation. Figure 9.2 shows how the work on producing a new accounting system might be broken down into different tasks. Work on systems projects is usually broken down according to the different modules of the system. In this example, three levels of the WBS are shown for the accounts receivable module down to its printing function. All the other five modules of the system would also have similar tasks.

At the start of the project in the initiation or startup phase, an overview project plan is drawn up estimating the resources required to carry out the project. It is then possible to compare overall project requirements with available resources.

Projects can be **resource-constrained** (limited by the type of people or hardware resources available) or **time-constrained** (limited by the deadline).

The next step, after the project has been given the go-ahead, is a more detailed estimate of the resources needed to undertake the tasks identified in the work breakdown structure. If highly specialised resources are required (e.g. skilled analysts), then the project completion date may have to be set to ensure that these resources are not overloaded. This is a resource-constrained approach. Alternatively, there may be a need to complete a project in a specific timeframe (e.g. due date specified by customer). In this case, alternative resources (e.g. subcontractors) may have to be utilised to ensure timely project completion. This is a time-constrained approach. This information can then be used to plan what resources are required and what activities should be undertaken over the lifecycle of the project.

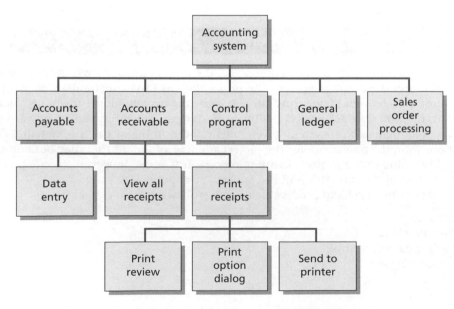

Figure 9.2 **Work breakdown structure (WBS) for an accounting system**

Effort time and elapsed time

When estimating the amount of time a task will take, it is important to distinguish between two different types of time that need to be estimated. **Effort time** is the total amount of work that needs to occur to complete a task. The **elapsed time** indicates how long in time (such as calendar days) the task will take (duration). Estimating starts by considering the amount of effort time that needs to be put in to complete each task. Effort time is then converted into elapsed time, which indicates how long the task will take through real-time measures such as months or days. Effort time does not usually equal elapsed time, since if a task has more than one worker the elapsed time will take less time than the effort time. Conversely, if workers on a task are also working on other projects, then they will not be available all the time and the elapsed time will be longer than the effort time. An additional factor is that different workers may have different speeds. A productive worker will need less elapsed time than an inexperienced worker. These constraints on elapsed time can be formalised in a simple equation:

$$Elapsed\ time = Effort\ time \times \frac{100}{Availability\ \%} \times \frac{100}{Work\ rate\ \%}$$

The equation indicates that if the availability or work rate of a worker is less than 100 per cent, the elapsed time will increase proportionally, since availability and work rate are the denominators on the right-hand side of the equation. The equation will need to be applied for each worker, who may have different availabilities and work rates. These factors can be entered into a project management package, but to understand the principles of estimation better the activity on project planning should be attempted (see p. 357).

From the example in the activity, it can be seen that several stages are involved in estimation:

1 Estimate effort time for average person to undertake task.
2 Estimate different work rates and availability of staff.
3 Allocate resources (staff) to task.
4 Calculate elapsed time based on number of staff, availability and work rate.
5 Schedule task in relation to other tasks.

Yeates (1991) provides the following techniques for estimating the human resource and capacity requirements for the different stages of an IS project:

1 *Estimating the feasibility study*. This stage will not usually be estimated in detail, since it will occur at the same time as or before a detailed project estimate is produced. The feasibility stage consists of tasks such as interviewing, writing up interview information and report writing in order to assess the financial, technical and organisational acceptability of the project. The estimate will depend greatly on the nature of the project, but also on the skills and experience of the staff involved. Thus it is important to keep records of previous performance of personnel for this activity in order to improve the accuracy of future estimates.

2 *Estimating analysis and design phases*. The analysis phase will typically involve collection of information about the operation of current systems and the specification of requirements for the new system. This will lead to the functional requirements specification, defining the new system in terms of its business specification. The design phase will specify the new computer-based system in terms of its technical content. This will need to take into account organisational policies on design methodologies and hardware and software platforms. In order to produce an accurate estimate of the analysis and design phases, it is necessary to produce a detailed description of each task involved. As in the feasibility stage, time estimates will be improved if timings are available for previous projects undertaken.

Effort and elapsed time

Effort time is the total amount of work that needs to occur to complete a task. The elapsed time indicates how long in time (such as calendar days) the task will take (duration).

3 *Estimating build and implementation*. This stage covers the time and resources needed for the coding, testing and installation of the application. The time taken to produce a program will depend mainly on the number of coding statements required and the complexity of the program. The complexity of the coding will generally increase with the size of the program and will also differ for the type of application. A lookup table can be derived from experience to give the estimated coding rate dependent on the complexity of the project for a particular development environment. This is discussed in more detail below.

Estimating tools

Statistical methods can be used when a project is large (and therefore complex) or novel. This allows the project team to replace a single estimate of duration with a range within which they are confident the real duration will lie. This is particularly useful for the early stage of the project when uncertainty is greatest. The PERT approach described later in this chapter allows optimistic, pessimistic and most likely times to be specified for each task – from these a probabilistic estimate of project completion time can be computed.

Constructive cost model (COCOMO)

A model used to estimate the amount of effort required to complete a project on the basis of the estimated number of lines of program code.

The most widely used economic model is the **constructive cost model (COCOMO)**, described by Boehm (1981) and first proposed by staff working at US consultancy Doty Associates. The constructive cost model is used to estimate the amount of effort required to complete a project on the basis of the estimated number of lines of program code. Based on an analysis of software projects, the model attempts to predict the effort required to deliver a project based on input factors such as the skill level of staff. A simplified version of the model is:

$$WM = C \times (KDSI)^K \times EAF$$

where: WM = number of person months,
C = one of three constant values dependent on development mode,
$KDSI$ = delivered source lines of code $\times$ 1000,
K = one of three constant values dependent on development mode,
EAF = effort adjustment factor.

The three development modes or project types are categorised as organic (small development teams working in a familiar environment), embedded (where constraints are made by existing hardware or software) and semi-detached, which lies somewhere between the two extremes of organic and embedded. In order to increase the accuracy of the model, more detailed versions of COCOMO incorporate cost drivers such as the attributes of the end product and the project environment. The detailed version of the model calculates the cost drivers for the product design, detailed design, coding and unit test, and integration and test phases separately.

These techniques may take a considerable amount of time to arrive at a reasonably accurate estimate of personnel time required. However, since the build phase will be a major part of the development budget, it is important to allocate time to undertake detailed estimation.

Function point analysis

A method of estimating the time it will take to build a system by counting up the number of functions and data inputs and outputs and then comparing to completed projects.

A problem with COCOMO is that the time estimates it produces are in turn dependent on an estimate of the number of lines of programming code to be written. To counter this problem, a method of estimating the number of lines of code was developed by Alan Albrecht of IBM (Albrecht and Gaffney, 1983). **Function point analysis** is based on counting the number of user functions the application will have. It is possible to do this in detail after the requirements for the application have been defined. The five user function categories are:

1 number of external input types;
2 number of external output types;
3 number of logical internal file types;
4 number of external interface file types;
5 external enquiry types.

Each of these types of input and output are then weighted according to their complexity and additional factors applied according to the complexity of processing. The function point estimate can be compared to the function point count of previous completed information systems to give an idea of the number of lines and code and length of time that are expected.

Note that both the COCOMO and function point analysis techniques were developed before the widespread use of applications with graphical user interfaces, interactive development environments for 'graphical programming', rapid applications development (RAD) and client/server databases to store information. These new techniques have made it faster to develop applications and the original data sets and principles on which these models are based have been updated to account for this.

Activity 9.1

Project planning exercise

The scenario

You are required to construct a project plan for the following BIS development project. Your objective is to schedule the project to run in the shortest time possible. The plan should include all activities, the estimated, elapsed and effort time, and who is to perform each activity. In addition, it is necessary to indicate the sequence in which all the tasks will take place. The programs can be scheduled in any order, but for each program the design stage must come first, followed by the programming and finally the documentation.

Within the context of the exercise, you can assume that the detailed systems analysis has already been carried out and that it is now necessary to perform the design, programming and documentation activities. For the purposes of this exercise, we will not include the testing and implementation phases.

Present your project plan in the form of a Gantt chart (see Figure 9.12) showing each task, the sequence in which tasks will be performed, the estimated effort and elapsed time and the resource allocated to each task.

The activities

There are five programs in the system. Each has a different level of difficulty:

- Program 1   Difficult
- Program 2   Easy
- Program 3   Moderate
- Program 4   Moderate
- Program 5   Difficult

For each level of difficulty, the design, programming and documentation tasks take different amounts of effort time:

Design

- Easy programs   1 day
- Moderate programs   2 days
- Difficult programs   4 days

▶

Programming

- Easy programs   1 day
- Moderate programs   3 days
- Difficult programs   6 days

Documentation

- Easy programs   1 day
- Moderate programs   2 days
- Difficult programs   3 days

Resources

In order to complete the project plan, you need to know what resources you have available. For each resource, there are two variables:

- *Work rate*. This describes the speed at which the resource works (i.e. a work rate of 1.0 means that a task scheduled to take one day should only take one day to complete satisfactorily; a work rate of 1.5 means that a task scheduled for three days should only take two days etc.).
- *Availability*. Each resource will be available for certain amounts of time during the week. 100% availability = 5 days per week, 50% availability = 2.5 days per week, etc.

In planning your project, work to units of half a day. For simplicity, any task which requires a fraction of half a day should be rounded up (e.g. 1.6 days should be rounded up to 2 days). Also, a resource can only be scheduled for one task at any one time!

Resource availability

System Designer 1 (SD1)

- Work rate   1.0
- Availability   100%

Systems Designer 2 (SD2)

- Work rate   1.5
- Availability   40%

Systems Designer 3 (SD3)

- Work rate   0.5
- Availability   50%

Programmer 1 (P1)

- Work rate   2.0
- Availability   40%

Programmer 2 (P2)

- Work rate   1.0
- Availability   100%

Programmer 3 (P3)

- Work rate   0.5
- Availability   60%

Technical Author 1 (TAl) (to do the documentation)
- Work rate   1.0
- Availability   60%

Technical Author 2 (TA2)
- Work rate   0.5
- Availability   100%

Technical Author 3 (TA3)
- Work rate   2.0
- Availability   40%

Tips

1 This exercise will be easier if you structure the information well. You could do this by producing three matrices for the design, programming and documentation tasks. Each of them should show across the columns three different tasks for easy, moderate and difficult programs. Each row should indicate how long the different types of workers will take to complete the task.

2 To calculate the length of elapsed time for each cell in the matrix, it is easiest to use this relationship:

$$Elapsed\ time = Effort\ time \times \frac{100}{Availability\ \%} \times \frac{100}{Work\ rate\ \%}$$

3 A calculator may help!

4 When drawing the Gantt chart, you may want to put your best people on the most difficult tasks, as you would on a real project.

▶ Scheduling and planning

Scheduling is determining when project activities should be executed. The finished schedule is termed the *project plan*.

Resource allocation is part of scheduling. It involves assigning resources to each task. Once the activities have been identified and their resource requirements estimated, it is necessary to define their relationship to one another. There are some activities that can only begin when other activities have been completed. This is termed a *serial relationship* and is shown graphically in Figure 9.3.

The execution of other activities may be totally independent and thus they have a *parallel relationship*, as shown graphically in Figure 9.4. Here, after the design phase, three activities must occur in parallel before implementation can occur.

For most significant projects there will be a range of alternative schedules which may meet the project objectives.

Scheduling
Scheduling involves determining when project activities should be executed. The finished schedule is termed the project plan.

Resource allocation
This activity involves assigning a resource to each task.

Figure 9.3 Serial relationship of activities

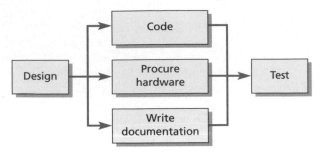

Figure 9.4 Parallel relationship of activities

▶ Software for project management

For commercial projects, computer software will be used to assist in diagramming the relationship between activities and calculating network durations. From a critical path network and with the appropriate information, it is usually possible for the software automatically to generate Gantt charts, resource loading graphs and cost graphs, which are discussed later in the chapter.

Project management software, such as Microsoft Project, CA SuperProject and Hoskyns Project Manager Workbench, can be used to assist in choosing the most feasible schedule by recalculating resource requirements and timings for each operation. The network analysis section of this chapter provides more information on project scheduling techniques.

A screen display for a Microsoft Project network chart is shown in Figure 9.5. This illustrates sequential activities such as from the START to activity A and parallel activities such as C, D and E which occur simultaneously. Note that activity A is on the critical path, since this is the activity that takes the longest time to complete. The critical path is shown by the bold lines for the arrows and dependencies.

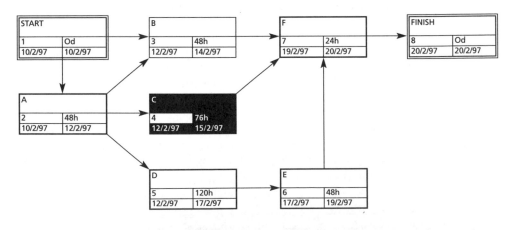

Figure 9.5 Network chart generated by Microsoft Project

❱ Monitoring and control

When a project is under way, its objectives of cost, time and quality in meeting targets must be closely **monitored**. Monitoring involves ensuring that the project is working to plan once it has started. This should occur daily for small-scale tasks or weekly for combined activities. **Control** or corrective action will occur if the performance measures deviate from plan. It is important to monitor and assess performance as the project progresses, in order that corrective action can be taken before it deviates from plan to any great extent. Milestones (events that need to happen on a particular date) are defined so that performance against objectives can be measured (e.g. end of analysis, production of first prototype).

Computer project management packages can be used to automate the collection of project progress data and production of progress reports.

Monitoring and control
....
Monitoring involves ensuring the project is working to plan once it is started. Control is taking corrective action if the project deviates from the plan.

Achieving time, cost and quality objectives

As stated earlier, the project should be managed to achieve the defined objectives of time, cost and quality. The time objective is met by ensuring that the project is monitored in terms of execution of tasks within time limits. Corrective action is taken if a variance between actual and planned time is observed. The cost objective is achieved by the use of human resource and computing resource budgets and, again, variation between estimated and actual expenditure is noted and necessary corrective action taken. To ensure that quality objectives are met it is necessary to develop a quality plan which contains a list of items deliverable to the customer. Each of these will have an associated quality standard and procedure for dealing with a variance from the required quality level defined in the quality plan.

Project structure and size

The type of project structure required will be dependent on the size of the team undertaking the project. Projects with up to six team members can simply report directly to a project leader at appropriate intervals during project execution. For larger projects requiring up to 20 team members, it is usual to implement an additional tier of management in the form of team leaders. The team leader could be responsible for either a phase of the development (e.g. analysis, design) or a type of work (e.g. applications development, systems development). For any structure it is important that the project leader ensures consistency across development phases or development areas as appropriate. For projects with more than 20 members, it is likely that additional management layers will be needed in order to ensure that no one person is involved in too much supervision.

Reporting project progress

The two main methods of reporting the progress of a project are by written reports and verbal reports at meetings of the project team. It is important that a formal statement of progress is made in written form, preferably in a standard report format, to ensure that everyone is aware of the current project situation. This is particularly important when changes to specifications are made during the project. In order to facilitate two-way communication between team members and team management, regular meetings should be arranged by the project manager. These meetings can increase the commitment of team members by allowing discussion of points of interest and dissemination of information on how each team's effort is contributing to the overall progression of the project.

◗ Documentation

Project documentation
....
Documentation is essential to disseminate information during project execution and for reference during software maintenance.

Ensuring adequate **project documentation** is a key aspect of the role of the project manager. Software development is a team effort and documentation is necessary to disseminate design information throughout the team. Good documentation reduces the expense of maintenance after project delivery. Also, when members of the team leave the department or organisation, the coding they have produced must be understandable to new project members. Often a development methodology will require documentation at stages during the project in a specific format. Thus documentation must be an identified task in the development effort and a standard document format should be used throughout the project (this may be a standard such as BS 5750 or ISO 9001).

Documents that may be required include the following:

- *Workplan/task list.* For each team member a specified activity with start and finish dates and relevant coding standard should be defined.
- *Requirements specification.* This should clearly specify the objectives and functions of the software.
- *Purchase requisition forms.* Required if new software and hardware resources are needed from outside the organisation.
- *Manpower budget.* A running total of personnel costs, including expenses and subsistence payments. These should show actual against predicted expenditure for control purposes.
- *Change control documents.* To document any changes to the project specification during the project. A document is needed to highlight the effect on budgets and timescales of a change in software specifications.

F *Focus on* a project management methodology: PRINCE

PRINCE
....
A project management methodology that has been developed to be compatible with the system development methodologies such as SSADM.

PRINCE, which stands for Projects in Controlled Environments, is a project management methodology that has been developed to be compatible with the system development methodologies used in government IT projects, such as SSADM. It has become the standard project management methodology used for the UK government and is also being used increasingly in commercial organisations in the UK. It will be evident that it offers a structure for a project which is only applicable to large projects involving teams of at least 10 people. Many of the in-built quality assurance checks are, however, appropriate to smaller projects.

PRINCE defines four main project aims:

1 to deliver the required end-product(s);
2 to meet the specified quality;
3 to stay within budget;
4 to deliver on schedule.

Thus the PRINCE methodology is built around the idea that a project is required to deliver product(s) within the time, cost and quality constraints imposed. The products are defined not just in the sense of the technical product of the delivered IT system, but including management products such as project plans and quality products such as quality reviews.

The planning process under PRINCE involves defining a list of products required to produce the end-product of the project and defining the sequence in which these products must be produced. From this can be derived the activities required to generate these products in terms of management tasks, technical requirements and quality criteria. In order to ensure that the aims of cost, time and quality are met, PRINCE provides controls that enable the progress of the project management and product management activities to be monitored against plan.

In order to ensure user involvement in the project, PRINCE provides an organisational **structure** and set of job descriptions that define responsibility for activities in a project and ensure a user role in major decisions during the project. The following sections summarise the PRINCE approach to project organisation and the planning and control functions.

PRINCE structure

PRINCE defines an organisational structure and standard set of job descriptors.

▶ Project organisation

PRINCE attempts to ensure user involvement and communication between members of the project by defining an organisational structure and standard set of job descriptions. PRINCE provides a precise definition of the organisational structure and the roles within it. Note that one individual may undertake multiple roles or a single role may be undertaken by several people at different stages of the project.

PRINCE identifies different steering committees to guide the project. These are:

- the *information systems steering committee (ISSC)*, which defines and assesses the feasibility of IS projects;
- the *information technology executive committee (ITEC)*, which is responsible for the implementation of these projects and resource allocation;
- an ITEC-appointed *project board (PB)*, which has the task of managing the implementation of the project. The PB is the top level of management defined within the PRINCE framework and so is defined in more detail in terms of the following roles.

The *senior user* role is to represent the department(s) affected by the project. This involves an understanding of the user issues, human factors and the implementation of change. The *senior technical* role mirrors the user role in that it represents the interests of the IS departments implementing the project. This role requires a knowledge of technical, user and quality issues. The *project manager* role assumes responsibility for the day-to-day management of the project throughout its stages, while *stage managers* who have specialist skills can manage particular stages or work packages. This means that a stage manager need only be associated with a project at a particular time when his or her skills are required. The actual activities of the project and the technical products of each stage are undertaken by stage teams under the supervision of a *team leader*. Finally, the project manager is supported by a *project assurance team* with the following roles:

- *business assurance coordinator* – to monitor progress against financial plan;
- *technical assurance coordinator* – to monitor and report on technical aspects of the project;
- *user assurance coordinator* – to monitor and report on user aspects of the project.

▶ Project plans

The planning structure

There are three levels of plan in PRINCE, each of which consists of a technical plan (detailing which activities are required) and a resource plan (giving which resources are needed). The three levels of plans are:

1 *Project plan.* This shows the main activities within the project, providing an overall schedule and identifying resources needed for project implementation.
2 *Stage plan.* A stage plan is produced at the end of each previous stage in the project. The project board reviews all progress against the plan and takes corrective action as necessary.

3 *Detailed plan*. If a project is already broken down into stages, a detailed plan may not be required. However, for large projects with few stages, a series of detailed plans may be needed.

There are also two additional types of plan to complete the planning structure:

4 *Individual work plan*. This provides the allocation of work of a project. This information is extracted from tasks listed in the stage plan or detailed plan.
5 *Exception plan*. Exception plans enable 'out-of-control' behaviour within a stage plan to be reported to the project board. This is required if the project moves outside tolerance margins set by the project board. The exception plan replaces the stage, detailed and individual work plan for that stage.

The idea of the planning structure is to ensure that control activities can be undertaken at a specific level. The project plan is created during the project initiation stage and provides an overall assessment of the cost, time and resources necessary to undertake the project. The stage, detailed and individual work plans are more detailed and provide a basis for day-to-day control of project activities. If the actions within the exception plan are accepted, then it will replace the stage plan for the remainder of that stage.

The planning process

The traditional method of developing a plan is to list the activities involved and arrange them in a work breakdown structure (WBS). However, the PRINCE approach begins with a list of the products or deliverables that will be produced from the project. Activities will then be described from these products. There are three main products, defined as:

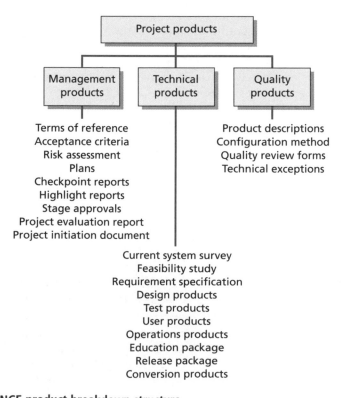

Figure 9.6 **PRINCE product breakdown structure**

1 management products;
2 technical products;
3 quality products.

Figure 9.6 shows how each class of product can be broken down into a number of elements through the product breakdown structure (PBS).

The technical products are defined as follows. We start with the final product to be delivered; this is broken down into the products that are required to produce that final product. These are then broken down further until a list of products required to produce the final product is generated. When this has been completed, the management and quality products can be defined. Management products will include such items as the project terms of reference, project plans and progress reports, while quality products will include the product descriptions and quality plans.

For each identified product, it is then necessary to create a product description which defines the finished product and can provide a guide to the resources needed to create the product. The next step is to develop a technical and a quality strategy for the project. The technical strategy may identify a standard software development methodology (e.g. SSADM) to be used for the project, while the quality strategy will consider the resources and techniques used to ensure that quality is maintained.

Once the technical, management and quality products have been identified for a particular project, a product flow diagram is developed which shows the sequence in which products are required over time (Fig. 9.7). Any products external to the project

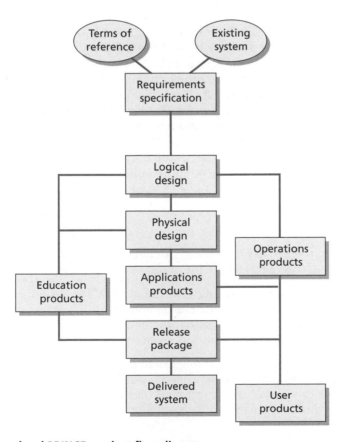

Figure 9.7 **A top-level PRINCE product flow diagram**

are shown in ellipses, while products created by the project are shown in boxes. Management and quality products will need to be examined to see if they should be brought into the flow as well as technical products. Any additional products contained within the product flow need to be added to the product breakdown structure.

Defining the activities

The lines joining the products in the product flow diagram represent the processes or activities that are needed to transform one product into another. Identification of these activities, their duration and dependence on other activities will allow the production of an activity-on-node (AON) network diagram, as described in the network analysis section of this chapter. This permits the identification of the network critical path and slack times for non-critical activities. The activity network also provides the earliest and latest start and finish times for each activity and the total elapsed time for the project.

Defining the plans

The next stage is to produce a bar chart (termed a 'Gantt chart' in network analysis) which allows the incorporation of resource constraints into the network and forms the basis of the technical plan. Resource allocation will need to take account of the availability of team members during the project. Their 100 per cent availability should not be assumed, and other necessary activities should be taken into account (e.g. telephone, administration, unplanned meetings). Once actual availability of resources has been determined, they can be allocated to activities in the project. Allocation should be to critical activities first (i.e. activities for which there is no slack time) and then to other parallel activities. The availability of individual resources can be measured over time using a capacity loading graph (see network analysis section). It may be found that due to the duration of activities or the fact that a resource is needed for more than one activity at a time (i.e. parallel activities), the project cannot be completed in the time shown by the activity network chart. This requires either the allocation of extra resources or an adjustment to the project completion time.

The previous resource allocation charts are supplemented by a plan description document to form the technical plans that are submitted to the project board. The plan description contains information regarding the proposed plan, assumptions made on aspects such as resource availability, skill levels and an assessment of risk at each plan level.

◗ Project control

Project control is the activity of ensuring that a project meets planned objectives. PRINCE attempts to ensure this by the use of business and technical integrity:

- *Business integrity* involves ensuring that the work is carried out to the schedule agreed within resource and cost constraints imposed.
- *Technical integrity* involves ensuring that the development system (i.e. the product) meets the goals of quality, reliability and maintainability.

Control is exercised by comparing performance to plan and taking action on any deviation that is outside the agreed tolerance. Management tolerances measure deviation from planned cost or schedule, while technical tolerances measure deviation in quality as defined by the user requirements and objectives.

▶ Management control

PRINCE provides management controls in the form of meetings of project staff that produce a set of predefined documents. These allow senior management to assess the status of the project before providing further expenditure.

The main control points in a PRINCE project are project initiation, stage assessment and project closure.

Project initiation

The outcome of this stage is a project initiation document that will include a high-level plan for the project and confirmation of the responsibilities of project members. There will also be a more detailed plan of the first stage of the project. The project manager, the first stage manager and members of the project assurance team prepare the document. The project initiation document should include the following elements:

- project organisation diagram;
- job descriptions;
- project brief including project definition and scope of work;
- project terms of reference;
- business case including cost–benefit analysis and risk assessment;
- project plan estimating development cost and duration (see planning section) at a high level, to include the following:
  (a) project technical plan
  (b) project resource plan
  (c) project quality plan
  (d) configuration management plan
  (e) first-stage plan.

For each stage of the plan the following are required:

- stage technical plan
- stage resource plan
- stage resource graphical summary
- stage plan description
- stage quality plan.

In addition, the following supporting documents for each stage are recommended:

- stage product breakdown structure
- stage product flow diagram
- stage activity network.

Stage assessment

There are *checkpoint meetings* held on a regular (e.g. weekly) time-related basis to review progress against plans, particularly in connection with individual work allocations. They are held at a team level and are usually run by the stage manager or team leader.

Highlight reports provide a regular (e.g. monthly) summary of progress to date to the project board.

The *end-stage assessment (ESA)* is not time-based but is triggered by the end of each project stage. Participants should include the project board, project manager, project assurance team, current team manager and next stage manager. The meeting's aims are to confirm delivery of the current stage of the project to specification and to ensure that a viable business case still exists for the project, as well as considering and approving the plan for the next stage. If necessary, corrective action must be taken or, if this is not thought possible, the project terminated.

The *mid-stage assessment (MSA)* is an optional event and may be triggered by the following:

- a need to check progress during a lengthy project stage;
- when stage tolerance levels have been exceeded;
- when it is felt necessary to begin the next stage before the end-stage assessment can be held for the present stage.

The mid-stage assessment follows the format of the end-stage assessment.

Exception plans

If a stage cannot be completed within its tolerances, the project manager must advise the project board immediately and present an exception plan as a mid-stage assessment. An exception plan consists of the technical plan covering remaining stage activities, a matching resource plan and additional information to describe the exception. This should include the impact of options considered in the stage plan, project plan and business case. If the project board agrees the exception plan, it becomes the stage plan for the remainder of that stage.

Project closure

The project closure meeting replaces the final end-stage assessment and confirms the signing of the system, user, operations, security and business acceptance letters by the appropriate board members. The acceptance criteria should have been clearly stated in the project initiation document.

The last act of a PRINCE project is a business assessment of the system provided by the project after a period of use, called a *post-implementation review*.

Product controls

Product controls ensure that quality is built into the development of the products during the project. Tasks involved include agreeing quality criteria for products with users, planning quality reviews, and detecting and correcting quality problems as early as possible. The measurement criteria for a product's quality are contained within the product description and as such are created during the planning stage, thus building in quality to the product design.

Quality reviews

The purpose of the quality review is to identify errors through a planned and documented process as early as possible in the development cycle. The quality review consists of three phases:

1 *Preparation*. This includes setting up a review team and distribution of appropriate documentation.
2 *Review*. The meeting is held and actions are listed and allocated to individuals.
3 *Follow-up*. This covers the correction of actions listed.

Every project managed using the methodology has a quality file containing details of all quality reviews and requests for changes.

The PRINCE methodology uses the following ways to document changes:

- *project issue reports (PIR)* – used by anyone to raise a quality issue;
- *off-specification reports (OSR)* – when systems fail to meet specification;
- *requests for change (RFC)* – propose a change following from a PIR or OSR.

If an RFC causes project budgets to exceed tolerance, an exception plan is created which is considered by the project board. The control document will probably be created by members of the maintenance team and system users and will be sent to the ITEC for signing.

Configuration management

Configuration management is needed because of the dependence between components within a project. Each component will have its own development cycle and during this development any of the components may be changed, which could make them incompatible with other components. Configuration management identifies each hardware, software or documentation component used and records the status of that component. The authorised version of each item is then issued for use. A configuration librarian is used to manage and control configuration management activities.

▶ Project management methodologies compared

Although PRINCE has a reputation for being applicable only to large projects it has been used on a variety of projects of small size. Also, it is recognised as a standard in the UK public sector and by large private sector companies. PRINCE was designed specifically for IT project management but a new version, PRINCE2 (www.prince2.com) provides a generic project management framework suitable for use in all types of projects. In addition to PRINCE many other project management methodologies (as opposed to development process methodologies such as SSADM, JSD and STRADIS) exist such as BPMM (www.bates.ca), IDEAL (www.sei.cmu.edu/ideal) and EUROMETHOD (Turner and Jenkins, 1996) (www.esi.es/Euromethod). In addition methodologies have been developed 'in-house' by companies for their own use or have been developed commercially and require a licence fee before more information is released.

Activity 9.2

An assessment of PRINCE

An important function of a company's information systems manager is to review which methodologies should be employed to improve the quality of its systems development processes. Some methodologies may add a structure to a company process which improves its efficiency. Others may enforce restrictions which reduce the efficiency of the process and increase the cost and duration of the project.

You are a project manager in a company of 400 people. The company has a history of developing systems that meet the needs of the end-users well, but can sometimes be over six months late. The managing director has decided that the project will be conducted by internal IS development staff. Your role as the owner of the system in which the project will be implemented is to manage the project using other resources, such as the IS department, as you see fit.

Question

From the information given in the preceding section and using any relevant books, decide whether to use a formal project methodology such as PRINCE, IDEAL or EUROMETHOD or a different approach. Justify your answer, giving a brief evaluation of what you perceive as the advantages and disadvantages of the methodology.

A project management tool: network analysis

Critical path
Activities on the critical path are termed critical activities. Any delay in these activities will cause a delay in the project completion time.

Critical path diagrams are used extensively during scheduling and monitoring to show the planned activities of a project and the *dependencies* between these activities. For example, network analysis will show that activity C can only take place when activity A and activity B have been completed. Once a network diagram has been constructed, it is possible to follow a sequence of activities, called a *path*, through the network from start to end. The length of time it takes to follow the path is the sum of all the durations of activities on that path. The path with the longest duration gives the *project completion time*. This is called the *critical path* because any change in duration in any activities on this path will cause the whole project duration to become shorter or longer. Activities not on the critical path will have a certain amount of slack time in which the activity can be delayed or the duration lengthened and not affect the overall project duration. The amount of *slack time* is the difference between the path duration the activity is on and the critical path duration. By definition, all activities on the critical path have zero slack. Note that there must be at least one critical path for each network and there may be several critical paths. The significance of the critical path is that if any node on the path finishes later than the earliest finish time, the overall network time will increase by the same amount, putting the project behind schedule. Thus any planning and control activities should focus on ensuring that tasks on the critical path remain within schedule.

Critical path network diagrams are sometimes called 'PERT charts', but the correct technical meaning of this term is detailed in a later section.

▶ The critical path method (CPM)

Once the estimation stage has been completed, the project activities should have been identified, activity durations and resource requirement estimated and activity relationships identified. Based on this information, the critical path diagrams can be constructed using either the activity-on-arrow (AOA) approach or the activity-on-node (AON) approach. The issues involved in deciding which one to utilise will be discussed later. The following description of critical path analysis will use the AON method.

Critical path method (CPM)
Critical path diagrams show the relationship between activities in a project.

The **critical path method (CPM)** uses critical path diagrams to show the relationships between activities in a project.

The activity-on-node (AON) method

In an activity-on-node network, the diagramming notation shown in Figure 9.8 is used. Each activity task is represented by a node with the format shown in the figure.

Earliest start	Duration	Earliest finish
Activity number/letter Activity description		
Latest start	Slack/float	Latest finish

Figure 9.8 **Activity on node notation**

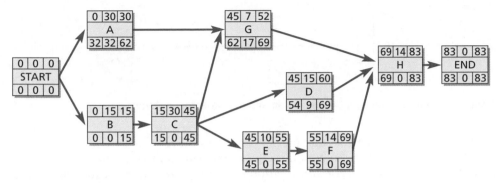

Figure 9.9 Activity on node network diagram

Thus a completed network will consist of a number of nodes connected by lines, one for each task, between a start and an end node, as shown in Figure 9.9.

Once the network diagram has been drawn using the activity relationships, the node information can be calculated, starting with the earliest start and finish times. These are calculated by working from left to right through the network, in the 'forward pass'. Once the forward pass has been completed, it is possible to calculate the latest start and finish times for each task. This is achieved by moving right to left along the network, backward through time, in the 'backward pass'. Finally, the slack or float value can be calculated for each node by taking the difference between the earliest start and latest start (or earliest finish and latest finish) times for each task.

The activity-on-arrow (AOA) method

The format for the activity-on-arrow method will now be described. The symbol used in this method is as shown in Figure 9.10.

Rather than considering the earliest and latest start and finish times of the activities directly, this method uses the earliest and latest event times, as below:

- *Earliest event time.* This is determined by the earliest time at which any subsequent activity can start.
- *Latest event time.* This is determined by the latest time at which any subsequent activity can start.

Thus for a single activity the format would be as shown in Figure 9.11.

Comparison of activity-on-arrow and activity-on-node methods

There has historically been a greater use of the activity-on-arrow (AOA) method, but the activity-on-node (AON) method is now being recognised as having a number of advantages, including the following:

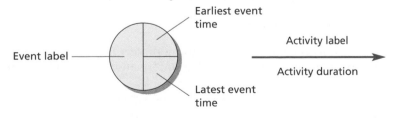

Figure 9.10 Activity-on-arrow notation

Figure 9.11 Calculating event times for an activity-on-arrow network

● Most project management computer software uses the AON approach.
● AON diagrams do not need dummy activities to maintain the relationship logic.
● AON diagrams have all the information on timings and identification within the node box, leading to clearer diagrams.

An example of the use of activity-on-node in Microsoft Project is shown in Figure 9.9. This illustrates *sequential activities* such as from the START to activity A and *parallel activities* such as C, D and E which occur simultaneously. Note that activity A is on the critical path, since this is the activity that takes the longest time to complete. The critical path is shown by the bold lines for the arrows and dependencies.

▶ Gantt charts

Gantt charts

Show the duration of parallel and sequential activities in a project as horizontal bars on a chart.

Although network diagrams are ideal for showing the relationship between project tasks, they do not provide a clear view of which tasks are being undertaken over time and particularly of how many tasks may be undertaken in parallel at any one time. **Gantt charts** are used to summarise the project plan by showing the duration of parallel and sequential activities in a project as horizontal 'time bars' on a chart. The Gantt chart provides an overview for the project managers to allow them to monitor project progress against planned progress and so provides a valuable information source for project control.

Milestone

This denotes a significant event in the project such as completion of a prototype.

Figure 9.12 shows a typical Gantt chart produced using Microsoft Project. Note that some phases such as 'Phase 1 – software evaluation' have *subactivities* such as 'consult and set criteria' and 'evaluate alternatives – report'. Each of these subactivities has a certain number of days and a corresponding cost assigned to it. **Milestones** are activities that are planned to occur by a particular day, such as 'Purchase hardware by 17/06'. These are shown as triangles. They are a significant event in the life of the project, such as completion of a prototype.

To draw a Gantt chart manually or using a spreadsheet or drawing package, follow these steps:

1 Draw a grid with the tasks along the vertical axis and the timescale (for the whole project duration) along the horizontal axis.
2 Draw a horizontal bar across from the task identifier along the left of the chart, starting at the earliest start time and ending at the earliest finish time.
3 Indicate the slack amount by drawing a line from the earliest finish time to the latest finish time.
4 Repeat steps 2 and 3 for each task.

If the network analysis is being conducted using project management software, then the Gantt chart is automatically generated from information in the network analysis.

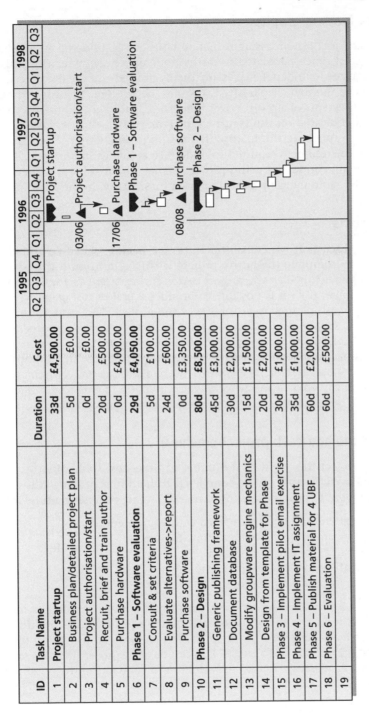

ID	Task Name	Duration	Cost	1995				1996				1997				1998		
				Q2	Q3	Q4	Q1	Q2	Q3	Q4	Q1	Q2	Q3	Q4	Q1	Q2	Q3	
1	Project startup	33d	£4,500.00														
2	Business plan/detailed project plan	5d	£0.00														
3	Project authorisation/start	0d	£0.00														
4	Recruit, brief and train author	20d	£500.00														
5	Purchase hardware	0d	£4,000.00														
6	Phase 1 – Software evaluation	29d	£4,050.00														
7	Consult & set criteria	5d	£100.00														
8	Evaluate alternatives->report	24d	£600.00														
9	Purchase software	0d	£3,350.00														
10	Phase 2 – Design	80d	£8,500.00														
11	Generic publishing framework	45d	£3,000.00														
12	Document database	30d	£2,000.00														
13	Modify groupware engine mechanics	15d	£1,500.00														
14	Design from template for Phase	20d	£2,000.00														
15	Phase 3 – Implement pilot email exercise	30d	£1,000.00														
16	Phase 4 – Implement IT assignment	35d	£1,000.00														
17	Phase 5 – Publish material for 4 UBF	60d	£2,000.00														
18	Phase 6 – Evaluation	60d	£500.00														
19																	

Figure 9.12 Gantt chart showing activities and milestones

❯ Capacity loading graphs

The basic network diagram assumes that all tasks can be undertaken when required by the earliest start times calculated from the node dependency relationships. However, resources required to undertake tasks are usually limited and the duration of an individual task or the number of parallel tasks may be limited. In order to calculate the capacity requirements of a project over time, the capacity requirements associated with each task are indicated on the Gantt chart. From this, a **capacity loading graph** can be developed by projecting the loading figures on a time graph. The capacity loading graphs show the resources required to undertake activities in a project. If the network analysis is being conducted using project management software, then the capacity loading graph is automatically generated from information in the network analysis.

Capacity loading graphs
Capacity loading graphs show the resources required to undertake activities in a project.

❯ Project costs

The previous discussion has concentrated on the need to schedule and control activities in order to complete the entire project within a minimum timespan. However, there are situations in which the project cost is an important factor. If the costs of each project are known, then it is possible to produce a **project cost graph** which will show the amount of cost incurred over the life of the project. This is useful in showing any periods when a number of parallel tasks are incurring significant costs, leading to the need for additional cashflow at key times. In large projects it may be necessary to aggregate the costs of a number of activities, particularly if they are the responsibility of one department or subcontractor. As a control mechanism, the project manager can collect information on cost to date and percentage completion to date for each task to identify any cost above budget and take appropriate action without delay.

Project cost graphs
Show the financial cost of undertaking the project.

❯ Trading time and cost: project crashing

Within any project there will be a number of time–cost trade-offs to consider. Most projects will have tasks that can be completed with an injection of additional resources, such as equipment or people. Reasons to reduce project completion time include:

● to reduce high indirect costs associated with equipment;
● to reduce new product development time to market;
● to avoid penalties for late completion;
● to gain incentives for early completion;
● to release resources for other projects.

Project crashing
Refers to reducing the project duration by increasing spending on critical activities.

The use of additional resources to reduce project completion time is termed **crashing** the network. The idea is to reduce overall indirect project costs by increasing direct costs on a particular task. One of the most obvious ways of decreasing task duration is to allocate additional labour to a task. This can be either an additional team member or through overtime working. To enable a decision to be made on the potential benefits of crashing a task, the following information is required:

● the normal task duration;
● the crash task duration;
● the cost of crashing the task to the crash task duration per unit time.

The process by which a task is chosen for crashing is by observing which task can be reduced for the required time for the lowest cost. As stated before, the overall project completion time is the sum of the task durations on the critical path. Thus it is always necessary to crash a task that is on the critical path. As the duration of tasks on the critical path is reduced, however, other paths in the network will also become critical. If this happens, it will require the crashing process to be undertaken on all the paths that are critical at any one time.

▶ Project evaluation and review technique (PERT)

PERT replaces the fixed activity duration used in the CPM method with a statistical distribution which uses optimistic, pessimistic and most likely duration estimates.

PERT
PERT replaces the fixed activity duration used in the CPM method with a statistical distribution which uses optimistic, pessimistic and most likely duration estimates.

The critical path method (CPM) described above was developed by Du Pont during the 1950s to manage plant construction. The PERT approach was formulated by the US Navy during the development of the Polaris submarine-launched ballistic missile system in the same decade (Sapolsky, 1972). The main difference between the approaches is the ability of PERT to take into consideration uncertainty in activity durations.

The PERT approach attempts to take into account the fact that most task durations are not fixed, by using a beta probability distribution to describe the variability inherent in the processes. The probabilistic approach involves three time estimates for each activity:

● *Optimistic time*. The task duration under the most optimistic conditions.
● *Pessimistic time*. The task duration under the most pessimistic conditions.
● *Most likely time*. The most likely task duration.

As stated, the beta distribution is used to describe the task duration variability. To derive the average or expected time for a task duration, the following equation is used:

$$\textit{Expected duration = Optimistic + (4 × Most likely) + Pessimistic}$$

The combination of the expected time and standard deviation for the network path allows managers to compute probabilistic estimates of project completion times. A point to bear in mind with these estimates is that they only take into consideration the tasks on the critical path and discount the fact that slack on tasks on a non-critical path could delay the project. Therefore the probability that the project will be completed by a specified date is the probability that all paths will be completed by that date, which is the product of the probabilities for all the paths.

▶ Project network simulation

In order to use the PERT approach, it must be assumed that the paths of a project are independent and that the same tasks are not on more than one path. If a task is on more than one path and its actual completion time was much larger than its expected time, it is obvious that the paths are not independent. If the network consists of these paths and they are near the critical path time, then the results will be invalid.

Simulation can be used to develop estimates of a project's completion time by taking into account all the network paths. Probability distributions are constructed for each task, derived from estimates provided by such data collection methods as observation and historical data. A simulation then generates a random number within the probability distribution for each task. The critical path is determined and the project duration calculated. This procedure is repeated a number of times (possibly more than 100) until there are sufficient data to construct a frequency distribution of project times. This distribution can be used to make a probabilistic assessment of the actual project duration. If greater accuracy is required, the process can be repeated to generate additional project completion estimates which can be added to the frequency distribution.

▶ Benefits and limitations of the network analysis approach

The main benefit of using the network analysis approach is the requirement to use a structured analysis of the number and sequence of tasks contained within a project, so aiding understanding of resource requirements for project completion. It provides a number of useful graphical displays that assist understanding of such factors as project dependencies and resource loading, a reasonable estimate of the project duration and the tasks that must be completed on time to meet this duration (i.e. the critical path), and a control mechanism to monitor actual progress against planned progress on the Gantt chart. It also provides a means of estimating any decrease in overall project time by providing extra resources at any stage and can be used to provide cost estimates for different project scenarios.

Limitations to consider when using network analysis include remembering that its use is no substitute for good management judgement in such areas as prioritising and selecting suppliers and personnel for the project. Additionally, any errors in the network such as incorrect dependency relationships or the omission of tasks may invalidate the results. The tasks' times are forecasts and are thus estimates that are subject to error. PERT and simulation techniques may reduce time estimation errors, but at the cost of greater complexity which may divert management time from more important issues. Finally, time estimates for tasks may be greater than necessary to provide managers with slack and ensure that they meet deadlines.

Summary

1 Projects are unique, one-time operations designed to accomplish a specific set of objectives in a limited timeframe with a limited budget and resources.

2 Major roles in project organisation include the project sponsor, the project manager and the project user. The project sponsor provides a justification of the project to senior management. The project manager role is to provide clearly defined goals and ensure that adequate resources are employed on the project. The project user who will be utilising the system should be involved in the definition and implementation of the system.

3 The main elements in the project management process include estimate, schedule and plan, monitoring and control, and documentation.

4 A work breakdown structure splits the overall project task into a number of more detailed activities in order to facilitate detailed estimation of resources required.

5 Projects can be resource-constrained (limited by resource) or time-constrained (limited by the deadline).

6 Scheduling involves producing a project plan which determines when activities should be executed.

7 Once under way a project can be monitored against the defined objectives of time, cost and quality.

8 Documentation is essential in reducing the expense of project maintenance.

9 PRINCE is an example of a project management methodology. An example of a systems development methodology is SSADM.

10 Critical path analysis shows the activities undertaken during a project and the dependencies between them. The critical path is identified by making a forward and

then a reverse pass through the network, calculating the earliest and latest activity start/finish times respectively.

11 Gantt charts provide an overview of what tasks are being undertaken over time. This allows the project manager to monitor project progress against planned progress.

12 Capacity loading graphs provide an indication of the amount of resource needed for the project over time.

13 Cost graphs provide an indication of monetary expenditure over the project period.

14 Project crashing consists of reducing overall indirect project costs (e.g. by reducing the project duration) by increasing expenditure on a particular task.

15 The PERT approach provides a method of integrating the variability of task durations into the network analysis.

EXERCISES

Self-assessment exercises

1 What are the main elements of the project management process?
2 What are the main project aims of the PRINCE methodology?
3 What information is required for the construction of a critical path diagram?
4 What information do the Gantt chart and the PERT chart convey?
5 Define the term critical path.
6 What is the difference between effort time and elapsed time?

Discussion questions

1 Draw a Gantt chart for the following AON network.
2 'One of the most difficult parts of project management is getting the estimates right.' Discuss.

Essay questions

1 Explore the features of a project management computer package such as Microsoft Project. Evaluate its use in the project management process.

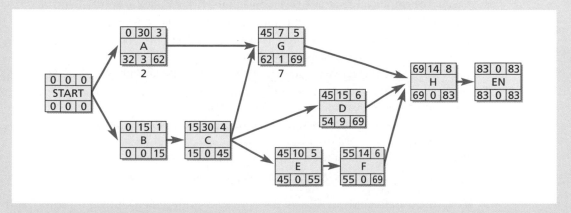

Figure 9.13 **Activity-on-node network**

2 Compare the different alternatives that are available for the critical path method of network analysis.

3 What is the most effective method of estimating the duration of an information systems development project?

Examination questions

1 Evaluate the roles undertaken by people in a project organisation.

2 What are the main elements in the project management process?

3 Evaluate the use of the PRINCE project management methodology.

4 Explain the difference between portraying a project plan as a Gantt chart and as a PERT chart.

5 What is the importance of conducting monitoring and control when managing a project?

6 Why is it difficult and often impossible for a software project manager to balance the three constraints of time, budget and quality? You should relate your answer to two different aspects of the quality of the delivered information system.

7 What is the difference between elapsed time and effort time? How are the two factors related in terms of the availability and work rate of different staff? Describe this in words, or using an equation or an example.

References

Albrecht, A.J. and Gaffney, J. (1983) 'Software function, source lines of code and development effort prediction', *IEEE Transactions on Software Engineering*, SE-9, 639–48

Bicknell, D. (1996) 'Managers blamed for record project failures', *Computer Weekly*, 18 January

Bicknell, D. (1998) 'Clark Kent holds keys to project success', *Computer Weekly*, 9 July, p. 14

Boehm, B.W. (1981) *Software Engineering Economics*, Prentice-Hall, Englewood Cliffs, NJ

Cadle, J. and Yeates, D. (2001) *Project Management for Information Systems*, 3rd edition, Pearson Education, Harlow

Kaye, J. (1997) 'Falling at the final hurdle', *Computer Weekly*, 8 May

Lytinen, K. and Hirscheim, R. (1987) 'Information systems failures: a survey and classification of the empirical literature', *Oxford Surveys in IT*, 4, 257–309

Mouler, J. (1996) 'UK tops project failure league', *Computing*, 8 February

PricewaterhouseCoopers (2001) Global Data Management Survey 2001, PricewaterhouseCoopers, New York. Available online at www.pwcglobal.com

www.pwcglobal.com/extweb/ncsurvres.nsf/DocID/E68F3408A463BD2980256A180064B96A

Sapolsky, H.M. (1972) *The Polaris System Development: Bureaucratic and Programmatic Success in Government*, Harvard University Press, Boston, MA

Turner, P. and Jenkins, T. (1996), *Euromethod and Beyond,* International Thomson Computer Press, London

Warren, L. (1996) 'Tales of the unexpected', *Computing*, 8 February

Yeates, D. (1991) *Project Management for Information Systems*, Financial Times Pitman Publishing, London

Further reading

Boehm, B.W. (1984) 'Software engineering economics', *IEEE Transactions on Software Engineering*, SE-10, 10–21

Brooks, F.P. (1995) *The Mythical Man-month: Essays on Software Engineering – Anniversary Edition*, Addison-Wesley, Reading, MA

Button, K. (1996) 'Thou shalt not . . .', *Computing Weekly*, 2 May

Dingle, J. (1997) *Project Management: Orientation for Decision Makers*, Edward Arnold, London

Leung, L. (1996) 'Leading a project', *Computing*, 6 June

Lock, D. (1996) *Project Management*, 6th edition, Gower, Aldershot

Maylor, H. (1996) *Project Management*, Financial Times Pitman Publishing, London

Whitten, N. (1990) *Managing Software Development Projects*, John Wiley, New York

Web links

Web sites with further information on project management methodologies are as follows:

www.strategictransitions.com/basicproject5steps.htm 5-STEPS

www.ogc.gov.uk/prince/index.htm PRINCE official site

www.bates.ca BPMM

www.sei.cmu.edu/ideal IDEAL

www.esi.es/Euromethod EUROMETHOD

Chapter 10

Systems analysis

LEARNING OBJECTIVES

After reading this chapter, readers will be able to:

● define the importance of conducting the analysis phase to the overall success of the system;
● choose appropriate techniques for analysing users' requirements for an information system;
● construct appropriate textual descriptions and diagrams to assist in summarising the requirements as an input to the design phase.

MANAGEMENT ISSUES

Careful systems analysis must be conducted on each BIS project to ensure that the system meets the needs of the business and its users. From a managerial perspective, this chapter addresses the following questions:

● Which different aspects of the system must be summarised in the requirements document?
● Which diagramming tools are appropriate to summarise the operation of the existing and proposed systems?

Links to other chapters

Links to other chapters

This chapter is directly related to Chapter 8, which describes the preceding stage of information systems development (initiation), and Chapter 11, which describes the next phase (systems design).

Introduction

Once it has been determined that it is desirable to proceed with the acquisition of a new BIS, it is necessary to determine the system requirements before any design or development work takes place. Systems analysis is about finding out *what* the new system is to do, rather than *how*. There are two basic components to the analysis process:

- *fact-finding* – an exercise needs to take place where all prospective users of the new system should contribute to determining requirements;
- *documentation* – detailed systems design follows the analysis stage and it needs to be based on unambiguous documentation and diagrams from the analysis stage.

Systems analysis involves the investigation of the business and user requirements of an information system. Fact-finding techniques are used to ascertain the user's needs and these are summarised using a range of diagramming methods.

Factors that will influence the use of fact-finding techniques and documentation tools will include:

- *The result of the 'make-or-buy decision'*. Made during the feasibility stage, a 'make' decision where bespoke software is developed will need more detailed analysis than a 'buy' decision where packaged software is purchased off-the-shelf, especially when the results of the analysis process are fed into the design stage.
- *Application complexity*. A very complex system or one where there are linkages to other systems will need very careful analysis to define system and subsystem boundaries, and this will lead to use of more formal techniques when compared with a simple or standalone application.
- *End-user versus corporate development*. End-user development does not lend itself to extensive use of formal analysis tools. However, basic analysis is required and there are certain analysis tools that end-user developers can use that increase the probability of success. Similarly, where application development by IS/IT professionals occurs there will be a need for a more formal approach, especially where systems cut across functional boundaries.

Any errors in systems development that occur during the analysis phase will cost far more to correct than errors that occur in subsequent stages. It is therefore essential that maximum thought and effort be put into the analysis process if unanticipated costs are not to arise in the later stages of development.

Systems analysis

The investigation of the business and user requirements of an information system. Fact-finding techniques are used to ascertain the user's needs and these are summarised using a requirements specification and a range of diagramming methods.

Identifying the requirements

The first task in analysis is to conduct a fact-finding exercise so that the information systems requirements can be determined. The methods an organisation uses in the analysis phase will depend, at least in part, on two factors:

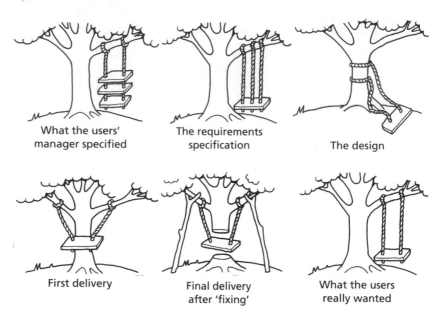

What the users'
manager specified

The requirements
specification

The design

First delivery

Final delivery
after 'fixing'

What the users
really wanted

Figure 10.1 Varying interpretations of a user's requirements at different stages in a project

- *Levels of decision making involved.* A new information system will be under consideration either to resolve a problem or to create an opportunity. In either case, the objective is to improve the quality of information available to allow better decision making. The type of system under consideration may include a transaction processing system, a management information system, a decision support system, a combination of these or some other categorisation of system (Chapter 6). So, for example, an information system that is purely geared towards the needs of management will require a different approach to fact-finding (for example, using one-to-one interviews with senior managers) from one that mainly involves transaction processing (for example, using observation of the existing process).
- *Scope of functional area.* A new information system may serve the needs of one functional business area (e.g. the HRM function), or it may cut across many functional areas. An information system that is restricted in scope may be faced with fewer of the problems that can affect new systems designed to meet the needs of many different areas. As before, the techniques of fact-finding may be similar, but how they are used and the findings presented may be radically different. Organisational culture, structure and decision-making processes will all have a part to play in selling the systems solution to all the affected parties.

Regardless of the scope and organisational levels involved, the objective of the fact-finding task is to gather sufficient information about the business processes under consideration so that a design can be constructed which will then provide the blueprint for the system build phase. We will now turn to a consideration of a number of fact-finding methods.

Although it might be thought that finding out the requirements for a system is straightforward, this is far from the case. Dissatisfaction with information systems, referred to in Chapter 9, is often due to the requirements for the information system being wrongly interpreted. Figure 10.1 shows an oft-quoted example of how a user's requirements for a swing might be interpreted, not only at the requirements analysis stage but throughout the project.

▶ Interviewing

During **interviewing**, a range of staff are interviewed using structured techniques to identify features and problems of the current system and required features of the future system.

Interviewing is one of the most widely used fact-finding methods. Success with this method involves careful planning, proper conduct of the interviews themselves and, finally, accurate recording of the interview findings. We can expand each of these to provide more detail.

Analysis technique – interviewing
Recommended practice: a range of staff are interviewed using structured techniques to identify features and problems of the current system and required features of the future system.

Planning

- Clear objectives need to be set to identify what needs to be achieved at the end of the interviewing process.
- Interview subjects must also be carefully selected so that the information gained will be relevant to the system being developed. For example, there may be little use in interviewing all the shopfloor workers in a manufacturing company if the system being developed is an executive information system (EIS) to assist with decision making at senior levels within the business. There may still be some merit in interviewing certain key personnel involved in operational decision making, since data produced may be useful in the proposed EIS.
- Customers should be involved in analysis if the use of a system affects them directly. For example, a customer of a phone-based ordering system or a telephone bank may well give an insight into problems of an existing system.
- The topics the interview is to cover need to be clearly identified and the place where interviews are to take place must be determined.
- Finally, it is necessary to plan how the interviews are to be conducted and the types of questions to be used.

Conduct

- The interviewer must establish a control framework for the interview. This will include the use of summarising to check the points being made and appropriate verbal and non-verbal signals to assist the flow of the interview.
- Interviewers must be good listeners. This is especially important when dealing with complex business processes which are the object of the systems development project.
- The interviewer must select a mix of open and closed questions which will elicit maximum information retrieval.
- Finally, the interview must be structured in an organised way. There are three main approaches to structuring an interview. The first is the *'pyramid structure'*, where the interview begins with a series of specific questions and during the course of the interview moves towards general ones. The second is the *'funnel structure'*, where the interviewer begins with general questions and during the course of the interview concentrates increasingly on specific ones. The third approach is the *'diamond structure'*, where the interview begins with specific questions, moves towards general questions in the middle of the interview and back towards specific questions at the end.

Open questions
Not restricted to a limited range of answers such as Yes/No (closed questions). Asked to elicit opinions or ideas for the new system or identify commonly held views amongst staff. Open questions are not typically used for quantitative analysis, but can be used to identify a common problem.

Regardless of which approach is taken, it will still be necessary to document carefully the findings of the interview.

Interviews should use a mixture of open and closed questions. **Open questions** are not restricted to a limited range of answers such as Yes/No (closed questions). They are asked to elicit opinions or ideas for the new system or identify commonly held views among staff. Open questions are not typically used for quantitative analysis, but can be used to identify a common problem.

Closed questions have a restricted choice of answers such as Yes/No or a range of opinions on a scale from 'strongly agree' to 'strongly disagree' (Lickert scale). This approach is useful for quantitative analysis of results.

Closed questions

Closed questions have a restricted choice of answers such as Yes/No or a range of opinions a scale from 'strongly agree' to 'strongly disagree' (Lickert scale). Approach is useful for quantitative analysis of results.

Recording

During the course of the interview, the interviewer will need to make notes to record the findings. It may also be useful to draw diagrams to illustrate the processes being discussed. Some interviewers like to use a tape recorder to be sure that no points are missed. Whichever methods are used, the requirement is to record three main attributes of the system under consideration:

● *Business processes.* A business process exists when an input of some kind (raw materials, for example) is transformed in some way so that an output is produced for use elsewhere in the business.
● *Data.* Data will be acquired and processed and information produced as a consequence of carrying out business processes. Data must be analysed so that data acquisition, processing needs and information requirements can be encapsulated in the new information system.
● *Information flows.* Functional business areas do not exist in isolation from each other and neither do different business processes within the same business function. It is necessary, therefore, to identify how data and information within one business process are necessary for other business processes to operate effectively.

We will look at some relevant tools and techniques which help to record the findings later in this chapter.

As an information-gathering tool, interviews have a number of advantages and disadvantages. On the positive side they include:

✓ the ability to gather detailed information through a two-way dialogue;
✓ the ability for candid, honest responses to be made;
✓ an open, spontaneous process which can lead to valuable insights, especially when open questions are used;
✓ responses that can easily be quantified, especially when closed questions are used;
✓ being one of the best methods for gathering qualitative data such as opinions, and subjective descriptions of activities and problems.

On the negative side, however, the following points can be made:

✗ The analyst's findings may be coloured by his or her perceptions of how other, similar, business operations work. Interviewers need to be especially skilled if this is to be avoided.
✗ The development of a new information system may represent a threat through the risk of deskilling, redundancy or perceived inability to cope with change. Interviewees may, therefore, not cooperate with the interview process, either by not taking part or by giving vague and incomplete replies.
✗ The interviewee may tell the analyst what he or she thinks should happen rather than what actually happens.
✗ An interview at lower organisational levels may not yield as much information as some other methods if staff in this area are not capable of articulating with sufficient clarity.

On balance, interviewing is an essential part of the information-gathering process. For maximum benefit, interviewing should be used in conjunction with other techniques and we will turn to these now.

▶ Questionnaires

Questionnaires are used to obtain a range of opinion on requirements by targeting a range of staff. They are open to misinterpretation unless carefully designed. They should consist of both open and closed questions.

Questionnaires can be a useful addition to the analyst's armoury, but are not in themselves enough to gather sufficient information for the later stages of the systems development process. That said, questionnaires can be very useful when used with other fact-finding methods, either to confirm the findings obtained elsewhere or to open up possible further areas for investigation. Typically, they are used before more detailed questions by interview.

Successful questionnaires have a number of characteristics:

✓ The questions will be framed by the analyst with a clear view of the information that is to be obtained from the completed questionnaires.
✓ The target audience must be carefully considered – a questionnaire designed for clerical or operational personnel should not contain questions that are not relevant to their level of work.
✓ The questionnaire should only contain branching (e.g. 'if the answer to Question 3 was "No", then go to Question 8') if it is absolutely necessary – multiple branches create confusion and may lead to unusable responses.
✓ Questions should be simple and unambiguous so that the respondent does not have to guess what the analyst means.
✓ Multiple-choice, Lickert-scale-type questions make the questionnaire easier to fill in and allow the results to be analysed more efficiently.
✓ The questionnaire should contain the required return date and name of the person to whom the questionnaire should be returned.

Difficulties that can be encountered with questionnaires include:

✗ the inability of respondents to go back to the analyst to seek clarification about what a question means;
✗ difficulty in collating qualitative information, especially if the questionnaire contains open-ended questions;
✗ the inability to use verbal and non-verbal signals from the respondent as a sign to ask other or different questions;
✗ low response rates – these can be lower than 20 to 25 per cent when sent to other organisations or customers, which means that a large sample size is needed if the results are to carry any weight. Response rate is not such a problem with internal staff.

By contrast, the questionnaire process also has a number of benefits:

✓ When large numbers of people such as customers or suppliers need to be consulted, a carefully worded questionnaire is more efficient and less expensive than carrying out large numbers of interviews.
✓ Questionnaires can be used to check results found by using other fact-finding methods.
✓ The use of standardised questions can help codify the findings more succinctly than other tools.

In summary, questionnaires can have a useful role to play in certain circumstances, but they should not be used as the sole data-gathering method.

Analysis technique – questionnaires
Used to obtain a range of opinion on requirements by targeting a range of staff. They are open to misinterpretation unless carefully designed. They should consist of open and closed questions.

▶ Documentation review

Documentation reviews target information about existing systems, such as user guides or requirements specifications, together with paper or on-screen forms used to collect information, such as sales order forms. They are vital for collecting detail about data and processes that may not be recalled in questionnaires and interviews.

All organisations have at least some kind of documentation that relates to some or all of the business operations carried out. A documentation review can be carried out at a number of different stages in the analysis process. If carried out at the beginning of a requirements analysis exercise, it will help provide the analyst with some background information relating to the area under consideration. It may also help the analyst construct a framework for the remainder of the exercise, and enable interviews to be conducted in a more effective way since the analyst has some idea of current business practices and procedures. If document review is carried out later, it can be used to cross-check the actual business operations with what is supposed to happen. The kinds of documentation and records that can be reviewed include the following:

✓ instruction manuals and procedure manuals which show how specific tasks are supposed to be performed;

✓ requirements specifications and user guides from previous systems;

✓ job descriptions relating to particular staff functions which may help identify who should be doing what;

✓ strategic plans both for the organisation as a whole and the functional areas in particular, which can provide valuable background data for establishing broad functional objectives.

While documentation review can provide a very useful underpinning for other fact-finding tasks, there are still a number of problems:

✗ There can be a large quantity of data for an analyst to process. This is especially true in large organisations and it may take the analyst a long time to identify the documentation that is useful and that which can be ignored.

✗ Documentation is often out of date. If there is an old computerised system, it is quite possible that the documentation has not been changed for years, even though the system may have changed considerably over that period. The same can be said for the documentation of activities and procedures.

▶ Observation

Observation is useful for identifying inefficiencies in an existing way of working, with either a computer-based or a manual information system. It involves timing how long particular operations take and observing the method used to perform them. It can be time-consuming and the staff who are observed may not behave normally.

This fact-finding method involves the analyst in directly observing business activities taking place so that they can see what is *actually* taking place rather than looking at documentation which states what *should* be taking place. One of the benefits of observation is that the analyst can see directly how something is done, rather than relying on verbal or written communication which may colour the facts or be the subject of misinterpretation by the analyst. Other benefits include:

✓ the ability to see how documents and records are actually handled and processed;

✓ observation may give a greater insight into actual business operations than simple paper documentation;

✓ identification of particular operations that take a long time;

✓ the opportunity to see how different processes interact with each other, thus giving the analyst a *dynamic* rather than a *static* view of the business situation under investigation.

On the downside, there are a number of difficulties associated with the observation technique:

✗ It is an extremely time-consuming exercise and therefore needs to be done as a supplementary rather than a principal fact-finding method.

✗ While observation allows an organisation to be dynamically assessed, it still does not allow attitudes and belief systems to be assessed. This can be a very important issue if the proposed information system is likely to encounter resistance to change among the workforce.

✗ Finally, there is the issue of the 'Hawthorne effect', where people tend to behave differently when they are being observed, thus reducing the value of the information being obtained. Of course, for the analyst, the problem is in determining whether those being observed are behaving differently or not!

This effect was first noticed in the Hawthorne plant of Western Electrics in the United States. Here, it was noted that production increased, not as a consequence of actual changes in working conditions introduced by the plant's management, but because management demonstrated an interest in improving staff working conditions.

Despite these difficulties, it is desirable for the analyst to conduct at least some observation to ensure that no aspect of the system being investigated is overlooked.

▶ Brainstorming

Brainstorming uses interaction within a group of staff to generate new ideas and discuss existing problems. It is the least structured of the fact-finding techniques.

> Analysis technique – brainstorming
> ....
> Brainstorming uses interaction within a group of staff to generate new ideas and discuss existing problems. It is the least structured of the fact-finding techniques.

This is the final fact-finding technique we will consider. The methods we have looked at so far are either passive or conducted on a one-to-one basis, or both. The brainstorming method involves a number of participants and is an active approach to information gathering. While the other methods allow for many different views to be expressed, those methods do not allow different persons' perceptions of the business processes and systems needs to be considered simultaneously. Brainstorming allows multiple views and opinions to be brought forward at the same time. If the proposed system's user community participates actively, it is more likely that an accurate view of current business processes and information systems needs will be reached.

Brainstorming sessions require careful planning by the analyst. Factors to consider include:

● which persons to involve and from which functional business areas;

● how many people to involve in the session – too few and insufficient data may be gathered; too many and the session may be too difficult to handle;

● terms of reference for the session – there may need to be more than one session to identify clearly areas of agreement and those that need further discussion;

● management involvement – a session for shopfloor workers, for example, may be far less successful if management personnel are involved than if they are not. It would be appropriate, however, for management groups to have their own brainstorming session so that tactical and strategic issues can be tackled rather than simply operational ones.

The main benefit of the brainstorming approach is that, through the dynamics of group interaction, progress is more likely to be made than from a simple static approach to information gathering. Brainstorming sessions, if they are handled properly, can result in the productive sharing of ideas and perceptions, while at the same time cultural factors, attitudes and belief systems can be more readily assessed. Also, when the outcomes are positive ones, a momentum for change is built among those who will be direct users of the new information system. Change management is therefore more easily facilitated.

The main danger of the approach is that in the hands of an inexperienced analyst, there is a risk that the sessions may descend into chaos because of poor structure, bad planning, poor control or a combination of all three.

However, if used properly, this fact-finding method can generate the desired results more quickly than any other information-gathering method. Even so, it still needs to be supplemented by one or more of the other methods discussed above.

Yeates et al. (1994) explains how structured brainstorming can be used to identify different options for a new system. This technique involves the following stages:

- Invite ideas which are written by individuals on separate sheets of paper or called out spontaneously and then noted on a whiteboard.
- Identify similarities between ideas and rationalise the options by choosing those which are most popular.
- Analyse the remaining options in detail, by evaluating their strengths and weaknesses.

It is important when brainstorming is undertaken that a facilitator be used to explain that a range of ideas is sought with input from everyone. Each participant should be able to contribute without fear of judgement by other members. When such an atmosphere is created this can lead to 'out-of-box' or free thinking which may generate ideas of new ways of working.

Brainstorming and more structured group techniques can be used throughout the development lifecycle. Brainstorming is an important technique in re-engineering a business, since it can identify new ways of approaching processes. Taylor (1995) suggests that once new business processes have been established through analysis, they should be sanity-checked by performing a 'talk-through, walk-through and run-through'. Here, the design team will describe the proposed business process and in the talk-through stage will elaborate on different business scenarios using cards to describe the process objects and the services they provide to other process objects. Once the model has been adjusted, the walk-through stage involves more detail in the scenario and the design team will role-play the services the processes provide. The final run-through stage is a quality check in which no on-the-spot debugging occurs – just the interactions between the objects are described. This method is similar to the class responsibility collaboration model proposed by Kent Beck, as cited by Kavanagh (1994).

Once the analyst has completed the requirements investigation, it will be necessary to document the findings so that a proposal can be put forward for the next stage of the project. Some of the documentation tools discussed below may be used at the same time as the fact-finding process. For example, information flow diagrams may be used by the analyst to check with the end-user that points have been properly understood.

▶ Pictures and brainstorming

Research has shown that new ideas and recall are improved by the use of pictures, which tend to prompt thought better than text. This point is well made by Buzan (1995), who describes a technique known as 'mindmapping' to record information and promote brainstorming. Mindmaps are a spontaneous means of recording information which are ideally applied to systems analysis, since they can be used to record information direct from user dialogues or summarise information after collection.

Another graphical technique which is useful to the system analyst is the 'rich picture'. The rich picture is an element of the soft systems methodology described later in this chapter.

Documenting the findings

In this section we will concentrate on three main diagramming tools: information flow diagrams (IFDs), dataflow diagrams (DFDs) and entity relationship diagrams (ERDs). These techniques are used by professional IS/IT personnel, partly as documentation tools and partly as checking tools with the user community. It is important, therefore, for non-IS/IT personnel to understand the fundamentals behind these diagramming tools so that communication between functional personnel and IS/IT experts is enhanced. Furthermore, tools such as ERDs can be applied by end-users to assist them in developing their own personal or departmental applications. As well as these tools, the requirements specification will also contain a text description of what the functions of the software will be. We will consider this first, and then consider the documentation tools.

◗ The requirements specification

The **requirements specification** is the main output from the systems analysis stage. Its main focus is a description of what all the functions of the software will be. These must be defined in great detail to ensure that when the specification is passed on to the designers, the system is what the users require. This will help prevent the problem referred to in Figure 10.1.

Requirements specification
....
The main output from the systems analysis stage. Its main focus is a description of what all the functions of the software will be.

The scope of the requirements specification will include:

- *data capture* – when, where and how often. The detailed data requirements will be specified using entity relationship diagrams and stored in a data dictionary. Dataflow diagrams will indicate the data stores required;
- *preferred data capture methods* – this may include use of keyboard entry, bar codes, OCR, etc. (it could be argued that this is a design point, but it may be a key user requirement that a particular capture method is used);
- *functional requirements* – what operations the software must be able to perform. For example, for the maps in a geographic information system, the functional requirements would specify: the ability to zoom in and out, pan using scroll-bars and the facility to change the features and labels overlaid on the map;
- *user interface layout* – users will want access to particular functions in a single screen, so the requirements specification will define the main screens of an application. Detailed layout will be decided as part of prototyping and detailed design;
- *output requirements* – this will include such things as enquiry screens, regular standard and ad hoc reports and interfaces to other systems.

One approach to documenting requirements is illustrated by the 'requirements catalogue' specified in SSADM (discussed in Chapter 7). Figure 10.2 illustrates a typical requirements catalogue entry.

The purpose of the requirements catalogue is to act as the repository of all requirements information. It can be used from the initiation stage when early thoughts are being gathered about the possible requirements, through to the design stage when user requirements may still be emerging (especially in such areas as system navigation and performance requirements).

There are three main aspects that need to be documented, usually from a user perspective:

- *Functional requirements*. Consist of requirements that perform the activities that run the business. Examples include updating master files, enquiring against data on file, producing reports and communicating with other systems.

REQUIREMENTS CATALOGUE ENTRY

Source	Owner	Requirement ID	Priority
Credit Control Clerk	Credit Control Manager	5.9	High

Functional Requirements

Link Sales Order Processing system in with accounting package so that online credit checking is an automatic process when new orders are being processed.

Non-functional requirements

Description	Target Value	Acceptable range	Comments
Response Time	Within 10 seconds	Within 20 seconds	
Service Hours	08:30 to 18:00 Monday to Friday		
Availability	97.5%	Above 92.5%	

Benefits

Will speed up order processing and enable account handlers to spend more time collecting cash rather than continually switching between computer systems when processing orders.

Comments / suggested solutions

Either provide a function key to perform the credit check function, or make it an automatic process when an order is entered. Do not allow order to be confirmed if credit check is failed.

Related documents

Required System DFD, process box 5.9

Related requirements

3.2. Improve cash collection process – more accurate sales ledger data
4.9. Reduce number of bad debts – link to improved aged debtors report

Resolution

3.2. Improve cash collection process – more accurate sales ledger data
4.9. Reduce number of bad debts – link to improved aged debtors report

Figure 10.2 **Example of a requirements catalogue entry**

- *Non-functional requirements*. Define the performance levels of the business functions to be supported. Examples include on line response times, turn-round time for batch processing, security, back up and recovery.
- *Quantification of requirements*. Refers to the need for a measure of quality if the benefits are to be properly evaluated. Examples might include reducing customer complaints by 75%, reducing the value of unsold stock by 85%, or increasing online sales by 25%.

Each entry in the requirements catalogue would typically consist of an A4 sheet that contains the details outlined above. Other elements such as requirements originator, date and links to other formal documentation would be included.

When reviewing the contents of a requirements catalogue, it is desirable to prioritise requirements so that the development effort concentrates on the most important features of the new system. For example, it is possible to categorise user requirements into three: the A list, the B list and the C list (or Priority 1 to 3). The A list should comprise all those requirements that the proposed system *must* support and without which it would not function. For example, an accounting system that does not produce customer statements may be seriously deficient. The B list would contain those requirements that are very desirable but are not vital to the successful operation of the system. For example, it may be very desirable for a sales order processing system to produce a list of all customers who have not placed an order for the last six months, but it is not essential. The C list would contain those things that are nice to have (the 'bells and whistles') but are neither essential nor very desirable. It might be nice in a stock control system, for example, if a screen 'buzzed' at the user if a certain combination of factors were present. However, this would not be classified as essential.

The requirements catalogue can be used to prioritise the 'very desirables' and the 'bells and whistles' so that at the design stage, most attention can be paid to those items that are perceived as having the highest priority. It may be, however, that if a low-priority item is seen to be very easy to implement, and a higher-priority item less so, the lower-priority item would be included in the development in preference.

It may be that in the case of a 'very desirable but hard to implement' feature, a simpler item might be included as an imperfect substitute. This would be more readily apparent at the design stage and it may be necessary to revisit the requirements catalogue at this point and consult the functional personnel again.

▶ Information flow diagrams

The **information flow diagram (IFD)** is one of the simplest tools used to document findings from the requirements determination process. It is used for a number of purposes:

- to document the main flows of information around the organisation;
- for the analyst to check that they have understood those flows and that none has been omitted;
- the analyst may use them during the fact-finding process itself as an accurate and efficient way to document findings as they are identified;
- as a high-level (not detailed) tool to document information flows within the organisation as a whole or a lower-level tool to document an individual functional area of the business.

The information flow diagram is a simple diagram showing how information is routed between different parts of an organisation. It has an information focus rather than a process focus.

An information flow diagram has three components, shown in Figure 10.3.

The ellipse in the diagram represents a source of information, which then flows to a destination location. In a high-level diagram, the source or destination would be a department or specific functional area of the business such as sales, accounting or manufacturing. In a lower-level (more detailed) diagram, one might refer to subfunctions such as accounts receivable, credit control or payroll (as you would normally find in an accounts department). The name of the source or destination should appear inside the ellipse. The source or destination is sometimes referred to as an 'internal' or 'external entity' according to whether it lies inside or outside the system boundary. The term

Information flow diagram (IFD)
A simple diagram showing how information is routed between different parts of an organisation. It has an information focus rather than a process focus.

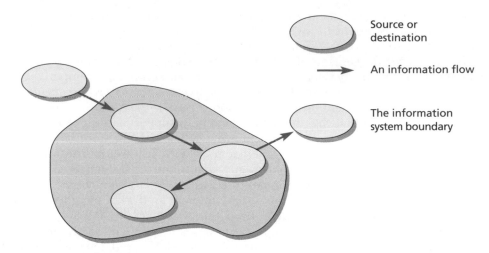

Figure 10.3 Information flow diagrams – the basic building blocks

'entity' is used frequently when constructing entity relationship diagrams and entities are described more fully later.

The information flow, as represented by the arrowhead line, shows a flow of information from a source location to a destination. In an IFD the line should always be annotated with a brief description of the information flow. So, for example, if a sales department sends a customer's order details to the accounts department for credit checking, the resulting flow might look like Figure 10.4.

Sources or destinations lying within the system's boundary imply that this information will be used directly by the system. The concept of the system boundary is explained further in Case Study 10.1.

We now need to give a more detailed example to illustrate how an IFD could be used in practice.

Figure 10.4 An illustration of a simple information flow

CASE STUDY 10.1

IFD drawing – a student records system

Suppose that a university wished to move from a manual, paper-based student records system to one that was computerised. The analyst would need to create a clear picture of the required information flows to help the system designer with the blueprint for the proposed system. We include some sample narrative to demonstrate the possible result of an interview between the analyst and the head of admissions.

'When a student enrols for the first time, they are required to fill in a form which has the following details:

● Forename.
● Surname.
● Date.
● Local authority.

- Home address.
- Term-time address.
- Home telephone number.
- Term-time telephone number.
- Sex.
- Course code.
- Course description.
- Module code (for each module being studied).
- Module description (as above).

When the forms have been completed, they are passed to the student information centre. A series of actions follows:

- The student information centre (SIC) allocates the student a unique code number which stays with the student until they complete their studies.
- The SIC creates a card index of the student's details down to and including course description, plus the new student code number.
- The SIC also creates a list of all students belonging to each local education authority (LEA).
- The SIC sends the LEA list to the finance department, which then invoices the LEAs for the tuition fees relating to the students from their area.
- The SIC creates a study record card (SRC), giving the student details and the modules being studied.
- The SIC groups the SRCs by course and for each course sorts the cards into student name order; the SRCs for each course are then sent to the department that runs that course.
- Each department will take the SRCs for its courses and produce a number of class lists, based around the modules that the student is studying, which are then passed to the relevant module leaders.
- The SIC will issue the student with an enrolment form which the student can use to obtain a library card.
- Finally, the SIC will pass a list of all new students to the library and the students' union so that the library can issue students with library cards and the students' union can issue students with their NUS cards.'

It is necessary to translate the above into a series of information flows and also define the systems boundary (i.e. the line that separates what is in the system under consideration from what is outside it).

In order to be successful in drawing IFDs, it is helpful to follow a few simple steps, since an attempt to draw a diagram from scratch may prove a little tricky:

Step 1   List all the sources of information for the system under consideration (in other words, places where information is generated).

Step 2   List all the destinations (receivers) of information for the system under consideration.

Step 3   Make a simple list of all the information flows.

Step 4   For each of the information flows identified in Step 3, add the source and destination that relate to it.

Step 5   Draw the IFD from your list that you produced from 3 and 4.

Tips

1   When you have gained experience in doing this, Steps 1 and 2 can be ignored and Steps 3 and 4 can be combined.

2   An information source/destination can appear more than once on an IFD – it can help to eliminate lots of crossed lines (and crossed lines are best avoided since the annotations can look rather jumbled).

3   Use A4 paper, or larger, in landscape mode.

The result of your efforts should look something like this:

Step 1 (information generators)
STUDENT
SIC
FINANCE
DEPARTMENT

Step 2 (information destinations)
STUDENT
SIC
LEA
TUTOR
LIBRARY
STUDENTS' UNION

Step 3 (information flows)
Student's personal and course information
LEA list
Invoices
Students on course
Class list
Enrolment form
List of all new students (times two)

Step 4 (adding sources and destinations to the information flows)

GENERATOR	FLOW	DESTINATION
STUDENT	Student's personal and course information	SIC
SILEA list	FINANCE	
FINANCE	Invoices	LEA
SIStudents on course	DEPARTMENT	
DEPARTMENT	Class list	TUTOR
SIEnrolment form	STUDENT	

▶

SIList of all new students (1)
SIList of all students (2)

STUDENTS' UNION   NUS card
LIBRARY   Library card

LIBRARY
STUDENTS'
UNION
STUDENT
STUDENT

Step 5 (the completed diagram)

It is almost certain that if you were to attempt this diagram your results would not be exactly the same. However, provided that all the flows are represented correctly and there are no crossed lines, the result will be perfectly acceptable. Also, note that the student appears twice on the diagram. This is not just because the student is important (which of course they are!), but because it helps avoid crossed lines.

What remains now is to consider the systems boundary. If this manual information system were to be replaced by a new computer-based information system, it would be necessary to identify what would be within the systems boundary and what would be external to the system and, hence, outside the system boundary. For the purposes of this example, we will make some assumptions:

● *Students* are external to the system – they provide information as an input to the system and receive outputs from the system but are not themselves part of it – students will, therefore, be outside the system boundary.

● The *student information centre* is clearly central to the whole system and, therefore, is an integral part of the system under consideration – the SIC will lie inside the system boundary.

● The *finance* area needs a further assumption to be made. Let us assume that the finance area operates a computer-based information system for its accounting records and that the proposed system is to interface directly with it; in this case, it would make sense to include the finance area inside the system boundary.

● Similarly, suppose that the *library* operates its own computerised lending system. In the new system, it may wish to use an interface between the student records system and its own system for setting up new students' details. Since the library system is a separate one and does not require development itself, we will place the library outside the system boundary.

● As with the library, we need to make an assumption about the students' union information systems. The students' union may be able to use an interface file from the student record system to generate NUS cards automatically; but, as with the library, that system would lie outside the scope of the area under consideration. Therefore, we will place the students' union outside the system boundary.

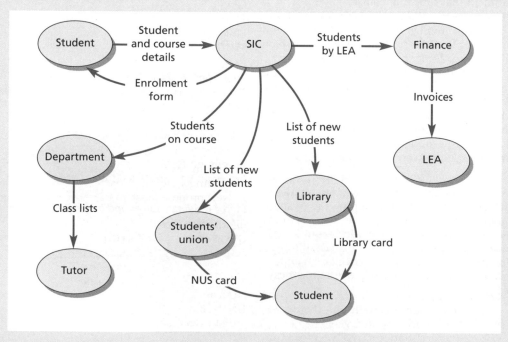

Figure 10.5 A simple, high-level IFD, excluding the system boundary

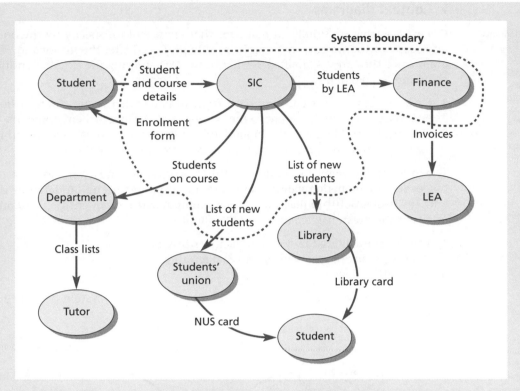

Figure 10.6 The completed IFD, including the system boundary

- It is reasonable to assume that the *tutor* is only to receive outputs from the system rather than carry out any processing of the data; it is reasonable, then, for the tutor to lie outside the system boundary.
- Finally, the local education authority is physically external to the university as well as not being part of the university itself; the LEA should, therefore, lie outside the system boundary.

We can see the result of this analysis in the final IFD, with the system boundary included (Fig. 10.6).

You will observe that there are three different types of information flow:

- The first crosses the system boundary from outside with its destination inside the boundary – it is thus an input to the system from the external environment.
- The second lies entirely within the system boundary and is, therefore, an output from one area in the system which then forms the input to another.

- The third begins inside the system boundary and its destination lies outside – it is, therefore, an output from the system into its external environment.

What we have now is a diagram that clearly identifies the context for the systems development under consideration. The diagram can be used by the analyst to check with the prospective system users that all areas have been covered. It also helps the user community build a picture of how a new computer system should help to make the processes more efficient. Two separate IFDs are often drawn:

1 System 'as-is' to identify inefficiencies in the existing system.
2 New proposed system to rectify these problems.

What is required is further work to identify the business processes and data needs for the proposed system and this is where the following tools come in.

Source: Simon Hickie, course notes

▶ Context diagrams

Context diagrams are simplified diagrams that are useful for specifying the boundaries and scope of the system. They can be readily produced after the information flow diagram since they are a simplified version of the IFD showing the external entities. They show these types of flow:

1 Flow crosses the system boundary from outside with its destination inside the boundary – it is thus an input to the system from the external environment.
2 Flow begins inside the system boundary and its destination lies outside – it is, therefore, an output from the system into its external environment.

The internal flows which lie entirely within the system boundary are not shown.

Context diagrams provide a useful summary for embarking on dataflow diagrams and entity relationship diagrams, since they show the main entities. The main elements of a context diagram are:

1 a circle representing the system to be investigated;
2 ellipses (or boxes) representing external entities;
3 information flows.

Figure 10.7 shows a context diagram for the student loan system described in Case Study 10.1

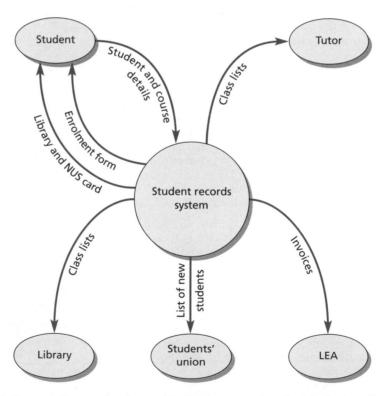

Figure 10.7 Context diagram for the student loan system described in Case Study 10.1

◗ Dataflow diagrams

Dataflow diagrams (DFDs) define the different processes in a system and the information that forms the input and output to the processes. They provide a process focus to a system. They may be drawn at different levels: level 0 provides an overview of the system with levels 1 and 2 providing increasing detail.

Dataflow diagrams of different types are one of the mainstays of many systems analysis and design methodologies. SSADM, for example, makes extensive use of DFDs, not only to document things as they are at the moment but also to document the *required* system. Whether the latter is really of any value is debatable. However, as a tool to document processes, data or information flows and the relationships between them for an existing system (computerised or paper-based), they are extremely valuable.

Dataflow diagrams build on IFDs by adding two new symbols as well as subtly redefining others.

The diagram conventions in Figure 10.8 are those that are in most common use in Europe. Differing methodologies adopt different symbols for some items (such a circle for a process), as you will see in some of the supplementary texts for this chapter.

Dataflow diagrams (DFDs)
Define the different processes in a system and the information that forms the input and output of the processes. They may be drawn at different levels. Level 0 provides an overview of the system with levels 1 and 2 providing progressively more detail.

Explanations of symbols

- *Sources and sinks*. An information source is one which provides data for a process and is *outside the system boundary*. A sink lies outside the system boundary and is a receiver of information. There is a clear distinction between the use of this symbol in the DFD and in the IFD that we looked at before, in that the symbol should not appear inside the system boundary.
- *Processes*. Processes convert data into either usable information or data in a different form for use in another process. The data that enter a process can come either from a datastore (see below) or from an external source.
- *Datastores*. A datastore can either provide data as input to a process or receive data that has been output from a process. The amount of time that data would spend in a datastore can vary from a very short time (e.g. fractions of seconds in the case of some work files) or much longer periods (e.g. months or years in the case of master files).
- *Dataflows*. A dataflow describes the exchange of information and data between datastores and processes and between processes and sources or sinks. Note that in this

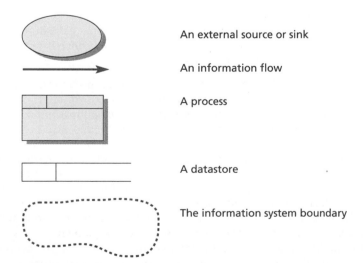

An external source or sink

An information flow

A process

A datastore

The information system boundary

Figure 10.8 Symbols used in data flow diagrams

context we are using data in a broad sense (to include information) rather than in the narrow sense used in Part 1 of the book.

● *Systems boundary*. This remains the same as for an IFD – it indicates the boundary between what lies inside the system under consideration and what lies outside.

Tips

It is unfortunate that many texts actually contain errors in the DFD examples used. This is mainly through having 'illegal' information flows. In a well-constructed diagram, you will note the following:

● Data do *not* flow directly between processes – the data that enter a process will come either from a source or from a datastore, they cannot exist in a vacuum!
● Data do *not* flow directly between datastores – there must be an intervening process that takes the input data and converts them into a new form and outputs them to either a datastore or a sink.
● Data do *not* flow directly from a datastore to a sink, or from a source to a datastore – there *must* be an intervening process.

To draw a basic high-level DFD, there are five steps required:

1 Identify and list all *processes* which take place in the system under consideration. A process is an event where an input of some kind, from either a source or a datastore, is transformed into an output (the output being either to a sink or to a datastore).
2 Identify all the datastores which you think exist in the system under consideration. A datastore will exist wherever a set of facts needs to be stored about persons, places, things or events.
3 For each process identified in Step 1, identify where the information used in the process comes from (this can be from a *source* or a *datastore* or both) and identify the output(s) from that process (which can be an information flow to a sink or to a datastore or to both).
4 Draw a 'mini-DFD' for each single process, showing the process box and any relevant sources, sinks or datastores.
5 Link the mini-DFDs to form a single diagram, using the datastores to link the processes together.

To help you to construct a diagram, the following tips are useful:

● Use A4 paper in landscape orientation.
● Aim to have no more than about six or seven processes on a page (ten maximum).
● Include the same datastores, sources and sinks more than once if required (to eliminate crossed lines or to make the flows clearer).

Before working through the student records example introduced in the previous section, it is necessary to introduce the concept of 'levelling' in DFDs. For anything other than a very small system with a handful of processes, it would be almost impossible to draw a single diagram with all the processes on it. It is necessary, therefore, to begin with a high-level diagram with just the broadest processes defined. Examples of high-level processes might be 'process customer orders', 'pay suppliers' or 'manufacture products'. Needless to say, each of the processes described can be broken down further until all the fundamental processes which make up the system are identified. It is usual to allow up to three or four levels of increasing detail to be identified. If there are any more levels of detail than this, it suggests that the system is too large to consider in one development and that it should be split into smaller, discrete subsystems capable of separate development.

To illustrate the levelling concept and also to demonstrate how process boxes should be used, we will take the simple example of checking a customer order. At Level 1, the process box will appear as in Figure 10.9.

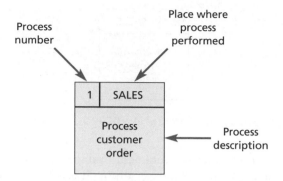

Figure 10.9 An example of a Level 1 process in a DFD

It is desirable to split this process up into smaller components. As an example, suppose the following are identified:

● Check customer credit limit – can the customer pay for the goods?
● Perform stock check – to see whether the desired goods are in stock.
● Create sales order – this may be a special order form that is needed for each order.
● Send order to warehouse – the warehouse will need to pick the stock ready for delivery.
● Dispatch customer order.
● Invoice customer.

This will give us six new processes to record at the next level. The process box for the first Level 2 process would be similar to this (Fig. 10.10).

Note that the process number is 1.1. This indicates that the process has been decomposed from the higher-level process numbered 1. Subsequent processes would be numbered 1.2, 1.3, 1.4 and so on. Also note that the process name begins with a verb. The choice of verb helps indicate more clearly the type of process that is being performed.

Suppose now that we still need to decompose the new process 1.1 further. For example, the credit check process may involve these steps:

● Calculate order value.
● Identify current balance.
● Produce credit check result.

We need to present the new processes as Level 3 processes, since they have been decomposed from the higher Level 2 process. The first of these would be represented as in Figure 10.11.

The new processes would be numbered 1.1.1, 1.1.2 and 1.1.3. This approach to numbering allows each of the low-level processes to be easily associated with the higher-level process that generated it. Thus, for example, processes 3.2.1, 3.2.2 and 3.2.3 could be tracked back to process 3.2, and thence to process 3.

Figure 10.10 An example of a Level 2 process in a DFD

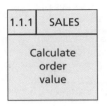

Figure 10.11 **An example of a Level 3 process in a DFD**

We will now return to the student enrolment example. We will concentrate on producing a Level 1 diagram for this procedure, although it will be clear that the example is a somewhat simplified one.

The first task is to identify all the processes which exist. Looking back to p. 395, we can identify the following:

1 Allocate unique student code.
2 Create student card index.
3 Create LEA list.
4 Invoice LEA.
5 Create student record card.
6 Create class list.
7 Issue enrolment form.
8 Issue new students list.

Step 2 requires us to identify all the datastores which might exist. Our example reveals the following:

● Student card index.
● LEA list.
● Student record card.
● Class list.
● New students list.

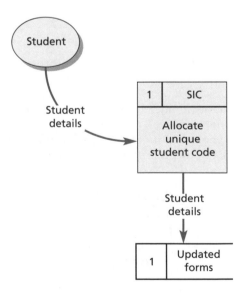

Figure 10.12 **Mini-DFD for process 1**

Step 3 requires us to construct a 'mini-DFD' for each of the eight processes identified above. We will restrict ourselves to the first three (see Figs 10.12, 10.13 and 10.14).

You will see from these figures that each of the processes we have considered has generated an output which forms an input to the next process. In the full diagram in Figure 10.15 you will see the complete picture, including all processes, datastores, sources and sinks. In this diagram, you will notice that the datastore 'card index file' appears more than once. This does not mean that there are two separate datastores with the same name, but that we have included it for a second time to make the diagram easier to draw. If we did not do this, there would have been either crossed lines or at least very tortuous ones. A system boundary is also included and you will note that sources and sinks lie outside the system boundary, while processes and datastores are inside. Many of the dataflows are inside the boundary, but you see where flows also cross the system boundary.

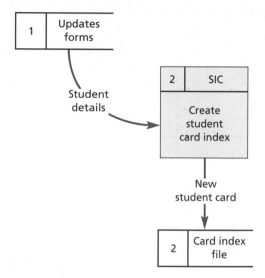

Figure 10.13 Mini-DFD for process 2

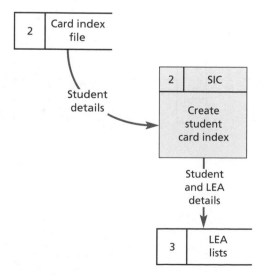

Figure 10.14 Mini-DFD for process 3

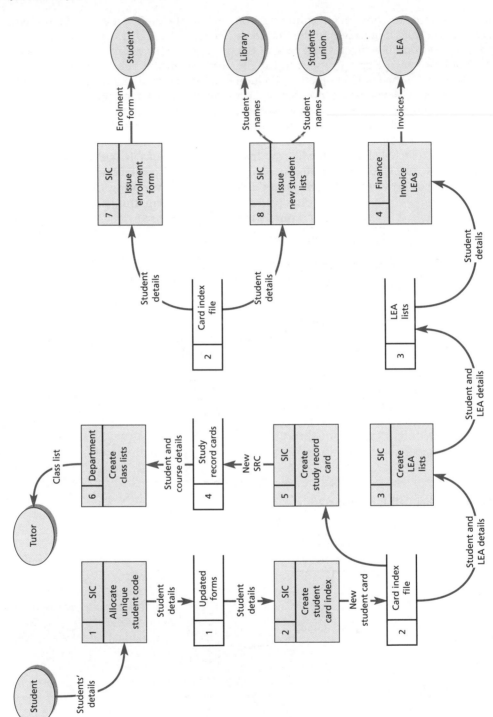

Figure 10.15 Completed DFD for the student record system

The final point to note is that a dataflow diagram is *time-independent*. This means that we are not trying to show the sequence in which things happen, but rather to show all the things that happen.

The benefits to an organisation of constructing a dataflow diagram can be summed up in the following 'three Cs':

● *Communication*. A picture paints a thousand words and DFDs are no exception. A diagram can be used by an analyst to communicate to end-users the analyst's understanding of the area under consideration. This is likely to be more successful than what Ed Yourdon describes as the 'Victorian novel' approach to writing specification reports.

● *Completeness*. A DFD can be scrutinised by functional area personnel to check that the analyst has gained a complete picture of the business area being investigated. If anything is missing or the analyst has misinterpreted anything, this will be clearer to the user if there is a diagram than if purely textual tools are used.

● *Consistency*. A DFD will represent the results of the fact-finding exercise conducted by the analyst. For the DFD to be constructed at all, the analyst will need to compare the fact-finding results from all the areas investigated and look for linkages between them. If the same processes are portrayed differently by different people, then the DFD will be hard to construct. In such an event, this will be a catalyst for the analyst to return to the fact-finding task, perhaps using brainstorming to get to the real facts.

▶ Entity relationship diagrams (ERDs)

Entity relationship diagrams (ERDs) provide a data-focused view of the main data objects or entities within a system such as a person, place or object and the relationships between them. It is a high-level view and does not consider the detailed attributes or characteristics of an object such a person's name or address.

In dealing with entity relationship diagrams, we must bear in mind that we are beginning to move away from the analysis stage of the systems development lifecycle towards the design stage. This is because we are beginning to think about how data are represented and how different sets of data relate to each other. For this chapter, we will concentrate on the fundamentals of entity relationships as they exist within a particular business situation, rather than on the detail of database design which follows directly from using this tool. Database design will be covered in much more detail in Chapter 12 where a technique called *data normalisation* will also be covered.

In any business situation, data (whether paper-based or computerised) are processed to produce information to assist in the decision-making processes within that business area. Processes may change over time and new ones be created to provide new or different information, but very often the types of data that underpin this remain relatively unchanged. Sometimes, data requirements change to allow new processes to be created. For example, a supermarket that moves to an EPOS system from a manual one will generate new data in the form of sales of specific products at specific times and in specific quantities. The data can then be linked to automated stock ordering systems and the like.

In order to produce good-quality information, two things are needed above all others. These are:

● accurate data;
● correct processing.

If data are inaccurate, correct processing will only result in the production of incorrect information. If data are accurate, but faults exist in the processing, the information will still be incorrect. However, in the second case, the capability exists for producing

Entity relationship diagrams (ERDs)
Provide a data-focused view of the main data objects or entities within a system such as a person, place or object and the relationships between them. It is a high-level view and does not consider the detailed attributes or characteristics of an object such as a person's name or address.

correct information if the processing is adjusted. With faulty data, it may not be so easy to rectify the situation.

In the analysis context, we need to engage in fact-finding activities that reveal the data that underlie all the relevant business processes, so that they can be captured and stored correctly and then processed to produce the required information. This process will reveal details of certain *entities* which exist within the business. One of the most useful methods that can be used here is the review of records and documentation (for example, order forms, stock control cards, customer files and so on).

Entity
....
An object such as a person, place, thing or event about which we need to capture and store data. An entity forms a data about a particular object.

An **entity** can be defined as *facts about a person, place, thing or event about which we need to capture and store data*. To take the example of a sales department, it would need to know facts about customers, orders, products and stock availability.

The essential symbols used in ERDs are very straightforward (Fig. 10.16). Note that additional symbols are used in some notations, but they are not necessary for the detail of analysis conducted in this chapter.

There are a number of possible relationships between entities.

One-to-one relationships

For each occurrence of entity A there is one and only one occurrence of entity B.

For example, let us assume that a lecturer may teach on only one module, and that module may be taught by only one lecturer (an unlikely situation) (Fig 10.17).

In Figure 10.17, we have added some additional information. This shows the nature of the relationship between the two entities. This information on the relationship is added to the line between the two entities. The relationship can be described in two ways according to which entity we refer to first. The relationships are:

- Lecturer *teaches* module.
- Module *is taught by* lecturer.

The practice of describing the relationship on the line is recommended since it helps others interpret the ERD more readily. However, the nature of the relationship is omitted on some subsequent diagrams for the sake of clarity.

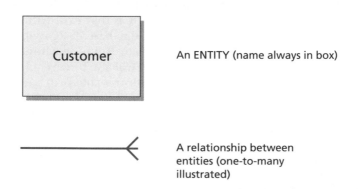

Figure 10.16 **Essential symbols in an entity relationship diagram**

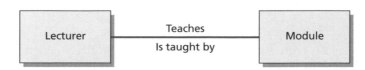

Figure 10.17 **A one-to-one relationship**

One-to-many relationships

For each occurrence of entity A, there may be zero, one or many occurrences of entity B. For example, a lecturer belongs to a single division, but that division *may* contain many lecturers (it may, of course, have no staff at all if it has only just been created or if all the staff decided to leave) (Fig. 10.18).

Many-to-many relationships

For each occurrence of entity A, there may be zero, one or many occurrences of entity B, *and* for each occurrence of entity B there may be zero, one or many occurrences of entity A.

For example, a course MODULE may be taken by zero, one or many STUDENTS and a student may take zero, one or many course modules (Fig. 10.19).

Unfortunately, especially in database design, many-to-many relationships can cause certain difficulties. Therefore, they are usually 'resolved' into *two* one-to-many relationships through the creation of a 'linking' entity. The decomposition is shown in Figure 10.20. The linking entity will contain an item of data from each of the other entities which allows the link to be made.

The following example shows a simple ERD which illustrates each of the above possibilities in more detail.

Suppose that a nation has a professional hockey league, comprising 16 clubs. Each club may only play in this one league. Each club may employ a number of professional players (although it is also possible for a team to consist completely of amateurs). Each professional player may only be contracted to one club at a time and may also experience periods of unemployment between contracts. Professional players are also eligible to play for their national team, but any one player may only ever play for one national team. Finally, suppose that professionals may have a number of sponsors and that each sponsor may sponsor a number of players.

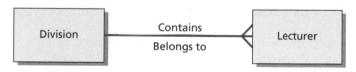

Figure 10.18 **A one-to-many relationship**

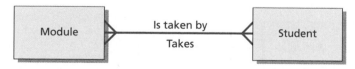

Figure 10.19 **A many-to-many relationship**

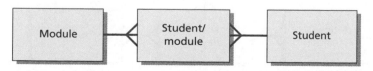

Figure 10.20 **A many-to-many relationship decomposed into two one-to-many relationships**

If we inspect the previous paragraph, we can identify the following entities:

LEAGUE
CLUB
PROFESSIONAL
NATIONAL TEAM
SPONSOR

Our first-cut ERD is shown in Figure 10.21.

The only obvious difficulty here is the many-to-many relationship between PROFES-SIONAL PLAYER and SPONSOR. We can resolve this by introducing a linking entity which contains something common to both an individual player and their sponsor. This can be seen in the next ERD of Figure 10.22.

We have introduced the linking entity SPONSORSHIP AGREEMENT to resolve the many-to-many relationship. Thus, any one player may have many sponsorship agreements, but any one sponsor agreement will belong to one player and to one sponsor.

This example was pretty straightforward. Others will be less so and it is therefore time to go back to our student records example from earlier in the chapter. In fact, we have already started the process of thinking about entities because the earlier DFD section required us to think about *datastores* – somewhere we store data, in other words a possible entity! Faced with a more complex set of possible relationships, it is useful to adopt a more structured approach to constructing ERDs.

There are six steps that can be helpful in producing an ERD, especially when one lacks experience in drawing them:

1 Identify all those things about which it is necessary to store data, such as customers and orders.
2 For each entity, identify specific data that need to be stored. In the case of a customer, for example, name, address and telephone number are all necessary.
3 Construct a cross-reference matrix of all possible relationships between pairs of entities and identify where a relationship actually exists. To do this, it is very helpful to identify some item of data which is common to the pair of entities under consideration.
4 Draw a basic ERD showing all the possible relationships, but not yet the *degree* of the relationship.
5 On the basic ERD, inspect each relationship and amend it to show whether it is a one-to-one, one-to-many or many-to-many relationship.
6 Resolve any many-to-many relationships by introducing an appropriate linking entity.

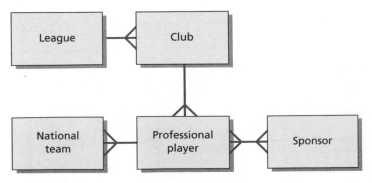

Figure 10.21 First ERD for the professional hockey example

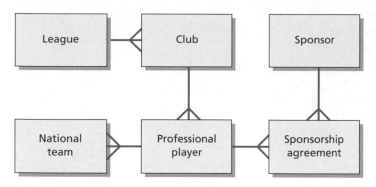

Figure 10.22 Final ERD for the professional hockey players

Step 1: Identify the entities

By going back to the example on p. 405 and the DFD on p. 402, it is possible to identify some possible candidate entities. The difficulty here is that the kind of documentation generated from the process obscures what we really need to hold data about. For example, there is a datastore called CARD INDEX FILE. This is hardly helpful! What really needs to be done is to ask the question: *'What things do we need to store data about?'* This may yield something rather different from the entities we thought we had before. As a starting point, we will begin with the following entities:

STUDENTS
COURSES
LEAS
DEPARTMENTS
MODULES

Step 2: Identify specific data for each entity

Each entity will be taken in turn, and a number of data attributes suggested.

STUDENTS
name
home address
sex
local education authority name
local education authority code
course code
term-time address
date of birth
next of kin

COURSES
course code
course description
department
course leader

LEAS
name
LEA code
address

contact name
telephone number
fax number

DEPARTMENT
department name
department location
office number
head of department

MODULES
module code
module leader
department
semester run
owning department

Step 3: Construct cross-reference matrix

This part of the process helps novice analysts identify where relationships exist between entities. It is necessary to identify where there is a common data attribute between pairs of entities, so indicating that a probable relationship exists between them. This is the hardest part of the whole exercise. The essence is to ask the question: *'For any occurrence of entity A, are there (now or likely to be in the future) any occurrences of B that relate to it?'* For example, is it likely that for a customer some orders exist that relate to it?

The cross-reference matrix in Figure 10.23 allows each pair of possible relationships to be examined for a link. In the cross-reference diagram, it is only necessary to identify each possible pair of relationships once. Also, there is no need to examine a relationship that an entity might have to itself. As a result, we are only interested in examining ten possible pairs of relationship for this small, five-entity example.

Steps 4 and 5: Construct first-cut ERD and add degree of relationship

Steps 4 and 5 will be combined, since there is nothing to be gained here from making separate diagrams. However, when drawing the diagram for Case Study 10.2, it would be wise to split the tasks as suggested.

The diagram in Figure 10.24 is almost correct, but there is still the question of the many-to-many relationship to resolve, so we must move to the final step.

	Student	Course	LEA	Department	Module
Student		Y	Y	N	Y
Course			N	Y	Y
LEA				N	N
Department					N
Module					

Figure 10.23 Cross-reference matrix for student records system

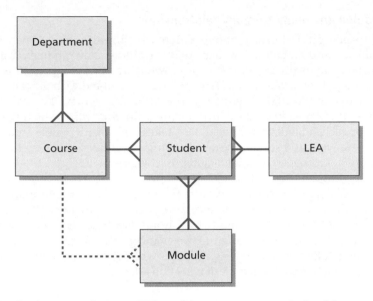

Figure 10.24 **Student record system ERD – with many-to-many relationship**

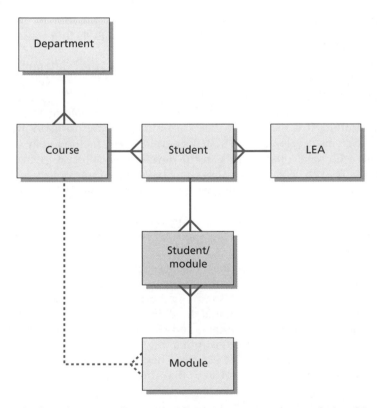

Figure 10.25 **Final student record system ERD – with many-to-many relationships decomposed**

Step 6: Resolve any many-to-many relationships

The many-to-many relationship about which we should be concerned is the one between students and modules. A student may enrol for many modules and any modules may be taken by many students. However, what we need to represent is the ability of students to enrol for as many or as few modules as required without causing complications in either the STUDENT entity or the MODULE entity. The many-to-many relationship is therefore resolved by introducing a linking entity which will have one occurrence for each module that one student takes and for the whole student population. So if there were 100 students each studying 8 modules, the new linking entity would contain 800 records. The final diagram is in Figure 10.25.

By working through the student record system example, we have moved from the process of identifying what the data requirements are for the system under consideration (the *analysis* part) and have made substantial progress on how a database might be constructed to hold the required data (which is a *design* task). This exercise is far from complete, however, as database design involves more than just looking at entity relationships. The detailed database design aspects will therefore be covered in the next chapter, where all aspects of system design are considered.

F *Focus on* soft systems methodology

Soft systems methodology

A methodology that emphasises the human involvement in systems and models their behaviour as part of systems analysis in a way that is understandable by non-technical experts.

Human activity system

A human activity system can be defined as 'notional system (i.e. not existing in any tangible form) where human beings are undertaking some activities that achieve some purpose' (Patching, 1990).

Soft systems methodology is a methodology that emphasises the human involvement in systems and models their behaviour as part of systems analysis in a way that is understandable by non-technical experts.

This methodology has its origins in Peter Checkland's (1981) attempt to adapt systems theory into a methodology which can be applied to any particular problem situation. From an information systems development perspective, it is argued that systems analysts often apply their tools and techniques to problems that are not well defined. In addition, it is also argued that since human beings form an integral part of the world of systems development, a systems development methodology must embrace all the people who have a part to play in the development process (users, IS/IT professionals, managers, etc.). Since these people may have conflicting objectives, perceptions and attitudes, we are essentially dealing with the problems caused by the unpredictability of human activity systems.

Human activity systems are 'notional system[s] (i.e. not existing in any tangible form) where human beings are undertaking some activities that achieve some purpose' (Patching, 1990).

Proponents of soft systems methodology (SSM) claim, therefore, that true understanding of complex problem situations (and in our case this means information systems development) is more likely if 'soft systems' methods are used rather than formal 'hard systems' techniques. This is not to say that 'hard' methods do not have a place. Rather, it is to suggest that the more traditional tools and techniques will have a greater chance of being used effectively if they are placed within a soft systems perspective.

Soft systems methodology has seven stages. They should be regarded as a framework rather than a prescription of a series of steps that should be followed slavishly.

▶ Stage 1: The problem situation: unstructured

This stage is concerned with finding out as much as possible about the problem situation from as many different affected people as possible. Many different views about the problem will surface and it is important to bring out as many of them as possible. The structure of the problem in terms of physical layout, reporting structure, and formal and informal communication channels will also be explored.

A soft systems investigator will often find that there is a vagueness about the problem situation being investigated and what needs to be done. There can also be a lack of structure to the problem and the situation that surrounds it.

▶ Stage 2 The problem situation: expressed

The previous stage was concerned with gathering an informal picture of the problem situation. This stage documents these findings. While there is no prescribed method for doing this, a technique that is commonly used is the drawing of 'rich pictures'. A rich picture can show the processes involved in the problem under consideration and how they relate to each other. The elements which can be included are the clients of the

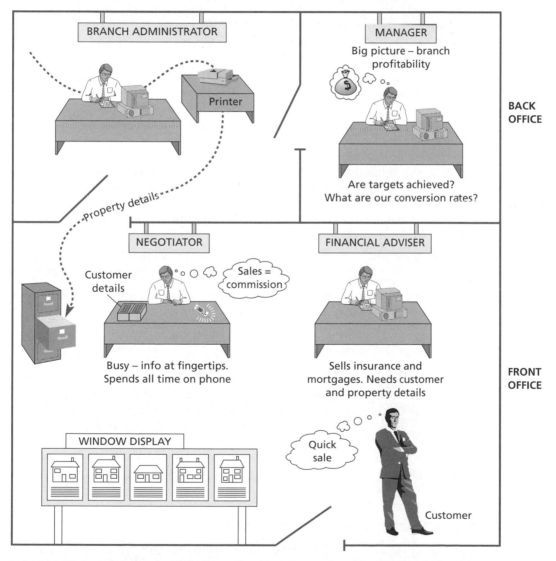

Figure 10.26 An example of a rich picture for an estate agency showing the needs and responsibilities of different staff

system (internal and external), the tasks being performed, the environment within which the system operates, the owners of the 'problem' and areas of conflict that are known to exist.

Rich pictures can act as an aid to discussion, between problem owner and problem solver or between analysts and users, or both. From a rich picture it then becomes possible to extract problem themes, which in turn provide a basis for further understanding of the problem situation. An example of a rich picture is shown in Figure 10.26. Such a diagram can be used in systems analysis to indicate the flows of information, the needs of staff and how the physical environment – in this case the office layout – affects the current way of working. This summary of the existing situation provides a valuable context for systems analysis and design.

▶ Stage 3: Root definitions of relevant systems

Checkland (1981) describes a root definition as a 'concise, tightly constructed description of a human activity system which states what the system is'.

A root definition is created using the CATWOE checklist technique. CATWOE is an acronym that contains the following elements:

- *Clients or Customers* – the person(s) who benefit, or are affected by or suffer from the outputs of the system and its activities that are under consideration.
- *Actors* – those who carry out the activities within the system.
- *Transformation* – the changes that take place either within or because of the system (this lies at the heart of the root definition).
- *Weltanchauung or Worldview* – this refers to how the system is viewed from an explicit viewpoint; sometimes this term is described as assumptions made about the system.
- *Owner* – the person(s) to whom the system is answerable: the sponsor, controller or someone who could cause the system to cease.
- *Environment* – that which surrounds and influences the operation of the system but which has no control over it.

The main use of the root definition is to clarify the situation so that it can be summed up in a clear, concise statement. An example of a root definition for a university might be:

> *To provide students with the maximum opportunity for self-development, while at the same time safeguarding academic standards and allowing the university to operate within its budgetary constraints.*

An alternative root definition might be:

> *A system to maximise revenue and the prestige of academic staff!*

If there are many different viewpoints to be represented, it is possible that a number of different root definitions may be constructed. These in turn will provide a basis for further discussion, so that a single agreed root definition can be produced. A single root definition that is hard to produce is indicative of sharp divisions between the CATWOE elements. From an information systems development perspective, if it is not possible to agree on a single root definition, then the systems development process is likely to be fraught with difficulties.

▶ Stage 4: Building conceptual models

A conceptual model is a logical model of the key activities and processes that must be carried out in order to satisfy the root definition produced in Stage 3. It is, therefore, a representation of what must be done rather than what is currently done.

Conceptual models can be shown on a simple diagram where activities and the links between them can be shown. Figure 10.27 shows a simple conceptual model of a student records system.

Where several alternative root definitions have been produced, it is usual to draw a conceptual model for each one. Successive iterations through the alternative models can then lead to an agreed root definition and conceptual model. When this has happened, it is possible to move on to the next stage.

▶ Stage 5: Comparing conceptual models with reality

Different alternative conceptual models that represent what should happen can be compared with the reality of what actually happens, as represented by the rich picture produced in Stage 2.

The purpose of this step is not to alter the conceptual models so that they fit more closely with what happens in reality. Instead, it is to enable the participants in the problem situation to gain an insight into the situation and the possible ways in which the change to reality can take place.

▶ Stage 6: Assessing feasible and desirable changes

From the output of Stage 5, an analysis of the proposed changes can be made and proposals for change drawn up for those that are considered feasible and desirable. Such changes may relate to information systems, but there is no restriction on the type or scope of the change.

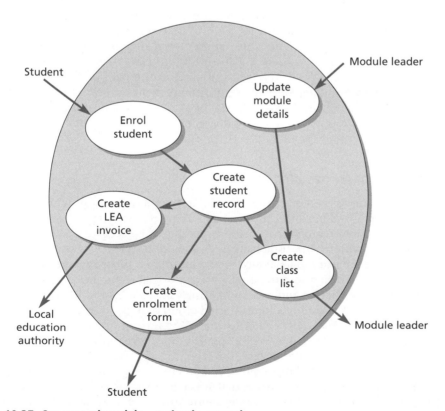

Figure 10.27 **Conceptual models – a simple example**

▶ Stage 7: Action to improve the problem situation

It is perhaps here that the application of the model is most evident. SSM does *not* describe methods for implementing solutions – that lies outside the scope of the methodology. What it *does* do is to provide a framework through which problem situations can be understood. In fact, there is no reason that SSM should not be used as a tool for assisting the implementation of the required solution – the steps can be repeated, but this time the problem situation under consideration is the implementation of the required solution. This in turn may throw up alternative methods such as SSADM or rapid applications development (Chapter 7) as the best approach to information systems development. Indeed, SSM has often been used as a 'front end' to more traditional structured development methodologies.

Systems analysis – an evaluation

Any systems development project will be confronted by issues such as system size, complexity and acquisition method. These factors affect the choice of fact-finding and documentation tools. It is appropriate, therefore, to consider three alternative acquisition methods and review fact-finding and documentation needs for each.

▶ Bespoke development

Bespoke software, which can be developed either internally or by a third party, presents the greatest scope for using the full range of analysis tools. Complex systems will require that the analyst gain a very clear and precise understanding of the business processes that take place, and all the tools at the analyst's disposal may need to be used. A combination of interviewing, documentation review and observation will yield much of the information that is needed, but if the system is a large one with many users, questionnaires may also need to be used. Brainstorming will be valuable, especially when linkages between different processes and subsystems are being investigated.

Complex projects will also require the use of all of the documentation tools we have discussed. Needless to say, the resulting diagrams will be more detailed and extensive than the ones given as examples in this chapter.

▶ Purchasing packages off-the-shelf

Even though there is no requirement to produce something from which the system designer can produce a blueprint for the build stage, it is still necessary to gain a clear understanding of user requirements before a package is considered. Therefore, the fact-finding process will still be undertaken, but will be geared towards gaining an understanding of the features a package must support and those that are only desirable.

One benefit of deciding to purchase a package is that a number of candidate packages can be initially selected and used by the analyst as a means of identifying real user needs. It is possible, for example, for a selected group of users to review the features of a small number of packages with a view to compiling an appropriate requirements catalogue. Also, when users actually have an opportunity to experiment with a package, the analyst can gain a much greater insight into what the users' *real* requirements are.

For the analyst, it may still be useful to construct information flow and dataflow diagrams to help ensure that the package that is finally selected will support the required linkages, both between processes in the business area under consideration and to other business areas (from sales to accounts, for example). It will also be useful for the analyst to construct an entity relationship diagram to be sure that the packaged software will support the data requirements of the organisation.

▶ End-user applications development

The situation here is somewhat different from the previous two acquisition methods. The end-user will have a clear idea of what the system is required to do. Also, it is less likely that the system will need to have linkages to other applications. The emphasis for the user, therefore, should be on identifying the data and processing requirements clearly so that they can be reviewed by others in the organisation, and an application can be produced which delivers good-quality information. Of the techniques discussed, the most relevant is the entity relationship diagram. By concentrating on data and how they are to be captured and represented, the user increases the probability that the data will be correct, while the use of fourth-generation language tools will help maximise the probability that the processing will also be correct.

Many end-user-developed applications suffer from poor database design and, as a consequence, the processing requirements are much more complex and prone to error. By taking care to consider carefully the relationships between the relevant data items, the probability of obtaining successful end-user developed applications is increased.

Software tools for systems analysis

Software tools are available to assist in the analysis phase. These usually focus on the diagramming rather than the enquiry stage, so much of the skill remains with the analyst in interpreting the users' requirements before producing meaningful diagrams showing the information flows and processes.

An important issue in using software tools to help the analyst is the degree to which the diagrams used to summarise processes can be converted easily into the system design and then into the final system. Traditionally, there have been separate tools for the analyst, designer and programmer. Since there is a strong overlap with the design phase, we will defer the examination of these tools to Chapter 12, which has a section on computer-aided software engineering or CASE tools. Integrated CASE tools are intended to bridge the gap between analysis, design and programming.

CASE STUDY 10.2

ABC case study

Background
The following scenario is typical of many companies in the retail/wholesale business. A number of information flows exist both internally within the organisation and also with people outside. This case study is used for exercises on information flow diagrams (IFDs), dataflow diagrams (DFDs) and entity relationship diagrams (ERDs).

The exercise continues in Chapter 11 when the reader is asked to produce a detailed database design based on the entity relationship diagram produced and the paper form examples.

ABC case study information
Andy's Bonsai Company (ABC) specialises in selling bonsai kits by mail order. The kits are made up of a number of elements, including soil, plant pots and seeds. Other products such as mini-garden tools are also sold.

Customers place orders by telephone or by mailing an order slip which is printed as part of an ABC advert. Customers pay by cheque, credit card or debit card.

When an order is received by ABC, it is directed to a sales clerk. Each sales clerk has responsibility for

▶

CUSTOMER ORDER FORM

CUSTOMER NUMBER

C234792

CUSTOMER ADDRESS

26 Vicarage Drive

Thorndyke

West Yorkshire

WF24 7PL

ORDER NUMBER

4214

DATE ORDERED

29 March 1999

TELEPHONE NUMBER

01482 7374

CODE	DESCRIPTION	PRICE	QTY	VALUE
1983	MINI-OAK	19.95	2	39.90
0184	MINI-MAPLE	24.50	2	49.00
2984	MINI GARDEN TOOLS (STAINLESS)	29.95	1	29.95
3775	MINI WATERING CAN (COPPER)	17.50	1	17.50

PAYMENT TYPE   Cheque   ORDER VALUE   136.35

WAREHOUSE CARD INDEX

LOCATION   J82   CARD No. 19

PRODUCT CODE   4151

PRODUCT DESCRIPTION   MINI-ASH

START QTY	TRANSACTION QTY	DATE	SIGNATURE
37	−5	2/6/99	RON
28	−3	4/6/99	JEFF
25	−15	9/6/99	LUCY
10	+50	17/6/99	ERIC
60			

MANUFACTURING ORDER FORM

MANUFACTURING ORDER NUMBER	7210
PRODUCT CODE	4151
PRODUCT DESCRIPTION	MINI-ASH
QUANTITY ORDERED	50
DATE ORDERED	3/6/99
DATE REQUIRED	13/6/99
DATE DELIVERED	17/6/99
SIGNATURE	BERYL

PURCHASE ORDER FORM

SUPPLIER NUMBER
S165

PURCHASE ORDER NUMBER
214

SUPPLIER ADDRESS

14 Wyke Trading Estate

Heckwhistle

West Yorkshire

WF9 5JJ

DATE ORDERED

29 March 1999

TELEPHONE NUMBER

01637 7346

CODE	DESCRIPTION	PRICE	QTY	VALUE
23	OAK CHIPPINGS	30.00	25	750.00
69	2" POTS	0.03	1000	300.00
84	SILVER SAND	1.77	10	17.70
75	MINI WATERING CAN (STAINLESS)	4.56	20	91.20

		ORDER VALUE	1158.90

a particular geographic region. The sales clerk will enter the details of the order onto a preprinted three-part order form. One part is retained by the sales clerk, one copy together with the payment is sent to the accounts department and the other is sent to the warehouse (on confirmation of the customer's creditworthiness).

On receipt of the customer orders and payment details, the accounts department ensures that the customer's payment is valid. If the payment is satisfactory, the department will inform the sales department and the order may proceed. An unsatisfactory payment situation is also communicated to the sales department, which then informs the customer of the problem.

The warehouse keeps a manual card-index system of stock and raw materials held together with copies of the customer orders. When an order is dispatched to the customer, the relevant order form is marked as having been dispatched. The warehouse also needs to keep track of the amount of product in stock and, when stock levels are low, it sends a manufacturing order to the manufacturing department.

The manufacturing department is responsible for ordering materials from various suppliers and then packaging them into products for sale to the customer. A three-part purchase order is made out: one part is sent to the supplier, one part is retained by the manufacturing department and the third part is sent to the accounts department. The accounts department holds copies of purchase orders for future matching with delivery notes and invoices. When the supplier delivers the ordered items, together with a delivery note, a check is made to ensure that the delivery matches the order. The supplier will send an invoice to the accounts department on confirmation that the delivery is correct so that payment can be made.

Questions

1 Using the ABC case study, produce an information flow diagram for the company by following the steps given earlier in the chapter. Does the diagram tell you anything about ABC's operations which may need some attention (such as missing or superfluous information flows)?

2 Using the ABC case study and the information flow diagram that you drew in answer to Question 1, produce a simple Level 1 dataflow diagram for the company by following the steps given earlier in the chapter. Compare your answer with that by one of your colleagues. Are the diagrams the same? If not, is it possible to say which is correct? If not, why not?

3 Using the ABC case study, including the sample forms included below the main text, construct an entity relationship diagram for the company. Make sure that you do a cross-reference matrix before attempting to draw the diagram. When you have drawn your first-cut diagram, check for many-to-many relationships and eliminate any that you find by using the appropriate technique described earlier in the chapter.

Summary

Stage summary: systems analysis

Purpose:	Define the features and other requirements of the information system
Key activities:	Requirements capture (interviews, questionnaires, etc.) diagramming
Inputs:	User's opinions, system documentation, observation
Outputs:	Requirements specification

1 The analysis phase of systems development is aimed at identifying *what* the new system will do.

2 Analysis will identify the business processes which will be assisted by the software, the functions of the software and the data requirements.

3 The results of the analysis phase are summarised as a requirements specification which forms the input to the design phase, which will define *how* the system will operate.

4 Fact-finding techniques used at the analysis stage include:

● questionnaires;
● interviews;

- observation;
- documentation review;
- brainstorming.

5 The results from the fact-finding exercise are summarised in a requirements specification and using different diagrams such as:

- information flow diagrams which provide a simple view of the way information is moved around an organisation;
- dataflow diagrams which show the processes performed by a system and their data inputs and outputs;
- entity relationship diagrams which summarise the main objects about which data needs to be stored and the relationship between them.

6 The depth of analysis will be dependent on the existing knowledge of requirements. An end-user development may have limited analysis since the user will have a good understanding of their needs. A software house will need to conduct a detailed analysis which will form the basis for a contract with the company for which it is developing software.

EXERCISES

Self-assessment exercises

1 What is the difference between the 'funnel' and 'pyramid' approaches to structuring an interview?

2 Why can closed questions still be useful in an interview?

3 Assess the relative effectiveness of interviews versus questionnaires when attempting to establish user requirements.

4 In an information flow diagram, why should we not record information flows that lie completely outside the system boundary?

5 What are the main differences between an information flow diagram and a dataflow diagram?

6 What is meant by the term 'levelling' in dataflow diagrams?

7 In a sales order processing system, which of the following are not entities? Customer, colour, size, product, telephone number, sales order, salesperson, order date.

8 Why might the construction of an ERD still be useful even if an off-the-shelf package was going to be purchased?

Discussion questions

1 Use a simple example with no more than five processes or ten information flows to examine the differences between the information flow diagram and the dataflow diagram. Which would be more effective for explaining deficiencies with an existing system to:

(a) a business manager;
(b) a systems designer?

Justify your reasoning.

2 Compare the effectiveness of 'soft' methods of acquiring information such as interviews and questionnaires and 'hard' methods of gathering information such as document analysis and observation of staff. In which order do you think these analysis activities should be conducted and on which do you think most time should be spent?

3 'For producing a database, the only type of diagram from the analysis phase that needs to be produced is the entity relationship diagram. Dataflow diagrams are not relevant.' Discuss.

Essay questions

1 Compare and contrast alternative fact-finding methods and analysis documentation tools as they might relate to bespoke software development and the purchase of off-the-shelf packages.

2 Errors in the analysis stage of a systems development project are far more costly to fix than those that occur later in the systems development lifecycle. Why do some organisations seem to devalue the analysis process by seeking to get to the system build as quickly as possible?

3 Compare and contrast the relative effectiveness of the use of information flow diagrams, dataflow diagrams and entity relationship diagrams by a business analyst to demonstrate inefficiency in a company's existing information management processes. Use examples to illustrate your answer.

Examination questions

1 Briefly review the arguments for and against using interviewing as a means of determining system requirements.

2 Explain the relationship between the initiation and analysis phases of the systems development lifecycle.

3 Briefly explain (in one or two sentences) the purpose of each of the following diagramming methods:
   (a) information flow diagram;
   (b) context diagram;
   (c) dataflow diagram;
   (d) entity relationship diagram.

4 Draw a diagram showing each of the following relationships on an ERD:
   (a) The customer places many orders. Each order is received from one customer.
   (b) The customer order may contain many requests for products. Each product will feature on many customer orders.
   (c) Each customer has a single customer representative who is responsible for them. Each customer representative is responsible for many customers.

5 The final examination question is based on a detailed case study for Megatoys and is to be found on the companion web site.

References

Buzan, I. (1995) *The Mind Map Book*, BBC Books, London

Checkland, P.B. (1981) *Systems Thinking, Systems Practice*, John Wiley, Chichester

Kavanagh, D. (1994) 'OMT development process, vintage 1994', in K. Spurr, P. Layzell, L. Jennison and N. Richards (eds) *Business Objects: Software Solutions*, John Wiley, New York, 90–105

Patching, D. (1990) *Practical Soft Systems Analysis*, Financial Times Pitman Publishing, London

Taylor, D. (1995) *Business Engineering with Object Technology*, John Wiley, New York

Yeates, D., Shields, M. and Helmy, D. (1994) *Systems Analysis and Design*, Financial Times Pitman Publishing, London

Further reading

Avison, D.E. and Fitzgerald, G. (1996) *Information Systems Development: Methodologies, Tools and Techniques*, Blackwell, Oxford

Eva, M. (1992) *SSADM Version 4: a User's Guide*, McGraw-Hill, Maidenhead

Flynn, D. (1992) *Information Systems Requirements: Determination and Analysis*, McGraw-Hill, Maidenhead

Griffiths, G. (1998) *The Essence of Structured Systems Analysis Techniques*, Prentice-Hall, Hemel Hempstead

Kendall, K. and Kendall, J. (1998) *Systems Analysis and Design*, Prentice-Hall, London

Lejk, M. and Deeks, D. (1998) *An Introduction to Systems Analysis Techniques*, Prentice-Hall, Hemel Hempstead

Robinson, B. and Prior, M. (1995) *Systems Analysis Techniques*, International Thompson Computer Press, London

Tudor, D. and Tudor, I. (1997) *Systems Analysis and Design: a Comparison of Structured Methods*, Macmillan, Basingstoke

Weaver, P.L., Lambrou, N. and Walkley, M. (1998) *Practical SSADM Version 4+: a Complete Tutorial Guide*, Financial Times Pitman Publishing, London

Whitten, J. and Bently, L. (1998) *Systems Analysis and Design Methods*, Irwin/McGraw-Hill, Boston, MA

Web links

www.cio.com CIO.com for Chief Information Officers and IS staff has many articles related to analysis and design topics in different research centres such as security (www.cio.com/research/security), CRM (www.cio.com/research/crm) and infrastructure (www.cio.com/research/infrastructure).

www.360.com *Computer Weekly* is a IS professional trade paper with UK/Europe focus which has many case studies on practical problems of analysis, design and implementation.

www.eds.com/case_studies/cs_home.shtml Case studies from major BIS consultant EDS illustrate many of the issues of systems analysis, design and implementation.

www.research.ibm.com/journal *IBM Systems Journal* and the *Journal of Research and Development* have many cases and articles on analysis and design related to e-business concepts such as knowledge management and security.

www.intranetjournal.com/itadvisor Intranet journal has case studies on systems analysis and design specific to intranets.

www.fdic.gov/regulations/information/index.html FDIC: The Federal Financial Institutions Examination Council (FFIEC) handbook for conducting examinations of banks' and savings associations' information systems is interesting since it recommends appropriate approaches and activities to different stages of building banking systems which also apply to other systems.

knowledge.wharton.upenn.edu/category.cfm?catid=14 Managing Technology at Wharton articles cover a range of technology management issues, including analysis, design and implementation issues.

Chapter 11

Systems design

LEARNING OBJECTIVES

After reading this chapter, readers will be able to:
- define the difference between analysis and design and the overlap between them;
- synthesise the relationship between good design and good-quality information systems;
- define the way relational databases are designed;
- evaluate the importance of the different elements of design for different applications.

MANAGEMENT ISSUES

Management issues

Design is also a critical phase of BIS development since errors at this stage can lead to a system that is unsatisfactory for the user. From a managerial perspective, this chapter addresses the following questions:

- What different types of design need to be conducted for a quality BIS to be developed?
- What are the key aspects of design for an e-business system?

Links to other chapters

This chapter is closely linked to Chapters 10 and 12, since the design phase receives input from the requirements specification of the analysis phase and the design specification acts as input to the implementation phase.

Introduction

The design phase of information systems development involves producing a specification or 'blueprint' of how the system will work. This forms the input specification for the final stage of building the system by programmers and database administrators. The design phase is also closely linked to the previous analysis phase, since the users' requirements directly determine the characteristics of the system to be designed.

The **systems design** is given in a design specification defining the best structure for the application and the best methods of data input, output and user interaction via the user interface. The design specification is based on the requirements collected at the analysis stage.

Design is important, since it will govern how well the information system works for the end-users in the key areas of performance, usability and security. The design specification will include the architecture of the system, how security will be implemented, and methods for entry, storage, retrieval and display of data.

Systems design
The design phase of the lifecycle defines how the finished information system will operate. This is defined in a design specification of the best structure for the application and the best methods of data input, output and user interaction via the user interface. The design specification is based on the requirements collected at the analysis stage.

Aims of system design

In systems design we are concerned with producing an appropriate design that results in a good-quality information system that:

- is easy to use;
- provides the correct functions for end-users;
- is rapid in retrieving data and moving between different screen views of the data;
- is reliable;
- is secure;
- is well integrated with other systems.

These factors are all likely to be important to the end-users. As well as these factors, we must think forward to future releases of the software. When the software is updated in the maintenance phase, it is important to have a system that can be easily modified. Good documentation is important to this, but equally important is that the design be flexible enough to accommodate changes to its structure. To achieve flexibility, simplicity in design is a requirement. Many designers and developers adopt the maxim 'KISS' or 'Keep It Simple, Stupid!'.

Whitten and Bentley (1998) point out that design does not simply involve producing an architectural and detailed design, but is also an evaluation of different implementation methods. For example, an end-user designing an application will consider whether to implement a system within an application such as Microsoft Access or develop a separate Visual Basic application. However, it is usually possible to take the 'make-or-buy' decision earlier in the software lifecycle, even when the detailed design constraints are unknown. The acquisition method is described in more detail in Chapters 7 and 8 on the startup phases of a project.

Constraints on system design

The system design is directly constrained by the user requirements specification, which has been produced as a result of systems analysis. This will describe the functions that are required by the user and must be implemented as part of the design. As well as the requirements mentioned in the previous section, there are environmental constraints on design which are a result of the hardware and software environment of implementation. These include:

- hardware platform (PC, Apple or Unix workstation);
- operating system (Windows 98, Windows 2000 Mac OS 10 or Unix);
- data links required between the application and other programs or a particular relational database such as Oracle or MS SQL Server;
- design tools such as CASE tools;
- methodologies or standards adopted by the organisation, such as SSADM;
- system development tools or development environments for programming, such as Microsoft Visual Studio;
- number of users to be supported and the performance required.

The relationship between analysis and design

As Yeates et al. (1994) point out, there is considerable overlap between analysis and design. To help ensure completion of the project on time, preliminary design of the architecture of the system will start while the analysis phase is progressing. Furthermore, the design phase may raise issues on requirements that may require further analysis with the end-users, particularly with the prototyping approach.

The distinction is often made between the *logical* representation of data or processes during the analysis stage and the *physical* representation at the design stage. Consider, for example, data analysis: here the entity relationship diagram of the analysis phase will be transformed into a physical database table definition at the design stage. A logical entity 'customer' will be specified as a physical database table 'Customer' in which customer records are stored. Similarly, the dataflow diagram will be transformed into a structure chart indicating how the different submodules of the software will interact at the design stage.

Elements of design

The different activities that occur during the design phase of an information systems project can be broken down in a variety of ways. In this section we consider different ways of approaching system design. These alternatives are often used in a complementary fashion rather than exclusively.

A common approach to design is to consider different levels of detail. In the next main section we start by considering an overall design for the architecture of the system. This is referred to as 'system design'. Once this is established, we then design the individual modules and the interactions between them. This is known as 'module design'. Through using this approach we are tackling design by using a functional decomposition or top-down approach, similar to that referred to in Chapter 9 on project management as the 'work breakdown structure'.

▶ Top-down or bottom-up?

Top-down design

The top-down approach to design involves specifying the overall control architecture of the application before designing the individual modules.

Since many systems are made from existing modules or pre-built components that need to be constructed, the design approach that is most commonly employed is a **top-down** strategy. In this approach, it is best to consider the overall architecture first and then perform the detailed design on the individual functional modules of the system. The 'divide and conquer' approach can then be used to assign the design and implementation tasks for each module to different development team members. The description here will follow this approach by looking at the overall design first and then at the detailed module design.

The **bottom-up** approach to design starts with the design of individual modules, establishing their inputs and outputs, and then builds an overall design from these modules.

Bottom-up design

The bottom-up approach to design starts with the design of individual modules, establishing their inputs and outputs, and then builds an overall design from these modules.

▶ Validation and verification

An aspect of the design which is quite easy to overlook and which is stressed by Budgen (1994) is testing that the design we produce is the right one. Checking the design involves validation and verification.

Validation

This is a test of the design where we check that the design fulfils the requirements of the business users which are defined in the requirements specification.

In **validation** we will check against the requirements specification and ask '*Are we building the right product?*' In other words, we test whether the system meets the needs of the end-users identified during analysis. This will occur during testing of the system by the end-users; it highlights the value of prototyping in giving immediate feedback of whether a design is appropriate.

When undertaking **verification** we will 'walk through' the design and ask '*Are we building the product right?*' Since there are a number of design alternatives, designers need to consult to ensure they are choosing the optimal solution. Verification is a test of the design to ensure that the one chosen is the best available and that it is error-free.

Verification

This is a test of the design to ensure that the design chosen is the best available and that it is error-free.

The two questions should be considered throughout the design process and also form the basis for producing a test specification to be used at the implementation stage.

▶ Scalability

Scalability

The potential of an information system, piece of software or hardware to move from supporting a small number of users to a large number of users without a marked decrease in reliability or performance.

Scalability is the potential of an information system, piece of software or hardware to move from supporting a small number of users to a large number of users without a marked decrease in reliability or performance.

When designing information systems, the design target must always be for the maximum anticipated number of users. Many implementations have failed, or have had to be redesigned at considerable cost, because the system used in the development and test environment with a small number of users does not *scale* to the live system with many more users. If the system does not scale, there may be major problems with performance which makes the system unusable. Volume testing (Chapter 12) in which the anticipated workload of the live environment is simulated, can help us foresee problems of scalability.

The increased popularity of three-tier client/servers considered later in the chapter results from their ability to scale better from departmental to enterprise-level systems. When purchasing or designing applications for the enterprise, it is necessary to check with vendors and other adopters on the scale of their implementations – what are the maximum number of users and transaction rates that are supported?

▶ Data modelling and process modelling

Another common approach to design is to consider data modelling and process modelling separately. The design of the data structures required to support the system, such as input and output files or database tables, are considered in relation to information collected at the analysis stage as the ERD and data requirements. In SSADM a separate stage is identified for data design which is followed by process design, although as Downs et al. (1992) point out, the two are often combined.

Process modelling is the design of the different modules of the system, each of which is a process with clearly defined inputs and outputs and a transformation process. Dataflow diagrams are often used to define system processes.

Data modelling considers how to represent data objects within a system, both logically and physically. The entity relationship diagram is used to model the data and a data dictionary is used to store details about the characteristics of the data, which is sometimes referred to as 'metadata'.

The processes or program modules which will manipulate this data are designed based on information gathered at the analysis stage in the form of functional requirements and dataflow diagrams. This approach is used, for example, by Curtis (2002). While this is a natural division, there is a growing realisation that for a more efficient design these two aspects cannot be considered in isolation. Object-oriented techniques, which are increasing in popularity, consider the design of process and associated data as unified software objects. These are considered in more detail at the end of this chapter.

Other elements of design are required by the constraints on the system. To ensure that the system is easy to use we must design the user interface carefully.

To ensure that the system is reliable and secure, these capabilities must be designed into the system. User interface and security design are elements of design that will be considered at both the overall or system design phase and the detailed design phase.

> **Process modelling**
> Involves the design of the different modules of the system, each of which is a process with clearly defined inputs and outputs and a transformation process. Data flow diagrams are often used to define processes in the system.

> **Data modelling**
> Data modelling involves considering how to represent data objects within a system, both logically and physically. The entity relationship diagram is used to model the data.

▶ What needs to be designed?

We will review the following different elements of systems design:

1 *Overall design or system design.* What are the best architecture and client/server infrastructure? The overall design defines how the system will be broken down into different modules and how the user will navigate between different functions and different views of the data.

2 *Detailed design of modules and user interface components.* This defines the details of how the system will operate. It will be reviewed by looking at user interface and input/output design.

3 *Database design.* How to design the most efficient structure using normalisation.

4 *User interface design.* How to design the interface to make it easy to learn and use.

5 *Security design.* Measures for restricting access data and safeguarding data against deletion.

System or outline design

System design involves specifying an overall structure or **systems architecture** for all the different components that will make up the system. It is a high-level overview of the different components that make up the architecture of a system and how they interact. The components include software modules that have a particular function such as a print module, the data they access, and the hardware components that may be part of the system. Hardware will include specifying the characteristics of the client PC and servers, plus any additional hardware such as an image scanner or specialised printer.

> **System or outline design**
> A high-level definition of the different components that make up the architecture of a system and how they interact.

> **Systems architecture**
> The design relationship between software applications, hardware, procss and data for an information system.

Designing the overall architecture involves specification of how the different hardware and software components of the system fit together. To produce this design, a good starting point is to consider the business process definition that will indicate which high-level tasks will be performed using the different components of the system.

▶ Designing applications infrastructure for the e-business

Management of an e-business applications infrastructure involves delivering appropriate applications and levels of service to all users of e-business services. The objective of the designer, at the behest of the IS manager, is to deliver access to effective, integrated applications and data that are available across the whole company. Traditionally businesses have tended to develop applications silos or islands of information as depicted in Figure 11.1(a). Figure 11.1(b) shows that these silos have three different levels of applications: (1) there may be different technology architectures or hardware used in different functional areas; (2) there may also be different applications and separate

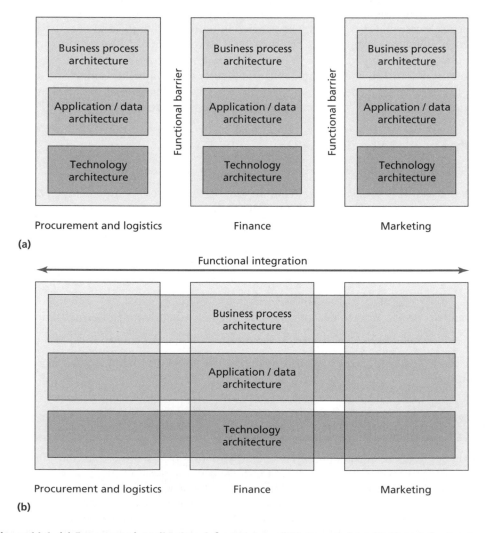

Figure 11.1 (a) Fragmented applications infrastructure, (b) integrated applications infrastructure
Source: Adapted from Hasselbring (2000)

databases in different areas; (3) processes or activities followed in the different functional areas may also be different.

These applications silos are often a result of decentralisation or poorly controlled investment in information systems, with different departmental managers selecting different systems from different vendors. An operational example of the problems this may cause is if a customer phones a B2B company for the status of a bespoke item they have ordered, the person in customer support may have access to their personal details, but not the status of their job which is stored on a separate information system in the manufacturing unit.

To avoid the problems of a fragmented applications infrastructure companies have been attempting, since the early 1990s, to achieve the more integrated position shown in Figure 11.1(b). Here the technology architecture, applications and data architecture and process architecture are uniform and integrated across the organisation. To achieve

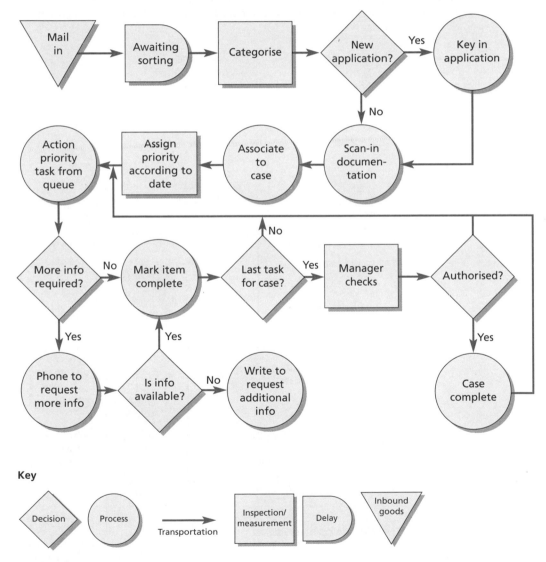

Figure 11.2 Flow process chart showing the main operations performed by users when working using workflow software

Enterprise resource planning (ERP) software.
....
A software system with integrated functions for all major business functions across an organisation such as production, distribution, sales, finance and human resources management. It is normally purchased as an off-the-shelf package which is tailored by a consultant. A single package typically replaces many different previous packages.

this many companies turned to **enterprise resource planning (ERP)** vendors such as SAP, Baan, PeopleSoft and Oracle. Here, they are effectively using a pre-existing design from the off-the-shelf package, and the design involves selecting appropriate modules and tailoring them for the revised business process.

Process modelling

Process modelling is used to identify the different activities required from a system, as explained in Chapter 10. These functions can be summarised using a flow process chart as shown in Figure 11.2. The process is described further in the case study on workflow systems.

Flow process charts such as Figure 11.2 can be used to inform the architectural design directly since they help to identify the different components needed and how they link. Figure 11.3 concentrates on hardware, but also describes location of data and applications.

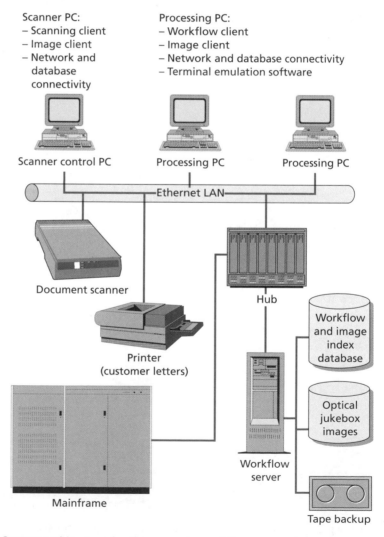

Figure 11.3 **System architecture for the example workflow processing system**

Use of flow process charts for design of workflow systems

Flow process charts are a tool commonly used in operations management applications to help in identifying the bottlenecks in manufacturing plants. They can also be usefully applied to some information systems applications to help represent the flow of information in an organisation. They represent a hybrid between information flow diagrams and dataflow diagrams.

Flow diagrams have been used for a long time in the design of programs. Recently, they have waned in popularity and tend to have been replaced by dataflow diagrams as a method of displaying structure, since this is less ambiguous and supports different levels of abstraction (detail). However, flow diagrams are described since they offer an alternative analysis method which helps in system design and is easy to understand for business users.

In this example, mortgage (loan) applications are received by post. It is then necessary to identify new applications and supporting documentation for applications already received. (This is a decision point indicated by a diamond-shaped decision box.) New applications are keyed into the workflow system as a new case and the original form scanned in for reference (these are processes shown as circles on the chart). Supporting material such as ID (driving licences) and letters from employers are also scanned in. A team member will then assign or associate all scanned images of material which have been scanned into a particular case. Assigning new documents (*assignment tasks*) is always the most important task, so these need to be placed by the software automatically at the head of the workflow queue. Once assigned, the documents will need to be actioned (*action tasks*) by the operator, so according to the type of document and when it needs to be chased, the workflow system will assign a priority to the task and place it on the workflow queue. Team members will then have to action tasks from the workflow queue which are prioritised according to date. Processing an action task will usually involve phoning the customer for clarification or writing a letter to request additional information. After this has been achieved, the operator will mark the item as complete and a new workflow task will be created if necessary: for example, to follow up if a letter is not received within ten days.

This diagram is useful to system designers since they can identify different modules of a system and the hardware and software necessary to support these modules. In this case some of the modules are:

- scan document (scanner and scanning software);
- associate document to customer case (link to customer database);
- prioritise document (specialised workflow module);
- review document (link to customer database);
- contact customer (link to phone system and letter printer).

From these modules, a system architecture will be developed as shown in Figure 11.3.

The overall architecture description will also include details of the navigation between the main screens or views of data in the application which can be based on this type of diagram.

Screen functions needed in this software are to categorise the type of mail received, associate it with a particular 'case' or customer and review items of work in the workflow queue, marking them as complete where appropriate. Table 11.1 summarises what is achieved during the different types of design.

Table 11.1 **Comparison between the coverage of system and detailed design**

Design function	System design	Detailed design
Architecture	Specification of different modules and communication between them; specification of hardware components and software tools	Internal design of modules
User interface	Flow of control between different views of data	Detailed specification of input forms and dialogues
Database	Data modelling of tables	Normalisation
File structure	Main file types and contents	Detailed 'record and field structure'
Security	Define constraints	Design security method

◗ The client/server model of computing

Client/server model

This describes a system architecture in which end-user computers access data from more powerful server computers. Processing can be split in various ways between the server and client.

The majority of modern information systems are designed with a client/server architecture. In the **client/server model**, the clients are typically desktop PCs which give the 'front-end' access point to business applications. The clients are connected to a 'back-end' server computer via a local- or wide-area network. As explained in Chapter 5, applications accessed through a web browser across the Internet are also client/server applications. These include e-commerce applications for online purchase and application service provider solutions such as remote e-mail management.

When it was introduced, the client/server model represented a radically new architecture compared with the traditional centralised processing method of a mainframe with character-based 'dumb terminals'.

Client/server is popular since it provides the opportunity for processing tasks to be shared between one or more servers and the desktop clients. This gives the potential for faster execution, as processing is shared between many clients and the server(s), rather than all occurring on a single server or mainframe. Client/server also makes it easier for end-users to customise their applications. Centralised control of the user administration and data security and archiving can still be retained. With these advantages, there are also system management problems which have led to an evolution in client/server architecture from two- to three-tier as described below. The advantages and disadvantages of client/server are discussed in Chapter 5.

When designing an information system for the client/server architecture, the designer has to decide how to divide tasks between the server and the client. These tasks include:

● data storage;
● query processing;
● display;
● application logic including the business rules.

In 1995 the Gartner Group produced a report defining five different ways in which application logic, data management and presentation could be partitioned between client and server. These include:

1 distributed presentation (three-tier client/server);
2 remote presentation (three-tier client/server);
3 distributed logic (three-tier client/server);
4 remote data management (two-tier client/server);
5 distributed database (two-tier client/server).

Since that time, descriptions of client/server design have followed just two main approaches: two-tier and three-tier client/server. Two-tier client/server is sometimes referred to as '*fat client*', the application running on the PC being a large program containing all the application logic and display code. It retrieves data from a separate database server. Three-tier client/server is an arrangement in which the client is mainly used for display, with application logic and the business rules partitioned on a server as a second tier and the database server the third tier. Here the client is sometimes referred to as a '*thin client*', because the size of the application's executable program is smaller. It is important to understand the distinctions between these, since they involve two quite different design approaches that can have significant implications for application performance and scalability. These are the 'thin client' approach where the client only handles display and the 'fat client' approach where a larger program runs on the client and handles both display and application logic. In the 'fat client' model the client handles the display and local processing, with the server holding the data (typically in a database) and responsible for handling processing of queries on the back end. This model, which is known as two-tier client/server, is still widely used, but more recently the three-tier client/server has become widespread due to problems with unreliability and lack of scalability with two-tier systems. Examples of recent successful three-tier implementations are described in the book by Edwards and DeVoe (1997). These include:

Two-tier client/server

Sometimes referred to as 'fat client', the application running on the PC being a large program containing all the application logic and display code. It retrieves data from a separate database server.

Three-tier client/server

The client is mainly used for display with application logic and the business rules partitioned on a second-tier server and a third-tier database server. Here the client is sometimes referred to as a 'thin client', because the size of the executable program is smaller.

- UK Employment Service record system;
- Peoplesoft enterprise resource planning;
- 3M Patient Care management system;
- Wells Fargo Internet banking;
- MCI telecommunications customer transaction management systems.

Figure 11.4 shows a simple two-tier client/server arrangement. In this, a client application directly accesses the server to retrieve information requested by the user, such as a report of 'aged debtors' in an accounting system. In many systems, this is mediated through SQL, with an SQL request being passed to the server as a parameter which is processed by the server and the result of the query returned to the client. In this

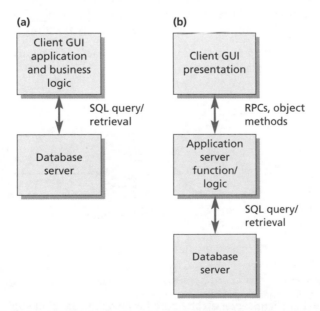

Figure 11.4 (a) Two-tier and (b) three-tier client/server architecture compared

two-tier model, the client handles all application logic such as control flow, the display of dialogues and formatting of views. Typically, the business rules will also be contained in the 'fat client' application, although these could also be held on the database as stored procedures. The two-tier model has the advantage of simplicity, but it has the main problem that the business rules become bound in with the user interface code. This makes maintenance difficult. It has also been found that two-tier client/server did not scale very well to larger implementations.

In a three-tier client/server model (Fig. 11.4), the GUI or 'thin client' forms the first tier, with the application and function logic separated out as a second tier and the data source forming the third tier. In this model there may be a separate application and database server, although these could reside on the same machine. Two-tier client/server may be the most rapid to develop in a RAD project, but it will not be the most efficient at runtime or the easiest to update. Through separating out the display coding and the business application into three tiers, it is much easier to update the application as business rules change (which will happen frequently). It also offers better security through fine-tuning according to the service required.

System architecture for e-commerce applications

Most e-commerce and application service provider applications use a three-tier client–server application with a thin client. If we take the example of online banking, a database server will hold customer and transaction details. Access to the data will be controlled by an application server that uses tools such as Active Server Pages (ASP) or Java servlets to mediate between the user interface and the database. Web browsers are here acting as a thin client that is mainly used for information display and user interaction. Some application control may occur in the browser using JavaScript for validation or a Java application for more complex data presentation, user interaction and managing security. Figure 11.5 summarises this arrangement.

Although the three-tier model of an e-commerce system suggests a relatively simple architectural design, the reality is more complex. Different servers are needed which combine applications logic and database storage for different requirements. These may be physically separate servers or combined. Figure 11.6 shows a typical e-commerce systems architecture for an e-tailer such as Jungle (www.jungle.com) or Land's End (www.landsend.com). The purpose of each of the servers is as follows:

● *Web server.* Manages http requests from client and acts as a passive broker to other servers. Returns or serves web pages.

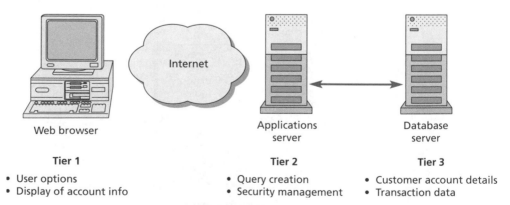

Figure 11.5 Three-tier client/server architecture for an online banking application
Source: Chaffey (2002)

- *Merchant server.* This is the main location of the application logic and integrates the entire application by making requests to the other server components.
- *Personalisation server.* Provides tailored content – may be part of commerce server functionality.
- *Payment commerce server.* Manages payment systems and secure transactions.
- *Catalogue server.* A document management server used to display detailed product information and technical specifications.
- *CRM server.* Stores information on all customer contacts.
- *ERP server.* Required for information on stock availability and pricing from the customer. Will also need to be accessed for sales order processing and histories. Logistics for distribution will also be arranged through the ERP server.

It is evident that designing the method of integration between different components to create a fully integrated e-commerce is not straightforward! The best approach to simplifying the design is often to reduce the number of suppliers of components to improve the ease of data and applications integration.

◗ Program and module structure

The module and program structure will also be outlined at the system design stage. There are various notations used by programmers to indicate the structure that will be used. The best known is the structure chart which is used in the design methodology JSD (Jackson system design – Jackson, 1983). An example of a structure chart is illustrated in Figure 11.7. A structure chart shows how the software will be broken down into different modules and gives an indication of how they will interact. Here the main control module is calling a variety of other modules with different functions. The interaction or exchange of data items between procedures is also shown. For example, the 'edit customer' module

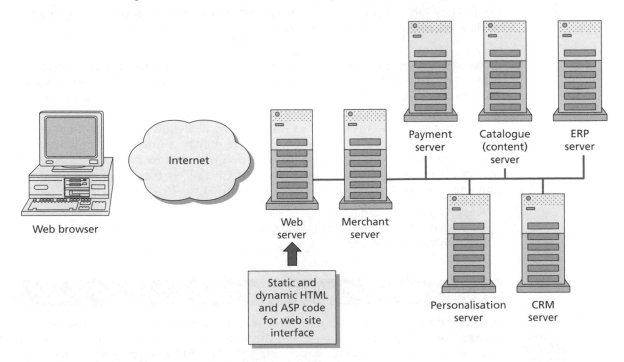

Figure 11.6 A typical e-commerce systems architecture for an e-tailer
Source: Chaffey (2002)

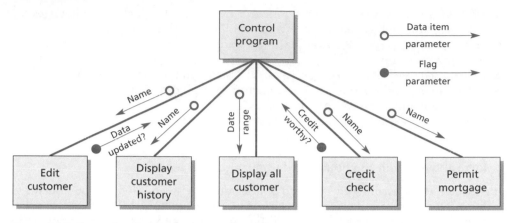

Figure 11.7 **Example of a program structure chart**

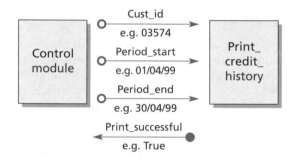

Figure 11.8 **Part of a structure chart showing how parameters are passed from a control module to a module to print a credit history**

is passed the name (or customer code) of the customer to edit and if the user changes the data a 'flag' (True or False) parameter is passed back to the control module, indicating that the data was updated. Similarly, the credit check module is passed the name of the customer and a flag indicates whether the customer is creditworthy or not.

The interactions between modules will normally be defined at this stage rather than at the detailed design stage. For example, there may be a function to produce a customer report of credit history. Here, the function will need to know the customer and the time period for which a report is required. Thus the system design will specify the function with three parameters as shown in Figure 11.8.

Function: Print_Credit_history
Parameters: Cust_id, Period_start, Period_end
Return value: Print Successful

Detailed or module design

Detailed design involves the specification of how an individual component of a system will function in terms of its data input and output, user interface and security.

Detailed design (module design)

Detailed design involves considering how individual modules will function and how information will be transferred between them. For this reason, it is sometimes referred to as *module design*. A modular design offers the benefit of breaking the system down into different units which will be easier to work on by the team developing the system. It will also be easier to modify modules when changes are required in the future.

Module design includes:

- how the user interface will function at the level of individual user dialogues;
- how data will be input and output from the system;
- how information will be stored by the system using files or a database.

Detailed design is sometimes divided further into external and internal design. The external design refers to how the system will interact with users, while the internal design describes the detailed workings of the modules.

Focus on relational database design and normalisation `F`

Business users are often involved in the design of relational databases, either in an advisory capacity (specifying what data they should contain) or when building a small personal database, perhaps of customer contacts. For this reason, the terminology used when working with databases and the process of producing a well-designed database are described in some detail.

Relational database terminology was introduced in Chapter 4, but it is restated here since understanding the terms is important to understanding the design process. This section uses the example of a sales order processing database for a clothing manufacturer, 'Clothez'.

▶ Databases – fundamental terms

Databases are used for the management of information and data within organisations. The functions of a database, whether it be a tiny address book on a phone or a corporate database supporting an entire organisation, are to enter, modify, retrieve and report information

The terms defining the structure of a relational **database** can be considered as a hierarchy or tree structure. A single database is typically made up of several **tables**. Each table contains many **records**. Each record contains several **fields**. These terms can be related to the Clothez example as follows:

1 *Database.* All information for one business application (normally made up of many tables). Example: *sales order* database.

2 *Table.* Collection of records for a similar entity. Example: all customers of the company within the sales order database. Other tables in the database are *product* and *order*.

3 *Record.* Information relating to a single instance of an entity (comprising many fields). Example: single customer such as *Poole*.

4 *Field.* An attribute of the entity. Example: *customer name* or *address* for a particular customer such as *Poole*.

Database
....
All information for one business application (normally made up of many tables).

Table
....
Collection of records for a similar entity.

Record
....
Information relating to a single entity (comprising many fields).

Field
....
An attribute of the entity.

This structure is represented as a diagram in Figure 11.9 for the Clothez database. It can be seen that the sales order processing database for Clothez could be designed and implemented as three tables: customer, order and product. Each table such as customer is made up of several records for different customers and then each record is divided down further into fields or attributes which describe the characteristics of the customers such as name and address.

Note that this example database is simplified and this structure only permits one product to be ordered when each order is placed. The reason for this restriction is that the database has not been fully normalised from order table into order-header and order-line tables. The normalisation process is described in a later section.

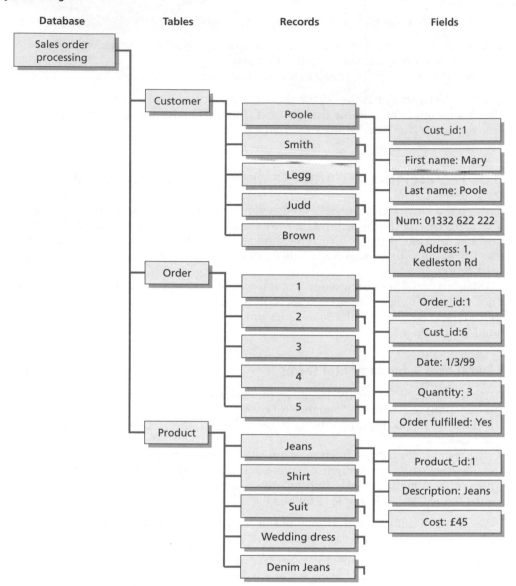

Figure 11.9 **Diagram illustrating the tree-like structure used to structure data within a relational database. This example refers to the Clothez database. The fields are only shown for the first record in each table**

If the data was entered into a database such as Microsoft Access, the tables and their records and fields would appear as in Fig. 11.10. All three tables are shown. Fields and records for the product table are shown in Fig. 11.11.

A further term that needs to be introduced is **key field**. This is the field by which each record is referred, such as customer number. The key field provides a *unique* code such as '001' or '993AXR', comprising numbers or letters or both. It is required to refer to each record to help distinguish between different customers (perhaps three different customers called Smith). Key fields are also used to link different tables, as explained in the next section.

Key field

This is a field with a unique code for each record. It is used to refer to each record and link different tables.

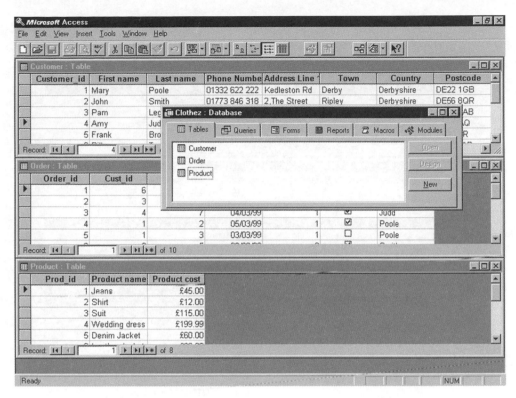

Figure 11.10 **Clothez database in Microsoft Access**

Figure 11.11 **Product table showing records and fields**

▶ What makes an Access database relational?

The term *relational* is used to describe the way the different *tables* in a database are linked to one another. Key fields are vital to this. In recognition of the importance of key fields, Microsoft uses the key as the logo or brand icon for the Access database.

In the Clothez databases, the key fields are: Customer_id, Product_id and Order_id (id is short for identifier; reference (ref) or code number (num) could also be used for these field names). These fields are used to relate the three tables, as shown in Figure 11.12.

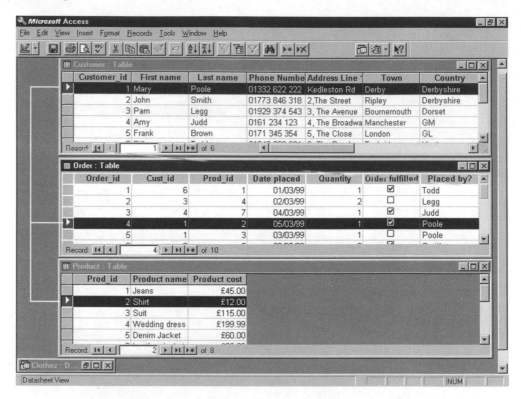

Figure 11.12 Clothez database in Microsoft Access, showing how the Order table is related to Customer and Product

Figure 11.12 shows how the highlighted record in the order table (Order_id = 4) uses key fields to refer to the customer, Mary Poole, who has placed the order (Cust_id = 1) and the product (Shirt) she has ordered (Prod_id =2).

To understand how the key fields are used to link different tables, two different types of fields need to be distinguished: primary and foreign keys.

Primary keys provide a unique identifier for each table which refers directly to the entity represented in the table. For example, in the product table, the primary key is Prod_id. There is only one primary key per table, as follows:

- Customer table: Customer_id
- Order table: Order_id
- Product table: Prod_id

Secondary or foreign keys are used to link tables by referring to the primary key of another table. For example, in the order table, the secondary key Cust_id is used to indicate which customer has placed the order. The order table also contains Prod_id as a foreign key, but neither of the other tables has secondary keys. There may be zero, one or more secondary key fields per table.

Figure 11.13 shows how the primary key fields in the customer and product tables are used to link to their corresponding foreign keys (Cust_id and Prod_id) in the order table when constructing a query in Microsoft Access. This is a summary query which summarises the details of orders by taking data from each table. The result of the query is shown in Figure 11.14. The highlighted record in Figure 11.14 is the example relationship which was used to illustrate the links between tables in Figure 11.12.

Primary key fields
These fields are used to uniquely identify each record in a table and link to similar secondary key fields (usually of the same name) in other tables.

Rules for identifying primary and secondary keys

1 **Primary keys**
● The primary key provides a unique identifier for each record.
● There is usually one primary key per table (unless a compound key of more several fields is used).
● The name of the field is usually the name of the entity or table followed by code, reference, identifier or id.

2 **Secondary key**
● The secondary key always links to a primary key in another table(s).
● There may be 0, 1 or several secondary keys in each table.

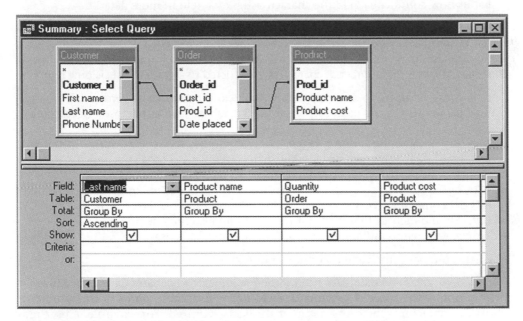

Figure 11.13 **Query design screen for the summary query in the Clothez database**

Last name	Product name	Quantity	Product cost	Date placed
Judd	Dungarees	1	£35.00	04/03/99
Legg	Wedding dress	2	£199.99	02/03/99
Poole	Shirt	1	£12.00	05/03/99
Poole	Suit	1	£115.00	03/03/99
Smith	Denim Jacket	3	£60.00	02/03/99
Todd	Denim Jacket	1	£60.00	28/02/99
Todd	Dungarees	1	£35.00	05/02/99
Todd	Jeans	1	£45.00	01/03/99
Todd	Leather Jacket	1	£89.00	03/03/99

Record: ◄◄ ◄ [3] ► ►► ►＊ of 9

Figure 11.14 **Summary query for orders placed from Clothez database**

▶ Defining field data types and sizes

A relatively straightforward aspect of database design is deciding on the field definitions. Fields need to be defined in terms of:

- field name;
- field data type;
- field data size;
- field validation rules.

These are defined when the database is created, since storage space for each field is pre-allocated in a database. During analysis and design, the field characteristics are managed in a **data dictionary**, often referred to as the *metadata* or 'data about data', particularly with reference to data warehouses (Chapter 6).

Let us now consider each of the characteristics of a field in more detail:

Data dictionary
A repository that is used
to store the details of the
entities of the database.
It will define tables,
relations and field details
which are sometimes
referred to as metadata
or 'data about data'.

1 *Field name*. Field names should clearly indicate the content of the field. It is conventional in some databases to use underscores rather than spaces to define the name, since some databases may not recognise spaces (e.g. Order_fulfilled rather than Order fulfilled). In some databases the number of characters is restricted to eight, but this is now rare.

2 *Field data type*. Data types define whether the field is a number, a word, a date or a specialised data type. The main data types used in a database such as Microsoft Access are:

- *Number*. Whole number or decimal. (Most databases recognise a range of numeric data types such as integer, real, double, byte, etc.)
- *Currency*. This data type is not supported for all databases.
- *Text*. Often referred to as character, string or alphanumeric. Phone numbers are of this data type, since they may need to include spaces or brackets for the area code.
- *Date*. Should include four digits for the year! Can also include time.
- *Yes/No*. Referred to as Boolean or true/false in other databases.

Key fields can be defined as either number or text.

3 *Field data size*. Field data sizes need to be pre-allocated in many databases. This is to help minimise the space requirements. Field size is defined in terms of the number of digits or characters which the designer thinks is required. For example, a user may define 20 characters for a first name and 40 characters for an address. It is better to overestimate than to risk having to modify the field later.

4 *Field validation rule*. Validation rules are necessary to check whether the user has entered valid data. Basic types of validation are:

- Is field essential? For example, postcodes are usually mandatory to help identify a customer's address.
- Is field format correct? For example, postcodes or ZIP codes usually follow a set format.
- Is value within range? For example, an applicant for a mortgage would have to be more than 18 years of age.
- Does field match a restricted list? An entry for marital status might need to be 'married', 'divorced' or 'single'. Restricted list choices can be defined in separate 'lookup tables'.

To maintain data quality validation is an important, but sometimes neglected, aspect of detailed design which is covered in more detail in the section on input design.

Table 11.2 shows how the field definitions for a table can be summarised. Note that setting the key fields to a field size of six allows a maximum number of customers of 999 999.

Table 11.2 Definition of field details for the order table in the Clothez database (with fields added to show range)

Field name	Field type	Field size	Validation rule	Key field
Order_id	Number	6	Mandatory	Primary
Cust_id	Number	6	Mandatory	Foreign
Prod_id	Number	6	Mandatory	Foreign
Date_placed	Date	10	Mandatory, must be valid date	
Order_fulfilled	Yes/No	3	Restricted, must be Yes/No	
Special_instructions	Text	120	Not mandatory	
Total_order_value	Currency	10	Not mandatory	

▶ What is normalisation?

Normalisation is a design activity that is used to optimise the logical storage of data within a database. It involves simplification of entities and removal of duplication of data.

It is one of the most important activities that occurs during database design. The main purpose of data normalisation is to group data items together into database structures of tables and records which are simple to understand, accommodate change, contain a minimum of redundant data and are free of insertion, deletion and update anomalies. These anomalies can occur when a database is modified, resulting in erroneous data. They are explained in the next section. Since this activity should be

Normalisation
This design activity is a procedure that is used to optimise the physical storage of data within a database. It involves simplification of entities and minimisation of duplication of data.

Table 11.3 Summary of terms used to describe databases and normalisation

Term	Definition
Normalisation	The process of grouping attributes into well-structured relations between records linked with those in other tables
Table	Used to store multiple records of different instances of the same type of entity such as customer or employee
Relation	Relational database terminology for a record
Attribute	The smallest named unit in a database; other names include 'data item' and 'field'
Update anomaly	The inability to change a single occurrence of a data item in a relation without having to change others in order to maintain data
Insertion anomaly	The inability to insert a new occurrence (record) into a relation without having to insert one into another relation first
Deletion anomaly	The inability to delete some information from a relation without also losing some other information that might be required
Functional dependency	A functional dependency is a relationship between two attributes and concerns determining which attributes are dependent on which other attributes: 'attribute B is fully functionally dependent on attribute A if, at any given point in time, the value of A determines the value of B' – this can be diagrammed as A → B
Determinant	An attribute whose value determines the value of another attribute
Primary key	An attribute or group of attributes that *uniquely* identifies other non-key attributes in a single occurrence of a relation
Foreign key	An attribute or group of attributes that can be used to link different tables; the foreign key will link to the primary key in another table
Composite key	A key made up of more than one key within a relation
Candidate key	A candidate key is a determinant that can be used for a relation; a relation may have one or more determinants; determinants can be either single attributes or a composite key

conducted when all databases are designed, and since databases are so widely used in business applications, we consider the process of normalisation in some detail.

Normalisation is essentially a simplifying process that takes complex 'user views' of data (such as end-user, customer and supplier) and converts them into a well-structured logical representation of the data.

Normalisation has its origins in the relational data model developed by Dr E.F. Codd from 1970 onwards and based on the mathematics of set theory. In this section we present a brief, straightforward explanation of the steps involved in normalising data, which can be applied to simple and complex data structures alike. The description of normalisation involves a series of stages which convert unnormalised data to normalised data. There are a series of intermediate stages which are referred to as first, second, third and fourth normal forms.

▶ Some definitions

Before commencing the steps of normalisation, it is worth providing some key definitions in order to simplify the flow of the following sections. These definitions are summarised in Table 11.3.

▶ Unnormalised data

Unnormalised data are characterised by having one or more repeating groups of attributes. Many user views of data contain repeating groups. Consider a customer order form for the Clothez company (Fig. 11.15): there might be such information as customer name, customer address and order date recorded at the top of the form; there might also be a section in the main body of the form that allows multiple items to be ordered.

It is possible to represent the user view described above in diagrammatic form which is equivalent to a physical database table. Note that the example in Figure 11.16 uses a subset of the information shown in the order form example.

Name:	Mary Poole	**Order date:**	5/3/99	**Order no:**	4
Address:	1 Kedleston Road	**Tel no:**	01332 622 222	**Cust no:**	1
	Derby				
Post code:	DE22 1GB				

Line no	**Product no**	**Product description**	**Quantity**	**Price**
1	2	Shirt	1	£12.00

Figure 11.15 Customer order form for the Clothez company

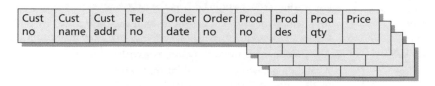

Figure 11.16 Repeating groups for the Clothez database

The possibility of entering multiple lines into a single order form is clearly a repeating group, i.e. order no. is being used to identify multiple order lines within the view and so, therefore, is not a unique determinant of each order line and its details.

It might also be argued that address also represents a repeating group, because there are two address lines. However, in practice a set number of address lines would be given a unique data name for each line and could be identified by a customer number. (Address is an example of a non-repeating 'data aggregate', whereas the line details are an example of a repeating data aggregate.)

By constructing such a diagram, it becomes much easier to identify repeating groups of data and thus pave the way to progressing to first normal form (1NF).

▶ Insertion/update/deletion anomalies

At this stage it is not obvious why repeating groups of data are a bad thing! If Figure 11.16 is transformed into a table, however, updating it could result in errors or inconsistencies. Each of the three different types of anomalies is now explained in turn with reference to Table 11.4.

Table 11.4 Table with example data for the structure shown in Figure 11.16

Cust no	Cust name	Cust addr	Tel no	Order date	Order no	Prod Num	Prod des	Prod Qty	Price
1	Poole	1, Ked	01332	5/03/99	4	2	Shirt	1	12
2	Smith	2, The	01773	2/03/99	6	5	Denim	3	60
3	Legg	3, The	01929	2/03/99	2	4	Weddin	2	199
3	Poole	1, Ked	01332	3/03/99	5	3	Suit	1	115

Insertion anomaly

If it was desired to enter a new customer into the table, it would not be possible without having an order to enter at the same time.

Update anomaly

An **update anomaly** indicates that it is not possible to change a single occurrence of a data item (a field) in a relation (table) without having to change others in order to maintain the correctness of data.

If a customer such as 'Poole' had several orders in the table and that customer moved to a new address, all the entries in the table where that customer appeared would have to be updated if inconsistencies were not to appear.

Deletion anomaly

A **deletion anomaly** indicates it is not possible to delete a record from a relation without also losing some other information which might still be required.

If a customer such as 'Smith' had only one order in the table and that table entry was deleted, information about the customer would also be deleted.

The way to get round some of these problems is by normalising the data. Stage one of this process is the removal of repeating groups of data, i.e. proceeding to **first normal form (1NF)**.

Insertion anomaly
It is not possible to insert a new occurrence record into a relation (table) without having to also insert one into another relation first.

Update anomaly
It is not possible to change a single occurrence of a data item (a field) in a relation (table) without having to change others in order to maintain the correctness of data.

Deletion anomaly
It is not possible to delete a record from a relation without also losing some other information which might still be required.

First normal form (1NF)
Transforming unnormalised data into its first normal form state involves the removal of repeating groups of data.

▶ First normal form (1NF)

In the example above, the repeating group comprises *product number, product quantity* and *price*. Removing these attributes into a separate table will not suffice, however. For example, how could each entry in the newly created table be related to the order to which it is attached? The answer lies in including a linking attribute (also known as a 'foreign key') which is present in both the modified table and the new table. In this case, a sensible attribute to use would be *order number*. The first step in normalisation has thus resulted in the transformation of one table into two new ones. The two new tables are shown in Figure 11.17. The example shows the relationship between fields at the top and example records below.

Removing insertion/update/deletion anomalies

Even though repeating groups have been removed by splitting the unnormalised data into two tables (relations), anomalies of all three types still exist.

Insert anomaly

- In the customer/order relation, an order cannot be entered without also entering the customer's name and address details, even though they may already exist on another order; a customer cannot be added if there is no order to be placed.
- In the order/product relation, an item cannot be added without also adding an order for that item.

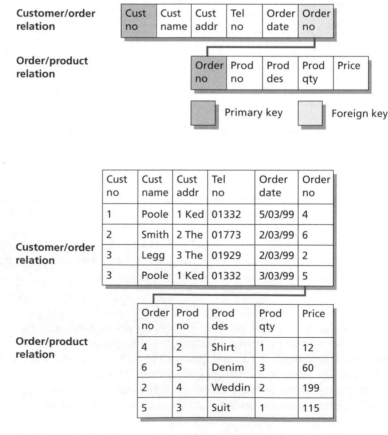

Figure 11.17 **The revised table structure and example data for two tables**

Update anomaly

- In the customer/order relation, a customer's name and address details cannot be amended without needing to amend all occurrences (where the customer has more than one order).
- In the order/product relation, an item description could appear on many order lines for many different customers – if the description of the item was to change, all occurrences where that item appeared would have to be changed if database inconsistencies were not to appear.

Deletion anomaly

- In the customer/order relation, an order cannot be deleted without also deleting the customer's details.
- In the order/product relation, an order line cannot be deleted without also deleting the item number and description.

Identification and removal of insertion, deletion and update anomalies

Activity 11.1

This activity shows a prototype database that has been produced by an employee of a toy manufacturer relating to its customers and sales activities. The designer, a business user, is not aware of the need for normalisation and has stored all the data in a single table.

Customer number	Customer name	Customer address	Order number	Product code	Product description	Quantity ordered	Price per item	Total cost	Order date	Salesperson number
100	Fred's Toys	7 High Street	10001	324	Action Man	3	13.46	40.38	7/10/99	007
100	Fred's Toys	7 High Street	10001	567	Silly Dog	6	5.15	30.9	7/10/99	007
100	Fred's Toys	7 High Street	10001	425	Slimy Hand	12	1.39	16.68	7/10/99	007
100	Fred's Toys	7 High Street	10001	869	Kiddy Doh	4	0.68	2.72	7/10/99	007
200	Super Toys	25 West Mall	13001	869	Kiddy Doh	12	0.68	8.16	7/17/99	021
200	Super Toys	25 West Mall	13001	637	Risky	3	17.42	52.26	7/17/99	021
200	Super Toys	25 West Mall	13001	567	Silly Dog	2	32.76	43.52	7/17/99	021
300	Cheapo Toys	61 The Arcade	23201	751	Diplomat	24	5.15	123.6	6/21/99	007

Questions

1 Identify an insertion anomaly which might cause a problem when adding a new product to the range.
2 Identify two deletion anomalies which would occur if Cheapo Toys cancelled its order and a record was removed.
3 Identify an update anomaly if the product Silly Dog was renamed Fancy Dog.
4 How could the table be split up to remove the anomalies? Define the fields which would be placed in each table and define the foreign keys which would be used to link the tables.

It is anomalies of this kind which indicate that the normalisation process needs to be taken a step further – that is, we must now proceed to second normal form (2NF).

▶ Second normal form (2NF)

Second normal form (2NF) states that 'each attribute in a record (relation) must be functionally dependent on the whole key of that record'. To continue the normalisation process to second normal form, it is necessary to explore further some of the terms defined in the introductory section.

Functional dependencies

Within each of the relations produced above, a set of functional dependencies exists. These dependencies will be governed by the relationships that exist between different data items, which in turn will depend on the 'business rules', i.e. the purposes for which data are held and how they are used.

Once the functional dependencies have been established, it is then possible to select a candidate key for the relation.

Candidate keys

The process of analysing the functional dependencies within a relation will reveal one or more possible candidate keys – a candidate key is the minimum number of determinants (key fields) which uniquely determines all the non-key attributes.

Part	Supplier	Supplier	Supplier	Price
no	no	name	details	

An example

Consider the following record. Note that this example is different from that given in first normal form, since it illustrates the principles better.

The functional dependencies are as follows:

Part no and supplier no → Price
Supplier no → Supplier name
Supplier no → Supplier details

A possible candidate key might be thought to be supplier number. However, supplier number alone cannot be a determinant of price, since a supplier may supply many items.

Similarly, part number alone cannot be a determinant of price, because a part may be supplied by many different suppliers at different prices.

The candidate key is, therefore, a composite key comprising part number and supplier number.

We can express this more clearly by employing a dependency diagram (Fig. 11.18). Two additional properties relating to candidate keys can now be introduced:

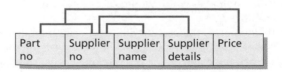

Figure 11.18 **Example of a dependency diagram for supplier example**

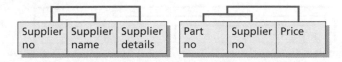

Figure 11.19 Revised dependency diagram for supplier example

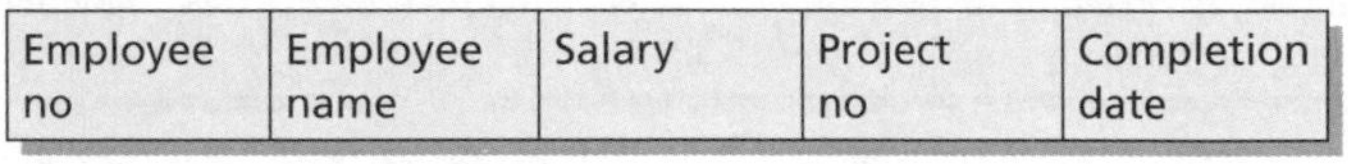

Employee no	Employee name	Salary	Project no	Completion date

Figure 11.20 Example of a structure diagram – employee details

1 For every record occurrence, the key must uniquely identify the relation.
2 No data item in the key can be discarded without destroying the property of unique identification.

The dependency diagram in Figure 11.18 indicates a number of problems:

● If supplier number is discarded, it will no longer be possible to identify the remaining attributes uniquely, even though part number remains.
● Details of a supplier cannot be added until there is a part to supply; if a supplier does not supply a part, there is no key.
● If supplier details are to be updated, all records which contain that supplier as part of the key must be accessed – i.e. there are redundant data.

This situation is known as a *partial key dependency* and is resolved by splitting the record into two or more smaller records (Fig. 11.19).

A record is, therefore, in *at least* second normal form when any partial key dependencies have been removed.

Removing insertion/update/deletion anomalies

Consider the record structure shown in Figure 11.20. If it is assumed that an employee only works on one project at a time; then employee number is a suitable candidate key, in that all other attributes can reasonably be said to be fully functionally dependent on it.

Note: the record is already in second normal form because there is only one key attribute (therefore partial key dependencies *cannot* exist). However, some problems still exist:

● *Insertion anomaly*: before any employees are recruited for a project, the completion date for a project cannot be recorded because there is no employee record.
● *Update anomaly*: if a project completion date is changed, it will be necessary to search *all* employee records and change those where an employee works on that project.
● *Deletion anomaly*: if all employees are deleted for a project, all records containing a project completion date would be deleted also.

To resolve these anomalies, a record in second normal form must be converted into a number of third normal form records.

◗ Third normal form (3NF)

Transitive dependency

A data item that is not a key (or part of a key) but which itself identifies other data items is a *transitive dependency*.

Third normal form (3NF). A record is in third normal form if each non-key attribute 'depends on the key, the whole key and nothing but the key'.

Third normal form (3NF)
....
A record is in third normal form if each non-key attribute 'depends on the key, the whole key and nothing but the key'.

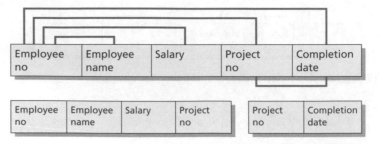

Figure 11.21 **Dependency diagram for employee example and revised structure**

An example

Consider the previous example. To convert the record into two third normal form records, any transitive dependencies must be removed. When this is done the result is the two records in Figure 11.21.

Removing insertion/update/deletion anomalies

If a record has only one candidate key and both partial key and transitive dependencies have been removed, then no insertion, update or deletion anomalies should result.

However, if a record has more than one candidate key problems can still arise. In this situation we can take the normalisation process still further.

▶ Fourth normal form (4NF) and fifth normal form (5NF)

Further normalisation may be necessary for some applications. In these normalisation can proceed to the fourth and fifth normal forms. These are described in Mcfadden and Hofer (1995): 'In 4NF multi-valued dependencies are removed. A multi-valued dependency exists when there are at least three attributes in a relation and for each value of A there is a well-defined set of values of B and a well-defined set of values of C. However, the set of values of B is independent of set C and vice versa.'

In 5NF it is necessary to account for the potential of decomposing some relations from an earlier stage of normalisation into more than two relations. In most practical applications, decomposition to 3NF gives acceptable database performance and is often easier to design and maintain.

▶ Other significant database design issues

As well as the logical design of the database there are aspects of physical database design that should be taken into account. These are specialised functions performed by a database administrator or DBA. A company which does not employ a specialist risks a poor performance system or, worse still, a loss or corruption of data. These design and database implementation tasks include:

1 *Design of optimal database performance.* Use of specialist techniques such as indexes or stored procedures will accelerate the display of common user views such as a list of all customer orders. Queries can also be optimised, but this is mainly performed automatically by the database engines such as Oracle, Microsoft SQL Server or Informix. To verify the design is good, volume testing is essential to ensure that the system can cope with the number of transactions that will occur.

2 *Designing for multi-user access.* When defining a new system, it is important to consider what happens when two users want to access the same data, such as the same

Database design exercise using the ABC case study

This activity builds on the ABC case study from Chapter 10. It is not necessary to have completed the Chapter 10 exercise to be able to undertake this one. You should use the extract in Chapter 10 describing ABC and in particular the paper forms of the existing system to identify which fields are required in the database.

Questions

1 Either:
  (a) Use normalisation to third normal form to identify tables and fields for an ABC database; or
  (b) Assume the following entities for the ABC database:
  - customer details;
  - salesperson details;
  - sales order header details;
  - sales order line details;
  - item details.

2 For each table in the database, define details of:
  - table names;
  - primary and foreign key fields for each table;
  - name of each field;
  - data type of each field;
  - size of each field;
  - any validation rules which may apply to each field (e.g. a limit on maximum price or quantity etc.).

You may find it most efficient to summarise the database definition using a table (in your word processor).

---

customer record. If access to records is unlimited, then there will be anomalous data in the database if users save data about the customer at a similar time. Since multi-user access will not be frequent, the best method for dealing with it will be to implement record locking. Here, the first user to access a record will cause the database to restrict subsequent users to read-only access to the record rather than read–write. Subsequent users should be informed that a lock is in place and access is read-only.

3 *Planning for failed transactions*. Recovery methods can be specified in the design for how to deal with failed transactions which may occur when there is a software bug or power interruption. Databases contain the facility to 'roll back' to the situation before a failure occurred.

4 *Referential integrity*. The database must be designed so that when records in one table are deleted, this does not adversely affect other tables. Impact should be minimal if normalisation has occurred. Sometimes it is necessary to perform a 'cascading delete', which means deleteing related records in linked tables.

5 *Design to safeguard against media, hardware or power failure*. A backup strategy should be designed to ensure that minimal disruption occurs if the database server fails. The main design decision is whether a point-in-time backup is required or whether restoring to the previous day's data will be sufficient. Frequently, a point-in-time backup will be required. Of course, a backup strategy is not much use if it cannot be used to restore the data, so backup and recovery must be well tested. To reduce the likelihood of having to fall back on a backup, using a fault-tolerant server is important. Specifying a

server with an uninterruptible power supply, disk mirroring or RAID level 2 is essential for any corporate system. The frequency of archiving also will be specified.

6 *Replication.* Duplication and distribution of data to servers at different company locations and for mobile users is supported to different degrees by different database vendors.

7 *Database sizing.* The database administrator will size the database and perform capacity planning to ensure that sufficient space is available on the server for the system to remain functional.

8 *Data migration.* Data migration will occur at the system build phase, but it must be planned for at the design stage. This will involve an assessment of the different data sources which will be used to populate the database.

Design of input and output

Most modern information systems use relational database management systems for the storage of data. RDBMS provide management facilities which means that programmers do not have to become directly involved with file management. Because of this, most business users will not hear these terms unless eavesdropping on systems designers and this section is therefore kept brief. However, some older systems and large-scale transaction processing systems requiring superior performance do not use RDBMS for data storage. Such systems use a terminology which is unfamiliar to most developers of PC-based information systems.

▶ File access methods

File-based systems will access data that is stored in a file using two main methods:

1 *Sequential access.* The program reading or writing a file will start processing the file record by record (usually from the beginning).

2 *Direct (random) access.* Access can occur to any point (record) in the file without the need to start at the beginning.

Sequential and random or direct file access methods
Sequential file access involves reading or writing each record in a file in a set order. Random or direct file access allows any record to be read or written.

Sequential access is often used when batch processing a file which involves processing each record. Sequential file access involves reading or writing each record in a file in a set order. **Direct access** is preferable when finding a subset of records such as in a query, since it is much faster. Random or direct file access allows any record to be read or written.

▶ Indexing

Index
A file index is an additional file which is used to 'point' to records in a direct access file for more rapid access.

To enable rapid retrieval of data in a random access file (and also a database table), it is conventional to use an **index** which will find the location of the record more rapidly. These files are sometimes referred to as 'indexed sequential files'. A file index is an additional file that is used to 'point' to records in a direct access file for more rapid access. An index file for a customer file would contain two fields only for each record – the indexed item such as a customer number and the number of the record in the parent file (also known as the 'offset' or 'pointer') which contains details on this customer. Indexes are also used to speed access to tables for RDBMS.

▶ File descriptions

In transaction processing systems which use standard native files rather than RDBMS, there are additional terms that are used to describe the types of files. These types include:

1 *The master file*. This is used to store relatively static information that does not change frequently. An example would be a file containing customer details. After a customer record has been created it will not need to be updated frequently unless details such as name and address change. New records will only be added as new customers are registered.
2 *The transaction file*. This contain records of particular exchanges, usually related to a transaction such as a customer placing an order or paying for an order, or an invoice being produced. This file has records added to it frequently.
3 *Archive file*. To reduce storage requirements and improve performance, transactions that occurred some time ago to which businesses are unlikely to wish to refer are removed from the online system as an archive which is usually stored on a tape or optical disk rather than a magnetic disk. It will be still available for reference, but access will be slower. Depending on the application, archiving may occur for records that are older than one day, one week, one month or one year.
4 *Temporary file*. These provide temporary storage space for the system which might be used during batch processing, when comparing data sets for example. The information would not be of value to a business user.
5 *Log file*. The log file is a system file used to store information on updates to other files. Its information would not be of value to a business user.

▶ File organisation

Information can be organised in file-based systems in a variety of ways, which are not of general relevance to the business user, so the terms are only summarised in tabular form (Table 11.5). Note that the indexed-sequential technique offers the best balance between speed of access to individual records and for achieving updates.

Table 11.5 **Methods of file organisation**

Organisation method	Access method	Application	Brief description
Sequential	Sequential	Batch process of a customer master file	An ordered sequential access file, e.g. ordered by customer number
Serial	Sequential		A sequential access file, but without any ordering
Random	Random + index	Querying data for decision support; unsuitable for frequent updates due to overhead of updating index	Organisation is provided by index
Indexed sequential	Sequential + index	Querying data for decision support and sequentia batch processing	Best compromise between methods above

▶ Batch and real-time processing

When designing information processing systems, designers have to decide which is the more appropriate method for handling transactions:

- Batch – data are 'post-processed' after collection, usually at times of low system workload.
- Real-time or online processing – data are processed instantaneously on collection.

Table 11.6 compares the merits of batch and real-time systems according to several criteria.

Batch system
A batch system involves processing of many transactions in sequence. This will typically occur over some time after the transactions have occurred.

Real-time system
In a real-time system processing occurs immediately data are collected. Processing follows each transaction.

Table 11.6 **A comparison of batch and real-time data processing**

Factor	Batch	Real-time
Speed of delivery to information user	Slower – depends on how frequently batch process is run – daily, weekly or monthly	Faster – effectively delivered immediately
Ability to deal with failure	Better – if a batch process fails overnight there is usually sufficient time to solve the problem and rerun the batch	Worse – when a real-time system is offline there is major customer disruption and orders may be lost
Data validation	Worse – validation can occur, but it is time-consuming to correct errors	Better – validation errors are notified and corrected immediately
Cost	Better – performance is less critical so cheaper hardware communications can be purchased	Worse – high-specification databases and infrastructure are necessary to achieve the required number of transactions per second
Disruption to users when data processing needs to be performed	Better – can occur in slack periods such as at weekends or overnight	Worse – can disrupt customers if time-consuming calculations occur as each record is processed

There is a general trend from batch systems to real-time processing, but it can be seen from the table that batch processing is superior in some areas, not least cost. For a system such as the National Lottery, a real-time system must be used, but it is expensive to set up the necessary infrastructure.

Batch systems are still widely used, since they are appropriate for data processing before analysis. For example, batch processing is used in data warehousing when transferring data from the operational system to the warehouse (Chapter 6). A batch process can be run overnight to transfer the data from one location to another and to perform aggregation such as summing sales figures across different market or product segments.

User interface design

The design of the user interface is key to ensuring that information systems are easy to use and that users are productive. User interface design involves three main parts: first, defining the different views of the data such as input forms and output tables; second, defining how the user moves or navigates from one view to another; and, third, providing options for the user.

Each module can be broken down into interface elements such as **forms** which are used to enter and update information such as a customer's details, **views** which tabulate results as a report or graphically display related information such as a 'to-do' list and **dialogs** which are used for users to select options such as a print options dialogue. **Menus** provide selection of different options. Figure 11.22 gives an example of these different interface components.

User interface design is a specialist field which is the preserve of graphic designers and psychologists. This field is often known as **human–computer interaction design (HCI)**. HCI involves the study of methods for designing the input and output of information systems to ensure they are 'user-friendly'. It is covered well in Preece et al. (1994) and Yeates et al. (1994). Many of the design parameters can be assisted by a knowledge of HCI. Since many information systems are now accessed through a web browser interface across an intranet,

Form

An on-screen equivalent of a paper form which is used for entering data and will have validation routines to help improve the accuracy of the entered data.

Data views

Different screens of an application which review information in a different form such as table, graph, report or map.

Dialog

An on-screen window (box) which is used by a user to input data or select options.

Menu

Provides user selection of options for different application functions.

Human–computer interaction (HCI) design

HCI involves the study of methods for designing the input and output of information systems to ensure they are 'user-friendly'.

Dialog box   Report data view   Onscreen form

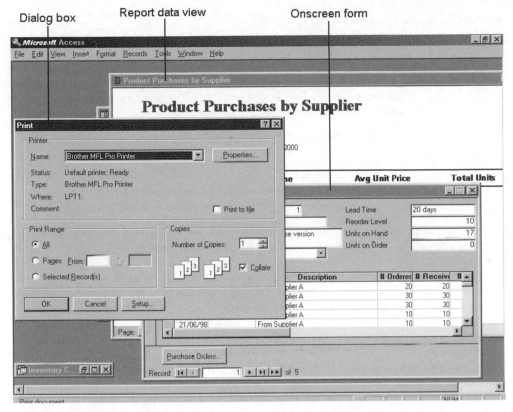

Figure 11.22 Microsoft Access showing key elements of interface design

extranet or the Internet, the next section describes some of the important design issues in developing interfaces for information systems with web-based interfaces.

Focus on user-centred design for e-business applications

User interface design has always been important to the effectiveness of information systems. Today, since e-business systems are often customer- or employee-facing systems, human–computer interaction is even more important. Referring to web site design, Nigel Bevan (1999a) says:

> Unless a web site meets the needs of the intended users it will not meet the needs of the organization providing the web site. Web site development should be user-centred, evaluating the evolving design against user requirements.

Noyes and Baber (1999) explain that **user-centred design** involves more than user interface design. It can be conceived as centring on the person using the system, but surrounded concentrically by factors that affect usability such as user interface, computers, workplace and the environment. Here we will be specifically looking at the user interface.

User-centred design starts with understanding the nature and variation within the user groups. According to Bevan (1999a), issues to consider for a web site include:

User-centred design

A design technique for the development of user interfaces for information systems which is primarily informed by user requirements.

● Who are the important users?
● What is their purpose in accessing the site?

- How frequently will they visit the site?
- What experience and expertise do they have?
- What nationality are they? Can they read the language (e.g. English) used in the site?
- What type of information are they looking for?
- How will they want to use the information: read it on the screen, print it or download it?
- What type of browsers will they use? How fast will their communication links be?
- How large a screen/window will they use, with how many colours?

Rosenfeld and Morville (1998) suggest four stages that also have a user-centred basis:

1 Identify different audiences.
2 Rank importance of each to business.
3 List the three most important information needs of the audience.
4 Ask representatives of each audience type to develop their own wish lists.

For an example of the principle of customer orientation in action visit retailer B&Q's DIY site (www.diy.com). This is targeted at a range of users of DIY products, so is designed around three zones: products, advice and inspiration. Experts who know what they want go straight to the product section and buy what they need. Less experienced users with queries on what to purchase can gain advice from an expert just as they would in-store, and novices may visit the inspiration zone which includes room mock-ups with lists of the products needed to create a particular look. An alternative approach is used by Guinness (www.guinness.com) which has three site zones 'like it, live it, love it'.

Bevan (1999b) also notes the importance of defining key scenarios of use, which is consistent with the use case approach described above. This stage, often known as 'knowledge elicitation', involves interviewing users and asking them to talk through their current or preferred way of working.

Once the scenarios have been established, card sorting techniques, as described by Noyes and Baber (1999), can be used. They describe how after interviewing users, typical tasks or actions were written down onto cards. These were then used to identify the sequence of actions users required from a menu system. They explain that the menu system devised was quite different from that envisaged by the software engineers. Card sorting techniques can also be used to check through that no stages have been missed during the **talk-through** – a **walk-through** the cards is performed. Talk-throughs do not require a physical setup, but walk-throughs do, in the form of a series of cards or use of a prototype of the system.

Evaluating designs

A test of effective design for usability is dependent on three areas according to Bevan (1999b):

1 *Effectiveness* – can users complete their tasks correctly and completely?
2 *Productivity* (efficiency) – are tasks completed in an acceptable length of time?
3 *Satisfaction* – are users satisfied with the interaction?

▶ Use-case analysis

The **use-case** method of process analysis and modelling was developed in the early 1990s as part of the development of object-oriented techniques. It is part of a methodology known as **Unified Modelling Language (UML)** which attempts to unify the approaches that preceded it such as the Booch, OMT and Objectory notations. Jacobsen

Talk-through

A user verbally describes their required actions.

Walk-through

A user executes their actions through using a system or mock-up.

Use-case

The sequence of transactions between an actor and a system that support the activities of the actor.

Unified modelling language (UML)

A language used to specify, visualise and document the artefacts of an object-oriented system.

et al. (1994) gives an accessible introduction to how object modelling can be applied to workflow analysis.

The following stages are identified by Schneider and Winters (1998) for analysis using the use-case method:

1 Identify actors

Actors are those objects that are involved in using or interacting with a system. They are not part of the system. The obvious actors are the users of a system. In a customer service application the actors may be a customer and the customer service person at the company. When performing process analysis to define use-cases we ask questions such as 'Who are the actors for this process?', 'What services do these actors provide?' and 'What are the actors' tasks?' and 'What changes do they make to the status of the overall process?'. Actors are typically application users such as customers and employers. They may add information to the system or receive it through reporting facilities. Note that an employee who has several roles such as a manager role and administrator would be represented by two different actors.

Schneider and Winters (1998) point out that other actors include software and hardware control devices that change the state of the process and external systems that interface with the system under consideration. These are effectively human actors who have been auto-

Actors
....
People, software or other devices that interface with a system. See *Use-case*.

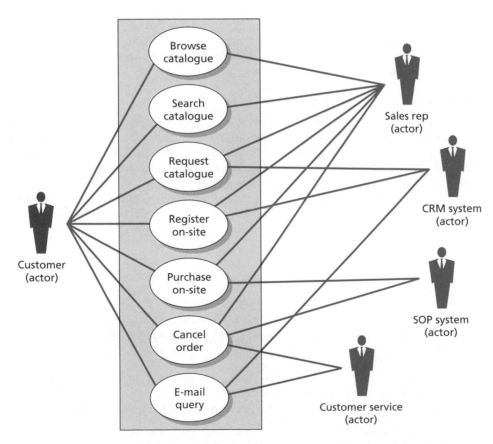

Figure 11.23 Relationship between actors and use-cases for a B2C company sell-side e-commerce site
Source: Chaffey (2002)

mated through other systems that interface with the current system under consideration. Actors are denoted using the straightforward approach shown in Figure 11.23.

2 Identify use-cases

Use-cases are the different things users of a system want it to perform. These can be described as activities or tasks that are part of a dialogue between an actor and the system. They summarise the requirements of a system from each actor since they describe the functionality that will be provided by the system. Common use-cases are:

- starting up, shutting down or amending a system;
- adding or amending information on a system. Examples include placing an e-commerce order or recording a complaint via e-mail;
- using a system for reporting or decision support.

Some use-cases for a typical e-commerce web application are shown in Figure 11.23.

3 Relate actors to use-cases

Figure 11.23 also shows how actors relate to use-cases. It can be used to identify responsibilities and check for missing activities. For example, 'Check order status' is a use-case that is missing and the company would have to discuss whether it was acceptable for a customer service representative to place an order for a customer who was complaining about a particular product. This probably would be desirable to avoid the customer's being transferred from a salesperson to a customer service person. One of the features of e-commerce is that the system that is used by the sales reps will typically have the same use-cases or features as that for the customer, but some may differ – for example, only a customer service representative or sales rep would be able to perform a 'give refund' use-case.

4 Develop use-case scenarios

Scenario
A particular path or flow of events or activities within a use-case.

A detailed **scenario** is then developed to detail the different paths of events and activities for each use-case. The primary scenario describes the typical case where nothing goes wrong. The use-case includes detail of activities or function, what happens when there is an alternative or decision, or if there is an error. Pre-conditions for entering and post-conditions for exiting the use-case are also specified.

Figure 11.24 shows a primary scenario for the complete e-commerce purchase cycle. A more detailed primary scenario for the particular use-case 'Register' written from the point of view of the customer actor from Figure 11.25 is as follows.

Pre-condition: A user is active on the web site
Scenario: Register.

Basic path:
1 Use-case starts when customer presses 'register'.
2 Customer enters their name, postal address and e-mail.
3 The postcode and e-mail address (@ symbol) will be checked for validity after entry and the user prompted if there is an error.
4 The customer will select 'submit'.
5 The system will check all fields are present and the customer information will be passed to the customer relationship management (CRM) system.
6 A redirect page will be displayed to thank the customer for registering and providing an option to return to the home page, and the use-case ends.

Post-condition. The customer details have been saved.

Alternative paths
The customer can cancel at stages 2 to 4 before pressing 'submit' and the use-case ends.

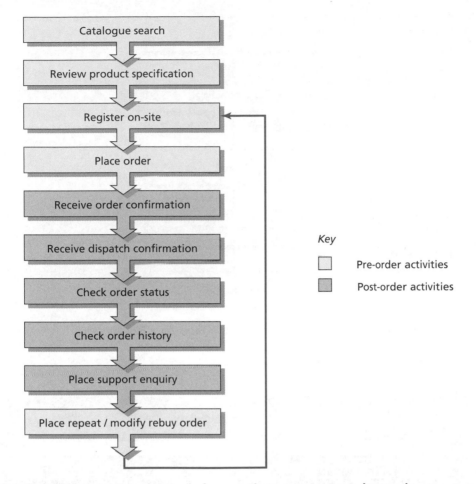

Figure 11.24 Primary use-case scenario for an entire e-commerce purchase cycle
Source: Chaffey (2002)

It can be seen that by stating the use-case in this way different issues can be clarified. For instance, should the validation at stage 3 occur when the entry field loses focus (i.e. tab to next field), or should it wait until step 4 which is perhaps more conventional. Another issue is whether we should display the customer details at stage 6 with the option to amend them if incorrect. Discussing the options before development saves time when coding prototyping. After the primary scenario is complete, second or alternative scenarios can be developed and added to the primary scenarios as alternatives. For the register scenario, cancel is a secondary scenario, others could include error conditions such as if the postcode is invalid.

Figure 11.26 illustrates an e-commerce site with clear menu options that is consistent with use case analysis.

▶ Customer orientation

A well-designed site will have been developed to achieve **customer orientation**. This involves the difficult task of trying to provide content and services to appeal to a wide range of audiences. As shown in Figure 11.27 for a B2B company, the three main types of audience are: customers, other companies and organisations, and staff. Visit the Dell web site (www.dell.com) to see how Dell segments its customer base on the home page into:

Customer orientation
Developing site content and services to appeal to different customer segments or other members of the audience.

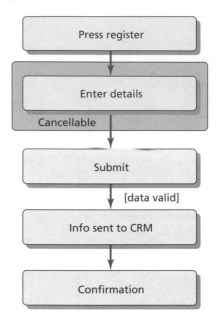

Figure 11.25 Primary scenario for the Register use-cases for a B2C company
Source: Chaffey (2002)

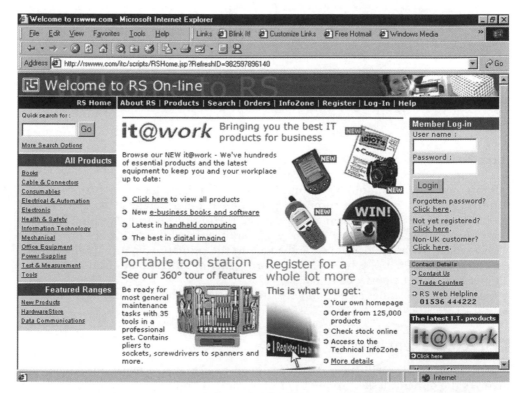

Figure 11.26 Clear user scenario options at the RS Components site (www.rswww.com)
Source: Copyright © 2000 RS Components Ltd.

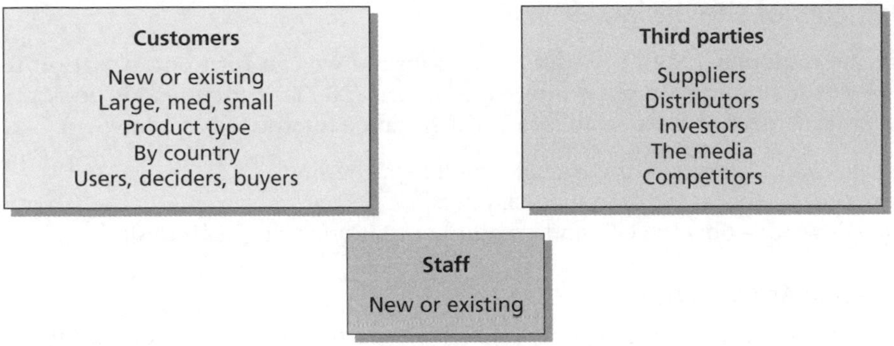

Figure 11.27 Different types of audience for the web site of a B2B company
Source: Chaffey (2002)

- small office and home users
- small businesses
- medium businesses
- large businesses
- corporates
- government organisations.

Think about how well this approach works. What would your reaction be to being classified as a mere small-business and home owner be? Do you think this is a valid approach? A similar approach, by Microsoft is to offer specialised content for IS managers to help them in their investment decisions. Is a more straightforward product-centred structure to the web site appropriate?

As well as customer segments, designers also need to take into account variations in the backgrounds of visitors to the site. These can be thought of as four different types of familiarity:

1 *Familiarity with the Internet* – are short-cuts provided for those familiar with the Internet and for novices to help to lead them through your site? Site design should try to accommodate this.
2 *Familiarity with organisation* – for customers who don't know an organisation, content is needed to explain who the company is and demonstrate credibility through 'About Us' options and customer testimonials.
3 *Familiarity with organisations' products* – even existing customers may not know the full range of your product offering.
4 *Familiarity with your site* – site maps, Search and Help options are not 'nice-to-have' options for an e-commerce site since you may lose potential customers if they cannot be helped when they are lost.

Jakob Nielsen (2000a) says this about novice users:

Web users are notoriously fickle: they take one look at a home page and leave after a few seconds if they can't figure it out. The abundance of choice and the ease of going elsewhere puts a huge premium on making it extremely easy to enter a site.

But he notes that we also need to take account of experts. He says we may eventually move to interfaces where the average site visitor gets a simplified design that is easy to learn and loyal users get an advanced design that is more powerful. But for now *'in-depth content and advanced information should be added to sites to provide the depth expected by experts'*.

▶ Elements of site design

Once the requirements of the user are established we can turn our attention to the design of the human–computer interface. Nielsen (2000b) structures his book on web usability according to three main areas, which can be interpreted as follows:

1 *site design and structure* – the overall structure of the site;
2 *page design* – the layout of individual pages;
3 *content design* – how the text and graphic content on each page is designed.

Site design and structure

The structures created by designers for web sites will vary greatly according to their audience and the site's purpose, but we can make some general observations about design and structure. We will review the factors designers consider in designing the style, organisation and navigation schemes for the site.

Site style

An effective web site design will have a style that is communicated through use of colour, images, typography and layout. This should support the way a product is positioned and its brand.

The style elements can be combined to develop a 'personality' for a site. We could describe a site's personality in the same way we can describe people, such as 'formal' or 'fun'. This personality has to be consistent with the needs of the target audience (Fig. 11.28). A business audience often requires detailed information and prefers an

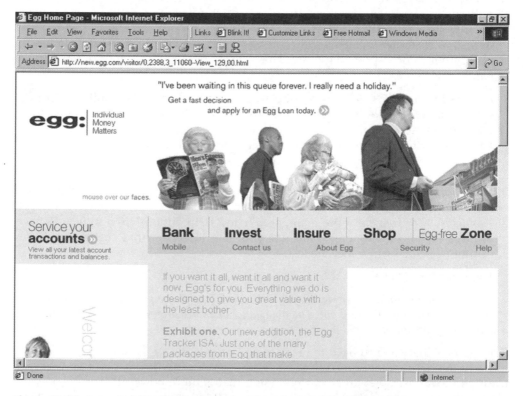

Figure 11.28 A personality that appeals to a broad audience at Egg.com
Source: Reproduced by kind permission of The Egg Group, Copyright © 2000 Egg plc.

information-intensive style such as that of the Cisco site (Fig. 11.31) (www.cisco.com) A consumer site is usually more graphically intensive. Before the designers pass on their creative designs to developers, they also need to consider the constraints on the user experience, such as screen resolution and colour depth, the browser used and download speed. The list of constraints which must be tested against is illustrated in Chapter 12.

Site organisation

In their book *Information Archictectures for the World Wide Web*, Rosenfeld and Morville (1998) identify several different information organisation schemes. These can be applied to different aspects of e-commerce sites, from the whole site through to the smallest parts of the site.

Rosenfeld and Morville identify the following information organisation schemes:

1 *Exact*. Here information can be naturally indexed. If we take the example of books, these can alphabetical, by author or title; chronological, by date; or for travel books, for example, geographical – by place. Information on an e-commerce site may be presented alphabetically, but this is not suitable for browsing.
2 *Ambiguous*. Here the information requires classification, again taking the examples of books, the Dewey decimal system is an ambiguous classification scheme since the librarians classify books into arbitrary categories. Such an approach is common on an e-commerce site since products and services can be classified in different ways. Other ambiguous information organisation schemes that are commonly used on web sites are where content is broken down by topic, by task or by audience. The use of metaphors is also common; a metaphor is where the web site corresponds to a familiar real-world situation. The Microsoft Windows Explorer, where information is grouped according to Folders, Files and Trash is an example of a real-world metaphor. The use of the shopping basket metaphor is widespread within e-commerce sites. It should be noted, though, that Nielsen (2000b) believes that metaphors can be confusing if the metaphor is not understood immediately or is misinterpreted.
3 *Hybrid*. Here there will be a mixture of organisation schemes, both exact and ambiguous. Rosenfeld and Morville (1998) point out that using different approaches is common on web sites, but this can lead to confusion, because the user is not clear what mental model is being followed. We can say that is probably best to minimise the number of information organisation schemes. To look at these, complete Activity 11.3.

Activity 11.3

Site architecture and content

The purpose of this activity is to assess different forms of information content on e-commerce sites.

Visit RS Components web site (www.rswww.com) and the Dell Computer site (www.dell.com) relevant to your country. Which information organisation schemes are used?

Site navigation schemes

Devising a site that is easy to use is critically dependent on the design of the site navigation scheme. Hoffman and Novak (1997) stress the importance of the concept of 'flow' in governing site usability. 'Flow' essentially describes how easy it is for the users to find the information they need as they move from one page of the site to the next, but it also includes other interactions such as filling in on-screen forms.

Most navigation systems are based upon a *hierarchical site structure*. When creating the structure, designers have to compromise between the two approaches shown in Figure 11.29. The 'narrow and deep' approach has the benefit of fewer choices on each page, making it easier for the user to make their selection, but more clicks are required to reach a particular piece of information. The 'broad and shallow' approach requires fewer clicks to reach the same piece of information, but the design of the screen potentially becomes cluttered. Figures 11.29(a) and 11.31 depict the narrow and deep approach and Figures 11.29(b) and 11.30 the broad and shallow approach. Note that in both these cases the approaches are appropriate for the non-technical and technical audiences. A rule of thumb is that site designers should ensure it only takes three clicks to reach any piece of information on a site. This implies the use of a broad and shallow approach on most large sites. Lynch and Horton (1999) recommend a broad and shallow approach and note that designers should not conceive of a single home page where customers arrive on the site, but of different home pages according to different audience types. Each of the pages in the second row of Figure 11.29(b) could be thought of as an example of a home page which the visitors can bookmark if the page appeals to them. Nielsen (2000b) points out that many users will not arrive on the home page, but may be referred from another site or according to a print or TV advert to a particular page such as www.b2b.com/jancomp. He calls this process 'deep linking' and site designers should ensure that navigation and context are appropriate for users arriving on these pages.

As well as compromises on depth of links within a site it is also necessary to compromise on the amount of space devoted to menus. Nielsen (1999) points out that some sites devote so much space to navigation bars that the space available for content is

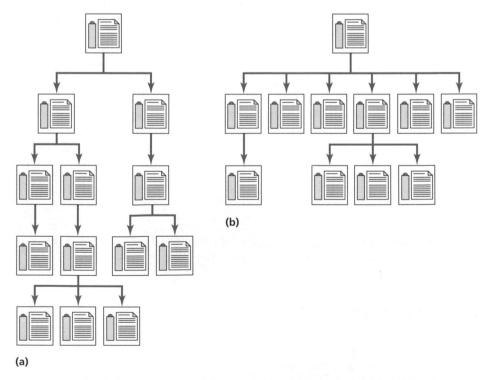

(b)

(a)

Figure 11.29 (a) Narrow and deep and (b) broad and shallow organisation schemes
Source: Chaffey (2002)

limited. He suggests that the designer of navigation systems should consider the following information that a site user wants to know:

- *Where am I?* The user needs to know where they are on the site and this can be indicated by highlighting the current location and clear titling of pages. Chaffey et al. (2000) refer to this as *context*. *Consistency* of menu locations on different pages is also required to aid cognition. Users also need to know where they are on the web. This can be indicated by a logo, which by convention is at the top or top left of a site.

- *Where have I been?* This is difficult to indicate on a site, but for task-oriented activities such as purchasing a product can show the user that they are at the *n*th stage of an operation such as making a purchase.

- *Where do I want to go?* This is the main navigation system which gives options for future operations.

To answer these questions, clear succinct labelling is required. Widely used standards such as Home, Main page, Search, Find, Browse, FAQ and Help and About Us are preferable. But for other particular labels it is useful to have what Rosenfeld and Morville (1998) call 'scope notes' – an additional explanation. These authors also argue against the use of iconic labels or pictures without corresponding text since they are open to misinterpretation and take longer to process.

Since using the navigation system may not enable the user to find the information they want rapidly, alternatives have to be provided by the site designers. These alternatives include search, advanced search, browse and site map facilities. Whatis.com (www.whatis.com) illustrates these features well.

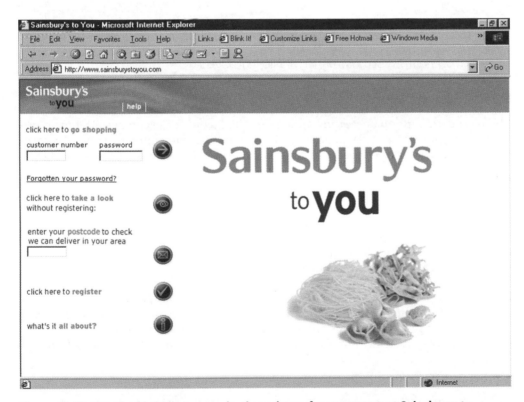

Figure 11.30 Broad and shallow organisation scheme for consumers at Sainsburys to You Site (www.sainsburys.co.uk)

Source: Reproduced by kind permission of Sainsbury's Supermarket Ltd.

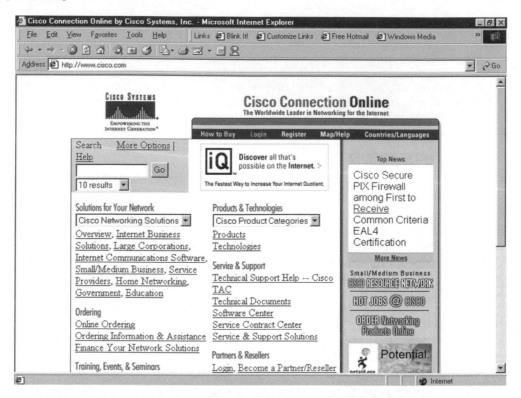

Figure 11.31 Broad organisation schemes and professional style at Cisco.com

Source: These materials have been reproduced by Pearson Education Limited with the permission of Cisco Systems, Inc. COPYRIGHT © CISCO SYSTEMS, INC. ALL RIGHTS RESERVED

◗ Page design

The page design involves creating an appropriate layout for each page. The main elements of a particular page layout are the title, navigation and content. Standard content such as copyright may be added to every page as a footer. Issues in page design include:

- *Page elements.* The proportion of page devoted to content compared to all other content such as headers, footers and navigation elements. The location of these elements also needs to be considered. It is conventional for the main menu to be at the top or on the left. The use of a menu system at the top of the browser window enables more space for content below.
- *The use of frames.* This is generally discouraged for the reasons given in Chapter 12.
- *Resizing.* A good page layout design should allow for the user to change the size of text or to work with different monitor resolutions.
- *Consistency.* Page layout should be similar for all areas of the site unless more space is required, for example for a discussion forum or product demonstration. Standards of colour and typography can be enforced through cascading style sheets.
- *Printing.* Layout should allow for printing or provide an alternative printing format.

◗ Content design

Copywriting for the web is an evolving art form, but many of the rules for good copywriting are the same as for other media. Common errors we see on web sites are:

- too much knowledge assumed of the visitor about the company, its products and services;
- using internal jargon about products, services or departments – using undecipherable acronyms.

Web copywriters also need to take account of the user reading the content on screen. Approaches to dealing with the limitations imposed by the customer using a monitor include:

- writing more concisely than in brochures;
- 'chunking' or breaking text into units of five or six lines at most, allowing users to scan rather than read information on web pages;
- use of lists with headline text in larger font;
- never including too much on a single page, except when presenting lengthy information such as a report which may be easier to read on a single page;
- using hyperlinks to decrease page sizes or help achieve flow within copy, either by linking to sections further down a page or linking to another page.

Hofacker (2000) describes five stages of human information processing when a web site is being used. These can be applied to both page design and content design to improve usability and help companies get their message across to consumers. Each of the five stages summarised in Table 11.7 acts as a hurdle, since if the site design or content is too difficult to process, the customer cannot progress to the next stage. It is useful to consider these stages in order to minimise these difficulties.

Table 11.7 A summary of information web stages described by Hofacker (2000)

Stage	Description	Applications
1 **Exposure**	Content must be present for long enough to be processed	Content on banner ads may not be on screen sufficiently long for processing and cognition
2 **Attention**	Users' eyes will be drawn towards headings and content, not graphics and moving items on a web page (Nielsen, 2000b)	Emphasis and accurate labelling of headings is vital to gain a user's attention. Evidence suggests that users do not notice banner adverts, but suffer from 'banner blindness'
3 **Comprehension and perception**	The user's interpretation of content	Designs that use common standards and metaphors and are kept simple will be more readily comprehended
4 **Yielding and acceptance**	Is information (copy) presented accepted by customers?	Copy should reference credible sources and present counterarguments as necessary
5 **Retention**	As for traditional advertising, this describe the extent to which the information is remembered	An unusual style or high degree of interaction leading to flow and user satisfaction is more likely to be recalled

Input design

User interface design can also be subdivided into **input design** and output design, but these terms are used more generally to refer to all methods of data entry and display, so they warrant a separate section.

Input design includes the design of user input through on-screen forms, but also other methods of data entry such as import by file, transfer from another system or specialised data capture methods such as bar-code scanning and optical or voice recognition techniques.

Data input design involves capturing data that have been identified in the user requirements analysis via a variety of mechanisms. These have been described in Chapter 3 and include:

- keyboard – the most commonly used method;
- optical character recognition and scanning;
- voice input;
- directly from a monitoring system such as a manufacturing process, or from a phone system when a caller line ID is used to identify the customer phoning and automatically bring their details on screen;
- input from a data file that is used to store data;
- import of data from another system via a batch process (for example a data warehouse will require import of data from an operational system).

❱ Validation

One of the key elements in input by all these methods is ensuring the quality of data. This is achieved through **data validation**. This is a process to ensure the quality of data by checking they have been entered correctly; it prompts the user to inform them of incorrect data entry.

Validation is important in database systems and databases usually supply built-in input validation as follows:

- *Data type checking*. When tables have been designed, field types will be defined such as text (alphanumeric), number, currency or date. Text characters will not be permitted in a number field and when a user enters a date, for example, the software will prompt the user if it is not a valid date.
- *Data range checking*. Since storage needs to be pre-allocated in databases, designers will specify the number of digits required for each field. For example, a field for holding the quantity of an item ordered would typically only need the range 1–999. So three digits are required. If the user made an error and entered four digits, then they would be warned that this was not possible.
- *Restricted value checking*. This usually occurs for text values that are used to describe particular attributes of an entity. For example, in a database for estate agents, the type of house would have to be stored. This would be a restricted choice of flat, bungalow, semi-detached, etc. Once the restricted choices have been specified, the software will ensure that only one of these choices is permitted, usually by prompting the user with a list of the available alternatives.

Some additional validation checks may need to be specified at the design phase which will later be programmed into the system. These include:

- *Input limits*. This is another form of range checking when the input range cannot be specified through the number of digits alone. For example, if the maximum number of an item that could be ordered is 5, perhaps because of a special offer, this would be specified as a limit of 1–5. Note that the user would not be permitted to enter 0.

● *Multiple field validation.* If there are business rules that mean that allowable input is governed by more than one field, then these rules must be programmed in. For example, in the estate agent database, there could be a separate field for commission shown as a percentage of house price, such as 1.5 per cent, and a separate field showing the amount, such as £500. In this situation the programmer would have to write code that would automatically calculate the commission amount depending on the percentage entered.

● *Checksum digits.* A **checksum** involves the use of an extra digit for ensuring the validity of long code numbers. The checksum digit is calculated from an algorithm involving the numbers in the code and their modulus (by convention modulus 11). These can be used to ensure that errors are not made in entering long codes such as a customer account number (although these would normally be generated automatically by the computer). They are often used in bar codes.

Checksum digits

A checksum involves the use of an extra digit for ensuring the validity of long code numbers. The checksum digit is calculated from an algorithm involving the numbers in the code and their modulus (by convention modulus 11).

Activity 11.4

Checksum digits example

The checksum digit is calculated using the modulus of the weighted products of the number, as follows:

1 Code number without check digit = 293643.

2 Calculate the sum of weighted products by multiplying the least significant digit by 2, the next by 3 and so on. For this example:

(7*2) + (6*9) + (5*3) + (4*6) + (3*4) + (2*3) = 14 + 54 + 15 + 24 + 12 + 6 = 125

3 Remainder when sum divided by 11 (modulus 11) = 125\11 = 11 remainder 4.

4 Subtract remainder from 11 to find check digit (11–4) = 7. (If the remainder is 0, check digit is 0; if 1, check digit is X.)

5 New code number with check digit = 2936437.

Output design

Output design specifies how production of on-screen reports and paper-based reports will occur. Output may occur to database or file for storing information entered or also for use by other systems.

Output data is displayed by three methods:

1 It may be directly displayed from input data.
2 It may be displayed from previously stored data.
3 It may be *derived* data that are produced by calculation.

Design involves specifying the source of data (which database tables and fields map to a point on the report), what processing needs to occur to display data such as aggregation, sorting or calculations, and the form in which the information will be displayed – graph, table or summary form.

Output design is important for decision support software to ensure that relevant information can be chosen, retrieved and interpreted as easily as possible. Given that output design involves these three factors, it will also relate to input design (to select the report needed) and database design (to retrieve the information quickly).

Output design

Output design involves specifying how production of on-screen reports and paper-based reports will occur. Output may occur to database or file for storing information entered or also for use by other systems.

Defining the structure of program modules

The detailed design may include a definition for programmers, indicating how to structure the code of the module. The extent to which this is necessary will depend on the complexity of the module, how experienced the programmer is and how important it is to document the method of programming. A safety-critical system (Chapter 4) will always be designed in this detail before coding commences. Structured English is one of the most commonly used methods of defining program structure. Standard flowcharts can be used, but these tend to take longer to produce.

▶ Structured English

Structured English
A technique for producing a design specification for programmers which indicates the way individual modules or groups of modules should be implemented.

Structured English is a technique for producing a design specification for programmers which indicates the way individual modules or groups of modules should be implemented. It is more specific than a flowchart. It uses keywords to describe the structure of the program, as shown in the example box. Structured English is sometimes known as 'pseudocode' or 'program design language'. Data action diagrams use a similar notation.

Structured English has the disadvantage that it is very time-consuming to produce a detailed design. But it has the advantage that to move from here to coding is very straightforward and the likelihood of errors is reduced.

Example: structured English

This example moves through each record of a database table totalling all employees' salaries. (Note that this could be accomplished more quickly using an SQL statement.)

```
DO WHILE NOT end of table
   IF hours_worked > basic_hours
        SET pay = (hours*basic_rate)+ (overtime_hours*overtime_rate)
   ELSE
        SET pay = (hours*basic_rate)
   END IF
   SET total_pay = total_pay + pay
   move to next record
ENDDO
```

Security design

Data security is of course a key design issue, particularly for information systems that contain confidential company information which is accessed across a wide-area network or the Internet. The four main attributes of security which must be achieved through design are:

1 *Authentication*. Authentication ensures that the sender of the message, or the person trying to access the system, is who they claim to be. Passwords are one way of providing authentication, but are open to abuse – users often tend to swap them. Digital certificates and digital signatures offer a higher level of security. These are available in some groupware products such as Lotus Notes.
2 *Authorisation*. Authorisation checks that the user has the right permissions to access the information that they are seeking. This ensures that only senior personnel managers can access salary figures, for example.

3 *Privacy*. In a security context, privacy equates to scrambling or encryption of messages so that they cannot easily be decrypted if they are intercepted during transmission. Credit card numbers sent over the Internet are encrypted in this way.

4 *Data integrity*. Security is also necessary to ensure that the message sent is the same as the one received and that corruption has not occurred. A security system can use a checksum digit to ensure that this is the case and the data packet has not been modified.

Data must also be secure in the sense of not being subject to deletion, or available to people who don't have the 'need to know'. Methods of safeguarding data are covered in more detail in Chapter 15.

Design tools: CASE (computer-aided software engineering) tools

CASE (computer-aided software engineering) tools are software that helps the systems analyst and designer in the analysis, design and build phases of a software project. They provide tools for drawing diagrams such as entity relationship diagrams (ERDs) and storing information about processes, entities and attributes.

CASE tools are primarily used by professional IS developers and are intended to assist in managing the process of capturing requirements, and converting these into design and program code. They also act as a repository for storing information about the design of the program and help make the software easy to maintain. The use of an engineering approach was intended to impose an engineering discipline on developing software which had been developed in an ad hoc way in many companies. CASE tools are based on a user graphically specifying a design using a diagram such as an ERD and this logical design is then converted into a physical database structure. CASE tools permit different approaches to the design technique such as dataflow diagrams or object-oriented diagramming techniques. They are often supplied as part of a database package such as Oracle, Informix or Sybase, and in these cases are used for managing the data dictionary.

CASE tools were introduced in the 1980s in response to the need to engineer software products more methodically. The underlying rationale behind CASE tools is to provide a software tool which can be used to assist throughout the software lifecycle. Previously there had been some tools to assist with analysis, tools for design, and programming tools for the build phase. CASE tools provide a mechanism for architects of systems to use a single tool across all these phases of the lifecycle. Such tools are sometimes described as ICASE or integrated CASE tools, since they can be used throughout the lifecycle and are integrated with databases or programming tools. CASE tools are also useful since they tend to enforce documentation of the detailed design, much of which can be generated automatically.

Different ways in which CASE tools can be used are:

- A CASE tool can be used to summarise the requirements of users from the system needed for data modelling. For example, the CASE tool will produce an entity relationship diagram that can be linked to a data dictionary describing the attributes of the entities. This is then used to produce the physical table automatically at the build phase. The Oracle database provides CASE tools that give this facility. A more limited facility also exists in Microsoft Access which enables all the relationships between tables to be defined. These are then used to form queries.
- A CASE tool can be used to assist in process modelling. A dataflow diagram can be produced at different levels which relates to a data dictionary and provides a structure to the application, i.e. data can be linked to process and process to program modules.

CASE (Computer-aided software engineering) tools
Software that helps the systems analyst and designer in the analysis, design and build phases of a software project. They provide tools for drawing diagrams such as ERDs and storing information about processes, entities and attributes.

CASE tools tend to be related to particular methodologies, for example SSADM Select helps users through the stages related to SSADM.

When they were first introduced it was thought that CASE tools would dramatically speed application development and also improve application quality. While they have helped in minimising the risk of project failure, dramatic improvements have not occurred. Intervention is still required by designers to produce a logical design and the need for skilled programmers has not been reduced. Since CASE tools tend to be expensive they are typically used by large companies only on major projects; they are less likely to be used for smaller-scale or end-user-developed systems.

Error handling and exceptions

The design will include a strategy for dealing with bugs in the system or problems resulting from changes to the operating environment, such as a network failure. When an error is encountered the design will specify that:

- Users should be prompted with a clear but not alarming message explaining the problem.
- The message should contain sufficient diagnostics that developers will be able to identify and solve the problem.

Help and documentation

It is straightforward using tools to construct a Windows help file based on a word-processed document. The method of generating help messages for users will also be specified in the design. Help is usually available as:

- an online help application similar to reading a manual, but with links between pages and a built-in index;
- context-sensitive help, where pressing the help button of a dialogue will take the user straight to the relevant page of the online user guide;
- ToolTip help, where the user places the mouse over a menu option or icon and further guidance is displayed in the status area;
- help associated with error messages; this is also context-sensitive.

Object-oriented design (OOD)

Object-oriented design
This is a design technique which involves basing the design of software on real-world objects which consist of both data and the procedures that process them rather than traditional design where procedures operate on separate data.

Object-oriented design is a design technique which involves basing the design of software on real-world objects that consist of both data and the procedures that process them, rather than traditional design where procedures operate on separate data. Many software products are labelled 'object-oriented' in a bid to boost sales, but relatively few are actually designed using object-oriented techniques. What makes the object approach completely different?

- Traditional development methods are *procedural*, dealing with separate data that are transformed by abstract, hierarchical programming code.
- OOD is a relatively new technique involving *objects* (which mirror real-world objects consisting of integrated data *and* code).

Examples of objects that are commonly used in business information systems include customer, supplier, employee and product. You may notice that these are similar to the entities referred to in Chapter 10, but a key difference is that an object will not only consist of different attributes such as name and address, but will also comprise procedures that process them. For example, a customer object may have a procedure (known as a 'method') to print these personal details.

SAP uses object-oriented structure for its R/3 ERP product

With its R/3 enterprise resource planning product, SAP provides several hundred standard business process modules for areas such as procurement or finance that can assist in rapid implementation of the system for new users. The business processes are defined as objects that are stored in an object repository. For example, an invoice is defined as an object with the standard methods:

- Create (constructor).
- Revise.
- Release.
- Post.
- Delete (destructor).

When executed, each of these methods will automatically generate an event that can be used for generating subsequent actions or monitoring workflow status. Although it is possible to tailor the objects somewhat, note that it is not practical to modify the standard objects to any great extent, so a consequence of this approach is that adopters of the SAP system tend to follow the standard processes provided by the software.

The main benefits of using object orientation are said to be more rapid development and lower costs which can be achieved through greater reuse of code. Reuse in object-oriented systems is a consequence of the ease with which generic objects can be incorporated into code. This is a consequence of inheritance, where a new object can be derived from an existing object and its behaviour modified (polymorphism).

Some further advantages of the object-oriented approach are:

- easier to explain object concepts to end-users since they are based on real-world objects;
- more reuse of code – standard, tested business objects;
- faster, cheaper development of more robust code.

Object-oriented design is closely linked to the growth in use of software components for producing systems. Developers writing programs for Microsoft Windows on a PC will now commonly buy pre-built objects with functionality such as displaying a diary, a project schedule or different types of graph. Such object components are referred to as Visual Basic controls and object controls (OCX). Through using these, developers can implement features without having to reinvent the wheel of writing graphical routines.

An example of a class hierarchy is shown in Figure 11.32. The base class is a person who attends the college. All other classes are derived from this person.

▶ How widely is the object-oriented approach used?

There was a rapid growth in the use of object-oriented techniques in the 1990s, although original research using the Simula language dates back to the late 1960s. This growth in interest is reflected by the increase in the number of jobs advertised by companies looking to develop software using object-oriented methods, such as Smalltalk, C++ and Java

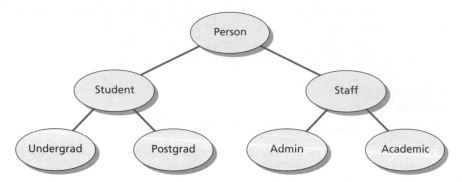

Figure 11.32 **A class hierarchy for different types of people at a university**

which is now one of the main methods for developing interactive web sites. Specialised methodologies exist for designing object-oriented systems. Some of the most commonly used are the object modelling technique (OMT), described by Kavanagh (1994) and the original text by Rumbaugh (1991), and hierarchical object-oriented decomposition (HOOD), based on work conducted by Booch (1986) relating to the Ada programming language. These share some elements with DFD and ERD, but differ in that a hierarchical class breakdown is an additional perspective on designing the system.

What are the main characteristics of an object-oriented system?

1 An object consists of *data* and *methods* that act on them. A customer object would contain data such as their personal details and methods to act on them such as 'print customer details'.

2 Objects communicate using *messages* which request a particular service from another object, such as a 'print current balance' service. These services are known as methods and are equivalent to functions in traditional programming.

3 Objects are created and destroyed as the program is running. For example, if a new customer opens an account, we would create a new instance of the object. If a customer closes an account, the object is destroyed.

4 Objects provide *encapsulation* – an object can have private elements that are not evident to other objects. This hides complex details and gives a simple public object interface for external use by other objects. A real-world analogy is that it is possible to use a limited number of functions on a television without knowing its inner workings. In object-oriented parlance the television controls are providing different public methods which can be used by other objects. 'Abstraction' refers to the simplified public interface of the object.

5 Objects can be grouped into classes which share characteristics. For example, an organisation might contain an employee class. The classes can be subdivided using a hierarchy to create subclasses such as 'manager' or 'administrator'. Classes can share characteristics with other classes in the hierarchy, which is known as *inheritance*. This refers to the situation when an object inherits the behaviour of other objects. A specialised part-time staff class could inherit personal details data items from the employee class. If the method for calculating salary was different, then the part-time staff could override its inherited behaviour to define its own method 'calculate salary'. This is known as *polymorphism*, where an object can modify its inherited behaviour.

Despite the growth of OOD, non-object or procedural systems vastly outnumber object systems. So if OOD is nirvana, why doesn't everyone use it? The following are all practical barriers to growth:

- Millions of lines of procedural legacy computer code exist in languages as COBOL.
- Many programmers' skills are procedural – OOD requires retraining to a different way of thinking.
- Methodologies, languages and tools are developing rapidly, requiring constant retraining and making reuse different when using different tools and languages. For example, the most popular object-oriented method has changed from Smalltalk to C++ to Java in just 10 years.
- Limited libraries are available for reuse.
- When initially designing projects, it is often slower and more costly – the benefits of OOD take several years to materialise.

The experience of early adopters has shown that the benefits do not come until later releases of a product and that initial object-oriented design and development may be more expensive than traditional methods.

Summary

Stage summary: systems design

Purpose: Defines *how* the system will work
Key activities: Systems design, detailed design, database design, user interface design
Input: Requirements specification
Output: System design specification, detailed design specification, test specification

1 The design phase of the systems development lifecycle involves the specification of how the system should work.

2 The input to the design phase is the requirements specification from the analysis phase. The output from the design phase is a design specification that is used by programmers in the build phase.

3 Systems design is usually conducted using a top-down approach in which the overall architecture of the system is designed first. This is referred to as the systems or outline design. The individual modules are then designed in the detailed design phase.

4 Many modern information systems are designed using the client/server architecture. Processing is shared between the end-user's clients and the server, which is used to store data and process queries.

5 Systems design and detailed design will specify how the following aspects of the system will work:

- its user interface;
- method of data input and output (input and output design);
- design of security to ensure the integrity of confidential data;
- error handling;
- help system.

6 For systems based on a relational database and a file-based system, the design stage will involve determining the best method of physically storing the data. For a database system, the technique for optimising the storage is known as normalisation.

7 Object-oriented design is a relatively new approach to design. It has been adopted by some companies attracted by the possibility of cheaper development costs and fewer errors, which are made possible through reuse of code and a different design model that involves data and process integration.

EXERCISES

Self-assessment exercises

1 Define systems design.

2 What distinguishes systems design from systems analysis?

3 Describe the purpose of validation and verification.

4 What are process modelling and data modelling? Which diagrams used to summarise requirements at the analysis phase are useful in each of these types of modelling?

5 Explain the client/server model of computing.

6 What parts of the system need to be designed at the detailed design stage?

7 Describe the purpose of normalisation.

8 Explain insertion, update and deletion anomalies.

9 What is the difference between the sequential and direct (random) file access methods? In which business applications might they be used? What is the purpose of a file index?

10 Explain the difference between a batch and a real-time system. Which would be the more appropriate design for each of the following situations:
   ● periodic updating of a data warehouse from an operational database;
   ● capturing information on customer sales transactions?

11 What are the different types of input validation that must be considered in the design of a user input form?

12 Describe the main differences between the analysis and design phases within the systems development lifecycle.

Discussion questions

1 'The client/server model of computing has many disadvantages, but these do not outweigh the advantages.' Discuss.

2 'The distinction between system design and detailed design is an artificial one since a bottom-up approach to design is inevitable.' Discuss.

Essay questions

1 Explain, using an example from a human resources management database, the normalisation process from unnormalised data to third normal form (3NF).

2 Table 11.8 from a relational database contains a number of rows and columns. When data are entered into the table, all columns must have data entered. Information about product descriptions, prices, product groups and rack locations is not held elsewhere. Explain how, because of its design, the table contains the potential for insertion, update and deletion anomalies. What is meant by these anomalies and what could be done to prevent them?

Table 11.8 **Table from a relational database**

Product code	Product description	Product group	Group description	Cost	Retail price	Rack location	Quantity
0942	Small Green	KD	Kiddy Doh	0.19	1.29	A201	16
0439	Large Red	KD	Kiddy Doh	0.31	1.89	W106	35
0942	Small Green	KD	Kiddy Doh	0.19	1.29	E102	0
0902	Small Green	KD	Kiddy Doh	0.19	1.29	J320	56
1193	Spinning Top	PS	Pre-School	1.23	12.49	X215	3
2199	Burger Kit	KD	Kiddy Doh	3.25	17.75	D111	0

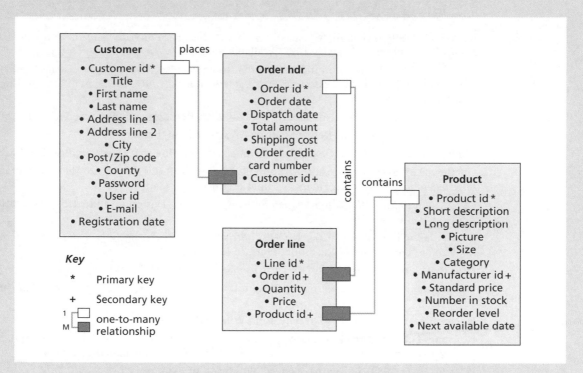

Figure 11.33 **The expanded ERD for a kitchenware retailer**

3 A business-to-consumer company (B2C), a kitchenware retailer, wants to set up an e-commerce site, but first wants to produce a prototype in Microsoft Access. The data analysis has been performed and is shown in the expanded entity relationship diagram in Figure 11.33 . Produce this database in Access based on the ERD. Include 4 or 5 sample records for each table.

Examination questions

1 Explain the difference between validation and verification. Why are they important elements of systems design?

2 What benefits does three-tier client/server offer over two-tier client/server?

3 What are the main elements of system design?

4 Explain normalisation and how it can help remove different types of anomaly when modifying a database.

5 Which criteria are important in deciding whether to use a batch or real-time system?

6 What are the important aspects of user interface design?

7 Which different types of validation need to occur on data input to a system to ensure information quality?

8 What are the four main attributes of information security which need to be attained in an information system?

9 What is meant by the terms 'input design', 'output design' and 'database design'? Illustrate each of them with an example.

References

Bevan, N. (1999a) 'Usability issues in web site design', *Proceedings of the 6th Interactive Publishing Conference, November 1999.* Available online at www.usability.serco.com

Bevan, N. (1999b) 'Common industry format usability tests', *Proceedings of UPA'98, Usability Professionals Association, Scottsdale, Arizona, 29 June – 2 July, 1999.* Available online at www.usability.serco.com

Booch, G. (1986) 'Object oriented development', *IEEE Transactions on Software Engineering*, SE12

Budgen, D. (1994) *Software Design*, Addison-Wesley, Wokingham

Chaffey, D. (2002) *E-Business and E-Commerce Management*, Financial Times Prentice Hall, Harlow

Chaffey, D., Mayer, R., Johnston, K. and Ellis-Chadwick, F. (2000) *Internet Marketing: Strategy, Implementation and Practice*, Financial Times Prentice Hall, Harlow

Curtis, G. (2002) *Business Information Systems*, Analysis, Design and Practice, 4th edition, Addison-Wesley, Harlow

Downs, E., Clare, P. and Coe, I. (1992) *Structured Systems Analysis and Design Method: Applications and Context*, 2nd edition, Prentice Hall, London

Edwards, J. and DeVoe, D. (1997) *3-Tier Client/Server at Work*, John Wiley, New York

Hasselbring, W. (2000) 'Information system integration', *Communications of the ACM*, June, 43, 6, 33–8

Hofacker, C. (2000) *Internet Marketing*, John Wiley, New York

Hoffman, D.L. and Novak, T.P. (1997) 'A new marketing paradigm for electronic commerce', *The Information Society*, Special issue on electronic commerce, 13 (Jan–Mar), 43–54

Jackson, M.A. (1983) *System Development*, Prentice Hall, London

Jacobsen, I., Ericsson, M. and Jacobsen, A. (1994) *The Object Advantage. Business Process Re-engineering with Object Technology*, Addison-Wesley, Wokingham

Kavanagh, D. (1994) 'OMT development process, vintage 1994', in K. Spurr, P. Layzell, L. Jennison and N. Richards (eds) *Business Objects: Software Solutions*, John Wiley, New York, 90–105

Lynch, P. and Horton, S. (1999) *Web Style Guide. Basic Design Principals for Creating Web Sites*, Yale University Press. Available online at info.med_yale.edu/caim/manual/contents.html

Mcfadden, F.R. and Hofer, J.A. (1995) *Database Management*, 4th edition, Benjamin Cummings Science, Menlo Park, CA

Nielsen, J. (1999) *Details in Study Methodology Can Give Misleading Results.* Jakob Nielsen's Alertbox, February 21, 1999 at www.useit.com/alertbox/990221.html

Nielsen, J. (2000a) *Novice vs. Expert Users.* Jakob Nielsen's Alertbox, 6 February, at www.useit.com/alertbox/20000206.html

Nielsen, J. (2000b) *Designing Web Usability*, New Riders Publishing, Indianapolis, IN

Noyes, J. and Baber, C. (1999) *User-centred Design of Systems*, Springer-Verlag, Berlin

Preece, J., Rogers, Y., Sharp, H., Benyon, D., Holland, S. and Carey, T. (1994) *Human Computer Interaction*, Addison-Wesley, Wokingham

Rosenfeld, L. and Morville, P. (1998) *Information Architecture for the World Wide Web*, O'Reilly & Associates, Sebastopol, CA

Rumbaugh, J. (1991) *Object Oriented Modelling and Design (OMT)*, Prentice-Hall, Englewood Cliffs, NJ

Schneider, G. and Winters, J. (1998) *Applying Use Cases. A Practical Guide*, Addison Wesley Longman, Reading, MA

Whitten, J.L. and Bentley, L.D. (1998) *Systems Analysis and Design Methods*, Irwin/McGraw Hill, Boston, MA

Yeates, D., Shields, M. and Helmy, D. (1994) *Systems Analysis and Design*, Financial Times Pitman Publishing, London

Further reading

Galitz, W.O. (1997) *The Essential Guide to User Interface Design: an Introduction to GUI Design*, John Wiley, Chichester

Heuring, V. (1997) *Computer Systems Design and Architecture*, Addison-Wesley, Menlo Park, CA

Jacobsen, I., Ericsson, M. and Jacobsen, A. (1994) *The Object Advantage: Business Process Reengineering with Object Technology*, Addison-Wesley, Wokingham

Kendall, K. and Kendall, J. (1998) *Systems Analysis and Design*, Prentice Hall, London

Skidmore, S. (1996) *Introducing Systems Design*, NCC Blackwell, Oxford

Stowell, F. and West, D. (1994) *Client Led Design: a Systemic Approach to Information Systems Definition*, McGraw-Hill, Maidenhead

Tudor, D. and Tudor, I. (1997) *Systems Analysis and Design: a Comparison of Structured Methods*, Macmillan, Basingstoke

Yourdon, E. and Constantine, L. (1979) *Structured Design Fundamentals of a Discipline of Computer Program and Systems Design*, Prentice-Hall, Englewood Cliffs, NJ

Web links

www.cio.com CIO.com for Chief Information Officers and IS staff has many articles related to analysis and design topics in different research centres such as security (www.cio.com/research/security), CRM (www.cio.com/research/crm) and infrastructure (www.cio.com/research/infrastructure).

www.360.com *Computer Weekly* is a weekly IS professionals trade paper with UK/Europe focus; has many case studies on practical problems of analysis, design and implementation.

www.eds.com/case_studies/cs_home.shtml EDS case studies from major BIS consultant EDS illustrate many of the issues of systems analysis, design and implementation.

www.research.ibm.com/journal IBM Journals *IBM Systems Journal* and the *Journal of Research and Development* have many cases and articles on analysis and design related to e-business concepts such as knowledge management, security.

www.intranetjournal.com/itadvisor Intranet journal has case studies on systems analysis and design specific to intranets.

www.fdic.gov/regulations/information/index.html FDIC The Federal Financial Institutions Examination Council (FFIEC) handbook for conducting examinations of banks' and savings associations' information systems is interesting since it recommends appropriate approaches and activities to different stages of building banking systems which also apply to other systems.

knowledge.wharton.upenn.edu/category.cfm? catid=14 Managing Technology at Wharton articles cover a range of technology management issues including analysis, design and implementation issues.

System build, implementation and maintenance

LEARNING OBJECTIVES

After reading this chapter, readers will be able to:

- state the purpose of the build phase, and its difference from changeover and implementation;
- specify the different types of testing required for a system;
- select the best alternatives for changing from an old system to a new system;
- recognise the importance of managing both organisational change and software change associated with introduction of a new BIS.

MANAGEMENT ISSUES

Effective systems implementation is required for a quality system to be installed with minimal disruption to the business. From a managerial perspective, this chapter addresses the following questions:

- How should the system be tested?
- How should data be migrated from the old system to the new system?
- How should the changeover between old and new systems be managed?

Links to other chapters

This chapter focuses on the build and implementation stage of a systems project before a system goes 'live' within a business. It is related to previous chapters (7–11) which describe preceding phases of systems development.

Introduction

System build occurs after the system has been designed. It refers to the creation of software using programming or incorporation of building blocks such as existing software components or libraries. Testing by programmers will occur alongside programming to check for any errors. End-user testing may also occur at this stage as part of prototyping, but it may be deferred until the implementation phase when the complete system can be tested. Writing of documentation to specify the design of the system and end-user documentation also occur during the build stage.

To emphasise the importance of testing in a systems development project, you are referred to Case Study 12.1 on the implementation problems the Woolwich encountered when introducing a new e-commerce system. The number of errors found in this system illustrate that testing can be a significant part of the systems development lifecycle. You should consider whether such problems in a system are inevitable and measures must be taken in the build phase to identify and solve them, or whether there are failures in earlier phases in the lifecycle which are responsible for them.

System implementation follows the build stage. It involves setting up the right environment in which the test and finished system can be used. This may involve setting up a network or purchasing new PCs to run the software. It will also involve preparing new data for the system to run on. This will often involve transferring data from a previous system. Once a test version of the software has been produced, this will be tested by the users and corrections made to the software followed by further testing and fixing until the software is suitable for use throughout the company. This transition is known as the *changeover* from the existing system to the new system. There are several different alternatives for this which are explored in the chapter.

System build and implementation are just as important as earlier stages in the systems development lifecycle, in that a technically good solution from the earlier stages can still fail if the implementation has not been planned adequately.

A key implementation decision that needs to be taken is how to manage the changeover from the old system to the new system. This decision will always need to be taken, whether a company is moving from an old paper-based system or from an existing information system.

We will consider the issues associated with the different activities of system build first in this chapter, then discuss how to manage change and the maintenance once the system is live.

System build
The creation of software by programmers involving programming, building release versions of the software and testing by programmers and end-users. Writing of documentation and training may also occur at this stage.

System implementation
Involves the transition or changeover from the old system to the new and the preparation for this such as making sure the hardware and network infrastructure for a new system are in place; testing of the system and also human issues of how best to educate and train staff who will be using or affected by the new system.

CASE STUDY 12.1

Woolwich Financial Services   FT

Terry Boldick had no time for present shopping in the week leading up to Christmas. A consultant with Unisys, the computer company, he was too busy working against the clock tackling problems with a new and critically important information technology system which had just been installed at the Woolwich financial services group.

The chief cause for concern was, as Mr Boldick puts it, 'instability when the system was running in a production environment'. In other words, it tended to fall over in an unpredictable manner when used for real world applications.

Companies frequently experience difficulties when bedding down new computer systems. In this case, the systems software was Microsoft's very recently introduced Distributed InterNet Architecture (DNA) running on Dell servers. So a few hiccoughs were to be expected.

A great deal, however, was riding on this system. It was fundamental to the successful introduction of The Woolwich's 'Open Plan' current account, designed to offer customers a range of attractive new technologically smart ways of getting at their money. In addition to traditional branches, it included the telephone, the cash machine, the internet, the mobile phone and interactive television. Customers would receive a single monthly statement of all their dealings with the bank. The Woolwich would have a comprehensive view of each of its customers.

The UK group's top brass were convinced of the value of technology as a key element in the future of the financial services business. By moving quickly to launch an online service, they believed they had stolen a march on the competition. Failure would be public, embarrassing and demoralising.

But the stability problems meant the pilot service was frequently and unexpectedly unavailable. At this point, with Christmas looming, Unisys, in the shape of Mr Boldick and colleagues, was called in. Within the week they were able to say the problem lay in the load balancing area – the controls necessary to fine tune the system the better to distribute processing loads across the available resources.

The solution was another matter. Technically, what Mr Boldick needed were new 'layer four' switches, the systems which control the transport layer of the network. These are responsible for ensuring that entire files or messages are safely delivered.

The DNA software was proprietary to Microsoft and not to be interfered with. Mr Boldick considered three possibilities, not one of which really appealed because they were software rather than hardware fixes: IBM Redirector, Cisco Local Director or Windows Load Balancing.

At this point luck and technology played a pivotal part. Mr Boldick discovered a new company, Alteon WebSystems of San Jose, California, on the internet. Alteon manufactures web switches, hardware devices which operate between web servers and the web itself, controlling, processing, tracking and forwarding web content – essentially network traffic police.

So Mr Boldick had discovered a hardware solution with the advantage of providing what he describes as 'health checks at the application level' – in other words, if a web server failed, you knew about it.

Option put to the test

On the other hand, Alteon and its products were an unknown quantity. He decided, based on gut feel, to persuade The Woolwich to test the Alteon option – 'if the salesman comes across as genuine, you tend to believe the product will do what he says it will do'.

In any case, he had Windows Load Balancing as a fall-back alternative. In the event, the Alteon switch proved up to the task. From one system in 1999, The Woolwich now operates some 12 to 15 of the switches to manage its intranets and extranets.

Tony O'Reilly, IT infrastructure manager, says the group now has some 550,000 Open Plan customers and expects to have 1m by the end of the year: 'We now have 99 per cent availability end-to-end', he claims. A Wap (wireless application protocol) capability enabling customers to bank over their mobile phones was added in six weeks.

The Woolwich order was a breakthrough for Alteon. It had already sold systems in the US to companies such as Lycos and Yahoo! but The Woolwich represented its first sale outside North America to a non-internet group. Now it has sold some 20,000–30,000 systems in Europe.

The company, founded in 1996, was acquired by Nortel Networks in July last year and its product line is being integrated into Nortel's offerings. The deal gives Alteon financial stability, a large direct sales force and the resources to compete with Cisco Systems, the internet leader.

The advantage to Nortel according to Dominic Orr, Alteon chief executive, is that web switching capabilities will be increasingly important to internet infrastructure manufacturers. He points out that web data centres are very different from conventional data centres, requiring a new architecture to keep the traffic moving at maximum speed.

▶

The Woolwich's experience tends to support that view. Mr Boldick says it has between 60 and 70 servers on each of two sites: 'It is an extremely complicated operation. But with the load balancing using the Alteon switches you can lose half the system and the service will still be available.'

Source: Alan Cane, 'Woolwich Group: switched-on route to fix a problem', *Financial Times*, 5 February 2001

Questions

1 How did these problems with the implementation affect the business?

2 Outline the problems and solutions.

3 Assess whether these problems could have been avoided by considering the whole of the SDLC.

Key system build activities

▶ System development

System development, which includes programming and testing, is the main activity that occurs at the system build phase.

The coverage of programming in this book will necessarily be brief, since the technical details of programming are not relevant to business people. A brief coverage of the techniques used by programmers is given since a knowledge of these techniques can be helpful in managing technical staff. Business users also often become involved in end-user development, which requires an appreciation of programming principles.

Software consists of program code written by programmers that is compiled or built into files known as 'executables' from different modules, each with a particular function. Executables are run by users as interactive programs. You may have noticed *application or executable files* in directories on your hard disk with a file type of '.exe', such as winword.exe for Microsoft Word, or '.dll' library files.

There are a number of system development tools available to programmers and business users to help in writing software. Software development tools include:

- Third-generation languages (3GLs) include Basic, Pascal, C, COBOL and Fortran. These involve writing programming code. Traditionally this was achieved in a text editor with limited support from other tools, since these languages date back to the 1960s. These languages are normally used to produce text-based programs rather than interactive graphical user interface programs that run under Microsoft Windows. They are, however, still used extensively in *legacy systems*, in which there exist millions of lines of COBOL code that must be maintained.
- Fourth-generation languages (4GLs) were developed in response to the difficulty of using 3GLs, particularly for business users. They are intended to avoid the need for programming. Since they often lack the flexibility for building a complex system, they are often ignored.
- Visual development tools such as Microsoft Visual Studio, Visual Basic and Visual C++ use an 'interactive development environment' that makes it easy to define the user interface of a product and write code to process the events generated when a user selects an option from a menu or button. They are widely used for prototyping and some tools such as Visual Basic for Applications are used by end-users for extending spreadsheet models. These tools share some similarities with 4GLs, but are not true application generators since programming is needed to make the applications function. Since they are relatively easy to use, they are frequently used by business users.
- **CASE or computer-aided software engineering tools** (see Chapter 11 for coverage of CASE tools) are primarily used by professional IS developers and are intended to assist in

Computer-aided software engineering (CASE) tools

Primarily used by professional IS developers to assist in managing the process of capturing requirements, and converting these into design and program code.

managing the process of capturing requirements, and converting these into design and program code.

▶ Assessing software quality

Software metrics are used by businesses developing information systems to establish the quality of programs in an attempt to improve customer satisfaction through reducing errors by better programming and testing practices. **Software quality** is measured according to its suitability for the job intended. This is governed by whether it can do the job required (Does it meet the business requirements?) and the number of bugs it contains (Does it work reliably?). The quality of software is dependent on two key factors:

1 the number of errors or bugs in the software;
2 the suitability of the software to its intended purpose, i.e. does it have the features identified by users which are in the requirements specification?

It follows that good-quality software must meet the needs of the business users and contain few errors. We are trying to answer questions such as:

● Does the product work?
● Does it crash?
● Does the product function according to specifications?
● Does the user interface meet product specifications and is it easy to use?
● Are there any unexplained or undesirable side-effects to using the product which may stop other software working?

The number of errors is quite easily measured, although errors may not be apparent until they are encountered by end-users. Suitability to purpose is much more difficult to quantify, since it is dependent on a number of factors. These factors were referred to in detail in Chapters 8 and 11 which described the criteria that are relevant to deciding on a suitable information system. These quality criteria include correct functions, speed and ease of use.

What is a bug?

Problems, errors or defects in software are collectively known as 'bugs', since they are often small and annoying! Software bugs are defects in a program which are caused by human error during programming or earlier in the lifecycle. They may result in major faults or may remain unidentified. A major problem in a software system can be caused by one wrong character in a program of tens of thousands of lines. So it is often the source of the problem that is small, not its consequences.

Computing history recalls that the first bug was a moth which crawled inside a valve in one of the first computers, causing it to crash! This bug was identified by Grace Hopper, the inventor of COBOL, the first commercial programming language.

Software quality also involves an additional factor which is not concerned with the functionality or number of bugs in the software. Instead, it considers how well the software operates in its environment. For example, in a multitasking environment such as Windows 95 or Windows NT, it assesses how well a piece of software coexists with other programs. Are resources shared evenly? Will a crash of the software cause other software to fail also? This type of interaction testing is known as 'behaviour testing'.

Software metrics

Software metrics have much in common with measures involved with assessing the quality of a product in other industries. For example, in engineering or construction, designers want to know how long it will take a component to fail or the number of errors in a batch of products. Most measures are defect-based, measuring the number and type of errors. The source of the error and when it was introduced into the system are also important. Some errors are the result of faulty analysis or design and many are the result of a programming error. By identifying and analysing the source of the error, improvements can be made to the relevant part of the software lifecycle. An example of a comparison of three projects in terms of errors is shown in Table 12.1. It can be seen that in Project 3, the majority of errors are introduced during the coding (programming) stage, so corrective action is necessary here.

Software metrics
Measures which indicate the quality of software.

Table 12.1 Table comparing the source of errors in three different software projects

	Project 1	Project 2	Project 3
Analysis	20%	30%	15%
Design	25%	40%	20%
Coding	35%	20%	45%
Testing	20%	10%	20%

While the approach of many companies to testing has been that bugs are inevitable and must be tested for to remove them, more enlightened companies look at the reasons for the errors and attempt to stop them being introduced by the software developers. This implies that longer should be spent on the analysis and design phases of a project. Johnston (1995) suggests that the balance between the phases of a project should be divided as shown in Table 12.2, with a large proportion of the time being spent on analysis and design.

Table 12.2 Ideal proportions of time to be spent on different phases of a systems development project, focusing on details of build phase

Project activities	Suggested proportion
Definition, design and planning	20%
Coding	15%
Component test and early system test	15%
Full system test, user testing and operational trials	20%
Documentation, training and implementation support	20%
Overall project management	10%

In software code the number of errors or 'defect density' is measured in terms of **errors per 1000 lines of code (or KLOC for short)**. The long-term aim of a business is to reduce the defect rate towards the elusive goal of 'zero defects'.

Errors per KLOC is the basic defect measure used in systems development. Care must be taken when calculating defect density or productivity of programmers using KLOC, since this will vary from one programming language to another and according to the style of the programmer and the number of comment statements used. KLOC must be used consistently between programs, and this is usually achieved by only counting executable statements, not comments, or by counting function points.

Errors per KLOC
Errors per KLOC (thousands of line of code) is the basic defect measure used in systems development.

The technical quality of software can also be assessed by measures other than the number of errors. Its complexity, which is often a function of the number of branches it contains, is commonly used.

Another metric, more commonly used for engineered products, is the mean time between failures. This is less appropriate to software since outright failure is rare, but small errors or bugs in the software are quite common. It is, however, used as part of outsourcing contracts or as part of the service-level agreement for network performance.

A more useful measure for software is to look at the customer satisfaction rating of the software, since its quality is dependent on many other factors such as usability and speed as well as the number of errors.

◗ Data migration

Data migration
....
Data migration is the transfer of data from the old system to the new system. When data are added to a database, this is known as populating the database.

A significant activity of the build phase is to transfer the data from the old system to the new system. **Data migration** is the transfer of data from the old system to the new system. When data are added to a database, this is known as 'populating the database'. One method of transferring data is to rekey manually into the new system. This is impractical for most systems since the volume of data is too large. Instead, special data conversion programs are written to convert the data from the data file format of the old system into the data file format of the new system. Conversion may involve changing data formats, for example a date may be converted from two digits for the year into four digits. It may also involve combining or aggregating fields or records. The conversion programs also have to be well tested because of the danger of corrupting existing data. Data migration is an extra task which needs to be remembered as part of the project manager's project plan. During data migration data can be '**exported**' from an old system and then '**imported**' into a new system.

Import and export
....
Data can be 'exported' from an old system and then 'imported' into a new system.

When using databases or off-the-shelf software, there are usually tools provided to make it easier to import data from other systems.

◗ Testing information systems

Testing is a vital aspect of implementation, since this will identify errors that can be fixed before the system is live. The type of tests that occur in implementation tend to be more structured than the ad hoc testing that occurs with prototyping earlier in systems development.

Note that often testing is not seen as an essential part of the lifecycle, but as a chore that must be done. If its importance is not recognised, insufficient testing will occur. Johnston (1995) refers to the '*testing trap*', when companies spend too long writing the software without changing the overall project deadline. This results in the amount of time for testing being 'squeezed' until it is no longer sufficient. This type of problem is evident from the case study on insurance. As an indication of the amount of testing that needs to occur, Cornhill Insurance recently reported that 80 per cent of the budget for its year 2000 project was spent on testing. *Computer Weekly* reported that the project controller, Sue Pellatt, said:

> *Testing is often pushed to the end of the project, especially when there is a fixed deadline. But it should be a routine part of any project, especially after this project.*

During prototyping, the purpose of testing is to identify missing features or define different ways of performing functions. Testing is more structured during the implementation phase in order to identify as many bugs as possible. It has two main purposes: the first is to check that the requirements agreed earlier in the project have been implemented, the second to identify errors or bugs. To achieve both of these objectives, testing must be conducted in a structured way by using a **test specification** which details tests in different areas. This avoids users' performing a general usability test of the system where they only use common functions at random. While this is valid, and is necessary since it mirrors real use of the software, it does not give a good coverage of all the areas of the system. Systematic tests should be performed using a test script which covers, in detail, the functions to be tested.

Test specification
A detailed description of the tests that will be performed to check the software works correctly.

MINI CASE STUDY

Insurance – testing, testing

If Cornhill Insurance has learnt anything from the engineer management project it would be the importance of testing. IT project manager Peter Williamson says given a second chance he would undoubtedly do a lot more testing than he actually did. 'We had some fairly tight, pretty ambitious timescales, and basically the area that got compounded at the end of the day was testing. There were lots of points of failure and I guess what I would have felt more comfortable with is if we could have done a complete and thorough test. We did a lot of unit testing, but the thing we did a bit of a flyer on was the actual overall link testing.'

Source: Courtesy of *Computer Weekly*, 24 April 1997

Given the variety of tests that need to be performed, large implementations will also use a **test plan**, a specialised project plan describing what testing will be performed when, and by whom. Testing is always a compromise between the number of tests that can be performed and the time available.

Test plan
Plan describing the type and sequence of testing and who will conduct it.

The different types of testing that occur throughout the software lifecycle should be related to the earlier stages in the lifecycle against which we are testing. This approach to development (Fig. 12.1) is sometimes referred to as the 'V-model of systems development', for obvious reasons. The diagram shows that different types of testing are used to test different aspects of the analysis and design of the system: to test the requirements specification a user acceptance test is performed, and to test the detailed design unit testing occurs.

We will now consider in more detail the different types of testing that need to be conducted during implementation. This review is structured according to who performs the tests.

Developer tests

There are a variety of techniques that can be used for testing systems. Jones (1996) identifies 18 types of testing, of which the most commonly used are subroutine, unit, new function, regression, integration and systems testing. Many of the techniques available are not used due to lack of time, money or commitment. Some of the more common techniques are summarised here.

- **Module tests.** These are performed on individual modules of the system. The module is treated as a 'black box' (ignoring its internal method of working) as developers check that expected outputs are generated for given inputs. When you drive a car this can be thought of black box testing – you are aware of the inputs to the car and their effect as outputs, but you will probably not have a detailed knowledge of the mechanical aspects of the car and whether they are functioning correctly. Module testing involves considering a range of inputs or test cases, as follows:

Module or unit testing
Individual modules are tested to ensure they function correctly for given inputs.

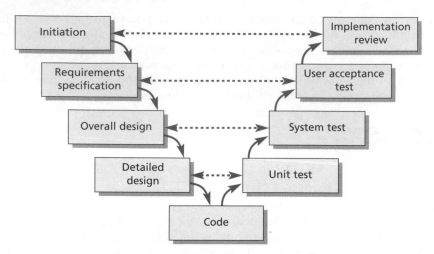

Figure 12.1 The V-model of systems development relating analysis and design activities to testing activities

(a) Random test data can be automatically generated by a spreadsheet for module testing.

(b) Structured or logical test data will cover a range of values expected in normal use of the module and also values beyond designed limits to check that appropriate error messages are given. This is also known as 'boundary value testing' and is important, since many bugs occur because designed boundaries are exceeded. This type of data is used for regression testing, explained below.

(c) Scenario or typical test data uses realistic example data, possibly from a previous system, to simulate day-to-day use of the system.

These different types of test data can also be applied to system testing.

- Integration or module interaction testing (black box testing). Expected interactions such as messaging and data exchange between a limited number of modules are assessed. This can be performed in a structured way, using a top-down method where a module calls other module functions as stubs (partially completed functions which should return expected values) or using a bottom-up approach where a driver module is used to call complete functions.

- New function testing. This commonly used type of testing refers to testing the operation of a new function when it is implemented, perhaps during prototyping. If testing is limited to this, problems may be missed since the introduction of the new function may cause bugs elsewhere in the system.

System testing

When all modules have been completed and their interactions assessed for validity, links between all modules are assessed in the system test. In system testing, interactions between all relevant modules are tested systematically.

Volume testing

Testing assesses how system performance will change at different levels of usage.

- **System testing.** When all modules have been completed and their interactions assessed for validity, links between all modules are assessed in the system test. In system testing, interactions between all relevant modules are tested systematically. System testing will highlight different errors to module testing, for example when unexpected data dependencies exist between modules as a result of poor design.

- Database connectivity testing. This is a simple test that the connectivity between the application and the database is correct. Can a user log in to the database? Can a record be inserted, deleted or updated, i.e. are transactions executing? Can transactions be rolled back (undone) if required?

- **Database volume testing.** This is linked to capacity planning of databases. Simulation tools can be used to assess how the system will react to different levels of usage anticipated from the requirements and design specifications. Methods of indexing may need to be improved or queries optimised if the software fails this test.

- Performance testing. This will involve timing how long different functions or transactions take to occur. These delays are important, since they govern the amount of wasted time users or customers have to wait for information to be retrieved or screens refreshed. Maximum waiting times may be specified in a contract, for example.
- Confidence test script. This is a short script which may take a few hours to run through and which tests all the main functions of the software. It should be run before all releases to users to ensure that their time is not wasted on a prototype that has major failings which mean the test will have to be aborted and a new release made.
- Automated tests. Automated tools simulate user inputs through the mouse or keyboard and can be used to check for the correct action when a certain combination of buttons is pressed or data entered. Scripts can be set up to allow these tests to be repeated. This is particularly useful for performing regression tests.
- **Regression testing.** This testing should be performed before a release to ensure that the software performance is consistent with previous test results, i.e. that the outputs produced are consistent with previous releases of the software. This is necessary, as in fixing a problem a programmer may introduce a new error that can be identified through the regression test. Regression testing is usually performed with automated tools.

Regression testing

Testing performed before a release to ensure that the software performance is consistent with previous test results i.e. that the outputs produced are consistent with previous releases of the software.

End-user tests

The purpose of these is twofold: first, to check that the software does what is required; and second, to identify bugs, particularly those that may only be caused by novice users.

For ease of assessing the results, the users should be asked to write down for each bug or omission found:

1 module affected;
2 description of problem (any error messages to be written in full);
3 relevant data – for example, which particular customer or order record in the database caused the problem;
4 severity of problem on a three-point scale.

Different types of end-user tests that can be adopted include:

- *Scenario testing*. In an order processing system this would involve processing example orders of different types, such as new customers, existing customers without credit and customers with a credit agreement.
- **Functional testing.** Users are told to concentrate on testing particular functions or modules such as the order entry module in detail, either following a test script or working through the module systematically.
- *General testing*. Here, users are given free rein to depart from the test specification and test according to their random preferences. Sometimes this is the only type of testing used, which results in poor coverage of the functions in the software!
- **Multi-user testing.** The effect of different users accessing the same customer or stock record. Software should not permit two users to modify the same data at the same time. Tests should also be made to ensure that users with different permissions and rules are treated as they should be, e.g. that junior staff are locked out of company financial information.
- *Inexperienced user testing*. Staff who are inexperienced in the use of software often make good 'guinea pigs' for testing software, since they may choose an illogical combination of options that the developers have not tested. This is a surprisingly effective and recommended method of software testing. The staff involved often also like the power of being able to 'break' the software.
- **User acceptance testing.** This is the final stage of testing which occurs before the software is signed off as fit for purpose and the system can go live. Since the customer will want to be sure the software works correctly, this may take a week or more.

Functional testing

Testing of particular functions or modules either following a test script or working through the module systematically.

Multi-user testing

The effect of different users' accessing the same customer or stock record is tested. Software should not permit two users to modify the same data at the same time.

User acceptance testing

This is the final stage of testing which occurs before the software is signed off as fit for purpose and the system can go live.

- *Alpha and beta testing.* These terms apply to user tests which occur before a packaged software product is released. They are described in the section on configuration management.

Benefits-based testing

An alternative approach to testing is not to focus only on the errors when reviewing a system, but rather to test against the business benefits that the system confers. A system could be error-free, but if it is not delivering benefits then its features may not have been implemented correctly. This approach can be used with prototyping, so that if a system is not delivering the correct features it can be modified. When undertaking structured testing, the software will be tested against the requirements specification to check that the desired features are present.

Testing environments

Testing occurs in different environments during the project. At an early stage prototypes may be tested on a single standalone machine or laptop. In the build phase, testing will be conducted in a *development environment*, which involves programmers' testing data across a network on a shared server. This is mainly used for module testing. In the implementation phase, a special **test environment** will be set up which simulates the final operating environment for the system. This could be a room with three or more networked machines accessing data from a central server. This test environment will be used for early user training and testing and for system testing. Finally, the **production or live environment** is that in which the system will be used operationally. This will be used for user acceptance testing and when the system becomes live.

When a system goes live, it is worth noting that there may still be major problems despite extensive testing. An example of this is provided by the case study on a bank network. Here a critical customer-facing banking system failed, apparently because of a problem in the underlying operating system (although this point is disputed by Microsoft).

❱ Documentation

Producing **documentation** occurs throughout the software lifecycle, such as when requirements are specified at the analysis stage, but it becomes particularly important at the implementation and maintenance stages of a project. At this stage user guides will be used as part of user acceptance testing and system developers will refer to design documents when updating the system. The main types of documentation required through the project are referred to in Figure 12.1. The important documentation used at the testing stage includes:

- the requirements specification produced at the analysis stage; this is used in the user acceptance test, to check that the correct features have been implemented;
- the user manual, which will be used during testing and operational use of the system by business users;
- the design specification, which will be used during system testing and during maintenance by developers;
- the detailed design, which will be used in module testing and during maintenance;
- the data dictionary or database design, which will be used in testing and maintenance by database administrators and developers;
- detailed test plans and test specifications, which will be used as part of developer and user testing;
- quality assurance documents such as software change request forms, which will be used to manage the change during the build and implementation phases.

Test environment

A specially configured environment (hardware, software and office environment) used to test the software before its release.

Live (production) environment

The term used to described the setup of the system (hardware, software and office environment) where the software will be used in the business.

Documentation

Software documentation refers to end-user guidance such as the user guide and technical maintenance documentation such as design and test specifications.

Code error floors bank network

An obscure code error has caused NatWest Bank's brand new Windows NT branch network almost a week's worth of delays and disruptions.

The software glitch prevented the bank from processing customers' queries at all of its 1750 branches, and brought down thousands of branch workstations.

Customers who called branches with basic queries, such as checking account balances, were told the task would take 24 hours and customers were advised to use ATM machines.

The disaster struck after the bank upgraded 5000 PCs and 300 servers with an in-house application, which suffered a handle leak. This type of fault causes an application to repeatedly request services from the server until the system crashes, or the application fails to release system resources such as virtual memory.

According to information on Microsoft's Web site, Windows NT has a history of difficulties operating alongside some third-party applications. Rather than revert to a previous version of the new application, NatWest opted to wait for a quiet period at the weekend to fix the fault. NatWest's head of retail information systems Catherine Doran said the bank had no plans to revamp software testing procedures as a result of the incident.

'There's not a system in the industry that hasn't got problems. You can test and test to destruction,' she said. Microsoft denied the problem was due to a fault in Windows NT itself, but added it had released service packs to solve handle leaks in all versions of the operating system.

Source: Computing, 1 July 1998

The writing of documentation is often neglected, since it tends to be less interesting than developing the software. To ensure that it is produced, strong project management is necessary and the presence of a software quality plan will make sure that time is spent on documentation, since a company's quality standard is assessed on whether the correct documentation is produced.

Example of a user guide structure

User guides are normally structured to give a gradual introduction to the system, and there may be several guides for a single system. A common structure is:

1 A *brief introductory/overview guide*, often known as 'Getting started'. The aim of this is to help users operate the software productively with the minimum of reading. The introductory section will also explain the purpose of the system for the business.

2 *Tutorial guide*. This will provide lessons, often with example data to guide the user through using the package. These are now often combined with online 'guided tours'.

3 *Detailed documentation* is often structured according to the different screens in an application. However, it is usually better to structure such guides according to the different functions or applications a business user will need. Chapter titles in such an approach might include 'How to enter a new sales order' or 'How to print a report'. This guide should also incorporate information on troubleshooting when problems are encountered.

4 *Quick reference guide, glossary and appendix*. These will contain explanations of error messages and a summary of all functions and how to access them.

User guides

The user guide has become a less important aspect of systems documentation with the advent of online help such as the help facility available with Windows applications and web-site-based help. Online help can give general guidance on the software, or it can give more specific advice on a particular screen or function – when it is known as 'context-sensitive'. It is often a good idea to ask business users to develop the user guide, since if programmers write the guide it will tend to be too technical and not relevant to the needs of users. Since business users are sometimes charged with producing a user guide, approaches to structuring these is covered in a little more detail.

Change management

The main activities undertaken by a manager of systems development projects are essentially concerned with managing change. Managing change takes different forms. First, we will look at managing technical changes to the software requirements as the system is developed through prototyping and testing. We will then look at how organisations can manage the transition or changeover to a new information system from an old system. Another important aspect of change we will review is how the introduction of a new system can affect the business users and action that can be taken to manage this organisational change. The role of organisational culture in influencing this will also be considered.

◗ Software change management

Change (modification) requests
························
A modification to the software thought to be necessary by the business users or developers.

At each stage of a systems development project, change requests or variations to requirements will arise from business managers, users, designers and programmers. These requests include reports of bugs and of features that are missing from the system as well as ideas for future versions of the software.

These requests will occur as soon as users start evaluating prototypes of a system and will continue through to the maintenance phase of the project when the system has gone live. As the users start testing the system in earnest in the implementation phase, these requests will become more frequent and tens or possibly hundreds will be generated each week. This process of change needs to be carefully managed, since otherwise it can develop into *requirements creep*, a problem on many information systems projects. As the number of requirements grows, more developer time will be required to fix the problems and the project can soon spiral out of control. What is needed is a mechanism to ensure, first, that all the changes are recorded and dealt with, and second, that they are reviewed in such a way that the number of changes does not become unmanageable.

The main steps in managing changed requirements are:

1 Record the change requests, indicating level of importance and module affected.
2 Prioritise them with the internal or external customer as *must have, nice to have or later release (Priority 1, 2 or 3)*. This will be done with reference to the project constraints of system quality, cost and timescale.
3 Identify responsibility for fixing the problem, since it may lie with a software house, internal IS staff, systems integrator or hardware vendor.
4 Implement changes that are recorded as high-priority.
5 Maintain a check of which high-priority errors have been fixed.

When a system is being implemented, it is useful to have a three-way classification of errors to be fixed, since this highlights the errors or missing features that must be implemented and avoids long discussions of the merits of each solution.

When the system is live, a more complex classification is often used to help in deciding how to 'escalate' problems up the hierarchy according to their severity. This could be structured as follows:

1 Critical problem, system not operational. This may occur due to power or server failure. Level 1 problems need to be resolved immediately, since business users cannot access the system at all. With customer-facing applications such as e-commerce systems, this type of problem needs to be corrected as soon as possible since every minute the system isn't working transaction revenue is lost.
2 Critical problem, making part of the system unusable or causing data corruption. These would normally need to be resolved within 12 to 24 hours, depending on the nature of the problem.
3 Problem causing intermittent system failure or data corruption. Resolve within 48 hours.
4 Non-severe problem not requiring modification to software until next release.
5 Trivial problem or suggestion which can be considered for future releases.

If the system has been tailored by a systems integrator, these will be their responsibility to fix and this will be specified in the contract or service-level agreement (SLA), together with the time that will be taken for the change to be made. If the system has been developed or tailored internally by the IS department or even within a department, an SLA is still a good idea. If the problem occurs from a problem with packaged software, you will have to hope that an update release that solves the problem is available; if not, you will have to lobby the supplier for one.

Software quality assurance

As we have seen, procedures should be followed throughout the software lifecycle to try to produce good-quality systems. These quality assurance (QA) procedures have been formalised in the British Standard BS 5750 Part 1 and its international equivalent ISO9001 (TickIT). These procedures do not guarantee a quality information system, but their purpose is to ensure that all relevant parts of the software lifecycle, such as requirements capture, design and testing, are carried out consistently. Business users can ask whether suppliers have quality accreditation as a means of distinguishing between them. QA procedures would not specify a particular method for design or testing, but they would specify how the change was managed by ensuring that all changes to requirements are noted and that review mechanisms are in place to check that changes are agreed and acted on accordingly.

If a business buys software services from a company that has achieved the quality standards, then there is less risk of the services' being inadequate. For a company to achieve a quality standard it has to be assessed by independent auditors and if successful it will be audited regularly.

Configuration management: builds and release versions

Configuration management is control of the different versions of software and program source code used during the build, implementation and maintenance phases of a project.

Throughout the implementation phase, updated versions of the software are released to users for testing. Before software can be used by users it needs to be released as an executable, built up from compiled versions of all the program code modules that make up the system. The process of joining all the modules is technically known as the *linking or build process*. The sequence can be summarised as:

1 Programmers *write* different code modules.
2 Completed code modules are *compiled* to form object modules.
3 Object modules are *linked* to form executables.

4 Executables are installed on machines.

5 Executables are loaded and run by end-users testing the software.

Each updated release of the software is therefore usually known as a new 'build'. With large software systems there will be hundreds of program files written by different developers that need to be compiled and then linked. If these files are not carefully tracked, then the wrong versions of files may be used, with earlier versions causing bugs. This process of version control is part of an overall process known as **configuration management**, which ensures that programming and new releases occur in a systematic way. One of the problems with solving the millennium bug was that in some companies configuration management was so poor that the original program code had been lost!

During the build phase, updated software versions will become more suitable for release as new functions are incorporated and the number of bugs is reduced. Some companies, such as Microsoft, call these different versions 'release candidates', others use the terminology alpha, beta and gold to distinguish between versions. These terms are often applied to packaged software, but can also be applied to bespoke business applications.

- *Alpha releases and alpha testing.* **Alpha releases** are preliminary versions of the software released early in the build phase. They usually have the majority of the functionality of the complete system in place, but may suffer from extensive bugs. The purpose of **alpha testing** is to identify these bugs and any major problems with the functionality and usability of the software. Alpha testing is usually conducted by staff inside the organisation developing the software or by favoured customers.
- *Beta releases and beta testing.* Beta releases occur after alpha testing and have almost complete functionality and relatively few bugs. **Beta testing** will be conducted by a range of customers who are interested in evaluating the new software. The aim of beta testing is to identify bugs in the software before it is shipped to all customers.
- *Gold release.* This is a term for the final release of the software which will be shipped to all customers.

▶ Selecting a changeover method

Choosing the method to be used for migrating or changing from the old system to the new system is one of the most important decisions that the project management team must make during the implementation phase. **Changeover** can be defined as moving from the old information system to the new information system. Note that this changeover is required whether the previous information system is computer- or paper-based. Before considering the alternatives, we will briefly discuss the main factors that a manager will consider when evaluating them. The factors are:

- *Cost.* This is of course an important consideration, but the quality of the new system is often more important.
- *Time.* There will be a balance between the time available and the desired quality of the system which will need to be evaluated.
- *Quality of new system after changeover.* This will be dependent on number of bugs and suitability for purpose.
- *Impact on customers.* What will be the effect on customer service if the changeover overruns or if the new system has bugs?
- *Impact on employees.* How much extra work will be required by employees during the changeover? Will they be remunerated for this?
- *Technical issues.* Some of the options listed below may not be possible if the system does not have a modular design.

There are four main alternatives for moving from a previous system to a new system. The options are shown in Figure 12.2 and described in more detail below.

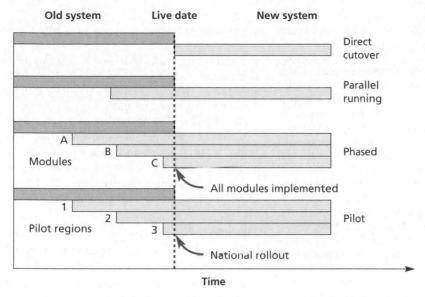

Figure 12.2 **Alternative changeover methods for system implementation**

Immediate cutover or big bang method

The **immediate cutover** method involves moving directly from the original system to the new system at a particular point in time. On a designated date, the old system is switched off and all staff move to using the new system. Clearly, this is a high-risk strategy since there is no fallback position if serious bugs are encountered. However, this approach is adopted by many large companies (such as Barclays in the Case Study 12.2), since it may be impractical and costly to run different systems in parallel. Before cutover occurs, the company will design the system carefully and conduct extensive testing to make sure that it is reliable and so reduce the risk of failure. The case study shows a relatively successful example of the cutover method and indicates why this is necessary for the implementation of large systems. The success factors of this project are described.

Immediate cutover (big-bang) changeover Immediate cutover is when a new system becomes operational and operations transfer immediately from the previous system.

CASE STUDY 12.2

Barclays Bank implements customer system using the 'big bang' approach

An example of a company adopting this approach for a major implementation is that of Barclays Bank, which switched over to a £110 million customer-facing system used in 2000 branches in 1997. This case study is described as an example of a successful implementation in the book *Crash* by Tony Collins and David Bicknell (1997). The bank decided on this approach since it was thought that it would not be possible for the old and new systems to run simultaneously with the hardware available. Furthermore, the cost of running two parallel systems was estimated at millions of pounds, which would reduce the cost savings made by implementing the new system. One of the biggest problems in this imple-

mentation, as with all changeovers, was migrating the data from the old system to the new. In this case, it involved transferring 25 million customer names and their account details – all held on various databases in thousands of different locations – into a single IBM DB2 database. One of the benefits of undertaking this migration was that erroneous data such as accounts that had been closed would be removed in this data-cleaning operation. The information from this database was then made available to every branch through nearly 2000 RS/6000 UNIX-based servers.

The day for the system going live was Monday 10 October 1994. This date had been set 18 months earlier and designers and developers from Andersen Consulting had been working towards this target. Transfer of the customer records began on Wednesday 5 October, with a plan to bring 1000 branches online with the new system by noon on Monday 10 October. Compared to many other implementations, this scheme was a great success, with 800 branches going live by noon. The implementation was not without problems and those encountered show the types of errors that can cause big-bang implementations to fail. On the Thursday before the live data, a hard disk head failed and a software bug delayed the schedule by two hours. To recover from this, the bank prevented more than 1000 branches from logging into the branch systems for two hours on the Thursday morning before live Monday, which did cause some disruption to customers. The implications of a more serious error which could not be fixed in two hours are clear.

Collins and Bicknell (1997) consider that the reasons for the success of this system are as follows:

- Artificial deadlines were not imposed and all staff were encouraged to be open about problems so that they could be solved.

- The scale of the problem was recognised so a realistic budget was set.
- Contingency plans were put in place to deal with problems such as the hard disk crash.
- Although changeover was targeted for a single day, the process of data migration started almost a week earlier and the whole project over 18 months had focused on a direct changeover through meticulous analysis, design and testing.
- Changes to users' requirements were kept under control, with only vital reviewed changes being incorporated.

Questions

1 What benefits and risks do you think Barclays faced by undertaking a big bang implementation?

2 What were the main problems faced in the cutover between the two systems?

3 Why do you think the project was successful? Consider other factors as well as those described in the case study.

Parallel running

Parallel running
This changeover method involves the old and new system operating together at the same time until the company is certain the new system works.

With **parallel running** the old and new systems are operated together for a period until the company is convinced that the new system performs adequately. This presents a lower risk than the immediate cutover method, since if the new system fails, the company can revert to the old system and customers will not be greatly affected. Parallel running sometimes also involves using a manual or paper-based system as backup in case the new system fails.

The cost of running two systems in parallel is high, not only in terms of maintaining two sets of software and possibly hardware, but also in the costs of the human operators repeating operations such as keying in customer orders twice. Indeed, the increase in workload may be such that overtime or additional staff may be required. The parallel method is only appropriate when the old and new systems perform similar functions and use similar software and hardware combinations. This makes it unsuitable for business re-engineering projects where completely new ways of working are being introduced that involve staff in working on different tasks or in different locations.

Phased implementation

Phased implementation
This changeover method involves introducing different modules of the new system sequentially.

A **phased implementation** involves delivering different parts of the system at different times. These modules do not all become live simultaneously, but rather in sequence. As such, this alternative is part-way between the big-bang and parallel running approaches. Each module can be introduced as either immediate cutover or in parallel. In a modular accounting system, for example, the core accounting functions, such as accounts payable, accounts receivable and general ledger, could be introduced first, with a sales order processing and then inventory control module introduced later. This gives staff the opportunity to learn about the new system more gradually and problems encountered on each module can be fixed as they are introduced.

Although this may appear to be an attractive approach, since if a new module fails the other modules will still be available, it is difficult to implement in practice. To achieve a phased implementation requires that the architecture of the new system and old system be designed in a modular way, and that the modules can operate independently without a high degree of coupling. For all systems, however, data exchange will be required between the different modules and this implies that common data exchange formats exist between the old and the new systems. This is often not the case, particularly if the software is sourced from different suppliers. Designers of systems are using techniques such as object-oriented design to produce modules with fewer and clearer dependencies between them. This should help in making phased implementations more practical. In the example given for the modular accounting system, modules in the old and new systems would have to have facilities to transfer data.

Pilot system

In a **pilot implementation**, the system will be trialled in a more limited area before it is deployed more extensively. This could include deploying the system in one operating region of the company, possibly a single country, or in a limited number of offices. This approach is common in multinational or national companies with several offices. Such a pilot system usually acts as a trial before more extensive deployment in a big-bang implementation.

Pilot system
The system is trialled in a more limited area before it is deployed more extensively across the business.

Using combinations of changeover methods

The different changeover methods are often used in conjunction for different stages of an implementation. For example, in a national or international implementation it is customary to trial the project in a single region or country using a pilot of the system. If a pilot system is considered successful there is then a choice of one of the following:

- immediately implementing the system elsewhere using the big bang approach;
- running the new and old systems in parallel until it is certain that the new system is stable enough;
- if the new system is modular in construction, it is possible for the implementation to be phased, with new modules gradually being introduced as they are completed and the users become familiar with the new system;
- parallel running will probably also occur in this instance, in case there is a need to revert to the old system in the event of failure of the new system.

Once the system is proved in the first area, then further rollout will probably occur through the big bang approach.

The advantages and disadvantages of each of these changeover methods are summarised in Table 12.3.

Table 12.3 **Advantages and disadvantages of the different methods of implementation**

Method	Main advantages	Main disadvantages
Immediate cutover	Rapid, lowest cost	High risk if serious errors in system
Parallel running	Lower risk than immediate cutover	Slower and higher cost than immediate cutover
Phased implementation	Good compromise between immediate cutover and parallel running	Difficult to achieve technically due to interdependencies between modules
Pilot system	Essential for multinational or national rollouts	Has to be used in combination with the other methods

Deployment planning

A **deployment plan** is necessary to get all 'kit' or hardware in place in time for user acceptance testing. A deployment plan is a schedule that defines all the tasks that need to occur in order for changeover to occur successfully. This includes putting in place all the infrastructure such as cabling and hardware. This is not a trivial task, because often a range of equipment will be required from a variety of manufacturers. A deployment plan should list every software deliverable and hardware item required, when it needs to arrive and when it needs to be connected. The deployment plan will be part of the overall project plan or Gantt chart. A deployment plan is particularly important for large implementations involving many offices, such as the Barclays system referred to earlier in the chapter. Several people may be responsible for this task on large projects.

When planning deployment, advanced planning is required due to possible delays in purchasing and delivery. The burden of purchasing will often be taken by a systems integrator, but it may be shared by the purchasing department of the company buying the new system. This needs careful liaison between the two groups.

With installation of new hardware, a particular problem is where changes to infrastructure are required – for example upgrading cabling to a higher bandwidth or installing a new router. This can take a considerable time and cause a great deal of disruption to users of existing systems.

▶ Organisational change management

The implementation of a new system will always cause disruption to staff, because changes to their patterns of working will occur. In some cases staff may be transferred to new roles. The change involved in the introduction of the new system needs management so staff motivation and productivity are not adversely affected.

The best approach to managing this change is to use education to communicate the purpose of the system to the staff – in other words, to sell the system to them. This education should target all employees in the organisation who will be affected by the change. It involves:

- explaining why the system is being implemented;
- explaining how staff will be affected;
- treating users as customers by involving them in specification, testing and review;
- training users in use of the software;
- above all, listening to users and acting on what they say.

Kurt Lewin and Edgar Schein suggested a model for achieving organisational change that involves three stages:

1. Unfreeze the present position by creating a climate of change through education, training and motivation of future participants.
2. Quickly move from the present position by developing and implementing the new system.
3. Refreeze by making the system an accepted part of the way the organisation works.

Note that Lewin and Schein did not collaborate on developing this model of personal and organisational change. Lewin developed the model in unpublished work and this was then extended by Edgar Schein who undertook research into psychology based on Lewin's ideas (Schein, 1956). Later, Kurt Lewin summarised some of his ideas (Lewin, 1972). More recently, Schein (1992) concluded that three variables are critical to the success of any organisational change:

1 the degree to which the leaders can break from previous ways of working;
2 the significance and comprehensiveness of the change;
3 the extent to which the head of the organisation is actively involved in the change process.

Change was defined by Kurt Lewin as a transition from an existing quasi-equilibrium to a new quasi-equilibrium. This model was updated and put into an organisational context by Kolb and Frohman (1970). Although this is now an old model, it remains relevant to the implementation of information systems today.

▶ Organisational culture

Understanding social relationships within an organisation, which are part of its **culture**, is also an important aspect of change management. The efficiency of any organisation is dependent on the complex formal and informal relationships that exist within it. Formal relationships include the hierarchical work relationships within and between functional business areas. Informal relationships are created through people working and socialising with each other on a regular basis and will cut across functional boundaries. Major change, such as the move to e-business, has the capacity to alter both types of relationships as it brings about change within and between functional business areas.

Schein (1992) also claims that the notion of organisational culture provides useful guidance on what must be changed within a corporate culture, if organisational change is to be successfully accomplished. He provides a threefold classification of culture that helps to identify what needs to be done:

- Assumptions are the invisible core elements of an organisation's culture such as a shared collective vision within the organisation. One of the challenges in change management is to question core assumptions where appropriate, especially if they are seen to be obstructing organisational change.
- Values are preferences that guide behaviour such as attitudes towards dress codes and punctuality within an organisation or ethics within a society. Often such values are transmitted by word of mouth rather than being enshrined in written documents or policy statements. As with organisational assumptions, values are hard to change, especially when the views that embody them are firmly held.
- Artefacts are tangible material elements of cultural elements. These will be identifiable from the language used in the policies, procedures and acronyms of the organisation, and the spoken word and dialects of the society. In some ways they are also the easiest to change. Policies can be created or rewritten, but it is the organisation's values and assumptions that will determine how they are perceived and acted upon.

The implications of organisational culture for information systems implementation are important. While the 'artefacts' associated with information systems developments may be clear, it is the 'assumptions' and 'values' that will ultimately determine the success of the implementation and it is to these that the change management process must be largely directed.

Boddy et al. (2001) summarise four different types of cultural orientation that may be identified in different companies. These vary according to the extent to which the company is inward-looking or outward-looking, in other words to what extent it is affected by its environment. They also reflect whether the company is structured and formal or has a more flexible, dynamic, informal character. The four cultural types of cultural orientation are:

1 *Survival (outward-looking, flexible)* – the external environment plays a significant role (an open system) in governing company strategy. The company is likely to be driven by customer demands and will be an innovator. It may have a relatively flat structure.

Culture
....
This concept includes shared values, unwritten rules and assumptions within the organisation as well as the practices that all groups share. Corporate cultures are created when a group of employees interact over time and are relatively successful in what they undertake.

2 *Productivity (outward-looking, ordered)* – interfaces with the external environment are well structured and the company is typically sales-driven and is likely to have a hierarchical structure.

3 *Human relations (inward-looking, flexible)* – this is the organisation as family, with interpersonal relations more important than reporting channels, a flatter structure and staff development, and empowerment is thought of important by managers.

4 *Stability (inward-looking, ordered)* – the environment is essentially ignored with managers concentrating on internal efficiency and again managed through a hierarchical stucture.

Different approaches to change management that may be required according to the type of culture are explored in the activity.

Activity 12.1

Changing the culture for e-business

The purpose of this activity is to identify appropriate cultural changes that may be necessary for e-business success.

Review the four general categories of organisational cultural orientation summarised by Boddy, *et al*. (2001) and take each as characterising four different companies and then suggest which will most readily respond to the change required for a move to an e-business. State whether you think the cultures are most likely to occur in a small organisation or a larger organisation.

◗ Achieving user involvement

Efforts should be made to involve as many staff as possible in the development. The following types of involvement (summarised by Regan and O'Connor, 1994) can occur in a systems development project:

1 *Non-involvement.* Here, users are unwilling to participate or are not invited to.
2 *Involvement by advice.* User advice is solicited through interviews or questionnaires during analysis.
3 *Involvement by signoff.* Users approve the results produced by the project team, such as requirements specifications.
4 *Involvement by design team membership.* Active participation occurs in analysis and design activities (including interviews of other users, creation of functional specifications and prototyping).
5 *Involvement by project team membership.* User participation occurs throughout the project since the user manages and owns the project.

System sponsors

System sponsors are senior managers or board members who are responsible for a system at a senior level in a company.

System owners

These are managers who are directly responsible for the operational use of a system.

Stakeholders

All staff who have a direct interest in the system.

While it will not be practical to involve everyone, representatives of all job functions should be polled for their requirements for the system at the analysis stage. As many user and manager representatives as possible should be involved in the active analysis and design involved in prototyping.

Promotion of the system can also be achieved by appointing particular managers to champion the new system:

● Senior managers or board members are used as **system sponsors**. Sponsors are keen that the system should work and will fire up staff with their enthusiasm and stress why introducing the system is important to the business and its workers.
● **System owners** are managers in the organisation who will use the system to create the business benefits envisaged.
● **Stakeholders** should be identified at every location in which the system will be used. These people should be respected by their co-workers and will again act as a source

of enthusiasm for the system. The user representatives used in specification and test-ing can also fill this role.

- Legitimisers protect the norms and values of the system; they are experienced in their job and regarded as the experts by fellow workers; they may initially be resist-ant to change and therefore need to be involved early.
- Opinion leaders are people whom others watch to see whether they accept new ideas and changes. They usually have little formal power, but are regarded as good 'ideas' people who are receptive to change, and again need to be involved early in the project.

❙ Resistance to change

Some resistance to change is inevitable, but this is particularly true with the introduction of systems associated with business process re-engineering, because of the way that work is performed and people's job functions will be changed. If the rationale behind the change is not explained, then all the classic symptoms of resistance to change will be apparent. Resistance to change usually follows a set pattern. For example, Adams et al. (1976) have used the transition curve in Figure 12.3 to describe the change from when staff first hear about a system to when the change becomes accepted.

While outright hostility manifesting itself as sabotage of the system is not unheard of, what is more common is that users will try to project blame on to the system and will identify major faults where only minor bugs exists. This will obviously damage the reputation of the system and senior managers will want to know what went wrong with the project. Another problem that can occur if the system has not been intro-duced well is avoidance of the system, with users working around the system to continue their previous ways of working. Careful management is necessary to ensure that this does not happen. To summarise the way in which resistance to change may manifest itself, the following may be evident:

- *aggression* – in which there may be physical sabotage of the system, deliberate entry of erroneous data or abuse of systems staff;
- *projection* – where the system is wrongly blamed for difficulties encountered while using it;
- *avoidance* – withdrawal from or avoidance of interaction with the system, non-input of data, reports and enquiries ignored, or use of manual substitutes for the system.

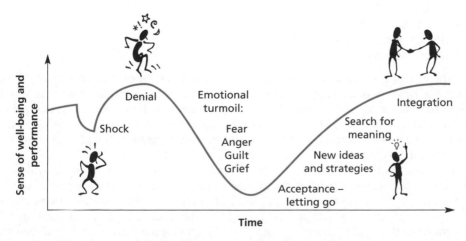

Figure 12.3 **Transition curve of showing reaction of staff through time from when change is first suggested**

There are many understandable reasons for people to resist the technological change that comes from the development of new information systems. These include:

- social uncertainty;
- limited perspectives and lack of understanding;
- threats to power and influence of managers (loss of control);
- perception that costs of new system outweigh the benefits;
- fear of failure, inadequacy or redundancy.

It is evident that training and education can be used to counter many of these issues. Additionally, other steps can be taken to reduce resistance to change, namely:

- Ensure early participation and involvement of users.
- Set realistic goals and raise realistic expectations of benefits.
- Build in user-friendliness to the new system.
- Don't promise too much and deliver what was promised!
- Develop a reliable system that is easy to maintain.
- Ensure support of the various stakeholders.
- Bring about agreement through negotiation.

Training

Appropriate education and training are important in implementation. Many companies make the mistake of not training staff sufficiently for a new system. This is often because of the cost of training or of taking staff away from their daily work for several days. If companies do provide training, it is often the wrong sort. Practical, operational training in how to use the software, such as which menu options are available and which buttons to press, is common. What is sometimes missing is ideological training: an explanation of why the system is being brought in – why are the staff's existing ways of working being overturned? This educational part of training is very important. Previous projects or examples of how systems have improved the business of competitors may be used here.

▶ A consolidated change model

Jay and Smith (1996) identify four phases in a change model:

- the initial orientation;
- preparation;
- implementation of the change;
- a supportive phase.

In the orientation phase, it is necessary that there is a clear understanding of the reasons for bringing about change. This would include a cost–benefit analysis and specific terms of reference for the project. A change strategy must be developed that includes an indication of how quality would be measured, the project milestones, and how objectives would be measured and the change project organised. A skilled change team should be established and committed change sponsors identified.

The preparation phase will involve an analysis of the environment within which the change is to take place. This includes an identification of the critical success factors for change along with a threat analysis. A work-plan for the change process must also be developed that includes detailed tasks and timings. The change direction must be announced to those affected and there should be an emphasis on maximising communication effectiveness. It is necessary to communicate the future position to a wider audience and the need to make the change and its potential consequences must be clearly specified. The final step in this phase is to provide direction, particularly through strong communication of the goals and how they will be achieved.

In the third phase, Jay and Smith suggest that the changes be implemented by piloting the change, introducing the new procedures, conducting training and finally rolling out the change. In cases where a new information system is being rolled out to the whole organisation at the same time, choosing a pilot department or site may be difficult. However, the organisational aspects as they relate to reporting relationships, job definitions, training schedules, working procedures and reward systems must be still be defined and communicated. Appropriate training should be completed and the implementation must be carried out using a roll out plan.

In the final phase, the change must be stabilised. This means that management must openly commit itself to the change and fine-tune or adjust procedures where necessary. Measuring acceptance and new behaviour and producing a formal report can be used to evaluate the effectiveness of the change. There must be prevention of a relapse, such as an attempt to revert to old systems and practices or even bypassing the new system altogether. Conducting regular review meetings along with continual training and procedure reviews can help this.

The absence of a change management approach can impede user acceptance of the system and many of the planned benefits (and hence return on investment) may not be realised. This suggests that there is a strong case to integrate a full change management programme into the systems development lifecycle. This was suggested in Chapter 7 when the SDLC diagram was shown as having project management and change management as a central part of the development process. Mapping the change model onto the SDLC provides project managers with the extra change activities required in the overall project work-plan. However, the result should be a system that is more likely to be accepted by the user community and, hence, the anticipated business benefits are more likely to be derived.

Maintenance

The maintenance phase of a project starts when the users sign off the system during testing and it becomes a live production system. After a system is live, there are liable to be some errors that were not identified during testing and need to be remedied. When problems are encountered, this presents a dilemma to the system manager, since they will have to balance the need for a new release of the system against the severity of an error. It is not practical or cost-effective to introduce a new release of the software for every bug found, since each release needs to be tested and installed and fresh problems may exist in the new system. Most systems managers would aim not to make frequent, immediate releases to correct problems because of the cost and disruption this causes. Instead, faults will be recorded and then fixed in a release that solves several major problems. This is known as a **maintenance release** and it might occur at monthly, six-monthly or yearly intervals according to the stability of the system. This is usually a function of the age of the system – new systems will have more errors and will need more frequent maintenance releases.

With the advent of customer-facing e-commerce systems that need to be available 24 hours a day, 7 days a week for 365 days a year, periodic maintenance releases are not appropriate. Significant problems must be rectified immediately with the minimum of disruption. In 2001 Barclays Bank was censured by the UK advertising standard authority for suggesting in their television adverts that their systems were continuously available 24 hours per day. In fact, some users of their system complained that it was not available for a short period after midnight each night due to maintenance.

Maintenance
....
Maintenance occurs after the system has been signed off as suitable for users. It involves reviewing the project and recording and acting on problems with the system.

Consequently Barclays had to change the advert, and may eventually change their approach to maintenance.

Maintenance releases will not only fix problems, but may also include enhancements or new features requested by users.

Major and minor releases are denoted by the release or version number. If a system changes from version 1.1 to 2.0, this will be a major release. When moving from version 2.0 to 2.1, some new features might be involved. From version 2.1 to 2.11 might represent a patch or interim release to correct problems.

To help make the decision of installing a new release to correct the problem, a scale of severity of the fault is used by companies to govern what action is required. Such a scale may form part of the contract if a company has outsourced its systems development to a third party. An example of such a scale is shown in Table 12.4.

Table 12.4 **Fault taxonomy described in Jorgenson (1995)**

Category	Example	Action
1 **Mild**	Misspelt word	Ignore or defer to next major release
2 **Moderate**	Misleading or redundant information	Ignore or defer to next major release
3 **Annoying**	Truncated text	Defer to next major release
4 **Disturbing**	Some transactions not processed correctly, intermittent crashes in one module	Defer to next maintenance release
5 **Serious**	Lost transactions	Defer to next maintenance release; may need immediate fix and release
6 **Very serious**	Crash occurs regularly in one module	Immediate solution needed
7 **Extreme**	Frequent, very serious errors	Immediate solution needed
8 **Intolerable**	Database corruption	Immediate solution needed
9 **Catastrophic**	System crashes, cannot be restarted – system unusable	Immediate solution needed
10 **Infectious**	Catastrophic problem also causes failure of other systems	Immediate solution needed

Most systems now have a modular design such that it is not necessary to reinstall the complete system if an error is encountered – rather the module where the error lies can be replaced. This is described in a rather primitive way as applying a **patch** to the system. Patches to off-the-shelf systems are now available for download over the Internet. Because of the competitive pressures of releasing software as soon as possible, a large number of off-the-shelf packages require some sort of patch. For example, web browser software such as Netscape Navigator and Microsoft Internet Explorer has required frequent patches to correct errors in the security of the browser which permit unauthorised access to the computer on which the browser is running.

Software patch

This is an interim release of part of an information system that is intended to address deficiencies in a previous release.

Post-implementation review

A meeting that occurs after a system is operational to review the success of the project.

▶ **Post-implementation review**

A **post-implementation review** or project closedown review occurs several months after the system has gone live. Its purpose is to assess the success of the new system and decide on any necessary corrective action. The review could include the following:

- faults and suggested enhancements with agreement on which need to be implemented in a future release;
- success of system in meeting its budget and timescale targets;
- success of system in meeting its business requirements – has it delivered the anticipated benefits described in the feasibility study?
- development practices that worked well and poorly during the project.

MINI CASE STUDY

Project closure summary for a software house

The form in Table 12.5 shows a real example of the output of a project closure meeting produced after implementation of a small project. It can be seen that the project was completed on time, but needed slightly more effort than estimated to achieve this. This led to a small budget overrun.

Table 12.5 **Project closure summary**

Project information				
Project	Bespoke module for client A			
Version	1.2			
Release date	18.12.02			

Performance: estimated against actual				
Measure	Estimated	Actual	Difference	Difference %
Budget	£7350	£8000	£650	+9%
Date	18/12/02	18/12/02	–	–
Total time (effort)	24.5 days	28 days	3.5 days	+12.5%
Elapsed time	5 weeks	5 weeks	–	–

Learning for next time		
Question	Answer	Improve by?
What went right?	Completed on time for client	–
What went wrong?	Delays caused by poor procedure for final build from program files Using existing library code which contained bugs	Develop better configuration management plans
What was underestimated?	Greater contingency should have been allowed; 5% appropriate contingency was insufficient	15–20% more
Suggestions for improvement next time?	Keep customer informed more regularly	–

An additional reason for performing a post-implementation review is so that lessons can be learnt from the project. Good practices can be applied to future projects and attempts made to avoid techniques which failed.

An example of a post-implementation review is shown in the case study on project closure summary.

Summary

Stage summary: systems build

Purpose: To produce a working system
Key activities: Programming (coding), system and user documentation, testing
Input: Design specification and requirements specification
Output: Preliminary working system which can be tested by end-users

Stage summary: systems implementation

Purpose: To install the system in the live environment
Key activities: Install computers and software, user acceptance test, changeover, sign off
Input: Preliminary versions of software
Output: Tested, release version of software

Stage summary: systems maintenance

Purpose: To ensure system remains available to end-users
Key activities: Monitoring errors, reviewing and fixing problems, releasing patches
Input: Tested, release version of software
Output: Revised version of software

1 The build stage of systems development involves programming, testing and transferring data from the old system to the new system.

2 The main types of testing are unit testing of individual modules, system testing of the whole system by developers and user acceptance testing by the business. Sufficient time for testing must be built in using a quality assurance system to ensure that the delivered system is of the right quality.

3 The implementation stage involves managing the changeover from the old system to the new system. There are several alternative changeover approaches that can be used together if required:

- run the old and new systems in parallel;
- a phased approach where different modules are gradually introduced;
- cutover immediately to the new system;
- pilot the system in one area or office before 'rolling out' on a larger scale.

4 Some of the main reasons that information systems projects may fail at the build or implementation stage include:

- *Forgetting the human issues.* New systems are usually accompanied by a new way of working, so managers need to explain through training why the change is occurring and then train people adequately in the use of the system.
- *Cutting corners through using RAD.* Some corners cannot be cut, especially in design, optimising system performance and testing. If insufficient time is spent on these activities, the system may fail. Documentation may also be omitted, which is serious during maintenance.
- *Computer resources are inadequate.* The project managers need staff to check, for example, that the server can handle the load at critical times of the day, such as when scanning is occurring or at peak times in a call centre. Checks will also be made to ensure that the system performance does not degrade as the number of users of the systems or customers' records held increase.
- *Poor management of change process.* Staff who are involved with the new system should be trained so that they can use the software easily and understand the reasons for its introduction.

- *Lack of support from the top or from stakeholders*. Top management and appropriate stakeholders must support the cultural changes necessary to introduce the new system.
- *Using a big bang method of changeover*. Using this approach is high risk unless there has been extensive testing and methodical design.

5 The maintenance phase is concerned with managing the system once it is live. This will involve responding to errors as they are found. If serious, the problems will have to be solved immediately through issuing a 'patch' release to the system; otherwise they will be recorded for a later release.

6 A post-implementation review will occur to assess the success of the systems development project so that lessons are recorded for future projects.

EXERCISES

Self-assessment exercises

1 What are the main activities that occur in the build and implementation phases of a systems development project?
2 What is the difference between unit and system testing?
3 How can resistance to change among staff affect a new information system?
4 What are the most important factors in reducing resistance to change?
5 Why is it important to manage software change requests carefully?
6 What is the difference between the direct changeover method and the parallel changeover method?
7 What is the best option for an end-user to program a system?
8 What is the purpose of a post-implementation review?

Discussion questions

1 'All the different project changeover methods are likely to be used on any large project'. Discuss.
2 The most important aspect of software quality assurance is to make sure that bugs are identified during the testing phase.
3 Companies should aim to minimise the number of patch releases, provided that no serious system errors occur.

Essay questions

1 You are a business manager responsible for the successful implementation of a new information system. What problems would you anticipate from staff when the new system is introduced? What measures could you take to minimise these?
2 Discuss the advantages and disadvantages of the different methods of changeover from an old system to a new one. Which is the optimal method?

Examination questions

1 Describe the direct changeover method. How does this differ from phased implementation?
2 What different classes of fault will a user be aiming to identify in a user acceptance test?
3 What are the three classical signs of resistance to change by end-users?
4 Distinguish between system testing and unit testing.

5 What different types of documentation will be used during the implementation phase of a project?

6 What elements of staff training should a new system receive?

7 What is the purpose of volume testing?

8 Which criteria should be used to measure the successful outcome of a systems development project?

9 In the maintenance phase of the systems development lifecycle, why might an information system need to be maintained?

10 Briefly outline the considerations that a company needs to take into account in deciding between the two main methods of changeover to a new information system: direct and parallel running.

References

Adams, J., Hayes, J. and Hopson, B. (1976) *Transitions: Understanding and Managing Personal Change*, Martin Robertson, London

Boddy, D., Boonstra, A. and Kennedy, G. (2001) *Managing Information Systems: An Organisational Perspective*, Financial Times, Prentice Hall, Harlow

Collins, T. and Bicknell, D. (1997) *Crash*, Simon and Schuster, London

Jay, K.E.. and Smith, D.C. (1996) 'A generic change model for the effective implementation of information systems', *South African Journal of Business Management*, September, 27, 3

Johnston, A.K. (1995) *A Hacker's Guide to Project Management*, Butterworth-Heinemann, Oxford

Jones, C. (1996) *Software Quality: Analysis and Guidelines for Success*, International Thomson Computer Press, London

Jorgenson, P. (1995) *Software Testing: a Craftsman's Approach*, CRC Press, Boca Raton, FL

Kolb, D.A. and Frohman, A.L. (1970) 'An organizational development approach to consulting', *Sloan Management Review*, 12, 51–65

Lewin, K. (1972) 'Quasi-stationary social equilibria and the problems of permanent change', in N. Margulies, and A. Raia (eds) *Organizational Development: Values, Process and Technology*, McGraw-Hill, New York, 65–72

Regan, E.A. and O'Connor, B.N. (1994) *End-user Information Systems: Perspectives for Managers and Information Systems Professionals*, Macmillan, New York

Schein, E (1956) 'The Chinese indoctrination program for prisoners of war', *Psychiatry*, 19, 149–72

Schein, E. (1992) *Organizational Culture and Leadership*, Jossey Bass, San Francisco

Further reading

Hallows, J. (1998) *Information Systems Project Management: How to Deliver Function and Value in Information Technology Projects*, Amacom, New York

Kerzner, H. (1995) *Project Management: A Systems Approach to Planning Scheduling and Controlling*, 5th edition, Van Nostrand Reinhold, New York

Kit, E. (1995) *Software Testing in the Real World: Improving the Process*, Addison-Wesley, Harlow

Lindgaard, G. (1994) *Usability Testing and System Evaluation: A Guide for Designing Useful Computer Systems*, Chapman & Hall, London

Lucas, H. (1990) *Information Systems Implementation: Testing a Structural Model*, Ablex, Norwood, NJ

Taylor, D (1992) *Object-oriented Information Systems: Planning and Implementation*, John Wiley, Chichester

Web links

www.cio.com CIO.com for Chief Information Officers and IS staff has many articles related to analysis and design topics in different research centres such as security (www.cio.com/research/security), CRM (www.cio.com/research/crm) and infrastructure (www.cio.com/research/infrastructure).

www.360.com *Computer Weekly* IS professionals' trade paper with UK/Europe focus has many case studies on practical problems of analysis, design and implementation.

www.eds.com/case_studies/cs_home.shtml Case studies from major BIS consultant EDS illustrate many of the issues of systems analysis, design and implementation.

www.research.ibm.com/journal/ IBM Journals *IBM Systems Journal* and the *Journal of Research and Development* have many cases and articles on analysis and design related to e-business concepts such as knowledge management, security.

www.intranetjournal.com/itadvisor Intranet journal has case studies on systems analysis and design specific to intranets.

www.fdic.gov/regulations/information/index.html FDIC The Federal Financial Institutions Examination Council (FFIEC) handbook for conducting examinations of banks' and savings associations' information systems is interesting since it recommends appropriate approaches and activities to different stages of building banking systems which also apply to other systems.

knowledge.wharton.upenn.edu/category.cfm?catid=14 Managing Technology at Wharton articles; these cover a range of technology management issues, including analysis, design and implementation issues.

PART 3

Business information systems management

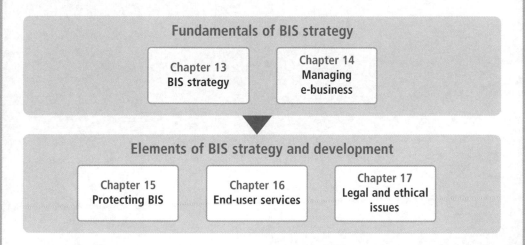

Fundamentals of BIS strategy

Chapter 13
BIS strategy

Chapter 14
Managing
e-business

Elements of BIS strategy and development

Chapter 15
Protecting BIS

Chapter 16
End-user services

Chapter 17
Legal and ethical
issues

Managing BIS within an organisation involves two main elements: strategic planning; and operational management of systems, to give reliable access to IS for end-users and third parties such as customers, suppliers and distributors. In Part 3, we start by reviewing approaches to IS strategy and then go on to describe key operational aspects of IS that need to be managed. These include:

● providing e-business services (Chapter 14);
● protecting IS from security breaches (Chapter 15);
● providing end-user services (Chapter 16);
● adhering to moral, legal and ethical constraints (Chapter 17).

The IS strategy will define the future applications portfolio of business information systems required to support the business objectives of the organisation. The IS strategy will also seek to improve the quality of information used by the company. Since information is an increasingly important asset of the company, it must be managed to ensure it is well protected and of suitable quality for decision making. IS management should also ensure that audits and appropriate follow-up actions occur to be certain that the company is complying with legal and ethical codes relating to the use of information systems. This will involve asking questions such as:

● Has the company's applications software been purchased legally?
● Is personal information accurate and well protected?

BIS strategy

LEARNING OBJECTIVES

After reading this chapter, readers will be able to:
● define approaches for integrating IS strategy with business strategy;
● apply simple strategic analysis tools to determine IS strategy;
● relate IS strategy to business process re-engineering;
● assess the arguments for and against outsourcing.

MANAGEMENT ISSUES

Annual investment in BIS is significant for many companies. But what return do organisations receive for this investment? To achieve more effective investment, a well-planned BIS strategy is required that supports the corporate goals. In this chapter we aim to answer the questions a newly installed manager seeking to develop an IS strategy would ask:

● Which process can we follow to develop an IS strategy?
● How can we ensure the IS strategy supports the business strategy?
● What analysis tools are available to assess current use of IS within the organisation and its environment and formulate IS strategy?
● Where should we locate the IS function and to what extent should some services be outsourced?

Links to other chapters

This chapter introduces some elements of IS strategy. It does not link directly to subsequent chapters in Part 3, since these describe specific aspects of managing information systems which are separate elements of strategy implementation. The aspects of business information systems management covered in Part 3 are managing e-business infrastructure (Chapter 14), protecting information quality (Chapter 15), managing end-user services in a business (Chapter 16), and professional issues such as data privacy and protection (Chapter 17). Chapter 8 in Part 2 covers cost–benefit analysis and investment appraisal for a single information system in more detail than the coverage In this chapter.

Introduction

Organisations that make the most effective use of business information systems (BIS) are those that make BIS strategy an integral part of their overall business strategy. The development of the e-business concept is intended to further support the integration of BIS with business strategy. This chapter looks at approaches an organisation can use to develop a strategy for putting information systems in place which will support and enhance its overall business strategy.

The productivity paradox

Productivity paradox
Research results indicating a poor correlation between organisational investment in information systems and organisational performance measured by return on equity.

Despite the large-scale investments in IS within organisations, it is still not clear the extent to which investment in information systems benefits organisations. This highlights the importance of effective development and implementation of an IS strategy which supports business goals.

Studies in the late 1980s and 1990s summarised by Brynjolfsson (1993) and Strassman (1997) suggest that, across companies, there is little or no correlation between a company's investment in BIS and its business performance measured in terms of profitability or shareholder value. Strassman's early work was based on a study of 468 major North American and European firms which showed a random relationship between IS spending per employee and return on equity (Fig. 13.1).

To the present day, there has been much dispute about the reality of the productivity paradox, with most authors such as Brynjolfsson and Hitt (1996) refuting the productivity paradox and concluding that it results either from mismeasurement, the lag occurring between initial investment and payback, or from the mismanagement of information systems projects. More recent detailed studies such as that by Sircar et al. (2000) confirm the findings of Brynjolfsson and Hitt (1996). They state that:

> Both IT and corporate investments have a strong positive relationship with sales, assets, and equity, but not with net income. Spending on IS staff and staff training is positively correlated with firm performance, even more so than computer capital.

In conclusion they state:

> The value of IS staff and staff training was also quite apparent and exceeded that of computer capital. This confirms the positions of several authors, that the effective use of IT is far more important than merely spending on IT.

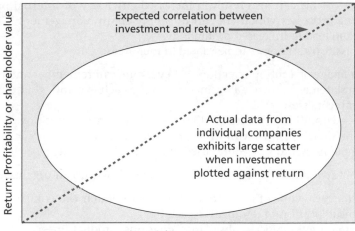

Figure 13.1 The productivity paradox

As these authors say, this will not be a surprise to many managers, but it is a reminder that it is not how much is spent on BIS, but the way in which it is spent that is important in delivering business benefits and achieving the e-business. This highlights the importance of business information strategy development and implementation.

The strategic context

In its original sense, 'strategy' referred to the development of plans for deceiving or outwitting an enemy. Today, corporate strategy is developed not to conquer a single competitor, rather to compete within a chosen market. Johnson and Scholes (1999) use a definition that places strategy in the context of the marketplace environment and stresses its role in utilising internal resources to be best able to compete in this environment. The elements of this environment are summarised in Figure 1.2 (p. 15). These authors define strategy as:

> *the direction and scope of an organization over the long-term: which achieves advantage for the organization through its configuration of resources within a changing environment to meet the needs of markets and to fulfil stakeholder expectations.*

Strategy

Definition of the future direction and actions of a company defined as approaches to achieving specific objectives.

BIS is one of the resources deployed to help meet the needs of the market by developing and promoting new, innovative products and services that increase customer value. Most companies use a **hierarchy of strategies** to support the business strategy. For example, a marketing strategy is developed to assist in implementing the business strategy and this in turn will inform a marketing communications strategy. Similarly an information strategy will support the business strategy and this will be achieved by implementing separate IS and IT strategies as explained in the next section.

Hierarchy of strategies
A collection of sub-strategies developed to help achieve corporate objectives.

Effective use of BIS can also result in increased efficiency of internal processes and outward-facing processes which are part of supply chain management. This can help reduce costs and lead to increased profitability.

Any organisation's strategy can be rooted in four areas:

- *vision* – an image of a future direction that everyone can remember and follow;
- *mission* – a statement of what a business intends to achieve and what differentiates it from other businesses;
- *strategies* – a conditional sequence of consistent resource allocations that defines an organisation's relationships with its environment over time;
- *policies* – guidelines and procedures used in carrying out a strategy.

These areas in turn can be applied at a number of levels within an organisation:

- *corporate strategy* – view of the lines of business in which the company will participate and the allocation of resources to each line;
- *strategic business units (SBU)* – subsidiaries, divisions, product lines;
- *functional strategy* – each functional area within a business unit must develop a course of action to support the SBU strategy Examples include marketing strategy and logistics strategy.

This straightforward definition masks an underlying complexity of strategy. Indeed, the way in which an organisation can formulate its strategy is the subject of some debate. Claudio Ciborra (Ciborra and Jelassi, 1994) contrasts the mechanistic or prescriptive approach to business strategy with more flexible and eclectic approaches. The former is characterised by such elements as:

- *Conscious and analytical thought*, where strategies emerge from a structured process of human thought and rigorous analysis; it is suggested that implementation can only follow when the strategy has been analytically formulated.
- *Top-down and control orientation*, where strategy is formulated at the peak of the managerial pyramid and responsibility for strategy lies with the organisation's chief executive officer.
- *Simple and structured models* of strategy formulation, where data analysis and internal and external scanning are undertaken so that the resulting model is clear and simple.
- *Separation* between the formulation of strategy and its implementation; diagnosis is followed by prescription and then by action; an organisation structure must therefore follow the formulation of the strategy rather than the other way round.

Flexible, eclectic or emergent approaches, on the other hand, are characterised by responsiveness to gradual changes through evolutionary decision-making processes that often prevail in organisations that profess to adhere to formal and mechanistic approaches to strategy formulation. Mintzberg (1990), as cited by Ciborra and Jelassi (1994), questions the mechanistic, prescriptive school of thought on three counts:

1 During strategy implementation, surprises occur that question previously developed plans. To be successful, the strategic plan needs to be modified to reflect the new situation and this contradicts the previously stated rationality and rigidity that characterise the mechanistic approach. Organisational learning is also hampered by an unduly inflexible approach.

2 While the mechanistic approach to strategy features the strategist as an impartial and independent observer and participant in the strategy development process, the reality in organisations is that organisational structure, culture, inertia and politics themselves influence the strategy development process. Strategy formulation is therefore profoundly influenced by the environment it is seeking to affect.

3 The mechanistic approach to strategy formulation is an intentional process of design. However, the reality is that organisations acquire knowledge on a continual basis and this knowledge can have a profound influence on the contents of strategy and, therefore, its formulation process.

Since both corporate and IS strategy formulation will always involve the need to react to unforeseen circumstances, resulting in sudden changes to overall corporate objectives, an effective strategy formulation process must embrace adaptation, organisational learning and incremental development that reflect a constantly changing business environment.

Introduction to BIS strategy

We have seen that all business strategies must be responsive to the external environment, but what are the elements of a strategy for managing BIS and how do they relate? Ward and Griffiths (1996) identify three different elements of IS strategy:

1 *Business information strategy*. This defines how information, knowledge and the applications portfolio will be used to support business objectives. Increasingly, a chief information officer (CIO) or chief knowledge officer (CKO) who is part of, or reports to the senior management team is appointed to be responsible for defining and implementing this strategy.

2 *IS functionality strategy*. This defines, in more detail, the requirements for e-business services delivered by the range of business applications (the **applications portfolio**).

3 *IT strategy (IS/IT strategy)*. This defines the software and hardware standards and suppliers which make up the e-business infrastructure.

These strategies are part of the organisation's hierarchy of strategies discussed in the previous section.

IT strategy determines the technological infrastructure of the organisation. It ensures the most appropriate technologies and best standards are used in terms of cost, efficiency and supporting the needs of the business users and integration with customers and other partners. A recent strategic decision taken by many companies is to use the Internet protocol (IP) to support deployment of business applications via an intranet. The hardware and software elements of the IT infrastructure were described in Chapters 3 to 6. Figure 13.2 summarises the main elements of technological infrastructure that must be determined by IT strategy. Approaches for controlling the total cost of ownership (TCO) of the IT infrastructure are described in Chapter 16.

IS Strategy determines how IT is applied within an organisation. It should ensure that the IT deployed supports business strategies and that the appropriate resources and processes are in place for the deployment to be effective.

Note that, in reality, there is some overlap between elements of IS and IT strategy. For example, it can be argued that the selection of the optimal portfolio of software applications is an aspect of both IS and IT strategy. For this reason a convention preferred by many authors such as Ward and Griffiths (1996) refer to both elements together (IS/IT strategy). This convention is used in this chapter.

The relationship between these elements is indicated in Figure 13.3. It is evident that these three elements can be considered to be hierarchical. Here, business information strategy should be driven by the objectives of the business strategy – by its information needs. IS functionality, delivered by BIS applications, should in turn be driven by the information requirements of the organisation, and finally IT strategy is the implementation of IS strategy through the delivery of IT infrastructure. Such a model is useful for debate. For example, does this model represent reality in most organisations? Do

Applications portfolio
The range of different types of business information systems deployed within an organisation.

IT strategy
Determination of the most appropriate technological infrastructure comprising hardware, networks and software applications.

IS strategy
Determination of the most appropriate processes and resources to ensure that information provision supports business strategy.

Examples

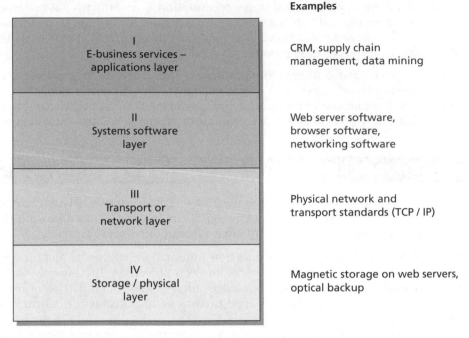

	Examples
I E-business services – applications layer	CRM, supply chain management, data mining
II Systems software layer	Web server software, browser software, networking software
III Transport or network layer	Physical network and transport standards (TCP / IP)
IV Storage / physical layer	Magnetic storage on web servers, optical backup

Figure 13.2 A four-layer model of an organisation's technological infrastructure
Source: Chaffey (2002)

organisations have separate information, IS and IT strategies? What are the benefits and disadvantages of this approach? Although the top-down approach implies strong control of IS and alignment with business strategy, it may have limited responsiveness in taking advantage of opportunities provided by IS. If IS strategy development identifies a business opportunity it is difficult to feed this back up the hierarchy to be incorporated

Figure 13.3 Relationship between business strategy and IS/IT strategies

into the business strategy. We return to this issue in a later section where we review the merits of business impacting and business aligning techniques.

The importance of a coherent strategy to manage information is highlighted by Willcocks and Plant (2000) who found in a study of 58 major corporations in the USA, Europe and Australasia that the leading companies were astute at *'distinguishing the contributions of information and technology, and considering them separately'*. They make the point that competitive advantage *'comes not from technology, but how information is collected stored, analysed and applied'*.

▶ IS/IT strategy and an organisation's environment

All organisations operate within an environment that influences the way in which they conduct business. Strategy development is strongly influenced by considering the environment the business operates in. Figure 1.2 (p. 15) illustrates some of the key elements that may influence the way in which an organisation operates. Environmental influences can be broken down into:

- the immediate competitive environment (**micro-environment**) which includes customer demand and behaviour, competitor activity, marketplace structure and relationships with suppliers and partners;
- the wider environment (**macro-environment**) in which a company operates includes economic development and regulation by governments in the forms of law and taxes together with social and ethical constraints such as the demand for privacy.

Micro-environment
Immediate environment includes customers, competitors, suppliers and distributors.

Macro-environment
Wider environment of social, legal, economic, political and technological influences.

For IS/IT strategy, the most significant environmental influences are those of the immediate marketplace which is shaped by the needs of customers and how services are provided to them through competitors and intermediaries and via upstream suppliers. We concentrate on managing these influences in Chapters 13 and 14. Wider influences are provided by local and international economic conditions and legislation together with what business practices are acceptable to society. Finally, technological innovations are vital in providing opportunities to provide superior services to competitors or through changing the shape of the marketplace. Chapters 15 to 17 look at issues involved in managing some of the external factors related to information systems.

Activity 13.1

Why are environment influences important?

Purpose

To emphasise the importance of monitoring and responding to a range of environment influences

Activity

For each of the environment influences shown in Figure 1.2, give examples of why it is important as part of IS/IT strategy to monitor and respond in an information systems strategy context. Environmental influences are clearest for a company operating an e-commerce service

◗ The environment and the modern management imperatives

Paul Lickert refers to seven 'modern management imperatives' (Lickert, 1997) summarised as the 'seven R's of strategy'. These highlight how an organisation must compete by using information systems strategy to respond to its external environment. Each of the seven R's is described below together with how IS can be used to respond to the influence.

- *Reach* – this recognises that businesses increasingly compete globally rather than locally or within national boundaries. As a result organisations need the ability to compete with everyone else, regardless of geographic constraints.

  IS/IT both allows global competition and is required to compete; organisations need information and the tools to process it to allow quick, accurate response, any time and anywhere; global competition implies information networks and inter-organisational systems

- *Reaction* – customers are becoming ever more demanding and customers will make their views known and wish to have them respected. This means that organisations need quick customer feedback on products and services in order to offer what customers are demanding.

  IS/IT is needed to access and interpret customer feedback. It can be used to keep track of customers, products and projects – it is particularly important to bring order to the data to facilitate fast and accurate response so that managers will be able to anticipate customer needs because they understand the customer. A consequence of this is that software needs to be flexible and quickly developed;

- *Responsiveness* – the process of turning an idea into a product or service that can be marketed is shortening – global reach means that there will be a greater probability that a competitor will be able to offer a good or service that more closely meets customers' requirements. The response to this situation is to shorten the concept-to-customer cycle time so that the organisation can tailor goods and services to meet customers' specific needs.

  There needs to be a rapid movement of product ideas to the market. Organisations need IS/IT to help manage this process: efficiency and speed as well as accuracy and reliability are required and information needs to be relevant and well formatted.

- *Refinement* – greater customer sophistication and specificity mean that customers are more able than ever to distinguish fine differences between products and compare them with their needs and desires.

  More customer sophistication means increased turbulence in the market, so more information and the tools to manage and manipulate it are needed. Customers are better at communicating precise requirements which means that niche markets appear, grow and disappear rapidly. As a result increased breadth of information is required to create and market products. Also, customers respond well to systems that respond well to them.

- *Reconfiguration* – as a consequence of changing customer needs and preferences, it may be necessary to re-engineer work patterns and organisational structures to change the structure of work and workflow from idea to product or service.

  As business processes need to evolve and adapt to market needs, there is a big impact on information resource requirements needed for organisational learning (crossing functional boundaries). Complex work structures generate complex data, and management support systems are needed to help manage continually evolving work patterns and structures. Also, new architectures (e.g. client–server) allow decentralisation of IS/IT and greater customer responsiveness.

- *Redeployment* – changing an organisation's configuration may require the reorganisation and redesign of the financial, physical, human and information resources that are required to create and market a product or service.

Rapid redeployment of resources is required to meet customer needs. An organisation needs to be able to visualise complex arrangements for resources and models to manage them. Therefore, it is necessary to maintain detailed, relevant information on resources at all times and be able to redeploy them. Information itself has become a competitive resource, as well as allowing more control over other resources.

● *Reputation* – an organisation's reputation will be determined, at least in part, by the satisfaction that a customer experiences. This will be enhanced when the product or service meets or exceeds expectations and requirements. Therefore, an organisation needs to pay attention to the quality and reliability of its products or services and processes by which they are produced.

IS/IT can be used to support product development, testing, marketing and customer post-sales service. It can also help to reduce the gap between expectation and performance. Organisations need to enhance the quality and reliability of the product, and information systems can help in such areas as quality benchmarks, measurement and group-based control techniques.

Figure 13.4 illustrates how an organisation's IS/IT strategy increasingly forms the bridge between the external business environment and internal business processes and activities. Consider an airline: the quality of all customer interactions, often referred to as 'moments of truth' by marketers, whether by phone, Internet or in person, require the support of IS. Similarly most supplier services will also be arranged and delivered through IS support.

An organisation's IS/IT capability will determine, at least in part, how well it can respond to demands placed on it by the external business environment and how it can manage and revise its internal business processes to meet those external demands.

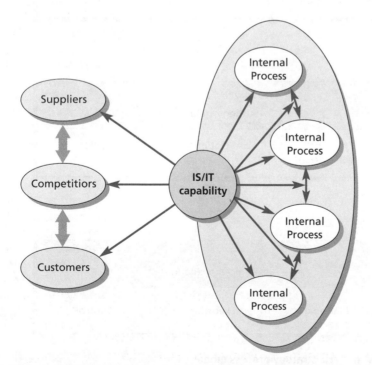

Figure 13.4 IS/IT capability positioning model showing IS/IT capability as the bridge between internally and externally focused business strategies

Strategy process models

Strategy process model

A framework for approaching strategy development.

A **strategy process model** provides a framework that gives a logical sequence to follow to ensure inclusion of all key activities of strategy development. It is typical of the mechanical, prescriptive approach to strategy development described in the introductory section. Such models are used to structure strategy formulation and development for a range of business areas whether corporate strategy (e.g. Lynch, 2000), marketing (McDonald, 1999; Smith, 2001), logistics (e.g. Hughes et al., 1998) or IS (e.g. Ward and Griffiths, 1996; Robson, 1997).

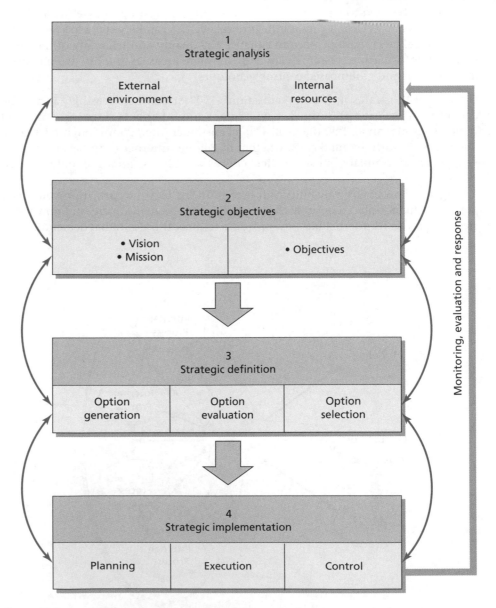

Figure 13.5 A generic strategy process model
Source: Chaffey (2002)

A review of the strategy process models developed by these different authors indicates these common features, which are summarised in Figure 13.5:

1 Continuous internal and external environment scanning or analysis is required to assess internal strengths and weaknesses and external opportunities and threats.
2 Clear statement of objectives is needed and a vision of the future direction of the organisation is required.
3 Strategy development can be broken down into formulation of different strategic options and then selection.
4 After strategy development, enactment of the strategy occurs as strategy implementation.
5 Control is required to detect problems and adjust the strategy accordingly.

In addition, the models suggest that these elements, although generally sequential, are also iterative and require reference back to previous stages. Such a strategy framework can be applied to each of the different strategies related in Figure 13.3, whether business strategy, information strategy, IS strategy or IT strategy. Each should have a situation analysis, objective setting, option selection and implementation stage. The four stages of this generic strategy process model are used to structure this chapter.

Note the use of two-way arrows in Figure 13.5 to indicate that each stage is not discrete, but rather involves referring backwards or forward to other strategy elements. Each strategy element will have several iterations. Kalakota and Robinson (2000) recommend a dynamic strategy process specific to e-business in which the business is responsiveness to its environment.

Tools for strategic analysis and definition

In this section we present six tools commonly used in BIS strategic analysis and definition. We start by considering tools that are mainly used to assess the external environmental constraints and options for strategy and then move on to tools that assess the existing internal situation and are used to generate options about future strategy. The tools selected form only a small proportion of those available, but those are covered provide a firm foundation for further analysis. In addition, each tool will be examined in the context of the way in which it can be used to help derive an IS strategy that is an integral part of an organisation's business strategy. We will review the application of these six tools:

1 *Porter and Millar's five forces model*. A model for analysing the different *external* competitive forces that affect an organisation and how information can be used to counter them.
2 *Porter's competitive strategies*. Assesses how *external* competitive forces can be harnessed.
3 *Nolan's stage model*. An evolutionary maturity model to assess the current development of information systems *within* an organisation.
4 *McFarlan's strategic grid*. A model for assessing the current and future applications portfolio *within* an organisation.
5 *Value chain analysis*. A tool for analysing the value-adding of information *within* an organisation. Note that value chain or value stream analysis can also be used to assess value-adding activities *outside* an organisation.
6 *Critical success factors (CSF) analysis*. A model assessing those factors *within* an organisation that are required to achieve strategic objectives.

1 Porter and Millar's five forces model

Porter and Millar's five forces model is a model for analysing the different external competitive forces that affect an organisation and how information can be used to counter them. The five forces are: rivalry between existing competitors, threat of new entrants, threat of substitutes, the power of buyers and the power of suppliers.

This model originated in 1985 and has remained one of the classic tools by which an organisation can assess its current competitive position in relation to a number of external factors:

- *Rivalry between existing competitors*. This will determine the immediate competitive position of the business and will depend principally on the number of firms already in the industry and the maturity of the industry itself. For example, a mature or declining industry will probably experience a high degree of rivalry, since survival is the key issue at stake.
- *Threat of new entrants*. A new entrant to an industry will cause the existing competitive situation to be disrupted. This has been evident in many countries over the last few years, where many of the formerly nationalised industries which were then privatised are now facing competition that they have never faced before.
- *Threat of substitutes*. The substitutes in question already exist within the industry, but because of differentiation they are not quite perfect substitutes for each other. The danger here, therefore, is that a company may lose market share if a rival can supply a substitute that more closely matches the needs of certain customers.
- *Power of buyers*. The phrase 'the customer is king' is never more true than here where buyers, especially in a business area where there are relatively few of them, can exert power by threatening to switch their purchasing to an alternative supplier. This is also true for businesses where the items being purchased are particularly high-value items (e.g. aero engines).
- *Power of suppliers*. This may appear a little odd given the previous point, since a business is going to be the customer to its suppliers. However, there are still competitive

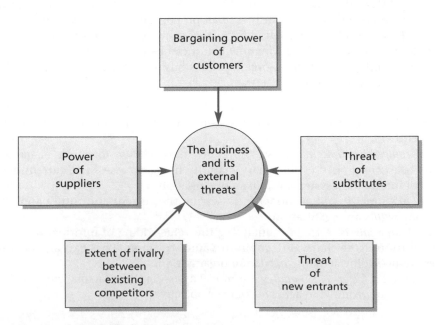

Figure 13.6 Porter and Millar's five forces model

pressures to be addressed. For example, in a situation where a material is in short supply, a business is going to be at risk from its competitors bidding up material prices and suppliers selling to the highest bidder. An illustration of this is the worldwide shortage of PC memory chips in the early 1990s, where computer manufacturers effectively had to endure a large hike in prices if they were still to manufacture and sell personal computers.

Figure 13.6 illustrates how the five forces outlined above provide the main external pressure on the successful operation of a typical business.

These five forces can exert a profound influence on how business is conducted. If the model is to be used successfully, it will require a thorough analysis of the industry under consideration. Of itself, the resulting information will not automatically generate a business strategy for the organisation. However, it will create a vivid picture of the market environments within which the organisation is operating and provide some pointers towards avenues of further investigation.

From an information systems strategy perspective, the tool provides further pointers towards how IS can be used to affect one or more of the five forces. Each one of the five forces will be taken and an illustration of how IS can be used to benefit the business will be given:

- *Rivalry between existing competitors*. The greater the extent of rivalry within the industry, the higher the costs that will be incurred by a business as it seeks to compete with its rivals. In addition, industry rivalry will be profoundly influenced by the positioning of its products in both the industry and product lifecycles. In a declining industry, for example, collaborative efforts between industry rivals may help reduce costs or raise the profile of the industry.
- *Threat of new entrants*. Businesses such as the financial services industry are competing increasingly on the basis of quality and service, and information systems are one enabler in this process. Investment in systems that support these two aspects of competition can deter potential entrants if they themselves have to make a significant investment in such systems before they can hope to compete successfully.
- *Threat of substitutes*. The threat here is greater if the substitute products are a close alternative. In the shape of CAD/CAM and computer-integrated manufacturing, IS can be used to speed up development of new products and therefore reduce the ability of competitors to provide products that are acceptable substitutes.
- *Power of buyers*. IS can be used to lock customers into a company's products and so reduce the risk of the customer switching to a rival. For example, a business specialising in organising corporate travel may locate terminals at its main corporate customers so that they will be more likely to book flights, hotels and car hire with that company rather than a competitor.
- *Power of suppliers*. If a supplier believes that its customers will always buy from it because there are few perceived alternatives, it is in a position to exert upward pressure on prices and to dictate trading terms to the customer rather than the other way round. Through external databases and now the Internet, IS can help businesses identify equipment and raw material suppliers much more efficiently than before and so reduce the bargaining power of suppliers. An example of this is provided in Chapter 17 by the BT Trading Places initiative, where the Internet is used to review PC prices from several manufacturers, which reduces the power of the individual supplier.

The value of this model is that it encourages an organisation to look at itself in the context of its external environment. It is not a methodology that a company can follow to transform itself. It is now appropriate to switch from an externally oriented view to an internal one, again courtesy of Michael Porter.

Using Porter and Millar's model to devise strategies for exploiting the Internet

Using the Internet as an example of a new information technology, examine how a business could apply information technology to counter each of Porter and Millar's competitive forces. This provides an easy-to-understand example of how this model can be applied to the competitive use of IS. If you are not familiar with business applications of the Internet, you are referred to Chapter 17.

Applications that you may wish to consider are: sales of existing products by electronic commerce to customers across the Internet; introducing new products available over the Internet; marketing of products across the Internet; reducing the cost and increasing the efficiency of dealing with suppliers through an extranet; and changes in the ease of switching and switching costs through using the Internet. Note that the new technologies may actually improve the power of the company you are dealing with in some instances. State where you feel this is the case.

2 Porter's competitive strategies

Related to his work on the five forces, Porter proposed three different competitive strategies that could be used to counter these forces, of which the organisation may be able to adopt one (Porter, 1980). Once a competitive strategy has been identified, all marketing efforts can be applied to achieving this and IS can help support the aim. The three competitive strategies, which are covered in more detail in Chapter 1, are:

● *Overall cost leadership.* Firm aims to become the lowest-cost producer in the industry. The strategy here is that, by reducing costs, one is more likely to retain customers and reduce the threat posed by substitute products. An example of how this might be achieved is to invest in systems that support accurate sales forecasting and therefore projected materials requirements so that good, long-term deals can be struck with suppliers, thus reducing materials costs.
● *Differentiation.* Creates a product perceived industry-wide as being unique. By being able to tailor products to specific customers' requirements or by offering an exceptional quality of service, the risk of customers' switching is reduced.
● *Focus or niche.* This involves identifying and serving a target segment very well (e.g. buyer group, product range, geographic market). The firm seeks to achieve either or both of 'cost leadership' and 'differentiation'.

There is also a possible undesirable outcome:

● *'Stuck in the middle'.* The firm is unable to adopt any of the above approaches and, therefore, is ultimately at the mercy of competitors that are able to offer these approaches.

3 Nolan's stage model

Nolan's stage model
This model is a six-stage evolutionary model of how IS can be applied within a business.

Nolan's stage model is a six-stage maturity model for the application of information systems to a business.

It must be stressed at the outset that this model dates back to the mainframe era and, therefore, provides a way of looking at an organisation's response to ongoing IS investment and management that is fundamentally influenced by this. However, the model does have value since it is simple to understand, provides an evolutionary view of business use of IS and demonstrates that an organisation's approach to the management of IS will change over time. The model demonstrates that, over time and with experience, an organisation's approach to computer applications, specialist IS personnel and methods of management will evolve to a level of maturity where the planning and development of information systems are embedded into the strategic planning process for the business as a whole.

The six-stage 1979 version of the model is the one on which we will focus here:

1 *Initiation*. The first cautious use of a strange technology, characterised by:
- low expenditures for data processing;
- small user involvement;
- lax management control;
- emphasis on functional applications to reduce costs.

2 *Contagion*. The enthusiastic adoption of computers in a range of areas:
- proliferation of applications;
- users superficially enthusiastic about using data processing systems;
- management control even more lax;
- rapid growth of budgets;
- treatment of the computer by management as just a machine;
- rapid growth of computer use throughout the organisation's functional areas;
- computer use is plagued by crisis after crisis.

3 *Control*. A reaction against excessive and uncontrolled expenditures of time and money on computer systems:
- IS raised higher in the organisation;
- centralised controls placed on the systems;
- applications often incompatible or inadequate;
- use of database and communications, often with negative general management reaction;
- end-user frustration.

4 *Integration*. Using new technology to bring about the integration of previously uninte-grated systems:
- rise of control by the users;
- large DP budget growth;
- demand for database and online facilities;
- DP department operates like a computer utility;
- formal planning and control within DP;
- users more accountable for their applications;
- use of steering committees, applications financial planning;
- DP has better management controls, standards, project management.

5 *Data administration*. There is a new emphasis on managing corporate data rather than information technology:
- identification of data similarities, their usage and meanings within the whole organisation;
- the applications portfolio is integrated into the organisation;
- DP (MIS) department serves more as an administrator of data resources than of machines;
- the emphasis changes to IS rather than DP.

6 *Maturity*. Information systems are put in place that reflect the real information needs of the organisation:
- use of data resources to develop competitive and opportunistic applications;
- MIS organisation viewed solely as a data resource function;
- MIS emphasis on data resource strategic planning;
- ultimately users and MIS department *jointly* responsible for the use of data resources within the organisation.

Data processing (DP) department

Commonly used in the 1970s and 1980s to describe the functional area responsible for management and implementation of information systems.

Data processing (DP) department is a term commonly used in the 1970s and 1980s to describe the functional area responsible for management of what is now referred to as information systems and applications development. It is interesting to note that the term focuses on the processing of data rather than the application of information. The head of this department was referred to as DP manager rather than chief information officer or IS manager.

There are a number of implications of Nolan's model which, if taken into account, may help provide a clearer path towards the maturity stage. Both general and IS management must:

- verify the state of IS development in order to plan for the future;
- recognise the fundamental organisational transition from computer management to information resource management;
- recognise the importance of and the future trends in information technology;
- introduce and maintain the appropriate planning and control devices for the IS function (steering committees etc.).

While it is clear that the model has value, there are clearly a number of shortcomings, particularly in respect of the lack of a human dimension. Galliers and Sutherland (1991) extended the model so that it is a socio-technical one rather than merely a technical one. They did this by including reference to the organisation's goals, culture, skills and structure. Nevertheless, we should not dismiss Nolan's model, despite its age, since it can still provide a useful framework for information systems planning. Indeed, the maturity stage implies what all organisations should aspire to: true integration between IS and business planning! Stage models for e-business are in Chapter 14.

4 McFarlan's strategic grid

McFarlan's strategic grid

This model is used to indicate the strategic importance of information systems to a company now and in the future.

Applications portfolio

The range of different types of business information systems deployed within an organisation.

McFarlan's strategic grid model is used to indicate the strategic importance of information systems to a company now and in the future. It is sometimes referred to as an **applications portfolio** model since it assesses the current mix of business information systems within an organisation.

This matrix model was developed by McFarlan and McKenney (1993) to consider the contribution made currently by information systems and the possible impact of future IS investments. It is suggested in the original model that any business will occupy one of the segments in the matrix (Fig. 13.7):

- The *strategic* segment indicates that the business depends on both its existing IS and its continued investment in new IS to sustain continued competitive advantage.
- The *turnaround* segment suggests that, while a business in this position does not currently derive significant competitive benefits from its current IS, future investment in this area has the potential to positively affect the business's competitive position.
- On the other hand, a business operating in the *factory* segment, while depending on its current IS to operate competitively, does not envisage further IS investment having a positive impact on its competitive position.
- Finally, a business in the *support* segment does not and believes it will not derive significant competitive advantage from information systems.

Note that it is not likely to be the aim for every company to move to a high strategic importance for IS. In some industries such as manufacturing, it is unlikely that IS will ever attain high importance. In others, such as retailing, it may become more important. Given the varying significance of IS in different industries, there are a number of ways in which this model can be applied:

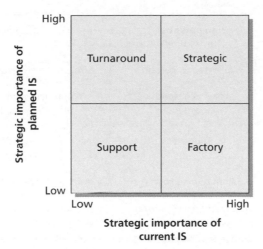

Figure 13.7 McFarlan's strategic grid
Source: McFarlan and McKenney (1993)

- across industries for analysing the strategic importance that particular industries attach to IS;
- within an industry, different competitors can be plotted according to the relative significance they attach to IS.
- within a company, different departments within an organisation can be classified and goals set in relation to the future planned importance of IS.

This model has been criticised by Hirscheim et al. (1988) as being too simplistic, since most companies have information systems that fall into all four categories. Ward and Griffiths' (1996) modified matrix provides a useful variation on this model by categorising information systems and their business contribution in terms of an applications portfolio. This model recognises that the information systems used by a single company will not fit into a single quadrant on such a matrix, but rather there will be a portfolio of IS, some of which may lie in different quadrants. The four sectors are shown in Figure 13.8.

The four sectors are:

- *Support*. These applications are valuable to the organisation but not critical to its success.
- *Key operational*. The organisation currently depends on these applications for success (mission-critical).
- *High potential*. These applications may be important to the future success of the organisation.
- *Strategic*. Applications that are critical to sustaining future business strategy.

Each of an organisation's applications will fall into one of these categories. It is quite feasible that applications will move from one sector to another over time (e.g. today's strategic application may become tomorrow's key operational one). It is quite possible, for example, that a current key operational system needs to be developed to replace an old legacy system that no longer meets all the organisation's requirements (e.g. in respect of year 2000 compliance).

The McFarlan matrix and its variant do not of themselves provide a methodology to assist an organisation with its information systems planning. However, especially in its Ward and Griffiths guise, the matrix can be effective in providing a framework through which an organisation can explore current and planned IS, both from an IS perspective and from that of functional business managers.

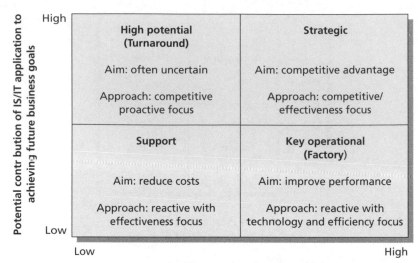

Figure 13.8 Ward and Griffiths' modified strategic grid
Source: Ward and Griffiths (1996)

5 Value chain analysis

Value chain
....
Michael Porter's value chain is a framework for considering key activities within an organisation and how well they add value as products and services move from conception to delivery to the customer.

This is an analytical framework for decomposing an organisation into its individual activities and determining the value added at each stage. In this way, the organisation can assess how effectively resources are being used at the various points on the **value chain**. Michael Porter's value chain is a framework for considering key activities within an organisation and how well they add value as products and services move from conception to delivery to the customer. The relevance for information systems is that for each element in the value chain, it may be possible to use IS to increase the efficiency of resource usage in that area. In addition, IS may be used between value chain activities to increase organisational efficiency.

Value chain analysis makes a distinction between *primary activities*, which contribute directly to getting goods and services closer to the customer (physical creation of a product, marketing and delivery to buyers, support and servicing after sale), and *support activities*, which provide the inputs and infrastructure that allow the primary activities to take place. Figure 13.9 shows the distinction between these activities.

Primary activities can be broken down into five areas:

● *Inbound logistics*. Receiving, storing and expediting materials to the point of manufacture of the good or service being produced.
● *Operations*. Transforming the inputs into finished products or services.
● *Outbound logistics*. Storing finished products and distributing goods and services to the customer.
● *Marketing and sales*. Promotion and sales activities that allow the potential customer to buy the product or service.
● *Service*. After-sales service to maintain or enhance product value for the customer.

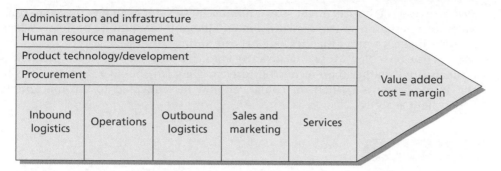

Figure 13.9 Michael Porter's internal value chain model, showing the relationship between primary activities and support activities to the value chain within a company
Source: Porter (1980)

Secondary activities fall into four categories:

- *Corporate administration and infrastructure.* This supports the entire value chain and includes general management, legal services, finance, quality management and public relations.
- *Human resource management.* Activities here include staff recruitment, training, development, appraisal, promotion and rewarding employees.
- *Technology development.* This includes development of the technology of the product or service, the processes that produce it and the processes that ensure the successful management of the organisation. It also includes traditional research and development activities.
- *Procurement.* This supports the process of purchasing inputs for all the activities of the value chain. Such inputs might include raw materials, office equipment, production equipment and information systems.

It is probably easier to see how IS can be applied within this model than in the five forces model that we looked at earlier. For example, sales order processing and warehousing and distribution systems can be seen to be very relevant to the inbound and outbound logistics activities. Similarly, accounting systems have an obvious relevance to administration and infrastructure tasks. What is perhaps less clear is how IS can be used between value chain elements. The case study on applying the value chain to a manufacturing organisation helps illustrate the use of IS to provide linkages between some of the value chain elements.

How can an organisation have a positive impact on its value chain by investing in new or upgraded information systems? Porter and Millar (1985) propose the following five-step process:

- *Step 1.* Assess the information intensity of the value chain (i.e. the level and usage of information *within* each value chain activity and *between* each level of activity). The higher the level of intensity and/or the higher the degree of reliance on good-quality information, the greater the potential impact of new information systems.
- *Step 2.* Determine the role of IS in the industry structure (for example, banking will be very different from mining). It is also important to understand the information linkages between buyers and suppliers within the industry and how they and competitors might be affected by and react to new information technology.
- *Step 3.* Identify and rank the ways in which IS might create competitive advantage (by affecting one of the value chain activities or improving linkages between them). High-cost or critical activity areas present good targets for cost reduction and performance improvement.

- *Step 4.* Investigate how IS might spawn new businesses (for example, the Sabre computerised reservation system spawned a multi-billion-dollar software company which now has higher earnings than the original core airline business).
- *Step 5.* Develop a plan for taking advantage of IS. A plan must be developed that is business-driven rather than technology-driven. The plan should assign priorities to the IS investments (which, of course, should be subjected to an appropriate cost–benefit analysis).

MINI CASE STUDY

Applying the value chain to a manufacturing organisation

A toy manufacturer has a range of integrated information systems, including sales order processing (SOP), warehousing and distribution, accounting systems, including sales, purchase and general ledgers, and finally a manufacturing system. The SOP system, which is used to store customer and order details, has a linkage to the accounting system for credit checking and processing accounts receivable. Thus there is an electronic linkage between the sales administration and infrastructure activities. The warehousing and distribution system keeps track of stock levels and actual and projected sales order levels. Information here can be used to generate automatically raw material orders and manufacturing orders. Here is a clear linkage between inbound logistics and operations and also procurement and inbound logistics. Finally, the warehouse and distribution system will generate a 'picking list' that is used to select stock from the warehouse for delivery to specific customers. This illustrates a linkage between the sales and outbound logistics functions. These activities are clearly operational in nature. However, the ability to have related information from a variety of systems also creates the possibility of management information, such as a weekly management report, which draws from all these sources.

Questions

1 Draw a diagram showing the role of information and information technology in assisting the value chain.

2 Give further ways in which the company could apply IT to improve efficiency.

---

6 Critical success factors (CSF) analysis

Critical success factors (CSFs)
Measures that indicate the performance or efficiency of different parts of an organisation and its processes.

Critical success factors (CSFs) are measures that indicate the performance or efficiency of different parts of an organisation. Good performance of processes measured by these factors is vital to the business unit or organisation.

This technique is one of the most useful for an organisation in pinpointing what are its precise information needs. The essence of CSF analysis is summarised in Figure 13.10.

Critical success factors will exist in every functional area of the business and they indicate those things which must be done right if that functional area in particular and the organisation as a whole are to flourish. CSFs will also relate to the level within each functional area. For example, in the sales function, a CSF for an account handler may be the accurate and speedy recording and retrieval of sales data. On the other hand, for a senior manager, a CSF may involve achieving the right mix of products.

Once CSFs have been determined across process and hierarchical levels, it is possible to consider the key decisions that have to be made if those CSFs are to be achieved.

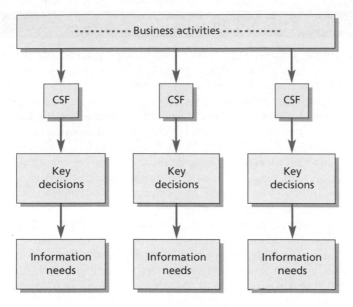

Figure 13.10 Critical success factors and deriving information needs

An example of the application of CSFs in sales order processing

When a customer places an order, a number of decisions need to be made, the results of which will determine the processing actions for the order and the effectiveness of the process. The critical success factor for this process will be to achieve a high conversion rate of orders received to orders fulfilled while minimising the risk of bad debts.

One of the first decisions will be whether to accept the customer order at all. Such a decision will hinge on the creditworthiness of the customer. Second, a decision will have to be made about when the customer can receive his or her order. This may be a complex process, depending on the size and importance of the customer, the size and complexity of the order and finally existing stock levels for the ordered items and planned manufacturing or purchasing lead times. If the order is delayed, the customer may seek an alternative supplier.

Having identified the range of key decisions that need to be supported, consideration must turn to the information needed to support the decision-making processes for each relevant functional business area or operational level. To pursue the sales example to its logical conclusion, one of the first information needs is, therefore, the creditworthiness of the customer as expressed by his or her credit line or limit and the current outstanding amount. Both of these items of information would normally be drawn from a mixture of existing sales and accounts receivable data. The sales account handler needs this information before a decision can be made to continue with the customer order. Second, information relating to order item availability needs to be known before a delivery date commitment can be made to the customer. This information will probably be drawn from:

1 Customer data (for example, is the customer an important one who needs to be looked after?).
2 Stock control data (is there sufficient stock in the warehouse to fulfil this customer's requirements?).
3 Production planning data (if there is currently insufficient stock on hand, will there be sufficient stock in time to meet the customer's requirements?).

Through improving the quality of information available to support decision making, it should be possible to improve the efficiency of sales order processing and achieve the CSF.

IS and business strategy integration

This section examines how strategic models can be applied to ensure that there is good congruence between business and IS strategies. The aim is to apply tools that enable us either to *align* the IS strategies with the business needs or use IT/IS to have a favourable impact on the business. Aligning techniques are top-down in nature, beginning with the organisation's generic business strategy and from this deriving information systems strategies that support business activities. Before these tools can be applied, it is necessary to consider the organisational strategy and the environment in which the business operates.

It is useful to consider tools for strategy definition in the context of whether they are intended to support an existing business strategy directly (**business alignment**), or whether they are intended to indicate new opportunities which may have a positive impact on a business strategy (**business-impacting**).

In a business-alignment IS strategy the IS strategy will be generated from the business strategy through techniques such as CSF analysis. In a business-impacting IS strategy the IS strategy will have a favourable impact on the business strategy through the use of innovative techniques and technologies, often as part of business process re-engineering. CSF analysis is fundamentally a business-aligning technique rather than an impacting one.

Business impacting could be achieved through the use of value chain analysis where an organisation, through an analysis of the potential for the use of IS within and between value chain elements, may seek to identify strategic IS opportunities. Perhaps the ultimate expression of using IS to impact business performance is through business process re-engineering.

Business-aligning IS strategy

The IS strategy is derived directly from the business strategy in order to support it.

Business-impacting IS strategy

The IS strategy is used to favourably impact the business strategy, perhaps by introducing new technologies.

▶ The importance of strategic alignment

Figure 13.11 attempts to illustrate one of the key problems in strategic information systems planning. T1 represents the point in time when it is recognised that the current IS/IT capability (C1) is insufficient to meet the needs of the organisation (represented

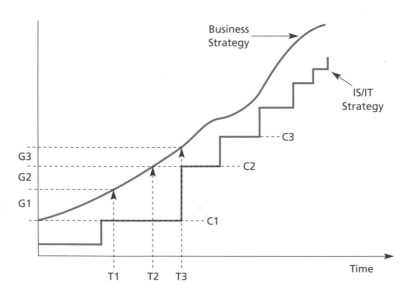

Figure 13.11 IS/IT capability/requirement model showing a strategic mismatch between IS/IT capability and business requirements

by the IS/IT capability gap G1). Plans are therefore developed to acquire the applications and/or infrastructure which will meet the needs of the business. At time T1 it is anticipated that a level of IS/IT capability represented by C2 will be sufficient when implemented at time T3 (thus making up the anticipated IS/IT capability gap G2). However, developments in an organisation's business strategy may mean that, by T3, IS/IT requirements are greater that those envisaged earlier on, thus resulting in a new IS/IT capability gap, G3. The response to this can be a shortening of the cycle time between new software releases so that the capability gap is smaller and for a shorter period. However, the implication of this is that IS/IT and business strategies run the risk of never being fully and consistently aligned.

It is possible to take the misalignment argument further (Fig. 13.12). At time T1, an organisation may anticipate significant demands for additional IS/IT development and construct an IS plan that will deliver capability C2 by time T2. However, it is possible that the organisation may only need part of that capability by T2 and will only be capable of using the IS/IT resource C2 by time T3. Therefore, the time from T2 to T3 may represent wasted resources. Furthermore, it may also represent a period of organisational change and upheaval while there is a misalignment of this type. In an extreme case, the resulting mismatch could result in business failure since the organisation's business strategy has been neglected at the expense of an over-emphasis on the perceived benefits of IS/IT investments alone.

These misalignment problems lie at the heart of IS planning and mean that there is a risk of ever-moving goalposts when attempting to specify, acquire and implement new computer based information systems.

▶ Balanced scorecards and strategic alignment

It has been suggested by van der Zee and de Jong (1999) that:

the continuously growing importance of IT requires organisations to integrate IT decisions with their common planning and decision-making processes at all organisational levels.

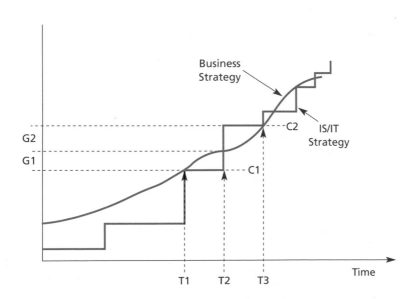

Figure 13.12 **IS/IT capability/requirement scenario 2 showing a strategic mismatch between IS/IT capability and business requirements**

They also suggest that it is inappropriate to attempt to align distinct business and IT management cycles. The balanced scorecard is suggested as a method of achieving integration.

Integrated metrics such as the balanced scorecard have become widely used as a means of translating organisational strategies into objectives and then providing metrics to monitor the execution of the strategy. The **balanced scorecard**, popularised in a 1993 *Harvard Business Review* article by Kaplan and Norton, can be used to translate vision and strategy into objectives. In part, it was a response to over-reliance on financial metrics such as turnover and profitability and a tendency for these measures to be retrospective rather than looking at future potential as indicated by innovation, customer satisfaction and employee development. In addition to financial data the balanced scorecard uses operational measures such as customer satisfaction, efficiency of internal processes and also the organisation's innovation and improvement activities including staff development.

We will now consider each of four main areas of the balanced scorecard (Fig. 13.13). Consider the influence of IS in contributing to each area:

Balanced scorecard
A framework for setting and monitoring business performance. Metrics are structured according to customer issues, internal efficiency measures, financial measures and innovation.

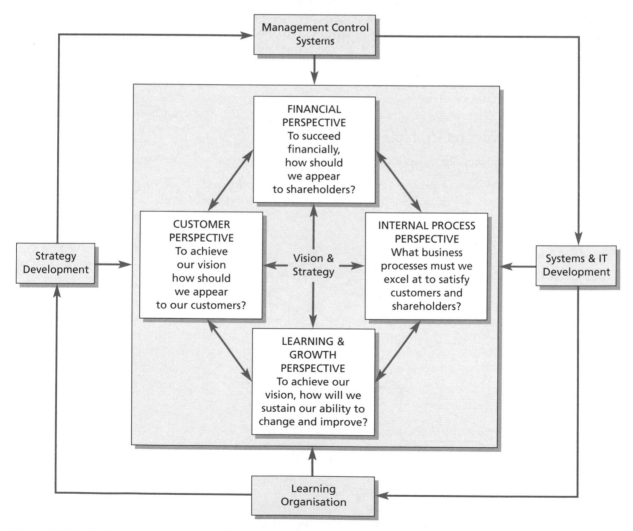

Figure 13.13 **The balanced scorecard process**

1 *Customer concerns.* These include time (lead time, time to quote, etc.), quality, perform- ance, service and cost. A measure for Halifax Bank from Olve et al. (1999) considers satisfaction of mystery shoppers visiting branches and from branch customer surveys. Customer satisfaction will be partly determined by the performance of customer-facing IS in branches and directly determined by the quality of online banking.

2 *Internal measures.* Internal measures should be based on the business processes that have the greatest impact on customer satisfaction: cycle time, quality, employee skills, productivity. Companies should also identify critical core competencies and try to guarantee market leadership. Example measures from Halifax: ATM availability (%), conversion rates on mortgage applications (%), arrears on mortgage (%). IS can be directly applied to improve these performance measures.

3 *Financial measures.* Traditional measures such as turnover, costs, profitability and return on capital employed. For publicly quoted companies this measure is key to shareholder value. Example measures from Halifax: gross receipts (£), mortgage offers (£), loans (£).

4 *Learning and growth: innovation and staff development.* Innovation can be measured by change in value through time (employee value, shareholder value, percentage and value of sales from new products). Examples: management performance, training performance, new product development. Some companies such as Skandia Life use measures such as staff IT skills or access to the IT to assess performance in this area.

For each of these four areas management teams will define objectives, specific meas- ures, targets and initiatives to achieve these targets. For some companies, such as Skandia Life, the balanced scorecard becomes much more than a performance measure- ment system but provides a framework for the entire business strategy process. Olve et al. (1999) make the point that a further benefit of the scorecard is that it does not solely focus on outcomes, but also considers measures that are performance drivers that should positively affect the outcomes. Examples of performance drivers are investment in technology and employee training.

Determining investment levels for information systems in an organisation

Chapter 8 describes the assessment of costs at the initiation phase of a single informa- tion systems project. In this chapter, we consider at an organisational level the amount of investment that should occur in information systems.

Managers in many organisations are concerned with the level of investment in infor- mation systems and whether they are getting value for money from that investment. One of the difficulties with measuring this is that while costs tend to be tangible in nature, benefits are often more difficult to quantify.

▶ Investment levels

One of the perennial questions surrounding corporate expenditure on IS is how much a business should spend on IS as a proportion of annual turnover. According to a report by Spikes Cavell (*Computing*, 19 December 1997), the top 500 companies in the USA invested an average of 2.9 per cent of their turnover in IS, while similar companies in Europe spent 2.1 per cent.

The Swedish research company Compass (*Computer Weekly*, 9 April 1998) suggests that as a proportion of total company costs, IS spending has increased from a typical 2–3 per cent in the 1980s to 7–10 per cent in 1998. The same source also suggests that

IS spending now makes up 40 per cent of capital investment by businesses in the USA, compared to 5–10 per cent twenty years earlier. The figures presented here imply that business operations are increasingly dependent on IS.

How much an organisation will spend on IS will depend both on the size of the organisation and on the nature of its business operations. Spending as a proportion of turnover will also vary over time, depending on the maturity of an organisation's systems and on the organisation itself. There is a tendency for the proportion of spending on IS to increase as organisations mature and have to maintain legacy systems. Regardless of any of these considerations, the task facing senior managers remains the same: can we be sure that investment in IS will deliver more benefit than the costs incurred?

▶ Information systems costs

As described in Chapter 8, costs can be both tangible and intangible. As you would expect, tangible costs are more easily identified than intangible ones. This leads to the observation that costs can also be classified as *expected* and *hidden*. Research by Keen indicates that there are differences between in-house developed and purchased software in the proportions of expected and hidden costs. This can be compounded by the complexity of the chosen method of software acquisition and the complexity of the system being acquired: the more complex the method and/or system, the more likely costs are to overrun what was anticipated in advance.

Hochstrasser and Griffiths (1990) produced a checklist which can help organisations identify, quantify and evaluate information system costs. The main cost elements include:

- hardware costs;
- software costs;
- installation costs;
- environmental costs;
- running costs;
- maintenance costs;
- security costs;
- networking costs;
- training costs;
- wider organisational costs.

Since every information system that is acquired incurs operational and maintenance costs, IS expenditure will always be split between *development* costs and *operational and maintenance* costs.

▶ Information system benefits

While information systems costs are relatively easy to identify, the benefits that accrue from IS investment are harder to quantify. This is because benefits are often intangible in nature and, therefore, harder to ascribe a financial value to. Broadly speaking, benefits from IS investment result from the capability of the organisation to do things that it could not do or did not do very well before. This must be supported by information of good quality, as defined in Chapter 2. This will include:

- Information relevance – is the information being provided relevant to the business decisions being made?
- Is accurate information available on which business decisions can be made?
- Speed of information delivery – does information reach the decision makers when they need it?

- The functionality of the IS to support decision making – will the system do what we want it to do?
- The reliability of the IS – can we rely on the system to give us the information we want when we want it?

If the above questions can be answered positively, then the investment in IS is providing benefits to the organisation and, therefore, allows it to do things that it could not do before.

In making an IS investment decision, the value that accrues from the above elements must be measured in some way. However, as noted above, value from IS investment can often be intangible in nature and, therefore, harder to measure. Such items of intangible benefit include:

- improved customer service;
- gaining competitive advantage and avoiding competitive disadvantage;
- support for core business functions;
- improved management information;
- improved product quality;
- improved internal and external communication;
- impact on the business through innovation;
- job enhancement for employees.

Each of these elements has a level of difficulty attached when we attempt to determine the value of the benefit. For example, impact on the business through innovation is very hard to measure quantitatively, while the benefit of improved product quality may be easier to measure.

▶ IS investment – balancing costs and benefits

We can deduce from the above discussion that the more accurately we can identify the contribution of IS towards the value of business gain, the more accurately we can identify the value accruing from IS investments. It follows from this that in order to assess the value of future investments in IS, we must come up with a framework that allows us to weigh up the relative costs and benefits and so enables us to make properly considered IS investment decisions.

There are a number of approaches that attempt to evaluate IS investment decisions. In essence, a proposed or ongoing investment should proceed if the benefits from the investment outweigh the costs incurred. However, as Robson (1997) indicates, one of the main difficulties is the intangible benefits, which can amount to at least 30 per cent of all benefits obtained. In addition, even if a benefit can be quantified (e.g. a new system speeds up customer response to queries from an average of 10 minutes to 10 seconds), it is not always easy to put a monetary value on it. This leads to a division in approaches between those that concentrate purely on financial measures and those that attempt a non-monetary evaluation.

Chapter 8 considers the basis of investment decisions taken at the feasibility assessment stage of the initiation of an individual project. It is the role of the IS manager to ensure that individual IS project decisions are consistent with the company's overall IS strategy.

Financial justification methods look at the relationship between the monetary costs of IS investment and the monetary benefits that might be obtained from it. There are a number of techniques that can be used, including:

- return on investment (RoI);
- discounted cashflow (DCF), such as net present value (NPV) and internal rate of return (IRR);
- payback period.

These are described in more detail in Chapter 8, which reviews how they are applied to a proposal for an individual system.

Risk assessment methods, on the other hand, look at a number of factors other than those related to pure financial return. Such considerations include:

- the benefits that are designed to accrue from investment in different categories of IS;
- the reasons that systems fail;
- categories of risk and their likely impact on systems success.

Information systems fail when they do not deliver the benefits they were intended to achieve. Clearly, the greater the investment in IS, the greater the impact of a failed project, especially as that investment could have been made in another part of the business (e.g. investment in additional plant, people or equipment) with much greater effect.

We will now look at an alternative approach for prioritising investment in IS.

Investment categories of the IS applications portfolio

Sullivan (1985) identified four investment categories for information systems that provide a framework within which the strategic value of the investment to the company can be placed. It is useful to identify in which category a new system lies within the IS portfolio, in order to assess its importance and allocate resources to it accordingly. The investment categories are:

1 *Strategic systems*. These are designed to bring about innovation and change in the conduct of business and so bring about a competitive edge. Business processes may need to be designed and relationships with customers and suppliers changed. Risk occurs because of the level of uncertainty associated with these kinds of systems (we are dealing with unstructured decision making, the results of which are often hard to quantify).

2 *Key operational systems*. Existing processes are rationalised, integrated or reorganised in order to carry out the activities of business more effectively. The risk occurs in the complexity of the systems in this category and the need to integrate them with other systems (externally as well as internally).

3 *Support systems*. Such systems support well-structured, stable and well-understood business processes (i.e. decisions are usually made in a climate of relatively high business certainty). Benefits derive either from eliminating unnecessary processes or from automating regular and routine procedures. In either case, the aim is to reduce cost and raise efficiency. The risks occur in selecting the right kind of software (often packaged) and implementing it effectively to gain the benefits.

4 *High-potential projects*. These are of research and development orientation and may have the capacity to deliver significant business benefits in the future. They are usually high-risk projects (in the sense that they may not deliver anything at all) and the main business risk lies in committing too much money to the project (i.e. the attitude that if we invest more, we must realise some benefits!).

The challenge for the organisation is to channel investment into the areas that are likely to yield the highest level of potential benefit at the lowest level of acceptable risk.

Risk factors

These have been summarised by Ward and Griffiths (1996). They should be considered at the start of a project to attempt to reduce the risk of project failure. Risk management is described in more detail in Chapter 8.

Focus on business process re-engineering

Business process re-engineering (BPR) involves identifying radical, new ways of carrying out business operations, often enabled by new IT capabilities.

Business process re-engineering has been the subject of much debate in recent years. On the one hand, it has been hailed as one of the most dramatic tools for achieving dramatic improvements in an organisation's performance. On the other hand, others regard it simply as a 'fad' responsible for many large-scale redundancies in the early 1990s, ultimately failing to confer major business benefits while at the same time providing management consultants with a great deal of revenue. It is not the purpose of this section to support either stance! Rather, it presents a review of how IS can fit into the BPR process. Before this is done, we will give an overview of the main BPR concepts and also consider the business framework within which BPR operates.

Business process re-engineering
Identifying and implementing radical new ways of carrying out work, often enabled by new IT capabilities.

◗ BPR fundamentals

BPR has its origins at the beginning of the 1990s and is closely associated with the work of Hammer and Champy (1993) and Davenport (1993). The essence of BPR is that there is a recognition that business processes and management structures can be fundamentally altered so that the business itself is better defined, focused, organised and run. Hammer and Champy defined BPR as: 'the fundamental rethinking and radical redesign of business processes to achieve dramatic improvements in critical, contemporary measures of performance, such as cost, quality, service, and speed.'

The key words of re-engineering are:

- *Fundamental rethinking.* Re-engineering usually refers to changing significant business processes such as customer service, sales order processing or manufacturing.
- *Radical process redesign.* Re-engineering is not involved with minor, incremental change or automation of existing ways of working. It involves a complete rethinking of the way in which business processes operate.
- *Dramatic improvements.* The aim of BPR is to achieve improvements measured in tens or hundreds of per cent. With automation of existing processes, only single-figure improvements may be possible.
- *Critical contemporary measures of performance.* This point refers to the importance of measuring how well the processes operate in terms of the four important measures of cost, quality, service and speed.

Information systems are often central to enabling the changes to take place. As we have seen earlier, IS has a capacity to allow communication within and between functional areas of the business much more quickly and efficiently than traditional manual methods. In *Reengineering the Corporation*, Hammer and Champy (1993) have a chapter giving examples of how IS can act as a catalyst for change. These include tracking technology, decision support tools, telecommunications networks, teleconferencing and shared databases. Hammer and Champy label these 'disruptive technologies' which can force companies to reconsider their processes and find new ways of operating.

Business process re-engineering is sometimes confused with less radical solutions to business problems. These have the benefit that they may have lower costs and risks, but the potential benefits may also be lower. The potential of each of these alternative strategic approaches is summarised in Table 13.1.

A problem with BPR is the historically high failure rate among BPR projects. It has been estimated that some 70 per cent of BPR projects fail, either completely or at least in delivering the benefits that were originally conceived. These figures have even been

Table 13.1 Alternative terms for using IS to enhance company performance

Term	Involves	Intention	Risk of failure
Business process re-engineering	Fundamental redesign of all main company processes	Large gains in performance (>100%?)	Highest
Business process improvement	Targets key processes in sequence for redesign	(<50%)	Medium
Business process automation	Automating existing process	(<20%)	Lowest

quoted by the original proponents of BPR such as Hammer. Given this, many companies are now adopting a more conservative approach by more gradually improving key business processes, perhaps one at a time. This is often referred to as 'business process improvement' or BPI – a less radical term than business process re-engineering. Note that BPI still involves a redesign of processes, but it does not involve disrupting the entire organisation.

Business process automation *is a misnomer that suggests radical change, but actually only involves using IS to automate existing ways of working. The introduction of a sales order processing system that mimics existing ways of working fits into this category. While such projects are likely to be easier to implement, they may not deliver sufficient benefits to pay for themselves.*

A further observation is that BPR has, in the past, been hampered by the lack of any really coherent methodology for carrying out BPR projects. For a broad framework, Davenport's stage approach to BPR offers a useful guide:

- Identify the process for innovation.
- Identify the change levers.
- Develop the process vision.
- Understand the existing processes.
- Design and prototype the new process.

- *Identify the process for innovation.* Emphasis here should be on major business processes. Commentators differ on how many major processes an organisation may have. It seems reasonable to equate a major business process with those from the organisation's value chain that add most to the value of the finished product or service.
- *Identify the change levers.* The main areas where emphasis can be placed include the organisation's information systems and its **organisational culture** and structure. As discussed earlier, BPR activities will be directed towards improving business processes either through better use of information, restructuring the organisation (physically and socially) or both.

    The concept of organisational structure includes shared values, unwritten rules and assumptions within the organisation as well as the practices that all groups share. Corporate cultures are created when a group of employees interact over time and are relatively successful in what they undertake.
- *Develop the process vision.* Before a BPR project can begin in earnest, it is necessary to generate a view of how and why business processes might be modified. The vision must be communicated to all parties in a way that acts as a motivator to all concerned.
- *Understand the existing processes.* Current business processes must be documented. This allows the performance of existing business processes to be benchmarked and so provides a means for measuring the extent to which a re-engineered process has improved business performance. In addition, a documented process provides a framework for discussion when process redesign is actually taking place.

Business process automation
Automating existing ways of working manually through Information Technology.

Organisational culture
This concept includes shared values, unwritten rules and assumptions within the organisation as well as the practices that all groups share.

- *Design and prototype the new process*. Here, the BPR team needs to be creative as it seeks to design the replacement processes – the vision must be translated into practical new processes that the organisation is going to be able to operate. Prototyping the new process operates on two levels. First, simulation and modelling tools can be used to check the logical operation of the process. Second, assuming that the simulation model shows no significant problems, the new process can be given a full operational trial. Needless to say, the implementation must be handled sensitively if it is to be accepted by all parties.

It is now appropriate to consider a possible framework that seeks to clarify how a number of factors can influence the BPR process itself.

▶ Success factors in BPR – the BPR diamond

Figure 13.14 shows a number of dimensions within which BPR must operate to be successful. Of these influences, the most important is the value chain, since BPR often seeks to affect this.

1 *Value chain activities*. BPR attempts fundamentally to alter processes *within* one or more of an organisation's value chain activities in order to improve business performance. It can also seek fundamentally to improve the effectiveness of relationships *between* value chain elements. It follows, therefore, that an organisation must fully understand its own value chain if it is to stand any chance of success with a BPR project. An important point here is the impact on the rest of the value chain of an improvement in one part of it. For example, substantial improvements in one value chain element (e.g. operations) may be pointless if another (inbound logistics, say) is incapable of expediting the necessary raw materials in time. ERP applications (Chapter 6) are often used when re-engineering the value chain.

2 *Management structure and organisational culture*. This will have a profound impact on the probability of success of a BPR project. Factors that are important here include:

- communication of the business vision by managers;
- corporate strategy formation;
- hierarchical structures – shallow structures may increase the likelihood of success, since they may indicate less bureaucratic management structures;
- senior management commitment is essential for success; many BPR projects fail because senior managers are not fully committed to the cause.

3 *Technical infrastructure and legacy systems*. The original proponents of BPR felt that IS was one of the key enablers of radical process redesign, not least because of its ability to transform working relationships within and between value chain elements. The ability of an organisation to act on this will be dependent on its existing IS infrastructure. For example, a business dominated by old mainframe legacy systems may actually be prevented from re-engineering business processes because the IS systems are too inflexible or are overloaded.

4 *Social relationships*. The efficiency of any organisation is dependent on the complex formal and informal relationships that exist within it. These can be formal in the sense of hierarchical work relationships within and between functional business areas. Informal relationships are created through people working with each other on a regular basis and will cut across functional boundaries. BPR has the capacity to alter both types of relationships, as it brings about change within and between functional business areas. Project management and a change management programme are clearly going to be essential if a BPR project is to succeed.

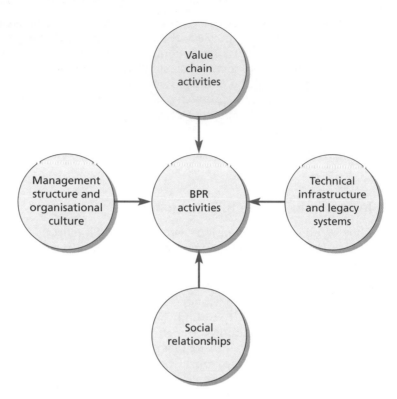

Figure 13.14 **The BPR diamond: influences on BPR activities**

▶ How to re-engineer

Many commentators exhort companies to re-engineer, but without giving detailed guidelines on how to achieve this. Nick Obolensky's book (1994) offers detailed guidelines for re-engineering with company case studies and is recommended reading. Figure 13.15 shows his recommended stages for re-engineering, which are consistent with a generic method of implementing business strategy. The first stages are involved with creating a vision for the company at a senior level and then planning the implementation. There follows the stage of undertaking re-engineering, which covers activities such as process analysis, design and implementation. Once the re-engineered system is operational, collecting metrics occurs so that the processes of the company can be continuously improved to keep up with or be one step ahead of the competition.

More detailed re-engineering methodologies have been developed by management consultancies, for example the Breakpoint BPR methodology developed by Coopers and Lybrand. This has three phases: discover, redesign and realise:

● Phase 1 is the initiation, in which the project vision and communications strategy is developed, processes for redesign are identified and teams are built.
● In Phase 2 the redesign modules are mobilise, analyse, innovate, engineer and commit.
● Phase 3 is mobilise, communicate, act, measure and sustain.

Case Study 13.1 reviews the results of re-engineering initiatives at companies such as British Airways, SmithKline Beecham and Siemens Nixdorf. It illustrates some of the problems faced by companies on this path and some of the solutions that have been tried.

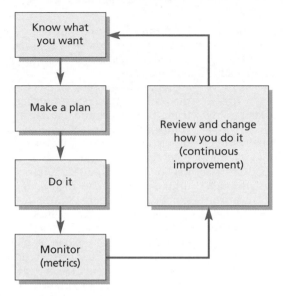

Figure 13.15 Stages in re-engineering
Source: Adapted from Obolensky (1994)

CASE STUDY 13.1

Corporate re-engineering – managing the change process

Five re-engineering practitioners explain why these factors hold the key to performance improvement.

Turning a vision of radical performance improvement into hard results can test management to the limit. Potential difficulties can be encountered at all stages of the cycle. Targets may be too modest to stimulate breakthrough solutions. But by far the greatest set of problems cluster round the management of change and corporate culture.

'The more projects I have done, the more I have come to realise the importance of change management', says Martin Boiling, a partner with PriceWaterhouse with extensive experience of re-engineering. 'Once you start tackling major projects you end up with a much more complex programme of change, and that means handling the people problems. It has been a traditional blind spot for most companies', says Boiling.

Typically, it is at the implementation phase that re-engineering starts to show the stresses and strains of change. But if diagnosed and treated in time, the symptoms need not be fatal.

In 1993 SmithKline Beecham set itself the goal of establishing a single supply chain process supported by appropriate information technology systems to replace the jumble of incompatible systems and practices that linked its 150-plus trading units worldwide. In the end, its project turned out to be a success. Initial indications are that the group is likely to achieve a 60 per cent improvement in cycle times, 40 per cent improvement in inventory, and error rates close to zero. But this was one re-engineering project that could easily have been added to the log of failure stories.

'There are always peaks and troughs in projects', says Robert Abel, director and vice-president, intercompany trade, SmithKline Beecham. 'But in this case the trough was deeper than anticipated.' The reason why was not immediately clear, although it was apparent the project was lacking the support and commitment it needed to be driven forward.

It was around this time that Abel became aware of the change management concepts and techniques pioneered by ODR, an American-based company that had started out in the 1970s studying success factors in corporate change. Relating their framework to the problem showed where the main problem lay. Executive sponsors had been inadequately involved in the initiative. While he now understood how the re-engineering programme should be managed, Abel was saddled with a difficult situation. There had been a change of ownership and senior executives. 'When the new owners asked what was going on, the perception from the business was not very positive', he says. 'It was that much harder to get started again, we had to go back to basics. It was a hard sell.'

By this stage, the project had not entirely fizzled out but had gone underground. 'It was kept going through the personal network, more or less as a favour', says Abel. Its revival hinged on the readiness of the new executive to take up the sponsor's role and provide active support. Abel successfully put the case for continuation by demonstrating that, although patchy, some progress had been made. Given the green light again, Abel applied the ODR tools and techniques to the project. This provided the means for engaging people to play their essential roles. That included senior executives as sponsors and front-line staff as change agents, individuals prepared to play an active role in facilitating change over and above their regular commitments. Just as selling sponsorship to senior executives had been difficult, winning others to play their part in the change management process presented challenges.

'Change agents were hard to find', says Abel. 'We did it through education by looking at the issue from the "what's in it for me?" angle, and people signed up for it.'

As a result of getting the project back on track, Abel has now won himself the job of sorting out supply chain issues for the group and its external suppliers.

SmithKline Beecham's experience underlines the high-risk nature of re-engineering. 'If you can reach your goal through continuous improvement then this is always preferable because re-engineering is disruptive, risky and demands a high level of commitment', says Mark Maletz, managing director of Business Process Design Associates, whose career is rooted in process improvement at Xerox and American Airlines. The choice depends on how wide the gulf is between current and target performance levels. It is this gap that has been key to persuading some companies that re-engineering is the only option.

Initially, British Airways Engineering believed poor information flows from the support areas of the business to aircraft maintenance staff was what was holding back performance. But it became apparent that there was a more basic problem to be tackled.

'Re-engineering is the vehicle for creating a new way of working within the engineering business', says Ray Claydon, project manager, British Airways Engineering. When the programme is completed, it will affect a workforce of 9500 people. The vision for the re-engineered organisation was signed off in June 1995 and work is now well advanced.

'Implementation has been a major challenge', says Claydon. 'It involves project management on a massive scale to coordinate change across the entire business.'

Central to the programme was the restructuring of the business to create a number of cross-functional teams to support and manage aircraft maintenance, component overhaul, design modifications and supply chain logistics. Processes and product groups have replaced departments as the principle for the new organisational structure. Self-sufficient business units will each have their own integrated technical support, production, engineering, planning and other management support facilities.

British Airways Engineering has placed great emphasis on the change management side of the project. Audio-visual presentations for all staff have been a key feature of the structured communications programme. This was followed by an open job forum where staff had the opportunity to find out about the re-engineered organisation from the 'new world' managers and the new roles and responsibilities they will be required to take on. To date, the programme has affected 2500 support staff, most of whom have had to apply for these new jobs. Already, says Claydon, there is evidence of performance improvement. The re-engineering project deliberately tackled the people and organisational changes first, leaving the systems strategy review until now. 'In this way we can be sure our future systems are designed to support our new ways of working', he says. If strong sponsorship and project management are features of successful re-engineering projects, another factor is the close involvement of those most affected by the changes brought about by re-engineering.

For Roger Boyes, financial director of the Halifax [Bank, former building society], this is an essential ingredient in the society's Finance 2000 project, now about halfway through its two-year programme. 'I am asking the people involved to design the new systems. It's not me telling them what to do. I am empowering people to come up with new processes.'

Behind Finance 2000 is recognition that the changes that were begun in the 1980s with the deregulation of financial services require a new mindset and approach to serving the market. In the past, building societies tended to be inward-looking. But continuing rapid changes in financial services call for a different outlook.

'It is no good having a customer-facing branch network, if support does not recognise customers are both internal and external', says Boyes. The primary goal is to re-engineer financial processes and services so they support the business unit strategy that will enable the Halifax to develop into a broad-based financial services organisation.

'We will have focused self-accounting business units, responsible for strategy and financial control with upward consolidation into the group', he says. 'This gives you the opportunity to re-engineer all those processes.'

The programme of changes is extensive and will involve the introduction of fully loaded P&L reports at the business unit level, the application of leading-edge cost accounting techniques, distribution channel and customer profitability, the use of value engineering and the development of a balanced scorecard. But it is not only processes that will change. 'It doesn't make sense to have a customer-oriented branch network and inward looking support services', says Boyes. 'You've got to have one culture.'

According to Maletz, management should turn their attention to corporate culture to ensure it is aligned with the goals of the transformed organisation before embarking on any transformation programme. 'Unless that happens, you are unlikely to bring about the improvements you want.' In a re-engineering context, the values, beliefs and behaviour consistent with the desired changes can include a willingness to take risks and experiment with new ways of working, increased responsibility and accountability among those who deal directly with customers, and a more entrepreneurial approach to business.

Maletz argues it is possible to turn round corporate culture, even in international groups, within two years or so. 'If they are prepared to tackle the three main dimensions of corporate culture: strategic direction, organisational structure and organisational behaviour, as part of a timetabled programme of change, then the results can start to come through even faster than that. But it calls for a high level of commitment, time and energy.'

Siemens Nixdorf, one company with which he has been working, has bet its future on achieving a dramatic turnround in its corporate culture to give it the capacity to compete in the global information technology market. Inside two years, it started to win new business as a direct result of its transformation into a customer-focused, market-oriented company.

Organisationally, its switch to process-based operations has begun in conditions where the changes have the best chance of taking root.

Siemens Nixdorf and other companies are discovering that investing in what has been regarded in the past as the soft side of business pays off. The right corporate culture not only enables performance improvement to work well. It may be the only investment that can guarantee longer-term success.

Source: Adapted from David Harvey, VNU-NET, 1 October 1996

Questions

1 What are the success factors for the change process referred to in relation to SmithKline Beecham?

2 What new structures were created as part of the British Airways re-engineering?

3 Summarise the common solutions to problems faced by all companies in the case study.

▶ IS and BPR

As will have been clear from the preceding analysis, IS is a key enabler in the BPR process. This operates on four main levels:

1 *Potential impact of new IT*. In this context, IT includes hardware, communications technology, systems software and systems development tools (including development languages and database technologies). The ability of the organisation to use this will depend to a large extent on its existing hardware and systems software strategy. For example, a strategy based on preserving an old mainframe environment may create fewer opportunities than one based on a more modern, up-to-date one (such as a client/server architecture). To make the shift away from the mainframe environment will be more involved and therefore costly, not least in respect of old legacy systems.

2 *Potential impact of new information systems*. This will be constrained both by the ability of the information technology infrastructure to support new information systems and by the existence of legacy systems. For example, an information system solution to a requirement that would be enabled by a significant amount of end-user development may be impossible to implement if there is little history of this within the organisation. Similarly, an information systems development that depended on

taking advantage of relational database capability would be fundamentally constrained if existing legacy systems used non-database file storage techniques.

3 *Prototyping and IS support for BPR process.* As referred to above, software tools such as simulation and modelling applications make it possible to model both existing systems and the redesigned business processes. Such tools are frequently used in manufacturing applications where, for example, they may model operations and workflow, thus revealing bottlenecks within the production process that can then be removed by reorganising the process.

4 *Organisational culture and the ability to absorb new IS.* The culture of an organisation can have a profound impact on how it approaches IS investment decisions. For example, an organisation that can be categorised as conservative and thus valuing low-risk strategies, may well be reluctant to make IS investments which, although carrying an element of risk, could confer major competitive advantage if successful. Indeed, conflict will almost definitely occur if a dynamic MIS manager has an IS vision that conflicts with a fundamentally conservative organisational culture! It could be argued, of course, that an organisation in this position is unlikely to make a success of a BPR project even if it embarked on one in the first place. Perhaps this explains why BPR failure rates are so high!

Guidelines for supporting process improvement

1 Develop and maintain an IT strategy that is integrated and aligned with the company's business goals

Closely aligned business and IT strategies are necessary so that IT solutions are implemented to support business goals, not so that developers can use 'cool new technology'. Information resources should be made available through collaborative systems to support decision making at all levels within the company: strategic, tactical and operational.

2 Create and foster a customer focus for the IT organisation and personnel

The US company Action Technologies considers customer focus in processes so critical that its workflow process model is defined through specifying a customer and a supplier for each subprocess. This customer–supplier relationship puts the spotlight on customer service and can boost the quality of solutions delivered. Customer focus can apply to both internal or external customers.

3 Design an IT organisation that maximises support for the company's various business groups

This guideline indicates that although processes and their supporting teams may seem to operate independently, it would be a mistake to think there are no links between these processes. Groupware is important in allowing information to be shared between different teams as well as within teams.

4 Use a centralised IT function to set enterprise-wide architecture standards

This is important to ensure the adoption of common applications and standards throughout the company in order to reduce cost, but also to minimise technical problems of incompatibility between applications and promote information exchange throughout the organisation.

5 Develop a clearly communicated process for integrating new technology into the business

The final point emphasises the importance of explaining through training why new collaborative technologies are being introduced and developing a plan so that there are no surprises for employees as new technologies are brought in to support processes. A culture can be established where continuous change is familiar. It will then be no surprise when new technologies are introduced to support changing business needs.

Chaffey (1998) refers to five guidelines for integrating IS strategy with BPR. These are shown in the box. These guidelines indicate the responsibilities that the IS manager has in an organisation for making BPR work. In particular, he or she is responsible for achieving standardisation across the processes and developing systems that are accepted by users, so easing the change process.

▶ IT infrastructure and BPR

Broadbent and Weill (1999) undertook a study on the relationship between information technology infrastructure and business process redesign. In a study of four organisations they found that all firms needed at least a basic level of IT infrastructure if they were to be able to implement BPR. They also found that:

The firms that had developed a higher level of IT infrastructure capabilities, before or concurrent with undertaking business process redesign, were able to implement extensive changes to their business processes over relatively short time frames. The higher level of infrastructure capability was provided in the form of (1) a set of infrastructure services that spanned organisational boundaries such as those between functions, business units, or firms, and (2) the ability of the infrastructure to reach particular constituencies inside and outside the firm to transfer information and process complex transactions.

The research used the generic list of IT infrastructure services developed by Broadbent and Weill as a framework for analysing infrastructure capability. The list is split between core and additional IT infrastructure services, with those in bold being 'boundary-crossing where they are clearly and actively integrative supporting information flows beyond one functional area'.

A. Core Information Technology Infrastructure Services
1. Manage firm-wide communication network services
2. **Manage group-wide or firm-wide messaging services**
3. Recommend standards for at least one component of IT architecture (e.g. hardware, operating systems, data, communications)
4. Implement security, disaster planning, and business recovery services for firm-wide installations and applications
5. Provide technology advice and support services
6. Manage, maintain, support large-scale data processing facilities (e.g. mainframe operations)
7. **Manage firm-wide or business-unit applications and databases**
8. Perform IS project management
9. Provide data management advice and consultancy services
10. Perform IS planning for business units

B. Additional Information Technology Infrastructure Services
11. **Enforce IT architecture and standards**
12. Manage firm-wide or business-unit workstation networks (e.g. LANs, POS)
13. Manage and negotiate with suppliers and outsourcers
14. Identify and test new technologies for business purposes
15. Develop business-unit-specific applications (usually on a chargeback or contractual basis)
16. Implement security, disaster planning, and recovery for business units
17. **Electronically provide management Information (e.g. EIS)**
18. Manage business-unit-specific applications
19. **Provide firm-wide or business-unit data management, including standards**
20. **Develop and manage electronic linkages to suppliers or customers**

21. **Develop a common systems development environment**
22. Provide technology education services (e.g. training)
23. Provide multimedia operations and development (e.g. video-conferencing)

IT infrastructure can constrain or enable what is possible in a BPR effort.
Enabling factors include:

● providing increased flexibility;
● improved communication;
● integration of different functions and organisations.

Constraining factors include situations where:
● systems are not compatible;
● inconsistent data models have been used in different parts of the business;
● there are very significant investments in systems that are based on old or inappropriate processes, business design, or structure assumptions;
● data and systems architectures are built to serve local, functional needs, rather than the needs of the whole organisation.

In their analysis of the four firms (all of which had completed the redesign of at least one business process and had some firm-wide IT infrastructure), Broadbent and Weill drew the following conclusions:

● The firms had infrastructure capabilities that allowed implementation of some type of BPR and also had some form of online or EDI linkage to suppliers or customers.
● The firms had experience in creating boundary-crossing capabilities (within the firm and with other firms). They also suggest that 'the lack of such infrastructure services will be a potential barrier to implementation of BPR'.
● 'Infrastructure range that crosses business unit boundaries is important for BPR ... the firms that completed more extensive BPR had infrastructure range that at least enabled complex transactions across multi-site business units.'

Two different types of BPR were identified:

● process simplification that required a medium level of IT infrastructure because the process changes are limited in scope;
● process innovation that was 'facilitated by extensive IT infrastructure capabilities with a high number of infrastructure services and high reach and range extending across functions and business units'.

Finally, IT infrastructure capability has an impact on successful BPR implementation with higher levels of capability enabling a more dramatic business process redesign and more radical change.

The implications of the research are clear. Organisations with an inadequate or limited IT infrastructure that attempt BPR projects are more likely to be limited to simple redesign tasks. In this case, substantial investment in IT infrastructure may, therefore, be necessary if radical change is to be brought about. This has, of course, all sorts of implications for justifying and financing the cost of the IT investment as well the change management exercise that will also be necessary.

Mische and Bennis (1996) make a number of claims about the potential for IT in the re-engineering (or redesign) process:

1 *Information technology will replace manual processes, paper forms, and traditionally structured operations.*
2 *Information technology will consolidate and eliminate many traditional tasks, human resources, and associated costs.*

3 *Information technology will enable trans-national expansion and virtual enterprises and employees.*

4 *Information technology will enable the consolidation of functionality and creation of cross-functional organisations and integrated processes.*

5 *Information technology will create and support a common standard and framework for managing shareholder resources for enhanced competitiveness, not greater management control.*

They also claim that 'in the re-engineered enterprise, reinvented information technology has six differentiating characteristics:

1 Applications and computing platforms that are demassed, decoupled, and scalable to specific business needs and their constituents.
2 Applications and data that are cross-platform functional.
3 Data that is accessible, rationalised, and consolidated in warehouses.
4 Applications that are built to common standards using a variety of productivity tools.
5 Applications and platforms that are portable and shared among various process constituencies and organisations.
6 Technology resources that are logically consolidated and physically distributed.'

None of this is unreasonable! However, the IT function needs to be managed carefully if these objectives are to be achieved and it is the management of the IS/IT function that we turn to now.

Locating the information systems management function

There are two basic approaches to locating the information system function in an organisation that operates at more than one location. These are the centralisation of all IS services at one office (usually the head office) and decentralisation. It is unusual for a company to choose one extreme or the other; typically, the approach will vary for the different types of services. The approach chosen is significant, since it will have a direct correspondence to the quality of service available to the end-user departments and the cost of providing this service.

◗ What needs to be managed?

It is useful to make a distinction between information systems and information technology. As has been stated before, we can view IT as the infrastructure and an enabler, while information systems give a business the applications that produce the information for decision-making purposes. IS cannot exist without the IT to support it, but IT on its own does not of itself confer any business benefits.

For information technology the following must be managed:

- *Hardware platforms.* These need to be selected and supported (for example, it may be decided only to operate a client/server environment using Unix workstations).
- *Network architectures.* An organisation currently operating a mixture of AS/400 computers and PCs may wish to focus on a particular network architecture for the PCs in order to facilitate easier integration with the AS/400 systems.
- *Development tools.* It may be desirable to adopt tools that permit more rapid development of new information systems. Such tools will need to be able to run on the selected hardware platform and also be compatible with chosen database management systems.
- *Legacy systems.* These systems may run on old hardware platforms and be difficult to integrate with planned systems development. While strictly an IS issue rather than

an IT one, it may still be necessary in the short-to-medium term to provide the necessary IT support to allow these systems to continue to operate.

- *Operations management*. This covers a number of areas, including hardware management, capacity planning, security (backups, access control, error detection, archiving), technical support (for hardware and systems software), telecommunications and network management.

The areas that relate to information systems management are:

- *Business systems development*. Applications development falls into two broad categories: those applications that deal with corporate data and those that are departmental or personal in nature.
- *Migration and conversion strategy*. While strictly being part of the systems development process, migration from one system to another involves specialists from both IS/IT and functional business areas. For corporate information systems, many functional areas may be involved.
- *Database administration*. Today's information systems depend very much on database management systems (such as DB2, Oracle, Informix and Access).
- *User support and training*. All applications software users require support at some point. The objective is to get the right support to the right people at the right time.
- *End-user application development*. This is becoming increasingly popular, especially in medium-to-large organisations. Such development will not only require support (e.g. advice on appropriate development tools) but will require explicit management to ensure that wheels are not being invented and bug-ridden software not being produced.
- *Shared services*. Recent innovations such as e-mail and collaborative work systems have both local and corporate application. The objective should be to maximise local flexibility while at the same time ensuring that organisation-wide standards are adhered to (the same could be said of end-user development).
- *IS/IT staffing*. While this is more of a human resources issue than an IT one, it is, nevertheless, important to stress that for an IT strategy to be implemented, there need to be staff with expertise in hardware, communications, systems software and development software. Naturally, for a small business this expertise will be limited.

This analysis indicates that there are some aspects of IS/IT that need central control and management, but at the same time there are local needs that have to be addressed within individual functional areas of the business. Therefore, we should now move from *what* needs to be managed to *where* IS/IT needs to be managed and the factors that influence this.

▶ Structuring information systems management

In a large company with several sites, IS/IT management must be organised and located in such a way as to ensure full integration of business and IS/IT strategies, as well as full support for the IS/IT needs of each functional area of the business.

Questions that should be asked when ascertaining the best approach include:

- *Is information systems management (ISM) in tune with corporate strategy?* Structures need to exist in such a way that an organisation's information systems strategy is fully embedded within its business strategy. This means that mechanisms must exist that embrace all functional areas of the business as well as the most senior management.
- *Is ISM in tune with organisational shape?* A heavily centralised approach to managing all aspects of IS/IT may conflict with a geographically dispersed organisation, or with one where individual functional areas enjoy a high degree of local autonomy.

- *Is the focus of ISM inward-looking on managing technology?* If this is the case, it suggests that IS/IT is operating mainly in a support capacity rather than a strategic one. An alternative, less palatable explanation is that the IS/IT department is rooted in the past and does not see IS/IT as being an integral part of business strategy.
- *Is the focus of ISM outward-looking on helping the business plan the best use of technology?* A positive answer to this question indicates a modern approach to IS/IT management. One can look at all aspects of IS/IT, from getting the best management information from existing transaction processing systems to implementing a company-wide communications strategy to enable business processes to be re-engineered and facilitate better links to customers and suppliers.

There are a number of additional factors that will influence the structuring of information systems management. An organisation that operates in a single geographic location will have different needs from one that is spread over many sites (perhaps over many countries). Similarly, a business that has a diverse range of products and business operations may need an ISM different from that of a single-product company. If a large organisation has a number of discrete strategic business units, it may be appropriate to treat each distinct SBU as a separate entity in its own right for ISM purposes.

One must also not ignore the impact of organisational culture and management style on ISM structure. An organisation that has a **decentralised** management philosophy may find it easier to decentralise certain ISM functions than one that is highly **centralised**. King (1983) discusses these issues.

> **Decentralised IS management**
> Management of some IS services in individual operating companies or at regional offices, but with some centralised control.

There are two approaches to IS/IT management. The centralised approach will concentrate all aspects of IS/IT management at a single point within the organisation, such as the data processing or management information systems (MIS) department. An MIS department may either report into a single functional business area (traditionally, the accounting department has been a popular choice) or it may report directly at board level. The modern trend is for MIS managers or chief information officers (CIOs) to report directly at board level in the same way as heads of functional areas such as HRM, sales and finance.

> **Centralised IS management**
> The control of all IS services from a central location, typically in a company head office or data centre.

The decentralised approach recognises that some aspects of IS/IT management are best located close to the point of use. If any degree of decentralisation exists, the inference is that there will be staff located within the parts of the organisation that enjoy a degree of local autonomy. In some cases, the staff will be IS/IT professionals who might otherwise be located in a more centralised structure.

Alternatively, there may be 'hybrid' personnel who have both functional area expertise and good IS/IT skills. Aspects of IS/IT that lend themselves well to a degree of decentralisation are the development of end-user applications, use of report generators with corporate data as the main input, and information systems in functional areas that carry out discrete activities not connected with primary business functions (such as plant maintenance or HRM systems).

For centralised and decentralised approaches there are advantages. With the centralised approach, it is suggested that it is possible to:

✓ achieve and control consistent IS/IT strategy without having to worry about what individual functional business areas are doing;
✓ coordinate IS/IT activities more easily;
✓ implement simpler control systems, since it will not be necessary to monitor the quality of the distributed IS/IT activities;
✓ allocate resources more efficiently, using the benefit of economies of scale and eliminating the risk of similar applications being developed in different parts of the organisation;
✓ achieve speedier strategic decision making because of fewer parties being involved.

Supporters of the decentralised approach also claim a number of advantages:

✓ The presence of IS/IT expertise at a functional level allows for a rapid response to local problems without the competition for resources that exists with the centralised approach.

✓ Where local decisions can be made about IS/IT that directly affects that area, improved motivation and commitment among staff to their information systems is likely.

✓ The cumbersome overhead associated with purely centralised systems is reduced.

The decentralised approach also has a number of problems associated with it:

✗ Where responsibilities are split (e.g. between operational and strategic matters), they need to be very carefully defined if matters are not to be forgotten.

✗ Central management may become frustrated by what they perceive as an idiosyncratic approach being adopted within the functional business areas (and vice versa).

✗ Split responsibilities may result in complicated control procedures which make decision making more difficult and time-consuming. No one location will be correct for all organisations. Indeed, as an organisation moves towards the maturity stage, it will evolve different locations for different areas of information systems management.

For those who get the balance right between centralised and decentralised services, they can expect to enjoy:

✓ rapid information systems development;
✓ harmonious IS and business relationships;
✓ an IS service that is tailored for the user community;
✓ a cost-effective IS/IT function;
✓ development of technology infrastructures that support the required information systems;
✓ business success through successfully implemented IS/IT strategies;
✓ adoption of appropriate IS strategies;
✓ effective change management processes;
✓ encouragement of end-user computing where appropriate;
✓ accurate assessment of IS/IT costs and benefits, thus ensuring value for money from IS/IT investments.

On the other hand, those organisations that fail can expect:

✗ continual conflict between functional business areas and the IS/IT function;
✗ continual complaints about information systems management as a whole;
✗ business decline or inefficient service provision;
✗ lack of interest in information systems by non-IS/IT personnel;
✗ skills problems – either shortages in certain areas or wasteful duplication;
✗ high staff turnover;
✗ gaps and overlaps in the provision of IS/IT services.

Activity 13.3 **Location of the IS function at Security Services Limited (SSI)**

This is an additional case study on the companion web site. You should suggest an appropriate strategy for SSL which is distributed over several sites in the UK.

Outsourcing

Outsourcing occurs when a function of a company that was traditionally conducted internally by company staff is instead completed by a third party. The main reasons for doing this are usually cost reduction and to enable focus on the core business. Functions that are commonly outsourced include catering, cleaning, public relations and information systems.

Outsourcing is a major trend in the development and management of information systems. Analysts IDC say that the global outsourcing market was worth $56 (which doesn't include application services, consulting services, business process management, network management and desktop outsourcing) in the year 2000, with outsourcing exhibiting a compound annual growth rate of between 15 and 20 per cent. Major public and private organisations in the UK such as the Inland Revenue and Rolls-Royce have outsourced their IS management to Electronic Data Systems (EDS). Outsourcing is currently most popular in central government and the financial services industries (Table 13.2).

Table 13.2 UK outsourcing market by sector for the year 2000

Market by sector	Percentage of sector
Central government	34%
Financial services	16%
Engineering	15%
Transport and communications	11%
Wholesale and Retail	10%
Other	14%

Source: Reproduced from *ITNET Index*, www.itnetplc.com, by kind permission of ITNET plc

The ITnet survey (2001) suggests that the UK outsourcing market is continuing to grow with the total outsourcing market in 2000 being worth £4.3bn in annual contract value, a figure that is up 37 per cent from 1999. Interestingly, the survey also shows a trend towards fewer but larger value contracts with the total number of contracts in the year down by 35 per cent on the previous year.

▶ Types of outsourcing

There are different degrees of outsourcing, varying from total outsourcing to partial management of services. It is best to consider the types of outsourcing services offered rather than specifics such as facilities management and time sharing, which are open to different interpretations. The main categories of services that can be managed include:

1 *Hardware outsourcing.* This may involve renting time on a high-capacity mainframe computer. Effectively, the company is sharing the expense of purchasing and maintaining the network with other companies that are also signed up to an outsourcing contract. This arrangement is sometimes known as a **time-sharing** contract.
2 *Network management.* Network management may also be involved when managing hardware: here a third party is responsible for maintaining the network. This is often referred to as **facilities management** or FM, and may also include management of PC and server hardware.
3 *Outsourcing systems development.* When specialised programs are required by a business, it is necessary either to develop bespoke software or to modify existing systems. This is also a significant outsourcing activity. When EDS undertook its contract with

Information systems outsourcing
All or part of the information systems services of a company are subcontracted to a third party.

Time sharing
The processing and storage capacity of a mainframe computer is rented to several companies using a leasing arrangement.

Facilities management (FM)
The management of a range of IT services by an outsourcing provider. These commonly include network management and associated software and hardware.

the Inland Revenue in the UK, one of its main tasks was to write the software to deal with changes to the way in which tax forms were submitted.

4 *IS support.* A company helpdesk can be outsourced to a third party. This could cover answering queries about operating systems, office applications or specific company applications. It could also include fixing problems, in which case an on-site presence would be required. Microsoft outsources much of its support for Windows 95 and 98 to third parties such as Digital.

5 *Management of IS strategy.* Determining and executing the information systems strategy is less common than the other types of outsourcing outlined above, because many companies want to retain this control. A great deal of trust will be placed in the outsourcing partner in this arrangement and it is most common in a total outsourcing contract.

6 *Total outsourcing.* An example of total outsourcing is the 1996 agreement between Thorn Europe and IBM Global Services. This five-year contract involves IBM taking over all IT operations on hardware from five different vendors, managing 90 staff and defining and implementing the IT strategy as well.

A 1996 report by Olivetti on outsourcing among 700 UK MIS managers at large sites (more than 1000 PCs) showed that a mix of in-house and outsourced functions is most common. Only 19 per cent rely exclusively on in-house services. An example of a company that uses a mixed approach is Rolls-Royce and Associates, which has customers in the defence sector. While functions such as accounting and management reporting systems have been outsourced to EDS, the specialised IS functions and confidential work involving mathematical modelling and product design have been kept in-house.

Lacity and Willcocks (1998) in an investigation of information technology sourcing practices analysed 61 IT sourcing decisions in 40 organisations. In their research, they analysed the outcomes from the three sourcing options that can be taken: total outsourcing, selective outsourcing and total insourcing. Their findings make interesting reading.

For total insourcing the following were noted:

- expected cost savings were less likely to be achieved than with selective outsourcing
- excess fees were charged for services beyond contract
- excess fees had to be paid for services participants assumed were in the contract
- hidden costs existed, for example software licence transfer fees
- fixed prices for services could exceed market prices for the same service two or three years into the contract
- there were difficulties in adapting the contract for minor changes in business or technology without triggering additional costs

Total insourcing, on the other hand, exhibited the following characteristics:

- they were generally successful; expected cost savings could be determined by comparing IT budgets before and after decision not to outsource
- there is a risk that internal IT monopolies can promote complacency and thus reduced performance when compared with outsourcing some functions
- organisational obstacles to continuous improvement may be erected

Finally, selective outsourcing was examined where between 20% and 80% of an organisation's IT budget was transferred to an external IT provider. With this option, it was noted that:

- selective outsourcing generally achieved expected cost savings more frequently than 'all-or-nothing' approaches
- selective outsourcing helped to overcome the problem where vendors or internal IT departments do not have all the expertise needed to perform all IT tasks most efficiently.

Outsourcing is no licence to save money, DVLA learns

Companies often have unrealistic expectations of outsourcing deals because the wrong people are consulted when contracts are drawn up.

The recent news that EDS struggled to deliver a proposed 30% cost saving to the Driver and Vehicle Licensing Agency (DVLA) after implementing a new system for registering vehicle details should serve as a reminder to companies about the harsh realities of outsourcing contracts.

The anticipated cost reduction was a key feature of a proposal for the £5m Vehicle System Software (VSS) prepared by EDS in January 1997. The saving was to be delivered 'once VSS was implemented' in October 1999, according to the outsourced services giant.

Experts believe that it is too simple to point the finger at outsourcing companies and accuse them of under-performing. Robert Morgan, chief executive of outsourcing consultancy Morgan Chambers, said, 'We see this all the time. In 80% of the cases it is the client who is wholly responsible for the savings not being achieved.'

He estimates that less than 10% of the problems that occur in outsourcing contracts can actually be blamed on the outsourcing company.

Charles Symons, director of Software Measurement Services, highlighted the need for IT experts to become involved in drawing up the contracts.

He said, 'Generally the problem is that when organisations outsource, the contract is drawn up by lawyers and accountants who haven't a clue about controlling value for money in the likes of software acquisition.'

According to Morgan, one of the biggest problems in outsourcing deals is that clients do not have sufficient control mechanisms to cope with changes in their contracts with outsourcing companies. With his company undertaking in the region of 40 outsourcing audits for businesses each year, Morgan feels that users need to push for more transparent contracts to prove that the supplier really has delivered what was ordered.

There is a pressing need for companies to devise procedures to measure the effectiveness of outsourcing deals. Even some of the biggest deals are not without their problems.

Last year a report from the National Audit Office (NAO) on EDS's £2.4bn 10-year deal with the Inland Revenue warned that it was difficult to prove that the contract had delivered value for money. The report, which was generally positive about the partnership between the two organisations, also suggested that benchmarking against other IT service providers could give an indication of the comparative value offered by EDS.

This is an important point; the report advocated the use of external expertise to address what it described as 'difficulties in obtaining usable comparative information from other information technology providers'. Companies should be prepared to compile information from a range of sources to help work out the ongoing value of outsourcing deals.

For long-term deals such as the one between EDS and the Inland Revenue, it goes without saying that companies need to do some serious forward planning. The NAO warned, 'Although there are incentives in the contract to improve efficiency, these may be insufficient to keep pace with the market over the 10-year life of the partnership.'

Businesses should always set up their contracts to ensure that they are getting the value for money they originally envisaged. Symons argued that there are a number of procedures that businesses can employ to guarantee this, especially where software is concerned. He believes that there are three main components of value that need to be measured and controlled, namely productivity, speed of delivery and quality. Symons admits that productivity usually gets the most attention but warns that businesses need to measure and control all three parameters.

When it comes to measuring the value for money delivered by a specific software, Symons advocates the use of a technique called function point analysis. First developed in the late 1970s, the system involves classifying the components of the software requirements and specifications, and weighting them according to specific rules. 'In a long-term outsourcing contract, use of these methods combined with checking performance against external benchmarks is the only way to ensure continuing and improving value for money', Symons said. There is no excuse for not doing so, especially when large sums of public money are at stake, he said.

On a more basic level, companies should make sure that they have done all their homework before a deal is even signed. There are many eventualities to consider before putting pen to paper. These range from delays in the project delivery to external factors such as unforeseen events that could affect the project. Morgan said, 'Preparation and understanding are pivotal to what you are trying to achieve.'

If businesses don't prepare properly there is a good chance that they will end up with egg on their faces.

For its part, the DVLA argued that it seeks value for money in all its contracts. A spokesman explained that the agency rigorously scrutinises all IT proposals to ensure that the solutions provide 'value for money and fitness for purpose'.

And a spokesman for EDS told Computer Weekly last week that the original contract for the VSS system was not predicated on the 30% potential reduction.

Source: James Rogers, courtesy of *Computer Weekly*, 6 September 2001

▶ Why do companies outsource?

The main reasons for IS outsourcing are to achieve the following:

- *Cost reduction*. An outsourcing vendor can share its assets, such as mainframes and staff, between different companies and achieve economies of scale. It is also argued by outsourcing vendors that lower costs are achieved since they are in a contractual relationship, unlike most internal providers of IT services.
- *Quality improvements and customer satisfaction*. Through outsourcing IS functions to a company that is expert in this field, it should be possible to deliver better-quality services to internal and external customers. Better quality could be in the form of systems that are more reliable and have appropriate features, a more reliable company network and better phone support.
- *Enables focus on core business*. A company can concentrate its expertise on what it is familiar with, i.e. its market and customers, rather than being distracted by information systems development. This particular argument is weak in some industries such as the financial services sector where information systems are critical to operating in a particular market.
- *Reduce risk of project failure*. Owing to the contract, there is more pressure on the supplier compared with internal developers to deliver a quality product on time, hence it is more likely to succeed.
- *Implementation of a strategic objective*. To implement a strategic objective may involve considerable risk if it is undertaken internally or resources are not available. For example, in the mid-1990s many companies undertook outsourcing to ensure that the 'millennium bug' could be fixed by using a third party with the expertise to solve the problem. Similarly, in the mid-1990s many companies were undertaking business process re-engineering initiatives that often involved major changes to information systems.

Reasons for outsourcing

The top 10 reasons companies outsource (in alphabetical order), according to the Outsourcing Institute:

1 Accelerate re-engineering benefits.
2 Access to world-class capabilities.
3 Cash infusion.
4 Free resources for other purposes.
5 Function difficult to manage or out of control.
6 Improve company focus.
7 Make capital funds available.
8 Reduce operating costs.
9 Reduce risk.
10 Resources not available internally.

Source: Reproduced by kind permission of The Outsourcing Institute, Copyright © 1998 The Outsourcing Institute, Jericho, NY

Whether these benefits are achievable is currently the subject of a great deal of debate, with the detractors of outsourcing arguing that although costs may be reduced, the quality of the service will also decline. Since outsourcing is a relatively new phenomenon, it is not clear whether the promises are achieved, but the number of companies signing up to outsourcing contracts indicates that it is a major industry trend. Other problems that may occur are that IT staff are likely to be unhappy, as they are transferred to a third-party company with new contracts. To summarise this section, reasons given by companies as to why they have outsourcing are given in Table 13.3.

Table 13.3 **Main reasons for outsourcing**

Reason	Percentage mentioning
Cost savings	57%
Improved quality of service	40%
Access to specialist expertise	37%
Increased flexibility	27%
Strategic business decision	21%
Free management time	19%
Lack of resources	11%
Improved financial control	8%

Activity 13.4

Activity

Examine Table 13.3 and assess which of the reasons for outsourcing would be important to the following:

1 Financial manager (chief finance officer).
2 Information systems manager.
3 Managing director.
4 Departmental manager in human resources, marketing or production.

▶ Problems of outsourcing

Strassmann (2002) checked on some of the largest recent multi-year contracts for firms that outsourced more than half their computing resources. An analysis of detailed financial information from 1996 to 2000 that was available for eight firms revealed that each of them had delivered declining returns on shareholder equity (ROE), with the average ROE for the entire group declining from 18.2% in 1996 to 2.5% in 2000.

This observation raises an interesting question: is it the outsourcing of computing resources that is cause of the decline, or is it a symptom of outsourcing being used by a business in trouble as an attempt to reduce costs?

Collins and Millen (1995) cite the following concerns over outsourcing:

- loss of control of IS;
- loss or degradation of internal IS services;
- corporate security issues;
- qualifications of outside personnel;
- negative impact on employee morale.

In addition to these problems, case studies seem to suggest that the principal objective of undertaking outsourcing, cost reduction, may not be achieved in many cases. Cost reduction is usually thought to occur because of a reduction in the number of staff employed and savings on the cost of acquisition of hardware and software through discounts available through economies of scale. For example, the UK National Audit Office reported in 1996 that through outsourcing Home Office IT to Sema Group, savings of £23.6 million would occur. However, a survey from the UK National Computing Centre reported that only 15 per cent of managers with experience in dealing with external suppliers thought that outsourcing was a good way to save money, while 46 per cent didn't agree that outsourcing reduced service costs.

Lacity and Hirscheim (1995), in their classic study of outsourcing, identify the following reasons for escalating costs:

- not identifying present and future requirements fully, and leaving loopholes in the contract;
- failing to identify the full costs and service levels of existing in-house operations, with the result that contracts turn out to cost more than originally anticipated because in-house calculations were too low;
- change of character clauses prompting excess fees for any changes in service or functions;
- software licence transfer clauses making customers responsible for fees;
- fixed prices that soon exceed market prices because the cost of IT is decreasing;
- fluctuations in data processing volumes not covered by fixed limits under the contract, and incurring significantly higher fees.
- paying extra for services that the customer assumed were included in the fixed price, because of poor analysis beforehand of services provided by the in-house group leading to a limited fixed-price contract;
- subsidising the vendor's learning curve;
- changes in technology: vendors offer services on existing platforms and subsequent moves into new technology often cost more than anticipated.

These types of problems are illustrated by the *1998 Global Survey of Chief Information Executives* by Deloitte and Touche Consulting Group (Table 13.4). This survey seems to suggest that what are perceived as the desired benefits of outsourcing often turn out to be the biggest disappointment, suggesting that in many, but not all, cases, outsourcing fails to deliver the anticipated benefits.

Table 13.4 **Summary of perceptions of outsourcing**

Objective	% who perceived as most desired benefit of outsourcing	% who perceived as greatest disappointment of outsourcing
Cost reduction	33%	59%
Transition to new technology	41%	42%
Improved quality	47%	51%
Focus on core competencies	49%	41%
Supplier expertise	52%	59%

Source: Reproduced by kind permission of Deloitte and Touche Consulting Group

To avoid some of the problems outlined above, the design of the contract is critical to ensure that the supplier provides a full service. For network management this can be achieved through service-level agreements (SLAs) that specify minimum acceptable values for availability of the network, such as 99.8 per cent access, or give the maximum number of failures per month. It is more difficult to specify in a contract services to be provided for developing software. As a result of this, the costs of outsourced software development can spiral. Further details on defining contracts for information systems development are given in the final section of this chapter.

▶ Human factors and outsourcing

Outsourcing IS developments will have a direct impact on information systems staff and this needs to be managed. In the worse case staff may be made redundant, but in the majority of cases the outsourcing company will agree to employ existing IS staff while a core of IS staff remain with the company to manage the contract or functions that have not been outsourced. Redundancies tend not to occur, because this is part of the agreement between the company and the outsourcer to avoid resistance to change. Additionally, due to shortages of IS staff it is usually possible for the outsourcing company to redeploy staff if necessary.

Even if staff are not made redundant, transfer of staff will cause major disruption and often resentment. One main cause of this is that staff will be forced to sign a new contract when they transfer. While remuneration may be better, terms and conditions will change. For example, there may be no paid overtime, or staff may be asked to work elsewhere in the country on other outsourcing contracts. The Lloyds/TSB case study shows the types of problems that can arise when outsourcing occurs if it is not managed sensitively. As well as disputes on terms and conditions such as remuneration, staff are not happy about the need to relocate. This particular problem has been compounded by the merger of the two banks (TSB and Lloyds).

MINI CASE STUDY

Lloyds/TSB staff say 'yes' to strike action

Finance union Bifu has received a unanimous 'yes' response to its postponed strike action ballot of Lloyds/TSB workers outsourced to IT services company Sema. All of the 91 ballot papers received from staff were in favour of action, and armed with that mandate, union official Hugh Roberts met with Sema representatives.

Now it has a yes vote, the Bifu can give Lloyds/TSB bank just seven days' notice before commencing a strike. The ballot of 103 staff at datacentres in Crawley and Andover was originally due to close at the end of February, but was retaken after the union found it had more members at the sites than it previously thought.

It is understood that staff have received improved compensation offers on those made by Lloyds/TSB and Sema two weeks ago. So far Sema has offered staff a goodwill payment of £1200 and a pay rise of 5% on top of the 3.5% received in January.

The bank has offered the staff employment, but cannot confirm which jobs are available or if they would be in Peterborough or London. If Bifu was to launch strike action now it would occur over the Easter period, and could cause severe problems for Lloyds/TSB customers trying to withdraw money from their accounts.

Source: Courtesy of *Computer Weekly*, 20 March 1997

Positive aspects of outsourcing for staff may include:

- improved rates of pay;
- better training;
- greater career opportunities for improving knowledge and promotion through working in a range of companies.

◗ Making outsourcing work

The critical role of the contract in ensuring that an outsourcing initiative will work has already been mentioned. In addition to this, other factors must be incorporated. These include:

- Outsourcing strategy must be consistent with the business and information management strategy.
- Level of outsourcing should be appropriate to the business: selective outsourcing for most businesses or total outsourcing where information systems play a mainly supporting role.
- A method of retaining control and leverage over the suppliers is necessary. This could include a shorter-term contract, a risk and reward contract, and not including strategic planning in the services to be outsourced.
- Human factors involved in outsourcing must be considered in conjunction with the human resources department, particularly where staff may be displaced or made redundant.
- If a company does not have previous experience of outsourcing, it may be valuable to get an independent specialist to assist in drawing up the outsourcing agreement.
- Allocating time and using measurement systems to manage the outsourcing contract.

Feeny et al. (1995) have identified alternative scenarios to help an organisation decide whether to stay in-house or to outsource. These are summarised in Table 13.5.

Table 13.5 Decision matrix for deciding which IS services stay in-house

Business characteristics	Outsource	Don't outsource
Business positioning impact	Low	High
Links to business strategy	Low	High
Future business uncertainty	Low	High
Technological maturity	High	Low
Level of IT integration	Low	High
In-house v market expertise	Low	High

The same authors cite the following statistics from the organisations they surveyed:

- 80 per cent had considered outsourcing;
- 47 per cent outsourced some or all of their information systems;
- 70 per cent did not have formal outsourcing policy in place;
- only 43 per cent of organisations that had outsourced actually have an outsourcing policy;
- few organisations approach outsourcing in a strategic manner.

These rather alarming statistics clearly show that more than half of those organisations that outsource some of their information systems provision do not have a formal outsourcing policy in place. Perhaps it is not surprising then, that Paul Strassmann has described outsourcing as a 'game for losers'.

Summary

1 Business strategy will embrace business decisions, the broad objectives and direction of the organisation and how it might cope with change – in other words, where the business is going and why. IS has an impact on this and provides potential for competitive advantage.

2 A company needs an information systems strategy that is rooted in business needs, meets the demand for information to support business processes and provides applications for key functional areas of the business.

3 If an organisation does not have a clear picture of what its strategy is, it is difficult to see how the right information systems can be put in place. In turn, if the information needs are unclear, it is difficult to see how the right technology can be put in place to satisfy those needs.

4 Since business strategies have the potential to be subjected to sudden and unpredictable change (or even evolutionary change), the IS and IT strategies that are needed to support changing business strategies must themselves be capable of adaptation and change if they are to continue to reflect the existing business strategy at any time. In reality, IS strategy must be embedded in an organisation's business strategy and be a fundamental part of it. Separation between the two is likely to result in a suboptimal solution, with organisations failing to gain the full benefits that information systems and the technology associated with them can bring.

5 Business process re-engineering involves the radical redesign of business processes. It is often supported and enabled by information systems based on groupware, workflow and relational database systems. While many companies have attempted re-engineering, the failure rate is high and there is a move to less radical process improvement programmes.

6 The alternatives for structuring or locating IS within an organisation range from centralised to decentralised. A hybrid approach is often used with some aspects of IS management, such as IS strategy and security centralised and others such as user support decentralised.

7 Outsourcing is a significant trend in IS management. It involves a third party undertaking some or all of the following IS activities:

- hardware outsourcing;
- network management or facilities management (FM);
- systems development;
- IS support;
- management of IS strategy.

When all activities are performed by the external company, this is known as 'total outsourcing'. When some activities are performed, this is known as 'selective outsourcing'. Outsourcing is driven by a desire to reduce costs while improving the quality of IS and user services. The debate on whether this is frequently achieved is still raging!

EXERCISES

Self-assessment exercises

1 When information systems costs are being considered, what kinds of costs would be considered *development* costs and what would be considered *operations/maintenance* costs?

2 How do strategic systems differ from high-potential projects?

3 Why do information systems projects fail?

4 Explain the difference between *project size* and *project complexity* when evaluating information systems risk.

5 Why might the mechanistic approach to strategy formulation be considered inadequate?

6 How might Porter's five forces model be helpful in determining information systems requirements?

7 Explain how a fast-food restaurant may use Porter's value chain analysis to help determine its information systems needs.

8 How might Nolan's stage model be useful to an organisation that is struggling with spiralling IS costs?

9 Identify three critical success factors for the maternity department of a busy hospital. How do those CSFs translate into key decisions and then information requirements?

10 Distinguish between IS as a key enabler of BPR and as a support tool for the BPR process itself.

11 Using the 'Corporate re-engineering – managing the change process' case study above, evaluate the importance of the change management process within BPR.

12 What are the main different types of outsourcing?

Discussion questions

1 'The millennium bug has demonstrated that organisations, more often than not, take a short-term view in their approach to information systems rather than a strategic one.' Discuss.

2 'Public-sector organisations such as the police and health service are incapable of delivering good-quality information systems because they are dominated by the need to demonstrate tangible benefits before any investment decisions are made.' Discuss.

3 'Far from being the "greatest thing since sliced bread", BPR is simply a vehicle for consultants to sell expensive services that ultimately confer no major business benefits.' Discuss.

4 Would you outsource the HRM or accounting functions of a company? If not, what is so different about IS/IT?

Essay questions

1 Why do many new information systems seem to deliver poor value for money?

2 'Far from being the ultimate enabler of business performance, BPR in reality is only undertaken by businesses that are desperate to turn round a loss-making situation.' Is this view correct or are there wider benefits to be gained?

3 It has been said that when making IS investment decisions, organisations are dominated by organisational politics. Is this really true or are there other, more important issues at stake?

4 Top-down and bottom-up approaches to formulating information systems strategy are fine as far as they go. However, is there a case for a more eclectic or selective approach to the strategy formulation process?

5 What do you see as the main problems with outsourcing, and how can they be overcome?

Examination questions

1 Explain the concept of Porter's value chain and how it can be used to identify a company's information needs.

2 What are the two main alternatives for a company's location of its information systems? Summarise the benefits and disadvantages in terms of cost and control.

3 What is a legacy system? What problems do legacy systems present to IS managers?

4 How can McFarlan's strategic grid be used to define an information systems strategy for a company?

5 Explain the difference between a business impacting and business aligning approach to a company's IS strategy. Give examples of strategy tools that can help support each method.

6 Using the potential business applications of the Internet, show how Porter's five forces model can help identify opportunities for deploying information systems.

7 What information systems management activities would occur with a total outsourcing contract?

References

Broadbent, M. and Weill, P. (1999) 'The implications of information technology infrastructure for business process redesign', *MIS Quarterly*, June, 23, 2

Brynjolfsson, E. (1993) 'The productivity paradox of information technology', *Communications of the ACM*, 36, 12, 67–77

Brynjolfsson, E. and Hitt, L. (1996) 'Beyond the productivity paradox', *Communications of the ACM*, 41, 8, 49–55

Chaffey, D.J. (1998) *Groupware, Workflow and Intranets: Re-engineering the Enterprise with Collaborative Software*, Digital Press, Woburn, MA

Chaffey, D. (2002) *E-Business and E-Commerce Management*, Financial Times Prentice Hall, Harlow

Ciborra, C. and Jelassi, T. (1994) *Strategic Information Systems: a European Perspective*, John Wiley, Chichester

Collins, J.S. and Millen, R.A. (1995) 'Information systems outsourcing by large American firms: choices and impacts', *Information Resources Management Journal*, Winter, 8, 1, 9–14

Davenport, T.H. (1993) *Process Innovation: Re-engineering Work through Information Technology*, Harvard Business School Press, Boston

Feeny, D., Fitzgerald, G. and Willcocks, L. (1995) 'Outsourcing IT: the strategic implications', *Long Range Planning*, October, 28, 5, 59–71

Galliers, R.D. and Sutherland, A.R. (1991) 'Information systems management and strategy management and formulation: the stages of growth model revisited', *Journal of Information Systems*, 1, 2, 89–114

Hammer, M. and Champy, J. (1993) *Reengineering the Corporation: a Manifesto for Business Revolution*, HarperCollins, New York

Hirscheim, R., Earl, M.J., Feeny, D. and Lockett, M. (1988) 'An exploration into the management of the IS function: key issues and an evolving model', *Proceedings of the Joint International Symposium on IS*, March

Hochstrasser, B. and Griffiths, C. (1990) *Regaining Control of IS Investments: a Handbook for Senior UK Management*, Kobler Unit, Berlin

Hughes, J., Ralf, M. and Michels, B. (1998) *Transform Your Supply Chain*, International Thomson Business Press

Johnson, G. and Scholes, K. (1999) *Exploring Corporate Strategy*, Prentice Hall Europe, Hemel Hempstead

Kalakota, R. and Robinson, M. (2000) *E-business. Roadmap for Success*. Addison-Wesley, Reading, MA

Kaplan, R.S. and Norton, D.P. (1993). 'Putting the balanced scorecard to work', *Harvard Business Review*, Sep–Oct, 134–42

King, J.L. (1983) 'Centralised versus decentralised computing: organisational considerations and management options', *Computing Survey*, 15, 4, 319–49

Lacity, M. and Hirscheim, R. (1995) *Beyond the Information Systems Outsourcing Bandwagon – the Insourcing Response*, John Wiley, Chichester

Lickert, Paul S. (1997) *Management Information Systems: A Strategic Leadership Approach*, Dryden Press, London

Lynch, R. (2000) *Corporate Strategy*, Financial Times Prentice Hall, Harlow

McDonald, M. (1999) 'Strategic marketing planning: theory and practice', in M. Baker (ed.), *The CIM Marketing Book*, 4th edition, Butterworth-Heinemann, 50–77

McFarlan, F. and McKenney, J. (1993) *Corporate Information Systems Management*, Prentice Hall, London

Mintzberg, H. (1990) 'The design school: reconsidering the basic premises of strategic management', *Strategic Management Journal*, 11, 171–95

Mische, M.A. and Bennis, W. (1996) 'Reinventing through re-engineering – a methodology for enterprisewide transformation', *Information Systems Management*, Summer 1996

Nolan, R. (1979) 'Managing the crisis in data processing', *Harvard Business Review*, Mar–Apr, 115–26

Obolensky, N. (1994) *Practical Business Re-engineering: Tools and Techniques for Achieving Effective Change*, Kogan Page, London

Olve, N., Roy, J. and Wetter, M. (1999) *Performance Drivers. A Practical Guide to Using the Balanced Scorecard*, John Wiley, Chichester

Porter, M.E. (1980) *Competitive Strategy*, Free Press, New York

Porter, M.E. and Millar, V.E. (1985) 'How information gives you competitive advantage', *Harvard Business Review*, July/August, 149–60

Robson, W. (1997) *Strategic Management and Information Systems: An Integrated Approach*, Financial Times Pitman Publishing, London

Sircar, S., Turnbow, J. and Bordoloi, B. (2000) 'A framework for assessing the relationship between information technology investments and firm performance', *Journal of Management Information Systems*, Spring, 16, 4, 69–98

Smith, P. (2001) *Marketing Communications: An Integrated Approach*, 3rd edition, Kogan Page, London

Smith, S. (1997) 'Outsourcing: better out than in?', *Computer Weekly*, 29 May

Strassmann, P. (1997) *The Squandered Computer*, Information Economics Press, New Canaan, CT

Sullivan, C.H. (1985) 'Systems planning in the information age', *Sloan Management Review*, Winter, 3–12

van der Zee, J. and ke Jong, B. (1999) 'Alignment is not enough: integrating business and information technology management with the balanced business scorecard', *Journal of Management Information Systems*, Fall, 16, 2, 137–57

Ward, J. and Griffiths, P.M. (1996) *Strategic Planning for Information Systems*, John Wiley, Chichester. This book provides an excellent review of current thinking on IS strategy. The strategic analysis and planning coverage is mainly restricted to the first eight chapters, with latter chapters dealing with implementation issues. Chapter 1 offers a strategic overview from a historical perspective. Chapter 2 outlines important concepts in business strategy with particular relevance to IS. Chapter 3 describes what is involved in the IS planning process. Chapters 4 and 5 explore methods of strategic analysis. Chapter 8 describes management of organisational issues including the management of change and the placement or location of IS within an organisation

Willcocks, L. and Plant, R. (2000) 'Business Internet strategy – moving to the Net', in L. Willcocks and C. Sauer (eds) *Moving to E-business*, 19–46, Random House, London

Further reading

Callon, D. (1996) *Competitive Advantage through Information Technology*, McGraw-Hill, London

Curtis, G. (1995) *Business Information Systems: Analysis, Design and Practice*, 2nd edition, Addison-Wesley, Harlow

Hammer, M. (1990) 'Reengineering work: don't automate, obliterate', *Harvard Business Review*, July/August, 104–12

Johnson, G. and Scholes, K. (1999) *Exploring Corporate Strategy*, Prentice Hall Europe, Hemel Hempstead

Kalakota, R. and Robinson, M. (2000) *E-business. Roadmap for Success*, Addison-Wesley, Reading, MA

Kaplan, R.S. and Norton, D.P. (1993) 'Putting the balanced scorecard to work', *Harvard Business Review*, Sep–Oct, 134–42

Kendall, K.E. and Kendall, J.E. (1995) *Systems Analysis and Design*, 3rd edition, Prentice-Hall, Englewood Cliffs, NJ

Lewis, P. (1994) *Information-Systems Development*, Financial Times Pitman Publishing, London

Lickert, Paul S. (1997), *Management Information Systems: A Strategic Leadership Approach*, Dryden Press, London

Patching, D. (1990) *Practical Soft Systems Analysis*, Financial Times Pitman Publishing, London

Van der Zee, J. and de Jong, B. (1999) 'Alignment is not enough: integrating business and information technology management with the balanced business scorecard', *Journal of Management Information Systems*, Fall, 16, 2, 137–57

Willcocks, L. and Plant, R. (2000) 'Business Internet strategy – moving to the Net', in L. Willcocks and C. Sauer (eds) *Moving to E-business*, 19-46, Random House, London

Web links

itpapers.com A digest of papers published concerning IS/IT on the web. Can be searched by topic, e.g. strategy, measurement, process.

www.warwick.ac.uk Business Processes Resource Centre at Warwick University. A good resource for software tools and techniques used for re-engineering.

www.outsourcing.com Outsourcing Institute web site.

www.strassmann.com The web site of Paul Strassmann includes many of his articles on the Vale of Information and issues such as outsourcing and IS investment.

www.prosci.com Consultancy ProSci provides articles and tutorials relating to BPR and process metrics.

www.brint.com The business researchers' interests site gives thorough coverage of strategic issues such as business process re-engineering, workflow technology, knowledge management and organisational learning.

Managing e-business

LEARNING OBJECTIVES

After reading this chapter, readers will be able to:

● outline alternative strategic approaches to achieve e-business;

● evaluate the relevance of key decisions for e-business strategy definition to an organisation;

● define the main control issues in managing an e-business infrastructure.

MANAGEMENT ISSUES

E-business is a relatively new management term, based on more well-established concepts. This chapter explores strategic issues such as how the Internet is integrated into existing management and implementation issues with creating and maintaining service levels such that the competitiveness of the business does not suffer through problems with the e-business infrastructure.

This chapter is supported by previous chapters that introduce the concept of e-business and strategy:

Chapter 4   provides a brief introduction to the features of software used to access the Internet, such as e-mail and web browsers.

Chapter 5   introduces the Internet – its history and standards.

Chapter 6   introduces e-business and the Internet applications of the e-business.

Chapter 13   defines a traditional approach to information systems strategy.

Chapter 15   describes some of the methods of securing information transmitted over inter-organisational networks.

Introduction

The rapid adoption of the Internet for business use is one of the most dramatic changes in the short history of computing. The use of Internet technologies for e-business support of internal business processes and to manage relationships with customers, suppliers and other partners is now an integral part of business operations (see Fig. 6.1). This chapter explores the management issues involved with creating and managing the e-business. It addresses two main issues: first, how should a strategy be developed to integrate the use of the Internet-based technologies into an organisation? Secondly, what are the practical issues involved with creating and maintaining the e-business?

The concept of e-business was explained in the 'introducing e-business' section of Chapter 6. **E-business** is the use of information and communications technology to manage the full range of its internal processes and their interface with external partners. Its scope, which includes buy-side e-commerce, sell-side e-commerce and internal processes is summarised in Figure 6.1.

E-business
....
All electronically mediated information exchanges, both within an organisation and with external stakeholders supporting the range of business processes.

E-business strategy

Developing an e-business strategy requires a fusion of existing approaches to business and information systems strategy development. In addition to elements of traditional strategy approaches, innovative techniques to achieve competitive advantage must also be incorporated. This innovative element of strategy is, perhaps, the most difficult to achieve since, at the time of writing, few businesses have completed the transformation to an e-business. The issues involved in developing an e-business strategy are based around the four-stage prescriptive strategy process model introduced in Chapter 13:

1 strategic evaluation;
2 strategic objectives;
3 strategy definition;
4 strategy implementation.

To what extent then can this traditional strategy process approach be applied to e-business? We will now review some suggestions for how e-business strategy should be approached.

1 *Hackbarth and Kettinger (2000)* suggest a four stage 'strategic e-breakout' model with stages of:

1. initiate.
2. diagnosis of the industry environment.

3. breakout to establish a strategic target.
4. transition or plotting a migration path.

This model emphasises the need to innovate away from traditional strategic approaches by using the term 'breakout' to show the need for new business/revenue models which are considered later in this chapter. A weakness of this approach is that it does not emphasise objective setting and control. However, Hackbarth and Kettinger's paper is valuable in detailing specific e-business strategy development activities. For example, in keeping with traditional approaches to strategy, the authors suggest that company analysis and diagnosis should review the firm's capabilities with respect to the customers, suppliers, business partnerships and technologies.

2 *The UK Institute of Directors (2000)* suggest the following differences between traditional business strategy and e-business strategy;

- *Planning horizon.* Traditional business strategy is based on predictability, assuming it is possible to forecast the future and to then develop business plans in 1-, 3-, 5- or 10-year spans while e-business strategy focuses on adaptability and responsiveness with implementation time of three months or less and limited predictability.
- *Planning cycles.* From one-time development effort to iterative strategic development since competitive advantage is very fleeting and the pace of technological change is rapid.
- *Power base.* From positional power or strength in the marketplace to informational power where success is based on access, control and manipulation of critical information.
- *Core focus.* From factory and production goods to customer focus.

3 *Chaston (2000)* presents a marketing-oriented approach to 'selecting e-strategies and constructing an e-plan'. This approach can be usefully applied to e-business since it relates to electronic commerce resources, market position and financial performance. His ten-step e-marketing plan is:

1. A situation review.
2. A SWOT analysis.
3. A summary of key issues.
4. A statement of future objectives.
5. A strategy to achieve future objectives.
6. A marketing mix for delivering strategy.
7. An action plan.
8. Financial forecasts.
9. Control systems.
10. Contingency plans.

4 *Deise et al. (2000)* present a novel approach to developing e-business strategy. Their approach is based on work conducted for clients of management consultants PricewaterhouseCoopers. They suggest that the focus of e-business strategy will vary according to the evolutionary stage of e-business. Initially the focus will involve the enhancement of the selling channels (sell-side e-commerce), which then tends to be followed by value-chain integration (buy-side e-commerce), and creation of a value network.

5 *Venkatraman (2000)* suggests a five-stage strategy process for what he describes as a 'dot-com strategy', for existing businesses intending to make use of new digital media. The five stages are presented as five questions for a management team:

1. *What is your strategic vision?* This includes consideration of business models and how to achieve differentiation.
2. *How do you govern dot-com operations?* Governance is divided into operational decisions (production, sourcing, logistics, marketing and human resources) and the trade-off

with financial decisions (investment logic, funding sources and performance criteria (i.e. objectives)).

3. *How do you allocate key resources for the dot-com operations?* To operationalise the e-business which techniques are used for resourcing: commit internal resources, form strategic alliances or outsource?
4. *What is your operating infrastructure for the dot-com operations?* Venkatraman emphasises the importance of the infrastructure in adding value to the customer through functionality, personalisation and ensuring privacy.
5. *Is your management team aligned for the dot-com agenda?* This considers the responsibilities and structures used for executing the other aspects of the strategy such as vision, resourcing and infrastructure.

It could be argued that 2 to 5 are more about strategy implementation than definition. The importance of resourcing and structuring for the move to e-business is a characteristic of e-business

Venkatraman (2000) also highlights the need to continuously scan the environment and so revise the strategy. He says

> *We need to abandon calendar-driven models of strategy perfected under the predictable conditions of the Industrial Age. We should embrace the philosophy of experimentation since the shape of future business models is not obvious.*

The speed at which change may occur in e-business is indicated by the speed at which new access technologies are adopted. Figure 14.1 shows how for the UK, the time which it takes for new technologies to reach a million adopters is rapidly declining. Retailers who can not adapt to make use of the new technologies described in Chapter 5 will lose market share to more nimble competitors and may never recover.

6 *Plant (2000)*, following examination of 40 US and European organisations, suggests that the e-commerce strategy (buy-side and sell-side) should devise approaches for seven dimensions made up of four positional factors (technology, service, market, brand) and three bonding (internal) factors (leadership, infrastructure, organisational learning).

Bringing together the ideas of these pioneering authors on e-business we can note that it does appear that existing strategy elements such as environment analysis, objective

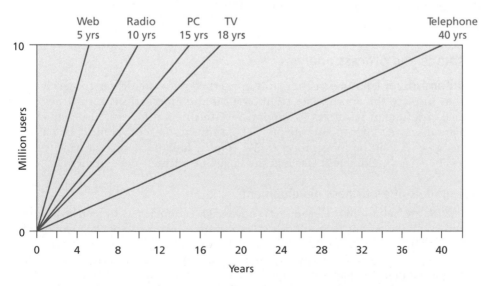

Figure 14.1 Time taken for different technologies to reach 1 million adopters in the UK
Source: Online Research Agency

setting and strategy definition are naturally still required. However, there is greater emphasis on restructuring and resourcing through using new technology to build an infrastructure and supporting knowledge management to achieve quality customer service.

Strategic analysis

Strategic analysis

Collection and review of information about an organisation's internal processes and resources and external marketplace factors in order to inform strategy definition.

As we saw at the start of Chapter 13, **strategic analysis** or situation analysis involves review of:

- the internal resources and processes of the company and a review of its activity in the marketplace;
- the immediate competitive environment (micro-environment) including customer demand and behaviour, competitor activity, marketplace structure and relationships with suppliers and partners;
- the wider environment (macro-environment) in which a company operates, which includes economic development and regulation by governments in the forms of law and taxes together with social and ethical constraints such as the demand for privacy.

The elements of situation analysis for the e-business are summarised in Table 14.1. For the effective, responsive e-business, it is essential that situation analysis or environmental scanning be a continuous process with clearly identified responsibilities for performing the scanning and acting on the knowledge acquired. In this chapter we start with the internal perspective of how a company currently uses technology and then we then review the competitive environment.

Table 14.1 **Factors in the macro- and micro-environment of an organisation**

Macro-environment	Micro-environment (e-marketplace)
Social	The organisation
Legal, ethical and taxation	Its customers
Economic	Its suppliers
Political	Its competitors
Technological	Intermediaries
Competitive	The public at large

▶ Resource and process analysis

Resource analysis

Review of the technological, financial and human resources of an organisation and how they are utilised in business processes.

Resource analysis for e-business is primarily concerned with the degree to which a company has in place the appropriate technological and applications infrastructure and financial and human resources to support it. E-business infrastructure management issues are discussed later in this chapter. These internal resources must be harnessed together give efficient business processes. We start by looking at current resources for e-business by reviewing different stages at the stage of e-business development.

Stage models of e-business development

Stage models

Used to assess the current and future application of technology in an organisation.

Stage models are helpful in reviewing how advanced a company is in its use of information and communications technology (ICT) to support its processes. Stage models have traditionally been popular in the analysis of the current application of business information systems (BIS) within an organisation. For example, the six-stage model of Nolan (1979) referred to in the previous chapter describes the development of use of information systems within an organisation from initiation with simple data processing through to a mature adoption of BIS with controlled, integrated systems. Note that companies will not necessarily progress through all stages in a definite sequence. We will now consider more recent stage models which look at the development of e-business services within an organisation.

Quelch and Klein (1996) developed a five-stage model referring to the development of sell-side e-commerce. For existing companies the stages are: (1) image and product information, (2) information collection, (3) customer support and service, (4) internal support and service and (5) transactions. Considering sell-side e-commerce, Chaffey et al. (2003) suggest there are six choices for a company deciding on which *marketing services* to offer via an online presence.

- *Level 0. No web site or presence on web.*
- *Level 1. Basic web presence.* Company places an entry in a web site listing company such as www.yell.co.uk to make people searching the web aware of the existence of the company or its products. There is no web site at this stage.
- *Level 2. Simple static informational web site.* Contains basic company and product information sometimes referred to as 'brochureware'.
- *Level 3. Simple interactive site.* Users are able to search the site and make queries to retrieve information such as product availability and pricing. Queries by e-mail may also be supported.
- *Level 4. Interactive site supporting transactions with users.* The functions offered will vary according to company. They will usually be limited to online buying. Other functions might include an interactive customer service helpdesk which is linked into direct marketing objectives.
- *Level 5. Fully interactive site supporting the whole buying process.* Provide relationship marketing with individual customers and facilitating the full range of marketing exchanges.

Note that the typical stage models of sell-side e-commerce such as those above are most appropriate to companies whose products can be sold online through transactional e-commerce. In fact, stage models can be developed for a range of different types of online presence and business models each with different objectives. Four of the major different types of online presence are:

1 *Transactional e-commerce site.* Stage models as described above. Examples: a car manufacturer such as Vauxhall (www.buypower.vauxhall.co.uk) or retailers such as Tesco (www.tesco.com).
2 *Services-oriented relationship building web site.* For companies such as professional services companies, online transactions are inappropriate. Through time these sites will develop increasing information depth and question-and-answer facilities. Examples: PricewaterhouseCoopers (www.pwcglobal.com), Accenture (www.accenture.com) and Arthur Andersen KnowledgeSpace (www.knowledgespace.com).
3 *Brand-building site.* These are intended to support the offline brand by developing an online experience of the brand. They are typical for low-value, high-volume fast-moving consumer goods (FMCG brands). Examples: Tango (www.tango.com), Guinness (www.guinness.com).
4 *Portal site.* Information delivery as described in Chapter 2. Examples: Yahoo! (www.yahoo.com) and Vertical Net (www.verticalnet.com).

Similar stage models have been developed for e-business by Hackbarth and Kettinger (2000) and Willcocks and Sauer (2000). In these, the sell-side e-commerce perspective of Quelch and Klein (1996) occupies the early stages, but with greater organisational transformation and involvement of the upstream supply chain at later stages. Considering buy-side e-commerce, the corresponding levels of *product sourcing applications* can be identified:

- *Level I.* No use of the web for product sourcing and no electronic integration with suppliers.
- *Level II.* Review and selection from competing suppliers using intermediary web sites, B2B exchanges and supplier web sites. Orders placed by conventional means.
- *Level III.* Orders placed electronically through EDI, via intermediary sites, exchanges or supplier sites. No integration between organisation's systems and supplier's systems. Rekeying of orders necessary into procurement or accounting systems.
- *Level IV.* Orders placed electronically with integration with company's procurement systems.
- *Level V.* Orders placed electronically with full integration of company's procurement, manufacturing requirements planning and stock control systems.

A stage model that focuses on these buy-side applications of e-commerce based on the research results of an international benchmarking study (DTI, 2000) is shown in Figure 14.2. The authors liken the process of adoption as similar to moving up the steps of a ladder. Companies start off using e-mail to communicate internally and with suppliers (step 1) before moving to offering product information and availability checking (step 2), online ordering (step 3), online payment (step 4), online progress tracking (step 5), and finally when the e-business is achieved all stages are integrated (step 6).

As a summary to this section Table 14.2 presents a synthesis of stage models for e-business development. Organisations can assess their position on the continuum between stage 1 and 4 for the different aspects of e-business development shown in the column on the left.

When companies devise the strategies and tactics to achieve their objectives they may return to the stage models to specify which level of innovation they are looking to achieve in the future.

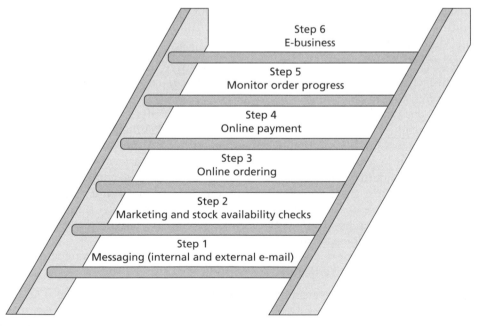

Figure 14.2 Adoption steps of e-business services
Source: DTI (2000)

Table 14.2 A stage model for e-business development

Aspect	1. Web presence	2. E-commerce	3. Integrated	4. E-business e-commerce
Services available	Brochureware or interaction with product catalogues and customer service	Transactional e-commerce on buy-side or sell-side	Buy- and sell-side integrated with ERP or legacy systems. Personalisation of services	Full integration between all internal organisational processes and elements of the value network
Organisational scope	Isolated departments, e.g. marketing department	Cross-organisational	Cross-organisational	Across the enterprise and beyond (extraprise)
Transformation	Technological infrastructure	Technology and new responsibilities identified for e-commerce	Internal business processes and company structure	Change to e-business culture, linking of business processes with partners
Strategy	Limited	Sell-side e-commerce strategy, not well integrated with business strategy	E-commerce strategy integrated with business strategy using a value-chain approach	E-business strategy incorporated as part of business strategy

Applications portfolio analysis

Analysis of the current portfolio of business applications within a business is used to assess current information systems capability and also to inform future strategies, e.g. Tjan (2001). A widely applied framework, introduced in the previous chapter, is that of McFarlan and McKenney (1983) with the modifications of Ward and Griffiths (1996). Figure 14.3 illustrates the results of a portfolio analysis for a typical B2B company applied within an e-business context. It can be seen that current applications such as human resources, financial management and production-line management systems will continue to support the operations of the business and will not be a priority for future investment. In contrast, to achieve competitive advantage, applications for maintaining a dynamic customer catalogue online, online sales and collecting marketing intelligence about customer buying behaviour will become more important. Applications such as procurement and logistics will continue to be of importance in an e-business context. Of course, the analysis will differ greatly according to the type of company; for a professional services company or a software company, its staff will be an important resource and systems that facilitate the acquisition and retention of quality staff will be strategic applications.

A weakness of the portfolio analysis approach is that today applications are delivered by a single e-business software or enterprise resource planning application. Given this, it is perhaps more appropriate to define the *services* that will be delivered to external and internal customers through deploying information systems.

In addition to portfolio analysis, organisations should also review the capability of their technology infrastructure such as hardware and networking facilities to deliver these applications.

Human and financial resources

Resource analysis will also consider these two factors:

1 *Human resources.* To take advantage of the opportunities identified in strategic analysis the right resources must be available to deliver e-business solutions. This requires an effective approach for the recruitment and retention of appropriate staff . The need for new structures and cultures to achieve e-business is covered later in this chapter.

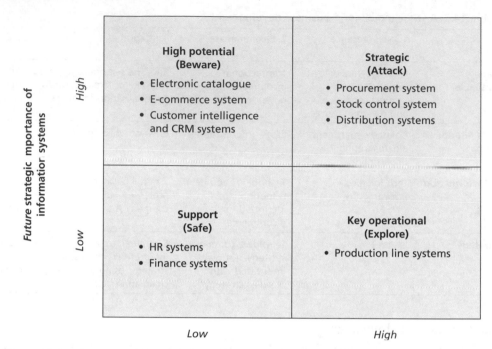

Figure 14.3 **Summary applications portfolio analysis for a B2B company**
Source: Chaffey (2002)

2 *Financial resources*. Assessing financial resources for information systems is usually conducted as part of investment appraisal and budgeting for enhancements to new systems as described in the previous chapter.

▶ Competitive environment analysis

As well as assessing the suitability of the internal resources of an organisation for the move to e-business, external factors are also assessed as part of strategic analysis. In the previous chapter we have already considered some of the external opportunities and threats for a business, but here we consider demand analysis and look at competitive threats in more detail.

Demand analysis

Demand analysis for e-business
....
Assessment of the demand for e-commerce services amongst existing and potential customer segments.

A key factor driving e-business strategy objectives is the current level and future projections of customer usage of sell-side e-commerce services, the demand analysis.

Figure 14.4 summarises the type of picture the strategist needs to build up for each target market. The questions that need to be asked as part of the analysis are:

● What percentage of customer businesses have access to the Internet?
● What percentage of members of the buying decision in these businesses have access to the Internet? How do these vary for different segments?
● What percentage of customers are prepared to purchase your particular product online?
● What percentage of customers with access to the Internet are not prepared to purchase online, but are influenced by web-based information to buy products offline?
● What are the barriers to adoption amongst customers and how can we encourage adoption?

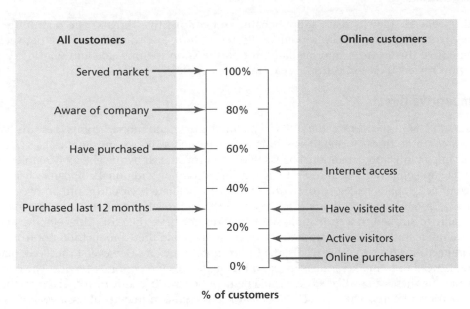

Figure 14.4 Customer demand for e-marketing services for The B2B Company
Source: Chaffey (2002)

For buy-side e-commerce a company also needs to consider the e-commerce services its suppliers offer. How many suppliers offer services for e-commerce and where are they located (e.g. direct with suppliers, tenders at customer sites or marketplaces)?

▶ Assessing competitive threats

Michael Porter's classic 1980 model of the five main competitive forces that impact a company still provides a valid framework for reviewing threats arising in the e-business era. Figure 14.5 shows the main threats updated to place emphasis on the competitive threats to the e-business. Threats have been grouped into buy-side (upstream supply

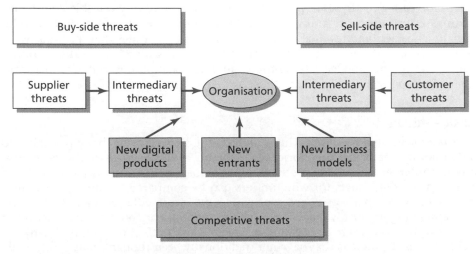

Figure 14.5 Competitive threats acting on the e-business
Source: Chaffey (2002)

chain), sell-side (downstream supply chain) and competitive threats. The main differences from the five forces model of Porter (1980) are the distinction between competitive threats from intermediaries (or partners) on the buy-side and sell-side. We will now review these e-business threats in more detail.

Competitive threats

1 *Threat of new e-commerce entrants.* For traditional 'bricks and mortar' companies this has been a common threat for retailers selling products such as books and financial services. For example, in Europe, traditional banks have been threatened by the entry of completely new startup competitors such as First-e (www.first-e.com) or traditional companies from a different geographic market who use the Internet to facilitate their entry into an overseas market. Citibank (www.citibank.com) has used this approach. These new entrants have been able to succeed in a short time since they do not have the cost of developing and maintaining a distribution network to sell their products and these products do not require a manufacturing base. In other words, the *barriers to entry* are low. However, to succeed, new entrants need to be market leaders in executing marketing and customer service. The costs of achieving these will be high. These could perhaps be described as *barriers to success* rather than barriers to entry. This competitive threat is less common in vertical business-to-business markets involving manufacture and process industries such as the chemical or oil industry since the investment barriers to entry are much higher.

2 *Threat of new digital products.* This threat can occur from established or new companies. The Internet is particularly good as a means of providing information-based services at a lower cost. The greatest threats are likely to occur where product fulfilment can occur over the Internet, as is the case with delivering share prices, industry-specific news or software. This may not affect many business sectors, but is vital in some such as newspaper, magazine and book publishing, music and software distribution. In photography, Kodak has responded to a major threat of reduced demand for traditional film by increasing its range of digital cameras to enhance this revenue stream and by providing online services for customers to print and share digital photographs.

3 *Threat of new business models.* This threat can also occur from established or new companies. It is related to competitive threat 2 in that it concerns new methods of service delivery. The threats from existing competitors will continue, with the Internet perhaps increasing rivalry since price comparison is more readily possible and the rival e-businesses can innovate and undertake new product development and introduce alternative business and revenue models with shorter cycle times than previously. This again emphasises the need for continual environment scanning. See the section on business and revenue models later in this chapter for examples of strategies that can be adopted in response to this threat.

Sell-side threats

Commoditisation

The process whereby product selection becomes more dependent on price than differentiating features, benefits and value-added services.

1 *Customer power and knowledge.* This is perhaps the single biggest threat posed by electronic trading. The bargaining power of customers is greatly increased when they are using the Internet to evaluate products, and compare prices. This is particularly true for standardised products for which offers can be compared for different suppliers through price comparison engines provided by intermediaries such as Easyshop (www.easyshop.com) or MySimon (www.mysimon.com). For commodities, auctions on business-to-business exchanges can also have a similar effect of driving down price. Purchase of some products that have not traditionally been thought of as commodities, may become more price-sensitive. This process is known as **commoditisation**. Examples of goods that are becoming commoditised include electrical goods and cars.

In the business-to-business arena too, the bargaining power of customers is likely to be increased since the customers will become aware of alternative products and services that they may previously have been unaware of, and customers will then use this knowledge to negotiate. A further issue is that the ease of use of the Internet channel makes it easier for customers to swap between suppliers. With a specific EDI link that has to be set up between one company and another, there may be reluctance to change this arrangement. With the Internet, which offers a more standard method for purchase through web browsers, the barriers to swapping to another supplier will be lower. It should be noted, however, that there are still barriers to swapping since once a customer invests time in understanding how to use a web site to select and purchase products, they may not want to learn another service. This is the reason why it is a competitive advantage for a company to offer a web-based service before its competitors.

2 *Power of intermediaries*. A significant downstream channel threat is the potential loss of partners or distributors if there is a channel conflict resulting from disintermediation (see Chapter 5). For example, a car distributor could switch to an alternative manufacturer if its profitability were threatened by direct sales from the manufacturer. *The Economist* (2000) reported that to avoid this type of conflict, Ford US are now using dealerships as part of the e-commerce solution and are still paying commission when sales are achieved online. This also helps protect their revenue from the lucrative parts and services market.

An additional downstream threat is the growth in the number of intermediaries (another form of partners) to link buyers and sellers. This threat links to the rivalry between competitors. If a company's competitors are represented on a portal while the company is absent or, worse still, are in an exclusive arrangement with a competitor, then this can potentially exclude a substantial proportion of the market.

Buy-side threats

1 *Power of suppliers*. This can be considered as an opportunity rather than a threat. Companies can insist, for reasons of reducing cost and increasing supply chain efficiency, that their suppliers use electronic links such as EDI or Internet EDI to process orders. Additionally, the Internet tends to reduce the power of suppliers since barriers to migrating to a different supplier are reduced, particularly with the advent of business-to-business exchanges. However, if suppliers insist on proprietary technology to link companies, then this creates 'soft lock-in' (creating an overhead of switching suppliers) due to the cost or complexity of changing supppliers.

2 *Power of intermediaries*. Threats from buy-side intermediaries such as business-to-business exchanges are arguably less than those from sell-side intermediaries, but risks arising from using these services should be considered. These include the cost of integration with these intermediaries, particularly if different standards of integration are required for each. They may pose a threat from increasing commission once established.

From the review above, it should be apparent that the extent of the threats will be dependent on the particular market a company operates in. Generally the threats seem to be greatest for companies that currently sell through retail distributors and have products that can be readily delivered to customers across the Internet or via post or courier. The test of Kumar (1999) described in the section on strategic objectives can be applied.

▶ Competitor analysis

Competitor analysis is also a key aspect of e-business situation analysis.

Deise et al. (2000) suggest an 'equation' that can be used in combination to assess competition when benchmarking:

Competitor analysis for e-business
Review of e-business services offered by existing and new competitors and adoption by their customers.

$$Competitive\ capability = \frac{Agility \times Reach}{Time\ to\ market}$$

Agility refers to the speed at which a company is able to change strategic direction and respond to new customer demands. Reach is the ability to connect to, or to promote products and generate new business in new markets. Time to market is the product life-cycle from concept through to revenue generation. Companies can also turn to benchmarking organisations such as Gómez (www.gomez.com) to review e-commerce scorecards such as that of Table 14.3. It should be noted that this is an adaptation and summary and that the full criteria number is 175 items per scorecard.

Deise et al. (2000) also suggest a further 'equation' that can be used to appraise competitors from their customer's viewpoint. This is

$$Customer\ value\ (brand\ perception) = \frac{Product\ quality \times Service\ quality}{Price \times Fulfillment\ time}$$

These elements are also evident from Table 14.3.

Table 14.3 Gómez scorecard criteria for rating competitors within the e-tail (electronic retail) sector

Scorecard category	Scorecard criteria
1 Ease of use	• Demonstrations of functionality • Simplicity of account opening and transaction process • Consistency of design and navigation • Adherence to proper user interaction principle • Integration of data providing efficient access to information commonly accessed by consumers
2 Customer confidence	• Availability, depth, and breadth of customer service options, including phone, e-mail, and branch locations • Ability to accurately and readily resolve a battery of telephone calls and e-mails sent to customer service, covering simple technical and industry-specific questions • Privacy policies, service guarantees, fees, and explanations of fees • Each ranked web site is monitored every five minutes, seven days a week, 24 hours a day for speed and reliability of both public and secure (if available) areas • Financial strength, technological capabilities and independence, years in business, years online, and membership organisations
3 On-site resources	• Availability of specific products • Ability to transact in each product online • Ability to seek service requests online
4 Relationship services	• Online help, tutorials, glossary and FAQs • Advice • Personalisation of data • Ability to customise a site • Re-use of customer data to facilitate future transactions • Support of business and personal needs such as tax reporting or repeated buying • Frequent buyer incentives
5 Overall cost	• A basket of typical services and purchases • Added fees due to shipping and handling • Minimum balances • Interest rates

Source: Gómez, Inc.

Resource-advantage mapping

Once the external opportunities and internal resources have been reviewed, it is useful to map the internal resource strengths against external opportunities, to identify, for example, where competitors are weak and can be attacked. To identify internal strengths, definition of **core competencies** is one approach. Lynch (2000) explains that core competencies are the resources, including knowledge, skills or technologies that provide a particular benefit to customers, or increase **customer value** relative to competitors. Customer value is defined by Deise et al. (2000) as dependent on product quality, service quality, price and fulfilment time. So, to understand core competencies we need to understand how the organisation is differentiated from competitors in these areas.. The cost-base of a company relative to its competitors is also important since lower production costs will lead to lower prices. Lynch (2000) argues that core competencies should be emphasised in objective setting and strategy definition.

Core competencies
Resources, including skills or technologies that provide a particular benefit to customers.

Customer value
Dependent on product quality, service quality, price and fulfillment time.

Strategic objectives

Defining and communicating an organisation's **strategic objectives** is a key element of any strategy process model since (1) the strategy definition and implementation elements of strategy must be directed at how best to achieve the objectives and (2) the overall success of e-business strategy will be assessed by comparing actual results against objectives and taking action to improve strategy. Note that objective setting typically takes place in parallel with strategic analysis and strategy definition as part of an iterative process.

Strategic objectives
Statement and communication of an organisation's mission, vision and objectives.

▶ Defining vision and mission

Corporate vision is defined in Lynch (2000) as 'a mental image of the possible and desirable future state of the organisation'. It provides a backdrop for the development of purpose and strategy of the organisation.

The Institute of Directors (2000) suggests that a coherent vision is a critical part of developing an e-business strategy. They suggest the following elements as part of this vision:

● *Relevance* – the company must understand the potential of new technology to impact the business.
● *Change* – the company must be prepared to revise its business model and processes more frequently in the light of the changing business environment.
● *Value* – the timeframe for returns must be determined so that stakeholder value can be protected and increased.
● *People* – competencies must be acquired and developed to help achieve the vision.

Simons (2000a), in referring to the vision of Barclays Bank, illustrates the change in thinking required for e-business vision. He reports that to execute the vision of the bank 'a high tolerance of uncertainty' must be introduced. The group CEO of Barclays (Matt Barrett) said:

our objective is to use technology to develop entirely new business models ... while transforming our internal structure to make us more efficient and effective. Any strategy that does not achieve both is fundamentally flawed.

From a sell-side e-commerce perspective, a key objective is whether the Internet will primarily *complement* the company's other channels or whether it will *replace* other channels. Vision also encompasses the timeframe or the rate of change of replacement;

will replacement happen over a period of 2 years or 10 years? Whether the vision complements or replaces, it is important to communicate this to staff and other stakeholders such as customers, suppliers and shareholders. The clarity of such vision, backed up by realistic plans and actions has been shown to have a major impact on the stock market value of companies.

Clearly, if it is believed that the e-commerce will primarily replace other channels, then it is important to invest in the technical, human and organisational resources to achieve this. Kumar (1999) suggests that replacement is most likely to happen when:

1 customer access to the Internet is high;
2 the Internet can offer a better value proposition than other media (i.e. propensity to purchase online is high);
3 the product can be delivered over the Internet;
4 the product can be standardised (user does not usually need to view to purchase).

If at least two of Kumar's conditions are met there may be a replacement effect. For example, purchase of travel services or insurance online fulfils criteria 1, 2 and 4. As a consequence physical outlets for these products may no longer be viable since the service can be provided in a cheaper more convenient form online. The closure of British Airways travel retail units and AA shops is indicative of this change, with the business being delivered completely by phone or online sales channel. The extent to which these conditions are met will vary through time, for example as access to the Internet and propensity to purchase online increases.

A similar vision of the future can be developed for buy-side activities such as procurement. A company can have a vision for how e-procurement and e-enabled supply chain management (SCM) will complement or replace paper-based procurement and SCM over a future time period.

▶ Objective setting

The relationship between objectives, strategies and performance measures is illustrated by the e-business strategic plan of a typical company in Table 14.4. Each of the performance indicators should also have a timeframe in which to achieve these objectives. Despite the dynamism of e-business, some of the goals that require processes to be re-engineered cannot be achieved immediately. Prioritisation of objectives, in this case from 1 to 6, can help in communicating the e-business vision to staff and also when allocating resources to achieve the strategy.

Organisations must consider the relative importance of objectives for revenue generation and improving internal process or supply chain efficiency. Consider what Oleson (2000) says:

> IDC places most weight in identifying sources of income in the areas of organizational impact and greater process efficiency, believing that too much emphasis has been placed on being first to market in the assessment of income resulting from gaining a competitive advantage.

The online revenue contribution

Online or Internet revenue contribution
An assessment of the direct or indirect contribution of the Internet to sales, usually expressed as a percentage of overall sales revenue.

By considering the demand analysis, competitor analysis and factors such as those defined by Kumar (1999) an Internet or **online revenue contribution** objective can be set. This key e-business objective states the percentage of company revenue *directly* generated through online transactions. However, for some companies such as B2B service companies, it is unrealistic to expect a high direct online contribution. In this case, an *indirect* online contribution can be stated; this is where the sale is influenced by the

Table 14.4 Objectives, strategies and performance indicators for a B2B company (in order of priority)

Objectives					
1 Develop revenue from new geographical markets	2 Increase revenue from smaller-scale purchases from retailers	3 Ensure retention of key account customers	4 Improve efficiency of sourcing raw materials	5 Reduce time to market and costs for new product development	6 Protect and increase efficiency of distributor and partner network
Strategies to achieve goals					
Create e-commerce facility for standard products and assign agents to these markets	Create e-commerce facility for standard products	Soft lock-in by developing extranet facilities. Continued support from sales reps	Develop e-procurement system	Use collaboration and project management tools	Create partner extranet and aim for paperless support
Key performance indicators (critical success factors)					
Achieve combined revenue of £1m by year-end. Online revenue contribution of 70%	Increase sales through retailers from 15% to 25% of total by year 2. Online revenue contribution of 30%	Retain five key account customers. Online revenue contribution of 100% from these five	Reduce cost of procurement by 5% by year-end, 10% by year 2. Achieve 80% of purchasing online	Reduce cost and time to market by average of 10% by year 3	Reduce cost of sales in each of five main geographical markets by 30%

online presence but purchase occurs using conventional channels: for example a customer selecting a product on a web site and then phoning to place the order. Online revenue contribution objectives can be specified for different types of products, customer segments and geographic markets. They can also be set for different digital channels such as web, mobile or interactive digital TV. Large variations exist in online revenue contributions for different businesses (Table 14.5). Clearly the impact of e-business is significantly greater on some sectors than others.

An example of objective setting within a particular company is provided by Goodwin (2000) who reports that UK retail group Kingfisher, owners of Woolworth, B&Q,, Superdrug and many less well-known brands, has set the objective of growing its e-commerce sales from £40 million in 2000 to £1.5 billion by 2004, this representing 10% of group sales. To achieve this it has created a separate e-business division known as eKingfisher. Company sites such as DIY retailer B&Q have moved up the technology adoption ladder from an informational site to a transactional site. The company has

Table 14.5 Variations in online revenue contribution

Organisation	Sector	Online contribution	Overall turnover
Cisco	Networking hardware	90%	$19bn
EasyJet	Air travle	85%	£264m
Dell	Computers	48%	$25bn
Lands End Clothing	Clothing	11%	$1.3bn
Book Club Associates	Books	10%	£100m
Electrocomponents	Electronics	7%	£761 group
Domino's Pizza	Food	3.4%	£76m
Tesco	Grocery	1.4%	£18.4 bn
Thomas Cook	Travel	<1%	£1.8bn

Source: Company web sites, end 2000

also set objectives for using IT further up its supply chain. Woolworth is installing a SAP system to link its web site and interactive TV channels with its financial and stock management systems and B&Q is using a similar approach. In 2001, Kingfisher had to revise these objectives due to disappointing results from new channels suggesting deficiencies in the analysis for this particular sector.

Activity 14.1

Assessing the significance of digital channels

Purpose

To illustrate the issues involved with assessing the suitability of the Internet for e-commerce

Table 14.6 Vision of online revenue contribution for different sectors

Products/services	Now	2 years	5 years	10 years
Example. Cars, US				
Direct online sales	5%	10%	25%	50%
Indirect online sales	50%	70%	90%	95%
Financial services				
Direct online sales				
Indirect online sales				
Clothing				
Direct online sales				
Indirect online sales				
Business office supplies				
Direct online sales				
Indirect online sales				

Activity

For each of the products in Table 14.6, assess the suitability of the Internet for delivery of the product or service and position it on the grid in Figure 14.6 with justification and make estimates in Table 14.6 for the direct and indirect online revenue contribution in 5 and 10 years' time for different products in your country. Choose specific products within each category.

An equivalent buy-side measure to the online revenue contribution is the proportion of procurement that is achieved online. Deise et al. (2000) note the three business objectives for procuring materials and services should be improving supplier performance, reducing cycle time and cost for indirect procurement and reducing total acquisition costs. Metrics can be developed for each of these.

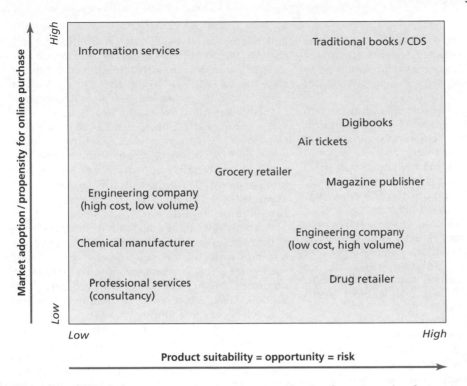

Figure 14.6 **Grid of product suitability against market adoption for transactional e-commerce (online purchases)**

Source: Chaffey (2002)

CASE STUDY 14.1

Sandvik Steel – the challenge of becoming an e-business

When dotcom mania was at its height, so-called old economy companies, such as Sweden's Sandvik, tended to be overshadowed as the brash new online stars took the limelight.

But now that the collapse of Internet and other technology stocks has injected a harsh dose of reality into the stock market and business scene, many established names are back in favour again.

As the experience of Sandvik, founded in 1862, shows, skilful use of the Internet can lead to huge improvements in links with customers and suppliers, bringing considerable cost savings.

Based north of Stockholm in Sandviken, the company's activities seem remote from the virtual world of the Internet. It makes cutting tools, specialty steels and mining and construction equipment.

However, the group – which last year raised turnover by 12 per cent to SKr44bn ($4.3bn) and earnings per share by 34 per cent – is a long-time advocate of IT. Its annual IT budget is some SKr1bn.

'We first formulated our IT strategy in 1969', says Clas Ake Hedstrom, the chief executive. 'We didn't foresee the Internet.' Only recently, he adds, has IT moved from serving the company to benefiting customers.

Transferring its 30-year-old IT experience to the age of the web requires more than a deep understanding of technology, says Arnfinn Fredriksson, director of Internet business development at the group's Coromant tooling business.

'The major challenges are not IT and systems, but "soft" things such as attitudes, insights and getting people to understand and accept that this is part of their daily work.' This means focusing hard on business needs and cutting through the Internet hype.

Sandvik Steel, the specialty steel operation, also goes beyond transactions to find solutions for its customers. Its extranet enables users to obtain worldwide stock information, catalogues and training aids, as well as take part in online discussions.

▶

At both Coromant and Sandvik Steel, e-business activities are mainly directed towards enhancing links with customers. 'Customer value comes when our product is used, not when it is purchased', Mr Fredriksson says.

Thus, Coromant allows customers not only to buy tools over the web but also to design their own products – within parameters set by Coromant – and receive advice on how best to use them.

Choosing the right cutting tools and using them effectively can save around 10 per cent of the total cost of manufactured components. The e-business strategy had to take account of this.

It also had to avoid channel conflict, the bypassing of its traditional sales outlets. Most Coromant tools are sold directly to customers, but 40 per cent goes through resellers. Moreover, there are big regional variations; more than 80 per cent of sales in the Nordic region are direct, while most North American sales are indirect.

The company's approach was to work with the traditional sales channels. 'So many companies try to bypass traditional channels and lose sales and relationships', Mr Fredriksson says.

It is the relationship with the customer – including greater personalisation and an extended reach into global markets – which will be the most important pillar of its e-business strategy in the long term, he says.

This is what provides real competitive advantage. Shifting existing customers to the Internet, winning new ones and saving costs are also important. But other companies will be doing the same.

At present, only a small part of Coromant's orders are transacted over the web. Nordic countries are leading the way. Around 20 per cent of all orders from Denmark are online and 31 per cent of those from Sweden.

The proportion in the US, however, is only 3 per cent, since most business goes through distributors and is conducted by EDI (electronic data interchange), the pre-Internet means of e-commerce.

Over the next six months, the company hopes to raise the US figure to 40 per cent. Mr Fredriksson hopes that in two years, between 40 and 50 per cent of total orders will come via the web.

To enhance its online service to customers, Coromant plans to offer each one a personalised web page. This will enable the company to offer new products, materials and advice on productivity improvements. Training will also be part of this expanded web offering, which Coromant aims to have in place later this year.

For both Coromant and Sandvik Steel, the value of the web lies in strengthening and expanding relationships with customers. In the case of Coromant, with some 25,000 standard products, there are numerous customers buying low volumes. With Sandvik Steel, however, a small number of customers buys a high volume of products.

'Our aim is to have 200 key customers using the extranet at the end of June 2001', says Annika Roos, marketing manager at Sandvik Steel. 'By the end of December, 2001, we want a confirmation from at least 80 per cent of key customers that they consider the extranet to be a major reason to deal with Sandvik.'

By putting the Internet at the heart of its business, the Sandvik group intends to penetrate deeply into the minds and ambitions of its customers. 'The challenge is not just doing e-business, it is *becoming* an e-business', she adds.

Questions

1 Summarise how Sandvik Steel has been transformed through e-business.

2 What are some of the risks of e-business that need to be managed that are highlighted by the article?

Source: Andrew Fisher, *Financial Times*, 4 June 2001

Strategy definition

Strategy definition
....
Formulation, review and selection of strategies to achieve strategic objectives.

The **definition of strategy** is driven by the objectives and vision referred to in the previous sections. As strategy is formulated based on vision and objectives it is necessary to frequently revisit and revise them.

In this section the key strategic decisions faced by a management team developing e-business strategy are reviewed. For each the areas of strategy definition that we cover, managers will generate different options, review them and select the most appropriate. As you read through the seven key decisions, think about how these decisions are going to vary according to the many different organisational characteristics such as B2C or

B2B, physical products or intangible services or mixed, size of organisation, stage in product lifecycle, market penetration, not-for-profit, etc.

▶ Decision 1: E-business priorities

The e-business strategy must be directed according to the priority of different strategic objectives such as those in Table 14.4. If the priorities are on the sell-side, as are objectives 1 to 3 in Table 14.4, then the strategy must be to direct resources at these objectives. For a B2B company that is well known in its marketplace worldwide and cannot offer products to new markets an emphasis on *buy-side* e-commerce and the value chain may be more appropriate.

E-business strategy priorities can be summarised, as Gulati and Garino (2000) have said, by *'Getting the right mix of bricks and clicks'*. This expression usually refers to sell-side e-commerce. The general options for the mix of 'bricks and clicks' are shown in Figure 14.7. This shows that strategic e-commerce alternatives for companies should be selected according to the percentage of the target market using the channel and the commitment of the company. The idea is that the commitment should mirror the readiness of consumers to use the new medium. If the objective is to achieve a high online revenue contribution of over 70% then this will require fundamental change for the company to transform to a 'bricks and clicks' or 'clicks only' company.

In the terminology of de Kare-Silver (2000) the strategic alternatives given in Figure 14.7 range from those where there is a limited response to the medium such as 'information only' or 'subsume' in business through to spinning off the electronic commerce part of a company into a 'separate business' or even 'switching fully' to an Internet-based business. Internet-only businesses, particularly startups, are sometimes referred to as **Internet pure-plays**. Although the 'switch-fully' alternative may seem unlikely for

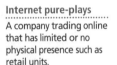

Internet pure-plays
A company trading online that has limited or no physical presence such as retail units.

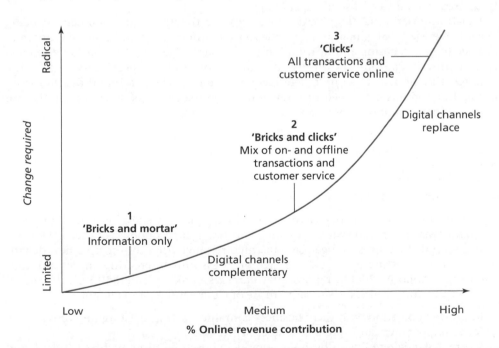

Figure 14.7 Strategic options for a company in relation to the importance of the Internet as a channel
Source: Chaffey (2002)

many businesses, it is already happening. In the UK, the Automobile Association and British Airways have closed the majority of their retail outlets since orders are predominantly placed via the Internet or by phone. However, the transition to a service that is clicks-only is unlikely for the majority of companies. Both of these examples require the phone channel, indeed dot-coms such as Lastminute.com have set up a call centre because this is what customers require, and others such as Amazon have developed a limited high-street presence.

▶ Decision 2: Restructuring

Closely related to Decision 1 is whether the company should restructure in order to achieve the priorities set for e-business. Gulati and Garino (2000) identify a continuum of approaches from integration to separation. The choices are:

1 *In-house division. (Integration).* Example: RS Components Internet Trading Channel (www.rswww.com).
2 *Joint venture. (Mixed).* The company creates an online presence in association with another player.
3 *Strategic partnership. (Mixed).* This may also be achieved through purchase of existing dot-coms, for example, in the UK Great Universal Stores acquired e-tailer (electronic retailer) Jungle.com for its strength in selling technology products and strong brand, while John Lewis purchased the Buy.coms UK operations.
4 *Spin-off. (Separation).* Example: Egg bank is a spin-off from Prudential financial services company.

Referring back to Figure 14.6, the in-house division or joint venture will be typical for the clicks and mortar approach while the strategic partnership or spin-off is more likely to be used to create a clicks-only operation.

Gulati and Garino (2000) give the advantages of the integration approach as being able to leverage existing brands, to be able to share information and achieve economies of scale (e.g. purchasing and distribution efficiencies). They say the spin-off approach gives better focus, more flexibility for innovation and the possibility of funding through flotation. For example, Egg has been able to create a brand distinct from Prudential and has developed new revenue models such as retail sales commission. They say that separation is preferable in situations where:

● a different customer segment or product mix will be offered online;
● differential pricing is required between online and offline;
● if there is a major channel conflict;
● if the Internet threatens the current business model;
● if additional funding or specialist staff need to be attracted.

Additionally, from a technology viewpoint it may be quicker to develop a new infrastructure rather than integrating with an existing one, but again economies of scale are lost.

It is seen that changes in organisation structure range from setting up a new department, through setting up a new strategic business unit to creating an autonomous companies. Simons (2000b) reports that Barclays Bank considered four different e-business structures which are similar to those of Gulati and Garino (2000):

1 integrated operation with the e-business contained within existing line of business, for example American Express or Charles Schwab;
2 separate standalone line of business, a model chosen by firms such as Citibank and Sears and Roebuck;
3 spin-off with the the e-business established as a separate entity, a model chosen by firms such as Procter and Gamble and Bank One;

4 portfolio/incubator, a model where the e-business is managed as an investment. This approach has been adopted by Du Pont and UPS.

Barclays Bank selected the integrated model, which they felt would 'allow stand-alone e-activities in each line of business, while ensuring coordination and integration'. However, this model still requires fundamental restructuring of Barclays operations and IT infrastructure with substantial outsourcing.

Goodwin (2000) reports that Kingfisher have used approach 2 and have set up eKingfisher, a new business unit.

Organisation restructuring has also been considered by Parsons et al. (1996) from a sell-side e-commerce perspective. They recognise four stages in the growth of what they refer to as the 'digital marketing organisation'. These are:

1 *Ad hoc activity*. At this stage there is no formal organisation related to e-commerce and the skills are dispersed around the organisation. At this stage it is likely that there is poor integration between online and offline marketing communications. The web site may not reflect the offline brand, and the web site services may not be featured in the offline marketing communications. A further problem with ad hoc activity is that the maintenance of the web site will be informal and errors may occur as information becomes out of date.
2 *Focusing the effort*. At this stage, efforts are made to introduce a controlling mechanism for Internet marketing. Parsons et al. (1996) suggest that this is often achieved through a senior executive setting up a steering group which may include interested parties from marketing and IT with legal experts. At this stage the efforts to control the site will be experimental, with different approaches being tried to build, promote and manage the site.
3 *Formalisation*. At this stage the authors suggest that Internet marketing will have reached a critical mass and there will be a defined group or separate business unit within the company who manage all digital marketing.
4 *Institutionalising capability*. This stage also involves a formal grouping within the organisation, but is distinguished from the previous stage in that there are formal links created between digital marketing and a company's core activities. It could be argued that a separate e-commerce department may be needed as the company may need to be restructured in order to provide the necessary levels of customer service over the Internet if existing processes and structures do not do this.

Although this is presented as a stage model with evolution implying all companies will move from one stage to the next, many companies will find that true formalisation with the creation of a separate e-commerce or e-business department is unnecessary. For small and medium companies with a marketing department numbering a few people and an IT department perhaps consisting of two people, it will not be practical to have a separate group. Even large companies may find it is sufficient to have a single person or small team responsible for e-commerce with their role being to coordinate the different activities within the company using a matrix management approach.

An example of a company that has implemented major organisational change is Oticon (www.oticon.com), a Danish hearing aid company that is described by Boddy et al. (2001) on the basis of a study conducted by Bjorn-Anderson and Turner (1994). In the early 1990s the company was rapidly losing market share, and its profitability was declining. The board appointed a new chief executive, Lars Kolind, and he took a radical approach to the problem by trying to create an organisation that could respond better to customer needs. Some of the changes he made were:

- Creation of a project-centred approach where senior management appointed project leaders rather than projects being run within a department. Project leaders then recruit from within the company using electronic advertising.
- Elimination of traditional departments – staff worked on projects rather than in a department – this is a process-oriented approach.
- Introduction of staff mobility. Staff would typically contribute to several projects
- Use of hot-desking or mobile caddies, each with a PC.
- Elimination of paper through the use of electronic document management systems for project documents and resulting meetings.

It can be seen that this company was forward-thinking, and implemented in 1994 many of the concepts that we today refer to as e-business.

Activity 14.2

Which is the best organisation structure for e-commerce?

Purpose

To review alternative organisational structures for e-commerce.

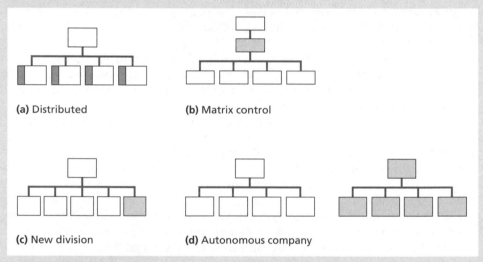

(a) Distributed   **(b)** Matrix control

(c) New division   **(d)** Autonomous company

Figure 14.8 Summary of alternative organisational structures for e-commerce suggested in Parsons et al. (1996)

Source: Chaffey (2002)

Activity

1 Match the four types of companies and situations to the structures (a) to (d) in Figure 14.8.
   i) A separate operating company. Example: Prudential and Egg (www.egg.com).
   ii) A separate business unit with independent budgets. Example: RS Components Internet Trading Company (www.rswww.com).
   iii) A separate committee or department manages and coordinates e-commerce. Example: Derbyshire Building Society (www.derbyshire.co.uk).
   iv) No formal structure for e-commerce. Examples: many small businesses.

2 Under which circumstances would each structure be appropriate?

3 Summarise the advantages and disadvantages of each approach.

▶ Decision 3: Business and revenue models

Another aspect of e-business strategy formulation is review of opportunities from new **business and revenue models**. Evaluating new models is important since if companies do not innovate then competitors and new entrants will and companies will find it difficult to regain the initiative. Equally, if inappropriate business or distribution models are chosen, then companies may make substantial losses.

Timmers (1999) defines a 'business model' as:

> *An architecture for product, service and information flows, including a description of the various business actors and their roles; and a description of the potential benefits for the various business actors; and a description of the sources of revenue.*

It can be suggested that a business model for e-commerce requires consideration of the marketplace from several different perspectives:

- Does the company operate in the B2B or B2C arena, or a combination?
- How is the company positioned in the value chain between customers and suppliers?
- What is its value proposition and for which target customers?
- What are the specific revenue models that will generate different income streams?
- What is its representation in the physical and virtual world, e.g. high street presence, online only, intermediary, mixture?

Timmers (1999) identifies no less than eleven different types of business model that can be facilitated by the web as follows:

1 *e-shop* – marketing of a company or shop via the web;
2 *e-procurement* – electronic tendering and procurement of goods and services;
3 *e-malls* – a collection of e-shops such as Barclays Square (www.barclays-square.com)
4 *e-auctions* – these can be for B2C, e.g. Ebay (www.ebay.com), or B2C, e.g. QXL (www.qxl.com);
5 *virtual communities* – these can be B2C communities such as Xoom (www.xoom.com) or B2B communities such as Vertical Net (www.vertical.net);
6 *collaboration platforms* – these enable collaboration between businesses or individuals, e.g. E-groups (www.egroups.com), now part of Yahoo! (www.yahoo.com) services;
7 *third-party marketplaces*;
8 *value-chain integrators* – offer a range of services across the value chain;
9 *value-chain service providers* – specialise in providing functions for a specific part of the value chain such as the logistics company UPS (www.ups.com);
10 *information brokerage* – providing information for consumers and businesses, often to assist in making the buying decision or for business operations or leisure;
11 *trust and other services* – examples of trust services include Which Web Trader (www.which.net/webtrader) and Truste (www.truste.org) which authenticate the quality of service provided by companies trading on the web.

Pant and Ravichandran (2001) have also produced a similar list of business models.

Revenue models specifically describe different techniques for generation of income. For existing companies, revenue models have revolved largely around the income from sales of products or services. This may be either for selling direct from the manufacturer or supplier of the service or through an intermediary who will take a cut of the selling price. Both of these revenue models are, of course, still crucial in online trading. There may, however, be options for other methods of generating revenue, perhaps a manufacturer may be able to sell advertising space or sell digital services that were not previously possible.

One example of how companies can review and revise their business models is provided by Dell Computer. Dell gained **early-mover advantage** in the mid-1990s when it became one of the first companies to offer PCs for sale online. Its sales of PCs and peripherals grew from the mid-1990s with online sales of $1 million per day to 2000

Business model

A summary of how a company will generate revenue identifying its product offering, value-added services, revenue sources and target customers.

Revenue models

Describe methods of generating income for an organisation.

Early- (first-) mover advantage

An early entrant into the marketplace.

sales of $50 million per day. Based on this success it has looked at new business models it can use in combination with its powerful brand to provide new services to its existing customer base and also to generate revenue through new customers. In September 2000, Dell announced plans to become a supplier of IT consulting services through linking with enterprise resource planning specialists such as software suppliers, systems integrators and business consulting firms. This venture will enable the facility of Dell's Premier Pages to be integrated into the procurement component of ERP systems such as SAP and Baan, thus avoiding the need for rekeying and reducing costs.

In a separate initiative, Dell launched a B2B marketplace aimed at discounted office goods and services procurements including PCs, peripherals, software, stationery and travel (www.dellmarketplace.com). To see the importance of taking the right business model decision review Case Study 14.2. This article is informative since it shows how the online marketplace for car sales has changed during its five-year infancy from the initial success of new intermediaries to the increasing influence of the car manufacturers as they develop their e-business strategies. It again emphasises the need for a dynamic strategy that produces new strategies to deal with changes in the marketplace.

To sound a note of caution, flexibility in business model should not be to the detriment of retaining focus on the core business. An example of business model flexibility is the diversification of Amazon from books and CDs to a range of products more typical of a department store. It remains to be seen whether this results in more profitability. A 2000 survey of CEOs of leading UK Internet companies such as Autonomy, Freeserve, NetBenefit and QXL (Durlacher, 2000) indicates that although flexibility is useful this may not apply to business models. The report states:

> A widely held belief in the new economy in the past, has been that change and flexibility is good, but these interviews suggest that it is actually those companies who have stuck to a single business model that have been to date more successful. … CEOs were not moving far from their starting vision, but that it was in the marketing, scope and partnerships where new economy companies had to be flexible.

So with all strategy options, managers should also consider the 'do nothing option'. Here a company will not risk a new business model, but adopt a 'wait and see' approach to see how competitors perform. The benefit of such an approach is that it is possible to learn from other companies' mistakes and also gauge the market potential without incurring any costs. The counter-argument is that once a company has fallen behind its competitors it may prove impossible for it to regain lost customers or catch up in terms of how to use the new technologies and how to revise business processes.

CASE STUDY 14.2

Evolving business models in the Internet car sales market

Some of internet retail's magic-wand promises of an instant revolution appear to be drying up, and perhaps nowhere is this more apparent than in the US auto retail market. Car web retailing is in the midst of change – again.

Take, for example, this headline from the industry trade magazine, *Automotive News*, published in August: 'Reports of the dealer's demise appear to have been premature'.

The first wave of web retailing of cars is already past with some very notable casualties, including the cessation of operations at carOrder.com and doom-and-gloom parting shots by the former head of Priceline.com's auto sales.

Nevertheless, selling cars via the world wide web is far from dead. The model has simply shifted back in favour of the traditional strengths of dealers, manufacturers and some mega auto retail sites: access to a network of cars to sell.

▶

The internet was supposed to help consumers to bypass, if not to kill off, the unpleasantness in buying a car: haggling with the car dealers.

Buyers would log on to the internet, configure a car to their own specification, or just browse and negotiate anonymously in serenity.

The promises came fast and furious. Venture capital was thrown at new ideas designed to sell cars over the internet.

Hopes were high all around except at the dealers, who became defensive at the thought of their business being undermined. Many started to use the web for themselves.

Many harboured the suspicion that the big car manufacturers were manoeuvring to use the internet as a way of pushing dealers out in order to increase profits.

However, as many dotcom companies and ideas fall to earth, the shakeout has also changed the initial perceptions of how cars would sell and who would sell them over the internet.

The new thinking was crystallised by the recent resignation of Maryann Keller as the head of Priceline.com's auto business. Ms Keller, a former Wall Street auto analyst, who joined the site with hopes of 'revolutionising' car retail, left on a more disillusioned note.

'For car buying, the internet is an idea whose time has not yet come and may never', she says.

Many industry analysts, however, see a bright future in online car retail on sites that can actually improve the buying process, something not achieved by the web brokering or price-naming model of Priceline.com.

That improvement could come with offering a searchable, unlimited virtual warehouse of cars.

This process, called Locate-To-Order (LTO), allows consumers to search an inventory of dealers and the factory to find a match close to their desired specifications.

Transactions could occur through dealerships still, but demand could move close to supply with customers able to reserve cars still on the factory line.

'We think we are going to see an evolution of this process over the next few years', says Baba Shetty, senior automotive analyst at Forrester Research. 'The internet enables some fundamental process improvements, but that doesn't blow up the existing retail distribution system.'

Both General Motors and Ford have offered dealers an olive branch and started to build systems heading in this direction. GM's BuyPower.com launched in October a Minneapolis pilot programme, where it linked Oldsmobile dealerships and offered e-prices. It plans to expand its testing of this system.

Ford has launched a site, FordDirect.com, in which its dealers own an 80 per cent stake and offer combined inventories with e-prices that vary according to region. Other early leaders include, AutoNation.com, and its AOL partnership, and Microsoft's auto portal, CarPoint.com.

AutoNation, the US's largest dealer holding group, says it will sell Dollars 1.5bn in new cars online this year, and is now running a system that could be considered a prototype for the larger-scale LTO.

CarPoint.com has established 3,000 dealer links with a relationship with Ford and has the highest traffic of car sites to date.

Right now it only refers customers to dealers, but is likely to change early next year.

Another big referral site, Autobytel.com, is thought likely to struggle if it does not change, while direct sellers, such as Greenlight.com – which is linked with Amazon.com and finds cars for buyers – also could gravitate to this model to compete.

In five years, Forrester Research estimates that 6.5 per cent of new vehicle sales, or $33bn, will happen over the internet, compared with about 1 per cent, or $2.8bn, currently.

Also, by 2005, internet research is expected to influence 55 per cent of car sales, with 40 per cent of buyers at least visiting an online selling site.

In the meantime, data about vehicles being sold on the internet should be more detailed.

Source: Christopher Bowe, *Financial Times*, 8 December 2000

Questions

1 Evaluate the overall success of the Internet as a mechanism for car sales.

2 Which business models and revenue models appear to be effective on the Internet? Can other success factors be identified?

3 Summarise the approach taken by the car manufacturers to the Internet marketplace.

❯ Decision 4: Marketplace restructuring

A related issue to reviewing new business and revenue models is to consider the options created through disintermediation and reintermediation (Chapter 5) within a marketplace. These can be options can be taken from both a buy-side and a sell-side perspective.

Sell-side

- disintermediation (sell-direct);
- create new online intermediary (countermediation);
- partner with new online or existing intermediaries;
- do nothing!

Buy-side

- disintermediation (buy-direct, bypassing distributors);
- buy through new intermediaries such as B2B exchanges;
- do nothing!

Prioritising strategic partnerships as part of the move from a value chain to a value network (Chapter 5) should also occur as part of this decision.

For all options tactics will be needed to manage the channel conflicts that may occur as a result of restructuring

◗ Decision 5: Market and product growth strategies

Managers of e-business strategy also have to decide whether to use new technologies to expand the scope of their business into new markets and products. As for Decision 1 the decision is a balance between fear of the do-nothing option and fear of poor return on investment for strategies that fail. The model of Ansoff (1957) is still useful as a means for marketing managers to discuss market and product development using electronic technologies. The four options summarised in Figure 14.9 are, from an e-business context:

1 *Market penetration*. Digital channels can be used to sell more existing products into existing markets. Online channels can help consolidate or increase market share by providing additional promotion and customer service facilities amongst customers in an existing market. The Internet can also be used for customer retention management. This is a relatively conservative use of the Internet.

2 *Market development*. Here online channels are used to sell into new markets, taking advantage of the low cost of advertising internationally, without the necessity for a supporting sales infrastructure in the customers' country. This is a relatively conservative use of the Internet, but is a great opportunity for SMEs to increase exports at a low cost, but it does require overcoming the barriers to exporting.

A less evident benefit of the Internet is that, as well as selling into new geographical markets, products can also be sold to new market segments or different types of customers. This may happen simply as a by-product of having a web site. For example, RS components (www.rswww.com) a supplier of a range of MRO (maintenance, repairs and operations) items, found that 10 per cent of the web-based sales were to individual consumers rather than traditional business customers. The UK retailer Argos found the opposite was true with 10 per cent of web site sales from businesses, whereas their traditional market was consumer-based. The Internet may offer further opportunities for selling to market subsegments that have not be previously targeted. For example, a product sold to large businesses may also appeal to SMEs, or a product targeted at young people could also appeal to some members of an older audience.

3 *Product development*. New digital products or services can be developed that can be delivered by the Internet. These are typically information products, for example online trade magazine *Construction Weekly* has diversified to a B2B portal Construction Plus (www.constructionplus.com) which has new revenue streams. This is innovative use of the Internet.

4 *Diversification.* In this sector, new products are developed which are sold into new markets. For example, Construction Plus is now international, while formerly it had a UK customer-base.

The benefits and risks of adopting a market and product development approach are highlighted by the creation of Smile (www.smile.co.uk), an Internet-specific bank by the Co-operative Bank of the UK. Smile opened for business in October 1999 and its first year added 200 000 at a rate of 20 000 per month. Significantly, 80 per cent of these customers were market development in the context of the parent, since they were not existing Co-op customers and typically belonged to a higher-income segment. As well as the new online banking products available from Smile, a secure shopping zone had been developed which is a new revenue model since each purchase made from the site will provide affiliate revenue (a small percentage of sales price paid by the retailer to Smile). Retailers also pay Smile for placing advertisements and promotions within the shopping zone. The risks of the new approach are highlighted by the costs of these innovations. It is estimated that in its first year, costs of creation and promotion of Smile increased overall costs of the Co-op bank by 5 per cent. However, overheads are relatively low since Smile only employs 130 people and it is targeted for profit 3 years from launch.

The danger of diversification into new product areas is illustrated by the fortunes of Amazon, which is infamous for not delivering profitability despite multi-billion dollar sales. Philips (2000) reported that for books and records, Amazon sustained profitability through 2000, but it is following a strategy of product diversification into toys, tools, electronics and kitchenware. This strategy gives a problem through the cost of promotion and logistics to deliver the new product offering. Amazon is balancing this against its vision of becoming a 'one-stop shop' for online retailers.

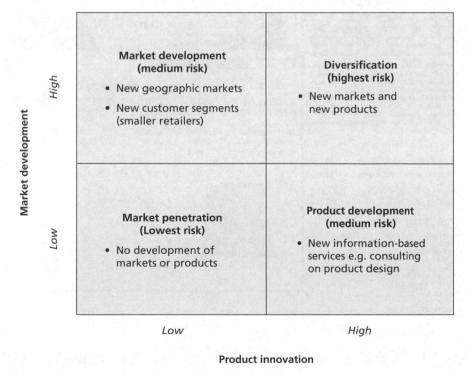

Figure 14.9 Strategic options for market development and product innovation
Source: Chaffey (2002)

❿ Decision 6: Positioning and differentiation strategies

Companies can position their products relative to competitor offerings according to four main variables: product quality, service quality, price and fulfilment time. As mentioned earlier, Deise et al. (2000) suggest it is useful to review these as an equation of how they combine to influence customer perceptions of value or brand.

$$Customer\ value\ (brand\ perception) = \frac{Product\ quality \times Service\ quality}{Price \times Fulfillment\ time}$$

Strategies should review the extent to which increases in product and service quality can be matched by decreases in price and fullfilent time. We will now look at some other opinions of positioning strategies for e-businesses. As you read through, refer back to the customer value equation to note similarities and differences.

Chaston (2000) argues that there are four options for strategic focus to position a company in the online marketplace. He says that these should build on existing strengths, but can use the online facilities to enhance the positioning as follows:

- *Product performance excellence*. Enhance by providing online product customisation.
- *Price performance excellence*. Use the facilities of the Internet to offer favourable pricing to loyal customers or to reduce prices where demand is low (for example, British Midland Airlines use auctions to sell underused capacity on flights).
- *Transactional excellence*. A site such as software and hardware e-tailer Dabs.com (www.dabs.com) (Fig. 14.10) offers transactional excellence through combining pricing information with dynamic availability information on products listing number in stock, number on order and when expected.

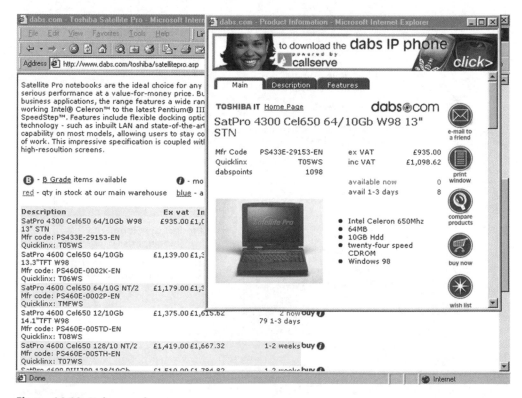

Figure 14.10 Dabs.com home page

Source: www.dabs.com

• *Relationship excellence*. Personalisation features to enable customers to review sales order history and place repeat orders. Example: RS Components (www.rswww.com).

These positioning options have much in common with Porter's competitive strategies of cost leadership, product differentiation and innovation (Porter, 1980). Porter has been criticised since many commentators believe that to remain competitive it is necessary to combine excellence in all of these areas. It can be suggested that the same is true for sell-side e-commerce.

▶ Decision 7: Restructuring the value chain (partner management)

Electronic commerce has implications for whether value-chain activities are achieved internally or externally. These changes have been referred to as value-chain *disaggregation* (Kalakota and Robinson, 2000) or *deconstruction* (Timmers, 1999) and value-chain *reaggregation* (Kalakota and Robinson, 2000) or *reconstruction* (Timmers, 1999). Value-chain disaggregation can occur through deconstructing the primary activities of the value chain. Each of the elements can be approached in a new way, for instance by working differently with suppliers. In value-chain reaggregation the value chain is streamlined to increase efficiency between each of the value-chain stages. Indeed Timmers (1999) notes that the conventional wisdom of the value chain as a series of discrete steps may no longer be tenable as steps such as inbound logistics and operations become more tightly integrated through technology. We have only touched upon changes to the structure of the value chain here, since there is great similarity to the changes possible in the structure of the supply chain.

Reduced time to market and increased customer responsiveness are not simply the result of reviewing the efficiency of internal processes and how information systems are deployed, but also through consideration of how partners can be involved to outsource some processes that have traditionally been considered to be part of the internal value chain of a company. Porter's original work considered both the internal value chain, but also the external value chain or network. Since the 1980s there has been a tremendous increase in outsourcing of both core value-chain activities and support activities. As companies outsource more and more activities, management of the links between the company and its partners become more important. Deise et al. (2000) describe **value network** management as: '*the process of effectively deciding what to outsource in a constraint-based, real-time environment based on fluctuation'*.

Electronic communications have enabled this shift to outsourcing to take place and, as a consequence, the transfer of information necessary to create, manage and monitor partnerships. These links are not necessarily mediated directly through the company, but also through intermediaries known as 'value-chain integrators' or directly between partners. As a result the concept of managing a value network of partners has become commonplace.

Figure 14.11, which is adapted from the model of Deise et al. (2000), shows some of the partners of a value network that characterises partners as:

1 supply-side partners (upstream supply chain) such as suppliers, business-to-business exchanges, wholesalers and distributors;
2 partners who fulfil primary or core value-chain activities. The number of core value-chain activities that will have been outsourced to third parties will vary with different companies and the degree of virtualisation of an organisation. In some companies the management of inbound logistics may be outsourced, in others different aspects of the manufacturing process. In the virtual organisation all core activities may be outsourced;

Value network

The links between an organisation and its strategic and non-strategic partners that form its external value chain.

3 sell-side partners (downstream supply chain) such as business-to-business exchanges, wholesalers, distributors and customers (not shown, since they are conceived as distinct from other partners);

4 value-chain integrators or partners who supply services that mediate the internal and external value chain. These companies typically provide the electronic infrastructure for a company and include strategic outsourcing partners, system integrators, ISP/WAN providers and ASP providers. A strategic decision is required on whether to outsource key applications to APSs.

The similarity between elements of the value network of Figure 14.11 and the traditional value chain will be apparent. But the value network offers a different perspective that is intended to emphasise:

- the electronic interconnections between partners and the organisation and directly between partners that potentially enable real-time information exchange between partners;
- the dynamic nature of the network. The network can be readily modified according to market conditions or in response to customer demands. New partners can readily be introduced into the network and others removed if they are not performing;

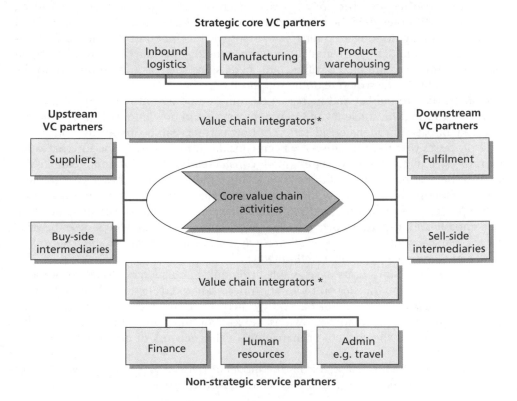

Figure 14.11 Members of the value network of an organisation
Source: Chaffey (2002)

- different types of links can be formed between different types of partners. For example, EDI links may be established with key suppliers, while e-mail links may suffice for less significant suppliers.

In this section, we refer to wholesale outsourcing the elements of a value network to third parties. In fact, the options are more complex than this. The different types of partnership that can be formed are described in more detail in the later section on managing partnerships. Remember also that outsourcing does not simply imply cost reduction. Michael Dell relates that Dell do not see outsourcing as getting rid of a process that does not add value, rather they see it as a way of *'coordinating their activity to create the most value for customers'* (Magretta, 1998). Dell has improved customer service by changing the way it works with both its suppliers and distributors to build a computer to the customer's specific order within just six days.

▶ Towards the virtual organisation

The implication of increasing outsourcing of core activities is that companies will move towards the virtual organisation. Benjamin and Wigand (1995) state that *'it is becoming increasingly difficult to delineate accurately the borders of today's organisations'*. A further implication of the introduction of electronic networks such as the Internet is that it becomes easier to outsource aspects of the production and distribution of goods to third parties (Kraut et al., 1998). This can lead to the boundaries between and within organisations becoming blurred. Employees may work in any time zone and customers are able to purchase tailored products from any location. The absence of any rigid boundary or hierarchy within the organisation should lead to a more responsive and flexible company with greater market orientation.

Davidow and Malone (1992) describe the virtual corporation as follows:

> *To the outside observer, it will appear almost edgeless, with permeable and continuously changing interfaces between company, supplier and customer. From inside the firm, the view will be no less amorphous, with traditional offices, departments, and operating divisions constantly reforming according to need. Job responsibilities will regularly shift.*

Kraut et al. (1998) suggest that the features of a **virtual organisation** are:

1 Processes transcend the boundaries of a single form and are not controlled by a single organisational hierarchy.
2 Production processes are flexible with different parties involved at different times.
3 Parties involved in the production of a single product are often geographically dispersed.
4 Given this dispersion, coordination is heavily dependent on telecommunications and data networks.

All companies tend to have some elements of the virtual organisation. As these characteristics increase this is known as **virtualisation**. Malone et al. (1987) argued that the presence of electronic networks tends to lead to virtualisation since the governance and coordination of business transaction can be conducted effectively at lower costs.

Strategy implementation

Strategy implementation includes all tactics used to achieve strategic objectives. The main aspect of implementation from an IS perspective is the completion of projects to build e-business applications and the management of the infrastructure. The project management issues of the different stages of system development have been described in Part 2. In the following section, we review e-business infrastructure management.

Virtual organisation
An organisation that uses information and communications technology to allow it to operate without clearly defined physical boundaries between different functions. It provides customised services by outsourcing production and other functions to third parties.

Virtualisation
The process of a company developing more of the characteristics of the virtual organisation.

Strategy implementation
Planning, actions and controls needed to achieve strategic goals.

Managing e-business infrastructure

The management of e-business infrastructure can be informed by reviewing two different perspectives of the infrastucture. These are:

1 *Technology infrastructure*. This refers mainly to the hardware and networking infrastructure. This includes the provision of servers, clients, networks and also systems software such as operating systems and browsers (Layers II and III and IV in Figure 13.2).

2 *Applications infrastructure*. This refers mainly to the how the software provision of the infrastructure. This is the applications software used to deliver services to employees, customers and other partners (Layer I in Fig. 13.2).

Alternative models of the infrastructure of an organisation have been proposed by Zwass (1998) and Kampas (2000). Zwass (1998) describes a framework for the Internet consisting of three main levels which are:

I *Infrastructure*. The hardware, software, databases and telecommunications.

II *Services*. Software-based services such as search engines, digital money and security systems.

III *Products and services*. The web sites of individual companies and marketplaces.

◗ Managing technology infrastructure

Management of the technology infrastructure requires decisions on Layers II, III and IV in Figure 13.2.

- *Layer II. Systems software*. The key management issue is standardisation throughout the organisation. Standardisation leads to reduced numbers of contacts for support and maintenance and can reduce purchase prices through multi-user licences. Systems software choices occur for the client, server and network. On the client computers, the decision will be which browser software to standardise on, for example Microsoft Explorer, Netscape Communicator or more specialised software such as the Lotus Notes client or the Opera browser. Standardised plug-ins should be installed across the organisation. The systems software for the client will also be decided on; this will probably be a variant of Microsoft Windows, but alternatives such as Sun Microsystems Solaris may also be considered. For the server, there may be many servers in the global organisation, both for the Internet and intranets. Using a standardised web server software such as Apache will help maintenance. Networking software will also be decided on; this could be Microsoft-sourced or from other suppliers such as Sun Microsystems or Novell.

- *Layer III. Transport or network*. Decisions on the network will be based on the internal company network, which for the e-business will be an intranet, and the external network, either an extranet or VPN or links to the public Internet. The main management decision is whether internal or external network management will be performed by the company or outsourced to a third party. Outsourcing of network management is common. Standardised hardware is also needed to connect clients to Internet, for example a modem card or external modem in home PCs or a network interface card (NIC) to connect to the company network (LAN) for business computers.

- *Layer IV*. Storage. The decision on storage is similar to that for the transport layer. Storage can be managed internally or externally. This is not an either/or choice. For example, intranet and extranet are commonly managed internally while Internet storage such as the corporate web site is commonly managed externally or at an application service provider.

We will now consider decisions involving third-party service providers of the technology infrastructure.

Internet service providers

Service providers are usually referred to as ISPs or **internet service providers**. Providers who also provide some specialised web content to users such as America Online or Compuserve are sometimes distinguished as OSPs or 'online service providers'. ISPs are telecommunications companies that provide access to the Internet for home and business users. ISPs have two main functions. First, they can provide a link to a company or individual which enables them to access the World Wide Web and send Internet E-mail. Secondly, they can host web sites or provide a link from a company's web servers to enable other companies and consumers access to a corporate web site. Note that as well as these basic services many ISPs have extended their services to become applications service providers.

Internet service provider (ISP)
Companies that provide home or business users with a connection to access the Internet and hosting of web sites.

Issues in managing ISPs

The primary issue in managing ISPs is to ensure a satisfactory service quality at a reasonable price. Organisations hosting an event's web site have to have the capacity to deal with large increases in traffic volume. The official site of the Wimbledon tennis tournament (www.wimbledon.org) in 2000 received 2.3 billion hits in a fortnight compared to 942 million hits the previous year, with the site busiest during the fifth set of the semi-final between André Agassi and Pat Rafter, registering 963 948 hits a minute. The official Euro 2000 web site (www.euro2000.org) recorded around 1 billion hits during this football tournament. For these large sites, a single server is not used – the Euro 2000 site was hosted in 10 locations with traffic balanced so that each user went to the closest and fastest location. We will now examine the elements of service quality – speed, availability and security.

Speed of access

Speed of access of a customer, employee or partner to services on an e-business server is determined by both the speed of server and the speed of the network connection to the server. The speed of the site governs how quick the response is to a request for information from the end user. This will be dependent on the speed of the server machine on which the web site is hosted and how quickly the server processes the information. If there are only a small number of users accessing information on the server, then there will not be a noticeable delay on requests for pages. If, however, there are thousands of users requesting information at the same time then there may be a delay and it is important that the combination of web server software and hardware can cope. Web server software will not greatly affect the speed at which requests are answered. The speed of the server is mainly controlled by the amount of primary storage (e.g. 1024 Mb RAM memory is faster than 512 Mb RAM) and the speed of the magnetic storage (hard disk). Many of the search engine web sites now store all their index data in RAM since this is faster than reading data from the hard disk. Companies will pay ISPs according to the capabilities of the server. An important point is whether the server is **dedicated** or shared. Clearly if content on a server is shared with other sites hosted on the same server then performance will be affected by demand loads on these others sites. For high-traffic sites servers may be located across several computers with many processors to spread the demand load. Such arrangements are sometimes referred to as 'web farms'. New methods of hosting content summarised by Spinrad (1999) have been introduced to improve the speed of serving web pages. These methods involve distributing content on servers around the globe. Two rival schemes emerging are Akamai Freeflow (www.akamaitech.net) and Sandpiper Networks

Dedicated server
Server only contains content and applications for a single company.

Footprint (www.sandpiper.com). These are used by companies such as Yahoo, Apple and other 'hot spot' sites likely to receive many hits.

The speed is also governed by the speed of the network connection, commonly referred to as the network **bandwidth**. The bandwidth of a web site's connection to the Internet and the bandwidth of the customer's connection to the Internet will affect the speed with which web pages and associated graphics load onto the customer's PC. The term is so called because of the width of range of electromagnetic frequencies an analogue or digital signal occupies for a given transmission medium.

Bandwidth gives an indication of the speed at which data can be transferred from a web server along a particular medium such as a network cable or phone line. In simple terms bandwidth can be thought of as the size of a pipe along which information flows. The higher the bandwidth, the greater the diameter of the pipe, and the faster information is delivered to the user.

The bandwidth required for acceptable quality of service is proportional to the complexity of the data. For example, more bandwidth is required to download a graphical image in one second compared to downloading a page of text in one second.

Bandwidth measures are in bits per second, where one character or digit, such as the number '1' would be equivalent to 8 bits. So a modem operating at 57 600 bits per second (57.6 kbps) will transfer information at 7200 characters per second (57 600/8). When selecting an ISP it is important to consider the bandwidth of the connection between the ISP and the Internet. Choices may be:

- ISDN – 56 kbps up to 128 kbps;
- frame relay – 56 kbps up to T1 (1.55 Mbps);
- dedicated point-to-point – 56 kbps up to T3 (45 Mbps): connected to the Internet backbone.

A medium-to-large business connects to an ISP using a high-speed phone line such as T1 line. A T1 line can handle approximately 1.5 million bits per second, while a smaller business will use a normal phone line using a modem which can usually handle a maximum of 56 600 bits per second or ISDN which is up to twice as fast.

Some ISPs are not connected directly to the Internet backbone but are linked to it via other providers. Their service will be slower than those directly connected to the main Internet backbone since information has to 'jump' several different network links.

Figure 14.12 shows that there is a large variation in speed of service delivery by ISPs, so it is important that managers monitor their site's performance in comparison to industry standards.

Availability

'Availability' refers to the amount of time that a web site is available to customers. For a company offering 24 × 7 services, it should be 100 per cent. However, inspection of Table 14.7 shows this is often not the case. For an e-commerce site, such as a travel site, a large amount of revenue could be lost if availability drops below 100 per cent. Of course, this will not only be revenue lost from customers unable to complete their transactions, but also revenue lost from potential or current customers who are unlikely to use the site in the future because of the disruption they have faced.

Service-level agreements

To ensure the best speed and availability a company should check the **service-level agreements (SLAs)** carefully when outsourcing web-site hosting services. The SLA will define confirmed standards of availability and performance measured in terms of the *latency* or network delay when information is passed from one point to the next (meas-

Bandwidth
Indicates the speed at which data is transferred using a particular network medium. It is measured in bits per second (bps).

Service-level agreements
A contractual specification of service standards a contractor must meet.

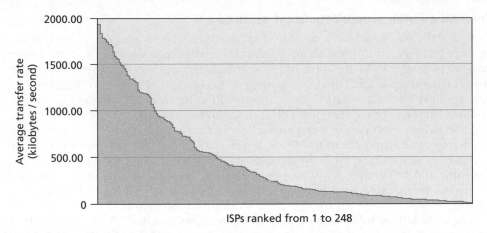

Figure 14.12 Variation in average transfer rate of data from a web server, compilation of UK ISPS from Zeus (www.webperf.net)

Source: Chaffey (2002)

Table 14.7 Variation in download and availability of top UK sites, February 2002

Site	Download (secs.)	Availability (%)
Yahoo	0.37	99.74
Go-Fly	0.47	99.68
BT	0.49	98.95
Iceland	0.59	99.74
Easyjet	0.62	99.10
Worst	7.65	93.13

Source: Copyright © 2002 Keynote Systems, Inc., San Mateo, CA, The Internet Performance Authority®

ured between London and New York: length of time – average). The SLA also includes notification to the customer, detailing when the web service becomes unavailable with reasons why and estimates of when the service will be restored. Further information on SLAs is available at www.uk.uu.net/support/sla. The activity below gives sources where individuals or companies can monitor the performance of their ISP and the case study summarises some of the management issues involved with hosting.

Security

Security is another important constraint on the service quality of e-business systems. How to control security is referred to in more depth in Chapters 5 and 15.

▶ Managing applications infrastructure

Management of the **e-business applications infrastructure** concerns delivering the right applications for users of e-business services. Managers specifying the e-business applications infrastructure need to introduce a system that enables information exchange for both the internal and the external value chain. We will consider these issues separately, but it is a further strategic decision as to whether a single solutions provider is used for both.

E-business applications infrastructure
Applications that provide access to services and information inside and beyond an organisation.

Internal e-business applications infrastructure

Traditionally businesses have developed applications silos or islands of information as depicted in Figure 11.1(a). This shows that these silos may develop at three different levels: (1) there may be different technology architectures used in different functional areas giving the problems discussed in the previous section; (2) there will also be different applications and separate databases in different areas; (3) process or activities followed in the different functional areas may also be different.

To avoid the problems of a fragmented applications infrastructure, companies have been attempting throughout the 1990s to achieve more integrated position where the technology architecture, applications and data architecture and process architecture are uniform and integrated across the organisation. To achieve this many companies turned to **Enterprise resource planning (ERP)** vendors such as SAP, Baan, PeopleSoft and Oracle.

The approach of integrating different applications is entirely consistent with the principle of e-business, since applications services must integrate the whole supply chain and value chain. It is noteworthy that many of the ERP vendors such as SAP have repositioned themselves as suppliers of e-business solutions! The difficulty for those managing e-business infrastructure is that there is not, and probably can never be a single solution of components from a single supplier. For example, to gain competitive edge, companies may need to turn to solutions from innovators who, for example, support new channels such as WAP, provide knowledge management solutions or sales management solutions. If these are not available from their favoured current supplier, do they wait until these components become available or do they attempt to integrate new software into the application? Thus managers are faced with a precarious balancing act between standardisation or core product and integrating innovative systems where applicable. Figure 14.13 illustrates this dilemma. It shows how different types of applications tend to have strengths in different areas. ERP systems were originally focused on achieving integration at the operational level of an organisation. Solutions for other applications such as business intelligence in the form of data warehousing and data mining tended to focus on tactical decision making based on accessing the operational data from within ERP systems. Knowledge management software also tends to cut across different levels of management. Figure 14.13 only shows some types of applications, but it shows the trial of strength between the monolithic ERP applications and more specialist applications looking to provide the same functionality.

Enterprise resource planning applications (ERP)

Software providing integrated functions for major business functions such as production, distribution, sales, finance and human resources management.

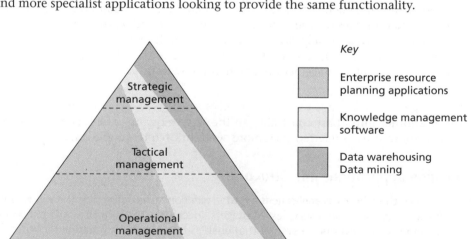

Figure 14.13 Differing use of applications at levels of management within companies
Source: Chaffey (2002)

External e-business applications infrastructure

The emergence of the e-business concept has modified the emphasis of ERP from a mainly internal perspective of improving internal information flows to management of both internal and external value chains. Although tools for linking to partners have always been available, there is now more emphasis on these. Providers such as SAP have repositioned themselves as e-business solutions providers with approaches such as MySAP that are intended to facilitate the exchange of purchase and inventory information with third parties since SAP provides a common interface.

The alternatives for integrating internal systems with supplier systems for **e-procurement** are outlined in Table 14.8.

Electronic procurement (e-procurement)
....
The electronic integration and management of all procurement activities including purchase request, authorisation, ordering, delivery and payment between a purchaser and a supplier.

Table 14.8 Assessment of the procurement model alternatives for buyers

Procurement model	Advantages to buyer	Disadvantages to buyer
Sell-side, e.g. many catalogue-based B2B suppliers such as. www.rswww.com	● Searching ● Onus of maintaining data on supplier	● Different interface on each site (catalogue and ordering) ● Restricted choice ● Poor integration with ERP/ procurement systems ● Limited purchase control
Buy-side, e.g. solutions developed by www.sap.com, www.ariba.com	● Simplicity – single interface ● Wider choice than sell-side ● Integration with ERP/ procurement systems ● Good purchase control	● Onus of maintaining data is on buyer ● Software licence costs ● Retraining
Marketplace, e.g. www.itoi.com, www.vertical.net, www.chemdex.com	● Simplicity – single interface ● Potentially widest choice of suppliers, products and prices ● Often unified terms and conditions and order forms	● Difficult to know which marketplace to choose (horizontal and vertical) ● Poor purchase controls* ● Uncertainty on service levels from unfamiliar suppliers ● Interfacing with marketplace data format* ● Relatively poor integration with ERP*

* Note that these disadvantages of the marketplace will disappear as marketplaces develop ERP integration

Different approaches may be preferred for different types of goods. For example, Kaplan and Sawhney (2000) have developed a taxonomy of B2B marketplaces by applying existing classifications of corporate purchasing, namely *how* businesses buy (systematic purchasing or spot purchasing) and *why* businesses buy (manufacturing inputs or operating resource inputs). They identify different types of marketplace to serve these needs as shown in Table 14.9. Note that manufacturing input marketplaces tend to be vertical marketplaces set up for a particular industry such as steel, construction or chemical while operating resources tend to be horizontal marketplaces offering a range of products to differing industries

A final strategic decision for e-business is required on whether to outsource key applications to ASPs. ASPs are reviewed in Chapter 5. Case Study 5.1 explains how ASPs give SMEs the opportunity to access applications such as ERP which were once only possible for corporate budgets.

Table 14.9 Types of B2B marketplaces identified by Kaplan and Sawhney (2000) with examples

How businesses buy?	What businesses buy?	
	Operating resources	**Manufacturing resources**
Systematic sourcing	MRO hubs ● Commerce One (www.commerceone.net)	Catalogue hubs ● Chemdex (www.chemdex.com)
Spot sourcing	Yield managers ● www.elance.com	Exchanges ● www.itoi.com ● www.vertical.net Chemicals ● www.plastics.net

Summary

1 In this chapter four elements of e-business strategy development were reviewed in the areas below.

2 *Strategic analysis.* Continuous scanning of the micro- and macro-environment of an organisation are required, with particular emphasis on the changing needs of customers, actions and business models of competitors and opportunities afforded by new technologies. Techniques include resource analysis, demand analysis and competitor analysis, applications portfolio analysis, SWOT analysis and competitive environment analysis.

3 *Strategic objectives.* Organisations must have a clear vision on whether digital media will complement or replace other media and their capacity for change. Clear objectives must be defined and, in particular, goals for the online revenue contribution should be set.

4 *Strategy definition.* Seven key elements of e-business strategy that were reviewed are:

● 1. E-business priorities – significance to organisation (replace or complement) and emphasis on buy-side or sell-side.
● 2. Form of restructuring required.
● 3. Business and revenue models.
● 4. Marketplace restructuring.
● 5. Market and product development strategies.
● 6. Positioning and differentiation strategies.
● 7. Revised value chain

5 Strategy implementation. Detailed in the remainder of Part 3.

6 *Management of the e-business infrastructure* involves providing an appropriate technology infrastructure and applications infrastructure to provide reliable, appropriate e-business services.

EXERCISES

Self-assessment exercises

1 What are the key characteristics of an e-business strategy model?

2 Select a retailer or manufacturer of your choice and describe what the main elements of its situation analysis should comprise.

3 For the same retailer or manufacturer suggest different methods and metrics for defining e-business objectives.

4 For the same retailer or manufacturer assess different strategic options to adopt for e-business.

5 Describe the characteristics of an effective e-business infrastructure.

Discussion questions

1 Analyse the reasons for the failure of the original boo.com. Research and assess the sustainability of the new boo.com business model.

2 Discuss this statement by David Weymouth, Barclays Bank chief information officer (Simons, 2000b), who says:

There is no merit in becoming a dot-com business. Within five years successful businesses will have embraced and deployed at real-scale across the whole enterprise, the processes and technologies that we now know as dot-com.

Essay questions

1 Evaluate the range of restructuring options for an existing 'bricks and mortar' organisation to move to a 'bricks and clicks' or 'clicks only' contributing a higher online revenue.

2 Explain the main strategy definition options or decisions available to an organisation intending to become an e-business.

3 Discuss the merits and disadvantages of locating company e-business services inside a company, in comparison with outsourcing to an ISP or ASP.

4 Between 1994 and 1999 Amazon lost more than $500m, but at the end of this period its valuation was still more than $20bn. At the start of 2000 Amazon.com underwent its first round of job cuts, sacking 150 staff or 2 per cent of its worldwide workforce. Later in 2000 its valuation was more than halved. Write an essay on the strategy of Amazon.com exploring its history, different criteria for success and its future. See the *Wired* magazine archive for profiles of Amazon (www.wired.com).

Examination questions

1 Define the main elements of an e-business strategy.

2 You are an incumbent e-business manager for a domestic airline. What process would you use to create objectives for the organisation? Suggest three typical objectives and how you would measure them.

3 What choices do executives have for the scope and timeframe of implementing e-business?

4 Explain why the e-business coordinator of a company might investigate the use of applications service providers.

5 Describe the relevance of a service-level agreement to an organisation that has outsourced its e-mail service. Outline four performance criteria on which the service-level agreement could be based.

References

Ansoff, H. (1957) 'Strategies for diversification', *Harvard Business Review*, September–October, 113–24

Benjamin, R. and Wigand, R. (1995) 'Electronic markets and virtual value-chains on the information superhighway', *Sloan Management Review*, Winter, 62–72

Bjorn-Anderson, N. and Turner, J. (1994) 'Creating the Twenty-First century organisation: the metamorphsis of Oticon', in Baskerville et al. (eds) *Transforming the Organisations with Information Technology*, Elsevier Science, Amsterdam

Boddy, D., Boonstra, A. and Kennedy, G. (2001) *Managing Information Systems: An Organisational Perspective*, Financial Times Prentice Hall, Harlow

Chaffey, D. (2002) *E-Business and E-Commerce Management*, Financial Times Prentice Hall, Harlow

Chaffey, D., Mayer, R. Johnston, K. and Ellis-Chadwick, F. (2003) *Internet Marketing: Strategy, Implemetation and Practice*, 2nd edition, Financial Times Prentice Hall, Harlow

Chaston, I. (2000) *E-marketing Strategy*, McGrawHill, Maidenhead

Davidow, W.H. and Malone, M.S. (1992) *The Virtual Corporation. Structuring and Revitalizing the Corporation for the 21st Century*, HarperCollins, London

Deise, M., Nowikow, C., King, P., Wright, A. (2000) *Executive's Guide to E-business. From Tactics to Strategy*, John Wiley, New York

de Kare-Silver, M. (2002) *eShock 2000*, Macmillan, Basingstoke

DTI (2000) *Business in the Information Age – International Benchmarking Study 2000*, UK Department of Trade and Industry. Based on 6000 phone interviews across businesses of all sizes in eight countries. Statistics update available online at: www.ukonlineforbusiness.gov.uk

Durlacher (2000) 'Trends in the UK new economy', *Durlacher Quarterly Internet Report*, November, 1–12

Economist (2000) 'Enter the ecosystem', 11 November

Goodwin, R. (2000) 'IT vital to high-street e-commerce boost', *Computer Weekly*, 13 July, 6

Gulati, R. and Garino, J. (2000) 'Getting the right mix of bricks and clicks for your company', *Harvard Business Review*, May–June, 107–14

Hackbarth, G. and Kettinger, W. (2000) 'Building an e-business strategy', *Information Systems Management*, Summer, 78–93

Institute of Directors (2000) *E-business – Helping Directors to Understand and Embrace the Digital Age*, Director Publications, London

Kalakota, R. and Robinson, M. (2000) *E-business. Roadmap for Success*, Addison-Wesley, Reading, MA

Kampas, P. (2000) 'Road map to the e-revolution', *Information Systems Management Journal*, Spring, 8–22

Kaplan, S. and Sawhney, M. (2000) 'E-hubs: the new B2B marketplaces', *Harvard Business Review*, May–June, 97–103

Kraut, R., Chan, A., Butler, B. and Hong, A. (1998) 'Coordination and virtualisation: the role of electronic networks and personal relationships', *Journal of Computer Mediated Communications*, 3(4)

Kumar, N. (1999) 'Internet distribution strategies: dilemmas for the incumbent', *Financial Times Special Issue on Mastering Information Management*, No 7. Electronic Commerce

Lynch, R. (2000) *Corporate Strategy*, Financial Times Prentice Hall, Harlow

McFarlan, F. and McKenney, J. (1983) *Corporate Information Systems Management*, Prentice-Hall, London

Magretta, J. (1998) 'The power of virtual integration. An interview with Michael Dell', *Harvard Business Review*, March–April, 72–84

Malone, T., Yates, J. and Benjamin, R. (1987) 'Electronic markets and electronic hierarchies: effects of information technology on market structure and corporate strategies', *Communications of the ACM*, 30(6), 484–97

Nolan, R. (1979) 'Managing the crisis in data processing', *Harvard Business Review*, March–April, 115–26

Oleson (2000) The return on investment Associated with eBusiness and eCommerce. Research report. IDC W21462. www.idcresearch.com

Pant, S. and Ravichandran, T. (2001) 'A framework for information systems planning for e-business', *Logistics Information Mangement*, 14, 1, 85–98

Parsons, A., Zeisser, M. and Waitman, R. (1996) 'Organising for digital marketing', *Mckinsey Quarterly*, No 4, 183–92

Phillips, S. (2000) 'Retailer's crown jewel is a unique customer database', *Financial Times*, 4 December

Plant, C. (2000) *E-commerce*, Financial Times Prentice Hall, Harlow

Porter, M. E. (1980) *Competitive Strategy*, Free Press, New York

Quelch, J.A. and Klein, L.R. (1996) 'The Internet and international marketing', *Sloan Management Review*, Spring, 60–76

Simons, M. (2000a) 'Barclays gambles on web big bang', *Computer Weekly*, 13 July, 1

Simons, M. (2000b) 'Setting the banks alight', *Computer Weekly*, 20 July, 6

Spinrad, P. (1999) 'The new cool. Akamai overcomes the Internet's hotspot problem', *Wired*, 7.08, August, 152–4

Timmers, P. *(1999) Electronic Commerce Strategies and Models for Business-to-business Trading*, John Wiley, Chichester

Tjan, A. (2001) 'Finally, a way to put your Internet portfolio into order', *Harvard Business Review*, February, 76–85

Venkatraman, N. (2000) 'Five steps to a dot-com strategy: how to find your footing on the web', *Sloan Management Review*, Spring, 15–28

Ward, J. and Griffiths, P.M. (1996) *Strategic Planning for Information Systems*, John Wiley, Chichester

Willcocks, L. and Sauer, C. (2000) 'Moving to e-business: an introduction', in L. Willcocks and C. Sauer (eds) *Moving to e-business*, 1–18, Random House, London

Zwass, V. (1998) 'Structure and macro-level impacts of electronic commerce: from technological infrastructure to electronic marketplaces', in K. Kendall, *Emerging Information Technologies*, Sage, Thousand Oaks, CA

Further reading

Deise, M., Nowikow, C., King, P. and Wright, A. (2000) *Executive's guide to e-business. From tactics to strategy*, John Wiley, New York. An excellent practitioner's guide

Gulati, R. and Garino, J. (2000) 'Getting the right mix of bricks and clicks for your company', *Harvard Business Review*, May–June, 107–14. A different perspective on the six strategy decisions given in the strategic definition section, with a road map through the decision process

Hackbarth, G. and Kettinger, W. (2000) 'Building an e-business strategy', *Information Systems Management*, Summer, 78–93. An information systems perspective to e-business strategy

Willcocks, L. and Sauer, C. (2000) 'Moving to e-business: an introduction', in L. Willcocks and C. Sauer (eds) *Moving to E-business*, 1–18. Random House, London. Combines traditional IS strategy based approaches with up-to-date case studies

Web links

www.brint.com BRINT.com. A business researcher's interests. Extensive portal with articles on e-business, e-commerce, knowledge management, change management and IS strategy.

www.cio.com/forums/ec CIO Magazine E-commerce resource centre. One of the best online magazines from a business/technical perspective – see other research centres also, e.g. intranets, knowledge management.

www.ecommerce.ac.uk E-commerce innovation centre at Cardiff University. Interesting case studies for SMEs and basic explanations of concepts and terms.

www.ecommercetimes.com E-commerce Times. An online newspaper specific to e-commerce developments.

www.ft.com/ftit *Financial Times* IT surveys. Excellent monthly articles based on case studies. Also see Connectis for more European examples.

http://ecommerce.about.com E-commerce About.com. Portal about all aspects of e-commerce.

http://www.internet.com/sections/marketing.html Internet.com. Good collection of articles for professionals (mainly technically oriented).

www.ittoolbox.com IT Toolbox. Guidelines, articles on e-business, ERP, CRM and data warehousing.

www.ebusiness.mit.edu US Center for e-business. Useful collection of articles.

www.netacademy.org Net Academy. Business resources, including e-business articles.

Chapter 15

Managing information security

LEARNING OBJECTIVES

The learning objectives for this chapter are that readers should:
● be able to understand and assess potential threats to a computer-based information system;
● propose an overall strategy for ensuring the security of a computer-based information system;
● identify specific techniques that might be used to protect a computer-based information system against damage or unauthorised access.

MANAGEMENT ISSUES

The concept that information is an important and valuable business asset has been stressed throughout this text. The responsibility for ensuring the security of organisational information systems is one that cannot be taken too lightly. In addition to ensuring that the organisation has uninterrupted access to its information resources, managers must also deal with the threat of outsiders attempting to gain access to those same resources. From a managerial perspective, this chapter addresses the following areas:

● An understanding of approaches towards information systems security will help managers to develop and implement an overall strategy for security.
● An understanding of the threats to information systems will help in predicting and anticipating acts such as denial of service attacks.
● Knowledge of specific techniques for protecting information systems will help in the development of effective countermeasures.
● As organisations turn to the Internet for business purposes, it becomes important to understand some of the new threats that must be faced.

Chapter 14	deals with managing the Internet- and intranet-based information systems.
Chapter 17	deals with ethical issues of relevance to the developers and managers of computer-based information systems.

Introduction

The first section of this chapter discusses the need for controls on information systems, paying particular attention to unauthorised access. Having established some of the threats facing modern computer-based systems, several strategies are introduced for ensuring the integrity of an information system. A brief description of some of the controls that can be placed on information systems is followed by a more detailed examination of two areas of contemporary interest: computer viruses and threats to Internet services.

After studying this chapter, readers should have obtained:

- an understanding of the need to control information systems;
- an overview of the strategies that can be employed in order to maintain the security of an information system;
- an overview of some methods that can be used to control access to and operation of information systems;
- an understanding of the nature of crime in relation to information technology;
- a more detailed understanding of some common forms of computer-related crime.

The need for controls

Controls upon information systems are based upon two underlying principles:

- the need to ensure the accuracy of the data held by the organisation;
- the need to protect against loss or damage.

Although this chapter is largely concerned with unauthorised access and the physical security of information systems, it should be noted that many of the issues raised are also relevant to the discussion of accuracy and privacy that is provided in Chapter 17.

The most common threats faced by organisational information systems can be placed into the following categories:

- accidents
- natural disasters
- sabotage (industrial and individual)
- vandalism
- theft
- unauthorised use (hacking)
- computer viruses

Table 15.1 charts a number of major incidents that made national or international headlines over 2000. As can be seen, there has been a marked increase in threats related to the Internet and organisational intranets.

Table 15.1 Why do we need controls? A catalogue of major computer-related security incidents for 2000

January

● The World Intellectual Property Organisation forced to close web site after hackers replaced its pages with the lyrics of a Bruce Springsteen song.

February

● Reed Executive reviewed security on its web site, after it was revealed that customers' CVs could be accessed without a password.

May

● Computer services group Bull blamed human error for a security flaw that left details about its customers' contracts, including the French and Russian police and Barclays Bank, exposed on the web.

June

● Hacker placed an offensive message on the Visa.com web site.

July

● Seven thousand people were advised to cancel their credit card accounts after it emerged that confidential details were freely accessible on the Powergen web site.
● Confidence in Barclays' online banking site was dealt a blow when customers found they could look at other people's financial details.

August

● An organised criminal gang attempted fraudulently to gain hundreds of thousands of pounds from the Egg online bank.
● Names and work addresses of customers registered on the BT.com web site were left exposed by a password error.
● Woolworths shut down its web site after customers found they could read each others' credit card and telephone numbers.

September

● Web hosting company Netcetera was forced to repair a server after it was reported that a security error allowed corporate customers to view each others' confidential files, including customer credit card details.
● Online auction broker E-Trade fixed a security glitch that allowed users to recover names and passwords of other customers.
● Western Union blamed human error after a hacker copied debit information about 15 700 customers.

October

● A glitch on the Buy.com retail site exposed names, addresses and telephone numbers of customers.
● The MBA International business school web site was attacked by pro-Palestinian hackers.

November

● A well-known American credit card company threatened to sue a UK university student after he discovered and informed customers of a major security flaw on its web site. The company, which had failed to fix the site despite warnings from the student, backed down after a report in *Computer Weekly*.
● Hackers gained entry to Microsoft servers. They viewed, and possibly copied, Microsoft source code, believed to be of a forthcoming product release.
● Arab Internet users gained control of several Israeli government web sites. Companies with business links with Israel, including Lucent, were also attacked.

December

● Hacker claimed a successful attack against the British Technology Group, replacing the web site with the message, 'Pathetic security like this makes me sick'.

Source: Reproduced from *Computer Weekly*, *11 January 2001*, Copyright © 2001 Reed Business Information

Figure 15.1 shows a breakdown of security threats that were faced by UK companies in 2000.

▶ Accidents

A number of estimates suggest that 40–65% of all damage caused to information systems or corporate data arises as a result of human error. The DTI's Information Security Breaches Survey, for example, reported that 40% of organisations had suffered security breaches as a result of human error in 2000. Some examples of the ways in which human errors can occur include:

- *Inaccurate data entry.* As an example, consider a typical relational database management system, where update queries are used to change records, tables and reports. If the contents of the query are incorrect, errors might be produced within all of the data manipulated by the query. Although extreme, significant problems might be caused by adding or removing even a single character to a query.
- *Attempts to carry out tasks beyond the ability of the employee.* In smaller computer-based information systems, a common cause of accidental damage involves users attempting to install new hardware items or software applications. In the case of software applications, existing data may be lost when the program is installed or the program may fail to operate as expected.
- *Failure to comply with procedures for the use of organisational information systems.* Where organisational procedures are unclear or fail to anticipate potential problems, users may often ignore established methods, act on their own initiative or perform tasks incorrectly.
- *Failure to carry out backup procedures or verify data backups.* In addition to carrying out regular backups of important business data, it is also necessary to verify that any backup copies made are accurate and free from errors.

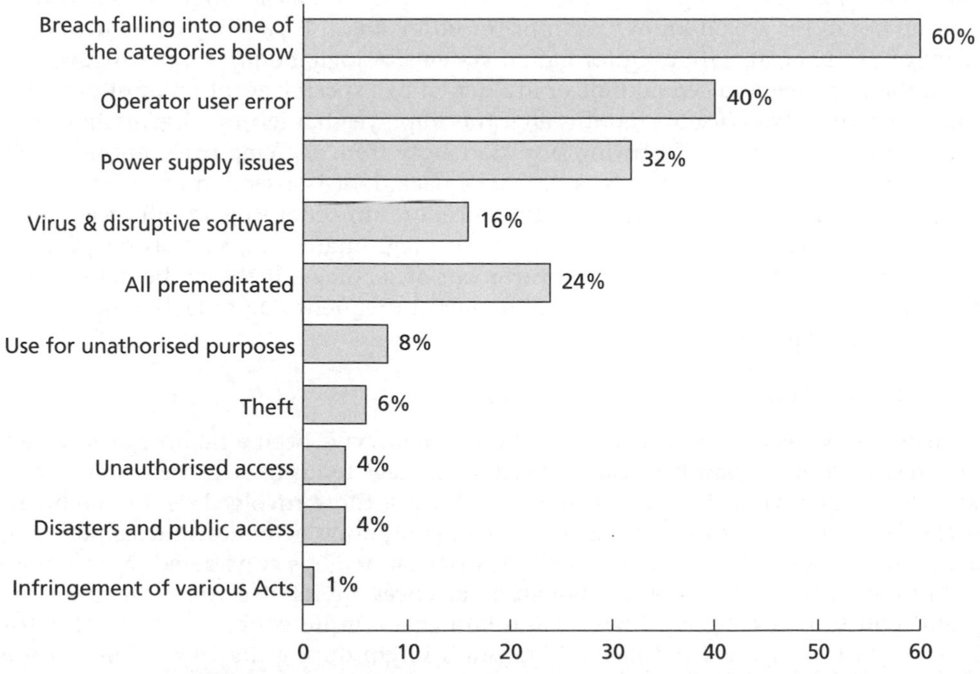

Security breach.
A deliberate or unintentional act that leads to unauthorised access to or loss or damage to information or an information system.

Update query
Used to change records, tables and reports held in a database management system.

Figure 15.1 Breakdown of breaches of security reported by UK companies in 2000
Source: Information Security Breaches Survey 2000, DTI (www.dti.gov.uk)

> In 2000, 40% of companies reported security breaches due to operator or user error.
>
> *Source*: Information Security Breaches Survey, 2000 www.dti.gov.uk/cii/datasecurity/survey2000techreport/
> headline_news.shtml

▶ Natural disasters

Safety-critical system
Where human lives rely the correct operation of a computer-based information system.

> Where human lives rely on the proper operation of an information system, this is usually known as a critical system. Perhaps a better way of describing a critical system is to suggest that it is an information system that must not fail. A good example of a critical system is an air traffic control system.

All information systems are susceptible to damage caused by natural phenomena, such as storms, lightning strikes, floods and earthquakes. In Japan and the United States, for example, great care is taken to protect critical information systems from the effects of earthquakes. Although such hazards are of less concern in much of Europe, properly designed systems will make allowances for unexpected natural disasters.

▶ Sabotage

With regard to information systems, sabotage may be deliberate or unintentional and carried out on an individual basis or as an act of industrial sabotage.

Individual sabotage

Logic bomb
Sometimes also known as a time bomb, a logic bomb is a destructive computer program that activates at a certain time or in reaction to a specific event.

Back door
A section of program code that allows a user to circumvent security procedures in order to gain full access to an information system.

Individual sabotage is typically carried out by a disgruntled employee who wishes to exact some form of revenge upon their employer. The **logic bomb** (sometimes known as a 'time bomb') is a well-known example of how an employee may cause deliberate damage to the organisation's information systems. A logic bomb is a destructive program that activates at a certain time or in reaction to a specific event. In most cases, the logic bomb is activated some months after the employee has left the organisation. This tends to have the effect of drawing suspicion away from the employee. Another well-known example is known as a **back door**. The back door is a section of program code that allows a user to circumvent security procedures in order to gain full access to an information system. Although back doors have legitimate uses, such as for program testing, they can also be used as an instrument of sabotage. It should be noted, however, that individual sabotage is becoming more infrequent due to legislation such as the Computer Misuse Act.

Industrial sabotage

Industrial sabotage is considered rare, although there have been a number of well-publicised cases over the past few years. Industrial sabotage tends to be carried out for some kind of competitive or financial gain. The actions of those involved tend to be highly organised, targeted at specific areas of a rival organisation's activities, and supported by access to a substantial resource base. Industrial sabotage is considered more serious than individual sabotage since, although occurrences are relatively few, the losses suffered tend to be extremely high. A well-known example concerns the legal battle between British Airways and Richard Branson's Virgin during the 1990s, where it was alleged that BA gained access to Virgin's customer databases and used this information to 'poach' Virgin's customers.

Unintentional sabotage

An intent to cause loss or damage need not be present for sabotage to occur. Imagine the case of an organisation introducing a new information system at short notice and without proper consultation with staff. Employees may feel threatened by the new system and may wish to avoid making use of it. A typical reaction might be to enter data incorrectly in an attempt to discredit the new system. Alternatively, the employee might continue to carry out tasks manually (or with the older system), claiming that this is a more efficient way of working. In such cases, the employee's primary motivation is to safeguard their position – the damage or loss caused to the organisation's information systems is incidental to this goal.

▶ Vandalism

Deliberate damage caused to hardware, software and data is considered a serious threat to information systems security. The threat from vandalism lies in the fact that the organisation is temporarily denied access to some of its resources. Even relatively minor damage to parts of a system can have a significant effect on the organisation as a whole. In a small network system, for example, damage to a server or shared storage device might effectively halt the work of all those connected to the network. In larger systems, a reduced flow of work through one part of the organisation can create bottlenecks, reducing the overall productivity of the entire organisation. Damage or loss of data can have more severe effects since the organisation cannot make use of the data until it has been replaced. The expense involved in replacing damaged or lost data can far exceed any losses arising from damage to hardware or software. As an example, the delays caused by the need to replace hardware or data might result in an organisation's being unable to compete for new business, harming the overall profitability of the company.

In recent years, vandalism has been extended to the Internet. A number of incidents have occurred where company web sites have been defaced. Table 15.1 provides some examples of such incidents.

▶ Theft

As with vandalism, the loss of important hardware, software or data can have significant effects on an organisation's effectiveness. Theft can be divided into two basic categories: physical theft and data theft.

Between 1995 and 1996, thefts of equipment from government offices in the UK grew by 400%, from £100,000 to £400,000.

Physical theft, as the term implies, involves the theft of hardware and software. **Data theft** normally involves making copies of important files without causing any harm to the originals. However, if the original files are destroyed or damaged, then the value of the copied data is automatically increased.

Service organisations are particularly vulnerable to data theft since their activities tend to rely heavily upon access to corporate databases. Imagine a competitor gaining access to a customer list belonging to a sales organisation. The immediate effect of such an event would be to place both organisations on an essentially even footing. However, in the long term, the first organisation would no longer enjoy a competitive edge and might, ultimately, cease to exist.

Data theft
....
This can involve stealing sensitive information or making unauthorised changes to computer records.

> In 1998 some £300 million of computer equipment was stolen from industry and the public sector in the UK. However, this value represents only the insured value of equipment and it is estimated that uninsured losses were in the region of £1 billion.
> *Source*: Circle Security Ltd October 1998

Both data theft and physical theft can take a number of different forms. As an example, there has been growing concern over the theft of customer information, such as credit card details, from company web sites.

▶ Unauthorised use

One of the most common security risks in relation to computerised information systems is the danger of unauthorised access to confidential data. Contrary to the popular belief encouraged by the media, the risk of hackers, gaining access to a corporate information system is relatively small. Most security breaches involving confidential data can be attributed to the employees of the organisation. In many cases, breaches are accidental in that employees are unaware that particular sets of information are restricted. Deliberate breaches are typically the result of an employee's wishing to gain some personal benefit from using the information obtained. A good example concerns the common myth of the police officer using the Police National Computer to check up on a car they wish to buy. In reality, strict guidelines cover the use of the Police National Computer and a log is kept of all enquiries made.

However, we must consider that the threat posed by hackers is starting to increase as more organisations make use of the Internet for business purposes. In addition, it should be noted that even a relatively small number of hacking incidents can account for significant losses to industry. As an example, Datamonitor estimates that security breaches related to web sites cost more than £10 billion per year in repair costs and lost revenue (*Computer Weekly*, 11 January 2001).

Hacker

Hackers are often described as individuals who seek to break into systems as a test of their abilities. Few hackers attempt to cause damage to systems they access and few are interested in gaining any sort of financial profit.

Cracker

A person who gains access to an information system for malicious reasons is often termed a cracker rather than a hacker. This is because some people draw a distinction between 'ethical' hackers and malicious hackers.

A **hacker** is a person who attempts to gain unauthorised access to a computer-based information system, usually via a telecommunications link. However, this is the *popular* use of this term and is considered incorrect by many IT professionals. Traditionally, 'hacking' referred to the process of writing program code, so hackers were nothing more than skilled computer programmers. Even today, many people consider themselves to be 'hackers' of the traditional kind and dislike being associated with the stereotype of a computer criminal. Furthermore, many people draw distinctions between those who attempt to gain unauthorised access to computer-based information systems for malicious reasons and those with other motivations. A person who gains access to an information system for malicious reasons is often termed a **cracker** rather than a hacker. Similarly, many people claim to use hacking for ethical purposes, such as helping companies to identify security flaws or assisting law enforcement agencies in apprehending criminals. These people tend to be referred to as 'white-hat hackers' and their counterparts are termed 'black-hat hackers'. However, for the purposes of this chapter, we will continue to use the term 'hacker' in its popular sense.

In general, most people consider hackers to fall into one of three catgeories:

- those who wish to demonstrate their computer skills by outwitting the designers of a particular system;
- those who wish to gain some form of benefit (usually financial) by stealing, altering or deleting confidential information;
- those who wish to cause malicious damage to an information system, perhaps as an act of revenge against a former employer.

Understandably, the most common crime committed by hackers involves telecommunications fraud. Clearly, the first task carried out by most hackers is to obtain free telephone calls, so that the time-consuming task of breaking into a given system can be carried out without incurring a great deal of expense. However, the growth of digital communications technology means that it is possible to implement countermeasures against hacking.

An excellent example concerns a 1989 case, where a hacker managed to access information systems in more than 35 military bases across the United States. The hacker's intention was to steal information on the Strategic Defence Initiative (SDI) – the so-called Star Wars project. The hacker was traced on the basis of an anomaly found by Clifford Stoll in telephone records. The unauthorised use of 75 cents of telephone time led to an investigation that lasted more than 18 months. Finally, following a number of failed attempts to trace the hacker via the telecommunications system, he was caught and sentenced to imprisonment.

A single hacker's web site recorded more than 100 successful hacks within the first four days of 2001.

Source: Courtesy of *Computer Weekly*, 11 January 2001

▶ Computer viruses

Whilst some methods, such as logic bombs, are beginning to decline, others are becoming more common. The release of the 'virus construction kits' and 'virus mutation engines' places the construction of a new computer virus within the hands of most users. Additionally, whilst methods such as virus scanning provide a degree of protection against virus infection, no completely secure prevention technique has yet been found.

Computer viruses are considered in more detail later on.

Control strategies

In the previous section it was shown that there is a need to:

- control access to information systems;
- maintain the integrity of the information held within a computer-based information system;
- implement procedures to ensure the physical security of equipment;
- safeguard the overall security of an information system.

In this section, strategies for reducing threats to information systems are discussed. In general, there are four major approaches that can be taken to ensure the integrity of an information system. These are containment, deterrence, obfuscation and recovery. Although each strategy is discussed separately, it is important to note that an effective security policy will draw upon a variety of concepts and techniques.

▶ Containment

The strategy of containment attempts to control access to an information system.

One approach involves making potential targets as unattractive as possible. This can be achieved in several ways but a common method involves creating the impression that the target information system contains data of little or no value. It would be pointless, for example, attempting to steal data that had been encrypted – the data would effectively be useless to anyone except the owner.

A second technique involves creating an effective series of defences against potential threats. If the expense, time and effort required to gain access to the information system is greater than any benefits derived from gaining access, then intrusion becomes less likely. However, defences must be continually improved and upgraded in order to keep up with advances in technology and the increasing sophistication of hackers. Thus, such as approach tends to be expensive in terms of organisational resources.

A third approach involves removing the target information system from potential threats. Typical ways in which this might be achieved include distributing assets across a large geographical area, distributing important data across the entire organisation or isolating important systems.

▶ Deterrence

A strategy based upon deterrence uses the threat of punishment to discourage potential intruders. The overall approach is one of anticipating and countering the motives of those most likely to threaten the security of the system.

A common method involves constantly advertising and reinforcing the penalties for unauthorised access. It is not uncommon, for example, to dismiss an employee for gaining access to confidential data. Similarly, it is not uncommon for organisations to bring private prosecutions against those who have caused damage or loss to important information systems. Attempts to breach the security of the information system are discouraged by publicising successful actions against employees or other parties.

A second approach involves attempting to detect potential threats as early as possible, for example by monitoring patterns of information system usage and investigating all anomalies. However, although such a technique can prevent some attacks and reduce the damage caused by others, it can be expensive in terms of organisational resources.

The third technique used commonly involves predicting likely areas of attack and then implementing appropriate defences or countermeasures. If an organisation feels, for example, that it is particularly vulnerable to computer viruses, it might install virus scanning software across the entire organisation.

▶ Obfuscation

Obfuscation concerns itself with hiding or distributing assets so that any damage caused can be limited.

One means by which such a strategy can be implemented is by monitoring *all* of the organisation's activities, not just those related to the use of its information systems. This provides a more comprehensive approach to security than *containment* or *deterrence* since it also provides a measure of protection against theft and other threats.

Audit
The process of monitoring an organisation's hardware and software resources. In general, audits are used as a deterrent against theft and the use of illegal software.

A second method involves carrying out regular audits of data, hardware, software and security measures. In this way, the organisation has a more complete overview of its information systems and can assess threats more accurately. A regular software audit, for example, might result in a reduction in the use of illegal software. In turn, this might reduce the number of virus infections suffered by the organisation, avoid potential litigation with software companies and detect illegal or unauthorised use of programs and data.

The dispersal of assets across several locations can be used to discourage potential intruders and can also limit the damage caused by a successful attack. The use of other techniques, such as backup procedures, can be used to reduce any threats further.

▶ Recovery

A strategy based upon **recovery** recognises that, no matter how well defended, a breach in the security of an information system will eventually occur. Such a strategy is largely concerned with ensuring that the normal operation of the information system is restored as quickly as possible, with as little disruption to the organisation as possible.

The most important aspect of a strategy based upon recovery involves careful organisational planning. The development of emergency procedures that deal with a number of contingencies is essential if a successful recovery is to take place.

In anticipating damage or loss, a great deal of emphasis is placed upon backup procedures and recovery measures. In large organisations, a **backup site** might be created, so that data processing can be switched to a secondary site immediately in the event of an emergency. Smaller organisations might make use of other measures, such as **RAID** facilities or **data warehousing** services.

Types of controls

There are five major categories of controls that can be applied to information systems. These are: physical protection, biometric controls, telecommunications controls, failure controls and auditing.

▶ Physical protection

Physical protection involves the use of physical barriers intended to protect against theft and unauthorised access. The reasoning behind such an approach is extremely simple: if access to rooms and equipment is restricted, risks of theft and vandalism are reduced. Furthermore, by preventing access to equipment, it is less likely that an unauthorised user can gain access to confidential information. Locks, barriers and security chains are examples of this form of control.

▶ Biometric controls

These controls make use of the unique characteristics of individuals in order to restrict access to sensitive information or equipment. Scanners that check fingerprints, voice prints or even retinal patterns are examples of biometric controls.

Until relatively recently, the expense associated with biometric control systems placed them out of reach of all but the largest organisations. In addition, many organisations held reservations concerning the accuracy of the recognition methods used to identify specific individuals. However, with the introduction of more sophisticated hardware and software, both of these problems have been largely resolved. Many organisations have now begun to look at ways in which biometric control systems can be used to reduce instances of fraud. Within five years, for example, banks are expected to introduce automated teller machines (ATM) that use fingerprints and retinal patterns to identify customers.

▶ Telecommunications controls

These controls help to verify the identity of a particular user. Common types of communications controls include passwords and user validation routines.

As an example, when a new network account is created for a given user, they may be asked to supply several pieces of personal information, such as the name of their spouse

Recovery.
The process which is used to restore backup data.

Backup site
This houses a copy of the organisation's main data processing facilities, including hardware, software and up-to-date data files. In the event of an emergency, processing can be switched to the backup site almost immediately so that the organisation's work can continue.

RAID
This stands for 'redundant array of inexpensive disks'. Essentially, identical copies of important data files are kept upon a number of different storage devices. If one or more of the storage devices fails, additional devices are activated automatically, allowing uninterrupted access to the data and reducing the possibility of losing transactions or updates.

or their date of birth. When the user attempts to connect to the network system via a modem, they will be asked to confirm their identity by providing some of the information given when the account was created.

▶ Failure controls

Failure controls attempt to limit or avoid damage caused by the failure of an information system. Typical examples include recovery procedures and regular backups of data. Backups are explained in more detail later on.

▶ Auditing

Auditing involves taking stock of procedures, hardware, software and data at regular intervals.

With regard to software and data, audits can be carried out automatically with an appropriate program. Auditing software works by scanning the hard disk drives of any computers, terminals and servers attached to a network system. As each hard disk drive is scanned, the names of any programs found are added to a log. This log can then be compared to a list of the programs that are legitimately owned by the organisation. Since the log contains information concerning the whereabouts of each program found, it is relatively simple to determine the location of any unauthorised programs. In many organisations, auditing programs are also used to keep track of software licences and allow companies to ensure that they are operating within the terms of their licence agreements.

> A **software licence** enables a company to make several copies of a program, allowing it to acquire important programs at reduced cost. Typically, a company will purchase a single copy of the program and install this on as many computers as required. Since only one copy of the program and any accompanying documentation is required, costs are reduced for both the company and the supplier. The terms of the software licence will determine how many copies of the program can be made. A ten-user licence, for example, allows a company to make up to ten copies of a program for use by its employees.

Some techniques for controlling information systems

Some of the most common techniques used to control computer-based information systems are:

- formal security policies;
- passwords;
- file encryption;
- organisational procedures governing the use of computer-based information systems;
- user validation techniques;
- backup procedures.

The following describes each of these techniques in more detail.

▶ Formal security policy

Perhaps the simplest and most effective control is the formulation of a comprehensive policy on security. Amongst a wide variety of items, such a policy will outline:

In 2000, only one in seven UK organisations had a formal information management security policy in place.

Source: Information Security Breaches Survey, 2000 (www.dti.gov.uk/cii/datasecurity/survey2000techreport/headline_news.shtml)

- what is considered to be acceptable use of the information system;
- what is considered unacceptable use of the information system;
- the sanctions available in the event that an employee does not comply with the security policy;
- details of the controls in place, including their form and function and plans for developing these further.

Once a policy has been formulated, it must be publicised in order for it to become effective. In addition, the support of management is essential in order to ensure that employees adhere to the guidelines contained within the policy.

It is worth noting that many European countries have national standards that can be used to develop and assess organisational security policies. In the UK, for example, compliance with BS 7799 demonstrates that a company has established an effective information security management infrastructure. Standards such as BS 7799 are extemely useful in that they provide a framework that can be used to develop a series of policies and procedures in order to maintain the security of computer-based information systems.

In 2000, only 37% of organisations interviewed had undertaken a risk assessment where a systematic approach was taken to assess the security risks faced by the organisation.

Source: Information Security Breaches Survey, 2000 (4)

▶ Passwords

The password represents one of the most common forms of protection for computer-based information systems. In addition to providing a simple, inexpensive means of restricting access to equipment and sensitive data, passwords also provide a number of other benefits. Amongst these are the following:

- Access to the system can be divided into levels by issuing different passwords to employees based on their positions and the work they carry out.
- The actions of an employee can be regulated and supervised by monitoring the use of their password.
- If a password is discovered or stolen by an external party, it should be possible to limit any damage arising as a result.
- The use of passwords can encourage employees to take some of the responsibility for the overall security of the system.

▶ Encryption

An additional layer of protection for sensitive data can be provided by making use of encryption techniques. Modern encryption methods rely upon the use of one or more keys. Without the correct key, any encrypted data is meaningless – and therefore of no value – to a potential thief.

Passwords

Contrary to popular belief, most computer fraud is not technically sophisticated, and is often due to a lack of basic controls.

'A company's head of IT needs to keep abreast with the latest developments and have regular security revisions', says Mark Morris, senior manager of UK-based Computer Forensics Investigations.

Many fraudsters, he says, rely on human behaviour rather than technology. 'Social engineers', for example, are often temporary workers who will telephone the accounts department with a bogus tale about a computer crash that has deleted the password files. The fraudster will ask for the passwords, so that employees can gain access to their computers.

'Dumpster divers', meanwhile, search rubbish bins for notes with passwords scribbled on them.

'Shoulder surfers' look over the shoulder of someone entering a password on a computer. There are also password-cracking programs that can search through vast dictionary databases to find passwords. 'Passwords should be alphanumeric, and they should only mean something to you', says Mr Morris.

Another UK company, Priority Data Group (PDG), whose clients include Citibank, computer services company EDS, the computer services company, and General Motors, has developed a system that auto-matically blanks a PC screen when the user is away from it. The screen is reactivated by using a password. 'People can leave sensitive data on a computer screen while they go to the coffee machine or leave the office', says Alec Florence, PDG's chief executive.

US based Finjan has developed SurfinShield Corporate, designed to protect computers against rogue programs attached to ActiveX or Java-created programs. SurfinShield monitors the behaviour of the downloaded program and if it attempts to breach the computer's security system, the program is eliminated.

Source: 'Computer fraud: screen out divers and surfers', *Financial Times*, 8 April 1998

Questions

1 Why should an organisation use passwords to protect equipment and sensitive data from unauthorised users?

2 The case study describes several ways in which fraudulent users are able to obtain important passwords. What measures can an organisation take to protect against some of the methods described?

3 Describe the password protection features provided by a typical operating system, such as Windows NT.

Pretty Good Privacy (PGP)

Using the Internet as a resource, locate information related to a well-known product called Pretty Good Privacy (PGP). Describe how PGP works and explain why you think the system is so popular.

▶ Procedures

Under normal circumstances, a set of procedures for the use of an information system will arise from the creation of a formal security policy. Such procedures should describe in detail the correct operation of the system and responsibilities of users. Additionally, the procedures should highlight issues related to security, should explain some of the reasoning behind them and should also describe the penalties for failing to comply with instructions.

User validation

Checks made to ensure the user is permitted access to a system. Also known as access control systems, they often involve user names and passwords, but can also include biometric techniques.

▶ User validation

Of relevance to telecommunications is the use of **user validation** techniques. It is necessary to verify the identity of users attempting to access the system from outside of the organisation. A password is insufficient to identify the user since it might have been stolen or accidentally revealed to others. However, by asking for a date of birth, National Insurance number or other personal information, the identity of the user can be confirmed. Alternatively, if the location of the user is known, the system can attempt to call the user back at their current location. If the user is genuine, the call will be connected correctly and the user can then access the system. Although such methods do not offer total security, the risk of unauthorised access can be reduced dramatically.

▶ Backup procedures

The effects of a sudden loss of data can affect a company's activities in a variety of ways. The disruption caused to a company's normal activities can result in significant financial losses due to factors such as lost opportunities, additional trading expenses and customer dissatisfaction.

The cumulative effects of data loss can prove detrimental to areas as diverse as corporate image and staff morale. Perhaps the single most compelling reason for introducing effective backup procedures is simply the expense involved in reconstructing lost data.

One of the most common methods of protecting valuable data is to use the 'grandfather, father, son' technique. Here, a rotating set of backup disks or tapes are used so that three different versions of the same data are held at any one time.

To illustrate this method, imagine a single user working with a personal computer and using three floppy disks to store their data on. Each day, all of the data being worked on is copied onto the disk containing the oldest version ('grandfather') of that data. This creates a continuous cycle that ensures that the oldest backup copy is never more than three days old.

Table 15.2 illustrates the operation of the 'grandfather, father, son' method. As can be seen, each disk or tape moves through three generations. Since three copies of the data are maintained, the risk of data loss is reduced considerably. In the event of the original data becoming corrupted or damaged in some way, only the changes made since the last backup copy was made would be lost. In most cases, this would amount to new or altered data produced during the previous day. In addition, since only three sets of reusable media are required in order to make backups, the costs involved can be considered low.

It is worth noting several general points concerning backups of data:

> **Grandfather, father, son**
> A common procedure used for creating backup copies of important data files.

Table 15.2 The 'grandfather, father, son' backup method

Day 1	Day 2	Day 3
Disk 1 Grandfather	Disk 2 Grandfather	Disk 3 Grandfather
Disk 2 Father	Disk 3 Father	Disk 1 Father
Disk 3 Son	Disk 1 Son	Disk 2 Son

- The time, effort and expense involved in producing backup copies will be wasted unless they are made at regular intervals. How often backups are made depends largely upon the amount of work processed over a given period of time. In general, backups will be made more frequently as the number of transactions carried out each day increases.
- Backup copies of data should be checked each time they are produced. Faulty storage devices and media may sometimes result in incomplete or garbled copies of data. In addition, precautions should be taken against computer viruses, in order to prevent damage to the data stored.

- The security of backup copies should be ensured by storing them in a safe location. Typically, an organisation will produce two sets of backup copies; one to be stored at the company premises, the other to be taken off the premises and stored at a separate location. In this way, a major accident, such as a fire at the company premises, will not result in the total destruction of the organisation's data.
- It is worth noting that not all data need be backed up at regular intervals. Software applications, for example, can normally be restored quickly and easily from the original media. In a similar way, if a backup has already been made of a given item of data, the production of additional copies may not be necessary.

Incremental backup

Includes only those files that have changed in some way since the last backup was made.

Full backup

A method of producing copies of important data files by including all data files considered to be important.

In order to reduce the time taken to create backup copies, many organisations make use of software that allows the production of **incremental backups**. Initially, a backup copy of all data files is made and care is taken to ensure the accuracy of the copy. This initial, complete backup is normally referred to as a **full backup** (sometimes also known as an archival backup). From this point on, specialised backup software is used to detect and copy only those files that have changed in some way since the last backup was made. In the event of data loss, damaged files can be replaced by restoring the full backup first, followed by the incremental backups. One of the chief advantages of creating incremental backups is that it is possible to trace the changes made to data files over time. In this way, any version of a given file can be located and restored.

 ## *Focus on* the computer virus

▶ What is a computer virus?

Computer virus

This is a computer program that is capable of self-replication, allowing it to spread from one 'infected' machine to another.

The origin of the term '**computer virus**' is credited to Fred Cohen, author of the 1984 book *Computer Viruses: Theories and Experiments*. However, 'natural' computer viruses were reported as early as 1974 and papers describing mathematical models of the theory of epidemics were published in the early 1950s.

▶ Types of computer virus

There are several different types of **computer virus**. Some examples include:

- The *link virus* attaches itself to the directory structure of a disk. In this way, the virus is able to manipulate file and directory information. Link viruses can be difficult to remove since they become embedded within the affected data. Often, attempts to remove the virus can result in the loss of the data concerned.
- *Parasitic viruses* (sometimes known as 'file infectors') insert copies of themselves into legitimate programs, such as operating system files, often making little effort to disguise their presence. In this way, each time the program file is run, so too is the virus. Additionally, the majority of viruses are created as **terminate and stay resident** (TSR) programs. Once activated, the virus remains in the computer's memory performing various operations in the background. Such operations might range from creating additional copies of itself to deleting files on a hard disk.

Terminate and stay resident (TSR)

A program that is stored in the computer's memory and functions as a background task, receiving only a small share of the processor's time.

> By dividing processor time amongst a number of tasks, it is possible to run several applications simultaneously. Users will normally be unaware that more than one program is running at a time since the application that receives the largest share of the processor's time (known as the *foreground task*) disguises the operation of any other *background tasks*. A *terminate and stay resident* program is one that is stored in the computer's memory and functions as a background task.

- *Macro viruses* (sometimes called 'script viruses') are created using the high-level programming languages found in e-mail packages, web browsers and applications software, such as word processors. Technically, such viruses are extremely crude but are capable of causing a great deal of damage.

> In May 2000, the 'I Love You' or 'Love Bug' virus received international attention when it infected millions of personal computers across the world. Once the virus infected a user's e-mail package, it copied itself by sending infected messages to every person in the user's address book. The intriguing subject line of the e-mail message caused many people to open it and immediately infect their own systems. In all, it is estimated that the virus infected more than 45 million data files. Losses caused by the virus are difficult to estimate – some estimates suggest worldwide losses as low as $2.5 million, whilst others claim figures as high as $500 million.

With the possible exception of **anti-viruses** (described in more detail later), all viruses must be considered to be harmful. Even if a virus program does nothing more than reproduce itself, it may still cause system crashes and data loss. In many cases, the damage caused by a computer virus might be accidental, arising merely as the result of poor programming.

There is also evidence to suggest that viruses may be capable of causing physical damage to hardware components. It is possible, for example, to construct a virus that instructs a disk controller to attempt to read a non-existent track, causing immediate and irreparable damage to the hard disk drive.

Until quite recently, it was thought that computer viruses could not be attached to data files, such as word processing documents or e-mail messages. However, the built-in programming languages featured within many modern applications mean that data files may now be used to transmit viruses. A typical example are the Word for Windows macro viruses, which attach themselves to a document template and duplicate each time a new document is created. Using an infected document on another machine automatically infects the user's copy of Word for Windows. However, it remains true that viruses cannot be transmitted by a conventional e-mail message. A virus can only be transmitted as an attachment to a message, or if the e-mail package being used allows active content.

Two other kinds of programs are related to computer viruses; worms and Trojans. A **worm** is a small program that moves through a computer system randomly changing or overwriting pieces of data as it moves.

A **Trojan** appears as a legitimate program in order to gain access to a computer system. Trojans are often used as delivery systems for computer viruses. A good example of this was McAfee Scan V84, originally released in 1991. This program appeared to be a genuine version of a popular virus detection utility but was actually the delivery system for a particularly destructive computer virus. By assuming the identity of a new version of the world's most popular virus detection program, the Trojan was able to gain an extremely wide distribution in a very short time.

▶ The transmission of computer viruses

A number of reports suggest that consultants, maintenance engineers and employees are responsible for approximately 40 to 60 per cent of all virus infections. Often, a virus infection occurs as a result of employees bringing disks into work from their machines at home. Other ways in which viruses may be transmitted include through the use of illegal software, software downloaded via the Internet and, occasionally, through commercial software and magazine cover-mounted discs.

Anti-virus

An anti-virus is a benevolent virus program that copies itself to the boot sectors of unprotected floppy disks. If another virus attempts to overwrite the anti-virus it displays a message on the screen warning the user of infection.

Worm

A small program that moves through a computer system randomly changing or overwriting pieces of data as it moves.

Trojan

A Trojan presents itself as a legitimate program in order to gain access to a computer system. Trojans are often used as delivery systems for computer viruses.

It can be argued that computer users themselves are often responsible for damage arising as a result of virus infections. Few users take adequate security measures, such as backing up data. It is estimated that fewer than five per cent of computer users are capable of carrying out backup procedures. Furthermore, inadequate training and incorrect responses to virus infections often exaggerate the problem, since anxious users may cause more damage than the virus itself.

There are few estimates of the financial loss caused by computer viruses each year. This is undoubtedly due to the reluctance of major companies to disclose the fact that their systems have been compromised. However, various surveys suggest that 65–90 per cent of major corporates come into contact with computer viruses each year. However, the real rate of infection may be substantially higher since companies are unlikely to admit any major losses arising as a result of computer virus infections. In the UK, the DTI's Information Security Breaches Survey 2000 reports that 16 per cent of all security breaches suffered by companies were related to computer viruses. In considering the seriousness of virus infections, they were seen as 'very serious', being comparable to other threats, such as theft and unauthorised access (Fig. 15.2).

◗ Detecting and preventing virus infection

The risk of virus infection can be reduced to a minimum by implementing a relatively simple set of security measures:

- unauthorised access to machines and software should be restricted as far as possible;
- machines and software should be checked regularly with a virus detection program;
- all new disks and any software originating from an outside source should be checked with a virus detection program before use;
- floppy disks should be kept write-protected whenever possible since it is physically impossible for a virus to copy itself to a write-protected disk;
- regular backups of data and program files must be made in order to minimise the damage caused if a virus infects the system.

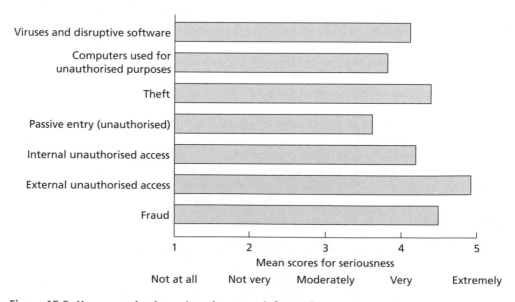

Figure 15.2 **How organisations view threats to information systems**
Source: Information Security Breaches Survey 2000, DTI (www.dti.gov.uk)

Virus scanners are intended to detect and then safely remove virus programs from a computer system. The most common method of detection used by these programs involves scanning for the **signatures** of particular viruses. It is often possible to locate a virus by simply searching every file on an infected disk for these identifying characteristics. However, since new viruses are discovered quite frequently, the list of signatures contained within a detection program quickly becomes dated. For this reason, most software developers insist that regular program updates are essential. However, the introduction of new kinds of viruses, such as **polymorphic** and **stealth** viruses, mean that signature checking alone can no longer be regarded as a completely secure method of detection. For this reason, most virus scanners use a combination of techniques to enhance their efficiency. Amongst the methods used are checksums, virus shields, anti-viruses, **heuristics** and inoculation.

Virus shields are TSR programs that constantly monitor and control access to a system's storage devices. Any unusual attempt to modify a file or write to a disk drive will activate a message asking the user to authorise the operation. A similar task is performed by hardware virus detection devices. Modern hardware protection devices can be extremely sophisticated, featuring their own processors, disk controllers and other expensive components. However, despite the claims of the manufacturers of these devices, there is little evidence to suggest that they are any more effective than software solutions.

Once a virus has been detected there are three methods of removing it. The first, *disinfection*, attempts to restore damaged files and directory structures to their original condition. However, disinfection is not possible in all cases. The second technique involves *overwriting* the virus program so that it is permanently and irrevocably deleted from the disk. The third and final method of removing a virus is by restoring a backup of the infected disk to the system. The process of writing files to the disk effectively overwrites the virus and restores the system to its original state.

> A distinction is made between **erasing** and **deleting** a file. Erasing a file merely removes its entry in the disk's directory structure: the file remains intact until another file overwrites it. For this reason, virus killers delete the virus completely by overwriting it with new data.

Despite the sophistication of scanning programs, none is capable of offering complete protection against infection. Many tests have been carried out to determine the efficiency of specific virus-scanning programs. In all of these tests, no program has yet achieved a perfect score. In some cases, the detection rate of some programs was found to be as low as 50 per cent.

> The action that a virus carries out when activated is normally referred to as the **payload**. An example of a payload might be issuing the command to delete all of the files from the user's hard disk drive when a certain condition is met, such as when a particular date or time is reached.

▶ Trends

In 1989, it was believed that there were fewer than 50 viruses in circulation. Recent reports estimate that as many as 5000 viruses exist at present. Furthermore, other estimates suggest that new viruses are being discovered at a rate of more than 50 per month.

Virus scanner

Intended to detect and safely remove virus programs from a computer system.

Signature

Unique features of a virus such as the unique series of values in its program file or message displayed on screen or hidden text.

Polymorphic virus

Capable of altering its form, so that the 'standard' signature of the virus is not present. This means that a virus scanner may not always identify the virus correctly.

Stealth virus

Specifically designed to avoid detection. Such programs are normally written with the intention of defeating common or well-known virus-scanning programs.

Heuristics

Involves monitoring a system to detect common behaviours associated with computer viruses, such as attempts to access certain areas of the hard disk drive.

Virus shield

Virus shields are programs that constantly monitor and control access to a system's storage devices. Any unusual attempt to modify a file or write to a disk drive will activate a message asking the user to authorise the operation.

Improved access to technology, an increase in the use of networks and new communications technology has increased the vulnerability of many users to virus infections. At most risk are universities and other large sites, such as public services. The ICL case study demonstrates some of the risks posed by new computer viruses and explains how virus infections can impact on a company's operations.

MINI CASE STUDY

ICL and e-security

Like many multi-national companies, global IT services company ICL believed that its anti-virus strategy provided comprehensive protection, until a new breed of virus came on to the scene during 1999.

The company became infected with the W97M/Ethan, a macro virus which affects Word 97 documents and disables some of the options relating to anti-virus security. ICL's anti-virus software, Dr Solomon's Toolkit from Network Associates, could recognise the virus but could not actually deal with it.

While the company reacted quickly to close systems down to stop the virus spreading, there was nothing it could do to help those systems already affected, which meant that all appropriate resources were immediately diverted to the project. Network Associates also stepped in to help.

'In some cases the cure was worse than the infection because workstations had to be completely rebuilt', says John Colley, head of information security. 'We lost work, time and productivity from this event.'

To protect against the virus in the future, ICL arranged to upgrade to the latest, more comprehensive Virus Scan software. But just as the upgrade was being installed, ICL became the victim of a second virus that struck many companies last year – Melissa.

This virus is technically known as a worm since it spreads by copying itself to e-mail addresses in the system and then mailing itself out to unsuspecting recipients. 'This was a completely new way of spreading viruses and no-one in the industry knew how to deal with it', says Colley. 'It had a bigger impact on us than the Ethan virus because we had to stop our mail delivery system worldwide for about eight hours while we cleaned the systems manually, to prevent infecting our external trading partners.'

ICL spent hundreds of man-hours racing to implement its new anti-virus software, which could cope with Melissa.

'Because we had to implement the software very quickly across the rest of the company, this virus incident escalated to being flagged a "corporate red alert" within ten minutes', says Colley.

'We had an advantage in that we had a quick fix partially installed, but we were still anxious that we might spread Melissa outside our company, so we put some rough-and-ready protection on our mail gateway while we were cleaning up the system.'

Today, ICL has installed additional protective products at the edge of its infrastructure, and on its mail gateways, desktops and Exchange servers. Colley is confident that no known or new virus can get in or out of ICL without being spotted and dealt with quickly.

He concludes, 'The overriding lesson we've learned is that no matter how well you think you know and understand the security threat environment, something new will always come along.'

Source: Courtesy of *Computer Weekly*, 6 April 2000

CASE STUDY 15.2

Hackers

One cold and windy afternoon in January, I first learned what it takes to become a computer hacker. I attended a class at hacking school.

In one of the nondescript buildings that typify New York's financial district, I was shown into a room of earnest men.

They were eager to show me the weakness in corporate firewalls, the origin of computer viruses and even how to disable an entire computer network through a 'distributed denial of service' attack.

Yet, the people around the table were not the criminals and hooligans who have brought down respected internet sites such as Yahoo.com, or committed billions of dollars of fraud using credit card information stolen online.

To begin with, they were far too well dressed. Amid the neat haircuts and corporate casualwear, there was not a dreadlock or nose-ring to be seen.

Second, they were all employed by Ernst & Young, the professional services firm, to help large corporations prevent their computer systems from being infiltrated.

Yet, the IT security team at E&Y are not that far removed from the unscrupulous elements they are paid to thwart.

They even describe themselves as hackers, although they are quick to point out that they are the 'ethical' or 'white hat' variety, as opposed to the 'black hat' hackers they are constantly battling.

What's more, in their struggle to ensure that computer systems can withstand the latest threat, the E&Y team will often behave like hackers to test the defences set up by a company.

'We are going to go in and do what the bad guys are going to do', says Thomas Klevinsky, a former US Army engineer.

In order to demonstrate the point, Mr Klevinsky and his colleagues then showed me the methods used by hackers to infiltrate a company's computer system. Sometimes, hackers will simply attempt to break into a company's external internet site in order to steal sensitive information or, more often, just to create havoc.

An alternative is to attempt to dial in through an external phone line to a computer which is connected to the company's network.

This is mostly done by randomly dialling all the possible extensions in a block of numbers owned by a company. Once they have found such a computer, hackers are close to gaining access to the computer network.

Other approaches are more intricate: much fraud is caused by disgruntled employees or external contractors who are familiar with the setup of a company's computer network. Even more devious is what Mr Klevinsky calls social engineering.

This involves hackers phoning people in a company and extracting valuable information by pretending to be employees from another. For example, that person from Human Resources calling to ask about your social security number might actually be a hacker.

Another favourite technique is to call the IT department pretending to be an employee who has forgotten his or her password.

'If you are inside a company you can call tech support and say you are anyone you like. Mostly, you will get your password reset', says Scott Laliberte, an E&Y consultant. From then on, the hacker has access to the network.

In order to test a company's resilience to such attacks, the 'white hat' team will attempt to mimic the actions of 'black hat' hackers.

This is mostly done with the knowledge of the company's IT department, though sometimes just one or two senior executives in the organisation will know of the pending attack.

Amazingly, much of the material used in setting up an attack is freely available on the internet. With just a few clicks of the mouse, the E&Y team downloaded a package which identifies the software a particular server is running.

They also accessed a program which generates random passwords and tests them against encoded information which can be downloaded from any computer's hard drive.

As a result, the 'white hat' and 'black hat' hackers are locked in an eternal struggle, with the former constructing newer and more formidable defences to the weaknesses that the latter find. 'Just staying current with the technology is a full-time job', says Mr Klevinsky.

According to Mr Laliberte, most companies are caught out by believing two fallacies: first, that if their computer network is protected by a firewall, they are safe. Second, that their internal protection systems will warn them if a hacker has infiltrated the system.

In fact, firewalls are 'like putting a steel door on a cardboard house', says Mr Klevinsky, who holds the E&Y hacking record for bringing down a corporate computer system in just 42 seconds.

Most warning systems, meanwhile, are not properly set up.

Once a security breach has taken place, a whole new group of specialists moves in to conduct forensic analysis of the computer system. This can provide valuable evidence which can be used to track down and sometimes convict the culprits.

According to Kristopher Sharrar, a former US Air Force investigator who conducts forensic studies, the most important rule is not to touch the original system which has been hacked.

Instead, Ernst & Young's analysts will create an identical copy for their research. All my white-hatted tutors insist that they have never, in the past, used their knowledge for anything other than helping companies protect themselves.

Indeed, former 'black hat' hackers hoping to join the other side will find that they are unwelcome.

'We do a background search on everybody we hire. We won't hire people whose integrity has been questioned', says Mr Klevinsky.

After several hours, the class was over.

As I walked outside, I vowed to change all the passwords on my computer at once. In the building behind me, the struggle resumed.

Source: P. Larsen, 'The black arts of "white hat" hackers', *Financial Times*, 10 April 2001

Questions

1 Why are firewalls 'like putting a steel door on a cardboard house'?

2 What methods can be used to defeat techniques such as the use of programs that generate passwords or calling the IT department to have a password reset?

3 Should we distinguish between 'white hat' and 'black hat' hackers, or are all hackers the same?

Threats related to Internet services

Since 1999, a number of significant new threats to organisational information systems have emerged. Many of these threats reflect an increasing reliance on intranets and the Internet as basic tools for conducting transactions with partners, suppliers and customers. Although the following material focuses on the Internet, much of it is also relevant to company intranets.

▶ Denial of service (DoS)

Denial of service (DoS)
This is a form of attack on company information systems that involves flooding the company's Internet servers with huge amounts of traffic. Such attacks effectively halt all of the company's Internet activities until the problem is dealt with.

As companies begin to rely on network technology to reduce costs, they become more vulnerable to certain risks. For example, more harm can be caused if an individual gains access to a network server than if they merely gain access to a single PC. Similarly, companies relying on the Internet for business communications may find themselves subject to **denial of service** attacks. Typically, these attacks involve blocking the communications channels used by a company. For example, an e-mail system might be attacked by sending millions of lengthy messages to the company. Other techniques involve altering company web pages or attacking the systems used to process online transactions. In these cases, companies are usually forced to shut down services themselves until the problem can be dealt with. Such attacks were almost unheard of before 1999 but have recently started to become more common.

The impact of a denial of service attack can be extremely severe, especially for organisations that rely heavily on the Internet for e-commerce. As an example, an attack on Yahoo in 2000 involved servers being flooded with 1 billion hits per minute. The attack was estimated as costing £300,000 in lost advertising revenue alone (*Financial Times*, 17 November 2000).

Activity 15.2

Using the Internet as a resource, locate three examples of recent denial of service attacks. For each example, describe how the attack occurred and the losses suffered by the victim.

▶ Trojans

In the past two years, the use of Trojans to disrupt company activities or gain access to confidential information has grown sharply. Most of the Trojans encountered by business organisations are designed to gather information and transmit regular reports back to the owner. Typically, a Trojan will incorporate a *key logging* facility (sometimes called a 'keystroke recorder') to capture all keyboard input from a given computer. Capturing keyboard data allows the owner of the Trojan to gather a great deal of information, such as passwords and the contents of all outgoing e-mail messages.

Some Trojans are designed to give owners control over the target computer system. Effectively, the Trojan acts as a remote control application, allowing the owner to carry out actions on the target computer as if they were sitting in front of it. Sometimes, the owner of the Trojan will make no effort to conceal their activities: the victim sees actions being carried out but is unable to intervene, short of switching off the computer. More often, however, the Trojan operates silently and the victim is unaware that their computer is running programs, deleting files, sending e-mail, and so on. Back Orifice is an example of a Trojan that can be used in both of these ways. The program was designed to target Microsoft's operating systems and is arguably the most famous program of its kind.

Some programs are designed to disrupt company activities by initiating denial of service attacks or by attacking company servers. However, incidents involving these kinds of Trojan are rare since they often require very high levels of access to company systems.

▶ Identity theft and brand abuse

Identity theft involves using another person's identity to carry out acts that range from sending libellous e-mail to making fraudulent purchases. It is considered relatively easy to impersonate another person in this way, but far harder to prove that communications did not originate from the victim.

For business organisations, there is a threat that employees may be impersonated in order to place fraudulent orders. Alternatively, a company may be embarrassed if rumours or bogus press releases are transmitted via the Internet.

The term **brand abuse** is used to cover a wide range of activities, ranging from the sale of counterfeit goods, for example software applications, to exploiting a well-known brand name for commercial gain. As an example, the name of a well-known company might be embedded into a special web page so that the page receives a high ranking in a search engine. Users searching for the name of the company are then likely to be diverted to the special web page where they are offered a competitor's goods instead. Some estimates suggest that a typical company may lose between £2 million and £100 million per year as a result of brand abuse. Various estimates suggested that the global cost of brand abuse in 2001 would be £20 billion.

Brand abuse
This describes a wide range of activities, ranging from the sale of counterfeit goods (e.g. software applications) to exploiting a well-known brand name for commercial gain.

▶ Extortion

Various approaches can be used to extort money from companies. Two examples include cybersquatting and the threat of divulging customer information.

Cybersquatting involves registering an Internet domain that a company or celebrity is likely to want to own. Although merely registering a domain is not illegal in itself, some individuals attempt to extort money from companies or celebrities in various ways. Typically, the owner of the domain will ask for a large sum in order to transfer the domain to the interested party. Sometimes, however, demands for money may be accompanied by threats, such as the threat the domain will be used in a way that will

Cybersquatting
The act of registering an Internet domain with the intention of selling it for profit to an interested party. As an example, the name of a celebrity might be registered and then offered for sale at an extremely high price.

harm the victim's reputation unless payment is forthcoming. Although there is an established mechanism for dealing with disputes over domain names, many victims of cybersquatting choose not to use these procedures since they do not wish to attract negative publicity.

A more common form of extortion usually occurs after a security breach in which sensitive company information has been obtained. Often, the threat involves making the information available to competitors or the public unless payment is made. As an example, the *Financial Times* (17 November 2000) reports an incident when an online music retailer's e-commerce systems were compromised and the details of some 300 000 credit cards were obtained. When a demand for a payment of $100,000 was not met, 25 000 credit card numbers were published on the Internet.

◗ Abuse of resources

Organisations have always needed to ensure that employees do not take advantage of company resources for personal reasons. Whilst certain acts, such as sending the occasional personal e-mail, are tolerated by most companies, the increased availability of Internet access and e-mail facilities increases the risk that such facilities may be abused. Two examples of the risks associated with increased access to the Internet involve libel and cyberstalking.

Cyberstalking

This refers to the use of the Internet as a means of harassing another individual. A related activity is known as corporate stalking, where an organisation uses its resources to harass individuals or business competitors.

Cyberstalking is a relatively new form of crime that involves the harassment of individuals via e-mail and the Internet. Of interest to business organisations is the fact that many stalkers make use of company facilities in order to carry out their activities. There have also been cases of 'corporate stalking' where an organisation has used its resources to harass individuals or business competitors. For an organisation, the consequences of cyberstalking can include a loss of reputation and the threat of criminal and civil legal action.

A number of cases where employees have abused company e-mail facilities have received a great deal of publicity. As an example, the *Financial Times* (17 November 2000) reported that Norwich Union was forced to pay £450,000 in damages after staff libelled a competitor in internal e-mails. In another case, some 80 members of staff were suspended by Royal & Sun Alliance after an internal investigation uncovered a series of lewd e-mails circulating. Ten of these individuals were later dismissed as a result of an internal investigation (*Financial Times*, 25 January 2001). These cases demonstrate that allowing Internet resources to be used inappropriately can have serious repercussions for organisations. In addition to the legal and financial consequences of libel and harassment, a great deal of harm can be caused to a company's public image and its relationships with customers and suppliers.

◗ Other risks

Cyberterrorism

This describes attacks made on information systems that are motivated by political or religious beliefs.

Online stock fraud

Most online stock fraud involves posting false information to the Internet in order to increase or decrease the values of stocks.

A thorough discussion of the risks to organisations that arise from increased reliance on the Internet is beyond the scope of this chapter. However, in closing this section we provide two additional examples of emerging threats: cyberterrorism and stock fraud.

Cyberterrorism describes attacks made on information systems that are motivated by political or religious beliefs. Organisations involved in the defence industries are often the victims of such attacks. As an example, the US Department of Defense recorded more than 22 000 attacks on its systems during 1999, many of which were politically motivated. However, many other companies are also at risk from politically motivated attacks. For example, companies trading in countries that are in political turmoil or companies with business partners in these countries also face the risk of such attacks.

A number of recent cases have highlighted the danger of allowing inaccurate or misleading information to propagate across the Internet. **Online stock fraud** involves artificially increasing or decreasing the values of stocks by spreading carefully designed rumours across bulletin boards and chat-rooms. Whilst such activities may seem relatively harmless, companies can suffer significant losses. As an example, the *Financial Times* (7 February 2001) reported the following: 'In separate incidents, Lucent Technologies, the telecoms network equipment giant, and Emulex, a computer network hardware vendor, saw $7.1bn and $2.6bn wiped off their respective stock market values within hours of bogus press releases appearing on the web.'

Incidences of online stock fraud highlight an extremely important issue: organisations are at risk from the distribution of false information across the Internet. It is important to note that the effects of online stock fraud are not limited only to influencing stock prices. Imagine, for example, what might happen if bogus press releases began to appear when a company was in the process of negotiating a merger or strategic alliance. Preventing inaccurate or misleading information from appearing on the Internet is fraught with difficulty. The sheer size of the Internet means that monitoring web sites, chat-rooms and news services places an unacceptable burden on the resources of even the largest organisations. However, the use of intelligent agents, offline readers and meta-search tools, as described in Chapter 4, can go some way towards helping an organisation monitor how it is being portrayed on the Internet.

▶ Managing threats to Internet services

In general terms, threats to information systems that originate from the Internet can be managed using the basic approaches and techniques outlined in this chapter.

Of the four basic strategies outlined earlier, an emphasis is likely to be placed on containment, obfuscation and recovery. Whilst an approach based on deterrence is likely to reduce problems associated with staff abuse of facilities, it is unlikely to discourage threats originating from outside the organisation. For example, it would be extremely difficult to take legal action against an attacker based in another country.

In terms of the specific techniques used to control access to information systems, whilst a great deal of emphasis will usually be placed on telecommunications controls, other methods are also of value. Encryption, for example, is used in a variety of circumstances to ensure that any information transmitted via the Internet is only of value to its intended recipient.

> 82 per cent of UK companies with external links do not use any firewall protection. 59 per cent of UK companies with a web site have yet to implement any method of web site protection.
>
> *Source*: Courtesy of *Computer Weekly*, 10 October 2000

It is also important to remember that a formal security policy will play a key role in ensuring that an organisation is prepared to deal with Internet-based threats. Unfortunately, as evidenced by the DTI's Information Security Breaches Survey 2000, only one in seven organisations has a formal security policy in place, and only one in three organisations actually recognises that the information held by the company is a valuable business asset.

Recently, a range of specialised software applications have appeared that help individuals and companies maintain the security of their systems. Examples include:

● **Firewalls.** Firewalls act as a barrier between an information system and the Internet. The software attempts to monitor and control all incoming and outgoing traffic in an attempt to prevent outsiders gaining access to the information system.

Firewalls
....
A specialised software application mounted on a server at the point the company is connected to the Internet to prevent unauthorised access into the company from outsiders.

- *Intrusion detection software.* This type of software monitors activity on a network in order to identify intruders. Typically, the software will look for characteristic patterns of behaviour that might identify the fact that someone has gained access to the network.
- *Trojan scanners.* Trojan scanners work in much the same way as virus scanners but with the aim of detecting and removing Trojan horse programs.
- *AI software.* Many organisations have begun to develop applications that use artificial intelligence in order to detect intrusion attempts or unusual activity that might indicate a breach in security. As an example, Searchspace has developed an application that a system that detects unusual activity on the London Stock Exchange in order to detect attempts at insider trading.

Chapter 4 describes firewalls and intrusion detection software in more detail.

Summary

1 Controls upon computer-based information systems are needed to ensure the accuracy of data held by an organisation and to prevent loss or damage.

2 The most common threats to computer-based information systems include accidents, natural disasters, sabotage, vandalism, theft, unauthorised use and computer viruses.

3 Accidental damage to computer-based information systems can arise from a number of sources including: inaccurate data entry, attempts to carry out tasks beyond the ability of the employee, failure to comply with procedures for the use of organisational information systems and failure to carry out backup procedures or verify data backups.

4 In some cases, a computer-based information system may be vulnerable to damage caused by natural disasters, such as flooding.

5 Computer-based information systems should be protected against deliberate or unintentional sabotage. The damage or loss caused by unintentional sabotage is often incidental to the actions taken by an employee in pursuit of a different goal.

6 Vandalism can result in an organisation's being deprived of critical hardware, software and data resources.

7 Theft can involve the physical theft of equipment or data theft. Whilst problems caused by physical theft can normally be overcome quickly and easily, data theft can result in significant long-term losses to an organisation.

8 The threat of unauthorised access to confidential data can arise from internal or external sources. Most security breaches involving confidential data can be attributed to the employees of the organisation.

9 There are four basic control strategies that can be applied to the security of computer-based information systems: containment, deterrence, obfuscation and recovery. Containment attempts to control access to an information system and often involves making potential targets as unattractive as possible. A strategy based upon deterrence uses the threat of punishment to discourage potential intruders. Obfuscation concerns itself with hiding or distributing assets so that any damage caused can be limited. A strategy based upon recovery recognises that, no matter how well defended, a breach in the security of an information system will eventually occur. Such a strategy is largely concerned with ensuring that the normal operation of the information system is restored as quickly as possible.

10 Types of control for computer-based information systems include: physical protection, biometric controls, telecommunications controls, failure controls and auditing. Physical protection involves the use of physical barriers intended to protect against theft and unauthorised access. Biometric controls make use of the unique characteristics of individuals, such as fingerprints, in order to restrict access to sensitive information or equipment. Telecommunications controls, such as user validation routines, help to verify the identity of a particular user. Failure controls attempt to limit or avoid damage caused by the failure of an information system. Auditing involves taking stock of procedures, hardware, software and data at regular intervals.

11 Techniques used to control computer-based information systems include: formal security policies, passwords, file encryption, organisational procedures governing the use of computer-based information systems and user validation techniques.

12 A formal security policy should be supported by management and widely publicised. The policy will outline what is considered to be acceptable use of the information system and the sanctions available in the event that an employee does not comply with the policy.

13 Encryption involves encoding data so that it is meaningless to anyone except the rightful owner.

14 Backup procedures enable an organisation to protect sensitive files by making copies that can be stored at a safe location. The 'grandfather, father, son' technique is one of the most popular methods of making backups. An incremental backup provides a means of copying only those files that have changed in some way since the last backup was made. This provides a number of benefits, such as the ability to trace the changes that a given file has undergone over time.

15 Computer viruses, worms, Trojans and logic bombs represent a growing threat to information systems security. A computer virus is a computer program that is capable of self-replication, allowing it to spread from one 'infected' machine to another. All computer viruses are considered harmful and steps should be taken to protect valuable data from infection.

16 As organisations begin to rely on the Internet as a means of conducting business transactions, new threats to the security of information systems have begun to emerge. Some of these threats include denial of service attacks, brand abuse, identity theft, extortion and online stock fraud.

EXERCISES

Self-assessment exercises

1 What are the two basic reasons for the need to control computer-based information systems?

2 List some of the advantages and disadvantages of using passwords to protect equipment and sensitive data from unauthorised users.

3 What types of controls can be used to protect a computer-based information system against vandalism, theft and unauthorised access?

4 What are the advantages and disadvantages of an approach to controlling computer-based information systems that is based on containment?

5   Describe some of the ways in which accidental damage can occur to a computer-based information system.

6   Explain why virus scanning software and anti-virus programs are often of only limited value in detecting and removing computer viruses.

Discussion questions

1   What motivates an individual or organisation to create a computer virus?

2   'No computer-based information system can be considered completely secure – all organisations should base their control strategies on recovery.' Make a case in favour or against this argument.

3   'An increased reliance on the Internet exposes organisations to increased risk in terms of threats to information systems security.' Make a case in favour or against this argument.

Essay questions

1   Conduct any research necessary and produce a formal security policy governing student access to the computer systems at the institution that you attend. In addition to providing details of any controls already in place, your work must also address the areas listed below. For each of these areas, you should also justify any decisions or choices made:

   (a) what activities are considered acceptable;
   (b) what activities are considered unacceptable;
   (c) the sanctions that may be used against those failing to comply with the policy.

2   Select an organisation that you are familiar with, such as a university or bank. Conduct any research necessary to address the following tasks:

   (a) Describe the potential impact of infection by computer viruses on the organisation's computer-based information systems.
   (b) Consider the effectiveness of tools, methods and procedures designed to protect computer-based information systems from computer viruses.
   (c) Evaluate the level of risk posed to the organisation by computer viruses and produce a set of recommendations that may assist the organisation in reducing this risk.

3   Outline some of the threats to information systems that arise as a result of doing business via the Internet. Illustrate your response with appropriate examples and indicate how the risks you identify can be mitigated.

Examination questions

1   Computer viruses represent a significant threat to the security of organisational computer-based information systems. It is estimated that as many as 500 new computer viruses appear each month. You are required to:

   (a) Provide a definition of the term 'computer virus'.
   (b) Using relevant examples, describe the ways in which computer viruses can be transmitted.
   (c) Discuss some of the ways in which organisations can protect against computer viruses. Highlight some of the advantages and disadvantages of each method described.

2   With regard to the control of computer-based information systems, answer the following:

   (a) Describe some of the common security threats facing organisational computer-based information systems.
   (b) Explain the four basic approaches to controlling computer-based information systems. Highlight the advantages and disadvantages of each approach.
   (c) 'More effective protection for a computer-based information system can be achieved by

▶

employing a combination of the four basic approaches to control.' Using relevant examples, discuss this statement.

3 A formal security policy can provide an effective means of protecting an organisation's computer-based information systems against theft, damage and other hazards.

(a) Provide an overview of the areas that will be outlined by a typical formal security policy document.

(b) Describe the ways in which a formal security policy can help to protect an organisation's computer-based information systems.

(c) A number of factors will determine whether or not a security policy works effectively. Using relevant examples, provide a brief discussion of some of these factors.

Further reading

Bernstein, T. (ed.) (1996) *Internet Security for Business*, John Wiley, New York. A somewhat technical but comprehensive treatment of security

Burger, R. (1989) *Computer Viruses – A High-Tech Disease*, 3rd edition, Data Becker, Newton, MA

Fites, P., Johnston, P. and Kratz, M. (1992) *The Computer Virus Crisis*, 2nd edition, Van Nostrand Reinhold, New York

Forrester, T. and Morrison, P. (1995) *Computer Ethics*, 2nd edition, MIT Press, Cambridge, MA

Gralla, P. (1999) *The Complete Idiot's Guide to Protecting Yourself Online*, Idiots Guide, Indianapolis, IN. As with all 'Idiot's Guides' this is a highly informative and accessible text

Levy, S. (1994) *Hackers: Heroes of the Computer Revolution*, Penguin, London. An investigation into the behaviour of computer hackers, including Steve Wozniak, who later formed Apple Computers

Mungo, P. and Clough, B. (1993) *Approaching Zero*, Faber and Faber, London. This is often credited as the book that introduced the notion of information warfare and brought computer crime to the public's attention. Although a little dated in places, much of the material is still relevant today

Stein, L. (1997) *Web Security: A Step-by-Step Reference Guide*, Addison-Wesley, Reading, MA

Web links

www.elsevier.com/inca/publications/store/4/0/5/8/7/7 *Computers and Security* (international journal). Includes full articles and a search facility.

www.acm.org/pubs/contents/journals/tissec *ACM Transactions on Information and System Security*. Various articles are available to download.

datamation.earthweb.com *Datamation* is a publication aimed at IS professionals with sections dedicated to security and e-commerce.

www.alw.nih.gov/Security/security.html Wide range of documents, publications, FAQs and other materials related to security.

www.intelbrief.com/compusec.htm IntelBrief provides a huge range of resources related to computer security, including a comprehensive news section.

www.lockdown.co.uk LockDown is a site aimed at home computer users. It provides information on security threats rated by severity. This site gives an excellent overview of the very large and diverse range of security problems that computer users face. Note that many of the problems listed in the site's database also apply to business computer users.

www.cert.org The Computer Emergency Response Team provides up-to-date information on security issues related to the Internet. The site publishes some interesting statistics concerning the number of incidents investigated.

www.infosyssec.org Information Systems Security Alert. This is a highly respected site that contains links to literally hundreds of resources. Of particular interest is a sophisticated search facility that allows information to be located on all aspects of security.

www.mountainwave.com Computer Security News provides a daily digest of news. Many of the articles are of specific interest to business users.

www.boran.com/security The IT Security Cookbook. A set of documents that provide detailed information on security management. There is a particularly good section on firewalls.

www.mcafee.com McAfee publishes Virus Scan, widely regarded as the best virus detection package available. The site contains a great deal of information on individual computer viruses.

www.askbub.com Bub claims to answer any question related to computer security or hacking.

csrc.nist.gov/nistpubs NIST publishes a range of official documents dealing with aspects of computer security. Amongst these are various guides and handbooks including an introductory guide to computer security.

www.vmyths.com This site sheds light on common myths related to viruses and computer security.

End-user computing – providing end-user services

LEARNING OBJECTIVES

After reading this chapter, readers will be able to:
- define the range of services that must be delivered to support end-users effectively;
- distinguish between the general term end-user computing and the more specific end-user development;
- analyse the risks associated with pursuing end-user development of information systems as part of a company's IS strategy;
- recommend policies for the effective management of end-user computing within an organisation;
- recommend new information systems applications that could reasonably be developed by end-user staff within an organisation.

MANAGEMENT ISSUES

End-user computing plays a significant role in the majority of organsations since, as we have seen throughout the book, many business users regularly use BIS as an essential part of their role. Managerial issues involved with controlling the use of information systems by end-users include:
- Assessing the emphasis to be placed on end-user software development activities.
- Providing a suitable support function to assist end-users in their use of computers.
- Ensuring the appropriate skill levels for end-users through staff development and training.
- Controlling the cost of end-user activities and support.

Links to other chapters

Protecting information, another key role of the IS manager, is covered in Chapter 15. Attributes of good-quality data were covered in Chapter 1.

End-user computing and the location of support services are elements of overall IS strategy which is described in Chapter 13.

Issues involved with employeee monitoring described in Chapter 17.

Introduction

This chapter considers some of the many tasks to support end-users that need to be performed by an information systems manager in the modern organisation. At the top of the list of priorities is the management of user information within the organisation – ensuring that it is secure, that backups are made and that its quality is maintained. A further important aspect of managing the information quality is ensuring that it is delivered to the user in a reliable and timely way. The management of the network is key to achieving this, but ensuring reliable access to the applications needed to work with the data is also important. This is particularly true with mission-critical applications – the operational systems used to deal with customers for taking orders and reservations. When a new version of the EuropCar car reservation system failed, for example, it is estimated to have cost the company $300,000 in lost orders over three days.

The protection of information is one type of end-user service that was covered in the previous chapter. As well as managing information, the network and applications, the IS manager has to manage other services provided to end-users to help them work with this application. These 'soft' services include advice, troubleshooting various problems and assisting users in developing their own applications. End-user development is an increasingly important activity with the move to PCs from a central mainframe and dumb terminal arrangement, giving more opportunities for tailoring of applications. This chapter will focus on the management of these 'soft' services and examine how they should be integrated into a company's overall IS strategy.

End-user service provision is often considered under the heading 'end-user computing'. This covers a wide range of activities. In this chapter, the distinction is made between the use of applications created by others by the end-user (**end-user computing**) and the *creation* of applications by the end-user (**end-user development**). The chapter considers how to provide services to support both classes of activity. Supporting both activities is certainly important – Robson (1997) suggests that what she defines as user-controlled computing has increased from 25 per cent of IS budgets in the early 1980s to 75–90 per cent in the 1990s.

End-user computing (EUC)

All uses of computers by business people who are not information systems professionals.

End-user development (EUD)

Systems development and programming undertaken by non-IS staff.

End user IS services

All services required to support end users in running their PCs and developing and using applications.

End-user IS services

The main **end-user services** that the information systems manager has to provide are as follows:

1 *Provide a help-desk service*. This will solve problems that users are having in using their software. This will involve troubleshooting to work out the source of the problem, which could be caused by:

- the way the user is using the software;
- a problem with the way the software has been installed;

- a bug in the software;
- an underlying hardware or networking problem.

This service must be delivered as rapidly as possible, but this is often difficult to achieve since a help desk will have to juggle many requests, some of which may be quite time-consuming to solve.

2 *Achieve standardisation of software.* Applications used across departments should be standardised to reduce the cost of purchase through volume discounts and to ensure easy transfer of information through the organisation (Chapter 3).

3 *Ensure network efficiency.* Users should not experience 'downtime' when the network is unavailable (Chapter 5).

4 *Provide training.* Users require training in the use of standard and company applications and where necessary in how to develop applications or manage information when end-user development is undertaken.

5 *Delivering services to end-users cost-effectively.* This is referred to as 'minimising the total cost of ownership', which includes both the initial cost of purchase of hardware and software and the ongoing cost of maintenance.

At a more strategic level, the IS manager will be responsible for:

- setting the organisation's IS strategy covering issues such as integration with business strategy, investment levels and whether services are centralised or decentralised (Chapter 14);
- establishing IS infrastructure (networks, hardware and software services);
- implementation of corporate strategy through developing line-of-business systems;
- ensuring that the company follows ethical or legal codes for health and safety and data protection (Chapter 18).

Managing network services

▶ Network management services

Network management services are part of the goal of integrated information management. This will include the following end-user services that are normally managed centrally:

- maintaining servers, including file (document) servers, database servers and web servers for intranets (Chapter 5 describes types of servers);
- ensuring availability of end-user applications;
- backup and restoration of information;
- network maintenance.

In many companies, the magnitude of the cost of managing user services is not recognised. To start with, the number of PCs and the different applications they run must be audited. The number of PCs that have been purchased and applications being used may be a surprise. For example, on completing its first audit, Nottinghamshire County Council discovered 6500 PCs across 830 sites. A recent survey in the UK of 500 IT and finance directors by market research company Banner discovered that 47 per cent had no tools to help in auditing the software applications used or for troubleshooting. This shows that network management and end-user services can be neglected in some organisations.

▶ Cost-effective delivery of IS services

A growing realisation among many IS and financial managers is that the total cost of ownership of each PC in a company is significant when summed across all PCs in the organisation. Traditionally, companies have costed PCs on the initial purchase price or the cost of leasing, without explicitly costing the other services required to support a PC and its users. These other costs are all the end-user services referred to above, such as running a help desk to solve end-user problems and managing user information. It also includes other costs such as:

- the loss of productive work time when users are unable to use their computer;
- the loss of productive work time when someone is trying to fix a colleague's problem (this type of unofficial support can be very costly);
- the cost of consumables such as paper and toner for printing.

Total cost of ownership (TCO)
TCO refers to the total cost for a company operating a computer. This includes not only the purchase or leasing cost, but also the cost of all the services needed to support the end-user.

This issue was highlighted in the USA in the mid-1990s by studies by the Gartner Group which have shown that the annual cost of servicing a PC, known as the **total cost of ownership (TCO)**, runs at $8000 per year.

Figure 16.1 shows the breakdown of the TCO. Costs in these categories can be attributed to 'desktop costs', related to the PC hardware and software, and 'network costs', related to managing communications and the network operating system. Desktop costs account for about two-thirds of the TCO. Note the relatively small proportion that is spent on capital and that all the other costs can be considered as aspects of supporting end-user computing. Further studies have shown that if companies carefully manage their PC resources, they can achieve cost savings of up to $3100 per PC per annum.

In 1996, US PC manufacturer Compaq launched a marketing initiative based on the cost of ownership that claims that Compaq 'costs you less than other computers' due to tools bundled with the computer to reduce TCO. Microsoft's initiative of Zero Administration Windows (ZAW) and tools such as Systems Management Server (SMS) are aimed at reducing the cost of distributing and maintaining software. SMS provides:

- automated software distribution and upgrades;
- metering of which applications are being used;
- hardware and software inventory for each machine;

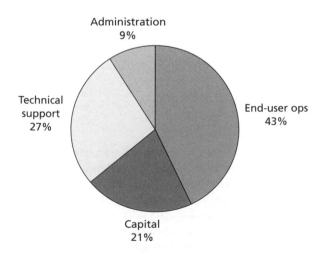

Figure 16.1 Breakdown of the total cost of ownership
Source: Gartner Group (1996)

● troubleshooting diagnostics of each machine from a remote location (i.e. users' machines can be monitored from a help desk).

The TCO can also be reduced by using simpler, less expensive hardware, which is the idea behind the network computer and NetPC. The case study on using network computers shows how the savings can be achieved.

MINI CASE STUDY

Using network computers to reduce the total cost of ownership

A further response to reducing TCO is to treat the problem at its root cause – the complexity of the PC. By reducing the options to configure each PC and its software individually, there is less risk of its failing and the need for support. This has led to the idea of the network computer (introduced in Chapter 3). This is a simplified computer that runs the software on a network server. This reduces the purchase cost, since the computer needs less RAM memory, no hard disk, no floppy disk and a less powerful processor than a PC. It also reduces the cost of ownership, since there are fewer hardware items to fail and the software can be managed by central support staff rather than the end-user. Of course, simplifying the maintenance of the computer in this way also reduces the flexibility of options available for the end-user.

Since the NC concept was first discussed in 1995, a number of companies have purchased large numbers of NCs to help reduce the TCO. For example, in the UK retailer Safeway and insurer Eagle Star have each bought several hundred, and in the US Boeing has committed to buying several thousand. Despite large individual purchases, it should be noted that the market for NCs is still less than 1 per cent of the desktop computer market.

The network computer concept was chiefly promoted by Oracle and IBM. It represents a threat to rival companies Microsoft and Intel, since typically it would not use Windows for the operating system or Intel processors. To counter this, several counterinitiatives have been launched. These include a hardware initiative through the concept of a Net PC, which can be thought of as a hybrid between a PC and an NC, with the aim again being to reduce the TCO, but without removing all the flexibility of the PC. There are two main software initiatives to date. The first is Hydra, included in Windows NT 5.0 to allow Windows-based applications to be run on a server while the user only uses a relative low-cost Windows terminal from a manufacturer such as Wyse. The second is to build tools into the operating system to make central administration of PCs, NCs and Windows terminals more effective. This is known as ZAW or Zero Administration Windows.

▶ Managing employee access to the Internet

A further TCO issue is the level of staff access to the Internet. Governments incite employers to empower employees by widening access in order to increase competitiveness. However, is it practical to give all employees access or should it be limited? An extreme example of the type of problem that can arise is highlighted by the case of Lois Franxhi, a 28-year-old IT manager who was sacked in July 1998 for making nearly 150 searches over 4 days in office hours for a holiday. As with many unfair dismissals, the case was not clearcut, with Mrs Franxhi claiming the company sacked her because of sex discrimination – she was pregnant at the time of the dismissal. The tribunal dismissed these claims, finding that the employee had lied about the use of the Internet, saying she had only used it for one lunchtime when, in fact, records showed she had used it over four days. More recently hundreds of employees have been sacked for access to and distribution of material interpreted as 'lewd' by their employers. Complete Activity 16.1 for a discussion of actions a company can take to deal with these problems of employee access.

Activity 16.1

Controlling employee access to the Internet

Purpose

To consider the issues involved with granting employees access to the Internet and personal e-mail addresses.

Activity

In this scenario, you are a senior manager at the B2B company who has just read the latest International Benchmarking study commissioned by the DTI (DTI, 2000) which presents data from across Europe and North America and Japan on access levels (Figs 16.2 and 16.3). Employee access to the Internet for your company is limited. You want to remain competitive, but are concerned about the issues of staff time wasting indicated by an article you read in the *Guardian* and the cost and possible problems with employee relations of monitoring staff access.

Questions

Referring to Figures 16.2 and 16.3,

1 prepare a list of advantages and disadvantages of enabling widespread employee access;

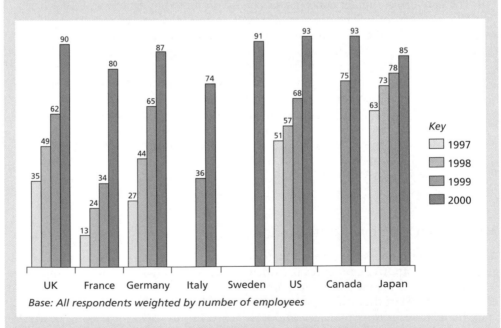

Base: All respondents weighted by number of employees

Figure 16.2 Business access to the Internet between 1997 and 2000
Source: DTI (2000)

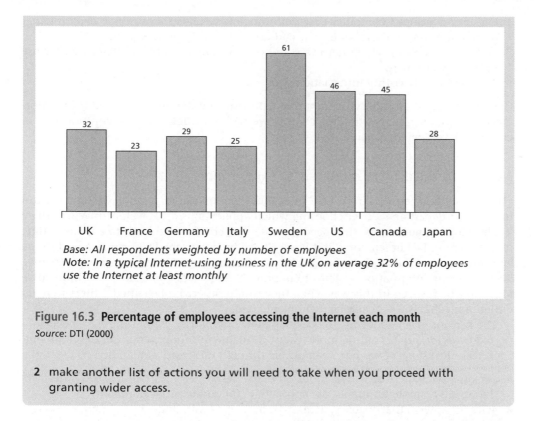

Base: All respondents weighted by number of employees
Note: In a typical Internet-using business in the UK on average 32% of employees
use the Internet at least monthly

Figure 16.3 Percentage of employees accessing the Internet each month
Source: DTI (2000)

2 make another list of actions you will need to take when you proceed with granting wider access.

End-user computing

▶ What is end-user computing?

The term *end-user computing* has different meanings according to the context in which it is used. The following statements could all refer to end-user computing:

- all tools by which non-data processing staff handle their own problems without professional programmers;
- creative use of data processing by non-data-processing experts;
- complex computing by non-data-processing professionals to answer organisational information needs;
- non-technical end-users using user-friendly, fourth-generation languages (4GLs) and PCs to generate reports or build decision support systems;
- the use of computer hardware and software by people in organisations whose jobs are usually classified as net users of information systems rather than net developers of information systems.

The common theme is that staff whose main job function is not building information systems are doing some system development. The definitions vary in what is meant by 'system development'. For some staff this may mean just that: developing a complete information system. More frequently, it will mean users' building their own spreadsheet model or using a report generator. The three main types of end-user computing can be defined as:

1 end-user-developed computer-based information systems for personal, departmental or organisation-wide use, where the end-user is a non-IT professional;

2 end-user control of which hardware and package applications are purchased for use in their department;

3 end-user use of existing information systems.

Clearly, each type of end-user computing represents a different challenge for the information systems manager. In this chapter we will consider end-user computing and end-user development separately.

◗ What are the drivers for end-user computing?

The primary business driver for EUC from the *organisational perspective* is greater control in end-user departments over choosing which applications are developed. Where there is a backlog of applications that need to be developed, this also leads to a reduced time for a system to be implemented if it is developed by end-users. EUC can also lead to the empowerment of staff in functional areas of an organisation to follow through creative ideas for using information systems to improve the efficiency of their work. Innovative ideas may be fostered in this way when they would otherwise be stifled if there were no outlet or mechanism for their being implemented.

The reasons given above for the development of end-user computing have been supported by *technology* becoming more readily available to support end-user development. Such technical support has become possible through increased availability of:

● personal computers or workstations on users' desktops with graphical user interfaces that (unlike simple terminals) are appropriate for end-user development;
● 4GLs (Chapter 4) that enable systems to be developed with limited programming skills;
● visual development tools such as Visual Basic, PowerBuilder and Delphi, which make it easier to prototype application screen layouts and navigation between data views – these tools also enable screen elements such as tables to be readily integrated with information from a database;
● support for extending productivity applications. For example, Microsoft Word or Excel can be extended to an end-user application using the Visual Basic for Applications tools.

Finally, EUC has also been enabled by IS skills among the workforce increasing as the overall standard of IT familiarity grows through staff using IT throughout their education and into the workplace.

◗ Which company staff are involved in end-user computing?

A common method of describing end-user computing is according to the skills of the end-user. This method was described in a paper from the early 1980s by Rockart and Flannery, summarised in Table 16.1. Some of the terms used have been superseded (updated equivalents are shown in brackets), but the basic definition remains valid. The classification does not represent a continuum from Class 1 to 6, but rather two different groupings: first, business users of different skills levels in Classes 1 to 3, and then support personnel in Classes 4 to 6. Blili et al. (1996) present a more recent review of how end-user computing can be defined, grouping work into types of user, types of application and end-user behaviour.

A further important method of describing end-user computing is according to the way in which it is controlled. This will typically vary in line with the maturity of end-user computing in an organisation. Initially there will be no control and an organic

Table 16.1 **Different types of end-user personnel. Updated descriptions based on original classes of Rockart and Flannery (1983).**

Class	Term	Description
1	**Non-programming end-users**	These are users of software developed by others
2	**Command-level end-users (power users)**	These are users who use more sophisticated functions of a package, such as formulas and macros in a spreadsheet such as Excel
3	**Programming-level end-users**	Here users write their own functions using add-on application languages such as Visual Basic for Applications
4	**Functional support personnel (business analysts and developers)**	These are support staff who work in one area of the business to provide end-user development and support
5	**End-user computing support personnel (help-desk staff)**	These are the support staff who exist to troubleshoot hardware and software problems that are encountered by users in Classes 1 to 3
6	**Data-processing programmers (application developers)**	This type of programming staff has traditionally worked on company operational or reporting systems

growth of EUC. As EUC becomes more prevalent, problems caused by the lack of control will occur and a need will be identified by business and IS managers to take measures to control it. Control measures are referred to below.

The information centre

Information centre (IC) is an American term that has arisen from a concept developed by IBM in the 1980s. Typical information centres developed at this time are described by White and Christy (1987). In the UK and Europe, the equivalent is usually referred to by the less grand terms 'IT support' or 'help desk'. However, the IC or modern IT support centre offers much more than phone support to users – it provides all the services required for end-users to use and develop applications.

The range of services offered by a typical information centre are:

1 *Help desk support for user problems.* Case Study 16.1 on Pfizer's help desk illustrates the different levels of support that are offered.
2 *Advice on software purchase.* This ensures that the software is suitable for its purpose and is compatible with hardware, other software and company purchasing schemes.
3 *Advice on hardware purchase.* This will usually be a centralised standard, again to take advantage of discounts and limiting support contracts.
4 *Advice on how end-user development should be approached.* The support person will suggest the best approaches for developing software, such as following the main parts of the lifecycle. These can be defined through more detailed training.
5 *Application development.* For larger systems, the IC staff may be involved in performing the systems analysis and design or more difficult aspects of the programming.
6 *Training.* In particular, on packages or development techniques.
7 *Data management.* Management and supply of data to end-users or explanations of formats used.

The main difficulty with information centres is getting the balance right between providing a flexible service and exerting controls that are too restrictive. The information

Information Centre (IC)
....
A central facility in an organisation which provides end-user help-desk services such as phone support for troubleshooting end-user software and hardware problems, training, guidance on end-user development and management of user information.

centre can be valuable in providing controls to prevent the type of problems that are described in the following section.

As part of the trend to outsourcing of IS described in Chapter 14, many help desks are now outsourced to other companies. For example, within Rolls-Royce UK, user support is now provided by EDS staff. Microsoft outsources its help desk for its applications and operating systems to companies such as Digital (now part of Compaq). The case study on Pfizer's help desk illustrates how a company has taken steps to avoid the problems that could occur through outsourcing. It highlights a common three-tier method of profiling user problems so that they can be dealt with efficiently. The case study also illustrates how a company is evolving the strategy for its help desk.

CASE STUDY 16.1

Levels of end-user support at Pfizer

In recent years computer service departments have come under increasing pressure from business units to significantly raise the level of support they provide. As a result, service level agreements have become an accepted way of life. Yet at the same time, as many companies look to focus their internal expertise on core business rather than support services, these departments are under the constant threat of outsourcing as well as pressure to contain, if not reduce, ongoing costs.

Key to providing that service is an integrated and efficient help desk. Pfizer Central Research, part of pharmaceutical giant Pfizer, has recently been awarded Help Desk of the Year by the Help Desk User Group. Steve Ladyman, head of computer user support at Pfizer, attributes the award to the company's 'very professional approach to the help desk'. He says, 'We have an innovative approach to resolving help desk problems'. A key element of that innovative approach has been the adoption of a co-sourcing agreement for the staffing of the help desk. As Ladyman explains, most firms in this competitive market are concentrating on core business. 'Pfizer employees are focused on drug discovery and development rather than IT', he says. Pfizer, like many rivals, initially took the contracting approach to help desk staff. 'We found they were not fully committed to us which created a morale problem', Ladyman says. With average staff turnover hitting six months, the obvious lack of training programmes and a career development path was significantly affecting the ongoing level of service the help desk could provide Pfizer employees.

So Pfizer adopted a co-sourcing strategy. 'The help desk staff are not Pfizer employees, but are full time for DCS [the outsourcing firm which holds the contract]', he says. And, to overcome that morale problem, the contract between Pfizer and DCS stipu-

lates a training plan and clear career development must be in place. 'They work to similar terms and conditions of both pay and holiday as Pfizer employees', he says.

Since this strategy was implemented early in 1995, the help desk has lost only one staff member – a clear indication, says Ladyman, of the success of co-sourcing. But, to ensure the help desk is still under Pfizer's firm managerial control, each of the three tiers of the help desk is managed by a Pfizer employee. This three-tier help desk architecture is, according to Ladyman, Pfizer's other innovative solution for creating a truly supportive help desk.

The first tier attempts to solve the user's problem there and then, usually over the phone. These are calls relating to recognised, standard problems that are documented and have a clear, predefined response. Pfizer's target is to solve 60% of calls this way and the company is already achieving a 50% resolution rate. The second tier is also for recognised problems, but those that require actual physical work on the system – and a visit to the user's site. The third tier deals with unrecognised problems. 'The third tier expert is given time not only to find and fix the problem, but to document it and train second tier staff to solve it themselves in a predefined manner should that problem occur again', Ladyman says.

The target is to ensure a third tier problem should arise once only – once solved it has a standard fix and can be handled by one of the first two tiers. Pfizer has not yet attained this goal. 'We are trying to capitalise learning within a documented solution and contain support costs', says Ladyman. Controlling staff turnover on the help desk is key to attaining these targets: previously without good documentation and follow-up training, rapid staff turnover meant problems were having to be regularly resolved. 'Rapid staff turnover means that, without adequate documentation of problems, when a problem recurs you have to go back to the beginning', says Ladyman. 'We are trying to be much more careful in our documentation of solutions, which means we have a greater likelihood of the expertise being on site if a problem returns.'

Underpinning this new strategy has been the replacement of the firm's existing help desk software with Utopia from Utopia. As one of the new breed of client/server help desk products, Utopia enables Pfizer to build an extensive database of user problems, providing the opportunity to spot trends and track problem resolution to ensure a satisfactory response to user demands.

Ladyman says, 'Our target is to contain costs.' He says, 'Pfizer has a highly technical user population. They are very bright and tend to be pushing IT to the limits. We don't want users trying to solve problems that we can solve more quickly for them. The strategy is not about reducing calls to the help desk, but increasing the efficiency with which they are solved.' Ladyman cites two recent trends spotted by help desk staff where specific departments were logging a higher-than-average number of calls. One department had many calls about cc:mobile which, after analysis, the help desk team was able to link to the fact that members of that department are constantly on the road. 'The other department is clearly pushing technology to the limit', he explains.

Using this information, Pfizer is starting to work out specific training programmes for cc:mobile users to help them with problem solving. In addition, Ladyman says the information will prove critical in negotiations with user departments about service level agreements. 'The previous help desk software gave us no information to help us to put agreements in place. It was a driving reason for replacing the help desk software', says Ladyman.

Having achieved the first phase of the implementation, Pfizer will now look to setting up an improved asset register for asset management in the next phase which will, eventually, be followed by change management. 'Effective asset management is a big target', he concedes. 'We have 2300 PCs to support and if we do an audit one day, you can guarantee the next day some of those PCs will have moved. This has always been a headache.' Despite the early success of the help desk strategy, Ladyman remains pragmatic. 'I don't think anyone has help desks right yet. The demand for support services is always ahead of what you can economically provide and there is always someone who needs help quicker than you can provide it. But with our three tier model, co-sourcing and the tools set we have implemented, we have an advantage over other organisations running help desks in this environment'.

Source: 'IT help desk: questions and answers', courtesy of *Computer Weekly*, 12 September 1996

Questions

1 Explain the three-tier method used for targeting the type of enquiry being made.

2 How has Pfizer attempted to keep the help desk staff well integrated with business users, despite their being employed by another company?

3 Summarise the future strategy that Pfizer has developed for managing its help desk.

▶ Help desk technologies

In this section we briefly review the way in which information systems are used to support the use of other information systems within a company!

1 *Asset management software.* Help desk staff need to know the technical details of the systems being used in the company and the software loaded on them. This is achieved by asset management software such as Microsoft Systems Management server. This can also distribute new software automatically.

2 *Computer telephony integration (CTI).* CTI gives automatic phone number identification and the system will then load up the details of the computer, its current user and configuration. This allows first-tier calls to be answered much faster.

3 *Case-based reasoning.* These systems use artificial intelligence techniques (Chapter 6) to guide the user or help desk staff through the process of solving the problem.

4 *Web-based intranet access.* Users can access frequently asked questions, send an e-mail or type in keywords describing their problems. Problems solved this way will save help desk staff the time spent dealing with straightforward queries.

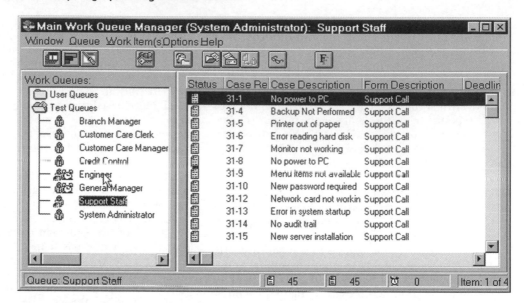

Figure 16.4 **Workflow system from Staffware being used to prioritise support calls**

5 *Workflow*. Workflow systems can be used to prioritise user queries and assign them to the staff best placed to deal with them. An example of a workflow queue used in a help desk is shown in Figure 16.4.

Further details on the type of facilities available in help desk software are provided by Utopia, one of the most frequently used products worldwide (see **www.utosoft.com**).

End-user development

End-user development of applications represents a major trend in the use of information technology in organisations. An increasing number of users are writing their own software or spreadsheet models to help in decision making. This was not possible before there was a PC on every desktop. The user was then reliant on the IS department writing applications. Because the IS department focused on strategic applications, the users' requests for small-scale applications would often be ignored.

▶ Applications and tools for end-user development

There is a wide range of possible applications for end-user developed software listed below. Typically it is the smaller-scale, departmental applications that are most appropriate for end-user development. The development tools reflect these. These tools are usually high-level reporting and programming tools. It is rare for the end-user to program using a lower-level language such as C++ or Java, which would require extensive training. Possible types of applications include:

- reports from a corporate database using standard enquiries defined by the IS/IT function;
- simple ad hoc queries to databases defined by the user. For someone in an airline, for example, these might include access to a frequent flier database, customer reservation system or crew rostering system to monitor performance of each;
- what-if? analysis using tools such as spreadsheet models or more specialised tools such as risk or financial management packages or business intelligence software,

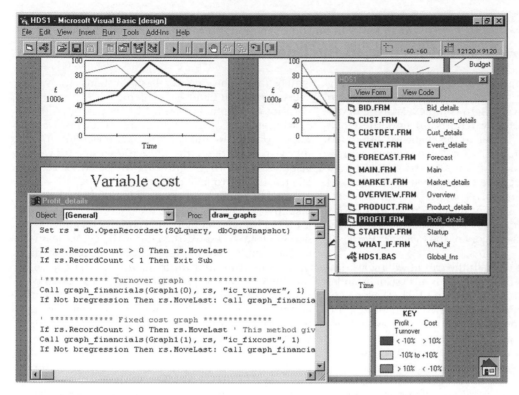

Figure 16.5 Visual Basic development tool showing onscreen forms and development code

used for monitoring sales and marketing performance of information stored in a data warehouse;
- writing company information for a company intranet;
- development of applications such as a job costing tool or production scheduling system, using easy-to-use, high-level tools such as application generators, PC database management systems such as Microsoft Access or Borland, or visual programming environments such as Microsoft Visual Basic, Borland Delphi, Powerbuilder or Centura.

An example of a visual programming environment is shown in Figure 16.5. The user has easy-to-use tools to draw graphs and tables and to populate these with information from a database. Program code (shown in the window) may be required to achieve this.

❿ Reasons for the growth of end-user development

The reason for the increase in end-user-developed applications is a combination of two main factors. The first is that it only became practical for end-users to develop software with the introduction of the PC and graphical systems development tools. With earlier mainframe and minicomputer systems, it was not practical for people who were not in the IS department to develop software; neither the tools nor the access were available.

The second reason is that users were not receiving the required response from the IS department in terms of building systems for them. This is often known as the **applications backlog**. The IS department has rightly to focus on corporate, mission-critical applications such as production, financial and customer services applications. It follows that they will not have the resources available to develop smaller-scale systems required in departments. As an example of this, one UK travel industry organisation has a

Applications backlog
The demand for new applications by users exceeds the capacity of the IS department or IS outsourcing company to develop them.

End-user development training at the Open University

In the fast-changing world of Windows, training staff can quickly rise from providing guidance on simple word processing to complex database development. Jason Hobby reports on how the Open University not only rose to the challenge, but found wider recognition in CW's coveted training awards. A team of just two systems analysts working on a shoestring budget have transformed more than 200 staff at the Open University (OU) from mere PC users to amateur systems developers. In the process they scooped for the university the End User Training Award, a category of the *Computer Weekly* IT Training Awards.

The hard graft on both the part of willing learners and the two experienced systems analysts falls under the mantle of the university's End User Development (EUD) Scheme, specifically geared to adapting IT to meet local needs directly. Essentially, it allows individuals or departments to develop the applications they choose without waiting for the IT department to do it for them.

The OU defines six levels of end-user computing, ranging from basic word processing to complex multi-user relational databases. It is at levels four and five that the EUD support team steps in, providing instruction in the development of simple, single-table databases to more complex office-modelling procedures. This is restricted to PC hardware, stopping short of university-wide systems.

The administrative staff at whom the scheme is aimed are expected to do much of the local data manipulation. Sandra Evans, one of the two systems analysts involved in the training project, explains. 'The basic word processing skills were already catered for, but there was this higher level where people started wanting to use tools such as Microsoft Access. They needed to write their own databases.'

In the beginning the trainers concentrated on teaching how to use only Microsoft Access but, 'Then we also realised they would need to do a small amount of systems analysis', Evans says. 'Something slightly different from using Word and Excel – actually learning how to design a database properly.' So Evans set up a one-day Basic Systems Analysis course, classroom-based and with the intention of teaching the rudiments of systems development and providing guidance on key issues such as security, back-ups and data protection.

The trainees are taken step-by-step through the development process with a case study exercise. Next follows the two-day Microsoft Access course, which unlike the one-day Basic Systems Analysis course has a high hands-on content.

'A lot of people don't want to come and do the systems analysis course', says Evans. 'They just want to get straight on and work with the PC. But once they've been through the course they realise it's very valuable, before they start using the PC, to be actually taught how to do it properly.'

The Microsoft Access course for the developers takes the system designed in the analysis course and leads the learner through the techniques required to develop it in Access. At the end of the course learners have built a five-table relational database with query, reporting and forms facilities. The course, says the OU, is designed for varying levels of ability with step-by-step instructions for the less confident and things to try for the more advanced who want to experiment. Afterwards, if the developers ask for something called 'mentor support', one of the support team is allocated to their particular project to assist in the development. 'People enjoyed the training', says Evans, 'I think mainly because they actually wanted to do it. They know that back in the office they have to deal with a large amount of data and they can't teach themselves.'

In the beginning funding was hard to come by. 'We had to put a bid in ourselves to get funding for the course', says Evans. 'We set up the training ourselves on a very, very limited budget to begin with.' So far, more than 200 staff have attended the courses and there are over 60 successful developments, with more currently under way. The major benefits, says the OU, have been found in regional offices where their particular requirements have never been met by central services. Applications include tutorial timetabling, exam deferrals, invigilator allocation and exam special needs. Several systems have been written in one department, and they have been so successful that the systems are adopted by others. Examples include an inventory database, holiday bookings, contacts database and tutor enquiries. There have also been examples of staff using the scheme to further their careers: one progressed to a project management job on the university's major student registration systems development.

'A lot of the paperwork has gone', says Evans. 'People are more aware that they can get hold of data and do things with it instead of asking us. They are quite happy to have a go and do it themselves, a lot faster and a lot more efficiently, and not to have to wait several weeks for a programmer from the IT

▶

department to come along and do it for them.' Plans for the future include offering more than just training on Access because the newly confident developers are thinking of using other tools. 'There are quite a lot of requirements other than just databases', Evans says. 'We are also hoping to start encouraging departments to build up their own expertise in end-user development; to have their own local expert rather than keep coming to us for support.'

Source: OU Study, courtesy of *Computer Weekly*, 1996

Questions

1 What different types of end-user computing does the Open University recognise?

2 What types of end-user developed systems have been produced?

3 What benefits has the scheme brought?

4 Why do you think staff didn't want to take the systems analysis course? Should it be compulsory, in your opinion?

backlog of nearly 100 systems required by users to add to over 120 existing systems. Any new system requested will almost certainly not be authorised by the IS department. For example, if the marketing department requires a new system to analyse sales performance and it requests this from the central IS, it will almost certainly be of a lower priority than items that were requested a year ago. As a result, the *only* option may be for it to be developed in the marketing department or to ask an outside consultant to develop it. Viewed in this way, end-user development could be considered as a failure of the IS department and IS strategy.

Less significant reasons for the growth of end-user development are:

- the desire by users to query and analyse data and generate reports from information stored on databases available across the corporate network;
- a trend to decentralisation of computing to user departments for systems to support departmental activities;
- reduced expense of application development when conducted by end-users (from departmental rather than information systems budget);
- better fit between end-user-developed software and their requirements (since no requirements translation is needed between the users and third-party developers). End-users are also less likely to 'over-engineer' a solution to a basic problem than an IS professional who will want to treat every problem with rigour.

▶ Benefits of end-user development

There are many benefits claimed for end-user development. Some are those experienced by the end-users, such as more varied work and being able to use applications sooner. Additionally, IS personnel can concentrate on key, mission-critical applications. Improvements in both these areas also accrue benefits to the organisation as a whole. The full range of benefits includes:

- reduction in the number of professional analysts and programmers and IS employed by a company (and reduced cost of employing outside consultants);
- reduction in communications overheads of users explaining requirements to IS professionals and also reduced risk of mistranslation of requirements;
- help in reducing the applications development backlog associated with centralising applications development in an IS department;
- IS staff can focus on tasks requiring their expertise, such as the maintenance of corporate systems;
- it allows applications in departments to be developed more quickly, so the business can benefit from new facilities more quickly and gain competitive advantage;
- it can encourage innovation and creativity in the use of IS/IT, since bureaucratic barriers can be removed.

To balance these benefits, there are many potential problems. These include lack of standardisation, which leads to different software tools being selected by different users, giving rise to incompatible software and data sources. Users may also take short cuts during development, such as missing out application design or testing, which will give rise to poor-quality software with bugs in it. These problems, and how to counter them, are described in more detail below.

MINI CASE STUDY

Delcam uses end-user developers to help internal communication using an intranet

Delcam is a Birmingham-based software house with over 200 staff producing CAD software that is sold in more than 40 countries. It has developed an intranet which is used for corporate communication from directors to staff, and is also used extensively in the marketing department. Examples of the use of the intranet include:

- company newsletter;
- company phone directories;
- reviews of client meetings and exhibitions attended;
- price lists used by agents in different countries;
- technical information on products for prospective customers;
- support information for existing customers.

The intranet web pages are produced by end-user developers mainly based in the marketing department, who write them in Microsoft Word before converting them to HTML pages that are read through a web browser. The advantages of end-users developing these pages are:

- The pages can be updated immediately by end-users as soon as the need arises – there is no need to wait for the IS department to make the changes.
- The pages have a distinctive, informal 'look and feel' that is consistent with the mindset of the staff who use them.
- The cost of changes to web pages can be borne by the marketing staff and does not have to be charged out.
- Confidential data is only seen by marketing staff with the access permissions to view it.

▶ The development of EUD in an organisation

The stage model of Huff et al. (1988) indicates how the use of end-user computing might develop in a typical organisation. This is loosely based on Nolan's stage model of computing use in organisations (Chapter 14). The stages of development are:

1 *Isolation*. A few scattered pioneers of EUD develop small-scale business tools within their area. Initially, little support from central IS.
2 *Standalone*. Larger-scale applications are developed that may be of importance to a department. Examples might include a staff rostering system or an application for anticipating demand for raw materials. At this stage, an information centre may be developed to support an increase in demand for user computing services.
3 *Manual integration*. Here, different end-user applications need to exchange data. This happens through manual intervention, with files being transferred by floppy disk or across the network or even with rekeying of information. Information centre devel-

opment has continued to support the needs of these larger-scale applications by providing training and skills and specifying standards for hardware, software and the development process.

4 *Automated integration.* Users start to link into corporate applications to gain seamless access to information. For example, end-users may download information from a central data warehouse, which is then used to profile customers for a new product launch or marketing campaign.

5 *Distributed integration.* At this stage of development, there is a good level of integration between different end-user applications and corporate systems. Good standards of metadata (or data describing data in a data dictionary) are required to help achieve this.

Since this model was proposed, experience indicates that although a natural progression can be seen in many organisations, the development beyond Stage 3 may not be practical or desirable. Once end-user-developed applications become important or 'mission-critical' to a department or an organisation, the question that must be asked is: 'Are end-users the right people to maintain an application of this importance?' The answer will usually be 'no', since end-users will not have the skills to develop such an application, and if they are trained to levels necessary to do this, they will no longer be end-users fulfilling their original function, but specialist application developers!

◗ Problems of end-user development

The problems of end-user development are usually the result of a lack of sufficient training in software development or the inability of management to ensure that this training occurs. This can manifest itself in different ways. Perhaps the best way to consider these problems is to review where they may occur over the course of end-user development using the software lifecycle model as a framework (Table 16.2).

Table 16.2 Review of problems associated with EUD and where they occur in the systems development lifecycle (SDLC)

Stage of SDLC	Typical problem
Initiation	*Absent or limited feasibility study.* If omitted, the user may be developing a system that is not required or solving a problem that has been solved before. *Insufficient review of cost–benefit and acquisition alternatives.* Other end-user software with the same function may be available elsewhere in the organisation. Off-the-shelf software may also be available.
Analysis	*Limited analysis.* Since the end-user may know their own requirements, they may not consult others in the company who may have a different perspective. This may alienate potential users and mean that the software is unsuitable for its application.
Design	*Omitted completely!* This stage is often omitted and programming will occur straightaway. This may occur since users may not have the design skills or understand the importance of design. This will adversely affect the usability, speed and security of the software.
Build	Programming will occur as normal; the problem is that ancillary activities may be omitted. *Documenting* the work and *testing* are areas that should not be omitted.
Implementation	Implementation becomes more difficult for large systems. For a standalone piece of end-user-developed software, there should not be too many problems.
Maintenance	Problems at this stage are minor compared to those that may have happened before. Users may not keep an adequate list of problems that need to be fixed. There is also a tendency to release updates to the software without good version control.

The problems referred to in Table 16.2 could have serious consequences if they occurred during the development of a large, new information system. However, for small-scale end-user-developed software that will only be used by a limited number of staff and is not vital to the business, such errors are less important.

Note that Table 16.2 is based on assuming that end-user development follows a similar pattern to a large-scale systems development. However, some authors, such as Lally (1995), note that additional stages of promotion or dissemination of information about the product are required. The product may then need to evolve for it to be adopted more widely in a company.

Among the general risks or misuse of information associated with end-user-developed information systems are:

- using information that is out of date;
- information requires export from other information systems before it can be analysed by the end-user application;
- corruption of centrally held data by uploading erroneous data;
- development of insecure systems without password control that are vulnerable to accidental and deliberate damage.

A final problem to be mentioned is the hazard of personal or private systems that are unreadable, undocumented and not transferable to any other users. This is a particular problem if the developer of the software leaves. This can be a common scenario with end-user-developed software. The only solution to this problem is often to rewrite the software, since the source code and documentation may be impossible to follow or non-existent.

Managing EUC as part of IS strategy

It could be argued that the IS manager has two basic choices when considering the relationship between IS strategy and end-user computing. These could be paraphrased as 'ignore it or embrace it'. The 'ignore it' option may be appealing to the IS manager who sees EUC as a threat that is eroding their control. In reality, they will not ignore it completely, rather they will not take any steps to encourage it. Those IS managers who wish to embrace it will probably have realised that EUC is inevitable, given the reasons mentioned earlier in the chapter such as insufficient availability of staff to develop applications, increasing skills among staff and availability of tools to produce the applications. EUC should be encouraged to reduce the applications backlog and will help in ensuring that the requirements of end-users are well understood and are met by the software developed.

We have seen that quite serious problems can develop with EUC due to inexperience in systems development and management among the end-users and their managers. Given this, it is vital that there be a strategy to support *and* control EUC, whether the IS manager is ignoring it or embracing it. Many of these risks and problems arise through a lack of experience of system development, coupled with a lack of training for end-users. End-user development should be recognised as part of the IS strategy and guidelines should be developed that cover the techniques below. Techniques that could be used to improve control of end-user development include:

1 *Training.* Provision of relevant training courses both in how to program and in how to approach systems development in a structured way (the second of these is often omitted). This happened at the Open University, where many of the end-users wanted to omit the analysis course.
2 *Suitability review.* Authorisation of major end-user new developments by business and IS managers to check that they are necessary (this should not be necessary for smaller-scale developments since otherwise creativity may be stifled).

3 *Standards for development*. Such standards will recommend that documentation and structured testing of all user-developed software occurs. Detailed standards might include clear data definitions, validation rules, backup and recovery routines and security measures.

4 *Guidance from end-user support personnel*. IC or help desk staff can provide training in techniques used to develop software.

5 *Software and data audits*. Regular audits should occur of software produced by end-users for data and application quality. There is an apocryphal story of a company that had an end-user-developed spreadsheet for making investment decisions which had an error in a formula that lost the company millions of pounds each year!

6 *Ensuring corporate data security*. Ensure that users are not permitted to enter data directly into central databases except via applications especially written for the purpose by the IS department which have the necessary validation rules to ensure data quality. For analysis of corporate data, data should regularly be downloaded from the central database to the PC for analysis, where they can be analysed without causing performance problems to the corporate system.

It will be apparent from the list of potential measures that a careful balance has to be struck between being over-restrictive, which may cause a stifling of innovation, or too open, which will result in the type of problems referred to above.

Summary

1 End-user computing (EUC) describes the use of information systems by non-IT staff.

2 Providing end-user services is an important function of the IS department, since many company staff rely on analysing data for decision making.

3 End-user development (EUD) is one type of EUC that is significant in many organisations, since it provides a low-cost method of reducing the applications backlog.

4 The key benefits of end-user development are:

- shorter wait for system before it can be used in the organisation;
- users understand their requirements better than IS specialists;
- lower cost than paying a third party.

5 The principal problem with end-user development is that users may omit some essential activities in software development, such as assessing the best solution, documenting their work, design or thorough testing.

6 An information centre or help desk is provided by many medium and large organisations to provide guidance, support and troubleshooting for end-users.

7 Given the potential problems of end-user-developed applications, they are most appropriate for small-scale applications within departments.

8 The cost of providing end-user services can be high, which is partly responsible for the high total cost of ownership (TCO) of PCs in many organisations and a trend to using thin clients to reduce this.

9 EUC and EUD have great potential, but enthusiasm can be misdirected due to inexperience. EUC must be an element of overall IS strategy to ensure that it is effectively controlled and supported.

EXERCISES

Self-assessment exercises

1 What are the principal end-user services that must be provided by the information systems manager?

2 What is the significance of the total cost of ownership?

3 What is the role of the network computer and other thin clients in reducing the total cost of ownership (see Chapter 3)?

4 What is the difference between end-user computing and end-user development?

5 What are the different types of end-user development?

6 What are the main reasons for the growth in end-user development?

7 Which activities in the software development lifecycle are often omitted by end-users?

8 What facilities can be provided to support end-user development?

Discussion questions

1 It has been argued that end-user computing has been driven by a failure of central information systems departments to develop applications quickly enough (the applications backlog). Is this statement true or is there an alternative explanation?

2 Examine the reasons for the growth of end-user computing in companies of all sizes. You should consider the balance between practical necessity and strategic planning.

3 What do you see as the future for end-user computing? Will the growth continue, or will there be a backlash against the problems experienced by some companies using this approach?

Essay questions

1 End-user applications development poses a new set of management problems in companies that adopt this approach. Identify the nature of these problems and suggest measures to overcome them.

2 Intranets are now widely used by many companies. Examine the suitability of end-users for the control, development and maintenance of intranets.

3 End-user computing can only be successful if users have a knowledge of the software lifecycle and the activities required to produce good-quality information systems. Which activities do you consider essential to achieving this, and which are likely to be omitted?

4 Imagine that you are the IS manager of a medium-to-large company with 500 staff. Explain the strategy you would develop to encourage end-user computing, while seeking to control any problems that may arise.

Examination questions

1 What are the main benefits provided by end-user computing?

2 Why are end-user-developed applications unsuitable for cross-enterprise applications?

3 What factors contribute to the total cost of ownership? Why is it significantly higher than the purchase cost?

4 How does the network computer differ from the personal computer? Why might this appeal to:

(a) the IS manager;
(b) the finance manager;
(c) the end-user.

▶

5 Name and explain three services that can be provided by an information centre.

6 What is the applications backlog and how is end-user development significant in relation to this?

7 Give three reasons why it is important for end-user computing to be part of a company's overall IS strategy. Briefly justify each.

References

Blili, S., Raymond, L. and Rivard, S. (1996) 'Definition and measurement of end user computing sophistication', *Journal of End User Computing*, Spring, 8, 2, 13–23

DTI (2000) *Business in the Information Age – International Benchmarking Study 2000*, Department of Trade and Industry, UK. Available online at www.ukonlineforbusiness.gov.uk

The Gartner Group (1996) *Total Cost of Ownership: Reducing PC/LAN Costs in the Enterprise*, 9 February, The Gartner Group, Boston

Huff, S., Munro, M. and Martin, B. (1988) 'Growth stages of End-User Computing', *Communications of the ACM*, 31, 5, 542–50

Lally, L. (1995) 'Supporting appropriate user-developed applications: guidelines for managers', *Journal of End User Computing*, Summer, 7, 3, 3–11

Robson, W. (1997) *Strategic Management and Information Systems: An Integrated Approach*, Financial Times Pitman Publishing, London

Rockart, J. and Flannery, L. (1983) 'The management of End-User Computing', *Communications of the ACM*, 26, 10, 776–84

White, C.E. and Christy, D.P. (1987) 'The Information Centre concept: A normative model and a study of six installations', *MIS Quarterly*, December, 450–8

Further reading

Alavi, M.R., Nelson, R. and Weiss, I.R. (1988) 'Strategies for end-user computing: an integrative framework', *Journal of Management Information Systems*, 4, 3

Brancheau, J. and Brown, C. (1993) 'Management of end-user computing', *ACM Computer Surveys*, 437–82

Computing special issue on help desks, 3 June 1998 – contains many case studies

Nelson, R. (1989) *End-User Computing: Concepts, Issues and Applications*, John Wiley, Chichester

Regan, E.A. and O'Connor, B.N. (1994) *End-user Information Systems: Perspectives for Managers and Information Systems Professionals*, Macmillan, New York

Tourniaire, F. and Farrell, R. (1996) *The Art of Software Support: Design and Operation of Support Centres and Help Desks*, Prentice Hall, London

Web links

www.helpdeskinst.com This site provides resources for practitioners to manage held desks. It includes articles on measuring help desk effectiveness and how to improve service levels.

www.vnunet.co.uk *Computing*. Special issue on help desks has many case studies, 3 June 1998.

Ethical, legal and moral constraints on information systems

LEARNING OBJECTIVES

The learning objectives for this chapter are that readers should be able to:

● analyse decisions and courses of action from professional, ethical and moral perspectives,

● select appropriate and legal courses of action in keeping with professional codes of conduct,

● understand and respond to issues of concern, such as personal privacy.

MANAGEMENT ISSUES

This chapter illustrates the huge number of demands that must be balanced in order to ensure that an organisation functions efficiently, responsibly and legally. From a managerial perspective, this chapter addresses the following areas:

● Managers must deal with moral, ethical, professional and legal issues that often conflict with one another.

● Responsible organisations must show an awareness of issues that cause concern for employees and the public such as monitoring of employees.

● An understanding of legislation is required to ensure that the organisation operates within the law.

Links to other chapters

Chapter 13   deals with a number of issues relevant to this material, such as managing organisational change.

Chapter 15   considers common threats to the security of computer-based information systems, such as unauthorised access.

Introduction

This chapter considers the moral, legal and ethical responsibilities of those involved in designing, developing and managing computer-based information systems.

After studying this chapter, readers should have obtained an understanding of:

- legislation relevant to the management and use of computer-based information systems;
- the social and professional responsibilities of those involved in the management, development and use of computer-based information systems;
- major and contemporary social issues related to computer-based information systems, such as the impact of technology on employment and personal privacy.

Professionalism, ethics and morality

We expect the developers, managers and users of computer-based information systems to behave in a professional manner at all times. They are expected to balance the needs of their employer and the requirements of their profession with other demands such as a responsibility to society. The terms ethics, morality and professionalism are often used to describe our expectations of managers and employees:

- **Professionalism** can be described as acting to meet the standards set by a profession in terms of individual conduct, competence and integrity.
- **Ethics** describes beliefs concerning right and wrong that can be used by individuals to guide their behaviour.
- **Morality** is concerned with an individual's personal beliefs of what is right and wrong.

The IS professional is in a difficult position when undertaking their work since there are a number of constraints affecting their behaviour. These constraints are indicated on Figure 17.1. These constraints may not necessarily conflict, but the employer may place demands on the manager which go against any of the constraints in Figure 17.1.

Professionalism
Acting to meet the standards set by a profession in terms of individual conduct, competence and integrity.

Ethics
In general terms, describes beliefs concerning right and wrong that can be used by individuals to guide their behaviour.

Morality
Individual character or personality and beliefs governing right and wrong.

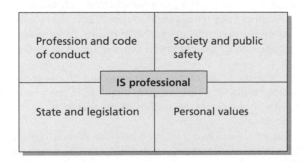

Figure 17.1 Constraints and potential areas of conflict related to the duties and responsibilities of the IS professional

What should a project manager do, for instance, if the company asks them to reduce the time taken for testing on a project (in order to meet a deadline) which may affect public safety? The sections that follow examine some of the responsibilities and values on the IS manager in each of these areas.

Codes of conduct

In addition to personal beliefs concerning right and wrong, professionals must also ensure that they obey the law and meet the standards set by their professional association.

A professional association is entitled to set entrance requirements that govern minimum levels of experience and qualifications for new members. Gaining membership affords status to the member and implies that they have achieved a high level of competence in their field. Membership also provides a variety of other benefits, such as training and official representation. However, in return for membership, the individual accepts a duty to meet certain standards of conduct and behaviour. All professional associations expect members to adhere to a **code of conduct** that sets out a number the association's principles.

In the UK, the **British Computer Society (BCS)** is regarded as the leading professional association for those involved in the design, use and management of computer-based information systems. The BCS code of conduct provides clear and firm guidance concerning a member's duties and responsibilities.

Code of conduct

Members of professional associations are expected to abide by a set of principles that sets out minimum standards of competence, conduct and behaviour.

British computer society (BCS)

Widely regarded as the UK's leading professional association for those involved the management and development of computer-based information systems.

British Computer Society – Code of Conduct

The Public Interest
1 Members shall in their professional practice safeguard public health and safety and have regard to protection of the environment.
2 Members shall have due regard to the legitimate rights of third parties.
3 Members shall ensure that within their chosen fields they have knowledge and understanding of relevant legislation, regulations and standards and that they comply with such requirements.
4 Members shall in their professional practice have regard to basic human rights and shall avoid any actions that adversely affect such rights.

Duty to employers and clients
1 Members shall carry out work with due care and diligence in accordance with the requirements of the employer or client and shall, if their professional judgment is overruled, indicate the likely consequences.
2 Members shall endeavour to complete work undertaken on time and to budget and shall advise their employer or client as soon as practicable if any overrun is foreseen.
3 Members shall not offer or provide, or receive in return, inducement for the introduction of business from a client unless there is full prior disclosure of the facts to the client.
4 Members shall not disclose or authorise, to be disclosed, or use for personal gain or to benefit a third party, confidential information acquired in the course of professional practice, except with prior written permission of the employer or client, or at the direction of a court of law.
5 Members should seek to avoid being put in a position where they may become privy to or party to activities or information concerning activities which would conflict with their responsibilities in 1–4 above.

6 Members shall not misrepresent or withhold information on the capabilities of products, systems or services with which they are concerned or take advantage of the lack of knowledge or inexperience of others.

7 Members shall not, except where specifically so instructed, handle client's monies or place contracts or orders in connection with work on which they are engaged where acting as an independent consultant.

8 Members shall not purport to exercise independent judgment on behalf of a client on any product or service in which they knowingly have any interest, financial or otherwise.

Duty to the profession

1 Members shall uphold the reputation of the Profession and shall seek to improve professional standard through participation in their development, use and enforcement, and shall avoid any action which will adversely affect the good standing of the Profession.

2 Members shall in their professional practice seek to advance public knowledge and understanding of computing and information systems and technology and to counter false or misleading statements which are detrimental to the Profession.

3 Members shall encourage and support fellow members in their professional development and, where possible, provide opportunities for the professional development of new entrants to the Profession.

4 Members shall act with integrity towards fellow members and to members of other professions with whom they are concerned in a professional capacity and shall avoid engaging in any activity which is incompatible with professional status.

5 Members shall not make any public statements in their professional capacity unless properly qualified and, where appropriate, authorised to do so, and shall have due regard to the likely consequences of any statement on others.

Professional Competence and Integrity

1 Members shall seek to upgrade their professional knowledge and skill and shall maintain awareness of technological developments, procedures and standards which are relevant to their field, and shall encourage their subordinates to do likewise.

2 Members shall seek to conform to recognised good practice including quality standards which are in their judgment relevant, and shall encourage their subordinates to do likewise.

3 Members shall only offer to do work or provide a service which is within their professional competence and shall not claim to any level of competence which they do not possess, and any professional opinion which they are asked to give shall be objective and reliable.

4 Members shall accept professional responsibility for their work and for the work of their subordinates and associates under their direction, and shall not terminate any assignment except for good reason and on reasonable notice.

5 Members shall avoid any situation that may give rise to a conflict of interest between themselves and their client and shall make full and immediate disclosure to the client if any conflict should occur.

Professional associations

Activity 17.1

Using the Internet as a resource, locate some of the other professional associations that help to regulate the activities of those employed in the IT industry. You should attempt to locate both national and international associations. In addition, you should try to compare what you locate in terms of entrance requirements, codes of conduct and the benefits offered to members.

❱ Professional responsibilities

Another way in which the responsibilities of managers, developers and users can be described is by considering some of their obligations to their employers, the public and the state. In this way, we can illustrate some of the areas in which conflicts of interest might occur.

Employers and employees

Both managers and employees are expected to balance a number of duties and responsibilities in the course of their activities. These can be divided into two broad areas: the responsibilities of all staff to the employer and the responsibilities of managers to the staff they supervise.

Some of the responsibilities employers expect their staff to assume include:

- All employees should look for ways in which they can help the company to achieve its aims. In many cases, this will involve finding new or more efficient ways to complete their work.
- All staff should take responsibility for their actions and the quality of their work.
- Managers should assess projects carefully, considering areas such as cost and risk in relation to the aims of their employer.
- Staff should work to ensure the security of equipment, software and data.
- All employees should attempt to protect and maintain the accuracy of the data held by the company.
- All employees should only attempt work they feel competent to perform. In the event that they feel unable to manage a task correctly, they should seek appropriate help and advice.
- All employees should maintain an up-to-date knowledge of their area of expertise and seek training when required.

In addition to their responsibilities to their employer, managers must also assume additional responsibilities for the staff under their supervision. Some of these responsibilities include:

- Managers should assign tasks to employees based on skills and experience. Staff should not feel that their skills are being under-employed, nor should they feel pressured into attempting work they are not capable of carrying out competently.
- Managers should ensure that their staff are adequately trained and should assign responsibilities carefully and fairly.
- Resources should be applied in the most efficient ways possible. Managers should be accountable for how the resources they control are used.

These points should help to illustrate some of the difficulties that can arise in the workplace. As an example, consider a manager charged with completing a complex technical project with only a limited budget. Some of the possible approaches to the task might be as follows:

(a) The manager might approach a superior and ask for additional resources or could continue with the work knowing that the assigned budget would be exceeded.
(b) The manager could attempt to distribute the work amongst staff members, potentially placing them under extreme stress by asking them to complete work that might be beyond their capabilities.
(c) The manager could use part of the budget to provide additional training for staff. This would enable the work to be completed but might affect the timescale allowed for the project and cause difficulties for the company later on.

In each of these cases, there is a clear conflict between the manager's responsibilities to the employer and their responsibilities towards staff. In attempting to seek a solution to such a problem, the manager must deal with a number of professional and ethical issues, often relying upon personal judgement and experience.

The public

The responsibilities of managers, developers and users to the public can also raise a number of ethical and professional issues. Two of the most important obligations placed upon professionals concern the duty to protect confidential information and a duty towards public safety.

The duty to protect sensitive or confidential information is normally described in terms of developing security measures to prevent hackers and other unauthorised users from gaining access to company data. However, in terms of a duty to the public, this responsibility can be extended to encompass areas relevant to civil liberties, such as censorship, the right of individuals to view personal data held on them and the privacy of e-mail messages and other communications.

In a similar way, the duty to maintain public safety is not to be restricted to simply ensuring that **safety-critical systems** function correctly. Managers and developers must also take responsibility for the quality of the systems they work with.

Safety-critical system
Where human lives rely on the correct operation of a computer-based information system, this is normally referred to as a critical system.

Many computer-based information systems can have an indirect impact on public safety by producing inaccurate or incomplete information that is relied upon by users. As an example, many companies publish medical software programs designed to help home users find information related to illnesses and their treatment. Despite the prominent warnings displayed by these programs, there is clearly a danger that users may accept a suggested diagnosis or treatment and act upon the information.

If some people can place too much reliance upon computer-based information systems, then the opposite is also true. An unreliable or ineffective system can also have consequences for public safety. A well-known example concerns a case in 1990 where the pilot of a British Airways aircraft, Captain Tim Lancaster, was nearly sucked out of his cockpit window after the bolts securing the windscreen gave way. It was later found that an engineer had used the wrong bolts when fitting the windscreen. Although the engineer had access to a computer-based information system that could have been used to identify and select the correct bolts, he had chosen not to use it since it was considered unreliable and inaccurate (*Independent on Sunday*, 15 November 1992).

A controversial aspect of public safety involves issues related to child pornography and information that could be used to support criminal and terrorist activities. Whilst some argue that all information should be freely available, others are concerned that steps should be taken to control potentially dangerous information and protect the vulnerable, such as children.

The state

The state attempts to maintain standards and behaviour by enacting legislation to regulate the behaviour of companies and employees. Although specific pieces of legislation, such as the Computer Misuse Act (1990), are aimed directly at those working in the field of computer-based information systems, companies and employees must also observe more general laws. As an example, the Health and Safety at Work Act (1974) means that all employees are responsible for safety in the workplace. Staff are required to take immediate action in response to any hazard or danger to health. Furthermore, employers are expected to ensure that the workplace is safe through actions such as providing safety equipment.

Other aspects of legislation relevant to those working in the field of computer-based information systems are described in more detail later on.

Social issues

The **information society** is a term that has been coined to describe a modern population that is conversant with – and reliant upon – information and communications technology. In this section, we consider a selected range of social issues that concern both individuals and organisations.

▶ Employment

There can be no doubt that technology has made a significant impact on patterns of employment. In the office environment, the positions and tasks of many employees have been taken over by computer-based information systems. Where a number of clerks may have been needed to maintain records or handle everyday transactions, many tasks are now carried out automatically through technologies such as EDI and computer telephony. In manufacturing organisations, industrial robots and automated manufacturing processes have replaced many thousands of skilled workers.

However, whilst it is certainly true that technology has been responsible for the loss of many jobs within manufacturing and service industries, it is also apparent that a wealth of new employment opportunities have been created in their place:

● As the demand for highly skilled IS professionals continues to grow, new positions have opened up in areas such as computer training and higher education.
● As more companies adopt IT on a larger scale, demand increases for people to develop, maintain and manage the software and equipment used.
● The Internet has created a huge demand for people skilled in areas such as web page design, e-commerce and networking.

At present, the demand for skilled IS professionals far outstrips supply. In the UK, some estimates suggest that there may be more than 100 000 unfilled vacancies in the IT industry at any given time. Worldwide, staff shortages have become so severe that 'headhunting' agencies can command fees of hundreds of thousands of pounds when recruiting an experienced manager for a large IS department. In some cases, the situation has become so severe that some companies, such as John Lewis, have begun to monitor staff e-mail in order to learn when an employee is approached by another company or a recruitment agency (*Computer Weekly*, 10 May 2001). A secondary effect of staff shortages has been to increase salaries across the entire industry.

> Europe's IT industry continues to experience a skills shortage, with 44 per cent of companies in the region unable to fill IT positions.
> *Source*: NUA Internet Surveys, 20 March 2001 (www.nua.com/surveys)

▶ Skilling versus deskilling

A subject of great debate over the past ten years has been whether or not technology leads to the deskilling of employees. In general, the debate concerns a single central question: Are employees being given the opportunity to develop new skills in depth, or are they developing a broader range of skills, but failing to develop any real expertise in one or more specific areas?

Some people have expressed concerns about the development of a labour force made up of a large proportion of relatively unskilled employees and just a small number of 'elite' (highly skilled) employees. The belief is that we will eventually rely and depend on a very small number of highly competent people to manage companies, develop new products, and so on.

It is certainly true that there are relatively few employees in the IT industry who could be described as highly skilled. For example, the British Computer Society has approximately 40 000 members, but the total number of people involved in the UK IT industry is estimated at more than 2 million. However, we should recognise that there may be many highly skilled people in the labour force who go unrecognised because they have not joined a professional association or come to our attention in other ways. In addition, society always has the opportunity to produce more skilled employees by investing in training and education.

Case Study 17.1 highlights issues related to skills shortages in the IT industry.

CASE STUDY 17.1

Recruitment

FT

At a time when much of the IT industry is laden with gloom and jobs are being shed around the globe, it might seem insensitive or bizarre to talk about a skills shortage. But despite stock market depression and the dotcom fallout, many companies are struggling to find the right people.

Their desperation stems from the upsurge in e-business and online corporate activities. They are looking for experts in networks, e-business applications, software development for the web, and numerous other aspects of the internet-based changes sweeping through the whole of industry.

Such employees have become increasingly hard to find as IT has moved from being a separate function within corporations – generally regarded as a cost rather than a profit centre – to one which forms a crucial element of business in the 21st century.

The IT skills shortage affects all industries, not just IT itself. It has now become clear to even the least technology-minded companies that e-business – stretching from the supply chain to customer service and beyond to external partners – can deliver impressive cost-savings and revenue opportunities.

Thus, businesses around the world are expected to invest more than $5,000bn over the next four years to develop and run e-businesses, according to IDC, the US-based IT market analysts. But it says companies are facing difficulties in finding and keeping talent.

Nor does the economic slowdown offer much relief. 'The difference with this global economic downturn is that the role of IT has become much more ingrained in the way economies around the world work', says Michael Boyd, a human resources expert at IDC.

The people being laid off – many of them in failed internet consumer ventures – are not necessarily the ones other companies need. The skills shortage could thus impede efforts towards e-business efficiency.

'I worry about the whole growth of the industry being curtailed', says Nicholas Donofrio, senior vice president for technology and manufacturing at IBM. 'I am very optimistic about the future. But it won't happen if we can't fill all the shortages we are facing.'

Just how severe is the IT skills shortage? Mr Donofrio calls it 'chronic'. Peter Radley, chairman of the UK operation of Alcatel, the French telecoms group, is 'concerned about the shortage of the right skills'. At Cisco, the US networking equipment company, Mike Couzens, head of corporate communications and training for Europe, calls it a 'major problem'.

Microsoft started raising the alarm three years ago, says Bernard Vergnes, chairman of European operations at the US software giant. 'The problem is still around. It is still difficult to find people with the right IT skills.'

In the US, Meta Group, the IT market analysts, estimates that some 850,000 IT staff positions are unfilled – more than double the figure of two years ago. As a result, IT salaries – including sign-on bonuses and other incentives – are rising by between 8 and 15 per cent a year, says Maria Schafer, head of Meta's executive services division.

At some US companies, salary reviews now take place twice a year rather than every 12 months. 'There is a lot of pressure on the compensation side of the scale', she adds. 'Many companies are struggling with compensation above the base salary.'

IT pay has been rising less steeply in Europe, where IT salary levels are lower than in the US anyway, but the skills shortage is no less acute. Both in the US and Europe, according to Ms Schafer, 'if you ask companies if they plan to cut back on projects and people, they say "not at all" '.

Instead, these businesses would hire 25 per cent more people if they could find them.

IDC puts the shortage of IT people in Europe at more than 1m, rising to 1.7m in 2003. This means demand will outstrip supply by 13 per cent in that year, though the shortage should then diminish as demand eases, companies' own training efforts bear fruit and national educational systems catch up with industry's needs.

The European Commission is certainly concerned about the problem. 'The shortage of qualified ICT (information and communications technology) professionals is now generally recognised as a serious handicap for the European economy', it says in the foreword to a new report by IDC and the Frankfurt-based European Informational Technology Observatory, (EITO).

Taking a broad view of ICT – including call centres and e-business – the report says jobs in this sector will account for 13.4 per cent of employment in western Europe in 2003 against 8.3 per cent at present.

Today's ICT labour shortage is around 1.9m people. But by 2003, this will have grown to 3.8m. In Germany, where the problem is most marked because of the country's economic weight, the shortage is seen likely to increase from 444 000 to 723 000 in two years' time.

Even if it turns out to be less acute than forecast – and the current economic weakness has certainly taken some of the sting out of the problem – there seems little doubt that companies will have to search hard to find the right people.

They are pursuing three main strategies: stepping up training; lobbying governments and educational establishments; and employing the immigrant IT specialists (notably from India) now being wooed in the US, Europe and elsewhere.

However, they could also make better use of the resources they have. 'They can do more with less', says Kazim Isfahani, a senior industry analyst at Giga Information Group, the US-based IT market analysts.

Using sophisticated software programmes, companies can improve their knowledge of internal skills and ensure that these are used to best effect. They can track who is doing what and 'get the right people at the right time onto the right project'.

More companies are now starting to use such methods, Mr Isfahani says. 'They can either over-pay (for new IT staff) or become more efficient.' They are not laying off 'their best and brightest' as the surrounding IT climate grows chillier. But they have to enhance the productivity of those they keep.

Outsourcing is another way of easing the skills problem. Businesses can shift non-core activities to application service providers (ASPs) and other service companies in areas such as storage and web hosting, enabling them to concentrate on their main operations. Yet this can only be a partial solution. ASPs can absorb some of the load by handling the IT operations of a number of companies, but basic network, e-business, Java programming, infrastructure and related consultancy and other skills are still in strong demand.

This is forcing companies to look outside the IT sector. When Alcatel needed 500 new people to assemble electro-optic equipment for undersea cables at its plant in south-east London, it had to cast its net wide.

It selected people through interviews and aptitude tests – such as reading an engineering drawing and threading a needle – and put them through a six-week training course. The recruits included former lorry drivers and car assembly workers.

Alcatel UK has also used such 'cross training' methods to find sales and marketing people. Stockbrokers and coffee salesmen are among those it has taken on in this way, training them over several months in the basics of telecoms before putting them to work.

One company which is particularly energetic on the training and education front is Cisco Systems, the US network equipment group. Mr Couzens sees potential for training IT workers from the ranks of the military, where numbers are being reduced across Europe, and the sports world. Not all budding sports professionals, whether in football, golf or basketball, make the grade. Why not train some of them as IT staff?

Cisco is discussing this with sports organisations in Europe and the US. It is also talking with churches and prison services about schemes to draw the unemployed and young offenders into IT. But its main efforts are directed at encouraging schools, colleges and universities to produce more people with IT abilities. Its Cisco Networking Academy Programme has provided some 200 000 students in 120 countries with the skills to design, build and maintain computer networks.

The programme is delivered over the web and includes the course, online testing, performance tracking and instructor training and support. Cisco also provides its curriculum to commercial training companies.

'Industry has to get involved with governments and the academic world', says Mr Couzens. The statistics show the urgency of the problem. In Europe, the shortage of qualified networking professionals will approach 600 000 by next year, IDC estimates.

Many governments, seeing an employment opportunity, have helped take up the challenge of developing more information technology specialists. A raft of educational and promotional initiatives has been launched in the UK, Germany and other European countries.

The lack of skills would also be alleviated if more women could be attracted to IT.

IBM's Mr Donofrio says: 'We discourage young women from liking maths and science – there's a nerdy nature to it.' Schools need to make courses more appealing and companies must do more to show teenagers that a career in IT can be interesting.

Rebecca George, European director of staffing at IBM, says IT suffers from an image problem among women. It is not regarded as a lively and fun career. Women account for less than 25 per cent of total employment in the IT sector, though IBM is slightly above this at 30 per cent.

▶

But whether it is a question of attracting more women into the sector, looking beyond traditional recruitment areas or lobbying governments, companies have to be far more innovative in the way they hire people. 'There are multiple causes of the skills shortage. So, de facto, there need to be multiple solutions', says Ms George.

One further remedy is immigration. But most executives and analysts see this as only a quick fix. 'It's valid as long as it's backed up with training', says Chriss Andrews, managing director of Church International, a UK recruitment consultancy.

The US has increased the number of immigration visas to attract more IT specialists, mostly from India, as have European countries such as Germany.

However, Indian sensitivities were bruised when an opposition politician – ironically, a former education and technology minister, Jurgen Ruttgers – criticised the visa policy with the clumsy slogan Kinder statt Inder ('Children not Indians' – meant to stress training over immigration) in a local election campaign.

Most Indians prefer to go to the US – where California's Silicon Valley has benefited considerably from immigrants – rather than Europe, anyway. 'The US is more diverse and heterogeneous', says Sudip Nandy, head of European operations at Wipro, the Indian software group. It is also home to the big names of the IT industry.

India, moreover, needs to keep as many people as it can to serve its own fast-growing software industry. Mr Nandy says the educational system has stepped up its efforts to train more computer and software engineers and is confident that the country's needs will be met.

But it will be a hard slog. Around 1,000 IT companies have been established in India in the past six years. Technology training institutes will need to raise their intake of students by around 100 000 a year if the country is to meet its estimated need for 800 000 software professionals by 2005 and 2.2m in 2008.

Mr Nandy expects the global skills shortage to become less of an issue in coming years, however, as supply catches up with demand. Others agree. 'After 2005, we should start to see a decline in the skills problem', says Andrew Milroy, a European analyst at IDC.

But there will still be a gap. As technology continues its advance, skills will inevitably lag behind to some extent. Companies will have to stay on the alert to find the right people, keep them happy and make sure their training matches the constantly shifting demands of the internet age.

Source: Andrew Fisher, 'Skills shortage puts job market out of balance', *Financial Times*, 2 May 2001

Questions

1 How can we explain the existence of an international skills shortage?

2 How can technology be used to make up for a lack of skilled IT personnel? Illustrate your response with appropriate examples.

3 It can be argued that some IT personnel enjoy excellent employment conditions since employers are keen to attract and retain skilled staff. What kinds of benefits can new entrants into the industry expect to receive?

▶ The digital divide

Concern is growing that society may eventually become divided into two distinct groups. One group will be made up of those who have access to technology and are able to obtain information via the Internet. The other will be made up of those who are unable to gain access to technology and information.

The concept of a digital divide can be viewed from a national and international perspective. From an international point of view, consider the availability of Internet access across different countries. In Africa, for example, Somalia has only 200 Internet users from a total population of more 7 million. However, in South Africa there are 1.8 million Internet users, representing approximately 60 per cent of all Internet users on the continent (Global Internet Liberty Campaign, 4 May 2001 – www.gilc.org).

The existence of a digital divide can be illustrated further by looking at Internet access across continents. As a whole, only 0.2 per cent of the population of Africa have Internet access. In contrast, the total number of Internet users in Europe is expected to reach more than 230 million by 2004, representing approximately 60 per cent of the population (Nua Internet Surveys, 8 May 2001 – www.nua.com/surveys). In the UK alone, there are an estimated 13.5 million Internet users, amounting to approximately 32 per cent of homes.

There is also evidence that a digital divide exists within individual countries. In the UK, for example, a recent survey reported that: 'More than 60% of the most well-off homes have Internet access while only 10% of the bottom 40% can surf from home – and the numbers are growing far more quickly among the wealthier sections' (*Computer Weekly*, 20 December 2000). The government's concern over this issue has led to a number of new initiatives aimed at widening access to technology and the Internet. For example, a pilot scheme resulted in 12 000 personal computers being given to families living in the poorer parts of Liverpool.

For business, the implications of a digital divide provide cause for concern. For example, attempts to open new premises in certain parts of the country could be hindered by an inability to recruit suitably qualified and experienced staff from the local area.

▶ Personal privacy

It has long been recognised that technology enables companies, government departments and other organisations to collect large amounts of personal information. Although the use of such information is controlled by various mechanisms, such as legislation, many people are concerned by the potential threat to personal privacy.

The threat to personal privacy is perceived to arise from the basic functions of computer-based information systems, namely their ability to store, process and retrieve data quickly and efficiently. Two examples can be used to illustrate common concerns related to privacy:

- The use of computer-based information systems enables an organisation to combine or analyse data in ways not previously possible with manual systems. As an example, a bank might build up profiles of its customers by analysing their spending, borrowing and saving habits. This information could then be supplied to other organisations involved in marketing relevant goods or services.
- Communications technology allows organisations to share data, allowing them to develop a comprehensive pool of information regarding individuals. An insurance company, for example, might gather medical information before deciding whether or not to offer a policy to an individual.

A further issue related to privacy concerns the quantity and accuracy of the personal data held on individuals. It is estimated that an average adult may be listed on as many as 200 computer files. Furthermore, there may be a 2 per cent error rate in the information held (*Guardian*, 12 May 1997). Other estimates suggest that up to 43 per cent of consumer credit files may contain errors. Holding inaccurate personal data on an individual can result in a number of problems, for example an incorrect health service number might result in an error in a person's treatment.

Another area of concern is the use of computer monitoring to gather information concerning the behaviour of people in the workplace. Although such monitoring has legitimate uses, for example measuring workflow and productivity, it can also be used to violate an employee's privacy. The monitoring of e-mail and Internet use is described in more detail a little later.

Computer monitoring

The use of computer and communications technology to monitor the activities of individuals.

Computer monitoring is also used in a number of other areas, for example a security firm may use a combination of computers, video cameras, sensors and other devices to maintain the security of a large building.

The monitoring of communications, such as telephone calls and e-mail messages is also a major area of concern for many users. Although there seems little evidence to suggest that all communications are monitored at all times, many companies and indi-

An individual is likely to be filmed by up to 300 cameras a day. Furthermore, the number of surveillance cameras in Britain is set to double over the next three years to 2m. This will be largely due to the impact of mobile communications technology on monitoring devices. It is estimated that removing the need to install expensive cabling can reduce the cost of devices such as surveillance cameras by up to 80 per cent.

Source: Sunday Times, 11 March 2001

viduals have turned towards methods such as encryption in order to protect sensitive business or personal information.

In the UK, the introduction of legal measures that allow government agencies to monitor e-mail messages has sparked a huge controversy. Businesses have expressed concern that such measures will harm competitiveness and damage business relations. Other people are concerned that the ability to gather this kind of information could be abused, causing untold harm to industry and individuals. In early 2000, for example, it was alleged that American intelligence agencies were sharing information – such as the contents of e-mail messages – with certain companies, giving them an unfair advantage in international markets.

Echelon

Many people are concerned at what appears to be the indiscriminate monitoring of communications, the majority of which are almost certain to be both innocent and legitimate.

Echelon is a global surveillance system that monitors communications around the world. The project is operated by the USA, the UK, Canada, Australia and New Zealand. Each day, millions of telephone calls, faxes and e-mail messages are intercepted and scanned for key words and phrases. Messages matching the search criteria used are collected and sent to the United States for further analysis.

In May 2000, allegations were made that US intelligence services were found to be passing sensitive information to American companies, effectively giving them an unfair advantage over British and European competitors.

It should be noted that some of the fears surrounding Echelon may not be valid. For instance, it is unlikely that Echelon is capable of monitoring the sheer volume of messages sent around the world each day. In the UK alone, for example, it is estimated that more 360 million e-mails are sent each day (*Financial Times*, 2 February 2001). Similarly, given the sophistication of modern encryption techniques, it is highly unlikely that Echelon would be capable of decrypting even a tiny fraction of the messages transmitted every day.

Personal privacy

Activity 17.2

As mentioned in this section, it is estimated that a typical adult may be listed in as many as 200 computer files.

1   How many organisations hold data on you? List as many organisations as possible and describe the data held.
2   Imagine that you have access to all of this data and wish to build a profile of the characteristics of a person. Describe what such a profile would contain and what other assumptions could be made.
3   If a government department or commercial organisation were given access to all of this information, what uses could they put it to?

▶ Crime

As the use of technology has become more widespread, so too have the incidences of computer crime. Acts such as theft, fraud, unauthorised access and vandalism have become almost commonplace and the losses or damage caused by such acts have increased dramatically.

> In 2000, the UK suffered the highest levels of electronic security fraud in Europe.
> *Source: Financial Times*, 29 March 2001

Computer criminals

Those who commit computer-related crimes can be divided into three basic categories:

Computer criminals
Make use of technology to perform a variety of criminal acts, ranging from vandalism and sabotage to hacking and fraud.

1 **Computer criminals** are well-educated, white-collar workers who feel undervalued or bear some resentment to an employer or former employer (Parker, 1976). Such individuals resort to sabotage, vandalism or theft as a means of revenge against the employer. Other computer criminals may stumble upon ways of compromising system security and take advantage of these in order to steal money, goods or services.

Information warrior
Seeks to obtain data by any means necessary. Such people may resort to illegal methods, such as hacking, in order to obtain the information they require.

2 Schwartau (1994) describes **information warriors** as those who seek to obtain data by any means necessary. Such people may resort to illegal methods, such as hacking, in order to obtain the information they require. It is worth noting that the information obtained may not necessarily be used in pursuit of criminal activities, for example a police officer might feel the need to resort to such methods in order to gather evidence against a suspect.

Hacker
Individuals who seek to break into systems as a test of their abilities. Few hackers attempt to cause damage to the systems they access and few are interested in gaining some sort of financial profit.

3 **Hackers** are often described as individuals who seek to break into systems as a test of their abilities. As the points below demonstrate, we can make distinctions between different kinds of hackers and the terms used to describe them. This area was considered briefly in Chapter 15. Comparatively few hackers attempt to cause damage to the systems they access and few are interested in gaining any sort of financial profit. It can be argued that there are four basic motives behind the actions of hackers (Johnson, 1994).

(a) Some hackers hold the belief that all information should be free. Such individuals feel a duty to ensure free access to information held by government departments and private companies.

(b) Many hackers believe that they provide an important service to companies by exposing flaws in security.

(c) Some people believe that hacking serves an educational purpose by helping them to improve their knowledge and skills. Since no harm is caused to any systems accessed, their actions are acceptable and should not be considered threatening.

(d) A final motive for hacking is simply for enjoyment or excitement. Many hackers find stimulation in the challenge of defeating the designers of the security measures used by a given system.

Types of computer crime

Computer crime can be divided into a number of different categories:

Theft
In terms of computing, theft normally, but not always, involves altering computer records to disguise the theft of money. The theft of services can include a variety of acts, such as the unauthorised use of a company's information systems.

● **Theft** normally, but not always, involves altering computer records to disguise the theft of money. An employee of an insurance company, for example, might create a number of fictitious clients and then make claims on their behalf.

- The *theft of services* can include a variety of acts, such as the unauthorised use of a company's information systems. Although many of these acts may appear innocuous, it should be noted that their effect can lead to significant losses. Making intensive use of a company's computer systems, for example, can temporarily deprive the organisation of its resources, leading to financial losses through decreased productivity.
- **Software theft** involves making unauthorised copies of software applications. This topic is described in more detail later on.
- **Data theft** can involve stealing sensitive information or making unauthorised changes to computer records.
- The *destruction of data and software*, for example by creating and disseminating computer viruses, can lead to significant losses.

> Ernst & Young's 1999 global survey of information security found that 28 respondent companies had each lost more than $25 million in the last five years.
>
> Source: *Financial Times*, 2 June 2000

Chapter 15 describes some of the emerging trends in computer crime with a particular emphasis on activities related to the Internet.

Software theft
....
Software theft, also known as software piracy, involves making unauthorised copies of software applications.

Data theft
....
Data theft can involve stealing sensitive information or making unauthorised changes to computer records.

Legal issues

In this section, we consider some of the legislation relevant to managers, users and developers of computer-based information systems.

It is worth noting that whilst this section is primarily concerned with UK legislation, many other countries have similar laws and guidelines that deal with the same issues. In general, the majority of the material in this section will be relevant to all European Union members, the United States and other nations, such as South Africa, Australia and New Zealand.

▶ Data Protection Act (1984, 1998)

The full title of the Data Protection Act 1998 is:

An Act to make new provision for the regulation of the processing of information relating to individuals, including the obtaining, holding, use or disclosure of such information.

As can be seen, the Act tries to ensure that organisations use personal information in a responsible way. The Act gives individuals limited rights concerning how information on them is gathered, stored and used. Any company that makes use of personal information must register under the Act.

The **Data Protection Act** is based upon a number of general principles. These include:

- Information shall be obtained and processed 'fairly and lawfully'.
- Information shall be held only for one or more specific and lawful purposes.
- Companies should not hold information that is excessive or not relevant to the purposes the company has registered under the Act.
- Information held on individuals should be accurate and up-to-date.
- Information should not be held for longer than needed.
- Individuals have the right to see the data held on them and have corrections made where necessary.
- Companies must take measures to protect information from unauthorised access.

Data Protection Act (1984)
....
Legislation setting out the rights of organisations and individuals in terms of how personal information is gathered, stored, processed and disclosed.

The penalty for failing to comply with the Act is a fine of up to £2,000. However, to date, there have been relatively few prosecutions brought under the Act and the majority of these have been for the failure to register as a data user.

There are three major criticisms levelled at the Data Protection Act:

● It is considered fairly easy for companies to obtain exemption from the conditions set out in the Act.
● It is sometimes very difficult for individuals to gain access to the information held on them.
● It is sometimes difficult for users to ensure that corrections are made to the information held on them.

The adoption of EU regulations dealing with the processing of personal data has brought the UK's legislation in line with the rest of the Union. However, the changeover has not been without difficulty and UK companies have now started to share some of the problems of their European counterparts. Examples of the difficulties now faced by UK and other European organisations include:

● *Conflicts with other legislation.* For example, the adoption of the Human Rights Act (1998) has provided UK citizens with a set of fundamental rights, including a right to privacy. Already there have been a number of cases where the requirements of the Human Rights Act have come into conflict with the activities permissable under the Data Protection Act. Note that such a situation is not unique to the UK: the basic principles set out in UK legislation apply to all EU members.
● *Difficulty in trading across international boundaries.* EU regulations place strict controls on the transfer of personal data to organisations based outside of the EU. Since many organisations have close relationships with companies in the United States and Asia, this has served to constrain some business activities. Of particular importance is the impact of restrictions on areas such as e-commerce. Again, this issue impacts upon all EU members.
● *Lack of clear guidance.* Many organisations have found it difficult to incorporate new data protection legislation into existing company policies and procedures. Although the amended Data Protection Act came into force in 1998, there have also been a number of new developments, such as the introduction of the Human Rights Act in 2000. Unfortunately, clarification of some of the issues raised by these changes has been slow to arrive. For instance, government guidance on implementing data protection policies arrived in late 2001, several years after the introduction of the new legislation. Recent revisions to the Data Protection Act with reference to e-mail can be reviewed at Marketing Law (www.marketinglaw.co.uk).

▶ Computer Misuse Act (1990)

Computer Misuse Act (1990)

Legislation intended to protect sensitive equipment and data from unauthorised access, alteration and damage.

The full title of the **Computer Misuse Act (1990)** can be used to clarify its intent:

An Act to make provision for securing computer material against unauthorised access or modification; and for connected purposes.

A number of offences are covered by the Act. Amongst these are the following:

(a) unauthorised access to computer material;
(b) unauthorised access with the intention of carrying out or assisting others with the commission of further offences;
(c) unauthorised modification of computer material;
(d) impairing the operation of a program or the reliability of data;
(e) preventing or hindering access to any program or data.

It is worth noting several general points in relation to the offences outlined here. First, the Act makes it clear that offences need not be directed at any particular program, data or computer system. This provides the Act with far-reaching authority, allowing action to be taken in a wide variety of circumstances.

Secondly, the Act states that an individual is guilty of an offence if they have the 'requisite knowledge and intention', meaning that individuals must be aware that their actions are unauthorised and they must have the intention to cause some form of damage or harm. This offers a measure of protection to those users who unintentionally gain unauthorised access to a computer system or cause accidental damage.

Thirdly, the Act makes no distinction between acts that cause permanent or temporary changes to programs or data. In this way, even a practical joke, such as changing a user's password without their permission, could be considered a criminal act.

The Act deliberately makes no attempt to define what is meant by a computer. It was recognised very early on that it would be impossible to create a definition that could encompass the technological changes likely to occur over the next few decades. Instead, it was decided that the courts should use the common, everyday meaning of the term. It was felt that this would enable the Act to remain relevant for longer by allowing it to keep pace with technology. However, the Act is already seen as being outdated since it fails to take into account developments such as the growth of the Internet. As an example, the Act fails to cover certain acts, such as denial of service attacks (*Computer Weekly*, 5 April 2001).

The focus of the Computer Misuse Act is on the protection of computer systems, not the data they hold. It can be argued that only by protecting computer systems can the data held be safeguarded.

Oddly, the Act does not extend to damage caused to data held on offline storage media, such as compact discs and magnetic tapes. However, other legislation can be used to provide additional protection. It is an offence under the Criminal Damage Act (1971), for example, to destroy or damage any property. This legislation has been extended to cover storage media by suggesting that certain actions, such as deleting data from a floppy disk, can be said to cause damage by reducing the value or usefulness of the media.

Other notable omissions from the Act include electronic eavesdropping, software piracy and the writing of viruses. Although relatively uncommon at the time the Act was passed, incidences of electronic eavesdropping have grown rapidly over the past five years. Much of this growth can be attributed to increased sales of mobile telephones and the rapid development of e-commerce. Software piracy is considered to be covered adequately by existing counterfeiting and copyright legislation. Although the dissemination of computer viruses has become illegal, the act of creating a computer virus is not covered by the Act.

Electronic eavesdropping describes the act of gaining access to confidential information by intercepting or monitoring communications traffic. Some examples include:

- Calls made using cellular telephones can be monitored using relatively inexpensive radio receivers.
- Police, emergency services and air traffic control radio transmissions can be monitored using a domestic radio receiver.
- Material sent via the Internet, such as e-mail messages, can be intercepted at a number of different points. This allows individuals to gain access to any sensitive information transmitted in this way, such as credit card numbers.
- Comparatively inexpensive receivers can be used to view the display shown on a computer monitor being used in another location. Although monitors can be shielded to prevent this, relatively few organisations seem aware of the risk.

The penalties for offences covered by the Act can include a fine of up to £2,000 and up to six months' imprisonment. More serious offences can result in an unlimited fine and up to a maximum of five years' imprisonment.

▶ Copyright, Designs and Patents Act (1988)

Copyright, Designs and Patents Act (1988)
Legislation that can be used to provide organisations and software developers with protection against unauthorised copying of designs, software, printed materials and other works.

The **Copyright, Designs and Patents Act** provides organisations and software developers with protection against unauthorised copying of designs, software, printed materials and other works. In general, most countries have legislation that mirrors the principles of the Copyright, Designs and Patents Act.

Copyright legislation allows a company to safeguard its *intellectual property rights (IPR)* against competitors and others who might wish to profit from the company's research and investment.

Intellectual property
A generic term used to describe designs, ideas and inventions. In general, intellectual property covers the following areas: patents, trade marks, designs and copyright.

> Intellectual property is a generic term used to describe designs, ideas and inventions. In general, intellectual property covers the following areas: patents, trade marks, designs and copyright.

▶ Copyright

Copyright exists automatically as soon as a given work is completed and no action is necessary to gain copyright. The copyright to a given work can exist for up to 50 years following the author's death. Authors of copyrighted works can transfer their rights to others, selling or leasing them if they wish.

For managers involved with computer-based information systems, copyright legislation raises a number of important issues. We will now describe the two most significant.

Ownership of bespoke software developed for the company by a consultant

The possibility of disputes means that organisations should introduce procedures that can be used to establish ownership of copyright. Quite a common problem is when a bespoke system is developed for a company by a consultant. Unless specified in the contract, the copyright or IPR will reside with the consultant. The consultant can then sell the same software (which was of course paid for) to a competitor of the first company. This is obviously undesirable and needs to be included in the contract for development of the system.

Consider a dispute concerning two writers claiming ownership over the contents of a book or article. Unless one of the authors can prove that they were the original creator of the material, it may not be possible to resolve the argument. For a company, such copyright disputes might result in lengthy and expensive legal battles, leading to lost revenues and adverse publicity. A common solution to this problem is to register all copyright materials with an agency, government department or legal firm. However, this requires organisations to set procedures in place in order to ensure that all important materials are protected in this way.

Source escrow
An arrangement where a third party stores software that can be used for maintenance purposes if the original developer of the software becomes insolvent.

In the UK it is worthwhile including an **source escrow** clause in a contract for bespoke software. Under this arrangement software (both media and source code instructions) is stored at the National Computing Centre in Manchester and if the company developing the software becomes insolvent the company who originally contracted them can still attempt to use the source code to fix maintenance problems.

Many countries allow companies to lodge materials with a government department in order to register copyright. In the United States, for example, materials can be lodged with the US Copyright Office for a small fee.

Employee 'takes' software to another company

Another problem concerning ownership of copyright involves materials produced by the employees of an organisation. Although many organisations assume automatic ownership to the copyright of any materials produced by their employees, this may not necessarily be the case. Unless specifically stated by the employee's contract, or implied on the basis of the employee's usual work for the organisation, the company may have no rights to any materials created.

Activity 17.3

Copyright

You are employed as a clerk in a large sales organisation. In your spare time, for example during lunch breaks, you develop a computer program that could be of significant value to your employer. Your employer claims ownership of the program on two grounds: that the program is related to your normal activities as an employee and that you used their equipment when creating the program. You dispute this on the grounds that the work was carried out during your own time and that the majority of the work was completed at home, using your own personal computer.

1 What legal, moral and ethical issues are involved in this case?
2 Who owns the program?

An example may help to make this point clearer. A computer programmer moves to another company, taking with them a program that was under development. The programmer argues that they are entitled to take the program since the contract they worked under made no reference to ownership of copyright. However, since the programmer was formerly employed to produce computer programs, the original employer has implied rights concerning the uncompleted program. In such a case, it is likely that the original employer would be successful if they took legal action against the employee.

This example should help to illustrate the importance of ensuring that employees' contracts take account of copyright issues. Many organisations routinely issue employment contracts containing clauses that concern copyright to all employees, regardless of their position or function.

Note that copyright protection applies only to materials that have been recorded in some way and cannot be used to protect ideas or concepts. The operation of a computer program, for example, is not normally protected by copyright legislation; although the actual source code may be subject to copyright, there may be little to stop a competitor creating a similar program to fulfil the same purpose.

In general, breach of copyright involves making a direct copy of part or the whole of a given work, such as an article. However, copyright can sometimes be extended to include the expression of a work and derivative works. As an example consider what might happen if a programmer developed a program that produced precisely the same screen displays, in terms of content and presentation, as an existing commercial product. Copyright infringement could be argued on the basis that the new program was merely an expression of the original commercial product. However, if the displays produced by the program were sufficiently different from the original, it might not be possible to prove infringement.

For business organisations, these aspects of copyright legislation can present a major dilemma. Although copyright legislation can be used to gain a measure of protection for certain works, for example computer programs, such protection is often limited and may not be sufficient in the case of particularly valuable or important works. As a result, large amounts of expense and time can be involved in pursuing copyright infringement via legal action.

Software piracy

Copyright is also infringed when software is copied by employees in the organisation so that it can be installed on more machines than licences have been paid for. This is an important topic and a later section describes some of the consequences of copyright theft in the form of software piracy.

▶ Patents

Patent

Provides its owner with a monopoly allowing them to exploit their invention without competition. The protection offered by a patent lasts for a number of years but does not begin until the patent has been granted.

A **patent** provides its owner with a monopoly allowing them to exploit their invention without competition. The protection offered by a patent lasts for a number of years but does not begin until the patent has been granted. The application process for a patent can take as long as five years. During this time, the applicant must not disclose the details of the invention or the application will be rejected.

A patent can only be granted for original inventions that are considered to be 'non-obvious'. A simple modification to an existing item, for example, would be considered obvious and unoriginal.

Since the patent application will describe the method used to create the item and the way in which it functions, the owner's work is protected in its entirety. Once the patent has been granted, competitors are prohibited from duplicating the item.

Unlike copyright, where international agreements provide automatic protection for an author's work in other countries, separate applications may need to be made to patent offices in other countries. It is common, for example, for companies to register patents in the UK, Europe and the United States in order to protect these potential markets from competitors.

Cross-licensing agreement

Agreements allow companies to share patents so that each can produce and market a wider range of products.

The rights assigned by a patent can be sold or licensed to others. This enables smaller companies to form partnerships with others in order to exploit foreign markets. **Cross-licensing agreements** allow companies to share patents so that each can produce and market a wider range of products.

In many countries, patents can be used to protect computer programs by registering the methods and techniques used in their creation. As an example, PKZIP is a leading data compression utility that uses a number of specialised techniques to compress data quickly and efficiently. It is these techniques that distinguish the program from others, allowing it to provide an original and non-obvious approach to data compression. In the UK, patents are not granted for computer programs, although this is may change in the near future. In the EU, the European Patent Convention prohibits the patenting of software programs, although it is possible to patent the function of the software (*Computer Weekly*, 22 March 2001).

Reverse engineering

Attempts to recreate the design of software or hardware by analysing the final product.

Reverse engineering represents one of the ways in which companies attempt to circumvent the restrictions imposed by copyright and patent legislation. Reverse engineering attempts to recreate the design of an item by analysing the final product. This can be compared to the 'black box' approach to systems analysis, where the outputs from the system are analysed in order to determine the inputs and processes involved.

Microprocessors compatible with Intel's range of Pentium processors are often created using reverse engineering methods. Typically, a team of developers is assembled and made to work in a 'clean room', that is, an environment where there is no access to information concerning the item to be reproduced. The development team is then given information concerning the functions performed by the processor to be dupli-cated and works to reproduce all of these functions. Since the developers have no access to the original processor and information concerning its operation, the new processor design cannot be claimed to be an identical copy. However, this does not nec-essarily mean that reverse engineering is considered an acceptable activity; this area continues to be a subject of legal controversy.

▶ Registered designs

The aesthetic aspects of items such as clothing, furniture, electrical goods and jewellery can be protected by registering their designs. Registered designs can be thought of as similar to patents except that they deal only with the appearance of a given item.

▶ Trademarks

A trademark distinguishes a company's goods or services from those of its competitors. The 'Intel Inside' campaign is an excellent example of how a trademark can help to establish a strong product or brand identity. As with patents and designs, trademarks can be protected by formally registering them.

▶ Regulation of Investigatory Powers Act (2000)

The Regulation of Investigatory Powers Act (2000) – known as the RIP Act – is likely to have a profound effect on business organisations. The Act introduced measures that allow electronic communications to be monitored by government agencies. In some circumstances, companies can be obliged to comply with requests to supply informa-tion considered confidential. Companies may also be required to provide agencies with the encryption keys they use, so that information can be decoded.

Whilst it is unlikely that these measures will have a direct effect on companies, it has been suggested that there may be some *indirect* effects. For example, it has been claimed that the Act will discourage the adoption of e-commerce, leading to lost business opportunities of up to £2 billion each year. As a relatively new piece of legislation, it will take some time before the impact of the Act can be evaluated.

> One in five employers monitor staff e-mails without their knowledge or consent.
> *Source: Financial Times*, 17 January 2001

The Act has already caused difficulties for some organisations since it appears to con-done certain acts that are illegal under the Data Protection Act and Human Rights Act. As an example, there is a great deal of confusion over the monitoring of employees. Whilst many people believe that an organisation has the right to monitor e-mail mes-sages and Internet use, others argue that this is an infringement of privacy and is therefore illegal under Human Rights legislation. For many companies, this is a dilemma that is not easily resolved. A great deal of productive time can be lost if employees are allowed free use of e-mail and Internet facilities. Consider the words of Ian Wells, the managing director of a company called Mediapps: 'If a typical company employee, earning £18,000 per year, views six known Web pages per day, for five min-utes each, they will waste an average of 96 hours a year logging onto the Web pages alone. This amounts to a cost to the company of over £1,000 per employee per year' (*Computer Weekly*, 7 December 2000). In addition, companies expose themselves to other risks, for example there is the possibility of legal action if employees libel a competitor within e-mail messages. However, monitoring e-mail messages and Internet use can also lead to significant problems. In addition to the threat of legal action, for example, companies must consider the expense involved in monitoring employees.

A recent CIPD report found that UK companies are losing up to £2.5m each year due to non-work related surfing. A survey in 1999 found that 50% of workers were using the Web to visit 'adult' sites.

Source: Courtesy of *Computer Weekly*, 7 December 2000

Case Study 17.2 highlights some of the issues related to personal privacy and the monitoring of e-mail in the workplace.

CASE STUDY 17.2

Employee monitoring

A personal assistant was looking through a colleague's e-mail account – standard practice when people were away or off sick at the consultancy where she worked. But instead of the client e-mail she was hunting for, she found an 'unpleasant and defamatory' message about herself. She complained – and was promptly sacked for accessing a confidential record.

The dispute is one of hundreds of cases involving staff privacy that are waiting to be heard by employment tribunals. Employers are hoping not to join this queue face a mass of new, potentially conflicting, regulation.

The government last week gave a legal green light to snooping on staff e-mails and phone calls. Proposals to force companies to seek the consent of both the senders and recipients have been abandoned.

Instead, rules coming into force on October 24 will allow employers 'routine access' to messages to check whether they are business-related. The only important caveat is that companies must make 'all reasonable efforts' to inform staff and the outside recipients of the messages that they may be monitored.

'They have effectively given in to all of the pressures from industry', says James Davies, an employment partner at Lewis Silkin, the law firm. But this apparent victory for employers may prove a somewhat Pyrrhic one. A draft code on workplace surveillance being published this week by the Data Protection Commissioner, the privacy watchdog, places much tighter constraints on employers.

Companies engaging in unreasonable or blanket snooping could face enforcement action from the Commissioner. They also risk being taken to court. The unions have threatened to back an early challenge to surveillance by using the Human Rights Act, which enshrined the right to respect for privacy into UK law on October 2.

This new legal right might appear to sit uneasily with the mass of surveillance techniques used by business. Insurers routinely employ private detectives to snoop on people they suspect of fraud, citing cases such as the man claiming chronic back pain who was videoed mending his roof. Employers use similar techniques to catch staff on long-term sickness leave who are moonlighting as taxi drivers or window cleaners.

New technology allows companies to keep tabs on their employees in Orwellian ways. Hidden cameras, smart-card identification badges that track where people are in a building and software that analyses duration and destination of telephone calls are only part of the armoury.

Drugs testing of employees has spread from the US to Europe. Genetic testing – used by 15 per cent of big American companies, according to a survey earlier this year – is expected to be next.

But the question of which parts – if any – of this activity will be curtailed by the Human Rights Act appears an open one. The new right to privacy is not absolute. It can be overridden if the intrusion is necessary to, among other things, protect public safety or health, prevent disorder or crime, or protect 'the rights and freedoms of others'.

This gives a broad range of possible defences. But cases decided by the European Court of Human

▶

Rights give little guidance on which defences will persuade the UK courts. The most prominent case concerned Alison Halford, a senior police officer who argued successfully that her right to privacy had been breached at work.

But the Halford decision may have stemmed from the fact the police had secretly bugged a phone line they had installed for her use in a discrimination case she was fighting against them. Such a blatant intrusion of privacy is a long way from monitoring work calls with the knowledge and implied consent of employees.

The lack of certainty is compounded by the fact that no one yet knows the extent to which the Human Rights Act will bite on the employment policies of private companies. Only public sector bodies can be sued for breaching the Act. But the courts and employment tribunals have to interpret laws in accordance with the new Act.

So a ruling on whether a private sector employer has acted fairly and reasonably – a core question in many tribunal decisions – could turn on the Act's requirements.

'Human rights are great for lawyers and a nightmare at the same time, because who knows what will happen?', says Catherine Taylor, an employment partner at Olswang, the law firm. 'Companies can either be ultra cautious and get the best practice in place now, or they can take a commercial view and wait and see what happens.'

Amid the uncertainty, there are two practical steps lawyers strongly advise all companies to take. The first is to ensure there is a reasonable justification for the surveillance.

'I believe insurers will win rights challenges on covert surveillance, provided they can offer some sort of rational explanation for using it, such as evidence of suspected fraud', says Kevin Fletcher, a partner at Weightmans, the law firm. 'Where people fall into difficulties is where they act on gut instinct.'

The second step is to make anyone affected by the monitoring aware of it, unless there are bulletproof reasons against such disclosure.

BP Amoco scored a public relations own goal last year when it emerged that the oil company had installed secret microphones in some of its Scottish petrol station forecourts. The aim was to catch thieves, rather than snoop on staff or customers. But the press furore persuaded BP to put up signs warning of the possible surveillance.

Many employers have lost tribunal challenges when it became clear the employee had not been given any rules on e-mail or internet use, or told they might be monitored. Companies appear to have been slow to absorb this fact.

'There has been an upsurge in people wanting us to look at their computer and e-mail policies in the last couple of weeks', says Catherine Prest, an employment lawyer at Hammond Suddards Edge, the law firm. 'So many employers have got nothing at all, or what they have is wholly inadequate.'

Source: Jean Eaglesham, 'Staff privacy in the spotlight', *Financial Times*, 9 October 2000

Questions

1 Why do employers feel the need to monitor e-mail, telephone calls and Internet access?

2 What problems might occur if an employer is found to have been monitoring staff secretly?

3 Do employers have a right to ensure that their resources are being used appropriately?

◗ Other legislation

We conclude this section by describing some of the other legislation that may have an impact on organisations and individuals working in the technology industry.

● The Human Rights Act (1998) provides UK citizens with a set of fundamental rights, including a right to privacy. The provisions made in the Human Rights Act are important since the principles described by the Act apply to the whole of the European Union.

● The government has recently announced plans to introduce a Freedom of Information Act, similar to that used in the United States. Such an Act will, for the first time, set out the specific rights of UK citizens in terms of personal privacy. Although other legislation, such as the Human Rights Act (1998) deals with areas such as personal privacy, many people feel that additional legislation is needed. A Freedom of Information Act will also serve to make government agencies and other organisations more accountable to the public since there will be a statutory duty to meet requests for information.

- The Police Act (1997) set up the National Criminal Intelligence Centre, a specialised police organisation charged with preventing and detecting computer-related crime. As with the RIP Act, this Act gives the police and other agencies the power to monitor communications. However, unlike the RIP Act, this Act has received a better welcome since it has been seen as less intrusive in terms of personal privacy.
- The Official Secrets Act (1911–1989) prevents individuals from disclosing any information related to national security. In addition, both individuals and organisations are required to take appropriate measures in order to prevent such information from being disclosed. This legislation is of particular importance to companies and individuals that work in areas related to defence.
- The Obscene Publications Act (1959) and the Protection of Children Act (1978) prohibit the publication of material considered pornographic or excessively violent. This legislation would deal with issues such as copying pornographic materials from the Internet.
- The Malicious Communications Act (1988) makes it an offence to send any message that might be considered obscene or threatening.
- The Defamation Act (1996) is concerned with slander and libel. This legislation extends to comments made in e-mail messages and material displayed on web sites.
- The Electronic Communications Act (2000) is intended to support the growth of e-commerce in the UK. Amongst other things, the Act serves to make electronic signatures legally binding.

F *Focus on* software piracy

Copyright theft, in the form of software piracy, continues to be one of the most common crimes associated with computer systems. This section considers software piracy from several perspectives with a view to improving understanding of this complex area.

▶ Background

The recognition of software theft as a major problem to software companies and distributors can be traced back to the early 1980s. During this period, the personal computer 'boom' began with the launch of the original IBM personal computer in the United States and the launch of a series of inexpensive home computers by Sir Clive Sinclair in the UK. The sudden popularity of personal computers created a huge demand for software applications and resulted in the creation of thousands of small software companies around the world. However, as the number of applications increased, so too did incidence of illegal copying.

Prior to the widespread adoption of CD-ROM, most software applications were distributed via floppy disk and magnetic tape. Programs distributed via magnetic media, such as the floppy disk, were relatively simple to copy since few software companies made use of copy protection methods. However, even the use of copy protection techniques did little to deter users. A number of companies existed that supplied various hardware and software items that could be used to circumvent common copy protection techniques. Such items were often sold as legitimate products, for example special utility programs designed to help users to duplicate copy protected software were often sold as legitimate backup utilities.

As more sophisticated personal computers became available, the cost of software began to increase and the problem of software theft grew even greater. Many individuals saw an

Copy protection describes a number of methods that can be used to prevent unauthorised copies being made of a software package. The most common form of copy protection is the use of passwords and registration codes; unless the user possesses the correct registration information, the software will not function. It is worth noting that some software companies make use of hardware copy protection devices. Specialised programs are sometimes supplied with a hardware key, often called a dongle. The hardware key must be connected to the computer in order for the software to function. This provides a highly effective, if inconvenient, means of preventing illegal copies of the program from being made.

opportunity to profit by distributing counterfeit versions of popular programs. Organised groups began to sell counterfeit software through a number of different channels, for example via mail order. New programs were obtained through a variety of different methods. As an example, *cracking groups* were made up of users who gained satisfaction by defeating the copy protection methods used by software companies. Collections of programs where all copy protection had been disabled were created and sold on to others. In some cases, individuals imported software from countries without effective copyright legislation or where software theft was regarded as unimportant.

The advent of CD-ROM as a distribution medium in the early 1990s briefly obstructed the making of illegal copies. The sheer quantity of data held on a CD made it impractical for individuals to transfer data onto magnetic tape or floppy disk. In addition, the costs involved in duplicating large numbers of disks or tapes also served to hinder the activities of the organised groups. However, the introduction of inexpensive CD-recordable (CDR) units reversed the situation by making it possible to store and distribute numerous applications on a single CD.

As DVD (digital versatile disc) units become widespread, the problem of software theft is likely to decline. The DVD format offers a number of features designed to prevent illegal copying of software and data. However, as recordable DVD units become more affordable, we see software piracy begin to grow once more.

◗ The growth of software piracy

Produced on behalf of the **Business Software Alliance (BSA)** and the **Software Publishers Association (SPA)**, the annual *Global Software Piracy Report* charts changes and trends in software piracy across the world.

The report provides a number of statistics that illustrate the severity of the problem of software piracy:

- Worldwide losses from software piracy were estimated at $12 billion in 1999, a 34 per cent increase from 1998.
- The highest losses due to software piracy in 1999 were attributed to Western Europe ($3.6 billion)
- In the United Kingdom, the piracy rate for 1999 was estimated at 26 per cent.

Figure 17.2 and Table 17.1 illustrate selected software piracy rates by region and country.

◗ Perspectives on software piracy

In this section, we consider software piracy from three perspectives: a typical end-user, software development companies and business organisations.

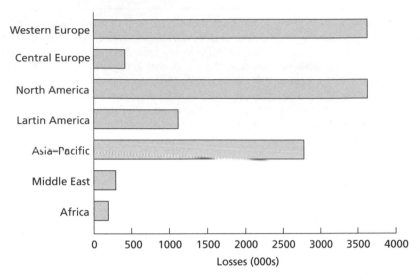

Figure 17.2 1999 global software piracy rates by region

End-users

On an individual basis, making illegal copies of computer programs holds a number of attractions:

● Software packages can be acquired at a very low cost. After an initial outlay for any specialised software or hardware needed, users face only the ongoing costs of blank media.
● Many users collect software applications in order to trade with others or create a library of applications that can be used to support their activities. It us not unusual, for example, for a person interested in programming to acquire a collection of editors, compilers and interpreters.
● Many users consider software piracy a trivial offence; some even believe that making copies of software is perfectly legal. In truth, since software piracy is extremely widespread, individual users who make copies of programs for their own use are unlikely to be pursued by agencies such as **FAST** (the Federation against Software Theft). In the event that a user is caught in possession of illegal software, prosecution is unlikely because of the time and expense involved in taking legal action.
● A significant minority of users produce and distribute illegal copies of software in order to generate an income that can be used to support their hobby. In many cases, the distribution of software is seen as a business venture and used as a source of revenue.

Federation Against Software Theft (FAST)
An organisation formed to act against software piracy.

There are several common arguments put forward by individuals who advocate the copying of software and associated materials, such as manuals.

One argument suggests that software houses provide too little information concerning their products. Software houses and retailers are also seen as being reluctant to provide demonstrations or allow users to purchase products on a trial basis. These factors can sometimes mean that the software chosen for a particular task proves to be unsuitable. In some cases, the user may not be able to reclaim the cost of the software since retailers and manufacturers are sometimes reluctant to offer refunds. In view of these factors, many users feel that it is unfair to ask them to bear the full cost of a decision made on the incomplete or inaccurate information provided by the retailer or software house. Copying a given package, some argue, allows a full and careful evaluation to be made of the software. If it is felt that the package is appropriate to their needs, users are likely to purchase a genuine copy of the program in order to receive manuals, technical support and other

Table 17.1 **Software piracy rates by country and region**

Western Europe	Piracy rate	Losses (000s)
Austria	36%	$66,929
Belgium/Luxembourg	36%	$77,371
Denmark	29%	$59,184
Finland	30%	$50,594
France	39%	$548,408
Germany	27%	$652,379
Greece	71%	$67,708
Ireland	51%	$117,892
Italy	44%	$421,434
Netherlands	44%	$264,400
Norway	37%	$87,568
Portugal	47%	$49,920
Spain	53%	$247,650
Sweden	35%	$131,358
Switzerland	33%	$107,068
UK	26%	$679,506
Eastern Euorpe		
Bulgaria	80%	$11,245
CIS less Russia	90%	$43,520
Czech Republic	42%	$36,897
Hungary	52%	$37,262
Poland	60%	$164,914
Romania	81%	$12,132
Russia	89%	$165,515
Slovakia	46%	$9,653
Slovenia	70%	$10,366
Other Eastern Europe	52%	$13,708
North America		
Canada	41%	$440,101
USA	25%	$3,191,111
Asia/Pacific		
Australia	32%	$150,390
China	91%	$645,480
India	61%	$214,557
Indonesia	85%	$42,106
Israel	44%	$72,487
Japan	31%	$975,396
Korea	50%	$197,269
Malaysia	71%	$84,154
New Zealand	31%	$19,656
Pakistan	83%	$18,913
Singapore	51%	$61,758
Taiwan	54%	$122,946
Thailand	81%	$82,184
Turkey	74%	$98,257
UAE	47%	$7,624

benefits. On the other hand, if the software is considered unsuitable, the user will delete any copies made since they are of little or no value.

A second argument in favour of copying software involves the sometimes restrictive licence conditions adopted by software houses. When a user purchases a software package, they are merely buying the right to make use of the package for an unspecified period of time. In general, the software house retains ownership of the software, all accompanying documentation and the distribution medium itself. A licence agreement may also forbid users from making a backup copy of a package and the software may incorporate *copy protection* in order to prevent users from making copies. In addition, licence agreements often include statements that disclaim responsibility if the software does not function correctly or if the distribution media become damaged or corrupt. If the terms set out in the software licence agreement are broken, the user may be required to return all of the materials supplied at their own expense. Many users believe that they should have the right to safeguard their investment in a software package by making one or more backup copies. Such users will see the terms of the licence agreement as being unreasonable and will often disregard any clauses regarding backup copies.

A third argument concerns the pricing policies adopted by software companies. Some users argue that software companies have deliberately inflated their prices, placing some packages out of the reach of individuals and small companies. Copying software, it is argued, causes no harm to the software companies involved since the software would never have been purchased in the first place.

Software developers

Software companies make a number of powerful arguments against the copying of software.

Perhaps the simplest and most compelling argument made by software companies is that software is protected under international copyright laws. In most countries, the copying of software is regarded as theft and exposes the individual to both criminal and civil liability.

A second argument involves a defence of the pricing policies adopted by many software companies. The costs involved in the development of a sophisticated, comprehensive application program can be extremely high. The effort involved in developing an application is normally measured in terms of labour hours. A word processing program, for example, may take several years to develop and can involve the efforts of hundreds of staff. Such a program might require many millions of labour hours before it is released to the public. Since the cost of development must be recovered, it is reflected within the price of the application. In addition, the cost of the software also includes sums that support the continued development of the application and research into new products. Copying software, it is argued, reduces the revenues generated from the sale of the software and jeopardises new developments.

This leads to a related argument concerning the pricing of software. As incidences of illegal copying increase, software companies face a need to safeguard profit margins and recover development costs as quickly as possible. In order to do this, prices must be increased so that the losses made due to illegal copying can be recovered. In this way, it is argued, those that make illegal copies of software are directly responsible for the higher prices faced by legitimate customers.

Business organisations

The preceding sections should make clear some of the problems that face modern business organisations.

Smaller organisations, with limited budgets, are sometimes tempted to make additional copies of a given software package. As mentioned earlier, although the risk of detection is relatively low, the use of illegal software can lead to a number of repercussions. Some examples include:

- Organisations found in breach of copyright can suffer severe financial penalties. It is not uncommon for an organisation to be required to purchase licences for all illegal programs found on the company's premises. In addition, the company may face criminal or civil proceedings that result in significant fines.
- By encouraging employees to make use of illegal software, the company exposes itself to action from unions, employees and other parties. As an example, an employee accused of using illegal software in the course of their duties might take legal action against the employer. In addition, staff morale might be reduced, leading to productivity losses and labour disputes.
- Action taken by organisations such as the Business Software Alliance often result in negative publicity for an organisation. This could have a major impact on relationships with customers and suppliers.
- The organisation's profitability can be damaged if it is deprived of the applications software needed to support day-to-day activities. In some companies, even a temporary disruption might lead to long-term effects. As an example, relationships with clients could be harmed if a sales organisation were unable to offer high levels of customer service.

It is worth noting that, as the size of the organisation increases, so too does the risk of detection and the severity of the possible consequences. Organisations such as the Federation against Software Theft (FAST) and Business Software Alliance (BSA), for example, encourage employees to report software piracy by their employers, sometimes offering a substantial reward for information leading to a successful prosecution.

Large organisations must also recognise a number of issues and responsibilities that influence the way in which they operate. A key issue facing many organisations is the need to reduce or eliminate the use of illegal software within their computer-based information systems. Only by taking an active stand against software piracy can a company gain a measure of protection against prosecution and the other losses outlined in this section. In addition, only such a stance can protect the company's reputation and industry status.

At the simplest level, an organisation seen to be making an effort to control how software is used in its computer systems is likely to be dealt with less severely than one that takes no action at all. However, such an approach can also lead to a number of other, somewhat more tangible benefits. Consider some of the benefits to be gained by using methods such as regular software audits in order to control which software applications are used by a company's computer-based information systems:

- In the UK and many other countries, an employer, ultimately the managing director, is held responsible for the actions taken by employees during the course of their work. In this way, the employer could be held jointly responsible if an employee uses illegal software with the company's computer-based information systems. The use of methods such as software audits can help to reduce instances where employees install or use illegal programs on the company's systems. In turn, this acts to reduce the risk of the company facing prosecution due to the employee's actions.
- By reducing the number of illegal or unauthorised programs used with the company's systems, employees can be encouraged to focus on their work more closely. Games and Internet browsers, for example, are well-known distractions that cost organisations many millions of labour hours each year.
- With a reduction in the use of unauthorised or illegal software also comes a reduction in the risk of infection by computer viruses. In turn, this decreases the costs and damage associated with virus infection.
- By preventing the use of unauthorised or illegal software, employees can be encouraged to adhere to organisational standards for the use of the company's

computer-based information systems. This can provide a number of benefits related to the way in which the organisation produces, manages and makes use of its data. As an example, if only programs that have been approved by the organisation are used, then the accuracy of data can be maintained or improved.

Activity 17.4

The ASP software model

A new approach to the distribution of software may help to reduce levels of software piracy whilst ensuring that legitimate users gain benefits such as improved support and access to the very latest applications. Using the Internet as a resource, locate information related to application service providers (ASP) and answer the following questions.

1 How does this model of software distribution work?
2 What are the benefits of ASP to business organisations?
3 What are the benefits of ASP to software companies?

Summary

1 Managers, developers and users of computer-based information systems are required to balance the needs of their employer and the requirements of their profession with other demands such as a responsibility to society.

2 Membership of a professional association brings with it the requirement to abide by a professional code of conduct. The code of conduct provides guidance related to the individual's legal, social and professional responsibilities.

3 An alternative view of the responsibilities of managers, developers and users involves considering some of their obligations to their employers, the public and the state. Conflicts of interest can arise from the need to serve the duties and responsibilities imposed upon the individual.

4 The impact of technology on personal privacy has manifested itself in many different ways. A contemporary issue related to personal privacy is the increase in the use of computer monitoring techniques. Computer monitoring can involve a wide variety of activities, from observing the behaviour of employees in the workplace to intercepting private e-mail messages.

5 Acts of computer crime can include theft of goods or services, software theft, data theft, damage to data or software, and hacking.

6 Some of the legislation relevant to those involved in managing or developing computer-based information systems include

● The Copyright, Designs and Patents Act (1988) provides limited protection for an organisation's intellectual properties. Such legislation also places a responsibility upon companies to ensure that they do not infringe the copyright of others, for example by making or using unauthorised copies of computer programs.
● The Computer Misuse Act (1990) attempts to prevent unauthorised access to computer-based information systems. In addition, such legislation also makes it an offence to cause damage to hardware, software or data.
● The Data Protection Act (1998) defines the way in which companies may gather, store, process and disclose personal data. In addition, the Act provides individuals

with a number of rights allowing them to view or modify the personal data held on them.

- The Human Rights Act (1998) has implications for personal privacy, including the privacy of employees.
- The Regulation of Investigatory Powers Act (2000) has caused concern for many business organisations since, under certain circumstances, it allows confidential e-mail traffic and business data to be monitored by security forces.

7 Software developers see software piracy as a major threat to their business activities and the continued growth of the software industry. Business organisations face severe penalties unless they take an active stand against software piracy.

EXERCISES

Self-assessment exercises

1 Describe the offences are covered by the Computer Misuse Act (1990).

2 What is meant by computer monitoring?

3 What are eight guiding principles of the Data Protection Act?

4 What are the most common types of computer crime?

5 Identify the legislation that covers the following actions:

 (a) distributing a computer virus
 (b) making an unauthorised copy of a computer program;
 (c) gaining unauthorised access to a computer-based information system;
 (d) vandalising computer hardware;
 (e) creating a computer virus;
 (f) placing an unauthorised computer program on a network system;
 (g) stealing a backup copy of a data file;
 (h) photocopying a software manual.

6 For each of the following acts, state whether or not they are permissible under the Computer Misuse Act (1990) or Data Protection Act (1998):

 (a) storing inaccurate or misleading personal data;
 (b) damaging data held on offline storage media;
 (c) electronic eavesdropping;
 (d) preventing access to personal data held in manual files, such as microfilm;
 (e) software piracy;
 (f) accidental damage to hardware, software or data;
 (g) disclosing personal data without the permission of the individual;
 (h) preventing access to personal data.

7 What is reverse engineering?

8 What is a professional code of conduct?

Discussion questions

1 You are given the responsibility of managing a technical project that may result in hundreds of job losses. Decide whether or not you should continue with the project and justify your decision on professional, moral and ethical grounds.

2 Do the security services and government departments have the right to monitor personal communications, such as e-mail messages? Justify your answer.

3 'The cost of software applications leaves some users no choice but to make illegal copies.' Make a case in favour or against this argument.

4 What new developments are likely to have a beneficial impact on software piracy?

5 Is there a digital divide?

Essay questions

1 Discuss changes in employment patterns brought about by increased levels of automation and the introduction of computer-based information systems.

2 What are some of the moral, ethical and professional issues faced by the managers of information systems? Illustrate your answer with relevant examples.

3 Using relevant examples, critically review the major pieces of legislation relevant to the ways in which organisations use computer-based information systems. Your discussion should refer to areas such as copyright, unauthorised access, the use of personal data and any other relevant issues.

Examination questions

1 The Data Protection Act (1988) regulates the ways in which organisations may gather, store, process and disclose personal information. You are required to:
   (a) Describe the principles upon which the Act is based.
   (b) Discuss some of the responsibilities placed on organisations by the Act.
   (c) Critically evaluate the strengths and weaknesses of the Act in terms of the right given to individuals to view and amend any personal data held on them.

2 The ability of computer-based information systems to store, process and retrieve data quickly and efficiently raises concerns related to the privacy of individuals. You are required to:
   (a) Explain the meaning of 'personal privacy'.
   (b) Describe some of the ways in which technology can allow an individual's personal privacy to be invaded.
   (c) Using relevant examples, discuss the moral and ethical issues involved in gathering, storing and making use of personal data.

3 Members of associations, such as the British Computer Society, are required to abide by a professional code of conduct.
   (a) Describe the areas that a professional code of conduct is likely to include.
   (b) Using relevant examples, discuss some of the ways in which a manager's ethical and professional responsibilities can conflict.
   (c) 'An individual's professional and legal obligations always take precedence over moral and ethical concerns.' Adopt a position in favour or against this argument and justify your response.

References

Johnson, D.G. (1994) *Computer Ethics*, 2nd edition, Prentice-Hall, Englewood Cliffs, NJ

Parker, D.B. (1976) *Crime by Computer*, Charles Scribner's Sons, New York

Schwartau, W. (1994) *Information Warfare*, Thunder's Mouth Press, New York

Further reading

Bainbridge D. (1995) *Introduction to Computer Law*, Pitman Publishing, London. Coverage of legal issues related to computer-based information systems. Includes the Computer Misuse Act and discusses areas such as reverse engineering

Bowyer, K. (ed.) (1996) *Ethics and Computing*, 2nd edition, IEEE Computer Society Press, Washington, DC

Currie, W. (2000) *The Global Information Society*, John Wiley, Chichester. An interesting look at the information society, with good coverage of the Internet

Forrester, T. and Morrison, P. (1995) *Computer Ethics*, 2nd edition, MIT Press, Cambridge, MA

Hoffman, W. and Frederick, R. (1995) *Business Ethics: Readings and Cases in Corporate Morality*, 3rd edition, McGraw-Hill, New York

Hussain, K. and Hussain, D. (1995) *Information Systems for Business*, Prentice Hall International, Hemel Hempstead. Chapter 16 describes issues related to privacy and security

Langford, D. (1995) *Practical Computer Ethics*, McGraw-Hill, New York. This is an ideal introductory text for students. In addition to plenty of case studies, there is good coverage of codes of conduct

Langford, D. (1999) *Business Computing Ethics*, Addison-Wesley, Harlow. This is a comprehensive text that covers ethics in relation to areas such as legislation, networks and the Internet

Lynch, J. (1996) *Cyberethics: Managing the Morality of Multimedia*, Rushmere Wynn, Bedfordshire

O'Brien, J. (1997) *Introduction to Information Systems*, 8th edition, Richard D. Irwin, Homewood, IL. This is an accessible and structured text. Chapter 12 deals with information systems security and ethics

Post, G. and Anderson, D. (2000) *Management Information Systems: Solving Business Problems with Information Technology*, 2nd edition, McGraw-Hill, New York. Although this text has a very strong US bias, it provides a slightly different perspective on some of the material covered here. Chapter 14 deals with social aspects of technology

Schwartau, W. (1994) *Information Warfare*, Thunder's Mouth Press, New York. Regarded as one of the classic texts on information warfare

Schwartau, W. (2000) *Cybershock: Surviving Hackers, Phreakers, Identity Thieves, Internet Terrorists and Weapons of Mass Disruption*, Thunder's Mouth Press, New York. Winn Schwartau's latest book covers a broad range of interesting ideas

Web links

www.bsa.org Business Software Alliance. Provides reports and information on international software piracy.

http://cyberethics.cbi.msstate.edu Good selection of resources on computer ethics, including case studies.

www.wired.com HotWired is the electronic sister of *Wired* magazine. It carries a range of popular articles and covers areas such as anonymity, freedom of speech and so on.

www.nd.edu/~rbarger/cases.html A large range of case studies related to ethics. These pose some interesting questions and make excellent discussion points.

http://eserver.org/cyber/mainfram.html A body of articles and other materials covering a wide range of issues related to privacy, software theft, hacking and other issues.

http://library.thinkquest.org/26658 An interactive guide to computer ethics. A little simplistic, but offers a good introduction to this area and provides links to other resources.

http://library.hilton.kzn.school.za/Computers/compethics.htm The 10 Commandments of computer ethics, taken from the Computer Ethics Institute.

www.infosyssec.org/infosyssec/compcrim1.htm Information Systems Security Provides a huge array of links and resources related to computer ethics.

http://http.cs.berkeley.edu/~bh/hackers.html An interesting paper from the University of California that looks at how and why individuals become hackers.

http://gasnet.med.yale.edu/software/EthicsDescription.html An interactive ethics tutorial. This poses some interesting questions for students and supplies discussion material for them to consider.

www.smartbooks.com/b9811/bw811fightcompcrime.htm Details of a book called *Fighting Computer Crime*. An excerpt from the book can be accessed from this page. This sample chapter looks at some of the characteristics of those who engage in computer crime.

http://fly.hiwaay.net/~pspoole/echelon.html A good range of information (including links to press articles) concerning Echelon.

www.aclu.org/echelonwatch/resources.html A site devoted to monitoring Echelon. Links to news stories and articles.

www.gilc.org/privacy/survey Information on privacy legislation around the world.

www.legislation.hmso.gov.uk/acts/acts1998/19980029.htm The text of the Data Protection Act (1998) from HMSO.

www.official-documents.co.uk/document/hoffice/rights/rights.htm The Human Rights Bill. Contains information on the European Union's Data Protection Directive.

www.hmso.gov.uk/acts/acts1997/1997050.htm The Police Act (1997). Describes the role of the National Criminal Intelligence Service, which is entitled to authorise activities such as tapping telephone lines.

www.official-documents.co.uk/document/caboff/foi/foi.htm A White Paper detailing proposals for a Freedom of Information Act.

www.privacy.org/pi/countries/uk Privacy International. News and information related to privacy issues in the UK.

www.homeoffice.gov.uk/oicd/ripbill.htm Information on the Regulation of Investigatory Powers Bill. This Bill deals with issues such as electronic surveillance. A controversial aspect of the Bill is that it will require people to supply encryption keys upon receiving an appropriate request. Failure to do so may result in imprisonment. Another controversial aspect of the Bill is that Internet Service Providers will be forced to allow access to communications passing through their servers.

www.eff.com The Electronic Frontier Foundation A respected organisation that campaigns for free speech and the right to privacy. The web site contains some general information and news related to these issues.

www.ifi.uio.no/iris20/proceedings/12.htm A lengthy but comprehensive paper entitled: 'Computer ethics – the most vital social aspect of computing: some themes and issues concerning moral and ethical problems of IT'.

www.ifs.univie.ac.at/~pr2gq1/rev4344.html International review of criminal policy – United Nations Manual on the prevention and control of computer-related crime.

www.cynatech.co.uk/links/legislation.htm This site contains information on legislation and government policy related to e-commerce and digital signatures.

www.hmso.gov.uk/acts/acts1988/Ukpga_19880027_en_1.htm A link to the full text of the Malicious Communications Act 1988.

www.legislation.hmso.gov.uk/acts/acts1996/1996031.htm A link to the full text of the Defamation Act 1996.

www.hmso.gov.uk/acts/acts2000/20000007.htm A link to the full text of the Electronic Communications Act 2000.

www.hmso.gov.uk/acts/acts2000/20000023.htm A link to the full text of the Regulation of Investigatory Powers Act 2000.

www.hmso.gov.uk/acts/acts1998/19980042.htm A link to the full text of the Human Rights Act 1998.

Glossary

3DFx graphics card. A type of graphics card that features a sophisticated coprocessor used to manipulate an image so that it appears more realistic. Complicated calculations are required in order to perform actions such as smoothing jagged shapes or showing the shadows that an object might cast.

Access control. See *User validation.*

Access time. In terms of storage devices, the access time refers to the average time taken to locate a specific item of data. Access times are normally given in milliseconds, for example a typical hard disk drive might have an access time of 11 ms.

Active content. Describes a method by which a browser can restrict access to WWW pages that have been rated for their content.

Active-X. A programming language standard developed by Microsoft which permits complex and graphical customer applications to be written and then accessed from a web browser. An example might be a form for calculating interest on a loan. A competitor to Java.

Actors. People, software or other devices that interface with a system. See *Use-case.*

Ad clicks. An IFABC standard indicating the number of audited occasions a web banner or interstitial has been clicked on by a user to view an advert.

Adaptive system. In general, an adaptive system has the ability to monitor and regulate its own performance. In many cases, an adaptive system will be able to respond fully to changes in its environment by modifying its behaviour.

Address book. A folder that contains frequently used e-mail addresses. Rather than identifying other users by their e-mail addresses, individuals or groups can be given aliases or nicknames. E-mail addressed to an alias is automatically sent to the user(s) associated with that name.

Adoption levels. The proportion of the population/businesses that have access to the Internet, are influenced by it or purchase using it.

Agent. The term agent is used to describe a specialised program that automatically searches the Internet for information meeting a user's requirements.

Alias. The process of sending e-mail messages to specific individuals or groups of users can be simplified by making use of aliases. An alias – sometimes known as a nickname – usually consists of a description and the e-mail addresses of those grouped under the alias.

Alpha release and alpha testing. Alpha releases are preliminary versions of the software released early in the build process. They usually have the majority of the functionality of the system in place, but may suffer from extensive bugs. The purpose of 'alpha testing' is to identify these bugs and any major problems with the functionality and usability of the software. Alpha testing is usually conducted by staff inside the organisation developing the software or by favoured customers.

Analogue. Analogue data is continuous in that an infinite number of values between two given points can be represented. As an example, the hands of a clock are able to represent every single possible time of the day.

Annotation. A note or message that can be attached to a document. Voice annotations are spoken messages that can be embedded within a document.

Anti-virus. An anti-virus is a benevolent virus program that copies itself to the boot sectors of unprotected floppy disks. If another virus attempts to overwrite the anti-virus, it displays a message on the screen warning the user of infection. See *Computer virus.*

Apple Macintosh. A family of personal computers produced by Apple Computers. Although less popular than IBM-compatible personal computers, the Apple Macintosh is widely used for professional desktop publishing applications, graphics and animation.

Applets. Small programs with limited functions typically running from within a web browser.

Applications backlog. An applications backlog occurs when the demand for new applications by users exceeds the capacity of the IS department or IS outsourcing company to develop them. Over a period of a year a large number of applications are in the queue of required new work.

Applications generator. An applications generator performs an action or creates a computer program based on a set of requirements given by the user. Many applications generators allow users to define a series of actions or requirements by arranging icons on a special design screen. The resulting design is then converted into a series of instructions or an executable program.

Applications portfolio. The range of different types of business information systems deployed within an organisation.

Artificial intelligence (AI). Artificial intelligence (AI) methods attempt to make a computer system behave in the same way a human being. One application for AI is in natural language processing, where users can communicate with a computer system using English-like statements.

Assembly language. Assembly language represented an attempt to simplify the process of creating computer programs. Symbols and abbreviations were used to create sequences of instructions. An assembler was used to translate a completed assembly language program into the machine code required by the computer.

Asymmetric digital subscriber line (ADSL). A relatively new development in telecommunications, ADSL makes use of conventional telephone lines to provide extremely high data transmission rates.

Asynchronous. When collaborators send messages that can be accessed at a later time these are known as asynchronous. Asynchronous exchange occurs with e-mail or discussion groups.

Attributes of information quality. A group of characteristics by which the quality of information can be assessed. These attributes are normally grouped into three categories: time, content and form. Examples of attributes of information quality include accuracy, reliability and timeliness.

Audits. This describes the process of monitoring an organisation's hardware and software resources. In general, audits are used as a deterrent against theft and the use of illegal software.

Autoresponder. This describes a program that automatically responds to incoming e-mail messages by scanning for key words or phrases and returning an appropriate reply.

Backbones. High-speed communications links used to enable Internet communications across a country and internationally.

Back door. The back door is a section of program code that allows a user to circumvent security procedures in order to gain full access to an information system.

Backup site. A backup site houses a copy of the organisation's main data processing facilities, including hardware, software and up-to-date data files. In the event of an emergency, processing can be switched to the backup site almost immediately so that the organisation's work can continue.

Balanced scorecard. A framework for setting and monitoring business performance. Metrics are structured according to customer issues, internal efficiency measures, financial measures and innovation.

Bandwidth. The term bandwidth is often used to describe how many pieces of data can be transmitted or received at one time by a given device. Bandwidth is usually expressed in hertz (Hz) or in bits or bytes per second.

Banner. A rectangular graphic displayed on a web page for the purposes of advertising. It is normally possible to perform a click-through to access further information. Banners may be static or animated.

Bar code. A bar code is a means of displaying a unique identification number as a series of thick and thin lines. The sequence and width of the lines in the bar code can be translated into a sequence of digits. Bar code numbers are normally produced according to specific method. The Universal Product Code, for example, is a standard method for creating and using bar codes.

Bar code reader. A bar code reader measures the intensity of a light beam reflected from a printed bar code to identify the digits making up a unique identification number. The digits making up the identification number are also printed at the foot of the bar code. If a label containing a bar code becomes damaged or cannot be read for some other reason, it may still be possible to enter the identification number manually.

Batch processing. Data is 'post-processed' following collection, often at times when the workload on the system is lower. Batch processing usually occurs without user interaction as a 'background job'.

Baud. A simple means of measuring the performance of a modem or other device. Early modems operated at speeds of 1200 baud, the equivalent of approximately 100 characters per second. Data transmission rates can also be expressed in bits per second (bps). In general, the higher the baud rate or bps value, the faster and more efficient the device.

Benchmarks. This describes the process of testing the performance of computer equipment. Having carried out a series of benchmark tests, the results can be compared against similar items in order to make the best selection.

Bespoke development. An IS is developed 'from scratch' by an IS professional to suit the business requirements of the application.

Beta release and beta testing. Beta releases occur after alpha testing and have almost complete functionality and relatively few bugs. Beta testing will be conducted by a range of customers who are interested in evaluating the new software. The aim of beta testing is to identify bugs in the software before it is shipped to a range of customers.

Big-bang changeover. Immediate cutover when a new system becomes operational and operations transfer immediately from the previous system.

BIOS (Basic Input/Output System). Housed in a memory chip on the computer's motherboard, the BIOS contains software that controls all of the computer's most basic activities. It is the BIOS that allows the keyboard, display, hard disk drives, serial ports and other devices to function. The BIOS is stored in ROM so that it is always available and cannot be accidentally damaged or erased.

Bit. A single binary digit representing a (0) zero or a 1.

Bit map image. A bit map image is made up of small dots (pixels) arranged in a grid. The finer the grid, the higher the resolution of the image.

Bookmarks. All web browsers allow users to maintain a directory of WWW sites. The directory will enable users to add, edit, delete and organise addresses in the form of bookmarks.

Bottom-up design. The bottom-up approach to design starts with the design of individual modules, establishing their inputs and outputs and then builds an overall design from these modules.

Boundary. This describes the interface between a system and its environment. Everything within the boundary forms part of the system, everything outside the boundary forms part of the external environment.

Brainstorming. Uses the interaction between a group of staff to generate new ideas and discuss existing problems. It is the least structured of the fact-finding techniques.

Brand abuse. This describes a wide range of activities, ranging from the sale of counterfeit goods (e.g. software applications) to exploiting a well-known brand name for commercial gain.

British Computer Society (BCS). The British Computer Society is widely regarded as the UK's leading professional association for those involved the management and development of computer-based information systems.

Bubble jet printer. A bubble jet printer works in similar manner to an inkjet printer, but transfers the character by melting the ink droplets onto the paper.

Bug. Software bugs are defects in a program which are caused by human error during programming or earlier in the lifecycle. They may result in major faults or may remain unidentified.

Bulk e-mailer. The use of mass e-mail programs, called bulk e-mailers, enables an organisation to issue documents, such as questionnaires, at a fraction of the cost of traditional methods.

Bus width. Describes how many pieces of data can be transmitted or received at one time by the bus connecting the processor to other components of the PC.

Business-aligning IS strategy. The IS strategy is used to support the business strategy.

Business-impacting IS strategy. The IS strategy is used to favourably impact the business strategy, perhaps by introducing new technologies.

Business information systems. This describes information systems used to support the functional areas of business. For example, an organisation might use specialised information systems to support sales, marketing and human resource management activities.

Business intelligence (BI) software. BI software is a general term used to describe analysis software which makes use of functions available in data warehouses, data marts and data mining.

Business model. A summary of how a company will generate revenue identifying its product offering, value-added services, revenue sources and target customers.

Business process automation (BPA). Automating existing ways of working manually through information technology.

Business process re-engineering (BPR). Identifying and implementing radical new ways of carrying out work, often enabled by new IT capabilities.

Business resource base. The resources that a company has available to it are known collectively as the business resource base. The business resource base is made up of physical and conceptual resources (also known as tangible and intangible assets).

Business rule. A rule defines the actions that need to occur in a business when a particular situation arises. For example a business rule may state that if a customer requests credit and they have a history of defaulting on payments, then credit will not be issued. A business rule is broken down into an event which triggers a rule with test conditions which result in defined actions.

Business Software Alliance (BSA). An organisation formed to act against software piracy. See *Software theft*.

Business-to-business (B2B). Commercial transactions are between an organisation and other organisations.

Business-to-consumer (B2C). Commercial transactions are between an organisation and consumers.

Buy-side e-commerce. E-commerce transactions between a purchasing organisation and its supplier.

Byte. Made up of eight bits and represents the amount of space required to hold a single character.

Cable modem. These devices allow users to make use of the fibre-optic cables that have been installed in most major cities by cable television companies. Cable modems offer very high data transfer rates, up to a theoretical maximum of 30 Mbps.

Cache (browser). In order to increase the speed and efficiency with which a web browser functions, a temporary storage space is used to store copies of any pages that the user has viewed. If the user returns to a given location, the web browser retrieves the required page from the temporary storage space (known as a cache), rather than transfer a fresh copy from a remote computer.

Cache memory. In a computer system, cache memory is used to improve performance by anticipating the data and instructions that will be needed by the processor. The required data are retrieved and held in the cache, ready to be transferred directly to the processor when required.

Call centre. An office which is devoted to answering telephone enquiries from customers, call centres are commonly used for financial services and retail customer support.

Capacity loading graphs. Capacity loading graphs show the resources required to undertake activities in a project.

CD-R (CD-recordable). This describes a variation on the traditional CD-ROM. CDR drives can not only read conventional compact discs but can also write data to special 'gold' discs. Compact discs produced in this way are known as write-once discs, that is, once data has been stored on the disc it can not be altered or erased. See *CD-ROM*.

CD-ROM. A computer storage device offering a relatively high capacity. The acronym CD-ROM stands for compact disc – read only memory, denoting the fact that CD-ROM discs are read-only devices; data cannot be written to a CD-ROM by a conventional player.

CDRW. A more recent development in terms of compact disc storage are CD re-writable drives. In addition to providing the functionality of the CDR drive, the CDRW drive also allows the use of special compact disc media that can be written and erased many times. However, discs produced in this way are not compatible with standard CD-ROM drives and can only be used with a CDRW unit. See *CDR* and *CD-ROM*.

Central processing unit (CPU). This describes the microprocessor found in a computer system. The CPU controls all of the computer's main functions and enables users to execute programs or process data.

Centralised IS management. Centralised IS management will involve the control of all IS services from a central location, typically in a company head office or data-centre.

CGI (common gateway interface). CGI offers a way of providing interactivity through the web. With a form-type HTML document, a user type in information and structured information or queries sent using the web.

Change (modification) requests. A modification to the software thought to be necessary by the business users or developers.

Changeover. The term used to describe moving from the old information system to the new information system.

Channels. Channels (sometimes described as netcasting) enable users to subscribe to particular sites on the Internet, in much the same way that one might subscribe to a newspaper or magazine. The use of channels allows both the user and the information provider to select the information to be sent and schedule its transmission.

Checksum digits. A checksum involves the use of an extra digit for ensuring the validity of long code numbers. The checksum digit is calculated from an algorithm involving the numbers in the code and their modulus (by convention modulus 11).

Chip theft. Chip theft describes a relatively new phenomenon involving the removal of small but valuable components from computers, such as memory modules and processors.

CISC. (complex instruction set computer) is a specific type of microprocessor which has a wide range of instructions to enable easy programming and efficient use of memory. CISC processors are best known as the Intel processors from 8086 to 80486 and the Motorola 68000 used in early Apple Macintoshes.

Client/server. The client/server architecture consists of client computers such as PC s sharing resources such as a database stored on a more powerful server computers. Processing can be shared between the clients and the servers.

Client/server model. This describes a system architecture in which end-user computers access data from more powerful server computers. Processing can be split in various ways between the server and client.

Closed questions. Closed questions have a restricted choice of answers such as Yes/No or a range of opinion on a scale of strongly agree to strongly disagree (Lickert scale). Approach is useful for quantitative analysis of results.

Closed system. No or limited interaction occurs with the environment.

Code of conduct. Members of professional associations, such as the British Computer Society, are expected to abide by a set of principles that set out minimum standards of competence, conduct and behaviour.

Cognitive style. This describes the way in which a manager absorbs information and reaches decisions. A manager's cognitive style will fall between analytical and intuitive styles.

Comma-separated values (CSV). A CSV file is a simple text file made up of items enclosed within quotation marks and separated by commas. The use of commas and quotation marks enables a program reading the file to identify individual items.

Command line interpreter (CLI). A CLI is used to pass instructions from a user to a computer program. The CLI accepts instructions from a user in the form of brief statements entered via the keyboard.

Commercial languages. This category of programming languages is intended to create applications that meet the basic information processing requirements of business organisations.

Commoditisation. The process whereby product selection becomes more dependent on price than differentiating features, benefits and value-added services.

Compact disc (CD). This describes the media used by CD-ROM players. The data on a compact disc are encoded as a series of dips and raised areas. These two states represent binary data – the same number system used by microprocessors. The CD-ROM player shines a laser beam onto the surface of the disc and measures the light that is reflected back. The intensity of the light that is reflected back enables the player to distinguish individual binary digits. See *CD-ROM*.

Competitive advantage. In order to survive or expand, organisations must seek to gain dominance over their competitors in the marketplace. This can be achieved by using a variety of strategies to gain control of a market or prevent others from gaining control.

Compiler. The instructions that make up a computer program are often stored as a simple text file, usually called a source code file. A compiler produces an executable program by converting instructions held as source code into machine language.

Compound key. In a relational database, it is possible to retrieve data from several tables at once By using record keys in combination, often known as a compound key. See *Record key* and *Primary key*.

Computer-aided design (CAD). Provides interactive graphics that assist in the development of product and service designs. Connects to a database allowing designs to be recalled and developed easily.

Computer-aided manufacture (CAM). CAM involves the use of computers directly to control production equipment and indirectly to support manufacturing operations.

Computer-aided software engineering (CASE) tools. CASE tools are software which helps the systems analyst and designer in the analysis, design and build phases of a software project. They provide tools for drawing diagrams such as ERDs and storing information about processes, entities and attributes.

Computer criminals. In general, computer criminals are well-educated, white-collar workers who feel undervalued or bear some resentment to an employer or former employer. Computer criminals make use of technology to perform a variety of criminal acts, ranging from vandalism and sabotage to hacking and fraud.

Computer Misuse Act (1990). This legislation is intended to protect sensitive equipment and data from unauthorised access, alteration and damage.

Computer monitoring. The use of computer and communications technology to monitor the activities of individuals.

Computer network. A computer network can be defined as: 'a communications system that links two or more computers and peripheral devices and enables transfer of data between the components'.

Computer output to microfilm (COM). COM, also known as computer output microfilm, is often used to archive large quantities of information for future reference. Information is processed via a personal computer and sent directly to a device that produces microfilm negatives.

Computer system. A computer system consists of a number of interrelated components that work together with the aim of converting data into information. In a computer system, processing is carried out electronically, usually with little or no intervention from a human user. The components of a computer system include hardware and software.

Computer virus. A computer virus is a computer program that is capable of self-replication, allowing it to spread from one 'infected' machine to another.

Computer-based information system. This describes an information system that makes use of information technology in order to create management information.

Conceptual resources. Conceptual resources describe the non-physical resources owned by a company. Conceptual resources are also known as intangible assets. Examples include knowledge, experience and judgement.

Configuration management. Procedures which define the process of building a version of the software from its constituent program files and data files.

Constructive cost model (COCOMO). A model used to estimate the amount of effort required to complete a project on the basis of the estimated number of lines of program code.

Contact manager. This describes a software application that can be used to maintain lists of information relating to customers, suppliers and other important individuals or organisations.

Content. Content is the design, text and graphical information which forms a web page.

Content dimension. This describes several characteristics of information quality related to the scope and contents of the information. Amongst these characteristics are the accuracy, relevance and conciseness of information. As an example, information may be considered to be of high quality if it is accurate. Other dimensions of information characteristics include time and form. See *Time dimension, Form dimension.*

Context diagrams. A simplified diagram which is useful for specifying the boundaries and scope of the system. They can be readily produced after the information flow diagram since they are a simplified version of the IFD showing the external entities.

Control. If alterations are needed to the system, adjustments are made by some form of control mechanism. The function of a control mechanism is to ensure that the system is working to fulfil its objective.

Copyright, Designs and Patents Act (1988). Legislation that can be used to provide organisations and software developers with protection against unauthorised copying of designs, software, printed materials and other works.

Copy protection. This describes a number of methods that can be used to prevent unauthorised copies being made of a software package.

Core competencies. Resources, including skills or technologies that provide a particular benefit to customers.

Cost of ownership. The cost of ownership describes a range of different expenses incurred by purchasing and maintaining a computer system. Such costs include the original cost of the hardware and software, upgrades, maintenance, technical support and training.

Cost per megabyte. The cost per megabyte presents a simple means of gauging the costs associated with a given storage device.

Cost per page. The cost per page provides a simple means of determining the overall running costs of a given printer. The figures given usually refer to the costs of consumables such as ink and replacement components (toner cartridges, drums and so on).

Countermediation. Creation of a new intermediary by an established company.

Coupling. Defines how closely linked different subsystems are. Loose coupling means that the modules pass only the minimum of information between them and do not share data and program code. Close-coupled systems are highly dependent on each other.

CPM. Cost for advertising is specified as CPM or cost per thousand page impressions.

Cracker. A person who gains access to an information system for malicious reasons is often termed a cracker rather than a hacker. This is because some people draw a distinction between 'ethical' hackers and malicious hackers.

Critical path. Activities on the critical path are termed critical activities. Any delay in these activities will cause a delay in the project completion time.

Critical path method (CPM). Critical path diagrams show the relationship between activities in a project.

Critical success factors (CSFs). CSFs are measures which indicate the performance or efficiency of different parts of an organisation.

Cross-licensing agreement. Cross-licensing agreements allow companies to share patents so that each can produce and market a wider range of products. See *Patent*.

Customer relationship management (CRM). CRM involves a company forming a long-term business relationship with its customers for mutual benefit. The essential aim of CRM is to improve customer service without harming company profitability. Typically, information technology is used to obtain and analyse information on customer behaviour. Such an analysis might result in various actions, such as improving the products and services offered to customers.

Customer value. Dependent on product quality, service quality, price and fulfilment time.

Cybermall. A single web site which gives online access to goods from a range of shops in a similar way to how physical shopping malls enable shoppers to make purchases in one location.

Cybersquatting. The act of registering an Internet domain with the intention of selling it for profit to an interested party. As an example, the name of a celebrity might be registered and then offered for sale at an extremely high price.

Cyberspace. The prefix cyber indicate a blurring in distinction between humans, machines and communications. Cyberspace is a synonym for Internet.

Cyberstalking. This refers to the use of the Internet as a means of harassing another individual. A related activity is known as corporate stalking, where an organisation uses its resources to harass individuals or business competitors.

Cyberterrorism. This describes attacks made on information systems that are motivated by political or religious beliefs.

Daisywheel printer. The daisywheel printer functions in much the same way as a conventional typewriter. Characters are mounted on hammers arranged in the shape of a wheel. The wheel is rotated until the correct character is in the correct position for printing. As one of the earliest forms of printing technology, daisywheel printers are considered slow and noisy. However, they are also considered inexpensive and reliable. It should be noted that daisywheel printers are unable to print graphics.

Data. Data can be described as a series of facts that have been obtained by observation or research and recorded.

Data dictionary. A repository which is used to store the details of the entities of the database. It will define tables, relations and field details which are sometimes referred to as metadata or 'data about data'.

Data entry form. In an electronic database, a data entry form provides a convenient means of viewing, entering, editing and deleting records.

Data marts. These are small-scale data warehouses which do not hold information across an entire company, but rather focus on one department.

Data migration. Data migration is the transfer of data from the old system to the new system. When data are added to a database, this is known as populating the database.

Data mining. This involves searching organisational databases in order to uncover hidden patterns or relationships in groups of data. Data mining software attempts to represent information in new ways so that previously unseen patterns or trends can be identified.

Data modelling. Data modelling involves considering how to represent data objects within a system, both logically and physically. The entity relationship diagram is used to model the data.

Data process. A process used to convert data into information. Examples include summarising, classifying and sorting.

Data processing. This describes the process of handling the large volumes of data that arise from an organisation's daily activities. Although data processing describes a wide range of activities, the most common are transaction processing and process control.

Data processing (DP) department. The data processing (DP) department was a term commonly used in the 1970s and 1980s to describe the functional area responsible for management of what is now referred to as information systems and applications development. It is interesting to note that the term focuses on the processing of data rather than the application of information. The head of this department was referred to as DP manager rather than Chief Information Officer or IS manager.

Data Protection Act (1984). This legislation sets out to define the rights of organisations and individuals in terms of how personal information is gathered, stored, processed and disclosed. One of the most important aspects of the Act is a focus on the individual's rights to view the information stored on them and ensure that it is accurate.

Data validation. Data validation is a process to ensure the quality of data by checking they have been entered correctly.

Data warehouses. Data warehouses are large database systems (often measured in gigabytes or terabytes) containing detailed company data on sales transactions which are analysed to assist in improving the marketing and financial performance of companies.

Data theft. Data theft can involve stealing sensitive information or making unauthorised changes to computer records. See also *Software theft* and *Theft*.

Data transfer rate. In terms of storage devices, the data transfer rate describes how quickly a device is able to read continuous blocks of data. This figure is normally expressed in terms of kilobytes or megabytes.

Data views. Different screens of an application which review information in a different form such as table, graph, report or map

Database. A database can be defined as a collection of related information. The information held in the database is stored in an organised way so that specific items can be selected and retrieved quickly. See *Database management system*.

Database management system (DBMS). The information held in an electronic database is accessed via a database management system. A DBMS can be defined as one or more computer programs that allow users to enter, store, organise, manipulate and retrieve data from a database. For many users, the terms *database* and *database management system* are interchangeable. A *relational database management system (RDBMS)* is an extension of a DBMS and allows data to be combined from a variety of sources.

Dataflow diagrams (DFD). Define the different processes in a system and the information which forms the input and output datastores to the processes. They may be drawn at different levels. Level 0 provides an overview of the system with levels 1 and 2 providing progressively more detail.

Decentralised IS management. Decentralised IS management involves management of some services in individual operating companies or at regional offices.

Decision behaviour. Describes the way in which people make decisions.

Decision support systems. Decision support systems provide managers with information needed to support semi-structured or unstructured decisions.

Decision table. A matrix showing all the alternative outcomes of different decisions which occur when certain input conditions occur.

Decision tree. A diagram showing the sequence of events, decisions and consequent actions that occur in a decision making process.

Deletion anomaly. It is not possible to delete a record from a relation without also losing some other information which might still be required.

Denial of service (DoS). This is a form of attack on company information systems that involves flooding the company's Internet servers with huge amounts of traffic. Such attacks effectively halt all of the company's Internet activities until the problem is dealt with.

Deployment plan. A deployment plan is a schedule which defines all the tasks that need to occur in order for changeover to occur successfully. This includes putting in place all the infrastructure such as cabling and hardware.

Desktop computer. The desktop computer is intended for office use and supports the day-to-day activities of an organisation's employees. These machines tend to be placed in a fixed location and connected permanently to items such as printers, scanners and other devices. The desktop computer is the most common type of microcomputer and is found in the majority of organisations.

Detailed design. Detailed design involves the specification of how an individual component of a system will function in terms of its data input and output, user interface and security.

Development programs. Development programs allow users to develop their own software in order to carry out processing tasks.

Dial-up networking (DUN). Dial-up networking software allows users to access a network at a remote location via a modem. Most home computer users, for example, access the Internet via dial-up networking.

Dialog. An onscreen window (box) which is used by a user to input data or select options.

Digital. Digital data can only represent a finite number of discrete values. For example, at the most basic level, a computer recognises only the values 0 (zero) and 1. Any values *between* 0 and 1, for example 0.15, cannot be represented.

Digital audio tape (DAT). A storage medium that combines some of the characteristics of magnetic tape and compact disc. Digital audio tape couples high storage capacities with improved speed and reliability.

Digital camera. A digital camera captures and stores still images in much the same way as a traditional camera. Images are held in the camera's memory or stored on disk until they can be transferred to a personal computer. The image is recorded using a charge-coupled device which recognises the different colours and intensity of light in the image.

Digital certificates. A method of ensuring privacy on the Internet. Certificates consist of a private key for encrypting data or documents and a corresponding public key for reading the data. An independent certification authority issues public and private keys. Basis for SET.

Digital ID. A digital ID provides a means of confirming the identity of a specific user through the use of a small data file called a personal certificate. The certificate contains encrypted information relating to the user's identity.

Digital versatile disc (DVD). Although superficially similar to CD-ROM, DVD devices offer two important benefits to users. First, the discs used by a DVD player offer extremely high storage capacities, typically between 4 Gb and 7 Gb. Secondly, data

held on DVD can be accessed at very high speeds. One of the most common applications for DVD as a distribution medium for full-length feature films. See *CD-ROM*.

Disaster recovery company. These maintain copies of important data on behalf of an organisation. They may also provide a service which can immediately supply replacement systems.

Disintermediation. The removal of intermediaries such as distributors or brokers that formerly linked a company to its customers.

Direct capture. This describes a method of acquiring and storing data automatically with little or no human intervention. As an example, the sensors on an automated production line can be described as direct capture devices.

Direct file access. Random or direct file access allows any record to be read or written.

Document image processing (DIP). DIP systems are used in industry to convert printed documents into an electronic format so that they can be stored, organised and retrieved more easily.

Documentation. Software documentation refers to end-user guidance such as the user guide and technical maintenance documentation such as design and test specifications.

Documentation review. Uses information on existing systems such as user guides, or requirements specifications together with paper or on-screen forms used to collect information such as sales order forms.

Domain name. Refers to the name of the web server and is usually selected to be the same as the name of the company and the extension will indicate its type. The extension is also commonly known as the Global Top Level Domain (gTLD).

http://www.domain-name.extension/filename.htm

Dongle. This describes a hardware device used to prevent unauthorised copies of a program being made. The hardware 'key' must be connected to the computer in order for the software to function.

Dot-matrix printer. The dot-matrix printer arranges a series of pins to form the shape of a required character. The character is transferred to the paper by striking the pins against an ink ribbon. The greater the number of pins used, the more detailed the character can be produced. As one of the earliest forms of printing technology, dot-matrix printers are considered slow and noisy. However, they are also considered inexpensive and reliable.

Dot-pitch. This describes a common method of gauging the quality of a monitor's display and involves measuring the distance – known as the dot-pitch – between the pixels on the screen. The smaller the distance between pixels, the finer the image will appear.

Dots per inch (DPI). The quality of a printer's output is normally measured in dots per inch. This describes the number of individual dots that can be printed within a space of one square inch. Quality is normally compared against professional typesetting, such as the equipment used to produce a book or magazine.

Dynamic systems development methodology (DSDM). A methodology which describes how RAD can be approached.

Dynamic web page. A page that is created in real time, often with reference to a database query, in response to a user request.

Early adopter. Early adopters are companies or departments that invest in new technologies when they first become available in an attempt to gain a competitive advantage despite the risk in deploying new systems.

Economic feasibility. An assessment of the costs and benefits of different solutions to select that which gives the best value. (Will the new system cost more than the expected benefits?)

Editing. The process of entering or correcting text is known as editing.

Effort time. Effort time is the total amount of work that needs to occur to complete a task.

EISA (Extended Industry Standard Architecture). This describes a common standard governing the way in which an expansion card interacts with a computer's motherboard and CPU. See *Expansion card* and *Motherboard*.

Elapsed time. Elapsed time indicates how long in time (such as calendar days) the task will take (duration).

Electronic business. All electronically mediated information exchanges, both within an organisation and with external stakeholders, supporting the range of business processes.

Electronic commerce. Transactions of goods or services for which payment occurs over the Internet or other wide-area networks.

Electronic data interchange (EDI). The electronic exchange of information between businesses using wide-area network. EDI transactions transfer structured data such as an electronic payment and also documents.

Electronic document management software (EDMS). Systems that convert documents into a digital format which allows storage, retrieval and manipulation of the document on computer.

Electronic eavesdropping. This describes the act of gaining access to confidential information by intercepting or monitoring communications traffic. See also *Computer monitoring*.

Electronic funds transfer. Automated digital transmission of money between organisations and banks.

Electronic mail (e-mail). E-mail can be defined as the transmission of a message over a communications network.

Electronic meeting systems. This describes a category of office automation systems that seek to improve communications between individuals and groups. Examples of these systems include those that support teleconferencing, teleworking and groupwork. See *Office automation systems*.

Electronic publishing systems. This describes a category of office automation systems that supports the production of documents, such as letters, reports and catalogues. Some of the typical programs used include word processors and desktop publishing packages. See *Office automation systems*.

End-user computing (EUC). End-user computing includes all uses of computers by business people who are not information systems professionals. This may range from use of business applications through spreadsheet modelling to developing programs to solve specific problems.

End-user development (EUD). End-user development is programming undertaken by non-IS staff. It typically involves development of small applications for solving departmental problems rather than cross-departmental applications.

End-user IT services. These include all services required to support end-users in running their PCs and applications.

Enterprise resource planning (ERP) software. A software system with integrated functions for all major business functions across an organisation such as production, distribution, sales, finance and human resources management. It is normally purchased as an off-the-shelf package which is tailored by a consultant. A single package typically replaces many different previous packages.

Environment. This describes the surroundings of a system. The environment of a system can contain other systems and external agencies.

EPROM (eraseable programmable read-only memory). This is a form of ROM that retains its contents until changed using a special device known as a 'burner'. See *Read-only memory*.

Error rate. In many cases, it may be acceptable if an input device generates a certain number of errors. This is often referred to as the error rate and the acceptable level will vary according to the input device being used and the business application. Optical character recognition, for example, is generally considered a comparatively unreliable means of entering data. At present, a typical OCR software package will have an error rate of between five and ten per cent.

Errors per KLOC. Errors per KLOC (thousands of line of code) is the basic defect measure used in systems development.

Estimation. Estimation allows the project manager to plan for the resources required for project execution through establishing the number and size of tasks that need to be completed in the project.

Ethics. In general terms, ethics describes beliefs concerning right and wrong that can be used by individuals to guide their behaviour. See *Morality* and *Professionalism*.

Executive information systems. These systems are used by senior management to select, retrieve and manage information that can be used to support the achievement of an organisation's business objectives. They need not be directly concerned with decision-making activities, but can help senior managers to become more efficient and productive in a number of other ways, for example by helping them to manage their time more efficiently.

Expansion card. Expansion cards can be used to extend a computer's capabilities by adding new devices to the system. An expansion card usually takes the form of a small circuit board that can be inserted into an expansion slot on the computer's motherboard. Some examples of expansion cards include modems, graphics cards and sound cards.

Expert systems. Expert systems are used to represent the knowledge decision-making skills of specialists so that non-specialists can take decisions. They encapsulate the knowledge of experts by providing tools for the acquisition of knowledge and representation of rules and their enactment as decisions.

Explicit knowledge. Knowledge that can be readily expressed and recorded within information systems.

Export. The process of saving a file in a format compatible with another software package is known as exporting.

Extensible markup language. See *XML*.

Extranet. An intranet with restricted access which is extended to suppliers, collaborators or customers.

Fax-modem. A fax-modem combines the capabilities of a modem with the ability to send and receive fax transmissions.

Fax-on-demand. A service that allows users to select from a range of documents by using the keys on the telephone handset. Once a document has been selected, the system automatically telephones the user's fax machine and transmits the document.

Feasibility study. The feasibility study is the activity that occurs at the start of the project to ensure that the project is a viable business proposition. The feasibility report analyses the need for and impact of the system and considers different alternatives for acquiring software. Input: Idea for initiation of a new information system. Output: Feasibility report and recommendation to proceed.

Federation against Software Theft (FAST). An organisation formed to act against software piracy. See *Software theft*.

Feedback. A feedback mechanism provides information on the performance of a system. An example of feedback might include quality control measurements taken on a production line.

Feedback control. In feedback closed-loop control systems the control loop compares the output of the process to the desired output and if a difference is found, adjusts the input or process accordingly.

Feedforward control. Feedforward incorporates a prediction element in the control feedback loop.

Field. The data in an electronic database is organised by fields and records. A field is a single item of information, such as a name or a quantity.

File attachment. E-mail messages can be used to transmit data files to other users. Files can be attached to messages and transmitted in the usual way. All types of data can be sent in this way including word processor files, spreadsheet data, graphics and database files.

Filter. In a spreadsheet or database, a filter can be used to remove data from the screen temporarily. This allows users to work with a specific group of records. Filters do not alter or delete data but simply hide any unwanted items.

Financial EDI. Aspect of electronic payment mechanism involving transfer of funds from the bank of a buyer to a seller.

Firewalls. This is a specialised software application mounted on a server at the point the company is connected to the Internet. Its purpose is to prevent unauthorised access into the company from outsiders. Firewalls are essential for all companies hosting their own web server.

First normal form (1NF). Transforming unnormalised data into its first normal form state involves the removal of repeating groups of data.

Flat file database. A flat file database can be described as being self-contained since it contains only one type of record – or table – and cannot access data held in other database files.

Flexible manufacturing systems (FMS). A group of machines with programmable controllers linked by an automated materials handling system and integrated by an IS that enables a variety of parts with similar processing requirements to be manufactured.

Floppy disk. Consists of a plastic disk, coated with a magnetic covering and enclosed within a rigid plastic case.

Font. The typeface used in a document is referred to as the font. The size of the characters used is referred to as the point size.

Foreign (secondary) key fields. These fields are used to link tables together by referring to the primary key in another database table.

Form. An on-screen equivalent of a paper form which is used for entering data and will have validation routines to help improve the accuracy of the entered data.

Formal communication. Formal communication involves presenting information in a structured and consistent manner. Such information is normally created for a specific purpose, making it likely to be more comprehensive, accurate and relevant than information transmitted using information communication. An example of formal communication is an accounting statement. See *Informal communication*.

Form dimension. This describes several characteristics of information quality related to how the information is presented to the recipient. Amongst these characteristics are clarity, level of detail and the order of information. As an example, information may be considered to be of high quality if it is presented in a clear and consistent fashion (clarity). Other dimensions of information characteristics include time and content. See *Time dimension, Content dimension*.

Formula. In a spreadsheet, a formula is a calculation that is entered by the user and performed automatically by the spreadsheet program.

Free-form database. A free-form database allows users to store information in the form of brief notes or passages of text. Each item held can be placed within a category or assigned one or more key words. Information is organised and retrieved by using categories or key words.

FTP file transfer. The file transfer protocol is used as a standard for moving files across the Internet. The most common use is for releasing fixes to software applications. Documents can be transferred by this means. FTP is available as a feature of web browsers for downloading files.

Function. In a spreadsheet, a function is a built-in command that carries out a calculation or action automatically.

Functional testing. Testing of particular functions or modules either following a test script or working through the module systematically.

Functionality. A term used to describe whether software has the features necessary to support the business requirements.

Function point analysis. A method of estimating the time it will take to build a system by counting up the number of functions and data inputs and outputs and then comparing to completed projects.

Full backup. A method of producing backup copies of important data files. A full backup includes all data files considered to be important. See also *Incremental backup*.

Gantt charts. Show the duration of parallel and sequential activities in a project as horizontal bars on a chart.

GIF (graphics interchange format). A graphics format and compression algorithm best used for simple graphics.

Gigabyte (Gb). A measure of storage capacity. Approximately 1000 Mb, of the equivalent of one billion characters.

Geographical Information System (GIS). Uses maps to display information about different geographic locations such as catchments or branches. They are commonly used for performance analysis by marketing staff.

Global business. The global business is a company that operates in several countries and uses information technology to assist in the control of operation and performance in each country.

Goal seeking. In a spreadsheet, goal seeking describes a way of automatically changing the values in a formula until a desired result is achieved.

Grandfather, father, son. A common procedure used for creating backup copies of important data files.

Graphics accelerator card. A type of graphics card containing its own memory and featuring a coprocessor. The coprocessor reduces the burden placed on the CPU by taking over the intensive calculations needed to produce complex graphical displays.

Graphics tablet. A graphics tablet is used in the same way as a writing pad. A stylus is used to draw images on a rigid pad located near to the computer. As the user draws with the stylus, the image is duplicated on the computer's display.

Graphical user interface (GUI). A graphical user interface allows the user to control the operation of a computer program or item of computer hardware using a pointing device, such as a mouse. In general, commands are issued by selecting items from menus, buttons and icons.

Groupware. Software which enables information and decision making to be shared by people collaborating within and between businesses.

H

Hacker. Hackers are often described as individuals who seek to break into systems as a test of their abilities. Few hackers attempt to cause damage to systems they access and few are interested in gaining any sort of financial profit.

Hardware. Describes the physical components of a computer system. The hardware of a computer system can be said to consist of: input devices, memory, central processing unit, output devices and storage devices.

Hard data. See *Quantitative data.*

Hard disk. A magnetic media that stores data upon a number of rigid platters that are rotated at very high speeds.

Hierarchical systems. Systems that are hierarchical in nature, being made up of subsystems that may themselves be made up of other subsystems.

Hierarchy of strategies. Sub-strategies developed to help achieve corporate objectives.

Hits. A measure of individual files delivered to the browser when requesting a URL. Hits usually overstate access to a web page. Page-impressions and ad-impressions are more accurate.

Hot plugging. This describes the ability to add or remove new devices whilst the computer is running and have the operating system automatically recognise any changes made.

HTML (hypertext markup language). HTML is the method used to create web pages and documents. The HTML code used to construct pages has codes or tags such as <TITLE> to indicate to the browser what is displayed.

Human activity system. A human activity system can be defined as a 'notional system (i.e. not existing in any tangible form) where human beings are undertaking some activities that achieve some purpose'.

Human–computer interaction (HCI) design. HCI involves the study of methods for designing the input and output of information systems to ensure they are 'user-friendly'.

Hypertext. Hypertext is highlighted words or phrases that represent links to other documents activated by clicking the mouse.

Hypertext database. In a hypertext database information is stored as series of objects and can consist of text, graphics, numerical data and multimedia data. Any object can be linked to any other, allowing users to store disparate information in an organised manner.

I

IBM-compatible. The modern personal computer found in most business organisations developed from a family of personal computers launched by IBM in the early 1980s. The IBM-compatible computer is considered the standard for general business use.

If Then Else statement. These are common within programs since they govern the different actions taken by the program according to a condition. They are usually in the form:
IF Condition Then.
Action if condition is TRUE
Else.
Action if condition is FALSE
End If.

Image processing systems. This describes a category of office automation systems that allows users to create, edit, store and retrieve documents in electronic format. Document image processing (DIP) is an example of an image processing systems. See *Office automation systems*.

Immediate cutover (big-bang) changeover. Immediate cutover is when a new system becomes operational and operations transfer immediately from the previous system.

Import. The process of loading a file created with another package is known as importing

Incremental backup. A method of producing backup copies of important data files. An incremental backup includes only those files that have changed in some way since the last backup was made. See *Full backup*.

Index. In an electronic database, an index stores information concerning the order of the records in the database. The index lists the locations of records but does not alter the actual order of the database.

Informal communication. This describes information that is transmitted by informal means, such as casual conversations between members of staff. The information transmitted in this way is often less structured and less detailed than information transmitted by formal communication. In addition, the information may be inconsistent or may contain inaccuracies. Furthermore, the information may also include a subjective element, such as personal opinions. See *Formal communication*.

Information. Data that have been processed so that they are meaningful.

Information centre (IC). An IC is a central facility in an organisation which provides end-user services such as phone support for troubleshooting end-user software and hardware problems, training, guidance on end-user development and management of user information.

Information flow diagram (IFD). A simple diagram showing how information is routed between

different parts of an organisation. It has an information focus rather than a process focus.

Information kiosk. A multimedia system usually integrated with a touch screen to provide information for retail or community applications such as libraries or local government is known as information kiosk.

Information leadership. Information leadership involves enhancing a product or service with an organisation's specialised information or expertise. In many cases, organisations achieve information leadership by selling information or expertise in the form of a separate product. A good example might be selling a mailing list created from an organisation's customer database.

Information need. The object of producing information is to meet a specific purpose or requirement.

Information reporting systems. These systems are used to generate reports containing information that can be used to support managerial decision making.

Information society. The information society is a term that has been coined to describe a modern population that is conversant with – and reliant upon – information and communications technology.

Information system. This describes a system designed to produce information that can be used to support the activities of managers and other workers.

Information systems acquisition. Acquisition describes the method of obtaining an information system for a business. The main choices are off-the-shelf (packaged), bespoke applications developed by an in-house IT department or a software house, and end-user developed systems.

Information systems strategy. Determination of the most appropriate processes and resources to ensure that information provision supports business strategy.

Information technology strategy. Determination of the most appropriate technological infrastructure comprising hardware, networks and software applications.

Information warrior. Information warriors seek to obtain data by any means necessary. Such people may resort to illegal methods, such as hacking, in order to obtain the information they require. However, the information obtained may not necessarily be used in pursuit of criminal activities.

Initiation phase. The startup phase in an IS development project. Its aims are to establish whether the project is feasible and then prepare to ensure the project is successful. Input: Creative thought and/or systematic evaluation of IS needs. Output: Idea for initiation of a new information system.

Inkjet printer. An inkjet printer uses a print-head containing 50 or more small nozzles. Each nozzle can be controlled individually by electrostatic charges produced by the printer. Characters are formed by squirting small droplets of directly onto the paper. Inkjets are considered relatively inexpensive, near silent in operation and capable of producing good quality results. It should be noted that inkjet printers also represent an economical means of printing in colour.

Input. The input to a system can be thought of as the raw materials for a process that will produce a particular output. Examples of inputs might include data, knowledge, raw materials, machinery and premises.

Input design. Input design includes the design of user input through on-screen forms, but also other methods of data entry such as import by file, transfer from another system or specialised data capture methods such as bar-code scanning and optical or voice recognition techniques.

Input device. Input devices are used to enter data, information or instructions into a computer-based information system.

Insertion anomaly. It is not possible to insert a new occurrence record into a relation (table) without having to also insert one into another relation first.

Intangible assets. Intangible assets describe the non-physical resources owned by a company. Intangible assets are also known as conceptual resources. Examples include knowledge, experience and judgement.

Intangible value. A value or benefit that is difficult or impossible to quantify.

Intellectual property. Intellectual property is a generic term used to describe designs, ideas and inventions. In general, intellectual property covers the following areas: patents, trade marks, designs and copyright.

Intelligent agent. An intelligent agent is a semi-autonomous computer program capable of carrying out one or more tasks specified by the user. You can think of an intelligent agent as a software 'robot' capable of being programmed to carry out a wide variety of tasks.

Interoperability. A general term used to describe how easily different components of a system can be integrated.

Interactive kiosk. A typical application for touch screen systems, an interactive kiosk allows a user to purchase items or browse through a list of products by pressing buttons or other controls shown on the screen. Such kiosks are often found in banks, music stores and large catalogue stores. Many bookings systems, such as those used by airlines, theatres and travel agents, also make use of touch screens. See *Touch screen*.

Interdependence. Interdependence means that a change to one part of a system leads to or results from changes to one or more other parts.

Interface. In terms of systems, the interface describes the exchanges between a system and its environment or the system and other systems. In the field of information technology, the interface describes ways in which information is exchanged between users and computer software or hardware.

Interlaced. An interlaced display is one where each complete image shown on a monitor's display is drawn in two steps. A non-interlaced monitor refreshes the display in a single pass. A good-quality monitor is normally capable of supporting a non-interlaced display at a refresh rate of 70 Hz or more.

Internal rate of return (IRR). A discounted cash flow technique used to assess the return of a project by considering the interest rate which would produce an NPV of zero.

Internet. The Internet refers to the physical network that links computers across the globe. It consists of the infrastructure of servers and communication links between them which is used to hold and transport the vast amount of information on the Internet.

Internet EDI. Use of EDI data standards delivered across non-proprietary Internet protocol networks.

Internet pure-plays. A company trading online that has limited or no physical presence such as retail units.

Internet relay chat (IRC). This is a synchronous communications tool which allows a text-based 'chat' between different users who are logged on at the same time. It is not used for many business applications since asynchronous discussions are more practical – not all team members need to be present at the same time.

Internet service provider (ISP). Companies which provide access to the Internet and web page hosting for home and business users. Online service providers give access to the Internet plus their own content.

Interpreted. An interpreted computer program can be run directly, without the need for compilation. As the program runs, each instruction is taken in turn and converted into machine language by a command interpreter.

Interstitial. A small, rectangular area within a web page used for advertising. May be animated or static.

Interviewing. Recommended practice: a range of staff are interviewed using structured techniques to identify features and problems of the current system and required features of the future system.

Intranet. An intranet uses web servers, browsers and e-mail within a company to share company information and software applications. The intranet is only accessible to company employees.

IP address. The unique numerical address of a computer.

ISA (Industry Standard Architecture). This describes a common standard governing the way in which an expansion card interacts with a computer's motherboard and CPU. See *Expansion card* and *Motherboard*.

ISDN (integrated services digital network). ISDN represents a standard for communications that allows data transfer rates that are up to five times faster than a 56 600 bps modem. An ISDN telephone line provides two separate 'channels' allowing simultaneous voice and data transmissions. Since ISDN lines transmit digital data, a modem is not required to make use of the service. Instead, a special terminal adapter (often called an ISDN modem) is used to pass data between the computer and the ISDN line. See *Modem* and *Baud rate*.

Java. An object-oriented programming language standard supported by Sun Microsystems which permits complex and graphical customer applications to be written and then accessed from a web browser. An example might be a form for calculating interest on a loan. A competitor to Active-X.

Javascript. A simple scripting programming language, which offers a subset of the features of the Java programming language.

JPEG (joint photographics experts group). A graphics format and compression algorithm best used for photographs.

Justification. In a word processor, the alignment of text with the left and right margins can be controlled by specifying the justification. Text can be left-justified, right-justified or fully justified.

Kilobyte (kb). A measure of storage capacity. Approximately 1000 bytes, or the equivalent of 1000 characters.

Knowledge. Applying managerial experience to problem solving. See *Explicit knowledge* and *Tacit knowledge*.

Knowledge management. Techniques and tools for collecting, managing and disseminating knowledge within an organisation.

Label printers. These are small units specifically designed to print on rolls of self-adhesive labels. Although various kinds of label printer exist, one of the most common types is used for printing bar codes.

Laser printer. The laser printer is commonly used for business applications requiring a combination of speed with high print quality.

Legacy system. When a new computer-based information system is developed, it may be necessary to retain hardware – but more often software – from the earlier system. In these cases, the software that has been retained is referred to as a legacy system.

Lightpen. A lightpen is a pointing device that can be used to control applications by pointing to items on the screen. Lightpens are also used for applications involving graphics, such as drawing packages, since images can be drawn directly onto the screen. See *Pointing device*.

Line printer. A line printer processes a document one line at a time. In contrast, a page printer processes a document one entire page at a time.

Live (production) environment. The term used to described the setup of the system (hardware, software and office environment) where the software will be used in the business.

Local-area network (LAN). A LAN is a computer network that spans a limited geographic area, typically a single office or building. A LAN consists of a single network segment or several connected segments which are limited in extent.

Logic bomb. Sometimes also known as a time bomb, a logic bomb is a destructive computer program that activates at a certain time or in reaction to a specific event.

Low-level language. A low-level programming language requires the programmer to work directly with the hardware of the computer system. Instructions are normally entered in machine code or assembly language.

Machine language. This describes the natural language of a computer. Machine language instructions are made up of binary digits and use only the values of 0 (zero) and 1.

Machine-oriented. A machine-oriented programming language focuses on the requirements of the computer hardware being used, where programs are produced in a form that suits the way in which the microprocessor functions.

Macro. A macro is a sequence of instructions that can be used to automate complex or repetitive tasks. Macros can be used to emulate a sequence of keys pressed on the keyboard or can be programmed so that they can carry out more complicated processes.

Macro-environment. Wider environment of social, legal, economic, political and technological influences.

Magnetic ink character recognition (MICR). This involves capturing data that have been printed using a special magnetic ink. This technology is normally associated with the banking industry, especially cheque processing. Some of the details on a cheque, such as the cheque number, are printed a special typeface using magnetic ink. The shape of each character means that it can be recognised by its magnetic field.

Mainframe. A traditional view of computing saw three main categories of computers: mainframes, minicomputers and microcomputers. Mainframes were considered the most powerful computers and were used for large-scale data processing.

Management information systems. These systems provide feedback on organisational activities and help to support managerial decision making.

Materials requirements planning (MRP) software. MRP software is used to plan the production of goods in a manufacturing organisation by obtaining components, scheduling operations and controlling production. MRP II integrates the information system with other functional areas in the business such as finance and marketing.

McFarlan's strategic grid. This model is used to indicate the strategic importance of information systems to a company now and in the future.

Megabyte (Mb). A measure of storage capacity. Approximately 1000 kb, or the equivalent of one million characters.

Megapixel. A measurement that is often used to describe the quality of the image captured by a digital camera. A megapixel represents one million individual picture elements – the dots that make up an image. Early digital cameras produced images at a quality of 0.5 megapixels. Modern devices can produce images at a quality of 3.5 megapixels or higher.

Memory. Computer memory is used as a temporary means of storing data and instructions. Memory is used to store data awaiting processing, instructions used to process data or control the computer system, and data or information that has been processed.

Metadata. Reference data describing the structure and content of data in a data warehouse are known as metadata.

Milestone. This denotes a significant event in the project such as completion of a prototype.

Minicomputer. A traditional view of computing saw three main categories of computers: mainframes, minicomputers and microcomputers. Minicomputers offered an intermediate stage between the power of mainframe systems and the relatively low cost of microcomputer systems.

Microcomputer. A traditional view of computing saw three main categories of computers: mainframes, minicomputers and microcomputers. Microcomputers were considered less powerful than other types of computer but were more flexible and relatively inexpensive to purchase.

Micro-environment. Immediate environment including customers, competitors, suppliers and distributors.

Middleware. A type of software that acts as a layer between other software to assist in data transfer between incompatible systems.

Modelling. Modelling involves creating a numerical representation of an *existing* situation or set of circumstances, whilst simulation involves *predicting* new situations or circumstances. In both cases, a model is produced that provides a numerical representation of the situation or circumstances being studied. Modelling and simulation are common activities carried out with the use of spreadsheet software. See *Spreadsheet*.

Modem (modulator–demodulator). A modem is a communications device that allows users to send and receive data via an ordinary telephone line. See also *Fax-modem*.

Module design. Detailed design involves the specification of how an individual component of a system will function in terms of its data input and output, user interface and security.

Module or unit testing. Individual modules are tested to ensure they function correctly for given inputs.

Monitoring and control. Monitoring involves ensuring the project is working to plan once it is started. Control is taking corrective action if the project deviates from the plan.

Morality. In general terms, morality is concerned with individual character or personality and beliefs governing right and wrong. See *Ethics* and *Professionalism*.

Motherboard. The motherboard is the main circuit board within a computer and houses the processor, memory, expansion slots and a number of connectors used for attaching additional devices, such as a hard disk drive.

Multidimensional data. Data broken down in analysis for a data warehouse into dimensions such as time period, product segment and the geographical location. Dimensions are broken down into categories. For time these could be months, quarters or years.

Multimedia. Multimedia can be defined as the combination of several media under the control of an interactive computer program. Such media can include text, graphics, sound, video and animation. In terms of computer hardware, a multimedia computer will incorporate a CD-ROM drive and sound card. In addition, current standards for multimedia computers specify minimum graphics capabilities and processor speed.

Multi-user testing. The effect of different users accessing the same customer or stock record is tested. Software should not permit two users to modify the same data at the same time.

Mouse. A pointing device found on most modern personal computers. Moving the mouse over a flat surface causes a corresponding movement to a small pointer on the screen. Selections, such as menu items, are made by clicking one of the buttons on the mouse. See *Pointing device*.

Natural keyboard. A variation on the conventional computer keyboard, a natural keyboard has the keys arranged so that users can locate them more quickly and easily. The keyboard itself is often shaped in a way that makes prolonged use more comfortable.

Navigating. The act of moving from one section of the Internet to another.

Net present value (NPV). A measure of the return from a system which takes into account the variation in monetary value through time.

Net PC. A hybrid between a traditional PC and a network computer, it will usually feature no floppy or hard drive and limited memory and processor since it will use the power of the server to provide applications.

Network computer (NC). The purpose of the network computer is to provide access to a network system, such as the Internet, at minimal cost. A typical network computer will feature limited disk storage, memory and expansion potential. In addition, the computer may also feature an older, less powerful processor than its desktop counterpart. Network computers are often associated with the thin client architecture and the concept of zero administration. See *Thin client* and *Zero administration*.

Network interface card. A network interface card is an expansion card that allows a personal computer to be connected to a network. The network card deals with all communications between the network and the computer.

Network operating system (NOS). This describes the software needed to operate and manage a network system.

Network topology. The physical layout of a LAN is known as a network topology. Bus, star, ring and combinations are most common.

Neural networks. These systems use a similar process to biological intelligence to learn problem-solving skills by 'training' or exposure to a wide range of problems. The learning occurs through interactions between nodes which are similar to the neurons of the brain.

Node name. The name used to identify a particular computer system on the Internet.

Nolan's stage model. This model is a six-stage maturity model for the application of information systems to a business.

Non-interlaced. An interlaced display is one where each complete image shown on a monitor's display is drawn in two steps. A non-interlaced monitor refreshes the display in a single pass. A good quality monitor is normally capable of supporting a non-interlaced display at a refresh rate of 70 Hz or more.

Non-volatile memory. The memory found in a personal computer is considered volatile, that is, anything held in memory is lost once the power to the computer system is switched off. However, non-volatile memory retains its contents until altered or erased.

Normalisation. This design activity is a procedure which is used to optimise the physical storage of data within a database. It involves simplification of entities and minimisation of duplication of data.

Notebook. A small portable computer, which is approximately the size of an A4 sheet of paper.

O

Object-oriented database. An object-oriented approach to database design employs the concept of reusable objects in order to develop sophisticated or complex applications. An object combines data structures with any functions needed to manipulate the object or the data it holds.

Object-oriented design. This is a design technique which involves basing the design of software on real-world objects which consist of both data and the procedures that process them rather than traditional design where procedures operate on separate data.

Observation. This analysis technique is useful for identifying inefficiencies in an existing way of working with either a computer-based or a manual information system. It involves timing how long particular operations take and observing the method used to perform them. It can be time-consuming and the staff who are observed may behave differently from normal.

Office management systems. This describes a category of office automation systems that assists users in scheduling projects and tasks. Examples of office management systems include personal information managers (PIM) and project management software. See *Office automation systems*.

Off-the-shelf purchase or packaged software. An acquisition method which involves direct purchase of a pre-written application used by more than one company.

Office automation systems. In business organisations, productivity software is often used to reduce the time needed to complete routine administrative tasks, such as producing documents or organising meetings. By attempting to automate many of the activities carried out within a typical office, organisations seek to improve efficiency, reduce costs and enhance internal communications. Computer-based information systems used in this way are generally referred to as office automation systems.

Offline. When a user is not connected to their Internet account, they are said to be offline.

Offline reader. Sometimes called an offline browser. An offline reader allows a single page, a group of pages, or an entire web site to be copied to the user's hard disk drive so that the material can be viewed at a later date.

Online. When a user is connected to their Internet account, usually by a modem link, they are said to be online.

Online analytical processing (OLAP). OLAP can be considered to be a synonym for a data warehouse. It refers to the ability to analyse in real time the type of multidimensional information stored in data warehouses. The term 'online' indicates that users can formulate their own queries compared to standard paper reports. The originator of OLAP, Dr E. Codd, defines OLAP as the dynamic synthesis, analysis, and consolidation of large volumes of multidimensional data

Online or Internet revenue contribution. An assessment of the direct or indirect contribution of the Internet to sales, usually expressed as a percentage of overall sales revenue.

Online stock fraud. Most online stock fraud involves posting false information to the Internet in order to increase or decrease the values of stocks.

Open profiling standard. A standard method of collecting personal details about customers. An initiative, begun by Netscape and Firefly, now supported by many players including Microsoft. www.firefly.net/OPS/OPS.html.

Open questions. Not restricted to a limited range of answers such as Yes/No (closed questions). Asked to elicit opinions or ideas for the new system or identify commonly held views amongst staff. Open questions are not typically used for quantitative analysis, but can be used to identify a common problem.

Open source. An alternative approach towards software development and acquisition. Open source applications are made available free of charge to individuals and organisations.

Open system. Interaction occurs with elements beyond the system boundary

Open systems interconnection (OSI) model. An international standard defining connectivity of links between computers at different levels.

Open-loop control system. An open-loop control system is one in which there is an attempt to reach the system objective, but no control action to modify the inputs or process is taken once the process has begun.

Operating environment. This describes a number of programs intended to simplify the way in which users work with the operating system. Early versions of Windows, for example, provided a graphical user interface that removed the need for users to work with the more complex aspects of MS-DOS.

Operating system (OS). The operating system interacts with the hardware of the computer at a very low level in order to manage and direct the computer's resources. The basic functions of the operating system include: allocating and managing system resources, scheduling the use of resources and monitoring the activities of the computer system.

Operational feasibility. An assessment of how the new system will affect the daily working practices within the organisation. (Is the system workable on a day-to-day basis?)

Operations information systems. These systems are generally concerned with process control, transaction processing, communications (internal and external) and productivity.

Optical character recognition (OCR). Optical character recognition involves using software that attempts to recognise individual characters. An optical scanner is normally used to capture an image of a document. As the image is processed, the OCR program creates a text file containing all of the characters recognised. This file can then be edited further using a word processor, text editor or other suitable program. See *Optical scanner*.

Optical mark recognition (OMR). A variation on optical character recognition is optical mark recognition, which involves detecting and recognising simple marks made on a document. See *Optical character recognition*.

Optical scanner. The optical scanner can be used to capture graphics and text from printed documents. A photograph, for example, can be captured and converted into a form suitable for use with a

number of different applications. Images captured in this way are normally incorporated into word processing or desktop publishing documents.

Organisational culture. This concept includes shared values, unwritten rules and assumptions within the organisation as well as the practices that all groups share. Corporate cultures are created when a group of employees interact over time and are relatively successful in what they undertake.

Organisational feasibility. Reviews how well the solution meets the needs of the business and anticipates problems such as hostility to the system if insufficient training occurs. (Considers the effect of change given a company's culture and politics.)

Outline design. A high-level definition of the different components that make up the architecture of a system and how they interact.

Output. An output is a finished product that is created by a system. Examples include information, products and services.

Output design. Output design involves specifying how production of on-screen reports and paper-based reports will occur. Output may occur to database or file for storing information entered or also for use by other systems.

Output devices. Output devices translate the results of processing – output – into a human-readable form.

Outsourcing. Outsourcing occurs when all or part of the information systems services of a company are subcontracted to a third party.

Packaged software. An acqusition method that involves direct purchase of a pre-written application used by more than one company

Packets. Units of data that are exchanged between different devices over communications media. The entire message to be sent is broken down into smaller packets since if an error occurs in transmission, only the packet with the error needs to be retransmitted.

Page impressions. Number of occasions a single page has been delivered to a user. Several hits may be recorded during one page impression according to the number of separate graphics and text blocks that need to be downloaded.

Page printer. A page printer processes a document one entire page at a time. In general, page printers are capable of printing documents quickly and at high quality. In contrast, line printers process a document one line at a time.

Pages per minute (ppm). This describes a simple means of measuring the speed of a printer. The speed of a page printer, such as a laser printer or modern inkjet model, is measured in terms of pages per minute.

Pages per month (ppm). Manufacturers often provide ratings for their printers that describe the typical workload appropriate for a given model. This value is often described in terms of pages per month.

Page requests. See *Page impressions*.

Paint programs. Paint programs serve the same purpose as a sketch pad or easel and enable users to produce drawings using a variety of different techniques.

Parallel port. A type of connector that allows various devices to be attached to a computer system. Examples of common parallel devices include printers and external storage devices.

Parallel running. This changeover method involves the old and new system operating together at the same time until the company is certain the new system works.

Patent. A patent provides its owner with a monopoly allowing them to exploit their invention without competition. The protection offered by a patent lasts for a number of years but does not begin until the patent has been granted.

Payback period. The period after the initial investment before the company achieves a net benefit.

PCI (peripheral component interconnect). This describes a common standard governing the way in which an expansion card interacts with a computer's motherboard and CPU. PCI devices often support the Plug and Play installation of devices. See *Expansion card*, *Plug and Play* and *Motherboard*.

Peer-to-peer network. A simple type of local-area network which provides sharing of files and peripherals between PCs.

Personal certificate. A data file containing encrypted information relating to the user's identity.

Personal digital assistant (PDA), can be thought of as a sophisticated personal organiser. A PDA is normally a hand-held device, often no larger than a pocket calculator. The purpose of the PDA is to help users manage their time more efficiently and effectively. The typical functions of a PDA can include: address book, appointment scheduler, calculator, expenses tracking, currency conversion, alarm clock, world

time display and a variety of other features that allow users to store notes, such as to-do lists.

Personal information manager (PIM). A PIM can be thought as an electronic personal organiser. The program allows users to store, organise and retrieve personal information such as appointments, personal expenses, telephone numbers and addresses, reminders and to-do lists.

PERT. Sometimes used to refer to a critical path network diagram (PERT charts), but more accurately PERT replaces the fixed activity duration used in the CPM method with a statistical distribution which uses optimistic, pessimistic and most likely duration estimates.

Phased implementation. This changeover method involves introducing different modules of the new system sequentially.

Photo-editing packages. Photo-editing packages enable users to capture, view and edit scanned images.

Physical resources. Physical resources are the tangible resources owned by a company. Examples include land, buildings and plant. Physical resources are also known as tangible assets.

Pilot system. The system is trialled in a limited area before it is deployed more extensively across the business.

Plotter. A plotter uses a number of different coloured pens to draw lines upon the paper as it moves through the machine. Although capable of producing characters, the quality of the text created is often very poor. Plotters are primarily used to create technical drawings, such as engineering diagrams but can also be used to record the results of the continuous monitoring of various events by creating charts. Some cardiac monitors, for example, use a simple plotter device to produce charts showing a patient's heart activity over time.

Plug and Play (PnP). This describes a means by which expansion cards can be added to a computer system and configured automatically without the user needing to enter settings or make other changes. See *Expansion card*.

Plug-in. A plug-in is a small program or accessory that can be used to extend a web browser's capabilities. For example, a number of different plug-ins exist that allow a web browser to display video or animation sequences.

Pointing device. An input device that allows the user to control the movement of a small pointer displayed on the screen. The pointer can be used to carry out actions by selecting items from a menu or manipulating icons.

Portable computer. The portable computer is largely self-contained, featuring its own power supply, keyboard, pointing device and visual display unit. Variations on the portable computer include the notebook and sub-notebook.

Portal. Sites which provide the main method of access to other web sites through providing services to locate information on the WWW are now commonly referred to as portals. Such portals are often set to the default or home page of the user's web browser. Examples of portals include Yahoo (www.yahoo.com), Microsoft's MSN (www.msn.com) and the Netscape Netcenter (home.netscape.com).

Porter and Millar's five forces model. Porter and Millar's five forces model is for analysing the different competitive forces which impact on an organisation. The five forces are: rivalry between existing competitors, threat of new entrants, threat of substitutes, the power of buyers and the power of suppliers.

Positive and negative feedback. Negative feedback is used to describe the act of reversing any discrepancy between desired and actual output. Positive feedback responds to a variance between desired and actual output by increasing that variance

Post-implementation review. A meeting that occurs after a system is operational to review the success of the project and learn lessons for the future.

Power supply unit (PSU). All modern personal computers feature a power supply unit used to convert AC current into DC current. The PSU regulates the amount of power supplied to the motherboard and any other devices installed within the case.

Presentation software. Presentation software enables users to create, edit and deliver presentations via a computer system.

Primary key fields. These fields are used to uniquely identify each record in a table and link to similar secondary key fields (usually of the same name) in other tables.

Primary storage. Data and instructions are loaded into memory such as random access memory. Such storage is temporary.

PRINCE. A project management methodology that has been developed to be compatible with system development methodologies such as SSADM.

PRINCE structure. PRINCE defines an organisational structure and standard set of job descriptors.

Print preview. The print preview feature displays a document exactly as it will be printed, enabling users to check and correct the document without making unnecessary printouts.

Printer sharer. A printer sharer allows several computers to be attached to a single printer.

Private branch exchange (PBX). Enables switching between phones or voice and data using existing telephone lines.

Problem-oriented. A problem oriented language focuses on the expression of a problem or set of information processing requirements. The language will provide a variety of features that allow programmers to express their requirements in a natural form.

Process. Inputs are turned into outputs by using a transformation process.

Processor. Uses instructions from software to control the different components of a PC.

Process control systems. These systems deal with the large volume of data generated by production processes.

Process modelling. Involves the design of the different modules of the system, each of which is a process with clearly defined inputs, outputs and a transformation process. Data flow diagrams are often used to define processes in the system.

Production (live) environment. The term used to described the setup of the system (hardware, software and office environment) where the software will be used in the business.

Productivity paradox. Research results indicating a poor correlation between organisational investment in information systems and organisational performance measured by return on equity.

Productivity software. This describes a category of computer software that aims to support users in performing a variety of common tasks.

Professionalism. In general terms, professionalism can be described as acting to meet the standards set by a profession in terms of individual conduct, competence and integrity. See *Ethics* and *Morality*.

Programming language. Programming languages enable users to develop software applications in order to carry out specific information processing tasks.

Project constraints. Projects can be resource-constrained (limited by the type of people, monetary or hardware resources available) or time-constrained (limited by the deadline).

Project costs graphs. Show the financial cost of undertaking the project.

Project crashing. Refers to reducing the project duration by increasing spending on critical activities.

Project documentation. Documentation is essential to disseminate information during project execution and for reference during software maintenance.

Project plan. This shows the main activities within the project, providing an overall schedule and identifying resources needed for project implementation.

Projects. Projects are unique, one-time operations designed to accomplish a specific set of objectives in a limited time frame.

Protocols. The Internet functions using a series of standard protocols which allow different computers to communicate with each other. Passing of data packets around the Internet occurs via the TCP/IP protocol which stands for transfer control protocol/Internet protocol. The HTTP (hypertext transfer protocol) is used to allow computers to transfer and process HTML files.

Prototyping. A prototype is a preliminary version of part or a framework of all of an information system which can be reviewed by end-users. Prototyping is an iterative process where users suggest modifications before further prototypes and the final information system are built.

Push technology. Push is used to deliver web pages to the user's desktop PC without specifically requesting each page. It is the Internet equivalent of a TV channel, hence it is sometimes also known as NetCasting. Important players are Marimba, Pointcast, Microsoft (Internet Explorer 4.0) and Netscape (Netcaster).

Pull technology. Information sent out as a result of receiving a specific request, for example a page is delivered to a web browser in response to a request from the user.

Qualitative data. Also known as *soft data*, qualitative data describes the qualities or characteristics of an object or situation. Such data are often collected in order to help achieve a better understanding of a given situation. An interview, for example, might help the interviewer to understand an individual's personal beliefs and opinions.

Quantitative data. Also known as *hard data*, quantitative data tend to make use of figures, such as statistics. These data are often collected in order to measure or quantify an object or situation.

Query. In a spreadsheet or database, a query can be used to extract data according to a set of conditions specified by the user. The results of a query can be stored in another part of the worksheet or database so that the original data remain intact.

Questionnaires. Used to obtain a range of opinion on requirements by targeting a range of staff. They are open to misinterpretation unless carefully designed. They should consist of both open and closed questions.

RAID. RAID stands for redundant array of inexpensive disks. Essentially, identical copies of important data files are kept upon a number of different storage devices. If one or more of the storage devices fail, additional devices are activated automatically, allowing uninterrupted access to the data and reducing the possibility of losing transactions or updates.

Random access memory (RAM). RAM is used as working storage by a computer, holding instructions and data that are waiting to be processed. The contents of RAM are volatile, that is, any data held are lost when the power to the computer system is switched off. See *Volatile memory*.

Random file access. Random or direct file access allows any record to be read or written.

Rapid applications development (RAD). A method of developing information systems which uses prototyping to achieve user involvement and faster development compared to traditional methodologies such as SSADM.

Ratings. Many web browsers support the use of ratings in order to restrict access to inappropriate content, for example pornography. When a web browser is used to access a site belonging to a given ratings scheme, the site's ratings are checked against the list of criteria set within the browser. If a site does not meet the criteria specified within the browser, access to the site is denied.

Read-only memory (ROM). The contents of ROM are fixed and cannot be altered. ROM is also non-volatile, making it ideal as a means of storing the information needed for a device to function properly. In a computer system, for example, the basic information needed so that the computer can access disk drives and control peripherals is stored in ROM. See *Non-volatile memory*.

Read-only. In terms of storage devices, a read-only device can only be used to access data that are already present on the medium. A CD-ROM player, for example, is unable to write data to a compact disc and can only read from it. See also *Read-only memory*.

Real-time processing. Data are processed immediately on collection.

Record. In an electronic database, a record is a collection of *related* fields. See *Field*.

Record key. In order to identify a specific item of information within a database, all records must contain an identifier, normally called the record key. The record key usually takes the form of a number or code and will be different for each record in the database.

Recovery. The process which is used to restore backup data.

Refresh rate. This describes a common method of gauging the quality of a monitor's display and involves measuring the number of times the image is drawn upon the screen each second. The refresh rate is normally measured in Hz, for example a refresh rate of 60 Hz means that the image will be drawn upon the screen 60 times each second.

Regression testing. Testing performed before a release to ensure that the software performance is consistent with previous test results, i.e. that the outputs produced are consistent with previous releases of the software.

Re-intermediation. The creation of new intermediaries between customers and suppliers providing services such as supplier search and product evaluation.

Relational databases. Data are stored within a number of different tables with each dealing with different subjects that are related (linked) using key fields.

Relational database management system (RDBMS). This is an extension of a DBMS and allows data to be combined from a variety of sources.

Relationship. In a relational database, data can be combined from several different sources by defining relationships between tables.

Remote access. Remote-access describes a means of accessing a network from a distant location. A modem and specialised software allow users to send and receive information from home or an office when travelling.

Replication (server). A process in which information on server computers at different locations is transferred and synchronised so users in different locations can view the same data.

Replication (virus). The process by which a virus copies itself.

Request for proposals (RFP). A specification drawn up to assist in selecting the supplier and software.

Requirements specification. The main output from the systems analysis stage. Its main focus is a description of what all the functions of the software will be.

Resolution. The resolution of the monitor describes the fineness of the image that can be displayed. Resolution is often expressed in terms of pixels (picture elements) – the individual dots that make up an image on the screen.

Resource allocation. This activity involves assigning a resource to each task.

Response time. Many organisations make use of external companies to provide maintenance and technical support for their computer-based information systems. In such cases, the organisation may require the maintenance provider to guarantee a minimum response time for important repairs.

Return on investment (RoI). An indication of the returns provided by an IS. Calculated by dividing the benefit by the amount of investment. Expressed as a percentage.

Revenue models. Describe methods of generating income for an organisation.

Reverse engineering. Reverse engineering attempts to recreate the design of an item by analysing the final product. This can be compared to the 'black box' approach to systems analysis, where the outputs from the system are analysed in order to determine the inputs and processes involved. Reverse engineering can be used to duplicate both hardware and software.

RISC (reduced instruction set computer) processor. Designed so that it has to perform fewer instructions than a CISC processor and it can then operate at a higher speed. The IBM RS/6000 workstation is a well known example of a computer that uses the PowerPC RISC processor. As new designs of Pentium processor are produced these are incorporating RISC features and are also making use of parallel processing.

Risk management. Risk management aims to anticipate the future risks of an information systems project and to put in place measures to counter or eliminate these risks.

Safety-critical system. Where human lives rely on the correct operation of a computer-based information system, this is normally referred to as a critical system.

Scalability. The potential of an information system, piece of software or hardware to move from supporting a small number of users to a large number of users without a marked decrease in reliability or performance.

Scenario. A particular path or flow of events or activities within a use case.

Scientific languages. Scientific programming languages are designed to serve scientific and mathematical applications.

Scoring system. A means of selecting hardware, software and suppliers using a point-scoring system. Each item or supplier is assigned scores against a number of selection criteria. Final selection is based upon the total score achieved by each item or supplier. The relative importance of the selection criteria can be recognised through the use of weighting factors, resulting in the creation of a weighted ranking table.

Script. All modern web browsers are capable of executing special commands that have been embedded within the body of a WWW page. These scripts can be used to control the appearance of the page or can provide additional facilities, such as on-screen clocks and timers.

SCSI (small computer system interface). This describes a common standard governing the way in which an expansion card interacts with a computer's motherboard and CPU. Up to seven separate devices can be attached to a single SCSI interface simultaneously. Connecting several devices in sequence is known as daisy-chaining. See *Expansion card*, *Plug and Play* and *Motherboard*.

Search engine. Search engines provide an index of all words stored on the World Wide Web. Keywords typed in by the end-user are matched against the index and the user is given a list of all corresponding web pages containing the keywords. By clicking on a hyperlink the user is taken to the relevant web page.

Second normal form (2NF). Second normal form states that 'each attribute in a record (relation) must be functionally dependent on the whole key of that record'.

Secondary key fields. These fields are used to link tables together by referring to the primary key in another database table.

Secondary storage. Floppy disks and hard disks are secondary storage which provides permanent storage.

Security breach. A security breach is a deliberate or unintentional act that leads to unauthorised access to or loss or damage to information or an information system.

Secure Electronic Transactions (SET). A method developed by Visa and Mastercard proposed for enabling credit-card-based electronic commerce based on digital certificates.

Secure sockets layer (SSL). A standard used within web browsers to encrypt data such as credit-card details sent over the Internet.

Sell-side e-commerce. E-commerce transactions between a supplier organisation and its customers.

Sensing device. Modern personal computers are capable of communicating with external devices via a number of different means. This allows them to be connected to a variety of sensing devices. Amongst these are motion detectors, light sensors, infra-red sensors (which can detect heat), microphones and many others.

Serial port. A type of connector that allows various devices to be attached to a computer system. Examples of common serial devices might include mouse, modem and printer.

Sequential access method. Sequential file access involves reading or writing each record in a file in a set order.

Server. A server is a powerful computer used to control the management of a network. It may have a specific function such as storing user files or a database or managing a printer.

Service-level agreements. A contractual specification of service standards a contractor must meet.

Signature. Most computer viruses contain a message to be displayed on screen or a hidden piece of text. Additionally, a virus program may also contain a unique series of values in its program file. These unique features are known as the signature of the virus.

Signature file. A signature file contains information such as an address and phone number that can be automatically added to the end of an e-mail message.

Site certificate. A site certificate contains information regarding the identity of a particular site on the Internet. The site certificate is encrypted to protect the information it contains. When a user's web browser accesses a given site on the Internet, the corresponding certificate is checked to ensure the authenticity of the site.

Soft systems methodology. A methodology that emphasises the human involvement in systems and models their behaviour as part of systems analysis in a way that is understandable by non technical experts.

Software. A series of detailed instructions that control the operation of a computer system. Software exists as programs that are developed by computer programmers.

Software bug. Software bugs are defects in a program which are caused by human error during programming or earlier in the lifecycle. They may result in major faults or may remain unidentified.

Software metrics. Measures which indicate the quality of software.

Software Publishers Association (SPA). An organisation formed to act against software piracy. See *Software theft*.

Software quality. Measured according to its suitability for the job intended. This is governed by whether it can do the job required (does it meet the business requirements?) and the number of bugs it contains (does it work reliably?).

Software theft. Software theft, also known as software piracy, involves making unauthorised copies of software applications. Software theft represents a serious and growing problem for the software industry. Global losses due to software piracy were estimated at more than $11 billion in 1996.

Sound card. A sound card allows a personal computer to play speech, music and other sounds. A sound card can also be used to capture sound, music and speech from a variety of sources.

Source escrow. An arrangement where a third party stores software that can be used for maintenance purposes if the original developer of the software becomes insolvent.

Spam. Unwanted messages, such as advertisements, are received by most e-mail users. The act of sending out these messages is usually called spamming.

Speech synthesis. Speech synthesis software allows text to be converted into speech. The contents of spreadsheet files, e-mail messages, word processing documents and other files can be converted into speech and played back via a sound card or other device.

Spiral model. An iterative systems development model developed by Boehm in which the stages of analysis, design, code and review repeat as new features for the system are identified.

Spreadsheet. A spreadsheet can be described as a program designed to store and manipulate values, numbers and text in an efficient and *useful* way. The work area in a spreadsheet program is called the worksheet. A worksheet is a grid made up of cells. Each cell is uniquely identifiable by its horizontal (row) and vertical (column) coordinates. A cell can contain text, numbers or a formula that relates to information held in another cell.

Stage models. Used to assess the current and future application of technology in an organisation.

Stakeholders. All who have a direct interest in the system.

Storage devices. Storage devices provide a means of storing data and programs until they are required.

Strategy. Definition of the future direction and actions of a company defined as approaches to achieving specific objectives.

Strategy process model. A framework for approaching strategy development.

Static web page. A page on the web server that is invariant.

Streaming media. Sound and video that can be experienced within a web browser without the need to download a complete file.

Structured decisions. Structured decisions tend to involve situations where the rules and constraints governing the decision are known. They tend to involve routine or repetitive situations where the number of possible courses of action is relatively small.

Structured English. A technique for producing a design specification for programmers which indicates the way individual modules or groups of modules should be implemented.

Structured query language (SQL). This describes a form of programming language that provides a standardised method for retrieving information from databases.

Sub-notebook. A small portable computer which is usually significantly smaller than a notebook due to its small screen and keyboard.

Subsystem. Large systems can be composed of one or more smaller systems. These smaller systems are known as subsystems.

Suprasystem. This describes a larger system that is made of one or more smaller systems (subsystems).

Synchronous. When people exchange information simultaneously as is the case with real time chat or a telephone conversation this is known as synchronous.

Synergy. Synergy means that the whole is greater than the sum of the parts.

System. A system can be defined as a collection of interrelated components that work together towards a collective goal.

System build. System build is the term used to describe the creation of software by programmers. It involves writing the software code (programming), building release versions of the software, constructing and populating the database and testing by programmers and end users. Writing of documentation and training may also occur at this stage. Inputs: Requirements and design specification. Outputs: Working software, user guides and system documentation.

System implementation. Implementation covers practical issues such as making sure the hardware and network infrastructure for a new system are in place; testing of the system and also human issues of how best to educate and train staff who will be using or affected by the new system. Implementation also involves the transition or changeover from the old system to the new. Input: Working system, not tested by users. Output: Signed off, operational information system installed in all locations.

System maintenance. Maintenance occurs after the system has been signed off as suitable for users. It involves reviewing the project and recording and acting on problems with the system.

System objective. All systems are created to meet a specific objective or purpose. All of the components of system are related to one another by a common objective. When the components of a system no longer share the same objective, a condition of sub-optimality is said to exist.

System or outline design. A high-level definition of the different components that make up the architecture of a system and how they interact.

System owners. These are managers who are directly responsible for the operational use of a system.

System sponsors. System sponsors are senior managers or board members who are responsible for a system at a senior level in a company.

System testing. When all modules have been completed and their interactions assessed for validity, links between all modules are assessed in the system test. In system testing interactions between all relevant modules are tested systematically.

Systems analysis. Systems analysis refers to the capture of the business requirements of a system from talking to or observing end-users and using other information sources such as existing system documentation. Input: Terms of reference in feasibility report describing outline requirements.

Output: Detailed requirements specification summarising system functions. Supported by diagrams showing the information flow and processes that are required.

Systems analysis and design method (SSADM). A methodology that defines the methods of analysis and design that should occur in a large-scale software development project. It is used extensively in the UK, particularly in government and public organisations.

Systems design. The systems design phase defines how the system will work in key areas of user interface, program modules, security and database transactions. Input: Requirements specification. Output: Detailed design specification.

Systems dynamics. Based on the view that the world can be regarded as a set of interdependent systems, it usually uses simulation models to try to understand why systems behave as they do.

Systems software. This form of software manages and controls the operation of the computer system as it performs tasks on behalf of the user.

Systems theory. The study of the behaviour and interactions within and between systems.

Table. In an electronic database, data are organised within structures known as tables. A table defines the structure of a specific record.

Tacit knowledge. Mainly intangible knowledge that is typically intuitive and not recorded since it is part of the human mind.

Talk-through. A user verbally describes their required actions.

Tangible assets. Tangible assets are the physical resources owned by a company. Examples include land, buildings and plant.

Tangible value. A value or benefit that can be measured directly, usually in monetary terms. With regard to information, tangible value is usually calculated as: value of information minus cost of gathering information.

Tape streamer. A common form of storage device that uses magnetic tape as a storage medium.

TCP/IP. The transmission control protocol is a transport layer protocol that moves data between applications. The Internet protocol is a network layer protocol that moves data between host computers.

Technical feasibility. Evaluates to what degree the proposed solutions will work as required and whether the right people and tools are available to implement the solution. (Will it work?)

Telecommunications. Telecommunications is the method by which data and information are transmitted between different locations.

Telecommunications channels. The media by which data are transmitted. Cables and wires are known as guided media and microwave and satellite links are known as unguided media.

Teleworking. The process where company staff work remotely from their company office. Most commonly it is applied to 'home workers' who spend at least three days a week working in this way.

Telnet. This allows remote access to computer systems. For example, a system administrator on one site could log-in to a computer elsewhere to check it is running successfully. Telnet is widely used in the retail industry. For example, a retailer could check to see whether an item was in stock in a warehouse using a telnet application. Such telnet applications will not usually be run over the public Internet, but rather over secure lines.

Tender document. A document used as an invitation to suppliers, asking them to bid for the right to supply an organisation's hardware, software and other requirements.

Terminate and stay resident (TSR). A program that is stored in the computer's memory and functions as a background task, receiving only a small share of the processor's time.

Test environment. A specially configured environment (hardware, software and office environment) used to test the software before its release.

Test plan. Plan describing the type and sequence of testing and who will conduct it.

Test specification. A detailed description of the tests that will be performed to check the software works correctly.

Theft. In terms of computing, theft normally, but not always, involves altering computer records to disguise the theft of money. The theft of services can include a variety of acts, such as the unauthorised use of a company's information systems. See also *Software theft* and *Data theft*.

Thermal printer. Thermal printers operate by using a matrix of heated pins to melt ink from a ribbon directly onto the paper.

Thin client. In a network system, this describes an architecture where the bulk of the processing is carried out by a central server. The results of the processing are then relayed back to a terminal or network computer. See *Network computer*.

Third normal form (3NF). A record is in third normal form if each non-key attribute *'depends on the key, the whole key and nothing but the key'*.

Three-tier client/server. The client is mainly used for display with application logic and the business rules partitioned on a second tier server and a third-tier database server. Here the client is sometimes referred to as a 'thin client', because the size of the executable program is smaller.

Time dimension. This describes several characteristics of information quality related to the time period that the information deals with and the frequency at which the information is received. Amongst these characteristics are the timeliness, currency and frequency of information. As an example, information may be considered to be of high quality if it is received in good time (timeliness). Other dimensions of information characteristics include content and form. See *Content dimension, Form dimension.*

Top-down design. The top-down approach to design involves specifying the overall control architecture of the application before designing the individual modules.

Total cost of ownership (TCO). TCO refers to the total cost for a company operating a computer. This includes not only the purchase or leasing cost, but also the cost of all the services needed to support the end-user.

Touch screen. The touch screen is a transparent, pressure-sensitive covering that is attached to the screen of a monitor. Users make selections and control programs by pressing on the screen. Although touch screens are simple to use, they are comparatively expensive and require special software to operate.

Trackball. A trackball is a pointing device that is controlled by rotating a small ball with the fingertips or palm of the hand. Moving the ball causes corresponding movement to a small pointer on the screen. Buttons are used to select items in the same way as the mouse. See *Pointing device.*

Transaction log files. A web server file that records all page requests from site visitors.

Transaction processing. This involves dealing with the sales and purchase transactions that an organisation carries out in the course of its normal activities. Banks, for example, handle millions of deposits and withdrawals each day.

Transaction processing systems (TPS). Transaction processing systems (TPS) manage the frequent external and internal transactions such as orders for goods and services which serve the operational level of the organisation.

Transformation process. A transformation process is used to convert inputs into outputs. A power station, for example, converts fuel into electricity.

Trojan. A Trojan presents itself as a legitimate program in order to gain access to a computer system. Trojans are often used as delivery systems for computer viruses.

Two-tier client/server. Sometimes referred to as 'fat client', the application running on the PC is a large program containing all the application logic and display code. It retrieves data from a separate database server.

Unified modelling language (UML). A language used to specify, visualise and document the artefacts of an object-oriented system.

Uniform (universal) resource locators (URL). A web address used to locate a web page on a web server.

Unit testing. Individual modules are tested to ensure they function correctly for given inputs.

Universal product code. A standard for defining bar codes used frequently in retailing.

Universal serial bus (USB). This describes a relatively new standard that governs the way in which an expansion card interacts with a computer's motherboard and CPU. In addition to offering very high data transmission speeds, USB also supports Plug and Play, the connection of up to 127 devices and hot plugging. See *Expansion card*, *Plug and Play*, *Hot plugging* and *Motherboard*.

Unstructured decisions. Unstructured decisions tend to involve complex situations, where the rules governing the decision are complicated or unknown. Such decisions tend to be made infrequently and rely heavily on the experience, judgement and knowledge of the decision maker.

Update anomaly. It is not possible to change a single occurrence of a data item (a field) in a relation (table) without having to change others in order to maintain the correctness of data.

Update query. An update query can be used to change records, tables and reports held in a database management system.

Use-case. The sequence of transactions between an actor and a system that support the activities of the actor.

Use-case modelling. A user-centred approach to modelling system requirements.

Usenet newsgroups. Usenet is mainly used by special interest groups such as people discussing their favourite pastimes. They are not used much by businesses, unless it is as a means of studying consumer behaviour.

User acceptance testing. This is the final stage of testing which occurs before the software is signed off as fit for purpose and the system can go live.

User-centred design. Design based on optimising the user experience according to all factors, including the user interface, which affect this.

User validation. Checks made to ensure the user is permitted access to a system. Also known as access control systems, they often involve user names and passwords, but can also include biometric techniques.

Utility programs. Utility programs provide a range of tools that support the operation and management of a computer system.

Validation. This is a test of the design where we check that the design fulfils the requirements of the business users which are defined in the requirements specification.

Value-added networks (VAN). Value-added networks (VAN) give a subscription service enabling companies to transmit data securely across a shared network.

Value chain. Michael Porter's value chain is a framework for considering key activities within an organisation and how well they add value as products and services move from conception to delivery to the customer.

Value network. The links between an organisation and its strategic and non-strategic partners that form its external value chain.

Vector image. Vector graphics are made up of shapes, rather than individual dots. Mathematical formulae determine the size, position and colour of the shapes that make up a given image.

Verification. This is a test of the design to ensure that the design chosen is the best available and that it is error-free.

VGA (Video graphics array). A common standard for graphics cards. All graphics cards support the VGA standard which specifies a maximum image size of 640 by 320 pixels, displayed in 16 colours.

Video capture card. The video capture card records and stores video sequences (motion video). A playback device, for example a video cassette recorder, is connected to the video capture card and special software is used to capture, edit and manipulate video sequences. Once a motion video sequence has been processed, it can then be output to a television, video cassette recorder or other device.

Video projector. A computer system can be connected directly to a projector so that output is directed to a projection screen. Some projectors convert the computer's output into a television picture before displaying it.

Virtual organisation. An organisation which uses technologies to allow it to operate without clearly defined physical boundaries between different functions. It provides customised services for customers by linking different human resources and suppliers at different locations.

Virtual private network (VPN). A data network that makes use of the public telecommunication infrastructure and Internet, but information remains secure by the use of a tunnelling protocol and security procedures such as firewalls.

Virtual reality (VR). An interactive, artificial reality created by the computer. Users perceive the environment in three dimensions and are able to interact with objects and people. Using virtual-reality goggles, for example, a user might interact with a body of data that appears as a three-dimensional model.

Virus. See *Computer virus*.

Virus scanner. Virus scanners are intended to detect and then safely remove virus programs from a computer system. The most common method of detection used by these programs involves scanning for the signatures of particular viruses. See also *Signature*.

Virus shield. Virus shields are TSR programs that constantly monitor and control access to a system's storage devices. Any unusual attempt to modify a file or write to a disk drive will activate a message asking the user to authorise the operation. See also *Terminate and stay resident*.

Visual display unit (VDU). This is normally used to describe the monitor connected to a computer system, but can also refer to any other form of display device.

Visualisation. This describes a variety of methods used to produce graphical representations of data so that it can be examined from a number of different perspectives.

Voice annotations. These can be described as spoken notes or reminders that can be inserted into data files, such as word processing documents. Annotations are created and played back via a sound card. See *Sound card*.

Voice modem. Voice modems offer greater flexibility than conventional modems by combining voice, fax and data facilities. At a simple level, a voice modem can be used as a speaker phone or answering machine.

Voice recognition. This describes the facility to control a computer program or carry out data entry through spoken commands. The user issues instructions via a microphone connected to a sound card. Specialised software then attempts to interpret and execute the instruction given.

Voice–data integration. Sometimes known as *computer telephony*. A combination of different communications technologies that provide a range of sophisticated facilities, for example automated call-switching, telephone answering services and fax-on-demand. See *Fax-on-demand*.

Volatile memory. The memory found in a personal computer is considered volatile, that is, anything held in memory is lost once the power to the computer system is switched off. However, non-volatile memory retains its contents until altered or erased.

Volume testing. Testing assesses how system performance will change at different levels of usage.

Walk-through. A user executes their actions through using a system or mock-up.

Waterfall model. Outlines the series of steps that should occur when building an information system. The steps usually occur in a predefined order with a review at the end of each stage before the next can be started.

Wax printers. Printers which employ a ribbon with a coloured wax coating to form images by heating sections of the ribbon and pressing it against the paper (dye-sublimation).

Web addresses. Web addresses refer to particular pages on a web server which are hosted by a company or organisation. The technical name for these is uniform resource locators, so you often see them referred to as URLs.

Web browsers. Browsers such as Netscape Navigator and Microsoft Explorer provide an easy method of accessing and viewing information stored as web documents on different servers. The web pages stored as HTML files on the servers are accessed through a particular standard supported by the web browsers (this is the hypertext transfer protocol (http), which you will always see preceding the web address of a company). For example http://www.derby.ac.uk defines the university home page at Derby.

Web directories or catalogues. Web directories provide a structured listing of web sites. They are grouped according to categories such as business, entertainment or sport. Each category is then subdivided further, for example into football, rugby, swimming, etc.

Web servers. Web servers such as Microsoft Internet Information Server are used to store the web pages accessed by web browsers. They may also contain databases of customer or product information which can be queried and retrieved from the browser.

What if? analysis. This describes the ability to see the predicted effect of a change made to a numerical model. See *Modelling* and *Spreadsheet*.

Wide-area network (WAN). These networks cover a large area to connect businesses in different parts of the same city, different parts of a country or different countries.

WIMP (windows, icons, mouse and pull-down menus). Often used to describe a GUI environment.

Wireless application protocol (WAP). WAP is a technical standard for transferring information to wireless devices, such as mobile phones.

Wireless markup language (WML). Standard for displaying mobile pages such as transferred by WAP.

Word processor. A word processor provides the ability to enter, edit, store and print text. In addition, word processing packages allow users to alter the layout of documents and often provide a variety of formatting tools.

Word wrap. In a word processor, as users type text and move towards the end of a line, the program automatically moves to the beginning of a new line.

Workbook. In a spreadsheet program, this describes a collection of worksheets.

Work breakdown structure (WBS). This is a breakdown of the project or a piece of work into its component parts (tasks).

Workflow management (WFM). Systems for the automation of the movement and processing of information in a business according to a set of procedural rules.

Workgroup. A workgroup can be defined as a group of individuals working together on a given task. Each member of the workgroup will be attached to the organisation's network system so that tasks can be organised and information can be shared with other members.

Worksheet. An individual area or sheet for entering data in a spreadsheet program.

Workstation. This describes a powerful terminal or personal computer system, usually applied to specialised applications, such as computer-aided design (CAD) and animation.

World Wide Web. The World Wide Web is a medium for publishing information on the Internet. It is accessed through web browsers which display web pages and can be used to run business applications. Company information is stored on web servers which are usually referred to as web sites.

WORM (write once, read many). A WORM (write once, read many) storage device allows data to be written only once. Once the data have been written, they cannot be changed or erased.

Worm (virus). A worm is a small program that moves through a computer system randomly changing or overwriting pieces of data as it moves.

XML (extensible markup language). A relatively new development, XML describes a standard for creating documents that can store almost any kind of data. XML is extremely flexible since it offers the ability to create new language elements – or whole new languages – using standard XML elements. XML is seen as a key technology in the area of business-to-business communications since it provides a simple and effective way for organisations to share data. XML is also seen as a key technology for areas such as e-commerce and distributed databases. Finally, XML forms part of Microsoft's .Net strategy, which is intended to shape the future of operating systems, applications software, software development and the use of the Internet.

Zero administration. In a network system, zero administration describes a point where the centralised management and control of the computers attached to a network server makes administration costs almost negligible. Zero administration is often associated with network computers. See *Network computer*.

Index